# Antislavery Newspapers and Periodicals

**Reference Publications in Afro-American Studies**

# Antislavery Newspapers and Periodicals

## Volume III
## (1836-1854)

**Annotated Index of Letters in the *Friend of Man, Pennsylvania Freeman, Advocate of Freedom,* and *American & Foreign Anti-Slavery Reporter***

**Edited by**
**John W. Blassingame, Mae G. Henderson and Jessica M. Dunn**

**G.K. HALL & CO. BOSTON, MASSACHUSETTS**

**The preparation of this volume of the** ***Antislavery Newspapers and Periodicals: Annotated Index of Letters*** **was made possible through grants from the Research Tools Program of the National Endowment for the Humanities and Yale University.**



*Library of Congress Cataloging in Publication Data* (Revised)
Main entry under title:
Antislavery newspapers and periodicals.
(Reference publications in Afro-American studies)
Includes indexes.
Contents: v. 1. Annotated index of letters in the Philanthropist, Emancipator, Genius of universal emancipation, Abolition intelligencer, African observer, and the Liberator, 1817-1845—v. 2. Annotated index of letters in the Liberator, Anti-slavery record, Human rights, and the Observer, 1835-1865—v. 3. Annotated index of letters in the Friend of man, Pennsylvania freeman, Advocate of Freedom, and American & foreign anti-slavery reporter, 1836-1854.
1. Slavery—United States—Anti-slavery movements—Periodicals—Indexes. 2. United States—Social conditions—To 1865—Periodicals—Indexes. 3. Afro-American newspapers—Indexes. 4. Afro-American periodicals—Indexes. 5. American newspapers—Indexes. 6. American periodicals—Indexes.
I. Blessingame, John W., 1940- II. Henderson, Mae. III. Series.
Z1249.S6A57 [E449] 326′.05 79-20230
ISBN 0-8161-8163-2 (v. 1) AACR2
ISBN 0-8161-8434-8 (v. 2)
ISBN 0-8161-8558-1 (v. 3)

*This publication is printed on permanent/durable acid-free paper.*
MANUFACTURED IN THE UNITED STATES OF AMERICA

**To Harriet W. Sheridan**

*a teacher of teachers*

# Contents

# Illustrations

# Preface

Most scholars agree that Charles Sainte-Beuve stated the obvious when he observed: "The details of history, in truth, can only be gathered from a study of the immense and varied surface which the literature of newspapers presents." At the same time, most scholars view newspapers and magazines, especially those from the nineteenth century, as labyrinths without a clue because there are no comprehensive journal indexes. We set out in the fall of 1977 to provide some clues to an extensive body of newspaper literature by establishing the Black and Reform Newspaper Indexing Project.

Funded by the National Endowment for the Humanities, the objective of the Project was the preparation of a multivolumed annotated list of letters appearing in selected nineteenth-century abolitionist, black, and reform journals. Unfortunately, we were only able to complete work on abolitionist newspapers and magazines. We chose to concentrate on letters because we felt they contained more of the personal details of history than did editorials, signed articles, book reviews, advertisements, and the like.

The letters in the journals reflect the spirit of the times, the fluctuating interests of blacks, reformers, and others, and represent a valuable tool in reconstructing the past. Until the first decades of the twentieth century Americans were addicted to writing letters to newspapers and magazines. As a result, nineteenth-century black and reform-oriented journals generally filled one-fifth of their columns with letters. Reports of conventions and social affairs, extended debates and discussions of controversial issues, accounts of foreign travel, and narratives of political campaigns were frequent. The body of the letters constitutes an incomparable source for genealogists, historians, and students of nineteenth-century American literature, black life and culture, the abolitionist movement, women's rights, music, education, social problems, urbanization, folklore, health and science, social mobility, alcoholism and temperance, pacifism, electoral politics, religion, migration, marriage and family life, immigration, slavery, the Civil War and Reconstruction, interracial violence, prisons and prison reform, emigration, drama, journalism, Indian life and culture, labor, agriculture, and diplomacy.

This published list of letters in newspapers and magazines gives scholars a key to the correspondence of individuals needed for writing biographies. It elucidates many of the intellectual, social, and political currents of the nineteenth century and expands the data available for studying local communities. A surprisingly large number of nineteenth-century journals contained correspondence from all parts of the United States. Often, the only extant letters either written by antebellum blacks or containing descriptions of Afro-Americans in widely scattered cities in the United States were printed in abolitionist newspapers.

Although focussing primarily on their own constituencies, abolitionist journals reprinted letters of correspondents catholic in their interests. Abolitionist newspapers frequently contained letters from Greece, Great Britain, Haiti, Russia, France, Latin America, Africa, and other parts of the world. Famous politicians, stung by editorial attacks, published letters on various topics in the journals. Generally not found in manuscript collections, but often published in abolitionist journals, the letters of such individuals become more accessible to their biographers through the publication of this annotated list.

An overwhelming majority of the correspondents are obscure individuals. Collectively, however, their letters provide a perspective on an almost unlimited range of topics and simplify the task of writing collective sketches and compiling biographical encyclopedias and directories of such groups as nineteenth-century women, abolitionists, Southern and Northern black politicians, novelists, poets, musicians, educators, and others.

Nineteenth-century abolitionist journals are among the most elusive of sources. Standard bibliographies and general histories of American journalism furnish few clues to either the number of journals published or the location of extant copies. There are no central repositories for the journals. Consequently, systematic research is required even to compile a list of nineteenth-century abolitionist periodicals. While some of the titles we discovered have been more elusive than others, we made a concerted effort to locate all of the extant issues of the journals we indexed. Because of the large number and historical dispersion of abolitionist and reform journals published in the nineteenth century, we were unable to locate all of the potential titles. We did, however, search systemically for them. Given limited resources, we tried to index all of the key abolitionist journals, while attempting to ensure geographical and ideological representativeness.

As important as abolitionist journals were during the nineteenth century, contemporary Americans know little about their editors, the financial struggles involved in keeping the journals afloat, or how frequently mobs destroyed them. The story of these journals is an exciting but neglected chapter of American journalism. Although their combined circulation figure was higher than that of such better known contemporaries as the *New York Times* in the nineteenth century, it is the *Times* which has attracted historians and students of journalism. Dozens of histories of the *Times* have been published; there is not only no book-length study of an abolitionist newspaper, but even articles on them are rare. Because so little is known about these journals, it is necessary for us to explain briefly why we concentrated on certain categories of newspapers and magazines.

We were interested in compiling an index of abolitionist newspapers and periodicals because in few general interest journals can the black and reform angle of vision on the nineteenth century be found. All too often when Afro-Americans and reformers sent letters to metropolitan newspapers they were rejected. Willis Hodges, a New York black, narrated a typical experience in the 1840s when he objected to an article in the New York *Sun* attacking Afro-Americans:

> I prepared a reply to this article and took it to the editor of the *Sun,* but he would not publish it unless I paid him $15. He then put my article away down in the corner out of the sight of nine out of ten of the readers. I went to him and demanded to know why? He said because it was "a paid advertisement." I then said, "Well, you told me that you would not put it in unless I paid you, and I, therefore, expected to see it in some other part of the paper. You are only giving light on one side of the case, and your paper says that it 'shines for all.' "
>
> [The editor replied:] "The *Sun* shines for all white men, not black men. You must get up a paper of your own if you want to tell your side of the story to the public. Good morning."

The editors of practically all nineteenth-century abolitionist journals included a "Correspondents" section in their papers to insure that the sun would also shine on the oppressed, black and white.

Even the most liberal papers carried relatively few communications from blacks because their letters often lacked literary polish. In contrast, black and reform journals often published the letters of the semiliterate in an effort to encourage the development of literary skills in the black community. One correspondent in *Frederick Douglass' Paper*, for instance, observed in 1851 that "it should not be forgotten, that *Frederick Douglass' Paper* has afforded the most extensive opportunity for a free and full expression of sentiments by the illiterate as well as the learned." A year later, Douglas stated an editorial position on publishing letters which was typical of nineteenth-century black and reform editors:

> We sometimes publish letters, which, when viewed apart from the writers, do very little credit to the literary character of our paper. The motive for such publication is

> to encourage those for whose special development and elevation this paper was established. Our readers must bear with them and give *our people* a chance to be great as well as themselves.

Open to a much broader spectrum of the reading public than general interest journals edited by whites, abolitionist periodicals contain an indispensable record of nineteenth-century Afro-American life and culture. Many blacks who rarely sent missives to general interest newspapers published dozens of letters in abolitionist newspapers and periodicals.

The early abolition journals have been included in the index because they differed in many ways from those published after 1830. Abolitionist editors in the 1820s, for instance, were far more tolerant and less militant than their successors. Published in Tennessee, Missouri, Kentucky, and Maryland, the early journals reflected the gradualist antislavery stance of many Southern abolitionists. John Finley Crowe's 1822 editorial declaration in the Shelbyville (Ky.) *Abolition Intelligencer* that the aim of the paper was "to *prepare* the public mind for taking the necessary *preparatory* measures for the *gradual* abolition of slavery," contrasted sharply with the objectives of William Lloyd Garrison's *Liberator*. Writing in his first issue in 1831, Garrison asserted:

> I shall strenuously contend for the immediate enfranchisement of our slave population. . . . I am aware that many object to the severity of my language; but is there not cause for severity? I *will* be as harsh as truth, and as uncompromising as justice. On this subject, I do not wish to think or speak, or write, with moderation. No! no! Tell a man whose house is on fire to give a moderate alarm; tell him to moderately rescue his wife from the hands of the ravisher; tell the mother to gradually extricate her babe from the fire into which it has fallen; —but urge me not to use moderation in a cause like the present.

Slaveholders appeared in the *Liberator* as sinners; in the earlier journals they were often depicted as ordinary men saddled with a complex social problem by their forefathers. The *Liberator* rejected African colonization; many of the earlier abolitionist journals contended that the only way blacks could obtain equality was by leaving the United States.

Because many of the early abolitionist journals were more moderate in tone than the later ones and were published in the South and Southwest (Tennessee, Missouri, Maryland, and Kentucky) they contain many letters from Southern reformers, colonizationists, and slaveholders. Confronting slavery as a reality rather than an abstraction, Southern correspondents publishing letters in periodicals between 1817 and 1830 present a portrait of the peculiar institution differing in many ways from that drawn by many historians. Southern planters appeared, for instance, quite ready to acknowledge guilt over holding slaves. Southern interest in temperance and other reforms also emerges in letters published in such journals as the *Genuis of Universal Emancipation* and the *Abolition Intelligencer.*

We begin by publishing indexes of the letters in abolitionist and reform journals which started publication between 1817 and 1831. The newspapers and magazines indexed in Volume One were published in Tennessee, Maryland, Kentucky, Washington, D.C., Pennsylvania, Ohio, Illinois, and Massachusetts and include the Mount Pleasant (Oh.) *Philanthropist,* 1817-18; Tennessee *Emancipator,* 1820; Shelbyville (Ky.) *Abolition Intelligencer,* 1822-23; *Genius of Universal Emancipation,* 1821-39; *African Observer,* 1827-28 and the Boston (Ma.) *Liberator,* 1831-65. The index of each journal is presented in its entirety with the exception of the long-running *Liberator*. Volume One includes the first fifteen years of the *Liberator,* 1831-45. Volume Two includes the second part of the *Liberator,* 1846-65; New York *Anti-Slavery Record,* 1835-38; New York *Human Rights*, 1835-38; and the Alton (Il.) *Observer,* 1835-38. Volume Three includes the Utica (N.Y.) *Friend of Man,* 1836-42; *Pennsylvania Freeman*, 1836-54; Hallowell (Me.) *Advocate of Freedom,* 1838-41; and the New York *American & Foreign Anti-Slavery Reporter,* 1840-46.

The annotated list of letters is presented chronologically by date of appearance in each journal and the entries are numbered consecutively throughout the volume. The list of letters in each journal is published in its entirety before beginning those appearing in another. A journal data sheet appears before the list of letters in each journal and presents its history in capsule form, indicating places where issues are located, whether or not there is a microform, names of editor(s), and place(s) of publication. Whenever they could be located, we have reprinted prospectuses of the journals to give readers some sense of their purpose. For the same reasons, we have included short biographical sketches, autobiographical statements, and reminiscences of the editors, the people who inevitably put their stamp on the journals. We have drawn these sketches, whenever possible, from nineteenth-century newspapers, books, pamphlets, and periodicals because biographies written by contemporaries and associates frequently include little known and especially revealing personal anecdotes and facts.

As a general rule, we attempted to present a rough characterization of the letters in as brief a form as was consistent with clarity and utility. Though we would have liked to publish a more detailed précis of each letter, we had to be realistic about the economics of research and printing. Consequently, we sought entries of manageable compactness and clarity. When the material being summarized is from an extract of a letter, this fact is noted. Boldface type is used to denote senders and recipients, dates and places of letters. Each entry has been assigned a number to facilitate indexing.

The entries vary in character and detail and partially reflect the different styles of several dozen graduate and undergraduate students who did the basic research. We tried throughout the project to have researchers write précis of between fifteen and twenty-five words. But as researchers became more familiar with the topics explored by correspondents (or bored with their repetitiveness), they began writing extremely short summaries. In some instances, they were originally so cryptic that we had to expand them during our proofreading and copyediting. Often a cryptic entry will appear because the annotated letter was part of a series in which the earlier entries give fuller detail. On the other hand, some of our researchers consistently wrote such long "abstracts" that we spent a great deal of time at the copyediting stage trying to reduce them to manageable size. Undoubtedly we have not always succeeded in our search for uniformity.

Despite our best efforts, we occasionally ended up with microfilm of journals where issues were illegible. We have indicated in our summaries those letters which were partially illegible. Illegible issues were much easier for us to handle than those rare instances when we began annotating a journal only to find months later that an entire reel of microfilm was illegible. In such cases we first explored the possibility of a second photocopying of the run. Secondly, when the original newspaper was so faded that we could not obtain a readable microfilm, we tried to locate other repositories having runs that we could photocopy. Finally, when we had exhausted all of the possibilities without being able to obtain complete runs, we decided to include the index of the partial run of such journals. We will note those journals with incomplete runs.

While perfection is perhaps more devoutly to be wished for in a reference tool than in any other work a scholar does, it is also the most difficult of tasks. In the final analysis, we can only tell readers how we tried to ensure accuracy and comprehensiveness and beg their indulgence for any errors of commission or omission.

People indexing newspapers and magazines eventually reach the point where they feel they are the object of the "error conspiracy." Nineteenth-century printers were notorious for mutilating names; inevitably their errors are replicated by researchers. Even with a minimum of errors in the journals being indexed, our typists sometimes fought a losing battle in trying to decipher the script of dozens of researchers. The frequent resort to pseudonyms and initials by nineteenth-century correspondents and idiosyncratic recording of place names made it impossible to verify certain items by turning to other sources.

Generally, we have recorded personal and place names as they appeared in the journals rather than trying to standardize or to modernize them. However strange such spellings as "Porto Rico" and "Mohamet" may appear to contemporary readers, they were acceptable according to nineteenth-century usage. Since we generally recorded names as they appeared in the newspapers and magazines, we have rarely used "*sic*" in our entries.

Occasionally newspapers and magazines committed errors in dating issues and enumerating pages. To indicate such errors, we have normally cited the dates and page numbers as they appeared in the journal and then added the correct information in brackets.

Many of the letters we have annotated covered two or more columns or pages in a journal. Our entries indicate only where each letter begins. Some letters were so long that they were printed in part in one issue of a journal and concluded in another one. We have usually noted when a letter continues from one issue to another.

In a number of cases, correspondents wrote long letters themselves while enclosing other letters which they suggested that an editor also publish. The editors did not always follow such suggestions. Consequently, some of our entries may indicate that a correspondent enclosed a letter while we have no précis of the enclosure.

Nineteenth-century newspapers and magazines were inconsistent in how they defined and treated letters. Letters often appeared in columns labelled "Correspondence," "Exchanges," or with headlines, with and without salutations, and were frequently clipped from other journals. Many editors favored the use of intitials by correspondents while others adopted such typographic practices that it was often difficult to separate letters from signed articles. Whatever the practices of the editors, we tried to err on the side of generosity in our annotation of the newspapers and magazines by adopting a broad definition of what constituted a "letter."

In an effort to ensure as high a degree of accuracy as possible, we first proofread the typescripts against the notecards and secondly against the journals. Systematically proofreading our original entries against the newspapers and magazines, we verified the names of correspondents and places, dates, page and column numbers, and the completeness and adequacy of annotations.

The entries are most reliable and useful as guides to the public letters written by individuals to the newspapers and magazines included in these volumes. Although we were unable to expand all of the cryptic entries, they can still often provide useful clues to the creative researcher. For example, it is frequently the case that entries preceding and following a cryptic one will provide enough detail to shed light on it. Thus, an entry on "nonresistance" might be followed by others indicating correspondents' reactions to a recent meeting of the New England Non-Resistance Society. In other words, those readers interested in specific subjects rather than individuals would be well served by checking those cryptic entries indicating larger categories under which their more limited topic might have been subsumed.

In order to avoid confusion, we should say a word about the index. Different correspondents who used the same initials and pseudonyms or who had identical names are included in the same entries in the index. It was, unfortunately, impossible to separate them with any confidence solely on the basis of data appearing in the journals.

The Black and Reform Newspaper Indexing Project was singularly fortunate in being able to build upon the work done by the staff of the Frederick Douglass Papers project between 1973 and 1977. By the latter date, the Douglass staff had compiled more than 60,000 notecards in the course of their search for Douglass letters and speeches published in nineteenth-century journals. Between 1973 and 1977, Yale undergraduates Donald Woodall, Mitchell Crusto, Wendy Jones, Marcia Finkelstein, James Singleton, Peter Bollier, Bart Steinfeld, Teresa McAlpine, Michelle Anderson, Ruth Good, Devon Miller, Carter Eskew, Marsha Moseley, Joanne Payton, Bruce Piersawl, Brent Raulerson, Kenneth Noble, Judith Hall, Phyllis Eckhaus, Christine Eng, Mark Gallegos, Elizabeth Hillyer, Nan Helm, and Klara Glowczewski set the tone for dedication and accuracy. Patricia Bates of Spelman College and Yale graduate students Harold Cooke, Glenn May, Carla Carr, Julie Jones, Horace Porter, and Barbara Riley also spent part of their summers annotating letters in nineteenth-century journals. In October 1977 the voluminous periodical files of the Douglas staff were turned over to the Black and Reform Newspaper Indexing Project. It was the work of these researchers which created the foundation upon which the Black and Reform Newspaper Indexing Project was built.

We were blessed throughout the life of the Black and Reform Newspaper Indexing Project with a remarkably talented and committed group of researchers. Jennifer Pruett of the University of New Mexico, David Curtis of Harvard University, Joan Reiss of New Haven, and Kurt Kaboth of Yale were the quintessential researchers during the first year of the project. Our Assistants in Research during the latter stages of the project, Amy Mantell, David Barnett, Richard Kramer, Lois Jameson, Carolyn Cott, Diane Peterson, John Caulfield, Joel Cornwell, Roy Nirschel, La Tanya Bailey, Michael Betz, Delgra Childs, and Ronald Matz, proofed, copyedited, and indexed the volumes. Their work substantially improved the accuracy and consistency of the entries. Our undergraduate researchers spent several months helping us to complete the research begun by the Douglass staff. The work of Stephen Schwanauer, Amy Wierczorowski, Maria Celichowski, Neeka Harris, Joseph

Liken, Daryl Warder, Ruth Copeland, Patricia Granger, Eric Koranteng, Peter Eckerstrom, Michael Cutler, Carlos McDade, Peter Borten, Steven Morris, Jefferson Morley, Cephas Ocloo, and Dorothy Trench helped to make the project more comprehensive than it was originally.

We owe special thanks to Dorothy Trench for translating and proofing French-language newspapers and magazines.

Carl Mallard of Philadelphia contributed greatly to the project with his fine reproductions of our photographs of editors.

The penetrating questions raised by the staff of the Research Tools Division of the National Endowment for the Humanities, especially George Farr, Cathy Fuller, and Maben Herring, forced us to entertain alternative perspectives and to examine our priorities in a more systematic fashion than we otherwise would have. We gained much from critiques of the project by Arthur Link of Princeton University and Joel Myerson of the University of South Carolina. Our editors at G.K. Hall encouraged our efforts to make the project comprehensive and utilitarian. Ultimately, they saved us from making many mistakes in design and execution of our research.

Our typists, Eileen Bell, Sharon Adams, Delgra Childs, Robert Reilly, Ruth Krigbaum, Anne Granger, Pamela Y. Price, Fabienne Moore, Katherine Harris, Kim Caron, and Jacqueline Shea did yeoman service in standardizing the entries and maintaining a remarkably high level of accuracy in transcribing thousands of notecards. Janet Giarratano's cheerfulness as she kept track of all of our drafts and addenda and in the face of our impossible demands inspired all of us.

No large-scale newspaper project can achieve even minimal success without the cooperation of thousands of librarians. We gratefully acknowledge all of those who graciously answered our letters seeking information on nineteenth-century journals, suggested unlikely repositories we might contact, and cheered us on by their enthusiasm for our project. Susan Steinberg of the Yale University Library deserves much of the credit for the success of the project. Suggesting research strategies, warning us of pitfalls in our attempts to locate elusive journals, and acquiring many obscure periodicals, Susan was our best critic, friend, and booster.

Because of the large commitment of time and energy which such projects demand, we must give the greatest credit to our friends and families for their patience and understanding in the face of the long hours we had to devote to the Black and Reform Newspaper Indexing Project. We hope that their sacrifice has helped to provide scholars with some clues to the details of history in nineteenth-century abolitionist newspapers and magazines.

JOHN W. BLASSINGAME
MAE G. HENDERSON
JESSICA M. DUNN
*New Haven*
*December 1980*

# List of Symbols

| | |
|---|---|
| **AAS** | American Anti-Slavery Society |
| **ACS** | American Colonization Society |
| **AS** | Anti-Slavery Society |
| **CS** | Colonization Society |
| **n.p.** | no place |
| **n.n.** | no name |
| **n.d.** | no date |
| **(*)** | Whenever printing errors which are not self-correcting result in a repeated page number, an asterisk (*) is placed next to the misleading pagination. The asterisk is used both for a single repeating page number and throughout a series. |

# State Abbreviations

Alabama—Al.
Alaska—Ak.
Arizona—Az.
Arkansas—Ar.
California—Ca.
Colorado—Co.
Connecticut—Ct.
Delaware—De.
Florida—Fl.
Georgia—Ga.
Hawaii—Hi.
Idaho—Id.
Illinois—Il.
Indiana—In.
Iowa—Ia.
Kansas—Ks.
Kentucky—Ky.
Louisiana—La.
Maine—Me.
Maryland—Md.
Massachusetts—Ma.
Michigan—Mi.
Minnesota—Mn.
Mississippi—Ms.
Missouri—Mo.
Montana—Mt.
Nebraska—Ne.
Nevada—Nv.
New Hampshire—N. H.
New Jersey—N. J.
New Mexico—N. M.
New York—N. Y.
North Carolina—N. C.
North Dakota—N. D.
Ohio—Oh.
Oklahoma—Ok.
Oregon—Or.
Pennsylvania—Pa.
Rhode Island—R. I.
South Carolina—S. C.
South Dakota—S. D.
Tennessee—Tn.
Texas—Tx.
Utah—Ut.
Vermont—Vt.
Virginia—Va.
Washington—Wa.
West Virginia—W. V.
Wisconsin—Wi.
Wyoming—Wy.

# **Utica (N.Y.)**
## *Friend of Man*

**Figure 1. William Goodell**

# William Goodell

## [Editor of The *Friend of Man,* 1836-39]

Frederic Goodell and Rhoda Guernsey were married in the fall of 1788, and, sometime after, removed to Coventry, where they lived a pioneer life of great privation and hardship, from the effects of which both died at a comparatively early period.

Of their six sons, William, the third, the subject of this sketch, was born October 25, 1792, in a log house in the woods. Being in delicate health in his early childhood, he was kept much within doors, with his mother, and her scanty library, consisting of the Bible, Watts' Psalms and Hymns, Hart's Hymns, the Methodist Pocket Hymn Book, Bunyan's Pilgrim's Progress, the writings of Mrs. Elizabeth Rowe, Wesley's Sermons, Fletcher's Appeal, and a volume or two of the *Spectator* and *Guardian,* as his early companions. His feebleness and long confinement, during these forming years of his life, fostered his taste for thought and study, and even for composition, which he commenced before he was eight years old; his first efforts being, as was natural under the circumstances, the scribbling of religious verses on bits of bark. Religious impressions were then made, and aspirations kindled which moulded his character for life. His parents were both devoted Christians, and he dated his own conversion from his seventh year. Church privileges were scanty and highly prized in that new settlement; families trudged afoot, or were drawn on ox-sleds, through the woods for miles, to religious meetings held in log school houses or dwellings. Methodist circuits were early established in the neighborhood; a "class" was formed, and joined by Frederic Goodell, who was educated a Presbyterian, and by his wife, who had been a Baptist. This fact indicates little sectarian prejudice on their part. The name of William was soon added. This was the beginning of a "Society" which is still in existence [in 1879], with a church near the Goodell homestead, where still resides Rev. Ezekiel Goodell, a local preacher, the only surviving son of Frederic and Rhoda Goodell. Here, in the dense forests, amid the howling of wolves (where now is heard the carwhistle) were laid, in a degree, the moral foundations of whatever has been of value in the life and labors of William Goodell. . . .

The youthful William early attracted attention for his faculty for "making verses," and his singing; his childish voice being unusually sweet and clear. These gifts earned for him the soubriquet of "nightingale," and were encouraged by his parents and relatives, who united to the practical caste of character which their lives of toil had imparted, a taste for the refinements of intellectual and moral culture.

In his eleventh year came his first great sorrow, the loss of his mother, who died of a slow nervous fever, brought on by toil and privations. A comfortable frame house had succeeded the log hut of her earlier wedded life, but she only entered it to die, at the early age of thirty-seven, leaving five sons surviving her. . . .

In 1804, William was sent to his uncle, John Guernsey, in Amenia, Dutchess County. He was at this time a pale, delicate, thoughtful boy, small for his age, shy, fond of books, studious and industrious. Here he attended the common school, and assisted some in the light labors of the farm. He joined the Methodist "class," though his uncle was a Baptist. A year later, his father sent him to the old Goodell homestead, in Pomfret, Conn., to live with his widowed grandmother Goodell, and several uncles and aunts, her children. Here his father once visited him, during the first year of his stay; and this was the last time he ever saw his father. . . .

William resided in Pomfret nearly five years, attending the common school winters; working on the farm summers, gradually improving in health and strength. Here he attended the Congregational Church, and enjoyed the advantages of two good libraries, the contents of which he eagerly devoured during the long winter evenings. But among his most valued literary and religious privileges he numbered the society of his grandmother, the Hannah Cheney whom we have described as, "one of the strong minded women of her times". . . .

The young William ardently longed for a collegiate education, but in this hope he was disappointed, and at the age of eighteen accepted a mercantile opening in Providence, R. I. Later, he returned to his Pomfret home to teach a winter school; but we soon find him again in Providence, an active, energetic, hopeful young man of twenty, a clerk in a store, an officer among the "cadets," who were training for possible military duty, rendered imminent by the War of 1812; and a boarder in the family of deacon Josiah Cady, with whose blue-eyed daughter of sixteen he found it the most natural thing in the world to walk home from church. About this time we find him writing a breezy, cheerful letter to one of his Connecticut aunts, commencing—

"From the noisy wharves and dusty streets of Providence, to the retired and peaceful valley of Abington, William Goodell sendeth greeting."

With the aunts still living in his old Pomfret home, he kept up a brisk correspondence for those times, and appears to have acted as their agent for the sale of various farm products, and the purchase of household commodities. In 1815 he appears to have been in business for himself, for he speaks of having suffered much loss by the terrible inundations of that year. "The water," he says, "was about four feet deep in my store, and the whole building must have been crushed to atoms, but for two small trees that warded off the ships. I remained in my store as long as possible, securing my goods to the best advantage, and then, with some difficulty, retreated to a building opposite."

In 1816 he writes: "The honorable legislature of Rhode Island convenes in town to-day; a circumstance, the recurrence of which I have learned to dread, as they are in the regular habit of extending the 'benefit of the act of insolvency' to about half of my delinquent customers at every session, not at all to my benefit or convenience."

In December he accepted an offer from Cyrus Butler and E. Carrington & Co., to act as super-cargo of one of their ships, bound to the East Indies, China and the European markets. He accordingly embarked on a sloop at Providence, December 21, and reached New York the 26th; sailing in the *Integrity* from N. Y., January 1, 1817. He returned to America in May, 1819, after a long, but prosperous and instructive voyage. . . .

Returning to Providence in 1819, he entered the counting house of Cyrus Butler, where, with the exception of a winter of commercial life in Wilmington, N. C., he remained until he formed a partnership with William Butler, nephew and prospective heir of Cyrus Butler, and engaged in the flour trade in Alexandria, Va.

On the 4th of July, 1823, the long attachment between himself and Miss Clarissa Cady, of Providence, culminated in marriage, and his first *home*, since that of his early childhood in the forest cabin of N. Y., was made in Alexandria, amid far different scenes; for he was now a successful merchant, and able to surround himself with comforts and luxuries. . . .

In Alexandria was born their first daughter, Clarissa Virginia, who died in infancy. Owing to unexpected fluctuations in trade, the firm of Wm. Butler & Co., for a time successful, lost heavily; and Wm. Goodell returned to Providence. Wm. Butler died young. He was the uncle of Wm. Butler Duncan, the New York banker and capitalist. Soon after Mr. Goodell found employment as book-keeper in the counting house of Phelps & Peck, of New York; the same firm afterwards known as Phelps, Dodge & Co., and later as Wm. E. Dodge & Co. While in New York at this time he aided in forming and conducting the Mercantile Library Association of New York, of which in 1826, he was chosen a Director, an office which he held till his removal from the city.

But Wm. Goodell grew restive over his day book and ledger. To his vision a terrible conflict was being waged between the Hosts of Heaven and the Powers of Darkness, and he longed to plunge into the thickest of the fight. What to him were the daily balancing of profit and loss over paltry bales of cotton, when slavery was creeping stealthily onward, threatening to enchain the nation; when the Drink Demon was slaying its thousands yearly; when lottery gambling was at its height, unrebuked by Church or State; and when fraudulent schemes of banking and insurance institutions, skillfully adapted and notoriously designed to amass fortunes by swindling the people were rife, and predecessors of Tweed and Credit Mobilier operators controlled judges and legislators, till even the Senate of the State of New York, acting as a high Court of Appeal, declared that "a conspiracy to defraud is no indictable offense". . . .

In 1827 he returned to Providence and commenced his weekly "Investigator," determined to lift up a standard against the tide of demoralization. This was at about the same time that Arthur Tappan, afterwards his co-laborer, started the *Journal of Commerce*, in New York, with the same end in view. Here it was, at the age of thirty-five, that William Goodell, ever after dated the commencement of his life-work. Writing of it, years afterward, he said:

"All my previous life was preparatory to this. When providentially debarred from acquiring a Collegiate education, I had cheerfully acquiesced, trusting that my life and destiny were under the oversight and direction of a wisdom high above my own. When and how this should appear I could not foresee. It might be by the early acquisition of means sufficient to carry me through College, or it might be by the accumulation of ample wealth, which, contributed to religious and benevolent enterprises, then just coming into existence, might effect more good than I could expect to accomplish by learning. These dreams were dispelled. Evidently I was not destined to be rich. What good could I, then, do in the world? Was there not much needing to be done, which colleges, with all their important uses and benefits, could not do; which the college-learned in Church and State, with all their indispensable services, had scarcely, or rarely, thought of attempting? Nothing that needed processes of education widely diverse from those with which they were familiar? Had I received no educational training for a much needed work? For seventeen years I had been mingling in the busy scenes of active life, where men are ever acting out themselves, and betraying the moral or immoral maxims by which they are really governed. In America, in Europe, and in Asia, the map of commercial life, usages, and maxims had passed under my inspection. Intellectually, if I had lost much that is taught in colleges, I had gained much that is not taught in them; nautical astronomy; theoretical and practical navigation, and seamanship; and, in the counting house, finances, accountancy by double entry, in itself a science comparable, for mental training, with most of the demonstrative sciences. Long sea passages of ninety to over one hundred days each, had afforded me enviable opportunities, not unimproved, for miscellaneous reading, and secluded meditation and study; in which the pen was not idle."

Nor, from this date, was his pen ever idle till he dropped it over an unfinished article in his eighty-sixth year, just one week before he breathed his last. . . .

The *Investigator* drifted so largely into temperance work that in 1829 it was removed to Boston and connected with the "National Philanthropist." Here Mr. Goodell attended the preaching of Dr. Lyman Beecher, then in his prime. A year later his paper was again removed to New York, where it was continued under the name of the "Genius of Temperance." As is usual with all papers of which the first aim is a moral and not a financial one, this periodical had a hard struggle for existence. Again and again its indefatigable editor was forced into the lecture field to awaken or keep alive the popular interest in the reforms advocated, and obtain subscribers, and donations, to keep it afloat. Bitterly disappointed, at times, in the apathy of professed Christian men from whom he had a right to expect aid and sympathy, he was well nigh despairing, but never *quite* willing to give up. To one who hinted that he was in danger of neglecting his family, in his zeal for the public good, he wrote: "I know I have a duty to my family and friends, as well as to my country; and that there may be danger of my neglecting the former in my zeal for the latter. But the question is how I shall better discharge my duty to my family and friends, and to myself by relinquishing this business? Providence, indeed, seems to have closed up every other avenue—to have thwarted me on every other course, and to have driven me and confined me to this work, which has been pent up as a fire in my bones for a quarter of a century. Jonah declined his embassy and fled to Tarshish, but the winds and the waves, and the monsters of the deep, saw well to it that he returned and accomplished his task. And the winds and the waves of adversity, since September 1815, have been against me. Not *once* to Tarshish, but *twice* to utmost India, (4,000 miles beyond Tarshish) have I vainly fled. And if the gourd which has sheltered my head while delivering my message, and watching the results, should wither and leave me defenseless, I ought not to murmur, nor to pray that Nineveh may be spared, though she ill requites my labors, and quotes her impunity to proclaim me a false alarmist for warning her.*** I rejoice to know that my last year's labor has *not* been in vain, though the unworthy instrument should be thrown aside, either in mercy or in judgment to this people. I have prayed—'send, Lord, by *whom* thou wilt send, yet command deliverances for Jacob;' and I have stayed myself on the promise—'Trust in the Lord and do good; so shalt thou dwell in the land; yea, verily, thou shalt be fed.' 'Though there be no herd in the stall, and the flock be cut off from the fold,' yea, 'though He slay me, yet will I trust in Him.'*** For the sake of my wife and child, and friends, I will do what will add to their comfort, if I can know what it is. But for myself, 'I count not my life dear unto me,' so that I can 'fulfill as an hireling my day.' There will be rest enough in the grave. And 'what mean ye to weep and to break my heart, for I am ready not only to labor and suffer perplexity and want, but indeed to wear my life out' in this cause, if I may be instrumental in saving my country."

Six years of severe labor in the city of New York followed, including the terrible cholera summer of 1832, when William Goodell was of the few who did not leave the city, but sending his family to a place of safety, boarded at the Graham boarding house, and toiled early and late in his editorial office, scarcely stopping to eat his meals, but munching his Graham crackers while his pen sped rapidly over his paper, warning the people against the terrible effects of liquor drinking, especially at that trying time. Nor were intemperance and slavery the only vices assailed. Lottery gambling, masonry, political corruption and immorality were severely attacked by his active pen. The new movement for "moral reform," inaugurated by Rev. J. R. McDowall, and opposed—incredible as it may seem—not only by the ignorant or indifferent multitude, but by a majority of professing Christians, was warmly espoused by him. The movement of McDowall, briefly explained, was this; the reformation of fallen women, a severer condemnation of vice in men, placing the sin in either sex upon the same moral plane, and labor for the eradication of the social evil. The persecutions of the devoted and self-denying McDowall in the inauguration of this new reform would hardly be accredited if told to-day. Mr. Goodell not only warmly defended him, and heartily espoused his cause, but besides advocating his principles in the "Genius of Temperance," published for two years a small semi-monthly paper, the "Female Advocate," of which moral reform, as well as temperance, was an important feature. He also published during a portion of this time, the "Youth's Temperance Lecturer," probably the first child's temperance paper ever published.

It was at this time that Mr. Goodell, together with Lewis and Arthur Tappan, and other temperance reformers, became interested in the lectures of Sylvester Graham, and partially followed his teachings, giving up tea and coffee, meats, and high seasoning, and using the unbolted (or Graham) flour bread. They boarded for a considerable time at the Graham boarding house kept by Mrs. Nicholson, at which Horace Greeley, then a bashful young man, saying little or nothing, imbibed anti-slavery principles from the conversation of those around him at the table. Mr. Goodell adhered to the simple diet adopted at this time, through life, excepting that he never strictly abstained from meats.

More and more the question of slavery loomed up, overshadowing every other. In December, 1833, the American Anti-Slavery Society was formed in Philadelphia. Mr. Goodell attended, and assisted in organizing it. In 1834, the "Genius of Temperance" was succeeded by the "Emancipator," of which, as its name indicated, opposition to slavery was the leading feature. At this time the feeling on both sides of the slavery question was at a white heat. Abolitionists were persecuted, mobbed, their lives threatened, and their names cast out as evil.

Mr. Goodell was at one time obliged to leave his home in Brooklyn, with his family, and seek shelter in an obscure locality of New York, till the fury of the mob-oligarchy had spent itself; at another time he barely escaped the grasp of an incoming mob, who clamorously offered a price for his head, as they put to rout an anti-slavery meeting being quietly held in a public hall in New York. In 1836, the Legislatures of several of the Southern States sent communications to the northern Legislatures, desiring them to enact laws, prohibiting the formation of anti-slavery societies, or the expression of anti-slavery sentiments, under severe penalties. The governor of Massachusetts, in his inaugural address, took occasion to severely censure the abolitionists, intimating that they were guilty of an offense punishable at common law. In view of these facts, the Massachusetts anti-slavery society requested a hearing before the Legislature, which was granted. Mr. Goodell was one of the speakers on this occasion, and the red-hot-lava of his indignation poured forth in a torrent of burning logic and fiery eloquence, under which the Legislative Committee, to whom the question had been referred, sat uneasily, till he characterized the communications of the Southern States as "fetters for nothern freemen;" and turning to the chairman of the committee, demanded—"Sir: Are you prepared to attempt putting them on?" when he was peremptorily ordered to sit down, and no further hearing was allowed. Writing almost night and day, Mr. Goodell was able, three days later, to put the plea of abolitionists, in pamphlet form, into the hands of every member of the Legislature, and to circulate it broadcast through the country. The Legislature took no action on the subject.

But it is impossible, in these few brief pages, to give any adequate idea of the severe labors of Mr. Goodell in this exciting moral warfare. We must pass on.

In 1836 he was strongly urged, by the Executive Committee of the N.Y. State Anti-Slavery Society, and personally by Alvan Stewart, Beriah Green, and Theodore D. Weld, to come to Utica and take charge of a weekly anti-slavery paper to be called "The Friend of Man." This offer he accepted, and edited "The Friend of Man" in Utica and Whitesboro, six years. Here also he issued his monthly "Anti-Slavery Lecturer" for one year, and commenced his "Christian Investigator" for discussing the religious and ecclesiastical questions involved in the moral struggles before the country. During these years he labored by voice as well as pen; frequently making lecturing tours through New York and the New England States. Nor were his labors confined to the enunciation of general principles. He took a sympathetic *personal interest* in the humblest being who needed his help. His home was not only open to the intellectual, the cultured, and the philanthropic, but to the ragged fugitive slave hiding from his pursuers; or the robbed and bewildered traveler without money, friends, or credit. The outcast, the suffering, even the *sinning*, but repentant, found a friend in him.

He bore a prominent part in the formation of the Liberty Party in Albany in the spring of 1840, a party which the year of its formation polled 7,000 votes for James G. Birney for President, and four years later gave the same candidate 60,000 votes, which later lowered its standard and became the "Free-Soil," and finally the Republican Party.

During the winter of 1843, he lectured on Church reform, endeavoring to induce churches in complicity with slavery to take action against it, and advocating other reforms in church organizations. A convention was held in Whitesboro to consider the duty of the churches in relation to slavery. Two delegates attended from Honeoye, Ontario County, who brought with them a cordial and pressing invitation to Mr. Goodell to take up his abode with them, and found a church upon the basis of the principles he advocated. This he decided to do, and when past his fiftieth year entered upon his labors as a minister, without seeking or desiring human ordination, and rejecting to the last all titles indicative of the profession. His church was organized on temperance, anti-slavery, and church union principles, and was composed of seceders from the Presbyterian and Methodist churches of the town of Richmond. Later it received further accessions by profession of faith. Among the distinctive features of this church was the fact that its members subscribed to no creed but the Bible, and that the afternoon service was devoted to a discussion of the subject of the morning's discourse, in which every variety of honest conviction was allowed free expression, and which proved a wonderful stimulus to thought. In these meetings there was "neither bond nor free, male nor female". . . .

During his residence in Honeoye, Mr. Goodell made frequent short lecturing tours through neighboring towns and counties; sometimes speaking every evening during the week. He occasionally went further, attending conventions at a distance. In 1846 he bore a prominent part in forming the American Missionary Association, at Albany, and wrote the "Address" issued by the Convention there assembled, which Wm. W. Patton, D.D., has since characterized as "full of seed-thoughts on every part of the Missionary work." It was about this time that he wrote his argument on the unconstitutionality of slavery, writing in the heat of summer, in feeble health, sitting at the bedside of a sick child, whom he fanned, or soothed, with one hand, while he wrote with the other. The argument has been pronounced unanswerable by some of the best minds in the country. For the purpose of writing on the legal aspect of the slavery question, he read elementary law works carefully, till he became so well versed in the science, that he was urged to apply for admission to the bar, being assured that there would be no difficulty in securing admission. But he cared too little for the empty honor to make the attempt.

It was during his residence in Honeoye that he wrote his "Democracy of Christianity," in two volumes; his history of "Slavery and Anti-Slavery," in the United States, and his "American Slave Code," which described the tenor and effects of the slavery legislation of the South.

In 1851 he made a lecturing tour through the Western States as far as Chicago.

In 1852 he went to New York to attend to the publication of his books, and was induced by friends to remain there permanently and edit an anti-slavery paper. This seemed the *then* most needed work, as the aggressions of slavery, by the repeal of the Missouri compromise, were threatening to inundate the entire country. He edited a monthly paper entitled the "Radical Abolitionist," in which he advocated the ability, duty, and necessity of the Federal Government to abolish slavery in the Southern States. He also wrote a series of able and masterly articles on the "Legal Tenure of Slavery," for the *National Era,* in which he showed conclusively that slavery, being contrary to the common law, and never legalized by statutory enactment in this country, (though statutes had been enacted recognizing and upholding it) was absolutely illegal, as well as unconstitutional. His paper was, after a time, enlarged, converted into a weekly, and called the "Principia," Dr. Geo. B. Cheever being, during a portion of the time, his associate in editorial labor. This paper was continued during the war, and until after the abolition of slavery, for which object it earnestly and unceasingly labored. The evening before the issuing of the Emancipation Proclamation, Mr. Goodell, Dr. Cheever, and Dr. Brown of New York were with President Lincoln until midnight, urging the measure upon him, lest, as some feared, his resolution might falter. They went to him with the fervor and enthusiasm, one might almost say with the *inspiration* of the Old Testament prophets; and a "Thus saith the Lord," rang through all their utterances, till the President remarked, with the dry humor for which he was distinguished, "Really, gentlemen, this is the first time that I ever had the honor of being waited on by a delegation from the Lord!" Mr. Goodell quickly responded, "President Lincoln, believest thou the prophets? I know that thou believest!" and proceeded to quote passage after passage of the Old Testament denunciations of oppression, and commands to let the oppressed go free, to execute justice, and to show mercy. He afterwards had the satisfaction of seeing some of his own expressions embodied in the Proclamation, which was issued the next day at noon.

During his residence in New York, or rather in the eastern district of Brooklyn, where his home was situated, he was a member of a small Congregational Church of radical anti-slavery and temperance principles, of which Rev. S.S. Jocelyn, of the American Missionary Association, was pastor. He preached frequently, though not statedly, in this and other pulpits; at one time supplying the pulpit of Dr. Cheever, during his absence. He made occasional lecturing tours through New York and New England; one of marked success through Vermont, in 1858, under the leadership of Governor Fletcher of that State.

In the spring of 1865 he removed, in feeble health, to the town of Lebanon, in Connecticut, where he and his wife boarded in the family of a relative. Here the fresh country air and farm living, together with the quiet and freedom from care, restored him to vigorous health, for a man of his years. He had ever been an ardent lover of nature, and greatly enjoyed his long country rambles, gathering berries and wild flowers, and very probably composing, as he strolled along, the article which he dashed off so rapidly on his return. For he did not drop his pen with abolition of slavery, but wielded it vigorously in favor of total abstinence and prohibition, woman suffrage, and religion. During his five years residence in Connecticut he was a frequent contributor to the *National Temperance Advocate,* and many other temperance and some local papers; also to the Hartford *Religious Herald,* the "Panoplist" of Boston, and "Good News" of New York.

He also wrote a theological work entitled "The Highest Good;" re-wrote and enlarged the poem of his youth, "The Christian Warfare;" and commenced a work on the "Life and Teachings of Christ." He filled the pulpit of the Congregational Church at Bozrahville for more than a year, and was a frequent supply in other pulpits. He attended various temperance conventions at easy distances, in which he participated; and in September, 1869, went to Chicago, by pressing invitation of prominent temperance workers, where he aided in forming the National Prohibition Party.

In June 1870, he removed, with his wife, to Janesville, Wisconsin, where his daughter, Mrs. Frost, resided; and where he was joined in the fall of 1871, by his younger daughter. Here he took great pleasure in the society of his daughters and grandsons, and entered as heartily into the passing events of the city and State, as in his younger days in the East; frequently attending conventions and ministers' meetings in different localities. He was a constant attendant of the Y. M. C. A. morning prayer meetings, through summer's heat and winter's cold, frequently leading the meetings. He occasionally supplied the Congregational pulpit, and spoke at public temperance and religious meetings. Here he finished his voluminous work on the *Life and Teachings of Christ,* and wrote a prize essay on the social aspect of the temperance question. He wrote for the local papers, and continued his contributions to temperance and religious journals; besides contributing occasional articles to the literary clubs of Janesville. . . .

He attended the re-union of Abolitionists in Chicago, in June, 1874, and participated in the proceedings; but came home quite fatigued from the exertion and excitement, and never left Janesville again. His mind remained active to the last, and he continued to write for the press to within a week of his death, being engaged in a series of articles on the history and results of the Maine law, which he had nearly completed. He was interested in every new reform, and ever hopeful for the future, having a firm faith in the coming of that day when "the kingdoms of this world shall become the kingdoms of our Lord and of his Christ." The proper treatment of the Indian and the Chinese, the questions of prison reform, and of peace and international arbitration, of free-trade, and civil service reform, all received his hearty interest and sympathy. . . .

It can be truly said of William Goodell that he "lived as seeing Him who is invisible." His character was all that might be inferred from his writings, *and more.* Of rare and wonderful elevation and purity of thought and motive, high purpose, undaunted courage, unwavering faith in the Infinite Goodness, he was an inspiration to all who knew him and were capable of understanding and appreciating his character. No public man was ever less actuated by ambition, or any form of self-seeking, than he. Modest, almost to diffidence, yet fearless in battling for the Right; strong, yet tender; his character bore the scrutiny of familiar and long continued intimacy, and those who knew him best loved and admired him most. As a reformer, he was radical, and in advance of the thought of the masses; he was pre-eminently a leader of thought. He taught the necessity of total abstinence at a time when moderate drinking was considered good temperance doctrine; and was among the first to advocate prohibitory legislation. He was among the earliest, if not the very earliest, to advance the theory of the right and duty of the Federal Government to abolish slavery in the States, and to claim that slavery was both illegal and unconstitutional, that its speedy abolition was intended by the framers of the Constitution, and was authorized by the words, "Congress shall guarantee to every State in the Union a republican form of Government." These theories he argued in the works which we have already named, and which were read and privately concurred in by such men as Charles Sumner, S. P. Chase, and Abraham Lincoln. In this view he differed from Wm. Lloyd Garrison and Wendell Phillips, his early co-laborers, who, regarding the Federal Constitution as pro-slavery, denounced it as a "covenant with death and an agreement with hell," and advocated a dissolution of the Union as the only consistent course for conscientious northerners opposed to slavery. His co-adjutors in the work of advocating the abolition of slavery by the Federal Government, under the Constitution, were Gerrit Smith, Alvan Stewart, Beriah Green, Arthur and Lewis Tappan, and their associates. Yet while differing with abolitionists of the Garrisonian school in methods, his personal friendship with them continued through life.

He was a courageous leader, a tender friend, a devoted Christian. Those who knew him were made better and happier, the world was made richer, for his life.

*"In Memoriam, William Goodell"* (Chicago: Guilbert and Winchell, 1879).

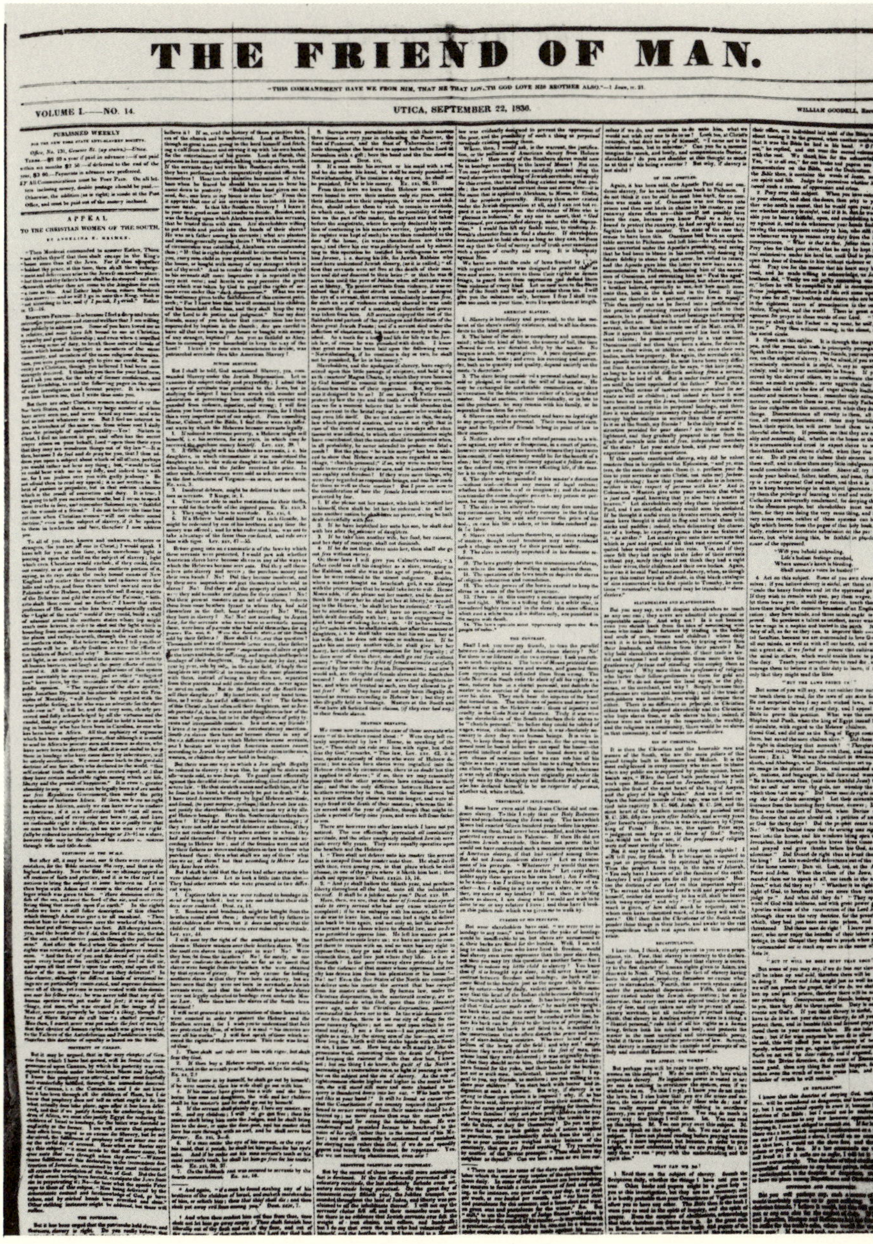

# THE FRIEND OF MAN.

"THIS COMMANDMENT HAVE WE FROM HIM, THAT HE THAT LOVETH GOD LOVE HIS BROTHER ALSO."—1 John, iv. 21.

VOLUME I.—NO. 14. UTICA, SEPTEMBER 22, 1836. WILLIAM GOODELL, Editor.

PUBLISHED WEEKLY

APPEAL TO THE CHRISTIAN WOMEN OF THE SOUTH.

BY ANGELINA E. GRIMKE.

**Figure 2**

# Journal Data

TITLE: The *Friend of Man* (23 June 1836–11 January 1842)

MOTTO: "This Commandment have we from Him, that He that loveth God love his Brother also"

INCLUSIVE DATES OF PUBLICATION: 23 June 1836–11 January 1842

PLACE OF PUBLICATION: Utica, New York

SUPERSEDES: *Standard and Democrat*

SUPERSEDED BY: *Liberty Press* (1843–1849)

FREQUENCY OF PUBLICATION: Weekly

DAY OF WEEK PUBLISHED: not indicated (23 June 1836–8 February 1837); Wednesday (15 February 1837–24 July 1839); Tuesday (9 November 1841–11 January 1842)

AVERAGE NUMBER OF PAGES PER ISSUE: 4

NUMBER OF COLUMNS PER PAGE: 6–7

EDITORS: William Goodell (23 June 1836–24 July 1839); Stanley Hough (by 9 November 1841–11 January 1842)

PUBLISHERS: J. P. Bishop (19 April 1837–22 March 1838); W. C. Rogers (by 17 October 1838–24 July 1839); Wm. J. Savage (by 9 November 1841–11 January 1842)

FEATURES: letters; editorials; local, national and foreign news; poetry; advertisements

PRICE PER ANNUM: $2.00

LANGUAGE: English

PERSPECTIVE: Abolitionist; published for the New York State Anti-Slavery Society

REPOSITORY: Cornell University. 23 June 1836–11 January 1842.

# Prospectus

Ever since God created man in his own image, his fundamental law has required every man to regard every other man as his equal, and love him as he loves his own soul. And ever since Cain sought the favor of his Maker by a pretended worship, without love to his brother, the progeny of Cain have dreamed themselves religious, while saying in their hearts, "Am I my brother's keeper?"

The second table engraved by the finger of God on Sinai, contained a solemn re-enactment of that original law; a decisive testimony against such selfish and spurious religion. Century after century holy men were inspired to tune the harp of melody and sweep the lyre of prophecy, in unison with the statutes of righteousness. Of their testimony, the fiftieth Psalm, with the first and fifty-eighth chapters of Isaiah, may be adduced as incidental, yet glowing specimens. But the religion of Cain had corrupted and well nigh displaced the religion of the law and the prophets, when Jesus Christ himself appeared among men to "magnify and make honorable" its requirements. For this cause his Sermon on the Mount unfolded its long forgotten principles, and vindicated from perversion its oft misconstrued enactments. For this cause he "went about doing good" to the bodies as well as the souls of men, that his followers might imitate his example. For this cause he put forth the parable of the good Samaritan, which teaches us to be neighbor to him who is fallen among thieves. For this cause he tested the religion of the rich young man, who imagined he had "kept" the law "from his youth up" by a requirement which sent him "away sorrowful." For this cause he drove the extortioners, as thieves, with a scourge of cords, from the house of prayer. For this cause he denounced woes upon the orthodox and high professing Scribes and Pharisees, whose hypocrisy was attested by their oppressions. For this cause he announced his fixed determination to distribute the awards of the last Judgment upon the principle of considering the good or ill treatment of one of the least of his earthly brethren to be virtually the treatment of his own person.

Christianity, while it remained such, was emphatically the *Friend of Man*. It could only become otherwise by a corruption which should extinguish its vital principle of equality and impartial love. The mystery of Iniquity began early to work. The Apostles themselves were "in perils among false brethren," who "loved to have the preeminence," and "lord it over God's heritage." In this spirit was revealed the *Man of Sin* who exalted himself above all that is called God. Christianity degraded became the ally of despotism. Tyranny dreaded the light that shone upon its own deformity, and deemed it unsafe to entrust to the injured poor the privilege of reading the Bible that condemned their own grievous wrongs!

This was the slumber of "the dark ages." Luther illumined its dungeons with a few gleams of day light. But we live in an age in which Protestants—so called—are redoubling its horrors, and becoming clamorous for the perpetuity of its darkness. In our own country, (so boastful of its liberties) they not only withhold the Bible from their brethren, but claim, and hold, and buy, and sell their souls and bodies as goods and "chattels personal." They "forbid to marry," and put asunder whom God hath joined together. They expunge, not the second merely, but every command of the Decalogue, particularly the first, the fifth, the seventh, and the eighth. They effectually say to their brother, "thou shalt have no other God before thy earthly master." They annul the law of obedience to the parent and of instruction to the child. They declare the wife and husband "not entitled to the conditions of matrimony." They sanctify and legalize "the highest kind of theft," the robbery of the labor of a whole life—the person of the laborer himself. They extort, not the unwilling tithe of the reaper's toil, but the hire itself, and the reaper with his hire! They "use their neighbor's service without wages, and give him not for his work." They judge not the cause of the widow, neither doth the cry of the needy come before them.

Such, to an alarming extent, is the religion of the nineteenth century, in America—a religion which claims to be the religion of Protestants, and of the Bible! It prates of the horrors of the inquisition, and erects gibbets for the defenders of the truth—the advocates of the poor! It builds the tombs of the reformers, and accounts it insanity and treason to ask for the oppressed American the occupancy of so elevated a condition as that *from* whose degradation it was the labor of the Reformers to redeem the benighted peasantry of Europe!

A remonstrance has been raised against these accumulated wrongs; a rebuke has been uttered against these unparalleled sins. Satan is roused from his seat, and wages war against the throne of God and of the Lamb.—Lawless violence has been wielded by the boasted guardians of the law. The National Constitution has been trampled in the dust, under the plea of preserving the Constitution. The bands of society have been severed under the pretext of preventing disunion. The contemners of law have been clamorous for despotic legislation. A corrupted christianity looks complacently on, and cautions the transgressor, not against his sin, but against its *too sudden abandonment*! Its anathemas, so charitably withheld from *iniquity,* are thundered fiercely upon the heads of its reprovers. Instead of calling to her children in the confines of Babylon,—"Come out of her, my people, that ye partake not her sins, and that ye receive not her plagues,"—she is heard proclaiming that all who 'in any way impair her powers,' are justly liable to the highest civil penalties and ecclesiastical censures."

Such is the crisis in which it is proposed to publish, in the heart of our "empire state," a weekly paper to be called "THE FRIEND OF MAN." Its object will be to maintain the equality and inalienable rights of all men:—To plead for the down trodden slave:—To support republican freedom:—To assert and *exercise* the right of free discussion—the right to investigate *truth*,—to proclaim and practice duty. In doing this it will seek to restore and promote *the religion of the Bible*—the religion of supreme love to God, the Father of all men, and of equal and impartial love to all his offspring, without respect of persons.

The promotion of "pure and undefiled religion" as defined by the apostle James, we propose as the beginning and the ending, the means and the object of our labors. Men will never "walk humbly with God" while they walk arrogantly towards man. "If a man love not his brother which he hath seen, how can he love God, whom he hath not seen?" When the solemnity of man's inalienable rights are duly appreciated, then, and not until then, will men begin to conceive the nature and magnitude of his claims in whose sight the nations of the earth are as the small dust of the balance.

Our labors, therefore, will not be confined to the subject of SLAVERY. INTEMPERANCE, GAMING AND WAR are giant enemies of our race, closely allied to slavery, and demanding the ceaseless opposition of the *Friend of Man*.—Violence will oppress men, so long as men avenge themselves by violence. The dishonesty that covets wealth without earning it, and seeks gain without an equivalent, is the same principle that fattens upon the unrequited labor of the slave. And so long as our rulers "drink wine, and our princes strong drink," so long will they "forget the law, and pervert the judgment of the afflicted." There is no escape from slavery, but by the freedom of virtue—no charter of human liberty, but the law of the Creator.

"THE FRIEND OF MAN," by seeking to cultivate and extend the religion of holy love and of the Bible, may hope, in some good measure, to escape the trammels of narrow bigotry; avoiding at the same time, the spurious liberality that deems it heavenly charity to shake hands with sin. By supporting the principles of liberty and the practices of righteousness—by rebuking lordly iniquity in high places—by thwarting the selfish purposes of partizan rivals of every name, we may hope to escape the polluting infection of party politics, and (while seeking to secure the liberties of the people) afford some guarantee that we will not become the tools of demagogues or of men in power.

Our departments of religious and secular intelligence, and miscellaneous reading selections, will receive constant attention, and vary in extent, from time to time, according to the amount of interesting matter afloat, and according to the wants and exigencies of the great cause in which we chiefly labor.

*Friend of Man*,
23 June 1836, p.1, c1.

## [1836]

1 **H. ELMER** *to* **MR. WILLIAM GOODELL. 21 June 1836. Oneida Institute.** Reports the establishment of the Missionary Band of Oneida Institute. 23 June 1836. p.2, c2.

2 **BERIAH GREEN** *to* **THE EDITOR OF THE** ***FRIEND OF MAN*** **[WILLIAM GOODELL]. n.d. n.p.** Stresses importance of influence of the Gospel on abolitionists; commends the principles of *Friend of Man.* 23 June 1836. p.2, c2.

3 **n.n.** *to* **n.n. [extract from the** ***Journal of Commerce*****] 27 May 1836. Near Palmyra.** Recounts the argument between Colonel Muldino and Dr. Bosley. 23 June 1836. p.3, c1.

4 **A. C. GARRATT** *to* **BROTHER LEAVITT. 21 May 1836. Quincy, Il.** Discusses violent opposition to abolitionists in Marion County, Missouri, and to prospective colored students at Marion College. 23 June 1836. p.3, c2.

5 **THEODORE D. WELD** *to* **BROTHER POTTER. [from the** ***Pawtucket Record*****] 11 June 1836. Troy.** Reports disturbance in Troy resulting from lecture on slavery and emancipation delivered by Theodore Weld. 23 June 1836. p.3, c4.

6 **BERIAH GREEN** *to* **SIR. n.d. n.p.** Responds to a request for suggestions concerning the responsibility of the ministry towards slavery by forwarding a letter written to a minister. 30 June 1836. p.6, c5.

7 **BERIAH GREEN** *to* **REV. AND DEAR SIR. n.d. n.p.** Explains why it is a minister's duty to preach against slavery. 30 June 1836. p.6, c5.

8 **GEORGE THOMPSON** *to* **MR. GARRISON. [extract from the** ***Boston Liberator*****] 13 April. Glasgow.** Provides account of his recent travels in England, where he delivered speeches advocating abolition and temperance. 7 July 1836. p.9, c5.

9 **GEORGE THOMPSON** *to* **MR. HENRY E. BENSON. [extract from the** ***Boston Liberator*****] 29 April. Glasgow.** Notes the favorable reception of his report before the Committee for the British and Foreign AS; reports on his meeting with Dr. Cox. 7 July 1836. p.9, c6.

10 **WM. D. LUSHER** *to* **MESSRS. CHESTER AND BARNES. [from the** ***Cincinnati Journal and Luminary*** **] 19 May 1835. Pontotoc, Ms.** Refuses to accept future editions of the *Cincinnati Journal and Luminary* because of its pronounced abolitionist viewpoint. 7 July 1836. p.11, c3.

11 **NATHAN SMITH AND CALVIN G. MUNGER** *to* **MESSRS. BARBER AND JEWETT. [from the** ***Free Press*****] 4 June 1836. Monkton.** Denounce slavery as sinful; submit resolutions adopted by the Shelburn Circuit Quarterly Conference of the Church. 21 July 1836. p.17, c3.

12 **BERIAH GREEN** *to* **MR. S. E. MORSE, EDITOR OF THE** ***NEW YORK OBSERVER*****. July 1836. Whitesboro'.** Notes that the views expressed at the recent AAS anniversary were no different than "those which have always prevailed in the North." 21 July 1836. p.17, c5.

13 **SENEX** *to* **MR. EDITOR [WILLIAM GOODELL]. n.d. n.p.** Discusses the meaning of liberty; argues that slavery is a sin. 21 July 1836. p.18, c1.

14 **IMPARTIAL JUSTICE** *to* **MR. EDITOR [WILLIAM GOODELL]. n.d. n.p.** Stresses the supremacy of the law and the need for an impartial judiciary process to respond to the recent violence in Oneida County. 21 July 1836. p.18, c1.

**15 GEO. STORRS** *to* **MR. KIMBALL. [from the** *Herald of Freedom***] 1 July 1836. Newbury, Vt.** Reports on the trial and conviction of those who disrupted his anti-slavery speech in November. 21 July 1836. p.18, c3.

**16 PETER SNYDER AND GEO. L. LEROW** *to* **BROTHER GOODELL. 12 July 1836. Union College, Schenectady.** Report the establishment of an auxiliary chapter to the New York State AS; forward the preamble and constitution. 21 July 1836. p.19, c1.

**17 S. J. MAY** *to* **BROTHER PHELPS. 4 July 1836. Brooklyn.** Details proceedings of the meeting held on 4 July to discuss the deplorable condition of slaves in America. 21 July 1836. p.19, c2.

**18 GENERAL THOMSON** *to* **GENERAL CALL. [from the** *Cleveland Whig***] 27 April 1835. Seminole Agency.** Opposes granting permission to friends of General Call to purchase Negroes from the Seminole Indians. 21 July 1836. p.19, c2.

**19 GENERAL THOMSON** *to* **GENERAL CALL. [from the** *Cleveland Whig***] 17 June 1835. Seminole Agency.** Criticizes the decision of the department to remove the Indians and allow General Call to purchase the Negroes. 21 July 1836. p.19, c2.

**20 WM. APES** *to* **MR. GARRISON. [from the** *Liberator***] n.d. n.p.** Encloses notice of a camp meeting in Marshpee, to be inserted in the *Liberator*. 21 July 1836. p.19, c4.

**21 DAVID G. BURNET** *to* **JEREMIAH BROWN, ESQ., COMMANDER OF SCHOONER** *INVINCIBLE*. **[from the** *New Orleans Commercial Bulletin***] 20 June 1836. Velasco.** Requests that he sail to Vera Cruz to meet the Mexicans and await further orders. 21 July 1836. p.19, c5.

**22 n.n.** *to* **THE REV. ---. June 1836. Oneida County, N.Y.** Considers him hypocritical in recognizing slavery as a sin yet censuring expressions of such opinions in sermons. 28 July 1836. p.21, c2.

**23 G. W. M'ELROY** *to* **MR. EDITOR. [from the** *Emancipator***] 10 June 1836. n.p.** Refutes the paper's charge that the New York and Kentucky CSs resort to forcible removal of emigrants. 28 July 1836. p.21, c5.

**24 FRANKLIN** *to* **MR. EDITOR. [WILLIAM GOODELL]. n.d. n.p.** Argues that a postmaster should be elected, rather than appointed, to his position. 28 July 1836. p.22, c3.

**25 S. H. ADDINGTON** *to* **MR. EDITOR [WILLIAM GOODELL]. 23 July 1836. Utica, N.Y.** Forwards resolutions adopted by the grand jury of Oneida County regarding recent mob violence, in reply to a letter from "Impartial Justice." 28 July 1836. p.22, c3.

**26 A LOVER OF HIS COUNTRY** *to* **THE EDITOR [WILLIAM GOODELL]. n.d. [Norway].** Reports the death of Alexander Corp from gunshot wounds received during a Fourth of July celebration; condemns the violence of such celebrations. 28 July 1836. p.22, c3.

**27 JOHN WESLEY** *to* **MR. WILBERFORCE. [extract] 26 February 1791. n.p.** Declares his determination to see slavery banished from America. 28 July 1836. p.22, c6.

**28 SAMUEL HOUSTON** *to* **GENERAL R. G. DUNLAP, NASHVILLE, TN. 3 July 1836. Near Sabine.** Discusses the role of the United States in the war between Texas and Mexico. 28 July 1836. p.23, c3.

**29 n.n.** *to* **n.n. [extract from the** *United States Gazette***] n.d. n.p.** Discusses debates in the French Chamber of Deputies concerning emancipation of West Indies Negroes. 28 July 1836. p.23, c5.

**30 n.n.** *to* **n.n. [extract] 11 July 1836. Fort Heileman (Black Creek).** Reports progress in battle against the Indians. 28 July 1836. p.23, c5.

**31 n.n.** *to* **THE EDITORS. [extract from the** *National Intelligencer*] **30 June 1836. Natchitoches.** Informs that the Mexicans are approaching the border and that General Gaines is considering an invasion of Nacogdoches. 11 August 1836. p.29, c4.

**32 Q. IN THE CORNER** *to* **MR. EDITOR. [from the** *Union Village Banner*] **n.d. n.p.** Asks whether by forbidding one action he sanctions another equally dangerous action. 11 August 1836. p.29, c5.

**33 n.n.** *to* **MR. EDITOR [WILLIAM GOODELL]. n.d. n.p.** Encloses extracts from the preamble and resolutions adopted during a public meeting in Clinton, Mississippi, expressing hostility to the abolitionist cause. 11 August 1836. p.29, c5.

**34 MR. GURLEY** *to* **n.n. [extract] 27 May 1836. New Orleans.** Observes the favorable attitude toward African colonization in Mississippi, Alabama and Louisiana. 11 August 1836. p.29, c5.

**35 T. T. BRADFORD AND H. S. REDFIELD** *to* **MR. GOODELL. 30 July 1836. Auburn.** Report the resolutions of the AS of the Auburn Theological Seminary. 11 August 1836. p.30, c3.

**36 CHAUNCEY D. GOODRICH** *to* **EDITOR [WILLIAM GOODELL]. 25 July 1836. Fly Creek, Otsego County, N.Y.** Forwards resolutions adopted by the Otsego County AS at its first annual meeting. 11 August 1836. p.31, c4.

**37 SECRETARY OF WAR [LEWIS CASS]** *to* **MAJOR GAINES. [extract] 11 July 1836. War Department.** Describes the hostility of Indian tribes in Texas; advocates government intervention to protect the safety of the frontier. 11 August 1836. p.31, c4.

**38 LEWIS CASS** *to* **MAJ. GEN. E. P. GAINES, FORT JESSUP, LOUISIANA. 11 May 1836. War Department.** Issues orders not to advance into Texas beyond official United States territory unless United States territory is endangered by hostile Indian tribes. 11 August 1836. p.31, c5.

**39 COLUMBUS** *to* **MR. EDITOR [from the** *Philadelphia National Gazette*] **May 1836. Philadelphia.** Reviews the origin and cause of the Texas insurrection. 18 August 1836. p.33, c1.

**40 F. C. WOODWORTH** *to* **MR. GOODELL. 17 August 1836. Oneida Institute.** Reports on the establishment of the Peace Society of Oneida Institute. 18 August 1836. p.34, c1.

**41 A SUBSCRIBER** *to* **MR. GOODELL. 11 August 1836. New York Mills.** Requests that he explain the relationship between slavery and the Texan war. 18 August 1836. p.34, c3.

**42 L. T.** *to* **MR. GOODELL. 8 August 1836. New York.** Forwards extract from letter from Cincinnati giving an account of a mobbing. 18 August 1836. p.34, c5.

**43 n.n.** *to* **n.n. [extract] n.d. n.p.** Describes the mobbing of the houses of Birney and Donaldson on 30 July in Cincinnati. 18 August 1836. p.34, c5.

**44 JACOB BURNET** *to* **J. G. BIRNEY, ESQ. [extract] 25 July 1836. n.p.** The committee of an anti-abolition meeting requests a meeting with Birney and associates of the *Philanthropist*. 18 August 1836. p.34, c6.

**45 J. G. BIRNEY** *to* **THE COMMITTEE OF THE ANTI-ABOLITION MEETING HELD IN THE LOWER MARKET, JULY 23D. [extract] n.d. n.p.** Explains that he is merely the editor of the *Philanthropist;* refers them to the executive committee of the Ohio AS, which owns the paper. 18 August 1836. p.34, c6.

**46 JACOB BURNET** *to* **J. G. BIRNEY. [extract] 27 July 1836. n.p.** Clarifies the earlier request of the anti-abolition committee; explains that their interest was to convince him that his present course is not the most expedient means of attaining his goals. 18 August 1836. p.34, c6.

**47 JAMES C. LUDLOW AND ISAAC COLBY** *to* **J. BURNET. 29 July 1836. Cincinnati.** Explain why the *Philanthropist* will continue to be published. 18 August 1836. p.35, c1.

**48 B. F. WHITNER** *to* **THE EDITOR OF THE** *AUGUSTA SENTINEL.* **18 July 1836. Hickstown, Fl.** Describes a battle with Indians. 18 August 1836. p.35, c3.

**49 A FEMALE** *to* **THE EDITOR OF THE** *AUGUSTA SENTINEL.* **19 July. Florida.** Reports the raid by Indians on Colonel Whitner's plantation. 18 August 1836. p.35, c3.

**50 n.n.** *to* **SIR. [extract from the** *New Orleans Bulletin*] **1 July 1836. Matamoras.** Informs that General Urrea, the Mexican commander in chief, has enlisted the aid of several Indian chiefs against Texas. 18 August 1836. p.35, c4.

**51 n.n.** *to* **n.n. [extract from the** *New Orleans Commercial Bulletin*] **29 July 1836. Matamoras.** Asserts that 8,000 Indians are already engaged to aid the Mexicans against Texas. 18 August 1836. p.35, c4.

**52 JOSE MARIA TORNEL [SECRETARY OF THE WAR DEPT.]** *to* **DON VINCENTE FILISOLA [GENERAL IN CHIEF OF THE MEXICAN ARMIES]. n.d. n.p.** States that the army favors the appointment of a dictator, who would take office until Texas is restored to Mexico; notes that the anarchy and weakness of the government threaten supplies of money and men for the military. 18 August 1836. p.35, c4.

**53 D. F.** *to* **FRIEND KIMBALL. [from the** *Herald of Freedom*] **20 July 1836. Tamworth, N.H.** Relates a small conflict regarding the formation of the Tamworth AS. 25 August 1836. p.37, c4.

**54 MOSES BROWN** *to* **ELDER RAY POTTER. 11 August 1836. Providence, R.I.** Forwards an issue of the *Friend* containing an article on the colored people of Providence. 25 August 1836. p.38, c1.

**55 RECHAB** *to* **MR. EDITOR [WILLIAM GOODELL]. n.d. n.p.** Advocates temperance, citing biblical examples. 25 August 1836. p. 38, c4.

**56 J. C. MERWIN** *to* **SIR. 10 August 1836. Albany.** Attests to the truthfulness of statements by Mrs. Showers concerning the circumstances of her daughter's disappearance. 25 August 1836. p.38, c4.

**57 GEO. STORRS.** *to* **MR. KIMBALL. [from the** *Herald of Freedom*] **10 August 1836. Exeter.** Recounts the hostile reaction to his anti-slavery lecture. 25 August 1836. p.39, c3.

**58 DAVID BURNET** *to* **ALL TO WHOM THESE PRESENTS SHALL COME. 21 July 1836. Valasco.** Declares that the port of Matamoras, Mexico is in a state of blockade; informs how the blockade will be executed and what the penalty for violation will be. 25 August 1836. p.39, c4.

**59 LEWIS CASS** *to* **N. CANNON, GOVERNOR OF TENNESSEE. [from the** *Baltimore American*] **4 May 1836. War Department.** Requests that additonal troops be placed at the disposal of General Gaines. 25 August 1836. p.39, c5.

**60 C. A. HARRIS, ACTING SECRETARY OF WAR** *to* **N. CANNON, GOVERNOR OF TENNESSEE. [from the** *Baltimore American*] **25 July 1836. War Department.** Informs that dispatches received by General Gaines have been forwarded to the president, and that funds requested will be disbursed immediately upon approval. 25 August 1836. p.39, c5.

**61 ANDREW JACKSON** *to* **GOV. N. CANNON. [from the** *Herald of Freedom*] **6 August 1836. Hermitage.** Acknowledges receipt of previous correspondence; discusses conditions of neutrality toward Texas and Mexico. 25 August 1836. p.39, c5.

**62** *N. Y. EVANGELIST* *to* **THE FRIENDS OF SOUTHERN RIGHTS. [from the** *Newark Daily Advertiser*] **10 August 1836. Morgan County, Ga.** Describes W. Kitchell and his actions, requesting that Southern newspapers aid in his capture. 25 August 1836. p.39, c5.

**63 MAINE FARMER** *to* **MR. HOLMES. n.d. n.p.** Doubts whether Holmes's contention that farmers are the most learned and influential men could be proven true. 25 August 1836. p.40, c1.

**64 SIR JAMES MACKINTOSH** *to* **n.n. [extract] n.d. n.p.** Describes an example of female excellence. 25 August 1836. p.40, c3.

**65 DR. DAVID NELSON** *to* **n.n. [from the** *Illinois Patriot*] **n.d. n.p.** Recounts mistreatment of himself and his family in Missouri and Illinois because of his abolitionist activities; supplies letters from citizens requesting that Nelson and family leave area. 1 September 1836. p.41, c4.

**66 WM. BLAKELY** *to* **DR. NELSON. n.d. n.p.** Informs him on behalf of citizens of Palmyra that he must either leave the county immediately or suffer the consequences. 1 September 1836. p.41, c6.

**67 WM. G. OVERTON, R. W. MILES, L. J. EASTIN, [AND EIGHTY-THREE OTHERS]** *to* **DR. NELSON. n.d. Palmyra and Marion County.** Demand that Nelson leave Palmyra as soon as his child's health improves. 1 September 1836. p.41, c6.

**68 n.n.** *to* **THE CHAIRMAN OF THE DEMOCRATIC COUNTY CONVENTION TO MEET AT HARTFORD ON AUG. 4, 1836. n.d. n.p.** Charges them with excluding him from their committee because of his anti-slavery views; asserts that they have no right to dictate views on matters not concerned with party politics. 1 September 1836. p.42, c1.

**69 ALVAN STEWART, C. STUART, WM. GOODELL, [AND EIGHT OTHERS]** *to* **THE EXECUTIVE COMMITTEE OF THE OHIO STATE AS IN CINCINNATI. 26 August 1836. Utica, N.Y.** Lend their support and encouragement in this time of mobbings and other outrages. 1 September 1836. p.42, c3.

**70 C. STUART** *to* **FRIEND AND BROTHER. 17 August 1836. n.p.** Encloses correspondence concerning the question of whether the Constitution sanctions slavery. 1 September 1836. p.42, c4.

**71 LORENZO NEELY** *to* **REV. C. STUART. 15 August 1836. Oneida Institute.** Contends that the Constitution sanctions slavery by guaranteeing the rights of slaveholders to maintain slavery where it exists. 1 September 1836. p.42, c4.

**72. C. STUART** *to* **MR. LORENZO NEELY. 16 August 1836. Oneida Institute.** Refutes Neely's contention that the Constitution sanctions slavery. 1 September 1836. p.42, c5.

**73 C.** *to* **MR. EDITOR [WILLIAM GOODELL]. n.d. n.p.** Decries the prejudice displayed by a minister in church. 1 September 1836. p.42, c5.

**74 JUSTICE** *to* **n.n. [extract] n.d. n.p.** Compliments lectures by Mr. Graham in Albany. 1 September 1836. p.43, c1.

**75 MR. GOULD** *to* **n.n. [from the** ***Emancipator*****] n.d. Pennsylvania.** Announces the formation of several new ASs, commenting that there are now too many to keep track of them. 1 September 1836. p.43, c1.

**76 E. WEED** *to* **n.n. [from the** ***Emancipator*****] 10 August 1836. Hillsborough.** Reports on his recent lectures; feels that the mobbing of Birney's press has opened the public's eyes. 1 September 1836. p.43, c1.

**77 JAMES G. BIRNEY** *to* **BROTHER. 10 August 1836. Cincinnati.** Condemns the destruction of the *Philanthropist* office; discusses the lack of support for the abolitionist movement in Ohio. 1 September 1836. p.43, c2.

**78 n.n.** *to* **n.n. [extract from the** ***N. Y. Commercial Advertiser*****] 12 August. St. Augustine, Fl.** Reports on the poor condition of the army fighting the Indian war. 1 September 1836. p.43, c3.

**79 MAJOR GENERAL GAINES** *to* **n.n. [extract] 18 July 1836. Camp Sabine, Tx.** States that his troops are healthy and that the Sabine will be navigable within eight months. 1 September 1836. p.43, c3.

**80 ANDREW JACKSON** *to* **MR. MOREHEAD, GOVERNOR OF THE STATE OF KENTUCKY. 7 August 1836. Hermitage.** Disapproves of General Gaines's requisition of 1,000 men from the states of Tennessee, Kentucky, Mississippi and Louisiana; explains his opposition and requests discharge of men if the requisition has already been filled. 1 September 1836. p.43, c4.

**81 LESLIE COMBS** *to* **n.n. 11 August 1836. Lexington.** Announces unofficially President Jackson's annulment of General Gaines's requisition. 1 September 1836. p.43, c4.

**82 J. B. DUSENBURY** *to* **COL. L. COMBS. 18 August 1836. Louisville, Ky.** Sends him a letter from President Jackson denying General Gaines's requisition for volunteers; advises delaying the discharge of troops until they are paid. 1 September 1836. p.43, c4.

**83 EDWARD HITCHCOCK** *to* **THE EDITOR OF THE** ***HAMPSHIRE GAZETTE*****. [extract] n.d. n.p.** Discusses the geology of Mount Holyoke. 1 September 1836. p.44, c3.

**84 n.n.** *to* **n.n. [extract from the** ***Buffalo Spectator*****] 14 August 1836. Cleveland, Oh.** Describes the unexpected good treatment that he, a colored man, received on his westward journey. 8 September 1836. p.45, c1.

**85 CHARLES H. LADD** *to* **MR. WHITTIER. [from the** ***Essex Gazette*****] 18 August 1836. East Bradford.** Quotes resolution adopted by the Young Men's Association assailing those who took part in the disturbances of the 15 August anti-slavery meeting. 8 September 1836. p.45, c3.

**86 WM. H. JOHNSON** *to* **WM. LLOYD GARRISON. [from the** ***Liberator*****] 27 July 1836. Buckingham, Bucks County, Pa.** Announces the establishment of the Bucks County AS. 8 September 1836. p.45, c4.

**87 LYDIA B. CAPRON, SARAH W. GROSVENOR, SARAH JUDSON, MARTHA WHIPPLE, AND OLIVE CHAPMAN** *to* **PROFESSING CHRISTIAN WOMEN OF KENTUCKY. n.d. n.p.** Remind them of the Christian's duty to aid the cause of abolition. 8 September 1836. p.45, c6.

**88 L. NEELY** *to* **REV. CHARLES STUART. n.d. Oneida Institute.** Contends that slavery is sanctioned by the Constitution. 8 September 1836. p.46, c1.

**89 H. C. W.** *to* **MR. EDITOR [WILLIAM GOODELL]. n.d. n.p.** Discusses the non-violent principles of the Peace Society of Oneida Institute. 8 September 1836. p.46, c2.

**90 J. CROSS** *to* **BROTHER GOODELL. 25 August 1836. Camden.** Forwards a note sent him by an advocate of slavery. 8 September 1836. p.46, c3.

**91 n.n.** *to* **J. CROSS. n.d. n.p.** Warns him of dire consequences if he continues his abolitionist work. 8 September 1836. p.46, c3.

**92 ALVAN STEWART** *to* **THE ABOLITIONISTS OF THE STATE OF NEW YORK. 8 September 1836. Utica.** Reports the formation of the New York AS; asks for support. 8 September 1836. p.46, c3.

**93 CORRESPONDENT** *to* **n.n. 14 August 1836. Hebronville, Ma.** Discusses C. C. Burleigh's successful speech. 8 September 1836. p.46, c4.

**94 n.n.** *to* **THE EDITOR [WILLIAM GOODELL]. [extract] n.d. Lockport.** Reports that the cause is advancing rapidly in Lockport. 8 September 1836. p.46, c4.

**95 n.n.** *to* **n.n. [extract from the** *Columbia Texas Telegraph***] 29 July 1836. Galveston Island.** Foresees victory in the coming battles with Mexicans. 8 September 1836. p.47, c3.

**96 S. F. AUSTIN** *to* **SIR. 4 August 1836. Columbia.** Reports that he will be a candidate for president of Texas in the forthcoming election. 8 September 1836. p.47, c3.

**97 A. S.** *to* **SIR. [from** *Zion's Herald***] n.d. Utica, N.Y.** Describes his excursion to Trenton Falls. 8 September 1836. p.48, c1.

**98 AFRICA** *to* **BROTHER GOODELL. n.d. n.p.** Denounces the Methodist and Presbyterian churches for refusing to pronounce slaveholding a sin at their recent conferences. 15 September 1836. p.50, c3.

**99 JAMES G. BIRNEY** *to* **PRESIDENT GREEN. [extract] 3 September 1836. Cincinnati.** Concludes that public interest in abolition has increased since the latest disturbance. 15 September 1836. p.50, c5.

**100 n.n.** *to* **n.n. [extract from the** *London Patriot***] 20 June 1836. Cadiz.** Notes the failure of treaties between England and Spain to end the slave trade. 15 September 1836. p.51, c5.

**101 CORRESPONDENT** *to* **THE** *COMMERCIAL ADVERTISER***. 30 July 1836. London.** Discusses current economic conditions, noting the increasing value of the principal articles of commerce. 15 September 1836. p.51, c6.

**102 J. F.** *to* **MR. EDITOR [WILLIAM GOODELL]. 6 September 1836. Elmira.** Eulogizes Mrs. Grace Doolittle, the widow of Gen. George Doolittle, who died on 27 August at the age of 70. 15 September 1836. p.51, c6.

**104 L. NEELY** *to* **MR. EDITOR [WILLIAM GOODELL]. n.d. Oneida Institute.** Rejects the principles of absolute non-violence advocated by the Peace Society of Oneida Institute. 22 September 1836. p.54, c3.

**105 OLIVER WETMORE** *to* **ABOLITIONISTS OF THE STATE OF NEW YORK. September 1836. n.p.** Announces the annual meeting of the New York State AS, to be held in Utica. 22 September 1836. p.54, c4.

**106 ELI S. BAILEY** *to* **SIR. [extract] 16 September. Brookfield.** Informs that the General Conference of the Seventh Day Baptists adopted a resolution condemning slavery as sinful. 22 September 1836. p.54, c5.

**107 n.n.** *to* **MR. EDITOR [WILLIAM GOODELL]. [extract] 15 September 1836. Stillwater.** Encloses twenty-five dollars for the New York State AS and the *Friend of Man*. 22 September 1836. p.54, c5.

**108 AN ARMY OFFICER** *to* **n.n. [extract from the** ***National Intelligencer*****] 4 August 1836. Camp Nacogdoches.** Describes the march to Nacogdoches and their reception there. 22 September 1836. p.55, c4.

**109 J. MITRE** *to* **BROTHER PHELPS. [from the** ***Emancipator*****] n.d. n.p.** Informs of the establishment of a Moral Reform Society by the colored people of Troy, auxiliary to the American Moral Reform Society; quotes its preamble and constitution. 29 September 1836. p. 57, c6.

**110 n.n.** *to* **n.n. [extract from the** ***New York Evangelist*****] 6 August 1836. Kentucky.** Praises Kentucky, whose beauty, he feels, is marred only by the fact that she is not a free state. 29 September 1836. p.58, c2.

**111 SAMUEL STILLMAN** *to* **MOSES BROWN. 14 February 1786. Boston.** Acknowledges receipt of pamphlets sent by Brown; encourages his abolition efforts. 29 September 1836. p.58, c2.

**112 H. B. STANTON** *to* **n.n. [extract from the** ***Emancipator*****] n.d. n.p.** Details discussion of English anti-slavery sentiment during an AS meeting in Fall River. 29 September 1836. p.58, c2.

**113 H. B. STANTON** *to* **n.n. [extract from the** ***Emancipator*****] n.d. n.p.** Gives an account of his labors in New Bedford, Fair Haven, East Bradford, Andover, Lowell, Haverhill and Ipswich. 29 September 1836. p.58, c3.

**114 n.n.** *to* **MR. PHELPS. [from the** ***Emancipator*****] 31 August 1836. Huntington, L.I.** Recounts a recent disturbance in Huntington resulting from an anti-slavery lecture. 29 September 1836. p.58, c3.

**115 N. P. ROGERS** *to* **MR. KIMBALL. 14 September 1836. Plymouth, N.H.** Sketches the proceedings of the Grafton County Anti-Slavery Convention. 29 September 1836. p.58, c4.

**116 MR. GOULD** *to* **BROTHER WRIGHT. [from the** ***Emancipator*****] 30 August 1836. Warren, Trumbull County, Oh.** Gives an account of the annual meeting of Beaver Baptist Association. 29 September 1836. p.58, c4.

**117 n.n.** *to* **REV. SIR. 23 May 1836. Logansport, Cass County, In.** Reports that an uproar was caused by the establishment of an AS in Logansport. 29 September 1836. p.58, c5.

**118 ONE WHO MEANS TO ATTEND THE MEETING OF THE STATE SOCIETY** *to* **THE ABOLITIONISTS OF THE STATE OF NEW YORK. n.d. n.p.** Explains why he supports abolition. 29 September 1836. p.58, c5.

**119 n.n.** *to* **GERRIT SMITH. [extract] 31 August 1836. Kentucky.** Attests to the enormity of the sin of slavery; observes that Southerners who have grown up within the system are unaware of the extent of their crimes. 29 September 1836. p.50 [59], c1.

**120 TH. S. JESUP** *to* **HON. LEWIS CASS. 5 September 1836. Montgomery, Al.** Reports on movement of Indians at Wetumpka and the dispersement of the Tennessee volunteers. 29 September 1836. p.50 [59], c4.

**121 LEVI WOODBURY** *to* **n.n. [from the** ***Washington Globe*****] 19 September 1836. Treasury Department.** Clarifies the procedure for payment of the Neapolitan indemnity. 29 September 1836. p.50 [59], c4.

**122 C. C. F.** *to* **BROTHER GOODELL. 20 September 1836. Oneida Institute.** Describes the pastor's recent sermon to the children of the congregation. 29 September 1836. p.60, c4.

**123 DUKE DE BROGLIE** *to* **REV. DR. HEUGH. n.d. n.p.** Regrets having missed an opportunity to meet with agents of the Glasgow Emancipation Society; offers assistance in establishing relations between the Scottish group and the Paris Society for the Abolition of Slavery. 6 October 1836. p.61, c6.

**124 O. SCOTT** *to* **MR. EDITOR. [from** ***Zion's Watchman*****] 6 September 1836. Lowell, Ma.** Denies that the New England conference has been insubordinate; explains that a committee report was kept from a vote by the work of a few. 6 October 1836. p.62, c1.

**125 S. S. S.** *to* **BRO. GOODELL. 27 September 1836. Fayetteville.** Urges those attending the forthcoming state AS meeting to subordinate personal needs to the cause of abolition and to bring contributions with them. 6 October 1836. p.62, c2.

**126 OLIVER WETMORE** *to* **THE ABOLITIONISTS OF THE STATE OF NEW YORK. September 1836. n.p.** Announces the annual meeting of the New York State AS at Utica; urges attendance. 6 October 1836. p.62, c2.

**127 A.** *to* **MR. EDITOR [WILLIAM GOODEL]. n.d. n.p.** Compliments the Junior Exhibition at the Oneida Institute, which comprised an essay competition based on knowledge of Scriptures, a mock trial of an abolitionist in a Southern court and other events. 6 October 1836. p.62, c3.

**128 F. ROOM** *to* **SIR. n.d. n.p.** Requests that he attend that evening's meeting. 6 October 1836. p.62, c4.

**129 C.P. GROSVENOR** *to* **BROTHER WRIGHT. [from the** ***Emancipator*****] 16 September 1836. Rutland, Ma.** Writes that he has just returned from a 200-mile tour and that he was invited to speak before the Westfield Baptists for two weeks in succession. 6 October 1836. p.62, c5.

**130 JOHN RANKIN** *to* **BROTHER WRIGHT. 6 September 1836. Ripley.** Gives account of his recent anti-slavery lecture tour. 6 October 1836. p.62, c6.

**131 JOHN SCOBLE** *to* **REV. ELIZUR WRIGHT. [from the** ***Emancipator*****] 19 August 1836. London.** Reports on George Thompson's anti-slavery speech at a public meeting in Exeter hall; encloses resolutions adopted. 6 October 1836. p.63, c1.

**132 LT. COL. HENRY STAUNTON** *to* **THE EDITORS OF THE** ***NORFOLK BEACON*****. 8 September 1836. Muskegee [*****sic*****], Al.** Announces the end of hostilities in the Creek Nation; congratulates the officers for the manner in which they carried out their orders. 6 October 1836. p.63, c3.

**133 n.n.** *to* **n.n. [extract] 27 August 1836. Vera Cruz.** Reports movement of Mexican vessels; sees little chance of victory over Texas. 6 October 1836. p.63, c4.

**134 ELIZABETH B. CHACE AND SARAH G. BUFFUM** *to* **BROTHER GARRISON. [from the** ***Liberator*****] 5 September 1836. Fall River.** Announce the establishment of a women's AS at Fall River; forward resolutions. 6 October 1836. p.64, c3.

**135 LADIES AS OF CONCORD** *to* **THE WOMEN OF NEW HAMPSHIRE. 9 September 1836. n.p.** Request that they circulate the enclosed anti-slavery petition to Congress. 13 October 1836. p.65, c5.

**136 E. REYNOLDS** *to* **SIR. [from the** ***Temperance Intelligencer*****] 12 July 1836. n.p.** Discusses the founding principles of the Temperance Society of Oneida Institute. 13 October 1836. p.66, c1.

**137 H.B. STANTON** *to* **BROTHER WRIGHT. [from the** ***Emancipator*****] 26 September 1836. Boston.** Details the lectures he has given and the money he has raised for the abolitionist cause. 13 October 1836. p.66, c4.

**138 JOHN NASH** *to* **MR. EDITOR [WILLIAM GOODELL]. 3 October 1836. Walton, Delaware County, N.Y.** Reports the establishment of an AS in Walton; inquires where the publication entitled, "Enemies of the Constitution Discovered" can be found. 13 October 1836. p.66, c5.

**139 PENN.** *to* **MR. EDITOR [WILLIAM GOODELL]. 27 September 1836. Oneida Institute.** Refutes the accusation that Oneida Institute Peace Society propagates unscriptural principles. 13 October 1836. p.66, c6.

**140 OLIVER WETMORE** *to* **THE ABOLITIONISTS OF THE STATE OF NEW YORK. September 1836. n.p.** Gives notice of the annual meeting of the New York State AS, to be held 19 October in Utica. 13 October 1836. p.66, c6.

**141 W. C. ROGERS** *to* **n.n. [extract] 7 October 1836. Rochester.** Believes that a lecture series by Brother Weld would be welcomed in Rochester. 13 October 1836. p.67, c1.

**142 A.** *to* **MR. KIMBALL. [from the** ***Herald of Freedom*****] n.d. n.p.** Sends an extract from a letter. 13 October 1836. p.67, c1.

**143 n.n.** *to* **A. [from the** ***Herald of Freedom*****] n.d. n.p.** Observes that abolitionist efforts are influencing the consciences of Southern slaveholders. 13 October 1836. p.67, c1.

**144 ALEXANDRE DE LABORDE** *to* **WILLIAM LLOYD GARRISON. [from the** ***Liberator*****] 23 July 1836. Paris.** Announces that the French Society for the Abolition of Slavery has elected Garrison as its United States corresponding member. 13 October 1836. p.67, c5.

**145 n.n.** *to* **MR. PORTER. [from the** ***New England Spectator*****] n.d. n.p.** Recalls a visit to Rev. Dr. Emmons, the oldest living graduate of Yale College and a champion of liberty. 13 October 1836. p.68, c3.

**146 n.n.** *to* **SAMUEL CROTHERS. [from the** ***Philanthropist*****] n.d. n.p.** Reports the murder of a man in Yazoo County for having spoken to a Negro slave. 20 October 1836. p.70, c2.

**147 MANY SOUTHERNERS** *to* **MR. EDITOR. [from the** *New York Evangelist*] **n.d. n.p.** Request that money be offered for the best essay on the morality of treating men as property. 20 October 1836. p.70, c3.

**148 J. B. B.** *to* **BROTHER. [from** *Zion's Watchman*] **n.d. Lockport, N.Y.** Forwards the preamble, constitution and resolutions of the Lockport-Wesleyan AS. 20 October 1836. p.70, c4.

**149 MR. WILCOX** *to* **SIR. 9 September 1836. Allegany County, Portageville.** Reports the favorable reactions to his anti-slavery lectures; comments that in some towns, many do not understand the purpose of ASs. 20 October 1836. p.70, c4.

**150 MR. GOULD** *to* **BROTHER PHELPS. n.d. n.p.** Reports on the third anniversary meeting of the French Creek Baptist Association; forwards resolutions adopted by the association. 20 October 1836. p.70, c4.

**151 EMANCIPATOR** *to* **MR. R. G. WILLIAMS. 26 September 1836. Caroline.** Informs of the increase in the number of abolitionists in his town. 20 October 1836. p.70, c6.

**152 CORRESPONDENT AT NACOGDOCHES** *to* **n.n. [from the** *Army and Navy Chronicle*] **n.d. Nacogdoches, Tx.** Describes the actions of an infantry company, revealing the deceptiveness and immorality of war. 20 October 1836. p.70, c6.

**153 AN OFFICER OF GEN. CHAMBER'S ARMY OF RESERVE** *to* **BROTHER. [from the** *Louisville City Gazette*] **13 August 1836. Nacogdoches, Tx.** Discusses the cause of the disturbance in Texas. 20 October 1836. p.71, c2.

**154 n.n.** *to* **n.n. [extract from the** *Savannah Georgian*] **28 September 1836. Jacksonville, Fl.** Reports the maneuvers of Governor Call and General Jesup. 20 October 1836. p.71, c5.

**155 JUDGE WILLIAM JAY** *to* **REV. SIR OLIVER WETMORE. 26 September 1836. Bedford.** Informs of his resignation as president of the New York AS; comments on the anti-slavery struggle. 27 October 1836. p.73, c1.

**156 SIMEON S. JOCELYN** *to* **REV. BERIAH GREEN. 15 October 1836. New York.** Regrets that he cannot attend the New York State AS meeting; hopes this meeting will improve the treatment of colored people; offers suggestions. 27 October 1836. p.74, c2.

**157 A REPUBLICAN** *to* **MR. EDITOR [WILLIAM GOODELL]. n.d. n.p.** Declares that the nominations of Rutger B. Miller and David Wagner are unworthy of the support of the Republican Party. 27 October 1836. p.74, c2.

**158 SENEX** *to* **MR. EDITOR [WILLIAM GOODELL]. n.d. n.p.** Testifies that the despicable character of Rutger B. Miller makes him an unworthy candidate for congressional office. 27 October 1836. p.74, c3.

**159 EDMUND P. GAINES** *to* **GOV. N. CANNON. [from the** *National Intelligencer*] **28 August 1836. Camp Sabine.** Reprimands the president of the United States for denying his requistion for additional men, explaining why they are necessary. 27 October 1836. p.75, c2.

**160 n.n.** *to* **MESSRS. EDITORS. 28 August 1836. Natchitoches, La.** Discusses United States relations with Texas; believes that Texans will vote for statehood in the coming elections. 27 October 1836. p.75, c3.

**161 C. W. BONNELL** *to* **THE EDITORS OF THE** ***MISSISSIPPI CHRISTIAN HERALD.*** **[extract] 4 September 1836. Nacogdoches.** Comments on the similarities between the miserable land in Texas and her inhabitants; criticizes the cowards who fled Texas when the fighting began and now claim that they own large tracts of land. 27 October 1836. p.75, c4.

**162 ELLEN B. LADD** *to* **MR. GARRISON. [from the** ***Liberator*****] 12 October 1836. East Bradford, Ma.** Reports the establishment of a female AS in that city. 3 November 1836. p.78, c2.

**163 MR. TILLINGHAST** *to* **n.n. [from the** ***Emancipator*****] n.d. Long Island.** Discusses his lecturing activities in Long Island. 3 November 1836. p.78, c2.

**164 MR. HAZELTON** *to* **n.n. [from the** ***Emancipator*****] 8 October 1836. New Hampshire.** Details his lecture tour; remarks that people are eager to read all of the printed material with which he can supply them. 3 November 1836. p.78, c3.

**165 MR. CODDING** *to* **n.n. [from the** ***Emancipator*****] 27 September 1836. Sudbury, Vt.** Notes that the ASs are growing. 3 November 1836. p.78, c3.

**166 MR. PRITCHETT** *to* **n.n. 5 October 1836. Champlain, N.Y.** Informs of the favorable response to abolition. 3 November 1836. p.78, c3.

**167 G. R. H. STUMWAY** *to* **THE EDITOR OF THE** ***FRIEND OF MAN*** **[WILLIAM GOODELL]. 17 October 1836. Palmyra, Wayne County.** Reports the proceedings of the Palmyra AS meeting and the advancement of the abolitionist cause. 3 November 1836. p.78, c4.

**168 JUNIOR** *to* **BROTHER GOODELL. n.d. n.p.** Stresses the importance of circulating petitions for the abolition of slavery. 3 November 1836. p.78, c4.

**169 H. C. W.** *to* **FRIEND GOODELL. 26 October 1836. Warren.** Attacks the depravity of principle behind the enclosed advertisement offering a reward for the capture of a runaway slave. 3 November 1836. p.78, c4.

**170 HENRY C. WRIGHT** *to* **FRIEND GOODELL. 25 October 1836. Bristol.** Discusses his lectures on abolition; describes a slight interruption. 3 November 1836. p.78, c5.

**171 O. SCOTT** *to* **BROTHER SUNDERLAND. 11 October 1836. Lowell, Ma.** Reproaches an alleged abolitionist and Methodist preacher for his refusal to acknowledge the cause of abolition in church and to pray publicly for slaves. 3 November 1836. p.78, c5.

**172 JAMES G. BIRNEY** *to* **GERRIT SMITH. [extract] n.d. n.p.** Believes that next year will witness a strong growth in the anti-slavery cause and that Southerners will be forced to admit that their system is not perpetual. 3 November 1836. p.78, c6.

**173 CORRESPONDENT OF THE** ***BALTIMORE AMERICAN*** *to* **n.n. [from the** ***Baltimore American*****] 9 October 1836. Apalachicola, Fl.** Encloses an article from the *Apalachicola Gazette* discussing the current state of war in Florida. 3 November 1836. p.79, c5.

**174 GEN. FELIX HOUSTON** *to* **COL. LOUIS P. COOK. [extract from the** ***New Orleans Bee*****] Headquarters, Texan Army.** Advocates pursuing the war to the Rio Grande to ensure the safety of future American settlers. 3 November 1836. p.79, c6.

**175 PAUL** *to* **MR. EDITOR. [from the** ***Boston Recorder*****] n.d. n.p.** Regrets that congregations fail to choose pious men for preachers. 3 November 1836. p.80, c3.

**176 A GIRL SEVEN YEARS OLD** *to* **SCHOOLMATES. n.d. Cincinnati.** States that her family will buy a farm; mourns the 200 slaves who were drowned when a boat went down. 3 November 1836. p.80, c4.

**177 A SCHOLAR TEN YEARS OLD** *to* **SIR. n.d. Cincinnati.** Informs that he has two enslaved cousins; asks for advice on how to aid them. 3 November 1836. p.80, c4.

**178 A SCHOLAR ELEVEN YEARS OLD** *to* **n.n. n.d. Cincinnati.** Asks the Lord to bless the cause of abolition. 3 November 1836. p.80, c4.

**179 A SCHOLAR TWELVE YEARS OLD** *to* **SCHOOLMASTER. n.d. Cincinnati.** Explains that the education of children will help the abolitionist movement. 3 November 1836. p.80, c4.

**180 n.n.** *to* **GERRIT SMITH, ESQ. [extract] 20 September 1836. British West India Island.** Discusses the emancipation of slaves in the British West Indies, stating that the horror stories circulated in the United States are myths and that emancipation has improved their society. 10 November 1836. p.81, c1.

**181 C. STUART** *to* **MR. EDITOR [WILLIAM GOODELL]. 24 October 1836. Whitesboro'.** Comments on the letter from Rev. R. J. Breckinridge to Rev. R. Wardlaw. 10 November 1836. p.81, c2.

**182 n.n.** *to* **BRETHREN. [from the** ***Pawtucket Record*****] 12 September 1836. n.p.** Argues the question of whether or not slaveholders should be permitted to take communion. 10 November 1836. p.82, c2.

**183 B. G. PADDOCK** *to* **BROTHER SUNDERLAND. [from** ***Zion's Watchman*****] n.d. Cazenovia.** Reports the conversion of many to the abolitionist cause. 10 November 1836. p.83, c3.

**184 DYAR FOOTE** *to* **REV. JOSHUA LEAVITT. 8 October 1836. Ludlowville, N.Y.** Encloses a resolution against slavery adopted by the meeting of the Synod of Geneva at Penn Yan. 10 November 1836. p.83, c3.

**185 CORRESPONDENT** *to* **BROTHER LEAVITT. 28 October 1836. Boston.** Reports on the proceedings of the Temperance Convention of People of Color. 10 November 1836. p.83, c4.

**186 BENJAMIN F. COOPER** *to* **N.Y. STATE AS. 19 October 1836. Utica.** Relates events of the 1835 state anti-slavery convention, commenting on the disturbance caused. 17 November 1836. p.85, c2.

**187 AMOS DRESSER** *to* **MR. EDITOR. n.d. n.p.** Observes that Southern Christians remain silent on the issue of abolition, for fear of offending the public; encloses a letter from a Tennessee minister. 17 November 1836. p.86, c1.

**188 MINISTER IN TENNESSEE** *to* **BRO. DRESSER. n.d. n.p.** Acknowledges receipt of Dresser's letters and advises Dresser on the course to take to mitigate the hostilities against him. 17 November 1836. p.86, c2.

**189 AMOS DRESSER** *to* **SIR [REV. JAMES SMITH]. September 1835. Cincinnati.** Replies to the minister's suggestions, offering a detailed refutation of the minister's account of the disturbance. 17 November 1836. p.86, c2.

**190 REV. JAMES SMITH** *to* **FRIEND [AMOS DRESSER]. 5 August 1835. Nashville.** Acknowledges receipt of a letter written by Dresser; praises Dresser's work. 17 November 1836. p.86, c3.

**191 JAMES SMITH** *to* **TRUMAN AND SMITH. n.d. n.p.** States that Reverend Smith had no knowledge of anti-slavery books in Dresser's possession; clarifies his anti-abolitionist stance. 17 November 1836. p.86, c3.

**192 MEMBER OF SMITH FAMILY** *to* **A. DRESSER. 10 September 1835. Nashville.** Warns that Smith's family is in danger of being lynched for harboring Dresser; comments on Southern attitudes and the lynch law. 17 November 1836. p.86, c4.

**193 RICHARD MORAN** *to* **AMOS DRESSER. 5 September 1835. Near Lawrenceburg, In.** Expresses concern for Dresser's trouble in Nashville; admires his abolitionist activities. 17 November 1836. p.86, c4.

**194 H. C. W.** *to* **BROTHER. 10 November 1836. Providence.** Encloses the resolutions passed by the Rhode Island State AS; comments on the contradiction between professing Christianity and owning slaves. 17 November 1836. p.86, c5.

**195 n.n.** *to* **A RELATIVE OF CAPT. LANE. [extract from the** *New York American*] **23 October 1836. St. Augustine.** Relates the details of Captain Lane's suicide. 17 November 1836. p.87, c4.

**196 JOHN B. ROBINS** *to* **MR. JOHN POWERS OR SAMUEL WHITE. 19 May 183 [illegible]. St. Martins.** Discusses the sale of Samuel White; offers to make White a free man for a fee of sixty dollars. 17 November 1836. p.87, c6.

**197 S. P. H.** *to* **MR. EDITOR [WILLIAM GOODELL]. n.d. n.p.** Explains that after learning that only white citizens were allowed to contribute to the construction of the Washington Monument, he decided to give his money to the New York State AS; urges other white men to do the same. 24 November 1836. p.90, c5.

**198 LORENZO NEELY** *to* **FRIEND GOODELL. 4 November 1836. Galway.** Reports on his lectures in East and West Galway. 24 November 1836. p.91, c2.

**199 CHARLES DICKINSON** *to* **BROTHER GOODELL. 16 November 1836. Haddam, Ct.** Reports the formation of the Middlesex County AS in Middletown. 24 November 1836. p.91, c3.

**200 BAXTER** *to* **BROTHER SUNDERLAND. 21 October 1836. Mount Morris, N.Y.** Praises a recent New York State AS meeting at Utica. 24 November 1836. p.91, c4.

**201 ALVAN STEWART** *to* **WM. GOODELL, ESQ. 14 November 1836. Burlington.** Reports on progress of abolitionism in Westford, Vermont; notes that Congress has the power to abolish the internal slave trade, and the existence of this power has lent hope to the cause. 1 December 1836. p.93, c5.

**202 ELISHA LORD** *to* **WILLIAM HUTCHINS, M.D. [from the** *Emancipator*] **15 September 1836. Abington.** Discusses the abolition of slavery and the dissolution of the Union. 1 December 1836. p.94, c1.

**203 MR. WEED** *to* **BROTHER WRIGHT. 24 October 1836. Circleville, Oh.** Declares that he is indeed alive, contrary to reports; describes his lectures in Sandy Spring, Decatur, Mount Leigh, West Liberty and Hillsboro', and his attendance at a meeting of the Cincinnati Synod. 1 December 1836. p.94, c2.

**204 MR. BIRNEY** *to* **BROTHER WRIGHT. [from the** *Emancipator*] **1 November 1836. Cincinnati, Oh.** Recounts his lectures in Dayton, Troy, Pique and Milton. 1 December 1836. p.94, c4.

**205 GEORGE S. BULL** *to* **ARTHUR TAPPAN, ESQ. 7 September 1836. Parsonage House, Byerley, W. Bradford, Yorkshire, England.** Reports on lecture of George Thompson; offers support to the AAS. 1 December 1836. p.94, c4.

**206 CHAS. F. LAYNE** *to* **THE** ***FRIEND OF MAN.*** **1 November 1836. Rochester.** Condemns slavery, defending the need to speak harshly of Southerners. 1 December 1836. p.94, c5.

**207 J. R. M'DOWALL** *to* **REV. J. LEAVITT. [from the** ***N.Y. Evangelist*****] n.d. n.p.** Informs that his suspension has been annulled by a superior ecclesiastical court; declares that persecuters will not deter his efforts to serve God. 1 December 1836. p.96, c4.

**208 SAMUEL TUKE** *to* **THE YEARLY MEETING OF FRIENDS OF INDIANA. [from the** ***National Enquirer*****] n.d. London.** Sympathizes with their efforts against slavery; reports that the abolition of slavery in all dependencies of the British Empire has been delayed one term. 8 December 1836. p.97, c6.

**209 J.** *to* **THE EDITOR OF THE** ***UNION HERALD.*** **n.d. n.p.** States that the British clergy is doing all in its power to end the slave trade. 8 December 1836. p.98, c3.

**210 n.n.** *to* **THE** ***FRIEND OF MAN.*** **n.d. n.p.** Lists resolutions adopted during the first meeting of the Johnstown AS. 8 December 1836. p.98, c4.

**211 MR. WRIGHT** *to* **BROTHER. [from the** ***Emancipator*****] 3 November 1836. Warren, R.I.** Finds it difficult to interest local residents in abolitionist work. 8 December 1836. p.98, c5.

**212 MR. BLANCHARD** *to* **n.n. 8 November 1836. Harrisburgh, Pa.** Describes the success of his anti-slavery lectures in Harrisburg. 8 December 1836. p.98, c5.

**213 REV. WILCOX** *to* **n.n. 14 November 1836. Warsaw, N.Y.** Reports that he has encountered much anti-abolitionist sentiment in the towns surrounding Warsaw. 8 December 1836. p.98, c5.

**214 n.n.** *to* **THE** ***FRIEND OF MAN.*** **2 December 1836. Lewis County.** States that anti-slavery almanacs can be purchased at the Utica Anti-Slavery Depository. 8 December 1836. p.98, c6.

**215 M. E. DE GOROSTIZA** *to* **ASBURY DICKENS. 15 October 1836. Washington.** Discusses the invasion of Mexico by the United States. 8 December 1836. p.99, c3.

**216 ASHBURY [*****sic*****] DICKENS** *to* **M. E. DE GOROSTIZA. 20 October 1836. Washington.** Encloses passports requested by Mr. Gorostiza. 8 December 1836. p.99, c4.

**217 n.n.** *to* **n.n. [from the** ***Jacksonville Courier*****] 8 October 1836. Micanopy.** Reports on a confrontation between Creek Indians and the United States Army. 8 December 1836. p.99, c4.

**218 n.n.** *to* **n.n. 20 September. St. Marks, Fl.** Describes an attack on United States troops by an Indian tribe. 8 December 1836. p.99, c5.

**219 n.n.** *to* **BROTHER EDGAR. [from the** ***American Presbyterian*** **via the** ***New York Evangelist*****] 13 August 1836. Alabama.** Believes that slaves do not receive enough religious instruction. 8 December 1836. p. 100, c2.

**220 J.R. McDOWALL** *to* **n.n. 6 March 1836. New York.** Reminds of the importance of reading the Bible regularly. 8 December 1836. p.100, c3.

**221 n.n.** *to* **n.n. 4 December 1836. New Haven.** Describes the hostile reception given Reverend Rand, an abolitionist, by Southern Yale students. 15 December 1836. p.103, c4.

**222 A. GRANT, M.S.** *to* **REV. JOHN B. SHAW. 5 July 1836. Oormiah, Persia.** Praises the work of missionaries in Persia. 15 December 1836. p.104, c1.

**223 ANDREW HARRIS** *to* **n.n. 21 November 1836. Troy, N.Y.** Lists resolutions adopted during a general meeting of the free colored people of Troy. 22 December 1836. p.105, c6.

**224 THOMAS VAN RENSSALAER** *to* **HON. RICHARD RIKER. n.d. n.p.** Disagrees with Riker's opinion that emancipation would be a curse rather than a blessing for the people of color. 22 December 1836. p.106, c1.

**225 GEN. EATON** *to* **MRS. EATON. [from the** ***Herald of Freedom*****] 6 April 1799. Tunis.** Discusses the barbaric treatment of American slaves. 22 December 1836. p.106, c1.

**226 MR. CROCKER** *to* **n.n. [extract] 21 June 1836. Edina.** Comments on the poor living conditions in Liberia. 22 December 1836. p.106, c2.

**227 O. SCOTT** *to* **BROTHER BROWN. [from** ***Zion's Herald*****] 16 December. Lowell.** Describes the hostile reception of abolitionists at Harvard, Massachusetts. 29 December 1836. p.110, c2.

**228 B. GREEN** *to* **ANGELINA E. GRIMKE. December 1836. Oneida Institute.** Considers the value and importance of education. 29 December 1836. p.110, c3.

**229 DR. WM. E. CHANNING** *to* **JAMES G. BIRNEY. n.d. n.p.** Criticizes abolitionists for their strong language and measures, but commends them for their perseverance in a good cause. 29 December 1836. p.111, c2.

## [1837]

**230 DR. WM. E. CHANNING** *to* **JAMES G. BIRNEY. 1 November 1836. Boston.** Comments upon the merits and faults of abolitionists. 5 January 1837. p.113, c1.

**231 BAPTIST UNION** *to* **THE BOARD OF THE TRIENNIAL CONVENTION OF BAPTIST CHURCHES IN THE UNITED STATES. 13 September 1836. London.** Lists resolutions debated and adopted during a meeting of the Baptist Union. 5 January 1837. p.113, c6.

**232 A. N.** *to* **MR. GOODELL. 13 December 1836. New York.** Details the cause and the circumstances of the death of Mr. M'Dowall. 5 January 1837. p.114, c3.

**233 B. LUNDY** *to* **WM. GOODELL. December 1836. Philadelphia.** Announces the death of Dr. Atlee. 5 January 1837. p.114, c3.

**234 AN ABOLITIONIST THAT IS NOT DISCOURAGED** *to* **BRO. GOODELL. 12 December 1836. Farmington, Ontario County.** Believes that abolitionists must pray for slaveholders even though they are their enemies. 5 January 1837. p.114, c4.

**235 B. GREEN** *to* **INNES GRANT. n.d. n.p.** Discusses the symbolic nature of language. 5 January 1837. p.114, c5.

**236 HENRY C. WRIGHT** *to* **BROTHER. [from the** ***New York Evangelist*****] n.d. n.p.** Emphasizes the importance of juvenile ASs and mentions his appointment as children's antislavery agent. 5 January 1837. p.115, c5.

**237 ALVAN STEWART** *to* **EZEKIEL WEBB, THOMAS CHANDLER AND DARIUS C. JACKSON. 20 September 1836. Utica.** Expresses his enthusiasm for the cause of abolition and apologizes for being unable to attend the Michigan Convention. 12 January 1837. p.117, c1.

**238 WM. GOODELL** *to* **EZEKIEL WEBB, THOMAS CHANDLER AND DARIUS C. JACKSON. 27 September 1836. Utica.** Thanks them for an invitation to attend the Michigan Convention. 12 January 1837. p.117, c1.

**239 JAMES G. BIRNEY** *to* **EZEKIEL WEBB, THOMAS CHANDLER AND DARIUS C. JACKSON. 6 October 1836. Cincinnati.** Discusses the work to be done by abolitionists and regrets that he cannot attend the Michigan Convention. 12 January 1837. p.117, c2.

**240 D. RUGGLES** *to* **THE EDITOR OF THE** *EMANCIPATOR.* **n.d. n.p.** Reports that the vigilance committee will need more money if it is to meet its operational costs. 12 January 1837. p.117, c6.

**241 B. GREEN** *to* **PROFESSOR GRANT. n.d. n.p.** Asserts that Latin is not as important a language as the professor believes it is; favors instruction in French and German. 12 January 1837. p.118, c6.

**242 C.** *to* **THE EDITOR OF THE** *FRIEND OF MAN* **[WILLIAM GOODELL]. n.d. n.p.** Declares that slavery contradicts the Constitution. 12 January 1837. p.119, c1.

**243 ANDREW JACKSON** *to* **THE UNITED STATES SENATE. 21 December 1836. Washington.** Discusses the difficulty in recognizing Texas as independent. 12 January 1837. p.119, c3.

**244 T. MERRITT** *to* **REV. N. BANGS, D.D. [from** *Zion's Herald***] 12 December. Lynn.** Believes that slavery is a great sin and that abolitionists should work towards its abolition. 19 January 1837. p.121, c3.

**245 MARY CLARK OF THE LADIES AS IN CONCORD** *to* **ANGELINA E. GRIMKE. November 1835. Concord, N.H.** Responds favorably to Miss Grimké's letter to William L. Garrison. 19 January 1837. p.122, c1.

**246 A. E. GRIMKE** *to* **THE LADIES AS OF CONCORD. 16 March 1836. n.p.** Thanks the Ladies AS for its letter and encourages its members to work hard for the abolition of slavery. 19 January 1837. p.122, c1.

**247 P. CRANDALL** *to* **n.n. [from** *Zion's Herald***] 10 November 1836. New Bedford, Ma.** Discusses the inconsistencies and contradictions of anti-abolitionists. 19 January 1837. p.122, c2.

**248 B. GREEN** *to* **WILLIAM GOODELL. January 1837. Oneida Institute.** Believes that one can understand English without understanding Latin. 19 January 1837. p.122, c4.

**249 D. K.** *to* **THE EDITOR OF THE** *FRIEND OF MAN* **[WILLIAM GOODELL]. n.d. n.p.** Rejects the notion that it would be unconstitutional for Congress to abolish slavery. 19 January 1837. p.122, c5.

**250 MR. BURLEIGH** *to* **n.n. [extract] n.d. n.p.** Mentions that while visiting Hartford County he met an unnamed abolitionist judge from Maryland; comments on the success of his anti-slavery lecture in Philadelphia. 19 January 1837. p.123, c2.

**251 C. S. RENSHAW** *to* **BROTHER WRIGHT. [from the** *Emancipator***] 6 December 1836. West Mendon, Monroe County.** Accepts appointment as an agent for the AAS and discusses his activities while visiting Rochester. 19 January 1837. p.123, c2.

**252 MR. RAND** *to* **MR. WRIGHT. 20 December 1836. Chester Village, Ms.** Comments on the successes and failures of his lecture tour through New York. 19 January 1837. p.123, c2.

**253 MR. PRITCHETT** *to* **n.n. [from the *Emancipator*] 22 December 1836. Blairsville, Pa.** Discusses various subjects including the temperance of Negroes and the whipping of a slave for alleged carelessness. 19 January 1837. p.123, c3.

**254 REV. O. SCOTT** *to* **BRO. WRIGHT. [from the *Emancipator*] 13 December 1836. Lowell.** Apologizes for not attending the agents' meeting and notes the success of his anti-slavery lectures in Springfield, Natick and Middlebury, Massachusetts. 19 January 1837. p.123, c3.

**255 GERRIT SMITH** *to* **THE EDITOR OF THE *LIBERATOR*. 13 December 1836. New York.** Praises the *Liberator* and encloses a check for fifty dollars to help in the paper's financial difficulties. 19 January 1837. p.123, c3.

**256 MATTHEW FORSTER** *to* **WILLIAM L. GARRISON. [from the *Liberator*] 3 November 1836. Newcastle-Upon-Tyne.** Describes the success of George Thompson's abolitionist lecture tour through England. 19 January 1837. p.123, c4.

**257 SILAS C. BROWN** *to* **BRO. LEAVITT. [from the *New York Evangelist*] n.d. n.p.** Encloses the minutes of the last meeting of the First Church of West Bloomfield, New York. 19 January 1837. p.123, c5.

**258 JUDGE C. HAYDEN** *to* **MR. NORTHWAY. 6 January 1837. n.p.** Condemns the exaggeration of slave atrocities and relates the story of a slaveholder's unsuccessful attempt to capture two runaway slaves. 26 January 1837. p.125, c1.

**259 DAVID RUGGLES** *to* **THE EDITOR OF THE *EMANCIPATOR*. 29 December 1836. New York.** Describes an incident involving a police officer named Boudinot who allegedly possessed a warrant issued by Governor Marcy in 1832 allowing him to arrest any black and send him South. 26 January 1837. p.125, c6.

**260 G. BECKLEY** *to* **BRO. SUNDERLAND. [from *Zion's Herald*] 30 November 1836. New York.** Recalls a meeting of the New York Conference during which an unnamed friend was embarrassed and humiliated. 26 January 1837. p.126, c3.

**261 B. GREEN** *to* **THE FRIENDS OF SOUND LEARNING AND TRUE RELIGION. January 1837. n.p.** Criticizes the American Education Society for withdrawing support from the Oneida Institute after it dropped Latin from its curriculum. 26 January 1837. p.126, c3.

**262 WM. YATES** *to* **BROTHER. [from the *Emancipator*] 12 December 1836. Flushing, Long Island.** Reports on the successful establishment of a Sunday school for blacks in Flushing. 26 January 1837. p.128, c3.

**263 ALVAN STEWART** *to* **WM. GOODELL. 17 January 1837. Williamstown, Oswego County.** Discusses the importance and the progress of the temperance and abolitionist movements. 1 February 1837. p.129, c1.

**264 AMOS DRESSER** *to* **BROTHER GOODELL. 31 January 1835. Uxbridge, Ma.** Describes the hostile reception he and H. B. Stanton received in Worcester. 1 February 1837. p.129, c2.

**265 S. COLE** *to* **BROTHER. 29 December 1836. Oberlin.** Describes the escape of thirteen slaves from Ohio to Canada. 1 February 1837, p.129, c4.

**266 S. COLE** *to* **n.n. 30 December 1836. Oberlin.** Expresses astonishment at the fact that not all ministers are engaged in anti-slavery work. 1 February 1837. p.129, c4.

**267 J. M. BLAKESLEY** *to* **BROTHER. 17 December 1836. Sardinia, Eric County, N.Y.** Describes the success of his anti-slavery lectures in East Hamburg, Boston and Sardinia. 1 February 1837. p.129, c5.

**268 A NEW ENGLAND ABOLITIONIST** *to* **BROTHER LEAVITT. [from the** *New York Evangelist***] n.d. n.p.** Rejects the new radical posture of abolitionists and calls for a more realistic approach to the problems of emancipation. 1 February 1837. p.129, c6.

**269 WM. P. RUSSELL** *to* **BROTHER. [from the** *Emancipator***] 17 December 1836. Hume.** Discusses the presentation of anti-slavery lectures and the founding of ASs in Erie and Allegheny counties. 1 February 1837. p.129, c6.

**270 REV. GEORGE STORRS** *to* **BROTHERS. 15 December 1836. Utica.** Recalls the success of his anti-slavery lectures in Westmoreland, Hampton, and Andover. 1 February 1837. p.129, c6.

**271 MR. W. T. ALLAN** *to* **BROTHER WRIGHT. 27 December 1836. Parma, N.Y.** Notes the appeal of his anti-slavery lectures in Trumbull, Ontario, and Monroe counties. 1 February 1837. p.130, c1.

**272 REV. A. SEDGWICK** *to* **BROTHER WRIGHT. 30 December 1836. Rome, N.Y.** Comments on the enthusiastic response to his anti-slavery lectures in Rome, Black Creek, Verona, Lee, Holland Patent and Trenton. 1 February 1837. p.130, c1.

**273 REV. JOHN [***sic***] McKIM** *to* **MR. E. WRIGHT. 2 January 1837. Holmesburg, Phila[delphia] County.** Reports on the popularity of his anti-slavery lectures in Newtown, Falsington, Sullyville, Lower Wakefield, and Purvis Manor. 1 February 1837. p.130, c1.

**274 LIBERTY** *to* **BROTHER BROWN. [From** *Zion's Herald***] n.d. n.p.** States that although the North may be anti-slavery, it is not necessarily pro-abolitionist. 1 February 1837. p.130, c1.

**275 B. GREEN** *to* **THE FRIENDS OF SOUND LEARNING AND TRUE RELIGION. n.d. n.p.** Rejects the American Education Society's belief that instruction in Latin is essential to an education. 1 February 1837. p.130, c4.

**276 R. R. GURLEY** *to* **AUXILIARY CSS. 6 January 1837. Washington.** Lists resolutions debated and adopted during the latest meeting of the ACS. 1 February 1837. p.130, c6.

**277 GEN. ANTONIO LOPEZ DE SANTA ANNA** *to* **ANDREW JACKSON. 4 July 1836. Columbia, Tx.** States that he is being held prisoner by Samuel Houston but wishes to be freed in order to help in the organization of peaceful negotiations between the United States, Mexico and Texas. 1 February 1837. p.131, c1.

**278 ANDREW JACKSON** *to* **GEN. ANTONIO LOPEZ DE SANTA ANNA, PRESIDENT OF THE MEXICAN REPUBLIC. 4 September 1836. Hermitage.** States that the Mexican government has declared that no action taken by Santa Anna during his imprisonment will be considered binding, thereby preventing President Jackson from initiating political negotiations. 1 February 1837. p.131, c1.

**279 n.n.** *to* **THE EDITORS OF** *N. Y. EXPRESS.* **17 January 1837. Bangor.** Reports on the extent of the damage done by a fire in New Brunswick. 1 February 1837. p.131, c5.

**280 SEC. GENERAL OF THE REPUBLIC OF HAYTI, B. INGINAC** *to* **BENJAMIN LUNDY OF PHILADELPHIA. 17 November 1836. Port au Prince.** Thanks Lundy for sending abolitionist publications and encourages him to continue working for slavery's abolition. 1 February 1837. p.131, c6.

**281 JOHN, BISHOP OF NEW YORK** *to* **THE EDITOR OF THE** *CATHOLIC DIARY.* **n.d. n.p.** Criticizes the editor for promoting the organization of a religious society without first receiving the Church's permission and approval. 1 February 1837. p.132, c2.

**282 HENRY C. WRIGHT** *to* **THE EDITOR OF THE** *EMANCIPATOR.* **9 January 183[7]. Newark, N.J.** Discusses the formation of the Newark Juvenile AS and lists resolutions adopted during its first meeting. 1 February 1837. p.132, c3.

**283 D. K.** *to* **THE EDITOR OF THE** *FRIEND OF MAN* **[WILLIAM GOODELL]. n.d. n.p.** Discusses the unpopularity of Governor McDuffie's successor. 8 February 1837. p.133, c1.

**284 JOHN CROSS** *to* **THE EDITOR OF THE** *FRIEND OF MAN* **[WILLIAM GOODELL]. 10 January 1837. Wilkes-Barre.** Condemns the unruly behavior of individuals opposed to the ideas presented during an abolitionist address in Wilkes-Barre. 8 February 1837. p.133, c4.

**285 MR. BELDEN** *to* **BROTHER. [from the** *Emancipator***] 12 January 1837. Pennsborough, Lycoming County, Pa.** Reports on the favorable reception of abolitionist lectures given in Milesburg, Bald Eagle and Bellefonte. 8 February 1837. p.133, c6.

**286 MR. BURLEIGH** *to* **BROTHER WRIGHT. 12 January 1837. Lampeter, Lancaster County.** Notes the progress made by abolitionists in Delaware County, Chester County and Philadelphia. 8 February 1837. p.133, c6.

**287 I. BLANCHARD** *to* **BROTHER PHELPS. 2 January 1837. Harrisburgh.** Recalls the organized opposition to abolitionism encountered in Carlisle and mentions the founding of an AS in Harrisburg. 8 Feburary 1837. p.133, c6.

**288 MR. S. F. PORTER** *to* **BROTHER. 3 January 1837. Harrisville, Oh.** Comments on the popularity of his lectures and the formation of ASs as a result of them in Cedar Creek, Moorfield, Wooster and Millbrook. 8 February 1837. p.134, c1.

**289 MR. FOOTE** *to* **BROTHER WRIGHT. 11 January 1837. Warren, Trumbull County, Oh.** Reports favorable responses to abolitionist lectures in Hartford, Brookfield, Hubbard, Youngstown and Ashtabula County. 8 February 1837. p.134, c1.

**290 A COLORED GENTLEMAN OF LANCASTER COUNTY, PENNSYLVANIA** *to* **THE EDITOR OF THE** *NATIONAL ENQUIRER.* **n.d. n.p.** Stresses the importance of the work done by ASs. 8 February 1837. p.134, c2.

**291 AN AGED MINISTER** *to* **MR. WALTON. [from the** *Vermont Watchman and Journal***] n.d. n.p.** States that Congress has the power to abolish slavery, but expresses impatience with Congress's inability to take steps to stop the American slave trade. 8 February 1837. p.134, c2.

**292 B. GREEN** *to* **THE FRIENDS OF LEARNING AND RELIGION. February 1837. Oneida Institute.** Criticizes the American Education Society for withdrawing support from Oneida Institute after the latter dropped Latin from its curriculum; upholds the beneficial effects of manual labor on mind and body. 8 February 1837. p.134, c3.

**293 GERRIT SMITH** *to* **MR. GOODELL. 30 January 1837. Peterboro'.** Encloses a letter by John Gladding, a laborer and an abolitionist, in the hopes that it will inspire others to take up the cause of abolitionism. 8 February 1837. p.134, c4.

**294 JOHN GLADDING** *to* **GERRIT SMITH. 28 January 1837. Pharsalia, Chenango County.** Describes steps he took to establish an AS in his community after reading an issue of the *Friend of Man.* 8 February 1837. p.134, c4.

**295 STARR CLARK** *to* **BROTHER GOODELL. 24 January 1837. Mexico, Oswego County.** Lists election results and resolutions adopted during the latest meeting of the Oswego County Anti-Slavery Convention. 8 February 1837. p.134, c4.

**296 F. RICE** *to* **WM. GOODELL. 4 February 1837. Cazenovia.** Discusses the annual meeting of the AS in Hamilton; lists resolutions adopted and officers elected. 8 February 1837. p.134, c5.

**297 HENRY CLAY** *to* **R.R. GURLEY, SEC. OF THE ACS. 22 December 1836. Washington.** Accepts his election as president of the ACS. 8 February 1837. p.134, c6.

**298 OLIPHANT AND SKINNER** *to* **THURLOW WEED. 22 January 1837.** ***Journal*** **Office, Auburn.** Describe the damage done by a fire in Auburn. 8 February 1837. p.135, c6.

**299 W. H. J.** *to* **FRIEND. [from the** ***National Enquirer*****] 11 January 1837. Buckingham, Bucks County.** Reports on the progress of anti-slavery work in Buckingham. 15 February 1837. p.137, c3.

**300 THOMAS JEFFERSON** *to* **DR. PRICE. 7 August 1785. Paris.** States that he has received Price's anti-slavery pamphlets and suggests areas of the United States in which they should be distributed. 15 February 1837. p.137, c5.

**301 THOMAS JEFFERSON** *to* **EDWARD COLES, ESQ. [GOVERNOR OF ILLINOIS]. 25 August 1814. Monticello.** Reaffirms his position on slavery and acknowledges Cole's letter. 15 February 1837. p.137, c6.

**302 THEOPHILUS** *to* **MESSRS. EDITORS. [from the** ***Philanthropist*****] 9 January 1837. Mansfield, Oh.** Urges readers to pray for abolitionists and their cause. 15 February 1837. p.138, c1.

**303 AN EYE WITNESS** *to* **BROTHER GOODELL. n.d. n.p.** Reports on the mobbing of abolitionists after an anti-slavery address in Floyd. 15 February 1837. p.138, c1.

**304 MR. HUNTSMAN** *to* **SIR [WM. GOODELL]. 6 January 1837. Washington City.** Chastizes Goodell for forwarding him a copy of the *Friend of Man* and forbids him to send any more abolitionist publications. 15 February 1837. p.138, c2.

**305 WILLIAM GOODELL** *to* **SIR [MR. HUNTSMAN]. 8 February 1837. Utica.** Promises to stop sending Huntsman the *Friend of Man*; explains that he sent Huntsman an issue of the paper because he felt it important that Huntsman know the views of abolitionists. 15 February 1837. p.138, c3.

**306 N. SOUTHARD** *to* **n.n. [from** ***Zion's Watchman*****] n.d. n.p.** Reports on the rise of abolitionist activity at Martha's Vineyard. 15 February 1837. p.139, c6.

**307 H. C. WRIGHT** *to* **MR. EDITOR. [from the** ***Emancipator*****] n.d. n.p.** Cites varied responses of children to the issues of colonization and anti-slavery. 15 February 1837. p.140, c3.

**308 JOHN G. WHITTIER** *to* **THE EDITOR OF THE** *NEW YORK EVANGELIST.* **30 January 1837. Harrisburg.** Reports on proceedings and resolutions of the Pennsylvania State Anti-Slavery Convention. 22 February 1837. p.142, c1.

**309 JAMES B. ELDRIDGE** *to* **THE EDITOR OF THE** *FRIEND OF MAN.* **13 February 1837. Hamilton.** Encloses new information to correct the mistaken impression of events during the anti-slavery convention in Hamilton. 22 February 1837. p.142, c2.

**310 JOHN R. DODGE** *to* **THE** *FRIEND OF MAN.* **n.d. n.p.** Relates the story of a woman who neglected her child to the point of death because of her interest in romance novels, and concludes that the reading and enjoyment of fiction is harmful. 22 February 1837. p.144, c1.

**311 NATHANIEL WEST** *to* **THE PRESIDENT AND MEMBERS OF THE ANTI-SLAVERY CONVENTION OF PENNSYLVANIA, ASSEMBLED AT HARRISBURG. [from the** *Emancipator***] 25 January 1837. Meadville, Crawford County, Pa.** Explains that he will not be able to attend the convention; encloses discussion topics for the delegates. 1 March 1837. p.145, c1.

**312 DANIEL L. MILLER, JR. AND SAMUEL J. LERIK** *to* **THE HARRISBURG ANTI-SLAVERY CONVENTION. [from the** *Emancipator***] 28 January 1837. Philadelphia.** Regret that members of the Junior AS of Philadelphia will not be able to attend the anti-slavery convention in Harrisburg. 1 March 1837. p.145, c1.

**313 ALVAN STEWART** *to* **MEMBERS OF ANTI-SLAVERY CONVENTION AT HARRISBURG. [from the** *Emancipator***] 22 January 1837. Utica.** Believes that slavery is a great evil and should be abolished. 1 March 1837. p.145, c1.

**314 WILLIAM GOODELL** *to* **BRETHREN. [from the** *Emancipator***] 20 January 1837. Utica.** States that he will not be able to attend the convention and encourages those who will attend to be productive and serious. 1 March 1837. p.145, c2.

**315 WILLIAM JAY** *to* **THE MEMBERS OF THE ANTI-SLAVERY CONVENTION. [from the** *Emancipator***] 25 November 1836. Bedford.** Regrets that he cannot attend the convention; describes the difficulties to be faced by abolitionists. 1 March 1837. p.145, c2.

**316 LA ROY SUNDERLAND** *to* **THE MEMBERS OF THE ANTI-SLAVERY CONVENTION. [extract from the** *Emancipator***] n.d. n.p.** Expresses horror that slavery exists in a supposedly free and democratic country. 1 March 1837. p.145, c3.

**317 REV. LUMUND WILCOX** *to* **SIR. [from the** *Emancipator***] 16 January 1837. Hamilton, N.Y.** Discusses the success of his anti-slavery lectures in Smyrna, Sherburne, Edmeston, Westford, Milford and Hartwick. 1 March 1837. p.145, c5.

**318 JOS. HORACE KIMBALL** *to* **BROTHER. 7 December 1835. St. Thomas.** Discusses slavery and other issues on the islands, including the status of free blacks, morals, the apprenticeship system in British colonies, and St. Croix slaveholders. 1 March 1837. p.145, c5.

**319 A. E. GRIMKE** *to* **n.n. 21 January 1837. New York.** Raises a number of issues including education in America and women's rights. 1 March 1837. p.146, c2.

**320 A. STEWART** *to* **WILLIAM GOODELL. 11 February 1836. Annsville, Oneida County.** Comments on issues raised in his lectures on temperance and abolitionism. 1 March 1837. p.146, c2.

**321 YOUR FELLOW LABORER** *to* **WILLIAM GOODELL. 17 February 1837. Albany.** Notes the courteous treatment of abolitionists by the House of Assembly of New York with regard to anti-slavery petitions. 1 March 1837. p.146, c3.

**322 GERRIT SMITH** *to* **BERIAH GREEN. 8 February 1837. Peterboro'.** Discusses the Unitarian concept of human nature and the dangers of the theory of a natural aristocracy. 8 March 1837. p.149, c5.

**323 D. K.** *to* **JUDGE ELDRIDGE OF HAMILTON. n.d. n.p.** Disagrees with Eldridge's statement that the Bible sanctions slavery, and argues that slavery in any form is immoral and must be abolished. 8 March 1837. p.150, c1.

**324 n.n.** *to* **WILLIAM GOODELL. n.d. n.p.** Encloses several letters addressed to Judge Eldridge, Rev. Beriah Green and Mr. Goodell, asking that they be published in the *Friend of Man*. 8 March 1837. p.150, c1.

**325 n.n.** *to* **BROTHER GOODELL. n.d. n.p.** Encloses a letter addressed to Rev. Beriah Green in which he discusses the problems of immediate emancipation. 8 March 1837. p.150, c2.

**326 DAVID R. GILLMER** *to* **REV. BERIAH GREEN. n.d. n.p.** Asks several questions of Reverend Green, including whether emancipation should be gradual or immediate, and what will be done to provide for the needs of the freedmen. 8 March 1837. p.150, c2.

**327 BERIAH GREEN** *to* **REV. DAVID R. GILLMER. 25 February 1837. Whitesboro'.** Answers Gillmer's letter, stating that although plans have not been drawn up, the newly emancipated Negro would not be left to fend for himself; stresses the Negro's ability to look after himself. 8 March 1837. p.150, c2.

**328 F. A. SPENCER** *to* **BRO. GOODELL. 20 February 1837. Verona.** Discusses the founding of the Verona AS and the opposition it has encountered from local residents. 8 March 1837. p.150, c4.

**329 ARISTIDES** *to* **MR. EDITOR. [from** *Zion's Watchman***] n.d. n.p.** Compares the leaders of the American Revolution with the abolitionists, concluding that both groups fought for a just but unpopular cause. 8 March 1837. p.152, c2.

**330 C. L.** *to* **WM. GOODELL. 24 February 1837. Rome.** States that Negroes are opposed to colonization and that the average Christian is not an abolitionist because of a lack of religious conviction. 15 March 1837. p.153, c1.

**331 A. S.** *to* **JOHN WILKINSON. 1 March 1837. Skaneateles.** Disagrees with Wilkinson's belief that slavery is right; argues that universal emancipation could occur safely. 15 March 1837. p.153, c3.

**332 P. B. J.** *to* **MR. EDITOR [WILLIAM GOODELL]. n.d. n.p.** Argues that every slave is a man, and that no man can hold another in slavery. 15 March 1837. p.153, c4.

**333 LYDIA MARIA CHILD** *to* **GERRIT SMITH. 14 February 1837. South Natick, Ma.** Describes the progress of abolitionist work in South Natick and mentions an unfriendly encounter with pro-slavery forces. 15 March 1837. p.153, c5.

**334 JOHN RANKIN** *to* **BRO. LEAVITT. [from the** *New York Evangelist***] 17 February 1837. Ripley.** Criticizes benevolent societies for accepting contributions from slaveholders. 15 March 1837. p.153, c5.

**335 JAMES W. DUFFIN** *to* **THE** ***FRIEND OF MAN.*** **10 February 1837. Geneva.** Reports that a black AS has been formed in Geneva; lists resolutions adopted and the amount of funds raised during its first meeting. 15 March 1837. p.154, c2.

**336 A BAPTIST** *to* **WM. GOODELL. 13 March 1837. Whitesboro'.** Praises Reverend Gould for his anti-slavery work in the United States and abroad. 15 March 1837. p.154, c2.

**337 T. MERRITT** *to* **THE METHODISTS IN THE NON-SLAVE-HOLDING STATES, ESPECIALLY IN NEW ENGLAND. [from** ***Zion's Herald*****] 1 March 1837. Lynn.** Argues that slavery cannot be defended and that it must be abolished. 22 March 1837. p.157, c1.

**338 J. H. KIMBALL, EDITOR OF THE** ***HERALD OF FREEDOM*** *to* **n.n. 10 December 1836. St. Thomas.** Describes the appearance of St. Thomas, the condition of blacks there, and the morality of the people; includes descriptions of Antigua, Tortola and St. Kitts, along with an account of visits to Nevis and Montserrat. 22 March 1837. p.157, c4.

**339 JOHN HUNTER** *to* **BROTHER. [from the** ***Emancipator*****] 5 January 1837. Mission Institute, Quincy, Il.** Relates the unsuccessful efforts of a Mr. Williams to bring legal action against John Humphrey for trying to sell two black boys into slavery. 22 March 1837. p.158, c3.

**340 E. WRIGHT, JR.** *to* **ASs. 3 March 1837. 143 Nassau Street, New York City.** Requests that all county ASs send him a list of all minor societies in each county. 22 March 1837. p.158, c3.

**341 WILLIAM T. ALLAN** *to* **WM. GOODELL. 8 March 1837. Middleport, N.Y.** Describes the success of his anti-slavery lectures in Middleport, Monroe and Niagara County. 22 March 1837. p.158, c4.

**342 C. STUART** *to* **BROTHER. n.d. n.p.** Describes the formation of the Onondaga County AS. 22 March 1837. p.158, c5.

**343 J. HORTON** *to* **MR. EDITOR. [from** ***Zion's Watchman*****] 15 February 1837. Boston.** Relates the story of a slaveholder who converted to abolitionism during an evening of prayer. 22 March 1837. p.160, c3.

**344 JOS. HORACE KIMBALL, EDITOR** *to* **n.n. n.d. Antigua, West Indies.** Continues his discussion of life on Antigua after emancipation, concluding that considerable progress has been made. [continued from 22 March 1837] 29 March 1837. p.155 [161], c1.

**345 WILLIAM JAY** *to* **THE EDITOR OF THE** ***WESTCHESTER HERALD.*** **21 January 1837. Bedford.** Encloses a letter from Jay to the mayor of New York City protesting the kidnapping and selling of a free colored man, Peter Lee. 29 March 1837. p.155 [161], c3.

**346 WILLIAM JAY** *to* **HON. W. C. LAWRENCE, MAYOR, CITY OF NEW YORK. 4 January 1837. Bedford, Westchester County.** Condemns the New York City Police Department for arresting Peter Lee, a colored man, on a three-year-old warrant and sending him South; demands an investigation of the police department. 29 March 1837. p.155 [161], c3.

**347 C. W. LAWRENCE** *to* **HON. WILLIAM JAY. 9 January 1837. New York.** Answers Jay's letter and states that he has no jurisdiction over two of the officers involved in the kidnapping of Peter Lee, and that the third is out of town; insists, however, that the men should be severely punished if they are guilty. 29 March 1837. p.155 [161], c3.

**348 C. W. LAWRENCE** *to* **HON. WILLIAM JAY. 1[?] January 1837. New York.** States that Tobias Boudinot, constable of the Third Ward, possessed several warrants issued in 1833 by the governor of New York, with Peter Lee's name appearing on one of the warrants as Henry. 29 March 1837. p.155 [161], c4.

**349 A. M. HUNTER** *to* **BRO. LOVEJOY. [from the** *Alton Observer***] 27 January 1837. Mission Institute.** Encloses a letter by Dr. D. Nelson concerning the immorality of slavery. 29 March 1837. p.155 [161], c4.

**350 DR. NELSON** *to* **MEMBERS OF HIS CONGREGATION. n.d. Missouri.** Urges his congregation to examine their slaveholding practices; reminds them that property means nothing in Heaven. 29 March 1837. p.155 [161], c4.

**351 JUNIOR GENESEE** *to* **MR. EDITOR. [from** *Zion's Watchman***] 14 January 1837. E---, N.Y.** Emphasizes the importance of prayer in anti-slavery work. 29 March 1837. p.155 [161], c6.

**352 GEORGE THOMPSON** *to* **n.n. [from the** *Liberator***] 21 January 1837. Edinburgh.** Reports on the state of his health after an attack of influenza; describes the progress made by abolitionists in England. 29 March 1837. p.155 [161], c6.

**353 n.n.** *to* **MESSRS. EDITORS. [from the** *Philanthropist***] n.d. n.p.** Denounces the concept of slavery as a divine institution sanctioned by the Bible; includes excerpts from a letter by a North Carolina farmer. 29 March 1837. p.156 [162], c3.

**354 GEORGE STORRS** *to* **BROTHER SUNDERLAND. [from** *Zion's Watchman***] n.d. Mexico, Oswego County, N.Y.** Reports on the success of his anti-slavery addresses in Oswego and Fulton counties; relates the story of two male runaways who escaped from a Virginia plantation to Philadelphia. 29 March 1837. p.156 [162], c3.

**355 REV. J. CROSS** *to* **MR. WM. GOODELL. 20 March 1837. Leyden.** Notes the success of his anti-slavery lectures in Collinsville, Constableville and Talcottville; mentions a minor encounter with anti-abolitionist forces in Copenhagen, Lewis County. 29 March 1837. p.157 [163], c4.

**356 REV. A. T. RANKIN** *to* **MESSRS. EDITORS. [from the** *Philanthropist***] 25 February 1837. n.p.** Discusses the mobbing of abolitionists in Dayton; observes that anti-abolitionist sentiment in Dayton is related to the large number of slaveholders in Dayton, the poor progress of colonizationists, and opposition from the Masonic fraternity. 29 March 1837. p.157 [163], c6.

**357 CLARKSON** *to* **SARAH M. AND ANGELINA E. GRIMKE [from the** *Intelligencer***] 11 February 1837. New Haven.** Requests that the Grimké sisters present a definite, practicable means by which the people of the North can put an end to slavery in the South. 5 April 1837. p.159 [165], c1.

**358 SARAH M. AND ANGELINA E. GRIMKE** *to* **CLARKSON. [from the** *Intelligencer***] n.d. n.p.** Reply to Clarkson, stating that the North could aid in the abolition of slavery by petitioning Congress, withdrawing political support from politicians who support slavery, and protesting the use of jails as holding pens for slaves. 5 April 1837. p.159 [165], c1.

**359 REV. J. M. McKIM** *to* **FRIEND LUNDY. [from the** *National Enquirer***] 7 March 1837. Pottsgrove.** Describes the success of anti-slavery lectures in Carlisle, Reading, Maiden Creek and Douglassville. 5 April 1837. p.159 [165], c5.

**360 J. BLANCHARD** *to* **BROTHER LUNDY. [from the** *National Enquirer*] **6 March 1837. Washington, Pa.** Describes a debate between abolitionists and pro-slavery forces in Washington, Pennsylvania, which resulted in victory for the pro-slavery forces. 5 April 1837. p.159 [165], c6.

**361 JAMES COX** *to* **BROTHER. 9 February 1837. St. Johns, Antigua.** Lists resolutions adopted during a meeting of the Wesleyan missionaries of the Antigua District. 5 April 1837. p.160 [166], c1.

**362 MR. C. S. RENSHAW** *to* **BROTHER. 2 February 1837. Palmyra.** Describes the success of his anti-slavery lectures in West Bloomfield, Ontario County. 5 April 1837. p.160 [166], c3.

**363 J. CROSS** *to* **MR. W. GOODELL. 1 April 1837. Camden.** Introduces further evidence supporting the story of W. C. Guildersleeve, an abolitionist, who claims that his home is being vandalized by pro-slavery forces. 5 April 1837. p.160 [166], c5.

**364 JOHN McVICCER** *to* **THE** *FRIEND OF MAN.* **n.d. n.p.** Describes the formation of the Onondaga County AS; lists the results of officer elections and resolutions adopted during its first meeting. 5 April 1837. p.160 [166], c5.

**365 ANSEL CHADWICK** *to* **WM. GOODELL. 28 March 1837. Genoa Five Corners.** Praises an anti-slavery lecture delivered by Rev. S. Hawley to the residents of Genoa Five Corners, which resulted in the formation of the Genoa Five Corners AS. 5 April 1837. p.160 [166], c6.

**366 JOHN A. BILLING AND JONATHAN A. S. PEASE** *to* **MR. EDITOR OF THE** *FRIEND OF MAN* **[WILLIAM GOODELL]. 25 March 1837. West Leyden.** Discuss the history of the formation of the West Leyden AS; list the resolutions adopted during its first meeting. 5 April 1837. p.160 [166], c6.

**367 ANTONIO LOPEZ DE SANTA ANNA** *to* **THE MINISTER OF WAR AND MARINE. 20 February 1837. Vera Cruz.** States that his journey from Texas to Baltimore was safe and enjoyable and that as soon as he returns to his home in Mexico, he will write an account of his experiences with the American and Mexican armies. 5 April 1837. p.161 [167], c4.

**368 JUAN N. ALMONTE** *to* **GENERAL DON JOSE MARIA TORNEL. 20 February 1837. Vera Cruz.** Informs that he is now free after being held prisoner in Texas and that he will see his family and friends soon. 5 April 1837. p.161 [167], c4.

**369 D. K.** *to* **JUDGE ELDRIDGE OF HAMILTON. n.d. n.p.** Emphasizes the importance of loving God and of loving each man as a brother. 12 April 1837. p.163 [169], c4.

**370 J. BLANCHARD** *to* **THE PUBLIC. [from the** *Harrisburg Chronicle*] **n.d. n.p.** Compares the old and new abolition societies of Pennsylvania; criticizes the residents of Harrisburg for refusing their town hall to abolitionists but permitting colonizationists to use it. 12 April 1837. p.164 [170], c2.

**371 WM. RICH** *to* **THE COLORED PEOPLE OF ALBANY, TROY, LANSINGBURGH, WATERFORD, SCHENECTADY, GREENBUSH AND VICINITY. [from the** *Daily Whig*] **29 March 1837. Troy.** Describes the formation of the Union Society of Albany, Troy and vicinity for the improvement of the colored people in morals, education and mechanical arts; includes a copy of the society's constitution and lists resolutions adopted during its first meeting. 12 April 1837. p.164 [170], c5.

**372 DYAR FOOTE** *to* **ALVAN STEWART. [extract] 22 March 1837. Ludlowville.** States that slavery, like intemperance, is an evil that should be abolished, and that all men should be free and treated equally. 12 April 1837. p.164 [170], c6.

**373 n.n.** *to* **ALVAN STEWART, ESQ. 20 March 1837. Virginia.** Describes the circumstances surrounding the death of a Mrs. Geyer, a wealthy slaveholder, and the sale of all of her slaves except two who escaped from Virginia to Utica, New York. 12 April 1837. p.165 [171], c1.

**374 n.n** *to* **WM. KIDD. [extract] 28 February 1837. Tampico.** Describes the preparations made to stave off another attack on Texas by Mexico. 12 April 1837. p.165 [171], c5.

**375 P. B. J.** *to* **MR. EDITOR [WILLIAM GOODELL]. n.d. n.p.** States that the common schools are deficient in moral as well as intellectual training. 12 April 1837. p.164 [172], c1.

**376 LEONARD BACON** *to* **GERRIT SMITH. [from the** *New Haven Religious Intelligencer***] 8 March 1837. New Haven.** Denounces the New York AS for accusing the Northern ministers of being pro-slavery and indifferent to the sufferings of slaves. 19 April 1837. p.167 [173], c1.

**377 WILLIAM GOODELL** *to* **REV. LEONARD BACON. n.d. n.p.** Replies to Bacon, stating that he accepts responsibility for publishing the New York State AS pamphlet which accused Northern ministers of being pro-slavery; apologizes for the misunderstanding which followed. 19 April 1837. p.167 [173], c5.

**378 A SPECTATOR** *to* **MR. MIDDLETON. [from the** *Gettysburg Star* **and the** *Republican Banner***] 5 April 1837. Millerstown.** Describes the opposition to an anti-slavery lecture delivered by Mr. Blanchard to the residents of Millerstown. 19 April 1837. p.168 [174], c6.

**379 STEPHEN ATWATER** *to* **WM. GOODELL. 4 April 1837. Lockport.** Believes that it is important to present anti-slavery lectures in schools and in remote towns; praises the work done by abolitionists in Niagara County. 19 April 1837. p.169 [175], c1.

**380 J. N. T. T[UCKER]** *to* **WM. GOODELL. 5 April 1837. Clockville.** Attributes the rise of anti-slavery sentiment in Clockville to the circulation of such anti-slavery publications as the *Friend of Man*. 19 April 1837. p.169 [175], c1.

**381 n.n.** *to* **n.n. [extract] n.d. n.p.** States that he is praying for the abolition of slavery and for everyone who is working toward that goal. 19 April 1837. p.169 [175], c2.

**382 R. PRATT** *to* **SIR. 10 April 1837. Marshall.** Provides a brief history of the formation of the Marshall AS. 19 April 1837. p.169 [175], c2.

**383 L. BOOMER** *to* **WM. GOODELL. 10 April 1837. Floyd.** Reports on the formation of an AS in Floyd. 19 April 1837. p.169 [175], c2.

**384 A. SEDGWICK** *to* **WM. GOODELL. 8 April 1837. Rome.** Reports on the formation of an AS in Waterville and describes a violent encounter with Waterville's pro-slavery forces. 19 April 1837. p.169 [175], c2.

**385 JAMES PRESTON** *to* **WM. GOODELL. 8 April 1837. Hadley.** Provides the history of the formation of the Hadley AS; includes a copy of its constitution and the names of officers elected during its first meeting. 19 April 1837. p.169 [175], c3.

**386 n.n.** *to* **MR. EDITOR OF THE** ***FRIEND OF MAN*** **[WILLIAM GOODELL]. n.d. n.p.** Criticizes the present common school system for its lack of moral and intellectual guidance; asserts that the purpose of an education is to teach the individual to think. 19 April 1837. p.170 [176], c1.

**387 D. K.** *to* **JUDGE ELDRIDGE. n.d. n.p.** States that God's love of man is a supreme love and that man must grow to understand the meaning of brotherly love. [continued from 12 April 1837] 26 April 1837. p.177, c1.

**388 C. STUART** *to* **WM. GOODELL. 11 April 1837. Whitesboro'.** Examines passages from Leviticus and Exodus in order to prove that slavery is not sanctioned by the Bible. 26 April 1837. p.177, c2.

**389 WILLIAM GOODELL** *to* **REV. LEONARD BACON. 26 April 1837. Utica.** States the goals of abolitionism, and elaborates upon a report from the New York State AS and the General Association of Connecticut regarding the objectives, value and importance of abolitionism. 26 April 1837. p.177, c6.

**390 CLARK LOCKWOOD** *to* **WM. GOODELL. 10 April 1837. Maltaville.** Discusses the formation of the Saratoga County AS and includes a copy of its preamble and constitution. 26 April 1837. p.179, c1.

**391 A LAWYER** *to* **MR. HAMMOND. [from the** ***Cincinnati Daily Gazette*****] n.d. n.p.** Disagrees with a ruling by Judge Este concerning the status of slaves in free territory, stating that slaves should be considered free in free territory regardless of their reasons for being there. 26 April 1837. p.179, c5.

**392 MR. A. WALKER** *to* **SIR. 28 March 1837. Boston.** Discusses the side effects of Dr. Graham's "Graham diet." 26 April 1837. p.180, c4.

**393 WM. GOODELL** *to* **REV. LEONARD BACON OF NEW HAVEN. 28 April 1837. Utica.** Restates issues which were raised in his letter to Rev. Bacon in the previous issue of the *Friend of Man.* 3 May 1837. p.181, c1.

**394 WM. GOODELL** *to* **REV. LEONARD BACON. 3 May 1837. Utica.** Continues to discuss the issues raised in his first and second letters to Reverend Bacon; mentions examples of mob violence directed toward abolitionists, and stresses the need for abolitionists to take a firm, uncompromising stand on slavery issues. 3 May 1837. p.182, c2.

**395 P. B. J.** *to* **MR. EDITOR OF THE** ***FRIEND OF MAN*** **[WILLIAM GOODELL]. n.d. n.p.** States that teachers in common schools are generally prepared to teach but are not encouraged to excel in their profession. 3 May 1837. p.184, c1.

**396 GRANT THORBURN** *to THE DAILY EXPRESS.* **n.d. n.p.** States that the theater has an evil and immoral effect upon one's character and believes that theater productions should be closely monitored. 3 May 1837. p.184, c2.

**397 C. STUART** *to* **THE EDITOR OF THE** ***COMMON SCHOOL ASSISTANT,*** **STATE STREET, ALBANY. 21 April 1837. Whitesboro'.** Stresses the importance of the teacher as a model for his students; condemns slavery and color prejudice. 10 May 1837. p.185, c3.

**398 D. K.** *to* **JUDGE ELDRIDGE OF HAMILTON. n.d. n.p.** Continues his debate with Eldridge in which he argues that slavery is not sanctioned by the Bible. 10 May 1837. p.185, c5.

**399 H. C. WRIGHT** *to* **THE** ***FRIEND OF MAN.*** **24 April 1837. Court room, New York.** Describes the proceedings of the trial of William Dixon of New York and criticizes the American judicial system which forces a man to stand trial in order to prove that he is a man. 10 May 1837. p.186, c1.

**400 G. RATRIE PARBURT** *to* **E. TAYLOR. 8 May 1837. Oneida Institute.** Believes that one must abstain from wine as well as other alcoholic beverages. 10 May 1837. p.186, c2.

**401 W. T. ALLAN** *to* **WM. GOODELL. n.d. n.p.** Describes the opposition encountered by abolitionists in Niagara County. 10 May 1837. p.186, c3.

**402 J. M. BLAKESLEY** *to* **BROTHER WRIGHT. [from the** ***Emancipator*****] 23 March 1837. Oberlin.** Notes the success of anti-slavery in Chatauque and Erie counties. 10 May 1837. p.186, c4.

**403 A. DRESSER** *to* **BROTHER. [from the** ***Emancipator*****] 21 March 1837. Boston.** Describes the success of his anti-slavery lectures in Hinsdale, Peru, and Goshen counties. 10 May 1837. p.186, c4.

**404 J. B. WATSON** *to* **BROTHER. [from the** ***Emancipator*****] 28 March 1837. Jay, N.Y.** Mentions the appeal of his anti-slavery lectures in Essex County and recalls anti-slavery conferences attended in Massachusetts and in England. 10 May 1837. p.186, c5.

**405 REV. J. BLANCHARD** *to* **BROTHER. [from the** ***Emancipator*****] 1 April 1837. Gettysburgh, Adams County, Pa.** Describes a debate on abolitionism in which the party opposed to abolitionism was victorious. 10 May 1837. p.186, c5.

**406 REV. C. P. GROSVENOR** *to* **BROTHER. [from the** ***Emancipator*****] 30 March 1837. Rutland, Ma.** Notes the success of his anti-slavery lectures in Brookfield, West Brookfield and Middlesex counties, Massachusetts. 10 May 1837. p.186, c5.

**407 WM. R. SAXTON** *to* **MR. EDITOR. [from the** ***Emancipator*****] n.d. n.p.** Provides a history of the formation of the Lebanon AS and includes a list of elected officers. 10 May 1837. p.186, c5.

**408 n.n.** *to* **n.n. [extract] n.d. Massachusetts.** Expresses enthusiasm over the rise of abolitionism and predicts that it will spread. 10 May 1837. p.186, c6.

**409 H. W. COBB** *to* **WM. GOODELL. 14 April. Camden.** States that this is an important era in the cause of human rights; calls upon abolitionists to be uncompromising in their battle against slavery. 10 May 1837. p.186, c6.

**410 A LOOKER ON** *to* **WM. GOODELL. n.d. n.p.** Relates a story involving Gerrit Smith, who was invited to Kirkland to deliver an anti-slavery lecture, but upon arrival was denied a hall in which to deliver his lecture. 10 May 1837. p.187, c1.

**411 D. K.** *to* **JUDGE ELDRIDGE OF HAMILTON. n.d. n.p.** Cites Biblical passages pointing to the great evil of American slavery. [continued from 10 May 1837] 17 May 1837. p.189, c5.

**412 DR. FISK** *to* **THE** ***LONDON CHRISTIAN ADVOCATE.*** **[from the** ***Philanthropist*****] August 1836. Birmingham, England.** Discusses the progress in the West Indies since emancipation and analyzes the differences between the AS of England and the Anti-Slavery Agency of England. 17 March 1837. p.189, c6.

**413 n.n.** *to* **DR. FISK. [from the** ***London Christian Advocate*****] n.d. n.p.** States that Dr. Fisk was misinformed in regard to the present situation in the West Indies; questions his source of information. 17 May 1837. p.192 [190], c1.

**414 WM. GOODELL** *to* **J. P. BISHOP. 8 May 1837. New York.** States that while visiting New York, he was the guest of several prominent abolitionists and he attended several abolitionist meetings. 17 May 1837. p.192 [190], c2.

**415 WM. GOODELL** *to* **SIR. 9 May 1837. New York.** Describes the opening ceremonies of the fourth annual meeting of the AAS; lists the names and topics of each speaker. 17 May 1837. p.192 [190], c3.

**416 GERRIT SMITH** *to* **THE PEOPLE OF CLINTON, ONEIDA CO. 4 May 1837. n.p.** Expresses astonishment at his hostile reception in Clinton, noting that he had been invited by the residents of Clinton to deliver an anti-slavery lecture. 17 May 1837. p.192 [190], c4.

**417 n.n.** *to* **MR. EDITOR OF THE** *FRIEND OF MAN.* **n.d. n.p.** Describes the proceedings of a convention of abolitionists in Harrisburg, Pennsylvania; includes a list of resolutions adopted by the convention and the names and topics of each speaker. 17 May 1837. p.192 [190], c5.

**418 G. RATRIE PARBURT** *to* **E. TAYLOR. 15 May 1837. Oneida Institute.** Believes that wine is as dangerous and as intoxicating as any hard liquor. 17 May 1837. p.192 [190], c6.

**419 H. C. WRIGHT** *to* **BROTHER. [from the** *Emancipator*] **n.d. n.p.** Discusses the dismissal of a Mr. Lane as superintendent of Laight Street Church Sunday School in New York because Lane defied his pastor by promoting total abstinence from alcoholic drinks and introducing abolitionist literature. 17 May 1837. p.191, c1.

**420 COLD WATER** *to* **THE** *FRIEND OF MAN.* **5 May 1837. Sauquoit.** Describes the proceedings of a meeting of the Sauquoit Temperance Association, during which the members discussed the evils of intoxication. 17 May 1837. p.191, c2.

**421 n.n.** *to* **n.n. n.d. Vermont.** States that abolitionism is spreading in Vermont, pointing to the organization of ASs in Calais, Berlin and Barnard as proof. 17 May 1837. p.191, c5.

**422 A MAGISTRATE IN JAMAICA** *to* **n.n. [extract from the** *London Christian Advocate*] **n.d. n.p.** Relates an incident involving a pregnant slave who was forced to do hard labor. 17 May 1837. p.191, c5.

**423 C. O. SHEPARD** *to* **THE ASSEMBLY OF THE STATE OF NEW YORK. 29 April 1837. Assembly Chamber, Albany.** Criticizes the faculty of Hamilton College for representing him as indifferent to slavery when he actually opposes it. 24 May 1837. p.193, c6.

**424 C. CALKINS** *to* **SIR. 11 April 1837. Hamilton College.** States that Shepard did not encourage Hamilton students to petition the state legislature to abolish slavery, noting that the idea originated within the Hamilton student body. 24 May 1837. p.193, c6.

**425 EXECUTIVE COMMITTEE OF HAMILTON COLLEGE AS** *to* **THE** *FRIEND OF MAN.* **12 May 1837. Hamilton College.** Describes the formation of the Hamilton College AS; forwards resolutions adopted during its first meeting. 24 May 1837. p.194, c1.

**426 G. RATRIE PARBURT** *to* **E. TAYLOR. 22 May 1837. Oneida Institute.** Provides historical evidence that wine is as intoxicating as whiskey or any other liquor. 24 May 1837. p.194, c2.

**427 H. C. WRIGHT** *to* **THE** *FRIEND OF MAN.* **11 May 1837. Boston.** Reports that a city in the vicinity of New York went bankrupt because certain Southern merchants and planters with whom the city dealt accumulated a debt of $5 million and then refused to repay it. 24 May 1837. p.194, c3.

**428 AUSTIN PUTNAM** *to* **WILLIAM GOODELL. 15 May 1837. Smithville, Jefferson County.** Reports on the formation of the Jefferson County AS. 24 May 1837. p.194, c4.

**429 A. SEDGWICK** *to* **WM. GOODELL. 15 May 1837. Rome.** Apologizes for statements made about a Mr. Husbands during an abolitionist meeting in Waterville. 24 May 1837. p.195, c2.

**430 A COLORED WOMAN** *to* **FRIENDS. 5 April 1837. A---.** Expresses sorrow over the death of Mary, a family member, and hopes that she accepted Christ as her savior before dying. 31 May 1837. p.195 [196], c1.

**431 G. A. F.** *to* **SISTER. n.d. n.p.** States that all things are possible if one believes in God; asks her to pray for an individual who showed her a special kindness. 31 May 1837. p.195 [196], c1.

**432 GERRIT SMITH** *to* **EDWARD C. DELAVAN. 10 April 1837. Peterboro'.** Invites Delavan to join the AAS and reviews Delavan's reasons for postponing his acceptance of membership. 31 May 1837. p.197, c4.

**433 MR. EDWARD C. DELAVAN** *to* **GERRIT SMITH. 10 May 1837. Ballston Centre, Saratoga County, N.Y.** Answers Smith's letter, stating that he has already joined the AAS and is proud to be associated with it. 31 May 1837. p.197, c6.

**434 J. BLANCHARD** *to* **BROTHER PHELPS. [from the** ***Emancipator*****] 5 May 1837. Harrisburg.** Describes the proceedings of the pro-slavery state convention held on 1 May in Harrisburg, Pennsylvania. 31 May 1837. p.197, c6.

**435 G. RATRIE PARBURT** *to* **E. TAYLOR. 29 May 1837. Oneida Institute.** Argues that the ancients were as intemperate as present-day men, pointing to various Old Testament characters as proof. 31 May 1837. p.198, c4.

**436 REHUM** *to* **WM. GOODELL. n.d. n.p.** Encourages abolitionists to hold more county conventions; wonders why so few have been organized in the past year. 31 May 1837. p.198, c5.

**437 J. GRIDLEY** *to* **MR. GOODELL. 2 May 1837. Pompey.** States that the men of Pompey have organized an AS; encloses the preamble of the constitution of the Pompey Ladies AS. 31 May 1837. p.198, c5.

**438 REHUM** *to* **WM. GOODELL. 25 May 1837. Utica.** Believes that the anti-slavery lectures which Mr. Southwick presented to the Young Men's Association should be published. 31 May 1837. p.198, c6.

**439 J. G. D.** *to* **WM. GOODELL. 17 May 1837. Schenectady.** Reports that two anti-slavery meetings were held in Schenectady and that Gerrit Smith lectured and was favorably received at both of them. 31 May 1837. p.199, c3.

**440 JOSE MARIA ORTIZ MONASTERIO** *to* **HIS EXCELLENCY, THE SECRETARY OF FOREIGN RELATIONS OF THE UNITED STATES OF AMERICA. [from the** ***National Enquirer*****] 31 March 1837. Palace of the National Government, Mexico.** Protests the United States' recognition of the independence of Texas. 31 May 1837. p.199, c4.

**441 P. B. J.** *to* **MR. EDITOR [WILLIAM GOODELL]. n.d. n.p.** Believes that beneficial reforms will occur in common schools only when the public is convinced that they are necessary. 31 May 1837. p.200, c1.

**442 JESSE CAMPBELL** *to* **THE** ***FRIEND OF MAN*****. n.d. n.p.** Reports that the Norway AS has been formed in Herkimer County. 7 June 1837. p.1, c2.

**443 GERRIT SMITH** *to* **REV. LEONARD BACON. [from the** *New York Observer***] 7 April 1837. Peterboro'.** Disagrees with Goodell's criticism of the anti-slavery efforts of the General Association of Connecticut, and apologizes to Bacon for Goodell's remarks. 7 June 1837. p.1, c3.

**444 WM. GOODELL** *to* **GERRIT SMITH. 18 May 1837. Utica.** Replies to Smith, stating that he will not retract his criticism of the General Association of Connecticut; emphasizes the need for constructive criticism within the abolitionist movement. 7 June 1837. p.1, c4.

**445 D. K.** *to* **JUDGE ELDRIDGE OF HAMILTON. n.d. n.p.** States that the American form of slavery has no biblical parallel; examines the biblical use of such terms as bondmen, bondmaids, handmaid and servant. [continued from 17 May 1837] 7 June 1837. p.2, c5.

**446 F.** *to* **MR. EDITOR [WILLIAM GOODELL]. 5 June 1837. Utica.** Criticizes a group of Presbyterian ministers who became anxious about their involvement in abolitionism and stopped supporting the abolitionist cause. 7 June 1837. p. 3, c1.

**447 n.n.** *to* **SIR. 1 May 1837. Matamoras.** States that the *Champion,* an American war ship, has been captured by the Mexican government and its crew tried for an unnamed offense. 7 June 1837. p.3, c6.

**448 N. SHERWOOD, MASTER, SCHOONER** *CHAMPION to* **J. B. MINCE. 3 May 1837. Matamoras.** Describes the overcrowded conditions and the lack of food in the Mexican jails. 7 June 1837. p.3, c6.

**449 n.n.** *to* **MR. EDITOR OF THE** *FRIEND OF MAN.* **n.d. n.p.** Notes that an institution has been established to treat and cure stammering. 7 June 1837. p.104,[4], c2.

**450 ELIJAH P. LOVEJOY** *to* **BROTHER LEAVITT. [from the** *Emancipator***] 3 October 1837. Alton.** Describes several attempts made on his life by pro-slavery groups in Alton and St. Charles. 8 November 1837. p.81, c3.

**451 G. RATRIE PARBURT** *to* **THE FRIENDS OF TEMPERANCE IN WHITESBORO'. October 1837. Junius, Seneca County, N.Y.** Stresses the importance of temperance and discusses the quantity of wine consumed at the Last Supper. 8 November 1837. p.81, c6.

**452 J. CROSS** *to* **WM. GOODELL. 18 October 1837. Waterloo.** Relates the story of a retired minister of the Methodist Episcopal church who was hard of hearing, but was forbidden by church officials to sit near the front of the church. 8 November 1837. p.82, c2.

**453 W. H. P.** *to* **WM. GOODELL. 23 October 1837. Adams, Jefferson County.** Praises an article on slavery by Alvan Stewart, entitled "Constitutional Argument"; suggests that abolitionists submit a petition to Congress forbidding slave trade between the United States and Texas. 8 November 1837. p.82, c3.

**454 W.** *to* **MR. EDITOR OF THE** *FRIEND OF MAN* **[WILLIAM GOODELL]. n.d. n.p.** Proposes that one individual from each district circulate petitions at the New York polls against the annexation of Texas to the United States. 8 November 1837. p.82, c3.

**455 n.n.** *to* **FRIEND. [extract] 17 October 1837. Meriden, Ct.** Describes the proceedings of an anti-slavery lecture in Meriden during which the lecturers were insulted and egged. 8 November 1837. p.82, c4.

**456 J. P. BISHOP** *to* **WM. GOODELL. 26 October 1837. Utica.** Notes the attempts made by the AAS to establish anti-slavery libraries throughout New York. 8 November 1837. p.82, c4.

**457 GULIAN C. VERPLANCK** *to* **W. L. CHAPLIN. 24 October 1837. New York.** A senatorial candidate from New York answers questions from the New York AS regarding his position on slavery. 8 November 1837. p.82, c5.

**458 SAMUEL HULL** *to* **W. L. CHAPLIN. 30 October 1837. Angelica.** States that he opposes slavery in all its forms, and refers them to his Utica speech in which he expressed his anti-slavery views. 8 November 1837. p.82, c6.

**459 AVERY SKINNER** *to* **W. L. CHAPLIN. 20 October 1837. Union Square.** A senatorial candidate from New York answers questions from the New York AS regarding his position on slavery. 8 November 1837. p.82, c6.

**460 LYMAN CURTISS** *to* **A. BLAIR, PRESIDENT OF THE ONEIDA COUNTY AS. 25 October 1837. Camden.** A candidate for county sheriff answers questions from the New York AS regarding his position on slavery. 8 November 1837. p.83, c1.

**461 JAMES DEAN** *to* **DR. A. BLAIR, PRES., ONEIDA COUNTY AS. 21 October 1837. Utica.** A candidate for county clerk answers questions from the New York AS regarding his position on slavery. 8 November 1837. p.83, c1.

**462 ANSON KNIBLOE** *to* **A. BLAIR, PRES., ONEIDA COUNTY AS. 30 October 1837. Trenton.** A candidate for county clerk refuses to answer questions from the New York AS regarding his position on slavery. 8 November 1837. p.83, c1.

**463 HENRY HEARSEY** *to* **A. BLAIR. 27 October 1837. Waterville.** A candidate for assemblyman answers questions from the New York AS regarding his position on slavery. 8 November 1837. p.83, c1.

**464 R. FULLER** *to* **A. BLAIR. 30 October 1837. Steuben.** A candidate for assemblyman answers questions from the New York AS regarding his position on slavery. 8 November 1837. p.83, c2.

**465 J. S. T. STRANAHAN** *to* **W. L. CHAPLIN. 24 October 1837. New York.** A candidate for assemblyman answers questions from the New York AS regarding his position on slavery. 8 November 1837. p.83, c2.

**466 INGHAM TOWNSEND** *to* **A. BLAIR. 31 October 1837. Floyd.** A candidate for assemblyman refuses to answer questions from the New York AS regarding his position on slavery. 8 November 1837. p.83, c2.

**467 NATHANIEL SHERRILL** *to* **A. BLAIR. 25 October 1837. Hampton.** A candidate for assemblyman answers questions from the New York AS regarding his position on slavery. 8 November 1837. p.83, c2.

**468 F. C. WHITE** *to* **A. BLAIR. 26 October 1837. Whitesboro'.** A candidate for assemblyman answers questions from the New York AS regarding his position on slavery. 8 November 1837. p.83, c2.

**469 A. ROOD** *to* **ISAAC HOUSTON. 5 August 1837. Middlebury.** Encloses copies of the *People's Press* for circulation within Middlebury. 8 November 1837. p.83, c3.

**470 n.n.** *to* **MR. EDITOR OF THE *EMANCIPATOR*. n.d. n.p.** Encloses a letter from James S. Bulloch to the editor of the *Georgian,* along with his comments on the letter. 8 November 1837. p.83, c4.

**471 JAMES S. BULLOCH** *to* **THE EDITOR OF THE** *SAVANNAH GEORGIAN.* **[from the** *Emancipator***] 7 August 1837. Hartford, Ct.** Mentions a case before the Connecticut Court of Appeals concerning his runaway slave; notes the rise of abolitionist sentiment in Connecticut. 8 November 1837. p.83, c4.

**472 SOPHIA L. LITTLE** *to* **BELOVED BROTHER. [from the** *Liberator***] 20 August 1837. Newport.** Criticizes the ministers of Newport for failing to read anti-slavery notices from their pulpits. 8 November 1837. p.84, c1.

**473 A SOUTHERNER** *to* **JAMES G. BIRNEY, ESQ. n.d. n.p.** Describes her conversion to abolitionism and rejoices that she has taken up the slave's cause. 8 November 1837. p.84, c3.

## [1838]

**474 A. STEWART** *to* **WILLIAM GOODELL. 26 February 1838. Westford, Vt.** Describes his visit to Albany and the proceedings of the annual meeting of the Vermont AS. 14 March 1838. p.150, c4.

**475 HIRAM WILSON** *to* **WM. GOODELL. 20 February 1838. Manlius.** Describes the poor living conditions of Wilberforce, a colony of Negroes near London, Upper Canada, adding that little of the $30,000 collected recently for the colony has reached its intended destination. 14 March 1838. p.150, c5.

**476 JOSEPH C. HATHAWAY** *to* **FRIEND. February 1838. Farmington.** Encloses information concerning a misunderstanding between himself and a Pharcellus Clay on the tactics of temperance supporters. 14 March 1838. p.150, c5.

**477 WILLIAM POUND** *to* **n.n. 24 February. Wayne County.** Lists resolutions adopted during a meeting of the Wayne County AS at Poultneyville. 14 March 1838. p.150, c6.

**478 W. L. CHAPLIN** *to* **BRO. GOODELL. 12 March 1838. Utica.** Announces the appointment of John D. Lawyer and Isaac M. Duryee as agents for the New York AS. 14 March 1838. p.351 [151], c1.

**479 JOHN MURRAY** *to* **CAPTAIN BIGLEY. [from the** *Glasgow New Liberator***] 12 May 1837. Bowling Bay, near Glasgow.** Relates an incident involving a colored gentleman who was refused first-class accommodations on a ship bound for New York; notes the rise of color prejudice in Scotland. 14 March 1838. p.351 [151], c5.

**480 CHA'S L.** *to* **WM. GOODELL. n.d. n.p.** Discusses his trip to South Carolina and Washington, D.C., and recalls his conversation with John Q. Adams on the great and good work of abolitionism. 22 March 1838. p.153, c4.

**481 J. J. THOMAS** *to* **WM. GOODELL. 5 March 1838. Palmyra, Wayne County.** Discusses the attempt by Walworth residents to establish an AS, and the opposition encountered from residents opposed to anti-slavery work. 22 March 1838. p.153, c5.

**482 JAMES CANNINGS FULLER** *to* **WM. GOODELL. 3 March 1838. n.p.** Relates the story of George Robinson, a freeman who was kidnapped and sold to a slaveholder in Louisiana but succeeded in escaping to New York. 22 March 1838. p.154, c2.

**483 W. L. CHAPLIN** *to* **WM. GOODELL. n.d. n.p.** Announces the appointment of A. Judson and J. M. Blakesley as agents of the New York State AS. 22 March 1838. p.155, c5.

**484 GEORGE STORRS** *to* **BROTHER SUNDERLAND. n.d. n.p.** Describes the opposition encountered by abolitionists in Elmira during an anti-slavery meeting. 17 October 1838. p.277, c6.

**485 SIMEON KEMP** *to* **THOMAS JOHNSON. [from the** *Emancipator***] n.d. n.p.** States that he has imprisoned Moses Johnson, a suspected runaway who claims to be free, and that he and Johnson's son will hold Moses Johnson until he hears from Johnson. 17 October 1838. p.277, c6.

**486 JOHN QUINCY ADAMS** *to* **THE EDITOR OF THE** *QUINCY PATRIOT.* **21 September 1838. Quincy.** States that he has received letters calling for the abolition of slavery and opposing the admission of new slave states. 17 October 1838. p.278, c1.

**487 H.** *to* **MR. EDITOR. [from the** *American Citizen***] n.d. n.p.** Feels that it is important to petition Congress and local representatives to draft legislation which will lead to the abolition of slavery. 17 October 1838. p.278, c3.

**488 GERRIT SMITH** *to* **WM. GOODELL. 9 October 1838. Peterboro'.** Encloses a letter received from a slaveholder. 17 October 1838. p.278, c5.

**489 n.n.** *to* **GERRIT SMITH. 22 June 1838. Georgia.** A slaveholder in Georgia states that he wishes to take his slaves North and free them; asks Smith's advice on how he should proceed. 17 October 1838. p.278, c5.

**490 E. W. GOODWIN** *to* **WM. GOODELL. 8 October 1838. Auburn.** Reports proceedings and resolutions of a recent meeting of the Cayuga County AS. 17 October 1838. p.278, c6.

**491 n.n.** *to* **n.n. [extract] 24 October. Oswego County.** States that pro-slavery Whigs are supportive of President Green; alleges that the *Friend of Man* has been bought by the Van Buren party. 29 November 1838. p.1, c5.

**492 n.n.** *to* **n.n. [extract] 24 October. Oswego County.** Requests confirmation of the rumor that the Utica abolitionists are supporting C. P. Kirkland; declares that abolitionists who choose to become involved in politics should act judiciously. 29 November 1838. p.1, c5.

**493 n.n.** *to* **n.n. [extract] 2 November. Oswego County.** Complains that abolitionists in Oswego County do not have a press and are consequently uninformed of outside developments. 29 November 1838. p.1, c5.

**494 SILVANUS HOLMES** *to* **SIR. 30 October 1832. Utica.** Defends the reputation of a Mr. Stewart, a candidate for Congress, against his detractors. 29 November 1838. p.2, c2.

**495 STEPHEN F. KLINE, EDWIN W. CLARKE, JAMES C. JACKSON, [AND TWENTY OTHERS]** *to* **THE ABOLITION ELECTORS OF OSWEGO COUNTY. 26 October 1839. Oswego County.** Oppose the nomination of Charles Kirkland to Congress because of his indifference to the plight of the slave. 29 November 1838. p.2, c4.

**496 GERRIT SMITH** *to* **MR. GOODELL. 17 November 1838. Peterboro'.** Explains that he has neither been a member of the Whig Party nor sympathized with its views. 29 November 1838. p.3, c1.

**497 A NEW YORK DEMOCRAT** *to* **MR. EDITOR. [from the** *Emancipator***] n.d. n.p.** Opposes the nomination of W. H. Seward to Congress because of his indifference to the plight of the slave. 29 November 1838. p.3, c5.

## [1839]

**498 S. OSGOOD** *to* **REV. RALPH EMERSON. [from the** *Boston Recorder***] n.d. n.p.** Opposes resolutions adopted during the last meeting of the General Association of Connecticut. 6 February 1839. p.1, c5.

**499 THOMAS AUSTIN** *to* **BROTHER LEAVITT. [from the** ***Emancipator*****] 28 November 1838. Poughkeepsie.** Reports on the success of the convention of the Dutchess County AS in Pleasant Valley; lists the resolutions adopted during the convention. 6 February 1839. p.2, c2.

**500 GERRIT SMITH** *to* **WM. GOODELL. 26 January 1839. Peterboro'.** Encloses a letter from Judge Henry Brewster for publication. 6 February 1839. p.2, c5.

**501 HENRY BREWSTER** *to* **GERRIT SMITH, ESQ. 21 January 1839. Le Roy.** Explains why he made the mistake of voting for Seward in the recent New York election; regrets dissent that has arisen among abolitionists as a result of the elections. 6 February 1839. p.2, c5.

**502 n.n.** *to* **BRO. GOODELL. January 1839. Utica.** Encloses an extract of a letter for publication. 6 February 1839. p.2, c6.

**503 n.n.** *to* **n.n. [extract] n.d. n.p.** Relates the story of a Virginia slave who succeeded in escaping from his master, a minister. 6 February 1839. p.2, c6.

**504 J.S. BUCKINGHAM** *to* **THE EDITOR OF THE** ***PROVIDENCE JOURNAL*****. 30 November 1838. Providence.** Advocates the drafting of legislation to restrict sale of alcohol. 6 February 1839. p.4, c1.

**505 THE FACTORY GIRLS** *to* **REV. CHAUNCEY RICHARDSON. [from** ***Zion's Watchman*****] n.d. n.p.** Challenge Richardson's statement that the condition of slaves is less wretched than that of factory girls, and invite Richardson to reply. 6 February 1839. p.4, c3.

**506 IRA PETTIBONE** *to* **THE EDITOR OF** ***ZION'S WATCHMAN*****. n.d. n.p.** Agrees with the authors of the letter signed "Factory Girls," who assert that factory workers fare better than slaves. 6 February 1839. p.4, c3.

**507 JOHN E. ROBIE** *to* **THE EDITOR OF** ***ZION'S WATCHMAN*****. 13 November 1838. New York Mills.** Agrees with Reverend Pettibone and the "Factory Girls," who assert that factory workers fare better than slaves. 6 February 1839. p.4, c4.

**508 J. N. T. T[UCKER]** *to* **FRIEND GOODELL. n.d. n.p.** Encloses an editorial from the *New York Baptist Register* on temperance and the progress of the temperance movement. 5 June 1839. p.195, c4.

**509 THOMAS B. WATSON** *to* **BROTHER. 13 May 1839. Westport.** Describes a violent encounter with pro-slavery supporters in Westport. 5 June 1839. p.195, c5.

**510 A PLEBIAN** *to* **MR. GOODELL. 22 May 1830. Madison County.** Defends the reputation of Henry Clay, who had been under attack from local ministers for his drinking and duelling; states that abolitionists should vote only for representatives who support abolitionism. 5 June 1839. p.195, c6.

**511 LUTHER LEE** *to* **MR. EDITOR OF THE** ***FRIEND OF MAN*** **[WILLIAM GOODELL]. 25 May 1839. Ballston Spa.** Reports on the success of his anti-slavery lectures in Troy and Sand Lake, New York. 5 June 1839. p.196, c1.

**512 W. C. CHURCH** *to* **WILLIAM GOODELL. 25 May 1839. Madison.** States that at a recent meeting of the Madison AS, it was resolved that Henry Clay was unworthy of the trust and respect of the American people. 5 June 1839. p.196, c1.

**513 THE MANAGERS OF THE MASSACHUSETTS AS** *to* **THE ABOLITIONISTS OF MASSACHUSETTS. 24 May 1839. Boston.** Assure that Elizur Wright's fear that the Massachusetts AS has accepted William L. Garrison's theories on religion and government is groundless. 5 June 1839. p.196, c5.

**514 THOS. MORRIS** *to* **DR. BAILEY. [from the** *Cincinnati Philanthropist***] n.d. n.p.** Asserts that Congress does not have the power to abolish slavery, and that when slaves are discovered in free states they should be returned to their masters. 12 June 1839. p.200, c3.

**515 M.** *to* **MR. EDITOR. [from the** *Leroy Gazette***] n.d. n.p.** Criticizes abolitionists for being more interested in politics than in the condition of the slave. 12 June 1839. p.200, c4.

**516 A. A. PHELPS** *to* **BROTHER GOODELL. 3 June 1839. Boston.** Discusses the formation of the Massachusetts Abolition Society; encloses a copy of its preamble and constitution. 12 June 1839. p.200, c4.

**517 UN.** *to* **WM. GOODELL. 3 June 1839. Utica.** Praises the anti-slavery addresses presented at the Junior Exhibition of the Oneida Institute. 12 June 1839. p.200, c5.

**518 JOHN QUINCY ADAMS** *to* **THE CITIZENS OF THE UNITED STATES. 21 May 1839. Quincy.** Discusses the usefulness and influence of petitions and Congress's responsibility to respond to them. 19 June 1839. p.1, c1.

**519 JAMES G. BIRNEY** *to* **BROTHER LEAVITT. [from the** *Emancipator***] 31 May 1839. Putnam, Oh.** Describes the spirit of camaraderie which pervaded a meeting of the Ohio AS. 19 June 1839. p.3, c2.

**520 W. S. P.** *to* **BRO. TYLER. [from the** *Connecticut Observer***] n.d. n.p.** Insists that slaves be given the right to marry and notes that such a right would undermine the institution of slavery. 24 July 1839. p.22, c3.

**521 n.n.** *to* **MR. EDITOR. [from the** *Voice of Freedom***] n.d. n.p.** Encloses a letter from the emperor of Morocco to Henry Clay. 24 July 1839. p.22, c4.

**522 HAMET [***sic***], THE EMPEROR OF MOROCCO** *to* **HENRY CLAY. [from the** *Voice of Freedom***] n.d. n.p.** Agrees with Clay in defending slavery by viewing property as defined by law. 24 July 1839. p.22, c4.

**523 HIRAM WILSON** *to* **BRO. GOODELL. 12 July 1839. Toronto.** Warns abolitionists near Clinton County of a colored man who earns his living by presenting himself to various anti-slavery meetings as a fugitive slave, and soliciting donations. 24 July 1839. p.22, c6.

**524 JAMES C. BROWN** *to* **MR. GOODELL. 12 July 1839. Toronto, Canada.** Comments on Immanuel Andrews, a colored man who allegedly obtains money by claiming to be a fugitive slave whose sons are still in bondage. 24 July 1839. p.22, c6.

**525 RUTH SOUTHWORTH** *to* **WM. GOODELL. 15 July 1839. Madison.** Encloses a report from the Madison Female AS. 24 July 1839. p.22, c6.

**526 E. R. McGREGOR** *to* **EDITOR [WILLIAM GOODELL]. 17 July 1839. Watertown.** Discusses the formation of the Watertown AS and stresses the need for the involvement of young men in anti-slavery work. 24 July 1839. p.23, c1.

**527 S. FISK** *to* **MR. GOODELL. 12 July 1839. Canandaigua.** States that he has never pretended to be an agent for the New York AS and that he is an independent anti-slavery lecturer. 24 July 1839. p.23, c1.

**528 S. FISK** *to* **MR. ROGERS. n.d. n.p.** States that he is unable to send the money collected in the counties because he has spent it. 24 July 1839. p.23, c1.

**529 MARGARET A. MACOMBER** *to* **FRIEND GOODELL. 13 July 1839. Farmington.** Reaffirms the commitment of the Farmington Female AS to work for the abolition of slavery; discusses issues raised during the society's last meeting. 24 July 1839. p.23, c2.

## [1841]

**530 GERRIT SMITH** *to* **THE EDITOR OF THE** ***FRIEND OF MAN*** **[STANLEY HOUGH]. n.d. n.p.** Praises Beriah Green's book on abolitionism entitled, *Green's Miscellanies.* 9 November 1841. p.5, c5.

**531 BERIAH GREEN** *to* **THE PATRONS OF THE ONEIDA INSTITUTE; TO MY FORMER PARISHIONERS; AND TO MY PERSONAL FRIENDS. n.d. n.p.** Encourages friends and associates to buy *Green's Miscellanies,* the proceeds of which will be donated to the Oneida Institute. 9 November 1841. p.5, c5.

**532 REV. WM. H. ANDERSON** *to* **[ILLEGIBLE]. [from the** ***Natchez Courier*****] [date and place illegible].** Supports the religious instruction of slaves, but states that slaves must have their master's permission before joining his church. 9 November 1841. p.5, c6.

**533 n.n.** *to* **[ILLEGIBLE]. [date and place illegible].** Describes the hardships caused by the depression in Tennessee; praises the work of Mr. Clarke, an abolitionist from Knoxville. 9 November 1841. p.5, c1.

**534 J. FROST** *to* **MR. HOUGH. 4 November 1841. Whitesboro'.** Reports on the success of his anti-slavery lectures in Oswego, Ithaca, Binghamton and Salina. 9 November 1841. p.6, c2.

**535 A.** *to* **MR. EDITOR OF THE** ***FRIEND OF MAN*** **[STANLEY HOUGH]. n.d. n.p.** Comments on the anniversary exercises of the Oneida Institute, held at the Presbyterian Church of New York Mills. 9 November 1841. p.6, c4.

**536 LEWIS TAPPAN** *to* **MESSRS. EDITORS. [from the** ***Congregational Observer*****] n.d. New York.** Solicits contributions to aid Cinque and crew in their return to Sierra Leone. 9 November 1841. p.7, c2.

## [1842]

**537 E. WRIGHT, JR.** *to* **THE EDITOR OF THE** ***TOCSIN OF LIBERTY.*** **24 December 1841. Washington.** Describes Washington, D.C., as an ugly slave capital, antithetical to the nation's ideals. 11 January 1842. p.41, c4.

**538 ONE OF GERRIT SMITH'S TENNESSEE CORRESPONDENTS** *to* **THE** ***FRIEND OF MAN.*** **27 November 1841. East Tennessee.** Believes that East Tennessee should withdraw from the rest of Tennessee and become a separate and free state. 11 January 1842. p.41, c5.

**539 G.** *to* **MR. EDITOR OF THE** ***FRIEND OF MAN*** **[STANLEY HOUGH]. n.d. n.p.** Describes his meeting with an unnamed bank clerk who was obsessed with money. 11 January 1842. p.42, c1.

**540 HIRAM WILSON** *to* **THE** ***FRIEND OF MAN.*** **28 December 1841. Toronto.** Reports on the progress of abolitionists in Canada and the construction of a building for the British American Institute of Science and Industry, a benevolent institute to aid colored, Indian and white persons. 11 January 1842. p.42, c2.

**541 DAN'L P. COOK** *to* **H. WARREN. 12 February 1820. Washington.** Reports on the debate between Rufus King of New York, John Sargent of Pennsylvania, and Henry Clay of Kentucky, concerning the extension of slavery into Missouri. 11 January 1842. p.42, c6.

*Pennsylvania Freeman*

**Figure 3. Oliver Johnson**

# Oliver Johnson

## [Editor of The *Pennsylvania Freeman,* 1851-53]

The great work of Oliver Johnson's life was his part in the anti-slavery conflict. At the age of twenty-three he was one of the twelve men, who under the lead of William Lloyd Garrison organized the New England Anti-Slavery Society. That was a famous meeting on New Year's Day of 1832 when the constitution of this first anti-slavery society was signed by William Lloyd Garrison with Oliver Johnson's name following next. They were all young men, at first mostly conservative in the religious faith, who knew how to put their religion into the greatest of all public questions and who were ready to announce:

"We believe that slavery is an evil *now*: and of course the slave ought to be *now* emancipated. If a thief is found in possession of stolen property he is required *immediately* to restore it. Every principle which proves slavery unjust, an evil and a curse, equally demonstrates the duty of *immediate* emancipation."

That Oliver Johnson, scarce more than a boy, should have floated down from the Vermont hills to the city of Boston to ally himself with the great reform of the age, when that reform was unpopular and called for martyrs, is proof what the man was. . . .

Mr. Johnson was a journalist by profession but he devoted his life from boyhood up to the anti-slavery cause. This is what Henry Ward Beecher said of him in a letter written in December, 1884, on the occasion of Mr. Johnson's seventy-fifth birthday:—

I rank Mr. Johnson among the best men that our time has produced, the men who have enriched the world, and of whom "the world was not worthy." Mr. Johnson belongs to the band—almost gone—of those who fought the battle of liberty and who have lived to see the victory. All his life long he has subordinated ease, gain and reputation to the great duty of this age. Closely associated with Garrison and Phillips, he was a worthy member of the triad—for, if he was in speech less able, by his pen he was more able than they. A devout man though outside of the church, a true Christian though not a follower of prevalent theology, his name will be precious in all time.

Many other letters of congratulation were received by Mr. Johnson from distinguished men in all parts of the country.

Mr. Johnson was born at Peacham, Vt., on December 27, 1809. He spent his boyhood on his father's farm, obtaining an elementary education at the district school, and at the age of sixteen started out in life by apprenticing himself in the office of the *Vermont Watchman*, owned by General Ezekiel P. Walton and published at Montpelier.

From there he journeyed to Boston and started the *Christian Soldier,* which opposed the spread of Universalism and advocated very strong anti-slavery views.

Mr. Johnson made the acquaintance of William Lloyd Garrison in 1830 and the two men were fast friends ever afterward. Mr. Johnson, as has been said, was the youngest of twelve men who organized the New England Anti-Slavery Society on January 6, 1832, under Mr. Garrison's leadership. From it sprung the American Anti-Slavery Society, which was formed on December 4, 1833.

During Mr. Garrison's absence in Europe Mr. Johnson was in charge of the abolition leader's paper. On September 6, 1832, Mr. Johnson married Mary Annie White, the daughter of the Rev. Broughton White, of Westmoreland, N. H. From this time until 1837 Mr. Johnson worked on various newspapers and lectured through the East and Pennsylvania against slavery. In Philadelphia he met James and Lucretia Mott.

He was appointed general agent of the Rhode Island State Anti-Slavery Society in 1837 and held the office until 1839. During this period he was mobbed in Greenville by the pro-slavery people, and narrowly escaped tar and feathers. He lectured in and around Boston with the Grimké sisters. In 1839 and 1840 he was one of the most energetic adherents of Garrison, whom the pro-slavery churches tried to drive from office.

Mr. Johnson edited the *National Anti-Slavery Standard* in 1840. The following year he lectured in Eastern Indiana and Western New York. In 1842 he printed the *Liberty Bell* in Boston, and accompanied by his wife made a tour of the North, stopping, among other places, at the little town where she was born. He became assistant editor of the *Tribune* in 1844, but ill health compelled him shortly afterward to abandon the undertaking. He was induced to start the Blackstone *Chronicle* in Massachusetts, but the paper died in six months. In 1848 Mr. Johnson edited the *Republic*, the free soil organ in Philadelphia, and then went to the Hopedale Community at Milford, Mass., where he edited the *Practical Christian*. In 1849 he was appointed editor of the *Anti-Slavery Bugle* at Salem, Ohio, and in 1851 joined the *Tribune* staff again while Mr. Greeley was in Europe.

Mr. Johnson next joined Sydney Howard Gay as editor of the *National Anti-Slavery Standard* in New York, and was thus engaged until the close of the war. . . . During all these years before the War he had one thought and purpose, and that was to pronounce the curse of God upon slavery. Like those with whom he associated, he was so disgusted with the position of the Church that he gave up the faith in which he was educated, allying himself with the early Comeouters, Theodore Parker and the Progressive Friends. During these years before the War, the followers of Garrison separated themselves from the growing body of anti-slavery men who believed that it was through political methods that slavery must be abolished. They kept apart from the churches and from political parties, contenting themselves with the prophetic work of a John the Baptist in the wilderness, proclaiming the judgment of God.

One can now hardly appreciate what was the hostility which then existed between Abolitionists, as they were called, who followed Garrison, and those who through the Church and through political action, sought the same end. But when the little Liberty Party had grown into the powerful Free Soil Party, and the Free Soil Party into the dominant Republican Party, and the South, seeing that slavery was doomed in the Union, seceded from the Union, and a terrible war united all parties together in the defense of the nation—then all anti-slavery ranks fused together. When the War closed there was no more Comeouterism or Abolitionism to attack or be attacked: all was patriotism: and so Garrison and Johnson gave influence and labor to help THE INDEPENDENT, which on its side forgot that it had ever criticised them. Joshua Leavitt, of the old *Emancipator*, and Oliver Johnson, of the old *Liberator*, were fellow editors of THE INDEPENDENT. As one of the editors of THE INDEPENDENT Johnson had two ideas to which he devoted himself: one was the elevation of the Negro slaves and the other was female suffrage. His reading, his thinking and his writing followed one or the other of these two lines.

Oliver Johnson was one of the most transparent of men. He knew what his purpose was, and he knew no way to accomplish it but to hammer at it. He was simple-hearted, kindly, earnest, passionate, but as quick to apologize as he was to attack. Our memory of him is wholly gratifying, that of a man who feared God, and had a purpose, and obeyed his conscience. He was the last survivor of the twelve heroes who formed that first anti-slavery society, as he was the youngest of them. During his last years withdrawn from active labor, he could be called from his retirement by any one who offered a criticism of the wisdom or the methods of Garrison and his associates. He was always ready to put on the old armor, and to prove that it was that old New England Anti-Slavery Society and its work which had educated public conscience and destroyed slavery. . . .

After leaving the *Standard* he became managing editor of the New York *Independent*, and continued in that position until 1870. In January, 1871, at Mr. Greeley's request, he became editor of the *Weekly Tribune*. When Greeley died Mr. Johnson was managing editor of the *Christian Union* for three years under Henry Ward Beecher. In 1876 Mr. Johnson purchased the Orange (N. J.) *Journal*, and published it for three years, when he sold it.

Mr. Johnson was author of a book, entitled "William Lloyd Garrison and His Times," which was published January 1, 1880.

Mr. Johnson was twice married. His second wife. . . was the daughter of the Rev. J. S. C. Abbott. [Oliver Johnson died in December, 1889.]

*New York Herald,* 11 December 1889,
p.5, c5 and *New York Independent,*
19 December 1889, p.13, c3.

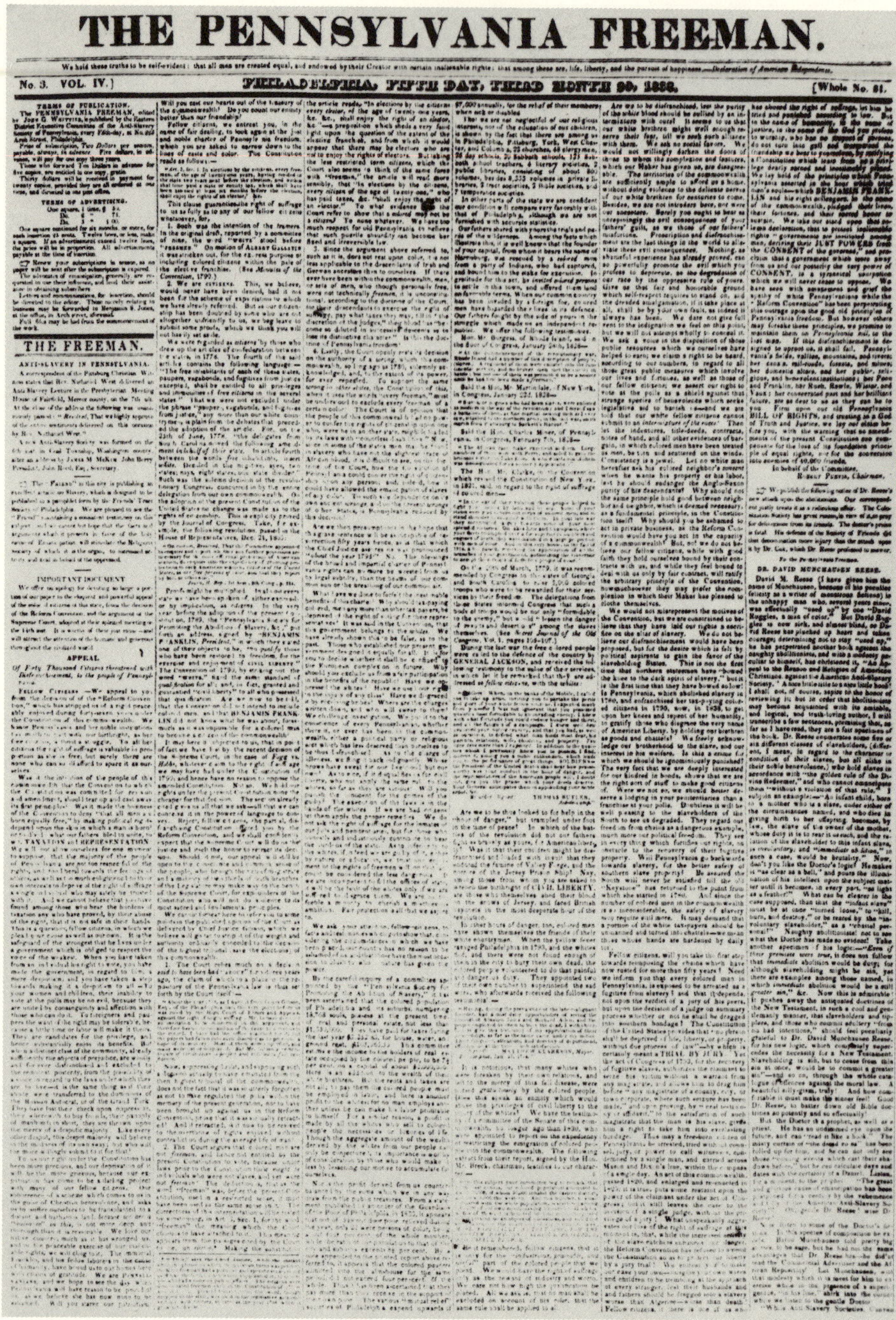

# THE PENNSYLVANIA FREEMAN.

We hold these truths to be self-evident: that all men are created equal, and endowed by their Creator with certain inalienable rights; that among these are life, liberty, and the pursuit of happiness.—*Declaration of American Independence.*

No. 3. VOL. IV.] PHILADELPHIA, FIFTH DAY, THIRD MONTH 29, 1838. [Whole No. 81.

**Figure 4**

# Journal Data

TITLES: *National Enquirer and Constitutional Advocate of Universal Liberty* (3 August 1836–8 March 1838); The *Pennsylvania Freeman* (15 March 1838–29 June 1854)

MOTTO: "We hold these truths to be self-evident: that all men are created equal, and endowed by their Creator with certain inalienable rights; that among these are, life, liberty, and the pursuit of happiness."—Declaration of American Independence (3 August 1836–29 June 1854 issues)

INCLUSIVE DATES OF PUBLICATION: 3 August 1836–29 June 1854 (publication suspended between 29 December 1841 and 18 January 1844)

PLACE OF PUBLICATION: Philadelphia, Pa.

FREQUENCY OF PUBLICATION: Weekly (3 August 1836–29 December 1841); Every two weeks (18 January 1844–18 December 1845); Weekly (1 January 1846–29 June 1854)

DAY OF WEEK PUBLISHED: Wednesday (3 August 1836–31 August 1836); Saturday (8 October 1836–15 July 1837); Thursday (20 July 1837–7 January 1841); Wednesday (10 February 1841–29 December 1841); Thursday (13 January 1844–3 June 1852); Saturday (12 June 1852–18 November 1852); Thursday (25 November 1852–29 June 1854)

AVERAGE NUMBER OF PAGES PER ISSUE: 4

NUMBER OF COLUMNS PER PAGE: 6–7

EDITORS: Charles C. Burleigh (30 April 1840–30 June 1841, 18 January 1844–13 August 1846); Cyrus M. Burleigh (30 September 1847–23 October 1851, 24 March 1853–18 May 1854?); Mary Grew (20 November 1845–13 August 1846?, 30 September 1847–23 October 1851); Oliver Johnson (30 October 1851–17 March 1853); James Russell Lowell (16 January 1845–13 August 1846?); Benjamin Lundy (3 August 1836–8 March 1838); James M. McKim (7 July 1841–29 December 1841, 18 January 1844–27 April 1848); John Greenleaf Whittier (15 March 1838–20 February 1840)

PUBLISHERS: Benjamin Lundy (3 August 1836–11 March 1837); The Executive Committee of the Anti-Slavery Society for the Eastern District of Pennsylvania (18 March 1837–29 December 1841); Pennsylvania Anti-Slavery Society (16 January 1845–29 June 1854)

FEATURES: letters, editorials; local, national and foreign news; poetry; essays; advertisements; illustrations

PRICE PER ANNUM: $2.00 (1836); $.75 (1844); $1.00 (1847); $1.50 (1851); $2.00 (1852)

LANGUAGE: English

PERSPECTIVE: Abolitionist

REPOSITORY: Friends Historical Library, Swarthmore College, and the Historical Society of Pennsylvania. 3 August 1836–29 June 1854.

# Prospectus of the
## *National Enquirer, And Constitutional Advocate of Universal Liberty*

This work has recently been established, with the view of advocating the cause of UNIVERSAL EMANCIPATION. The Editor, having publicly devoted more than eighteen years of his life to this important subject, – and having, nearly the whole of this period, superintended the editorial department of another publication of similar character and views, – conceives it to be unnecessary, at present, to give an exposition of his particular sentiments in relation to it. Yet it may not be improper to state explicitly, that the principal aim and leading object of the work will be THE IMMEDIATE AND TOTAL ABOLITION OF SLAVERY IN AMERICA, by the most efficient moral, judicious, and *Constitutional* means.

The time *was* – and well indeed is it *remembered* – when but a solitary voice (except its own occasional echo) was heard throughout the land, in favor of a restoration of the "inalienable rights," and redress for the innumerable wrongs, of the American bondman. It was a dreary *night* of hopeless, soul-depressing toil and care! – But within the period above mentioned, a marked and visible change has been effected; a wonderful impetus has been given to the progress of the holy cause; and the brightest cheering rays of hope and confidence in success, are beaming around us. It is true that much yet remains to be done, in order to guard against and ward off the awful, impending calamity, which has long threatened the peace and safety of our country. – A severe contest is yet to be waged with the demon of oppression, ere the vengeful arm of Justice shall be stayed, and the power of moral truth established, and the renovation of our social system effected. We must, therefore, buckle on the armor of righteous persevering energy – renew our zeal and activity in the vineyard of labor – plead with more earnestness the cause of the suffering and the enslaved – engage with more fervor in supplication, at the Throne of Almighty Power, for the successful termination of our arduous, yet glorious undertaking.

With such views as are here expressed, the editor of this work has assumed the station which he now occupies. He long since entered with alacrity this great arena of moral warfare, and yields to none, in the disposition to sustain the principles which he has for many years reduced to practice.

"In [Slavery's] field advancing his firm foot,
He plants it on the line that Justice draws,
And will prevail or perish in her cause."

The co-operation of all, who are friendly to the object of the work, is desired; and their patronage is generally solicited. Every exertion will be made to render it instructive and entertaining, while the appropriate motto will be ever recollected – *"Fiat Justitia Ruat Coelum."*

*National Enquirer,*
5 November 1836, p.4, c5.

# Prospectus of The *Pennsylvania Freeman*

At a meeting of the Executive Committee of the Eastern Pennsylvania Anti-Slavery Society, held December 21st, 1843, the following resolutions were unanimously adopted:

"Resolved, That the interests of the Anti-Slavery cause in this State require that the *Pennsylvania Freeman*, instead of being issued as it now is, gratuitously, and at irregular intervals, should be published as a regular monthly or semi-monthly paper, to be issued at stated periods, and sustained by a regular subscription list.

"Resolved, That for the sake of convenience and economy, and the better to ensure success in the measure, an arrangement be made, if practicable, with J. M. McKim, our Publishing Agent, and C. C. Burleigh, our Corresponding Secretary and travelling agent, by which they shall become the editors and publishers of the paper, and have the sole responsibility of its management."

In pursuance of the above resolutions, an arrangement has been made by which the undersigned have agreed to revive the *Pennsylvania Freeman* as a regular semi-monthly paper, and to assume the entire control and responsibility of its publication.

The first number will be issued in the second week in January. It will be published on a medium sheet, handsome paper, and in neat type. The price will be 75 cents per annum, in advance.

The character of the paper will not differ from that of the Anti-Slavery papers, except it be in the fact that it will allow, perhaps, a wider range of discussion, and a greater amount of freedom, than would be tolerated in any mere organ of a Society, or in any paper not conducted on individual responsibility.

The subjects which shall mainly occupy our attention will be the Church, the Clergy, Political parties and Political partizans; their present position in respect to the Anti-Slavery cause, and the duties of abolitionists in regard to them.

There are other topics of perhaps equal importance, though they may not occupy the same prominence, which shall claim our notice. Among these may be mentioned the duty of abstinence from slave-labor products, and the iniquitous disfranchisement by this commonweath of 40,000 of her honest citizens.

The columns of the paper will be open to all classes of abolitionists, without partiality, and the proceedings of Anti-Slavery meetings of every description will be freely published.

J. M. McKim
C. C. Burleigh
*Pennsylvania Freeman,*
18 January 1844, p.1, c1.

## [1836]

**542 B. LUNDY** *to* **THE PUBLIC. n.d. n.p.** Discusses plans for a new anti-slavery publication. 3 August 1836. p.2, c1.

**543 n.n.** *to* **n.n. 25 July. Augusta.** States that war has broken out near Fort M'Creary between Georgia troops and the Creek Indians. 3 August 1836. p.3, c5.

**544 n.n.** *to* **n.n. 20 July. New Orleans.** States that 1,300 Creek Indians have arrived in New Orleans and are waiting for the boat to take them west of the Mississippi; notes that forty Indians have died since their arrival because of heavy rains. 3 August 1836. p.3, c5.

**545 n.n.** *to* **n.n. [from the** *London Times*] **26 June. Paris.** Announces an assassination attempt against the king of France. 3 August 1836. p.3, c6.

**546 n.n.** *to* **n.n. [from the** *London Times*] **38 [sic] June. London.** States that the attempt to assassinate the French king has "no particular influence upon the British Funds." 3 August 1836. p.3, c6.

**547 DAVID RUGGLES** *to* **n.n. [from the** *Sun*] **n.d. n.p.** Describes the arrest in New York City and return to slavery of George Jones, a free black man. 3 August 1836. p.3, c6.

**548 LYDIA B. CAPRON, SARAH W. GROSVENOR, SARAH JUDSON, MARTHA WHIPPLE, AND OLIVE CHAPMAN** *to* **PROFESSING CHRISTIAN WOMEN OF KENTUCKY. n.d. n.p.** Encourage anti-slavery sentiment among Christians. 17 August 1836. p.5, c1.

**549 n.n.** *to* **n.n. 20 July 1836. Mobile, Al.** Describes two boats holding 2,600 Indians in chains on their way to Arkansas. 17 August 1836. p.7, c6.

**550 B. B. DAVIS, SECRETARY OF THE NEW GARDEN AS** *to* **THE EDITOR OF THE** ***LIBERATOR*****. 14 June 1836. New Garden, Oh.** Reports on the meeting of the New Garden AS, which plans to petition Congress. 17 August 1836. p.8, c6.

**551 WM. H. JOHNSON** *to* **FRIEND. n.d. Bucks County.** Describes newly formed AS in Bucks County and names the officers. 24 August 1836. p.9, c3.

**552 B. GREEN** *to* **BROTHER GOODELL. [from the** *Friend of Man*] **2 August 1836. n.p.** Reports on an anti-slavery meeting at New York Mills. 24 August 1836. p.12, c2.

**553 A FREEMAN** *to* **THE EDITOR OF THE** ***CENTREVILLE*** **(MD.)** ***TIMES*****. n.d. n.p.** Objects to a letter in the previous issue which promoted the expulsion of all free Negroes from the state. 24 August 1836. p.12, c2.

**554 VETO** *to* **n.n. [extract from the** *New York Evening Post*] **29 July 1835. Bombay.** Reports that the cotton cultivation in India is "just now taking a wonderful start." 24 August 1836. p.12, c3.

**555 A PATRIOT** *to* **MR. EDITOR. [from the** *Philadelphia Gazette*] **n.d. n.p.** Suggests that Americans eager to purchase land go to Upper Canada, where there is plenty of it. 24 August 1836. p.12, c5.

**556 COL. STEPHEN AUSTIN** *to* **THE** AYUNTAMIENTO **OF SAN FELIPE DE AUSTIN. 17 January 1834. Monterrey.** States that he does not blame the Mexican government for his arrest; declares that Texas is in a good position, and explains the advice he gave to Mexican revolutionaries. 31 August 1836. p.13, c1.

**557 STEPHEN F. AUSTIN** *to* **THE PUBLIC. 4 August 1836. Columbia.** Announces that he will accept the office of president of Texas, if he is elected; states that he favors the annexation of Texas. 31 August 1836. p.14, c2.

**558 WILLIAM H. JACK** *to* **THE PUBLIC. 5 August 1836. Columbia.** Announces his support of the annexation of Texas. 31 August 1836. p.14, c2.

**559 JAMES G. BIRNEY** *to* **BROTHER. [from the** *New York Evangelist***] 10 August 1836. Cincinnati.** Describes the looting of the *Philanthropist*'s office; states that some were converted to anti-slavery sentiment by their reading of anti-slavery literature found in the office. 31 August 1836. p.14, c4.

**560 STEPHEN DILLET** *to* **JUNIUS C. MOREL. 9 August 1836. Nassau.** Forwards some newspapers to Morel. 31 August 1836. p.14, c6.

**561 n.n.** *to* **n.n. [extract from the** *Buffalo Spectator***] 11 August. Cleveland, Oh.** A colored gentleman travelling in Ohio states that he has received good treatment everywhere he has been. 31 August 1836. p.15, c4.

**562 AMERICAN CONSUL AT MATAMORAS** *to* **n.n. n.d. n.p.** Announces that the Mexican government has opened its port to "all kinds of importations" during the war with Texas and that the efforts to blockade the port have been unsuccessful. 31 August 1836. p.15, c5.

**563 n.n.** *to* **n.n. n.d. Lonja.** States that the Gonzales party has been reduced to six men. 31 August 1836. p.15, c5.

**564 n.n.** *to* **THE EDITOR OF THE** *NATIONAL ENQUIRER* **[B. LUNDY]. n.d. n.p.** Comments on a pamphlet entitled, "The Origin and True Cause of the Texas Insurrection." 8 October 1836. p.19, c1.

**565 n.n.** *to* **THE EDITOR OF THE** *NATIONAL ENQUIRER* **[B. LUNDY]. n.d. n.p.** Condemns "Texian Patriots" for their "abominable conspiracy against the rights of man." 8 October 1836. p.19, c2.

**566 A GENTLEMAN** *to* **FRIEND. n.d. n.p.** Regrets that the slave states have ruled the United States; believes that the rest of the nation should think for themselves. 8 October 1836. p.19, c2.

**567 CORRESPONDENT** *to* **n.n. n.d. Michigan.** Believes that the effort to "wrest the Texas country from the government of Mexico is the last desperate effort for prolonging the trade in human blood." 8 October 1836. p.19, c2.

**568 GENERAL HOUSTON** *to* **GENERAL DUNLAP. [extract from the** *New York Sun***] n.d. n.p.** Urges the annexation of Texas to the United States. 8 October 1836. p.19, c3.

**569 A TRAVELLER** *to* **MR. EDITOR [B. LUNDY]. n.d. Philadelphia.** Praises the treatment of colored children in a school in Philadelphia. 8 October 1836. p.19, c6.

**570 JOHN SCOBLE** *to* **PROFESSOR ELIZUR WRIGHT. [from the** *Emancipator***] 19 August 1836. London.** Describes a meeting on slavery held in Exeter Hall; lists resolutions adopted. 15 October 1836. p.22, c2.

**571 GENERAL EDMUND P. GAINES** *to* **GOVERNOR N. CANNON. [from the** *National Intelligencer***] 28 August 1836. Camp Sabine.** States that he cannot protect frontiers against the Mexicans without the men promised him by the president. 15 October 1836. p.22, c5.

**572 n.n.** *to* **THE EDITORS OF THE** *NATIONAL INTELLIGENCER.* **28 August 1836. Natchitoches, La.** Discusses his journey into Texas; states that Texas is said to be "millions in debt"; discusses military activity there. 15 October 1836. p.22, c6.

**573 n.n.** *to* **THE** *NATIONAL ENQUIRER.* **[extract] n.d. n.p.** Reports on the African School in Nantucket. 15 October 1836. p.23, c3.

**574 n.n.** *to* **n.n. 13 September 1836. Velasco.** Reports on the positions of the American and Mexican armies; states that Bartholomon Pages will be tried as a spy because he attempted to rescue Santa Anna. 15 October 1836. p.23, c6.

**575 n.n.** *to* **n.n. [extract] 2 September. Matamoras.** Informs that 6,000 men will be ready to march into Texas by 1 November. 15 October 1836. p.23, c6.

**576 n.n.** *to* **n.n. [extract] n.d. n.p.** Informs that the Lepan Indians have killed many people on both sides of the Colorado River. 15 October 1836. p.23, c6.

**577 n.n.** *to* **n.n. [extract] 16 September. Matamoras.** States that the motto of the Mexican Legion is "the Law, Government, and Texas, or death." 15 October 1836. p.23, c6.

**578 SAMUEL HOUSTON** *to* **n.n. [from the** *New York Evening Post***] n.d. Texas.** Informs that Cherokee Indians and a Mexican force are about to attack; pleads for arms and reinforcements. 22 October 1836. p.26, c3.

**579 A GENTLEMAN** *to* **THE EDITOR OF THE** *NATIONAL ENQUIRER* **[B. LUNDY]. 12 October 1836. Bucks County, Pa.** Gives an account of the arrest and trial of an alleged fugitive slave in Bucks County. 22 October 1836. p.27, c3.

**580 A YOUNG MAN FROM OHIO** *to* **SAMUEL CROTHERS. [from the** *Cincinnati Philanthropist***] n.d. Ross County, Oh.** Reports the lynching of a man seen talking to a black. 22 October 1836. p.28, c2.

**581 AN OLD MAN** *to* **THE EDITOR OF THE** *VERMONT STATE JOURNAL.* **n.d. n.p.** Opposes the annexation of Texas, which would constitute a victory for the slave states. 29 October 1836. p.29, c6.

**582 C. H. JOHNSON** *to* **FRIEND. 14 July. Shelbyville, Ky.** Expresses his disappointment with the inhospitality of the people of Texas. 29 October 1836. p.30, c6.

**583 ALLEN** *to* **n.n. 14 July. Kentucky.** Informs that the Cabinet of Texas is very unpopular among the army and citizens of Texas. 29 October 1836. p.30, c6.

**584 n.n.** *to* **n.n. [from the** *Louisville City Gazette***] 13 August. Nacogdoches, Tx.** Expresses dissatisfaction with the forthcoming congressional election; condemns land speculators in Texas. 29 October 1836. p.30, c6.

**585 GENERAL HUGHES** *to* **PETER H. BURNET, THE EDITOR OF THE** *FAR WEST.* **17 September 1836. Fort Leavenworth.** Announces the conclusion of the Indian Treaty. 29 October 1836. p.31, c5.

**586 A GENTLEMAN** *to* **THE** *GLOBE.* **n.d. n.p.** Reports that the Mexican ports are now open to ships bearing the Spanish flag. 29 October 1836. p.31, c6.

**587 n.n** *to* **n.n. n.d. New York.** Announces the defeat of the Carlist army in Madrid under the command of General Gomez. 29 October 1836. p.31, c6.

**588 n.n.** *to* **SLAVE-HOLDERS AND SLAVE-DEALERS. [from the** ***Emancipator*****] n.d. n.p.** Discusses certain slaveholders who justified slavery for most of their lives, but repented their crime on their deathbeds. 29 October 1836. p.32, c3.

**589 A.** *to* **MR. KIMBALL. [extract from the** ***Herald of Freedom*****] n.d. n.p.** Forwards a letter for publication. 29 October 1836. p. 32, c4.

**590 n.n.** *to* **A. [extract from the** ***Herald of Freedom*****] n.d. n.p.** Reports on the effects of the abolition movement on Southerners. 29 October 1836. p.32, c4.

**591 CORRESPONDENT** *to* **THE** ***NATIONAL ENQUIRER*****. n.d. n.p.** Notes that the reading room of Wesleyan University carries many abolitionist newspapers. 29 October 1836. p.32, c5.

**592 ALVAN STEWART, C. STUART, W. GOODELL [AND EIGHT OTHERS]** *to* **THE OHIO AS COMMITTEE. 26 August 1836. Utica.** Encourage their efforts in the cause of abolition. 5 November 1836. p.33, c1.

**593 A GENTLEMAN IN KENTUCKY** *to* **GERRIT SMITH. [extract] 31 August 1836. n.p.** Expresses his disgust with the "depravity" of slavery in the South. 5 November 1836. p.33, c4.

**594 JOHN B. ROBINS** *to* **JOHN POWELL OR SAMUEL WHITE. 19 May 1831. St. Martins.** Discusses the sale of a Negro man named Sam. 5 November 1836. p.34, c2.

**595 MR. WEED** *to* **n.n. 29 September. West Union, Oh.** States that he has been lecturing and preaching on "great principles of action" for three months. 5 November 1836. p.35, c1.

**596 n.n.** *to* **n.n. [extract] 12 September 1836. n.p.** Reports on the activities of an artillery company on Galveston Island which is involved in the Texas war for independence. 5 November 1836. p.35, c1.

**597 W. H. J.** *to* **B. LUNDY. 1 November 1836. Buckingham.** Reports on the abolitionist activities of James M. McKim in Buckingham. 5 November 1836. p.35, c3.

**598 AN OFFICER IN THE TEXIAN ARMY** *to* **FRIEND. [extract] 21 September 1836. Rio La Baco.** States that Captains Carnes and Teal have arrived in the camp and bring news that the Mexicans expect to leave Mexico for Texas this month. 5 November 1836. p.35, c5.

**599 n.n.** *to* **n.n. [extract] 12 September 1836. Dimmitt's Landing, Tx.** States that S--- is leaving the camp and that remnants of his corps wish to return to their compatriots. 5 November 1836. p.35, c5.

**600 n.n.** *to* **n.n. [extract] n.d. Tampico.** Reports that Messrs. Mora, Parres, and Villa Uritis have embarked on diplomatic missions to Havana and Madrid. 5 November 1836. p.35, c6.

**601 REVEREND R. J. BRECKINRIDGE** *to* **DR. WARDLAW. [extract] n.d. n.p.** Charges the British nation with supporting and upholding the system of slavery in its colonies. 12 November 1836. p.37, c1.

**602 JUDGE WILLIAM JAY** *to* **THE SECRETARY OF THE NEW YORK AS. 26 September 1836. Bedford.** Resigns from the presidency of the New York AS. 12 November 1836. p.37, c6.

**603 W. H. J.** *to* **THE EDITOR [B. LUNDY]. 11 November 1836. Buckingham.** Describes the trial of a slave arrested for escaping. 12 November 1836. p.39, c1.

**604 LEWIS C. GUNN** *to* **LUNDY. n.d. n.p.** Introduces a summary of remarks made by him at the Young Men's AS about the purchasing of slaves. 12 November 1836. p.39, c1.

**605 A YOUNG ABOLITIONIST** *to* **THE EDITOR [B. LUNDY]. n.d. n.p.** Announces the formation of a Junior AS in Philadelphia. 12 November 1836. p.39, c4.

**606 THEODORE S. WRIGHT** *to* **REVEREND ARCHIBALD ALEXANDER, D.D. 11 October 1836. New York.** Describes events surrounding an attack which was made on him because he is colored. 12 November 1836. p.40, c3.

**607 RICHE** *to* **THE PRESIDENT OF HAYTI. n.d. n.p.** Reports on agriculture in the arrondissement of St. Jean. 12 November 1836. p.40, c4.

**608 BONNET** *to* **THE PRESIDENT OF HAYTI. 27 March 1836. St. Marc.** Reports on agriculture in the arrondissement of St. Marc. 12 November 1836. p.40, c5.

**609 A RESIDENT OF BARBADOES** *to* **GERRIT SMITH. 20 September 1836. n.p.** Describes the benefits of emancipation in the West Indies. 19 November 1836. p.41, c1.

**610 R. STANDISH** *to* **MARQUIS OF SLIGO. [extract] 25 June 1835. Chapelton, District of Clarendon.** Comments on the good conduct of Negroes in the district. 19 November 1836. p.41, c4.

**611 W. H. ALLEN** *to* **THE MARQUIS OF SLIGO. [extract] 1 July 1835. Mile Gulley.** Reports on the excellent disposition and conduct of Negroes in Mile Gulley. 19 November 1836. p.41, c4.

**612 THE FRIENDS IN ENGLAND** *to* **THE YEARLY MEETING OF FRIENDS IN INDIANA. n.d. n.p.** Encourage their anti-slavery efforts. 19 November 1836. p.41, c6.

**613 ESTHER MOORE, LUCRETIA MOTT, SARAH PUGH, [AND FOURTEEN OTHERS]** *to* **THE AS AND FRIENDS OF THE OPPRESSED. 10 November 1836. Philadelphia.** Encourage anti-slavery efforts; praise Angelina E. Grimké's work for the cause. 19 November 1836. p.42, c2.

**614 AN OFFICER IN THE UNITED STATES ARMY** *to* **n.n. [from the** ***Army and Navy Chronicle*****] n.d. n.p.** Reports that Gaines's troops have advanced into Nacogdoches. 19 November 1836. p.42, c6.

**615 NEUTRALITY** *to* **n.n. 14 September 1836. Nacogdoches, Tx.** Declares his allegiance to Texas, swearing to kill anyone in whose veins "circulates Mexican blood"; reports on the progress of the Texas revolution. 19 November 1836. p.43, c1.

**616 CORRESPONDENT** *to* **THE** ***NATIONAL INTELLIGENCER.*** **2 September. Nacogdoches.** Reports that peace in Texas has been disturbed by interference from the United States. 19 November 1836. p.43, c2.

**617 n.n.** *to* **n.n. [from the** ***Louisville City Gazette*****] 13 August. Texas.** States that "there are two parties in this country, the speculators, and the orderly farmers and volunteers." 19 November 1836. p.43, c3.

**618 n.n.** *to* **n.n. n.d. Boston.** Believes that the abolitionist vote may decide the forthcoming election. 19 November 1836. p.43, c4.

**619 GENERAL FELIX HOUSTON** *to* **COLONEL LOUIS P. COOK. 18 September. Texas.** States that in his opinion the war between Texas and Mexico is not yet ended. 19 November 1836. p.43, c5.

**620 AN OFFICER IN THE UNITED STATES ARMY** *to* **n.n. [from the** *Arkansas Gazette***] 21 September. Camp Nacogdoches, Tx.** Reports widespread sickness in Camp Nacogdoches. 19 November 1836. p.43, c5.

**621 n.n.** *to* **n.n. [extract] 14 October 1836. Brazoria, Tx.** Reports that no Mexican vessels have been seen off the coast; notes that the Congress of Texas met the previous Monday but decided little. 19 November 1836. p.43, c6.

**622 n.n.** *to* **n.n. 28 October 1836. New Orleans.** Reports on the election of Houston and Lamar as president and vice-president; states that the vote for annexing Texas to the United States was unanimous. 19 November 1836. p.43, c6.

**623 GENTLEMAN IN KENTUCKY** *to* **GENTLEMAN IN NEW YORK. [from the** *New York Evangelist***] 6 August 1836. Kentucky.** Describes the beauty of Kentucky; deplores slavery. 19 November 1836. p.44, c4.

**624 ANOTHER YOUNG ABOLITIONIST** *to* **THE** *NATIONAL ENQUIRER.* **n.d. n.p.** Discusses the efforts of the young in the anti-slavery cause. 26 November 1836. p.45, c2.

**625 J. G. W. W.** *to* **MR. EDITOR [B. LUNDY]. n.d. n.p.** Describes a panorama, "Grotto of Antiparos," constructed by a colored woman in Philadelphia. 26 November 1836. p.45, c3.

**626 THOS. VAN RENSSALEAR** *to* **RICHARD RIKER, RECORDER OF THE CITY OF NEW YORK. n.d. n.p.** Rebuts Riker's recent speech in which he asserted that emancipation would prove a curse. 26 November 1836. p.45, c4.

**627 JAMES G. BIRNEY** *to* **THE SLAVE-HOLDERS OF THE SOUTH. [from the** *Cincinnati Philanthropist***] n.d. n.p.** Condemns the institution of slavery. 26 November 1836. p.46, c3.

**628 M. E. GOROSTIZA** *to* **HON. ASBURY DICKENS. 15 October 1836. Washington.** Condemns the president of the United States for claiming the right to violate Mexican territory for the purpose of protecting the frontier of the United States. 26 November 1836. p.46, c6.

**629 JUNIOR** *to* **BROTHER GOODELL. [from the** *Friend of Man***] n.d. n.p.** Urges him to circulate anti-slavery petitions in Oneida County. 26 November 1836. p.47, c4.

**630 CORRESPONDENT** *to* **THE** *NEW YORK COURIER.* **5 November. New Orleans.** Reports that two Mexican commissioners visited Havana with the intent to renew friendly relations between the Mexican and Cuban governments. 26 November 1836. p.47, c6.

**631 MR. CROCHER** *to* **n.n. [extract from the** *Baptist Missionary Magazine***] n.d. n.p.** States that Liberia is in a state of starvation and distress. 26 November 1836. p.47, c6.

**632 L.** *to* **MR. EDITOR [B. LUNDY]. n.d. n.p.** Forwards a poem by E. M. Chandler. 26 November 1836. p.48, c1.

**633 n.n.** *to* **THE FRIENDS OF JUSTICE AND HUMANITY. [from the** *Pittsburgh Times***] 15 November 1836. Pittsburg.** Forwards memorials to the Senate and House of Representatives. 3 December 1836. p.49, c1.

**634 MEMORIALISTS** *to* **THE SENATE AND HOUSE OF REPRESENTATIVES. 20 October 1836. Pennsylvania.** Condemn the enslavement of any human being, regardless of skin color. 3 December 1836. p.49, c1.

**635 n.n. [INHABITANTS OF PENNSYLVANIA]** *to* **THE SENATE AND HOUSE OF REPRESENTATIVES OF THE COMMONWEALTH OF PENNSYLVANIA. n.d. n.p.** Believe that trial by jury is a privilege of inestimable value. 3 December 1836. p.49, c2.

**636 J. P.** *to* **THE EDITOR OF THE** ***EMANCIPATOR*****. n.d. n.p.** Criticizes Reverend J. A. Collins for using strong language in his condemnation of Northern abolitionists. 3 December 1836. p.49, c5.

**637 MR. BLANCHARD** *to* **THE** ***NATIONAL ENQUIRER*****. 8 November 1836. Harrisburg.** Describes the progress of his abolitionist lecture tour in Harrisburg. 3 December 1836. p.50, c2.

**638 JOHN BLACK, JOHN HULL, ROBERT BRUCE, [AND 163 OTHERS]** *to* **n.n. n.d. n.p.** State that they disapprove of the postponement of the Pennsylvania Anti-Slavery Convention; encourage those involved in the cause. 3 December 1836. p.50, c3.

**639 DEARBORN, SECRETARY OF WAR** *to* **GENERAL WILSON. 6 May 1806. n.p.** Reports that there is evidence of hostile intention by the officers of "His Catholic Majesty" at the New Orleans frontier, and declares that the United States should take precautionary measures. 3 December 1836. p.51, c3.

**640 JEFFERSON** *to* **MR. BURWELL. 17 September 1806. Monticello.** States that Burwell is to follow his previous instructions; comments that he has a special interest in St. Bernard's Bay because La Salle's first settlement was founded there. 3 December 1836. p.51, c4.

**641 JEFFERSON** *to* **MR. BOWDOIN. 10 June 1806. Washington.** Questions whether La Salle actually disembarked at St. Bernard's Bay. 3 December 1836. p.51, c5.

**642 THE LADIES AS OF CONCORD** *to* **ANGELINA E. GRIMKE. November 1835. Concord, N.H.** Express their admiration of Grimké and their hope for the future of abolition. 10 December 1836. p.53, c1.

**643 A. E. GRIMKE** *to* **THE LADIES AS OF CONCORD. 16 March 1836. n.p.** Encourages their abolitionist efforts and thanks them for their letter. 10 December 1836. p.53, c2.

**644 MR. WEED** *to* **BROTHER WRIGHT. [from the** ***Emancipator*****] 24 October 1836. Circleville.** Describes his recent anti-slavery lecture tour in Ohio. 10 December 1836. p.53, c4.

**645 ANT. LOPEZ DE SANTA ANNA** *to* **PRESIDENT D. G. BURNET. [from the** ***Texas Telegraph*****] 9 June 1836. n.p.** Protests violations of the recent agreement between Mexico and Texas concerning exchange of prisoners and treatment of prisoners of war. 10 December 1836. p.53, c5.

**646 PRESIDENT BURNET** *to* **GENERAL SANTA ANNA. n.d. n.p.** Acknowledges that Santa Anna has legitimate complaints, but regrets that he can do nothing for him. 10 December 1836. p.53, c6.

**647 CORRESPONDENT** *to* **THE** ***NEW YORK DAILY EXPRESS*****. [extract] 22 October. Mexico.** States that it is not improbable that Mr. Ellis, the American chargé at Mexico, will soon demand his passports and go home. 10 December 1836. p.55, c6.

**648 ELENORA** *to* **ERNEST. n.d. n.p.** Implores Ernest to come and meet a man who seems to be "sent on a message from heaven." 10 December 1836. p.56, c3.

**649 WM. YATES** *to* **BRO. LUNDY. 8 December 1836. New York.** Describes his work among free colored people; appeals for Lundy's help. 17 December 1836. p.58, c5.

**650 J. P.** *to* **FRIEND LUNDY. n.d. n.p.** Gives a biographical sketch of Moses Brown. 17 December 1836. p.58, c6.

**651 n.n.** *to* **n.n. [extract] 5 December 1836. Gettysburg.** Discusses the formation of an AS in Adams County, and opposition to its formation. 17 December 1836. p.58, c6.

**652 W. WHITEHEAD** *to* **MR. LUNDY. 1 December 1836. West Chester.** Reports on a meeting of the West Chester Abolition Society. 17 December 1836. p.58, c6.

**653 n.n.** *to* **n.n. 8 December 1836. Harrisburg.** Praises the governor of Pennsylvania for delivering an anti-slavery message before both houses of the Pennsylvania legislature. 17 December 1836. p.59, c4.

**654 COL. MILLS** *to* **n.n. [extract from the** *Jacksonville Courier***] n.d. n.p.** Confirms the verbal report of "two actions with the Seminoles." 17 December 1836. p.59, c6.

**655 CORRESPONDENT** *to* **THE** *NEW YORK COURIER AND ENQUIRER.* **[extract] 3 December 1836. New Orleans.** Reports that 150 Mexican cavalry have taken possession of the Alamo. 17 December 1836. p.59, c6.

**656 n.n.** *to* **MR. EDITOR. [from the** *Gettysburg Star***] n.d. n.p.** Criticizes the circular, "American Literary Company," which appeared recently in the *U. S. Telegraph.* 17 December 1836. p.60, c2.

**657 A FREEMAN** *to* **MR. EDITOR. [from the** *Norristown Free Press***] n.d. n.p.** Condemns citizens of Norristown, Pennsylvania who advocate returning blacks to Africa. 24 December 1836. p.62, c2.

**658 ADAM WERT, WM. YOUNG, SAMUEL DURBORAW, PETER BERCAW, AND JAMES McALLISTER, JR.** *to* **THE TWO CANDIDATES FOR CONGRESS FROM ADAMS AND FRANKLIN COUNTIES. 17 September 1836. Two Taverns, Adams County, Pa.** Solicit their opinions regarding slavery and the power of Congress to abolish it in Washington, D.C. 24 December 1836. p.62, c4.

**659 JAMES McSHELLY** *to* **ADAM WERT, WM. YOUNG, SAMUEL DURBORAW, PETER BERCAW, AND JAMES McALLISTER, JR. 22 September 1836. Littlestown.** States that he is in favor of abolishing slavery in Washington, D.C., and upholds Congress's power to do so. 24 December 1836. p.62, c4.

**660 DANIEL SHEFFER** *to* **ADAM WERT, WM. YOUNG, SAMUEL DURBORAW, PETER BERCAW, AND JAMES McALLISTER, JR. 26 September 1836. York Springs, Adams County.** States that he is in favor of abolishing slavery in Washington, D.C. 24 December 1836. p.62, c4.

**661 LEWIS TAPPAN** *to* **THE EDITOR OF THE** *EMANCIPATOR.* **5 December 1836. New York.** Encloses a letter he received from T. Oglethorpe. 24 December 1836. p.63, c3.

**662 THOMAS OGLETHORPE** *to* **LEWIS TAPPAN. 20 November 1836. Montgomery, Al.** Sends Tappan a slave's ear to add to his collection of natural curiosities. 24 December 1836. p.63, c3.

**663 A GENTLEMAN** *to* **n.n. [extract] 14 December 1836. Pittsburgh.** Informs of preparations for the coming convention. 24 December 1836. p.63, c3.

**664 CORRESPONDENT** *to* **THE** *NEW YORK COURIER*. **n.d. Washington.** Considers it unlikely that Texas will obtain recognition of its independence from Congress. 24 December 1836. p.63, c3.

**665 n.n.** *to* **n.n. [from the** *New York Courier and Enquirer*] **12, 13 December. New Orleans.** Reports on the strength of the Mexican army; discusses the release of Santa Anna and his projected visit to Washington; encloses letters. 24 December 1836. p.63, c4.

**666 n.n.** *to* **n.n. [extract] n.d. n.p.** States that troops "are in march from all the states towards Matamoras" to be employed in the expedition against Texas. 24 December 1836. p.63, c4.

**667 SUPERIOR OFFICER IN COMMAND** *to* **n.n. 18 November. San Luis, Potosi.** Reports on the number of cavalry men in San Luis. 24 December 1836. p.63, c4.

**668 n.n.** *to* **n.n. 10 November. Mexico.** Discusses measures taken to prevent Santa Anna from Landing at Vera Cruz; comments on the coming presidential election; reports that the troops at Matamoras have dwindled to 1,300 men. 24 December 1836. p.63, c6.

**669 n.n.** *to* **n.n. 10 December 1836. New Orleans.** Reports military preparations of the Mexicans on the coast of Matamoras. 24 December 1836. p.63, c6.

**670 CORRESPONDENT** *to* **THE** *NEW YORK COURIER AND ENQUIRER*. **n.d. New Orleans.** Reports that General Tacon is in possession of "positive information" respecting the plot which the Creoles have formed to proclaim the independence of Cuba. 24 December 1836. p.63, c6.

**671 DAVID RUGGLES** *to* **THE EDITOR OF THE** *EVENING POST*. **13 December 1836. New York.** Complains of authorities' refusal to acknowledge the presence of a slave-trading boat in their midst. 24 December 1836. p.64, c3.

**672 MR. BRECK[I]NRIDGE** *to* **DR. WARDLAW. [extract from the** *Birmingham Philanthropist*] **n.d. n.p.** Discusses the "national offences and sins of England." 24 December 1836. p.64, c5.

**673 WM. E. CHANNING** *to* **JAMES G. BIRNEY. 1 November 1836. Boston.** Defends the methods employed by abolitionists in promoting their cause. 31 December 1836. p.65, c1.

**674 ANDREW JACKSON** *to* **THE HOUSE OF REPRESENTATIVES. 21 December 1836. Washington.** Discusses political, military and civil conditions in Texas. 31 December 1836. p.65, c6.

**675 A FRIEND** *to* **B. LUNDY. n.d. Bucks County, Pa.** Accuses Pennsylvanians of negligence in moral matters; encourages the formation of more anti-slavery organizations. 31 December 1836. p.66, c5.

**676 COLORED FRIEND** *to* **B. LUNDY. n.d. Pittsburgh.** Advocates education and moral elevation of black people. 31 December 1836. p.66, c6.

**677 SECRETARY OF THE WESTMORELAND AS** *to* **A GENTLEMAN IN PHILADELPHIA. [extract] 13 December 1836. n.p.** Reports on the progress of the anti-slavery cause in New Alexandria. 31 December 1836. p.66, c6.

**678 S. L. GOULD** *to* **n.n. [extract] 23 December 1836. Pittsburgh.** Expects a good turnout for the state convention; notes that he has received a letter from Brother Johnson, who is lecturing to responsive audiences in Bedford. 31 December 1836. p.66, c6.

**679 GEORGE SCOTT** *to* **n.n. 16 November 1836. Beaver County.** Names delegates to the Harrisburg Anti-Slavery Convention. 31 December 1836. p.66, c6.

**680 n.n.** *to* **n.n. [extract] 21 October. Rio Grande.** Reports that the revolutionary forces near Porto Alegre have been defeated. 31 December 1836. p.67, c6.

**681 A GENTLEMAN** *to* **FRIEND IN PHILADELPHIA. [extract] 8 June 1831. Virginia.** Records a speech made by Captain Logan, an Indian warrior, following the slaying of Col. Charles Lewis. 31 December 1836. p.68, c5.

## [1837]

**682 HENRY C. WRIGHT** *to* **BROTHER. [from the** *New York Evangelist***] n.d. n.p.** Believes that it is easier to keep those who are "abolitionists by birth" from becoming slaveholders than to try to convert slaveholders to abolitionism; announces his appointment as children's anti-slavery agent. 7 January 1837. p.69, c3.

**683 LEWIS TAPPAN** *to* **THE FRIENDS OF THE CAUSE. n.d. n.p.** Announces the appointment of seventy abolitionist agents; requests donations. 7 January 1837. p.69, c3.

**684 OUR COUNTRY** *to* **MESSRS. EDITORS. [from the** *Belmont Chronicle***] n.d. n.p.** Believes that only if Texas remains under Mexican control can there be hope for the abolition of slavery. 7 January 1837. p.69, c5.

**685 AMOS GILBERT** *to* **DE LORMA BROOKS. [from the** *New Lisbon Aurora***] n.d. n.p.** Believes that the constitutional legality of slavery is unclear, but that the immorality of the system is unquestionable. 7 January 1837. p.70, c3.

**686 CHARLES E. WILSON** *to* **ADAM SLEMMER, JOSIAH EVANS AND OTHERS. 26 December 1836. Norristown.** Explains why he no longer supports African colonization. 7 January 1837. p.70, c4.

**687 GRACE HUNTLEY AND DESDEMONA** *to* **SIR. 7 November 1836. n.p.** State that they have borrowed his copy of *National Enquirer,* and thank him for the loan. 7 January 1837. p.70, c4.

**688 A GENTLEMAN OF HIGH POLITICAL STANDING** *to* **THE** *NATIONAL ENQUIRER.* **30 December 1836. Washington.** Reports on the "discordant proceedings" between the governor and legislature of South Carolina concerning the recognition of Texas. 7 January 1837. p.71, c2.

**689 A FRIEND IN THE INTERIOR OF PENNSYLVANIA** *to* **A FRIEND IN PHILADELPHIA. n.d. Pennsylvania.** Instructs him to tell Friend Lundy not to give "that ravenous gang of Texas marauders" too much notoriety because a "good size newspaper" would wrap them up. 7 January 1837. p.71, c3.

**690 LEWIS WOODSON** *to* **THE EDITOR [B. LUNDY]. 27 December 1836. Pittsburgh.** Forwards minutes of a recent meeting of the Pittsburgh Moral Reform Society. 7 January 1837. p.71, c3.

**691 A GENTLEMAN IN CHESTER COUNTY** *to* **A FRIEND IN PHILADELPHIA. [extract] 30 December 1836. Moore Hall, Chester County.** Praises an abolitionist speaker he recently heard. 7 January 1837. p.71, c4.

**692 M.** *to* **MR. EDITOR [B. LUNDY]. n.d. n.p.** Encloses a letter from John Wesley for publication. 7 January 1837. p.71, c4.

**693 JOHN WESLEY** *to* **SIR. 26 February 1791. London.** Exhorts him to labor in God's name against slavery. 7 January 1837. p.71, c4.

**694 F. JULIUS LEMOYNE** *to* **THE EDITOR [B. LUNDY]. [extract] 26 December 1836. Washington, Pa.** Informs that there is considerable interest in the emancipation cause in his county. 7 January 1837. p.71, c5.

**695 DAVID RUGGLES** *to* **MR. EDITOR. [from the** *New York Daily Express***] 29 December 1836. New York.** States that he was not involved in the "outrage, riot and assault" on the slave brig *Brilliante*; admits that he did try to free the slaves by legal means. 14 January 1837. p.73, c3.

**696 WM. H. SCOTT** *to* **JOSEPH RITNER. 5 January 1837. Philadelphia.** Encloses the preamble and resolutions unanimously adopted at a meeting of the Young Men's AS. 14 January 1837. p.74, c4.

**697 FRANKLIN** *to* **THE** *EMANCIPATOR.* **24 December 1836. Washington.** States that Northern abolitionists are having little effect in Washington. 14 January 1837. p.76, c2.

**698 A.S.** *to* **n.n. [from the** *Friend***] n.d. n.p.** Describes the beating of a slave by a master. 14 January 1837. p.76, c5.

**699 A LADY RESIDING IN A SLAVE STATE** *to* **FRIEND IN THE EAST. [extract from the** *New York Evangelist***] n.d. n.p.** Discusses the evils of slavery. 14 January 1837. p.76, c5.

**700 BERIAH GREEN** *to* **ANGELINA GRIMKE. [from the** *Friend of Man***] December 1836. Oneida Institute.** Expresses his views on education, noting that formal instruction is but one means of fostering development. 21 January 1837. p.77, c1.

**701 B. INGINAC** *to* **BENJAMIN LUNDY. 17 November 1836. Port au Prince.** Commends him on behalf of the president of Haiti for his abolitionist efforts. 21 January 1837. p.78, c4.

**702 C. C. BURLEIGH** *to* **FRIEND LUNDY. 11 January 1837. Lampeter, Lancaster County, Pa.** Describes the success of his anti-slavery lecture tour in Pennsylvania. 21 January 1837. p.78, c4.

**703 W. H. J.** *to* **B. LUNDY. 11 January 1837. Buckingham, Bucks County.** Describes the progress of the abolitionist movement in Bucks County. 21 January 1837. p.78, c5.

**704 n.n.** *to* **n.n. n.d. Harrisburg.** Discusses his anti-slavery lectures in and around Harrisburg. 21 January 1837. p.78, c5.

**705 GENTLEMAN** *to* **THE EDITOR OF THE** *NATIONAL ENQUIRER* **[B. LUNDY]. [extract] 16 January 1837. Coatesville.** Reports on his anti-slavery lectures in Chester and Lancaster counties. 21 January 1837. p.78, c5.

**706 GENTLEMAN** *to* **THE EDITOR [B. LUNDY]. [extract] n.d. Lancaster County, Pa.** Believes that the day when slavery is abolished is not far away. 21 January 1837. p.78, c6.

**707 GENTLEMAN** *to* **THE EDITOR [B. LUNDY]. [extract] 14 January 1837. Harrisburg.** Discusses the coming anti-slavery convention; believes that opposition to the convention is purely political, and not directed at the abolitionist movement. 21 January 1837. p.78, c6.

**708 FRIEND** *to* **THE EDITOR [B. LUNDY]. [extract] 1 January 1837. Ohio.** Informs that anti-slavery petitions to both national and state legislatures are being circulated. 21 January 1837. p.78, c6.

**709 E.** *to* **THE** *NATIONAL ENQUIRER.* **17 January 1837. n.p.** Discusses several questions concerning colonization, abolition and emancipation. 21 January 1837. p.79, c1.

**710 CORRESPONDENT** *to* **THE** *NATIONAL ENQUIRER.* **n.d. Maryland.** Forwards an article from a Baltimore paper on the laws concerning those who advocate the rights of Negroes. 21 January 1837. p.79, c4.

**711 n.n.** *to* **n.n. [extract from the** *New Orleans Courier***] 15 December 1836. Tampico.** Reports several arrests in connection with citizens supporting the former federal government. 21 January 1837. p.79, c6.

**712 CORRESPONDENT** *to* **THE** *U. S. GAZETTE.* **23 December 1836. Washington.** Discusses a letter from Mr. M'Duffie about Texas. 21 January 1837. p.79, c6.

**713 ANTONIO LOPEZ DE SANTA ANNA** *to* **ANDREW JACKSON. 4 July 1836. Columbia, Tx.** States that he is imprisoned and is willing to negotiate peace between Mexico and Texas. 28 January 1837. p.81, c6.

**714 ANDREW JACKSON** *to* **ANTONIO LOPEZ DE SANTA ANNA. 4 September 1836. Hermitage.** Acknowledges the receipt of his letter; regrets to inform that he has received word from the Mexican minister that no act of Santa Anna will be considered binding by the Mexican authorities. 28 January 1837. p.82, c1.

**715 A SUBSCRIBER** *to* **B. LUNDY. 23 January 1837. Philadelphia.** Advises him not to criticize the Van Buren party. 28 January 1837. p.82, c4.

**716 CORRESPONDENT** *to* **THE** *PENNSYLVANIA INQUIRER.* **18 January 1837. Washington.** Reports on the resolution to end discussion of slavery in Congress. 28 January 1837. p.83, c1.

**717 CORRESPONDENT** *to* **THE** *UNITED STATES GAZETTE.* **[extract] 22 January 1837. Washington.** Announces the release of Santa Anna from prison. 28 January 1837. p.83, c2.

**718 n.n.** *to* **THE EDITOR OF THE** *PENNSYLVANIA INQUIRER.* **[extract] 23 January 1837. Washington.** Discusses the likelihood of war with Mexico following the return of Mr. Ellis, minister to Mexico, to Washington. 28 January 1837. p.83, c2.

**719 A MEMBER OF CONGRESS** *to* **n.n. [extract] 20 January. Washington.** Discusses the resolution by the House that all abolition memorials shall be ignored. 28 January 1837. p.83, c3.

**720 J. BLANCHARD** *to* **THE PUBLIC. 8 January 1837. Harrisburg.** Discusses the beliefs and intentions of abolitionists. 28 January 1837. p.83, c4.

**721 n.n.** *to* **n.n. 11 January. New Orleans.** Informs that Santa Anna has been declared an outlaw by those presently in power in Mexico. 28 January 1837. p.83, c5.

**722 n.n.** *to* **n.n. 12 January. New Orleans.** Warns that the United States has a powerful enemy in Mexico and should not underestimate its strength. 28 January 1837. p.83, c5.

**723 WILLIAM WHIPPER, ALFRED NIGER, AND AUGUSTUS PRICE** *to* **THE AMERICAN PEOPLE. n.d. n.p.** Discuss American culture and the beliefs and aims of the American Moral Reform Society. 28 January 1837. p.84, c2.

**724 H. CLAY** *to* **REV. R. R. GURLEY. n.d. n.p.** Accepts the office of president of the ACS; promises to continue to uphold the society's principles. 28 January 1837. p.84, c5.

**725 PHILADELPHIA LADIES AS** *to* **THE BOSTON FEMALE AS. 18 November 1836. Philadelphia.** Inquires about the proposed formation of an executive committee for female ASs. 18 February 1837. p.89, c1.

**726 BOSTON FEMALE AS** *to* **PHILADELPHIA LADIES AS. 12 January 1837. Boston.** Proposes a national convention to determine how future ASs should be organized. 18 February 1837. p.89, c1.

**727 G.** *to* **SIR. 3 February. Harrisburg, Pa.** Gives an account of the abolition convention held in Harrisburg. 18 February 1837. p.91, c2.

**728 LEWIS C. GUNN** *to* **SARAH M. GRIMKE. 14 February 1837. Philadelphia.** Clarifies facts of a case regarding the attempted return of a slave to Virginia. 18 February 1837. p.91, c3.

**729 JUSTICE** *to* **MR. SARGENT. [from the** ***Commercial Herald*****] n.d. n.p.** Refutes criticism of Elliot Cresson's address on colonization from the Harrisburg correspondent of the *Commercial Herald.* 18 February 1837. p.91, c3.

**730 H. C.** *to* **MR. EDITOR OF THE** ***COMMERCIAL HERALD.*** **13 February. Harrisburg.** Criticizes Elliot Cresson for "reproaching and misrepresenting" abolitionists in his recent speech. 18 February 1837. p.91, c4.

**731 n.n.** *to* **THE SENATE AND HOUSE OF REPRESENTATIVES. [from the** ***Pittsburg Christian Witness*****] 1 February 1837. Pittsburg.** Informs of an increase in the number of unlawfully indentured slaves in Pennsylvania. 18 February 1837. p.91, c4.

**732 n.n.** *to* **THE EDITORS OF THE** ***COURIER AND ENQUIRER.*** **[extract] n.d. Frederick, Md.** Reports that "the Court has exonerated General Scott from all censure and decided that the failure of the campaign is attributable to causes over which he had no control." 18 February 1837. p.91, c6.

**733 CORRESPONDENT** *to* **THE** ***COURIER AND ENQUIRER.*** **1 February 1837. New Orleans.** Reports the arrival of General Bravo and his staff at Matamoras on 9 January. 18 February 1837. p.91, c6.

**734 CORRESPONDENT** *to* **THE** ***COURIER AND ENQUIRER.*** **5 February 1837. New Orleans.** Reports that General Bustamente's troops have abandoned plans for an expedition into Texas; states that Santa Anna plans on retiring from public affairs. 18 February 1837. p.91, c6.

**735 A CONSTANT READER** *to* **THE EDITOR [B. LUNDY]. n.d. n.p.** Encloses a poem by John G. Whittier for publication. 18 February 1837. p.92, c1.

**736 n.n.** *to* **THE EDITOR OF THE** ***NEW YORK EVANGELIST.*** **n.d. n.p.** Encloses a poem by a slave named Austin. 18 February 1837. p.92, c1.

**737 JOHN REYNOLDS** *to* **THE HARRISBURG ANTI-SLAVERY CONVENTION. 25 January 1837. Meadville.** Explains why the representative for the Crawford County AS is from another county. 18 February 1837. p.92, c2.

**738 NATHANIEL WEST** *to* **THE HARRISBURG ANTI-SLAVERY CONVENTION. 25 January 1837. Meadville.** Apologizes for having missed the convention and offers advice for the success of their efforts. 18 February 1837. p.92, c2.

**739 DANIEL L. MILLER, JR. AND SAMUEL J. LEVICK** *to* **THE HARRISBURG ANTI-SLAVERY CONVENTION. 28 January 1837. Philadelphia.** Apologize for failing to attend the convention; discuss the interest in abolitionism felt by the youth of Philadelphia. 18 February 1837. p.92, c3.

**740 WILLIAM JAY** *to* **THE HARRISBURG ANTI-SLAVERY CONVENTION. 25 November 1836. Bedford.** Thanks them for their invitation to the convention and expresses his regret for not attending; stresses the need for such a convention. 18 February 1837. p.92, c3.

**741 ALVAN STEWART** *to* **THE HARRISBURG ANTI-SLAVERY CONVENTION. 22 January 1837. Utica.** Commends the Harrisburg Anti-Slavery Convention. 18 February 1837. p.92, c4.

**742 WM. GOODELL** *to* **THE HARRISBURG ANTI-SLAVERY CONVENTION. 20 January 1837. Utica.** Thanks them for their invitation, but states that commitments in New York will not permit him to attend. 18 February 1837. p.92, c5.

**743 LA ROY SUNDERLAND** *to* **THE HARRISBURG ANTI-SLAVERY CONVENTION. [extract] n.d. n.p.** Asserts that the practice of "man-stealing" should receive more attention from friends of the anti-slavery cause. 18 February 1837. p.92, c5.

**744 SAMUEL J. MAY** *to* **THE HARRISBURG ANTI-SLAVERY CONVENTION. [extract] n.d. n.p.** States that the convention should set forth its principles in a plain fashion and thus convince the world of the evils of slavery. 18 February 1837. p.92, c5.

**745 ABRAHAM L. COX** *to* **THE HARRISBURG ANTI-SLAVERY CONVENTION. [extract] n.d. n.p.** Believes that the convention should address the illegality of capturing fugitive slaves. 18 February 1837. p.92, c6.

**746 ROWLAND T. ROBINSON** *to* **ORSON. [from the** *Vermont Telegraph***] 14 January 1837. n.p.** Requests publication of an enclosed anti-slavery memorial to Congress. 25 February 1837. p.93, c1.

**747 H. E. GAZZAM AND R. W. LAMBDIN, IN BEHALF OF THE FEMALE AS OF PITTSBURGH** *to* **THE FEMALE AS OF PHILADELPHIA. 26 December 1836. Pittsburgh.** Describe progress made by the Female AS of Pittsburgh. 25 February 1837. p.95, c2.

**748 ELIZABETH PEASE AND JESSE WEMYSS IN BEHALF OF THE LADIES OF DARLINGTON** *to* **THE MEMBERS OF THE LADIES ANTI-SLAVERY ASSOCIATION IN NEW ENGLAND. 14 December 1836. n.p.** Resolve that slavery is evil; commend the association's anti-slavery progress. 4 March 1837. p.97, c1.

**749 CHRISTOPHER RUSH, ISAAC BARNEY, TIMOTHY ETOE, JAMES SIMMONS, JOHN RAYMOND, WM. CORNISH, THEODORE WRIGHT, AND SAMUEL CORNISH** *to* **MINISTERS AND PASTORS OF COLORED CONGREGATIONS IN NEW YORK, THE FREE COLORED CITIZENS IN THE UNITED STATES, AND THEIR CHRISTIAN BRETHREN AND FRIENDS. [extract from the** *Zion's Watchman***] n.d. n.p.** Encourage the anti-slavery movement. 4 March 1837. p.97, c2.

**750 L.** *to* **THE** *NATIONAL ENQUIRER***. n.d. n.p.** Gives an account of the quarterly meeting of the Frankfort AS. 4 March 1837. p.98, c1.

**751 C. C. BURLEIGH** *to* **FRIEND LUNDY. 1 March 1837. n.p.** Describes his recent anti-slavery lecture tour in Pennsylvania. 4 March 1837. p.98, c3.

**752 A MERCHANT** *to* **n.n. n.d. n.p.** Reports that New Orleans newspapers remain silent regarding the misunderstanding which exists between the United States and Mexico. 4 March 1837. p.98, c6.

**753 AN AGENT OF THE TEXAS LAND SPECULATORS** *to* **n.n. [extract) n.d. New Orleans.** Gives an account of Santa Anna's reception in Mexico. 4 March 1837. p.99, c1.

**754 CORRESPONDENT** *to* **THE** *UNITED STATES GAZETTE.* **n.d. n.p.** Reports on Mr. Penrose's speech in favor of trial by jury and in opposition to the doctrines of the abolitionists. 4 March 1837. p.99, c2.

**755 A VISITOR** *to* **FRIEND LUNDY. n.d. n.p.** Describes a newly formed colored Sabbath school. 4 March 1837. p.99, c3.

**756 ARNOLD BUFFUM** *to* **n.n. [extract] n.d. n.p.** Stresses the necessity of education for Negroes. 4 March 1837. p.99, c5.

**757 THEODORE S. WRIGHT** *to* **n.n. [extract] n.d. n.p.** Recounts efforts of colored clergymen. 4 March 1837. p.99, c5.

**758 GEORGE BOURNE** *to* **n.n. [extract] n.d. n.p.** Recommends establishing a boundary between slave and free states. 4 March 1837. p.99, c5.

**759 AMERICAN CONSUL AT SANTA MARTHA** *to* **n.n. [extract] 3 February 1837. n.p.** Reports the presence of a British fleet off Carthagena and a frigate off Santa Martha; believes that the difficulties between Mexico and the United States may be settled amicably. 4 March 1837. p.99, c6.

**760 ABRAHAM BYRD** *to* **THE EDITOR OF THE** *ALTON OBSERVER.* **[extract] 26 January 1837. Jefferson City.** Opposes the *Alton Observer* because of its anti-slavery stance. 4 March 1837. p.100, c2.

**761 J. BLANCHARD** *to* **THE PUBLIC. [from the** *Harrisburg Chronicle***] n.d. n.p.** Compares abolitionists of 1774 to those of 1837. 4 March 1837. p.100, c2.

**762 THE BOARD OF MANAGERS OF THE EDUCATION SOCIETY** *to* **AMERICAN PHILANTHROPISTS. January 1837. Cincinnati.** Appeals for funds for a new high school. 4 March 1837. p.100, c4.

**763 MR. LIVINGSTON** *to* **MR. VAN BUREN. [extract] 5 December 1831. n.p.** Reports the wreck of a slave ship in the Bahamas, in which the slaves were rescued and set free by the governor of the island of Providence, and their owners were forbidden to claim them; considers this a violation of owners' rights. 11 March 1837. p.101, c4.

**764 CHIEF CLERK OF DEPARTMENT OF STATE** *to* **MR. VAIL. [extract] 28 September 1832. n.p.** Informs that British officials are reviewing the decision of the governor of Providence to free the slaves involved in the recent shipwreck. 11 March 1837. p.101, c5.

**765 MR. LIVINGSTON** *to* **MR. VAIL. [extract] 26 February 1833. n.p.** Asserts that the shipwreck in the Bahamas would not have happened if lights had been put in the Bahama channel. 11 March 1837. p.101, c5.

**766 MR. FORSYTH** *to* **MR. VAIL. 2 August 1834. n.p.** Regrets the delay by the British government in acting upon the emancipation of the slaves involved in the shipwreck in the Bahamas three years earlier. 11 March 1837. p.101, c5.

**767 JOHN FORSYTH** *to* **MR. VAIL. 26 March 1835. Washington.** Declares it an outrage that American-owned slaves were liberated by the governor of the island of Providence and the owners' rights thereby violated. 11 March 1837. p.101, c6.

**768 MR. VAN BUREN** *to* **MR. LIVINGSTON. [extract] 28 February 1832. n.p.** Encloses a copy of his letter to Lord Palmerston. 11 March 1837. p.101, c6.

**769 MR. VAN BUREN** *to* **LORD PALMERSTON. 25 February 1832. Stratford Place.** Submits the claims of several United States citizens against the British government for "injuries they have sustained" in consequence of the emancipation of their slaves in the Bahamas without their consent. 11 March 1837. p.101, c6.

**770 CORRESPONDENT** *to* **B. LUNDY. 6 March 1837. Harrisburg.** Reports that the Senate has rejected the bill to grant fugitive slaves trial by jury; refutes the *United States Gazette* correspondent's account of Senator Penrose's speech, stating that Penrose advocates the rights of the oppressed. 11 March 1837. p.102, c6.

**771 CORRESPONDENT** *to* **THE** *NATIONAL ENQUIRER.* **n.d. Washington.** Encloses a pamphlet on slavery; queries whether the United States intends to go to war with Great Britain over the "illegal" emancipation of American-owned slaves in the Bahamas. 11 March 1837. p.103, c1.

**772 W. H. J.** *to* **B. LUNDY. 26 February 1837. Buckingham.** Praises a speech given by C. C. Burleigh before the quarterly meeting of the Bucks County AS. 11 March 1837. p.103, c1.

**773 PHILADELPHUS** *to* **FRIENDS AND FELLOW CITIZENS. n.d. n.p.** Condemns slavery; urges increased efforts to oppose it. 11 March 1837. p.103, c6.

**774 SAMBO** *to* **GENTLEMEN. [from the** *Bucks County Intelligencer***] n.d. n.p.** Discusses a colored man's opposition to colonization. 11 March 1837. p.104, c2.

**775 WILLIAM SLADE** *to* **GENTLEMEN. [from the** *National Intelligencer***] 22 February 1837. n.p.** Requests publication of his article on the right of slaves to petition. 11 March 1837. p.104, c3.

**776 WILLIAM SLADE** *to* **THE EDITORS OF THE** *INTELLIGENCER.* **15 February 1837. Washington.** Discusses resolutions concerning slaves' rights to petition. 11 March 1837. p.104, c3.

**777 J. H.** *to* **n.n. [from the** *Herald of Freedom***] n.d. n.p.** Informs that thirty women have signed a petition to abolish slavery in the District of Columbia. 11 March 1837. p.104, c5.

**778 THE PHILADELPHIA FEMALE AS** *to* **THE FEMALE ASs OF PENNSYLVANIA. 15 February 1837. n.p.** Solicits support for a female anti-slavery convention in New York. 18 March 1837. p.1, c1.

**779 W. H. J.** *to* **THE EDITOR [B. LUNDY]. n.d. n.p.** Gives an account of a farmer in Solebury, Pennsylvania, who hired both white and colored men who worked and ate side by side; describes the horror of a white newcomer upon witnessing this. 18 March 1837. p.1, c3.

**780 REV. J. M. McKIM** *to* **FRIEND LUNDY. 7 March 1837. Pottsgrove.** Reports on his anti-slavery lecture tour. 18 March 1837. p.2, c1.

**781 J. BLANCHARD** *to* **BROTHER LUNDY. 6 March 1837. Washington, Pa.** Reports on a discussion between opponents and supporters of abolitionism. 18 March 1837. p.2, c2.

**782 SARAH M. GRIMKE AND ANGELINA E. GRIMKE** *to* **CLARKSON. [from the** *National Intelligencer***] n.d. n.p.** Rebut his letter which accuses them of impracticality, and propose a "practicable means" by which the North can abolish slavery in the South; encourage anti-slavery efforts. 18 March 1837. p.2, c4.

**783 CLARKSON** *to* **SARAH M. AND ANGELINA E. GRIMKE. [from the** *National Intelligencer***] 11 February 1837. New Haven.** Challenges them to present a practical plan for ending slavery. 18 March 1837. p.2, c4.

**784 C. C. BURLEIGH** *to* **n.n. [extract] 9 March 1837. Kimberton, Pa.** Gives an account of his speech which was interrupted by someone who had sprinkled pepper around the room, causing members of the audience to choke; reports on his lectures in Lionville. 18 March 1837. p.3, c3.

**785 A GENTLEMAN IN THE CHOCTAW NATION** *to* **THE EDITOR OF THE** *ARKANSAS GAZETTE.* **[extract] 20 January. n.p.** Discusses an agreement reached by the Chickasaw delegation and the Choctaws. 18 March 1837. p.3, c5.

**786 n.n.** *to* **n.n. [extract] 17 February 1837. Texas.** Reports that the United States troops in Texas are in good condition. 18 March 1837. p.3, c6.

**787 MR. KIDD** *to* **n.n. [extract] 8 February 1837. Vera Cruz.** Reports that one of the Mexican brigs bound for Matamoras is carrying arms from England. 18 March 1837. p.3, c6.

**788 MR. KIDD** *to* **n.n. [extract] 22 January 1837. n.d.** Reports that four brigs and two schooners of Mexico are "under sailing orders." 18 March 1837. p.3, c6.

**789 L.** *to* **THE** *NATIONAL ENQUIRER.* **n.d. n.p.** Encloses an article by E. M. Chandler about the interactions of Europeans and Africans. 18 March 1837. p.4, c1.

**790 H.** *to* **THE** *NATIONAL ENQUIRER.* **n.d. n.p.** Encloses a poem by Elizabeth M. Chandler. 18 March 1837. p.4, c2.

**791 MR. VAIL** *to* **MR. LIVINGSTON. [extract] 15 July 1832. n.d.** Discusses his interview with Lord Palmerston about the slaves emancipated after a shipwreck in the Bahamas. 18 March 1837. p.4, c3.

**792 MR. VAIL** *to* **MR. LIVINGSTON. [extract] 14 November 1832. n.p.** Reports that the case of the slaver shipwrecked in the Bahamas remains to be examined by British authorities. 18 March 1837. p.4, c3.

**793 MR. VAIL** *to* **MR. LIVINGSTON. [extract] 30 March 1833. n.p.** Reports that the case of the shipwreck of the slave brig in the Bahamas has not been examined by British authorities; encloses a copy of a note to Lord Palmerston. 18 March 1837. p.4, c3.

**794 A. VAIL** *to* **LORD PALMERSTON. 25 March 1833. n.p.** Reminds Palmerston that the British government has not yet responded to charges brought against it by the United States for emancipating American-owned slaves in the Bahamas after a shipwreck. 18 March 1837. p.4, c3.

**795 MR. VAIL** *to* **THE SECRETARY OF STATE. [extract] 6 April 1833. n.p.** Encloses Lord Palmerston's reply to Mr. Vail; includes his own comments. 18 March 1837. p.4, c3.

**796 LORD PALMERSTON** *to* **MR. VAIL. 30 March 1833. n.p.** Acknowledges the receipt of Vail's note concerning American claims on England arising from the seizure of slaves by the colonial authorities of the Bahamas. 18 March 1837. p.4, c4.

**797 A. VAIL** *to* **LORD PALMERSTON. 4 April 1833. n.p.** Provides, under instructions from the president, additional reasons for the indemnification of slaveowners whose slaves had been seized by British authorities in the Bahamas. 18 March 1837. p.4, c4.

**798 MR. VAIL** *to* **MR. LIVINGSTON. [extract] 29 April 1833. n.p.** Encloses a note from Lord Palmerston regarding the case of slaves seized by British authorities in the Bahamas. 18 March 1837. p.4, c5.

**799 LORD PALMERSTON** *to* **MR. VAIL. 24 April 1833. n.p.** Acknowledges the receipt of Mr. Vail's note of 4 April, and states that the note has been submitted to the king's law officers. 18 March 1837. p.4, c5.

**800 MR. VAIL** *to* **MR. McLANE. [extract] 28 September 1833. n.p.** Reports the failure of the British to arrive at a final decision in the case of slaves seized by colonial authorities in the Bahamas. 18 March 1837. p.4, c5.

**801 MR. VAIL** *to* **MR. McLANE. [extract] 14 January 1834. n.p.** Reports on an interview with Lord Palmerston in which the case of slaves seized by British authorities in the Bahamas was discussed; encloses a memorandum on the subject which was left with Lord Palmerston. 18 March 1837. p.4, c5.

**802 MR. VAIL** *to* **THE SECRETARY OF STATE OF THE UNITED STATES. [extract] 6 August 1834. n.p.** Reports that he has reminded Lord Palmerston repeatedly of the failure of the British government to respond to charges brought against it by the United States concerning American-owned slaves emancipated in the Bahamas. 18 March 1837. p.4, c5.

**803 A. VAIL** *to* **LORD PALMERSTON. 1 August 1834. n.p.** Urges him to endeavor to bring the case of slaves seized in the Bahamas to a speedy conclusion, in accordance with Palmerston's own promises to do so. 18 March 1837. p.4, c6.

**804 NO LONGER A FRIEND TO COLONIZATION** *to* **THE** ***NATIONAL ENQUIRER*****. n.d. n.p.** Reviews Captain Stockton's speech before a meeting of the CS in Trenton, New Jersey; condemns the colonizationists' acquiescence to slavery. 25 March 1837. p.5, c2.

**805 J. P.** *to* **THE EDITOR [B. LUNDY]. n.d. n.p.** Encloses a letter from Anthony Benezet to Queen Charlotte. 25 March 1837. p.5, c5.

**806 ANTHONY BENEZET** *to* **CHARLOTTE, QUEEN OF GREAT BRITAIN. 25 August 1783. Philadelphia.** Encloses tracts describing the suffering of slaves in America; urges the queen to intercede in behalf of the slaves. 25 March 1837. p.5, c5.

**807 A CLERGYMAN IN BEAVER COUNTY** *to* **HIS BROTHER IN PHILADELPHIA. [extract] 6 March 1837. n.p.** Describes an aborted attempt by colonizationists to disrupt his speech in New Castle. 25 March 1837. p.5, c6.

**808 A JUNIOR ABOLITIONIST** *to* **THE EDITOR [B. LUNDY]. 24 March 1837. Philadelphia, Pa.** Encloses an extract of a letter from a young correspondent. 25 March 1837. p.5, c6.

**809 A YOUTHFUL CORRESPONDENT** *to* **A JUNIOR ABOLITIONIST. [extract] n.d. Pennsylvania.** Asks whether hiring a slave and paying his master is not equivalent to buying the products of slave labor, and should not, therefore, be avoided by abolitionists. 25 March 1837. p.5, c6.

**810 ONE OF THE COMMITTEE** *to* **THE FRIENDS OF IMMEDIATE EMANCIPATION. n.d. n.p.** Pleads for financial support for the *Enquirer,* as the executive committee of the AS cannot run in debt to support it. 25 March 1837. p.6, c1.

**811 A VETERAN IN THE CAUSE OF EMANCIPATION** *to* **n.n. n.d. n.p.** Urges young people to take a leading role in the anti-slavery movement; responds to an address delivered before the Junior AS of Philadelphia and states that slaveholders cannot be virtuous men. 25 March 1837. p.6, c2.

**812 ANTONIO LOPEZ DE SANTA ANNA** *to* **THE MINISTER OF WAR AND MARINE. 20 February 1837. Vera Cruz.** Promises to give the president a full account of the circumstances of his capture and release by the Americans; pleads innocence of any charges of disloyalty. 25 March 1837. p.6, c4.

**813 COLONEL JUAN N. ALMONTE** *to* **GENERAL DON JOSE MARIA TORNEL. 20 February 1837. Vera Cruz.** Reports his escape from the Texas bandits. 25 March 1837. p.6, c4.

**814 n.n.** *to* **THE SECRETARY OF THE PENNSYLVANIA AS. [extract] n.d. Bellefonte, Pa.** Reports on the progress of the anti-slavery cause in Bellefonte. 25 March 1837. p.6, c6.

**815 LYDIA MARIA CHILD** *to* **GERRIT SMITH. [extract] 14 February 1837. South Natick, Ma.** Describes the resurgence of abolitionism in Boston. 25 March 1837. p.7, c4.

**816 JAMES DELL** *to* **THE EDITOR OF THE** ***COURIER.*** **11 March 1837. Jacksonville.** Encloses a letter from his brother Bennett M. Dell. 25 March 1837. p.7, c5.

**817 BENNETT M. DELL** *to* **JAMES DELL. 10 March 1837. Black Creek.** Announces the end of the war with the Indians. 25 March 1837. p.7, c5.

**818 MR. VAIL** *to* **SECRETARY OF STATE OF THE UNITED STATES. [extract] 14 August 1834. n.p.** Reports that the case of the slaves detained by British authorities in the Bahamas is still unconcluded. 25 March 1837. p.8, c2.

**819 MR. VAIL** *to* **THE SECRETARY OF STATE OF THE UNITED STATES. 13 September 1834. n.p.** Announces his intention to address the British government concerning two seamen taken from the ship *Rosanna* and slaves detained by British authorities in the Bahamas from the brigs *Encomium* and *Comet.* 25 March 1837. p.8, c2.

**820 MR. VAIL** *to* **THE SECRETARY OF STATE OF THE UNITED STATES. 22 September 1834. n.p.** Encloses a copy of a note to Lord Palmerston. 25 March 1837. p.8, c2.

**821 A. VAIL** *to* **LORD PALMERSTON. 20 September 1834. n.p.** Requests a decision in favor of the claimants in the case of slaves detained in the Bahamas by British authorities. 25 March 1837. p.8, c2.

**822 A LOVER OF CONSISTENCY** *to* **THE EDITOR [B. LUNDY]. n.d. n.p.** Suggests that abolitionists turn their attention to the slaveholding states, rather than concentrating on Washington, D.C. and the territories. 1 April 1837. p.9, c1.

**823 A SUBSCRIBER** *to* **BENJ. LUNDY. n.d. n.p.** Suggests that the compilation of a book of heroic actions of slaves would be beneficial to their cause. 1 April 1837. p.9, c3.

**824 J. BLANCHARD** *to* **n.n. [extract] 10 March. Gettysburg.** Describes pro-slavery activity in Washington County and Pittsburgh. 1 April 1837. p.10, c2.

**825 C. C. BURLEIGH** *to* **FRIEND LUNDY. 24 March 1837. Uwchlan.** Describes the progress of his lecture tour. 1 April 1837. p.10, c3.

**826 MENTOR** *to* **THE FRIENDS OF ABOLITION. n.d. n.p.** Urges abolitionists to vote only for abolition men and to form ASs. 1 April 1837. p.10, c5.

**827 OFFICE OF THE** *BULLETIN to* **n.n. 20 March 1837. New Orleans, La.** Encloses an extract of a letter addressed to William Kidd. 1 April 1837. p.10, c6.

**828 n.n.** *to* **WM. KIDD. [extract] 28 February 1837. Tampico.** Announces Mexican preparations for battle against the Texans. 1 April 1837. p.10, c6.

**829 n.n.** *to* **A NEW YORK EDITOR. [extract] n.d. London.** Reports that the British are negotiating secretly to gain possession of Cuba. 1 April 1837. p.11, c1.

**830 n.n.** *to* **B. LUNDY. [extract] 16 March 1837. Indiana.** Urges increased abolitionist activity in Indiana. 1 April 1837. p.11, c1.

**831 n.n.** *to* **n.n. [extract] n.d. New Orleans, La.** Reports that Castillo, the Mexican chargé d'affaires at Washington, sent Santa Anna a letter condemning the latter's negotiations with the United States. 1 April 1837. p.11, c2.

**832 MR. VAIL** *to* **MR. FORSYTH. [extract] 14 January 1835. n.p.** Reports on a conversation with the Duke of Wellington concerning the claims of owners of slaves shipwrecked in the Bahamas in 1830 and 1834. 1 April 1837. p.12, c3.

**833 MR. VAIL** *to* **MR. FORSYTH. [extract] 22 January 1835. n.p.** Conveys assurances from the Duke of Wellington that the claims of owners of slaves shipwrecked in the Bahamas are under consideration. 1 April 1837. p.12, c3.

**834 MR. VAIL** *to* **MR. FORSYTH. [extract] 14 March 1835. n.p.** Reports that the Duke of Wellington stated that the case of the shipwrecked slaves would soon be decided. 1 April 1837. p.12, c3.

**835 MR. VAIL** *to* **MR. FORSYTH. [extract] 14 May 1835. n.p.** Encloses a note to Lord Palmerston. 1 April 1837. p.12, c3.

**836 A. VAIL** *to* **LORD PALMERSTON. 11 May 1835. n.p.** Protests the liberation of slaves from the brig *Enterprise* by British authorities in Bermuda. 1 April 1837. p.12, c3.

**837 MR. VAIL** *to* **MR. FORSYTH. [extract] 6 November 1835. n.p.** Reports on his discussion with Lord Palmerston of legal proceedings regarding the case of the shipwrecked slaves. 1 April 1837. p.12, c5.

**838 MR. VAIL** *to* **MR. FORSYTH. [extract] 14 November 1835. n.p.** Encloses a note from Lord Palmerston informing of the referral of the case of the shipwrecked slaves to the Privy Council. 1 April 1837. p.12, c6.

**839 LORD PALMERSTON** *to* **MR. VAIL. 13 November 183[5]. n.p.** Informs Vail that the case of the shipwrecked slaves has been referred to the Privy Council. 1 April 1837. p.12, c6.

**840 MR. STEVENSON** *to* **MR. FORSYTH. [extract] 14 July 1836. n.p.** Expresses his intention to press the claims of Americans whose slaves were seized by British colonial authorities. 1 April 1837. p.12, c6.

**841 MR. STEVENSON** *to* **MR. FORSYTH. [extract] 29 July 1836. n.p.** Reports his communication to Lord Palmerston, strongly expressing his regret over the delay in the case of the shipwrecked slaves. 1 April 1837. p.12, c6.

**842 MR. STEVENSON** *to* **MR. FORSYTH. [extract] 6 August 1836. n.p.** Transmits a copy of his communication to Lord Palmerston regarding the shipwrecked slaves. 1 April 1837. p.12, c6.

**843 JOHN QUINCY ADAMS** *to* **THE EDITORS OF THE** *QUINCY PATRIOT.* **1 February 1837. Washington.** Describes his efforts to submit anti-slavery petitions to Congress; encloses a letter on the subject to petitioners for the abolition of slavery in the District of Columbia. 8 April 1837. p.13, c1.

**844 JOHN QUINCY ADAMS** *to* **THE PETITIONERS FOR THE ABOLITION OF SLAVERY AND THE SLAVE TRADE IN THE DISTRICT OF COLUMBIA FROM THE TWELFTH CONGRESSIONAL DISTRICT OF MASSACHUSETTS, AND TO OTHER INHABITANTS OF THE DISTRICT. 31 January 1837. Washington.** Describes his efforts to present anti-slavery petitions to Congress. 8 April 1837. p.13, c1.

**845 CORRESPONDENT** *to* **THE** *NATIONAL ENQUIRER.* **[extract] 29 March. Washington.** Comments on Calhoun's presentation of the subject of the slaves shipwrecked in the British islands before the United States Senate. 8 April 1837. p.14, c5.

**846 n.n.** *to* **THE** *NATIONAL ENQUIRER* **[extract] n.d. Washington.** Reports the vote of the House of Representatives of Massachusetts in favor of petitioning Congress for the abolition of slavery in the District of Columbia. 8 April 1837. p.14, c5.

**847 n.n.** *to* **A COMMERCIAL HOUSE IN NEW ORLEANS. [extract] 18 March 1837. Tampico.** Reports events concerning French, English and American diplomatic relations with Mexico. 8 April 1837. p.15, c1.

**848 A ZANESVILLE EMIGRANT IN THE TEXAN ARMY** *to* **A GENTLEMAN IN ZANESVILLE. [extract from the** *Zanesville* **(Oh.)** *Gazette***] n.d. n.p.** Describes the opening of hostilities between the Texans and the Mexicans. 8 April 1837. p.15, c2.

**849 J. BLANCHARD** *to* **BENJAMIN LUNDY. 1 April 1837. Gettysburg, Pa.** Expresses hope for the anti-slavery movement in his area. 8 April 1837. p.15, c4.

**850 WM. HAMILTON** *to* **THE SECRETARY OF THE STATE SOCIETY. [extract] 27 March 1837. Bellefonte.** Finds pro-slavery spirit too strong in the area to allow much progress by the anti-slavery cause. 8 April 1837. p.15, c5.

**851 AMERICAN CITIZEN** *to* **THE** *NATIONAL ENQUIRER.* **n.d. n.p.** Describes the beating of two slaves. 8 April 1837. p.15, c5.

**852 L. NAU** *to* **BENJAMIN LUNDY. n.d. Port au Prince.** Proposes to establish an exchange between the *National Enquirer* or the *Genius of Universal Emancipation* and *Le Républicain.* 8 April 1837. p.16, c1.

**853 MR. STEVENSON** *to* **LORD PALMERSTON. n.d. n.p.** Urges the resolution of the case of the shipwrecked slaves in favor of the claims of the slaves' owners, citing British and American legal precedents. 8 April 1837. p.16, c2.

**854 OUR COUNTRY** *to* **THE EDITORS OF THE** *BELMONT* **(OH.)** *CHRONICLE.* **n.d. n.p.** Opposes the admission of Texas into the United States, which he feels would serve to perpetuate slavery in Texas. 15 April 1837. p.17, c2.

**855 J. Q. ADAMS** *to* **THE EDITORS OF THE** *QUINCY PATRIOT.* **18 March 1837. Washington.** Opposes abolitionism, but supports the right of abolitionists to petition Congress; describes his efforts to submit such petitions despite opposition in Congress. 15 April 1837. p.17, c4.

**856 JOHN QUINCY ADAMS** *to* **THE INHABITANTS OF THE TWELFTH CONGRESSIONAL DISTRICT OF MASSACHUSETTS. [from the** *Quincy Patriot***] 13 March 1837. Washington.** Describes attempts to censure him in the House of Representatives for an alleged attempt to present a petition from slaves. 15 April 1837. p.17, c5.

**857 M. R. K.** *to* **THE** *NATIONAL ENQUIRER.* **n.d. n.p.** Encloses extracts from notes of the proceedings of the Yearly Meeting of the Society of Friends in London in 1835 and 1836. 15 April 1837. p.18, c4.

**858 E. L.** *to* **THE** *NATIONAL ENQUIRER.* **n.d. n.p.** Examines the question of whether a citizen of another state or territory who enters Pennsylvania with a slave is entitled to the support of legal authorities in Pennsylvania in compelling the slave to return with him. 15 April 1837. p.18, c5.

**859 JUDGE WASHINGTON** *to* **n.n. [extract from the** *Genius of Universal Emancipation***] 1821. n.p.** Denies that he voluntarily caused the separation of slave families. 15 April 1837. p.19, c3.

**860 TORNEL** *to* **THE OFFICE OF THE SECRETARY OF WAR AND NAVY. [from the** *New Orleans Bee***] 9 February 1837. Mexico.** Orders the closing of ports on the coast of Texas to foreign ships. 15 April 1837. p.19, c5.

**861 MRS. CHILD** *to* **n.n. [extract] n.d. n.p.** Mourns the death of Ann G. Chapman, a member of the Female AS who died on 24 March. 15 April 1837. p.20, c2.

**862 A. STEVENSON** *to* **LORD PALMERSTON. n.d. n.p.** Denies Great Britain's right to interfere with slavery in other nations; concludes that the case of the shipwrecked slaves should be decided in favor of the slaves' owners. [continued from 8 April 1837] 15 April 1837. p.20, c3.

**863 MR. SECRETARY SPRING RICE** *to* **THE GOVERNORS OF THE WEST INDIA COLONIES. 4 November 1834. n.p.** States that the abolition of slavery by Great Britain does not confer upon British authorities the right to interfere with the practices of other nations. 15 April 1837. p.20, c3.

**864 MR. STEVENSON** *to* **MR. FORSYTH. [extract] 22 August 1836. n.p.** Reports that no answer has been received from Lord Palmerston on the subject of the shipwrecked slaves. 15 April 1837. p. 20, c5.

**865 MR. STEVENSON** *to* **MR. FORSYTH. [extract] 5 October 1836. n.p.** Reports that the British have not yet responded on the subject of the shipwrecked slaves. 15 April 1837. p.20, c5.

**866 MR. STEVENSON** *to* **MR. FORSYTH. [extract] 19 November 1836. n.p.** Reports that no answer has been received on the subject of the shipwrecked slaves. 15 April 1837. p.20, c5.

**867 MR. STEVENSON** *to* **MR. FORSYTH. [extract] 14 December 1836. n.p.** Encloses a note to Lord Palmerston. 15 April 1837. p.20, c5.

**868 A. STEVENSON** *to* **LORD PALMERSTON. 13 December 1836. n.p.** Urges a speedy decision in the case of the shipwrecked slaves to ensure that the case will not damage relations between the United States and Britain. 15 April 1837. p. 20, c5.

**869 J. R. C.** *to* **THE EDITOR OF THE** *NATIONAL ENQUIRER* **[B. LUNDY]. n.d. n.p.** Endorses abolitionism, rejecting his earlier anti-abolitionist views. 22 April 1837. p.21, c3.

**870 n.n.** *to* **n.n. [extract] n.d. Bucks County.** Reports on the case of a white man who intends to take two colored children apprenticed to him to Missouri, against the wishes of their mother. 22 April 1837. p.22, c1.

**871 W.** *to* **THE EDITOR [B. LUNDY]. n.d. Philadelphia.** Complains of the age restriction on members of the Philadelphia Literary Company of Colored Persons. 22 April 1837. p.22, c1.

**872 JOHN QUINCY ADAMS** *to* **HIS CONSTITUENTS. [extract from the** *Quincy Patriot***] n.d. n.p.** Denies the right of slavery to the protection of the national government. 22 April 1837. p.22, c3.

**873 C. C. BURLEIGH** *to* **FRIEND LUNDY. 19 April 1837. Philadelphia, Pa.** Describes his anti-slavery lecture tour through the counties of Chester and Philadelphia. 22 April 1837. p.22, c5.

**874 A LAWYER** *to* **MR. HAMMOND. [from the** *Cincinnati Gazette***] n.d. n.p.** Discusses constitutional aspects of the question of whether a slave brought into Ohio is free, a question which arose in the trial of Matilda. 22 April 1837. p.23, c4.

**875 JOHN QUINCY ADAMS** *to* **THE INHABITANTS OF THE TWELFTH CONGRESSIONAL DISTRICT. [from the** *Quincy Patriot***] 13 March 1837. Washington.** Discusses attempts in the House of Representatives to limit the right of petition of slaves. [continued from 15 April 1837] 22 April 1837. p.24, c3.

**876 ALICE ELIZA HAMBLETON, RUTH HAMBLETON, LINDLEY COATES, [AND SEVENTEEN OTHERS]** *to* **THE FRIENDS OF IMMEDIATE EMANCIPATION IN CHESTER COUNTY AND PARTS ADJACENT. 16 April 1837. n.p.** Officials of the Clarkson, East Fallowfield and Oxford ASs call for a convention to organize a Chester County AS. 29 April 1837. p.25, c1.

**877 DAVID L. CHILD** *to* **HIS WIFE. [extract] n.d. n.p.** Discusses French and Belgian views of American slavery. 29 April 1837. p.26, c6.

**878 J. BLANCHARD** *to* **THE EDITOR OF THE** *GETTYSBURG STAR AND REPUBLICAN BANNER*. **n.d. n.p.** Claims he was assailed by a mob because of his anti-slavery opinions. 29 April 1837. p.27, c2.

**879 LUCY TOWNSEND** *to* **BENJAMIN LUNDY. 21 March 1836. West Bromwich.** Announces her intention to retire as secretary to the Birmingham Ladies Negro Friends Society; supports the emigration of colored Protestants to Haiti. 29 April 1837. p.27, c3.

**880 REV. J. M. M'KIM** *to* **THE EDITOR OF THE** *NATIONAL ENQUIRER* **[B. LUNDY]. [extract] 25 April 1837. Hatborough.** Describes attempts to deliver an anti-slavery lecture in Hatborough. 29 April 1837. p.27, c3.

**881 J. R.** *to* **MR. WALTER. [from the** *Delaware County Republican***] n.d. n.p.** Describes an anti-slavery speech delivered by Charles C. Burleigh at the Upper Darby school house. 29 April 1837. p.27, c4.

**882 F. D. L.** *to* **BENJ'N LUNDY. 18 April 1837. Washington, Pa.** Attacks a biblical justification of slavery. 29 April 1837. p.27, c4.

**883 J. Q. ADAMS** *to* **THE INHABITANTS OF THE TWELFTH CONGRESSIONAL DISTRICT OF MASSACHUSETTS. [from the** *Quincy Patriot***] 20 March 1837. Washington.** Explains circumstances surrounding his censure by the House of Representatives; describes a debate on the right of petition of slaves; denies the right of slavery to the protection of the national government. 29 April 1837. p.28, c3.

**884 ISAAC T. HOPPER** *to* **THE MAYOR OF SAVANNAH, GA. 18 April 1836. New York.** Thanks him for intervening on behalf of his son, who was attacked by a mob who suspected that he was an agent of the AS. 6 May 1837. p.29, c1.

**885 W. H. J.** *to* **FRIEND LUNDY. 27 April 1837. Buckingham.** Reports the success of C. C. Burleigh's lecture tour in Bucks County. 6 May 1837. p.29, c3.

**886 B.** *to* **MR. EDITOR [B. LUNDY]. n.d. n.p.** Describes the beating of several colored men at a firemen's procession. 6 May 1837. p.29, c4.

**887 H. S. SPACKMAN** *to* **MESSRS. SLOAN, ORTH, AND OTHERS. 3 March 1837. Harrisburg, Pa.** Informs them, the committee of arrangements of a pro-slavery meeting in Harrisburg, of his intention to attend their meeting and to work for their cause. 6 May 1837. p.30, c1.

**888 A GENTLEMAN IN HAYTI** *to* **HIS FRIEND. [extract from** *Zion's Watchman***] 31 March 1837. Port au Prince, Hayti.** Reports the kidnapping of a man and his delivery to the sloop of war *St. Louis* on the grounds that he was the slave of one of the ship's officers. 6 May 1837. p.30, c2.

**889 n.n. [THE SON OF ISAAC T. HOPPER]** *to* **THE EDITOR OF THE** *NATIONAL ENQUIRER* **[B. LUNDY]. n.d. n.p.** Discusses the attack on him by a pro-slavery mob in Savannah, Georgia. 6 May 1837. p.30, c4.

**890 W. H. J.** *to* **BENJ. LUNDY. 30 April 1837. Buckingham.** Reports on the case of two colored children apprenticed to a white man who were to be taken to Missouri against the wishes of their mother. 6 May 1837. p.30, c5.

**891 J. R.** *to* **FRIEND LUNDY. n.d. n.p.** Describes a meeting of the Friends of the Union in Philadelphia. 6 May 1837. p.30, c6.

**892 D. L. CHILD** *to* **n.n. [extract from the** *Liberator***] n.d. n.p.** Discusses the economic consequences of emancipation in the West Indies. 6 May 1837. p.31, c1.

**893 A GENTLEMAN IN HARRISBURG** *to* **THE SECRETARY OF THE PHILADELPHIA AS. [extract] 2 May 1837. Harrisburg, Pa.** Describes the failure of anti-abolitionists at the Friends of the Union convention in Harrisburg. 6 May 1837. p.31, c2.

**894 n.n.** *to* **THE EDITOR OF THE** *PENNSYLVANIA SENTINEL.* **[extract] 2 May 1837. Harrisburg, Pa.** Reports resolutions adopted at the convention of the Friends of the Union in Harrisburg. 6 May 1837. p.31, c3.

**895 D. I. ROBINSON** *to* **BROTHER. [from the** *Herald of Freedom***] 4 April 1837. Plymouth.** Reports having heard from a member of Congress that the next Congress may vote to reject abolition petitions; urges abolitionist efforts to prevent the admission of Texas and Wisconsin as slave states. 6 May 1837. p.32, c4.

**896 J. BLANCHARD** *to* **BENJ'N LUNDY. 5 May 1837. Harrisburg.** Describes the attempt to expel Mr. Stevens from a convention of the Friends of the Union on the grounds that he was an abolitionist. 13 May 1837. p.33, c1.

**897 D. E. M.** *to* **THE EDITOR OF THE** ***NATIONAL ENQUIRER*** **[B. LUNDY]. n.d. n.p.** Encloses an extract of a letter for publication. 13 May 1837. p.33, c3.

**898 A GENTLEMAN** *to* **n.n. [extract] n.d. Harrisburg, Pa.** Describes Thaddeus Stevens's efforts to block pro-slavery resolutions at the convention of the Friends of the Union in Harrisburg. 13 May 1837. p.33, c3.

**899 C. C. BURLEIGH** *to* **FRIEND LUNDY. 4 May 1837. Falsington.** Describes his current lecture tour. 13 May 1837. p.34, c6.

**900 LEWIS TAPPAN** *to* **FRIEND LUNDY. n.d. n.p.** The assistant treasurer of the AAS acknowledges the receipt of five dollars from J. C. Morel which was collected among colored friends in Harrisburg, Pennsylvania. 13 May 1837. p.35, c2.

**901 BENJAMIN S. JONES** *to* **B. LUNDY. 10 May 1837. New York.** Reports on the annual meeting of the AAS. 13 May 1837. p.35, c3.

**902 A PHILADELPHIA DELEGATE TO THE ANNUAL MEETING OF THE AAS** *to* **THE EDITOR OF THE** ***NATIONAL ENQUIRER*** **[B. LUNDY]. 12 May 1837. n.p.** Commends the annual meeting of the AAS. 13 May 1837. p.35, c4.

**903 n.n.** *to* **n.n. [extract from the** ***National Intelligencer*****] n.d. New Orleans, La.** Reports that the Mexican army is in full march against the insurgents in Texas. 13 May 1837. p.35, c5.

**904 SANTA ANNA** *to* **J. V. GONZALEZ. [extract] n.d. n.p.** Declares his intention to remain in retirement. 13 May 1837. p.35, c6.

**905 A SUBSCRIBER** *to* **MR. EDITOR [B. LUNDY]. 10 May 1837. Germantown.** Encloses a poem entitled, "Toll! Curfew, Toll!" 13 May 1837. p.36, c1.

**906 D. L. M.** *to* **B. LUNDY. n.d. n.p.** Encloses a letter from E. Wright to the Junior AS of Philadelphia. 20 May 1837. p.37, c1.

**907 E. WRIGHT, JR.** *to* **THE JUNIOR AS OF PHILADELPHIA. 14 December 1836. New York.** Encourages them in their work despite their youth. 20 May 1837. p.37, c1.

**908 D.** *to* **FRIEND LUNDY. n.d. n.p.** Refutes Representative Joseph M'Ilvaine's speech which called abolitionists fanatics and aliens. 20 May 1837. p.37, c1.

**909 OFFICE OF THE** ***COMMERCIAL BULLETIN*** *to* **THE** ***EXPRESS MAIL.*** **5 May 1837. New Orleans, La.** Reports a confrontation between a Mexican ship and an American ship which resulted in the former's capture. 20 May 1837. p.39, c2.

**910 n.n.** *to* **n.n. 6 May 1837. New Orleans, La.** Predicts retaliation by the Mexican government for the capture of a Mexican ship by the United States. 20 May 1837. p.39, c2.

**911 CORRESPONDENT** *to* **THE** ***NEW YORK EXPRESS.*** **n.d. New Orleans, La.** Describes the military, economic and political situation in Texas. 20 May 1837. p.39, c2.

**912 JOSE MARIA ORTIZ MONASTERIO** *to* **THE SECRETARY OF FOREIGN RELATIONS OF THE UNITED STATES OF AMERICA. 31 March 1837. Palace of the National Government, Mexico.** The principal secretary of the Mexican Department of Foreign Relations protests the recognition of Texan independence by the United States Congress. 20 May 1837. p.39, c3.

**913 n.n.** *to* **THE EDITOR OF THE** ***COURIER AND ENQUIRER.*** **2 April 1837. New Orleans, La.** Describes the economic crisis in New Orleans and its causes. 20 May 1837. p.40, c4.

**914 n.n.** *to* **THE** *COURIER AND ENQUIRER.* **4 April 1837. New Orleans, La.** States that the economic crisis is endangering various large cotton houses which are presently solvent. 20 May 1837. p.40, c5.

**915 n.n.** *to* **THE** *NEW YORK COURIER AND ENQUIRER.* **2 May 1837. New Orleans, La.** Encloses extracts from Santa Anna's account of the circumstances surrounding his capture by the Texans and his subsequent decision to negotiate with the American government. 27 May 1837. p.42, c6.

**916 A FRIEND** *to* **THE EDITOR OF THE** *NATIONAL ENQUIRER* **[B. LUNDY]. [extract] n.d. n.p.** Describes the anniversary of the Ohio AS; commends the abolitionists who attended the meeting. 27 May 1837. p.43, c3.

**917 CORRESPONDENT** *to* **THE** *NEW ORLEANS BEE.* **[from the daily papers] n.d. Vera Cruz.** Speculates on the policies which Bustamente, the new Mexican president, will follow. 27 May 1837. p.43, c5.

**918 n.n.** *to* **THE** *NATIONAL INTELLIGENCER.* **16 May. New Orleans, La.** Discusses the military actions of the new Mexican government. 27 May 1837. p.43, c5.

**919 SUSAN** *to* **THE EDITOR OF THE** *NATIONAL ENQUIRER* **[B. LUNDY]. 1837. Adams County, Pa.** Encloses a poem by Mary K. Greer entitled, "An Elegy on the Death of Maria Louisa Reynolds, of Washington City." 27 May 1837. p.44, c1.

**920 n.n.** *to* **THE** *ALTON OBSERVER.* **n.d. Alton, Il.** Discusses the arrival of David Smith in Alton, accompanied by twelve colored men who were formerly his slaves. 27 May 1837. p.44, c3.

**921 J. H. KIMBALL** *to* **BROTHER WRIGHT. [from the** *Emancipator***] 11 March 1837. Barbadoes.** Reports meeting emancipated slaves in the West Indies; describes conversations with W. R. Hayes and the governor of Barbados. 27 May 1837. p.44, c4.

**922 A YOUNG ABOLITIONIST** *to* **FRIEND LUNDY. 21 May 1837. Philadelphia, Pa.** Encloses an extract from *Neander's Church History,* which states that slavery is foreign to the nature of Christianity. 3 June 1837. p.45, c1.

**923 M. R.** *to* **THE EDITOR OF THE** *NATIONAL ENQUIRER* **[B. LUNDY]. n.d. n.p.** Encloses an essay written by a young woman of Chester County condemning slavery. 3 June 1837. p.45, c2.

**924 EDWIN FUSSELL** *to* **DR. B. FUSSELL. 5 March 1837. Pendleton, In.** Condemns the war against the Indians of Florida; calls for anti-slavery activity. 3 June 1837. p.46, c2.

**925 A MEMBER OF THE CHESTER COUNTY ANTI-SLAVERY CONVENTION** *to* **THE** *NATIONAL ENQUIRER.* **n.d. n.p.** Reports on the proceedings of the convention. 3 June 1837. p.46, c4.

**926 EDWARD C. DELAVAN** *to* **GERRIT SMITH, ESQ. 10 May 1837. Ballston Centre, Saratoga County, N.Y.** Explains his delay in joining the AS. 3 June 1837. p.46, c4.

**927 TRUTH** *to* **THE EDITOR OF THE** *NATIONAL ENQUIRER* **[B. LUNDY]. n.d. n.p.** Defends George Thompson from charges that he recommended the use of violence. 3 June 1837. p.47, c1.

**928 CORRESPONDENT AT NEW ORLEANS** *to* **THE** *NATIONAL INTELLIGENCER.* **[extract] 6 May 1837. n.p.** Predicts retaliation by the Mexican government for the capture of a Mexican ship by the United States. [reprint of letter appearing 20 May 1837] 3 June 1837. p.47, c2.

**929 n.n.** *to* **n.n. [extract] 25 April 1837. New Orleans, La.** Describes the military, political and economic situation in Texas. 3 June 1837. p.47, c3.

**930 CORRESPONDENT** *to* **THE** *NEW YORK EXPRESS.* **13 May 1837. New Orleans, La.** Discusses the military situation in Texas. 3 June 1837. p.47, c3.

**931 N. SHERWOOD** *to* **J. B. MINCE. 3 May 1837. Matamoras.** Describes his condition as a prisoner of the Mexicans. 3 June 1837. p.47, c4.

**932 S.** *to* **THE EDITOR OF THE** *NATIONAL ENQUIRER* **[B. LUNDY]. n.d. n.p.** Encloses a poem entitled, "The Buried." 3 June 1837. p.48, c1.

**933 n.n.** *to* **THE** *NEW YORK COMMERCIAL ADVERTISER.* **20 May 1837. New York.** Encloses a poem written in response to an attack upon a women's anti-slavery convention. 3 June 1837. p.48, c2.

**934 FREE DISCUSSION** *to* **MR. EDITOR. [from the** *Belmont* **(Oh.)** *Chronicle***] n.d. n.p.** Discusses the affinity between the views and interests of the upper classes of the North and the slaveholders of the South. 3 June 1837. p.48, c3.

**935 ANNA BLACKWELL** *to* **JOHN QUINCY ADAMS. n.d. n.p.** Encloses a resolution of the Women's Anti-Slavery Convention commending Adams's efforts in behalf of the right to petition, and criticizing his failure to work for the abolition of slavery in Florida and the District of Columbia. 10 June 1837. p.49, c4.

**936 ANN WARREN WESTON, ABBY ANN COX, AND MARY GREW** *to* **THE ANTI-SLAVERY WOMEN OF GREAT BRITAIN. 12 May 1837. New York.** Express appreciation for their support and work, on behalf of the Anti-Slavery Convention of American Women. 10 June 1837. p.49, c4.

**937 THE ABOLITIONISTS OF AFRICAN ORIGIN** *to* **THE TWO CHAMBERS. n.d. Martinique.** Express gratitude for the support of the government for the abolition of slavery in the French colonies; condemn political *renegadoes.* 10 June 1837. p.50, c2.

**938 THE COLORED ABOLITIONISTS OF ST. PIERRE** *to* **THE TWO CHAMBERS. 25 November 1836. St. Pierre.** Express appreciation for the support of the government and of the Minister of Marine for the emancipation of the slaves. 10 June 1837. p.50, c3.

**939 ANTI-HUMBUG** *to* **THE EDITOR OF THE** *COMMERCIAL HERALD.* **2 June. n.p.** States that slavery is supported by the constitution of Texas and that General Houston's condemnation of the slave trade applies only to the trade conducted with Africa. 10 June 1837. p.50, c3.

**940 WOMAN** *to* **THE** *NATIONAL ENQUIRER.* **n.d. n.p.** Refutes Catherine Beecher's views on abolitionism and the proper place of women. 10 June 1837. p.50, c4.

**941 D.** *to* **FRIEND LUNDY. n.d. n.p.** Defends abolitionists against charges that they seek political power as a group. 10 June 1837. p.50, c4.

**942 n.n.** *to* **THE EDITOR OF THE** *NATIONAL ENQUIRER* **[B. LUNDY]. 22 February 1837. Arras, France.** Discusses European views of the state of affairs between the United States and Mexico. 10 June 1837. p.50, c5.

**943 C. C. BURLEIGH** *to* **THE** *NATIONAL ENQUIRER.* **n.d. n.p.** Describes the proceedings of the New England Anti-Slavery Convention. 10 June 1837. p.50, c5.

**944 REV. JAS. M. M'KIM** *to* **MR. B. LUNDY. 6 June 1837. Coatesville.** Describes anti-slavery meetings in Woodbury, New Jersey and Coatesville. 10 June 1837. p.51, c1.

**945 REV. JOHN P. CLEAVELAND** *to* **MR. BENJAMIN LUNDY. 7 June 1837. Philadelphia, Pa.** Declares that he was misquoted by the paper in its report of his view of George Thompson. 10 June 1837. p.51, c2.

**946 A FRIEND** *to* **THE EDITOR OF THE** *NATIONAL ENQUIRER* **[B. LUNDY]. [extract] n.d. n.p.** Reports on a pro-slavery speech by a member of the Presbyterian General Assembly. 10 June 1837. p.51, c3.

**947 JOHN HOPPER** *to* **THE EDITORS OF THE** *NEW YORK GAZETTE.* **n.d. n.p.** Asserts that he was attacked by a mob in Savannah, contrary to the claim of the editor of the *Savannah Republican.* 10 June 1837. p.51, c4.

**948 JOSE MARIA ORTIZ MONASTERIO** *to* **MINISTER OF WAR DON JOSE MARIA TORNEL. [from the** *Diario del Gobierno***] 5 April 1837. Mexico.** Encloses documents relating to the American government's condemnation of the language of Mr. Butler's letters to Tornel. 10 June 1837. p.51, c5.

**949 CHARGE D'AFFAIRES OF THE UNITED STATES POWHATTAN ELLIS** *to* **JOSE MARIA ORTIZ MONASTERIO. [from the** *Diario del Gobierno***] 1 April 1837. n.p.** Encloses a note from Secretary of State John Forsyth to the chargé d'affaires of the Mexican Republic, Señor Castillo, indicating the disapproval of the American government of the letters of Mr. Butler, American minister to Mexico, to General Tornel. 10 June 1837. p.51, c5.

**950 SECRETARY OF STATE JOHN FORSYTH** *to* **CHARGE D'AFFAIRES OF THE UNITED STATES MR. POWHATTAN ELLIS. [from the** *Diario del Gobierno***] 16 November 1836. Washington.** Orders Ellis to make known to the Mexican government the president's disapproval of Mr. Butler's letters to General Tornel. 10 June 1837. p.51, c5.

**951 CHARGE D'AFFAIRES OF THE MEXICAN REPUBLIC** *to* **SECRETARY OF STATE JOHN FORSYTH. [from the** *Diario del Gobierno***] 4 March 1837. Philadelphia, Pa.** Acknowledges the receipt of a note from Forsyth expressing the American government's disapproval of Mr. Butler's letters to General Tornel. 10 June 1837. p.51, c5.

**952 AN ABOLITIONIST** *to* **MR. EDITOR [B. LUNDY]. n.d. n.p.** Criticizes the unchristian tone of *The Slave; or, Memoirs of Archy Moore.* 10 June 1837. p.52, c1.

**953 GEO. STORRS** *to* **MR. EDITOR. [from the** *American Citizen***] 25 February 1837. Warsaw.** Cites the peace treaty between Great Britain and the United States signed in Ghent in 1814, which committed both nations to endeavor to abolish the slave trade. 10 June 1837. p.52, c4.

**954 H. C. WRIGHT** *to* **BROTHER. [from the** *Friend of Man***] 11 May 1837. Boston, Ma.** Describes the economic failure of New York City as a product of the inability or refusal of Southerners to pay their debts. 17 June 1837. p.53, c2.

**955 n.n.** *to* **MR. EDITOR. [from the** *Maryville* **(Tn.)** *Intelligencer***] n.d. n.p.** Responds to the Rev. J. W. Douglass's letter and condemns slavery. 17 June 1837. p.53, c4.

**956 NOT A MAN OF THE TIMES** *to* **n.n. [from the** *Baltimore Chronicle***] n.d. n.p.** Disagrees with the contention that Congress has the power to abolish slavery in the District of Columbia. 17 June 1837. p.54, c3.

**957 L.** *to* **THE** ***NATIONAL ENQUIRER.*** **n.d. n.p.** Criticizes Catherine Beecher's *Slavery and Abolitionism.* 17 June 1837. p.54, c5.

**958 S. H. GLOUCESTER, EBENEZER BLACK AND JOSEPH PARKER** *to* **BROTHER LUNDY. 13 June 1837. Philadelphia, Pa.** Announce the formation of the Leavitt AS of Philadelphia by members of a church of colored people; enclose a copy of the society's constitution and a list of its officers. 17 June 1837. p.54, c6.

**959 n.n.** *to* **MR. KIDD. [from the** ***New Orleans Commercial Bulletin*****] 10 May. Tampico.** Reports Mexican military actions. 17 June 1837. p.55, c5.

**960 n.n.** *to* **FRIEND. [extract from the** ***Texas Telegraph*****] 16 May. Nashville, Milam County.** Reports Indian military actions. 17 June 1837. p.55, c6.

**961 n.n.** *to* **n.n. [extract from the** ***Texas Telegraph*****] 15 May. Mustang Prairie.** Reports conflicts with the Indians. 17 June 1837. p.55, c6.

**962 EMMA** *to* **THE EDITOR OF THE** ***NATIONAL ENQUIRER*** **[B. LUNDY]. n.d. n.p.** Encloses a poem by "S. J." entitled, "To the Friends of Abolition." 17 June 1837. p.56, c1.

**963 J. G. B.** *to* **MR. EDITOR. [from the** ***Herald of Freedom*****] n.d. n.p.** Encloses a poem entitled, "Faith and Works." 17 June 1837. p.56, c2.

**964 A SPECTATOR** *to* **MR. EDITOR [B. LUNDY]. n.d. n.p.** Quotes a story of racial prejudice, as told by Jeremiah Bowers. 24 June 1837. p.57, c4.

**965 E. PATTERSON** *to* **n.n. [from the** ***Philanthropist*****] 26 May 1837. Cincinnati, Oh.** Describes a conversation with the Rev. Mr. John B. Pinney, in which Pinney defended slavery. 24 June 1837. p.57, c4.

**966 FREE DISCUSSION** *to* **MR. EDITOR. [from the** ***Belmont Chronicle*****] n.d. n.p.** Discusses the fundamental principles held by abolitionists. 24 June 1837. p.57, c5.

**967 n.n** *to* **SENATOR JOHN C. CALHOUN. [from the** ***Christian Register and Observer*****] 26 April 1837. n.p.** Urges him to promote abolitionism. 24 June 1837. p.57, c6.

**968 W. G.** *to* **THE EDITOR OF THE** ***NATIONAL ENQUIRER*** **[B. LUNDY]. n.d. New York.** Warns of imminent conflict between the North and South over the admission of Texas and "the general subject." 24 June 1837. p.58, c4.

**969 L.** *to* **THE** ***NATIONAL ENQUIRER.*** **n.d. n.p.** Continues his criticism of Catherine Beecher's *Slavery and Abolitionism.* [continued from 17 June 1837] 24 June 1837. p.58, c4.

**970 n.n.** *to* **THE EDITOR OF THE** ***NATIONAL ENQUIRER*** **[B. LUNDY]. [extract] n.d. n.p.** Accuses Southerners of violating the Constitution. 24 June 1837. p.58, c5.

**971 J. C. B.** *to* **THE EDITOR OF THE** ***NATIONAL ENQUIRER*** **[B. LUNDY]. n.d. n.p.** Opposes the formation of separate ASs by colored people, contending that such societies tend to perpetuate racial prejudice. 24 June 1837. p.58, c6.

**972 A FRIEND** *to* **THE** ***NATIONAL ENQUIRER.*** **[extract] 15 June 1837. n.p.** Describes an anti-slavery meeting held by J. M. McKim, which was disrupted by several pro-slavery men. 24 June 1837. p.59, c3.

**973 CORRESPONDENT** *to* **THE** ***NATIONAL GAZETTE.*** **n.d. n.p.** Describes the proceedings of a constitutional convention on 19 June 1837. 24 June 1837. p.59, c3.

**974 AN ABOLITIONIST** *to* **THE EDITOR. [extract] n.d. Chester County.** Declares that slavery in the District of Columbia is unconstitutional. 24 June 1837. p.59, c3.

**975 MARY S. PARKER** *to* **FEMALE ASs THROUGHOUT NEW ENGLAND. 7 June 1837. Boston, Ma.** A member of the Boston Female AS solicits aid for Sarah M. and Angelina E. Grimké in their efforts in the anti-slavery cause. 24 June 1837. p.59, c4.

**976 L. C. G.** *to* **MR. EDITOR [B. LUNDY]. n.d. n.p.** Forwards an account of Dr. Isaac Parrish's conversation with the steward of an almshouse, in order to dispel the notion that "colored people fill our almshouses." 1 July 1837. p.61, c1.

**977 L. C. G.** *to* **THE** ***NATIONAL ENQUIRER*****. n.d. n.p.** Responds to charges that a high proportion of crimes are committed by colored people, citing the triviality of many such offenses and the prejudice to which colored people are subjected. 1 July 1837. p.61, c1.

**978 OFFICE OF THE AAS** *to* **n.n. 1837. New York.** Encloses copies of anti-slavery petitions the AAS wishes to be sent to Congress. 1 July 1837. p.62, c3.

**979 ANGELINA E. GRIMKE** *to* **CATHERINE E. BEECHER. 12 June 1837. Brookline, Ma.** Refutes Beecher's book on abolitionism. 1 July 1837. p.62, c5.

**980 CORRESPONDENT** *to* **THE** *NATIONAL GAZETTE.* **[extract] n.d. n.p.** Reports the vote by a state constitutional convention on an amendment limiting the franchise to white males. 1 July 1837. p.63, c1.

**981 JOHN MURRAY** *to* **CAPTAIN BIGLEY. [extract from the** *Glasgow Argus***] n.d. Bowling Bay, near Glasgow.** Protests Bigley's refusal to take a colored man in his cabin; condemns American racial prejudice. 1 July 1837. p.63, c2.

**982 I. D. MAULSBY** *to* **THE** *BALTIMORE CHRONICLE.* **23 June 1837. Harrisburg, Pa.** Reports on a meeting of Governor Ritner and Secretary of State Burrows of Pennsylvania on the subject of fugitive slaves, and on the progress of the state constitutional convention. 1 July 1837. p.63, c3.

**983 J. M. M'KIM** *to* **MR. BENJ. LUNDY. 24 June 1837. Wilmington.** Describes anti-slavery lectures in Wilmington, St. Georges and Salem, New Jersey. 1 July 1837. p.63, c4.

**984 L.** *to* **THE** *NATIONAL ENQUIRER.* **n.d. n.p.** Continues criticism of Catherine Beecher's *Slavery and Abolitionism.* [continued from 24 June 1837] 1 July 1837. p.63, c5.

**985 OFFICE OF THE** *COURIER* *to* **n.n. 21 June. New Orleans, La.** Reports the military situation in Texas. 1 July 1837. p.63, c6.

**986 BENJAMIN S. JONES** *to* **n.n. 29 June 1837. n.p.** Acknowledges the receipt of several letters by the Anti-Slavery Office. 1 July 1837. p.63, c6.

**987 n.n.** *to* **MR. EDITOR. [from the** *Delaware County Republican***] n.d. n.p.** Encloses a poem inspired by Benjamin Lundy's account of his conversion to abolitionism, which appeared in the *Genius of Universal Emancipation.* 1 July 1837. p.64, c2.

**988 LEWIS C. GUNN** *to* **MR. EDITOR [B. LUNDY]. n.d. n.p.** States that many Old School Presbyterians oppose slavery, contrary to the claim of an article from the *New England Spectator* published in the *National Enquirer.* 8 July 1837. p. 65, c1.

**989 MARY S. PARKER AND ANGELINA E. GRIMKE** *to* **THE SOCIETIES OF ANTI-SLAVERY WOMEN IN THE UNITED STATES. n.d. n.p.** Advocate the submission of anti-slavery petitions to Congress, on behalf of the Anti-Slavery Convention of American Women. 8 July 1837. p.66, c2.

**990 VOX POPULI** *to* **THE EDITOR OF THE** ***QUINCY PATRIOT.*** **n.d. n.p.** Praises John Quincy Adams for his defense of the right of petition. 8 July 1837. p.66, c4.

**991 J. BLANCHARD** *to* **MR. BENJ. LUNDY. 30 June 1837. Path Valley, Franklin County.** Describes his lecture tour through Franklin County. 8 July 1837. p.66, c5.

**992 JOHN P. BURR, RT. REV. MORRIS BROWN, THOMAS BUTLER, F. A. HINTON, JOHN B. ROBERTS, JOSHUA BROWN, AND S. H. GLOUCESTER** *to* **SIR. 22 June 1837. n.p.** Officers of the American Moral Reform Society solicit attendance at the organization's first annual meeting and request information on colored people for the organization's first annual report. 8 July 1837. p.66, c6.

**993 n.n.** *to* **THE** ***NEW YORK COURIER AND ENQUIRER.*** **20 May 1837. New Orleans, La.** Describes the activities of those opposed to the annexation of Texas by the United States, in particular the attempt of Houston to present himself to the British consul as an opponent of slavery. 8 July 1837. p.67, c3.

**994 n.n.** *to* **MR. LUNDY. n.d. n.p.** Encloses a poem written in response to the Convention to Preserve the Integrity of the Union. 8 July 1837. p.68, c1.

**995 n.n.** *to* **n.n. [from the** ***National Gazette*****] n.d. Texas.** Describes opposition to President Houston. 15 July 1837. p.69, c2.

**996 H. C. WRIGHT** *to* **BROTHER. 6 June 1837. Boston, Ma.** Describes the harm resulting from slavery. 15 July 1837. p.69, c3.

**997 n.n.** *to* **THE** ***NATIONAL GAZETTE.*** **7 July 1837. Harrisburg, Pa.** Reports a discussion of the question of adjournment at the constitutional convention. 15 July 1837. p.69, c6.

**998 n.n.** *to* **THE** ***NATIONAL GAZETTE.*** **8 July 1837. Harrisburg, Pa.** Describes a debate at the constitutional convention concerning slaves' right to petition. 15 July 1837. p.69, c6.

**999 AUDIENCE** *to* **n.n. [from the** ***Salem*** **(Ma.)** ***Gazette*****] n.d. n.p.** Commends John Quincy Adams's stand against slavery. 15 July 1837. p.70, c1.

**1000 W. H. J.** *to* **B. LUNDY. 5 July 1837. Buckingham.** Describes a debate between C. C. Burleigh and John Titus which took place in Concord and Buckingham. 15 July 1837. p.70, c3.

**1001 E. K.** *to* **B. LUNDY. 5 July 1837. Uwchlan.** Describes meeting Francis James in Westchester County, and reports the activities of the AS in Westchester. 15 July 1837. p.70, c4.

**1002 JAMES G. BIRNEY** *to* **MESSRS. DANIEL L. MILLER, JR. AND OTHERS OF THE COMMITTEE OF ARRANGEMENTS FOR THE ANNUAL MEETING OF THE JUNIOR AS OF PHILADELPHIA. 22 June 1837. New York.** Exhorts them to continue their anti-slavery work. 15 July 1837. p.70, c6.

**1003 H. B. STANTON** *to* **D. L. MILLER, JR. 16 June 1837. New York.** Regrets his inability to attend the meeting of the Junior AS of Philadelphia. 15 July 1837. p.71, c1.

**1004 ROBERT W. LANDIS** *to* **n.n. 22 June 1837. Jeffersonville, Pa.** Regrets his inability to attend the meeting of the Junior AS of Philadelphia. 15 July 1837. p.71, c1.

**1005 A SUBSCRIBER** *to* **MR. EDITOR [B. LUNDY]. 11 July 1837. n.p.** Requests that the names of those voting in the debate at the Junior AS be published in the *National Enquirer.* 15 July 1837. p.71, c1.

**1006 ISAAC MENDENHALL** *to* **n.n. n.d. n.p.** The treasurer of the Chester County AS encloses an address for the benefit of fellow abolitionists. 15 July 1837. p.71, c1.

**1007 CORRESPONDENT** *to* **THE** *NATIONAL ENQUIRER.* **28 June 1837. Harrisburg, Pa.** Reports the debate on Benjamin Martin's proposition at the constitutional convention. 15 July 1837. p.71, c2.

**1008 LEWIS C. GUNN** *to* **B. LUNDY. [extract] 10 July 1837. East Fallowfield.** Describes his anti-slavery activities in Uwchlan, Downington and East Fallowfield. 15 July 1837. p.71, c2.

**1009 n.n.** *to* **SIR. [from the** *Savannah Republican*] **3 July 1837. Black Creek, Fl.** States that information published by the paper regarding the imminence of hostilities is incorrect. 15 July 1837. p.71, c5.

**1010 OFFICE OF THE** *NEW ORLEANS BEE to* **THE** *NATIONAL ENQUIRER.* **[extract] 5 July 1837. New Orleans, La.** Encloses a decree promulgated by the Mexican president concerning relations with the United States. 15 July 1837. p.71, c5.

**1011 CORRESPONDENT** *to* **MR. KIDD. [extract] 21 June 1837. Tampico.** Believes that the conflicts between the United States and Mexico will be resolved peacefully. 15 July 1837. p.71, c6.

**1012 A. E. GRIMKE** *to* **CATHERINE E. BEECHER. [from the** *Liberator*] **17 June 1837. Brookline, Ma.** Explains the doctrines of abolitionism. 15 July 1837. p.72, c1.

**1013 n.n.** *to* **FRIEND. [from the** *Vermont Telegraph*] **n.d. n.p.** Encloses a poem entitled, "Appeal for the Slave." 15 July 1837. p.72, c3.

**1014 W. H. J.** *to* **THE EDITOR OF THE** *NATIONAL ENQUIRER* **[B. LUNDY]. 6 July 1837. Buckingham.** Describes anti-slavery meetings and debates addressed by C. C. Burleigh in Buckingham. 20 July 1837. p.73, c1.

**1015 A MINISTER IN MISSOURI** *to* **n.n. [extract from the** *Alton Observer*] **n.d. Missouri.** Proposes the establishment of churches in slave states from which slaveholders would be excluded. 20 July 1837. p.73, c4.

**1016 MR. KIMBALL** *to* **n.n. [extract from the** *Herald of Freedom*] **n.d. Antigua.** Commends one Henry Armstrong, a planter of Antigua. 20 July 1837. p.73, c4.

**1017 MR. KIMBALL** *to* **A FRIEND. [extract from the** *Herald of Freedom*] **n.d. Antigua.** Describes the estate of Henry Armstrong, a planter of Antigua. 20 July 1837. p.73, c4.

**1018 HENRY ARMSTRONG** *to* **MESSRS. THOME AND KIMBALL. [extract from the** *Herald of Freedom*] **n.d. Fitch's Creek, Antigua.** Describes the changes in Antigua, particularly among the Negroes, resulting from emancipation. 20 July 1837. p.73, c5.

**1019 A QUAKER** *to* **THE SOCIETY OF FRIENDS. [from the** *Delaware County Republican*] **n.d. n.p.** Encourages Quakers to work for the abolition of slavery; cites the activities of English Quakers in behalf of abolition in England. 20 July 1837. p.73, c6.

**1020 E. H. PHELPS** *to* **SIR. [from the** *Alton* **(Il.)** *Observer*] **31 May 1837. Princeton, Il.** The secretary of the Princeton AS encloses copies of the society's constitution and the resolutions adopted at its first meeting. 20 July 1837. p.74, c2.

**1021 J. PRESTON** *to* **THE** *ALTON* **(IL.)** *OBSERVER.* **n.d. n.p.** The secretary of the Hadley AS forwards the proceedings of the meeting at which the society was formed. 20 July 1837. p.74, c2.

**1022 GEORGE RUSSELL** *to* **THE EDITOR OF THE** *QUINCY PATRIOT.* **n.d. n.p.** The secretary of the Old Colony AS of Plymouth County reports on the society's third annual meeting. 20 July 1837. p.74, c3.

**1023 JAMES G. BIRNEY** *to* **THE ASSISTANT EDITOR OF THE** *PHILANTHROPIST.* **[extract] n.d. n.p.** Fears that the annexation of Texas would lead to the dominance of the slave states; describes a visit with John Quincy Adams; describes anti-abolition efforts in Pennsylvania and New York. 20 July 1837. p.75, c1.

**1024 LEWIS C. GUNN** *to* **B. LUNDY. 17 July 1837. Barts, Lancaster County.** Describes anti-slavery meetings he has held in Coatesville, Kennett Square, Old Kennett, Penn's Grove and Wasteland. 20 July 1837. p.75, c3.

**1025 A GENTLEMAN** *to* **THE EDITOR OF THE** *NATIONAL ENQUIRER* **[B. LUNDY]. 6 July 1837. Kalamazoo County, Mi.** Describes the need for anti-slavery activity in Michigan. 20 July 1837. p.75, c4.

**1026 C. C. B.** *to* **FRIEND LUNDY. n.d. n.p.** Recommends the *Life of Gustavus Vassa, the African, Written by Himself.* 20 July 1837. p.75, c4.

**1027 OFFICE OF THE** *LOUISIANA ADVERTISER* *to* **THE** *NATIONAL ENQUIRER.* **[extract] 12 July 1837. Louisiana.** Reports the arrival of two Mexican brigs at Matamoras; reports the situation of Mr. Wharton and Captain Wheelwright, captives of the Mexicans. 20 July 1837. p.75, c6.

**1028 THE BUCKINGHAM FEMALE AS** *to* **THE EDITOR OF THE** *NATIONAL ENQUIRER* **[B. LUNDY]. n.d. n.p.** Encloses a poem addressed to the other Female ASs in the state. 20 July 1837. p.76, c1.

**1029 L.** *to* **THE** *NATIONAL ENQUIRER.* **n.d. n.p.** Continues criticism of Catherine Beecher's *Slavery and Abolitionism.* [continued from 1 July 1837] 20 July 1837. p.76, c1.

**1030 A. E. GRIMKE** *to* **CATHERINE E. BEECHER. [from the** *Liberator***] 23 June 1837. Lynn, Ma.** Describes the doctrines of American abolitionists, distinguishing them from those of the English abolitionists. 20 July 1837. p.76, c2.

**1031 H.** *to* **n.n. [from the** *Commercial Advertiser***] n.d. n.p.** Encloses a poem by an Indian named Bourassa, entitled, "Sacvacola Lamentation." 20 July 1837. p.76, c4.

**1032 W. H. J.** *to* **THE EDITOR OF THE** *NATIONAL ENQUIRER* **[B. LUNDY]. 18 July 1837. Buckingham.** Describes the arrest of a colored man as a fugitive slave near Bristol. 27 July 1837. p.77, c1.

**1033 CHARLES E. WILSON** *to* **MR. LUNDY. 18 July 1837. Norristown.** Explains his opposition to the ACS; calls for the establishment of national CS founded on abolitionist principles. 27 July 1837. p.77, c2.

**1034 ABRAHAM SHRINER** *to* **EMMOR KIMBER. 30 June 1837. Little Pips Creek, Md.** Requests that Kimber persuade Bill Bud, who he claims is his slave, to return home; informs that Ann Brooks, a woman Bud sent for, is the wife of another man, John Brooks. 27 July 1837. p.77, c3.

**1035 EMMOR KIMBER** *to* **ABRAHAM SHRINER. 7 July 1837. Kimberton.** Denies that Shriner's slave, Bill Bud, lives with him, but acknowledges having met Bud and given him assistance. 27 July 1837. p.77, c3.

**1036 MUTIUS** *to* **THE PUBLIC. [from the** *Norristown Herald and Free Press*] **n.d. n.p.** Urges opposition to the admission of Texas to the Union. 27 July 1837. p.77, c6.

**1037 WILLIAM H. PRITCHARD** *to* **THE EDITOR OF THE** *GEORGIA CONSTITUTIONALIST.* **20 December 1836. Aiken, S.C.** A district coroner reports the findings of an autopsy performed on the body of a runaway slave killed by his pursuers. 27 July 1837. p.78, c1.

**1038 JOHN EDGAR, D. D.** *to* **THE MEMBERS OF THE AMERICAN CHURCHES. [from the** *New York Evangelist*] **n.d. Belfast.** Writes on behalf of the Presbyterian Synod of Ireland, urging American Christians to work for the abolition of slavery. 27 July 1837. p.78, c3.

**1039 CORRESPONDENT** *to* **THE** *NEW YORK COURIER AND ENQUIRER.* **[extract from the** *Boston Atlas*] **n.d. New Orleans, La.** Reports that Houston is now said to be opposed to slavery. 27 July 1837. p.78, c4.

**1040 JOSEPH KINGSBURY** *to* **THE SECRETARY OF THE SALISBURY AND AMESBURY AS. [from the** *New England Spectator*] **n.d. n.p.** Declares his support for the cause of abolitionism. 27 July 1837. p.78, c5.

**1041 J. COFFIN** *to* **MR. EDITOR [B. LUNDY]. n.d. n.p.** Reports that the First Presbyterian Church of the Northern Liberties prohibits the burial of people of color in its cemetery. 27 July 1837. p.79, c3.

**1042 AN ABOLITIONIST** *to* **THE** *NATIONAL ENQUIRER.* **n.d. n.p.** Praises *The Memoirs of Archy Moore.* 27 July 1837. p.80, c1.

**1043 M. E. J.** *to* **MR. EDITOR. [from the** *New York Evangelist*] **n.d. n.p.** Encloses a poem inspired by a visit to the Laurel Hill Cemetery. 27 July 1837. p.80, c4.

**1044 FREE DISCUSSION** *to* **MR. EDITOR. [from the** *Belmont Chronicle*] **n.d. n.p.** Declares that the perpetrators of slavery are destined to suffer because of it. 27 July 1837. p.80, c5.

**1045 REV. MR. BLANCHARD** *to* **THE** *EMANCIPATOR.* **[extract] n.d. n.p.** Reports that the Church of the United Brethren has excluded slaveholders from membership. 27 July 1837. p.80, c6.

**1046 MR. FOLLET** *to* **n.n. [extract from** *Facts for the People*] **n.d. Texas.** Reports the enslavement of prisoners of war by the Texans. 3 August 1837. p.82, c2.

**1047 REV. JUSTIN SPAULDING** *to* **n.n. [extract] 6 May. Rio Janeiro.** Discusses slavery in Rio de Janeiro. 3 August 1837. p.82, c3.

**1048 T. SPROULL** *to* **THE FRIENDS OF IMMEDIATE EMANCIPATION. [from the** *Christian Witness*] **1 July 1837. Pittsburgh, Pa.** An officer of the Pennsylvania AS requests information on anti-slavery activity in western Pennsylvania. 3 August 1837. p.82, c4.

**1049 J. BLANCHARD** *to* **MR. BENJ. LUNDY. 29 July 1837. Mercersburgh, Franklin County.** Reports an attack made upon him by a mob. 3 August 1837. p.82, c5.

**1050 LEWIS C. GUNN** *to* **THE EDITOR [B. LUNDY]. 31 July 1837. Philadelphia, Pa.** Describes anti-slavery meetings in Lancaster, Chester and Montgomery counties. 3 August 1837. p.82, c5.

**1051 n.n.** *to* **THE EDITOR OF THE** *GENIUS OF UNIVERSAL EMANCIPATION.* **24 July 1837. n.p.** Encloses a late subscription fee. 3 August 1837. p.83, c2.

**1052 CORRESPONDENT** *to* **n.n. n.d. Woodbury, N.J.** Reports on the case of a counterfeiter, Mr. Sailer. 3 August 1837. p.83, c3.

**1053 A. RINCHERE** *to* **THE** *NATIONAL ENQUIRER.* **[extract] 18 June 1837. St. Marks, Hayti.** Encloses a prospectus of a *History of Hayti.* 3 August 1837. p.83, c4.

**1054 n.n. [BENJAMIN LUNDY'S BROTHER-IN-LAW]** *to* **THE EDITOR OF THE** *NATIONAL ENQUIRER* **[B. LUNDY]. [extract] n.d. Illinois.** Describes the area near his home in Illinois. 3 August 1837. p.83, c5.

**1055 CORRESPONDENT** *to* **THE** *NEW YORK EVENING STAR.* **n.d. Florida.** Reports the capture of hundreds of Negroes by the Indians. 3 August 1837. p.83, c6.

**1056 A. E. GRIMKE** *to* **CATHERINE E. BEECHER. July 1837. Danvers, Ma.** Enumerates the evils of slavery; claims that abolitionist activity in the North has affected the South. 3 August 1837. p.84, c2.

**1057 HUMANITAS** *to* **n.n. [from the** *Bucks County Intelligencer***] n.d. n.p.** Describes the capture of a runaway slave near Bristol. 3 August 1837. p.84, c4.

**1058 A VIRGINIAN** *to* **THE EDITORS OF THE** *CLEVELAND MESSENGER.* **n.d. n.p.** Warns of violent retribution if the editors send another copy of their paper to the South. 3 August 1837. p.84, c6.

**1059 AN OBSERVER OF BUCKS COUNTY** *to* **MR. EDITORY [B. LUNDY]. n.d. n.p.** States that colonization cannot solve the problems created by slavery; informs that abolition has more adherents in Bucks County than colonization. 10 August 1837. p.85, c1.

**1060 A QUAKER** *to* **THE SOCIETY OF FRIENDS. [from the** *Delaware County Republican***] n.d. n.p.** Encourages Quakers to work with members of other denominations for the abolition of slavery. 10 August 1837. p.85, c6.

**1061 CLARKSON** *to* **SARAH M. GRIMKE AND ANGELINA E. GRIMKE. [from the** *New Haven Religious Intelligencer***] n.d. n.p.** Quotes Judge Cranch in order to refute the Grimkés' charge that Congress licenses the buying and selling of American citizens. 10 August 1837. p.86, c1.

**1062 SARAH M. GRIMKE AND ANGELINA E. GRIMKE** *to* **CLARKSON. [from the** *Intelligencer***] n.d. n.p.** Respond to Clarkson's letter, restating their claim that Congress implicitly licenses the buying and selling of American citizens. 10 August 1837. p.86, c1.

**1063 n.n.** *to* **THE** *ALTON OBSERVER.* **[extract] n.d. n.p.** Favors the proposal of an anti-slavery convention. 10 August 1837. p.86, c4.

**1064 n.n.** *to* **THE** *ALTON OBSERVER.* **[extract] n.d. n.p.** Favors the proposal of an anti-slavery convention. 10 August 1837. p.86, c4.

**1065 n.n.** *to* **THE** *ALTON OBSERVER.* **[extract] n.d. n.p.** Favors the proposal of an anti-slavery convention. 10 August 1837. p.86, c4.

**1066 J. R.** *to* **THE EDITOR OF THE** *NATIONAL ENQUIRER* **[B. LUNDY]. 2 August 1837. Schuylkill, Chester County.** Describes an anti-slavery lecture delivered by Lewis C. Gunn. 10 August 1837. p.86, c6.

**1067 A GENTLEMAN** *to* **THE EDITOR OF THE** *NATIONAL ENQUIRER* **[B. LUNDY]. [extract] 21 July 1837. Ohio.** Reports on pro- and anti-slavery activity in Ohio. 10 August 1837. p.86, c6.

**1068 W. H. J.** *to* **THE** *NATIONAL ENQUIRER.* **1 August 1837. Buckingham.** Reports the conclusion of the trial of Basil Dorsey, an alleged fugitive slave, in favor of the defendant. 10 August 1837. p.87, c1.

**1069 R.** *to* **THE EDITOR OF THE** *NATIONAL ENQUIRER* **[B. LUNDY]. n.d. n.p.** Disagrees with those who claim that it would be inexpedient to allow colored people to join ASs. 10 August 1837. p.87, c1.

**1070 n.n.** *to* **THE** *NEW YORK EXPRESS.* **30 July 1837. New Orleans, La.** Reports the arrival of several ships bringing military and political information concerning Mexico and economic information concerning Texas. 10 August 1837. p.87, c6.

**1071 n.n.** *to* **n.n. [extract] 25 June. Guatemala.** Reports a cholera epidemic in Guatemala and San Salvador. 10 August 1837. p.87, c6.

**1072 n.n.** *to* **n.n. [extract] 4 June 1837. Birmingham.** Reports on the anti-Catholic movement in England, Ireland and Scotland. 10 August 1837. p.87, c6.

**1073 n.n** *to* **THE EDITOR OF THE** *NATIONAL ENQUIRER* **[B. LUNDY]. n.d. n.p.** Encloses two poems, "The Son of a Soldier" and "The Disciple of Christ." 10 August 1837. p.88, c1.

**1074 n.n.** *to* **THE EDITOR OF THE** *NATIONAL ENQUIRER* **[B. LUNDY]. n.d. n.p.** Encloses a poem entitled, "To the Friends of Immediate Emancipation." 10 August 1837. p.88, c1.

**1075 S. SESSIONS** *to* **BROTHER PEET. [from the** *Buffalo Spectator***] n.d. n.p.** Encloses a letter from his brother, who has become an advocate of abolitionism; urges the use of moral suasion to further the cause of abolitionism. 10 August 1837. p.88, c3.

**1076 n.n. [S. SESSIONS'S BROTHER]** *to* **S. SESSIONS. [from the** *Buffalo Spectator***] 26 May 1837. Massachusetts.** Declares his support for abolitionism and describes his activities for the cause. 10 August 1837. p.88, c3.

**1077 n.n.** *to* **n.n. [from the** *Arkansas Gazette***] n.d. n.p.** Reports the establishment of Texan land offices which claim jurisdiction over territory belonging to Arkansas. 10 August 1837. p.88, c5.

**1078 W. H. J.** *to* **THE** *NATIONAL ENQUIRER.* **8 June 1837. Buckingham.** Reports additional details of the trial of Basil Dorsey, an alleged fugitive slave. 17 August 1837. p.89, c1.

**1079 CHARLES E. WILSON** *to* **MR. LUNDY. 5 August 1837. Norristown.** Advocates the formation of a CS based on abolitionist principles, which he feels would help to civilize the African races. 17 August 1837. p.89, c2.

**1080 ABRAHAM SHRINER** *to* **EMMOR KIMBER. 26 July 1837. Little Pips Creek, Md.** Repeats his request that Kimber persuade Bill Bud, who he claims is his slave, to return to him, and his assertion that Ann Brooks, a woman Bud sent for, is the wife of John Brooks. 17 August 1837. p.89, c3.

**1081 EMMOR KIMBER** *to* **ABRAHAM SHRINER. 6 August 1837. Kimberton.** Refuses to grant Shriner's request concerning Bill Bud; condemns slavery. 17 August 1837. p.89, c3.

**1082 A. W.** *to* **FRIEND LUNDY. n.d. n.p.** Describes an assault by Capt. David S. Craven on a colored female passenger on board the steamboat *New Philadelphia.* 17 August 1837. p.89, c5.

**1083 J. N. BUFFUM** *to* **FRIEND HENSHAW. [from the** *Lynn Record***] n.d. n.p.** Reports having heard from a Georgian that Southerners are given advance notice from friends in the North when an abolitionist is due to visit the South. 17 August 1837. p.90, c2.

**1084 JOHN ROBERTS** *to* **R. C. STOCKTON. [from the** *Upper Canada Christian Guardian***] 8 July 1837. Toronto, Upper Canada.** Rejects Stockton's appeal through the *Rochester Democrat* that Roberts return to slavery. 17 August 1837. p.90, c4.

**1085 GERRIT SMITH** *to* **ED.** *PHIL.* **[extract from the** *Upper Canada Christian Guardian***] n.d. n.p.** Reports that Stockton signed papers emancipating John Roberts. 17 August 1837. p.90, c4.

**1086 AN ABOLITIONIST** *to* **n.n. [from the** *Philanthropist***] 8 June 1837. Richmond, In.** Reports on two anti-slavery meetings he held in Monrovia County, Indiana; encloses a letter written from Monrovia County. 17 August 1837. p.90, c5.

**1087 n.n.** *to* **AN ABOLITIONIST. [extract from the** *Philanthropist***] n.d. Morgan, Monrovia County, In.** Announces the formation of an AS, enclosing a list of officers. 17 August 1837. p.90, c5.

**1088 WM. M. CHACE** *to* **CANDIDATES FOR CONGRESS FROM RHODE ISLAND. 18 July 1837. Providence, R.I.** Submits questions concerning the candidates' stands on slavery, on behalf of the Executive Committee of the Rhode Island AS. 17 August 1837. p.91, c1.

**1089 W. H. J.** *to* **THE** *NATIONAL ENQUIRER.* **1 August 1837. Buckingham.** Comments on the case of Basil Dorsey, an alleged fugitive slave. [continued from 10 August 1837] 17 August 1837. p.91, c2.

**1090 A GENTLEMAN** *to* **THE** *WASHINGTON REFORMER.* **[extract] 25 July 1837. n.p.** Comments on the relative political strengths of North and South. 17 August 1837. p.91, c3.

**1091 LEWIS C. GUNN** *to* **THE** *NATIONAL ENQUIRER.* **n.d. n.p.** Informs of the presence of slaveholders among the Chester County delegates to the Pennsylvania constitutional convention. 17 August 1837. p.91, c4.

**1092 H. C. WRIGHT** *to* **FRIEND LUNDY. 10 August 1837. West Chester.** Describes a meeting of the citizens of Chester County to consider the annexation of Texas to the United States. 17 August 1837. p.91, c5.

**1093 R. DOUGLASS, JR.** *to* **MR. EDITOR [B. LUNDY]. n.d. n.p.** Encloses a poem entitled, "Portraits from Cowper,—with a sketch by Tyro." 17 August 1837. p.92, c1.

**1094 n.n.** *to* **FRIEND LUNDY. 12 August 1837. Kennet.** Describes a meeting of the Kennet AS. 24 August 1837. p.93, c1.

**1095 n.n.** *to* **FRIEND LUNDY. 13 August 1837. Kennet Square.** Describes a meeting he held in Kennet Square. 24 August 1837. p.93, c1.

**1096 H. C. WRIGHT** *to* **FRIEND LUNDY. 14 August 1837. Kennet Square.** Describes an anti-slavery meeting of youth and children in Kennet Square; discusses the Juvenile AS of Darby, advocating the instruction of youth in anti-slavery principles. 24 August 1837. p.93, c1.

**1097 A JERSEYMAN** *to* **MR. EDITOR [B. LUNDY]. n.d. n.p.** Criticizes Captain Seth Lore's view that support of abolitionism is contrary to the principles of the Constitution. 24 August 1837. p.93, c2.

**1098 n.n.** *to* **R. [extract] n.d. n.p.** Fears that his previous letters to "R." have been destroyed because of racial prejudice. 24 August 1837. p.93, c3.

**1099 VERITAS** *to* **MESSRS. EDITORS. [from the** ***Public Ledger*****] n.d. n.p.** Reports a mob attack in Carlisle on Johnson, a colored man wrongly accused of seducing a white girl. 24 August 1837. p.94, c1.

**1100 DUTTEE J. PEARCE** *to* **WM. M. CHACE. 20 July 1837. Newport.** Responds to questions for political candidates from the Rhode Island AS; believes that Congress has the right to abolish slavery in Washington, D.C. 24 August 1837. p.94, c2.

**1101 JESSE HOWARD** *to* **WM. M. CHACE. 25 July 1837. Cranston.** Supports the right of petition and the abolition of slavery in Washington, D.C.; opposes the annexation of Texas. 24 August 1837. p.94, c3.

**1102 JOSEPH L. TILLINGHAST** *to* **WM. M. CHACE. 19 July 1837. Providence, R.I.** Believes that Congress should take action on anti-slavery petitions; opposes the annexation of Texas. 24 August 1837. p.94, c3.

**1103 B. B. CRANSTON** *to* **WM. M. CHACE. 25 July 1837. Newport.** Believes that Congress is empowered to abolish slavery in Washington, D.C.; opposes the annexation of Texas. 24 August 1837. p.94, c4.

**1104 M.** *to* **B. LUNDY. 15 August 1837. Bordentown, N.J.** Describes the status of abolitionism in New Jersey; reports the establishment of a moral reform society among the colored people of Bordentown. 24 August 1837. p.94, c5.

**1105 CIVIS** *to* **THE** ***NATIONAL ENQUIRER*****. n.d. n.p.** Discusses the issue of slavery in the forthcoming presidential election. 24 August 1837. p.94, c5.

**1106 LEWIS C. GUNN** *to* **MR. EDITOR [B. LUNDY]. n.d. n.p.** Encloses a lecture on "Freedom of the Speech and of the Press." 24 August 1837. p.94, c6.

**1107 ELI HAMBLETON** *to* **THE EDITOR OF THE** ***NATIONAL ENQUIRER*** **[B. LUNDY]. 1 August 1837. Penn's Grove.** Describes the progress of the anti-slavery cause in Chester County; describes a meeting of the Clarkson AS. 24 August 1837. p.95, c1.

**1108 ELI HAMBLETON** *to* **THE** ***NATIONAL ENQUIRER*****. n.d. n.p.** Announces a meeting of the Clarkson AS. 24 August 1837. p.95, c1.

**1109 A.** *to* **MR. LUNDY. n.d. n.p.** Criticizes an editorial in the *National Enquirer* which called Thomas P. Hunt a "slaveite demagogue" instead of employing constructive criticism. 24 August 1837. p.95, c3.

**1110 n.n.** *to* **n.n. [extract from the** ***New Orleans Bee*****] 22 July. Tampico.** Reports the attempted arrest of Santa Anna by the troops of General Bustamente. 24 August 1837. p.95, c4.

**1111 SAMUEL H. DAVIS** *to* **THE EDITOR OF THE** *ST. LOUIS COMMERCIAL BULLETIN.* **4 July 1837. Catterse, Wisconsin Territory.** Reports hostilities from the Indians due to the government's failure to pay them in accordance with treaty provisions. 24 August 1837. p.95, c5.

**1112 SARAH M. GRIMKE** *to* **FRIEND. [from the** *New England Spectator***] 27 July 1837. Andover.** Believes that relationships between men and women should not focus exclusively on their sexual differences, but should be conducted on an intellectual plane as well. 24 August 1837. p.96, c1.

**1113 H. WILSON** *to* **SIR. [from** *Human Rights***] 26 January 1837. Toronto.** An agent of the AAS inquires into the condition of the colored people of Toronto. 24 August 1837. p.96, c4.

**1114 R. G. DUNLAP** *to* **HIRAM WILSON. 27 January 1837. Toronto.** Describes the colored people of Toronto as a "loyal, honest, industrious, temperate, independent class of citizens." 24 August 1837. p.96, c4.

**1115 W. L. MACKENZIE** *to* **HIRAM WILSON. 30 January 1837. Toronto.** Attests to the good conduct of the colored people of Toronto. 24 August 1837. p.96, c4.

**1116 JOHN H. DUNN** *to* **HIRAM WILSON. 28 January 1837. Toronto.** Attests to the good conduct of the colored people of Canada. 24 August 1837. p.96, c5.

**1117 A GENTLEMAN** *to* **THE** *LIBERATOR.* **17 August. Old Colony.** Reports the indictment of a sheriff by a grand jury for failure to intervene when a mob disrupted the speech of Mr. Codding in Plymouth. 31 August 1837. p.97, c6.

**1118 THOS. W. DORR** *to* **WM. M. CHACE. 27 July 1837. Providence, R.I.** Upholds Congress's right to abolish slavery in the District of Columbia; opposes the annexation of Texas. 31 August 1837. p.97, c6.

**1119 DAN KING** *to* **WM. M. CHACE. 25 July 1837. Charlestown.** Opposes the annexation of Texas; favors the right of petition and abolition of slavery in Washington, D.C. 31 August 1837. p.98, c1.

**1120 A.** *to* **THE** *NATIONAL ENQUIRER.* **19 August. Bristol.** Urges opposition to the admission of Texas. 31 August 1837. p.98, c5.

**1121 H. C. W.** *to* **FRIEND LUNDY. 28 August 1837. Gulf Mills.** Summarizes Elliot Cresson's speech in favor of colonization, delivered at a meeting of colonizationists and abolitionists in Gulf Mills. 31 August 1837. p.99, c1.

**1122 W. H. BURLEIGH** *to* **FRIEND LUNDY. 22 August 1837. Warwick Furnace, East Nantmeal, Pa.** Describes his lecture tour in Pennsylvania. 31 August 1837. p.99, c2.

**1123 A SUBSCRIBER** *to* **MR. LUNDY. n.d. Pikeland, Chester County, Pa.** States that petitions may be presented to Congress on any day after the election of officers. 31 August 1837. p.99, c3.

**1124 A GENTLEMAN** *to* **THE EDITOR OF THE** *NATIONAL ENQUIRER* **[B. LUNDY]. [extract] 10 August 1837. New England.** Condemns Pennsylvania congressmen who support slavery. 31 August 1837. p.99, c3.

**1125 A GENTLEMAN** *to* **THE EDITOR OF THE** *NATIONAL ENQUIRER* **[B. LUNDY]. [extract] 18 August 1837. New York.** Praises Governor Ritner and several Pennsylvania newspapers for their stands on slavery; commends the *National Enquirer* for its articles on the political aspect of the anti-slavery cause. 31 August 1837. p.99, c3.

**1126 n.n.** *to* **FRIEND LUNDY. [extract] 25 August 1837. n.p.** Doubles his subscription to the *National Enquirer.* 31 August 1837. p.99, c5.

**1127 n.n.** *to* **n.n. [extract] 10 August 1837. Black Creek, E.F.** Reports the peaceful resolution of the conflict with the Indians. 31 August 1837. p.99, c6.

**1128 n.n.** *to* **THE EDITOR OF THE** ***COMMERCIAL BULLETIN.*** **21 July 1837. Matamoras, Mexico.** Reports the poor treatment of W. Wharton, a prisoner of the Mexicans; urges the Texans to take military action against Mexico; discusses the military situation in relation to the Indians. 31 August 1837. p.99, c6.

**1129 S. S.** *to* **MR. EDITOR [B. LUNDY]. 23 August 1837. Bristol.** Encloses a poem entitled, "Slavery." 31 August 1837. p.100, c1.

**1130 MOSES BROWN** *to* **THE** ***PROVIDENCE DAILY ADVERTISER AND AMERICAN.*** **n.d. Providence, R.I.** Encloses a copy of an act of the Rhode Island colonial government dated 18 May 1652 declaring it illegal for one man to serve another for more than ten years. 31 August 1837. p.100, c3.

**1131 n.n.** *to* **n.n. [extract] n.d. Aux Cayes.** Describes the lack of food in Aux Cayes. 31 August 1837. p.100, c4.

**1132 HANCOCK** *to* **n.n. [from the** ***Montrose Spectator*****] 26 July 1837. Susquehanna County.** Describes Texan morals and intentions toward Mexico as dishonorable, citing an article from the *Georgetown Messenger* of 1819 and a letter of 2 July from New Orleans as evidence. 31 August 1837. p.100, c4.

**1133 n.n.** *to* **n.n. [extract] 2 July. New Orleans, La.** Decribes preparations for a Texan invasion of Mexico. 31 August 1837. p.100, c4.

**1134 JAMES McCRUMMILL AND JACOB C. WHITE** *to* **FRIEND LUNDY. n.d. Philadelphia, Pa.** Enclose a copy of the constitution of the Philadelphia Vigilant Association, of which they are officers. 7 September 1837. p.101, c3.

**1135 CORRESPONDENT** *to* **THE** ***NATIONAL ENQUIRER.*** **n.d. n.p.** Describes the celebration of the First of August by Sabbath schools with teachers of color. 7 September 1837. p.102, c2.

**1136 COSMOPOLITE** *to* **FRIEND LUNDY. 22 August 1837. n.p.** Encloses an article entitled, "Something New Under the Sun," which expresses his reaction to the first issue of the *Anti-Abolitionist.* 7 September 1837. p.102, c2.

**1137 H. C. W.** *to* **FRIEND LUNDY. 28 August 1837. Gulf Mills.** Continues his review of Elliot Cresson's speech in favor of colonization, delivered at a meeting of colonizationists and abolitionists in Gulf Mills, and describes the conclusion of the meeting. [continued from 31 August 1837] 7 September 1837. p.102, c3.

**1138 H. C. W.** *to* **THE** ***NATIONAL ENQUIER.*** **n.d. n.p.** Describes an anti-slavery meeting in Gulf Mills which rejected the doctrines of colonization. 7 September 1837. p.102, c5.

**1139 L. C. G.** *to* **THE** ***NATIONAL ENQUIRER.*** **n.d. n.p.** Describes an anti-slavery meeting in Haddonfield, New Jersey, at which he and Joshua Coffin spoke. 7 September 1837. p.103, c2.

**1140 A FREEMAN** *to* **n.n. n.d. n.p.** Opposes the election of M'Ilvaine and Spackman to the state legislature. 7 September 1837. p.103, c2.

**1141 PUGH DUNGAN** *to* **THE PUBLIC. [from a Doylestown paper]. 1 August 1837. n.p.** Defends his treatment of Charlotte, a colored woman he took from jail to reside with him in order to hire out her labor. 7 September 1837. p.104, c3.

**1142 A CITIZEN OF DOYLESTOWN** *to* **THE** *NATIONAL ENQUIRER.* **n.d. n.p.** Discusses the inquiry into the alleged mistreatment of Charlotte, a colored woman, by Pugh Dungan. 7 September 1837. p.104, c4.

**1143 ANTI-SLAVERY** *to* **MR. EDITOR [B. LUNDY]. n.d. n.p.** States that there are many who consider themselves abolitionists yet do not find it expedient to express themselves on the issue. 14 September 1837. p.1, c1.

**1144 H. C. W.** *to* **FRIEND LUNDY. 4 September 1837. Lower Makefield, Yardleyville.** Describes a speech he delivered in Yardleyville, in which he refuted Elliot Cresson's arguments in favor of colonization. 14 September 1837. p.1, c1.

**1145 B. C.** *to* **FRIEND LUNDY. 3 September 1837. West Marlborough.** Describes a meeting of the East Fallowfield AS; encloses a copy of the resolutions adopted and a list of the society's officers. 14 September 1837. p.1, c1.

**1146 JUSTICE** *to* **MR. EDITOR. [from the** *U. S. Gazette***] n.d. n.p.** Recommends *The War in Texas,* written by an American citizen; contends that the issue of Texas is the most important question facing the United States. 14 September 1837. p.2, c2.

**1147 REMEMBER THAT** *to* **FRIEND LUNDY. 5 September 18[3]7. Philadelphia, Pa.** States that a meeting of the American Moral Reform Society has declared the use of the designation "colored" inconsistent with the principles of the society. 14 September 1837. p.2, c3.

**1148 J. P., JR.** *to* **FRIEND. 8 September 1837. Burlington, N.J.** Describes an anti-slavery meeting in Burlington County which was addressed by James M. McKim, H. C. Wright and Timothy Jackson. 14 September 1837. p.2, c4.

**1149 ELIJAH P. LOVEJOY** *to* **THE FRIENDS AND SUBSCRIBERS OF THE** *ALTON OBSERVER.* **24 August 1837. Alton, Il.** Appeals for aid in repairing the damage caused by a mob attack on the *Observer.* 14 September 1837. p.3, c3.

**1150 MATHEW FOSTER** *to* **GARRISON. [extract] n.d. England.** Describes the preparations for the visit of the Rev. Edward Frazer, a former slave. 14 September 1837. p.3, c6.

**1151 E. A.** *to* **MR. EDITOR [B. LUNDY]. n.d. n.p.** Encloses an article from the *London Christian Advocate* condemning slavery. 14 September 1837. p.4, c2.

**1152 H. C. W.** *to* **FRIEND LUNDY. 9 September 1837. Norristown.** Describes an anti-Texas meeting in Norristown. 21 September 1837. p.5, c1.

**1153 BENJ. S. JONES** *to* **FRIEND BURLEIGH. n.d. n.p.** States that the abolitionist claim that colonizationists favor the admission of Texas may stem from Rev. Henry Miller's warning against signing memorials opposing the admission of Texas. 21 September 1837. p.5, c1.

**1154 J. H. KIMBALL** *to* **AN ANTI-SLAVERY CONVENTION OF THE YOUNG MEN OF NEW HAMPSHIRE. [extract] n.d. n.p.** Asserts that the fight against slavery must be based on religious principles. 21 September 1837. p.5, c4.

**1155 W. L. GARRISON** *to* **AN ANTI-SLAVERY CONVENTION OF THE YOUNG MEN OF NEW HAMPSHIRE. [extract] n.d. n.p.** Admonishes them never to forget the existence of oppression in the country. 21 September 1837. p.5, c6.

**1155 W. L. GARRISON** *to* **AN ANTI-SLAVERY CONVENTION OF THE YOUNG MEN OF NEW HAMPSHIRE. [extract] n.d. n.p.** Admonishes them never to forget the existence of oppression in the country. 21 September 1837. p.5, c6.

**1156 MARY JOHNSON** *to* **THE FEMALE AS OF PHILADELPHIA. 4 August 1837. Buckingham.** Inquires, on behalf of the Buckingham Female AS, whether AS members should abstain from buying products of slave labor. 21 September 1837. p.6, c5.

**1157 MARY GREW** *to* **THE BUCKINGHAM FEMALE AS. 12 September 1837. Philadelphia, Pa.** Believes that abolitionists should patronize free labor, but believes that the slaveholder should be won over through appeals to his conscience, rather than to his pecuniary interests. 21 September 1837. p.6, c6.

**1158 H.** *to* **MR. EDITOR [B. LUNDY]. n.d. n.p.** Reports the burial of a colored man, Sheldon Loafman, in the cemetery of the Eleventh Presbyterian Church. 21 September 1837. p.7, c1.

**1159 CORRESPONDENT** *to* **THE** *NATIONAL ENQUIRER.* **[extract] 18 July 1837. Washington.** Describes attempts in the House of Representatives to limit the right of petition. 21 July 1837. p.7, c2.

**1160 A MEMBER OF THE PENNSYLVANIA DELEGATION IN CONGRESS** *to* **A GENTLEMAN IN PHILADELPHIA. [extract] 19 September 1837. Washington.** Reports the presentation of petitions opposing the admission of Texas by Gov. Lincoln, Mr. Adams and himself. 21 September 1837. p.7, c2.

**1161 A MEMBER OF THE PENNSYLVANIA DELEGATION IN CONGRESS** *to* **A GENTLEMAN IN PHILADELPHIA. [extract] 19 September 1837. Washington.** Reports the presentation of petitions opposing the admission of Texas by Messrs. Adams, Sergeant, Tolard and himself; believes that Texas will not be annexed to the Union. 21 September 1837. p.7, c2.

**1162 CORRESPONDENT** *to* **THE** *NEW YORK PLAINDEALER.* **[extract] n.d. Alton, Il.** Describes the circumstances surrounding the mob attack on the office of the *Alton Observer.* 21 September 1837. p.7, c4.

**1163 WASHINGTON CORRESPONDENT** *to* **THE** *NATIONAL ENQUIRER.* **[extract] n.d. Washington.** Praises the "firm and consistent" supporters of human rights. 21 September 1837. p.7, c5.

**1164 ALVAN STEWART** *to* **n.n. [extract from the** *New York Evangelist*] **n.d. n.p.** Tells the story of a slave who escaped to St. Lawrence County, New York. 21 September 1837. p.8, c2.

**1165 A FREE WOMAN OF AMESBURY** *to* **MR. PAGE. n.d. Amesbury.** Denies Page's assertion that the condition of free Northern laborers is no better than that of Southern slaves. 21 September 1837. p.8, c3.

**1166 A SOUTHERNER** *to* **J. G. BIRNEY. [from the** *Philanthropist*] **n.d. n.p.** Announces his conversion to abolitionism. 21 September 1837. p.8, c3.

**1167 O. SCOTT** *to* **THE EDITOR OF THE** *ZION'S WATCHMAN.* **[extract] n.d. n.p.** Reports on anti-slavery meetings which he addressed in Pittsburgh and Westfield; describes a conversation with the Rev. Mr. Pinney, former governor of Liberia. 21 September 1837. p.8, c4.

**1168 S. D. B.** *to* **THE** *UNION HERALD.* **[extract] n.d. Kentucky.** Describes slavery in Kentucky; reports the existence of anti-slavery opinion in the state. 21 September 1837. p.8, c4.

**1169 DR. CHANNING** *to* **CLAY. [extract] n.d. n.p.** Argues against the annexation of Texas. 28 September 1837. p.9, c1.

**1170 LEITCH RITCHIE** *to* **THE EDITOR OF** *SLAVERY IN AMERICA.* **[from** *Human Rights***] 2 January 1837. London.** Condemns Christians who support slavery. 28 September 1837. p.9, c4.

**1171 JACOB C. WHITE** *to* **MR. EDITOR [B. LUNDY]. 19 September 1837. Philadelphia, Pa.** Encloses resolutions adopted at a meeting of the Vigilant Committee of Philadelphia. 28 September 1837. p.10, c3.

**1172 J. BLANCHARD** *to* **FRIEND LUNDY. 8 September 1837. Canal Boat,** ***Lehman,*** **Above Dauphin.** Describes the progress of the anti-slavery cause in Perry County and other regions of the state. 28 September 1837. p.10, c5.

**1173 GERRIT SMITH** *to* **REV. D. R. GILLMER. n.d. n.p.** Agrees to receive Carter Braxton's slaves as a test of his devotion to the anti-slavery cause. 28 September 1837. p.11, c3.

**1174 A MEMBER OF CONGRESS** *to* **A GENTLEMAN OF PHILADELPHIA. [extract] 25 September 1837. Washington.** Reports numerous signatures to petitions against the admission of Texas. 28 September 1837. p.11, c5.

**1175 E. W.** *to* **FRIEND LUNDY. [from the** *Genius of Universal Emancipation***] n.d. n.p.** Encloses a poem by his wife entitled, "A Wife Proselyted." 28 September 1837. p.12, c1.

**1176 ONE OF THE MISSIONARIES AMONG THE SOUTH WESTERN INDIANS** *to* **A FRIEND IN NEW YORK. [extract] July 1837. n.p.** States that his abolitionist convictions have forced him to abandon his missionary work. 28 September 1837. p.12, c4.

**1177 DR. CHANNING** *to* **CLAY. n.d. n.p.** Argues against the annexation of Texas. [continued from 28 September 1837] 5 October 1837. p.13, c1.

**1178 A RESPECTABLE MEMBER OF THE COMMUNITY** *to* **MR. RIND. [extract from the** *Virginia Gazette***] 19 March 1767. n.p.** Encloses an address to the members of "our Assembly" condemning slavery. 5 October 1837. p.13, c4.

**1179 W. H. BURLEIGH** *to* **FRIEND LUNDY. 19 September 1837. East Fallowfield, Chester County.** Describes anti-slavery meetings in Warwick Furnace, Waynesburgh, East Fallowfield, West Fallowfield, Upper and Lower Oxford, Colerain, Cambridge, Penn's Grove, West Grove, and Derry. 5 October 1837. p.14, c5.

**1180 H. C. WRIGHT** *to* **FRIEND LUNDY. 23 September 1837. Solebury.** Describes colonization as a "scheme of National Ruin." 5 October 1837. p.14, c6.

**1181 n.n.** *to* **THE** *UNITED STATES GAZETTE.* **30 September 1837. Washington.** Conveys Mr. Preston's regret that petitions opposing the annexation of Texas were presented in the Senate. 5 October 1837. p.15, c5.

**1182 A MEMBER OF THE UNITED STATES SENATE** *to* **A GENTLEMAN OF PHILADELPHIA. 29 September 1837. Washington.** States that he will present the gentleman's petition opposing the annexation of Texas, and that he hopes the issue will not become a partisan political matter. 5 October 1837. p.15, c5.

**1183 A MEMBER OF CONGRESS** *to* **HIS FRIEND IN PHILADELPHIA. [extract] 30 September 1837. Washington.** Informs of numerous petitions against the annexation of Texas presented in Congress. 5 October 1837. p.15, c5.

**1184 ISAAC PARRISH** *to* **n.n. 3 October 1837. Philadelphia, Pa.** Urges members of ASs to send petitions to Congress opposing the annexation of Texas. 5 October 1837. p.15, c6.

**1185 CORRESPONDENT** *to* **THE** *CLEVELAND JOURNAL.* **[extract] n.d. n.p.** Describes the Niagara Falls. 5 October 1837. p.16, c2.

**1186 A. B.** *to* **MR. EDITOR. [from the** *Herald of Freedom***] n.d. n.p.** Encloses an anti-slavery composition written by an eleven-year-old boy. 5 October 1837. p.16, c3.

**1187 ALEXANDER CAMPBELL** *to* **JAMES G. BIRNEY. 15 September 1837. Bethany, Va.** Expresses his views concerning slavery. 12 October 1837. p.17, c3.

**1188 n.n.** *to* **THE SECRETARY OF THE AAS. [from the** *Emancipator***] 2 October 1837. Washington.** Describes the struggle against the annexation of Texas, focusing on the petitions presented to Congress. 12 October 1837. p.17, c6.

**1189 HIRAM WILSON** *to* **BROTHER WRIGHT. [from the** *Emancipator***] 28 September 1837. Steamboat between Buffalo and the Falls.** Describes the arrest of Mosely in Niagara for the theft of a horse belonging to Mosely's former owner, Mr. Castleman of Lexington, Kentucky. 12 October 1837. p.17, c6.

**1190 DR. F. JULIUS LEMOYNE** *to* **THE SECRETARY OF THE AAS. [from the** *Emancipator***] 18 September 1837. Washington, Pa.** Announces the formation of the West Finley AS. 12 October 1837. p.18, c1.

**1191 PRESIDENT M. VAN BUREN** *to* **THE HOUSE OF REPRESENTATIVES OF THE UNITED STATES. 30 September 1837. Washington.** Encloses a report from Secretary of State John Forsyth concerning the annexation of Texas, and correspondence between Forsyth and General Memucan Hunt, envoy extraordinary and minister plenipotentiary of Texas. 12 October 1837. p.18, c1.

**1192 JOHN FORSYTH** *to* **THE PRESIDENT OF THE UNITED STATES. 30 September 1837. Washington.** Encloses correspondence between himself and General Memucan Hunt of Texas. 12 October 1837. p.18, c1.

**1193 JOHN FORSYTH** *to* **GENERAL MEMUCAN HUNT. 25 August 1837. Washington.** States that the United States cannot consider the annexation of Texas while the latter is at war with Mexico. 12 October 1837. p.18, c1.

**1194 GENERAL MEMUCAN HUNT** *to* **SECRETARY OF STATE JOHN FORSYTH. 12 September 1837. Washington.** Argues that Texans favor annexation to the United States, and that annexation would prove economically beneficial to the Union. 12 October 1837. p.18, c2.

**1195 n.n.** *to* **THE** *NEW YORK JOURNAL OF COMMERCE.* **12 September. Washington.** Discusses political aspects of the issue of the annexation of Texas. 12 October 1837. p.18, c4.

**1196 n.n.** *to* **THE** *BOSTON COURIER.* **15 September. Washington.** Discusses Southern political maneuvers concerning the issue of the annexation of Texas. 12 October 1837. p.18, c5.

**1197 S. P. H.** *to* **THE EDITOR OF THE** *NATIONAL ENQUIRER* **[B. LUNDY]. 1 October 1837. Buckingham.** Describes a lecture by H. C. Wright at the New-Prospect schoolhouse. 12 October 1837. p.18, c5.

**1198 TERROREM** *to* **THE** *NATIONAL ENQUIRER.* **n.d. n.p.** Requests publication of the names of the "Dough Faces" who voted with the pro-slavery faction on the Missouri question. 12 October 1837. p.18, c6.

**1199 E.** *to* **FRIEND LUNDY. 27 September 1837. n.p.** Describes a debate between abolitionists and colonizationists at a debating society in Spring Garden. 12 October 1837. p.18, c6.

**1200 n.n.** *to* **SIR [A RESIDENT OF PHILADELPHIA]. 28 September 1837. Washington.** Reports his presentation of the recipient's memorial against the annexation of Texas to the House of Representations. 12 October 1837. p.19, c2.

**1201 n.n.** *to* **SIR [A RESIDENT OF PHILADELPHIA]. 3 October 1837. Washington.** Reports his presentation of the recipient's memorial against annexation of Texas. 12 October 1837. p.19, c2.

**1202 n.n.** *to* **SIR [A RESIDENT OF PHILADELPHIA]. 4 October 1837. Washington City.** Reports his presentation of the recipient's memorial against the annexation of Texas. 12 October 1837. p.19, c2.

**1203 A MEMBER OF AN ANTI-SLAVERY MEETING IN ST. CLAIRSVILLE, BELMONT COUNTY, OH.** *to* **THE EDITOR OF THE** *NATIONAL ENQUIRER* **[B. LUNDY]. [extract] n.d. n.p.** Describes an anti-slavery meeting; discusses the political implications of abolitionism and the fight over the annexation of Texas. 12 October 1837. p.19. c4.

**1204 CORRESPONDENT** *to* **THE** *NATIONAL ENQUIRER.* **22 September 1837. Schoolkruft, Kalamazoo County, Mi.** Reports widespread support for memorials to Congress against the annexation of Texas; discusses political aspects of abolitionism. 12 October 1837. p.19, c5.

**1205 A GENTLEMAN** *to* **THE** *NATIONAL ENQUIRER.* **[extract] n.d. Eastern Michigan.** Reports support for memorials to Congress against the annexation of Texas and for the abolition of slavery in the District of Columbia. 12 October 1837. p.19, c5.

**1206 n.n.** *to* **n.n. [extract] 21 August 1837. Matamoras, Mexico.** Reports indications of hostilities between the United States and Mexico. 12 October 1837. p.19, c6.

**1207 REV. DR. JAMES BLYTHE** *to* **n.n. [extract from the** *Cincinnati Journal***] n.d. n.p.** Discusses the relationship between slavery and religion in England and America. 12 October 1837. p.20, c4.

**1208 n.n.** *to* **THE EDITOR OF THE** *NEW ORLEANS BULLETIN.* **[extract from the** *Diario del Gobierno***] 7 June. Matamoras, Mexico.** A Texan correspondent describes General Canalizo. 19 October 1837. p.21, c1.

**1209 W. L. CHAPLIN** *to* **THE PRESIDENT AND EXECUTIVE COMMITTEE OF THE SEVERAL COUNTY ASs IN THE STATE OF NEW YORK. [from the** *Friend of Man***] n.d. n.p.** Encloses a resolution of the New York AS and forwards questions on the issue of slavery for the candidates for the New York legislature. 19 October 1837. p.21, c2.

**1210 GENERAL MEMUCAN HUNT** *to* **SECRETARY OF STATE JOHN FORSYTH. 4 January 1837. Washington City.** Advocates the annexation of Texas by the United States. 19 October 1837. p.21, c3.

**1211 THE SPY IN WASHINGTON** *to* **n.n. [from the** *New York Courier and Enquirer***] 9 October 1837. Washington.** Discusses proposals made by Presidents John Quincy Adams and Andrew Jackson for the annexation of Texas. 19 October 1837. p.22, c2.

**1212 THE INHABITANTS OF THE TOWN OF NIAGARA** *to* **LIEUTENANT GOVERNOR OF UPPER CANADA SIR FRANCIS BOND HEAD. [from the** *Toronto Christian Guardian***] n.d. Niagara, Canada.** Protest against the delivery of Molesby, a fugitive slave, to the American authorities. 19 October 1837. p.22, c3.

**1213 LIEUTENANT GOVERNOR OF UPPER CANADA SIR FRANCIS BOND HEAD** *to* **THE INHABITANTS OF THE TOWN OF NIAGARA. [from the** *Toronto Christian Guardian***] n.d. n.p.** Denies their request to reconsider the delivery of Molesby, a fugitive slave, to the American authorities. 19 October 1837. p.22, c3.

**1214 THE REV. J. M. M'KIM** *to* **n.n. [extract] n.d. Harrisburg.** Describes a meeting he held in Harrisburg. 19 October 1837. p.22, c5.

**1215 W. H. J.** *to* **THE EDITOR OF THE** *NATIONAL ENQUIRER* **[B. LUNDY]. 30 September 1837. Buckingham.** Describes a "First Day School" for colored people in Buckingham. 19 October 1837. p.23, c2.

**1216 Q.** *to* **MR. EDITOR [B. LUNDY]. 30 September 1837. Lancaster County.** Asks whether Daniel Sheffer was not a traitor due to his vote in the House in favor of tabling a resolution of John Quincy Adams concerning Texas. 19 October 1837. p.23, c3.

**1217 SPIRIT OF 76—O. S. M.** *to* **MR. EDITOR [B. LUNDY]. n.d. n.p.** Proposes a plan for the regulation of currency. 19 October 1837. p.23, c3.

**1218 N.** *to* **THE** *NATIONAL ENQUIRER.* **9 October 1837. Philadelphia.** Accuses the *National Enquirer* of misrepresenting the statements of Joseph M'Ilvaine on the issue of slavery. 19 October 1837. p.23, c5.

**1219 OFFICE OF THE** *AMERICAN* *to* **n.n. 16 October. Baltimore, Md.** Reports the wreck of the steam-packet *Home.* 19 October 1837. p.23, c6.

**1220 A LADY IN THE COUNTRY** *to* **HER FRIEND IN PHILADELPHIA. 1837. Chester County.** Regrets the common lack of knowledge of anti-slavery principles; asserts that abolitionists should refrain from buying slave produce. 19 October 1837. p.24, c1.

**1221 OBSERVER** *to* **THE EDITOR OF THE** *NATIONAL ENQUIRER* **[B. LUNDY]. n.d. n.p.** Encloses extracts from the *London Anti-Slavery Reporter* of January 1834 discussing various debates of slavery in England. 19 October 1837. p.24, c1.

**1222 DANIEL THOMAS** *to* **n.n. [extract from the** *Friend of Man***] 22 July 1837. Greatfield, near Aurora.** States that the *Liberator*'s account of matters concerning Nathaniel Crenshaw is incorrect; encloses an extract of a letter from a friend in Virginia concerning Crenshaw and John Randolph's will. 19 October 1837. p.24, c4.

**1223 n.n.** *to* **DANIEL THOMAS. [extract from the** *Friend of Man***] 8 July 1837. Virginia.** States that the judge who handled the wills of Nathaniel Crenshaw and John Randolph altered one of them in order that the slaves of the deceased would be liberated. 19 October 1837. p.24, c4.

**1224 S. M. AND A. E. GRIMKE** *to* **n.n. 2 October 1837. East Boyleston.** Describe their connection with slavery in previous years. 26 October 1837. p.25, c1.

**1225 J. BLANCHARD** *to* **REV. J. LEAVITT. [from the** *Emancipator***] 18 September 1837. Waynesboro', Franklin County, Pa.** Encloses Thaddeus Stevens's remarks on the right of slaves to trial by jury and on the admission of Texas; reports on the case of Johnson, who was lynched at Carlisle. 26 October 1837. p.25, c3.

**1226 MARTIN VAN BUREN** *to* **THE HOUSE OF REPRESENTATIVES OF THE UNITED STATES. 2 October 1837. Washington.** Encloses a report from John Forsyth, secretary of state, concerning the boundary between the United States and Mexico and the possible cession of territory by Mexico. 26 October 1837. p.25, c5.

**1227 JOHN FORSYTH** *to* **THE PRESIDENT OF THE UNITED STATES. 2 October 1837. Washington.** Encloses correspondence between the governments of the United States and Mexico concerning the boundary between the two countries and the possible cession of territory by Mexico. 26 October 1837. p.25, c5.

**1228 MR. CLAY** *to* **MR. POINSETT. [extract] 26 March 1825. Washington.** Discusses the possible alteration of the boundary between the United States and Mexico. 26 October 1837. p.25, c5.

**1229 JOSE TORRENS** *to* **SECRETARY OF STATE JOHN QUINCY ADAMS. [extract] 15 February 1824. Washington.** Asks whether the United States is willing to fix the boundary between the United States and Mexico according to the treaty of 1819. 26 October 1837. p.25, c6.

**1230 MR. CLAY** *to* **MR. POINSETT. [extract] 24 September 1825. Department of State.** Reports the president's response to Mexican views concerning a road from Missouri to Santa Fe and the appointment of commissioners to survey the land under discussion by the United States and Mexico. 26 October 1837. p.26, c1.

**1231 MR. CLAY** *to* **JOEL R. POINSETT. [extract] 15 March 1827. Washington.** Discusses a possible alteration of the boundary between the United States and Mexico. 26 October 1837. p.26, c1.

**1232 DR. JOSEPH PARRISH** *to* **JOHN SERGEANT. [from the** *United States Gazette***] n.d. n.p.** Responds to resolutions proposed at the constitutional convention at Harrisburg prohibiting the immigration of free men of color and fugitive slaves and limiting the elective franchise to white male citizens. 26 October 1837. p.26, c4.

**1233 H. C. WRIGHT** *to* **FRIEND LUNDY. n.d. n.p.** Discusses an oration on the life and character of Thomas Shipley by Isaac Parrish. 26 October 1837. p.27, c2.

**1234 J. FULTON, JR.** *to* **THE PUBLIC. 19 October 1837. East Fallowfield.** Discusses the activities of Austin L. Stanton, former editor of the *Emancipator*. 26 October 1837. p.27, c3.

**1235 S. H. GLOUCESTER** *to* **BROTHER LUNDY. n.d. n.p.** Thanks those who contributed to the fair for the benefit of the Second Presbyterian Church, a congregation of colored people of New York. 26 October 1837. p.27, c3.

**1236 JOSEPH WOLFF** *to* **MY AMERICAN FRIENDS IN GENERAL. [from the** *United States Gazette***] 21 October 1837. Philadelphia, Pa.** Refuses the requests of colonizationists and abolitionists to advocate their causes. 26 October 1837. p.27, c4.

**1237 H. F. RODNEY** *to* **MR. J. COFFEE. [from the daily papers] 22 October 1837. Lewes.** Reports the capture of the packet ship *Susquehanna* by a "piratical schooner." 26 October 1837. p.27, c4.

**1238 A NORTH CAROLINA MEMBER OF CONGRESS** *to* **THE EDITOR OF THE** *PHILANTHROPIST.* **26 September 1837. House of Representatives.** Condemns the doctrines of Dr. Channing and Henry Clay; returns a copy of the *Philanthropist.* 26 October 1837. p.28, c2.

**1239 ANGELINA E. GRIMKE** *to* **C. E. BEECHER. [from the** ***Liberator*****] 2 October 1837. East Boylston.** Discusses the proper role of women regarding moral duties. 26 October 1837. p.28, c3.

**1240 REV. ELIJAH P. LOVEJOY** *to* **THE EDITOR OF THE** ***PHILANTHROPIST.*** **7 October 1837. Alton, Il.** Reports the circumstances of the destruction of his press in Alton; encloses a letter to the publisher of the *Telegraph.* 2 November 1837. p.29, c4.

**1241 ELIJAH P. LOVEJOY** *to* **THE PUBLISHERS OF THE** ***TELEGRAPH.*** **n.d. n.p.** Describes an attack upon him by a mob in St. Charles, Missouri. 2 November 1837. p.29, c4.

**1242 M. VAN BUREN** *to* **JOEL R. POINSETT. 25 August 1829. Washington.** Orders Poinsett to open negotiations with the Mexican government for the cession of part of Texas; explains United States policy on the matter. 2 November 1837. p.29, c6.

**1243 WILLIAM A. GIBBS** *to* **MR. EDITOR. [from the** ***Colored American*****] 20 September 1837. Matanzas.** Advises people of color to beware of the island of Cuba, where colored people and abolitionists are mistreated. 2 November 1837. p.30, c4.

**1244 n.n.** *to* **THE** ***BALTIMORE PATRIOT.*** **8 October 1837. Mercersburg, Franklin County, Pa.** Describes the escape of three slaves from Frederick County, Virginia, and an aborted attempt to capture them near Mercersburg. 2 November 1837. p.30, c5.

**1245 S. M. G.** *to* **THE** ***NATIONAL ENQUIRER.*** **[extract] n.d. n.p.** Encloses an extract of a letter from an abolitionist in the South. 2 November 1837. p.30, c6.

**1246 n.n.** *to* **S. M. G. [extract] n.d. [A slave state.]** Foresees the downfall of slavery and praises abolitionism. 2 November 1837. p.30, c6.

**1247 A RESIDENT OF BRISTOL** *to* **FRIEND LUNDY. 24 October 1837. n.p.** Describes a pro-colonization speech by Elliot Cresson in Bristol. 2 November 1837. p.30, c6.

**1248 AMICUS** *to* **FRIEND LUNDY. 30 October 1837. n.p.** Describes a lecture by H. C. Wright at the orphan asylum. 2 November 1837. p.30, c6.

**1249 JUNIUS C. MOREL** *to* **FREDERICK A. HINTON. 19 September 1837. Harrisburg, Pa.** Declares that those designated by the term "colored men" should not look upon the term as an indication of inferiority. 2 November 1837. p.31, c1.

**1250 A GENTLEMAN** *to* **HIS FRIEND IN PHILADELPHIA. [extract] 25 October 1837. Northumberland County.** Reports a mob disruption of a sermon by James M. McKim. 2 November 1837. p.31, c4.

**1251 OFFICE OF THE** ***NEW ORLEANS BULLETIN*** *to* **n.n. 10 October. New Orleans, La.** Describes the damage caused by a storm in New Orleans. 2 November 1837. p.31, c5.

**1252 N. E.** *to* **THE** ***NATIONAL ENQUIRER.*** **n.d. n.p.** Encloses a poem in celebration of the marriage of James Alford and Mary Moore. 2 November 1837. p.32, c1.

**1253 n.n.** *to* **n.n. [extract from the** ***Friend*****] n.d. n.p.** Describes a storm at sea. 2 November 1837. p.32, c3.

**1254 LINDLEY COATES** *to* **GARRISON. [from the** ***Liberator*****] 17 October 1837. Harrisburg, Pa.** Believes that sectarian religious beliefs should not interfere with the anti-slavery cause; urges Garrison to continue his work. 9 November 1837. p.33, c1.

**1255 JOHN G. WHITTIER** *to* **BRO. GARRISON. [from the** ***Liberator*****] n.d. n.p.** Objects to the financial support given the *Liberator* by the Massachusetts AS, and to the publication of a letter in the *Liberator* nominating Jesus Christ for president. 9 November 1837. p.33, c2.

**1256 n.n.** *to* **n.n. [from the** ***Nashville Banner*****] 25 August 1837. Franklin, Ms.** Reports economic conditions in Mississippi, including the decline in the number of slaves. 9 November 1837. p.33, c3.

**1257 MR. LIVINGSTON** *to* **MR. BUTLER. [extract] 20 March 1833. Washington.** Urges Butler to bring the negotiations concerning Texas to a speedy conclusion. 9 November 1837. p.33, c4.

**1258 LOUIS McLANE** *to* **ANTHONY BUTLER. 13 January 1834. Washington.** Informs that the president has directed Butler, chargé d'affaires of the United States, to negotiate with Mexico for an extension of the date set by the previous treaty of limits for the appointment of commissioners and surveyors. 9 November 1837. p.33, c4.

**1259 JOHN FORSYTH** *to* **ANTHONY BUTLER. [extract] 2 July 1835. Washington.** Informs Butler that no changes have been made in the president's instructions; urges him to conclude the negotiations with Mexico swiftly. 9 November 1837. p.33, c5.

**1260 JOHN FORSYTH** *to* **ANTHONY BUTLER. [extract] 6 August 1835. Washington.** Details the boundaries the United States seeks with Mexico; states that Butler should try to secure the port of San Francisco for the United States. 9 November 1837. p.33, c5.

**1261 J. R. POINSETT** *to* **MR. CLAY. [extract] 18 July 1825. Mexico.** Reports a conversation with the Mexican secretary of state concerning treaties of commerce and limits between the United States and Mexico. 9 November 1837. p.33, c5.

**1262 MR. POINSETT** *to* **MR. CLAY. [extract] 27 July 1825. Mexico.** Encloses correspondence between himself and Mexican Secretary of State Lucas Alaman. 9 November 1837. p.33, c6.

**1263 LUCAS ALAMAN** *to* **MR. POINSETT. 20 July 1825. Mexico.** Discusses the treaties of commerce and limits between the United States and Mexico. 9 November 1837. p.33, c6.

**1264 EDWARD DAVIS, WILLIAM JONES, WM. WILLIAMSON, AND ABOVE THIRTY OTHERS** *to* **THE WELCHMEN [*sic*] IN AMERICA. n.d. Wales.** Appeal to American Welshmen, on behalf of the Welsh people convened in county assemblies in Merionythshire, Carnarvonshire, and Montgomeryshire, to work for the abolition of slavery. 9 November 1837. p.34, c2.

**1265 AN ABOLITIONIST** *to* **MR. EDITOR. [from the** ***Conneaut*** **(Oh.)** ***Gazette*****] n.d. n.p.** States that the interest of abolitionists in electoral politics is limited to insuring that the candidates who receive their votes adhere to their principles. 9 November 1837. p.34, c3.

**1266 THE RELIGIOUS SOCIETY OF FRIENDS** *to* **THE SENATE AND HOUSE OF REPRESENTATIVES OF THE UNITED STATES. [from the** ***Friend*****] n.d. Indiana.** Opposes the annexation of Texas. 9 November 1837. p.35, c3.

**1267 A CITIZEN OF BUCKS COUNTY** *to* **THE EDITOR OF THE** ***NATIONAL ENQUIRER*** **[B. LUNDY]. n.d. n.p.** Discusses the recent election in Bucks County in relation to the issue of slavery and the votes of colored people. 9 November 1837. p.35, c5.

**1268 A SYMPATHIZER WITH THE SLAVE** *to* **THE OPPOSERS OF ABOLITIONISTS. n.d. n.p.** Argues against active opposition to abolitionism for moral and religious reasons. 9 November 1837. p.35, c5.

**1269 L. C. G.** *to* **MR. EDITOR [B. LUNDY]. n.d. n.p.** Praises the *Second Reading Book,* compiled by the Association for the Improvement of Juvenile Books, from which he encloses a section entitled, "A Short Account of the Life of Capt. Paul Cuffee." 9 November 1837. p.36, c1.

**1270 ELIJAH P. LOVEJOY** *to* **BROTHER LEAVITT. n.d. n.p.** Declares that much help is needed for the reestablishment of the *Observer.* 9 November 1837. p.36, c5.

**1271 DR. BLYTHE** *to* **THE EDITOR OF THE** *CINCINNATI JOURNAL.* **[extract] n.d. n.p.** Criticizes Dr. Baxter for associating the Old School Presbyterian church with the religious justification of slavery. 16 November 1837. p.37, c1.

**1272 J. R. POINSETT** *to* **MR. ALAMAN. 27 July 1825. Mexico.** Objects to Alaman's proposal to delay the matter of a road between Missouri and Santa Fe until after the conclusion of the treaties of commerce and limits between the United States and Mexico; agrees to separate the two treaties; opposes the appointment of commissioners to survey the land. 16 November 1837. p.37, c4.

**1273 MR. ALAMAN** *to* **MR. POINSETT. [extract] 10 August 1825. Mexico.** Announces the negotiators for the treaty of commerce; recommends again that the land be surveyed before negotiating the treaty of limits. 16 November 1837. p.37, c5.

**1274 MR. POINSETT** *to* **MR. CLAY. [extract] 20 September 1825. Mexico.** Describes a conversation with the Mexican secretary of state concerning the boundaries between the United States and Mexico. 16 November 1837. p.37, c5.

**1275 MR. POINSETT** *to* **MR. CLAY. [extract] 18 March 1825. Mexico.** Reports the resolution of a problem in the negotiations which arose due to a grant of land made by the state of Coahuila and Texas. 16 November 1837. p.37, c5.

**1276 MR. POINSETT** *to* **MR. CLAY. [extract] 12 July 1826. Mexico.** Reports the appointment of General Teran to examine the land near the frontiers. 16 November 1837. p.37, c6.

**1277 J. R. POINSETT** *to* **SECRETARY OF STATE H. CLAY. 10 April 1827. Mexico.** Reports the actions of the House of Deputies concerning the treaty of limits. 16 November 1837. p.37, c6.

**1278 MR. POINSETT** *to* **MR. CLAY. [extract] 6 October 1827. Mexico.** Reports the appropriation of funds by the Mexican congress for General Teran's expedition. 16 November 1837. p.37, c6.

**1279 MR. POINSETT** *to* **MR. CLAY. [extract] 8 January 1828. Mexico.** Informs of Mexican insistence that the treaty between Spain and the United States of 1819 is binding between Mexico and the United States. 16 November 1837. p.37, c6.

**1280 MR. POINSETT** *to* **MR. CLAY. [extract] 7 February 1828. Mexico.** Encloses a copy of the protocols of the first and second conferences between the plenipotentiaries of the United States and Mexico, held on 8 and 10 January 1828 to conclude a treaty of limits. 16 November 1837. p.38, c1.

**1281 MR. POINSETT** *to* **MR. CLAY. [extract] 24 April 1828. Mexico.** Reports a delay in the ratification of the treaty of limits. 16 November 1828. p.38, c1.

**1282 J. R. POINSETT** *to* **SECRETARY OF STATE H. CLAY. 26 April 1828. Mexico.** Reports the ratification of the treaty of limits by the Mexican senate, but states that the exchange of ratifications will be delayed. 16 November 1837. p.38, c1.

1283 **MR. POINSETT** *to* **THE SECRETARY OF STATE. [extract] 10 March 1829. Mexico.** Describes discussions with the Mexican government concerning the treaty of Washington between Spain and the United States. 16 November 1837. p.38, c2.

1284 **MR. POINSETT** *to* **MR. VAN BUREN. [extract] 22 July 1829. Mexico.** Describes discussions with the Mexican government concerning the treaty of Washington between Spain and the United States. 16 November 1837. p.38, c2.

1285 **WM. D. HOSSETER** *to* **n.n. [from the** ***Philanthropist*****] 4 September 1837. South Hanover, Ia.** Encloses the proceedings of an annual meeting of the Jefferson County AS; gives a brief history of the society, of which he is the secretary. 16 November 1837. p.38, c2.

1286 **ELIJAH P. LOVEJOY** *to* **THE EDITOR OF THE** *EMANCIPATOR*. **[extract] n.d. n.p.** Describes an attack made upon him by a mob in St. Charles, Missouri. 16 November 1837. p.38, c4.

1287 **PRESIDENT JOHN PETER BOYER OF HAYTI** *to* **HAYTIANS. 22 October 1837. Port-au-Prince, Hayti.** Describes negotiations with the French government concerning an indemnity to be paid to France by Haiti. 16 November 1837. p.39, c1.

1288 **L. NAU** *to* **MR. B. LUNDY. 13 October 1837. Port-au-Prince, Hayti.** Thanks Lundy for the papers and letters he sent; encloses a copy of *L'Union* and the prospectus of a biography of distinguished Haitians. 16 November 1837. p.39, c3.

1289 **L. G. HAMILTON** *to* **BENJAMIN LUNDY. 17 October 1837. Port-au-Prince, Hayti.** Encloses a copy of the proceedings of the anniversary of the Haitian Abolition Society; praises Lundy's work for the cause of abolitionism. 16 November 1837. p.39, c3.

1290 **HEZEKIAH GRICE** *to* **BENJAMIN LUNDY. [extract] 22 October 1837. Port-au-Prince, Hayti.** Intends to work to increase the circulation of the *National Enquirer;* encloses a copy of the president's proclamation concerning France. 16 November 1837. p.39, c4.

1291 **EMMOR KIMBER** *to* **BENJAMIN LUNDY. 30 October 1837. Kimberton.** Encloses a legal opinion of Nicholas Waln concerning the rights of the people of color in Pennsylvania and New Jersey, dated 15 August 1771. 16 November 1837. p.39, c4.

1292 **n.n.** *to* **FRIEND LUNDY. [extract] 25 October 1837. Burlington.** Reviews a lecture by Dr. Booth in favor of colonization, delivered in Burlington. 16 November 1837. p.39, c5.

1293 **MR. BUTLER** *to* **MR. VAN BUREN. [extract] 19 May 1830. Mexico.** Reports the appointment of commissioners by Mexico for the treaty negotiations. 23 November 1837. p.41, c5.

1294 **LUCAS ALAMAN AND RAFAEL MANJINO** *to* **ANTHONY BUTLER. 21 May 1830. Mexico.** Inform that they have been authorized by the vice-president to negotiate the treaties between the United States and Mexico. 23 November 1837. p.41, c5.

1295 **ANTHONY BUTLER** *to* **JOSEPH M. O. MONASTERIO. 25 July 1832. Mexico.** Reports that the treaty of limits between Mexico and the United States is now the law of the land of the latter country; suggests that the boundary line designated in the treaty may need to be altered. 23 November 1837. p.41, c5.

1296 **BERNARDO GONZALEZ** *to* **ANTHONY BUTLER. 14 February 1833. Mexico.** Announces the intention of the Mexican government to carry out the stipulations of the treaty of limits. 23 November 1837. p.41, c5.

**1297 A. BUTLER** *to* **BERNARDO GONZALEZ. 16 February 1833. Mexico.** Protests against violations by Mexico of the treaty of amity, commerce, and navigation between the United States and Mexico. 23 November 1837. p.41, c6.

**1298 BERNARDO GONZALEZ** *to* **ANTHONY BUTLER. 21 February 1833. Mexico.** Acknowledges Butler's letter, and declares the intention of the Mexican government to publish the treaties between the United States and Mexico. 23 November 1837. p.41, c6.

**1299 BERNARDO GONZALEZ** *to* **ANTHONY BUTLER. 27 February 1833. Mexico.** Encloses copies of the treaties of limits and of amity, commerce, and navigation between Mexico and the United States. 23 November 1837. p.41, c6.

**1300 ANTHONY BUTLER** *to* **CARLOS GARCIA. 6 September 1833. Mexico.** Requests that the Mexican government consider the matter of altering the boundaries between Mexico and the United States. 23 November 1837. p.42, c1.

**1301 CARLOS GARCIA** *to* **ANTHONY BUTLER. 25 September 1833. Mexico.** Reports that the Mexican vice-president has appointed a commissioner and a surveyor for the purpose of executing the treaty of limits between Mexico and the United States. 23 November 1837. p.42, c1.

**1302 MR. BUTLER** *to* **HON. LOUIS McLANE. [extract] 1 July 1834. Mexico.** States that it would be preferable for him to return to the United States before the ratification of a new agreement with Mexico on the subject of boundaries. 23 November 1837. p.42, c1.

**1303 ANTHONY BUTLER** *to* **MEXICAN SECRETARY OF STATE FOR FOREIGN AFFAIRS FRANCISCO M. LOMBARDO. 21 December 1834. Mexico.** Proposes a renewal of the treaty of boundary between the United States and Mexico. 23 November 1837. p.42, c1.

**1304 OFFICE OF THE** ***MISSOURI ARGUS*** *to* **n.n. 9 November 1837. St. Louis, Mo.** Reports the death of the Rev. E. P. Lovejoy at the hands of a mob in Alton, Illinois, who sought to destroy his printing press; encloses an article from the *Alton Telegraph* reporting the occurrence. 23 November 1837. p.42, c3.

**1305 n.n.** *to* **THE** ***NATIONAL GAZETTE.*** **n.d. Cincinnati, Oh.** Describes the events leading to the death of Elijah P. Lovejoy at the hands of a mob in Alton, Illinois. 23 November 1837. p.42, c4.

**1306 MAYOR JOHN M. KRUM** *to* **THE PUBLIC. 8 November 1837. City of Alton, Il.** Describes the events leading to the death of Elijah P. Lovejoy at the hands of a mob in Alton. 23 November 1837. p.42, c5.

**1307 CORRESPONDENT** *to* **THE** ***NATIONAL GAZETTE.*** **25 October. n.p.** States that a convention met in Philadelphia to discuss whether liberty of conscience shall be permitted to men. 23 November 1837. p.43, c1.

**1308 CORRESPONDENT** *to* **THE** ***NATIONAL GAZETTE.*** **[extract] 26 October. n.p.** Reports on discussion of the militia at the constitutional convention in Pennsylvania. 23 November 1837. p.43, c1.

**1309 CORRESPONDENT** *to* **THE** ***NATIONAL GAZETTE.*** **[extract] 27 October. n.p.** Reports on discussion of the judiciary at the constitutional convention in Pennsylvania. 23 November 1837. p.43, c1.

**1310 CORRESPONDENT** *to* **THE** ***NATIONAL GAZETTE.*** **[extract] 28 October. n.p.** Reports on discussion of judicial terms at the constitutional convention in Pennsylvania. 23 November 1837. p.43, c2.

**1311 CORRESPONDENT** *to* **THE** *NATIONAL GAZETTE.* **[extract] 3 November. n.p.** Discusses Mr. Ingersoll's speech on judicial corruption at the constitutional convention in Pennsylvania. 23 November 1837. p.43, c2.

**1312 CORRESPONDENT** *to* **THE** *NATIONAL GAZETTE.* **[extract] 8 November. n.p.** Reports on discussion of the judiciary at the constitutional convention in Pennsylvania. 23 November 1837. p.43, c2.

**1313 J. S. L.** *to* **HIS FRIEND IN PHILADELPHIA. 17 November 1837. Attleboro', Bucks County, Pa.** Defends Samuel Johnson, a colored man, against charges that he announced his intention to shoot any man who prevented him from voting. 23 November 1837. p.43, c2.

**1314 H. W.** *to* **THE** *EMANCIPATOR.* **n.d. Canada.** Reports the acquittal of five of six colored men who stood trial for felony in the rescue of Moseby, a fugitive slave. 23 November 1837. p.43, c3.

**1315 GEN. LUCAS** *to* **THE EDITOR OF THE** *FAR WEST.* **14 October. Independence.** Reports that his troops staved off an attack by the Osage Indians. 23 November 1837. p.43, c5.

**1316 ANDREW JACKSON** *to* **THE FREE COLORED INHABITANTS OF LOUISIANA. 1814. n.p.** Calls upon them to defend their country. 23 November 1837. p.44, c1.

**1317 ANDREW JACKSON** *to* **THE FREE COLORED INHABITANTS OF LOUISIANA. n.d. n.p.** Praises their conduct in battle. 23 November 1837. p.44, c2.

**1318 JOHN HANNEN AND SAMUEL WILLIAMS** *to* **THE REV. J. BLANCHARD. [from the** *Christian Witness***] 6 November 1837. Pittsburgh, Pa.** Representatives of the Pennsylvania AS commend Blanchard, agent of the AAS, for his successful debate with Governor Pinney on the subject of colonization. 23 November 1837. p.44, c4.

**1319 J. M. GUTIERREZ DE ESTRADA** *to* **ANTHONY BUTLER, CHARGE D'AFFAIRES OF THE UNITED STATES OF AMERICA. 7 February 1833. Mexico.** The Mexican secretary of state and of internal and foreign relations states that the Mexican chargé d'affaires in Washington has been instructed to negotiate the settlement of limits between the United States and Mexico. 30 November 1837. p.45, c4.

**1320 MR. BUTLER** *to* **THE PRESIDENT. [extract] 26 February 1835. Mexico.** Explains the delays in the negotiations on the boundary treaty. 30 November 1837. p.45, c4.

**1321 J. M. GUTIERREZ DE ESTRADA** *to* **ANTHONY BUTLER, CHARGE D'AFFAIRES OF THE UNITED STATES OF AMERICA. 20 March 1835. Mexico.** Desires to negotiate with Butler concerning the treaty of limits. 30 November 1837. p.45, c5.

**1322 PABLO OBREGON** *to* **HON. HENRY CLAY, SECRETARY OF STATE. 19 March 1828. Washington.** The envoy extraordinary of the Mexican Republic inquires whether a passport from the secretary of state is necessary for the members of the commission appointed to make surveys relating to the treaty of limits; encloses a list of members of the commission. 30 November 1837. p.45, c5.

**1323 HENRY CLAY** *to* **DON PABLO OBREGON, ENVOY EXTRAORDINARY AND MINISTER PLENIPOTENTIARY FROM THE UNITED MEXICAN STATES. 24 March 1828. Washington.** Grants the passport requested by Obregon to the Mexican surveying commission. 30 November 1837. p.45, c6.

**1324 H. CLAY** *to* **DON PABLO OBREGON. 30 April 1828. Washington.** Reports the ratification of the treaty of limits by the United States. 30 November 1837. p.45, c6.

**1325 PABLO OBREGON** *to* **MR. CLAY. 1 May 1828. Washington.** Acknowledges the receipt of Clay's note informing of the ratification of the treaty of limits; states that he has not yet received the treaty. 30 November 1837. p.45, c6.

**1326 PABLO OBREGON** *to* **MR. CLAY. 2 August 1828. Washington.** States that he has received the treaty and is ready for the exchange of ratifications. 30 November 1837. p.45, c6.

**1327 DANIEL BRENT** *to* **DON PABLO OBREGON, ENVOY EXTRAORDINARY AND MINISTER PLENIPOTENTIARY FROM MEXICO. 2 August 1828. Washington.** Explains the necessity of submitting the treaties of limits and of commerce, amity, and navigation once more to the Senate. 30 November 1837. p.45, c6.

**1328 J. M. MONTOYA** *to* **MR. VAN BUREN. 16 April 1829. Baltimore, Md.** Informs that he has been authorized by the Mexican government to effect the exchange of ratifications of the treaty of limits and inquires whether the United States is prepared to conduct the exchange. 30 November 1837. p.46, c1.

**1329 M. VAN BUREN** *to* **DON J. M. MONTOYA. 22 April 1829. Washington.** States, as secretary of state, that the treaty of limits was not submitted at the Senate's last session, but will be submitted during the next session. 30 November 1837. p.46, c1.

**1330 S.** *to* **FRIEND LUNDY. 22 November 1837. n.p.** Encloses an article condemning the murder of Elijah P. Lovejoy, taken from a paper published in a city school. 30 November 1837. p.46, c6.

**1331 CITIZENS OF THE COUNTY OF BUCKS** *to* **THE CONVENTION TO AMEND THE CONSTITUTION OF PENNSYLVANIA, NOW SITTING AT HARRISBURG. n.d. n.p.** Request that a clause denying Negroes the right to vote be inserted in the constitution. 30 November 1837. p.47, c2.

**1332 SAMUEL AARON** *to* **B. LUNDY. 20 November 1837. Burlington, N.J.** Suggests that arrangements be made to provide for Mr. Lovejoy's widow and orphans; foresees more deaths in defense of human rights. 30 November 1837. p.47, c5.

**1333 J. M. MONTOYA** *to* **HON. EDWARD LIVINGSTON, SECRETARY OF STATE. 26 March 1832. Washington.** Announces that he has been authorized by the Mexican government to effect the exchange of ratifications of the treaties of amity, commerce, and navigation and of limits and inquires whether the secretary of state is prepared to conduct the exchange. 7 December 1837. p.49, c6.

**1334 MR. LIVINGSTON** *to* **MR. MONTOYA, CHARGE D'AFFAIRES OF MEXICO. 30 March 1832. Washington.** Declares that he will be prepared to exchange the ratifications of the treaty of commerce and navigation on 4 April. 7 December 1837. p.49, c6.

**1335 J. M. MONTOYA** *to* **THE HON. EDWARD LIVINGSTON, SECRETARY OF STATE. 31 March 1832. Washington.** Regrets the American government's delay in proceeding to the exchange of ratifications of the treaty of limits. 7 December 1837. p.50, c1.

**1336 EDWARD LIVINGSTON** *to* **JOSE MONTOYA, CHARGE D'AFFAIRES OF THE UNITED MEXICAN STATES. 31 March 1832. Washington.** States that the American government cannot exchange the ratifications of the treaty of limits before the Senate again ratifies the treaty. 7 December 1837. p.50, c1.

**1337 J. M. MONTOYA** *to* **THE HON. EDWARD LIVINGSTON, SECRETARY OF STATE. 3 April 1822. Washington.** Regrets American delay in proceeding to the ratification of the treaty of limits; declares his unwillingness to exchange the ratifications of the treaty of amity, commerce, and navigation before those of the treaty of limits. 7 December 1837. p.50, c2.

**1338 J. M. MONTOYA** *to* **MR. LIVINGSTON. 27 April 1832. Washington.** Inquires when the commissioner designated in the treaty of limits will be appointed by the United States. 7 December 1837. p.50, c2.

**1339 R. S.** *to* **MR. CORNISH. [from the** ***New York Colored American*****] n.d. n.p.** Encloses an article from the *New York Sun* reporting the arrest of a free colored man in the District of Columbia. 7 December 1837. p.50, c3.

**1340 CHARLES E. WILSON** *to* **MR. LUNDY. 2 December 1837. Norristown.** Urges renewed efforts in the anti-slavery struggle despite Reverend Lovejoy's murder. 7 December 1837. p.51, c5.

**1341 n.n.** *to* **n.n. [extract] n.d. n.p.** Conveys the protest of the Mexican president against American recognition of the independence of Texas. 9 December 1837 [Extra]. p.2, c3.

**1342 A GENTLEMAN** *to* **THE EDITOR OF THE** *NATIONAL ENQUIRER* **[B. LUNDY]. n.d. n.p.** Reports that his trip to the Southwest convinced him of the validity of a pamphlet entitled, "The origin and true causes of the Texas Insurrection." 9 December 1837 [Extra]. p.2, c4.

**1343 A GENTLEMAN** *to* **n.n. n.d. New York.** Describes Southern assistance to the Texans. 9 December 1837 [Extra]. p.2, c4.

**1344 n.n.** *to* **THE EDITOR OF THE** *NATIONAL ENQUIRER* **[B. LUNDY]. [extract] n.d. n.p.** Condemns the "Texas Conspiracy." 9 December 1837 [Extra]. p.2, c4.

**1345 n.n.** *to* **THE** *UNITED STATES GAZETTE.* **n.d. Washington.** Describes the debate in Congress on the subject of Texas. 9 December 1837. p.2, c5.

**1346 A GENTLEMAN** *to* **THE EDITOR OF THE** *NATIONAL ENQUIRER* **[B. LUNDY]. 22 February 1837. Arras, France.** Describes French and British reactions to the events in Texas. 9 December 1837 [Extra]. p.3, c1.

**1347 REV. DR. WM. E. CHANNING** *to* **HENRY CLAY. n.d. n.p.** Condemns the Texan revolt and opposes the annexation of Texas by the United States. 9 December 1837 [Extra]. p.3, c2.

**1348 CORRESPONDENT** *to* **THE** *COURIER AND ENQUIRER.* **[extract] n.d. New Orleans, La.** Reports General Jackson's support for the annexation of Texas. 9 December 1837 [Extra]. p.3, c4.

**1349 WASHINGTON CORRESPONDENT** *to* **THE** *JOURNAL OF COMMERCE.* **[extract] n.d. Washington.** Calls for Southern opposition to abolitionism. 9 December 1837 [Extra]. p.3, c4.

**1350 CHARLES E. WILSON** *to* **MR. LUNDY. 2 December 1837. Norristown.** Urges renewed efforts on behalf of abolitionism in the wake of Reverend Lovejoy's death. 9 December 1837 [Extra]. p.4, c1.

**1351 EDWARD LIVINGSTON** *to* **JOSE MONTOYA, CHARGE D'AFFAIRES OF THE UNITED MEXICAN STATES. 30 July 1832. Washington.** Reports that the United States government is prepared to proceed to the designation of a boundary line between the United States and Mexico. 14 December 1837. p.53, c5.

**1352 J. M. DE CASTILLO Y LANZAS** *to* **MR. McLANE. 2 December 1833. Philadelphia, Pa.** The Mexican chargé d'affaires encloses a note he received from his government; inquires whether the United States has appointed a surveyor and a commissioner. 14 December 1837. p.53, c5.

**1353 n.n.** *to* **J. M. DE CASTILLO Y LANZAS. n.d. n.p.** Announces the appointment of a Mexican commissioner and surveyor. 14 December 1837. p.53, c5.

**1354 LOUIS McLANE** *to* **SEÑOR DON J. M. DE CASTILLO Y LANZAS, CHARGE D'AFFAIRES OF MEXICO. 21 December 1833. Washington.** Asks when the appointment of commissioners by the Mexican government was made. 14 December 1837. p.53, c5.

**1355 MR. CASTILLO** *to* **MR. McLANE. [extract] 9 January 1834. Philadelphia, Pa.** States that the dispatch reporting the appointment of the Mexican commissioner and surveyor was dated 25 September. 14 December 1837. p.53, c5.

**1356 J. M. DE CASTILLO Y LANZAS** *to* **THE HON. LOUIS McLANE, SECRETARY OF STATE. 26 May 1834. Washington.** Suggests an extension of the term designated in the treaty for the meeting of the commissioners, as a remedy for the delay in the execution of the treaty of limits. 14 December 1837. p.53, c6.

**1357 THE MINISTER OF FOREIGN AFFAIRS OF MEXICO FRANCISCO DE LOMBARDO** *to* **THE SECRETARY OF STATE OF THE UNITED STATES. 21 October 1834. Mexico.** Announces the authorization of J. M. de Castillo y Lanzas to arrange the meeting of the commissioners called for by the treaty of limits. 14 December 1837. p.53, c6.

**1358 J. M. DE CASTILLO Y LANZAS** *to* **HON. JOHN FORSYTH. 4 December 1834. Philadelphia, Pa.** Informs Forsyth of the appointment of new Mexican commissioners and of his own authorization to negotiate an additional article of the treaty of limits. 14 December 1837. p.53, c6.

**1359 JOHN FORSYTH** *to* **SEÑOR DON J. M. DE CASTILLO Y LANZAS, CHARGE D'AFFAIRES OF MEXICO. 11 December 1834. Washington.** States that the United States wishes to conduct the negotiations in Mexico and has authorized Mr. Butler to conduct them on behalf of the United States. 14 December 1837. p.54, c1.

**1360 E. P. LOVEJOY, CORRESPONDING SECRETARY, ILLINOIS STATE AS** *to* **BROTHER. [from the *Philanthropist*] 6 November 1837. Alton, Il.** Announces the formation of the Illinois State AS and encloses a list of its officers; reports anti-slavery speeches in Alton by President Beecher of Illinois College. 14 December 1837. p.54, c2.

**1361 n.n. [MEMBER OF THE PENNSYLVANIA LEGISLATURE]** *to* **n.n. [RESIDENT OF PHILADELPHIA]. [extract] 9 December 1837. Harrisburg, Pa.** Urges the submission of petitions to the legislature in support of a bill granting the right of trial by jury to persons arrested as fugitive slaves. 14 December 1837. p.55, c3.

**1362 WM. HARNED, CHAIRMAN** *to* **FRIEND LUNDY. 11 December 1837. n.p.** Reports the efforts of the committee of arrangements for a public religious meeting in connection with the Alton murder. 14 December 1837. p.55, c5.

**1363 n.n.** *to* **n.n. [extract from the London papers]. n.d. Mexico.** Reports the success of the Mexican government under Bustamente. 14 December 1837. p.56, c3.

**1364 J. M. DE CASTILLO Y LANZAS** *to* **MR. FORSYTH. 15 December 1834. Philadelphia, Pa.** Asks the United States government not to insist that the negotiations on the extension of the third article of the treaty of limits be conducted in Mexico. 21 December 1837. p.57, c5.

**1365 JOHN FORSYTH** *to* **SEÑOR DON J. M. DE CASTILLO Y LANZAS. 9 January 1835. Washington.** Repeats that the United States wishes to conduct the negotiations in Mexico and will not acquiesce to Mexico's request that they be conducted in the United States. 21 December 1837. p.57, c6.

**1366 J. M. DE CASTILLO Y LANZAS** *to* **THE HON. JOHN FORSYTH, SECRETARY OF STATE. 12 January 1835. Washington.** Argues that negotiations should be conducted in the United States. 21 December 1837. p.57, c6.

**1367 J. M. DE CASTILLO Y LANZAS** *to* **MR. FORSYTH. 29 April 1835. Philadelphia, Pa.** Announces the agreement of the Mexican president to conducting negotiations in Mexico. 21 December 1837. p.58, c1.

**1368 ASBURY DICKINS** *to* **SEÑOR DON J. M. DE CASTILLO Y LANZAS. 11 May 1835. Washington.** Acknowledges, as acting secretary of state, the receipt of Castillo's note of 29 April 1835 to Mr. Forsyth. 21 December 1837. p.58, c1.

**1369 J. M. DE CASTILLO Y LANZAS** *to* **HON. MR. ASBURY DICKINS. 2 June 1835. Philadelphia, Pa.** Reports the approval of the General Congress of Mexico of an article extending the term designated in the treaty of limits for the meeting of commissioners; encloses a copy of the article. 21 December 1837. p.58, c1.

**1370 AMY PRESTON, ALICE ELIZA HAMBLETON, MARTHA LAMBORN, THOMAS HAMBLETON, JONATHAN LAMBORN, AND ELI HAMBLETON, COMMITTEE** *to* **THE PHILADELPHIA COUNTY AS. 1837. Penngrove.** Request cooperation, on behalf of the Clarkson AS, in calling a convention to promote the sale of goods produced by free labor. 21 December 1837. p.58, c5.

**1371 A CITIZEN OF BUCKS COUNTY** *to* **THE EDITOR [B. LUNDY]. 4 December. n.p.** Reports that the commissioner and auditor elect of Bucks County have been ordered to show cause why their election should not be set aside due to the dependence of their victory on Negro votes; condemns those who wish to exclude Negroes from the polls. 21 December 1837. p.58, c5.

**1372 J. M. McKIM** *to* **n.n. [extract] 9 November 18[3]7. Lewisburg.** Describes anti-slavery lectures he delivered in Mifflinsburg and Lewisburg. 21 December 1837. p.58, c6.

**1373 J. M. McKIM** *to* **n.n. 19 November 1837. Lewisburg.** Describes a debate on slavery in Lewisburg in which he participated. 21 December 1837. p.58, c6.

**1374 CORRESPONDENT** *to* **THE** ***BALTIMORE AMERICAN.*** **19 December 1837. n.p.** Reports Mr. Preston's intention to introduce measures for the annexation of Texas. 21 December 1837. p.59, c2.

**1375 n.n.** *to* **THE** ***BALTIMORE AMERICAN.*** **[extract] 18 December. Washington.** Describes the presentation of petitions in the House requesting a limitation of slavery in various ways; describes a debate in the Senate concerning a petition calling for the abolition of slavery in the District of Columbia. 21 December 1837. p.59, c4.

**1376 CORRESPONDENT** *to* **THE** ***UNITED STATES GAZETTE.*** **[extract] n.d. n.p.** Describes a debate in the Senate concerning a petition calling for the abolition of slavery in the District of Columbia; informs of a forthcoming debate in the House concerning an abolition petition and a memorial of the Peace Society. 21 December 1837. p.59, c5.

1377 **ASBURY DICKINS** *to* **SEÑOR DON J. M. DE CASTILLO Y LANZAS. 4 June 1835. Washington.** Acknowledges the receipt of Castillo's note reporting the approval of an additional article to the treaty of limits by the negotiators and the Mexican congress; requests a copy of the article. 28 December 1837. p.62, c1.

1378 **J. M. DE CASTILLO Y LANZAS** *to* **MR. DICKINS. 6 June 1835. Philadelphia, Pa.** Encloses a copy of the additional article to the treaty of limits. 28 December 1837. p.62, c1.

1379 **J. M. DE CASTILLO Y LANZAS** *to* **HON. JOHN FORSYTH, SECRETARY OF STATE. 10 July 1835. Philadelphia, Pa.** Reports that he has been authorized by the Mexican government to conduct the exchange of ratifications of the treaty of limits; asks whether Forsyth is prepared to do the same. 28 December 1837. p.62, c1.

1380 **MR. GOROSTIZA** *to* **MR. FORSYTH. 18 April 1836. Washington.** Reports Mr. Castillo's arrival in Washington; asks Forsyth to name a date for the exchange of ratifications. 28 December 1837. p.62, c1.

1381 **MR. FORSYTH** *to* **MR. DE GOROSTIZA. 18 April 1836. Department of State.** Replies that he will be ready to exchange ratifications on the following Wednesday. 28 December 1837. p.62, c1.

1382 **CORRESPONDENT** *to* **THE** *NEW YORK COMMERCIAL ADVERTISER*. **[extract] n.d. n.p.** Outlines a plan whereby Texas would be annexed without a consideration of the constitutional problem involved in such an action. 28 December 1837. p.62, c4.

1383 **B.** *to* **MR. LUNDY. n.d. n.p.** Encloses an extract from an anti-slavery speech delivered by Rev. Nathan Perkins, pastor of the Second Presbyterian Church in Hartford. 28 December 1837. p.62, c5.

1384 **M.** *to* **MR. EDITOR [B. LUNDY]. n.d. n.p.** Relates a story of mistreatment of colored men working on the Schuylkill. 28 December 1837. p.62, c6.

1385 **CORRESPONDENT** *to* **THE** *BALTIMORE AMERICAN*. **21 December 1837. n.p.** Describes a meeting of the Southern delegation to Congress. 28 December 1837. p.63, c1.

1386 **W. MERVINE, COMMANDER U. S. NAVY** *to* **n.n. [from the** *New Orleans Bee*] **15 December 1837. United States Ship of War** *Natchez*, **off S. W. Pass, Ms.** Directs the attention of New Orleans merchants to information enclosed concerning the crossing of the Rio Grande by Mexican troops. 28 December 1837. p.63, c5.

1387 **OFFICE OF THE** *TRUE AMERICAN* *to* **n.n. 19 December. New Orleans, La.** Describes the military situation in Texas. 28 December 1837. p.63, c5.

1388 **n.n.** *to* **n.n. [RESIDENT OF PHILADELPHIA]. [extract] 16 November 1837. Florida.** Reports the imminent departure of the brig *America* to Haiti with over sixty colored passengers; discusses the state of "our great warlike preparations." 28 December 1837. p.63, c5.

1389 **n.n.** *to* **n.n. [extract from the** *Baltimore American*] **13 December 1837. Camp, Near Fort Mellon, E.F.** Discusses the prospects for the termination of hostilities with the Cherokee Indians. 28 December 1837. p.63, c6.

1390 **G.** *to* **MR. EDITOR [B. LUNDY]. n.d. n.p.** Condemns the purchase of slave produce. 28 December 1837. p.64, c1.

1391 **Z.** *to* **THE** *NATIONAL ENQUIRER*. **n.d. n.p.** Describes a conversation with a former Pennsylvania farmer who is now a slaveholding Louisiana cotton planter. 28 December 1837. p.64, c2.

## [1838]

**1392 CARTER BRAXTON** *to* **THE EDITOR OF THE** *RICHMOND ENQUIRER.* **[from the** *Friend of Man*] **28 November 1837. Middlesex, Va.** Denies newspaper reports that he has offered to surrender his slaves to Gerrit Smith. 4 January 1838. p.65, c1.

**1393 D. R. GILLMER** *to* **THE** *FRIEND OF MAN.* **[extract] 16 August 1837. Sauquoit.** Informs that Carter Braxton has offered to deliver his slaves to any abolitionist who will provide for them; challenges Gerrit Smith to respond to Braxton's offer. 4 January 1838. p.65, c2.

**1394 MR. GILLMER** *to* **MR. GERRIT SMITH. 12 October 1837. n.p.** States that Mr. Braxton requires that Smith sign an oath before a magistrate concerning the terms under which Braxton will deliver his slaves to Smith. 4 January 1838. p.65, c2.

**1395 D. R. GILLMER** *to* **GERRIT SMITH. [from the** *Friend of Man*] **n.d. n.p.** Requests one hundred dollars to enable him to go to Virginia and bring Carter Braxton's slaves to Smith in Peterboro', New York. 4 January 1838. p.65, c3.

**1396 GERRIT SMITH** *to* **REV. D. R. GILLMER. [from the** *Friend of Man*] **n.d. n.p.** States that due to Carter Braxton's published denial of any intention to surrender his slaves, the correspondence between himself and Gillmer is terminated. 4 January 1838. p.65, c3.

**1397 WILLIAM SLADE** *to* **n.n. [from the** *National Gazette*] **27 December 1837. Washington.** Defends himself against criticism of his anti-slavery speech in the House of Representatives. 4 January 1838. p.66, c1.

**1398 J. M. M'KIM** *to* **FRIEND LUNDY. 28 December 1837. Montrose, Susquehanna County, Pa.** Describes his efforts on behalf of abolitionism in Wilkesbarre, Henesdale, Bethany, Carbondale, Montrose, Choconut, Franklin, and Brooklyn. 4 January 1838. p.66, c6.

**1399 A CITIZEN OF BUCKS COUNTY** *to* **MR. LUNDY. n.d. n.p.** Describes the progress of the attempt to abolish Negro suffrage in Bucks County. 4 January 1838. p.67, c1.

**1400 JOHN QUINCY ADAMS** *to* **RESPECTED FRIEND. 29 December 1837. Washington.** Describes his efforts in the House of Representatives on behalf of the anti-slavery cause and in opposition to a war with Mexico. 4 January 1838. p.67, c4.

**1401 A MEMBER OF CONGRESS** *to* **n.n. [extract] 29 December 1837. Washington.** Informs that he intends, with Mr. Adams and others, to incorporate the substance of petitions concerning slavery into a resolution which the Speaker would be less likely to lay on the table. 4 January 1838. p.67, c5.

**1402 M. EARLE, SECRETARY** *to* **THE CHRISTIAN PUBLIC. n.d. n.p.** Appeals, on behalf of the Female Moral Reform Society of Philadelphia, for aid in the society's effort to combat the "tide of licentiousness" in the city. 4 January 1838. p.68, c2.

**1403 CORRESPONDENT** *to* **THE** *BALTIMORE PATRIOT.* **[extract from the** *Pennsylvania Telegraph*] **n.d. n.p.** Describes the vote in the House of Representatives on a resolution limiting the right of petition. 4 January 1838. p.68, c3.

**1404 DAVID BURNHAM** *to* **BROTHER MURRAY. [from the** *Vermont Telegraph*] **20 December 1837. East Williamstown.** Encloses resolutions adopted by the Baptist Church of East Williamstown condemning the restriction of anti-slavery activity at the Hamilton Theological Seminary. 4 January 1838. p.68, c4.

**1405 H. D. GILPIN, SOLICITOR OF THE TREASURY** *to* **N. WILLIAMS, ESQ. U. S. ATTORNEY, BALTIMORE. 17 November 1837. Office of the Solicitor of the Treasury.** Requests that he investigate allegations concerning the circulation of counterfeit coins in Baltimore. 4 January 1838. p.68, c5.

**1406 BENEZET** *to* **THE** ***NATIONAL ENQUIRER.*** **n.d. n.p.** Describes a meeting of the Methodist AS. 11 January 1838. p.69, c1.

**1407 THE CLAIMANT IN A CONNECTICUT SLAVERY CASE** *to* **THE EDITOR OF THE** ***SAVANNAH GEORGIAN.*** **[extract] 7 August. n.p.** Describes the sympathy he received from the citizens of Hartford and the latter's opposition to abolitionism. 11 January 1838. p.69, c5.

**1408 WILLIAM E. CHANNING** *to* **THE ABOLITIONISTS. 14 December 1837. Boston, Ma.** Urges abolitionists, in the wake of Lovejoy's death, to foreswear the use of violence in the furtherance of their cause. 11 January 1838. p.70, c2.

**1409 A CITIZEN OF BUCKS COUNTY** *to* **MR. LUNDY. n.d. n.p.** Describes the proceedings at a hearing on the constitutional right of Negroes to vote, held at the Court of Common Pleas of Bucks County. 11 January 1838. p.70, c4.

**1410 COSMOPOLITE** *to* **THE** ***NATIONAL ENQUIRER.*** **n.d. n.p.** Describes a visit with a colored farmer in Maryland. 11 January 1838. p.70, c5.

**1411 L---S** *to* **MR. EDITOR [B. LUNDY]. n.d. n.p.** Urges the North to resist the demands of the South concerning slavery; opposes the annexation of Texas. 11 January 1838. p.70, c5.

**1412 n.n.** *to* **THE LEGISLATIVE COUNCIL AND GENERAL ASSEMBLY OF NEW JERSEY. n.d. n.p.** Urge the Legislature to ask Congress to abolish the internal slave trade and slavery in the District of Columbia and the territories. 11 January 1838. p.70, c6.

**1413 ELI NICHOLS** *to* **B. LUNDY. 15 December 1837. Lloydsville, Oh.** Calls on Congress to make reparations to the widow and orphans of Mr. Lovejoy. 11 January 1838. p.71, c3.

**1414 CORRESPONDENTS** *to* **THE** ***NATIONAL GAZETTE*** **AND THE** ***BALTIMORE AMERICAN.*** **[extract] n.d. n.p.** Describe debates in the House of Representatives concerning Texas, and in the Senate concerning Texas, states' rights, and Canada. 11 January 1838. p.71, c4.

**1415 n.n.** *to* **n.n. [extract] 20 December 1837. Houston, Tx.** Reports rumors of the imminence of war in Texas. 11 January 1838. p.71, c6.

**1416 H. E.** *to* **COUSIN. 1837. Oaka Valley.** States that the abolitionist plan to establish a boycott of slave produce will ensure the defeat of slavery. 11 January 1838. p.72, c2.

**1417 J. R.** *to* **B. LUNDY. n.d. n.p.** Encloses an article originally published in the Paris *Journal des Debats* comparing Presidents Van Buren and Jackson and condemning slavery and American treatment of the Indians. 11 January 1838. p.72, c2.

**1418 JAMES G. BIRNEY, ELIZUR WRIGHT, JR., AND HENRY B. STANTON, CORRESPONDING SECRETARIES** *to* **THE FRIENDS OF EMANCIPATION. 5 January 1838. New York.** Appeal on behalf of the AAS for petitions to be sent to Congress and state legislatures protesting a congressional resolution which called for the tabling of all anti-slavery petitions. 18 January 1838. p.73, c3.

**1419 WILLIAM E. CHANNING** *to* **THE ABOLITIONISTS. 14 December 1837. Boston, Ma.** Urges abolitionists, in the wake of Mr. Lovejoy's death, to foreswear the use of violence in the furtherance of their cause; praises their devotion to the principles of freedom of the press and human liberty. [continued from 11 January 1838] 18 January 1838. p.73, c6.

**1420 OWEN LOVEJOY** *to* **n.n. [from the** ***Emancipator*****] 8 December 1837. Alton, Il.** Describes the events leading to the death of his brother, Elijah Lovejoy, at the hands of a pro-slavery mob; states that Lovejoy had the legal right to defend himself. 18 January 1838. p.74, c5.

**1421 W. H. J.** *to* **THE** ***NATIONAL ENQUIRER*****. 7 January 1838. Buckingham.** Praises Elizabeth Hardin, a colored woman who purchased the freedom of several members of her family. 18 January 1838. p.75, c3.

**1422 B. LUNDY** *to* **n.n. 16 January 1838. Harrisburg, Pa.** Describes the anniversary meeting of the Pennsylvania AS. 18 January 1838. p.75, c4.

**1423 n.n. [A PENNSYLVANIAN]** *to* **THE EDITOR OF THE** ***NATIONAL ENQUIRER*** **[B. LUNDY]. n.d. Pennsylvania.** Praises the *National Enquirer* and the cause of abolitionism; hopes for a "favorable decision" in the debate on Texas taking place in Washington. 18 January 1838. p.75, c5.

**1424 M. N. Q.** *to* **n.n. [from the** ***Darby Republican*****] 5 January. Washington.** Describes the debate in the Senate on the president's message concerning the "Canadian disturbances." 18 January 1838. p.75, c5.

**1425 ELA** *to* **T. W. B. [extract] n.d. n.p.** Argues against the purchase of produce of slave labor. 18 January 1838. p.76, c1.

**1426 REV. GEO. W. GALE** *to* **THE** ***FRIEND OF MAN*****. [extract] 23 November. Galesburg.** Describes events taking place in Alton as consequences of Mr. Lovejoy's death. 18 January 1838. p.76, c4.

**1427 WM. WHIPPER** *to* **THE EDITOR OF THE** ***COLORED AMERICAN*****. 1 January 1838. Columbia.** Complains of the editor's failure to publish his letter expressing his views on the American Moral Reform Society. 25 January 1838. p.77, c1.

**1428 P. TILLINGHAST, REC. SECRETARY** *to* **MRS. LOVEJOY. [from the** ***Liberator*****] n.d. n.p.** Conveys the sympathies of the Providence Female AS for Mrs. Lovejoy in her bereavement. 25 January 1838. p.77, c2.

**1429 INHABITANTS OF THE CITY OF BATH** *to* **THE HOUSE OF LORDS AND THE HOUSE OF COMMONS. [from the** ***Bath and Cheltenham Gazette*****] n.d. Bath, England.** Petition for an end to the apprenticeship system in the British colonies. 25 January 1838. p.77, c3.

**1430 THE DUBLIN LADIES ASSOCIATION, AUXILIARY TO THE HIBERNIAN NEGRO'S FRIEND SOCIETY** *to* **THEIR CHRISTIAN COUNTRYWOMEN. [from the** ***Dublin Literary Gazette*****] 21 August 1837. Black Rock, Near Dublin.** Urges them to fight against slavery in the British colonies. 25 January 1838. p.77, c4.

**1431 n.n.** *to* **THE EDITORS OF THE** ***NATIONAL ENQUIRER*** **[B. LUNDY]. 10 January 1838. Washington.** States that he intends to present the anti-slavery petitions which Lundy sent to him to the House of Representatives. 25 January 1838. p.78, c6.

**1432 n.n.** *to* **THE EDITOR OF THE** ***NATIONAL ENQUIRER*** **[B. LUNDY]. 10 January 1838. Washington.** States that he has given the anti-slavery petitions received from Lundy to Senator McKean of Pennsylvania, who will submit them to the Senate. 25 January 1838. p.78, c6.

**1433 A REPRESENTATIVE IN CONGRESS** *to* **n.n. [extract] 15 January 1838. Washington.** States that he has submitted the recipient's anti-slavery petition to the House. 25 January 1838. p.78, c6.

**1434 C. C. BURLEIGH** *to* **E. M. DAVIS. [extract] 14 December 1837. Turk's Island Passage.** Describes his voyage to Haiti. 25 January 1838. p.78, c6.

**1435 GEO M. SAVMAN** *to* **THE PRESIDENT OF THE ABOLITION CONVENTION NOW IN SESSION AT HARRISBURG. 18 January 1838. Portsmouth.** States that he will allow members of the convention to eat breakfast at his house, but that he forbids Negroes and white men to eat at the same table. 25 January 1838. p.79, c1.

**1436 LEONIDAS** *to* **THE CITIZENS OF THE SOUTHERN STATES. 25 December 1837. n.p.** States that he has recently abandoned abolitionist principles; describes and condemns those principles; urges the South to defend its interests. 25 January 1838. p.79, c1.

**1437 W. H. BURLEIGH** *to* **FRIEND LUNDY. 6 January 1838. Penn's Grove, Chester County.** Describes his lecture tour in Pennsylvania and Delaware. 25 January 1838. p.79, c4.

**1438 AGNES** *to* **THE** ***NATIONAL ENQUIRER.*** **[extract] n.d. n.p.** Describes the sufferings of a slave woman. 25 January 1838. p.80, c1.

**1439 D.** *to* **FRIEND GOODELL. [from the** ***Friend of Man*****] n.d. n.p.** Encloses a poem entitled, "Song of the Hussites," by Rev. B. W. Newell. 25 January 1838. p.80, c2.

**1440 C. PHINDLE** *to* **n.n. [from the** ***Zion's Watchman*****] 7 December 1837. n.p.** Encloses a poem entitled, "Inscription under the Picture of an Aged Negro Woman," by James Montgomery. 25 January 1838. p.80, c2.

**1441 E.** *to* **n.n. n.d. n.p.** States that he does not hate his country despite his concern over the oppression that exists in it. 1 February 1838. p.81, c5.

**1442 GEO. W. GALE** *to* **MR. GOODELL. [from the** ***Friend of Man*****] 16 November 1837. Galesburg, Il.** Describes the formation of the Farmington AS. 1 February 1838. p.81, c6.

**1443 JOSHUA TINSON** *to* **FRIEND. 25 September 1837. Utica.** Describes the condition of the colored people in the West Indies and the effect of the emancipation law passed by the British Parliament. 1 February 1838. p.82, c2.

**1444 W. H. BURLEIGH** *to* **FRIEND LUNDY. 18 January 1838. Harrisburg.** Describes a lecture he delivered in East Nottingham and a debate on the subject of colonization and abolition in which he participated in Oxford village. 1 February 1838. p.82, c5.

**1445 A COLORED BALTIMORIAN** *to* **THE** ***NATIONAL ENQUIRER.*** **10 January 1838. Baltimore.** Condemns the pro-slavery resolution of the Methodist Georgia Conference. 1 February 1838. p.82, c6.

**1446 DAN. L. MILLER, JR., SAM. J. LEVICK, HENRY T. CHILD, DELEGATION FROM THE JUNIOR AS OF PHILADELPHIA** *to* **THE FIRST ANNUAL MEETING OF THE PENNSYLVANIA AS. 15 January 1838. Philadelphia.** Regret their inability to attend the meeting. 1 February 1838. p.83, c1.

**1447 ISAAC PARRISH** *to* **THE PRESIDENT AND MEMBERS OF THE PENNSYLVANIA AS. n.d. n.p.** Regrets his inability to attend the society's meeting; asks to be relieved of his duties as corresponding secretary for the Eastern District; praises the activities of the abolitionists. 1 February 1838. p.83, c4.

**1448 THE AS OF PENNSYLVANIA** *to* **THE SENATE AND HOUSE OF REPRESENTATIVES OF THE UNITED STATES. n.d. n.p.** Opposes the annexation of Texas. 1 February 1838. p.83, c6.

**1449 D. L. M.** *to* **THE EDITOR OF THE** *NATIONAL ENQUIRER* **[B. LUNDY]. n.d. n.p.** Encloses a poem written in response to Patton's resolution which provided for the tabling of anti-slavery petitions. 1 February 1838. p.84, c1.

**1450 ANTI-SLAVETRADER** *to* **MR. GODDARD. [from the** *Pennsylvania Chronicle*] **n.d. n.p.** Encloses an article calling for an end to slavery and the slave trade. 1 February 1838. p.84, c1.

**1451 WM. LLOYD GARRISON** *to* **E. M. DAVIS. 8 January 1838. Boston.** Regrets his inability to attend the meeting of the Pennsylvania AS; draws an analogy between the fight against slavery and the struggle for American independence. [partially illegible] 8 February 1838. p.85, c5.

**1452 JOSHUA TINSON** *to* **FRIEND. 25 September 1837. Utica.** Describes the condition of the colored people in the West Indies and the effect of the emancipation law passed by the British Parliament. [continued from 1 February 1838] 8 February 1838. p.85, c6.

**1453 LEWIS C. GUNN** *to* **EDWARD NEEDLES. 19 December 1837. Port au Prince, Hayti.** Encloses the journal kept during his voyage to Haiti. 8 February 1838. p.86, c2.

**1454 J. G. W. W.** *to* **THE PEOPLE OF PENNSYLVANIA. 27 January 1838. Philadelphia.** Objects to the amendment adopted by the Pennsylvania constitutional convention which restricts suffrage to white citizens. 8 February 1838. p.86, c5.

**1455 W. H. WINDER, JOHN G. STICKET, D. E. WILSON, AND C. WILLING** *to* **THE CONVENTION TO PROPOSE AMENDMENTS TO THE CONSTITUTION OF PENNSYLVANIA. n.d. n.p.** Justify the exclusion of free Negroes from rights granted to white citizens. 8 February 1838. p.87, c1.

**1456 W. H. WINDER, JOHN G. STICKET, D. E. WILSON, AND C. WILLING** *to* **THE CONVENTION TO PROPOSE AMENDMENTS TO THE CONSTITUTION OF PENNSYLVANIA. n.d. n.p.** Propose an amendment requiring the legislature to appropriate an annual sum for the purpose of colonizing Pennsylvania Negroes in Africa. 8 February 1838. p.87, c2.

**1457 A MEMBER OF THE LEGISLATURE OF OHIO** *to* **THE** *NATIONAL ENQUIRER.* **[extract] 6 January 1838. Columbus, Oh.** Returns a copy of the *National Enquirer* and condemns the paper. 8 February 1838. p.87, c4.

**1458 SOUTH** *to* **THE** *NATIONAL ENQUIRER.* **n.d. Milledgeville, Ga.** Returns a copy of the *National Enquirer* and applauds the murder of Lovejoy. 8 February 1838. p.87, c5.

**1459 n.n.** *to* **BENJAMIN LUNDY. 20 January 1838. n.p.** Praises the *National Enquirer* of 9 December 1837, an issue devoted to the question of the annexation of Texas. 8 February 1838. p.87, c5.

**1460 J. COFFIN** *to* **MR. EDITOR [B. LUNDY]. n.d. n.p.** Encloses the letter from Mary Dyer to the court which condemned her, written the day before her execution in 1639. 8 February 1838. p.88, c1.

**1461 MARY DYER** *to* **n.n. 26 October 1639. Boston.** Pleads her innocence; asks for repeal of laws against the Quakers. 8 February 1838. p.88, c1.

**1462 n.n.** *to* **n.n. [extract] 29 October. Houston, Tx.** Describes the debate in Texas concerning the financial affairs of the government. 8 February 1838. p.88, c3.

**1463 n.n.** *to* **n.n. [extract from a New Orleans paper] n.d. Texas.** Describes the corruption among members of the government of Texas. 8 February 1838. p.88, c3.

**1464 ANDREW DREW, COMMANDER OF ROYAL NAVY** *to* **THE HONORABLE A. N. M'NAB, COLONEL COMMANDING HER MAJESTY'S FORCES. 30 December. Chippewa.** Describes the destruction by his fleet of a "piratical vessel which had been plying between Navy Island and the American shore." 8 February 1838. p.88, c4.

**1465 LEWIS C. GUNN** *to* **EDWARD NEEDLES. 30 December 1837. Port au Prince, Hayti.** Describes the social, economic, and religious situation in Port-au-Prince. 15 February 1838. p.89, c2.

**1466 REV. J. G. PIKE** *to* **n.n. [from the** *New York Evangelist***] n.d. Derby, England.** Hopes for the abolition of slavery in America. 15 February 1838. p.89, c5.

**1467 MARY S. WILSON** *to* **WM. GOODELL. [from the** *Friend of Man***] 27 December 1837. Macedon.** Urges a boycott of the products of slave labor. 15 February 1838. p.89, c5.

**1468 n.n.** *to* **THE EDITOR OF THE** *COURIER***. [from the** *Boston Courier***] n.d. n.p.** Encloses a letter from Chief Justice Ward. 15 February 1838. p.89, c6.

**1469 CHIEF JUSTICE WARD** *to* **A COMMITTEE OF GENTLEMEN. [extract] n.d. n.p.** Opposes slavery and discusses the legal and constitutional aspects of the issue. 15 February 1838. p.89, c6.

**1470 W. H. J.** *to* **THE** *NATIONAL ENQUIRER***. 6 February 1838. Buckingham.** Encloses a letter for publication. 15 February 1838. p.90, c5.

**1471 A CITIZEN OF LAMBERTSVILLE, N.J.** *to* **W. H. J. n.d. n.p.** Reports on the case of George Nixon, a colored man of Lambertsville, who was arrested for harboring a colored woman claimed as a slave. 15 February 1838. p.90, c5.

**1472 A CITIZEN OF HAYTI** *to* **THE EDITOR OF THE** *NATIONAL ENQUIRER* **[B. LUNDY]. [extract] 15 January. Port-au-Prince, Hayti.** Describes the Haitian and English military preparations for the arrival of the French fleet in Haiti. 15 February 1838. p.91, c6.

**1473 CH. F. MITCHELL** *to* **SIR. [from the** *New York American***] 1 January 1838. Washington.** States that he opposes Patton's resolution limiting the right of petition, although he was prevented by illness from voting against it in the House. 15 February 1838. p.92, c3.

**1474 n.n.** *to* **n.n. [extract] n.d. Albany, N.Y.** Reports that anti-slavery resolutions will be passed by the lower house of the New York legislature but will be killed in the senate. 15 February 1838. p.92, c4.

1475 **CHARLES W. GARDNER, CHAIRMAN, BISHOP M. BROWN, DANIEL SCOTT, SIMON MURRAY, AND WM. DOUGLASS** *to* **THE OPPRESSED AMERICANS IN THE STATE OF PENNSYLVANIA, AND ALL OTHERS WHO MAY FEEL CONCERNED. n.d. n.p.** Representatives of a public meeting in Philadelphia call for a day of fast and prayer in protest of the proposed amendment to the Pennsylvania constitution which would exclude colored citizens from the right of suffrage. 15 February 1838. p.92, c5.

1476 **OBSERVER** *to* **MR. LUNDY. n.d. n.p.** Encloses an extract from a memorial to the Reform Convention. 22 February 1838. p.93, c2.

1477 **W. H. WINDER, JOHN G. STICKET, D. E. WILSON, AND C. WILLING** *to* **THE REFORM CONVENTION. [extract from the** ***Commercial Herald*****] n.d. n.p.** Propose a constitutional amendment requiring the Pennsylvania legislature to appropriate money for the purpose of colonizing Pennsylvania Negroes in Africa. 22 February 1838. p.93, c2.

1478 **A PHILANTHROPIST** *to* **A COLORED GENTLEMAN IN PHILADELPHIA. 9 February 1838. Brooklyn, N.Y.** Condemns the amendment to the Pennsylvania constitution excluding colored citizens from the right of suffrage; opposes the plan of colonizationists. 22 February 1838. p.93, c2.

1479 **MARY GREW, CORRESPONDING SECRETARY** *to* **FEMALE AS. 8 February 1838. n.p.** Announces on behalf of the Philadelphia Female AS that the Annual Convention of American Anti-Slavery Women will take place in Philadelphia during the third week in May. 22 February 1838. p.94, c5.

1480 **L. G. HAMILTON, CORRESPONDING SECRETARY** *to* **MR. BENJAMIN LUNDY. 17 January 1838. Port-au-Prince, Hayti.** Thanks Lundy for copies of the *National Enquirer* and the *Genius of Universal Emancipation;* describes the favorable reception accorded Burleigh and Gunn in Haiti. 22 February 1838. p.95, c2.

1481 **A MEMBER OF CONGRESS** *to* **A MEMBER OF THE JUNIOR AS OF PHILADELPHIA. [extract] n.d. n.p.** States that he was unable to present his correspondent's petition against the annexation of Texas, due to the limited amount of time allotted in the House for such presentations. 22 February 1838. p.95, c3.

1482 **A MEMBER OF CONGRESS** *to* **A MEMBER OF THE JUNIOR AS OF PHILADELPHIA. [extract] n.d. n.p.** Acknowledges the receipt of his petition against the annexation of Texas; expresses confidence that the present Congress will not agree to the annexation. 22 February 1838. p.95, c3.

1483 **n.n.** *to* **n.n. [from the** ***National Gazette*****] 1 February 1838. Harrisburg.** Describes a debate in the Pennsylvania senate concerning slavery. 22 February 1838. p.95, c3.

1484 **L. G. H.** *to* **n.n. [extract] 27 January. Port-au-Prince, Hayti.** Describes the preparations being made in Haiti for the arrival of the French; encloses a copy of the proceedings of a meeting of the Haytian Abolition Society. 22 February 1838. p.95, c4.

1485 **QUERIST** *to* **MR. EDITOR. 17 February. n.p.** Inquires as to the identity of the group signified by the term, "oppressed Americans," to whom a recently published circular was addressed. 22 February 1838. p.95, c4.

1486 **n.n.** *to* **A MERCANTILE HOUSE IN PHILADELPHIA. [extract from the** ***Philadelphia Exchange Books*****] 15 January. Trinidad de Cuba.** Describes rioting in Trinidad de Cuba by a group of maroons. 22 February 1838. p.95, c5.

**1487 J. BLANCHARD** *to* **DR. J. A. ALLEN, SECRETARY VERMONT AS. [from the** *Vermont Telegraph***] 26 January 1838. Near Cincinnati, Oh.** Urges the passage of a law by the Vermont legislature granting a bounty to merchants who sell produce of free labor. 22 February 1838. p.96, c3.

**1488 W. H. WINDER, JOHN G. STICKET, D. E. WILSON, AND C. WILLING** *to* **THE REFORM CONVENTION. [extract from the** *Commercial Herald and Pennsylvania Sentinel***] n.d. n.p.** Propose amendments to the Pennsylvania constitution barring colored people from owning property and providing for their colonization in Africa; offer biblical justification for slavery. 1 March 1838. p.97, c1.

**1489 JOSEPH PARRISH, ISAAC BARTON, JAMES MOTT, AND EIGHT OTHERS** *to* **THE PEOPLE OF COLOR IN THE STATE OF PENNSYLVANIA. February 1838. Philadelphia.** Urge them to renew their efforts to become virtuous Christians in the wake of the limitation of their rights by the Reform Convention. 1 March 1838. p.97, c2.

**1490 CHAS. W. GARDNER AND FRED'K A. HINTON, COMMITTEE** *to* **THE DELEGATES OF THE PEOPLE OF PHILADELPHIA, IN CONVENTION AT PHILADELPHIA ASSEMBLED. n.d. n.p.** Protest the exclusion of colored people from the right of suffrage, on behalf of the people of color of Philadelphia. 1 March 1838. p.97, c4.

**1491 TYRO** *to* **MR. LUNDY. 5 February 1838. n.p.** Justifies the attempts of the people of his town to prevent Burleigh from delivering an anti-slavery lecture, stating that the town has no one qualified to engage in a debate with a man like Burleigh. 1 March 1838. p.97, c5.

**1492 LEWIS C. GUNN** *to* **E. M. DAVIS. 13 January 1838. Port au Prince, Hayti.** Discusses the dietary and economic customs in Haiti; discusses the preparations being made for the arrival of the French squadron sent to Haiti to settle the indemnity question. 1 March 1838, p.97, c6.

**1493 EVAN WILLIAMS, PRESIDENT AND JOHN HOGARTH, SECRETARY** *to* **THE PRESIDENT AND MEMBERS OF THE AS OF THE CITY AND COUNTY OF PHILADELPHIA. 5 January 1838. Port-au-Prince.** Officers of the Haitian Abolition Society acknowledge the receipt of the Philadelphia AS's letter; urge them to persevere in their anti-slavery efforts despite opposition in the United States; enclose a copy of the proceedings of a meeting of the Board of Managers of the Haitian Abolition Society. 1 March 1838. p.98, c3.

**1494 CHARLES** *to* **THE EDITOR [B. LUNDY]. February 1838. Philadelphia.** Describes an exhibition presented by the students at a colored school. 1 March 1838. p.98, c4.

**1495 W. C. B.** *to* **FRIEND LUNDY. 1838. Philadelphia.** Urges abolitionists to refrain from buying the products of slave labor if they wish their actions to be consistent with their principles. 1 March 1838. p.98, c5.

**1496 OPPRESSED AMERICAN** *to* **FRIEND LUNDY. February 1838. Bridgewater, Bucks County, Pa.** Replies to "Querist," asking whether he believes that colored Americans are oppressed. 1 March 1838. p.99, c1.

**1497 ANSWER** *to* **MR. EDITOR [B. LUNDY]. n.d. n.p.** Replies to "Querist," stating that the colored people and the Indians are oppressed; defends the Whigs. 1 March 1838. p.99, c1.

**1498 L.** *to* **MR. EDITOR [B. LUNDY]. n.d. n.p.** Encloses a notice announcing the forthcoming publication by the AAS of a work on the laws of American slavery, written by David Lee Child. 1 March 1838. p.99, c1.

**1499 W. H. WINDER, JOHN G. STICKET, D. E. WILSON, AND C. WILLING** *to* **THE** *UNITED STATES GAZETTE.* **n.d. n.p.** Defend their memorial to the Reform Convention, which called for barring Negroes from property ownership and for their colonization in Africa. 1 March 1838. p.99, c2.

**1500 CHARLES C. BURLEIGH** *to* **THE EDITOR OF THE** *DELAWARE COUNTY REPUBLICAN.* **[extract] 3,5 January 1838. Port-au-Prince, Hayti.** Describes the celebration of Haitian independence; encloses an account of the celebration from the *Union.* 1 March 1838. p.100, c2.

**1501 WASHINGTON CORRESPONDENT** *to* **THE** *NEW YORK AMERICAN.* **n.d. Washington.** Reports that an "incredible" number of petitions against slavery and the annexation of Texas have recently been sent to Congress. 1 March 1838. p.100, c6.

**1502 THE REV. JAMES M. M'KIM** *to* **THE EDITOR OF THE** *NEW YORK EMANCIPATOR.* **6 February 1838. Washington, D.C.** Describes a journey by stage from Harrisburg to Washington; describes W. H. Williams's "slave-factory" in Washington. 8 March 1838. p.101, c2.

**1503 D. LEE CHILD** *to* **MESSRS. GARRISON AND PHELPS. 23 January 1838. Boston.** States that America has lost favor with liberal Europeans due to slavery and the treatment of the Indians; praises American institutions which have permitted abolitionists to voice their ideas. 8 March 1838. p.102, c1.

**1504 WOOLMAN** *to* **FRIEND LUNDY. n.d. n.p.** Encloses a letter to Henry Clay. 8 March 1838. p.102, c2.

**1505 n.n.** *to* **HENRY CLAY. 28 January 1838. Chester County, Pa.** Disagrees with remarks made by Clay and Senator Hoare during the Senate debate of 18 December concerning anti-slavery petitions. 8 March 1838. p.102, c2.

**1506 QUERIST** *to* **MR. EDITOR [B. LUNDY]. n.d. n.p.** Replies to the letters of "Answer" and "Oppressed American" concerning the identity of those signified by the term "oppressed Americans," to whom a circular published in the *National Enquirer* was addressed. 8 March 1838. p.102, c5.

**1507 H. B. STANTON** *to* **THE EXECUTIVE COMMITTEE OF THE PENNSYLVANIA STATE AS FOR THE EASTERN DISTRICT. 25 February 1838. New York.** Describes the activities of the AAS which necessitate great expenditures. 8 March 1838. p.103, c6.

**1508 A SON OF THE PILGRIMS** *to* **n.n. [from the** ***Richmond Whig*****] 31 December 1837. Washington City.** Concurs with an article in the *Richmond Whig* which stated that Southerners do not realize the extent to which abolitionism has gained support in the North. 8 March 1838. p.104, c4.

## [Pennsylvania Freeman]

**1509 WILLIAM SLADE** *to* **STUDENTS OF LANE SEMINARY, OHIO. 13 January 1838. Washington.** Acknowledges a letter from twenty-two Lane students approving his "recent course in the House of Representatives on the abolition of slavery and slave trade in the District of Columbia." 15 March 1838. p.1, c2.

**1510 GOVERNOR KENT** *to* **THE** *LIBERATOR.* **[extract] 28 February 1838. Hallowell, Me.** Recounts anti-slavery meetings in several Maine towns. 15 March 1838. p.1, c3.

**1511 J.M. McKIM** *to* **REV. JOSHUA LEAVITT. [from the** ***Emancipator*****] 14 February 1838. Pittsburgh.** Discusses his visits to two slave prisons. 15 March 1838. p.1, c5.

**1512 WASHINGTON CORRESPONDENT** *to* **THE** *BOSTON COURIER*. **[from the** *Emancipator*] **n.d. n.p.** Considers the Senate's actions regarding abolition. 15 March 1838. p.2, c1.

**1513 CORRESPONDENT IN MEXICO** *to* **THE** *EMANCIPATOR*. **n.d. n.p.** Describes the death of a house slave. 15 March 1838. p.2, c1.

**1514 B. FUSSELL** *to* **FRIEND WHITTIER. 10 March 1838. West Vincent.** Commends the works of Benjamin Lundy. 15 March 1838. p.2, c3.

**1515 L. C. GUNN** *to* **ESTEEMED FRIEND. 29 January 1838. Cape Haitian, Hayti.** Describes the Haitian countryside and villagers. 15 March 1838. p.2, c3.

**1516 MEMBER OF CONGRESS** *to* **THE EDITOR [B. LUNDY]. [extract] 11 March 1838. Washington.** Admonishes Congress of the dangers of Texas annexation. 15 March 1838. p.3, c4.

**1517 FRED K. WATTS** *to* **MR. CRABB. 27 February 1838. Carlisle.** Discusses the Supreme Court opinion on Negro suffrage. 15 March 1838. p.4, c1.

**1518 WILLIAM JACKSON** *to* **FRANCIS JACKSON. 11 April 1836. Washington, D.C.** Informs of the acquittal of Dr. Reuben Crandall; states that Crandall's health was harmed by his imprisonment. 15 March 1838. p.4, c5.

**1519 L. C. GUNN** *to* **n.n. 2 February 1838. Cape Haitian.** Characterizes Cape Haitian, noting its history and current appearance. 22 March 1838. p.1, c4.

**1520 DEBORAH B. L. WADE** *to* **THE LADIES OF THE SEVERAL BAPTIST CHURCHES IN NEW YORK CITY AND BROOKLYN. [extract] n.d. Tavoy, Burma.** Urges American Baptists to pray for emancipation. 22 March 1838. p.2, c4.

**1521 n.n.** *to* **R. G. WILLIAMS. [from the** *Emancipator*] **24 February 1838. Maryville, Tn.** Relates abolition progress in eastern Tennessee; encloses six copies of *Human Rights*. 22 March 1838. p.3, c4.

**1522 A FRIEND OF MAN** *to* **n.n. [from the** *Richmond Enquirer*] **n.d. n.p.** Speculates on methods of dealing with John Quincy Adams. 22 March 1838. p.3, c4.

**1523 MAJOR GENERAL JESSUP [sic]** *to* **THE SECRETARY OF WAR. 11 February 1838. Florida.** Advises that the Florida War be ended by moving Indian tribes to reservations. 22 March 1838. p.3, c5.

**1524 THE SECRETARY OF WAR** *to* **MAJOR GENERAL JESSUP [sic]. 1 March 1838. Washington.** Gives Jesup permission to make temporary treaties with the Seminoles as a last resort for peace. 22 March 1838. p.3, c5.

**1525 E. SIBLEY** *to* **REVEREND AND DEAR SIR. 11 November 1837. Bardstown, Ky.** Discusses abolition sentiment in Kentucky. 22 March 1838. p.4, c4.

**1526 ROBERT PURVIS** *to* **THE PEOPLE OF PENNSYLVANIA. n.d. n.p.** Appeals to Pennsylvanians to support the right of suffrage for all citizens of the state. 29 March 1838. p.1, c1.

**1527 CLARKSON** *to* **THE** *PENNSYLVANIA FREEMAN*. **n.d. Chester County, Pa.** Informs Northerners that their use of slave produce is a critical factor in the perpetuation of slavery. 29 March 1838. p.2, c1.

**1528 J. S. GREEN** *to* **n.n. [from the** *New York Emancipator***] 29 May 1837. Honolulu, Sandwich Islands.** Encourages prayers for emancipation in the United States. 29 March 1838. p.2, c6.

**1529 BENJAMIN LUNDY** *to* **FRIEND WHITTIER. 27 March 183[8]. Hayti.** Encloses a letter from Hezekiah Grice. 29 March 1838. p.3, c4.

**1530 HEZEKIAH GRICE** *to* **BENJAMIN LUNDY. [from the** *Union***] 15 February 1838. Port-au-Prince.** Provides a translation of the treaty between Haiti and France. 29 March 1838. p.3, c4.

**1531 B.** *to* **JOHN WHITTIER. n.d. n.p.** Discusses a racial outrage committed against a black man in Schuylkill. 29 March 1838. p.3, c5.

**1532 B.** *to* **n.n. [from the** *Emancipator***] n.d. n.p.** Reports the abolition of the apprenticeship program on Montserrat. 29 March 1838. p.3, c6.

**1533 n.n.** *to* **n.n. [extract from the** *Christian Witness***] n.d. Lake Shore.** Discusses progress and business of the county AS. 29 March 1838. p.4, c2.

**1534 WILLIAM H. BURLEIGH** *to* **n.n. [from the** *Liberator***] n.d. n.p.** Appeals to Pennsylvanians to reject black colonization. 5 April 1838. p.1, c2.

**1535 n.n.** *to* **THE EDITOR OF THE** ***LIBERATOR*****. [extract] n.d. n.p.** Disparages the slaveholder's strength and morality. 5 April 1838. p.1, c2.

**1536 n.n.** *to* **ANGELINA E. GRIMKE. [from the** *Liberator***] n.d. n.p.** Repents having once participated in slaveholding; deplores the practice. 5 April 1838. p.1, c3.

**1537 LEWIS C. GUNN** *to* **FRIEND. 22 January 1838. St. Marc, Hayti.** Characterizes the status of St. Marc; comments on people and appearances. 5 April 1838. p.2, c2.

**1538 MARY LUKENS, JR. AND JAMES FULTON, JR.** *to* **BENJAMIN LUNDY. 18 March 1838. East Fallowfield.** Commend Lundy as a "friend of freedom", on behalf of the East Fallowfield AS. 5 April 1838. p.2, c5.

**1539 BENJAMIN WILSON** *to* **COLORED AMERICANS. 24 March 1838. Philadelphia.** Advises blacks to heed the words of the Philadelphia Association for the Mental Improvement of People of Color regarding common sense and dignity. 5 April 1838. p.2, c5.

**1540 A GENTLEMAN IN SUSQUEHANNA COUNTY** *to* **n.n. n.d. n.p.** Discusses the progress of the abolitionist cause; comments on public discussions; considers the organization of society. 5 April 1838. p.3, c1.

**1541 Q.** *to* **FRIEND WHITTIER. n.d. n.p.** Wonders if "Doctor of Divinity" is a slave dealer. 5 April 1838. p.3, c5.

**1542 WESTON** *to* **JOHN WHITTIER. 2 April 1838. n.p.** Comments on article in the *Liberator* by Judge Tucker on the death of David Mapps. 5 April 1838. p.3, c5.

**1543 WM. B. SNEAD** *to* **THE EDITOR OF** ***ZION'S WATCHMAN*****. n.d. n.p.** Encourages dissolution of the Union. 5 April 1838. p.3, c5.

**1544 REVEREND JAMES WILSON** *to* **n.n. [from the** *Boston Herald***] n.d. n.p.** Compares the Himalayas to the Alps and the Alleghenies. 5 April 1838. p.4, c2.

**1545 C. ANTHONY AND GEORGE J. SMITH** *to* **THOMAS MORRIS. 23 February 1838. Ohio.** Protest the annexation of Texas to the Union. 5 April 1838. p.4, c3.

**1546 CARTER B. HARLAN** *to* **MR. MORRIS. 24 February 1838. Columbus, Oh.** Forwards a copy of the resolution passed by the Ohio legislature concerning the annexation of Texas. 5 April 1838. p.4, c5.

**1547 CORRESPONDENT** *to* **n.n. [from the** *Pennsylvania Inquirer***] n.d. Washington.** Discusses the likelihood of arson in two recent fires in Washington, D.C. 12 April 1838. p.1, c1.

**1548 HIPPOLYTE DE ST. ANTHOINE** *to* **ELIZUR WRIGHT, JR. [from the** *Emancipator***] 22 February 1838. Paris.** Discusses French emancipation. 12 April 1838. p.1, c2.

**1549 LEWIS C. GUNN** *to* **FRIEND. 22 January 1838. St. Marc.** Discusses the condition of the Haitians. 12 April 1838. p.1, c2.

**1550 JACOB M. ELLIS** *to* **THE** *PENNSYLVANIA FREEMAN.* **n.d. n.p.** Announces the Northern Liberties AS delegates chosen for a number of local conventions. 12 April 1838. p.2, c2.

**1551 J. H.** *to* **JOHN WHITTIER. n.d. n.p.** Considers principles of peace among abolitionists. 12 April 1838. p.2, c3.

**1552 n.n.** *to* **n.n. 28 March 1838. Washington, D.C.** Discusses the treaty between the United States and the Cherokees; criticizes injustices suffered by the Cherokees and the fraudulent nature of the treaty. 12 April 1838. p.2, c5.

**1553 HARRISBURG CORRESPONDENT** *to* **n.n. [from the** *Harrisburg Keystone***] n.d. n.p.** Reports the vote of the Pennsylvania legislature on the Cherokee treaty. 12 April 1838. p.2, c6.

**1554 THOMAS CLARKSON** *to* **THE CHAIRMAN OF THE ANTI-SLAVERY MEETING HELD AT IPSWICH, ENGLAND. 12 January 1838. Ipswich, England.** Expresses his views on the apprenticeship system established in the British West Indian colonies. 12 April 1838. p.2, c6.

**1555 HENRY W. DUCACHET** *to* **WM. H. SCOTT, ISAAC PARRISH, WM. HARNED, DANIEL MEATT, PETER WRIGHT, EASTERN EXECUTIVE COMMITTEE, ETC. 2 April 1838. Philadelphia.** Acknowledges receipt of a copy of "Address of the AS to Ministers of the Gospel in the State of Pennsylvania"; criticizes the address and the AS. 12 April 1838. p.3, c2.

**1556 P.** *to* **THE** *PENNSYLVANIA FREEMAN.* **n.d. n.p.** Relates the story of a white father who brought his two mulatto daughters to the slave market. 12 April 1838. p.3, c4.

**1557 F. E. MIZELL** *to* **n.n. 12 March. Jacksonville.** Recounts a mass murder by Indians. 12 April 1838. p.3, c5.

**1558 BENJAMIN WILSON** *to* **n.n. n.d. n.p.** Requests that local delegates attend the Annual Council of the Philadelphia Association for the Moral and Mental Improvement of the People of Color. 12 April 1838. p.3, c6.

**1559 N.** *to* **n.n. [from the** *New Hampshire Observer***] 12 February 1838. n.p.** Laments having left New England for Louisiana. 12 April 1838. p.4, c2.

**1560 A LADY IN MISSOURI** *to* **A FRIEND IN BOSTON. [extract] n.d. n.p.** Encourages female involvement in the abolitionist movement. 12 April 1838. p.4, c2.

**1561 LEWIS C. GUNN** *to* **ESTEEMED FRIEND. 23 February 1838. Port au Platte, Hayti.** Continues his discussion of Cape Haitian, Gen. Louis Etienne Bottex and the president's plantation. 19 April 1838. p.1, c4.

**1562 AN ABOLITIONIST OF THE OLD SCHOOL** *to* **FRIEND. 11 April 1838. New York.** Relates an incident with a colonizationist; comments on the movement for colonization in the North. 19 April 1838. p.2, c2.

**1563 CHANDLER DARLINGTON** *to* **THE** *PENNSYLVANIA FREEMAN.* **8 April 1838. n.p.** Announces a list of delegates chosen by the Kennett AS to attend the Female AS convention in Philadelphia. 19 April 1838. p.2, c3.

**1564 A.** *to* **THE** *PENNSYLVANIA FREEMAN.* **n.d. n.p.** Reports on efforts to gain subscribers. 19 April 1838. p.2, c3.

**1565 GERRIT SMITH** *to* **n.n. [from the** *Friend of Man***] n.d. n.p.** Comments on a series of discussions of abolition in Utica between himself, James Fenimore Cooper and E. B. Moorehouse. 19 April 1838. p. 2, c4.

**1566 MRS. E. C. DELAVAN** *to* **FRIEND. 16 March 1838. Ballston Centre.** Extols James Williams's pamphlet, "Advocate of Moral Reform." 19 April 1838. p.2, c5.

**1567 MRS. E. C. DELAVAN** *to* **n.n. 2 April. n.p.** Recommends that every family in Saratoga County receive a copy of James Williams's pamphlet, "Advocate of Moral Reform." 19 April 1838. p.2, c5.

**1568 WILLIAM SPRAGUE** *to* **OLIVER JOHNSON, ESQ. 28 March 1838. Warwick, R.I.** Acknowledges receipt of a letter from the Rhode Island AS soliciting his opinion on various political topics concerning abolition, and expresses his support for abolition. 19 April 1838. p.2, c5.

**1569 JAMES CANNINGS FULLER** *to* **WM. GOODELL. 3 March 1838. Skaneateles, N.Y.** Relates the story of a fugitive slave named George Robinson, who was born free in Connecticut but sold into slavery for eight years. 19 April 1838. p.4, c2.

**1570 S.** *to* **RESPECTED FRIEND. 14 April 1838. Burlington, N.J.** Forwards an account of a trial in Trenton, New Jersey, of several prominent gentlemen charged with rescuing fugitive slaves. 26 April 1838. p.1, c1.

**1571 C. C. BURLEIGH** *to* **n.n. [from the** *Delaware County Republican***] n.d. n.p.** Describes his tour of Haiti. 26 April 1838. p.1, c4.

**1572 PERRY WARREN** *to* **THE** *PENNSYLVANIA FREEMAN.* **16 April 1838. Philadelphia.** Submits the resolutions passed at the latest meeting of the Vigilant Committee of Philadelphia. 26 April 1838. p.2, c3.

**1573 JOSEPH PARRISH, JR.** *to* **JOHN WHITTIER. 17 April 1838. Burlington, N.J.** Reports on the Burlington AS; forwards the preamble and the first and second articles of its constitution. 26 April 1838. p.2, c3.

**1574 AN ELDER OF THE GEORGIA HOPEWELL PRESBYTERY** *to* **n.n. [from the** *Richmond Telegraph***] n.d. n.p.** Admonishes George Bourne for his abolitionist views. 26 April 1838. p.3, c1.

**1575 WM. S. PLUMMER** *to* **THE PRO-SLAVERY COMMITTEE ON CORRESPONDENCE. 1836. n.p.** Attacks abolitionists. 26 April 1838. p.3, c4.

**1576 A PHILADELPHIA NEW SCHOOL MAN** *to* **THE REVEREND A. CONVERSE. n.d. n.p.** Calls attention to Converse's repeated statements that he is not an abolitionist. 26 April 1838. p.3, c5.

**1577 B.** *to* **SIR. [from the** ***Emancipator*****] 1838. Troy.** Encloses a memorial entitled, "The Views of Slaveholders as Regards Slavery and Colonization," taken from a Richmond paper. 26 April 1838. p.4, c4.

**1578 AN AGED MEMBER OF THE METHODIST EPISCOPAL CHURCH** *to* **DR. FISK. [from** ***Zion's Watchman*****] n.d. n.p.** Admonishes Fisk for his anti-abolition views. 3 May 1838. p.1, c1.

**1579 A GENTLEMAN IN ILLINOIS** *to* **A FRIEND IN NEW YORK. [extract from the** ***Utica Friend of Man*****] n.d. n.p.** Worries that the Presbyterian church continues to support slavery. 3 May 1838. p.1, c2.

**1580 A.** *to* **THE** ***PENNSYLVANIA FREEMAN.*** **18 July 1837. Plymouth.** Appeals to the North to help abolish slavery. 3 May 1838. p.1, c4.

**1581 GEORGE BOURNE** *to* **THE** ***PENNSYLVANIA FREEMAN.*** **n.d. n.p.** Responds to the letter from "An Elder of the Georgia Hopewell Presbytery," warning slave-trading ministers to stay away from Philadelphia. 3 May 1838. p.1, c5.

**1582 A MEMBER OF THE CONVENTION** *to* **BROTHER WHITTIER. n.d. n.p.** Criticizes the address of the Pennsylvania AS; refutes the criticism of Ducachet. 3 May 1838. p.1, c6.

**1583 B. LUNDY** *to* **FRIEND WHITTIER. 27 April 1838. Philadelphia.** Thanks readers for their support of his abolitionist views and encourages more of the same. 3 May 1838. p.2, c2.

**1584 DR. HENRY PERRINE** *to* **HON. LOUIS McLANE. 1834. Compeachy.** Explains why American slaves are more productive than Cuban and West Indian slaves. 3 May 1838. p.2, c4.

**1585 n.n.** *to* **BROTHER WHITTIER. 21 April 1838. Bethany.** Describes a meeting held to form a CS. 3 May 1838. p.2, c5.

**1586 n.n.** *to* **SIR. 25 April 1838. Cincinnati.** Describes the explosion of the steamboat *Mozelle*, in which many died. 3 May 1838. p.3, c5.

**1587 MARY** *to* **FRIEND. 17 April 1838. Montreal.** Wonders why she has had no word from her friend or son since she escaped to freedom in Canada. 10 May 1838, p.1, c1.

**1588 THE BAPTIST UNION OF GREAT BRITAIN AND IRELAND** *to* **THE MINISTERS AND MEMBERS OF THE BAPTIST CHURCH IN THE U.S. 19 January 1838. London.** Pledges support in the struggle against slavery. 10 May 1838. p.1, c2.

**1589 N. KING** *to* **MR. EDITOR. [from the** ***Friend of Man*****] 14 April 1838. Hamilton, N.Y.** Comments on the outcome of a two-day discussion of abolition. 10 May 1838. p.1, c4.

**1590 PRISCILLA** *to* **MR. EDITOR. [from the** ***Philanthropist*****] n.d. n.p.** Discusses the status of women compared to that of men. 10 May 1838. p.1, c5.

**1591 JOHN G. WHITTIER** *to* **n.n. 6 May 1838. New York.** Reports on the annual business meeting of the AAS. 10 May 1838. p.2, c5.

1592 **WASHINGTON CORRESPONDENT** *to* **n.n. [extract] n.d. n.p.** Discusses a plot to expel the Cherokees from their lands by invoking the fraudulent treaty of New Echota. 10 May 1838. p.2, c6.

1593 **GOV. EDWARD EVERETT** *to* **EDMUND QUINCY, ESQ. [from the *Boston Daily Advertiser*] 26 April 1838. Boston.** Commends Thome and Kimball's *Tour in the West Indies*; supports immediate emancipation. 10 May 1838. p.3, c2.

1594 **S. H. EVERITT** *to* **n.n. [from the *Texas Telegraph*] 21 April. n.p.** States that he has submitted the preamble and joint resolution for annexation of Texas to the Senate for consideration. 10 May 1838. p.3, c3.

1595 **B. LUNDY** *to* **n.n. n.d. n.p.** Predicts the annexation of Texas to the Union. 10 May 1838. p.3, c3.

1596 **LEWIS C. GUNN** *to* **FRIEND WHITTIER. 7 May 1838. Philadelphia.** Writes that he has concluded his trip to Haiti. 10 May 1838. p.3, c4.

1597 **M. HAMPTON** *to* **THE *PENNSYLVANIA FREEMAN*. n.d. n.p.** Forwards a copy of the proceedings of the recent meeting of the Buckingham Female AS. 10 May 1838. p.3, c5.

1598 **JAMES P. ELLIS** *to* **THE *PENNSYLVANIA FREEMAN*. n.d. n.p.** Discloses names of the new officers of the Spring Garden AS. 10 May 1838. p.3, c5.

1599 **H. WETHERALD** *to* **THE *PENNSYLVANIA FREEMAN*. n.d. n.p.** Presents the names of the officers of the Philadelphia City AS. 10 May 1838. p.3, c5.

1600 **JACOB M. ELLIS** *to* **THE *PENNSYLVANIA FREEMAN*. n.d. n.p.** Resolves to increase the number of delegates representing the Northern Liberties AS at the convention to form a county AS. 10 May 1838. p.3, c5.

1601 **A COLERAIN ABOLITIONIST** *to* **FRIEND WHITTIER. 26 April 1838. Lancaster County.** Advises abstinence from slave-produced goods. 17 May 1838. p.2, c3.

1602 **J. CROSS** *to* **FRIEND WHITTIER. 11 May 1838. Philadelphia.** Forwards an account of a steamboat trip from Delaware to Philadelphia during which discussion of slavery was prohibited. 17 May 1838. p.2, c3.

1603 **FRANCIS JAMES** *to* **SAMUEL WEBB AND WM. H. SCOTT. 22 December 1837. Harrisburg.** Acknowledges receipt of an invitation to attend the dedication of Pennsylvania Hall; commends the principles to which the building is dedicated. 17 May 1838. p.2, c4.

1604 **GERRIT SMITH** *to* **MESSRS. S. WEBB AND WM. H. SCOTT. 26 December 1837. Peterboro'.** Declines an invitation to speak before the stockholders and builders of Pennsylvania Hall. 17 May 1838. p.2, c5.

1605 **THADDEUS STEVENS** *to* **SAMUEL WEBB AND OTHERS. 4 May 1838. Gettysburg.** Regrets that he cannot attend the opening of Pennsylvania Hall; supports free discussion. 17 May 1838. p.2, c5.

1606 **THEODORE D. WELD** *to* **S. WEBB AND WM. H. SCOTT. 3 January 1838. New York.** Regrets that he cannot deliver an address at the opening of Pennsylvania Hall due to illness; remarks on misuse of the word "free." 17 May 1838. p.2, c5.

**1607 JOHN QUINCY ADAMS** *to* **SAMUEL WEBB AND WILLIAM H. SCOTT. 19 January 1838. Washington.** Declines to deliver an address at the opening of Pennsylvania Hall; believes that a native Philadelphian, rather than he, should address the audience. 17 May 1838. p.2, c5.

**1608 NATHAN S. S. BEMAN** *to* **RESPECTED FRIENDS. 8 January 1838. Troy, New York.** Accepts an invitation to deliver an address at the opening of Pennsylvania Hall. 17 May 1838. p.2, c6.

**1609 NATHAN S. S. BEMAN** *to* **RESPECTED FRIENDS. 12 April 1838. Troy, New York.** Regrets that illness will prevent him from delivering an address at Pennsylvania Hall. 17 May 1838. p.2, c6.

**1610 DAVID PAUL BROWN** *to* **S. WEBB AND WM. H. SCOTT, ESQS. 25 December 1837. n.p.** Accepts an invitation to deliver the first address in Pennsylvania Hall. 17 May 1838. p.3, c1.

**1611 WILLIAM JAY** *to* **SIR. 12 May 1838. Bedford, New York.** Reports on a colonization meeting at Bethany; corrects Mr. Torry's statements concerning Jay's estimate of the number of slaves colonized by the society. 17 May 1838. p.3, c3.

**1612 A CITIZEN OF NEW JERSEY** *to* **HONORABLE S. L. SOUTHARD. 1 May 1838. Woodbury, N.J.** Comments on Southard's conduct as the counsel of the slave catcher Donnahower and his associates at the recent Trenton trial. 17 May 1838. p.3, c3.

**1613 n.n.** *to* **THE EDITOR OF THE *EMANCIPATOR*. 18 November 1837. Kaluaaha, Sandwich Islands.** States that every missionary at that location supports immediate emancipation; requests copies of the *Emancipator*. 17 May 1838. p.3, c4.

**1614 HONORABLE THOMAS MORRIS** *to* **SAMUEL WEBB, J. M. TRUMAN AND WM. McKEE. 30 January 1838. Washington.** Acknowledges an invitation to speak at the opening of Pennsylvania Hall; remarks on the building of the hall. 24 May 1838. p.1, c1.

**1615 HONORABLE THOMAS MORRIS** *to* **JOSEPH M. TRUMAN, WILLIAM H. SCOTT, WILLIAM McKEE, AND SAMUEL WEBB. 11 May 1838. Washington.** Regrets that he cannot be present at the opening of Pennsylvania Hall; comments at length on the responsibility of Americans concerning the abolition of slavery. 24 May 1838. p.1, c1.

**1616 WALTER FORWARD** *to* **SAMUEL WEBB, G. M. [sic] SCOTT AND WM. McKEE. 7 February 1838. Philadelphia.** Agrees to attend the opening of Pennsylvania Hall; comments on "free discussion." 24 May 1838. p.1, c5.

**1617 WILLIAM A. ADAIR** *to* **CHRISTIAN FRIENDS AND FELLOW LABORERS. 5 February 1838. Northeast Pennsylvania.** Acknowledges an invitation to speak at the Pennsylvania Hall. 24 May 1838. p.1, c5.

**1618 FREDERICK W. GRAVES** *to* **COMMITTEE OF PENNSYLVANIA HALL ASSOCIATION. 2 March 1838. Alton.** Regrets that he cannot attend the opening of Pennsylvania Hall. 24 May 1838. p.1, c5.

**1619 WILLIAM JAY** *to* **MESSRS. WEBB AND SCOTT. 3 January 1838. Bedford, Westchester County, New York.** Acknowledges an invitation to speak at Pennsylvania Hall; remarks on the political power of abolitionists. 24 May 1838. p.1, c5.

**1620 WILLIAM SLADE** *to* **MR. SAMUEL WEBB. 2 January 1838. Washington.** Acknowledges an invitation to deliver an address at the opening of Pennsylvania Hall; regrets that congressional responsibilities will prevent his attending. 24 May 1838. p.1, c6.

**1621 HIRAM WILSON** *to* **FRIEND WHITTIER. 15 May 1838. Philadelphia.** Relates the incidents one slave encountered on his attempted escape. 24 May 1838. p.1, c6.

**1622 GEORGE WASHINGTON** *to* **ROBERT MORRIS. [extract] n.d. n.p.** Expresses his desire to see the slaves emancipated; states that it can be properly achieved only by legislative authority. 24 May 1838. p.2, c3.

**1623 GEORGE WASHINGTON** *to* **LAFAYETTE. [extract] n.d. n.p.** Commends Lafayette's recent purchase of an estate in order to emancipate the slaves; remarks that petitions were presented to Congress for abolition of slavery, "but they could scarcely obtain a hearing." 24 May 1838. p.2, c3.

**1624 GEORGE WASHINGTON** *to* **SIR JOHN SINCLAIR. [extract] n.d. n.p.** Details some reasons for depreciation of Southern land. 24 May 1838. p.2, c3.

**1625 GEORGE WASHINGTON** *to* **JOHN F. MERCER. [extract] n.d. n.p.** Recommends abolition. 24 May 1838. p.2, c3.

**1626 GEORGE WASHINGTON** *to* **PHYLLIS WHEATLEY. [extract] 28 February 1776. Cambridge.** Acknowledges receipt of a poem Miss Wheatley sent to him; thanks her for her tribute; invites her to visit him in Cambridge. 24 May 1838. p.2, c3.

**1627 DEMOCRATIC PARTY MEMBER** *to* **SIR. [extract] 20 May 1838. Washington, D.C.** Comments on the recent burning of Pennsylvania Hall; congratulates the Pennsylvania AS, declaring that the outrage will do them more good than harm. 24 May 1838. p.2, c4.

**1628 REVEREND EDWARD BEECHER** *to* **SIR. [extract] 11 March 1838. Illinois College.** Doubts that he will travel East in the spring but declares that if he does, he will attend the anniversary of the AAS. 24 May 1838. p.4, c2.

**1629 F. JULIUS LEMOYNE** *to* **LEWIS TAPPAN. 27 February 1838. Washington County, Pa.** Declines an invitation to participate in the anniversary of the AAS, due to other responsibilities. 24 May 1838. p.4, c2.

**1630 JOHN QUINCY ADAMS** *to* **LEWIS TAPPAN. 7 April 1838. Washington.** States that he will not be able to attend the anniversary of the AAS in May, due to other responsibilities. 24 May 1838. p.4, c2.

**1631 J. S.** *to* **MR. EDITOR. [from the** ***Ohio Philanthropist*****] n.d. n.p.** Recalls an attempt by five slave-owning clergymen to hold an auction on board a cotton boat. 24 May 1838. p.4, c3.

**1632 CHANDLER DARLINGTON** *to* **THE** ***PENNSYLVANIA FREEMAN.*** **n.d. n.p.** Announces the most recent resolutions passed by the Kennett AS. 31 May 1838. p.1, c5.

**1633 LEWIS TAPPAN** *to* **REVEREND THOMAS P. HUNT. [from the** ***Emancipator*****] 14 May 1838. New York.** Admonishes Hunt for neglecting to emancipate 1,000 slaves and commend them to Tappan's care, as he had promised three years earlier. 31 May 1838. p.2, c1.

**1634 BLAND** *to* **n.n. [extract from the** ***Richmond Enquirier*****] 10 November 1837. n.p.** Expresses his indignation at the picture of a woman on the front page of the *Richmond Enquirer*; advises parents to think critically about their children's books. 31 May 1838. p.2, c1.

**1635 JOHN G. WATMOUGH** *to* **THE PUBLIC. n.d. n.p.** Puts forward the reasons for his inability to protect both Pennsylvania Hall and the meeting with the Committee of Pennsylvania Hall. 31 May 1838. p.2, c5.

**1636 DANIEL NEALL, SAMUEL WEBB AND PETER WRIGHT** *to* **THE** ***PENNSYLVANIA FREEMAN.*** **n.d. n.p.** Reply to Sheriff Watmough concerning the order of events which took place before and during the mob attack on Pennsylvania Hall. 31 May 1838. p.2, c6.

**1637 T. D. PUERIFOY** *to* **BROTHER CAPERS. [from the** ***Southern Christian Advocate*****] n.d. n.p.** Informs of the murder of his family and slaves by Indians at the Alachua Mission. 31 May 1838. p.3, c4.

**1638 DANIEL NEALL AND SAMUEL WEBB** *to* **THE EDITOR OF THE** ***PENNSYLVANIA FREEMAN*** **[J. G. WHITTIER]. 25 May 1838. Philadelphia.** Request publication of a reply to an article in the *Public Ledger*, which the latter had refused to print. 31 May 1838. p.3, c5.

**1639 DANIEL NEALL AND SAMUEL WEBB** *to* **THE PUBLIC. 24 May 1838. Philadelphia.** Respond to attacks by many editors on the purpose of Pennsylvania Hall and its destruction by mob violence. 31 May 1838. p.3, c5.

**1640 WM. McKEE** *to* **SAMUEL WEBB. 24 May 1838. Philadelphia.** Affirms that a letter from the mayor has been delivered as promised. 31 May 1838. p.3, c5.

**1641 EUROPEAN CORRESPONDENT** *to* **n.n. [from the** ***New York American*****] 30 January 1838. Paris.** Discusses the French abolition societies. 31 May 1838. p.4, c2.

**1642 J. G. BIRNEY, ESQ.** *to* **F. H. ELMORE. 8 March 1838. Anti-Slavery Rooms, New York.** Replies to the fourteen questions Elmore put to him regarding the AAS. 7 June 1838. p.1, c1.

**1643 GEORGE M. ALSOP** *to* **n.n. 30 May 1838. Philadelphia.** Submits the resolutions passed by the Pennsylvania Hall Association. 7 June 1838. p.1, c6.

**1644 C. MARRIOTT** *to* **JOSHUA LEAVITT. [from the** ***Emancipator*****] 27 May 1838. Hudson, New York.** Describes the detainment of Prince Matice, a free Negro of New York who was held as a runaway slave in a Virginia jail. 7 June 1838. p.2, c1.

**1645 n.n.** *to* **n.n. [extract from the** ***New Haven Herald*** **via the** ***Massachusetts Spy*****] 30 April 1838. Barbadoes.** Affirms that apprentices in Barbados will be freed on 1 August. 7 June 1838. p.2, c1.

**1646 J. G. WHITTIER** *to* **n.n. 28 May 1838. New York.** Discusses the New York Yearly Meeting of the Society of Friends. 7 June 1838. p.2, c2.

**1647 J. G. WHITTIER** *to* **n.n. 29 May 1838. Boston.** Reports the proceedings of the New England Anti-Slavery Convention. 7 June 1838. p.2, c2.

**1648 J. G. WHITTIER** *to* **n.n. 1 June 1838. Boston.** Continues his report of the proceedings of the New England Anti-Slavery Convention. 7 June 1838. p.2, c2.

**1649 GEORGE W. LEWIS** *to* **n.n. 30 May 1838. Great Valley, Chester County.** Deplores the destruction of Pennsylvania Hall. 7 June 1838. p.3, c2.

**1650 G. W. B.** *to* **J. G. BIRNEY, ESQ. 29 May 1838. New Haven.** Reports on the proceedings of the Connecticut legislature. 7 June 1838. p.3, c3.

**1651 ELIZABETH PEARSON** *to* **THE PUBLIC. 1 June 1838. Philadelphia.** The secretary of the Association for the Care of Colored Orphans thanks the helpful citizens who came to their aid during the recent burning of the shelter for colored orphans. 7 June 1838. p.3, c4.

**1652 B. LUNDY** *to* **THE CITIZENS OF PHILADELPHIA. 4 June 1838. Philadelphia.** Describes the recent burning of Pennsylvania Hall; states that many of his books and papers were destroyed and scattered during the fire, and asks that any found be returned to him. 7 June 1838. p.3, c4.

**1653 n.n. [MEMBER OF CONGRESS]** *to* **n.n. [extract] 22 May 1838. Washington.** Regrets the destruction of Pennsylvania Hall. 7 June 1838. p.3, c5.

**1654 J. G. BIRNEY, ESQ.** *to* **HON. F. H. ELMORE. n.d. n.p.** Continues his response to questions posed by Elmore concerning the AAS. 14 June 1838. p.1, c3.

**1655 WILLIAM C. BETTS AND ALICE ELIZA HAMBLETON** *to* **THE** ***PENNSYLVANIA FREEMAN.*** **n.d. n.p.** Forward names of members of the new correspondence committee of the Requited Labor Convention. 14 June 1838. p.1, c5.

**1656 ELI HAMBLETON** *to* **THE** ***PENNSYLVANIA FREEMAN.*** **n.d. n.p.** Sends a list of resolutions passed by the Clarkson AS. 14 June 1838. p.1, c6.

**1657 SAMUEL WEBB** *to* **THE** ***PENNSYLVANIA FREEMAN.*** **n.d. Philadelphia.** Encloses a letter for publication. 14 June 1838. p.1, c6.

**1658 A FRIEND OF LIBERTY AND HUMANITY** *to* **n.n. 6 June 1838. Philadelphia.** Forwards a $100 donation for the Pennsylvania Hall Fund. 14 June 1838. p.1, c6.

**1659 HUMANITAS** *to* **BRETHREN. n.d. n.p.** Appeals to abolitionists to abstain from the purchase and use of products of unrequited toil. 14 June 1838. p.2, c3.

**1660 THOMAS M'CLINTOCK** *to* **n.n. [extract] 28 May 1838. Waterloo.** Comments on the burning of Pennsylvania Hall. 14 June 1838. p.2, c4.

**1661 STEPHEN H. GLOUCESTER** *to* **MY PHILADELPHIA FRIENDS. [from the** ***Colored American*****] June 1838. Philadelphia.** Announces that the new publishers of the *Colored American* are Messrs. Day, Bell and Gloucester and that there will now be a Philadelphia edition. 14 June 1838. p.2, c5.

**1662 J. G. WHITTIER** *to* **n.n. 3 June 1838. Boston.** Recounts the close of the New England Anti-Slavery Convention and the topics discussed. 14 June 1838. p.2, c6.

**1663 N. P. ROGERS, ESQ.** *to* **H. B. STANTON. 26 April 1838. Plymouth, N.H.** Recommends increased fervor in the anti-slavery cause, arguing that slavery should become a concern for all. 14 June 1838. p.4, c4.

**1664 L. M. SARGENT, ESQ.** *to* **n.n. [extract] 22 April 1838. Boston.** Describes two incidents regarding temperance. 14 June 1838. p.4, c5.

**1665 A SOUTHERNER AND AN EYE-WITNESS** *to* **THE EDITOR OF THE** ***NEW ORLEANS TRUE AMERICAN.*** **18 May 1838. Philadelphia.** Reports on the burning of Pennsylvania Hall and describes how firemen refused to put out the blaze. 21 June 1838. p.1, c1.

**1666 THOMAS LAFON** *to* **MR. LOVEJOY. [from the** ***Alton Observer*****] 28 September 1837. Sandwich Islands.** Discusses missions and slavery. 21 June 1838. p.1, c2.

**1667 J. G. BIRNEY, ESQ.** *to* **HON. F. H. ELMORE. n.d. n.p.** Continues answering questions asked by Elmore concerning the AAS. 21 June 1838. p.1, c3.

**1668 REASON** *to* **THE EDITOR [J. G. WHITTIER]. n.d. n.p.** Describes a sermon of Reverend Barnes on the "Supremacy of the Laws," in which he alluded to criticism of a sermon by another in a previous issue of the *Pennsylvania Freeman*. 21 June 1838. p.2, c3.

**1669 S. M. DOUGLASS** *to* **THE** ***PENNSYLVANIA FREEMAN*. n.d. n.p.** Reports on the meeting of the Philadelphia Female AS. 21 June 1838. p.2, c3.

**1670 JOSEPH YARDLEY** *to* **n.n. n.d. n.p.** Reports on the annual meeting of the Bucks County AS. 21 June 1838. p.2, c4.

**1671 SAMUEL WEBB** *to* **THE** ***PENNSYLVANIA FREEMAN*. 18 June 1838. 307 Mulberry Street.** Offers a new book about Pennsylvania Hall. 21 June 1838. p.2, c4.

**1672 JOHN WESLEY** *to* **MR. WILBERFORCE. 24 February 1781. n.p.** Condemns any form of oppression. 21 June 1838. p.2, c6.

**1673 n.n.** *to* **n.n. [extract from a London paper] 15 February. Port-au-Prince, Hayti.** Praises President Boyer of Haiti. 21 June 1838. p.4, c4.

**1674 A.** *to* **MR. JONES. 17 May 1838. Philadelphia.** Describes Pennsylvania Hall and its occupants on the morning of May 17; calls the hall a "tabernacle of mischief and fanaticism." 28 June 1838. p.1, c2.

**1675 A.** *to* **MR. JONES. 17 May 1838. Philadelphia.** Presents an account of the burning of Pennsylvania Hall; acknowledges that he took part in vandalizing the building. 28 June 1838. p.1, c2.

**1676 J. G. BIRNEY** *to* **F. H. ELMORE. n.d. n.p.** Continues correspondence on the questions asked by Elmore concerning the AAS. 28 June 1838. p.1, c.3.

**1677 W. L. RAKESTRAW** *to* **THE** ***PENNSYLVANIA FREEMAN*. 17 June 1838. Bart.** Forwards the most recent resolutions passed by the Colerain AS. 28 June 1838. p.2, c1.

**1678 A JUNIOR** *to* **J. G. WHITTIER. 21 June 1838. Philadelphia.** Discusses the "faithfulness" of a slave, in regard to an attack on Michillimackinac Island and the rescue of the body of an officer by a slave. 28 June 1838. p.2, c1.

**1679 WM. W. TAYLOR** *to* **THE** ***PENNSYLVANIA FREEMAN*. n.d. n.p.** Forwards the preamble and resolutions of the meeting of the citizens of Schuylkill Township. 28 June 1838. p.2, c1.

**1680 n.n.** *to* **MR. EDITOR [J. G. WHITTIER]. n.d. n.p.** Deplores a judge's manipulation of New Jersey law in a fugitive slave case. 28 June 1838. p.2, c2.

**1681 JAMES G. BIRNEY** *to* **REVEREND W. FISK. 10 May 1838. New York.** Challenges remarks made by Fisk before the CS of New York. 28 June 1838. p.2, c2.

**1682 J. G. BIRNEY** *to* **THE EDITOR [J. G. WHITTIER]. 19 June 1838. n.p.** Encloses his letter to Dr. Fisk, wondering why it had been returned with no response. 28 June 1838. p.2, c2.

**1683 THE FREE STATE** *to* **THE EDITOR. [from the** ***New York American*****] 16 June. n.p.** Recalls Van Buren's commitment to the South and the institution of slavery. 28 June 1838. p.2, c2.

**1684 J. R.** *to* **n.n. [from the** ***Emancipator*****] n.d. n.p.** Encloses an account of funds recently collected by the American Bible Society, in order to prove that the abolitionist cause is still thriving. 28 June 1838. p.2, c3.

**1685 D. RUGGLES** *to* **n.n. [from the** ***Emancipator*****] 19 June 1838. New York.** Appeals to the friends and families of three free blacks arrested and sold in New Orleans, asking them to provide testimony necessary for their release. 28 June 1838. p.2, c4.

**1686 J. CROSS** *to* **BROTHER JOHNSON. [from the** ***New York Evangelist*****] 9 June 1838. Chili.** Advises of the resolutions adopted by the Genesee Consociation for the abolition of slavery. 28 June 1838. p.2, c4.

**1687 JAMES G. BIRNEY** *to* **HON. F. H. ELMORE. n.d. n.p.** Concludes his answer of Elmore's questions on the AAS. 5 July 1838. p.1, c2.

**1688 F. H. ELMORE** *to* **JAMES G. BIRNEY, ESQ. 5 May 1838. Washington.** States that Birney has answered more than required, but thinks he is wrong on many points. 5 July 1838. p.1, c4.

**1689 J. G. BIRNEY** *to* **n.n. 24 May 1838. n.p.** Defends his answers against Elmore's most recent attack. 5 July 1838. p.1, c5.

**1690 JOHN BURR, REVEREND MORRIS BROWN, JOHN B. ROBERTS, THOMAS BUTLER, JAMES McCRUMMILL, JAMES P. CLAY, AND JAMES FORTEN, JR.** *to* **THE** ***PENNSYLVANIA FREEMAN*****. 12 June 1838. Philadelphia.** Forward a list of resolutions of the American Moral Reform Society and invite the public to attend their second anniversary meeting. 5 July 1838. p.1, c6.

**1691 H.** *to* **ESTEEMED FRIEND. 25 June. n.p.** Encloses a letter from a friend and asks that it be published. 5 July 1838. p.2, c1.

**1692 A FEMALE HEARER** *to* **RESPECTED SIR. 20 June 1838. Philadelphia.** Comments concerning Christian ministers and their obligation to pray for slaves. 5 July 1838. p.2, c1.

**1693 CORRESPONDENT** *to* **n.n. [from the** ***Baltimore Chronicle*****] n.d. n.p.** Discusses a debate between Clay and Calhoun. 5 July 1838. p.3, c1.

**1694 S. S. SCHMUCKER** *to* **THE EDITOR. [from the** ***Colonization Herald*****] 6 June 1838. Gettysburg.** States his reasons for declining the position of vice-president of the ACS. 5 July 1838. p.3, c2.

**1695 A. C. B.** *to* **FRIEND. [from the** ***Baltimore Sun*****] 25 June 1838. Baltimore.** Reports the death by drowning of a man suspected of being a fugitive slave. 5 July 1838. p.3, c3.

**1696 A. C. B.** *to* **FRIEND. 25 June 1838. Baltimore.** Relates an episode in which a fugitive was betrayed by another black and subsequently drowned in his attempt to escape. 5 July 1838. p.3, c3.

**1697 LEWIS TAPPAN** *to* **THE EDITOR. [from the** ***Liberator*****] 15 June 1838. New York.** Corrects a report of Tappan's recent interview with Vice-President Johnson. 5 July 1838. p.4, c2.

**1698 MATTHEW FORSTER** *to* **E. WRIGHT, JR. 10 May 1838. Newcastle upon Tyne.** Encloses a letter from Dr. J. Bowring; comments on the apprenticeship system in the British colonies; informs that the emancipation question will be put to the House of Commons on 22 May 1838. 5 July 1838. p.4, c3.

**1699 DR. BOWRING** *to* **MARIA. 2 December 1837. Grand Cairo, Egypt.** Describes his visit to Mahmoud Ali to ask him to end the slave trade. 5 July 1838. p.4, c3.

**1700 T. F.** *to* **BROTHER CHESTER. [from the** *Cincinnati Journal***] 11 June 1838. Palmyra, Marion County, Mo.** Discusses anti-slavery sentiment in Palmyra. 12 July 1838. p.1, c1.

**1701 J. P., JR.** *to* **THE** *PENNSYLVANIA FREEMAN***. 30 June 1838. Burlington, N.J.** Discusses the trial of two blacks as alleged fugitives from labor. 12 July 1838. p.2, c3.

**1702 AEQUALITAS** *to* **THE** *PENNSYLVANIA FREEMAN***. n.d. n.p.** Appeals for freedom of speech. 12 July 1838. p.2, c4.

**1703 B. L.** *to* **THE** *PENNSYLVANIA FREEMAN***. 10 July 1838. Philadelphia.** Rejoices that Texas failed to obtain statehood. 12 July 1838. p.3, c6.

**1704 N. P. ROGERS** *to* **THE READERS OF THE NEW HAMPSHIRE** *HERALD OF FREEDOM***. June 1838. Plymouth, N.H.** Informs that he will succeed the late J. H. Kimball as editor of the *Herald*. 12 July 1838. p.4, c1.

**1705 n.n.** *to* **n.n. [extract from the** *Emancipator***] 24 August 1837. Monrovia.** Shows concern for the hatred of whites exhibited by new Liberians. 12 July 1838. p.4, c3.

**1706 n.n.** *to* **n.n. [extract from the** *Emancipator***] 12 May 1838. Liberia.** Describes dismal conditions in Liberia. 12 July 1838. p.4, c3.

**1707 P.** *to* **FRIEND WHITTIER. n.d. n.p.** Encloses a letter from a slaveholder who asks the new employer of his runaway slave either to return her to Maryland or to send money for her children, who are left behind. 12 July 1838. p.4, c5.

**1708 C.** *to* **DR. SIR. n.d. n.p.** Expresses concern for her children, whom she left in the care of another slave when she escaped. 12 July 1838. p.4, c5.

**1709 JOSEPH VANCE** *to* **THE HONORABLE MR. GOODE. 24 February 1838. Columbus, Oh.** Protests the annexation of Texas. 19 July 1838. p.1, c2.

**1710 LEWIS C. GUNN** *to* **FRIEND WHITTIER. n.d. n.p.** Criticizes an article in the *Philadelphia Observer* entitled, "Renunciation of Presbyterianism." 19 July 1838. p.2, c3.

**1711 LIEUTENANT GOVERNOR WILLIAMS** *to* **n.n. [extract] 8 May 1838. Liberia.** Describes the status of emigrants in Liberia and the destructive policies of the ACS. 19 July 1838. p.2, c5.

**1712 J. B. JOHNSTON** *to* **n.n. n.d. n.p.** Considers the resolutions of the Western Presbytery of the Reformed Presbyterian Church of Cincinnati concerning slavery. 19 July 1838. p.3, c1.

**1713 J. C.** *to* **THE EDITOR [J. G. WHITTIER]. n.d. n.p.** Discloses the true status of agriculture in Liberia. 19 July 1838. p.3, c5.

**1714 CAPTAIN WILLIAM C. WATERS** *to* **THE REVEREND DOCTOR PROUDFIT. [from the** *Colonization Herald***] 21 June 1838. New York.** Details the advantages of life in Liberia, but warns of extreme hardships. 19 July 1838. p.4, c4.

**1715 MANY PLANTERS** *to* **JOHN B. RITTENHOUSE, ELISHA YOUNG, JOHN M. BATES, SOLOMON McALPIN, E. D. WHITEHEAD, AND JOHN J. WINTON, ESQS. [from the** *Emancipator***] 15 June 1838. Clinton.** Question the legislative candidates about their domestic policies. 19 July 1838. p.4, c5.

**1716 n.n.** *to* **n.n. [extract] n.d. n.p.** Promises to carry on the fight for abolition even though he has been dropped from the lecture circuit by the executive committee. 19 July 1838. p4, c6.

**1717 HENRY B. STANTON** *to* **BROTHER LEAVITT. [from the** ***Emancipator*****] 14 July 1838. New York.** Reports on his tour in western New York. 26 July 1838. p.2, c2.

**1718 GERRIT SMITH** *to* **PRESIDENT SCHMUCKER. 19 June 1838. Peterboro'.** Compares his and Schmucker's views on colonization and slavery. 26 July 1838. p.2, c4.

**1719 CORRESPONDENT** *to* **n.n. [from the** ***Friend of Man*****] n.d. New Milford, Ct.** Quotes the sentiments of an anti-abolition preacher. 26 July 1838. p.3, c3.

**1720 JOHN CROSS** *to* **BROTHER GOODELL. [from the** ***Friend of Man*****] n.d. n.p.** Relates an example of Southern lip service to emancipation. 2 August 1838. p.1, c1.

**1721 LUCIUS C. MATLACK** *to* **FRIEND WHITTIER. 27 July 1837. Howellville.** Defends rumors concerning his motives for being an agent for the AAS. 2 August 1838. p.2, c2.

**1722 J. C.** *to* **MR. EDITOR [J. G. WHITTIER]. n.d. n.p.** Describes Liberia and discusses colonization there; encloses statements from Governor Mechlin, Governor Matthias, Captain Waters and Henry Clay. 2 August 1838. p.2, c2.

**1723 J.** *to* **THE** ***PENNSYLVANIA FREEMAN*****. 18 July 1838. Chester County.** Reveals incidents concerning fugitive slaves. 2 August 1838. p.2, c3.

**1724 E. M. D.** *to* **FRIEND WHITTIER. 3 July 1838. London.** Informs of progress of English abolitionists; states that emancipation is expected to take place in eight West Indian islands on 1 August 1838. 2 August 1838. p.2, c4.

**1725 GOVERNOR JOSEPH RITNER** *to* **HENRY HANNAN AND GENERAL D. R. PORTER. [from the** ***Pittsburgh Christian Witness*****] 5 April 1838. Harrisburg.** Answers questions regarding his stand on slavery, the right to jury trial and the annexation of Texas. 2 August 1838. p.3, c5.

**1726 n.n.** *to* **THE SENATE AND HOUSE OF REPRESENTATIVES OF THE COMMONWEALTH OF PENNSYLVANIA. 11 January 1838. Harrisburg.** Encloses a list of resolutions adopted by the legislature of Rhode Island concerning the annexation of Texas to the Union. 2 August 1838. p.3, c6.

**1727 ORSON S. MURRAY** *to* **REVEREND ELI BALL. n.d. Brandon, Vt.** Rebukes Reverend Ball's pro-slavery sentiments. 9 August 1838. p.1, c2.

**1728 JAMES McCRUMMELL** *to* **n.n. [from the** ***Colored American*****] n.d. n.p.** Reports resolutions of a meeting gathered in Philadelphia to honor Benjamin Lundy. 9 August 1838. p.2, c1.

**1729 ALVAN STEWART** *to* **BRETHREN. 24 July 1838. Utica, N.Y.** Declines an invitation to attend a meeting commemorating the emancipation of slaves in the British West Indies. 9 August 1838. p.2, c2.

**1730 JOHN BLACK** *to* **MESSRS. GEO. H. STUART, SAMUEL D. HASTINGS, AND ROBERT E. PETERSON. 25 July 1838. Pittsburgh.** Declines an invitation to attend a meeting commemorating the emancipation of slaves in the British West Indies. 9 August 1838. p.2, c2.

**1731 THEODORE D. WELD** *to* **SAMUEL HASTINGS, GEORGE H. STUART, AND ROBERT E. PETERSON. 29 July 1838. Fort Lee, N.J.** Regrets that illness prevents him from attending the meeting to commemorate Emancipation Day in the British West Indies. 9 August 1838. p.2, c2.

**1732 REVEREND N. E. JOHNSON** *to* **SAMUEL D. HASTINGS, GEORGE H. STUART, AND ROBERT E. PETERSON. 31 July 1838. New York.** Regrets that he cannot attend the meeting to commemorate the emancipation of slaves in the British West Indies. 9 August 1838. p.2, c3.

**1733 J. C.** *to* **MR. EDITOR [J. G. WHITTIER]. n.d. n.p.** Discusses the origin and object of the CS. 9 August 1838. p.2, c4.

**1734 A PRESBYTERIAN MINISTER** *to* **THE EDITOR. [from the** ***Richmond Religious Telegraph*****] n.d. Georgia.** Questions the soundness of the views of the Presbyterian church regarding slavery. 9 August 1838. p.3, c2.

**1735 JOHN QUINCY ADAMS** *to* **EDMUND QUINCY, ESQ. 28 July 1838. Quincy.** Declines an invitation to attend the celebration of Emancipation Day in the British West Indies. 9 August 1838. p.3, c3.

**1736 R. EVERETT** *to* **SIR. [from the** ***New York Evangelist*****] n.d. Wales.** Discusses the temperance movement in Wales. 9 August 1838. p.4, c3.

**1737 J. C.** *to* **THE EDITOR [J. G. WHITTIER]. n.d. n.p.** Describes early attempts in New England to abolish slavery. 16 August 1838. p.1, c5.

**1738 J. P., JR.** *to* **THE** ***PENNSYLVANIA FREEMAN*****. 9 August 1838. Burlington, N.J.** Discusses events which occurred after the recent trial of two slaves in Mount Holly. 16 August 1838. p.3, c5.

**1739 J. QUINCY ADAMS** *to* **A. BRONSON, ESQ. 30 July 1838. Quincy.** Regrets that he cannot attend the Fall River AS celebration of West Indies Emancipation. 16 August 1838. p.4, c5.

**1740 GEO. W. WEISSENGER** *to* **J. B. CLARK. [from the** ***Selma Free Press*****] 6 July 1838. Louisville, Ky.** Believes that efforts to abolish slavery gradually in Kentucky are not supported by Henry Clay. 23 August 1838. p.1, c2.

**1741 n.n.** *to* **SIR. 18 July 1838. Kentucky.** Comments on W. L. Breckinridge and his views on slavery. 23 August 1838. p.1, c3.

**1742 SECRETARY OF THE UNION AS** *to* **n.n. 11 August 1838. Leicester.** Describes his lecture at Leicester Academy and his efforts to distribute anti-slavery material on steamboats. 23 August 1838. p.1, c4.

**1743 J. C.** *to* **MR. EDITOR [J. G. WHITTIER]. n.d. n.p.** Comments on the injustices endured by the Negroes. 23 August 1838. p.1, c5.

**1744 S.** *to* **FRIEND WHITTIER. n.d. n.p.** Informs of anti-slavery meetings all around Middletown. 23 August 1838. p.2, c1.

**1745 WM. S. FULTON** *to* **HON. BEN. C. HOWARD. 7 July 1838. Senate Chamber.** Encloses a copy of the letter written to Fulton in 1830 by General Jackson asking him for information concerning General Houston and the Texas war. 23 August 1838. p.2, c4.

**1746 EDWARD KENT, GOVERNOR OF MAINE** *to* **THE EXECUTIVE COMMITTEE OF THE SOMERSET AS. 27 July 1838. Bangor.** States that he is in favor of the right of petition, free discussion, and abolition. 23 August 1838. p.3, c2.

**1747 LEWIS C. GUNN** *to* **ABOLITIONISTS. n.d. Philadelphia.** Urges all abolitionists to attend an upcoming meeting of the County AS. 23 August 1838. p.3, c5.

**1748 n.n.** *to* **n.n. 31 July. Camp Wilds, Ga.** Describes the massacre of a family by Indians. 23 August 1838. p.3, c6.

**1749 SAMUEL D. HASTINGS** *to* **n.n. n.d. Philadelphia.** Requests information about all the delegations planning to attend the Philadelphia County AS Convention. 23 August 1838. p.3, c6.

**1750 HONORABLE WILLIAM SLADE** *to* **REVEREND J. LEAVITT. [from the** ***Emancipator*****] 7 August 1838. Middlebury, Vt.** Requests 100 copies of Thome and Kimball's *Journal,* which describes their tour of the West Indies; favors immediate emancipation. 23 August 1838. p.4, c3.

**1751 n.n.** *to* **MR. COWLES. [from the** ***Friend of Man*****] 2 August 1838. Hartford.** Discusses a meeting of the Hartford County AS. 23 August 1838. p.4, c4.

**1752 E. C. PRITCHETT** *to* **WILLIAM GOODELL, ESQ. 11 August 1838. n.p.** Describes an attempt to kidnap a black man from Whitesboro' on the pretence that he was a fugitive, and the success of students in stopping the attempt. 23 August 1838. p.4, c4.

**1753 WILLIAM D. PARRISH** *to* **n.n. n.d. n.p.** Informs the public that he had nothing to do with the publication of a card which pictured Pennsylvania Hall before its destruction. 30 August 1838. p.1, c1.

**1754 M. HAMPTON** *to* **THE** ***PENNSYLVANIA FREEMAN.*** **n.d. n.p.** Forwards an essay on abstinence from slave-labor produce, on behalf of the Buckingham AS. 30 August 1838. p.1, c2.

**1755 JOHN QUINCY ADAMS** *to* **FELLOW CITIZENS. 13 August 1838. Quincy.** Considers the resolutions adopted by a district convention of delegates on 23 August concerning the right of petition, the "gag law," and the annexation of Texas to the Union. 30 August 1838. p.1, c3.

**1756 J. C.** *to* **THE EDITOR [J. G. WHITTIER]. n.d. n.p.** Discusses the compulsory colonization law considered by the Virginia legislature in 1805. 30 August 1838. p.2, c3.

**1757 CHANDLER DARLINGTON** *to* **THE** ***PENNSYLVANIA FREEMAN.*** **n.d. n.p.** Forwards the latest resolutions of the Kennett AS. 30 August 1838. p.2, c4.

**1758 A VOICE FROM THE SOUTH** *to* **MR. EDITOR [J. G. WHITTIER]. 12 August 1838. Clinton, N.C.** Comments on the real objectives of abolitionists. 30 August 1838. p.2, c5.

**1759 M. A.** *to* **BROTHER GOODELL. [from the** ***Friend of Man*****] 10 August 1838. St. Lawrence County, N.Y.** Informs of his purchase of a slave on board the steamboat *United States,* and his subsequent emancipation of the slave. 30 August 1838. p.3, c4.

**1760 A. McCARDELL** *to* **READERS. [from the** ***Daily Telegraph*****] 4 August 1838. Darien.** Appeals to subscribers to pay their accounts, and apologizes that he has been forced to discontinue the *Darien Telegraph.* 30 August 1838. p.4, c6.

**1761 WM. WATKINS** *to* **J. P. BURR. 13 August 1838. Baltimore.** Discusses the appropriate use of the word "colored" in reference to black people, as proposed in a resolution by the American Moral Reform Society. 6 September 1838. p.1, c1.

1762 **WM. McKEE** *to* **THE** ***PENNSYLVANIA FREEMAN*****. 23 August 1838. Philadelphia.** Announces the next meeting and forwards the annual Treasurer's Report of the Union AS. 6 September 1838. p.1, c5.

1763 **J. C.** *to* **n.n. n.d. n.p.** Submits further information on the nature of colonization. 6 September 1838. p.2, c1.

1764 **LINDLEY COATES** *to* **ESTEEMED FRIEND. 29 August 1838. Sadsbury.** Describes the proceedings of the meeting of the Clarkson Anti-Slavery Association. 6 September 1838. p.2, c3.

1765 **BURLINGTON CORRESPONDENT** *to* **n.n. [extract from the** ***Mount Holly Herald*****] n.d. n.p.** Praises John G. Whittier. 6 September 1838. p.3, c2.

1766 **SAMUEL M. POND** *to* **n.n. [extract from the** ***Colored American*****] n.d. n.p.** Praises the stand taken by the *Colored American.* 6 September 1838. p.3, c4.

1767 **NORTH CAROLINIAN OFFICER** *to* **n.n. [extract] n.d. Florida.** Deplores the Indian wars in Florida. 6 September 1838. p.3, c5.

1768 **GENERAL GAINES** *to* **GOVERNOR CANNON. [extract] n.d. n.p.** Warns the Tennessee governor of general attacks on plantations and frontier settlements by Indians. 6 September 1838. p.3, c5.

1769 **n.n.** *to* **BROTHER WHITTIER. 30 August 1838. Bethany.** Encloses a list of resolutions passed by the Wayne County AS. 6 September 1838. p.3, c6.

1770 **EQUALITY** *to* **THE EDITOR. [from the** ***Herald of Freedom*****] n.d. n.p.** Commends the legislature for rejecting a law which would entitle fugitive slaves to trial by jury; argues that passage of such a law is unconstitutional since it would acknowledge right of masters to claim slaves as property. 13 September 1838. p.1, c2.

1771 **J. C.** *to* **THE EDITOR [J. G. WHITTIER]. n.d. n.p.** Attempts to prove that the idea of a national CS did not originate with Dr. Finley or Rev. Samuel Mills but with Gov. Charles F. Mercer. 13 September 1838. p.1, c6.

1772 **SARAH M. GRIMKE** *to* **SISTER. 20 July 1838. Fort Lee.** States her views on the subject of prejudice. 13 September 1838. p.2, c1.

1773 **JAMES G. BIRNEY** *to* **MR. EDITOR. [from the** ***Emancipator*****] n.d. n.p.** Describes some atrocities inflicted on slaves by owners. 13 September 1838. p.2, c2.

1774 **DARWIN CARFIELD** *to* **BROTHER GOODELL. [from the** ***Friend of Man*****] 23 August 1838. Albany.** Illustrates oppression and slavery in New Jersey. 13 September 1838. p.2, c2.

1775 **D. C.** *to* **BROTHER GOODELL. [from the** ***Friend of Man*****] n.d. n.p.** Describes recent advertisements for runaway slaves; comments concerning "contentment" of slaves. 13 September 1838. p.2, c3.

1776 **WM. R. HAYES** *to* **A FRIEND IN NEW HAVEN, CT. [from the** ***New Haven Herald*****] 2 August 1838. Barbadoes.** Describes Emancipation Day in Barbados. 13 September 1838. p.2, c4.

1777 **JOSEPH S. BARRIS** *to* **BROTHER. [from** ***Zion's Watchman*****] 22 August 1838. Meadville, Pa.** States that he is "unpledged to the new doctrine that when a man becomes a Methodist minister, he gives up his rights and his conscience." 13 September 1838. p.3, c2.

**1778 I. FLETCHER** *to* **C. L. KNAPP, ESQ. 10 August 1838. Lyndon.** Replies to a letter from the secretary of the AAS asking his views on abolition, the annexation of Texas to the Union, and the establishment of commercial relations with Haiti. 13 September 1838. p.3, c3.

**1779 NO QUIBBLER** *to* **n.n. n.d. n.p.** Takes issue with Joseph Tracy's characterization of George Washington. 13 September 1838. p.3, c4.

**1780 SCIO** *to* **FRIEND WHITTIER. n.d. n.p.** Discusses an article from the *Colonization Herald* concerning John Hickman of West Chester. 13 September 1838. p.3, c5.

**1781 CORRESPONDENT OF THE** *NEW YORK EVANGELIST to* **n.n. 15 June 1838. England.** Comments on the burning of Pennsylvania Hall. 13 September 1838. p.4, c3.

**1782 J. C.** *to* **THE EDITOR [J. G. WHITTIER]. n.d. n.p.** Considers the origins of colonization. 20 September 1838. p.1, c2.

**1783 SAMBO** *to* **MISTER PRINTER. [from the** *New York Courier*] **1817. n.p.** Criticizes Henry Clay's views on colonization. 20 September 1838. p.1, c3.

**1784 J. FULTON, JR.** *to* **THE** *PENNSYLVANIA FREEMAN.* **n.d. n.p.** Provides a complete report of the most recent meeting of the East Fallowfield AS. 20 September 1838. p.1, c4.

**1785 SAMUEL D. HASTINGS** *to* **THE** *PENNSYLVANIA FREEMAN.* **14 September 1838. Philadelphia.** Announces the establishment of several anti-slavery libraries by auxiliary chapters of the Philadelphia County AS. 20 September 1838. p.1, c6.

**1786 A TRAVELLER** *to* **FRIEND WHITTIER. [from the** *Journal of Commerce*] **n.d. n.p.** Considers the admission of Florida to the Union. 20 September 1838. p.2, c2.

**1787 E. WRIGHT, JR.** *to* **n.n. n.d. New York City.** Requests reports from all the anti-slavery societies in the United States. 20 September 1838. p.2, c4.

**1788 REVEREND J. BLANCHARD** *to* **n.n. [from the** *Philanthropist*] **n.d. n.p.** Describes his encounter with two slave owners in Baltimore. 20 September 1838. p.4, c4.

**1789 WM. UPHAM** *to* **HONORABLE C. L. KNAPP. 9 August 1838. Montpelier.** Answers questions concerning his views on abolition in Washington, termination of slave trade, annexation of Texas to the Union and recognition of the independence of Haiti. 27 September 1838. p.1, c1.

**1790 J. C.** *to* **THE EDITOR [J. G. WHITTIER]. n.d. n.p.** Provides additional proof of his theories on the origin of the concept of colonization. 27 September 1838. p.1, c5.

**1791 JOHN QUINCY ADAMS** *to* **THE EDITOR OF THE** *QUINCY PATRIOT.* **[extract] n.d. n.p.** Comments on the annexation of Texas. 27 September 1838. p.3, c3.

**1792 J. FULTON, JR.** *to* **FRIEND WHITTIER. 19 September 1838. Ercildown.** Discusses two lectures on slavery given by Reverend James Latta and Reverend Hamilton in place of ex-Governor Buchannan of Liberia. 27 September 1838. p.3, c4.

**1793 A JOURNEYMAN** *to* **MR. WHITTIER. n.d. n.p.** Relates his views on equality of the races; discusses prejudices of the working class. 4 October 1838. p.1, c4.

**1794 J. C.** *to* **THE EDITOR [J. G. WHITTIER]. n.d. n.p.** Considers the abomination of slavery. 4 October 1838. p.1, c4.

1795 **HUMANITAS** *to* **FRIEND WHITTIER. n.d. n.p.** Relates incidents which occurred on the journey of a fugitive slave. 4 October 1838. p.1, c6.

1796 **W. H. J.** *to* **FRIEND WHITTIER. 20 September 1838. Buckingham.** Relays the proceedings of a meeting of the Buckingham AS. 4 October 1838. p.2, c1.

1797 **CORRESPONDENT** *to* **n.n. [from the** ***Connecticut Charter Oak*****] n.d. n.p.** Reports the progress of the newly founded Litchfield County AS. 4 October 1838. p.2, c2.

1798 **J. HAMILTON** *to* **THOMAS RITCHIE, ESQ. [from the** ***Richmond Enquirer*****] 15 August 1838. Long's Hotel, London.** Relates an incident regarding the slaveholding American minister to England. 4 October 1838. p.2, c4.

1799 **n.n.** *to* **n.n. [from the** ***New York Evangelist*****] 7 August 1838. England.** Celebrates West Indian Emancipation and questions America's system of slavery. 4 October 1838. p.2, c5.

1800 **DANIEL SMITH** *to* **ELI DILLIN AND THOMAS EARLE. 26 September 1838. Spring Garden.** The Democratic candidate for high sheriff of Philadelphia answers questions asked by the Philadelphia AS concerning his views on free discussion. 4 October 1838. p.3, c2.

1801 **DANIEL FITLER** *to* **WILLIAM McKEE AND JOS. S. PICKERING. 24 September 1838. Philadelphia.** The Whig candidate for high sheriff of Philadelphia answers questions concerning free discussion asked by the Philadelphia AS. 4 October 1838. p.3, c3.

1802 **THOS. C. HAYWARD** *to* **REVEREND JOSHUA LEAVITT. [from the** ***Emancipator*****] 8 September 1838. Ashford, Ct.** Discusses Reverend Ezekiel Skinner's sermons and conversation on colonization. 4 October 1838. p.4, c2.

1803 **TRUTH** *to* **THE EDITOR. [from the** ***Christian Witness*****] n.d. n.p.** Characterizes missionary traders in West Africa. 4 October 1838. p.4, c5.

1804 **JAMES G. BIRNEY, ESQ.** *to* **THE EDITORS OF THE** ***NEW YORK COMMERCIAL ADVERTISER.*** **n.d. n.p.** Stresses the authenticity of the narrative of James Williams. 11 October 1838. p.1, c2.

1805 **THOMAS S. CAVENDER AND THOMAS FOULK** *to* **THE** ***PENNSYLVANIA FREEMAN.*** **n.d. n.p.** Present the semiannual report of the Junior AS. 11 October 1838. p.1, c3.

1806 **J. C.** *to* **THE EDITOR [J. G. WHITTIER]. n.d. n.p.** Details the history of the CS. 11 October 1838. p.1, c4.

1807 **n.n.** *to* **FRIEND WHITTIER. 26 September 1838. Chester County.** Comments on a conversation with a young man from New Orleans returning to Chester County. 11 October 1838. p.1, c5.

1808 **OLIVER JOHNSON** *to* **FRIEND KNAPP. [from the** ***Liberator*****] 2 October 1838. Worcester.** Presents an account of the first day of the Young Men's Anti-Slavery Convention. 11 October 1838. p.2, c2.

1809 **BENJAMIN LUNDY** *to* **A FRIEND IN PHILADELPHIA. [extract] n.d. Hennepin, Putnam County, Il.** Discusses abolitionist sentiment in Illinois. 11 October 1838. p.3, c1.

**1810 WM. BETTS AND ALICE ELIZA HAMBLETON** *to* **THE** *PENNSYLVANIA FREEMAN.* **n.d. Philadelphia.** Forward the preamble and resolutions of a meeting of the American Free Produce Convention in Philadelphia. 11 October 1838. p.3, c5.

**1811 VERITAS** *to* **DR. BAILEY. 18 September 1838. Ripley.** Criticizes the actions of the states of Ohio and Kentucky in forcing a free black minister into slavery. 11 October 1838. p.4, c1.

**1812 A FRIEND OF THE OPPRESSED** *to* **n.n. n.d. n.p.** Condemns the actions of the governors of Ohio and Kentucky for their apparently trumped-up charge against a free black minister. 11 October 1838. p.4, c3.

**1813 HEZEKIAH G. WELLS** *to* **D. E. HARBAUGH. n.d. n.p.** Promises to give his full attention to all petitions regarding slavery if he is elected to Congress. 18 October 1838. p.1, c1.

**1814 CHARLES STUART** *to* **GERRIT SMITH. [extract from the** *Friend of Man***] n.d. n.p.** Extols the virtues of men involved in the anti-slavery struggle. 18 October 1838. p.1, c1.

**1815 DANIEL O'CONNELL** *to* **THE EDITOR OF THE** *MORNING CHRONICLE.* **13 September 1838. Darrynane Abbey.** Explains the previously published correspondence concerning slavery between himself and the American ambassador Stevenson. 18 October 1838. p.3, c1.

**1816 E. D. BARBER** *to* **THE YOUNG MEN'S ANTI-SLAVERY CONVENTION. [extract from the** *Liberator***] n.d. n.p.** Reproaches Congress for its actions on the slave laws in Washington, D.C. 18 October 1838. p.3, c2.

**1817 N. P. ROGERS** *to* **BROTHER PHELPS. [from the** *Liberator***] 28 September 1838. Plymouth, N.H.** Regrets that he cannot attend the convention at Worcester; comments on abolition. 18 October 1838. p.3, c3.

**1818 W. O.** *to* **n.n. 14 October 1838. New York.** Denounces ambiguous statements made by C. P. Grosvenor, Dr. Cox, Dr. Hoby, and Joseph J. Gurney at the recent Young Men's Anti-Slavery Convention. 18 October 1838. p.3, c4.

**1819 n.n.** *to* **n.n. [from the** *Newark Sentinel***] 1838. Havana.** Details some conditions of the Cuban slave trade and treatment of slaves. 18 October 1838. p.4, c1.

**1820 JESSE CAMPBELL, ESQ.** *to* **BROTHER. [extract] 15 August 1838. Mineral Point, W.T.** Pities the slaveholders for their misguided views. 18 October 1838. p.4, c6.

**1821 SAMUEL S. PHELPS** *to* **RUFUS W. GRISWOLD. [from the** *Vergennes Vermonter***] 8 October 1838. Middlebury.** Answers questions concerning his views on slavery. 25 October 1838. p.1, c2.

**1822 REVEREND JOHN RANKIN** *to* **n.n. [extract from the** *Emancipator***] n.d. Ohio.** Praises the AAS. 25 October 1838. p.1, c3.

**1823 GOVERNOR JAS. CLARK** *to* **THE GOVERNOR OF OHIO. [from the** *Ohio Political Journal and Register***] n.d. n.p.** Demands, as governor of Kentucky, that an alleged fugitive now living as a freeman in Ohio be turned over to Kentucky authorities. 25 October 1838. p.1, c4.

**1824 A YOUNG MAN** *to* **HIS FRIEND. [extract from the** *Meadville* **(Pa.)** *Statesman***] n.d. n.p.** Mourns the breakup of slave families in an incident witnessed on the Ohio River. 25 October 1838. p.2, c1.

**1825 GERRIT SMITH** *to* **THE EDITOR OF THE** *FRIEND OF MAN.* **9 October 1838. Peterboro'.** Encloses a letter from a Southern slaveholder; comments on the character of anti-abolitionists. 25 October 1838. p.2, c3.

**1826 n.n.** *to* **GERRIT SMITH. n.d. Georgia.** Decries the immorality of slavery and encourages Smith to continue his work. 25 October 1838. p.2, c4.

**1827 SEVENTY-SIX** *to* **MR. EDITOR. [from the** *Massachusetts Spy*] **n.d. n.p.** Denies that the Constitution guarantees the right of Southerners to hold slaves. 25 October 1838. p.4, c1.

**1828 RICHARD WILLIAMS** *to* **n.n. [from the** *Friend of Man*] **n.d. n.p.** Disputes the notion that slaves are happy. 25 October 1838. p.4, c3.

**1829 RICHARD WILLIAMS** *to* **MR. EDITOR. [from the** *Friend of Man*] **n.d. n.p.** Believes that the increase in population in several states between the years 1820 and 1830 was due to the influence of slavery. 25 October 1838. p.4, c3.

**1830 n.n.** *to* **GERRIT SMITH. [extract from the** *Friend of Man*] **n.d. n.p.** Indicts the North's understanding of slavery and cavalier treatment of ex-slaves. 25 October 1838. p.4, c5.

**1831 R.** *to* **MR. COWLES. [from the** *Charter Oak*] **n.d. n.p.** Recalls an incident which almost prevented the latest county AS meeting. 25 October 1838. p.4, c5.

**1832 WILLIAM SLADE** *to* **MR. SAMUEL D. DARLING. 12 October 1838. Middlebury, Vt.** Answers questions about congressional responsibility regarding slavery. 1 November 1838. p.1, c3.

**1833 GEO. STORRS** *to* **n.n. [from** *Zion's Watchman*] **n.d. Connecticut.** Deplores a Connecticut minister's opposition to abolition. 1 November 1838. p.2, c2.

**1834 JOHN B. MAHAN** *to* **SIR. 26 September 1838. A Kentucky Prison.** Describes his imprisonment and prays for an early release. 1 November 1838. p.3, c2.

**1835 JOHN B. MAHAN** *to* **HIS WIFE. 22 September 1838. A Kentucky Prison.** Reveals his feelings about imprisonment and asks his wife to thank his friends for their support. 1 November 1838. p.3, c2.

**1836 JOHN B. MAHAN** *to* **A FRIEND. 1 October 1838. A Kentucky Prison.** Recounts his days in prison. 1 November 1838. p.3, c2.

**1837 JOHN B. MAHAN** *to* **HIS WIFE. 2 October 1838. A Kentucky Prison.** Despairs over his prison sentence but maintains faith in God. 1 November 1838. p.3, c2.

**1838 JOHN B. MAHAN** *to* **A FRIEND. n.d. A Kentucky Prison.** Describes his health and feelings while in prison. 1 November 1838. p.3, c2.

**1839 O. S. M.** *to* **THE EDITOR [J. G. WHITTIER]. n.d. n.p.** Requests that funds be raised to reimburse Benjamin Lundy for his losses incurred in the burning of Pennsylvania Hall and to enable him to continue publication of AS material. 1 November 1838. p.3, c2.

**1840 L. BRADISH** *to* **WILLIAM JAY AND GERRIT SMITH. 13 October 1838. Moira, Franklin County.** A Whig candidate for lieutenant governor responds to questions put to him by the AS committee. 1 November 1838. p.3, c4.

**1841 JOHN W. NEVINS AND JOHN C. COLE** *to* **n.n. [from the** *Christian Witness***] 17 September 1838. Elmira.** Describe a drunken mob scene at a Methodist Preachers' AS meeting. 1 November 1838. p.4, c4.

**1842 U. S. COMMERCIAL AGENT** *to* **MERCHANTS OF PHILADELPHIA. [extract] 24 September 1838. Port-au-Prince, Hayti.** Relays President Boyer's wishes regarding trade relations between the United States and Haiti. 8 November 1838. p.1, c1.

**1843 J. R. LOCK** *to* **SIR. [from** *Zion's Watchman***] 6 October 1838. West Greenville, Pa.** Requests a subscription to *Zion's Watchman*; comments on the Erie annual conference. 8 November 1838. p.1, c1.

**1844 WILLIAM H. SEWARD** *to* **JUDGE WM. JAY AND GERRIT SMITH. 22 October 1838. Auburn.** Answers several questions on issues related to abolitionism. 8 November 1838. p.1, c2.

**1845 GOVERNOR W. L. MARCY** *to* **GERRIT SMITH AND WILLIAM JAY. 18 October 1838. Albany.** Answers several questions on issues related to abolitionism. 8 November 1838. p.1, c5.

**1846 GENERAL HAMILTON** *to* **THE EDITOR OF THE** *RICHMOND ENQUIRER.* **[from the** *New York Gazette***] n.d. n.p.** Apologizes for his vehement attack on Daniel O'Connell, but insists that he is wrong about both George Washington and Mr. Stevenson. 8 November 1838. p.2, c6.

**1847 DANIEL O'CONNELL** *to* **MR. STEVENSON. 10 August 1838. Pall Mall.** Contends that the published reports of his speech concerning George Washington's policy on slavery are wrong. 8 November 1838. p.3, c1.

**1848 HENRY VANWART** *to* **GENERAL HAMILTON. 6 September 1838. n.p.** Agrees that O'Connell made the statements with which General Hamilton takes issue. 8 November 1838. p.3, c1.

**1849 J. HAMILTON** *to* **THOMAS RITCHIE. 10 October 1838. New York.** Holds fast to his indictment of O'Connell for his apparent maligning of Stevenson and Washington. 8 November 1838. p.3, c1.

**1850 PHILANTHROPIST** *to* **THE** *PENNSYLVANIA FREEMAN.* **n.d. New York State.** Contrasts friends of the slaves with slave-catchers. 8 November 1838. p.4, c2.

**1851 H. B. STANTON** *to* **n.n. 27 October 1838. Boston.** Regrets his inability to attend the meeting of the Pennsylvania State AS for the Eastern District at Coatsville. 15 November 1838. p.3, c1.

**1852 WENDELL PHILLIPS** *to* **n.n. 24 October 1838. Greenfield.** Regrets his inability to attend the meeting of the Pennsylvania State AS for the Eastern District at Coatsville. 15 November 1838. p.3, c1.

**1853 JAMES G. BIRNEY** *to* **n.n. 20 October 1838. New York.** Refuses an invitation to attend the meeting of the Pennsylvania State AS for the Eastern District at Coatsville. 15 November 1838. p.3, c1.

**1854 JOHN G. WHITTIER** *to* **BROTHER. 26 October 1838. Amesbury.** Discusses the moral evils of slavery; comments on the abolitionist cause. 15 November 1838. p.3, c4.

**1855 JOHN W. BROWNE** *to* **n.n. [extract] n.d. n.p.** Refuses the Whig nomination for senatorial candidate; advises all Americans to abolish slavery and unify their views. 15 November 1838. p.4, c4.

**1856 JOHN B. MAHAN** *to* **JOSEPH VANCE. 4 October 1838. Washington, Mason County, Ky.** Asserts his innocence of charges brought against him; deplores the injustice of his arrest. 22 November 1838. p.1, c1.

**1857 JOHN J. MITER** *to* **MR. STANTON. 4 October 1838. Knoxville.** Gives an account of the anniversary of the Illinois State AS. 22 November 1838. p.1, c2.

**1858 WILLIAM OSBORNE** *to* **n.n. 16 November 1838. n.p.** Detests the moral evils of slavery. 22 November 1838. p.2, c2.

**1859 DR. DUNCAN** *to* **n.n. [extract from the** ***Richmond Whig*****] n.d. n.p.** Warns of corruption and damnation for slaveholders. 22 November 1838. p.2, c3.

**1860 BRADFORD SUMNER** *to* **S. G. SHIPLEY. [extract] n.d. n.p.** Argues that slavery is contrary to the laws of God. 22 November 1838. p.2, c6.

**1861 HENRY WILLIAMS** *to* **n.n. [extract] n.d. n.p.** Advises Congress to abolish slavery in Washington, D.C. 22 November 1838. p.2, c6.

**1862 ALEXANDER H. EVERETT** *to* **n.n. [extract] n.d. n.p.** Sees hope for the United States in emancipation in the British West Indies. 22 November 1838. p.2, c6.

**1863 RICHARD FLETCHER** *to* **FRANCIS JACKSON, ESQ. n.d. n.p.** Opposes the admission of any new state to the Union whose constitution tolerates slavery. 22 November 1838. p.3, c1.

**1864 ORANGE SCOTT** *to* **BROTHER LEAVITT. 9 November 1838. Boston.** Gives an account of an anti-slavery meeting in Pittsburgh. 22 November 1838. p.3, c2.

**1865 AN AGENT OF THE CONNECTICUT AS** *to* **n.n. [extract] n.d. New Haven, Ct.** Describes a recent meeting of the New Haven Baptist Association. 22 November 1838. p.3, c2.

**1866 n.n.** *to* **WILLIAM BASSETT. [extract] 12 October 1838. n.p.** Reports on the progress of the Friends' various programs in the previous year. 22 November 1838. p.3, c3.

**1867 n.n.** *to* **n.n. [extract] 7 September 1838. England.** Contrasts West Indian Negroes and ex-masters; discusses the proposed visit of John Scoble and Charles Stuart to the West Indies. 22 November 1838. p.4, c5.

**1868 LUTHER LEE** *to* **MR. EDITOR. [from the** ***Friend of Man*****] 3 November 1838. Plattsburgh.** Denounces the distribution of a handbill announcing the continuing auction of slaves. 29 November 1838. p.1, c3.

**1869 SAMUEL D. HASTINGS** *to* **n.n. 22 November 1838. Philadelphia, Pa.** Describes the quarterly meeting of the Union AS of Philadelphia. 29 November 1838. p.1, c6.

**1870 WILLIAM McKEE** *to* **n.n. 22 November 1838. Philadelphia, Pa.** Reports on the financial status of the Union AS, calling on members to pay their dues, buy subscriptions and show more enthusiasm for the cause. 29 November 1838. p.2, c2.

**1871 WILLIAM PIERCE** *to* **n.n. n.d. n.p.** Presents the minutes from the recent quarterly meeting of the Union AS of Philadelphia. 29 November 1838. p.2, c3.

**1872 MANY MEMBERS** *to* **REVEREND MR. ---. n.d. n.p.** Rebuke the minister for his fear of public opinion on the issue of slavery. 29 November 1838. p.2, c3.

**1873 GERRIT SMITH** *to* **n.n. [from the** *Friend of Man***] n.d. n.p.** Recommends consistency for abolitionists. 29 November 1838. p.2, c6.

**1874 LEWIS TAPPAN** *to* **THE EDITOR [J. G. WHITTIER]. 24 November 1838. New York.** Criticizes the CS; comments on Louis Sheridan. 29 November 1838. p.3, c1.

**1875 LOUIS SHERIDAN** *to* **LEWIS TAPPAN. 16 July 1838. Edina, Liberia.** Condemns the deplorable conditions of blacks in Liberia. 29 November 1838. p.3, c3.

**1876 GERRIT SMITH** *to* **WILLIAM GOODELL. 7 November 1838. Peterboro'.** Denounces anti-slavery men who vote for pro-slavery candidates. 29 November 1838. p.4, c1.

**1877 R. M. PEARSON** *to* **THE EDITOR. [from the** *Emancipator***] 30 October 1838. Jacksonville.** Discusses the kidnapping of a black man in Illinois and the trial of the kidnapper. 29 November 1838. p.4, c3.

**1878 DAVID LEE CHILD** *to* **MR. GARRISON. [from the** *Liberator***] 7 November 1838. Northampton.** Considers the admission of Texas to the Union. 29 November 1838. p.4, c4.

**1879 S. L. POMROY** *to* **MESSRS. EDITORS. [from the** *Maine Advocate of Freedom***] 6 November 1838. Bangor.** Introduces a letter from Gov. Edward Kent of Maine regarding an article entitled, "Emancipation in the West Indies." 29 November 1838. p.4, c4.

**1880 GOVERNOR EDWARD KENT** *to* **S. L. POMROY. [from the** *Maine Advocate of Freedom***] 5 November 1838. Bangor.** Thanks Mr. Pomroy for sending him Thome and Kimball's article entitled, "Emancipation in the West Indies." 29 November 1838. p.4, c4.

**1881 ABRAHAM ALLEN** *to* **DR. BAILEY. 3 November 1838. Union Township, Clinton County, Oh.** Deplores man-hunting in Ohio. 29 November 1838. p.4, c5.

**1882 JUNIOR** *to* **FRIEND WHITTIER. n.d. n.p.** Describes problems encountered by a group of abolitionists who attempted to hold a meeting in a school building; encloses a letter denying the group use of the building. 6 December 1838. p.1, c6.

**1883 MORGAN CLIFT AND JACOB JOHNSON** *to* **DR. S. W. PICKERING. 23 November 1838. Holmesburg.** Advise Dr. Pickering to cancel his anti-slavery meeting because of excitement in the community. 6 December 1838. p.1, c6.

**1884 LINDLEY COATES** *to* **n.n. n.d. n.p.** Describes a meeting of the Clarkson Anti-Slavery Association. 6 December 1838. p.1, c6.

**1885 MORRIS BROWN** *to* **n.n. n.d. n.p.** Relates the proceedings of a meeting of the Bethel Church congregation. 6 December 1838. p.2, c1.

**1886 A JOURNEYMAN MECHANIC** *to* **FELLOW WORKMEN. n.d. n.p.** Advises working people to look closely and carefully at abolition before dismissing it. 6 December 1838. p.2, c1.

**1887 EQUITY** *to* **MR. EDITOR [J. G. WHITTIER]. n.d. n.p.** Declares that slavery is a sin. 6 December 1838. p.2, c2.

**1888 HONORABLE RICHARD FLETCHER** *to* **FRANCIS JACKSON, ESQ. [extract] n.d. n.p.** Expresses his anti-slavery beliefs. 6 December 1838. p.2, c3.

**1889 JOHN QUINCY ADAMS** *to* **n.n. [extract] n.d. n.p.** Apologizes for not being as zealous an abolitionist as some, and condemns the slaveholders. 6 December 1838. p.2, c6.

**1890 AMOS FARNSWORTH** *to* **FRIENDS OF THE SLAVE. n.d. n.p.** Calls for an anti-slavery convention in the Fourth Congressional District of Massachusetts. 6 December 1838. p.3, c1.

**1891 n.n.** *to* **n.n. [extract from the** *New York American*] **3 December 1838. Washington.** Comments on the suicide of a slave. 6 December 1838. p.3, c2.

**1892 H. WETHERALD** *to* **n.n. n.d. Philadelphia.** Describes a recent meeting of the Philadelphia City AS. 6 December 1838. p.3, c2.

**1893 C. C. BURLEIGH** *to* **FRIEND WHITTIER. 5 December 1838. Philadelphia.** Describes a tour of anti-slavery meetings. 6 December 1838. p.3, c3.

**1894 W. H. J.** *to* **FRIEND WHITTIER. 1 December 1838. Upper Makefield.** Describes a meeting of the Bucks County AS. 6 December 1838. p.3, c4.

**1895 A. L. POST, ESQ.** *to* **n.n. [extract] n.d. Coatsville.** Describes a session of the Coatsville AS. 6 December 1838. p.4, c5.

**1896 D. LEE CHILD** *to* **LEWIS C. GUNN. [extract] n.d. n.p.** Comments on the economy of Southern plantations, and pleads to others to abstain from using articles produced by slave labor. 13 December 1838. p.1, c1.

**1897 DAVID L. AND LYDIA MARIA CHILD** *to* **BROTHER. [extract from the** *Providence* **(R.I.)** *Journal*] **n.d. n.p.** Decline an invitation to attend a meeting of the Rhode Island AS, and encourage further action for the cause. 13 December 1838. p.1, c3.

**1898 MARIA W. CHAPMAN** *to* **n.n. [extract from the** *Providence* **(R.I.)** *Journal*] **n.d. n.p.** Rejoices in the cause of abolition. 13 December 1838. p.1, c3.

**1899 SAMUEL AARON** *to* **n.n. 3 December 1838. Burlington, N.J.** Encourages the cause of philanthropy. 13 December 1838. p.1, c4.

**1900 CORRESPONDENT** *to* **n.n. [from the** *Bangor* **(Me.)** *Whig*] **n.d. Southern Illinois.** Reproaches the women of Quincy, Illinois, as lazy. 13 December 1838. p.3, c2.

**1901 A PRESBYTERIAN** *to* **MR. EDITOR [J. G. WHITTIER]. n.d. n.p.** Requests that "One Who Knows" sign his true name to his next column. 13 December 1838. p.3, c4.

**1902 ONE WHO KNOWS** *to* **MR. J. G. WHITTIER. n.d. n.p.** Indicts members of the Presbyterian congregation as hypocritical and fundamentally immoral in supporting abolition, with which he disagrees. 13 December 1838. p.3, c4.

**1903 ONE WHO KNOWS** *to* **MR. WHITTIER. n.d. n.p.** Wishes to know the name of "A Presbyterian" in return for divulging his own. 13 December 1838. p.3, c5.

**1904 C. C. BURLEIGH** *to* **FRIEND WHITTIER. 12 December 1838. Philadelphia.** Describes a tour of anti-slavery meetings. 13 December 1838. p.3, c5.

**1905 JAMES S. POPE AND 325 OTHERS** *to* **REVEREND TURPIN. n.d. n.p.** Criticize Reverend Turpin's missionary activities among blacks. 13 December 1838. p.4, c3.

**1906 J. C. PATTERSON, STANMORE BROOKS, WILLIAM ENDINS, AND JAMES S. POPE** *to* **REVEREND MR. TURPIN. 14 June 1838. Cambridge.** Caution Reverend Turpin to cease his missionary work among blacks. 13 December 1838. p.4, c3.

**1907 n.n.** *to* **n.n. [from the** *Washington Globe***] 12 December 1838. Washington, D.C.** Describes the actions of the House of Representatives on resolutions involving abolition of slavery in Washington, D.C., constitutional equality of the races, and the right of Congress to exert authority over the states. 20 December 1838. p.1, c6.

**1908 CORRESPONDENT** *to* **n.n. [from the** *U. S. Gazette***] 13 December 1838. Washington, D.C.** Presents resolutions of Congress involving abolition in Washington, D.C., abolition of the slave trade, the right of petition, apprehension and trial of fugitive slaves, slave ownership in the territories, and slave traffic through free states. 20 December 1838. p.2, c3.

**1909 WILLIAM C. RIVES** *to* **THE EDITOR. [from the** *Richmond Enquirer***] 22 November 1838. Albemarle County.** Discusses the Pennsylvania election and the question of abolition. 20 December 1838. p.3, c3.

**1910 A NEW JERSEY FRIEND** *to* **n.n. [extract] 29 November 1838. Burlington, N.J.** Decries slavery. 20 December 1838. p.4, c1.

**1911 OLIVER JOHNSON** *to* **JOHN QUINCY ADAMS. 26 November 1838. Providence, R.I.** Thanks Adams for his humanitarian work and forwards a copy of resolutions from the last meeting of the Rhode Island AS. 27 December 1838. p.1, c1.

**1912 JOHN QUINCY ADAMS** *to* **OLIVER JOHNSON. 13 December 1838. Washington.** Acknowledges the resolutions sent by Johnson and stresses the need for continued support for the cause. 27 December 1838. p.1, c1.

**1913 CORRESPONDENT** *to* **n.n. [extract from the** *U. S. Gazette***] 20 December 1838. Washington.** Discusses J. Q. Adams's presentation of several petitions before Congress. 27 December 1838. p.1, c2.

**1914 n.n.** *to* **n.n. [from the** *Inquirer* **and** *Courier***] 18 December 1838. Washington City.** Describes the resolutions concerning Haiti read before the House of Representatives. 27 December 1838. p.1, c4.

**1915 n.n.** *to* **n.n. 18 December 1838. Washington City.** Comments on General Lincoln's presentation of petitions regarding international trade with Haiti. 27 December 1838. p.1, c5.

**1916 JOSEPH YARDLEY** *to* **n.n. n.d. Bucks County.** Discusses the last meeting of the Bucks County AS. 27 December 1838. p.1, c6.

**1917 WASHINGTON CORRESPONDENT** *to* **THE** *NEW YORK EXPRESS.* **n.d. Washington.** Praises John Quincy Adams. 27 December 1838. p.2, c4.

**1918 n.n.** *to* **MR. LA ROY SUNDERLAND. [from** *Zion's Watchman***] 17 December 1838. Washington, D.C.** Comments further on the slave who committed suicide after having been sold away from his family. 27 December 1838. p.2, c5.

**1919 n.n.** *to* **WHITTIER. 10 December 1838. Marlborough.** Corrects what he claims to be a misrepresentation by C. C. Burleigh of the Marlborough anti-slavery meeting. 27 December 1838. p.2, c6.

**1920 C. C. BURLEIGH** *to* **n.n. n.d. n.p.** Announces the appointment of James Fulton, Jr. as lecturer for the Eastern District AS. 27 December 1838. p.3, c3.

**1921 JAMES T. WOODBURY** *to* **n.n. 15 December 1838. Acton.** Criticizes both candidates running for Congress in the Massachusetts Fourth District. 27 December 1838. p.3, c3.

**1922 J. B.** *to* **MR. EDITOR. [from the** ***Liberator*****] 10 December 1838. Andover.** Discusses Elliot Cresson's and Louis Sheridan's views regarding colonization. 27 December 1838. p.4, c1.

**1923 PIERCE M. BUTLER** *to* **THE SHERIFF OF RICHLAND DISTRICT, SOUTH CAROLINA. 30 October 1838. Executive Office, Columbia.** Replies to the petition in behalf of Nazareth Allen, who was convicted of murdering a Negro boy. 27 December 1838. p.4, c2.

**1924 D. S. INGRAHAM** *to* **LEWIS TAPPAN. 2 November 1838. Shatwood Chapel, Jamaica.** Describes the success of emancipation in Jamaica and the educational progress being made. 27 December 1838. p.4, c4.

## [1839]

**1925 J. S. GREEN** *to* **THE PRESIDENT OF ONEIDA INSTITUTE. 29 January 1838. Wailuku, Maui, Sandwich Islands.** Characterizes the missionary activities in the islands. 3 January 1839. p.1, c1.

**1926 L. FLETCHER** *to* **FRIEND WHITTIER. 24 December 1838. Great Valley, Pa.** Discusses Christianity and slavery. 3 January 1839. p.1, c6.

**1927 WM. S. PIERCE** *to* **MR. SAMUEL D. HASTINGS. 26 December 1838. Philadelphia.** Encloses an extract of the resolutions passed at the recent Union AS meeting. 3 January 1839. p.2, c1.

**1928 WILLIAM M. SULLIVAN** *to* **BROTHER SUNDERLAND. 9 December 1838. Jacksonopolis, Mi.** Considers the cause of abolition among Methodists. 3 January 1839. p.2, c3.

**1929 EDMUND BURKE** *to* **n.n. [extract] n.d. n.p.** Avows hostility toward abolitionists and supports the existing system. 3 January 1839. p.2, c6.

**1930 PHINEAS HANDERSON** *to* **n.n. [extract] n.d. n.p.** Reminds Congress of the importance of ending the slave trade in Washington, D.C. 3 January 1839. p.2, c6.

**1931 A. COLBY** *to* **n.n. [extract] n.d. n.p.** Opposes the congressional "gag rule" and admission of Texas to the Union. 3 January 1839. p.2, c6.

**1932 JOEL EASTMAN** *to* **n.n. [extract] n.d. n.p.** Favors immediate emancipation in the United States. 3 January 1839. p.2, c6.

**1933 JAMES WILSON, JR.** *to* **N. P. ROGERS. 15 November 1838. Keene.** Offers his opinion on certain governmental policies regarding slavery. 3 January 1839. p.3, c1.

**1934 B. FUSSELL** *to* **n.n. [extract] n.d. n.p.** Determines to continue his opposition to colonization. 3 January 1839. p.3, c3.

**1935 C. C. BURLEIGH** *to* **FRIEND WHITTIER. 31 December 1838. Newtown.** Relates his anti-slavery labors in Eastern Pennsylvania. 3 January 1839. p.3, c4.

**1936 B. I. CONTULD** *to* **J. Q. ADAMS. 19 December 1838. Montgomery, Al.** Criticizes Adams for the slander of Mr. Stevenson, minister to England. 3 January 1839. p.3, c5.

**1937 DANIEL L. MILLER, JR.** *to* **DELEGATES OF THE REQUITED LABOR CONVENTION. n.d. n.p.** Announces that copies of the proceedings of the convention have been sent to delegates and corresponding members. 3 January 1839. p.3, c5.

**1938 SARAH ASH, J. M. JACKSON AND DILLWYN PARRISH** *to* **n.n. n.d. Philadelphia.** Appeal to Philadelphians for help in keeping the two Negro schools operating. 3 January 1839. p.3, c6.

**1939 J. RANKIN** *to* **DR. BAILEY. [from the** ***Philanthropist*****] n.d. n.p.** Encloses a letter from a resident of the far South. 3 January 1839. p.4, c1.

**1940 A RESIDENT OF THE FAR SOUTH** *to* **J. RANKIN. n.d. n.p.** Expresses admiration for the men engaged in the anti-slavery cause. 3 January 1839. p.4, c1.

**1941 A. L. POST** *to* **n.n. [from the** ***Montrose Spectator*****] n.d. n.p.** Describes resolutions passed by the Susquehanna County Anti-Slavery and Free Discussion Society. 3 January 1839. p.4, c2.

**1942 JOHN QUINCY ADAMS** *to* **A LITERARY SOCIETY IN BALTIMORE. [extract from the** ***Baltimore Chronicle*****] n.d. n.p.** Recommends the Bible as the only book worth reading. 3 January 1839. p.4, c2.

**1943 I. H. T.** *to* **THE EDITOR OF THE** ***PITTSBURGH CONFERENCE JOURNAL.*** **1838. Prestonburgh, Ky.** Describes a wedding in the Lewisburgh, Virginia Methodist Episcopal Church. 3 January 1839. p.4, c3.

**1944 HENRY B. STANTON** *to* **n.n. [extract from the** ***Liberator*****] n.d. n.p.** Replies to accusations brought against him by N. Brooks. 10 January 1839. p.1, c1.

**1945 THE FACTORY GIRLS** *to* **REVEREND CHAUNCEY RICHARDSON. n.d. n.p.** Contradict Richardson's view that Southern slaves are no worse off than the laboring poor of the North. 10 January 1839. p.1, c2.

**1946 VERITAS** *to* **RESPECTED FRIEND. 31 December 1838. Burlington, N.J.** Cautions the writer of a previous letter to the *Freeman* to think carefully before advocating rash changes. 10 January 1839. p.1, c3.

**1947 J. H. H.** *to* **FRIEND WHITTIER. 1 January 1839. Burlington, N.J.** Criticizes the colonization scheme. 10 January 1839. p.1, c4.

**1948 W. H. J.** *to* **FRIEND WHITTIER. 30 December 1838. Buckingham.** Announces an anti-slavery meeting and lectures in Bucks County, Pennsylvania. 10 January 1839. p.2, c2.

**1949 W. H. J.** *to* **FRIEND WHITTIER. 3 January 1839. Buckingham.** Describes an attempt made to break up an anti-slavery meeting in Bucks County, Pennsylvania. 10 January 1839. p.2, c3.

**1950 FORTY-SIX** *to* **n.n. n.d. n.p.** Discusses several anti-slavery memorials presented from Ohio, Indiana, Massachusetts, Maine, Vermont and New York, as well as many slave states. 10 January 1839. p.3, c5.

**1951 JOHN SEYS** *to* **REV. J. J. MATTHIAS. 7 December 1838. New York.** Refutes Louis Sheridan's letter on the poor conditions prevailing in Liberia. 10 January 1839. p.4, c2.

**1952 A RESIDENT OF KINGSTON, JAMAICA** *to* **REVEREND J. LEAVITT. 6 November 1838. Kingston.** Describes emancipation in Jamaica as a success, contrary to all rumors. 10 January 1839. p.4, c4.

**1953 BENEZET** *to* **n.n. n.d. n.p.** Condemns colonization and those who use it to justify abolition. 10 January 1839. p.4, c5.

**1954 ENGLISH FRIENDS** *to* **n.n. n.d. n.p.** Describe the speech of George Thompson in Paisley, Scotland. 17 January 1839. p.1, c1.

**1955 A NORTHERN LABORER** *to* **n.n. [from the** ***Haverhill*** **(Ma.)** ***Gazette*****] n.d. n.p.** Condemns the attitude of anti-abolitionists who claim that free Northern laborers are also slaves. 17 January 1839. p.1, c4.

**1956 CHARLES W. DENISON** *to* **FRIEND WHITTIER. 8 January 1839. Wilmington, De.** Comments on various anti-slavery matters in Delaware. 17 January 1839. p.1, c5.

**1957 A. W. T.** *to* **FRIEND WHITTIER. n.d. n.p.** Forwards a copy of the petition presented by John Quincy Adams to the House of Representatives calling for abolition in Washington. 17 January 1839. p.2, c1.

**1958 DR. HAWES** *to* **n.n. [extract] n.d. n.p.** Urges that the issue of slavery be brought out into the open and disposed of, rather than avoided by means of various "gag" measures. 17 January 1839. p.2, c5.

**1959 CALEB CUSHING** *to* **THE PEOPLE OF MASSACHUSETTS. [extract] n.d. n.p.** Comments on the passage of the "gag rule" in the House of Representatives which forbids all discussion of the slavery question. 17 January 1839. p.2, c6.

**1960 LUCIUS C. MATLACK** *to* **FRIEND WHITTIER. 14 January 1839. Philadelphia.** Discusses his recent labors in the abolition cause. 17 January 1839. p.3, c3.

**1961 WM. M. CHACE** *to* **WHITTIER. 14 January 1838. Philadelphia.** Informs of anti-slavery meetings in Bucks County, Pennsylvania. 17 January 1839. p.3, c3.

**1962 HENRY PETERSON** *to* **n.n. n.d. n.p.** Submits the annual report of the Board of Managers of the Junior Anti-Slavery League. 17 January 1839. p.4, c1.

**1963 JOHN B. MAHAN** *to* **BROTHER SUNDERLAND. 15 December 1838. Sardinia, Oh.** Forwards an ardent proclamation against slavery. 17 January 1839. p.4, c3.

**1964 JAMES McCUNE SMITH, M.D.** *to* **n.n. n.d. n.p.** Forwards a list of resolutions passed at a large meeting of the colored citizens of New York. 24 January 1839. p.1, c1.

**1965 CALEB CUSHING** *to* **CONSTITUENTS OF MASSACHUSETTS. [extract] 22 December 1838. Washington.** Gives his opinion on the Atherton resolutions dealing with slavery. 24 January 1839. p.1, c3.

**1966 W. H. JOHNSON** *to* **FRIEND WHITTIER. 7 January 1839. Buckingham.** Discusses several anti-slavery meetings led by Charles C. Burleigh and William M. Chace. 24 January 1839. p.1, c4.

**1967 CALEB CLOTHIER** *to* **n.n. n.d. n.p.** Encloses the results of the election of officers at a meeting of the Pennsylvania Society for Promoting the Abolition of Slavery. 24 January 1839. p.1, c5.

**1968 JAS. YARDLEY** *to* **n.n. n.d. n.p.** Lists the resolutions passed by the Bucks County AS. 24 January 1839. p.1, c6.

**1969 JACOB M. ELLIS** *to* **n.n. n.d. n.p.** Submits a list of resolutions passed and officers elected for the new year by the Liberties AS. 24 January 1839. p.2, c1.

**1970 ABNER H. FRANCIS** *to* **REVEREND SAMUEL E. CORNISH. [from the** *Colored American***] 9 January 1839. Flemington.** Advises against the colonization scheme; asks abolitionists to send representatives to New Jersey and other Northern states to enlighten the population. 24 January 1839. p.2, c4.

**1971 BENJAMIN B. DAVIS** *to* **n.n. 25 December 1838. Salem, Oh.** Condemns the use of produce of slave labor. 24 January 1839. p.3, c1.

**1972 N. P. ROGERS** *to* **STANTON. 10 January 1839. Plymouth.** Urges abolitionists to remain true to their principles when voting for a member of Congress. 24 January 1839. p.3, c4.

**1973 E. C. PRITCHETT, ESQ.** *to* **MR. EDITOR. [from the** *Friend of Man***] n.d. n.p.** Praises the letter by Henry Peterson of the Junior Anti-Slavery League. 24 January 1839. p.3, c6.

**1974 A. D. BARBER** *to* **DR. BAILEY. [from the** *Cincinnati Philanthropist***] n.d. n.p.** Informs of the kidnapping of a black man, Alexander Johnson. 24 January 1839. p.4, c3.

**1975 WILLIAM SLADE** *to* **MESSRS. EDITORS. [from the** *National Intelligencer***] 7 January 1839. Washington.** Defends the abolitionists against accusations brought against them by Samuel M. Semmes. 24 January 1839. p.4, c4.

**1976 CORRESPONDENT** *to* **MR. EDITOR. [from the** *Liberator***] n.d. n.p.** Criticizes the conduct of Senator Prentiss of Vermont in presenting his state's resolutions on slavery, the right of petition, and the annexation of Texas. 31 January 1839. p.1, c6.

**1977 BENEZET** *to* **FRIEND ROGERS. [from the** *Herald of Freedom***] n.d. n.p.** Criticizes the tactics of the CS in transporting recaptured slaves to Monrovia. 31 January 1839. p.2, c1.

**1978 THOMAS MORRIS** *to* **THE EDITOR OF THE COLUMBUS (OH.) DEMOCRATIC PAPER. [extract] n.d. n.p.** Comments on the recent election of Judge Tappan; explains his own views and principles on slavery. 31 January 1839. p.2, c5.

**1979 JAMES FULTON** *to* **J. G. WHITTIER. [extract] n.d. n.p.** Informs of an anti-slavery meeting in Denmore, Lancaster County, Pennsylvania. 31 January 1839. p.3, c2.

**1980 VERUS** *to* **n.n. n.d. n.p.** Assails the New Jersey legislature for qualifying its support of emancipation. 31 January 1839. p.3, c3.

**1981 J. FULTON, JR.** *to* **FRIEND WHITTIER. n.d. n.p.** Cautions against the colonization scheme. 7 February 1839. p.1, c6.

**1982 SARAH PUGH AND MARY GREW** *to* **BELOVED FRIENDS AND FELLOW LABORERS. n.d. n.p.** Invite all women interested in abolition to a gathering. 7 February 1839. p.2, c1.

**1983 AN ADVOCATE OF WOMEN'S RIGHTS** *to* **FRIEND WHITTIER. 31 January 1839. Wilmington, De.** Discusses the rights of women in the United States. 7 February 1839. p.2, c2.

**1984 A MARYLAND FARMER** *to* **n.n. [extract from the** *National Intelligencer***] n.d. n.p.** Praises John Quincy Adams. 14 February 1839. p.1, c2.

**1985 FRANCIS JACKSON** *to* **n.n. n.d. n.p.** Reports on a meeting of the friends of the *Liberator* and encloses a list of resolutions adopted. 14 February 1839. p.1, c2.

**1986 REVEREND W. R. HAYES** *to* **REVEREND H. G. LUDLOW. 26 December 1838. Barbadoes.** Considers the effect of emancipation in the West Indies. 14 February 1839. p.2, c2.

**1987 JOHN G. WHITTIER** *to* **n.n. 4 February 1839. Boston.** Explains the rising controversy over the *Liberator*'s editorial policy and the politics of its editor, W. L. Garrison. 14 February 1839. p.2, c6.

**1988 NEW YORK CORRESPONDENT** *to* **THE** *NATIONAL INTELLIGENCER.* **[extract] n.d. n.p.** Observes some differences between Northern and Southern racism. 14 February 1839. p.3, c2.

**1989 MARIA** *to* **n.n. 9 February. Philadelphia.** Denounces a resolution passed by the Delaware legislature recommending that women should attend only to domestic matters. 14 February 1839. p.3, c6.

**1990 WILLIAM BROSIUS** *to* **n.n. n.d. n.p.** Gives an account of the last meeting of the Oxford Free Produce Society. 21 February 1839. p.1, c2.

**1991 CHARLES MAGILL** *to* **n.n. n.d. n.p.** Reviews progress of the past year by the Buckingham AS. 21 February 1839. p.1, c2.

**1992 SARAH PUGH AND MARY GREW** *to* **BELOVED FRIENDS AND FELLOW LABORERS. n.d. Philadelphia.** Invite members of the Female ASs of the United States to attend their convention. 21 February 1839. p.1, c4.

**1993 JOHN G. WHITTIER** *to* **n.n. 12 February 1839. Amesbury, Essex County, Ma.** Characterizes the spirit of slavery. 21 February 1839. p.2, c4.

**1994 JAMES G. BIRNEY** *to* **SIR. 8 February 1839. Meriden.** Discusses a convention held for the organization of the New Haven County AS. 21 February 1839. p.3, c4.

**1995 WOOLMAN** *to* **JOHN G. WHITTIER. 14 February 1839. Montgomery County.** Encloses a check for $20 for the AS, and praises the abolitionists for their accomplishments. 21 February 1839. p.3, c5.

**1996 W.** *to* **MR. EDITOR [J. G. WHITTIER]. n.d. n.p.** Observes John C. Calhoun. 21 February 1839. p.3, c5.

**1997 WM. LLOYD GARRISON** *to* **JOHN QUINCY ADAMS. n.d. n.p.** Questions Adams's real views on slavery and emancipation. 21 February 1839. p.4, c1.

**1998 JAMES MUTCHER** *to* **n.n. [from the** *Philanthropist***] n.d. n.p.** Forwards a mocking account of a meeting of the Elizabethtown, Kentucky AS, an organization which apparently does not exist. 21 February 1839. p.4, c3.

**1999 n.n.** *to* **THE NEW YORK YEARLY MEETING OF FRIENDS. [extract] n.d. London.** Encourages the work of the abolitionists. 21 February 1839. p.4, c3.

**2000 n.n.** *to* **THE NEW YORK YEARLY MEETING OF FRIENDS. [extract] n.d. Rhode Island.** Believes that divine intervention will save the slaves. 21 February 1839. p.4, c3.

**2001 n.n.** *to* **THE NEW YORK YEARLY MEETING OF FRIENDS. n.d. Ohio.** Desire that "every proper exertion" be made to promote the cause of the oppressed. 21 February 1839. p.4, c4.

**2002 n.n.** *to* **THE NEW YORK YEARLY MEETING OF FRIENDS. [extract] n.d. Indiana.** Suggests that all prayers be united for the cause of abolition. 21 February 1839. p.4, c4.

**2003 n.n.** *to* **THE NEW YORK YEARLY MEETING OF FRIENDS. [extract] n.d. Virginia.** Encourages the fight for emancipation. 21 February 1839. p.4, c4.

**2004 n.n.** *to* **MESSRS. EDES AND GILL. [from the** ***Boston Gazette*****] 23 August 1773. n.p.** Advises men to look to God for an end to slavery. 21 February 1839. p.4, c4.

**2005 FRANKLIN** *to* **n.n. n.d. n.p.** Encloses a letter from William Dickey to his brother. 28 February 1839. p.1, c5.

**2006 WILLIAM DICKEY** *to* **HIS BROTHER. 3 October 1824. Bloomingsburg.** Describes the brutal murder of a slave by his master. 28 February 1839. p.1, c5.

**2007 BENJAMIN CLENDERSON** *to* **n.n. n.d. n.p.** Discusses the recent meeting of the Colerain AS. 28 February 1839. p.1, c6.

**2008 GERRIT SMITH** *to* **THE EDITOR OF THE** *FRIEND OF MAN*. **26 January 1839. Peterboro'.** Forwards a letter from Henry Brewster. 28 February 1839. p.2, c1.

**2009 HENRY BREWSTER** *to* **GERRIT SMITH. 21 January 1839. LeRoy.** Repents his betrayal of the cause of the slave for the sake of party politics. 28 February 1839. p.2, c1.

**2010 ALVAN STEWART** *to* **THE EDITOR OF THE** *FRIEND OF MAN*. **n.d. n.p.** Discusses the effects of adoption of the "gag rule" in the House; declares that it seems to strengthen the moral cause of abolitionism. 28 February 1839. p.2, c1.

**2011 WALTER DENDY** *to* **BROTHER CLARKE. [extract] 29 October 1838. Bethtephil, St. James.** Relates instances of low wages and inflated costs of living for emancipated slaves in the West Indies. 28 February 1839. p.2, c4.

**2012 REVEREND THOMAS BURCHELL** *to* **BROTHER CLARKE. [extract] 29 October 1838. Mount Carey, Parish of St. James.** Commends the work of free laborers in Jamaica. 28 February 1839. p.2, c4.

**2013 JOHN CLARKE** *to* **BROTHER CLARKE. [extract] 30 October 1838. Brown's Town, St. Ann's.** Rejoices in the progress made by missionaries among the recently emancipated slaves in Jamaica. 28 February 1839. p.2, c5.

**2014 THOMAS T. ABBOTT** *to* **BROTHER CLARKE. [extract] 6 November 1838. St. Ann's Bay.** Comments on the working of the new free labor system. 28 February 1839. p.2, c5.

**2015 WILLIAM KNIBB** *to* **BROTHER CLARKE. [extract] 29 October 1838. Falmouth, Parish of Trelawny.** Determines to end the cheating of ex-slaves by employers, and has found help to that end. 28 February 1839. p.2, c5.

**2016 JOHN CLARKE** *to* **BROTHER LEAVITT. n.d. n.p.** Encloses letters from West Indies missionaries and elaborates on post-slavery conditions. 28 February 1839. p.2, c5.

**2017 SAMUEL OUGHTON** *to* **BROTHER CLARKE. [extract] 6 November 1838. Seneca, Hanover.** Describes the problems in employer-employee relationships which have arisen since emancipation. 28 February 1839. p.2, c5.

**2018 AMOS TOWNSEND, JR.** *to* **A NEW HAVEN MERCHANT. 21 February 1839. New Haven.** Discusses the success of emancipation in the West Indies. 28 February 1839. p.3, c6.

**2019 L. G. W.** *to* **n.n. [from the** *Amesbury Morning Courier***] 11 February 1839. n.p.** Condemns the public reaction to the Lynn Petition, which asks for the repeal of all discriminatory laws in Massachusetts. 28 February 1839. p.4, c3.

**2020 D.** *to* **MR. EDITOR. [from the** *Philanthropist***] 22 December 1838. Delaware, Oh.** Relates the story of a kidnapping in Ohio. 28 February 1839. p.4, c4.

**2021 PARIS CORRESPONDENT** *to* **THE** *NEW YORK AMERICAN***. [from the** *Emancipator***] 6 November. Paris.** Describes the author Sismondi. 28 February 1839. p.4, c5.

**2022 DANIEL MILLER** *to* **THE ASSOCIATION OF FRIENDS. n.d. n.p.** Observes the conditions of education, employment, and socialization among free black people. 7 March 1839. p.2, c1.

**2023 C. C. BURLEIGH** *to* **THE EDITOR [J. G. WHITTIER]. 24 February 1839. Montrose.** Encloses a detailed account of an anti-slavery convention. 7 March 1839. p.4, c3.

**2024 W. R. HAYES** *to* **REVEREND H. G. LUDLOW. 26 December 1838. Barbadoes.** Discusses the success of emancipation on the island of Barbados. 7 March 1839. p.4, c5.

**2025 AMOS TOWNSEND, JR.** *to* **A MERCHANT IN NEW HAVEN. [extract] 21 February 1839. New Haven.** Comments on the unexpected efficiency of free labor. 7 March 1839. p.4, c6.

**2026 T. S. C.** *to* **FRIEND WHITTIER. n.d. n.p.** Describes several meetings of the Junior AS at which the question, "Is Southern slavery at variance with the interest of the Northern laborer?" was discussed. 14 March 1839. p.1, c2.

**2027 OLIVER JOHNSON** *to* **MR. GARRISON. [from the** *Liberator***] 21 February 1839. Middlebury, Vt.** Describes the proceedings of the annual meeting of the Vermont AS. 14 March 1839. p.1, c3.

**2028 W. S.** *to* **SIR. [from the** *Emancipator***] 18 February 1839. Washington, D.C.** Condemns the presence of slavery in Washington. 14 March 1839. p.1, c4.

**2029 MR. HAYES** *to* **n.n. [extract from the** *Vermont Telegraph***] n.d. Barbadoes.** Reminds opponents of abolition and God's commands concerning slavery. 14 March 1839. p.1, c6.

**2030 GERRIT SMITH** *to* **MR. GOODELL. [from the** *Friend of Man***] 15 February 1839. Peterboro'.** Encloses an extract of a letter describing a slave auction. 14 March 1839. p.1, c6.

**2031 n.n.** *to* **GERRIT SMITH. [extract] n.d. n.p.** Describes a slave auction in Richmond, Virginia. 14 March 1839. p.1, c6.

**2032 n.n.** *to* **THOMAS HULME, ESQ. 29 December 1838. Estherton Farm.** Describes an incident in Georgia involving a South Carolinian and a young black girl, which convinced the author of the need for free labor and emancipation. 14 March 1839. p.2, c2.

**2033 CHARLES STUART** *to* **THEODORE WELD. 11 December 1838. Bridgetown, Barbadoes.** Discusses the success of emancipation in Barbados and encloses extracts of a letter from John Scoble to friends in England. 14 March 1839. p.2, c3.

**2034 J. SCOBLE** *to* **FRIENDS IN ENGLAND. [extract] n.d. Barbadoes.** Discusses the changes in Barbados since emancipation. 14 March 1839. p.2, c3.

**2035 AUGUSTUS WATTLES** *to* **BROTHER. [from the** *Colored American***] November 1838. New Bremen, Mercer County, Oh.** Describes his work in New Bremen, the largest black settlement in Ohio. 14 March 1839. p.2, c4.

**2036 JOHN RIDEOUT, J. H. GILL, CALEB D. PENNIMAN, WILLIAM GILL, EBENEZER HEATH, OLIVER FLANDERS, ISAAC BEAN, SAMUEL WELLS, AND WILLIAM WELCH** *to* **BELOVED BRETHREN AND FRIENDS. [from the** *Herald of Freedom***] 18 February 1839. Plymouth.** Denounce the "party for democracy." 14 March 1839. p.2, c5.

**2037 BENJAMIN S. JONES** *to* **n.n. 8 March 1839. n.p.** Questions the North's involvement in the continuation of slavery. 14 March 1839. p.2, c6.

**2038 L. M. CHILD** *to* **MR. GARRISON. [from the** *Liberator***] 15 February 1839. Northampton.** Recounts a lecture delivered by Dr. Nelson on slavery. 14 March 1839. p.4, c2.

**2039 D. B. RANDALL** *to* **BROTHER COX. [from the** *Maine Wesleyan Journal***] 1 February 1839. New Sharon.** Encloses resolutions passed by the Quarterly Conference of Vienna and Mercer circuits. 14 March 1839. p.4, c4.

**2040 THOMAS BURCHELL, JOHN CLARK, WILLIAM KNIBB, B. B. DEXTER, THOMAS ABBOTT, SAMUEL OUGHTON, WALTER DENDY, AND J. HUTCHINS** *to* **LORD GLENELG. n.d. North Side Union, Jamaica.** Appeal to Glenelg to prevent further oppression of emancipated slaves by the courts. 21 March 1839. p.1, c2.

**2041 J. P.** *to* **n.n. 11 March 1839. Burlington, N.J.** Forwards an account of a meeting to form a local CS at which the speaker, Dr. Skinner of Liberia, was challenged by an abolitionist. 21 March 1839. p.1, c3.

**2042 C. C. BURLEIGH** *to* **FRIEND WHITTIER. 7 March 1839. Carbondale.** Includes reports on several anti-slavery meetings. 21 March 1839. p.1, c4.

**2043 A. G.** *to* **MR. ROGERS. [from the** *Herald of Freedom***] n.d. n.p.** Describes an abolitionist meeting at which the members decided to take political action. 21 March 1839. p.2, c3.

**2044 MOSES BATES, INCREASE S. COLEMAN, ALBERT C. MUNSON, JOHN B. WOOD, PETER HORNE, WM. C. FERNALD, CHARLES DORE, JOHN A. SMILIE, AND PELATIAH LITTLEFIELD** *to* **THE DEMOCRATS OF NEW HAMPSHIRE. [from the** *Herald of Freedom***] 27 February 1839. Somersworth.** Refuse to support the Democratic Party until it supports equality for all men. 21 March 1839. p.2, c3.

**2045 n.n.** *to* **THE EDITOR. [from the** *Mississippi Free Trader***] 30 June 1838. Adams County, Ms.** Informs of abolition activity in Mississippi. 21 March 1839. p.2, c4.

**2046 GERRIT SMITH** *to* **THE EDITOR OF THE** *FRIEND OF MAN***. 23 February 1839. Livingstone County, N.Y.** Discusses several local anti-slavery meetings. 21 March 1839. p.2, c4.

**2047 P. CHAMBERLAIN** *to* **n.n. [from the** *Mercer* **(Pa.)** *Luminary***] n.d. n.p.** Encloses a list of resolutions passed by the Erie, Pennsylvania Presbytery concerning slavery. 21 March 1839. p.2, c6.

**2048 J. G. WHITTIER** *to* **n.n. 9 March 1839. Amesbury.** Regrets that he is still too ill to work, but deplores the reaction of the House of Representatives regarding petitions for equal treatment of blacks and whites. 21 March 1839. p.3, c1.

**2049 JESSE STEDMAN** *to* **C. L. KNAPP, ESQ. 1 March 1839. Chester.** Describes the escape of a Kentucky slave. 21 March 1839. p.4, c1.

**2050 W. GOODFELLOW AND MILES NORTON** *to* **MR. SUNDERLAND. 1 February 1839. Wayne County, Oh.** Forward the resolutions passed at an anti-slavery meeting in Waynesburgh, Ohio. 21 March 1839. p.4, c2.

**2051 BISHOP SMITH** *to* **THE HON. H. WICKLIFFE. [extract from the** ***Philanthropist*****] n.d. n.p.** Offers reasons for the large number of murders in Kentucky each year. 21 March 1839. p.4, c4.

**2052 DAVID DAGGETT** *to* **BISHOP SMITH. [from the** ***Philanthropist*****] 29 September 1839. New Haven, Ct.** States that there have been thirty murders in New Haven in twelve years. 21 March 1839. p.4, c4.

**2053 JOHN BUSHFIELD, JOHN EMERY, JOHN GILMOR, ESQ., [AND FOURTEEN OTHERS]** *to* **THE EDITOR OF THE** ***WHEELING GAZETTE*****. January term 1839. Ohio County Court.** Challenge the scope of the language as well as the legality of the preamble and resolutions concerning the right to petition in Wheeling. 28 March 1839. p.1, c3.

**2054 JOHN GILMOR** *to* **THE WORSHIPFUL THE JUSTICES OF OHIO COUNTY. n.d. n.p.** Refuses, for a number of reasons, to resign as justice of the peace. 28 March 1839. p.1, c5.

**2055 AMICUS** *to* **FRIEND WHITTIER. n.d. n.p.** Questions the wisdom of T. S. C.'s use of strong language in a previous letter. 28 March 1839. p.1, c5.

**2056 JNO. COHOON** *to* **THE** ***PENNSYLVANIA FREEMAN*****. 21 March 1839. Philadelphia.** Describes a tense meeting between abolitionists and opponents in Wilkesbarre, Pennsylvania. 28 March 1839. p.3, c2.

**2057 C. C. BURLEIGH** *to* **n.n. 21 March 1839. Philadelphia.** Discusses the encounter with an anti-abolitionist mob in Wilkesbarre. 28 March 1839. p.3, c2.

**2058 SARAH PUGH AND MARY GREW** *to* **THE FEMALE ASs OF THE UNITED STATES. n.d. n.p.** Extend a general invitation to the annual AS Convention in Philadelphia. 28 March 1839. p.3, c6.

**2059 ELIAM** *to* **n.n. [from the** ***Michigan Observer*****] 23 February 1839. Detroit.** Praises the Detroit black schools. 28 March 1839. p.4, c1.

**2060 J. H. WIGGINS** *to* **BRO. GOODELL. [from the** ***Friend of Man*****]. 19 January 1839. Albany.** Encloses two advertisements for the sale of slaves, and warns the South that it will some day have to pay for its cruelty. 28 March 1839. p.4, c4.

**2061 A FRIEND TO VIRGINIA** *to* **n.n. [from the** ***Globe*****] n.d. Virginia.** Warns Virginia not to take up the cause of abolition. 4 April 1839. p.1, c2.

**2062 J. G. BIRNEY** *to* **n.n. [extract from the** ***Emancipator*****] n.d. n.p.** Discusses an interview between Birney and General Scott. 4 April 1839. p.1, c2.

**2063 SAMUEL D. HASTINGS** *to* **n.n. n.d. n.p.** Informs of the proceedings of the third quarterly meeting of the Union AS. 4 April 1839. p.1, c5.

**2064 BENJ. WILSON** *to* **n.n. 25 March 1839. n.p.** Announces the objectives of the Philadelphia Association. 4 April 1839. p.1, c6.

**2065 n.n.** *to* **ESTEEMED FRIEND. 29 March 1839. Philadelphia.** Encloses an article published in the early 1800s on abolition. 4 April 1839. p.2, c3.

**2066 C. C. BURLEIGH** *to* **n.n. 30 March 1839. Philadelphia.** Comments on Dr. Skinner's lectures on colonization. 4 April 1839. p.2, c3.

**2067 W. H. J.** *to* **n.n. [extract] n.d. Bucks County.** Describes a party of slave-hunters who arrived in Bucks County in search of runaways. 4 April 1839. p.2, c3.

**2068 C. D. CAHOON** *to* **THE EDITOR OF** ***ZION'S WATCHMAN*****. n.d. n.p.** Forwards a report on the crime of slavery taken at a conference held in Danville District, New Hampshire. 4 April 1839. p.2, c4.

**2069 SARAH PUGH AND MARY GREW** *to* **THE FEMALE ASs OF THE UNITED STATES. n.d. Philadelphia.** Invite members to their home for the annual convention. 4 April 1839. p.3, c6.

**2070 SARAH PUGH AND MARY GREW** *to* **THE FEMALE ASs OF THE UNITED STATES. 5 March 1839. Philadelphia.** Announce a change of dates for the convention. 4 April 1839. p.2, c6.

**2071 JOHN CLARKE** *to* **MR. SHELDON. 9 January 1839. Mount Hermon, Jamaica.** Discusses the results of emancipation in the West Indies. 4 April 1839. p.2, c6.

**2072 JOHN CLARKE** *to* **REVEREND J. LEAVITT. [from the** ***Emancipator*****] 19 December 1838. Jericho, St. Thomas in the Vale.** Discusses the success of emancipation in Jamaica. 4 April 1839. p.4, c2.

**2073 JOSHUA COFFIN** *to* **n.n. [from the** ***Liberator*****] 12 March 1839. Philadelphia.** Observes slave life in the South. 4 April 1839. p.4, c3.

**2074 O. S. C.** *to* **THE EDITOR. [from the** ***Christian Reflector*****] 9 February 1839. Boston.** Speaks out against slavery; supports the efforts of abolitionists. 4 April 1839. p.4, c4.

**2075 H. NYE** *to* **n.n. [extract from the** ***Emancipator*****] 8 March 1839. Putnam, Oh.** Decries the passage of a law in Ohio that would benefit slaveholders. 4 April 1839. p.4, c4.

**2076 A. A. JAYNE** *to* **MR. SUNDERLAND. [from** ***Zion's Watchman*****] n.d. n.p.** Discusses his excommunication because of his enrollment in an AS. 11 April 1839. p.1, c1.

**2077 S. D. FERGUSON** *to* **A. A. JAYNE. 8 March 1839. New York.** Gives his reasons for excommunicating Jayne, chief among which was his participation in an AS. 11 April 1839. p.1, c2.

**2078 WILLIAM SLADE** *to* **A. LIBOLT. 25 January 1839. Washington.** Commends the work of abolitionists. 11 April 1839. p.1, c3.

**2079 E. N.** *to* **THE FREE COLORED PEOPLE. 28 March 1839. Philadelphia.** Advises free colored people of the advantages of industry and sobriety. 11 April 1839. p.1, c6.

**2080 T. S. C.** *to* **FRIEND WHITTIER. 29 March 1839. n.p.** Defends his original report of the Junior AS, which "Amicus" considered to be strongly worded. 11 April 1839. p.2, c2.

**2081 E. WRIGHT, JR.** *to* **n.n. [from** *Human Rights***] n.d. New York City.** Requests the names of presidents and secretaries of all county ASs, as well as the names of all hard-working abolitionists. 11 April 1839. p.2, c5.

**2082 J. CABLE** *to* **n.n. [from the** *Philanthropist***] 1 March 1839. Columbus.** Announces the submission of a petition to the Senate and House of Representatives of Ohio which demands remuneration for time and expenses to all citizens forcibly taken out of Ohio. 11 April 1839. p.2, c5.

**2083 A FRIEND AT MOBILE** *to* **n.n. [from the** *Norfolk* **(Ma.)** *Democrat***] December 1838. Alabama.** Describes the quality of life in Mobile. 11 April 1839. p.2, c5.

**2084 J. C. HATHAWAY** *to* **n.n. [extract] 16 March 1839. Farmington, N.Y.** Characterizes abolitionists and political action. 11 April 1839. p.3, c4.

**2085 CORRESPONDENT** *to* **n.n. [extract] n.d. Cincinnati.** Expresses hope that the cause of abolition will soon be supported by all. 11 April 1839. p.4, c5.

**2086 THOMAS JEFFERSON** *to* **EDWARD COLES. 25 August 1814. Monticello.** Comments on slavery and emancipation. 18 April 1839. p.1, c6.

**2087 H. K. BURKELL** *to* **JOHN G. WHITTIER. 18 March 1839. Jamaica.** Informs of the successful results of emancipation in Jamaica. 18 April 1839. p.2, c1.

**2088 J. C.** *to* **MR. EDITOR [J. G. WHITTIER]. n.d. n.p.** Encloses a letter citing an unusual method of discipline. 18 April 1839. p.2, c2.

**2089 J. A. ALLEN** *to* **BROTHER MURRAY. [from the** *Vermont Telegraph***] 27 March 1839. Middlebury.** Describes how a successful black businessman in Lexington, Kentucky, ended his harrassment by slaves in the area. 18 April 1839. p.2, c2.

**2090 GEORGE BRADBURN** *to* **FRIEND WHITTIER. 11 April 1839. Boston.** Forwards the resolutions passed by the Massachusetts state legislature concerning the detainment or imprisonment of its citizens while in other states. 18 April 1839. p.2, c3.

**2091 JOHN CONANT** *to* **n.n. [extract from the** *Vermont Telegraph***] n.d. Brandon, Vt.** Defends Henry Clay. 18 April 1839. p.2, c4.

**2092 C. WHITE** *to* **MESSRS. EDITORS. [from the** *Montrose Spectator***] 29 March 1839. Wilkesbarre.** Defends himself after an argument in print with C. C. Burleigh. 18 April 1839. p.2, c6.

**2093 n.n.** *to* **n.n. [extract from the** *National Gazette* of Cuba**] n.d. n.p.** Describes the procession of newly arrived slaves in Havana. 18 April 1839. p.3, c4.

**2094 THOMAS C. PERRY** *to* **THE EDITOR OF** *ZION'S WATCHMAN***. 3 March 1839. n.p.** Describes an episode involving a runaway slave. 18 April 1839. p.3, c6.

**2095 WILLIAM BARDWELL** *to* **n.n. [from** *Zion's Watchman***] 4 March 1839. Sandwich, Ma.** Reports an episode involving a runaway slave. 18 April 1839. p.3, c6.

**2096 n.n.** *to* **THE** *FRANKLIN* **(TN.)** *REVIEW***. [extract from the** *Christian Reflector***] 19 February. Macon, Ga.** Condemns widespread arson in Macon, Georgia; warns of further trouble if slavery is allowed to continue. 18 April 1839. p.4, c3.

**2097 J. LE BOSQUET** *to* **MR. EDITOR. [from the** *N.H. Christian Panoply***] 1839. Nottingham.** Responds to a recently published letter on the horrors of slavery on the Sandwich and Marquesas Islands. 18 April 1839. p.4, c4.

**2098 ESTHER HAYES** *to* **FRIEND WHITTIER. 17 April 1839. East Caln, Chester County.** Forwards the preamble and constitution of the newly formed East Caln AS. 25 April 1839. p.2, c3.

**2099 JACOB M. ELLIS** *to* **THE** ***PENNSYLVANIA FREEMAN.*** **n.d. n.p.** Furnishes a list of delegates from the Northern Liberties AS to the county society and to the Convention of American Women. 25 April 1839. p.2, c5.

**2100 H. WETHERELD** *to* **THE** ***PENNSYLVANIA FREEMAN.*** **n.d. n.p.** Encloses the minutes of the annual meeting of the Philadelphia City AS and the names of the newly elected officers. 25 April 1839. p.2, c5.

**2101 W. C. GILDERSLEEVE** *to* **BROTHER POST. [from the** *Montrose Spectator***] 9 April 1839. Wilkesbarre.** Affirms his intention to prosecute a mob of powerful citizens for their disruptive actions. 25 April 1839. p.2, c6.

**2102 G. F. HORTON** *to* **n.n. [extract] n.d. Bradford County.** Offers encouragement to Chace and Burleigh after the failures at Towanda and Wilkesbarre; hopes the Church will divorce itself from slavery and follow the message of the Bible. 25 April 1839. p.3, c3.

**2103 W. H. J.** *to* **FRIEND. 21 April 1839. Buckingham.** Discusses C. C. Burleigh's recent lectures. 25 April 1839. p.3, c5.

**2104 BOSTON CORRESPONDENT** *to* **THE** ***NEW YORK EVANGELIST.*** **[extract] 5 March. n.p.** Discusses Dr. Venable's experiences as a missionary in South Africa. 2 May 1839. p.1, c4.

**2105 JAMES C. FULLER** *to* **WILLIAM GOODELL. [from the** *Friend of Man***] n.d. Skaneateles.** Affirms the claims made by Hall in his letter. 2 May 1839. p.1, c5.

**2106 n.n.** *to* **n.n. [from the** *Philanthropist***] n.d. n.p.** Offers two anecdotes on Southern brutality. 2 May 1839. p.1, c6.

**2107 J. A. ALLEN** *to* **C. L. KNAPP. [from the** *Voice of Freedom***] 28 February 1839. Middlebury.** Forwards a letter from Gov. D. M. Camp. 2 May 1839. p.2, c1.

**2108 D. M. CAMP** *to* **J.A. ALLEN. 13 February 1839. Derby.** Discusses certain constitutional clauses upon which Southerners base their claim for protection of slavery. 2 May 1839. p.2, c1.

**2109 DAVID HALL, JR.** *to* **WILLIAM GOODELL. [from the** *Friend of Man***] 19 April 1839. Skaneateles.** Discusses an anti-abolitionist riot directed against J. C. Fuller. 2 May 1839. p.2, c4.

**2110 CORRESPONDENT** *to* **THE** ***NEW BEDFORD REGISTER.*** **[extract] n.d. n.p.** Compliments W. L. Garrison's speech in New Bedford, Massachusetts. 2 May 1839. p.2, c4.

**2111 JOHN TRUAIR** *to* **MR. MYRICK. 17 April 1839. Apulia.** Introduces a narrative by J. C. Hodge concerning the treatment of slaves in the South. 2 May 1839. p.3, c2.

**2112 W. H. J.** *to* **FRIEND WHITTIER. 26 April 1839. Buckingham.** Reports the formation of a new AS in Bucks County. 2 May 1839. p.3, c5.

**2113 J. FULTON, JR.** *to* **FRIEND WHITTIER. 24 April 1839. Ercildoun.** Describes several anti-slavery meetings. 2 May 1839. p.3, c5.

**2114 JAMES P. ELLIS** *to* **THE** ***PENNSYLVANIA FREEMAN.*** **n.d. n.p.** Announces the names of the new delegates to represent the Spring Garden AS at the next meeting of the Philadelphia City and County AS. 2 May 1839. p.3, c6.

**2115 THOMAS M'CLINTOCK** *to* **n.n. [from the** *Friend of Man***] 2 March 1839. Waterloo.** Responds to Henry Clay's recent speech before the Senate. 2 May 1839. p.4, c4.

**2116 W. L.** *to* **MESSRS. EDITORS. [from the** *New York Observer***] 7 March 1839. New York.** Warns of the terrible consequences of a second war with England. 9 May 1839. p.1, c5.

**2117 J. H. H.** *to* **FRIEND WHITTIER. 29 April 1839. n.p.** Considers the subject of slavery and the forthcoming presidential election. 9 May 1839. p.1, c5.

**2118 JOSHUA COFFIN** *to* **WHITTIER. 29 April 1839. Albany.** Encloses a verbatim copy of a letter from Phillis Wheatley to Rev. Mr. Samuel Hopkins; discusses a session in the House of Representatives which considered a bill granting trial by jury to fugitive slaves. 9 May 1839. p.1, c5.

**2119 PHILLIS WHEATLEY** *to* **REVEREND MR. SAMUEL HOPKINS. 9 February 1774. Boston.** Forwards several of her books which have just arrived from England, and mourns the condition of the slave. 9 May 1839. p.1, c6.

**2120 C. S. S. GRIFFING** *to* **BROTHER SUNDERLAND. [from** *Zion's Watchman***] 23 March 1839. Cadiz, Oh.** Relays an account of a slave's escape to Ohio. 9 May 1839. p.2, c3.

**2121 A YOUNG MAN IN LOUISIANA** *to* **FRIENDS AT RIGA. 21 February 1839. New York.** Condemns the deplorable condition of humanity in the South. 9 May 1839. p.3, c1.

**2122 REVEREND D. N. MERRITT** *to* **THE** ***UNION HERALD.*** **10 April 1839. Riga, N.Y.** Encloses the letter of a young man to his friends deploring conditions in the South. 9 May 1839. p.3, c1.

**2123 C. C. BURLEIGH** *to* **WHITTIER. n.d. n.p.** Discusses a series of anti-slavery meetings and discussions on slavery with R. D. Morris. 9 May 1839. p.3, c3.

**2124 E. W. GOODWIN** *to* **n.n. 15 March 1839. Albany.** Discusses a session of the New York legislature spent deliberating various anti-slavery petitions. 9 May 1839. p.4, c5.

**2125 J. K. PAULDING** *to* **n.n. [extract from the** *Emancipator***] Summer 1812. New York.** Deplores the conditions to which slaves are submitted during transportation to various states in the South. 16 May 1839. p.1, c3.

**2126 AUGUSTUS WATTLES** *to* **FRIEND. [from the** *Christian Witness***] 12 April 1839. New Bremen, Mercer County, Oh.** Describes his labors to establish a manual labor school and a black settlement. 16 May 1839. p.1, c4.

**2127 TWO MEN IN TENNESSEE** *to* **AUGUSTUS WATTLES. [extract] n.d. n.p.** Wonder if Wattles can help them liberate twenty slaves, but are wary because one man was previously fined $1,200 in Illinois for attempting to settle a family there. 16 May 1839. p.1, c3.

**2128 n.n.** *to* **n.n. [extract from the** *Friend of Man***] 14 March 1839. Penn Yan.** Rejoices that the church has played such an important part in the Western AS Convention. 16 May 1839. p.1, c4.

**2129 C. C. BURLEIGH** *to* **WHITTIER. n.d. n.p.** Concludes his discussion of R. D. Morris's speech. 16 May 1839. p.1, c5.

**2130 AN EPISCOPAL CLERGYMAN** *to* **BRETHREN. 14 January 1839. Florence.** Relates the impressions made abroad by the mobs against abolitionists and others in the United States. 16 May 1839. p.2, c3.

**2131 C. C. BURLEIGH** *to* **THE TREASURER OF THE PENNSYLVANIA STATE AS. n.d. n.p.** Includes an extract of a letter from a friend in response to Henry Clay's speech to the Senate and a donation of $50 to the Pennsylvania State AS. 16 May 1839. p.3, c4.

**2132 WOOLMAN** *to* **n.n. 12 May 1839. Chester County.** Criticizes Henry Clay's recent speech to the Senate and condemns his candidacy for Congress. 16 May 1839. p.3, c4.

**2133 REVEREND D. S. INGRAHAM** *to* **MR. BENEDICT. [from the** ***Emancipator*****] 17 January 1839. Kingston, Jamaica.** Affirms the good results of emancipation in Jamaica. 16 May 1839. p.4, c2.

**2134 A FRIEND** *to* **n.n. [from** ***Zion's Watchman*****] n.d. n.p.** Encloses a copy of a letter from his nephew describing his involvement with slavery in Alabama. 16 May 1839. p.4, c3.

**2135 HARLEY BUSHNELL BROWNELL** *to* **n.n. 15 March 1839. Centerville, Bibb County, Al.** A "slave driver" describes his activities to his uncle, a Northern abolitionist. 16 May 1839. p.4, c3.

**2136 I. S. P.** *to* **MR. EDITOR [J. G. WHITTIER]. n.d. n.p.** Responds to Dr. Channing's pamphlet on Henry Clay's speech before the Senate. 23 May 1839. p.1, c5.

**2137 J. M. E.** *to* **FRIEND WHITTIER. n.d. n.p.** Encloses a record of the proceedings of the most recent meeting of the AS of the City and County of Philadelphia. 23 May 1839. p.2, c2.

**2138 GERRIT SMITH** *to* **MR. LEAVITT. [from the** ***Emancipator*****] 11 May 1839. New York.** Provides a brief account of a mob which broke up his anti-slavery meeting at Newburgh, New York. 23 May 1839. p.2, c2.

**2139 S.** *to* **WHITTIER. [from the** ***Emancipator*****] 16 May 1839. New Haven, Ct.** Describes a mob which disrupted an anti-slavery meeting in New Haven. 23 May 1839. p.2, c3.

**2140 WM. LEFTWICH** *to* **n.n. [from "Slavery as It Is"] 26 December 1838. n.p.** Characterizes the miserable conditions of slaves in Alabama. 23 May 1839. p.4, c2.

**2141 JAMES G. BIRNEY** *to* **BROTHER LEAVITT. 23 May 1839. Washington, Pa.** Describes in detail the beginning of his western anti-slavery tour. 13 June 1839. p.1, c1.

**2142 C. C. BURLEIGH** *to* **WHITTIER. 2 June 1839. Boston.** Forwards an account of the proceedings at the New England convention. 13 June 1839. p.1, c5.

**2143 J. LYBRAND** *to* **MR. WHITTIER. 13 May 1839. New Mexico, Green County, Wi.** Declares himself to be against slavery. 13 June 1839. p.2, c1.

**2144 BENJAMIN CLENDENON** *to* **FRIEND WHITTIER. 18 May 1839. n.p.** Encloses the most recent resolutions adopted by the Colerain AS. 13 June 1839. p.2, c2.

**2145 MITCHELL THOMPSON** *to* **LEWIS C. GUNN. 27 March. Port Royal, Jamaica.** Explains why emancipation has been difficult for blacks in Jamaica. 13 June 1839. p.3, c2.

**2146 AN OFFICER ON BOARD THE BRITISH MAN-OF-WAR** ***PELICAN to*** **n.n. [extract from a London paper] n.d. Jamaica.** Deplores a contract between an American and a Spanish ship that manipulates naval law to permit the traffic of slaves to Cuba. 13 June 1839. p.3, c3.

**2147 A.** *to* **FRIEND WHITTIER. n.d. n.p.** Questions the principles of George Fox, a candidate for public office. 13 June 1839. p.3, c4.

**2148 JAMES G. BIRNEY** *to* **MR. LEAVITT. 31 May 1839. Putnam, Oh.** Discusses a meeting of the Ohio AS. 20 June 1839. p.1, c2.

**2149 CONSISTENCY** *to* **MR. EDITOR. [from the** ***Emancipator*****] n.d. n.p.** Questions the sincerity of President Madison's will. 20 June 1839. p.1, c3.

**2150 C. C. BURLEIGH** *to* **MR. WHITTIER. 6 June 1839. Concord, N.H.** Describes an anti-slavery meeting held in Concord. 20 June 1839. p.1, c6.

**2151 n.n.** *to* **n.n. [from the** ***Christian Witness*****] n.d. n.p.** Remarks on Henry Clay's speech before the Senate. 20 June 1839. p.2, c6.

**2152 HIPPOLYTE DE SAINT ANTHOINE** *to* **E. WRIGHT, JR., ESQ. 13 February 1839. Paris.** Details the principles of the French Society for the Abolition of Slavery; discusses the inconsistency between liberty and slavery in the American Republic; states his observations on the American attitude toward slavery and emancipation. 20 June 1839. p.3, c1.

**2153 CORRESPONDENT** *to* **n.n. [extract from the** ***Liberator*****] n.d. Andover Theological Seminary.** Commends C. C. Burleigh. 20 June 1839. p.3, c2.

**2154 J. S. P.** *to* **MR. WHITTIER. n.d. n.p.** Responds to a pamphlet entitled "Slavery as It Is" with renewed fervor in the abolition cause. 20 June 1839. p.3, c3.

**2155 PROFESSOR RIPLEY** *to* **THE EDITOR OF THE** ***BOSTON CHRISTIAN REFLECTOR*****. n.d. Newton, Ma.** Explains that he is an unwilling slave owner, having become a master by marriage. 20 June 1839. p.3, c3.

**2156 J. FULTON, JR.** *to* **FRIEND WHITTIER. n.d. n.p.** Asserts that the members of his AS are in favor of political action and can always be relied on to vote. 20 June 1839. p.3, c4.

**2157 G. P.** *to* **FRIEND GARRISON. 5 June 1839. Andover.** Regrets that abolition is slipping in importance and that their society must fold for lack of support. 20 June 1839. p.3, c5.

**2158 JAMES G. BIRNEY** *to* **BROTHER. 11 May 1839. n.p.** Asserts that the cause of abolition is still strong, and intends to reprint Weld's "Slavery as It Is". 20 June 1839. p.4, c2.

**2159 ARTHUR TAPPAN** *to* **JOSHUA LEAVITT. 27 May 1839. New York.** Appeals to Leavitt for help in escalating abolition. 20 June 1839. p.4, c4.

**2160 FRANCIS T. ALLEN AND SIRRUS TRACY** *to* **MR. CLARK. [from the** ***Cleveland Observer*****] 8 May 1839. Mesopotamia.** Comment on the Underground Railroad from Russel to Cleveland. 27 June 1839. p.1, c4.

**2161 BIBLE** *to* **FRIEND. n.d. n.p.** Cites biblical passages which address the issue of slavery. 27 June 1839. p.2, c1.

**2162 J. H. B.** *to* **BROTHER MURRAY. 5 June 1839. Oberlin Collegiate Institute, Oh.** Describes the anniversary meeting of the Ohio AS. 27 June 1839. p.2, c2.

**2163 JAMES G. BIRNEY** *to* **BROTHER LEAVITT. 11 June 1839. Cincinnati.** Portrays an anti-abolition town and several anti-slavery meetings. 27 June 1839. p.4, c3.

**2164 CORRESPONDENT** *to* **SIR. [from the** *New York Courier and Enquirer***] 25 April 1839. Rio de Janeiro.** Reports on slave ships captured in the Caribbean. 27 June 1839. p.4, c3.

**2165 C. C. BURLEIGH** *to* **MR. WHITTIER. 20 June 1839. Plainfield, Ct.** Characterizes several anti-slavery meetings in Massachusetts and the Massachusetts AS. 4 July 1839. p.1, c1.

**2166 A TRAVELLER** *to* **BROTHER LEAVITT. [from the** *Emancipator***] n.d. n.p.** Describes his progress up the Ohio River. 4 July 1839. p.1, c5.

**2167 A GENTLEMAN IN A SLAVE STATE** *to* **SIR. [extract from the** *Philanthropist***] n.d. n.p.** Requests more information on the principles of abolition and wishes to subscribe to abolitionist papers. 4 July 1839. p.1, c6.

**2168 GEORGE S. BULL** *to* **n.n. [extract] 23 February 1839. Yorkshire, England.** Cautions against the American system of slavery. 4 July 1839. p.1, c6.

**2169 NEW YORK CORRESPONDENT** *to* **THE** ***BOSTON ATLAS*****. [extract from the** *Emancipator***] 11 June. n.p.** Comments on the vice-president of the United States. 4 July 1839. p.1, c6.

**2170 FRANCIS S. KEY, ESQ.** *to* **DR. TAPPAN. [extract] n.d. Washington, D.C.** Answers several questions concerning several justifications of slavery. 4 July 1839. p.2, c3.

**2171 D. DE VINNE** *to* **THE PRESIDENT OF THE GREEN COUNTY AS. 10 June 1839. Durham.** Expresses his views against slavery. 4 July 1839. p.3, c2.

**2172 JAS. A. THOME** *to* **DR. G. BAILEY. 23 May 1839. Oberlin.** Urges a repeal of the Black Laws. 4 July 1839. p.3, c3.

**2173 ANDOVER CORRESPONDENT** *to* **MR. GARRISON. [from the** *Liberator***] 22 June 1839. Andover Theological Seminary.** Gives an account of a lecture delivered by ex-Governor Pinney of Liberia. 4 July 1839. p.3, c6.

**2174 S. D. C.** *to* **BROTHER. [from the** *Oberlin Evangelist***] 10 June 1839. Oberlin.** Encloses an extract from a friend on the subtle effects of abolition. 4 July 1839. p.4, c3.

**2175 n.n.** *to* **SIR. [extract from the** *Oberlin Evangelist***] 14 May 1839. Arkansas.** Believes that the morality of slavery is questioned by more slaveholders than one would imagine. 4 July 1839. p.4, c3.

**2176 JOHN CLARK** *to* **MR. EDITOR [from the** *Philanthropist***] June 1838. Tanner's Creek.** Stresses the strength of the abolitionist cause in Indiana and says that several new societies have been formed. 4 July 1839. p.4, c5.

**2177 DR. PLINY EARLE** *to* **n.n. [extract] n.d. n.p.** Describes the association based on equality between blacks and whites in European cities. 11 July 1839. p.1, c3.

**2178 A YOUNG MAN OF MARYLAND** *to* **THE EDITOR [J. G. WHITTIER]. 29 June 1839. Maryland.** Assails the system of slavery and all its evils; urges speedy reform. 11 July 1839. p.1, c5.

**2179 E. H. C.** *to* **FRIEND WHITTIER. n.d. n.p.** Satirizes the South's loss as more slaves move North. 11 July 1839. p.1, c6.

**2180 A YOUNG FRIEND OF BALTIMORE** *to* **FRIEND WHITTIER. [extract] n.d. Baltimore.** Hopes that the address from the recent Female Anti-Slavery Convention has some effect toward bringing an end to slavery. 11 July 1839. p.1, c6.

**2181 A. B.** *to* **THE EDITOR. [from the** ***Ohio Free Press*****] n.d. n.p.** Urges the formation of a political organization which will resist the encroachment of slavery in general, in accordance with the principles and spirit of the Declaration of Independence and the Constitution, but will remain independent of abolitionists. 11 July 1839. p.2, c1.

**2182 HENRY H. LOOMIS** *to* **n.n. [from the** ***Union Herald*****] May 1839. New York City.** Deplores the squalid conditions under which slaves are forced to live in South Carolina and Kentucky. 11 July 1839. p.2, c4.

**2183 S. D. C.** *to* **BROTHER. [from the** ***Oberlin Evangelist*****] 10 June 1839. Oberlin.** Encloses an extract of a letter from a friend who feels some sympathy for slaveholders. 11 July 1839. p.2, c5.

**2184 n.n.** *to* **SIR. [extract from the** ***Oberlin Evangelist*****] 14 May 1839. Arkansas.** Insists that many slaveholders realize the cruelty of slavery, but are reluctant to initiate change in the system themselves. 11 July 1839. p.2, c5.

**2185 JOHN G. WHITTIER** *to* **MR. CARTLAND. 8 July 1839. Harrisburg, Pa.** Discusses the beginnings of his tour through western Pennsylvania, and an anti-slavery meeting held there. 11 July 1839. p.2, c6.

**2186 H. B. STANTON** *to* **BROTHER LEAVITT. 29 June 1839. New York.** Describes two great anti-slavery conventions held in Auburn and Union Village, New York. 11 July 1839. p.4, c1.

**2187 Y.** *to* **THE EDITOR. [from the** ***Atlas*****] 11 June 1839. New York.** Discusses Calhoun's slave policy. 11 July 1839. p.4, c4.

**2188 B. C. BACON** *to* **MR. EDITOR [J. G. WHITTIER]. n.d. n.p.** Encloses the resolutions recently adopted by the Union AS. 18 July 1839. p.2, c2.

**2189 n.n.** *to* **LUCIUS C. MATLACK, ESQ. 16 June 1839. Mexico.** Considers the present state of St. Domingo. 18 July 1839. p.2, c3.

**2190 C. C. BURLEIGH** *to* **MR. CARTLAND. n.d. n.p.** Discusses a meeting held near Norristown. 18 July 1839. p.2, c4.

**2191 J. FULTON, JR.** *to* **J. G. WHITTIER. 4 July 1839. Ercildoun.** Describes an anti-slavery meeting held in West Grove, Chester County. 18 July 1839. p.2, c4.

**2192 HERMAN FERRIS** *to* **DR. BAILEY. [from the** ***Philanthropist*****] n.d. n.p.** Speaks out against allying oneself with a particular political party, and condemns parties which lack true principles. 18 July 1839. p.3, c4.

**2193 L. H.** *to* **MR. BURLEIGH. 17 June 1839. Pittsburgh.** Deplores the religious deprivation of slaves which results from the proscription against their education. 18 July 1839. p.4, c2.

**2194 BRUSSELS CORRESPONDENT** *to* **THE** ***NEW YORK EVENING STAR*****. [extract] n.d. Brussels.** Regrets that the battlefield at Waterloo has become a tourist attraction, complete with sculpture and family memorials. 18 July 1839. p.4, c5.

**2195 DR. FINLEY** *to* **REVEREND ASA MAHAN. [extract from the** *New York Evangelist***] n.d. n.p.** Submits an eyewitness account of the horrors of slavery for a review of the pamphlet, "Slavery as It Is." 25 July 1839. p.1, c3.

**2196 G. SEIDENSTICKER** *to* **n.n. [extract] n.d. A German Prison.** Finds hope for humanity in the abolition efforts of men like Slade. 25 July 1839. p.2, c6.

**2197 n.n.** *to* **n.n. [extract from the** *New York Evening Star***] 1 July 1839. Havana.** Deplores the smuggling of new slaves into Cuba on American ships. 25 July 1839. p.3, c6.

**2198 REVEREND H. H. KAVANAGH** *to* **n.n. [extract from the** *Emancipator***] n.d. Kentucky.** Illustrates the need for schools in rural Kentucky. 1 August 1839. p.1, c5.

**2199 C. S. RENSHAW** *to* **MR. BAILEY. [from the** *Philanthropist***] 12 June 1839. Akron.** Submits a testimonial to the memory of Elijah P. Lovejoy, who died for the cause of the slave. 1 August 1839. p.2, c1.

**2200 L. G. HAMILTON** *to* **MADAM [MRS. ELIJAH P. LOVEJOY]. [extract] 27 August 1838. Port-au-Prince.** Sends condolences from the Haitian AS to the widow of the "martyr of Alton." 1 August 1839. p.2, c1.

**2201 ELIJAH P. LOVEJOY** *to* **HIS WIFE. [extract] n.d. n.p.** Reaffirms his faith in God and acknowledges that he may sacrifice his life for the abolitionist cause. 1 August 1839. p.2, c1.

**2202 n.n.** *to* **n.n. [extract from the** *Emancipator***] n.d. n.p.** Describes a slave child's fear of being sold upon the death of his mother. 1 August 1839. p.2, c2.

**2203 A GENTLEMAN IN MISSOURI** *to* **n.n. [from the** *American Citizen***] n.d. n.p.** Thanks his friend for sending Thome and Kimball's book; responds to the published speeches of Morris and Clay. 1 August 1839. p.2, c3.

**2204 THOMAS ATKINSON** *to* **MR. WHITTIER. 11 July 1839. Warwick.** Sends a copy of the declaration of sentiments and the constitution of the Concord AS. 1 August 1839. p.2, c4.

**2205 MARY S. PARKER AND M. V. BALL** *to* **THE WOMEN OF NEW ENGLAND. n.d. n.p.** Appeal to women to become engaged in the anti-slavery cause. 1 August 1839. p.3, c2.

**2206 LONDON CORRESPONDENT** *to* **n.n. [extract from the** *National Intelligencer***] 4 July. North and South American Coffee House, London.** Announces a war in the Middle East. 1 August 1839. p.3, c4.

**2207 GEORGE STACY** *to* **FRIENDS. 7 March 1834. London.** Urges continued efforts to promote abolition in America. 1 August 1839. p.3, c4.

**2208 JOSIAH FORSTER** *to* **n.n. [extract] 1829. London.** Entreats the Society of Friends to press for abolition. 1 August 1839. p.3, c5.

**2209 BRO. WATSON** *to* **n.n. [from the** *Emancipator***] 5 July. Keesville, N.Y.** Praises the New York State AS Convention held in Keesville on the Fourth of July. 1 August 1839. p.4, c5.

**2210 THOMAS EARLE, ESQ.** *to* **A. L. POST, ESQ. 1 July 1839. n.p.** Proclaims his belief in universal liberty. 1 August 1839. p.4, c5.

**2211 HONORABLE F. H. ELMORE** *to* **E. M. S. SPENCER. February 1838. Washington City.** Asks for information concerning Northern abolition societies. 8 August 1839. p.1, c1.

**2212 E. M. S. SPENCER** *to* **HONORABLE F. H. ELMORE. n.d. n.p.** Describes some of the activities and plans of the Northern abolitionists. 8 August 1839. p.1, c2.

**2213 W. H. MURCH, JOSEPH BELCHER, AND EDWARD STEANE** *to* **BROTHER. [from the** ***Boston Christian Watchman*****] 7 June 1839. London.** Regret that the churches of America continue to sanction slavery. 8 August 1839. p.2, c1.

**2214 JOHN SMITH, JR.** *to* **n.n. [extract from the** ***New York Evening Post*****] n.d. Arkansas.** Recommends that the South trust Martin Van Buren, rather than Henry Clay. 8 August 1839. p.2, c4.

**2215 J. M. McKIM** *to* **M. A. CARTLAND. 28 July 1839. Carlisle.** Considers a lecture delivered by C. C. Burleigh, and the work of abolitionists in the counties of Pennsylvania. 8 August 1839. p.2, c5.

**2216 AN OBSERVER** *to* **THE EDITOR [J. G. WHITTIER]. 27 July 1839. Baltimore.** Discusses a series of lectures delivered by Stephen H. Gloucester. 8 August 1839. p.2, c6.

**2217 EAVES DROPPER** *to* **MR. EDITOR [J. G. WHITTIER]. n.d. n.p.** Provides a satirical argument against racial prejudice. 8 August 1839. p.2, c6.

**2218 J. FULTON, JR.** *to* **THE ABOLITIONISTS OF CHESTER COUNTY. 3 August 1839. Ercildoun.** Comments on the financial concerns and problems of the AAS. 8 August 1839. p.3, c1.

**2219 J. G. WHITTIER** *to* **MR. CARTLAND. 1 August 1839. Albany, New York.** Discusses the progress of the National Anti-Slavery Convention. 8 August 1839. p.3, c1.

**2220 ZENAS BLISS** *to* **MR. TRACY. [from the** ***Vermont Chronicle*****] n.d. n.p.** Encloses an exchange between himself and Rev. Nathan Lord. 8 August 1839. p.4, c1.

**2221 ZENAS BLISS** *to* **REVEREND NATHAN LORD. [from the** ***Vermont Chronicle*****] 16 April 1839. Quechee.** Asks Reverend Lord for his views on abolitionism, and expresses his opposition to abolitionism. 8 August 1839. p.4, c1.

**2222 REVEREND NATHAN LORD** *to* **REVEREND ZENAS BLISS. [from the** ***Vermont Chronicle*****] 30 May 1839. Dartmouth College.** Discusses his anti-slavery sentiments and the relationship between the interests of the Church and abolitionism. 8 August 1839. p.4, c2.

**2223 J. KEES AND WM. DAVIES** *to* **BROTHER. [from the** ***Emancipator*****] 6 July 1839. London.** Discuss their trip to England and their impressions of several anti-slavery meetings and discussions there. 15 August 1839. p.1, c4.

**2224 HAMET [*****sic*****], EMPEROR OF MOROCCO** *to* **HENRY CLAY. [from the** ***Voice of Freedom*****] n.d. n.p.** Commends Clay's pro-slavery speech before the Senate, particularly his remark that property is defined by law. 15 August 1839. p.2, c1.

**2225 ALPHA** *to* **MR. EDITOR. [from the** ***Philanthropist*****] n.d. n.p.** Encloses two letters inspired by a rabid young abolitionist. 15 August 1839. p.2, c3.

**2226 n.n.** *to* **REVEREND MR. B. [extract] n.d. n.p.** Describes the halting of a lynching by abolitionists. 15 August 1839. p.2, c3.

2227 **n.n.** *to* **n.n. [extract] n.d. n.p.** Warns a young abolitionist to stay out of Kentucky or risk being hanged. 15 August 1839. p.2, c3.

2228 **L. C. GUNN** *to* **MR. CARTLAND. 12 August 1839. n.p.** Discusses several anti-slavery meetings conducted by John Scoble. 15 August 1839. p.2, c4.

2229 **JOHN G. WHITTIER** *to* **MR. CARTLAND. 6 August 1839. Saratoga Springs, N.Y.** Comments on the resolutions on abolitionists and political action, which occupied the last day's session of the National Anti-Slavery Convention. 15 August 1839. p.2, c5.

2230 **THOMAS MORRIS** *to* **N. SANFORD, ESQ. 22 July 1839. Cincinnati.** Discusses the anti-slavery movement and the men actively involved in it. 22 August 1839. p.1, c2.

2231 **THEODORE SEDGWICK** *to* **JOSHUA LEAVITT AND H. B. STANTON. 23 July 1839. Stockbridge.** Supports the idea that the abolition of slavery by peaceful and constitutional means is in the best political interest of the United States. 22 August 1839. p.1, c2.

2232 **EDWARD C. DELAVAN** *to* **n.n. 28 July 1839. Ballston Centre.** Comments on anti-slavery feelings in England. 22 August 1839. p.1, c3.

2233 **HENRY CLAY** *to* **MESSRS. JOHN C. CRUMP, THOS. H. P. GOODWIN, JOHN C. COHOON, ETC. 25 May 1839. Ashland.** Stresses the necessity of preserving domestic slavery, and condemns abolition. 22 August 1839. p.1, c4.

2234 **C. C. BURLEIGH** *to* **MR. CARTLAND. 5 August 1839. Washington, Pa.** Discusses several anti-slavery meetings and lectures. 22 August 1839. p.2, c5.

2235 **C. C. BURLEIGH** *to* **MR. CARTLAND. 8 August 1839. Cadiz, Oh.** Discusses several anti-slavery meetings and lectures. 22 August 1839. p.2, c6.

2236 **WILLIAM KENDRICK** *to* **THE EDITOR OF THE** ***FARMER'S REGISTER*****. 1 April 1839. Portsmouth, Va.** Considers the effect of slavery on the agriculture of Virginia. 22 August 1839. p.4, c2.

2237 **ISRAEL R. VAN BRAKLE** *to* **JOHN LEVY. [extract from the** ***Liberator*****] 1 July 1839. St. Croix.** Explains the ban on abolitionist newspapers in many of the islands and requests that no more be sent him, to avoid jeopardizing his safety. 22 August 1839. p.4, c4.

2238 **n.n.** *to* **n.n. [extract from the** ***Dedham Patriot*****] n.d. n.p.** Pleads for an honest president for the United States. 22 August 1839. p.4, c5.

2239 **G. D.** *to* **MR. EDITOR. [from the** ***Philanthropist*****] 27 May 1839. n.p.** Notes the removal of an anecdote about slavery from the later edition of a textbook, which he condemns as Northern interference. 29 August 1839. p.1, c5.

2240 **P. HAYMER** *to* **MR. WHITTIER. 19 August 1839. Chester County.** Describes his discussion of slavery and Northern abolitionism with a slaveholder in the South. 29 August 1839. p.2, c5.

2241 **W. G.** *to* **n.n. [extract] 22 August 1839. Rochester, N.Y.** Rejoices in the cause of abolition. 29 August 1839. p.3, c4.

2242 **HIPPOLYTE DE SAINT ANTHOINE** *to* **THE PRESIDENT OF THE ACADEMY OF MORAL SCIENCE. [from the** ***British Emancipator*****] 6 May 1839. Paris.** Attempts to expose the danger of making abolition a prize instead of a basic human right. 29 August 1839. p.4, c6.

**2243 WENDELL PHILLIPS** *to* **W. L. GARRISON. [from the** *Liberator***] 31 July 1839. London.** Reports the progress of the abolitionist movement in England. 5 July [September] 1839. p.1, c5.

**2244 DON JOSE RUIZ AND DON PEDRO MONTEZ** *to* **n.n. 29 August 1839. New London.** Express their thanks to the officers and crew of the United States surveying brig *Washington* for seizing the *Amistad* and protecting her crew. 5 September 1839. p.2, c6.

**2245 J. G. WHITTIER** *to* **THE SECRETARY OF THE PHILADELPHIA COUNTY AS. 27 August 1839. Amesbury.** Stresses the importance of continued petitioning to Congress as a means of accomplishing abolition. 5 September 1839. p.2, c6.

**2246 L. L.** *to* **MR. EDITOR [J. G. WHITTIER]. n.d. n.p.** Encloses a piece of anti-abolitionist hate mail and sneers at the wit of the sender. 5 September 1839. p.4, c3.

**2247 H. W. JOHNSON** *to* **L. L. [extract] 29 July 1839. Augusta, Ga.** Informs him that if he ever goes to Georgia he will be lathered with aquafortis and shaved with a handsaw. 5 September 1839. p.4, c3.

**2248 AUGUSTUS BEACH** *to* **BROTHER DENISON. [from the** *Christian Reflector***] 19 June 1839. Oppenheim, N.Y.** Rejoices in his ability to aid fugitive slaves. 5 September 1839. p.4, c4.

**2249 n.n.** *to* **BROTHER GOODELL. [from the** *Friend of Man***] 20 July 1839. New York.** Stands firm in his hatred of slavery after a trip through the South, and vows to continue the fight for abolition. 5 September 1839. p.4, c5.

**2250 J. A. ALLEN** *to* **MR. MAXHAM. [from the** *People's Press***] 13 July 1839. Middlebury.** Presents his definition of democracy and encloses a letter by Thomas Jefferson as a further illustration of his views. 12 September 1839. p.2, c1.

**2251 THOMAS JEFFERSON** *to* **GOVERNOR COLES. [from the** *People's Press***] 25 August 1814. Monticello.** Assures Coles that his hopes and sentiments are with the abolitionists, but insists that he is too old for active participation in the cause. 12 September 1839. p.1, c3.

**2252 J. S. P.** *to* **HONORABLE EDWARD KING. n.d. n.p.** Pleads with Judge King to stop enforcing slavery through the courts. 12 September 1839. p.1, c6.

**2253 JOHN J. BAKER** *to* **THE EDITOR [J. G. WHITTIER]. 27 August 1839. Willistown.** Informs him of the newly created Willistown AS. 12 September 1839. p.2, c1.

**2254 J. M. McKIM** *to* **JOSHUA LEAVITT. [from the** *Emancipator***] 28 August 1839. Gettysburg, Pa.** Describes an anti-slavery meeting in Gettysburg. 12 September 1839. p.2, c4.

**2255 JOSHUA LEAVITT** *to* **THE COMMITTEE ON BEHALF OF THE AFRICAN PRISONERS IN NEW HAVEN. [from the** *New York Evening Post***] 6 September 1839. n.p.** Describes the condition of the *Amistad* prisoners, their health, accommodations, and general demeanor. 12 September 1839. p.3, c1.

**2256 J. A. JAMES** *to* **n.n. [extract from the** *New York Evangelist***] n.d. Birmingham, England.** Defends the stability of emancipation in England; advises Americans who expect to have an impact on the English people either to be devoted abolitionists, or to stay in America. 12 September 1839. p.3, c4.

**2257 C.** *to* **n.n. [from the** *Liberator***] n.d. Northampton.** Predicts the complete abolition of slavery in the French colonies. 12 September 1839. p.4, c2.

2258 **E. S.** *to* **FRIEND GARRISON. [from the** *Liberator***] 24 July 1839. Providence, R.I.** Encloses a letter on the progress of abolition in Ohio from a Methodist minister. 12 September 1839. p.4, c3.

2259 **A METHODIST MINISTER** *to* **E.S. [extract from the** *Liberator***] n.d. Ohio.** Asserts that loyal abolitionists are still aiding fugitive slaves through Ohio despite the recently passed Black Laws. 12 September 1839. p.4, c3.

2260 **BENNETT ROBERTS** *to* **MR. EDITOR. [from the** *New York Evangelist***] n.d. Watertown, Oh.** Describes some of the injustices of slavery as recounted by two former slaves. 19 September 1839. p.1, c6.

2261 **LEWIS TAPPAN** *to* **THE COMMITTEE ON BEHALF OF THE AFRICAN PRISONERS. [from the** *New York Sun***] 9 September 1839. New Haven, Ct.** Describes the Africans of the *Amistad*. 19 September 1839. p.2, c1.

2262 **LEWIS TAPPAN** *to* **THE COMMITTEE ON BEHALF OF THE AFRICAN PRISONERS. 10 September 1839. Long Island Sound.** Describes the private examinations of the Africans from the *Amistad*, which is docked in New Haven. 19 September 1839. p.2, c3.

2263 **WILLIAM JAY** *to* **LEWIS TAPPAN. [from the** *Emancipator***] 7 September 1839. Bedford.** Comments on the *Amistad* incident; donates twenty dollars for care of the prisoners. 19 September 1839. p.2, c5.

2264 **n.n.** *to* **SIR. [from the** *Emancipator***] 31 August 1839. Greenfield, Ma.** Denounces Elliot Cresson's policy of colonization. 19 September 1839. p.2, c6.

2265 **J. C. DELONG** *to* **MR. SUNDERLAND. [from** *Zion's Watchman***] 16 August 1839. Utica, N.Y.** Describes Bishop Hedding's abolitionist sermon delivered in Utica. 19 September 1839. p.4, c4.

2266 **n.n.** *to* **n.n. [extract from the** *Massachusetts Abolitionist***] n.d. n.p.** Encourages continued efforts on the part of Northern abolitionists; believes that the South is slowly coming around. 26 September 1839. p.1, c3.

2267 **DEACON DANIEL GALPIN** *to* **JOHN QUINCY ADAMS. [extract from the** *Connecticut Observer***] n.d. Berlin, Ct.** Criticizes Adams's policy of turning a blind eye on slavery. 26 September 1839. p.1, c3.

2268 **n.n.** *to* **SIR. [from the** *Connecticut Observer***] 6 September 1839. Farmington.** Discusses the case of the Africans from the *Amistad*, who are being detained in New Haven. 26 September 1839. p.1, c4.

2269 **AGRICOLA** *to* **REVEREND SIR. [from the** *Christian Reflector***] August 1839. Sullivan, N.H.** Urges abolitionists to increase their efforts and avoid being distracted by side issues. 26 September 1839. p.2, c1.

2270 **n.n.** *to* **MR. ZIBA FERIS. 17 August 1839. Head of Sassafras.** Wonders if there are extradition laws in Delaware under which to prosecute the kidnappers of a free black woman. 26 September 1839. p.2, c3.

2271 **E. F. CHAMBERS** *to* **MR. ZIBA FERIS. 22 August 1839. Chestertown.** Asserts that the kidnappers of a free black woman are being sought for arrest and punishment. 26 September 1839. p.2, c3.

**2272 JAMES BUCKHAM** *to* **THE EDITOR OF THE** *VERMONT CHRONICLE.* **19 August 1839. n.p.** Discusses the reactions of religious men in England to West Indies emancipation. 26 September 1839. p.4, c1.

**2273 MR. KNIBB** *to* **MR. STURGE. [extract] 25 May 1839. Falmouth, Jamaica.** Commends the forgiveness and patience exhibited by ex-slaves of the West Indies toward their former masters. 3 October 1839. p.1, c5.

**2274 M. A. CARTLAND** *to* **THE EDITOR OF THE** *HERALD.* **28 June 1839. Philadelphia.** Speaks out against slavery; praises Philadelphia for its long tradition of freedom fighters. 3 October 1839. p.2, c1.

**2275 MR. B** *to* **MR. BIRNEY. n.d. Louisville.** Thanks Birney for helping him emancipate one of his slaves. 3 October 1839. p.2, c4.

**2276 J. K. KANE** *to* **WM. A. GARRIGUES. 27 September 1839. Philadelphia.** Answers questions on the issues of free discussion and mob violence. 3 October 1839. p.2, c6.

**2277 JOHN SWIFT** *to* **MESSRS. A. GARRIGUES, B. C. BACON, WILLIAM THOMPSON, JAMES WOOD, AND WILLIAM HARNED. 27 September 1839. Philadelphia.** Approves of free discussion, and opposes mob and lynch law. 3 October 1839. p.3, c1.

**2278 JOHN C. MONTGOMERY** *to* **MESSRS. WM. A. GARRIGUES, B.C. BACON, WILLIAM THOMPSON, JAMES WOOD, AND WILLIAM HARNED. 28 September 1839. Philadelphia.** Favors free discussion and compensation to owners whose property was destroyed by mob violence. 3 October 1839. p.3, c1.

**2279 ANDREW MILLER** *to* **WM. A. GARRIGUES, B. C. BACON, WILLIAM THOMPSON, JAMES WOOD, AND WM. HARNED. 26 September 1839. Philadelphia.** Defends free discussion and trial by jury; deplores mob and lynch law and slavery. 3 October 1839. p.3, c3.

**2280 G. W. LEWIS** *to* **THE EDITOR [J. G. WHITTIER]. 21 September 1839. n.p.** Discusses the annual meeting of the Wilberforce AS. 3 October 1839. p.3, c4.

**2281 n.n.** *to* **FRIEND. n.d. n.p.** Forwards news of individuals and abolitionists in the South. 10 October 1839. p.2, c1.

**2282 THE EDITOR OF THE** *CHRISTIAN WITNESS* *to* **n.n. 16 September 1839. North-East, Erie County.** Considers the progress of abolition sentiments in that region. 10 October 1839. p.2, c3.

**2283 n.n.** *to* **MR. EDITOR. [from the** *Advocate of Freedom***] n.d. n.p.** Speculates on some reasons for strife among abolitionists. 10 October 1839. p.2, c5.

**2284 O'CONNELL** *to* **JOSEPH STURGE. [from the** *Morning Chronicle***] n.d. n.p.** Advises Her Majesty to refrain from recognizing the statehood of Texas until or unless it passes emancipation laws; requests her intervention in seeking land in Mexico that might be used as asylum for free blacks. 10 October 1839. p.2, c6.

**2285 FRIEND** *to* **n.n. [extract from the** *Philanthropist***] n.d. n.p.** Informs of Christian abolitionists among the people of Virginia and Maryland. 10 October 1839. p.2, c6.

**2286 WENDELL PHILLIPS** *to* **GEORGE THOMPSON. [from the** *Glasgow Argus***] n.d. n.p.** Declines an invitation to speak on abolition before the annual meeting of the Glasgow Emancipation Society; comments on the progress of abolition throughout the world. 10 October 1839. p.4, c2.

**2287 WILLIAM S. HALL** *to* **THE EDITOR [J. G. WHITTIER]. 25 September 1839. Milestown.** Describes an incident whereby a church of over 100 members was converted to the principles of anti-slavery. 17 October 1839. p.1, c1.

**2288 H. S. SPACKMAN** *to* **GENTLEMEN. 3 October 1839. Philadelphia.** Responds to questions addressed to political candidates concerning their views on mob law, free discussion, slavery and trial by jury; assures of his intention to advance the interests of his constituents. 17 October 1839. p.1, c6.

**2289 B. M. HINCHMAN** *to* **GENTLEMEN. 2 October 1839. Philadelphia.** Assures his constituents that he will vote in favor of free discussion and trial by jury and against mob and lynch law and slavery, as long as it is consistent with the voting of his colleagues in the House of Representatives. 17 October 1839. p.1, c6.

**2290 WM. CRABB** *to* **GENTLEMEN. 5 October 1839. Philadelphia, Pa.** Asserts that he is in favor of free discussion, free assembly and the right to trial by jury; believes abolition must be carried out either peacefully or not at all. 17 October 1839. p.1, c6.

**2291 J. GRATE** *to* **GENTLEMEN. 4 October 1839. Philadelphia.** Favors trial by jury and free discussion; disapproves of mob or lynch law and slavery. 17 October 1839. p.1, c6.

**2292 E. A. PENNIMAN** *to* **GENTLEMEN. 2 October 1839. Spring Garden.** Favors trial by jury and free discussion; disapproves of mob and lynch law and slavery. 17 October 1839. p.1, c6.

**2293 THOMAS VAUGHAN, DEMOCRATIC CANDIDATE FOR COUNTY COMMISSIONER** *to* **GENTLEMEN. 3 October 1839. Kensington.** Favors free discussion and trial by jury; deplores mob and lynch law and slavery. 17 October 1839. p.1, c6.

**2294 SAMUEL HART, DEMOCRATIC CANDIDATE FOR PROTHONOTARY OF THE COURT OF COMMON PLEAS** *to* **GENTLEMEN. 27 September 1839. Spring Garden.** Favors free discussion and opposes the mob and lynch proceedings. 17 October 1839. p.2, c1.

**2295 GEORGE SMITH** *to* **GENTLEMEN. 30 September 1839. Philadelphia.** Affirms his belief in freedom of discussion and the right to assemble safely; opposes mob and lynch law and slavery. 17 October 1839. p.2, c1.

**2296 ROBERT F. CHRISTY, DEMOCRATIC CANDIDATE FOR CLERK OF ORPHAN'S COURT** *to* **GENTLEMEN. 2 October 1839. Philadelphia.** Expresses his support of free discussion, and disagreement with mob and lynch proceedings. 17 October 1839. p.2, c1.

**2297 THOMAS J. HESTON, DEMOCRATIC CANDIDATE FOR AUDITOR** *to* **GENTLEMEN. 6 October 1839. Blockley.** Favors free discussion and rejects mob and lynch law. 17 October 1839. p.2, c1.

**2298 DAVID EVANS, DEMOCRATIC CANDIDATE FOR COMMISSIONER OF THE NORTHERN LIBERTIES** *to* **SIR. 3 October 1839. Philadelphia.** Favors free discussion and disapproves of mob and lynch law. 17 October 1839. p.2, c1.

**2299 JAMES ENEU, JR. DEMOCRATIC CANDIDATE FOR CLERK OF QUARTER SESSIONS** *to* **GENTLEMEN. 2 October 1839. Philadelphia.** Favors free discussion and deplores mob and lynch law. 17 October 1839. p.2, c1.

**2300 n.n.** *to* **MR. LEAVITT. [from the** ***Emancipator*****] n.d. n.p.** Wonders why most Northern abolitionists are so passionate in espousing their convictions, while Southern slaveholders remain calm and coherent when discussing slavery. 17 October 1839. p.2, c2.

**2301 H. DICKEY** *to* **THE PUBLIC. 30 September 1839. n.p.** Describes the removal of Mr. Burleigh and Mr. Gloucester from his ship because of the former's insistence that his colored friend should be allowed to dine with the rest of the passengers. 17 October 1839. p.2, c2

**2302 E. H. PETTIS** *to* **THE PUBLIC. n.d. New York, N.Y.** Submits himself as an anti-abolitionist candidate for the assembly. 17 October 1839. p.2, c4.

**2303 A. L. POST** *to* **THE** *PENNSYLVANIA FREEMAN.* **[extract] n.d. n.p.** Includes an extract of a letter from Elder C. A. Fox discussing the anti-slavery sentiments of the Baptist Association of Guilford, New York. 17 October 1839. p.2, c4.

**2304 CORRESPONDENT OF THE** *NEW LISBON* **(OH.)** *AURORA to* **n.n. [extract] n.d. n.p.** Praises Arnold Buffum's ability as an abolitionist lecturer. 17 October 1839. p.2, c4.

**2305 KERSEY GRAVE** *to* **THE** *CINCINNATI PHILANTHROPIST.* **[extract] n.d. n.p.** Reports lectures given, commenting on the lack of dissenting views. 17 October 1839. p.2, c4.

**2306 SECRETARY OF THE JAY COUNTY SOCIETY** *to* **THE AAS. [extract] 7 September 1839. n.p.** Discusses the efforts of the poor farmers in the anti-slavery cause. 17 October 1839. p.2, c4.

**2307 A. L. POST** *to* **THE** *CHRISTIAN REFLECTOR.* **[extract] n.d. n.p.** Reports the Baptist Association's new resolutions declaring slavery to be a sin. 17 October 1839. p.2, c5.

**2308 W. R. RANNEY** *to* **DR. J. A. ALLEN. [extract] n.d. n.p.** Asserts his faith that God will help them in their fight for universal freedom and human rights. 17 October 1839. p.2, c5.

**2309 S. D. H.** *to* **MR. EDITOR. n.d. n.p.** Includes excerpts from an editorial in the *Louisville* (Ky.) *Bulletin* deploring the slave trade in Africa and Spain; comments that slavery in America is equally deplorable. 17 October 1839. p.3, c4.

**2310 JOHN BROWN** *to* **THE EDITOR. [from the** *Emancipator***] 21 September 1839. Adrian, Len. County, Michigan.** Recounts the method used by the town of Adrian to prevent the recapture of two escaped slaves who had fled from Kentucky three years earlier. 17 October 1839. p.3, c5.

**2311 n.n.** *to* **THE** *JOURNAL OF COMMERCE.* **24 September 1839. Havana.** Reports the sailing of slave ships for Africa. 17 October 1839. p.3, c6.

**2312 NATHANIEL COLVER** *to* **BROTHER GROSVENOR. [from the** *Christian Reflector***] 20 September 1839. Boston.** Discusses the anti-slavery sentiments of Baptists in Boston. 17 October 1839. p.4, c4.

**2313 RICHARD VAUX, DEMOCRATIC CANDIDATE FOR CITY ASSEMBLY** *to* **GENTLEMEN. 1 October 1839. Philadelphia.** Replies to questions put to political candidates; condemns slavery and mob rule and defends the rights of free discussion and trial by jury. 24 October 1839. p.1, c1.

**2314 TOBIAS BEEHLER, WHIG CANDIDATE FOR COUNTY ASSEMBLY** *to* **GENTLEMEN. 2 October 1839. Philadelphia.** Declares his support of freedom of speech and assembly and his opposition to slavery. 24 October 1839. p.1, c1.

**2315 AARON WATERS, DEMOCRATIC CANDIDATE FOR CITY ASSEMBLY** *to* **SIR. 30 September 1839. Philadelphia.** Declares his opposition to slavery and mob law; supports free discussion and trial by jury. 24 October 1839. p.1, c1.

**2316 JAMES GREGORY, WHIG CANDIDATE FOR CORONER** *to* **GENTLEMEN. 30 September 1839. Philadelphia.** Favors free discussion and trial by jury; opposes slavery; describes a riot following Kearny's murder. 24 October 1839. p.1, c2.

**2317 W. V. PETTIT, DEMOCRATIC CANDIDATE FOR PROTHONOTARY OF THE DISTRICT COURT** *to* **GENTLEMEN. 1 October 1839. Philadelphia.** Affirms his support of rights guaranteed by the Constitution. 24 October 1839. p.1, c2.

**2318 WILLIAM PEIRSOL, DEMOCRATIC CANDIDATE FOR REGISTER OF WILLS** *to* **GENTLEMEN. 3 October 1839. Philadelphia.** Supports free discussion and trial by jury; opposes slavery and lynch law. 24 October 1839. p.1, c2.

**2319 W. O. KLINE, DEMOCRATIC CANDIDATE FOR CLERK OF CRIMINAL COURT** *to* **GENTLEMEN. 2 October 1839. Kensington.** Favors free discussion and opposes mob and lynch law. 24 October 1839. p.1, c3.

**2320 JAMES HANNA, WHIG CANDIDATE FOR CLERK OF ORPHAN'S COURT** *to* **GENTLEMEN. 2 October 1839. n.p.** Favors free discussion and attacks mob and lynch law. 24 October 1839. p.1, c3.

**2321 P. A. KETSER, WHIG CANDIDATE FOR COMMISSIONER OF THE NORTHERN LIBERTIES** *to* **GENTLEMEN. 29 September 1839. Philadelphia.** Stresses the supremacy of the law and the protection of individual rights. 24 October 1839. p.1, c3.

**2322 JAS. M. McKIM** *to* **J. G. WHITTIER. 8 October 1839. York.** Relates the success of his anti-slavery activities. 24 October 1839. p.2, c1.

**2323 C. C. BURLEIGH** *to* **MR. WHITTIER. 17 October 1839. Philadelphia.** Corrects the favorable impression created by Captain Dickey's letter by relating his own account of the incident on the canal boat *Phoenix*. 24 October 1839. p.2, c1.

**2324 ELIZUR WRIGHT, JR.** *to* **MR. CODDING. 24 September 1839. Boston.** Encourages the abolitionists of Maine; expresses his faith in the ultimate success of the cause. 24 October 1839. p.2, c2.

**2325 N. P. ROGERS** *to* **REVEREND D. THORNTON. 13 September 1839. Concord.** Sends words of encouragement to the young abolitionists of Maine. 24 October 1839. p.2, c3.

**2326 BRO. DENISON** *to* **THE** ***CHRISTIAN REFLECTOR*****. [extract] 30 September 1839. Paterson, N.J.** Describes the anti-slavery sentiments of the town of Paterson. 24 October 1839. p.2, c4.

**2327 A MERCHANT IN MIDDLETOWN, OH.** *to* **AN ABOLITION FRIEND IN PENNSYLVANIA. n.d. Middletown, Columbia County, Oh.** Commends the efforts of twenty poor black families to establish themselves respectfully in the community. 24 October 1839. p.2, c4.

**2328 n.n.** *to* **SIR. [from the** ***Emancipator*****] n.d. n.p.** Relates an incident connected with the burning of barns at Fort Lee landing, commenting on a slave who escaped from the fire while his master burned in his sleep. 24 October 1839. p.2, c4.

**2329 GEORGE E. DAY** *to* **THE EDITORS OF THE** *JOURNAL OF COMMERCE.* **8 October 1839. New Haven.** Includes a narrative of African captives who had been cruelly treated. 24 October 1839. p.2, c4.

**2330 CORRESPONDENT** *to* **n.n. [extract from the** *Liberator*] **n.d. Ashburnham, Ma.** Praises the successful oratory of J. D. Lewis, a colored man. 24 October 1839. p.3, c3.

**2331 GEORGE THOMPSON** *to* **JOHN E. FULLER. [from the** *Massachusetts Abolitionist*] **20 September 1839. Manchester, England.** Expresses satisfaction at the reception given John Scoble in the United States; relays Scoble's plans for his abolition activities. 24 October 1839. p.3, c4.

**2332 HIRAM WILSON** *to* **WILLIAM GOODELL. 24 August 1839. Toronto, Upper Canada.** Rejoices at the number of slaves who have escaped to Canada; asks for help in the education of the fugitives, while describing the hardships frequently endured by such volunteers. 24 October 1839. p.3, c4.

**2333 n.n.** *to* **THE EDITOR. [from the** *Colored American*] **n.d. n.p.** Appeals for prayers and votes to aid the fight against slavery. 31 October 1839. p.1, c2.

**2334 C. C. BURLEIGH** *to* **MR. WHITTIER. n.d. n.p.** Describes his anti-slavery tour through Ohio. 31 October 1839. p.1, c2.

**2335 E. P.** *to* **FRIEND WHITTIER. n.d. n.p.** Questions a system that encourages 10,000 men to risk their lives to save David Crockett, yet ignores the plight of thousands of slaves; advocates immediate abolition. 31 October 1839. p.1, c4.

**2336 H. P.** *to* **MR. EDITOR [J. G. WHITTIER]. n.d. n.p.** Examines the "unsound" principles expressed by the American Free Produce Association. 31 October 1839. p.1, c5.

**2337 HENRY GREW, WILLIAM BASSETT, AND C. C. BURLEIGH (COMMITTEE)** *to* **BRETHREN. n.d. n.p.** Urge AS members to abstain from the purchase of goods produced by slavery; state that such purchases sanction the institution of slavery. 31 October 1839. p.2, c1.

**2338 JOSEPH STURGE** *to* **THE FRIENDS OF THE ABOLITION OF THE SLAVE TRADE. [from the** *Christian Reflector*] **18 September 1839. Birmingham, England.** Clarifies the situation in Texas and examines the question of the slave trade. 31 October 1839. p.2, c2.

**2339 CORRESPONDENT AT ST. AUGUSTINE** *to* **n.n [extract from the** *National Intelligencer*] **n.d. St. Augustine, Fl.** Describes the Florida wild lands and the cunning of its natives. 31 October 1839. p.2, c4.

**2340 n.n.** *to* **n.n. [from the** *Friend of Man*] **n.d. n.p.** Comments on the escape of J. Davenport's slave. 31 October 1839. p.3, c3.

**2341 GERRIT SMITH** *to* **DANIEL L. MILLER, JR. n.d. n.p.** Excuses his failure to attend the meeting of the American Free Produce Association. 31 October 1839. p.4, c1.

**2342 THOMAS PEART** *to* **DANIEL L. MILLER, JR. 6 October 1839. Meadville, Crawford County.** Apologizes for his inability to attend the meeting of the American Free Produce Association and discusses the problem of slavery in the West Indies. 31 October 1839. p.4, c1.

**2343 D. LEE CHILD** *to* **DANIEL L. MILLER, JR. 30 September 1839. Northhampton.** Regrets that he will not be able to attend the American Free Produce Association meeting. 31 October 1839. p.4, c1.

**2344 ALVAN STEWART** *to* **DANIEL L. MILLER, JR. 3 October 1839. Utica, N.Y.** Expresses faith in the objectives of the American Free Produce Association, but explains that previous commitments will keep him from attending the meeting. 31 October 1839. p.4, c1.

**2345 PLINY SEXTON** *to* **DANIEL L. MILLER, JR. 10 October 1839. Palmyra.** Excuses his inability to attend the meeting of the American Free Produce Association; expresses sympathy with their cause. 31 October 1839. p.4, c1.

**2346 AARON L. BENEDICT** *to* **CALEB CLOTHIER, LEWIS C. GUNN, AND DANIEL L. MILLER, JR. 10 October 1839. Peru, Oh.** Regrets his inability to attend the meeting of the American Free Produce Association; suggests that it cooperate with English abolitionists to further its objectives. 31 October 1839. p.4, c2.

**2347 JAMES CANNINGS FULLER AND WM. GOODELL OF THE EXECUTIVE COMMITTEE OF THE NEW YORK AS** *to* **AUXILIARIES AND MEMBERS. 16 October 1839. Syracuse.** Enclose address of the New York AS; advocate political measures. 31 October 1839. p.4, c2.

**2348 T. S. C.** *to* **FRIEND WHITTIER. n.d. n.p.** Disputes "H. P.'s" views in his review of the "Address to Abolitionists"; insists that the use of the products of slave labor sanctions the institution of slavery. 7 November 1839. p.2, c1.

**2349 H.** *to* **n.n. [extract from the** *New York Commercial Advertiser***] February 1839. St. Croix.** Cautions those interested in purchasing only the products of free labor of the deceptions practiced by slave owners; relates a case in point. 7 November 1839. p.2, c2.

**2350 WM. BURR** *to* **THE EDITOR OF THE** *PENNSYLVANIA FREEMAN***. 23 October 1839. Dover, N.H.** Forwards the anti-slavery resolutions of the General Conference of the Freewill Baptist Convention. 7 November 1839. p.2, c3.

**2351 HENRY B. STANTON** *to* **MR. WHITTIER. 26 October 1839. Cleveland, Oh.** Describes the meeting of the AAS in Cleveland. 7 November 1839. p.2, c5.

**2352 FREDERICK A. HINTON** *to* **JOHN G. WHITTIER, ESQ. 2 November 1839. Philadelphia.** Solicits the opinion of the *Pennsylvania Freeman* on the pamphlet, "Description of the Island of Trinidad." 7 November 1839. p.2, c6.

**2353 REV. E. O. HALL** *to* **MR. BIRNEY. 23 September 1839. Kendall, Orleans County, N.Y.** Describes his anti-slavery activities in Indiana. 7 November 1839. p.4, c4.

**2354 C. LENOX REMOND** *to* **FRIEND WILLEY. [from the Maine** *Advocate of Freedom***] 27 October 1839. Bangor.** Relates his efforts to establish an AS in Hampden and the outrages to which he was subjected. 14 November 1839. p.1, c2.

**2355 S. WILLIAMS** *to* **BROTHER GROSVENOR. 26 September 1839. Pittsburgh, Pa.** Discusses the slave trade in Virginia, commenting on the inconsistency of professing Christianity while owning slaves. 14 November 1839. p.2, c2.

**2356 JAMES B. WRIGHT** *to* **BROTHER. [from the** *Massachusetts Abolitionist***] 24 October 1839. Cleveland.** Details a special meeting of the AAS in Cleveland, Ohio. 14 November 1839. p.2, c3.

**2357 GERRIT SMITH** *to* **WM. GOODELL. 31 October 1839. Peterboro'.** Rejoices in the safe arrival of Mr. Davenport's escaped slave, Harriet, in Canada. 14 November 1839. p.2, c5.

**2358 FEDERAL DANA** *to* **GERRIT SMITH. 29 October 1839. Cape Vincent.** Recounts the escape of a slave, Harriet, to Canada; includes a description and biographical sketch of her. 14 November 1839. p.2, c6.

**2359 C. C. BURLEIGH** *to* **FRIEND WHITTIER. n.d. n.p.** Summarizes his anti-slavery meetings and lectures, primarily in Ohio. 14 November 1839. p.3, c4.

**2360 J. M. PHILLIPPO** *to* **THE EDITOR OF THE** *NEW YORK EMANCIPATOR*. **30 September 1839. Spanish Town, Jamaica.** Recounts the departure of former governor Sir Lionel Smith of Jamaica; mentions the progress of the Spanish Town AS. 14 November 1839. p.4, c2.

**2361 E. O. HALL** *to* **MR. BIRNEY. 29 September 1839. Kendall, Orleans County.** Discusses several anti-slavery meetings and lectures he has delivered. 21 November 1839. p.1, c4.

**2362 A YOUNG ILLINOIS BAPTIST** *to* **BROTHER GROSVENOR. 24 October 1839. Tuzewell County, Il.** Discusses the Illinois Baptists and their opposition to abolition. 21 November 1839. p.2, c1.

**2363 H. B. STANTON** *to* **FRIEND WHITTIER. 7 November 1839. Pittsburgh.** Relates the proceedings of the Western Pennsylvania AS. 21 November 1839. p.2, c2.

**2364 A. L. POST** *to* **FRIEND WHITTIER. n.d. n.p.** Includes an extract from an article on Siam; contrasts the piety of the Buddhists with the posture of piety assumed by slaveholders. 21 November 1839. p.2, c3.

**2365 CORRESPONDENT** *to* **THE** *LIBERATOR*. **n.d. Manchester, England.** Recounts a discussion between abolitionists and slaveholders during the course of a trip across the Atlantic; records the opinions of West Indian proprietors and shows how they were forced to admit that slavery is an evil. 21 November 1839. p.3, c3.

**2366 GOVERNOR L. W. BOGGS** *to* **GENERAL CLARK. 27 October 1837. Jefferson City, Mo.** Orders him to exterminate the Mormons or to drive them from the state. 21 November 1839. p.4, c3.

**2367 CORRESPONDENT** *to* **THE** *LIBERATOR*. **n.d. n.p.** Discusses the abolitionist activities of George Thompson and Joseph Sturge in England. 28 November 1839. p.1, c1.

**2368 GERRIT SMITH** *to* **MR. GOODELL. 12 November 1839. Peterboro'.** Comments on the progress of the abolitionist cause and on the formation of an abolitionist party. 28 November 1839. p.2, c1.

**2369 GEORGE THOMPSON** *to* **GARRISON. [from the** *Liberator***] 17 September 1839. Manchester.** Expresses his sympathy with the American abolitionist movement. 28 November 1839. p.2, c2.

**2370 W. O. DUVALL** *to* **MR. GOODELL. 9 November 1839. Port Byron.** Reports the election of anti-slavery candidate John W. McFadden in Cayuga County. 28 November 1839. p.2, c2.

**2371 DAVID THOMAS** *to* **H. H. COOLY, PRESIDENT OF THE CAYUGA COUNTY AS. 24 October 1839. Great Field, near Aurora.** Declares that congressional candidates should publicize their opinions on slavery and other important political issues. 28 November 1839. p.2, c2.

**2372 JOHN W. McFADDEN** *to* **H.H. COOLY, PRESIDENT OF THE CAYUGA COUNTY AS. 25 October 1839. Sterling.** Desires that New York be a free state in fact; demands trial by jury for all men. 28 November 1839. p.2, c2.

**2373 C. C. BURLEIGH** *to* **MR. WHITTIER. 18 November 1839. Newport.** Recounts his anti-slavery operations in Rhode Island; discusses the annual meeting of the Rhode Island State AS. 28 November 1839. p.2, c3.

**2374 HIRAM WILSON** *to* **FRIEND WHITTIER. 18 November 1839. Toronto, Upper Canada.** Requests permission to address the Society of Friends through the *Pennsylvania Freeman.* 28 November 1839. p.2, c4.

**2375 HIRAM WILSON** *to* **RESPECTED FRIENDS. 18 November 1839. Toronto, Upper Canada.** Addresses the Quakers, describing the conditions that black fugitives find in Canada and asking for aid. 28 November 1839. p.2, c4.

**2376 DR. NELSON** *to* **DR. BAILEY. [from the** *Philanthropist***] October 1839. Illinois Mississippi Institute.** Urges abolitionists to avoid party politics and to be wary of politicians who merely profess abolitionist ideas. 28 November 1839. p.3, c2.

**2377 WHALEY ARMITAGE** *to* **THE EDITOR OF THE** *EMANCIPATOR.* **10 June 1839. Aura, Coast of Africa.** Comments on his visit to the colony of Sierra Leone. 28 November 1839. p.3, c5.

**2378 ARNOLD BUFFUM** *to* **BROTHER LEAVITT. [from the** *Emancipator***] 12 November 1839. Marietta, Oh.** Describes his anti-slavery activities; attacks colonization. 5 December 1839. p.1, c1.

**2379 GERRIT SMITH** *to* **HON. SETH M. GATES. [extract] n.d. n.p.** Cautions against blind party loyalty; supports General Scott as a presidential candidate. 5 December 1839. p.2, c1.

**2380 A COLORED WOMAN** *to* **FREE WOMEN OF CONNECTICUT. [from the** *Charter Oak***] n.d. n.p.** Exhorts women to circulate petitions and voice their outrage against slavery. 5 December 1839. p.2, c3.

**2381 JOSHUA LEAVITT** *to* **THE COMMITTEE ON BEHALF OF THE AFRICAN CAPTIVES. [from the** *Emancipator***] n.d. n.p.** Reports on the suit brought by Lt. Gedney, U.S.N., and others against the owners of the schooner *Amistad* to reclaim expenses incurred in saving the *Amistad* and her cargo. 5 December 1839. p.2, c4.

**2382 A. W. LAMBETH** *to* **MR. SWAIM. [from the** *Southern Citizen***] 16 November 1839. Davidson County, N.C.** Reports the murder of Nathan Lambeth, identifying John Goss and Lee Wharton as two of the murderers. 5 December 1839. p.3, c3.

**2383 THE COMMITTEE OF COLORED CITIZENS** *to* **SIR LIONEL SMITH. [from the** *Colored American***] 15 November 1839. New York.** States resolutions presented to Sir Lionel Smith, ex-governor of Jamaica; praises his philanthropy and accomplishments during his administration. 5 December 1839. p.4, c1.

**2384 SIR LIONEL SMITH** *to* **GENTLEMEN. [from the** *Colored American***] 15 November 1839. New York.** Expresses appreciation for the address; encourages them in their struggle for freedom. 5 December 1839. p.4, c2.

**2385 n.n.** *to* **n.n. [extract from the (Ohio)** *Philanthropist***] n.d. n.p.** Comments on the rewards of teaching in colored schools despite abuse. 12 December 1839. p.1, c1.

**2386 SHUBAL CARVER** *to* **n.n. [extract from the (Ohio)** *Philanthropist***] n.d. Oberlin.** Testifies to the learning ability of colored children. 12 December 1839. p.1, c2.

**2387 n.n.** *to* **n.n. [extract from the (Ohio)** *Philanthropist***] n.d. Shelby.** Comments on the proficiency of his colored scholars. 12 December 1839. p.1, c2.

**2388 n.n.** *to* **n.n. [extract from the (Ohio)** *Philanthropist***] n.d. Dayton.** Relates progress of his students. 12 December 1839. p.1, c2.

**2389 n.n.** *to* **n.n. [extract from the (Ohio)** *Philanthropist***] n.d. Springfield.** States that his present students have made better progress than any of his previous students. 12 December 1839. p.1, c2.

**2390 n.n.** *to* **n.n. [extract from the (Ohio)** *Philanthropist***] n.d. Wayne, Jefferson County.** Asserts that her colored pupils learn as quickly as white children. 12 December 1839. p.1, c2.

**2391 n.n.** *to* **n.n. [extract from the (Ohio)** *Philanthropist***] n.d. Milton, Jackson County.** Comments on the eagerness and rapidity with which her colored pupils learn. 12 December 1839. p.1, c2.

**2392 n.n.** *to* **n.n. [extract from (Ohio)** *Philanthropist***] n.d. Cincinnati.** Discuss the rapid improvement of their students. 12 December 1839. p.1, c2.

**2393 n.n.** *to* **n.n. [extract from the (Ohio)** *Philanthropist***] n.d. Cabin Creek.** Reports on the progress of the school. 12 December 1839. p.1, c3.

**2394 n.n.** *to* **n.n. [extract from the (Ohio)** *Philanthropist***] n.d. Mercer County.** Remarks on the enthusiasm of the pupils. 12 December 1839. p.1, c3.

**2395 n.n.** *to* **n.n. [extract from the (Ohio)** *Philanthropist***] n.d. Red Oak, Brown County.** Compares the superior performance of her colored students to that of her previous students, both colored and white. 12 December 1839. p.1, c3.

**2396 n.n.** *to* **n.n. [extract from the (Ohio)** *Philanthropist***] n.d. Cincinnati.** Reports that the parents are often an obstacle to their pupils' learning. 12 December 1839. p.1, c3.

**2397 n.n.** *to* **n.n. [extract from the (Ohio)** *Philanthropist***] n.d. Wayne.** States that the ignorance of some parents as to the raising of their children is responsible for many problems of discipline. 12 December 1839. p.1, c3.

**2398 n.n.** *to* **n.n. [extract from the (Ohio)** *Philanthropist***] n.d. Dayton.** Complains about unwillingness of parents to buy books for their children. 12 December 1839. p.1, c3.

**2399 n.n.** *to* **n.n. [extract from the (Ohio)** *Philanthropist***] n.d. Wayne.** Describes the difficulty of getting to and from school. 12 December 1839. p.1, c3.

**2400 n.n.** *to* **n.n. [extract from the (Ohio)** *Philanthropist***] n.d. n.p.** Explains that the boarding problem for teachers in colored schools is solved. 12 December 1839. p.1, c3.

**2401 n.n.** *to* **n.n. [extract from the (Ohio)** *Philanthropist***] n.d. n.p.** Complains of not having been paid yet for teaching. 12 December 1839. p.1, c4.

**2402 n.n.** *to* **n.n. [extract from the (Ohio)** *Philanthropist***] n.d. n.p.** Explains the problem of boarding teachers at schools where donors have failed to fulfill pledges of support. 12 December 1839. p.1, c4.

**2403 n.n.** *to* **n.n. [extract from the (Ohio)** *Philanthropist***] n.d. Brown.** Concludes that there are insufficient funds to maintain a school. 12 December 1839. p.1, c4.

**2404 n.n.** *to* **n.n. [extract from the (Ohio)** *Philanthropist***] n.d. Chillicothe.** Comments that he is payed on a weekly basis. 12 December 1839. p.1, c4.

**2405 n.n.** *to* **n.n. [extract from the (Ohio)** *Philanthropist***] n.d. Springfield.** Notes that he has encountered no difficulties with payment for his work as a teacher. 12 December 1839. p.1, c4.

**2406 n.n.** *to* **n.n. [extract from the (Ohio)** *Philanthropist***] n.d. n.p.** Declares that she has yet to be paid for the previous quarter. 12 December 1839. p.1, c4.

**2407 n.n.** *to* **n.n. [extract from the (Ohio)** *Philanthropist***] n.d. n.p.** Explains that she is going to teach in a white school for a few months to earn enough money with which to live. 12 December 1839. p.1, c4.

**2408 n.n.** *to* **n.n. [extract from the (Ohio)** *Philanthropist***] n.d. n.p.** Describes the satisfaction she receives from her work. 12 December 1839. p.1, c4.

**2409 n.n.** *to* **n.n. [extract from the (Ohio)** *Philanthropist***] n.d. n.p.** Asserts that the spiritual rewards of teaching more than compensate for the absence of monetary rewards. 12 December 1839. p.1, c4.

**2410 n.n.** *to* **n.n. [extract from the (Ohio)** *Philanthropist***] n.d. Chillicothe.** Discusses the county's temperance society. 12 December 1839. p.1, c4.

**2411 n.n.** *to* **n.n. [extract from the (Ohio)** *Philanthropist***] n.d. Shelby.** Recounts the formation of a temperance society. 12 December 1839. p.1, c4.

**2412 n.n.** *to* **n.n. [extract from the (Ohio)** *Philanthropist***] n.d. Cabin Creek.** Remarks that most of the inhabitants are practicing Christians. 12 December 1839. p.1, c4.

**2413 n.n.** *to* **n.n. [extract from the (Ohio)** *Philanthropist***] n.d. Lexington.** Comments on the large membership of the local temperance society. 12 December 1839. p.1, c4.

**2414 n.n.** *to* **n.n. [extract from the (Ohio)** *Philanthropist***] n.d. Springfield.** Cautions against the tendency to seek revenge. 12 December 1839. p.1, c4.

**2415 A. L. BENEDICT** *to* **G. BAILEY. [from the (Ohio)** *Philanthropist***] 15 November 1839. Peru, Delaware County, Oh.** Reports the court's action against the rioters in Marion. 12 December 1839. p.1, c6.

**2416 GERRIT SMITH** *to* **BROTHER GOODELL. [from the** *Friend of Man***] 1 October 1839. Peterboro'.** Sends an extract of a letter from a man reputed to be one of the country's best poets. 12 December 1839. p.2, c1.

**2417 n.n** *to* **GERRIT SMITH. [extract] n.d. n.p.** Praises the abolitionist efforts of Benjamin Lundy. 12 December 1839. p.2, c1.

**2418 MR. KNIBB** *to* **JOSEPH STURGE, ESQ. [extract from the** *Emancipator***] n.d. n.p.** Attacks estate owners in Jamaica who are making things difficult for the recently emancipated slaves. 12 December 1839. p.2, c2.

**2419 CAPTAIN STUART** *to* **MR. STURGE. [from the** *Emancipator*] **n.d. n.p.** Cautions of the danger of "tampering" with the Negroes in Jamaica. 12 December 1839. p.2, c2.

**2420 JOHN CHANEY** *to* **WM. M. HOUSLEY. [from the** *Liberator*] **5 October 1839. Conneaut, Oh.** Informs Housley that he cannot be ordained a Freewill Baptist minister because he is a slaveholder. 12 December 1839. p.2, c2.

**2421 G. W. ALEXANDER, CHAIRMAN** *to* **LORD PALMERSTON, HER MAJESTY'S PRINCIPAL SECRETARY OF STATE FOR FOREIGN AFFAIRS. [from the** *Liverpool Mercury*] **28 September 1839. London.** Urges on behalf of the British and Foreign AS that Great Britain withhold recognition from Texas due to the legal status of slavery in Texas. 12 December 1839. p.2, c2.

**2422 MR. BIRNEY** *to* **THE** *EMANCIPATOR*. **n.d. n.p.** Describes legal and other aspects of slavery in Kentucky. 12 December 1839. p.2, c3.

**2423 C.** *to* **THE** *PENNSYLVANIA FREEMAN*. **n.d. n.p.** Replies that the friend of Buxton alluded to by Dr. Bethune offered to pay half of the expense of reprinting Buxton's work on the slave trade. 12 December 1839. p.2, c5.

**2424 FREDERICK A. HINTON** *to* **EDWARD M. DAVIS, ESQ. 9 December 1839. Philadelphia.** Thanks him for a contribution of Bibles for emigrants sailing to Trinidad. 12 December 1839. p.2, c5.

**2425 G.** *to* **MR. EDITOR [J. G. WHITTIER]. n.d. n.p.** Encloses an extract from the *Religious Telegraph and Observer* reporting the circulation of a petition in favor of a canal across the Isthmus of Darien; calls for the abolition of slavery. 12 December 1839. p.2, c5.

**2426 J. FULTON, JR., RECORDING SECRETARY** *to* **FRIEND WHITTIER. 7 December 1839. Ercildoun.** Encloses anti-slavery resolutions offered at a meeting of the East Fallowfield AS. 12 December 1839. p.2, c6.

**2427 R.R. MADDEN** *to* **DR. CHANNING. [extract] n.d. n.p.** Discusses the American interest in maintaining the slave trade through Cuba; cites evidence that the slave trade has received the protection of the American and Portugese flags and that N. P. Trist, American consul in Cuba, bears much of the responsibility for such protection. 12 December 1839. p.3, c1.

**2428 LIEUTENANT ARMITAGE, R. N.** *to* **MR. WILLIAM ALLEN. 1839. Ascension.** Reports that the slave trade has stopped in the Bowery and Benin but continues, under the Portugese, Brazilian, and American flags, around the Gallinas and "southward of the line." 12 December 1839. p.3, c5.

**2429 GEORGE WILLIAM ALEXANDER** *to* **THE KING OF DENMARK. [extract] n.d. n.p.** Urges that slavery be abolished in the Danish colonies. 12 December 1839. p.3, c5.

**2430 JOHN QUINCY ADAMS** *to* **GEORGE ALEXANDER OTIS. [from the** *Boston Courier*] **20 November 1839. Quincy.** Discusses the philosophical and rhetorical merits of Cicero. 12 December 1839. p.4, c1.

**2431 I. CODDING** *to* **BROTHER WILLEY. [from the** *Advocate of Freedom*] **15 November 1839. Bangor, Me.** Describes several anti-slavery meetings. 12 December 1839. p.4, c3.

**2432 ELLEN** *to* **BROTHER. [from the** *Emancipator*] **October 1839. Quincy.** Describes the anniversary meeting of the Illinois AS. 19 December 1839. p.1, c2.

**2433 CORRESPONDENT** *to* **THE** *MASSACHUSETTS SPY.* **n.d. Constantinople.** Describes his voyage to Constantinople. 19 December 1839. p.1, c4.

**2434 EDWARD ROSSETER, PRESIDENT, JONATHAN HILLMAN, HENRY RUSSELL, JOS. MUNRO, JOS. McMURRAY, GEORGE MOORE, RUSSELL E. GLOVER, WM. H. MARTIN–MEMBERS PRESENT, S. E. GLOVER, SECRETARY** *to* **DR. R. R. MADDEN. [from the** *Emancipator***] 23 November 1839. New York.** Thank Madden, as mariners and members of the Finance Committee, for his actions on behalf of American citizens in Havana; disclaim any connection with abolitionism. 19 December 1839. p.2, c1.

**2435 R. R. MADDEN** *to* **E. ROSSETER, J. HILLMAN, H. RUSSELL, J. MUNRO, J. McMURRAY, R. GLOVER, G. MOORE, WM. H. MARTIN, AND S. GLOVER, ESQS. [from the** *Emancipator***] 23 November 1839. New York.** Acknowledges the receipt of their letter of gratitude; hopes for the abolition of slavery in the West Indies. 19 December 1839. p.2, c1.

**2436 CORRESPONDENT** *to* **THE** *PENNSYLVANIA FREEMAN.* **n.d. n.p.** Reports that a gentleman of color from Jamaica will attend a London ball at Guildhall along with the "nobles of the realm." 19 December 1839. p.2, c2.

**2437 DR. STEBBINS** *to* **EDWARD NEEDLES. n.d. n.p.** Reports the mistreatment he received from a curator of the Chester County Cabinet, which forbids the admission of blacks to its halls. 19 December 1839. p.2, c4.

**2438 D.** *to* **C. n.d. n.p.** Discusses the offer of a "Friend of Buxton" to pay for the republication of the latter's work; encloses an extract from an abolitionist and anti-colonizationist "Protest" signed by Buxton in 1833. 19 December 1839. p.3, c4.

**2439 R. R. MADDEN** *to* **DR. CHANNING. [extract] n.d. n.p.** Describes the actions of N. P. Trist, American consul general in Havana, in favor of the slave trade; encloses extracts of a letter from Trist to members of a British commission for the suppression of the slave trade. 19 December 1839. p.4, c1.

**2440 N. P. TRIST** *to* **THE MEMBERS OF THE BRITISH COMMISSION FOR THE SUPPRESSION OF THE SLAVE TRADE. [extract] n.d. n.p.** Opposes the activity of the commissioners and defends the slave trade. 19 December 1839. p.4, c4.

**2441 JOHN KEEP, LONDON CORRESPONDENT OF THE** *EMANCIPATOR* *to* **BROTHER. 15 November 1839. London.** Condemns slavery in America; describes opposition to slavery in Great Britain. 26 December 1839. p.1, c1.

**2442 MAJOR JOHN B. COLSHURST, LATE SPECIAL AND POLICE MAGISTRATE IN THE ISLANDS OF BARBADOES AND ST. VINCENT** *to* **A GENTLEMAN OF BOSTON. [extract from the** *Liberator***] 10 November 1839. Coachford-Cork.** Foresees the success of the British abolition of slavery; hopes that the United States will abolish slavery. 26 December 1839. p.1, c5.

**2443 n.n.** *to* **SIR. [from the** *Boston Post***] 9 October 1839. Rio de Janeiro.** Describes the approach to Rio de Janeiro by sea and discusses Brazilian slavery. 26 December 1839. p.2, c1.

**2444 D. N.** *to* **BROTHER LEAVITT. [from the** *Emancipator***] 23 November 1839. Mission Institute.** States that many Christians in the East choose to remain silent on the issue of slavery; reports the murders of two slave women in Arkansas. 26 December 1839. p.2, c2.

**2445 n.n.** *to* **MR. EDITOR. [from the** *Voice of Freedom***] n.d. n.p.** Urges abolitionists not to let disagreements among them become a source of weakness in the face of the enemy. 26 December 1839. p.2, c6.

**2446 HIPPOLYTE D. DE SAINT ANTHOINE** *to* **ELIZUR WRIGHT, JR. 16 October 1839. Paris.** Discusses the anti-slavery movement in France and the major role played in it by M. Passy, President of the French Society for Abolition of Slavery. 26 December 1839. p.3, c1.

**2447 POST** *to* **n.n. [extract] n.d. Montrose.** States that due to the anti-slavery opinions of Harrison, Tyler, and Van Buren, abolitionists should support a third party. 26 December 1839. p.3, c4.

**2448 A CITIZEN OF ONE OF THE SLAVE STATES** *to* **THE** *AMERICAN CITIZEN.* **[extract] n.d. n.p.** Discusses prevailing opinions of slavery in his state. 26 December 1839. p.3, c4.

**2449 HENRY CLAY** *to* **THE WHIG CONVENTION AT HARRISBURG. [extract] n.d. n.p.** States that many have urged him not to seek the presidential nomination. 26 December 1839. p.3, c6.

**2450 ANTI-CASTE** *to* **FRIEND GARRISON. [from the** *Liberator***] n.d. n.p.** States that slavery leads to the degradation of the white laborer and cites an incident as evidence of this fact. 26 December 1839. p.4, c1.

**2451 S. A.** *to* **MR. EDITOR [J. G. WHITTIER]. n.d. n.p.** Encloses a mercantile circular concerning Indian and slave labor used in the planting of cotton. 26 December 1839. p.4, c2.

**2452 CORRESPONDENT** *to* **THE** *EMANCIPATOR***. n.d. n.p.** Reports the case of a colored barber in Laporte, Indiana, who was declared a slave by a judge despite his claim that he could prove his freedom. 26 December 1839. p.4, c2.

## [1840]

**2453 EDWARD NEEDLES** *to* **THE CHESTER COUNTY AS. 25 November 1839. Philadelphia.** Supports the anti-slavery cause on the basis of religious principles. 2 January 1840. p.1, c5.

**2454 CHARLES STUART** *to* **THEODORE. [from the** *Emancipator***] 10 October 1839. Parish of St. Andrews, Mt. Charles, Jamaica.** Describes the favorable and unfavorable aspects of the current social and economic condition of Jamaica; compares the advantages of the system of cultivation by the use of slave labor with those of the system of free labor. 2 January 1840. p.2, c1.

**2455 JAMES G. BIRNEY** *to* **MESSRS. MYRON HOLLEY, JOSHUA H. DARLING, AND JOSIAH ANDREWS. [from the** *Rochester Freeman***] 17 December 1839. New York.** Declines a nomination for president of the United States by a convention of abolitionists which met in Warsaw, New York, stating that the time has not yet come for independent abolitionist candidates. 2 January 1840. p.2, c6.

**2456 F. JULIUS LEMOYNE** *to* **MESSRS. HOLLEY, DARLING, AND ANDREWS. [from the** *Rochester Freeman***] 10 December 1839. Washington, Pa.** Declines a nomination for vice-president of the United States by a convention of abolitionists of western New York, stating that the time has not yet come for independent abolitionist candidates. 2 January 1840. p.2, c6.

**2457 JAMES D. CHAPMAN** *to* **MR. BIRNEY. [from the** *New York Emancipator***] 12 December 1839. Wolcott, Ct.** Discusses the burning of the abolitionist meetinghouse in Wolcott, Connecticut, by pro-slavery incendiaries. 2 January 1840. p.4, c4.

**2458 W. O. DUVALL, S.C. CUYLER, ASA B. SMITH, [AND ELEVEN OTHERS]** *to* **n.n. [extract from the** *Friend of Man***] 6 December 1839. n.p.** Call for anti-slavery meetings in the state of New York. 9 January 1840. p.1, c1.

**2459 H. C. H.** *to* **MR. EDITOR. [from the** *Christian Witness***] 23 November 1839. Allegheny.** Encloses a letter from his son relating the story of a Tennessee preacher who offered a reward for help in capturing a fugitive slave; condemns slaveholding Christians. 9 January 1840. p.1, c5.

**2460 n.n. [SON OF H. C. H.]** *to* **H. C. H. [extract from the** *Christian Witness***] n.d. Ohio.** Encloses a letter from Matthew W. Webber, a preacher in Tennessee, offering him a reward for help in capturing a fugitive slave. 9 January 1840. p.1, c5.

**2461 MATTHEW W. WEBBER** *to* **THE SON OF H. C. H. [extract from the** *Christian Witness***] n.d. Tennessee.** Offers him a reward for help in capturing a fugitive slave. 9 January 1840. p.1, c5.

**2462 J. CROSS** *to* **J. G. BIRNEY, ESQ. [from the** *New York Emancipator***] 16 November 1839. Chicago, Il.** Describes a series of personal misfortunes during his move to Illinois; discusses the racial prejudice which pervades the legal code and the opinions of many in the state. 9 January 1940. p.1, c6.

**2463 J. CROSS** *to* **BROTHER LEAVITT. [from the** *New York Emancipator***] 6 December 1839. Canton, Fulton County, Il.** Describes a session of the Illinois State AS Convention. 9 January 1840. p.2, c1.

**2464 S. THURSTON** *to* **BROTHER WILLEY. [from the** *Advocate of Freedom***] 19 December 1839. West Prospect.** Reports the growth of anti-slavery sentiment in West Prospect and the success of anti-slavery lectures delivered there by Mr. Remond and Mr. Codding. 9 January 1840. p.2, c4.

**2465 CORRESPONDENT** *to* **THE** *CINCINNATI PHILANTHROPIST***. [extract] n.d. n.p.** Describes a lecture by an agent of the CS delivered in Georgetown, Ohio. 9 January 1840. p.3, c2.

**2466 THE ABOLITIONISTS OF PITTSBURGH** *to* **THE CANDIDATES FOR MAYOR OF PITTSBURGH. n.d. Pittsburgh.** Ask about their views on slavery and racial prejudice. 9 January 1840. p.3, c4.

**2467 n.n.** *to* **FRIEND. 1 January 1840. Philadelphia.** Encloses a check for the benefit of the slaves. 9 January 1840. p.3, c4.

**2468 CORRESPONDENT** *to* **n.n. [extract] n.d. n.p.** Asks whether the colonizationists will circulate petitions asking Congress to take action to suppress the slave trade in the United States. 9 January 1840. p.3, c5.

**2469 GOVERNOR CAMPBELL** *to* **THE VIRGINIA LEGISLATURE. [extract from the** *Emancipator***] n.d. n.p.** Discusses the refusal of the governor of New York to surrender to Virginia three men accused of stealing a slave and transporting him to New York; encloses Governor Seward's letter to the lieutenant governor of Virginia informing of this refusal. 9 January 1840. p.4, c2.

**2470 GOVERNOR SEWARD OF NEW YORK** *to* **THE LIEUTENANT GOVERNOR OF VIRGINIA. [extract from the** ***Emancipator*****] n.d. n.p.** Explains his refusal to surrender three men accused of stealing a slave from Virginia and transporting him to New York. 9 January 1840. p.4, c3.

**2471 CORRESPONDENT** *to* **THE** ***PENNSYLVANIA INQUIRIER*****. 2 January 1840. Washington.** Reports that the "ultra men" in Congress from the South will consent to have abolition petitions referred to a select committee; states that the issue of emancipation "must be met" and that the people of the South are ready to do so. 16 January 1840. p.1, c1.

**2472 J. CROSS** *to* **BROTHER LEAVITT. [from the** ***Emancipator*****] 14 December 1839. Juliet, Will County, Il.** Gives an account of the kidnapping of a free black man and the series of trials and judicial decisions which followed, which culminated in a pro-slavery judgment. 16 January 1840. p.2, c2.

**2473 GOVERNOR FAIRFIELD OF MAINE** *to* **n.n. [extract] n.d. n.p.** Discusses the demand of the governor of Georgia for the surrender of two men from Maine charged with abducting a slave from Georgia; encloses an extract from the Georgia governor's message to the Georgia legislature discussing the refusal of the governor of Maine to comply with the demand. 16 January 1840. p.3, c3.

**2474 THE GOVERNOR OF GEORGIA** *to* **THE GEORGIA LEGISLATURE. [extract] n.d. n.p.** Discusses the refusal of the governor of Maine to comply with his demand for the surrender of two men accused of abducting a slave. 16 January 1840. p.3, c3.

**2475 GOVERNOR SEWARD** *to* **n.n. [extract] n.d. n.p.** Discusses his refusal to comply with the demand of the governor of Virginia for the surrender of three men accused of stealing a slave from Virginia. 16 January 1840. p.3, c4.

**2476 SAMUEL AARON** *to* **BROTHER GROSVENOR. 17 November 1839. Burlington, N.J.** Discusses a meeting of the New Jersey Baptist Association concerning slavery; encloses the minutes of the meeting. 16 January 1840. p.4, c1.

**2477 EUROPEAN CORRESPONDENT** *to* **THE** ***COMMERCIAL ADVERTISER*****. n.d. n.p.** Discusses the granting of a charter by Sultan Abdul Medjid of Turkey to his people. 16 January 1840. p.4, c5.

**2478 GERRIT SMITH** *to* **REVEREND JOSHUA LEAVITT. [from the** ***Emancipator*****] 24 December 1839. Peterboro'.** Discusses the advantages and disadvantages of nominating independent abolitionist candidates. 23 January 1840. p.1, c1.

**2479 A. L. POST, ESQ.** *to* **n.n. [extract] n.d. n.p.** Describes an anti-slavery convention at Binghamton, New York. 23 January 1840. p.2, c4.

**2480 AMOS KENDALL, POSTMASTER GENERAL OF THE UNITED STATES** *to* **THE POSTMASTER AT CHARLESTON, S.C. [extract] 1835. n.p.** States that he does not oppose the Charleston postmaster's action to detain abolitionist publications. 23 January 1840. p.2, c6.

**2481 AMOS KENDALL, POSTMASTER GENERAL OF THE UNITED STATES** *to* **S. L. GO[U]VERNEUR, POSTMASTER AT NEW YORK CITY. [extract] 1835. n.p.** States that he does not oppose Gouverneur's actions to exclude abolitionist publications from the Southern mails. 23 January 1840. p.2, c6.

**2482 AMOS KENDALL, POSTMASTER GENERAL OF THE UNITED STATES** *to* **n.n. [extract] n.d. n.p.** Condemns the railroad company for opening a trunk of letters carried by a messenger of the post office. 23 January 1840. p.3, c1.

**2483 HENRY G. LUDLOW OF NEW HAVEN, CT.** *to* **THE EDITOR OF THE** ***EMANCIPATOR*****. [extract] n.d. n.p.** Reports the decision in the trial of the *Amistad* prisoners; describes the prisoners' joy upon being informed of it. 23 January 1840. p.3, c6.

**2484 A TRAVELLER** *to* **n.n. [extract from the** *New York Journal of Commerce***] 18 December 1839. Trinidad de Cuba.** Reports the investigation by the American consul of a ship which landed in Casilda; asserts that the ship had engaged in the slave trade for thirteen years. 23 January 1840. p.4, c4.

**2485 T. S. C.** *to* **FRIEND WHITTIER. n.d. n.p.** Praises the activities of the Vigilance Committee of Philadelphia in the cause of immediate emancipation; urges that assistance be given to fugitive slaves. 30 January 1840. p.3, c1.

**2486 E. F. PENNYPACKER** *to* **JOHN G. WHITTIER. 22 January 1840. Schuylkill.** Gives an account of the proceedings of the Franklin AS annual meeting. 30 January 1840. p.3, c2.

**2487 CORRESPONDENT** *to* **THE** ***NEW YORK EXPRESS*****. [extract] 12 January. New Orleans.** Reports the efforts of the Whigs in Louisiana to "carry the state" in 1841. 30 January 1840. p.3, c3.

**2488 ABEL BROWN** *to* **SIR. [from the** *Massachusetts Abolitionist***] 6 January 1840. Springfield.** Gives an account of an attempt to set off an explosive to destroy an abolition meeting in East Longmeadow. 30 January 1840. p.4, c5.

**2489 THOMAS T. JOHNSTON, AGENT GENERAL OF IMMIGRANTS** *to* **R. S. BUCHANAN, ESQ. [extract from the** *Colored American***] 21 November 1839. Trinidad.** Reports the arrival of immigrants aboard the ship *Metamora* in Trinidad. 6 February 1840. p.1, c5.

**2490 THOMAS T. JOHNSTON, AGENT GENERAL OF IMMIGRANTS** *to* **R. S. BUCHANAN, ESQ. [extract from the** *Colored American***] 5 December 1839. Trinidad.** Praises Captain Lowe of the ship *Metamora* for his treatment of the immigrants aboard his ship. 6 February 1840. p.1, c5.

**2491 THOMAS T. JOHNSTON, AGENT GENERAL OF IMMIGRANTS** *to* **R. S. BUCHANAN, ESQ. [extract from the** *Colored American***] n.d. Trinidad.** Reports the arrival in Trinidad of German laborers aboard Captain Chevalier's ship; reports the successful employment of immigrants who arrived aboard the *Metamora.* 6 February 1840. p.1, c5.

**2492 W. C. B.** *to* **FRIEND WHITTIER. 3 February 1840. Philadelphia.** Encloses the minutes of the first abolitionist meeting in America of which there is any record, dated 14 April 1775, Philadelphia. 6 February 1840. p.2, c1.

**2493 MR. BUTTS** *to* **n.n. [from the** *Ohio Philanthropist***] n.d. n.p.** Describes the progress of the anti-slavery cause observed while on a lecture tour spent mainly in Columbiana and Trumbull counties. 6 February 1840. p.2, c5.

**2494 EDWARD N. BUXTON** *to* **GEORGE THOMPSON, ESQ. [extract] n.d. n.p.** Asserts that his father, Thomas Fowell Buxton, opposes the principles of the colonizationists. 6 February 1840. p.2, c6.

**2495 DR. HORTON OF TERRYTOWN** *to* **THE** ***PENNSYLVANIA FREEMAN*****. [extract] n.d. n.p.** Praises an anti-slavery convention held in Towanda, Bradford County, Pennsylvania. 6 February 1840. p.3, c3.

**2496 CORRESPONDENT** *to* **n.n. n.d. Trenton, N.J.** Condemns the violation of freedom of speech by a mob during a meeting of the New Jersey AS in the Supreme Court Room in the State House at Trenton. 6 February 1840. p.3, c3.

**2497 TRENTON CORRESPONDENT** *to* **THE** *CONSTITUTION AND FARMER'S ADVERTISER*. **n.d. Trenton, N.J.** Describes the disruption by a mob of a meeting of the New Jersey AS in the Supreme Court Room at the State House in Trenton. 6 February 1840. p.3, c4.

**2498 ELIJAH COFFIN, CLERK** *to* **ALL CHRISTIANS IN THE UNITED STATES. n.d. n.p.** Condemns slavery on religious grounds, on behalf of the Yearly Meeting of the Religious Society of Friends. 6 February 1840. p.3, c4.

**2499 A. BROWN** *to* **BROTHER WRIGHT. [from the** *Massachusetts Abolitionist***] 27 December 1839. Cranville.** Reports that many Northern men participate in the internal slave trade. 6 February 1840. p.3, c6.

**2500 ALVAN STEWART, ESQ.** *to* **WEBB. 29 January 1840. Utica, N.Y.** Criticizes the disorganization prevailing among political abolitionists; urges the nomination of independent abolitionist candidates. 13 February 1840. p.1, c5.

**2501 CORRESPONDENT** *to* **THE** *EMANCIPATOR*. **n.d. n.p.** Reports the progress of the trial of the Africans of the *Amistad*. 13 February 1840. p.2, c1.

**2502 ARNOLD BUFFUM** *to* **JOSHUA LEAVITT. [from the** *Emancipator***] 23 January 1840. Newport, Wayne County, In.** Describes his anti-slavery lecture tour in Indiana during the two preceeding months; discusses the prevailing opinions in Indiana on slavery, particularly among the Friends. 13 February 1840. p.2, c1.

**2503 ARNOLD BUFFUM** *to* **THE** *EMANCIPATOR*. **[extract] n.d. Richmond, In.** Reports the progress of the anti-slavery cause in Indiana; states that he has been able to hold meetings in Friends' meetinghouses. 13 February 1840. p.2, c2.

**2504 A SPECTATOR** *to* **MR. JOSEPH R. CHANDLER. [from the** *United States Gazette***] 28 January 1840. n.p.** Discusses the financial aspect of the slave trade in Mississippi. 13 February 1840. p.2, c2.

**2505 JAMES C. FULLER** *to* **WM. GOODELL. [from the** *Friend of Man***] 28 January 1840. Skaneateles, N.Y.** Describes a meeting of the Onondaga County AS in Baldwinsville, New York. 13 February 1840. p.2, c3.

**2506 LEWIS TAPPAN** *to* **n.n. [from the** *New York Evening Star***] n.d. n.p.** Describes the role of Mr. Ruiz in the affairs of the Africans of the *Amistad* case; denies allegations that he was responsible for Ruiz's arrest. 13 February 1840. p.2, c4.

**2507 n.n.** *to* **n.n. [from the** *North American***] 3 January 1840. Trinidad.** Describes the arrival of immigrants to Trinidad aboard the *Archer*. 13 February 1840. p.2, c4.

**2508 JUDGE WILKINSON** *to* **n.n. n.d. n.p.** Describes the preparations being made for the arrival of colored immigrants in Africa. 13 February 1840. p.3, c5.

**2509 COLUMBUS CORRESPONDENT** *to* **THE** *CINCINNATI GAZETTE*. **n.d. Columbus, Oh.** Reports a proposal in the Ohio legislature to remove Williams as a trustee of Miami University because he is an abolitionist. 13 February 1840. p.3, c6.

**2510 THE TREASURER OF THE PHILADELPHIA CITY AS** *to* **ITS PATRONS. n.d. n.p.** Urges full payment of the "Liberty Tax." 13 February 1840. p.3, c6.

**2511 VERUS** *to* **THE** *PENNSYLVANIA FREEMAN*. **n.d. n.p.** Encloses an anti-slavery memorial to the House of Representatives, which he suggests should be extensively circulated. 13 February 1840. p.3, c6.

2512 **n.n.** *to* **THE** ***NEW YORK EXPRESS*****. 13 February 1840. Washington.** Describes a debate in the Senate on the abolition of slavery and the right of petition. 20 February 1840. p.2, c4.

2513 **SPENCER KELLOGG, ESQ.** *to* **THE EXECUTIVE COMMITTEE OF THE NEW YORK STATE AS. n.d. n.p.** Informs the committee of his resignation from the executive board as a result of the controversy caused by his action at a political meeting. 20 February 1840. p.3, c3.

2514 **J. A. W.** *to* **THE** ***PENNSYLVANIA FREEMAN*****. 18 February 1840. n.p.** Describes a meeting of the Wilberforce AS held in Radnor township. 20 February 1840. p.3, c6.

2515 **J. FULTON, JR.** *to* **FRIEND WHITTIER. 9 February 1840. Ercildoun.** Describes speeches delivered at a meeting of the Union CS in Chester County. 20 February 1840. p.4, c1.

2516 **ARTHUR TAPPAN, JAMES G. BIRNEY, JOSHUA LEAVITT, [AND EIGHT OTHERS]** *to* **THE FRIENDS OF CONSTITUTIONAL FREEDOM. 13 February 1840. New York.** Argue against the prohibition of the presentation of abolitionist petitions in the House of Representatives. 27 February 1840. p.1, c1.

2517 **SENOR ALMONTE, MEXICAN SECRETARY OF WAR** *to* **THE NATIONAL CONGRESS OF MEXICO. [from the** ***Cosmopolita*****] n.d. n.p.** Requests that the president be granted the powers necessary to conduct an expedition against Texas. 27 February 1840. p.1, c6.

2518 **DUNCAN DUNBAR, CHARLES W. DENISON, ZELOTES GRENNELL, JOHN J. RAYMOND, AND RICHARD C. McCORMICK, CENTRAL CORRESPONDING COMMITTEE** *to* **BAPTIST ABOLITIONISTS OF THE UNITED STATES. [from the** ***Christian Reflector*****] 8 February 1840. New York.** Invite them to attend a Convention of Immediate Abolitionists to form an American Baptist AS. 27 February 1840. p.2, c1.

2519 **n.n.** *to* **THE** ***NEW YORK SUN*****. 27 January 1840. Galveston, Tx.** Reports the arrival of a British brig at Velasco which was sent to demand from Texas two Negroes imported from Jamaica two years earlier. 27 February 1840. p.2, c4.

2520 **JOSEPH S. ELLIS, CHAS. W. AINSWORTH, SAVILLE METCALF, [AND TWELVE OTHERS]** *to* **n.n. [from** ***Zion's Watchman*****] 10 February 1840. Worcester.** Protest against the refusal of the presiding elder to allow them to raise the issue of slavery at the last two meetings of the Quarterly Meeting Conference, Worcester Station, Methodist Episcopal Church. 27 February 1840. p.2, c5.

2521 **B. CLENDENON** *to* **FRIEND WHITTIER. 16 February 1840. n.p.** Discusses the moral and enterprising character of the free colored people in Maryland; condemns the colonizationists. 27 February 1840. p.3, c3.

2522 **L. M.** *to* **THE** ***PENNSYLVANIA FREEMAN*****. 15 February 1840. Philadelphia.** Describes a meeting of the colored Female Minervian Literary Society. 27 February 1840. p.3, c4.

2523 **A. L. POST** *to* **FRIEND WHITTIER. 14 February 1840. Montrose, Susqehanna County, Pa.** Supports the formation of an independent abolitionist political party. 27 February 1840. p.3, c4.

2524 **W. FOX STRANGWAYS** *to* **WILLIAM P. PATON. 23 December 1839. London.** Reports on behalf of Viscount Palmerston that the British minister in Washington and chargé d'affaires in Madrid have been instructed to intervene on behalf of the Negroes captured on board the *Amistad*. 27 February 1840. p.3, c5.

**2525 ANDREW T. JUDSON** *to* **A GENTLEMAN. [from the** *Connecticut Observer***] 13 February 1840. Canterbury, Ct.** States that, contrary to a report in the *Patriot and Democrat*, Martin Van Buren did not recommend that the Africans from the *Amistad* be taken to Havana and sold as slaves. 27 February 1840. p.3, c6.

**2526 A MINISTERING BROTHER** *to* **n.n. [from the** *Christian Reflector***] n.d. n.p.** Praises the *Christian Reflector*. 27 February 1840. p.3, c6.

**2527 WM. LEGGETT** *to* **n.n. [from the** *Emancipator***] 24 October 1838. Aylemere, New Rochelle.** Affirms his support for abolitionism; states that he will not hide his anti-slavery beliefs for the sake of being elected to Congress. 27 February 1840. p.4, c3.

**2528 BETA** *to* **n.n. [from the** *Emancipator***] n.d. New Haven.** Describes the condition of the captured *Amistad* Africans in jail. 27 February 1840. p.4, c4.

**2529 A LOCO FOCO** *to* **MR. EDITOR. [from the** *Lancaster Union***] n.d. n.p.** Refutes the claim of Mr. Forney, editor of the *Lancaster Intelligencer and Journal*, that all abolitionists support General Harrison for president. 27 February 1840. p.4, c5

**2530 GOVERNOR SIR WM. G. COLEBROOK** *to* **THE MARQUESS OF NORMANDY. [from the** *British Emancipator***] 12 June 1839. Antigua.** Encloses statistics indicating that the abolition of slavery in Antigua has not had adverse economic consequences. 5 March 1840. p.2, c1.

**2531 A WRITER** *to* **n.n. [extract from the** *Gazette***] n.d. n.p.** Reports the case of laborers in Demerara who were discharged by their employer when the latter was informed of their resistance to their previous employer's "roguish exactions." 5 March 1840. p.2, c1.

**2532 LIEUTENANT GOVERNOR MAJOR MacPHAIL** *to* **THE GOVERNOR GENERAL OF THE LEEWARD ISLANDS. [extract] 22 April 1839. Roseau.** Reports the improved social, economic, and spiritual condition of the peasantry. 5 March 1840. p.2, c2.

**2533 LIEUTENANT GOVERNOR MAJOR MacPHAIL** *to* **THE GOVERNOR GENERAL OF THE LEEWARD ISLANDS. [extract] 8 June 1839. Roseau.** Describes the social, economic, and moral condition of the peasantry. 5 March 1840. p.2, c2.

**2534 THE GOVERNOR OF ANTIGUA** *to* **LORD GLENELG. [from the** *British Emancipator***] 21 May 1839. n.p.** Reports the high moral and industrious character of the inhabitants of the "independent villages." 5 March 1840. p.2, c3.

**2535 H. C. CORBIT** *to* **EDWARD M. DAVIS. 31 December 1839. Paris.** Encloses a bull of Pope Gregory XVI against slavery. 5 March 1840. p.3, c1.

**2536 JUNIUS AMIS, ISAAC HALL, JOHN WALL, C. YELLOWBY, SAMUEL B. SPIRRILL, AND JAS. W. PUIZINN** *to* **MARTIN VAN BUREN. 23 February 1836. Jackson, N.C.** Ask whether he believes that Congress has the constitutional power to interfere with or to abolish slavery in the District of Columbia. 5 March 1840. p.3, c3.

**2537 MARTIN VAN BUREN** *to* **MESSRS. JUNIUS AMIS, ISAAC HALL, JOHN WALL, C. YELLOWBY, SAMUEL B. SPIRRILL, JAMES W. PUIZINN, OF JACKSON, N.C. 6 March 1836. Washington, D.C.** Believes that Congress is not empowered to interfere with or to abolish slavery in the District of Columbia. 5 March 1840. p.3, c3.

**2538 n.n.** *to* **n.n. [extract from the** *New Orleans Courier***] n.d. Mexico City.** Reports that the British are negotiating with Mexico for the Californias; believes that the success of these negotiations could strengthen the abolitionist cause in the United States. 5 March 1840. p.3, c6.

**2539 FRANCIS JACKSON, PRESIDENT AND WM. LLOYD GARRISON, CORRESPONDING SECRETARY** *to* **n.n. [extract from the** *Liberator***] n.d. n.p.** Representatives of the Board of Managers of the Massachusetts AS condemn the proposed National Anti-Slavery Convention for Independent Nominations to be held in Albany, New York. 12 March 1840. p.1, c1.

**2540 GERRIT SMITH** *to* **MR. GOODELL. [from the** *Friend of Man***] 8 February 1840. Peterboro'.** Describes meetings of the New York State AS in Arcade and West Bloomfield; describes the state of public opinion concerning slavery in Rochester; favors the nomination of independent abolitionist candidates. 12 March 1840. p.1, c1.

**2541 A. BROWN** *to* **BROTHER WRIGHT. [from the** *Massachusetts Abolitionist***] 6 February 1840. Springfield.** States that abolitionist views are held by most Baptist ministers in Hampden County; reports the pro-slavery bias of the *Christian Secretary* and the *Christian Watchman*. 12 March 1840. pl, c5.

**2542 ISAAC B. HOVEY, PRESIDENT AND JAMES M. H. DOW, SECRETARY** *to* **BROTHER ROGERS. [from the** *Herald of Freedom***] 19 February 1840. Atkinson.** Enclose a copy of the preamble and resolutions adopted at a meeting of the AS in Atkinson. 12 March 1840. p.1, c6.

**2543 GEORGE THOMPSON** *to* **E. M. DAVIS. [extract] 15 February 1840. Darlington, England.** Encloses a letter from Thomas Fowell Buxton concerning colonization. 12 March 1840. p.3, c1.

**2544 THOMAS FOWELL BUXTON** *to* **GEORGE THOMPSON. 27 December 1839. Rome.** Opposes the views of the CS but believes that colonization would help the peoples of Africa. 12 March 1840. p.3, c1.

**2545 n.n.** *to* **THE MEMBERS OF THE ANTI-ABOLITION SOCIETY. n.d. n.p.** Call upon them to assemble at the Woodbury courthouse to oppose an abolition meeting. 12 March 1840. p.3, c4.

**2546 n.n.** *to* **n.n. [extract from the** *New York Journal of Commerce***] n.d. St. Thomas.** Reports the prevalence in the West Indies of a belief in the imminent demise of slavery. 12 March 1840. p.3, c5.

**2547 S. S. FOSTER, J. B. CHANDLER, AND SIMEON TERRY, COMMITTEE** *to* **THE MINISTERS OF MERRIMACK COUNTY. [from the** *Herald of Freedom***] 21 January 1840. Concord, N.H.** Question them, on behalf of the Merrimack County AS, concerning their views on slavery. 12 March 1840. p.4, c2.

**2548 ELIJAH WATSON** *to* **SIR. [from the** *Herald of Freedom***] 29 January 1840. Andover.** Expresses his anti-slavery convictions, in response to the questions of the Merrimack County AS. 12 March 1840. p.4, c2.

**2549 JOS. M. HARPER** *to* **S. S. FOSTER, J. B. CHANDLER, AND SIMEON TERRY. [from the** *Herald of Freedom***] 30 January 1840. Canterbury.** Expresses his anti-slavery convictions, in response to their questions. 12 March 1840. p.4, c2.

**2550 RUFUS A. PUTNAM** *to* **S. S. FOSTER, J. B. CHANDLER, AND SIMEON TERRY. [from the** *Herald of Freedom***] 3 February 1840. Chichester.** Expresses his anti-slavery convictions, in response to their questions. 12 March 1840. p.4, c2.

**2551 W. H. HATCH** *to* **MR. J. B. CHANDLER. [from the** *Herald of Freedom*] **4 February 1840. Concord.** Expresses his anti-slavery convictions, in response to the questions of the committee of the Merrimack County AS. 12 March 1840. p.4, c4.

**2552 C. R. HARDING** *to* **S. S. FOSTER, J. B. CHANDLER, AND SIMEON TERRY. [from the** *Herald of Freedom*] **8 February 1840. Sanbornton Bridge.** Expresses his anti-slavery convictions, in response to their questions. 12 March 1840. p.4, c4.

**2553 PARKER PILLSBURY** *to* **S. S. FOSTER, J. B. CHANDLER, AND SIMEON TERRY. [from the** *Herald of Freedom*] **14 February 1840. London.** Expresses his anti-slavery convictions, in response to their questions. 12 March 1840. p.4, c4.

**2554 J. HOLCOMB** *to* **n.n. [extract from the** *Vermont Telegraph*] **n.d. n.p.** Expresses disappointment over Senator Tappan's abandonment of his anti-slavery beliefs. 19 March 1840. p.3, c1.

**2555 n.n. [CORRESPONDENT IN PENNSYLVANIA]** *to* **n.n. [extract] n.d. n.p.** Describes several of C. C. Burleigh's anti-slavery lectures. 19 March 1840. p.3, c2.

**2556 n.n.** *to* **n.n. [from the** *Jamaica Morning Journal*] **25 October. Hopewell Pen, St. Ann's.** Reports that a fire in his house was put out by Negroes. 19 March 1840. p.3, c6.

**2557 STEWARD** *to* **MR. GROSVENOR. [from the** *Christian Reflector*] **n.d. n.p.** Offers to donate the value of all his property to the American and Foreign Bible Society, provided that the funds be used for the distribution of Bibles among the slaves in the South. 19 March 1840. p.4, c2.

**2558 C. C.** *to* **BROTHER SPRINGER. [from the** *Western Journal*] **22 February 1840. Philadelphia.** Praises the aesthetic and moral virtues of Philadelphia; criticizes the amount of money spent in the construction of Girard College, a school for indigent orphans, and questions the propriety of the school's exclusion of religious subjects. 19 March 1840. p.4, c3.

**2259 EUROPEAN CORRESPONDENT** *to* **THE** *MASSACHUSETTS SPY*. **[extract] n.d. n.p.** Praises the social and moral character of the Turkish people. 19 March 1840. p.4, c3.

**2560 MRS. M. L. BAILEY, MRS. S. MILLER, AND MRS. S. B. EUSTIS** *to* **REV. WM. H. BRISBANE. [from the** *Philanthropist*] **15 February 1840. Cincinnati.** Thank him for the speech he delivered on 12 February before the Ladies' AS of Cincinnati; request a copy of the speech. 26 March 1840. p.1, c1.

**2561 WM. HENRY BRISBANE** *to* **MRS. M. L. BAILEY, MRS. S. MILLER, AND MRS. S. B. EUSTIS. [from the** *Philanthropist*] **17 February 1840. Cincinnati, Oh.** Encloses, in response to their request, a copy of the speech he delivered before the Ladies' AS of Cincinnati. 26 March 1840. p.1, c1.

**2562 WM. HENRY BRISBANE** *to* **EDWARD H. PEEPLES. [from the** *Philanthropist*] **4 January 1840. Cincinnati, Oh.** Offers to buy all the slaves he had sold to Peeples, in order to set them free. 26 March 1840. p.1, c4.

**2563 n.n.** *to* **n.n. [from the** *Cincinnati Philanthropist*] **n.d. Indiana.** Reports that the anti-slavery cause is gaining supporters in Indiana. 26 March 1840. p.2, c2.

**2564 GERRIT SMITH** *to* **BROTHER GOODELL. [from the** *Friend of Man*] **4 March 1840. Peterboro'.** Praises the convention in western New York which called for the nomination of independent abolitionist candidates; criticizes Garrison and Jackson for condemning the convention. 26 March 1840. p.2, c3.

**2565 ANDREW LEIGHTON** *to* **n.n. [extract from the** *Morning Star***] 3 September 1839. Virginia.** Describes the social, moral, and economic evils of slavery. 26 March 1840. p.2, c4.

**2566 JOHN G. WHITTIER** *to* **n.n. [extract] 16 March 1840. Amesbury, Essex County.** Reports the repeal of a Massachusetts law which prohibited interracial marriages. 26 March 1840. p.3, c1.

**2567 M. J. THOMAS, CORRESPONDING SECRETARY** *to* **THE** *PENNSYLVANIA FREEMAN.* **10 March 1840. Uwchlan.** Encloses a resolution adopted at a meeting of the Uwchlan AS. 26 March 1840. p.3, c5.

**2568 n.n.** *to* **THE** *JOURNAL DES DEBATS.* **[extract] n.d. Constantinople.** Reports the protest made by the French ambassador to Turkey against military cooperation between Russia and Turkey. 26 March 1840. p.3, c6.

**2569 n.n.** *to* **n.n. n.d. Vienna.** Reports financial negotiations between Baron Rothschild and Prince Metternich. 26 March 1840. p.3, c6.

**2570 ROBERT W. ANDERSON** *to* **THE SESSIONS OF WEST HANOVER PRESBYTERY. [from the** *Richmond Enquirer***] 3 September 1835. n.p.** Condemns abolitionist ministers. 26 March 1840. p.4, c1.

**2571 EDWARD C. DELAVAN** *to* **GENTLEMEN. [from the** *Albany Argus***] 5 February 1840. Ballston Centre.** Reports the progress of temperance reform in Ireland; encloses an account of Father Mathew's efforts on behalf of temperance in Waterford. 26 March 1840. p.4, c3.

**2572 THE MAYOR OF LIMERICK** *to* **FATHER MATTHEW [***sic***]. n.d. n.p.** Reports the reduction of crime resulting from Mathew's efforts on behalf of temperance in Limerick, Ireland. 26 March 1840. p.4, c5.

**2573 REV. J. A. JAMES** *to* **A NEW ENGLAND PASTOR. [from the** *New York Observer***] 19 December 1839. Birmingham.** Replies to the pastor's response to his letter in the *New York Evangelist*; reaffirms his contention that American Christians have not done all they should in the anti-slavery cause; encloses an extract from a letter by another New England pastor in support of his claims. 2 April 1840. p.1, c1.

**2574 A NEW ENGLAND PASTOR** *to* **REV. J. A. JAMES. [extract from the** *New York Evangelist***] n.d. n.p.** Confirms James's account of the apathy concerning slavery which prevails in the political, mercantile, and religious communities of New England. 2 April 1840. p.1, c3.

**2575 P.** *to* **n.n. [extract from the** *New York Express***] n.d. Bombay, East Indies.** Describes the poverty of the Indian population; encloses an article from *Alexander's East Indian and Colonial Magazine* describing slavery in India. 2 April 1840. p.1, c5.

**2576 n.n.** *to* **n.n. [extract from the** *Evangelist***] n.d. Havana.** Reports the punishing of two slaveholders, one for murdering a slave, the other for "abusing" a slave; concludes that "monarchial slavery" is more protective of the slave than "republican slavery." 2 April 1840. p.2, c1.

**2577 R. HARRISON BLACK** *to* **THE EDITOR OF THE** *BRITISH EMANCIPATOR.* **16 December 1839. Paris.** Discusses the planned anti-slavery congress to be held in London in June of 1840; describes M. de Saint Anthoine of the AS in Paris. 2 April 1840. p.2, c2.

**2578 n.n.** *to* **n.n. [extract] n.d. n.p.** A Southerner writes to a friend in Philadelphia that he supports the cause of abolitionism. 2 April 1840. p.2, c5.

**2579 MILES HOTCHKISS** *to* **HON. WILLIAM H. HARRISON. [from the** ***Oswego Palladium*****] 31 January 1840. Oswego.** Asks Harrison, on behalf of the Union Association of Oswego, whether he favors the abolition of slavery in the District of Columbia, a United States bank for disbursing public funds, and the passage of a general bankrupt law by Congress. 2 April 1840. p.2, c5.

**2580 DAVID GWYNNE, J. C. WRIGHT, O. M. SPENCER, AND E. H. SPENCER, CORRESPONDING SECRETARY** *to* **THE OSWEGO UNION ASSOCIATION. [from the** ***Oswego Palladium*****] 29 February 1840. Cincinnati.** Members of General Harrison's "confidential committee" state that Harrison's position on constitutional questions has been made public and remains unchanged. 2 April 1840. p.2, c6.

**2581 C. C. BURLEIGH** *to* **FRIEND. 19 March 1840. York.** Describes his anti-slavery lecture tour in Pennsylvania during the past winter. 2 April 1840. p. 3, c3.

**2582 C. C. BURLEIGH** *to* **FRIEND. 23 March 1840. York.** Expects successful results from his current anti-slavery lecture tour in Pennsylvania. 2 April 1840. p.3, c5.

**2583 JACKSON CORRESPONDENT** *to* **THE** ***NATCHEZ COURIER*****. [extract] n.d. n.p.** Relates the story of a woman who impersonated a boy while in search of her husband. 2 April 1840. p.4, c2.

**2584 n.n.** *to* **MR. EDITOR. [from the** ***Connecticut Observer*****] n.d. n.p.** Encloses a letter from the sultan of Turkey to Martin Van Buren. 2 April 1840. p.4, c3.

**2585 ABDUL MEDJID, SULTAN OF TURKEY** *to* **MARTIN VAN BUREN, PRESIDENT OF THE UNITED STATES. n.d. n.p.** Grants permission to Christian missionaries to pursue their work in Turkey; states that Moslems object to the Christian practices of drinking intoxicants, disrespecting elders, and enslaving men of color. 2 April 1840. p.4, c3.

**2586 MR. CAMPBELL** *to* **THE** ***PENNSYLVANIA FREEMAN*****. 28 February. Georgetown.** Encloses an extract from a letter from a Presbyterian preacher in Tennessee. 9 April 1840. p.2, c3.

**2587 A PRESBYTERIAN PREACHER** *to* **MR. CAMPBELL. [extract] n.d. Tennessee.** Reports that two slaveholders in Tennessee provided in their wills for their slaves' freedom. 9 April 1840. p.2, c3.

**2588 D. H.** *to* **MR. EDITOR. 30 March 1840. Baltimore.** States that reform of the Constitution should be the abolitionists' main concern. 9 April 1840. p.2, c4.

**2589 SENTINEL** *to* **n.n. 1 April 1840. Richland.** Appeals to the citizens of Richland to work for the abolition of slavery. 9 April 1840. p.2, c5.

**2590 B. CLENDENON** *to* **FRIEND McKIM. 23 March 1840. Colerain.** Describes two debates in Darlington, in which he participated, concerning the relative virtues of colonization and abolition. 9 April 1840. p.2, c6.

**2591 JOHN G. WHITTIER** *to* **BROTHER MYRICK. 6 March 1840. Amesbury, Ma.** Explains his view that independent nominations of anti-slavery candidates, the purpose of a convention to be held in April, would be inexpedient at this time. 9 April 1840. p.3, c3.

2592 **F. C. BROWN** *to* **SIR. 29 December 1839. London.** Condemns the British government for its plans to wage war with China to secure the opium trade; encloses an article by Rev. A. S. Thelwall, entitled "The Iniquities of the Opium Trade." 9 April 1840. p.3, c4.

2593 **F.C. BROWN** *to* **SIR. 2 January 1840. London.** Encloses a paper written by C. A. Bruce, superintendent of the Agricultural and Horticultural Society of India, urging the British government to act to stop the cultivation of opium in Assam. 9 April 1840. p.3, c5.

2594 **RAM GOPAUL GHOSE** *to* **WILLIAM ADAM, ESQ. July 1839. Calcutta.** Praises the British for their enthusiastic love of freedom and commends the formation of a British India Society. 9 April 1840. p.4, c2.

2595 **RAM GOPAUL GHOSE** *to* **WILLIAM ADAM, ESQ. 24 August 1839. Calcutta.** Describes the progress of education in India. 9 April 1840. p.4, c2.

2596 **GEN. HARRISON** *to* **A MEMBER OF CONGRESS. [extract from the** ***Charleston Courier*****] n.d. n.p.** Reaffirms the anti-abolitionist sentiments he expressed in a speech at Vincennes in July 1835. 16 April 1840. p.1, c1.

2597 **J.** *to* **THE** ***PENNSYLVANIA FREEMAN*****. 1 April 1840. Chester County, Pa.** Encloses a letter from Francis James; praises Slade's speech in Congress but criticizes Slade for supporting Harrison for president. 16 April 1840. p.2, c3.

2598 **FRANCIS JAMES** *to* **J. n.d. n.p.** States that John Quincy Adams was mistaken in his contention that no more than one member of Congress would vote for the immediate abolition of slavery in the District of Columbia. 16 April 1840. p.2, c3.

2599 **GERRIT SMITH** *to* **MR. GOODELL. [from the** ***Friend of Man*****] 5 March 1840. Peterboro'.** Comments on letters concerning the political aspects of abolitionism by William Bosmith and James C. Jackson. 16 April 1840. p.2, c5.

2600 **ARNOLD BUFFUM** *to* **DR. BAILEY. [extract from the** ***Philanthropist*****] 16 March 1840. Sommerville, Pheble County.** Describes his anti-slavery lectures in Wayne County, Indiana; reports the growth of the Wayne County AS. 16 April 1840. p.2, c5.

2601 **HENRY H. CANNON** *to* **THE PUBLIC. n.d. n.p.** States that the Young Men's CS of Wilmington, of which he is a member, is opposed to abolitionism. 16 April 1840. p.2, c6.

2602 **JOSEPH JOHN GURNEY** *to* **BENJAMIN LUCKOCK, ESQ. [from the** ***New York Journal of Commerce*****] 18 February 1840. n.p.** Describes the moral and economic benefits of the abolition of slavery in Tortola, St. Kitts, Antigua, and Dominica. 16 April 1840. p.3, c1.

2603 **C. C. BURLEIGH** *to* **n.n. [extract] 7 April 1840. Harrisburg.** Describes the hardships he suffered on an anti-slavery lecturing tour. 16 April 1840. p.3, c2.

2604 **H. P.** *to* **MR. EDITOR. n.d. n.p.** Disagrees with those who would pass abolitionist laws before the people have been persuaded of the justice of immediate abolitionism. 16 April 1840. p.3, c3.

2605 **ORTHODOX** *to* **THE MEMBERS OF THE SOCIETY OF FRIENDS. n.d. n.p.** Invites them to an anti-slavery meeting. 16 April 1840. p.3, c5.

2606 **n.n.** *to* **n.n. [extract] 18 January 1840. Paris.** Reports that a debate on the abolition of slavery will take place in the French Chamber of Deputies. 23 April 1840. p.1, c2.

**2607 THOMAS EARLE** *to* **THE NATIONAL ANTI-SLAVERY NOMINATING CONVENTION. [from the** ***Emancipator*****] 30 March 1840. Philadelphia.** Suggests that nominations by the convention would be valuable only if the convention's platform coupled anti-slavery principles with those of "the equal rights of all men, the effective sovereignty of the people, and the reduction of salaries [for public office]." 23 April 1840. p.2, c2.

**2608 JOHN G. WHITTIER** *to* **THE ANTI-SLAVERY CONVENTION AT ALBANY. [from the** ***Emancipator*****] 22 March 1840. Amesbury, Ma.** Questions the expediency of anti-slavery nominations due to the dissension they would cause among abolitionists. 23 April 1840. p.2, c3.

**2609 H. N. ROBINSON** *to* **WILLIAM GOODELL. [from the** ***Emancipator*****] 20 March 1840. Canandaigua.** Expresses the support of the anti-slavery electors of Ontario County for the nomination of anti-slavery candidates. 23 April 1840. p.2, c3.

**2610 COL. J. P. MILLER** *to* **THE PRESIDENT OF THE ANTI-SLAVERY CONVENTION AT ALBANY. [from the** ***Emancipator*****] 27 March 1840. Montpelier, Vt.** Opposes the formation of an abolitionist political party before the exact views on slavery held by the candidates nominated already by the other two parties are ascertained. 23 April 1840. p.2, c3.

**2611 LEVI SUTLIFF** *to* **THE CONVENTION AT ALBANY. [from the** ***Emancipator*****] March 1840. Johnson, Trumbull County, Oh.** Supports the nomination of anti-slavery candidates. 23 April 1840. p.2, c4.

**2612 OLIVER CLARK** *to* **THE NATIONAL ANTI-SLAVERY CONVENTION AT ALBANY. [from the** ***Emancipator*****] 19 March 1840. Austinburg, Oh.** Supports abolitionism but believes that independent abolitionist nominations would be inexpedient at the present time. 23 April 1840. p.2, c4.

**2613 WARNER JUSTICE, CHAIRMAN AND ELI DILLON, SECRETARY** *to* **THE PRESIDENT OF THE CONVENTION OF ABOLITIONISTS AT ALBANY. [from the** ***Emancipator*****] 26 March 1840. Philadelphia.** Express support, on behalf of a meeting of abolitionists in Philadelphia, for the nomination of independent abolitionist candidates. 23 April 1840. p.2, c6.

**2614 E. W. FAIRCHILD** *to* **n.n. [extract from the** ***Philanthropist*****] n.d n.p.** Reports that he was prevented by a Christian mob from delivering an anti-slavery lecture in a Methodist meetinghouse in Belmont County, Ohio. 23 April 1840. p.2, c6.

**2615 n.n.** *to* **n.n. [extract from the** ***Hollidaysburg Register*****] n.d. Cattaraugus County, N.Y.** Opposes the formation of an independent abolitionist political party. 23 April 1840. p.3, c2.

**2616 n.n.** *to* **THE** ***BALTIMORE PATRIOT*****. 8 April. New Orleans.** Encloses an article from the *Texas Sentinel* describing a conflict between the residents of San Antonio and the Comanche Indians. 23 April 1840. p.3, c3.

**2617 RICHARD M. JOHNSON, VICE PRESIDENT OF THE UNITED STATES** *to* **MESSRS. BARNABAS BATES, CHARLES F. LINEBACK, WILLIAM FREMENT, MARSHALL J. BACON, AND HENRY C. SPERRY. [extract] 14 March 1840. Washington.** Supports the principles of democracy and civil liberties. 23 April 1840. p.3, c4.

**2618 C. C. BURLEIGH** *to* **n.n. 20 April 1840. Sadsbury.** Describes his anti-slavery lecture tour. 23 April 1840. p.3, c4.

**2619 REV. J. B. ADGER** *to* **BROTHER GILDERSLEEVE. [extract from the** *Charleston Observer*] **28 February 1840. London.** Describes several democratic measures taken by the Turkish sultan in the areas of law, politics, and the economy. 23 April 1840. p.4, c2.

**2620 OBSERVER** *to* **MR. EDITOR. [from the** *Boston Post*] **n.d. n.p.** Reports that a new cure for the scrofula has been discovered by a physician in Boston. 23 April 1840. p.4, c4.

**2621 J. CROSS** *to* **n.n. [extract from the** *Emancipator*] **7 March. Michigan City.** Describes the disruption of his anti-slavery lecture in Michigan City by a mob. 30 April 1840. p.1, c2.

**2622 LOGAN** *to* **FRIEND BAILEY. [from the** *Ohio Philanthropist*] **n.d. n.p.** Condemns abolitionists who would vote for pro-slavery candidates. 30 April 1840. p.1, c3.

**2623 H. P.** *to* **THE** *PENNSYLVANIA FREEMAN.* **n.d. n.p.** Criticizes the comments made by the editor of the *Pennsylvania Freeman* concerning his correspondence published in the paper on 16 April. 30 April 1840. p.1, c4.

**2624 J.** *to* **THE** *PENNSYLVANIA FREEMAN.* **29 March 1840. Chester County, Pa.** Encloses an extract from a letter from Capt. James Riley. 30 April 1840. p.1, c6.

**2625 CAPTAIN JAMES RILEY** *to* **n.n. [extract] 27 March 1824. Willston, Vanwert County, Oh.** States that if his candidacy for Congress is successful, he will direct all his efforts to the abolition of slavery; describes scenes of a slave uprising in St. Domingo. 30 April 1840. p.1, c6.

**2626 I. P.** *to* **FRIEND. n.d. n.p.** Supports the resolutions adopted at an anti-slavery convention in Albany in July 1839, calling on abolitionists to vote only for candidates who support the abolition of slavery. 30 April 1840. p.2, c4.

**2627 C. C. BURLEIGH** *to* **THE READERS OF THE** *FREEMAN.* **29 April 1840. n.p.** Announces his assumption of the editorship of the *Pennsylvania Freeman.* 30 April 1840. p.2, c6.

**2628 J. S. GIBBONS** *to* **FRIEND BURLEIGH. n.d. n.p.** States that the *Emancipator*, the organ of the AAS, has been sold to the New York City AS. 30 April 1840. p.3, c2.

**2629 n.n.** *to* **n.n. 19 January. Austin.** Reports that Judge Robinson has been charged with murder. 30 April 1840. p.3, c4.

**2630 n.n.** *to* **n.n. [from the** *Emancipator*] **n.d. n.p.** States that an anti-slavery lecturer is needed in his section of the West. 30 April 1840. p.3, c6.

**2631 COL. RICHARD M. JOHNSON, VICE PRESIDENT OF THE UNITED STATES** *to* **LEWIS TAPPAN. [extract from the** *Friend of Man*] **n.d. n.p.** States that he did not submit an anti-slavery petition to Congress, due in part to the fact that the petitioners were ladies. 30 April 1840. p.3, c6.

**2632 MR. WALSH** *to* **THE EDITOR OF THE** *NATIONAL INTELLIGENCER.* **[extract] n.d. n.p.** Provides biographical information about the new French ministers. 30 April 1840. p.4, c1.

**2633 OUR SOUTHERN CORRESPONDENT** *to* **MR. EDITOR. [from the** *Charter Oak*] **3 Janaury 1840. n.p.** Describes the moral and intellectual condition of Southern slaves. 7 May 1840. p.1, c4.

**2634 HARRIET POWELL** *to* **REV. MARCUS SMITH. [from the** *Friend of Man*] **18 February 1840. Kingston.** Reports that she is content in Kingston, where she now resides after escaping from slavery in the United States. 7 May 1840. p.1, c6.

**2635 HON. W. O. RIVES** *to* **n.n. [extract] n.d. n.p.** Quotes from a speech delivered by General Harrison in 1838 denouncing the abolitionists. 7 May 1840. p.2, c1.

**2636 THEO. S. WRIGHT** *to* **BROTHER RAY. [from the** *Colored American*] **16 April 1840. New York.** Encloses a copy of the proceedings of a meeting of colored American immigrants to Trinidad; discourages the emigration of colored Americans to Trinidad or Guiana. 7 May 1840. p.2, c2.

**2637 F. A. HINTON** *to* **THE EDITOR OF THE** *PENNSYLVANIA FREEMAN* **[C. C. BURLEIGH]. 30 April 1840. Philadelphia.** Disagrees with the unfavorable description of the condition of colored immigrants in Trinidad published in the *Colored American*; encloses an article from the *Baltimore Sun* concerning immigration to Trinidad, including a letter from S. Stevenson to Harrison Webb. 7 May 1840. p.2, c3.

**2638 S. STEVENSON** *to* **HARRISON H. WEBB, OF BALTIMORE. [from the** *Baltimore Sun*] **13 January 1840. San Fernando.** Gives a favorable account of the economic conditions in Trinidad. 7 May 1840. p.2, c3.

**2639 S.** *to* **THE** *PENNSYLVANIA FREEMAN*. **n.d. n.p.** Denies the common assertion that the Society of Friends is an AS. 7 May 1840. p.2, c4.

**2640 ELLIS GRAY LORING** *to* **THE EDITOR OF THE** *PENNSYLVANIA FREEMAN* **[C. C. BURLEIGH]. 1 May 1840. Boston.** Encloses a letter from himself to the editor of the *Emancipator*. 7 May 1840. p.2, c5.

**2641 ELLIS GRAY LORING** *to* **THE EDITOR OF THE** *EMANCIPATOR*. **30 April 1840. n.p.** Defends the Massachusetts AS from charges that it has adopted non-resistance principles; discusses the controversies concerning non-resistance and independent abolitionist candidates, which are dividing the abolitionists. 7 May 1840. p.2, c5.

**2642 W.** *to* **MR. EDITOR [C. C. BURLEIGH]. n.d. n.p.** Gives the substance of an anti-slavery sermon preached by the Rev. Robert W. Lundis. 14 May 1840. p.1, c5.

**2643 JOSHUA COFFIN** *to* **MR. EDITOR [C. C. BURLEIGH]. n.d. n.p.** Supports the resolutions adopted at a recent meeting of the Eastern Pennsylvania AS concerning the nomination of independent abolitionist candidates. 14 May 1840. p.3, c5.

**2644 J. W.** *to* **n.n. [from the** *Emancipator*] **24 December 1839. Havre.** Reports that Girard, a man of color, won a prize at the Sorbonne; encloses an extract reporting the refusal of a Vermont college to allow Harris, a colored man, to receive a diploma. 14 May 1840. p.3, c5.

**2645 n.n.** *to* **n.n. [extract from the** *Liberator*] **n.d. Burlington, Vt.** Reports the refusal by a Vermont college to allow James Harris, a colored man, to receive his diploma. 14 May 1840. p.3, c5.

**2646 COL. RICHARD M. JOHNSON, VICE PRESIDENT OF THE UNITED STATES** *to* **LEWIS TAPPAN. [extract from the** *Friend of Man*] **n.d. n.p.** States that he did not submit an anti-slavery petition to Congress, due in part to the fact that the petitioners were ladies. 14 May 1840. p.3, c6.

**2647 n.n.** *to* **n.n. [from the** *Emancipator*] **10 April. n.p.** States that an anti-slavery lecturer is needed in his section of the West. 21 May 1840. p.1, c3.

**2648 A. K. HOWARD** *to* **BRETHREN. [from the** *American Wesleyan Observer*] **n.d. n.p.** Condemns the slaveholders for ignoring their consciences. 21 May 1840. p.1, c4.

**2649 n.n.** *to* **THE WOMEN OF ENGLAND. [from the** ***British and Foreign Anti-Slavery Reporter*****] n.d. n.p.** Urge them to work in behalf of slaves around the world. 21 May 1840. p.1, c5.

**2650 W.** *to* **n.n. [from the** ***Friend of Man*****] n.d. n.p.** Cites statistics indicating that the state of New York's political power in the national government is disproportionately small when compared with its population and economic power. 21 May 1840. p.2, c1.

**2651 EDMUND QUINCY** *to* **SAMUEL D. HASTINGS, CORRESPONDING SECRETARY, AS, EASTERN PENNSYLVANIA. 1 May 1840. Dedham, Ma.** Regrets his inability to attend the annual meeting of the Eastern Pennsylvania AS; urges abolitionists to persevere in their work. 21 May 1840. p.2, c3.

**2652 N. P. ROGERS** *to* **SAMUEL D. HASTINGS, CORRESPONDING SECRETARY OF THE AS, FOR EASTERN PENNSYLVANIA. 27 April 1840. Concord, N.H.** Regrets his inability to attend the annual meeting of the Eastern Pennsylvania AS; reports the existence of much pro-slavery sentiment in New Hampshire; urges abolitionists to persevere in their work. 21 May 1840. p.2, c3.

**2653 WM. HENRY BRISBANE** *to* **SAMUEL D. HASTINGS, CORRESPONDING SECRETARY OF THE AS, FOR EASTERN PENNSYLVANIA. 28 April 1840. Cincinnati, Oh.** Regrets his inability to attend the annual meeting of the Eastern Pennsylvania AS; describes his recent conversion to the cause of abolitionism. 21 May 1840. p.2, c4.

**2654 LEWIS TAPPAN** *to* **SAMUEL D. HASTINGS, CORRESPONDING SECRETARY OF THE AS, EASTERN PENNSYLVANIA. 24 April 1840. New York.** Regrets his inability to attend the meeting of the Eastern Pennsylvania AS; criticizes those who cause divisions among the abolitionists. 21 May 1840. p.2, c4.

**2655 WILLIAM GOODELL** *to* **SAMUEL D. HASTINGS, CORRESPONDING SECRETARY OF AS OF EASTERN PENNSLYVANIA. 24 April 1840. Utica.** Regrets his inability to attend the annual meeting of the Eastern Pennsylvania AS; urges abolitionists to persevere in their work. 21 May 1840. p.2, c4.

**2656 C. D. CLEVELAND** *to* **SAMUEL D. HASTINGS, CORRESPONDING SECRETARY OF AS OF EASTERN PENNSYLVANIA. 29 April 1840. Philadelphia.** Expresses his views against slavery, and offers regrets for not being able to attend all of the meetings of the Eastern Pennsylvania AS. 21 May 1840. p.2, c4.

**2657 WM. HENRY BRISBANE** *to* **n.n. 22 April 1840. Cincinnati, Oh.** Expresses his regrets for not being able to attend the Baptist National Anti-Slavery Convention. 21 May 1840. p.3, c1.

**2658 C. C. BURLEIGH** *to* **n.n. 16 May 1840. New York.** Describes the proceedings of the annual meeting of the AAS. 21 May 1840. p.3, c2.

**2659 C. STUART** *to* **n.n. 4 May 1840. New York.** Relates the conditions in the West Indies after emancipation. 28 May 1840. p.2, c1.

**2660 n.n.** *to* **MR. EDITOR [C. C. BURLEIGH]. n.d. n.p.** Reflects upon the tragedy of man's need to work in order to satisfy artificial desires. 28 May 1840. p.2, c4.

**2661 JAMES G. BIRNEY** *to* **MESSRS. MYRON HOLLEY, JOSHUA LEAVITT, AND E. WRIGHT, JR. 11 May 1840. New York.** Accepts the nomination for president made by the Albany AS Convention; argues for independent anti-slavery nominations as the most effectual way to emancipate the slaves. 28 May 1840. p.3, c1.

**2662 JOHN CLARK (PASTOR)** *to* **n.n. n.d. Jamaica.** Reports on the good conditions in Jamaica since emancipation. 4 June 1840. p.1, c1.

**2663 ROBERT TURNBULL, ROLLIN H. NEALE, J. W. SAWYER, GEORGE N. WAITT, AND PHILIP ROBERTS** *to* **THE BAPTIST CHURCHES IN THE NORTHERN PART OF THE UNITED STATES. n.d. n.p.** Call for the active participation of church leaders in anti-slavery activities. 4 June 1840. p.1, c2.

**2664 C. C. BURLEIGH** *to* **n.n. 21 May 1840. New Haven.** Recounts the meeting of the Connecticut AS. 4 June 1840. p.2, c2.

**2665 WM. LLOYD GARRISON** *to* **n.n. [from the** ***Liberator*****] 22 May 1840. On board the packetship** ***Columbus*****, near Sandy Hook.** Comments on the upcoming World's Anti-Slavery Convention to be held in London on 12 June. 4 June 1840. p.3, c4.

**2666 LEWIS TAPPAN** *to* **n.n. 27 May 1840. New York.** Encloses a copy of the new periodical entitled *American and Foreign Anti-Slavery Reporter*, published by the new society. 4 June 1840. p.3, c4.

**2667 JOSEPH A. MERRILL, JONATHAN HORTON, ORANGE SCOTT, [AND SEVENTEEN OTHERS]** *to* **THE AAS. 9 May 1840. Baltimore, Md.** Stress the urgency and importance of the anti-slavery movement. 11 June 1840. p.1, c1.

**2668 A. TAPPAN** *to* **REV. JOSHUA LEAVITT, RECORDING SECRETARY AAS. 12 May 1840. n.p.** Explains his forthcoming absence at the business meetings. 11 June 1840. p.1, c4.

**2669 n.n.** *to* **THE EDITOR [C. C. BURLEIGH]. n.d. n.p.** Believes a separate political anti-slavery party to be the most effective means to abolish slavery. 11 June 1840. p.2, c1.

**2670 n.n. [A BLACK YOUTH FROM PHILADELPHIA]** *to* **n.n. [HIS FAMILY]. 29 April 1840. London.** Describes the National Gallery in London. 11 June 1840. p.2, c3.

**2671 C. C. BURLEIGH** *to* **n.n. 29 May 1840. Brookline, Ma.** Reports the proceedings of the New England Anti-Slavery Convention. 11 June 1840. p.2, c3.

**2672 THOMAS BUCHANAN** *to* **DR. PROUDFIT. 12 April 1840. Monrovia.** Describes the conditions in Monrovia. 11 June 1840. p.3, c3.

**2673 BENJAMIN TURMAN** *to* **SIMON TURMAN. 26 February 1840. Live Oak Point, Tx.** Describes the great disadvantages and hardships of settling in Texas; discourages his brother from coming there. 11 June 1840. p.3, c4.

**2674 ANDREW SPILLARD** *to* **DR. BAILEY. 8 May 1840. Economy, Wayne County, Ia.** Gives an account of the efforts to secure the permanent freedom of thirty-eight slaves who had been emancipated by the will of the late Capt. John Hill. 11 June 1840. p.3, c5.

**2675 J. C. ROGERS** *to* **n.n. 15 April 1838. Richmond, Va.** Depicts the terrible conditions of slaves in the South. 18 June 1840. p.1, c5.

**2676 JOSHUA COFFIN** *to* **THE EDITOR OF THE** ***FREEMAN*****. n.d. n.p.** Describes the deeds of cruelty perpetrated by Thomas Christmas of North Carolina, and his subsequent hanging. 18 June 1840. p.2, c1.

**2677 C. C. BURLEIGH** *to* **n.n. 8 June 1840. Oxford, Ma.** Forwards an account of the annual meeting of the New Hampshire AS. 18 June 1840. p.2, c2.

**2678 THOMAS EARLE** *to* **MESSRS. MYRON HOLLEY, JOSHUA LEAVITT, AND E. WRIGHT. n.d. n.p.** Accepts his nomination for vice-president by the Albany Anti-Slavery Convention; speaks out against slavery and for the benefit which may result from independent anti-slavery nominations. 25 June 1840. p.1, c1.

**2679 THANKFUL SOUTHWICK AND LOUISA M. SEWALL FOR THE BOSTON FEMALE AS** *to* **THE EXECUTIVE COMMITTEE OF THE AAS. 22 May 1840. Boston.** Contribute a sum of $500 for the establishment of a paper as a national official organ. 25 June 1840. p.2, c4.

**2680 n.n.** *to* **REV. JOHN SEYS. 3 March 1840. Heddington.** Outlines the progress of revivals. 25 June 1840. p.3, c2.

**2681 R. D., JR.** *to* **HIS PARENTS. 3 June 1840. London, England.** Rejoices on the anniversary of the Society for the Suppression of the Slave Trade. 25 June 1840. p.3, c5.

**2682 JOHN FORSYTH** *to* **MESSRS. BARCLAY AND LIVINGSTON. 7 May 1840. Washington.** Acknowledges for the president the receipt of two letters and expresses the president's appreciation of the gifts sent by the sultan. 25 June 1840. p.4, c2.

**2683 SEYD SEID BIN SULTAN BIN AUMED** *to* **PRESIDENT MARTIN VAN BUREN. 25 December 1839. Muscat.** Wishes the president well and offers his services. 25 June 1840. p.4, c2.

**2684 M. VAN BUREN** *to* **SEYD BEN SULTAN. 8 May 1840. Washington.** Acknowledges the sultan's desire for amicable relations but declines his gifts according to United States law. 25 June 1840. p.4, c2.

**2685 D. S. INGRAHAM** *to* **MR. LEAVITT. 2 June 1840. New York.** Comments on the beneficial effects of emancipation in Jamaica. 2 July 1840. p.1, c5.

**2686 A.** *to* **THE EDITOR OF THE** ***HERALD OF FREEDOM*****, N.H. n.d. n.p.** Asks various questions aimed at evaluating the political strategy of New Hampshire abolitionists. 2 July 1840. p.2, c2.

**2687 WM. THOMPSON AND WM. A. GARRIGUES** *to* **THE PRESIDENT OF THE MEETING CALLED AT CLARKSON HALL IN FAVOR OF INDEPENDENT NOMINATIONS. 19 June 1840. Philadelphia.** Support an anti-slavery third political party with James G. Birney for president and Thomas Earle for vice-president. 2 July 1840. p.2, c2.

**2688 ISAAC PARRISH, DANIEL NEALL, CHARLES WISE, AND WM. C. BETTS** *to* **THE PENNSYLVANIA SOCIETY FOR PROMOTING THE ABOLITION OF SLAVERY. 25 June 1840. Philadelphia.** Report on the subscriptions collected on behalf of the Africans captured on the schooner *Amistad.* 2 July 1840. p.2, c3.

**2689 J. A. WINSLOW** *to* **n.n. 6 May 1840. U.S. Schr.** *Enterprize,* **Pernambuco.** Announces the discovery of a new island in the Southern Ocean. 2 July 1840. p.4, c4.

**2690 JOHN G. WHITTIER** *to* **MR. LEAVITT. 24 June 1840. Amesbury.** Deplores the strife and divisions among the abolitionists. 9 July 1840. p.2, c1.

**2691 n.n.** *to* **n.n. [extract] n.d. Demerara.** Testifies to the increasing prosperity of sugar plantations. 9 July 1840. p.2, c3.

**2692 n.n. [JAMAICAN CORRESPONDENT]** *to* **n.n. [extract] n.d. n.p.** Describes his arrival and observes the progress made by emancipation in two years. 9 July 1840. p.2, c3.

**2693 WILLIAM JAY** *to* **n.n. [extract] n.d. n.p.** Comments on the AAS's advancing the doctrine of equality of the sexes. 9 July 1840. p.2, c6.

**2694 J. BLANCHARD** *to* **n.n. [extract] n.d. n.p.** Gives his reasons for choosing to vote for Harrison in the approaching election. 9 July 1840. p.3, c3.

**2695 THOMAS CLARKSON** *to* **J. STURGE. [extract] n.d. n.p.** Explains that his daughter and grandson will accompany him to the anti-slavery conference to be held in London. 16 July 1840. p.1, c2.

**2696 C. W. GARDNER** *to* **J. B. PINNEY, GENERAL AGENT OF THE PENNSYLVANIA CS. 29 June 1840. Philadelphia.** Criticizes the colonization scheme. 16 July 1840. p.1, c3.

**2697 BALTIMORE CORRESPONDENT** *to* **THE** ***COLORED AMERICAN.*** **[extract] n.d. n.p.** Protests the resolution of the General Conference concerning colored witnesses in church trials. 16 July 1840. p.2, c3.

**2698 n.n. [PHILADELPHIA LADY]** *to* **n.n. [HER SON]. 15 June 1840. Lexington, Ky.** Compares the condition of free blacks with that of the poor white population. 16 July 1840. p.2, c4.

**2699 n.n.** *to* **n.n. n.d. n.p.** Notes the progress of liberal attitudes concerning abolitionism. 16 July 1840. p.3, c2.

**2700 THOMAS BARTON** *to* **DR. BAILEY. 7 June 1840. Cortsville.** Reports on the resolutions adopted by the Green Plain Abolition Society with regard to the equal rights for women. 16 July 1840. p.3, c5.

**2701 n.n.** *to* **THE EDITOR OF THE** ***CONNECTICUT CONGREGATIONALIST.*** **n.d. n.p.** Describes the feelings of the South toward abolitionism. 23 July 1840. p.1, c4.

**2702 BROUGHAM** *to* **n.n. Thursday. House of Lords.** Regrets he will not be able to attend the anti-slavery convention due to poor health. 23 July 1840. p.2, c2.

**2703 GERRIT SMITH** *to* **n.n. [extract from the** ***Friend of Man*****] n.d. n.p.** Gives the proceedings of a meeting of the Madison County AS. 23 July 1840. p.3, c2.

**2704 JOHN G. WHITTIER** *to* **CHARLES LEAVITT. 16 July 1840. Amesbury.** Discusses his affiliation with ASs. 30 July 1840. p.3, c3.

**2705 PUBLICOLA** *to* **HON. D. WEBSTER. n.d. n.p.** Condemns Webster for his speech at Alexandria. 6 August 1840. p.2, c2.

**2706 R. B. LITTLE** *to* **n.n. 13 July 1840. Sunbury.** Conveys the proceedings of a meeting held at Montrose where the nominations of James Birney for president and Thomas Earle for vice-president were approved. 6 August 1840. p.2, c4.

**2707 GENERAL HARRISON** *to* **LYONS. n.d. n.p.** Notes that the word abolition had a different meaning in 1822. 6 August 1840. p.3, c1.

**2708 J. S. GIBBONS** *to* **n.n. [extract] n.d. n.p.** Relates an incident in Poughkeepsie, where a group of school girls sheltered a fugitive slave. 6 August 1840. p.3, c4.

**2709 H.** *to* **THE EDITOR [C. C. BURLEIGH]. n.d. n.p.** Relates the events of the Pennsylvania Democratic State Convention which met at Lancaster. 13 August 1840. p.3, c4.

**2710 W.** *to* **THE EDITOR OF THE** ***CHRISTIAN WITNESS*****. n.d. n.p.** Comments on the nomination of electors for the state of Pennsylvania. 13 August 1840. p.3, c5.

**2711 P. R.** *to* **MR. SUNDERLAND. 15 June 1840. Lenox, Ash County, Oh.** Reports the murder of a slave by a minister. 13 August 1840. p.3, c5.

**2712 n.n.** *to* **n.n. n.d. n.p.** Terminates subscription to the *Pennsylvania Freeman* due to the misrepresentation of Whig politics. 20 August 1840. p.2, c2.

**2713 n.n.** *to* **n.n. [extract] n.d. n.p.** Comments on his travels in Kentucky. 20 August 1840. p.2, c5.

**2714 N. P. ROGERS** *to* **n.n. [extract] n.d. n.p.** Criticizes the London World's Anti-Slavery Convention for not allowing women to participate. 20 August 1840. p.2, c5.

**2715 CORRESPONDENT** *to* **THE** ***LIBERIA HERALD*****. [extract] n.d. n.p.** Observes the lawlessness and turmoil in Liberia. 20 August 1840. p.3, c2.

**2716 B. S. J.** *to* **BURLEIGH. n.d. n.p.** Requests republication of the abolitionist society's constitution. 27 August 1840. p.2, c1.

**2717 LONDON CORRESPONDENT** *to* **THE** ***NEW YORK AMERICAN*****. n.d. n.p.** Praises Mr. O'Connell. 27 August 1840. p.2, c2.

**2718 AN INQUIRER** *to* **FRIEND BURLEIGH. 18 August 1840. Philadelphia.** Disagrees with Alvan Stewart's position that "the selfishness of the human heart must be had as the basis of success in any reform." 27 August 1840. p.3, c3.

**2719 W. ADAM, JAMES MOTT, CHAS. E. LESTER, WENDELL PHILLIPS, JONA. P. MILLER, GEO. BRADBURN, AND ISAAC WINSLOW** *to* **n.n. 23 June 1840. London.** Protest against certain principles recognized and proceedings held in the anti-slavery convention. 3 September 1840. p.1, c3.

**2720 G. W. W.** *to* **FRIEND BURLEIGH. n.d. n.p.** Supports Alvan Stewart on his controversial statement that selfishness must be practiced for the success of abolitionism. 3 September 1840. p.2, c2.

**2721 DR. MITCHELL THOMPSON** *to* **n.n. [extract] 16 July 1840. Havana.** Relates the capture of slave ships in the West Indies, and describes missionary work in Africa. 3 September 1840. p.2, c4.

**2722 JAMES CANNINGS FULLER** *to* **JOSEPH [ORCHAD]. 15 July 1840. Bristol, England.** Discusses the stand of the Methodist church in America on slavery. 10 September 1840. p.1, c1.

**2723 THOMAS S. KENDALL, ANDREW HERNON, JAMES MARTIN, AND THOMAS BEVERIDGE, [FOR THE PRESBYTERY OF THE CAROLINAS]** *to* **BRETHREN. n.d. n.p.** Emphasize the importance of a moral emancipation as well as a legal one. 10 September 1840. p.1, c3.

**2724 n.n.** *to* **THE EDITOR [C. C. BURLEIGH]. [from the** ***South Carolinian*****] 12 August 1840. Fairfield District.** Expounds upon the activities of abolition missionary Thomas Kendall in a Southern state. 10 September 1840. p.1, c5.

**2725 C.** *to* **THE EDITOR OF THE** ***FREEMAN*** **[C. C. BURLEIGH]. n.d. n.p.** Contests the *Freeman*'s interpretation that the majority of Vermont abolitionists are adverse to an independent political party. 10 September 1840. p.2, c4.

**2726 A FRIEND** *to* **GENERAL HARRISON. n.d. n.p.** Questions whether Americans truly possess the rights of free speech and petition of the legislature. 10 September 1840. p.2, c6.

**2727 WM. C. BETTS** *to* **THE ASSOCIATION OF FRIENDS FOR PROMOTING THE ABOLITION OF SLAVERY. 4 September 1840. Philadelphia.** Urges boycott of goods produced by slave labor. 17 September 1840. p.2, c2.

**2728 THOS. HAMBLETON AND WM. JACKSON** *to* **THE SENATE AND HOUSE OF REPRESENTATIVES OF THE UNITED STATES IN CONGRESS ASSEMBLED. [extract] n.d. n.p.** Note the failure of the American government to solve the problem of slavery. 17 September 1840. p.2, c4.

**2729 n.n.** *to* **THE EDITOR [C. C. BURLEIGH]. n.d. n.p.** Reports on the proceedings of the fourth annual meeting of the American Moral Reform Society. 17 September 1840. p.2, c4.

**2730 A FREEMAN** *to* **MR. BURLEIGH. n.d. n.p.** Criticizes the Pennsylvania State Convention for resisting the progress of abolitionists. 17 September 1840. p.2, c5.

**2731 JONATHAN GREEN** *to* **n.n. [extract from the** ***Emancipator*****] n.d. Sandwich Islands.** Assures recipient that he and other missionaries support emancipation. 17 September 1840. p.3, c4.

**2732 HIRAM WILSON** *to* **n.n. [extract from the** ***Friend of Man*****] n.d. n.p.** Describes the aborted voyage of the Liberian-bound ship *Saluda*, which was forced by bad weather to land in Philadelphia. 17 September 1840. p.3, c5.

**2733 LUCRETIA MOTT** *to* **DANIEL O'CONNELL. 17 June 1840. London.** Wishes to know why women were rejected from the General Anti-Slavery Convention. 17 September 1840. p.4, c2.

**2734 DANIEL O'CONNELL** *to* **LUCRETIA MOTT. 20 June 1840. 16 Pall Mall.** Supports the admission of women, on an equal footing with men, to conferences. 17 September 1840. p.4, c2.

**2735 n.n.** *to* **n.n. [extract from the** ***Ohio Free Press*****] n.d. Smyrna, Rocky Creek, Chester.** Reports the tar and feathering of T. S. Kendall. 24 September 1840. p.1, c1.

**2736 J. M. McKIM** *to* **C. C. BURLEIGH. n.d. n.p.** Spurs abolitionists to political action, encouraging voting especially. 24 September 1840. p.2, c1.

**2737 GERRIT SMITH** *to* **MR. BURLEIGH. 19 September 1840. Philadelphia.** Outlines reasons why the letters written by J. J. Gurney on the West Indies will have a beneficial effect. 24 September 1840. p.2, c3.

**2738 Y. Z.** *to* **CHARLES. 15 September 1840. Chester County.** Discusses preparations for elections for state and county officers. 24 September 1840. p.2, c4.

**2739 A.** *to* **THE EDITOR [C. C. BURLEIGH]. n.d. n.p.** Responds to the paper's previous criticism of the proceedings of the New York Convention. 24 September 1840. p.2, c6.

**2740 DEMOCRAT IN CONNECTICUT** *to* **THE EDITOR OF THE** ***RICHMOND ENQUIRER*****. [extract from the** ***Advocate of Freedom*****] n.d. n.p.** Sets fourth Van Buren's claims on the South. 24 September 1840. p.3, c3.

**2741 CORRESPONDENT** *to* **THE** *EMANCIPATOR*. **[extract] n.d. n.p.** Reports an attempt to collect a debt. 24 September 1840. p.3, c4.

**2742 ROBERT NEWTON** *to* **J. H. TREDGOLD. 17 August 1840. Newcastle-upon-Tyne.** Supports the British AS on behalf on England's Wesleyan Ministers. 1 October 1840. p.1, c1.

**2743 D. N.** *to* **BROTHER LEAVITT. 5 May 1840. Mission Institute.** Urges the practice of preaching anti-slavery sentiment to religious slaveholders, not only to the slaves. 1 October 1840. p.1, c1.

**2744 G. M. DALLAS** *to* **JOHN WILLIS, ESQ. 29 August 1840. Philadelphia.** Reports on the position of the Democratic Party. 8 October 1840. p.1, c3.

**2745 CATHERINE HOLMES** *to* **SON. 10 February 1840. King and Queen Court House.** Pleads with her son not to do missionary work in Africa. 8 October 1840. p.1, c4.

**2746 E. N.** *to* **THE** *U.S. GAZETTE*. **24 September. Philadelphia.** Describes the slave market in Constantinople. 8 October 1840. p.1, c6.

**2747 G. F. HORTON** *to* **THE** *PENNSYLVANIA FREEMAN*. **25 September 1840. Terrytown (Bradford County).** Reports the resolutions adopted by the Bradford County Freeman's Convention. 8 October 1840. p.2, c2.

**2748 GERRIT SMITH** *to* **BURLEIGH. 28 September 1840. Philadelphia.** Stresses the duty of anti-slavery papers to dissuade freemen from voting for certain candidates favorable to keeping the slavery system alive. 8 October 1840. p.2, c2.

**2749 A.** *to* **THE EDITOR [C. C. BURLEIGH]. n.d. n.p.** Accuses the editor of misinterpreting his article. 8 October 1840. p.2, c3.

**2750 n.n.** *to* **THE EDITOR [C. C. BURLEIGH]. n.d. n.p.** Objects to correspondent "A"'s interpretation of politics; stresses the moral obligation behind any political action. 8 October 1840. p.2, c3.

**2751 ANDREW MILLER** *to* **JAMES WOOD, WM. THOMPSON, E. DILLIN, AND OTHERS. 24 September 1840. Philadelphia.** Clarifies his position on the slavery issue. 8 October 1840. p.2, c4.

**2752 WM. A. GARRIGUES** *to* **THE FRIENDS OF LIBERTY AND EQUAL RIGHTS, IN THE CITY AND COUNTY OF PHILADELPHIA. 23 September 1840. Philadelphia.** Calls for the support of James G. Birney and Thomas Earle as candidates for the presidency and vice-presidency of the United States. 8 October 1840. p.3, c1.

**2753 GEORGE SHANNOCK** *to* **CHARLES GARDNER. n.d. Port of Spain, Trinidad.** Discourages laborers from immigrating to Trinidad. 8 October 1840. p.3, c2.

**2754 n.n.** *to* **n.n. n.d. n.p.** Requests a lecture supporting the cause of freedom. 8 October 1840. p.3, c3.

**2755 WILLIAM EDMUNDSON** *to* **n.n. [extract] 19 July 1676. Newport.** Emphasizes the need to uplift the slaves from their degraded condition. 8 October 1840. p.3, c5.

**2756 CORRESPONDENT** *to* **THE** *NEW HAVEN HERALD*. **[extract] n.d. n.p.** Reports on the rapid advances which the Africans from the *Amistad* are making in school. 15 October 1840. p.1, c6.

**2757 AN OFFICER IN THE SERVICE IN FLORIDA** *to* **THE EDITOR OF THE** ***ARMY AND NAVY CHRONICLE.*** **n.d. n.p.** Presents a gloomy picture of the state of affairs in Florida. 15 October 1840. p.1, c6.

**2758 THOMAS CLARKSON** *to* **WILLIAM LLOYD GARRISON. [from the** ***Liberator*****] n.d. n.p.** Renounces the American Colonization Society, having concluded that more harm than good would be done by colonizing slaves in Africa. 15 October 1840. p.2, c1.

**2759 M. S. N.** *to* **C. C. BURLEIGH. 28 September 1840. Burlington.** Defends J. J. Gurney against criticism expressed by Gerrit Smith. 15 October 1840. p.2, c3.

**2760 A.** *to* **THE EDITOR. n.d. n.p.** Questions which is the most advantageous method of gaining support for abolition. 15 October 1840. p.2, c5.

**2761 BIRNEY** *to* **n.n. [extract from the** ***A. S. Reporter*****] n.d. n.p.** Recounts his labors in England with John Scoble. 15 October 1840. p.3, c3.

**2762 T. S. C.** *to* **BURLEIGH. n.d. n.p.** Supports independent anti-slavery nominations. 15 October 1840. p.3, c5.

**2763 n.n.** *to* **FRIEND BURLEIGH. n.d. n.p.** Notes the American public's increasing interest in amusement and recreation. 15 October 1840. p.4, c4.

**2764 CORRESPONDENT OF THE** ***DUBLIN WEEKLY HERALD*** *to* **n.n. [extract] n.d. n.p.** Describes Charles Lenox Remond as a well educated and respected "black negro." 22 October 1840. p.1, c1.

**2765 T. S. KENDALL** *to* **MR. EDITOR [C. C. BURLEIGH]. 7 September 1840. Monroe County, East Tennessee.** Recounts his mistreatment by South Carolinians while doing missionary work in that state. 22 October 1840. p.1, c3.

**2766 SAMUEL THOMPSON** *to* **n.n. [from the** ***National A. S. Standard*****] n.d. n.p.** Describes a condemnation of slavery by a Virginian. 22 October 1840. p.1, c5.

**2767 PUBLICOLA** *to* **J. WASHINGTON TYSON, ESQ. n.d. n.p.** Criticizes an address delivered by Tyson to a committee of abolitionists for its imprecision. 22 October 1840. p.2, c1.

**2768 J. K. PAULDING** *to* **JOHN FORSYTH. 2 January 1840. Navy Department.** Reports that the Negroes aboard the *Amistad* are being taken to the bay of New Haven. 22 October 1840. p.2, c3.

**2769 ISAAC T. HOPPER** *to* **RESPECTED FRIEND. 21 October 1840. New York.** Relates the suffering of slaves and their attempts to escape. 22 October 1840. p.2, c3.

**2770 JOHN FORSYTH** *to* **W. S. HOLABIRD, ESQ. 12 January 1840. Department of State.** Discusses the decision regarding the delivery of the Negroes aboard the *Amistad*. 22 October 1840. p.2, c3.

**2771 J. G. WHITTIER** *to* **n.n. 8 October 1840. Amesbury.** Redefines the purpose of the AAS. 22 October 1840. p.2, c4.

**2772 JAMES HAMBLETON AND MARY ANN UPDEGRAFF** *to* **THE MEMBERS OF THE SOCIETY OF FRIENDS. n.d. n.p.** Encourage support for the anti-slavery cause. 22 October 1840. p.2, c6.

**2773 JAMES K. POLK** *to* **HON. S. M. GATES. 2 October 1840. Nashville, Tn.** Criticizes Gates for his association with the World's Convention of Abolitionists. 22 October 1840. p.3, c1.

**2774 n.n.** *to* **FRIEND BURLEIGH. n.d. n.p.** Expresses distress about censorship in the *Friend*. 22 October 1840. p.4, c2.

**2775 A MEMBER** *to* **THE VOTING MEMBERS OF THE SOCIETY OF FRIENDS. n.d. n.p.** Notes spirit of martial enthusiasm in America; refers to the presidential candidates Harrison and Van Buren. 22 October 1840. p.4, c2.

**2776 JAMES MARTINEAU** *to* **THE EDITOR. [extract from the** ***Liverpool Mercury*****] 29 May 1840. n.p.** Praises Webster's dictionary as the most authoritative. 22 October 1840. p.4, c4.

**2777 n.n.** *to* **MR. EDITOR [C. C. BURLEIGH]. 4 June 1840. Monrovia.** Criticizes government expenditures. 22 October 1840. p.4, c5.

**2778 JOHN G. WHITTIER** *to* **SEWALL. 10 October 1840. Amesbury.** Presents a biographical sketch of Thomas Earle. 29 October 1840. p.1, c6.

**2779 REV. JACOB WESTON** *to* **A FRIEND. 11 August 1840. Jamaica, West Indies.** Relates the successful results of emancipation among Jamaican blacks. 29 October 1840. p.2, c4.

**2780 GERRIT SMITH** *to* **MR. GOODELL. 9 October 1840. Peterboro'.** Announces that he is submitting for publication an extract from one of Whittier's letters. 29 October 1840. p.2, c4.

**2781 JOHN G. WHITTIER** *to* **GERRIT SMITH. [extract] n.d. n.p.** Praises James G. Birney and Thomas Earle. 29 October 1840. p.2, c4.

**2782 T.** *to* **BURLEIGH. n.d. n.p.** Outlines a speech given by Joseph R. Ingersoll on Martin Van Buren. 29 October 1840. p.2, c5.

**2783 THOMAS EARLE** *to* **THE** ***PENNSYLVANIA FREEMAN*****. 26 October 1840. n.p.** Denies his support of Van Buren for the presidency. 29 October 1840. p.2, c6.

**2784 P. A.** *to* **MR. EDITOR. n.d. n.p.** Criticizes the logic employed by Brother Rogers in an article published in the *Herald of Freedom*. 29 October 1840. p.2, c6.

**2785 REV. WILLIAM WINANS** *to* **A COMMITTEE DECLINING AN INVITATION TO A "WHIG BARBECUE." 2 September 1840. Centerville, Amite County.** Gives reasons for wishing for the election of General Harrison. 29 October 1840. p.3, c2.

**2786 T. S. C.** *to* **BURLEIGH. n.d. n.p.** Stresses the importance of independent antislavery nominations. 29 October 1840. p.3, c4.

**2787 WILLIAM J. EYER** *to* **MESSRS. GAYLORD AND TUCKER. 7 July 1840. Cattawissa.** Relates a new method to preserve winter apples. 29 October 1840. p.4, c4.

**2788 LEVESON** *to* **THOMAS CLARKSON, ESQ. 22 August 1840. Foreign Office.** Acknowledges the receipt of communications respecting the London Anti-Slavery Convention. 5 November 1840. p.2, c1.

**2789 n.n.** *to* **THE EDITOR OF THE** ***KERRY*** **(IRELAND). [extract] n.d. n.p.** Observes O'Connell's popularity in France. 5 November 1840. p.2, c1.

**2790 WILLIAM PENNINGTON** *to* **THOMAS CLARKSON, ESQ. 30 July 1840. Newark, N.J.** Acknowledges the receipt of communications respecting the London Anti-Slavery Convention. 5 November 1840. p.2, c1.

**2791 SAMUEL D. HASTINGS** *to* **THE FRIENDS OF HUMANITY IN PENNSYLVANIA. n.d. Philadelphia.** Reprimands citizens of Pennsylvania for not contributing money to the anti-slavery cause. 5 November 1840. p.2, c3.

**2792 HARRIET MARTINEAU** *to* **THE BOSTON FEMALE AS. n.d. Tynemouth, Northumberland.** Expresses support of the Female AS. 5 November 1840. p.3, c1.

**2793 ANNE KNIGHT** *to* **THE BOSTON FEMALE AS. 4 August 1840. England.** Expresses her belief in women's potential in the anti-slavery cause. 5 November 1840. p.3, c1.

**2794 CORRESPONDENT** *to* **THE** ***LIBERATOR*****. n.d. n.p.** Reports on attitudes at Amherst College regarding abolitionism. 5 November 1840. p.3, c2.

**2795 A LOVER OF CONSISTENCY** *to* **MR. EDITOR. n.d. n.p.** Protests the celebration of the Fourth of July while the institution of slavery still exists. 5 November 1840. p.4, c3.

**2796 WILLIAM JAY** *to* **JAMES G. BIRNEY. 28 March 1840. New York.** Discusses the relationship of the American church to slavery. 12 November 1840. p.1, c3.

**2797 n.n.** *to* **n.n. [extract] 21 July 1840. Trinidad.** Notes that the value of property has not decreased with the abolition of slavery. 12 November 1840. p.2, c1.

**2798 W. C. B.** *to* **MR. EDITOR [C. C. BURLEIGH]. 9 November 1840. Philadelphia.** Accuses the *Freeman* of misinterpreting Whittier's article concerning Thomas Earle; requests that correction be made. 12 November 1840. p.2, c5.

**2799 n.n.** *to* **MR. BURLEIGH. 9 November 1840. Philadelphia.** Summarizes an address given by J. Miller McKim before the Philadelphia City and County AS. 12 November 1840. p. 2, c5.

**2800 J. R. DAILY** *to* **JAMES McCRUMMELL. 6 September 1840. Monrovia.** Gives a discouraging picture of affairs in Liberia. 12 November 1840. p.3, c2.

**2801 A FRIEND IN LANCASTER COUNTY** *to* **n.n. n.d. n.p.** Recounts the progress made by the abolitionists. 12 November 1840. p.3, c5.

**2802 JAMES R. CAMPBELL, A.M.** *to* **n.n. 14 October 1840. Montrose, N. Britain.** Requests publication of the enclosed address on the annual meeting of the Congregational Union of Scotland. 19 November 1840. p.1, c1.

**2803 RALPH WARDLAW, D.D., DAVID RUSSELL, D.D., AND JAMES R. CAMPBELL, A.M.** *to* **BRETHREN. 16 April 1840. Dundee, Scotland.** Support the abolitionist cause in America. 19 November 1840. p.1, c1.

**2804** *NATIONAL A. S. STANDARD to* **n.n. 1 November 1840. Boston.** Refers to the state of the campaign. 19 November 1840. p.1, c6.

**2805 J.** *to* **CHARLES. 9 November 1840. Chester County, Pa.** Opposes the nomination of an anti-slavery governor for Pennsylvania. 19 November 1840. p.2, c1.

**2806 THOMAS MORRIS OF OHIO** *to* **THE EDITOR OF THE** *PHILANTHROPIST.* **[extract from the** *National Anti-Slavery Standard***] n.d. n.p.** Proposes that the anti-slavery men in each state choose a delegate to attend the next session of Congress. 19 November 1840. p.2, c1.

2807 **SARAH M. GRIMKE** *to* **THE PHILADELPHIA AS. 22 November 1840. Belleville.** Declines an invitation to address the Philadelphia AS. 19 November 1840. p.2, c3.

2808 **JOHN G. WHITTIER** *to* *PENNSYLVANIA FREEMAN*. **24 September 1840. Amesbury.** Remarks on the World's Anti-Slavery Convention and British abolitionism. 19 November 1840. p.2, c4.

2809 **WHITTIER** *to* **n.n. [extract] 30 October 1840. n.p.** Corrects the *Freeman*'s inference that he proposed a change in the AS organization. 19 November 1840. p.3, c2.

2810 **B. S. J.** *to* **BURLEIGH. n.d. n.p.** Invites the public to participate in the state AS's meeting, which is to take place soon. 19 November 1840. p.3, c6.

2811 **J. F., JR.** *to* **ALL ANTI-SLAVERY PEOPLE. 15 November 1840. Philadelphia County.** Suggests flooding Congress with anti-slavery petitions. 19 November 1840. p.3, c6.

2812 **BENJ. S. JONES AND SAMUEL J. LEVICK** *to* **BURLEIGH. n.d. n.p.** Introduce the report of the second annual meeting of the American Free Produce Association, which was held on 20 October 1840. 26 November 1840. p.1, c1.

2813 **LUCRETIA MOTT AND SARAH PUGH** *to* **THE FREE PRODUCE ASSOCIATION. 20 October 1840. Philadelphia.** Protest the exclusion of women as delegates to the Anti-Slavery Society Convention held in London. 26 November 1840. p.1, c5.

2814 **JOHN THORBURN, GEORGE ALLISON, JOHN McCOLL, [AND THIRTY-THREE OTHERS]** *to* **ALL CHRISTIANS. [from the** *Glasgow Argus***] n.d. n.p.** Proclaim the incompatibility of slavery with Christianity and true humanity. 26 November 1840. p.2, c4.

2815 **DR. U. HUBBE** *to* **LEWIS TAPPAN, ESQ. 9 August 1840. New Castle.** Introduces a document respecting the attitude of the Lutheran Church toward the anti-slavery cause. 3 December 1840. p.1, c6.

2816 **McKIM** *to* **BURLEIGH. n.d. n.p.** Disagrees with a letter in the last issue of the *Freeman* written by "J," who opposes independent anti-slavery nominations. 3 December 1840. p.2, c3.

2817 **A.** *to* **THE AUTHOR OF THE TWO ARTICLES IN THE** *FREEMAN* **SIGNED J. n.d. n.p.** Questions his political opinion. 3 December 1840. p.2, c4.

2818 **SAMUEL D. HASTINGS** *to* **THE EDITOR [C. C. BURLEIGH]. 28 November 1840. Philadelphia.** Presents the official returns of the votes given for the Liberty ticket. 3 December 1840. p.2, c4.

2819 **n.n.** *to* **JOHN G. WHITTIER. n.d. n.p.** Comments on Whittier's letter published the previous week. 3 December 1840. p.2, c4.

2820 **[BENJAMIN FRANKLIN]** *to* **n.n. April 1777. Paris.** Recommends the bearer of the letter. 3 December 1840. p.4, c6.

2821 **G. BAILEY, JR.** *to* **THE MEETING OF THE MASSACHUSETTS AS. [extract] n.d. n.p.** Describes the evils brought about by the slave power. 10 December 1840. p.1, c1.

2822 **JAMES HAMBLETON AND MARY ANN UPDEGRAFF** *to* **THE MEMBERS OF THE SOCIETY OF FRIENDS. 31 August 1840. n.p.** Enumerate possible alternatives in considering the question of slavery. 10 December 1840. p.1, c3.

**2823 H. W. G.** *to* **THE EDITOR [C. C. BURLEIGH]. 31 October 1840. York.** Relates the successful efforts of York inhabitants to conceal a group of fugitive slaves from their pursuers. 10 December 1840. p.1, c6.

**2824 H. CREW** *to* **THE EDITOR [C. C. BURLEIGH]. n.d. n.p.** Corrects a misstatement which claimed he had foreited the confidence of the Free Produce Association because he did not vote for the admission of women to full membership in the London Convention. 10 December 1840. p.2, c1.

**2825 D.** *to* **BURLEIGH. 24 November 1840. Philadelphia.** Expresses enthusiastic approval of the jury trial granted to a fugitive slave in Vermont. 10 December 1840. p.2, c2.

**2826 W. H. J.** *to* **CHARLES [BURLEIGH]. 23 November 1840. Buckingham.** Discusses moral reform. 10 December 1840. p.2, c3.

**2827 E.** *to* **n.n. 24 November 1840. Newgarden, Chester County.** Supports independent anti-slavery nominations. 10 December 1840. p.3, c5.

**2828 J. S. H.** *to* **THE EDITOR [C. C. BURLEIGH]. 1 November 1840. Mercer County, Oh.** Describes Mercer County, Ohio, and its colored population. 17 December 1840. p.1, c1.

**2829 WILLIAM HARNED** *to* **HIRAM WILSON. 7 December 1840. Philadelphia.** Contributes twenty-five dollars to missionary funds in the name of the First Free Church of Philadelphia. 17 December 1840. p.2, c1.

**2830 HENRY BLYNN AND SAMUEL D. HASTINGS** *to* **THE EDITOR [C. C. BURLEIGH]. 10 December 1840. Philadelphia.** Introduce a letter by Rev. Robert W. Landis. 17 December 1840. p.2, c1.

**2831 ROBERT W. LANDIS** *to* **HENRY BLYNN AND SAMUEL D. HASTINGS. 31 August 1840. Allentown.** Regrets that he cannot accept the offer made by the First Free Church of Philadelphia, but identifies himself with the anti-slavery cause. 17 December 1840. p.2, c1.

**2832 J. B. PINNEY** *to* **THE EDITOR [C. C. BURLEIGH]. n.d. n.p.** Refers to a letter on the terrible conditions encountered by United States emigrants to Liberia, written by J. R. Daily; denounces Daily and his testimony as unjust, untrue, and unreliable. 17 December 1840. p.2, c3.

**2833 THOMAS CLARKSON** *to* **DR. JOSEPH PARRISH. [extract] n.d. n.p.** Opposes the institution of slavery, as well as its supporters and defenders. 17 December 1840. p.2, c3.

**2834 ALVAN STEWART** *to* **JAMES K. POLK, ESQ., GOVERNOR OF TENNESSEE. 18 November 1840. Utica, N.Y.** Reprimands the governor for his response to the Anti-Slavery Conference held in London. 24 December 1840. p.1, c1.

**2835 JACOB FERRISS** *to* **BURLEIGH. 6 December 1840. Marengo.** Stresses the importance of the anti-slavery cause. 24 December 1840. p.2, c2.

**2836 J.** *to* **CHARLES [BURLEIGH]. n.d. n.p.** Argues against the organization of abolitionists as such into a political party. 24 December 1840. p.2, c3.

**2837 ROBERT PURVIS** *to* **THE EDITOR. n.d. n.p.** Defends James R. Daily against the accusations levied against him by J. B. Pinney. 24 December 1840. p.2, c3.

**2838 J.** *to* **BURLEIGH. 12 December 1840. Chester County.** Responds to the questions asked by "A" in a previous communication. 24 December 1840. p.2, c3.

**2839 A. L. POST** *to* **BURLEIGH. 17 December 1840. Montrose, Susquehanna County.** Expresses regret that he is unable to attend the state AS meeting. 24 December 1840. p.3, c4.

**2840 JAMES HAUGHTON** *to* **THE IRISH PEOPLE. October 1840. Dublin.** Beseeches the Irish public to abstain from the use of tobacco procured by slave labor. 31 December 1840. p.1, c1.

**2841 S.** *to* **THE EDITOR [C. C. BURLEIGH]. n.d. n.p.** Expresses fears about abolitionist apathy. 31 December 1840. p.2, c1.

**2842 A MECHANIC** *to* **n.n. 12 December 1840. Philadelphia.** Complains of unemployment and ill treatment in Nashville. 31 December 1840. p.2, c6.

**2843 H. L. W.** *to PENNSYLVANIA FREEMAN.* **n.d. n.p.** Relates the conclusion of a slave case in Louisiana in which the court decided in favor of the slave in granting her freedom. 31 December 1840. p.3, c1.

**2844 JOHN BOWRING** *to* **WM. LLOYD GARRISON. 9 November 1840. London.** Supports the admission of women to anti-slavery conferences. 31 December 1840. p.3, c1.

**2845 JAMES CANNINGS FULLER** *to* **n.n. 24 December 1840. Skaneateles.** Discusses the education of "self-emanicipated" black people in Canada. 31 December 1840. p.3, c2.

## [1841]

**2846 THOMAS MORRIS** *to* **DR. BAILEY. n.d. n.p.** Requests donations for an anti-slavery committee to attend the next session of Congress. 7 January 1841. p.1, c3.

**2847 JOSEPH STURGE** *to* **THE EDITOR OF THE** *PATRIOT.* **November 1840. Birmingham.** Attacks Dr. Wayland, president of Brown University, for his support of slavery. 7 January 1841. p.1, c4.

**2848 HIRAM WILSON** *to* **W. L. GARRISON. [from the** *Liberator*] **12 December 1840. Toronto.** Discusses emigration of United States blacks to Canada and other parts of the world. 7 January 1841. p.1, c5.

**2849 G. F. HORTON** *to* **THOMAS EARLE. 17 December 1840. Terrytown.** Expresses his regrets for not being able to attend a special meeting of the East District Pennsylvania State AS. 7 January 1841. p.2, c3.

**2850 GEORGE TOLAND** *to* **SAMUEL D. HASTINGS. 1 January 1841. Washington.** Reports aborted attempts to present a petition before the House of Representatives. 7 January 1841. p.2, c3.

**2851 DAVID SMITH** *to* **SAMUEL D. HASTINGS. 12 December 1840. Baltimore.** Comments on the subject of political action. 7 January 1841. p.2, c4.

**2852 THOMAS EARLE** *to* **n.n. 14 December 1840. Philadelphia.** Corrects a statement claiming he voted the Van Buren presidential ticket. 7 January 1841. p.3, c5.

**2853 n.n.** *to* **CHARLES. 20 December 1840. Buckingham.** Reports on an address made before the Bucks County Temperance Society. 7 January 1841. p.4, c2.

**2854 R. M. JOHNSON** *to* **THOMAS EARLE. 4 January 1841. City of Washington.** Refuses to present any petition concerning slavery to the United States Senate. 10 February 1841. p.1, c3.

**2855 THOMAS EARLE** *to* **RICHARD M. JOHNSON, VICE PRESIDENT, AND PRESIDENT OF THE SENATE OF THE UNITED STATES. 4 February 1841. n.p.** Replies to Johnson's refusal to present a petition calling for the abolition of slavery. 10 February 1841. p.1, c4.

**2856 J.** *to* **BURLEIGH. 24 January 1841. Chester County.** Reports on anti-slavery affairs in Chester County, Pennsylvania. 10 February 1841. p.2, c4.

**2857 n.n.** *to* **n.n. [extract from the** ***Philanthropist*****] n.d. n.p.** Comments upon the anti-slavery convention which met at the federal courthouse in Columbus. 10 February 1841. p.3, c2.

**2858 THOMAS F. MARSHALL** *to* **n.n. [extract] December 1480 [*****sic*****]. n.p.** Speaks against repealing the law of 1833 which prohibits the transportation of slaves from other states to Kentucky. 17 February 1841. p.1, c1.

**2859 GEORGE TRUMAN** *to* **n.n. [extract] n.d. Tortola.** Reports on the success of emancipation and the energy of freedom. 17 February 1841. p.2, c5.

**2860 GEORGE GAMBLE** *to* **SAMUEL D. HASTINGS. 3 February. Braintrim, Luzerne County, Pa.** Urges the banishment of slavery and the promotion of equality for all. 24 February 1841. p.2, c2.

**2861 GEORGE GAMBLE** *to* **SAMUEL D. HASTINGS. 3 February 1841. Braintrim, Luzerne County, Pa.** Comments on local, national and international anti-slavery activities. 24 February 1841. p.3, c2.

**2862 n.n.** *to* **THE EDITOR. n.d. n.p.** Introduces an article against slavery from the *Boston Recorder*. 3 March 1841. p.1, c5.

**2863 EDITOR OF THE** ***EMANCIPATOR*** *to* **n.n. n.d. Washington.** Relates Giddings's speech on the causes of the Florida war. 3 March 1841. p.3, c2.

**2864 GEORGE TRUMAN** *to* **n.n. [extract] n.d. n.p.** Refers to his visit to Tortola island. 3 March 1841. p.3, c4.

**2865 GEORGE TRUMAN** *to* **n.n. n.d. St. Christopher's.** Describes the prison on St. Christopher island. 3 March 1841. p.3, c4.

**2866 GEORGE TRUMAN** *to* **n.n. n.d. St. Christopher's.** Recounts an interview with the governor of the island. 3 March 1841. p.3, c5.

**2867 GEORGE TRUMAN** *to* **n.n. [extract] 25 December. St. Christopher's.** Describes the Christmas celebration. 10 March 1841. p.2, c6.

**2868 GEORGE TRUMAN** *to* **n.n. n.d. Antigua.** Reports the emancipation of slaves and its effect. 10 March 1841. p.3, c1.

**2869 SAMUEL AND MARY NOTTINGHAM** *to* **GEO. 30 September 1782. Bristol.** Express concern for the well-being of ex-slaves. 10 March 1841. p.3, c2.

**2870 J. C. WATTLES** *to* **n.n. [extract from the** *Voice of Freedom***] n.d. Vermont.** Gives an account of the anti-slavery convention in Windsor County. 17 March 1841. p.1, c2.

**2871 JOSHUA LEAVITT [EDITOR OF THE** *EMANCIPATOR***]** *to* **n.n. 1 March 1841. Washington.** Comments upon Adams's argument in the *Amistad* case. 17 March 1841. p.1, c6.

**2872 GEORGE TRUMAN** *to* **n.n. [extract] n.d. n.p.** Reports the success of Joseph E. Philip, a reformed alcoholic. 17 March 1841. p.2, c4.

**2873 n.n.** *to* **THE OHIO LADIES' SOCIETY FOR THE EDUCATION OF FREE PEOPLE OF COLOR. 11 December 1840. Alabama.** Pleads for an increased effort to aid slaves. 17 March 1841. p.2, c4.

**2874 H. GARNET** *to* **n.n. n.d. n.p.** Addresses the problem of establishing equal rights for colored people. 17 March 1841. p.2, c5.

**2875 GEORGE TRUMAN** *to* **n.n. [extract] n.d. Antigua.** Reports the capture of two slave ships by a British cruiser off Puerto Rico. 17 March 1841. p.3, c1.

**2876 GEORGE TRUMAN** *to* **n.n. [extract] n.d. Grace Hill.** Describes an independent village of colored people. 17 March 1841. p.3, c1.

**2877 GEORGE TRUMAN** *to* **n.n. [extract] n.d. Antigua.** Recounts the finding of some remarkable petrifications. 17 March 1841. p.3, c3.

**2878 n.n.** *to* **n.n. [extract from the** *Richmond Enquirer***] 25 January 1841. Louisville.** Proclaims the advent of emancipation. 24 March 1841. p.1, c1.

**2879 RICHARD ALLEN** *to* **THE** *LIBERATOR***. 2 February 1841. Dublin.** Inquires into the state of slavery in the United States. 24 March 1841. p.1, c2.

**2880 JOHN J. MITER** *to* **THE EDITOR. [extract from the** *Genius of Liberty***] n.d. n.p.** Wishes to establish an anti-slavery paper in Kentucky. 24 March 1841. p.1, c3.

**2881 W. ADAM, SEC. OF THE BRITISH INDIA SOCIETY** *to* **THE ASSOCIATION OF FRIENDS. 30 December 1840. London.** Explains the nature and objectives of the British India Society. 24 March 1841. p.2, c2.

**2882 WILLIAM SMEAL** *to* **WM. LLOYD GARRISON. 1 February 1841. Glasgow.** Refers to Garrison's visit to Scotland. 24 March 1841. p.4, c3.

**2883 LEWIS TAPPAN** *to* **THE COMMITTEE ACTING FOR THE AFRICANS OF THE** *AMISTAD***. 19 March 1841. Long Island Sound.** Describes the events that took place after the Supreme Court decision concerning the captives of the *Amistad.* 31 March 1841. p.1, c6.

**2884 S. M. BOOTH** *to* **SIR. 9 March 1841. New Haven.** Reports on the progress made by the *Amistad* captives. 31 March 1841. p.2, c2.

**2885 KA-LE** *to* **J. Q. ADAMS. 4 January 1841. New Haven.** Describes his feelings about "Merika" and Mendi people. 31 March 1841. p.2, c3.

**2886 D. H.** *to* **BURLEIGH. 24 March 1841. Baltimore.** Notes numerous errors made in the *Reformed Presbyterian.* 31 March 1841. p.2, c4.

**2887 THE GENERAL AGENT OF THE BAPTIST HOME MISSIONARY SOCIETY** *to* **n.n. [extract from the** *Boston Christian Watchman***]. n.d. Alabama.** Remarks on Cesar Blackmoor, a colored minister. 31 March 1841. p.2, c6.

**2888 [GEORGE] TRUMAN** *to* **n.n. [extract] n.d. Antigua.** Comments upon society in Antigua. 31 March 1841. p.3, c2.

**2889 RICHARD ALLEN** *to* **GARRISON. [extract] n.d. n.p.** Reports progress in the temperance cause. 31 March 1841. p.4, c2.

**2890 n.n.** *to* **BURLEIGH. n.d. n.p.** Interprets the correspondence between George F. White and Oliver Johnson. 31 March 1841. p.4, c2.

**2891 RICHARD ALLEN** *to* **FRIENDS. [from the** *Dublin Morning Register***] n.d. n.p.** Opposes Britain's recognition of Texas as an independent state. 7 April 1841. p.1, c2.

**2892 LEVESON** *to* **RICHARD ALLEN. 12 February 1841. n.p.** Replies in favor of Britain's policy toward Texas, on behalf of Lord Palmerston. 7 April 1841. p.1, c3.

**2893 J. FULTON** *to* **BURLEIGH. 1 April 1841. Ercildoun.** Reports on anti-slavery activities in Ercildoun. 7 April 1841. p.2, c2.

**2894 WILLIAM H. SEWARD** *to* **THE LEGISLATURE. 26 March 1841. Albany.** Transmits resolutions of the legislature of Mississippi concerning the controversy between Virginia and New York. 7 April 1841. p.3, c1.

**2895 RICHARD ALLEN** *to* **n.n. n.d. n.p.** Introduces a letter to Lord Palmerston. 14 April 1841. p.1, c5.

**2896 RICHARD ALLEN** *to* **LORD PALMERSTON. 15 January 1841. Dublin.** Objects to Britain's recognition of Texas and requests additional justification. 14 April 1841. p.1, c5.

**2897 J. FULTON, JR.** *to* **CHARLES. 5 February 1841. Ercildoun.** Encloses a note from Ed. E. Law, chairman of the committee on the judiciary system, expressing reluctance to change any laws concerning slavery. 14 April 1841. p.2, c5.

**2898 n.n.** *to* **n.n. [extract] n.d. n.p.** Forwards a donation of 200 pounds sterling to aid O'Connell in effecting a repeal of the union between England and Ireland. 14 April 1841. p.2, c6.

**2899 GEORGE TRUMAN** *to* **n.n. n.d. Barbadoes.** Notes the hardships involved with emancipation. 14 April 1841. p.3, c2.

**2900 H. C. WRIGHT** *to* **n.n. n.d. n.p.** Disparages the Hanging Committee of the Artists' Fund Society for its refusal to display a portrait of Cinque, one of the Africans of the *Amistad.* 21 April 1841. p.2, c1.

**2901 WM. LEGGETT** *to* **n.n. 24 October 1838. New Rochelle.** Clarifies his participation in the abolitionist cause. 21 April 1841. p.2, c4.

**2902 n.n.** *to* **n.n. 27 February 1841. Port of Spain, Trinidad.** Observes the progress made by the emancipated slaves. 21 April 1841. p.3, c1.

**2903 H. G. AND M. W. CHAPMAN** *to* **FRIEND GARRISON. [from the** *Liberator***] 16 February 1841. Cape Haytien.** Introduce an article from the *Feuille du Commerce.* 21 April 1841. p.3, c3.

**2904 H. TEAGE** *to* **JUDGE WILKESON. [extract] n.d. n.p.** Apologizes for the offensiveness of a previous letter. 21 April 1841. p.3, c4.

**2905 THOMAS JEFFERSON** *to* **MRS. ADAMS. [extract] 1 October 1785. n.p.** Suggests that missionary work in England begin with the kitchen, not the church. 21 April 1841. p.4, c4.

**2906 J. C. McKISSICK** *to* **J. FULTON, JR. n.d. n.p.** Defends himself against verbal attacks made upon him by Fulton. 28 April 1841. p.1, c6.

**2907 AN IRISH FRIEND** *to* **THE** ***PENNSYLVANIA FREEMAN.*** **26 February 1841. Dublin.** Comments on the colonization enterprise. 28 April 1841. p.2, c4.

**2908 JACOB WESTON** *to* **n.n. 19 February 1841. Jamaica.** Discusses the advantages of liberty and equal rights. 28 April 1841. p.3, c1.

**2909 MC.** *to* **BURLEIGH. n.d. n.p.** Suggests an increased effort to expand the subscription list of the *Freeman.* 28 April 1841. p.3, c2.

**2910 JOHN TAPPAN** *to* **n.n. n.d. n.p.** Describes the processing of wine in Europe. 28 April 1841. p.4, c4.

**2911 B. GREEN** *to* **n.n. 31 January 1841. n.p.** Urges faith in religion. 12 May 1841. p.1, c1.

**2912 JOSEPH STURGE** *to* **n.n. 7 May 1841. Philadelphia.** Regrets he is unable to attend the anniversary meeting of the AS. 12 May 1841. p.3, c2.

**2913 ROWLAND T. ROBINSON** *to* **n.n. 25 April 1841. N. Ferrisburgh, Vt.** Refers to Elias Hicks, an early abolitionist. 12 May 1841. p.3, c3.

**2914 D. JENKINS, H. JOHNSON, J. BENNETT** *to* **JOHN QUINCY ADAMS. n.d. n.p.** Praise him for the example he set with his treatment of the *Amistad* captives. 19 May 1841. p.1, c2.

**2915 JOHN Q. ADAMS** *to* **CITIZENS. 15 April 1841. Washington.** Acknowledges letter and expression of gratitude. 19 May 1841. p.1, c3.

**2916 THEODORE SEDGEWICK** *to* **D. JENKINS. 4 April 1841. New York.** Acknowledges his letter and expression of gratitude for his services. 19 May 1841. p.1, c3.

**2917 CORRESPONDENT** *to* **GERRIT SMITH. n.d. n.p.** Notes the decrease of cruel treatment toward the slave due to abolitionists' efforts. 19 May 1841. p.2, c1.

**2918 THE EDITOR [C. C. BURLEIGH]** *to* **THE** ***PENNSYLVANIA FREEMAN.*** **n.d. n.p.** Relates the meeting of the AAS. 19 May 1841. p.2, c5.

**2919 n.n.** *to* **MR. STURGE. 25 December 1840. St. Lucia.** Describes the island as a peaceable and prosperous one. 19 May 1841. p.3, c6.

**2920 WILLIAM H. SEWARD** *to* **JOHN M. PATTON. 6 April 1841. Albany, N.Y.** Discusses the diplomatic relations between the state of New York and the state of Virginia. 26 May 1841. p.1, c1.

**2921 C. C. BURLEIGH** *to* **n.n. 21 May 1841. Hartford.** Recounts the proceedings of the Connecticut AS meeting. 26 May 1841. p.2, c2.

**2922 B.** *to* **ADAMS, JAMES, PARMENTIER [*sic*], [AND NINE OTHERS]. n.d. n.p.** Suggests resubmitting the "gag law" for vote in Congress. 26 May 1841. p.3, c6.

**2923 GEORGE W. LEWIS** *to* **BURLEIGH. 7 May 1841. n.p.** Corrects reasons previously given for the loss of membership to the Great Valley Baptist Church. 2 June 1841. p.2, c1.

**2924 DANIEL NEALL** *to* **n.n. 24 May 1841. Philadelphia.** Desires a more spiritual abolition. 2 June 1841. p.2, c2.

**2925 THE EDITOR [C. C. BURLEIGH]** *to* **n.n. 29 May 1841. Boston.** Reports on the proceedings of the legislative committee in Hartford. 2 June 1841. p.2, c4.

**2926 E. W. GOODWIN** *to* **LEAVITT. 25 May 1841. Albany.** Relates news that New York abolished the slave law. 2 June 1841. p.3, c1.

**2927 J. A. COLLINS** *to* **JAMES GIBBONS. [extract] 2 May 1841. Glasgow.** Describes the abject condition of the lower class in England. 2 June 1841. p.3, c3.

**2928 A SUNDAY SCHOOL TEACHER** *to* **THE EDITOR [C. C. BURLEIGH]. 29 May 1841. Philadelphia.** Protests the exclusion of the colored children from the anniversary celebration of the Philadelphia Sunday School Union. 2 June 1841. p.3, c3.

**2929 A POSTMASTER IN GEORGIA** *to* **W. GOODELL AND W. J. SAVAGE. 28 February 1841. Georgia.** Refuses to receive anti-slavery papers. 10 June 1841. p.1, c5.

**2930 POSTMASTER** *to* **BRO. SAVAGE. 15 April 1841. Georgia.** Declares slavery beneficial to the North as well as the South. 10 June 1841. p.1, c5.

**2931 WENDELL PHILLIPS** *to* **GARRISON. 12 April 1841. Naples.** Reports on the religious fervor of the Italian Catholics. 10 June 1841. p.1, c6.

**2932 BURLEIGH** *to* **n.n. 29 May. Boston.** Reports on the North East Convention. 10 June 1841. p.2, c3.

**2933 O. JOHNSON** *to* **n.n. 29 May 1841. New York.** Contradicts report that he attended the Yearly Meeting of Friends in Ohio. 10 June 1841. p.2, c6.

**2934 W. J. A.** *to* **M. J. RHEES. 19 May 1841. Burlington.** Praises Rev. Samuel Aaron. 10 June 1841. p.3, c2.

**2935 AMERICUS** *to* **THE EDITOR OF THE** ***WHIG*****. n.d. n.p.** Supports Adams's opposition to the measures of the abolitionists. 16 June 1841. p.3, c2.

**2936 SAMUEL AARON** *to* **THE EDITOR OF THE** ***BAPTIST RECORD*****. 27 May 1841. Norristown, Pa.** Reports the resolutions passed by the Central Union Baptist Association. 16 June 1841. p.3, c4.

**2937 E. G. L.** *to* **FRIEND. 2 June 1841. Boston.** Reports on the anti-slavery movement in England; discusses the feasibility of free labor competing with slave labor. 23 June 1841. p.1, c3.

**2938 G. F. HORTON** *to* **BURLEIGH. 18 June 1841. Terrytown, Pa.** Refers to Burleigh's intended tour through northern Pennsylvania. 30 June 1841. p.1, c3.

**2939 n.n.** *to* **n.n. n.d. n.p.** Requests further information on C. J. Ingersoll's speech. 30 June 1841. p.1, c3.

**2940 DR. ROBERT MOORE** *to* **CHARLES [BURLEIGH]. 10 June 1841. Philadelphia.** Announces cancellation of his subscription to the *Public Ledger*. 30 June 1841. p.2, c5.

**2941 ISAAC T. HOPPER** *to* **N.P. ROGERS. 16 June 1841. New York.** Expresses support for the Society of Friends. 30 June 1841. p.3, c2.

**2942 n.n.** *to* **n.n. [extract] n.d. n.p.** Condemns the institution of slavery. 30 June 1841. p.3, c5.

**2943 JOSHUA LEAVITT** *to* **PIERCY AND REED. 26 June 1841. Washington City.** Changes his previous opinion concerning the "gag law." 7 July 1841. p.2, c4.

**2944 HENRY G. AND MARIA W. CHAPMAN** *to* **n.n. [extract from the** *National Anti-Slavery Standard*] **n.d. n.p.** Remarks upon American emigrants' fondness for C. C. Burleigh. 7 July 1841. p.2, c5.

**2945 A WRITER** *to* **THE** *EMANCIPATOR*. **n.d. n.p.** Remarks on a letter believed to be written by Joseph Tracy concerning the possibility of sending missionaries to accompany the Mendians on their return to Africa. 7 July 1841. p.3, c1.

**2946 JOHN M. BOTTS** *to* **JOHN M. PLEASANTS. 3 July 1841. Washington.** Discusses the political aspects of the slave issue. 14 July 1841. p.1, c1.

**2947 CYRUS P. GROSVENOR** *to* **WM. HENRY BRISBANE. 2 June 1841. Worcester.** Relays accusations made against Brisbane. 14 July 1841. p.1, c6.

**2948 W. H. BRISBANE** *to* **CYRUS P. GROSVENOR. 9 June 1841. Cincinnati, Oh.** Denies accusations detailed by Grosvenor. 14 July 1841. p.1, c6.

**2949 A JEFFERSON FARMER** *to* **n.n. n.d. n.p.** Considers the cultivation of the Irish potato. 14 July 1841. p.4, c4.

**2950 HARRIET MARTINEAU** *to* **n.n. n.d. n.p.** Recommends the book, *The Hour and the Man*. 21 July 1841. p.1, c6.

**2951 F. MALLORY** *to* **THE** *BEACON*. **30 June 1841. House of Representatives.** Realizes the impossibility of regaining lost human property. 21 July 1841. p.2, c4.

**2952 A. E. DOUGHERTY** *to* **THE HONORABLE JUDGES OF THE COURT OF GENERAL SESSIONS FOR THE CITY AND COUNTY OF PHILADELPHIA. 10 July 1841. Philadelphia.** Dissents from the report given by the jury concerning the damages done to Pennsylvania Hall. 21 July 1841. p.3, c2.

**2953 PARIS CORRESPONDENT** *to* **THE** *NATIONAL INTELLIGENCER*. **[extract] n.d. n.p.** Discusses Countess Merlin's anti-slavery literature in the *Review of Two Worlds* of Paris. 21 July 1841. p.4, c2.

**2954 D. H.** *to* **McKIM. 16 July 1841. Baltimore.** Comments upon colonization schemes of Marylanders. 28 July 1841. p.1, c6.

**2955 C. C. BURLEIGH** *to* **THE** *PENNSYLVANIA FREEMAN*. **15 July 1841. Oswego, N.Y.** Sketches his movements and operations in the upstate regions of Pennsylvania and New York. 28 July 1841. p.2, c6.

**2956 PUBLICOLA** *to* **McKIM. n.d. n.p.** Describes the treatment and suffering of slaves. 4 August 1841. p.2, c1.

**2957 NORTH CAROLINA CORRESPONDENT** *to* **n.n. [extract] n.d. n.p.** Discusses the abolition of slavery and encourages free labor. 4 August 1841. p.2, c2.

**2958 ALVAN STEWART** *to* **MR. HOUGH. [from the** *Friend of Man*] **July 1841. Utica.** Comments on the Congress of 1841. 11 August 1841. p.1, c3.

**2959 G.** *to* **BROTHER BENNETT. n.d. n.p.** Describes the trial of the Rev. Edward Smith in Pittsburgh. 11 August 1841. p.1, c5.

**2960 J. P. MAGILL** *to* **CHARLES. n.d. n.p.** Introduces poetry written by the late Martha Smith. 11 August 1841. p.2, c3.

**2961 C. C. BURLEIGH** *to* **THE** *PENNSYLVANIA FREEMAN.* **July 1841. Cerres, McKean County.** Recounts anti-slavery activities in upstate New York. 11 August 1841. p.2, c4.

**2962 I. T. HOPPER** *to* **n.n. [extract] n.d. Philadelphia.** Urges the exercise of patience. 11 August 1841. p.3, c3.

**2963 WM. T. ALLAN** *to* **n.n. [extract from the** *National Anti-Slavery Standard*] **n.d. n.p.** Upholds individuality and independence. 11 August 1841. p.3, c3.

**2964 NEW ORLEANS CORRESPONDENT** *to* **THE** *NEW YORK TRIBUNE.* **n.d. n.p.** Reports the location of a slaver. 11 August 1841. p.3, c4.

**2965 BENJAMIN SHAW** *to* **THE** *PENNSYLVANIA FREEMAN.* **26 July 1841. Philadelphia.** Calls for political action against slavery. 11 August 1841. p.3, c5.

**2966 EUROPEAN CORRESPONDENT** *to* **THE** *NATIONAL INTELLIGENCER.* **10 July 1841. Paris.** Details the moral and economic benefits of the abolition of slavery. 11 August 1841. p.4, c1.

**2967 JOSEPH STURGE** *to* **U. S. SOCIETY OF FRIENDS. 17 July 1841. New York.** Outlines activities of the Friends of England. 18 August 1841. p.1, c1.

**2968 S. M. BOOTH** *to* **THE** *CHARTER OAK.* **17 July 1841. Farmington.** Relays the *Amistad* prisoners' description of their native land. 18 August 1841. p.1, c3.

**2969 I. ROBERTS** *to* **McKIM. 14 August 1841. Norristown.** Relates the minutes of a meeting of the voting abolitionists of Montgomery County. 18 August 1841. p.2, c3.

**2970 SAMUEL D. HASTINGS** *to* **McKIM. 12 August. Fulton, Oswego County, N.Y.** Notes the physical and spiritual state of the *Amistad* Africans; includes notes from other New England cities and towns. 18 August 1841. p.2, c5.

**2971 JONATHAN DAVIS** *to* **n.n. [extract] n.d. Philadelphia.** Reports on his debating success in Utica. 18 August 1841. p.2, c5.

**2972 F. JULIUS LEMOYNE** *to* **SAMUEL D. HASTINGS. 31 July 1841. Washington, Pa.** Accepts the nomination for governor of Pennsylvania. 18 August 1841. p.3, c2.

**2973 RICHARD ALLEN** *to* **n.n. 16 July 1841. Dublin.** Communicates the success of temperance in Ireland. 18 August 1841. p.3, c3.

**2974 THE EUROPEAN CORRESPONDENT** *to* **THE** *NATIONAL INTELLIGENCER.* **8 July 1841. Paris.** Comments upon Parisian society and notes its advances in art and medicine. 18 August 1841. p.4, c2.

**2975 BENEVOLENCE** *to* **THE** *PENNSYLVANIA FREEMAN.* **13 August 1841. Baltimore.** Remarks on the proceedings of the late colonization convention held in Baltimore. 25 August 1841. p.2, c2.

**2976 D. H.** *to* **McKIM. n.d. n.p.** Attacks all voters, including abolitionists, for implicitly upholding slavery by upholding the Constitution. 25 August 1841. p.2, c3.

**2977 B. SHAW** *to PENNSYLVANIA FREEMAN.* **17 August 1840. Philadelphia.** Speculates on the ignorance of certain members of the clergy regarding abolitionism. 25 August 1841. p.2, c5.

**2978 J. MILLER McKIM** *to* **n.n. 20 August 1841. Carlisle.** Recounts his travels in upstate Pennsylvania. 25 August 1841. p.3, c1.

**2979 JOSHUA COFFIN** *to* **THE PUBLIC. n.d. n.p.** Explains his removal from the office of letter carrier. 25 August 1841. p.3, c3.

**2980 GEO. A. ALLEN, N. LOVELY, JAMES MITCHELL, AND D. A. BRAMAN** *to* **COL. CHARLES PAINE. 16 July 1841. Burlington, Vt.** Solicit Paine's views on slavery. 25 August 1841. p.3, c5.

**2981 CHARLES PAINE** *to* **GEO. A. ALLEN, N. LOVELY, JAMES MITCHELL, AND D. A. BRAMAN. 30 July 1841. Northfield, Vt.** States that he opposes slavery. 25 August 1841. p.3, c5.

**2982 JAMES W. SEWARD** *to* **n.n. 7 July 1841. St. Louis.** Thanks Gerrit Smith for his concern and generosity. 1 September 1841. p.1, c4.

**2983 A. B. CHAMBERS** *to* **n.n. 16 July 1841. St. Louis.** Forwards a letter by James W. Seward. 1 September 1841. p.1, c4.

**2984 A. F. WILLIAMS** *to* **TAPPAN. 30 June 1841. Farmington.** Reports the drowning of M. Chamberlain, a resident of Farmington. 1 September 1841. p.1, c5.

**2985 ELIZABETH PEASE** *to* **n.n. n.d. Darlington, England.** Discusses the small but noticeable presence of supporters of non-resistance and abolitionism. 1 September 1841. p.1, c6.

**2986 J. MILLER McKIM** *to* **n.n. 26 August 1841. Bellefonte.** Relates Underground Railroad activities in and around Bellefonte. 1 September 1841. p.2, c6.

**2987 C. C. BURLEIGH** *to* **THE** *PENNSYLVANIA FREEMAN.* **18 August 1841. Washington, Pa.** Describes his lecture tour in Pennsylvania. 1 September 1841. p.3, c3.

**2988 JUSTITIA** *to PENNSYLVANIA FREEMAN.* **August 1841. Pittsburgh, Pa.** Considers slavery unjust in the eyes of God. 8 September 1841. p.1, c1.

**2989 W. C. BRADLEY** *to* **FRIENDS OF THE SLAVE IN THE CITY AND CO. OF PHILA. 26 August 1841. Philadelphia.** Criticizes the Church as the "Bulwark of Slavery." 8 September 1841. p.1, c4.

**2990 JOHN G. WHITTIER** *to* **SAMUEL WEBB. [extract] 26 August. Amesbury, Essex County.** Supports Dr. Lemoyne's nomination for governor. 8 September 1841. p.1, c6.

**2991 J. M. McKIM** *to* **THE** *PENNSYLVANIA FREEMAN.* **27 August 1841. Milesburgh.** Describes the meeting held in Bellefonte. 8 September 1841. p.2, c3.

**2992 C. C. BURLEIGH** *to PENNSYLVANIA FREEMAN.* **18 August 1841. Washington, Pa.** Remarks on a debate held at Cannonsburg. 8 September 1841. p.2, c5.

**2993 H. C. W.** *to* **n.n. [from the** *Liberator***] 30 August 1841. Boston.** Asks whether a slaveholder can also be a Christian. 15 September 1841. p.1, c3.

**2994 THE PEOPLE OF IRELAND** *to* **THEIR COUNTRYMEN AND COUNTRYWOMEN IN AMERICA. n.d. n.p.** Stresses the necessity of abolishing slavery. 15 September 1841. p.1, c5.

**2995 W. H. J.** *to* **n.n. n.d. n.p.** Comments on the report made by the committee on slavery at the Yearly Meeting of the Society of Friends. 15 September 1841. p.1, c6.

**2996 G.** *to* **THE EDITOR. n.d. n.p.** Praises temperance societies. 15 September 1841. p.4, c1.

**2997 ALVAN STEWART** *to* **DAVID L. CHILD, ESQ., ASSISTANT EDITOR OF THE** *NATIONAL ANTI-SLAVERY STANDARD.* **[extract] n.d. n.p.** Supports the third party with James G. Birney and Thomas Morris as candidates. 22 September 1841. p.1, c1.

**2998 G.** *to* **THE EDITOR [C. C. BURLEIGH]. n.d. n.p.** Refers to a letter published by the *Liberator* dated 27 August, which communicates Mr. Davis's debating success at Utica. 22 September 1841. p.1, c6.

**2999 C. C. BURLEIGH** *to PENNSYLVANIA FREEMAN.* **18 August 1841. n.p.** Continues to describe the debate held at Cannonsburg. 22 September 1841. p.2, c1.

**3000 S. W. MIFFLIN** *to PENNSYLVANIA FREEMAN.* **10 September 1841. Philadelphia.** Relates the hanging of a black man in Virginia. 22 September 1841. p.3, c5.

**3001 WM. WEBB** *to* **DR. J. W. THOMPSON. 25 September 1841. Wilmington.** Explains the manufacture of sugar from corn. 29 September 1841. p.1, c5.

**3002 C. C. BURLEIGH** *to* **THE** *PENNSYLVANIA FREEMAN.* **n.d. n.p.** Describes his travels from the time he left Washington, Pennsylvania, up to his arrival at New Lisbon, Ohio, on 18 September. 29 September 1841. p.2, c1.

**3003 AN IRISH FRIEND** *to PENNSLYVANIA FREEMAN.* **3 July 1841. Dublin.** Comments on abolitionism in Ireland. 29 September 1841. p.2, c4.

**3004 GERRIT SMITH** *to* **MADISON COUNTY ABOLITIONISTS. 21 September. Cazenovia.** Discusses the establishment of an anti-slavery weekly in Cazenovia. 29 September 1841. p.3, c4.

**3005 N. P. ROGERS** *to* **J. A. F. 9 August 1841. Plymouth.** Summarizes a sermon delivered by Brother Beach at Camptown. 29 September 1841. p.4, c4.

**3006 C. C. BURLEIGH** *to PENNSYLVANIA FREEMAN.* **16 September. New Lisbon, Oh.** Recounts anti-slavery affairs in Ohio. 6 October 1841. p.2, c1.

**3007 WM. JACKSON AND J. FULTON, JR.** *to* **THE ABOLITIONISTS OF CHESTER COUNTY. 2 October 1841. Chester County.** Appeal to abolitionists to abstain from voting for candidates who do not support abolition. 6 October 1841. p.3, c1.

**3008 JAMES CANNINGS FULLER** *to* **JOSEPH STURGE. n.d. n.p.** Describes his trip through Kentucky in search of a family of slaves. 6 October 1841. p.3, c2.

**3009 J. C.** *to* **n.n. 3 September 1841. Manchester, England.** Discusses the Corn Laws. 13 October 1841. p.2, c1.

**3010 ABINGTON** *to* **FRIEND McKIM. n.d. n.p.** Criticizes a gentleman who claims to be an abolitionist but opposes immediate emancipation and equal rights. 13 October 1841. p.3, c2.

**3011 ABBY KELLEY** *to* **UXBRIDGE MONTHLY MEETING OF FRIENDS. 22 March 1841. Herron, Ct.** Explains her reasons for withdrawal from the society. 13 October 1841. p.4, c2.

**3012 ABBY KELLEY** *to* **BRO. GARRISON. 20 September 1841. Westerly, R.I.** Discusses her withdrawal from the Society of Friends. 13 October 1841. p.4, c2.

**3013 n.n.** *to* **n.n. [extract] n.d. n.p.** Notes the humane treatment of many slaves. 20 October 1841. p.1, c1.

**3014 n.n. [A WOMAN IN PHILADELPHIA]** *to* **n.n. [A WOMAN IN VIRGINIA]. n.d. n.p.** Objects to the Southern woman's justification of slavery on the basis of humane treatment. 20 October 1841. p.1, c2.

**3015 J. FULTON, JR.** *to* **J. M. McKIM. 1 October 1841. Ercildoun.** Supports F. J. Lemoyne. 20 October 1841. p.1, c5.

**3016 J. FULTON, JR.** *to* **J. M. McKIM. 10 October 1841. Ercildoun.** Solicits support for Lemoyne. 20 October 1841. p.1, c6.

**3017 JOHN B. CHRISMAN** *to* **MESSRS. FULTON AND JACKSON. 2 October 1841. Springtown Forge.** Answers questions concerning his political position. 20 October 1841. p.1, c6.

**3018 W. BEARDSLEY** *to* **n.n. [extract] n.d. n.p.** Reveals the treatment received by three brethren awaiting trial for aiding runaway Negroes. 27 October 1841. p.1, c1.

**3019 GEORGE THOMPSON** *to* **THE** *OBERLIN EVANGELIST*. **15 September 1841. Palmyra Jail, Mo.** Describes his trial and imprisonment. 27 October 1841. p.1, c1.

**3020 S. S. JOCELYN, LEWIS TAPPAN AND JOSHUA LEAVITT** *to* **JOHN TYLER, PRESIDENT OF THE UNITED STATES. n.d. n.p.** Solicit aid to send the Mendian Africans back to Africa. 27 October 1841. p.1, c2.

**3021 FLETCHER WEBSTER** *to* **LEWIS TAPPAN. 6 October 1841. Department of State, Washington, D.C.** Informs that the law made no provision to cover the cost of sending the Mendian Africans home. 27 October 1841. p.1, c3.

**3022 CINQUE** *to* **THE MENDIAN COMMITTEE OF N.Y. 5 October 1841. Farmington.** Pleads to have the Mendians sent home to Africa. 27 October 1841. p.1, c4.

**3023 n.n.** *to* **n.n. 28 May 1841. Macao.** Reports on the Chinese attack on Canton. 27 October 1841. p.3, c4.

**3024 WM. H. ANDERSON** *to* **PERSONS WHO HAVE BEEN SENDING THEIR SERVANTS TO BAPTIST MEETINGS AT THE (NATCHEZ) COURT HOUSE. n.d. n.p.** Announces the discontinuation of such meetings. 3 November 1841. p.1, c3.

**3025 JOHN RANKIN** *to* **MR. EDWARDS. 13 September 1841. Ripley, Oh.** Relates the events concerning the recent attack made upon him by midnight assailants. 3 November 1841. p.1, c4.

**3026 S. S.** *to* **n.n. [extract] n.d. Chester County, Pa.** Describes the enthusiastic response to temperance. 3 November 1841. p.2, c1.

**3027 C.** *to* **THE EDITOR [C. C. BURLEIGH]. 30 October 1841. Philadelphia.** Stresses the need for adequate information concerning the state of the slaves. 3 November 1841. p.2, c2.

**3028 EMMOR ELTON** *to* **MESSRS. JAMES FULTON AND WM. JACKSON. 19 October 1841. East Goshen.** Embraces those who oppose slavery. 10 November 1841. p.2, c3.

**3029 E.** *to* **GEORGE F. WHITE. n.d. n.p.** Proves White's arguments and logic erroneous. 10 November 1841. p.2, c3.

**3030 JUDGE S. BENEDICT** *to* **DOCT. PROUDFIT. 14 September 1841. n.p.** Reports on agriculture in Liberia. 10 November 1841. p.2, c6.

**3031 AN IRISH FRIEND** *to* **n.n. 17 September 1841. Dublin.** Expresses hope for abolition in America. 10 November 1841. p.3, c1.

**3032 GERRIT SMITH, A. A. PHELPS, WM. DAWES, LEWIS TAPPAN, S. S. JOCELYN, AND WM. PATTON, JR.** *to* **n.n. n.d. n.p.** Solicit funds for missionary work. 10 November 1841. p.3, c2.

**3033 C. STEWART RENSHAW** *to* **THE FRIENDS OF THE COLORED RACE. 15 August 1841. Peterboro'.** Reports on the condition of the emancipated slaves of Jamaica. 10 November 1841. p.3, c2.

**3034 M.** *to* **THE** ***PENNSYLVANIA FREEMAN.*** **1 November 1841. Philadelphia.** Clarifies his position on abolitionism. 17 November 1841. p.2, c2.

**3035 S. D. H.** *to* **THE** ***PENNSYLVANIA FREEMAN.*** **5 November 1841. New Albany, Ia.** Describes a Kentucky abolitionist. 17 November 1841. p.2, c3.

**3036 ROBERT PURVIS** *to* **THE EDITOR [C. C. BURLEIGH]. n.d. n.p.** Exposes the unjust policy of the state of Pennsylvania toward her colored citizens. 17 November 1841. p.3, c3.

**3037 LONDON CORRESPONDENT** *to* **THE** ***NEW YORK EVENING POST.*** **21 October 1841. London.** Discusses bloodshed in Canton, the civil war in Spain, and the attempt to murder the son of the king of France. 17 November 1841. p.4, c2.

**3038 n.n.** *to* **n.n. [extract from the** ***London Examiner*****] n.d. Paris.** Describes the political, social, and economic situation in Lyons. 17 November 1841. p.4, c3.

**3039 W. D. ERSKINE, FIRST LIEUT. R. N.** *to* **n.n. 11 July 1841. H.M. Sloop** ***Acorn.*** Reports the capture of a Spanish slave brig by Capt. John Adams. 24 November 1841. p.1, c3.

**3040 ALVAN STEWART** *to* **MR. HOUGH. [from the** ***Emancipator*****] 18 October 1841. Utica.** Relates his travels between New York and Washington, D.C. 24 November 1841. p.2, c2.

**3041 C. C. BURLEIGH** *to* **THE** ***PENNSYLVANIA FREEMAN.*** **11 November 1841. Sandusky Township, Richland County, Oh.** Reports on his activities and lectures. 24 November 1841. p.2, c5.

**3042 JOSEPH STURGE** *to* **A PHILADELPHIAN. n.d. n.p.** Rejoices that the independence of Texas was not recognized. 1 December 1841. p.1, c3.

**3043 CORA** *to* **THE** ***LIBERATOR*****. 10 November 1841. Kingston.** Reports anti-slavery victory in the Jamaican election. 1 December 1841. p.1, c4.

**3044 GEO. THOMPSON, J. E. BERN, AND A. WORK** *to* **THE** ***GENIUS OF LIBERTY*** **[ILLINOIS]. 20 September 1841. Palmyra, Mo.** Describe the nature of their treatment by prison officials. 1 December 1841. p.1, c4.

**3045 AN OFFICER ON H. M. SHIP** ***ACORN*** *to* **n.n. [extract] 4 September 1841. St. Helena.** Describes the capture of a Portuguese slave ship. 1 December 1841. p.2, c2.

**3046 HIRAM WILSON** *to* **J. C. FULLER. [extract] 2 November 1841. Toronto.** Relates his encounter with runaway slaves and appeals for more aid. 1 December 1841. p.2, c2.

**3047 C. C. BURLEIGH** *to* **n.n. n.d. n.p.** Reports on his anti-slavery lectures and travels. 1 December 1841. p.2, c3.

**3048 A MEMBER OF NAZARETH M. E. CHURCH** *to* **THE EDITOR. [extract] n.d. n.p.** Objects to the unfair leasing of a public house for lectures. 1 December 1841. p.3, c2.

**3049 n.n.** *to* **n.n. n.d. n.p.** Urges support for the abolitionist cause. 1 December 1841. p.3, c2.

**3050 CINQUE, KINNA, AND KA-LE** *to* **HON. JOHN QUINCY ADAMS. 6 November 1841. Boston.** Thank Adams for arranging transportation to Africa for the Mendians. 1 December 1841. p.3, c3.

**3051 JOHN QUINCY ADAMS** *to* **LEWIS TAPPAN. 19 November 1841. Boston.** Praises Tappan for his success with the Mendians. 1 December 1841. p.3, c4.

**3052 JOHN QUINCY ADAMS** *to* **CINQUE AND THE THIRTY-TWO MENDIANS. 19 November 1841. Boston.** Bids farewell to the Mendians. 1 December 1841. p.3, c4.

**3053 RICHARD ALLEN** *to* **THOMAS CLARKSON. 22 October 1841. n.p.** Introduces Thomas Clarkson's letter. 1 December 1841. p.4, c1.

**3054 THOMAS CLARKSON** *to* **RICHARD ALLEN. 25 September 1841. Playford Hall.** Discusses the value of abstinence. 1 December 1841. p.4, c1.

**3055 ANGELINA G. WELD** *to* **n.n. [extract] August 1841. Belleville.** Contends that use of slave products supports the institution of slavery and must be halted. 8 December 1841. p.1, c1.

**3056 E. N.** *to* **THE** ***PENNSYLVANIA FREEMAN*****. 4 December 1841. Philadelphia.** Admonishes abolitionists to persist in the "arduous service" of the anti-slavery cause. 8 December 1841. p.2, c2.

**3057 PUBLICOLA** *to* **W. L. GARRISON. n.d. n.p.** Discusses war, intemperance and slavery. 8 December 1841. p.2, c3.

**3058 n.n.** *to* **n.n. 1841. Naples.** Refutes the general impression of Naples as a dirty, backward city. 8 December 1841. p.4, c5.

**3059 n.n.** *to* **DR. BAILEY. n.d. n.p.** Introduces a letter by Joseph Bryant. 15 December 1841. p.1, c2.

**3060 JOSEPH BRYANT** *to* **MY DEAR WIFE. 10 November 1841. Wheeling Jail.** Describes conditions in jail. 15 December 1841. p.1, c2.

**3061 ALVAN STEWART** *to* **n.n. n.d. n.p.** Condemns the Missouri court which imposed a twelve-year sentence on the three abolitionists who helped a slave to escape. 15 December 1841. p.1, c3.

**3062 JAMES S. GIBBONS** *to* **n.n. n.d. n.p.** Requests donations for the anti-slavery cause. 15 December 1841. p.1, c3.

**3063 C. STEWART RENSHAW** *to* **THE** *PENNSYLVANIA FREEMAN.* **7 December 1841. Philadelphia.** Introduces a letter on emancipation in Jamaica by Rev. Wm. Whitehorn. 15 December 1841. p.1, c4.

**3064 WM. WHITEHORN** *to* **n.n. 18 May 1841. Mount Charles.** Comments on the physical, moral and spiritual condition of freemen living at Mount Charles. 15 December 1841. p.1, c5.

**3065 n.n.** *to* **THE EDITOR [C. C. BURLEIGH]. n.d. n.p.** Disclaims the accusation that officials would not allow the subject of slavery to be discussed in the public house. 15 December 1841. p.2, c2.

**3066 C. C. BURLEIGH** *to* **n.n. n.d. Buffalo.** Continues to describe his travels and lecture tour. 15 December 1841. p.2, c3.

**3067 WILLIAM CANBY** *to* **THOS. JEFFERSON. 29 August 1813. n.p.** Stresses the importance of professing Christian beliefs. 15 December 1841. p.4, c3.

**3068 THOS. JEFFERSON** *to* **WM. CANBY. 18 September 1813. Monticello.** Declares acceptance in heaven of men of all Christian denominations. 15 December 1841. p.4, c4.

**3069 C. S. R.** *to* **THE EDITOR. n.d. n.p.** Comments on life in Jamaica. 22 December 1841. p.1, c5.

**3070 SAMUEL J. MAY** *to* **n.n. n.d. South Scituate, Ma.** Reminisces about the formation of the AAS in December 1833. 22 December 1841. p.1, c6.

**3071 J. T. B. [AMERICAN CONSUL AT NASSUA]** *to N.Y. JOURNAL OF COMMERCE.* **14 November 1841. Nassau.** Reports on a slave mutiny. 22 December 1841. p.2, c2.

**3072 A. L. POST** *to* **McKIM. 15 November 1841. Montrose.** Declines an invitation to attend a meeting of the Pennsylvania AS Eastern District. 22 December 1841. p.2, c3.

**3073 WENDELL PHILLIPS** *to* **n.n. 2 December 1841. Boston.** Declines an invitation to be present at an AS meeting. 22 December 1841. p.2, c4.

**3074 C. C. BURLEIGH** *to* **THE** *PENNSYLVANIA FREEMAN.* **5 December 1841. Buffalo, N.Y.** Recounts his travels in upstate New York and parts of Ohio. 22 December 1841. p.2, c5.

**3075 CORRESPONDENT** *to* **THE** *N. Y. EVENING POST.* **18 November. London.** Announces the birth of a new prince of Wales. 22 December 1841. p.4, c2.

**3076 SAMUEL J. MAY** *to* **n.n. 6 December 1841. South Scituate.** Reminisces about the formation of the AAS in December 1833. 29 December 1841. p.1, c3.

**3077 C. C. BURLEIGH** *to* **n.n. [extract] 16 December 1841. Geneva, N.Y.** Updates notices on his travels and activities. 29 December 1841. p.3, c2.

**3078 AN IRISH FRIEND** *to* **n.n. 18 November 1841. Dublin.** Reports on the widespread increase of anti-slavery support. 29 December 1841. p.3, c3.

**3079 L. M. C[HILD]** *to* **n.n. [extract from the** *National Anti-Slavery Standard*] **n.d. New York.** Describes some of the remarkable individuals of the colored population, primarily Cinque. 29 December 1841. p.4, c2.

## [1844]

**3080 JAMES FULTON, JR.** *to* **McKIM AND BURLEIGH. 1 January 1844. Chester County.** Urges the revival of the *Pennsylvania Freeman.* 18 January 1844. p.1, c1.

**3081 W. H. JOHNSON** *to* **THE** *PENNSYLVANIA FREEMAN.* **9 January 1844. Buckingham.** Celebrates the revival of the *Pennsylvania Freeman.* 18 January 1844. p.1, c3.

**3082 SAMUEL M. SEMMER** *to* **THE EDITORS. 23 December 1843. Cumberland.** Opposes congressional acceptance of abolitionist petitions. 18 January 1844. p.3, c1.

**3083 n.n.** *to* **n.n. n.d. Washington.** Relates an incident involving anti-abolitionists. 18 January 1844. p.3, c1.

**3084 AMASA WALKER** *to* **WM. LLOYD GARRISON. 29 December 1843. North Brookfield.** Recalls his first meeting with Henry C. Wright. 18 January 1844. p.4, c2.

**3085 FRANKLIN** *to* **THE EDITORS. n.d. n.p.** Proposes, as a solution to the problem of abolitionist unification, that no separate candidates be nominated by the third party until candidates of the old parties have been questioned. 1 February 1844. p.1, c3.

**3086 BENJ. S. JONES** *to* **McKIM. 23 January 1844. Solebury.** Remarks on a state Temperance Society meeting held at Trenton on 17 January. 1 February 1844. p.2, c1.

**3087 THOMAS EARLE** *to* **n.n. n.d. n.p.** Relates the events and activities of the Massachusetts meeting. 1 February 1844. p.2, c4.

**3088 S. W. MIFFLIN** *to* **THE EDITORS. 6 February 1844. Wrightsville.** Denies James Birney's alleged membership in a pro-slavery church. 15 February 1844. p.2, c1.

**3089 LAY** *to* **McKIM AND BURLEIGH. 28 January 1844. Chester County.** Calls for a convention of the Society of Friends. 15 February 1844. p.2, c2.

**3090 SAM'L HASTINGS, J. MILLER McKIM, WILLIAM HARNED, PETER WRIGHT, TH. S. CAVENDER, ROBERT HAYS, AND EDWARD LEWIS** *to* **THE** *PENNSYLVANIA FREEMAN.* **10 January 1844. Philadelphia.** Call for abolitionist nominations for national and state offices. 15 February 1844. p.2, c3.

**3091 CASSIUS M. CLAY** *to* **THE EDITOR OF THE** *TRIBUNE.* **November 1843. Lexington, Ky.** Urges complete emancipation. 29 February 1844. p.1, c1.

**3092 JAMES G. BIRNEY** *to* **THE HONORABLE LEICESTER KING. 1 January 1844. Saginaw, Mi.** Accepts nomination for the presidency by the Liberty Party's Buffalo convention. 29 February 1844. p.4, c1.

**3093 BEREZETT** *to* **THE** *PENNSYLVANIA FREEMAN.* **27 February 1844. Bucks County.** Disagrees with Lay's urgent suggestion to organize a convention, and notes the increase of abolitionist spirit. 14 March 1844. p.2, c2.

**3094 ISAAC S. FLINT** *to* **THE EDITORS. 17 February 1844. Brandywine, Chester County.** Describes opposition to an anti-slavery meeting. 14 March 1844. p.4, c2.

**3095 n.n.** *to* **n.n. [extract] 15 March 1844. Pendleton.** Reports Mr. Calhoun's acceptance of his recent appointment as secretary of state. 21 March 1844. p.2, c1.

**3096 JOHN THOMAS, EDWIN COATES, AND EDWIN FUSSELL** *to* **CHESTER CO. ABOLITIONISTS. 20 March 1844. Kimberton, [Pa.]** Plan to organize fifty anti-slavery conventions in the vicinity. 21 March 1844. p.3, c3.

**3097 J. E.** *to* **THE EDITOR. 4 March 1844. Buckingham.** Complains about the late arrival of anti-slavery papers to the Buckingham area. 21 March 1844. p.3, c3.

**3098 ISAAC PIERCE** *to* **THE** *PENNSYLVANIA FREEMAN.* **4 April 1844. Caln, Chester County.** Recounts an incident in which a group of men attempted to disrupt an anti-slavery lecture. 11 April 1844. p.1, c1.

**3099 C. T. T.** *to* **THE EDITORS. n.d. n.p.** Condemns Henry Clay and his proposal to annex Texas. 11 April 1844. p.1, c2.

**3100 n.n.** *to* **n.n. n.d. n.p.** Describes an address made to the people of Delaware by Jones Pusey on temperance reform. 11 April 1844. p.3, c2.

**3101 GRIFFITH M. COOPER** *to* **ROGERS. [from the** *Herald of Freedom***] 17 March 1844. Williamson, N.Y.** Remarks on a proposed lecture series in the free states. 11 April 1844. p.4, c1.

**3102 GERRIT SMITH** *to* **n.n. 12 March 1844. Peterboro'.** Condemns the clergy for failing to respond to abolitionism. 11 April 1844. p.4, c2.

**3103 J. FULTON, JR.** *to* **THE** *PENNSYLVANIA FREEMAN.* **April 1844. Ercildoun.** Comments on the upcoming convention to nominate anti-slavery men for office. 25 April 1844. p.1, c4.

**3104 CHESTER COUNTY** *to* **THE** *PENNSYLVANIA FREEMAN.* **20 April 1844. n.p.** Criticizes A. R. McIlvaine for voting against an anti-slavery bill presented before Congress. 25 April 1844. p.2, c1.

**3105 J. MILLER McKIM** *to* **n.n. 7 May 1844. New York.** Relates the proceedings of an anti-slavery meeting held in New York. 9 May 1844. p.2, c3.

**3106 FRANCIS PATRICK** *to* **THE CATHOLICS OF THE CITY AND COUNTY OF PHILADELPHIA. 7 May 1844. Philadelphia.** Mourns the deaths caused by the riot and warns those involved to humble themselves before God. 9 May 1844. p.3, c2.

**3107 LAY** *to* **THE** *PENNSYLVANIA FREEMAN.* **4 May 1844. Chester County.** Comments on the late Western Quarterly Meeting of Friends held in London Grove. 23 May 1844. p.2, c1.

**3108 S. A.** *to* **THE** *PENNSYLVANIA FREEMAN.* **6 June 1844. Philadelphia.** Corrects previous remarks concerning the Yearly Meeting of Friends. 23 May 1844. p.2, c1.

**3109 WILLIAM A. WHITE** *to* **THE FRIENDS OF FREEDOM IN THE UNITED STATES. n.d. n.p.** Defines the future role of the AAS. 23 May 1844. p.3, c1.

**3110 G. M. DALLAS** *to* **JOHN WILLIS. 29 August 1810. Philadelphia.** Notes the importance of Virginia's Democratic Party to Southern politics. 20 June 1844. p.3, c1.

**3111 J. FULTON, JR.** *to* **FRIEND PAINTER, EDITOR OF THE** *REGISTER.* **4 June 1844. Ercildoun.** Refutes A. R. McIlvaine's protest that the Chester County convention which censured him for his recent vote in Congress acted unjustly. 20 June 1844. p.3, c3.

3112 **J. FULTON, JR.** *to* **D. L. CHILD. n.d. n.p.** Informs Child of the *Standard's* influence in gaining support for Clay. 20 June 1844. p.3, c3.

3113 **C. M. CLAY** *to* **EDMUND QUINCY. 14 May 1844. Lexington, Ky.** Explains the difference between the AS and the Liberty Party. 4 July 1844. p.4, c1.

3114 **HENRY W. ALLEN** *to* **THE PUBLIC. 16 April 1844. Grand Bluff, Ms.** Attempts to clear Rev. Dr. Hunt of the irresponsible charges made by the *Vicksburg Sentinel.* 18 July 1844. p.1, c1.

3115 **JUNIUS** *to* **CITIZENS OF CHESTER CO. 14 July 1844. n.p.** Refutes the oft-repeated assertion that anti-slavery candidates are ignorant of all major political issues except slavery. 18 July 1844. p.1, c3.

3116 **CORRESPONDENT TO THE** ***HARTFORD*** **(CT.)** ***CHRISTIAN FREEMAN*** *to* **n.n. [extract] n.d. n.p.** Recounts his recent visit with Cassius M. Clay. 1 August 1844. p.1, c2.

3117 **D. McLAUGHLIN** *to* **THE EDITORS. 5 July 1844. n.p.** Responds to the queries of a grand jury concerning the importation and exportation of slaves. 1 August 1844. p.1, c4.

3118 **J.** *to* **THE CITIZENS OF CHESTER COUNTY. 27 July 1844. Chester County.** Claims that only the Independent Party fights the battles of liberty. 5 September 1844. p.1, c3.

3119 **A COVENANTER** *to* **McKIM. n.d. n.p.** Criticizes abolitionists for supporting the United States Constitution, which sanctions slavery. 5 September 1844. p.2, c1.

3120 **FREDERICK DOUGLASS** *to* **McKIM. n.d. n.p.** Describes his impressions of the anti-slavery meetings recently held in Chester County. 5 September 1844. p.2, c3.

3121 **n.n.** *to* **n.n. n.d. n.p.** Praises Anthony Benezet for his dedication to educating the Negro. 5 September 1844. p.4, c2.

3122 **WENDELL PHILLIPS** *to* **GARRISON. 30 August. Nahant.** Disparages Gerrit Smith, especially for supporting the United States Constitution. 19 September 1844. p.1, c3.

3123 **S. P.** *to* **M'KIM AND BURLEIGH. n.d. n.p.** Reports a resolution of the Philadelphia Female AS to abstain from voting for officers who refuse to swear to support the Constitution. 19 September 1844. p.2, c2.

3124 **EDWIN FUSSELL, COR. SEC.** *to* **n.n. n.d. n.p.** Comments on the annual meeting of the Chester County AS. 10 October 1844. p.4, c1.

3125 **DANIEL L. MILLER, JR.** *to* **THE EXECUTIVE COMMITTEE OF THE AMERICAN FREE PRODUCE ASSOCIATION. October 1844. Philadelphia.** Reports an increased demand for goods produced by free labor. 24 October 1844. p.1, c4.

3126 **E. M. DAVIS** *to* **THE ABOLITIONISTS OF EASTERN PENNSYLVANIA. n.d. n.p.** Favors free distribution of a monthly anti-slavery tract. 24 October 1844. p.3, c4.

3127 **PHILADELPHIA FEMALE AS: ANNA M. HOPPER, MARY GREW, SARAH A. McKIM, [AND THIRTY OTHERS]** *to* **THE ABOLITIONISTS OF EASTERN PENNSYLVANIA. n.d. n.p.** Request aid in preparation for the annual fair of 1844. 24 October 1844. p.3, c4.

**3128 HENRY GREW** *to* **THE FREE PRODUCE SOCIETY. 15 October 1844. Philadelphia.** Regrets that he is unable to attend a meeting of the society. 24 October 1844. p.4, c1.

**3129 ELI HAMBLETON** *to* **THE FREE PRODUCE SOCIETY. 12 October 1844. Chester County, Pa.** Supports the "no-union-with-slaveholders" movement. 24 October 1844. p.4, c1.

**3130 AURELIA A. WORK** *to* **THE** *GREEN MOUNTAIN FREEMAN*. **13 August 1844. Theopolis, Il.** Laments family troubles caused by the absence of her husband, who was among those abolitionists imprisoned in Palmyra, Missouri. 7 November 1844. p.1, c1.

**3131 JONATHAN WALKER** *to* **HIS WIFE AND CHILDREN. 20 July 1844. Pensacola.** Describes his imprisonment for transporting fugitive slaves. 7 November 1844. p.1, c2.

**3132 A. E.** *to* **McKIM. 30 October 1844. Plymouth.** Relates the proceedings of the Norristown Clay Club meeting. 7 November 1844. p.1, c3.

**3133 HENRY W. WILLIAMS** *to* **n.n. 25 October 1844. Boston.** Requests aid for the imprisoned abolitionist Captain Walker. 7 November 1844. p.3, c1.

**3134 W. N.** *to* **WM. LLOYD GARRISON. 15 October 1844. Westchester.** Specifies the differences between Garrisonian and Liberty Party principles. 7 November 1844. p.4, c1.

**3135 PARKER PILLSBURY** *to* **ROGERS. [extract from the** *Herald of Freedom*] **n.d. n.p.** Notes the success of the abolitionist cause in Milford. 21 November 1844. p.1, c1.

**3136 J. FULTON, JR.** *to* **McKIM AND BURLEIGH. n.d. n.p.** Examines the "no-voting" question. 21 November 1844. p.1, c4.

**3137 SARAH PUGH** *to* **THE ANTI-SLAVERY MEN AND WOMEN OF EASTERN PENNSYLVANIA. n.d. n.p.** Solicits contributions to support anti-slavery efforts in the area. 21 November 1844. p.3, c3.

**3138 O. S. MURRAY** *to* **n.n. [extract] 20 October 1844. Shore of Lake Erie, Evans, N.Y.** Describes a storm on Lake Erie. 21 November 1844. p.4, c1.

**3139 WASHINGTON CORRESPONDENT** *to* **THE** *LEDGER*. **n.d. n.p.** Assures the public that the Texas issue will be resolved shortly. 5 December 1844. p.3, c4.

**3140 C. W. DENNISON [***sic***]** *to* **J. G. WHITTIER. [extract] n.d. n.p.** Expresses doubt and concern for C. T. Torrey, an imprisoned abolitionist. 5 December 1844. p.4, c1.

## [1845]

**3141 ISAAC S. FLINT** *to* **McKIM. 9 January 1845. Wilmington.** Comments upon the Wilmington AS Convention. 16 January 1845. p.1, c1.

**3142 SPECTATOR** *to* **BURLEIGH AND McKIM. 29 December 1844. Norristown.** Criticizes the Liberty Party for antagonizing anti-slavery supporters and hopes a more tolerant attitude will prevail. 16 January 1845. p.1, c1.

**3143 WASHINGTON CORRESPONDENT** *to* **THE** *CHARLESTON MERCURY* **[extract] n.d. n.p.** Calculates the chances in favor of admitting Texas into the Union. 16 January 1845. p.2, c1.

**3144 WASHINGTON CORRESPONDENT** *to* **THE** *TRIBUNE***. [extract] n.d. n.p.** Reports that Mr. Hale of New Hampshire is against the annexation of Texas. 16 January 1845. p.2, c1.

**3145 OLIVER OLDSCHOOL** *to* **JOSEPH R. CHANDLER. 13 January 1845. Washington.** Conveys the particulars of the resolution for the annexation of Texas presented by Mr. Foster of Tennessee. 16 January 1845. p.2, c1.

**3146 J. FULTON, JR.** *to* **McKIM AND BURLEIGH. 22 January 1845. Ercildoun.** Describes a visit from Abby Kelley and abolitionist friends. 30 January 1845. p.2, c1.

**3147 B.** *to* **MR. EDITOR. n.d. n.p.** Criticizes an editorial published in the last issue of the *Freeman* on several points. 30 January 1845. p.2, c1.

**3148 THOS. W. BROWN** *to* **n.n. 26 January 1845. Harrisburg.** Recounts an attempted kidnapping. 30 January 1845. p.3, c3.

**3149 C. M. CLAY** *to* **T. B. STEVENSON. [from the** *Frankfort Commonwealth***] n.d. Frankfort.** Summarizes his views on slavery, concluding that the institution must be abolished. 30 January 1845. p.4, c3.

**3150 FREDRIKA BREMER** *to* **MRS. CHAPMAN. 25 August 1845. Stockholm.** Declines the offer to become a leader in the abolitionist cause. 30 January 1845. p.4, c3.

**3151 SPECTATOR** *to* **THE** *PENNSYLVANIA FREEMAN***. 1 February 1845. Norristown.** Sends a brief sketch of anti-slavery meetings held in the area. 13 February 1845. p.1, c3.

**3152 HIRAM WILSON** *to* **McKIM. 7 January 1845. Clinton, N.Y.** Acknowledges contributions for the Manual Labor Institute at Dawn, Canada West. 13 February 1845. p.1, c4.

**3153 n.n.** *to* **n.n. 31 January 1845. Abington.** Requests the return of Abby Kelley and Dr. Hudson. 13 February 1845. p.2, c1.

**3154 SIMON BERNARD** *to* **n.n. [extract] n.d. n.p.** Notes the increasing popularity of anti-slavery meetings. 13 February 1845. p.2, c1.

**3155 SIMON BERNARD** *to* **n.n. [extract] n.d. West Grove, Chester County.** Describes Abby Kelley's success in converting a politician to abolitionism. 13 February 1845. p.2, c1.

**3156 I. S. FLINT** *to* **n.n. [extract] n.d. n.p.** Proclaims the present as the time for abolitionists to take action. 13 February 1845. p.2, c2.

**3157 EDWARD P. MAGILL** *to* **n.n. n.d. n.p.** Requests anti-slavery lecturers for Bucks County. 13 February 1845. p.2, c2.

**3158 VIATOR [WASHINGTON CORRESPONDENT OF THE** *LEDGER***]** *to* **n.n. n.d. n.p.** Believes the Oregon Bill will be defeated in the Senate. 13 February 1845. p.3, c4.

**3159 CASSIUS M. CLAY** *to* **THE PEOPLE OF KENTUCKY. January 1845. Lexington, Ky.** Pleads for the emancipation of slaves in Kentucky. 27 February 1845. p.1, c1.

**3160 E. N.** *to* **n.n. 25 January 1845. Philadelphia.** Sympathizes with the violent spirit of abolitionists. 27 February 1845. p.1, c4.

**3161 B. S. JONES** *to* **n.n. [extract] n.d. n.p.** Reports turmoil in Bucks County caused by the anti-slavery issue. 27 February 1845. p.3, c3.

**3162 J. FULTON, JR.** *to* **THE EDITORS. n.d. n.p.** Describes the trial and acquittal of William Lukens, a pro-slavery agitator. 27 February 1845. p.4, c1.

**3163 C. M. CLAY** *to* **n.n. [extract] n.d. n.p.** Denounces the Texas alliance. 27 February 1845. p.4, c4.

**3164 BENJAMIN S. JONES** *to* **THE** ***PENNSYLVANIA FREEMAN*****. 25 February 1845. Edgemont.** Remarks on the *American Citizen*, an anti-slavery paper. 13 March 1845. p.2, c1.

**3165 R.** *to* **THE** ***PENNSYLVANIA FREEMAN*****. 18 February 1845. Norristown.** Examines the good and evil of the no-voting theory. 13 March 1845. p.2, c2.

**3166 B. S. J.** *to* **n.n. n.d. n.p.** Relates an incident in which a father admitted to his daughter that he had aided in legalizing the sale of little girls from their mothers. 13 March 1845. p.2, c4.

**3167 S. G. W. J. RANKIN** *to* **n.n. [extract from the** ***Cincinnati Herald*****] n.d. n.p.** Asserts that he can provide proof that Miss Webster aided Fairbank in the abduction of slaves. 13 March 1845. p.3, c4.

**3168 R.** *to* **McKIM. 15 March 1845. Norristown.** Reports on the anti-slavery movement in Norristown. 27 March 1845. p.2, c1.

**3169 ALVAN STEWART** *to* **MR. BAILEY. [from the** ***Utica Liberty Press*****] 28 February 1845. New York.** Comments on his recent visit to Philadelphia. 27 March 1845. p.3, c1.

**3170 LONDON CORRESPONDENT** *to* **THE** ***BOSTON ATLAS*****. n.d. n.p.** Describes Mr. Macaulay's speech against slavery. 10 April 1845. p.1, c1.

**3171 HUMANITAS** *to* **THE** ***PENNSYLVANIA FREEMAN*****. 27 March 1845. Buckingham.** Comments on actions of pro-slavery Quakers. 10 April 1845. p.1, c3.

**3172 B. S. JONES** *to* **THE** ***PENNSYLVANIA FREEMAN*****. 17 February. Westgrove, Chester County.** Describes a number of anti-slavery meetings. 10 April 1845. p.1, c4.

**3173 WM. JAY** *to* **EDWARD M. DAVIS. n.d. n.p.** Favors the dissolution of the Union upon the annexation of Texas. 10 April 1845. p.2, c4.

**3174 WM. JAY** *to* **H. I. BOWDITCH, M.D. [extract] n.d. n.p.** Advocates dissolution of the Union upon the annexation of Texas as a slave state. 10 April 1845. p.3, c1.

**3175 ABBY KELL[E]Y** *to* **n.n. [extract] 4 April. Harrisburg.** Describes the enthusiasm created in Harrisburg by the slavery question. 10 April 1845. p.3, c2.

**3176 JANE ELIZABETH HITCHCOCK** *to* **n.n. 7 April 1845. Harrisburg.** Reports on the progress made by abolitionists in Harrisburg. 10 April 1845. p.3, c2.

**3177 n.n.** *to* **O. N. WHITE. [from the** ***Pittsburg Gazette*****] 25 March 1845. n.p.** Reports on the spread of abolitionist sentiment. 10 April 1845. p.3, c3.

**3178 C. M. CLAY** *to* **GERRIT SMITH. 18 February 1845. Lexington, Ky.** Requests a list of names of those willing to subscribe to Clay's forthcoming newspaper. 10 April 1845. p.3, c3.

**3179 HENRY GREW** *to* **THE** ***PENNSYLVANIA FREEMAN*****. n.d. n.p.** Argues against women's right to speak publicly, on biblical grounds. 24 April 1845. p.1, c2.

**3180 JAMES RAMAGE** *to* **THE** ***PENNSYLVANIA FREEMAN*****. 14 April 1845. Norristown.** Defends the character of Mr. Foster. 24 April 1845. p.1, c3.

**3181 J. FULTON, JR.** *to* **THE** ***PENNSYLVANIA FREEMAN*****. 16 March 1845. Ercildoun.** Notes Quaker opposition to the holding of anti-slavery meetings in Pennsylvania. 24 April 1845. p.1, c4.

**3182 J. H. HAMMOND [GOVERNOR OF SOUTH CAROLINA]** *to* **THE PRESBYTERY OF THE FREE CHURCH OF GLASGOW, SCOTLAND. 21 June 1844. South Carolina.** Upholds slavery, citing the misconceptions surrounding the institution and its improvement of the lifestyle of the Negro. 24 April 1845. p.2, c1.

**3183 B. S. JONES** *to* **THE** ***PENNSYLVANIA FREEMAN*****. [9-27 April. Traveling from Carlisle to Philadelphia.]** Summarizes his anti-slavery lectures. 8 May 1845. p.1, c1.

**3184 SAMUEL AARON** *to* **THE** ***PENNSYLVANIA FREEMAN*****. 26 April 1845. Norristown, Pa.** Acknowledges the charges made against him by Mr. Ramage. 8 May 1845. p.1, c3.

**3185 B. S. J.** *to* **M. n.d. n.p.** Reports on the resolutions made at the Chester County Convention by the Kennet Square AS. 8 May 1845. p.1, c3.

**3186 E. MOORE** *to* **THE** ***PENNSYLVANIA FREEMAN*****. 30 April 1845. Salem.** Describes the capture of a group of runaway slaves. 8 May 1845. p.2, c1.

**3187 S. S. FOSTER** *to* **McKIM. n.d. n.p.** Defends himself against accusations made by Henry Grew. 8 May 1845. p.2, c2.

**3188 JAMES RAMAGE** *to* **THE** ***PENNSYLVANIA FREEMAN*****. 15 May 1845. Norristown, Pa.** Corrects Samuel Aaron's misrepresentation of Mr. Foster. 22 May 1845. p.2, c1.

**3189 HENRY GREW** *to* **THE** ***PENNSYLVANIA FREEMAN*****. n.d. n.p.** Accuses Mr. Foster of misrepresenting one Mr. Barnes. 22 May 1845. p.2, c1.

**3190 JONA. WALKER** *to* **LUTHER G. HEWINS. 1 April 1845. Pensacola Jail.** Expresses his gratitude to Hewins and others who contributed to the financial support of his wife. 22 May 1845. p.4, c2.

**3191 C. M. CLAY** *to* **THE** ***CINCINNATI GAZETTE*****. 2 May 1845. Lexington, Ky.** Explains why he sold one of his ex-slaves. 22 May 1845. p.4, c2.

**3192 BENJ. S. JONES** *to* **THE** ***PENNSYLVANIA FREEMAN*****. n.d. n.p.** Recounts his east coast travels. 5 June 1845. p.1, c1.

**3193 n.n.** *to* **n.n. [extract from the** *Spirit of Liberty***] n.d. n.p.** Perceives opposition to C. M. Clay's new paper. 5 June 1845. p.3, c4.

**3194 JAMES RAMAGE** *to* **McKIM. 29 May 1845. Norristown.** Encloses a letter written to the Baptist Church explaining his opinions. 19 June 1845. p.1, c4.

**3195 JAMES RAMAGE** *to* **THE BAPTIST CHURCH. 10 May 1845. n.p.** Acknowledges his refusal to comply with church doctrines because of their apparently unchristian attitude toward slaves. 19 June 1845. p.1, c4.

**3196 A CITIZEN** *to* **THE** ***RICHMOND WHIG*****. n.d. n.p.** Objects to Negro Sunday schools in Richmond. 19 June 1845. p.4, c1.

**3197 GEO. F. HORTON** *to* **McKIM. 20 June 1845. Terrytown, Pa.** Foresees little likelihood of slavery being abolished while the Church continues to sanction the system. 3 July 1845. p.1, c3.

**3198 C.** *to* **McKIM. 27 June 1845. n.p.** Reports on the Marlboro' Come-outer Conference. 3 July 1845. p.1, c4.

**3199 JAMES RAMAGE** *to* **McKIM. 22 June 1845. Norristown.** Describes the pro-slavery character of Southern Christians. 3 July 1845. p.2, c1.

**3200 B. S. JONES** *to* **THE** *PENNSYLVANIA FREEMAN.* **6 July 1840. Ashtabula County, Oh.** Comments on his travels and lectures in Ohio. 17 July 1845. p.2, c1.

**3201 C. M. CLAY** *to* **HORACE GREELEY. 4 July 1845. Lexington, Ky.** Pledges against supporting "dualism." 17 July 1845. p.3, c4.

**3202 SCRUTATOR** *to* **McKIM. 24 July 1845. Pequea.** Notes the widespread opposition to abolitionism. 31 July 1845. p.1, c4.

**3203 WM. LLOYD GARRISON** *to* **McKIM. [extract] 19 July 1845. Boston.** Declines an invitation to come to Philadelphia. 31 July 1845. p.2, c3.

**3204 CORRESPONDENT** *to* **THE** *TRIBUNE.* **2 August 1845. Boston.** Comments on anti-slavery events in Massachusetts; mentions Theodore Parker and W. L. Garrison. 14 August 1845. p.1, c3.

**3205 MARYLAND** *to* **H. GREELEY. 1 August 1845. Baltimore, Md.** Opposes emancipation, arguing that the condition of free blacks is worse than that of the slaves. 14 August 1845. p.2, c1.

**3206 n.n.** *to* **n.n. [from the** *Gettysburg Star***] 8 August 1845. Plainfield Farm.** Corrects the report of a kidnapping in Virginia. 14 August 1845. p.2, c2.

**3207 JOHN SHAW, JAMES ANDERSON JR., GEORGE HAYWARD, [AND EIGHTEEN OTHERS]** *to* **WHOM IT MAY CONCERN. 27 April 1845. Green Plain, Clark County, Oh.** Declare themselves independent from the Yearly Meeting of Indiana. 14 August 1845. p.2, c4.

**3208 ISAAC W. HALL, ROBERT SANDERS, JEREMIAH WEBSTER, [AND TWENTY-SIX OTHERS]** *to* **THE MEMBERS OF THE SOCIETY OF FRIENDS, CONSTITUTING THE QUARTERLY MEETING OF GREEN PLAINS, IN THE STATE OF OHIO. 28 August 1845. Mount Pleasant, Jefferson County, Oh.** Recognize the unkindness dealt to the society, and encourage their faith. 14 August 1845. p.2, c4.

**3209 J. FULTON, JR.** *to* **THE** *PENNSYLVANIA FREEMAN.* **4 August 1845. Ercildoun.** Announces the opening of Ercildoun's new hall. 14 August 1845. p.3, c4.

**3210 GERALD RALSTON** *to* **n.n. [extract from the** *American Railroad Journal***] n.d. n.p.** Reports on the increase in the consumption of iron. 14 August 1845. p.4, c3.

**3211 C. M. CLAY** *to* **CITIZENS OF LEXINGTON AND THE COUNTY OF FAYETTE. 18 August 1845. Lexington.** Attributes the publication of a controversial article in his paper to his illness at the time and his allowance of free discussion on the slavery issue. 28 August 1845. p.3, c2.

**3212 R. W. DUDLEY, THO. H. WATERS, AND JOHN W. HUNT** *to* **C. M. CLAY. 14 August 1845. Lexington.** Ask Clay to discontinue publishing his paper, the *True American.* 28 August 1845. p.4, c1.

**3213 C. M. CLAY** *to* **R. W. DUDLEY, THO. H. WATERS, AND JOHN W. HUNT. 15 August 1845. Lexington.** Refuses to comply with recipients' request to discontinue publishing the *True American* and accuses them of harboring anti-American sentiments. 28 August 1845. p.4, c1.

**3214 C. M. CLAY** *to* **KENTUCKIANS. 15 August 1845. Lexington.** Solicits support in anticipation of his upcoming trial. 28 August 1845. p.4, c2.

**3215 C. M. CLAY** *to* **THE CITIZENS OF FAYETTE CO. AND CITY OF LEXINGTON. 16 August 1845. n.p.** Outlines his plan for emancipation. 28 August 1845. p.4, c2.

**3216 n.n.** *to* **n.n. [extract from the *Herald*] 18 August. Lexington.** Conveys the proceedings of a meeting held by the citizens of Fayette County who were opposed to Mr. Clay. 28 August 1845. p.4, c3.

**3217 OBSERVER** *to* **HORACE GREELEY. 20 August 1845. Cincinnati.** Praises C. M. Clay for his leadership against slavery. 28 August 1845. p.4, c3.

**3218 HENRY GREW** *to* **THE *PENNSYLVANIA FREEMAN*. n.d. n.p.** Conveys the content of Garrison's discourse on the Sabbath. 11 September 1845. p.1, c1.

**3219 A. E.** *to* **McKIM. 18 August 1845. Plymouth.** Outlines Robert D. Morris's view on slavery. 11 September 1845. p.1, c2.

**3220 H. H.** *to* **THE *NEW HAVEN COURIER*. n.d. n.p.** Describes the events in Lexington surrounding Mr. Clay's predicament. 11 September 1845. p.2, c1.

**3221 MARYLAND** *to* **HORACE GREELEY. 13 August 1845. Baltimore.** Argues against unconditional emancipation. 11 September 1845. p.2, c4.

**3222 W. L. NEALE** *to* **n.n. 22 August 1845. Lexington.** Relates the damage done to Mr. Clay's press and his move to the Springs for his health. 11 September 1845. p.3, c4.

**3223 E. B.** *to* **THE *CHRISTIAN CITIZEN*. 9 August 1845. Worcester.** Regards statistics on European and American government spending. 11 September 1845. p.4, c2.

**3224 CORRESPONDENT** *to* **THE *HERALD TRIBUNE*. [extract] n.d. Baltimore.** Reports on the condition of the captured slaves arrested at Rockville. 11 September 1845. p.4, c3.

**3225 B.** *to* **HORACE GREELEY. 18 August 1845. Baltimore.** Discusses slavery in Maryland. 25 September 1845. p.1, c1.

**3226 C. M. CLAY** *to* **BENJ. URMER, JAMES GLASCOE, JACOB ERNST, OLIVER LOVELL, GEORGE W. PHILLIPS, R. J. MITCHELL, AND JAMES CALHOUN. 4 September 1845. Lexington, Ky.** Acknowledges the encouragement given by many supporters. 25 September 1845. p.1, c2.

**3227 MILO A. TOWNSEND** *to* **GARRISON. 8 September 1845. Mt. Pleasant, Oh.** Reports that Abby Kelley was dragged out of a Quaker meeting house. 25 September 1845. p.1, c3.

**3228 HENRY H. BROWN** *to* **BURLEIGH. 27 August 1845. Lebanon Springs.** Refers to the New York establishment of a hydropathic infirmary in Lebanon Springs. 25 September 1845. p.1, c4.

**3229 J. FULTON, JR.** *to* **McKIM. 15 September 1845. Ercildoun.** Reports on the proceedings of the Marlboro' Conference. 25 September 1845. p.1, c4.

**3230 n.n.** *to* **n.n. 17 September 1845. Salem, Columbiana County.** Discusses the proceedings of a yearly meeting. 25 September 1845. p.2, c1.

**3231 EDWARD N. WRIGHT** *to* **n.n. [extract] n.d. n.p.** Describes the mobbing of Frederick Douglass on an English ship by Southern slaveholders and pro-slavery Yankees. 25 September 1845. p.3, c1.

**3232 W. B.** *to* **McKIM. n.d. n.p.** Encloses minutes from the ninth annual meeting of the Bucks County AS. 25 September 1845. p.3, c4.

**3233 C. M. CLAY** *to* **LYMAN CLARY. 18 September 1845. Lexington, Ky.** Expresses his belief in the freedom of speech and press. 9 October 1845. p.1, c1.

**3234 J. FULTON, JR.** *to* **McKIM. 19 September 1845. Ercildoun.** Discusses the no-voting theory. 9 October 1845. p.1, c2.

**3235 BALTIMORE CORRESPONDENT** *to* **THE** ***ALBANY PATRIOT.*** **n.d. n.p.** Expresses hope for emancipation in Maryland. 9 October 1845. p.1, c2.

**3236 SPECTATOR** *to* **McKIM. 30 September 1845. Norristown.** Reports on anti-slavery in Norristown. 9 October 1845. p.1, c3.

**3237 ROBERT D. MORRIS** *to* **THE EDITOR. 6 October 1845. Newtown, Bucks County, Pa.** Corrects statements concerning a sermon he gave on slavery. 9 October 1845. p.1, c4.

**3238 J. FULTON, JR.** *to* **McKIM. 3 October 1845. Ercildoun.** Asks whether the twelve jurymen who presided at J. B. Mode's trial will ever have clear consciences. 9 October 1845. p.2, c1.

**3239 J. FULTON, JR.** *to* **McKIM. 5 October 1845. Ercildoun.** Forwards questions to political candidates from the Chester County Temperance Society concerning their views on temperance. 9 October 1845. p.2, c1.

**3240 MILTON SHORT** *to* **MR. A. CAMPBELL. n.d. n.p.** Announces that he has discontinued reading the *Harbinger* because of its failure to take a stand against slavery. 9 October 1845. p.2, c3.

**3241 n.n.** *to* **McKIM. 6 October 1845. n.p.** Reports on the proceedings of the Educational Convention. 9 October 1845. p.2, c3.

**3242 J. FULTON, JR.** *to* **McKIM. 30 September 1845. Ercildoun.** Explains the constitutional clauses regarding the return of fugitive slaves and the suppression of slaves' efforts to free themselves. 23 October 1845. p.1, c2.

**3243 J. K. ESHLEMAN** *to* **McKIM. 13 October 1845. Elms.** Conveys his objections to being nominated on a new ticket formed by Elwood Brown of Little Britain. 23 October 1845. p.2, c2.

**3244 J. M. McKIM** *to* **THE** ***PENNSYLVANIA FREEMAN.*** **[extract] 18 October 1845. Marlboro'.** Reports on the Marlboro' Conference. 23 October 1845. p.2, c4.

**3245 n.n.** *to* **THE EDITOR. n.d. n.p.** Encloses a sonnet by W. L. Garrison. 23 October 1845. p.3, c4.

**3246 C. M. CLAY** *to* **C. D. CLEVELAND, J. BOUVOIR, WM. ELDER, AND T. S. CAVENDER. 25 October 1845. Lexington, Ky.** Comments on the resolutions of the Friends of Free Discussion. 6 November 1845. p.2, c3.

**3247 n.n.** *to* **n.n. [extract from** ***Bennett's Herald*****] 25 October. St. Louis.** Solicits volunteers for the war with Mexico. 6 November 1845. p.3, c1.

**3248 HENRY H. WAY, ROBERT B. BAILEY, CHARLES OSBORN, [AND ELEVEN OTHERS]** *to* **WM. FORSTER, JOSIAH FORSTER, GEORGE STACY, AND JOHN ALLEN. 8 October 1845. Newport.** Object to the committee's purpose of reuniting the Yearly Meeting of Friends. 6 November 1845. p.4, c1.

**3249 BENJAMIN STANTON, LEVI COFFIN AND H. H. WAY** *to* **WILLIAM FORSTER, JOSIAH FORSTER, GEORGE STACY, AND JOHN ALLEN. n.d. n.p.** Express dissatisfaction with the committee's intention to dissolve the religious society of anti-slavery Friends. 6 November 1845. p.4, c3.

**3250 JAMES HAUGHTON** *to* **THE EDITOR. 26 September 1845. 33 Eccles Street.** Reports on Mr. Douglass's activities in Dublin. 20 November 1845. p.1, c4.

**3251 LYDIA WIERMAN** *to* **THE** ***PENNSYLVANIA FREEMAN*****. 2 November 1845. York Springs.** Discusses slavery in Virginia. 20 November 1845. p.2, c1.

**3252 ELWOOD BROWN** *to* **McKIM. 5 November 1845. Kirk's Mill, Lancaster County.** Replies to John K. Eshleman's statement about his erroneous nomination. 20 November 1845. p.2, c2.

**3253 JAMES RAMAGE** *to* **McKIM. 26 October 1845. Norristown.** Distrusts pro-slavery Christianity. 20 November 1845. p.2, c2.

**3254 P. H. BURNETT** *to* **HON. DAVID R. ATCHISON. [extract] 6 December 1844. Oregon.** States that Indians and whites have been living in harmony in Oregon, and advises against passage of Hughes's bill, which would restrict the rights of all but free white males. 4 December 1845. p.1, c1.

**3255 SAMUEL RODMAN, JOSEPH RICKETSON, DANIEL RICKETSON, [AND EIGHT OTHERS]** *to* **n.n. n.d. New Bedford.** Protest recent policy of the Lyceum not to sell tickets of admission to blacks. 4 December 1845. p.1, c2.

**3256 LEWIS TAPPAN** *to* **LEAVITT. 14 November 1839. New York.** Enumerates reasons for his opposition to forming an anti-slavery political party. 18 December 1845. p.1, c1.

**3257 A. L. DE SANTA ANNA** *to* **BENJAMIN LUNDY. 20 February 1834. Manga de Clava.** Thanks Lundy for sending him a portrait of George Washington. 18 December 1845. p.3, c2.

**3258 FREDERICK DOUGLASS** *to* **n.n. 28 October 1845. Cork.** Reports on his successful visit to Cork. 18 December 1845. p.4, c1.

**3259 JAS. N. BUFFUM** *to* **THE EDITOR OF THE** ***PIONEER*****. n.d. n.p.** Reports on the depraved condition of the Church in Hanley, England. 18 December 1845. p.4, c2.

## [1846]

**3260 HENRY C. WRIGHT** *to* **THE EDITOR OF THE** *BRITISH AND FOREIGN ANTI-SLAVERY REPORTER.* **12 September 1845. Roseneath.** Denounces the constitutional clauses which apportion congressional representation so as to include three-fifths of the number of slaves among the population to be represented, and which guarantee slaveholders the right to reclaim escaped slaves. 1 January 1846. p.1, c1.

**3261 H. G.** *to* **MR. EDITOR. n.d. n.p.** Discusses J. S. Green, a missionary in the Sandwich Islands, who encourages among the converted heathen the practice of "remembering those in bonds as bound with them," and praying for freedom for the oppressed. 1 January 1846. p.1, c3.

**3262 THOMAS GARRETT** *to* **THE EDITOR OF THE** *PENNSYLVANIA FREEMAN.* **16 December 1845. Wilmington.** Gives an account of the false arrest and subsequent release of a colored man, his wife, and six children, who were accused of being runaway slaves. 1 January 1846. p.1, c4.

**3263 CASSIUS M. CLAY** *to* **THE EDITORS OF THE** *NATIONAL INTELLIGENCER.* **December 1845. Lexington, Ky.** Criticizes the Southern press, and specifically Mr. R. M. Walsh, correspondent of the *National Intelligencer*, for misrepresenting his views and principles. 8 January 1846. p.1, c1.

**3264 n.n.** *to BENNETT'S HERALD.* **[extract] 30 December 1845. Washington.** Reports the excitement in Washington following the paper's disclosure of the situation in Haiti. 8 January 1846. p.1, c1.

**3265 n.n.** *to BENNETT'S HERALD.* **[extract] 31 December 1845. Washington.** Discusses the response in Washington to the situation in Haiti; argues that America should aid the white inhabitants there. 8 January 1846. p.1, c2.

**3266 B. C. C.** *to* **MR. SLEEPER. [from the** *Boston Journal***] n.d. n.p.** Asserts that an effort on the part of the United States to aid the Dominicans in the Haitian struggle would be considered by the world as "anti-Republican, ungenerous, and unjust." 8 January 1846. p.1, c3.

**3267 n.n.** *to* **THE** *NEW YORK TRIBUNE.* **[extract] n.d. n.p.** Seeks to correct false information concerning the countries of Haiti and Dominica; concludes that "the Haytians individually or as a nation, will compare most favorably with the people of any republic on the American continent, with the single exception of our own." 8 January 1846. p.2, c1.

**3268 JOHN M. HOGARTH** *to* **n.n. 5 December 1845. Port Republican, Hayti.** Expresses sorrow at the misrepresentation by the American press of the situation in Haiti. 8 January 1846. p.2, c3.

**3269 J. FULTON, JR.** *to* **FRIEND McKIM. 2 November 1845. Ercildoun.** Discusses the character of the United States Constitution, and asks whether the pledge of the federal government to protect each of the states from "domestic violence" is unconditional. 15 January 1846. p.1, c3.

**3270 SAMUEL AARON** *to* **THE EDITORS OF THE** *PENNSYLVANIA FREEMAN.* **30 December 1845. Norristown, Pa.** Discontinues his subscription to the *Pennsylvania Freeman*, and expresses his convictions regarding Church and state which dictate this action. 15 January 1846. p.1, c4.

**3271 JOHN HUNN** *to* **n.n. [extract] 5 January 1846. Near Cantwell's Bridge.** Supplies further details regarding the arrest of a family of colored persons on the suspicion that they were runaway slaves. 15 January 1846. p.2, c4.

**3272 EDWARD CURTIS, E. C. BENEDICT, R. M. BLATCHFORD, [AND TEN OTHERS]** *to* **CASSIUS M. CLAY. [from the** *New York Tribune***] 9 January 1846. New York.** Express hope that Mr. Clay will address a public assembly on the subject of slavery. 15 January 1846. p.3, c1.

**3273 CASSIUS M. CLAY** *to* **EDWARD CURTIS, E. C. BENEDICT, R. M. BLATCHFORD [AND TEN OTHERS]. [from the** *New York Tribune***] 9 January 1846. Astor House [New York].** Accepts the invitation to address the people of New York on the subject of human freedom. 15 January 1846. p.3, c1.

**3274 n.n.** *to* **n.n. [extract from the** *Salem Register***] 3 December 1845. Manchester, England.** Praises the Hutchinsons, a family of New England vocalists touring England. 15 January 1846. p.4, c1.

**3275 n.n.** *to* **n.n. [extract] n.d. n.p.** Fears that Great Britain, France, and "another European Power" are plotting to establish a constitutional kingdom in Mexico and place upon its throne a son of Louis Philippe. 15 January 1846. p.4, c1.

**3276 W. L. C.** *to* **CHARLES A. WHEATON. [from the** *Albany Patriot***] 30 December 1845. Washington.** Discusses the case of the Carter family, some thirteen persons sold abruptly by their master in the District of Columbia; describes the futile attempts of the father (a freeman) to regain his family. 22 January 1846. p.1, c1.

**3277 RALPH WALDO EMERSON** *to* **THE NEW BEDFORD LYCEUM. [extract] n.d. n.p.** Explains that he cannot speak before the lyceum due to the members' recent vote to exclude colored persons from membership. 22 January 1846. p.3, c2.

**3278 CHARLES SUMNER** *to* **THE NEW BEDFORD LYCEUM. [extract] n.d. n.p.** Declines to lecture at the lyceum, in protest of their recent resolution barring membership to colored persons. 22 January 1846. p.3, c2.

**3279 CASSIUS M. CLAY** *to* **MESSRS. WM. C. BLOSS, E. W. CHESTER, J. MILLER, &C. 16 January 1846. Philadelphia.** Declines an invitation to speak in Albany, using the occasion for a stern declaration of the injustice of human slavery. 22 January 1846. p.3, c3.

**3280 JNO. SCOBLE** *to* **G. W. HOPE, ESQ. [from the** *British and Foreign Anti-Slavery Reporter***] 13 November 1845. n.p.** Inquires about the state of slavery in the Kondian provinces of Ceylon, which is the last refuge of slavery in the British empire. 29 January 1846. p.1, c4.

**3281 JAS. STEPHEN** *to* **JNO. SCOBLE, ESQ. 13 November 1845. n.p.** Informs Scoble that the total abolition of slavery in Ceylon has been achieved. 29 January 1846. p.1, c4.

**3282 A. ROBINETTE, L. S. WIERMAN, AND W. W. WRIGHT** *to* **n.n. 12 January 1846. York Springs, Pa.** Discuss the recent resolution of the York Springs AS to petition the state legislature to declare it a penal offence for citizens of Pennsylvania to aid slaveholders or their agents in arresting fugitive slaves. 29 January 1846. p.2, c4.

**3283 n.n.** *to* **n.n. [extract from the** *London Non-Conformist***] n.d. Manchester.** Lauds the success of the Hutchinsons, a family of singers from New Hampshire, in their current tour of England. 29 January 1846. p.2, c4.

**3284 n.n.** *to* **n.n. [from the** *National Intelligencer***] 15 January 1846. New Orleans.** Reports that negotiations are in progress between England, France, and Spain with regard to establishing a consitutional monarchy in Mexico. 29 January 1846. p.3, c1.

**3285 C. M. CLAY** *to* **THE EDITOR OF THE** *TRIBUNE***. 18 January 1846. Philadelphia.** Responds to charges made by the *Courier and Enquirer* in the course of reporting events surrounding a mob assault on his office. 29 January 1846. p.3, c2.

**3286 J. E. SNODGRASS** *to* **THE EDITOR OF THE** *DAILY ARGUS***. 26 January 1846. Baltimore.** Refutes charges made against him by Mr. Clagett before the lower house of the Maryland legislature. 5 February 1846. p.1, c2.

**3287 C. M. CLAY** *to* **THE EDITOR OF THE** *SATURDAY VISITOR***. 26 January 1846. Baltimore.** States his views on the constitutional question of slavery and offers encouragement to the editor, who has fallen into disfavor with the Maryland legislature as a result of his stand against slavery. 5 February 1846. p.1, c3.

**3288 FREDERICK DOUGLASS** *to* **FRIEND GARRISON. [from the** *Liberator***] 1 January 1846. Belfast.** Contrasts his experiences in England and Ireland with experiences in the United States; notes that the British "measure and esteem men according to their moral and intellectual worth, and not according to the color of their skin." 5 February 1846. p.2, c1.

**3289 J. E. SNODGRASS** *to* **n.n. [extract] n.d. n.p.** Announces his resolve to carry on the work of his newspaper despite the threats of slaveholding legislators in Maryland. 5 February 1846. p.2, c4.

**3290 ISAAC S. FLINT** *to* **MESSRS. EDITORS. n.d. n.p.** Responds to James Fulton, Jr., clarifying his views on the obligation of the federal government to protect the states from domestic violence. 5 February 1846. p.3, c2.

**3291 n.n.** *to* **n.n. [extract] n.d. Brazil.** Reports on a battle in Brazil between the allied French and English forces and South American forces under Rosas. 5 February 1846. p.3, c4.

**3292 J. W.** *to* **n.n. n.d. n.p.** Examines the basic principles of phonography. 5 February 1846. p.4, c1.

**3293 S.** *to* **MESSRS. EDITORS. n.d. n.p.** Quotes a letter concerning Dr. Brigham, principal of the Insane Asylum at Utica, New York, and a letter from a matron of the prison at Sing Sing; concludes that the power of love assures ultimate victory over the "morally insane" slaveholder. 5 February 1846. p.4, c2.

**3294 n.n.** *to* **n.n. n.d. Washington.** Discusses the dispute surrounding the Oregon Territory and speculates whether the United States and Great Britain will go to war. 12 February 1846. p. 3, c1.

**3295 J. E. SNODGRASS** *to* **MESSRS. EDITORS. 9 February 1846. Baltimore.** Clarifies a portion of one of his personal letters quoted in the *Freeman* of 5 February. 12 February 1846. p.3, c3.

**3296 n.n.** *to* **n.n. [from the** *Tribune***] n.d. Savannah.** Gives an account of the murder of a slave by his master. 12 February 1846. p.4, c2.

**3297 NORTHROP** *to* **MR. GREELEY. [from the** *New York Tribune***] 26 January 1846. New Orleans.** Expresses his indignation after attending a slave auction in New Orleans. 19 February 1846. p.1, c1.

**3298 HENRY WILSON** *to* **FRIEND SCHOULER. [from the** *Lowell Journal*] **30 January 1846. Boston.** Gives an account of an anti-slavery meeting in Boston. 19 February 1846. p.1, c1.

**3299 GEORGE WASHINGTON** *to* **PHILLIS WHEATLEY. 28 February 1776. Cambridge.** Compliments Miss Wheatley on her talent for poetry, evidenced in a composition she had sent to him. 19 February 1846. p.1, c3.

**3300 n.n.** *to* **J. E. SNODGRASS. [from the** *Baltimore Saturday Visiter*] **3 February 1846. South Carolina.** Requests a copy of a prospectus, so that he can attempt to organize a club of subscribers to the *Visiter.* 19 February 1846, p.1, c3.

**3301 N. WALTON** *to* **MESSRS. EDITORS. 8 February 1846. Gum Tree, Chester County.** Reports on the recent visit of a party of fugitive slave hunters to the area. 19 February 1846. p.1, c4.

**3302 O.** *to* **MESSRS. EDITORS. 10 February 1846. Philadelphia.** Encloses a letter concerning Rev. Wylie which was refused a place in the columns of the *American Citizen.* 19 February 1846. p.2, c1.

**3303 O.** *to* **MR. EDITOR. n.d. n.p.** Challenges the contention that Rev. Dr. Wylie is an abolitionist. 19 February 1846. p.2, c1.

**3304 n.n.** *to* **n.n. [extract] 10 October 1845. Damascus.** Gives an account of a man's attempt to sell his daughter. 19 February 1846. p.2, c4.

**3305 J. M. McKIM** *to* **n.n. n.d. Baltimore.** Finds encouraging signs in Maryland for the advocates of emancipation; laments the failure of the American clergy to wield its influence to further the cause of liberty. 19 February 1846. p.3, c1.

**3306 n.n.** *to* **n.n. [extract from the** *Tribune*] **n.d. n.p.** Discusses a recent denunciation of American slavery in a sermon by the Rev. William Joy of Bath, England. 19 February 1846. p.3, c2.

**3307 n.n.** *to* **THE** *BALTIMORE AMERICAN.* **13 February 1846. Washington.** Reports on the proposal before Congress to return the city of Alexandria to the state of Virginia. 19 February 1846. p.3, c2.

**3308 J. E. SNODGRASS** *to* **THE EDITORS OF THE** *PENNSYLVANIA FREEMAN.* **16 February 1846. Baltimore.** Corrects a false impression created by his recent letter, which some took to be "a fling at a distinguished co-laborer in Kentucky." 26 February 1846. p.2, c4.

**3309 n.n.** *to* **DR. J. E. SNODGRASS. [from the** *Baltimore Saturday Visiter*] **13 February 1846. Potter County, Pa.** Encloses a three-dollar contribution to the *Baltimore Saturday Visiter*, and expresses his support for the views put forth in that publication. 26 February 1846. p.3, c4.

**3310 n.n.** *to* **DR. SNODGRASS. [from the** *Baltimore Saturday Visiter*] **14 February 1846. Baltimore County, Md.** Encloses two dollars and requests that his subscription be extended. 26 February 1846. p.3, c4.

**3311 HARSANOANDA [ELY S. PARKER]** *to* **HORACE GREELEY. [from the** *New York Tribune*] **9 February 1846. Aurora, N.Y.** Pleads the cause of Seneca Indians who are involved in a dispute with the Ogden Land Company which may oblige 700 Senecas to leave their lands in New York. 5 March 1846. p.1, c3.

**3312 n.n.** *to* **n.n. [extract] n.d. Virginia.** Reports that many people in Virginia are beginning to see the destructive influences of slavery upon their land. 5 March 1846. p.3, c2.

**3313 ELIHU BURRITT** *to* **MR. EDITOR. n.d. n.p.** Requests publication of enclosed addresses from the merchants, manufacturers, and other inhabitants of Great Britain to the merchants, manufacturers, legislators, citizens, and Christians in America. 12 March 1846. p.1, c3.

**3314 n.n.** *to* **MR. EDITOR. [extract from the** ***Southern Christian Advocate*****] n.d. n.p.** Rejoices in the spread of the Gospel among Southern Negroes. 19 March 1846. p.1, c3.

**3315 n.n.** *to* **MR. GARRISON. [from the** ***Liberator*****] n.d. n.p.** Encloses translations of papers from J. F. Dorvelas Dorval. 19 March 1846. p.1, c4.

**3316 J. F. DORVELAS DORVAL** *to* **MR. WILLIAM LLOYD GARRISON. [from the** ***Liberator*****] n.d. Hayti.** Encloses an address delivered to the people of Haiti. 19 March 1846. p.1, c4.

**3317 CYRUS M. BURLEIGH** *to* **FRIENDS. 10 March 1846. Wilmington.** Reports on the debate at a meeting of the Delaware State AS between a Mississippi slaveholder and Charles C. Burleigh; discusses the change in public sentiment in Wilmington toward toleration of abolitionists; reports on the effect of a recent address by Cassius M. Clay. 19 March 1846. p.2, c1.

**3318 CYRUS M. BURLEIGH** *to* **n.n. [extract] n.d. Shiloh, Salem County, New Jersey.** Discusses his work in New Jersey and the justness of the cause of emancipation. 19 March 1846. p.2, c3.

**3319 CHARLES H. BELL** *to* **THE HON. GEORGE BANCROFT. 16 December 1845. Kabinda, Africa.** The commander of the U. S. S. *Yorktown* offers the secretary of the Navy an account of the capture of the American barque *Pons* of Philadelphia, which had been carrying 896 slaves on board at the time. 19 March 1846. p.3, c1.

**3320 J. BERRY** *to* **G. B. GALLIANO. n.d. n.p.** The captain of the ship *Pons* addresses the owner in a letter found on board the ship, which adds to the evidence that it was legally an American vessel at the time of its capture. 19 March 1846. p.3, c3.

**3321 FREDERICK DOUGLASS** *to* **THE EDITOR OF THE** ***LIBERATOR*****. 27 January 1846. Perth, Scotland.** Responds to Mr. A. C. C. Thompson's published refutation of certain facts related in the *Narrative of Frederick Douglass*. 26 March 1846. p.1, c2.

**3322 n.n.** *to* **n.n. [extract from the** ***Picayune*****] n.d. Vera Cruz.** Reports that many are anticipating the establishment of a monarchy in Mexico, and that the government newspaper strongly favors this. 26 March 1846. p.3, c3.

**3323 n.n.** *to* **FRIENDS EDITORS. [from the** ***Anti-Slavery Bugle*****] n.d. n.p.** Denies the legitimacy of abolitionists who purchase products of slave labor. 26 March 1846. p.4, c1.

**3324 JOHN G. WHITTIER** *to* **GENTLEMEN. 18 March 1846. Amesbury, Ma.** Congratulates a group of independent Democrats in New Hampshire on their victory in the recent election. 2 April 1846. p.1, c3.

**3325 HORACE GREELEY** *to* **MESSRS. G. T. CLARK, D. CLARK, AND FULSOM. 18 March 1846. New York.** Regretfully declines an invitation to a celebration by independent Democrats in New Hampshire of their victory in the recent election; decries the annexation of Texas. 2 April 1846. p.1, c3.

3326 **WILLIAM GOODELL** *to* **n.n. [extract] n.d. New York.** States that the progress of the Liberty Party, both in the state of New York and elsewhere, is at a standstill. 2 April 1846. p.1, c4.

3327 **R. B. F.** *to* **MESSRS. EDITORS. n.d. Hartsville, Bucks County, Pa.** Asserts that the contradiction between Christianity and American slavery is not sufficiently insisted upon by some abolitionists. 2 April 1846. p.2, c1.

3328 **CYRUS M. BURLEIGH** *to* **n.n. 23 March 1846. Bridgton.** Describes his visit to Springtown, a community made up largely of former slaves. 2 April 1846. p.2, c2.

3329 **n.n.** *to* **THE** ***PENNSYLVANIA FREEMAN*****. n.d. Bucks County, Pa.** Submits for publication a poem by George S. Burleigh. 2 April 1846. p.4, c1.

3330 **A SUBSCRIBER** *to* **MR. EDITORS. 19 March 1846. Boston.** Encloses a copy of *Elementary Works on Phonography*, an art which "is about . . . to make a complete revolution in the republic of letters." 2 April 1846. p.4, c2.

3331 **HENRY C. WRIGHT** *to* **FRIEND. [from the** ***Liberator*****] 11 February 1846. Arbroath.** Discusses the controversy in Arbroath over the money accepted by the Free Church of Scotland from American slaveholders; relates the case of a local minister, Mr. Sorely, who has married a colored woman, "the cherished object of respect and affection among all the people of this town." 9 April 1846. p.1, c1.

3332 **J. E. SNODGRASS** *to* **PARK BENJAMIN, ESQ. [from the** ***Baltimore Saturday Visiter*****] 24 February 1846. Baltimore.** Accepts a challenge to debate publicly the question of slavery in its political and moral aspects. 9 April 1846. p.1, c4.

3333 **D. S. BRATTON** *to* **MESSRS. EDITORS. [extract] 27 October 1846. Mergui, India.** A missionary in India writes of the problem he anticipates in converting the Karens once they learn of the system of American slavery. 9 April 1846. p.2, c3.

3334 **n.n.** *to* **THE** ***PENNSYLVANIA FREEMAN*****. [extract] n.d. n.p.** In reference to the report of a slave purchased by the Alabama Baptist Association for the purpose of preaching the Gospel, the author satirically suggests that the American Board of Commissioners for Foreign Missions buy some clergyman for the mission fields. 9 April 1846. p.3, c1.

3335 **WILLIAM SAWYER** *to* **n.n. [extract] 9 March 1846. Washington.** The senator from Ohio expresses doubt concerning the passage of the Oregon Resolutions because of "traitors in the Senate who would sell their Country for a Bale of Cotton or a Negro." 9 April 1846. p.3, c3.

3336 **PARKER PILLSBURY** *to* **FRIEND ELA. [from the** ***Herald of Freedom*****] n.d. Andover.** Summarizes a lengthy debate between himself, an orthodox churchman, and Andover seminarians. 16 April 1846. p.1, c1.

3337 **JNO. SWIFT** *to* **FRANCIS TIMMONS, DENNIS MEALY, MICHAEL McGEOY, COMMITTEE. 16 March 1846. n.p.** Declines an invitation to a dinner of the St. Patrick's Beneficial Society. 16 April 1846. p.2, c4.

3338 **n.n.** *to* **n.n. [extract] n.d. Hayti.** Reports a change of government in Haiti after General Riche forced the resignation of President Pierrot. 16 April 1846. p.3, c1.

3339 **TRUTH** *to* **THE EDITORS OF THE** ***NORTH AMERICAN*****. n.d. n.p.** Reports on his visit to the Rev. Charles T. Torrey in prison. 16 April 1846. p.3, c2.

**3340 R. B. T.** *to* **BROTHER WATTLES. [from the** *Herald of Progression***] 1 February 1846. n.p.** Reports on an upcoming debate in his Southern town; claims that an astonishing number of persons in the area declare themselves in favor of general emancipation, and expresses his belief that nothing less than a division of the Union will accomplish this end. 16 April 1846. p.3, c3.

**3341 R. B. T.** *to* **n.n. [from the** *Herald of Progression***] 12 February 1846. n.p.** Encloses money for the mother of a recently emancipated family, and reports on the first meeting of a debating society in his Southern town, where "Almost everyone declared openly and without fear, he was in favor of freeing the Negroes." 16 April 1846. p.3, c3.

**3342 A BALTIMOREAN** *to* **THE EDITOR OF THE** *LIBERATOR***. 12 March 1846. Baltimore.** Denounces Park Benjamin's defense of slavery and appeals to the South for subscribers to the *Western Continent*, of which he is editor; reports that the imprisoned Charles Torrey is likely to die of consumption; rebukes the recent session of the Maryland legislature for enacting laws penalizing free Negroes. 16 April 1846. p.4, c2.

**3343 n.n.** *to* **n.n. [extract from the** *Liberator***] n.d. Bristol, England.** Expresses his interest in Frederick Douglass, noting that Douglass's *Narrative* is selling extremely well; anticipates a visit from Douglass when he journeys to Bristol. 16 April 1846. p.4, c2.

**3344 C. M. BURLEIGH** *to* **FRIEND. 20 April 1846. Mullica Hill.** Praises spring and rural living. 23 April 1846. p.3, c3.

**3345 WILLIAM JAY** *to* **n.n. [from the** *Non-Slaveholder***] 9 October 1846. Bedford.** Examines slavery in Egypt; concludes that Egyptian cotton may more justly be regarded as free produce than otherwise. 30 April 1846. p.1, c2.

**3346 S. M.** *to* **MR. C. M. CLAY. 2 April 1846. Richmond, Ky.** Maintains that God has sanctioned the institution of slavery and cautions against willfully flaunting the decrees of the Almighty. 30 April 1846. p.1, c4.

**3347 E. B.** *to* **MR. EDITOR. 22 April 1846. Worcester.** Criticizes what he sees as excessive government spending on the military establishment. 30 April 1846. p.2, c2.

**3348 NORTHROP** *to* **MR. GREELEY. [from the** *New York Tribune***] 26 January 1846. New Orleans.** Gives an account of a slave auction in New Orleans which aroused his indignation. 30 April 1846. p.3, c2.

**3349 JAMES N. BUFFUM** *to* **FRIEND GARRISON. [from the** *Liberator***] 31 March 1846. Bowling Bay, Scotland.** Reports on the anti-slavery meetings throughout Scotland led by himself and Frederick Douglass. 7 May 1846. p.1, c3.

**3350 ABBY K. FOSTER** *to* **n.n. [extract from the** *Herald of Freedom***] n.d. Ohio.** Reports on anti-slavery activities in Ohio, including the establishment of a newspaper and the sale of twelve hundred dollars' worth of books. 7 May 1846. p.3, c3.

**3351 STEPHEN S. FOSTER** *to* **n.n. [extract from the** *Herald of Freedom***] n.d. Ohio.** Reports on the highly successful anti-slavery meetings that he and his wife have directed in the past year. 7 May 1846. p.3, c3.

**3352 I.** *to* **FRIEND EDITORS. n.d. n.p.** Urges readers of the *Pennsylvania Freeman* to subscribe to the *Liberator* and the *National Anti-Slavery Standard* if they have not already done so. 14 May 1846. p.2, c1.

**3353 W. G. CATLETT** *to* **GENTLEMEN [A COMMITTEE IN GALVESTON]. 28 April 1846. On board Steamer** ***Monmouth*****, off St. Josephs.** Requests twenty companies of militia to reinforce General Taylor's position at Matamoras. 14 May 1846. p.3, c1.

**3354 CHARLES E. BERRY** *to* **FRIEND McKIM. n.d. Unionville, Chester County, Pa.** States his reasons for remaining an abolitionist despite pro-slavery influence surrounding him. 14 May 1846. p.4, c1.

**3355 FREDERICK DOUGLASS** *to* **MR. GREELEY. [from the** ***Tribune*****] 15 April 1846. Glasgow, Scotland.** Defends himself against the charge that he is "running amuck in greedy-eared Britain against America," and states the motives and object of his visit to that country. 21 May 1846. p.1, c1.

**3356 DAVID LEE CHILD** *to* **THE EXECUTIVE COMMITTEE, AAS. 10 May 1846. Northampton.** Denounces American slavery and the acts of Congress which have attended and prolonged the institution; sees no hope in American political parties, concluding that he "can find no congenial form of action except that assumed by the AAS." 21 May 1846. p.1, c2.

**3357 MARY GREW** *to* **THE EXECUTIVE COMMITTEE OF THE AAS. 11 May 1846. Philadelphia.** Encloses $200 on behalf of the Executive Committee of the Pennsylvania AS, and expresses the members' regrets that they are not represented at the annual meeting. 21 May 1846. p.2, c1.

**3358 DOUGLAS JERROLD** *to* **ELIHU BURRIT. [extract] n.d. n.p.** Ridicules a speech in Congress by John Quincy Adams regarding the question of the Oregon Territory. 28 May 1846. p.3, c3.

**3359 JOHN MURRAY AND WILLIAM SMEAL** *to* **WM. LLOYD GARRISON. [from the** ***Liberator*****] 2 May 1846. Glasgow.** Enclose a resolution of the Glasgow Emancipation Society praising Garrison's work and inviting him to Scotland; inform Garrison of Frederick Douglass's intention to present a formal plea before the leaders of the Free Church of Scotland urging them to return money received from American slaveholders. 4 June 1846. p.1, c1.

**3360 H. C. WRIGHT** *to* **WILLIAM LLOYD GARRISON. 1 May 1846. Edinburgh.** Urges Garrison to accept the invitation of the Glasgow Emancipation Society to visit Great Britain in the summer, and offers a tentative schedule of organizational meetings to take place in England, Scotland, and Ireland. 4 June 1846. p.1, c2.

**3361 GEORGE THOMPSON** *to* **WILLIAM LLOYD GARRISON. [from the** ***Liberator*****] n.d. n.p.** Urges Garrison to accept the invitation of the Glasgow Emancipation Society, offers a list of his activities over the past eleven days, and reports on the controversy within the Free Church of Scotland over the question of accepting money from slaveholders. 4 June 1846. p.1, c2.

**3362 MARY GREW** *to* **FRIEND. 29 May 1846. Boston.** Reports on the New England Convention of the American Peace Society. 4 June 1846. p.3, c2.

**3363 n.n.** *to* **n.n. [extract from the** ***Boston Pilot*****] 9 August 1845. Rome.** Reports that the indiscriminate association of blacks and whites on all occasions is regarded as a matter of course in Italy; illustrates this point with the example of a colored priest of his acquaintance. 4 June 1846. p.4, c1.

**3364 n.n.** *to* **THE** *SPIRIT OF THE TIMES.* **[extract] 19 April 1846. Camp opposite Matamoras.** An American army officer reflects on the curious lack of resistance among the Mexican people and army to the invasion of their territory by American troops. 11 June 1846. p.1, c2.

**3365 HENRY C. WRIGHT** *to* **W. L. GARRISON. [from the** *Liberator***] 2 May 1846. Edinburgh.** Encloses resolutions adopted overwhelmingly at two public meetings in Edinburgh which condemn the Free Church of Scotland for being in league with "man-stealers" and direct the Church to return all money received from American slaveholders. 18 June 1846. p.1, c1.

**3366 GERRIT SMITH** *to* **THE** *ALBANY PATRIOT.* **[extract] n.d. Peterboro'.** States that the Liberty Party of Madison County is in ruins due to its failure to hold to its principles and abstain from voting for pro-slavery candidates for public office. 18 June 1846. p.1, c3.

**3367 E. H. MAGILL** *to* **FRIEND McKIM. 1 June 1846. Solebury, Bucks County, Pa.** Praises Cyrus M. Burleigh for his addresses before several anti-slavery meetings in the county. 18 June 1846. p.1, c4.

**3368 ELIHU BURRIT** *to* **MESSRS. EDITORS. 29 May 1846. Worcester, Ma.** Introduces an appeal for peace among nations signed by 1623 women of Exeter, England, and sent to the women of Philadelphia. 18 June 1846. p.2, c1.

**3369 MARY GREW** *to* **FRIEND. 10 June 1846. Milton, Ma.** Reports on the anniversary meeting of the American Peace Society in Boston, condemning the timidity of their protest of the Mexican War. 18 June 1846. p.2, c2.

**3370 MARY GREW** *to* **n.n. [extract] n.d. n.p.** Reflects upon a bronze American eagle in Trinity Church, New York, the symbolism of which she finds at once incongruous and highly appropriate. 18 June 1846. p.3, c4.

**3371 GEORGE THOMPSON** *to* **HENRY C. WRIGHT. 7 May 1846. London.** Denounces those who attempt to justify slavery from the Bible and assert that the institution is compatible with the Christian religion. 25 June 1846. p.1, c1.

**3372 HENRY C. WRIGHT** *to* **GARRISON. 16 May 1846. Edinburgh.** Introduces a letter from George Thompson and comments on the excitement in Scotland generated by the Free church's fellowship with American slaveholders. 25 June 1846. p.1, c1.

**3373 HENRY GREW** *to* **MR. EDITOR. n.d. n.p.** Criticizes the report adopted by the New School Assembly of the Presbyterian Church for declaring that, "Separation and secession are not the method God approves for the reformation of His church," thus shielding slaveholders from excommunication. 25 June 1846. p.3, c2.

**3374 n.n.** *to* **FRIEND. [from the** *National Anti-Slavery Standard***] n.d. n.p.** Encloses resolutions of the New England Convention. 25 June 1846. p.4, c1.

**3375 S. M. B.** *to* **FRIEND GREELEY. 13 June 1846. New Haven.** Reports that the Connecticut State House of Representatives has voted to strike the word "white" from that part of the state constitution pertaining to suffrage. 25 June 1846. p.4, c4.

**3376 FREDERICK DOUGLASS** *to* **WM. LLOYD GARRISON. 23 May 1846. London.** Gives a lengthy account of his activities in London. 2 July 1846. p.1, c1.

**3377 C. M. BURLEIGH** *to* **FRIEND McKIM. n.d. n.p.** Gives an account of his journey to Wilmington and a meeting at Kennet Square held to protest the war with Mexico. 2 July 1846. p.1, c4.

**3378 E. M. D.** *to* **MR. EDITOR. n.d. n.p.** Expresses his desire to increase the amount of money given annually for anti-slavery papers and books in his section of Pennsylvania. 2 July 1846. p.2, c2.

**3379 HENRY GREW** *to* **MR. EDITOR. n.d. n.p.** Asserts that H. C. Wright and others are inconsistent in demanding that the Free Church of Scotland return all money received from slaveholders without demanding that abolitionists cease to purchase the products of slave labor. 2 July 1846. p.3, c1.

**3380 GEORGE MILLER** *to* **THE** ***TRUE AMERICAN*****. 30 June 1846. Providence, Delaware County, Pa.** Expresses disgust with C. M. Clay's volunteering to fight in the Mexican War, and even more disgust with Clay's apology for the action; terminates his subscription to the *True American*. 2 July 1846. p.3, c3.

**3381 n.n.** *to* **n.n. [extract] n.d. n.p.** States her intention to take up plain sewing for the benefit of the anti-slavery cause. 2 July 1846. p.3, c4.

**3382 J. S., JR.** *to* **FRIEND McKIM. 5 July 1846. n.p.** Encloses a poem published in the *North American* under the name of Jose de Saltillo as an example of Mexican poetry; informs that the poem is actually the work of J. G. Whittier. 9 July 1846. p.2, c3.

**3383 C. M. BURLEIGH** *to* **n.n. n.d. n.p.** Gives an account of an anti-slavery meeting in Nottingham Township, Pennsylvania, which is close to the Maryland border. [continued from 2 July 1846] 9 July 1846. p.3, c1.

**3384 J. CABLE** *to* **FRIEND. [from the** ***Mercer Luminary*****] n.d. n.p.** Discusses the practice of hiring out slaves to pay a minister's salary, demonstrated by several prestigious Virginia parishes. 9 July 1846. p.3, c3.

**3385 ISAAC C. HERITAGE** *to* **n.n. 12 July 1846. Greenwich, N.J.** Encloses resolutions of a recent meeting of the Eastern Seventh-Day Baptist Association, held at Marlborough, New Jersey. 16 July 1846. p.2, c1.

**3386 A. BAER, JR.** *to* **ESTEEMED FRIENDS. [from the** ***Bugle*****] 22 June 1846. Crawford County, Oh.** Gives an account of an anti-slavery meeting where an abolitionist was murdered by a mobocrat. 16 July 1846. p.3, c2.

**3387 n.n.** *to* **GERRIT SMITH. [extract] 2 March 1846. Tennessee.** Examines the economic and demographic decline of South Carolina. 16 July 1846. p.3, c3.

**3388 JUNIPER HEDGEHOG** *to* **JOHN ROBINSON. [from Douglas Jerrold's** ***Shilling Magazine*****] n.d. n.p.** Writes as "an ignorant cabman" to a private in Her Majesty's army, satirizing the British victory over the Sikhs. 16 July 1846. p.4, c1.

**3389 C. M. BURLEIGH** *to* **n.n. n.d. n.p.** Reports on a debate taking place near Little Elk, Pennsylvania, which addressed the question, "Have the citizens of free states a right to interfere with slavery in the South?" [continued from 9 July 1846] 23 July 1846. p.2, c3.

**3390 C. M. CLAY** *to* **MRS. CHAPMAN. 30 June 1846. Camp Owsley, near Louisville, Ky.** Expresses his sorrow that Mrs. Chapman and many others find themselves alienated by his decision to volunteer to fight in the Mexican war; defends his decision. 23 July 1846. p.3, c2.

**3391 AUGUSTUS WATTLES** *to* **FRIEND MURRAY. [from the** *Regenerator*] **1 June 1846. Mercer County, Oh.** Cites a case in Ohio which strengthens the contention that cold water is an effective cure for scalds when applied immediately following the injury. 23 July 1846. p.3, c2.

**3392 TRUE-HEARTED SOUTHERNER** *to* **FRIEND GREELEY. [from the** *New York Tribune*] **14 July 1846. Kentucky.** Reports turbulence in Lewis County, Kentucky, arising from a published invitation to C. M. Clay to deliver an address. 23 July 1846. p.3, c3.

**3393 ELIHU BURRITT** *to* **n.n. [from the** *Christian Citizen*] **n.d. England.** Relates his impressions of England, his exuberance at the repeal of the Corn Laws, and his pleasure in a concert by the Hutchinsons. 30 July 1846. p.1, c3.

**3394 MARTIN VAN BUREN** *to* **A MEMBER OF THE BALTIMORE CONVENTION. [extract from the** *Granite Freeman*] **1844. n.p.** States that "Texas was wrested from Mexico, and her independence established, through the instrumentality of the United States." 30 July 1846. p.1, c4.

**3395 SECRETARY UPSHUR** *to* **MURPHY. [extract from the** *Granite Freeman*] **8 August 1843. n.p.** States that a movement on the part of other powers to induce Mexico to enter terms of reconciliation with Texas would be injurious to the Union, and could not be permitted to succeed. 30 July 1846. p.1, c4.

**3396 SECRETARY UPSHUR** *to* **MURPHY. [extract from the** *Granite Freeman*] **8 August 1843. n.p.** Speculates that the establishment of an independent government in Texas forbidding the existence of slavery "could not fail to produce the same unhappy effects on both parties." 30 July 1846. p.1, c4.

**3397 SECRETARY UPSHUR** *to* **MURPHY. [extract from the** *Granite Freeman*] **8 August 1843. n.p.** Asserts that the establishment of a British influence and the abolition of domestic slavery in Texas would be calamitous to the United States. 30 July 1846. p.1, c4.

**3398 MURPHY** *to* **UPSHUR. [extract from the** *Granite Freeman*] **24 September 1843. n.p.** Stresses the importance of maintaining the present form of the Texas constitution, which guarantees the slaveholder the perpetual right to his slave and prohibits the introduction of slaves from outside of the United States. 30 July 1846. p.1, c4.

**3399 MURPHY** *to* **UPSHUR. [extract from the** *Granite Freeman*] **23 September 1843. n.p.** Warns that England is anxious to abolish the constitution of Texas, due to its guarantee of slavery; stresses the importance of taking action to ensure that Texas maintains its constitution. 30 July 1846. p.2, c1.

**3400 UPSHUR** *to* **MURPHY. [extract from the** *Granite Freeman*] **22 September 1843. n.p.** Expresses the desire of the United States government to aid Texas "in the most prompt and effectual manner," though he doubts there is much public support for such action outside the South. 30 July 1846. p.2, c1.

**3401 UPSHUR** *to* **MURPHY. [extract from the** *Granite Freeman*] **21 November 1843. n.p.** States that the United States government views the Texas question as crucial to the security of the South and to the strength and prosperity of the entire nation. 30 July 1846. p.2, c1.

**3402 UPSHUR** *to* **MURPHY. [extract from the** *Granite Freeman*] **16 January 1844. n.p.** Fears that if Texas does not become a part of the United States, it will be filled by emigrants from Europe who will abolish slavery. 30 July 1846. p.2, c1.

**3403 CALHOUN** *to* **PACKENHAM. [extract from the** ***Granite Freeman*****] 18 April 1844. n.p.** Informs the British minister that a treaty has been concluded between the United States and Texas regarding the latter's annexation, and shall be submitted for the Senate's approval without delay. 30 July 1846. p.2, c1.

**3404 CALHOUN** *to* **GREEN. [extract from the** ***Granite Freeman*****] 19 April 1844. n.p.** Informs the United States minister to Mexico that the annexation of Texas was an act of self-defense resulting from the policy adopted by Great Britain regarding the abolition of slavery in Texas. 30 July 1846. p.2, c1.

**3405 PACKENHAM** *to* **CALHOUN. [extract from the** ***Granite Freeman*****] 19 April 1844. n.p.** Acknowledges Calhoun's communication regarding the annexation of Texas; states that the United States' motive was to preserve slavery in Texas. 30 July 1846. p.2, c1.

**3406 CALHOUN** *to* **PACKENHAM. [extract from the** ***Granite Freeman*****] 27 April 1844. n.p.** Informs the British minister that the United States has concluded its treaty of annexation with Texas "in order to preserve domestic institutions placed under the guarantee of their respective constitutions, and deemed essential to their safety and prosperity." 30 July 1846. p.2, c1.

**3407 ROBERT PEEL** *to* **B. R. HAYDON. 16 June 1846. Whitehall.** The British prime minister answers the appeal of a painter in London with a contribution of fifty pounds. 6 August 1846. p.3, c3.

**3408 MARIA WESTON CHAPMAN** *to* **C. M. CLAY. [from the** ***Liberator*****] 25 July 1846. Weymouth, Ma.** Criticizes Clay's decision to volunteer for service in the Mexican War; concludes by urging Clay to "come out from the army—the whig party—the State of Kentucky—the slaveholding Union . . . and join yourself to the American Anti-Slavery Society." 13 August 1846. p.1, c1.

**3409 WM. LLOYD GARRISON** *to* **QUINCY. [from the** ***Liberator*****] 19 July 1846. Halifax.** Relates particulars of his journey to England; reflects on the desirability of a universal language; praises Theodore Parker's "Sermon on War." 13 August 1846. p.1, c2.

**3410 n.n.** *to* **n.n. [extract from the** ***Tribune*****] n.d. n.p.** Discusses the liberated slaves of John Randolph and current arrangements to send them to Liberia; praises a Negro artist whose work the author has recently viewed. 13 August 1846. p.1, c4.

**3411 JAMES N. BUFFUM** *to* **n.n. n.d. n.p.** Expresses regret that he cannot attend the annual meeting at Kennet, and gives his assurance that the religious sentiment in Scotland is highly favorable to the anti-slavery cause. 13 August 1846. p.3, c4.

**3412 B. R. HAYDON** *to* **MRS. HAYDON. [from a London paper] 22 June. London.** Asks for his wife's pardon prior to his suicide and requests the distribution of a small sum of money. 13 August 1846. p.4, c2

**3413 B. R. HAYDON** *to* **MR. FREDERICK HAYDON, R. N. [from a London paper] 22 June 1846. London.** On the verge of suicide, Haydon asks God's blessing upon his son, that he might be an honor to his country. 13 August 1846. p.4, c2.

**3414 B. R. HAYDON** *to* **MR. FRANK HAYDON. [from a London paper] 22 June 1846. London.** Bids his son to continue in virtue and honest deeds. 13 August 1846. p.4, c2.

**3415 B. R. HAYDON** *to* **MISS MARY HAYDON. [from a London paper] 22 June 1846. London.** Bids his daughter to be pious and trust in God. 13 August 1846. p.4, c2.

**3416 ROBERT PEEL** *to* **B. R. HAYDON. [from a London paper] 16 June. Whitehall.** Encloses a sum of fifty pounds "as a contribution for your relief from embarrassments." 13 August 1846. p.4, c2.

**3417 S. S. FOSTER** *to* **FRIENDS. [from the Ohio** *Anti-Slavery Bugle***] 10 July 1846. Mentor.** Gives a lengthy account of his and his wife's arrest and trial for Sabbath breaking. 20 August 1846. p.1, c1.

**3418 J. H. HOWE** *to* **ELIPHALET MILLS, ESQ. [from the Ohio** *Anti-Slavery Bugle***] 30 June 1846. Unionville.** States his intention to be present, along with others of pro-slavery sentiments, at an anti-slavery meeting in Geneva, Ohio. 20 August 1846. p.1, c1.

**3419 OPPRESSED JUSTICE** *to* **BRETHREN. [from the** *Christian Advocate and Journal***] July 1846. Peninsula, Va.** Reports on a Northern Methodist preacher who was victimized by mob violence. 20 August 1846. p.1, c4.

**3420 JAMES B. BROOKE** *to* **FRIEND McKIM. 14 August 1846. Marlboroughville, Pa.** Refers to the recent anti-slavery meeting at Kennett, suggesting that in the future there should be an annual statement of fees paid to each agent, and recommending the erection of a building near Kennett Square to house their meetings. 27 August 1846. p.1, c4.

**3421 EQUAL RIGHTS** *to* **J. M. McKIM. 14 August 1846. Bensalem, Pa.** Reports on the attempt in Bensalem to oust a man of African blood from a mutual protection company; views the incident as a contemptible exhibition of latent pro-slavery spirit. 27 August 1846. p.2, c1.

**3422 PLAIN SPEAKER** *to* **n.n. 24 August 1846. New York.** Reports on the state of the anti-slavery cause in New York City, the celebration of the anniversary of West Indian Emancipation in that city, and the political parties in New York state; discusses the phenomenon of Northern subservience to Southern demands. 27 August 1846. p.3, c1.

**3423 DR. SNODGRASS** *to* **n.n. [extract from the** *Saturday Visiter***] n.d. Berkley County, Va.** Confirms the story of a slave girl who, having attained free sanctuary, returned voluntarily to her master; also relates the story of a slave's recent suicide, in order to illustrate that not all slaves would refuse the offer of freedom. 3 September 1846. p.1, c4.

**3424 SUMNER STEBBINS** *to* **MR. EVANS. 26 July 1846. Kennett Square.** Criticizes Evans for failing to publish the proceedings of the late anti-war meeting at Kennett Square in his newspaper, the *Village Record* of West Chester; urges the editor to take a stand on the Mexican War. 3 September 1846. p.2, c1.

**3425 n.n.** *to* **n.n. [extract] n.d. California.** Discusses the desirability of enslaving American Indians, whom he judges to be less burdensome than African slaves. 3 September 1846. p.2, c3.

**3426 PLAIN SPEAKER** *to* **n.n. 31 August 1846. New York.** Reports on a speech by James E. Burr, who was imprisoned in Missouri for his assistance to fugitive slaves; discusses *Hochelaga; or, England in the New World*, by Eliot Warburton, and Warburton's misrepresentation of Frederick Douglass in this book; comments on the renomination of Mr. Giddings for Congress. 3 September 1846. p.3, c2.

**3427 JAMES RICHARDSON** *to* **JOHN SCOBLE, ESQ. 23 April 1846. Tripoli.** Reports to the secretary of the British and Foreign AS on the slave traffic of central and northern Africa, which he has witnessed firsthand. 10 September 1846. p.1, c2.

3428 **n.n.** *to* **THE** ***NEW YORK COURIER AND ENQUIRER*****. [extract] 1 August 1846. New Orleans.** Reports a high rate of sickness and death among volunteers for the Mexican War in New Orleans; concludes that the total monetary loss will amount to two or three million dollars, "all owing to the miserable counsels that govern at Washington." 10 September 1846. p.1, c4.

3429 **n.n.** *to* **THE** ***NEW YORK COURIER AND ENQUIRER*****. [extract] 1 August 1846. New Orleans.** Expresses his surprise that barrelled pork should be chosen for the army, instead of smoked meat divested of bone and packed in boxes. 10 September 1846. p.1, c4.

3430 **n.n.** *to* **n.n. [extract from the** ***Emancipator*****] n.d. n.p.** An army volunteer from Alabama writes home concerning his economic hardships. 10 September 1846. p.1, c4.

3431 **n.n.** *to* **n.n. [extract from the** ***Emancipator*****] n.d. New Orleans.** Informs of a cargo brought from Philadelphia for General Taylor's army, and the exorbitant price the government is paying for its transport. 10 September 1846. p.1, c4.

3432 **n.n.** *to* **THE** ***COMMERCIAL ADVERTISER*****. [extract] n.d. New Orleans.** Discusses the excessive fees the government is paying to charter vessels for transport. 10 September 1846. p.1, c4.

3433 **PLAIN SPEAKER** *to* **n.n. 7 September 1846. New York.** Praises an article by the Rev. Edward B. Hall in the *Christian Examiner* concerning the "Relation of the Christian Ministry to Reform"; criticizes an editorial in the *Cleveland Plain Dealer* favoring colonization; commends the *Boston Whig* for its coverage of the Texas annexation controversy, as well as the *People's Journal* of London. 10 September 1846. p.2, c3.

3434 **n.n.** *to* **FRIEND. 7 September 1846. Boston.** Expresses his pleasure in aiding the promotion and circulation of the *Freeman*; informs that mechanics in Middlesex County are refusing government orders for pontoons. 10 September 1846. p.3, c1.

3435 **JOSEPH STURGE** *to* **THE CHAIRMAN OF THE WORLD'S TEMPERANCE CONVENTION. 3 August 1846. n.p.** Expresses his belief that it would have been his duty to disassociate himself from the convention, had slaveholders been appointed delegates. 10 September 1846. p.3, c1.

3436 **A NEW-ENGLANDER** *to* **n.n. [from the** ***Tribune*****] n.d. n.p.** Discusses the World Temperance Convention's interest in the temperance cause in America, and the favored status given to American delegates as a result; upholds the value of the convention, which rested not so much in debate or resolutions, but in the fact that "Hearts were knit together in unity of spirit and purpose which before were unknown to each other." 10 September 1846. p.3, c2.

3437 **MONTEZUMA** *to* **n.n. [extract] 26 August 1846. Havana.** Denies the report that an agreement has been reached between Santa Anna and agents of the American and British governments to reestablish the Mexican federal government of 1824 under the guaranty of the United States. 10 September 1846. p.3, c4.

3438 **WILLIAM LLOYD GARRISON** *to* **QUINCY. [from the** ***Liberator*****] 1 August 1846. Liverpool.** Reports on his arrival in England; praises Richard D. Webb and Henry C. Wright. 17 September 1846. p.1, c3.

3439 **WILLIAM LLOYD GARRISON** *to* **n.n. [QUINCY]. [from the** ***Liberator*****] 14 August 1846. London.** Discusses affairs in London, and the various editors with whom he has made contact. 17 September 1846. p.1, c4.

**3440 WILLIAM LLOYD GARRISON** *to* **n.n. [QUINCY]. [from the** *Liberator***] 4 August 1846. London.** Comments on his arrival in London; praises George Thompson. 17 September 1846. p.1, c4.

**3441 WILLIAM LLOYD GARRISON** *to* **n.n. [QUINCY]. [from the** *Liberator***] 18 August 1846. London.** Reports on a meeting called to establish the Anti-Slavery League in London. 17 September 1846. p.1, c4.

**3442 PLAIN SPEAKER** *to* **n.n. 14 September 1846. New York.** Denounces the *New York Journal of Commerce* for its pro-slavery bent. 17 September 1846. p.3, c2.

**3443 C. M. BURLEIGH** *to* **n.n. 9 September 1846. Emmetsburg.** Reports on conditions in Maryland, where he is engaged in a series of anti-slavery lectures. 24 September 1846. p.1, c3.

**3444 n.n.** *to* **FRIENDS. 14 September 1846. Chester County, Pa.** Reports on the labors of several people in the county in circulating anti-slavery petitions and distributing tracts. 24 September 1846. p.1, c4.

**3445 PLAIN SPEAKER** *to* **n.n. n.d. New York.** Notes indignation aroused in Southern clerical delegates to the late Temperance Convention in London by the presence of Frederick Douglass; denounces C. F. Daniels, who has recently withdrawn from the *Courier and Enquirer*; discusses the refusal of Williams College to accept as a student the brother of the governor of Liberia, and the coming election in Maine. 24 September 1846. p.3, c1.

**3446 THOMAS SMYTH** *to* **MESSRS. DAVISON AND TORRENS. 28 July 1846. Dublin.** A South Carolina clergyman writes to the solicitors of Frederick Douglass to retract statements which were "injurious to his [Douglass's] moral and religious character." 24 September 1846. p.3, c3.

**3447 C. M. BURLEIGH** *to* **FRIENDS. 21 September 1846. Harrisburg.** Discusses his anti-slavery tour of central Pennsylvania among the towns of Petersburg, Monallen, and Gettysburg. 1 October 1846. p.1, c2.

**3448 COCHITUATE** *to* **n.n. n.d. Boston.** Discusses events in Boston, including an anti-slavery address by John P. Hale at Faneuil Hall, a sharp debate over anti-slavery resolutions at the Whig convention, and a meeting to consider "the Kidnapping case," chaired by J. Q. Adams. 1 October 1846. p.2, c4.

**3449 n.n.** *to* **n.n. [extract from the** *New York Tribune***] n.d. n.p.** Comments on various implements on display at the New York State Agricultural Fair at Auburn. 1 October 1846. p.4, c2.

**3450 n.n.** *to* **FRIEND. 27 September 1846. Boston.** Reports on a meeting in Faneuil Hall which was addressed by John P. Hale, and on a meeting held shortly thereafter "to testify indignation against the kidnappers of the slave Joseph, and to take measures for the prevention of illegal seizures in the future." 8 October 1846. p.3, c3.

**3451 WM. LLOYD GARRISON** *to* **QUINCY. [from the** *Liberator***] 18 September 1846. London.** Commends Quincy's work as editor pro tempore of the *Liberator;* reports with disdain on a meeting of the Evangelical Alliance which refused to condemn slavery, and on a meeting at Exeter Hall held to review the proceedings of the Evangelical Alliance. 15 October 1846. p.1, c1.

**3452 LUKE J. HANSARD** *to* **MESSRS. HOWE. [from the** ***Liberator*****] 15 September 1846. London.** Encloses a contribution of fifty pounds to the Christian Emancipation Society. 15 October 1846. p.1, c2.

**3453 GEO. THOMPSON** *to* **EDMUND QUINCY, ESQ. [from the** ***Liberator*****] n.d. n.p.** Denounces pro-slavery American divines who work against the cause of emancipation in England; states that the Evangelical Alliance is divided over the question of slavery. 15 October 1846. p.1, c2.

**3454 R. SMITH** *to* **THE EDITOR OF THE** ***LIBERATOR*****. 18 September 1846. London.** Discusses the division of the Evangelical Alliance and a meeting of the Anti-Slavery League in Exeter Hall. 15 October 1846. p.1, c3.

**3455 n.n.** *to* **WM. LLOYD GARRISON. [from the** ***Liberator*****] 19 August 1846. Islington.** Discusses the prospects of the recently organized Anti-Slavery League. 15 October 1846. p.1, c3.

**3456 n.n.** *to* **THE** ***NEW ORLEANS PICAYUNE*****. n.d. n.p.** Reports on the terms of capitulation of the city of Monterey to the American forces under General Taylor. 15 October 1846. p.2, c4.

**3457 ISAAC E. MORSE** *to* **THE EDITOR OF THE** ***NEW YORK HERALD*****. 12 October 1846. Baltimore.** Defends his pro-slavery speech before Congress, and comments further upon the subject. 22 October 1846. p.1, c2.

**3458 n.n.** *to* **n.n. n.d. Virginia.** Calls on the people of the free states to repeal all legal restrictions on the emigration of manumitted slaves; denounces the war with Mexico; reports a growing trend in public sentiment favoring emancipation. 22 October 1846. p.2, c3.

**3459 PLAIN SPEAKER** *to* **n.n. 18 October 1846. New York.** Comments on the advance of the anti-slavery cause in New England; laments the death of Nathaniel Peabody Rogers; disparages the Evangelical Alliance. 22 October 1846. p.2, c4.

**3460 NEMO** *to* **n.n. 18 October 1846. Baltimore.** Comments on the recent political contests in Maryland, the results of which indicate an advance for the cause of freedom. 22 October 1846. p.3, c1.

**3461 GERRIT SMITH** *to* **N. MOORE. [extract] 6 August 1846. n.p.** Explains his absence from a Liberty Party convention. 22 October 1846. p.3, c4.

**3462 n.n.** *to* **THE** ***TRIBUNE*****. [extract] 10 October 1846. Concord, N.H.** Criticizes the quarrelsome conduct of delegates to the state Democratic convention. 29 October 1846. p.1, c2.

**3463 JAMES S. JACKSON** *to* **n.n. [extract] 23 September 1846. Texas.** A soldier of a Kentucky regiment writes of the hardships endured due to the lack of money and supplies from the government. 29 October 1846. p.1, c4.

**3464 HENRY GREW** *to* **THE MEMBERS OF THE FREE PRODUCE ASSOCIATION. 20 October 1846. Philadelphia.** Upholds the duty to abstain from the products of slave labor. 29 October 1846. p.2, c1.

**3465 PLAIN SPEAKER** *to* **n.n. 26 October 1846. New York.** Discusses the case of George, a runaway slave from Georgia, and recent political movements in New Hampshire. 29 October 1846. p.3, c1.

**3466 n.n.** *to* **FRIEND. 17 October 1846. Boston.** Reports that Faneuil Hall has been procured for an anti-slavery fair; encloses a resolution supporting the formation of the Anti-Slavery League in Great Britain. 29 October 1846. p.3, c2.

**3467 WM. LLOYD GARRISON** *to* **n.n. [from the** ***Liberator*****] 3 October 1846. Belfast.** Relates news of his activities in Scotland and Ireland. 5 November 1846. p.1, c1.

**3468 JOHN REED** *to* **HON. CHARLES HUDSON. [from the** ***U. S. Gazette*****] n.d. n.p.** Accepts the Whig nomination for lieutenant governor of Massachusetts; calls upon all parties in the free states to unite against the injustice and oppression of the slave states. 5 November 1846. p.1, c3.

**3469 JAMES W. HANNUM** *to* **THE EDITORS OF THE** ***NEW ORLEANS PICAYUNE*****. 11 September 1846. Boston.** The master of the brig *Ottoman* relates that a runaway slave stowed away on his vessel from New Orleans to Boston, resulting in the captain's being branded a slave stealer by the South and a kidnapper by the North. 5 November 1846. p.1, c4.

**3470 PLAIN SPEAKER** *to* **n.n. 2 November 1846. New York.** Refers to the case of George Kirk, the fugitive slave, who has been set free by a court in New York. 5 November 1846. p.2, c4.

**3471 n.n.** *to* **n.n. [extract] 15 October 1846. Cumberland County.** A recent convert to the anti-slavery cause praises C. M. Burleigh and ridicules the American delegates to the Evangelical Alliance. 5 November 1846. p.3, c1.

**3472 THE DOCTOR** *to* **THE** ***NEW YORK HERALD*****. 30 October 1846. Washington.** Discusses military operations of Generals Taylor and Patterson in Mexico and prospects for peace. 5 November 1846. p.3, c3.

**3473 L. M. CHILD** *to* **n.n. [extract from the** ***Boston Courier*****] n.d. n.p.** Relates particulars surrounding the recent slave case in New York. 12 November 1846. p.1, c4.

**3474 PLAIN SPEAKER** *to* **n.n. 9 November 1846. New York.** Comments on the letters of a young man in Liberia, published by the *Journal of Commerce* in a garbled form; discusses Sylvester Graham's defense of the Massachusetts governor's call for enlistments for the war with Mexico, the recent elections in New York, and the defeat of the measure to grant colored suffrage in New York. 12 November 1846. p.3, c3.

**3475 n.n.** *to* **THE** ***TRIBUNE*****. 30 October 1846. Chicago.** Relates the facts surrounding the arrest of three men accused of being runaway slaves, the outrage of public opinion concerning this action, the escape of the three men, and a public meeting held afterward to discuss the case. 19 November 1846. p.1, c2.

**3476 n.n.** *to* **SIR. [from the** ***True Wesleyan*****] 25 October 1846. North Carolina.** Requests a copy of the *True Wesleyan* and a copy of the church discipline of the Wesleyan Methodists; adds that he has decided to separate himself from the Methodist Episcopal church because it maintains fellowship with slaveholders. 19 November 1846. p.1, c3.

**3477 GEORGE THOMPSON** *to* **THE EDITOR OF THE** ***PATRIOT*****. 30 September 1846. n.p.** Discusses the position of the late Thomas Clarkson in favor of disunion. 19 November 1846. p.1, c4.

**3478 n.n.** *to* **THE** ***NEW ORLEANS PICAYUNE*****. [extract] n.d. Monterey.** Reports fatigue and uneasiness among the American troops at Monterey. 19 November 1846. p.2, c2.

**3479 n.n.** *to* **n.n. [extract] n.d. Monterey.** An American army officer believes that the war with Mexico is far from a termination, and that his own troops are now too weak to meet a strong opposing force. 19 November 1846. p.2, c2.

**3480 PLAIN SPEAKER** *to* **n.n. 16 November 1846. New York.** Quotes a correspondent of the *Charleston Courier* who viewed the Mexican war as a means to expand the field of Southern power; comments on a movement to nominate Governor Wright for the presidency, the labors of Garrison, Douglass, and Wright in Great Britain, and the unfavorable coverage given them by the *Journal of Commerce*; reports that the Rev. J. G. Fee of Kentucky has been reappointed as a missionary by the American Home Mission Society. 19 November 1846. p.3, c1.

**3481 WM. LLOYD GARRISON** *to* **n.n. [from the** ***Liberator*****] 20 October 1846. Liverpool.** Offers an account of his travels and activities in England, Scotland, and Ireland. 26 November 1846. p.1, c1.

**3482 n.n.** *to* **n.n. [from the** ***New Orleans Picayune*****] 30 September 1846. Monterey.** Discusses the military occupation of Monterey and the American volunteers who commit vandalism and other wanton acts. 26 November 1846. p.1, c4.

**3483 n.n.** *to* **n.n. [from the** ***Boston Whig*****] n.d. n.p.** Relates that ship masters are disposed to vary their course in order to surrender fugitive slaves, and thus place the commercial interests of the vessel in jeopardy. 26 November 1846. p.1, c4.

**3484 PLAIN SPEAKER** *to* **n.n. 23 November 1846. New York.** Conveys his opposition to capital punishment after witnessing a public hanging; comments upon the conduct of the mayor in a recent slave case; praises the Hutchinsons, who have begun a new concert tour. 26 November 1846. p.3, c2.

**3485 n.n.** *to* **THE** ***NEW YORK HERALD.*** **19 November 1846. Washington.** Urges that the question of the settlement of land recently acquired on the Rio Grande and on the Pacific south of Oregon be decided at the next session of Congress, lest the settlement become an issue in a presidential election. 26 November 1846. p.3, c3.

**3486 n.n.** *to* **THE** ***NEW YORK OBSERVER.*** **n.d. Piqua, Oh.** Reports on the liberated slaves of John Randolph, who are now in Ohio awaiting settlement of legal barriers to the occupancy of their land. 26 November 1846. p.3, c4.

**3487 D.** *to* **THE** ***NEW YORK TRIBUNE.*** **25 September 1846. Off Vera Cruz.** Relates account of the hanging of an American sailor at sea. 26 November 1846. p.4, c1.

**3488 n.n.** *to* **THE** ***CHARLESTON COURIER.*** **[extract] n.d. n.p.** Reports that the runaway slave on the brig *Ottoman*, whose capture in Boston excited a great deal of public interest, has been returned to his master. 26 November 1846. p.4, c2.

**3489 FREDERICK DOUGLASS** *to* **SAMUEL HANSON COX, D.D. [from the** ***Liberator*****] 30 October 1846. Edinburgh.** Responds to charges by Cox regarding Douglass's conduct at the World's Temperance Convention. 3 December 1846. p.1, c1.

**3490 SAMUEL H. COX** *to* **THE** ***NEW YORK EVANGELIST.*** **[extract] n.d. London.** Offers a critical account of Frederick Douglass's appearance before the World's Temperance Convention in London. 3 December 1846. p.1, c1.

**3491 REV. MR. COLTON** *to* **n.n. [extract] n.d. Monterey.** A chaplain in the United States Navy reports a deepening interest in religion among the men of his ship. 3 December 1846. p.2, c3.

**3492 F.** *to* **n.n. 28 November 1846. New York.** Reports on the wreck of the *Atlantic*, which took the lives of thirty passengers; comments on Dr. Cox's Thanksgiving sermon and the Hutchinson's recent concerts. 3 December 1846. p.2, c3.

**3493 n.n.** *to* **n.n. 26 November 1846. Boston.** Reflects on the meaning of Thanksgiving and on the governor's proclamation of the holiday; relates the story of a fugitive slave rescued at sea; denounces the leaders of the Whig Party for their support of the war with Mexico. 3 December 1846. p.2, c4.

**3494 PLAIN SPEAKER** *to* **n.n. 7 December 1846. New York.** Reports on the Hutchinson family's Thanksgiving concert at Sing Sing prison, on H. P. Byram, who is threatened by mobs in Kentucky, and on the vote on the question of equal suffrage. 10 December 1846. p.3, c1.

**3495 n.n.** *to* **n.n. [extract from the** *Liberty Advocate***] n.d. n.p.** Praises the Rev. John Rankin of Indianapolis, who is attempting to form an anti-slavery Presbyterian church. 10 December 1846. p.3, c2.

**3496 A TRUE BLUE OF THE SOUTH** *to* **THE EDITORS OF THE** *PENNSYLVANIA FREEMAN***. 5 December 1846. n.p.** A Southerner denounces the institution of slavery and encourages the work of the *Freeman*. 10 December 1846. p.3, c3.

**3497 n.n.** *to* **n.n. [extract from the** *St. Louis Republican***] 20 October 1846. Santa Fe, N.M.** Discusses the atrocities committed by American troops against the Mexican populace in Santa Fe. 10 December 1846. p.4, c3.

**3498 PLAIN SPEAKER** *to* **n.n. 14 December 1846. New York.** Praises the Hutchinson family's final concert in New York; reports that the Rev. Henry Giles is delivering a series of lectures in the city; denounces a "monstrous" proposal of the governor of Virginia to expel from the state all free persons of color; expresses hope for the reestablishment of the *True American* under John C. Vaughan. 17 December 1846. p.3, c1.

**3499 A TRUE BLUE OF THE SOUTH** *to* **THE EDITORS OF THE** *PENNSYLVANIA FREEMAN***. 5 December 1846. n.p.** A Southerner denounces the institution of slavery and encourages the work of the *Freeman*. [reprint of letter appearing 10 December 1846] 17 December 1846. p.3, c2.

**3500 A WHIG SUBSCRIBER** *to* **MR. GREELEY. [from the** *Tribune***] 10 December 1846. New Haven, Ct.** Challenges the editorial position of the *Tribune*, which opposes the Mexican war. 17 December 1846. p.3, c3.

**3501 FREDRIKA BREMER** *to* **MR. DOWNING. [extract from the** *New York Tribune***] 23 October 1846. Arsta, Sweden.** Invites her friend to visit Sweden; expresses her desire to visit America. 17 December 1846. p.4, c1.

**3502 PLAIN SPEAKER** *to* **n.n. 21 December 1846. New York.** Reports that the British government has issued a statement prohibiting all British functionaries in slaveholding countries from administering the estates of deceased persons wherein slaves constitute a portion of the property; praises a sermon of W. P. Tilden on the Evangelical Alliance; comments on widespread opposition to the Virginia governor's proposal to expel free colored people from the state; criticizes a decision of Judge Krum in St. Louis, which led to the whipping of seven free colored persons. 24 December 1846. p.3, c3.

## [1847]

3503 **GERRIT SMITH** *to* **HON. STEPHEN C. PHILLIPS. 22 October 1846. Peterboro'.** Accuses Phillips of inconsistency for denouncing Captain Hannum, who captured a fugitive slave, while approving a slaveholder as a presidential candidate. 1 January 1847. p.1, c1.

3504 **EDMUND QUINCY** *to* **GERRIT SMITH, ESQ. 12 November 1846. Dedham, Ma.** Responds to Smith's criticism to Stephen Phillips, observing that anyone who pledges himself to the American Constitution places himself in fellowship with slaveholders. 1 January 1847. p.1, c3.

3505 **FRANKLIN PEALE** *to* **MESSRS. HUTCHINSON. 29 December 1846. n.p.** Announces on behalf of the trustees of the Musical Fund Hall that due to fears of a riot, colored persons will not be admitted to the Hutchinson's concerts. 1 January 1847. p.2, c5.

3506 **n.n.** *to* **n.n. 19 December 1846. Boston.** Reports that W. L. Garrison has held several public discussions of his European trip; denounces the Free Church of Scotland and the Evangelical Alliance; criticizes Daniel Webster and the Whig Party for their support of the Mexican war. 1 January 1847. p.3, c1.

3507 **PLAIN SPEAKER** *to* **n.n n.d. New York.** Reports that Governor Briggs of Massachusetts is denounced in the South for "cowardly truckling to the fell spirit of abolition"; criticizes the *Gotham Sun* for its report on the death of Thomas Clarkson and its support of the Mexican war. 1 January 1847. p.3, c2.

3508 **M. S. S.** *to* **MR. GREELEY. [from the *Tribune*] 22 December 1846. Philadelphia.** Discusses the recent annual fair sponsored by the Philadelphia Female AS. 1 January 1847. p.4, c1.

3509 **n.n.** *to* **THE *PHILADELPHIA LEDGER*. [extract] 13 December 1846. Washington.** Reports that peace with Mexico may be at hand; reflects on the disposition of America's newly acquired territory. 1 January 1847. p.4, c2.

3510 **JOHN QUINCY ADAMS** *to* **SIR. 9 November 1846. Quincy, Ma.** Declares that the act re-ceding the county of Alexandria to the state of Virginia is unconstitutional and void. 1 January 1847. p.4, c3.

3511 **GERRIT SMITH** *to* **EDMUND QUINCY, ESQ. [from the *Albany Patriot*] 23 November 1846. Peterboro'.** Refutes charges from Quincy that his position against slavery is inconsistent with his support of the United States Constitution. 7 January 1847. p.1, c1.

3512 **EDMUND QUINCY** *to* **GERRIT SMITH, ESQ. [from the *Liberator*] 11 December 1846. Dedham.** Argues further concerning the pro-slavery character of the United States Constitution. 7 January 1847. p.1, c4.

3513 **PLAIN SPEAKER** *to* **n.n. 4 January 1847. New York.** Reports that Rev. Drs. Cox and Patton denounced Frederick Douglass at a meeting held to consider the proceedings of the World's Temperance Convention; quotes a portion of a New York representative's speech to Congress favoring the annexation of land conquered from Mexico as free territory. 7 January 1847. p.3, c2.

3514 **n.n.** *to* **FRIEND. 26 January 1847. Boston.** Reports on the thirteenth National Anti-Slavery Bazaar in Boston. 7 January 1847. p.3, c3.

**3515 n.n.** *to* **n.n. [extract from the** *Richmond Whig***] n.d. South Carolina.** Discusses the defeated proposal to entrust the selection of presidential electors to the people of South Carolina, instead of the legislature. 7 January 1847. p.3, c3.

**3516 C. M. CLAY** *to* **SIR. [from the** *New York Tribune***] 10 December 1846. Camango, Mexico.** Explains his reasons for volunteering for military service in the Mexican war. 14 January 1847. p.1, c3.

**3517 ELLWOOD HARVEY** *to* **SIR. 26 December 1846. Chaddsford on Brandywine.** Relates an account of a slave auction in Virginia. 14 January 1847. p.1, c5.

**3518 PLAIN SPEAKER** *to* **n.n. 11 January 1847. New York.** Criticizes those newspapers of Philadelphia which have not rebuked the mayor for his action regarding the Hutchinsons' concert; praises the self-sacrifice of the Irish community, which has donated $800,000 for the relief of persons in Ireland; reports progress in prison reform at Sing Sing. 14 January 1847. p.2, c5.

**3519 n.n.** *to* **THE** *PHILADELPHIA LEDGER***. [extract] n.d. Washington.** Defends General Taylor against censure from his political opponents in Congress. 14 January 1847. p.2, c5.

**3520 n.n.** *to* **THE** *NEW YORK COURIER AND ENQUIRER***. [extract] n.d. Washington.** Comments on the formation of a Southern voting coalition which pleads "the necessity of a combination, in self-defence, of the states below Mason and Dixon," irrespective of party. 14 January 1847. p.3, c1.

**3521 n.n.** *to* **FRIEND. n.d. Boston.** Reports on lectures by Stephen and Abby Foster in Massachusetts, Caleb Cushing's proposal to grant twenty thousand dollars to aid volunteers in the Mexican war, and the case of a fugitive slave from Surinam. 21 January 1847. p.2, c5.

**3522 CHARLES C. BURLEIGH** *to* **M. 11 January 1847. Buckingham.** Reports on his speeches to various anti-slavery meetings concerning the debate on the relationship between slavery and support for the United States Constitution. 21 January 1847. p.3, c1.

**3523 INDEPENDENT** *to* **THE** *NORTH AMERICAN***. n.d. Washington.** Denounces Congressman Pettit of Indiana for opposing the appointment of a chaplain for the House of Representatives. 21 January 1847. p.3, c3.

**3524 OTTIWELL WOOD** *to* **THE EDITOR OF THE** *TRIBUNE***. 11 January 1845 Albany.** Challenges Preston King's claim that if slavery is kept out of the territories and the inhabitants are given the right to decide the issue of slavery when statehood is granted, they will be unlikely to choose slavery. 28 January 1847. p.1, c1.

**3525 SUMNER STEBBINS** *to* **DR. J. STEWART LEECH. 20 December 1846. Kennett Square.** Criticizes his call for volunteers to serve in the war with Mexico, which he considers an unjust war. 28 January 1847. p.1, c4.

**3526 JACOB M. ELLIS AND LYDIA GILLINGHAM** *to* **FRIEND. n.d. n.p.** Forward a memorial of the "Association of Friends for promoting the abolition of Slavery, and improving the condition of free people of color." 28 January 1847. p.2, c1.

**3527 n.n.** *to* **n.n. n.d. Boston.** Discusses lectures by Henry Bibb, a fugitive slave from Kentucky; Caleb Cushing's proposal to appropriate twenty thousand dollars as a gratuity to volunteers for the war with Mexico; and the convention of the Liberty Party. 28 January 1847. p.2, c5.

**3528 ISAAC S. FLINT** *to* **FRIEND. 22 January 1847. Oxford.** Reports that public sentiment in Chester County favors slavery as well as the war with Mexico; opposes further legislative compromise with slave states. 28 January 1847. p.3, c1.

**3529 JAMES N. BUFFUM** *to* **FRIEND GARRISON. [from the** ***Liberator*****] n.d. n.p.** Details proceedings of a Liberty Party convention and a Christian anti-slavery convention, both held in Boston. 4 February 1847. p.1, c1.

**3530 H. C. WRIGHT** *to* **FREDERICK DOUGLASS. [from the** ***Liberator*****] 12 December 1846. Doncaster.** Advises him against compensating his former master for his freedom. 4 February 1847. p.1, c3.

**3531 FREDERICK DOUGLASS** *to* **HENRY C. WRIGHT. 22 December 1846. Manchester.** Defends the purchase of his freedom from his former master. 4 February 1847. p.1, c4.

**3532 n.n.** *to* **n.n. [extract] n.d. n.p.** Condemns the expulsion of colored people from the Musical Fund Hall in Philadelphia, where the Hutchinsons were to perform. 4 February 1847. p.2, c5.

**3533 PLAIN SPEAKER** *to* **n.n. 1 February 1847. New York.** Reports on opinion in New York regarding the Wilmot Proviso, on a rupture in the American Peace Society, and on the pledge of the League of Universal Brotherhood to work for the abolition of war. 4 February 1847. p.3, c1.

**3534 n.n.** *to* **THE EDITOR OF THE** ***FREEMAN*****. n.d. n.p.** Discusses the case of Mrs. Rowand of Charleston, South Carolina, who is accused of causing the death of one of her slaves. 4 February 1847. p.3, c2.

**3535 CYRUS M. BURLEIGH** *to* **FRIEND. 1 February 1847. Milesburg, Centre County.** Reports on his anti-slavery lectures in Harrisburg, Bellefonte, Milesburg, and Bald Eagle. 11 February 1847. p.2, c1.

**3536 PLAIN SPEAKER** *to* **n.n. 8 February 1847. New York.** Criticizes the *Presbyterian Herald* for its silence regarding the issue of slavery; criticizes the *Cincinnati Gazette* for its support of the ACS; reports on slaveholding among the Cherokee Indians, offering an account of the murder of a fugitive slave. 11 February 1847. p.3, c1.

**3537 n.n.** *to* **THE** ***PHILADELPHIA LEDGER*****. n.d. Washington.** States that the Wilmot Proviso is "fairly up in both Houses" of Congress, but predicts that it will be defeated. 11 February 1847. p.3, c3.

**3538 H. V. VAN AMRINGE** *to* **THE** ***PITTSBURGH DISPATCH*****. [extract] n.d. New York.** Warns that Northern agents for slaveholders might easily perpetrate fraud by dealing in counterfeit certificates of slaves. 18 February 1847. p.1, c5.

**3539 DANIEL WEBSTER** *to* **JACOB HARVEY. 3 January 1847. Dublin.** Describes the wretched condition of the people of Ireland due to the famine. 18 February 1847. p.2, c2.

**3540 W.** *to* **FRIEND. n.d. n.p.** Suggests that I. T. Hopper's "Tales of Oppression" be published in the form of a book. 18 February 1847. p.2, c4.

**3541 PLAIN SPEAKER** *to* **n.n. 15 February 1847. New York.** Discusses the cause of temperance in New York City, the reaction to reports of suffering in Ireland, support for the Wilmot Proviso in Maine, and clerical responsibility for the war with Mexico. 18 February 1847. p.3, c1.

**3542 NO. 4** *to* **n.n. n.d. Boston.** Reports on a debate of the Massachusetts AS over the propriety of voting for candidates who would refuse, if elected, to take the required oath to support the Constitution of the United States. 18 February 1847. p.3, c2.

**3543 CYRUS M. BURLEIGH** *to* **FRIEND. 2 February 1847. Clearfield.** Reports on his visit to Clearfield, where the cause of temperance has made good progress, but where anti-slavery sentiment is still young. 25 February 1847. p.1, c4.

**3544 CYRUS M. BURLEIGH** *to* **FRIEND. 5 February 1847. Curwensville.** Reports on an anti-slavery meeting in Clearfield, and on two meetings in Curwensville. 25 February 1847. p.1, c4.

**3545 CYRUS M. BURLEIGH** *to* **FRIEND. 7 February 1847. Grampian Hills.** Reports that he has spoken before two groups in Grampion Hills, that his labors in Clearfield County are completed, and that he plans to proceed to Jefferson County. 25 February 1847. p.1, c5.

**3546 CHARLES C. BURLEIGH** *to* **FRIEND. 6 February 1847. Bristol.** Offers an account of his anti-slavery tour through Pennsylvania and New Jersey; discusses the ransom of Frederick Douglass; criticizes the *Pennsylvania Freeman* regarding its controversy with the *Charter Oak*. 25 February 1847. p.1, c5.

**3547 n.n.** *to* **J. R. CHANDLER, ESQ. 20 February 1847. Wilmington.** Announces that the Delaware House of Representatives has passed an act providing for the gradual abolition of slavery. 25 February 1847. p.2, c5.

**3548 PLAIN SPEAKER** *to* **n.n. 22 February 1847. New York.** Reports on a recent meeting in New York for the purpose of sustaining the president's war policy; fears that Daniel Webster will propose a compromise measure to replace the Wilmot Proviso; announces a series of lectures by associationists; reports that one Sylvester Graham is worth at least twenty-thousand dollars, not being a pauper, as was commonly supposed. 25 February 1847. p.3, c1.

**3549 NO. 4** *to* **n.n. n.d. Boston.** Praises the Pennsylvania legislature for approving the Wilmot Proviso; delineates various factions in the Massachusetts legislature; reports on a meeting at Faneuil Hall to consider relief for Ireland. 25 February 1847. p.3, c2.

**3550 ISAAC VAN ZANDT** *to* **HON. A. P. UPSHUR. 17 January 1844. Washington.** A minister of the government of Texas questions the United States secretary of state about the possibility of military aid to Texas prior to congressional ratification of a treaty of annexation. 4 March 1847. p.1, c3.

**3551 MURPHY** *to* **n.n. n.d. n.p.** Official communication of the United States Department of State, suggesting that the United States, having made secret overtures to Texas regarding annexation, should be prepared to aid in the protection of Texas in the event of renewed hostilities with Mexico. 4 March 1847. p.1, c4.

**3552 MR. NELSON** *to* **MR. MURPHY. 11 March. n.p.** The acting secretary of state responds to a communication from an agent in Texas, informing him that the president is not empowered to employ the army or navy against a foreign power with which the United States is at peace [Mexico]; suggests that steps might be taken to protect Texas in the event of an emergency, but not at the time specified in Murphy's communication. 4 March 1847. p.1, c4.

**3553 J. C. CALHOUN** *to* **MESSRS. I. VAN ZANDT AND J. P. HENDERSON [MINISTERS OF TEXAS]. 11 April 1844. Washington.** On behalf of the president of the United States, pledges protection of Texas from foreign invasion while the annexation treaty is pending. 4 March 1847. p.1, c4.

**3554 MR. MURPHY** *to* **MR. JONES. 12 April 1844. Galveston, Texas.** Informs the government of Texas that the president of the United States considers himself restrained by the Constitution from the employment of armed forces against a nation with whom the United States is at peace, and that therefore, forces cannot be deployed for Texas's assistance. 4 March 1847. p.1, c5.

**3555 ELIHU BURRITT AND JAMES L. L. F. WARREN** *to* **THE RIGHT HON. LORD JOHN RUSSELL [FIRST LORD OF THE BRITISH TREASURY]. 1 February 1847. London.** American citizens inquire whether the English government will defray the expense of shipping American contributions of food and clothing to Ireland. 4 March 1847. p.3, c4.

**3556 C. E. TREVELYAN** *to* **MESSRS. ELIHU BURRITT AND JAMES L. L. F. WARREN. 3 February 1847. London.** Replies that Her Majesty's Treasury will pay the freight of any provisions or clothing donated by Americans to Ireland or distressed districts in Scotland. 4 March 1847. p.3, c4.

**3557 THOMAS CARLYLE** *to* **COUSIN ALEX'R. 21 February 1844. Chelsea.** The poet praises his cousin's verses, but cautions him against any attempt to earn his living by writing. 4 March 1847. p.4, c2.

**3558 C. M. BURLEIGH** *to* **FRIEND. n.d. Ridgeway, Elk County.** Describes his speaking tour through Jefferson County. 11 March 1847. p.1, c3.

**3559 S.** *to* **FRIEND. 16 February 1847. Philadelphia.** Demonstrates that the Southern press is often silent concerning brutal crimes involving slaveholders. 11 March 1847. p.1, c3.

**3560 PLAIN SPEAKER** *to* **n.n. 8 March 1847. New York.** Encloses an extract from an article on war by the Rev. W. B. O. Peabody; criticizes Headley's *Napoleon and His Marshalls;* criticizes a ceremony honoring officers killed in the Mexican war; commends Pennsylvania's enactment of a law preventing fraudulent removal of free Negroes from the state; reports that a committee of the New York legislature favors the abolition of capital punishment; praises an anti-slavery sermon by the Rev. T. L. Harris. 11 March 1847. p.2, c5.

**3561 n.n.** *to* **n.n. [from the** *New Orleans Bulletin***] 1 February 1847. Saltillo, Mexico.** Reports the capture by Mexican forces of some eighty American cavalrymen, including Capt. C. M. Clay. 11 March 1847. p.3, c4.

**3562 n.n.** *to* **THE** ***TRIBUNE.*** **[extract] n.d. Washington.** Reports that a new apportionment of legislative districts in Illinois will place control of the state in the northern districts, which are not subject to the pro-slavery influences of the South. 11 March 1847. p.3, c5.

**3563 H. G.** *to* **MR. EDITOR. n.d. n.p.** Cites the *North American*'s failure to support abolitionist principles as an example of the betrayal of truth and righteousness by the popular American press. 18 March 1847. p.1, c5.

**3564 C. C. BURLEIGH** *to* **M. 11 March 1847. Kennett.** Reports on his recent speaking tour, and his arrest and imprisonment for breaking the Sabbath. 18 March 1847. p.2, c2.

**3565 n.n.** *to* **GEORGE P. MARSH, M. C. [extract from the** *Courier and Enquirer***] n.d. n.p.** A Southern slaveholder comments on the "inventions in morals" which prompt New Englanders to oppose slavery. 18 March 1847. p.3, c2.

**3566 n.n.** *to* **GEORGE P. MARSH, M. C. [extract from the** *Courier and Enquirer***] n.d. n.p.** Attributes differences in Northerners' and Southerners' character and convictions to the wide variation in latitude, concluding that the perpetuity of the American Union is doubtful. 18 March 1847. p.3, c2.

**3567 J. CILLEY** *to* **BENJ. S. JONES, ESQ. [from the** *National Anti-Slavery Standard***] 13 February 1847. Washington.** The Liberty Party senator from New Hampshire states that he is not yet in favor of a dissolution of the Union, and is therefore returning certain petitions sent to him to be presented to the Senate. 18 March 1847. p.3, c4.

**3568 n.n.** *to* **n.n. [from the** *North American***] 7 February 1847. Island of Lobos, Gulf of Mexico.** Describes the Island of Lobos, which is used as a rendezvous by army troops destined for Vera Cruz. 18 March 1847. p.4, c1.

**3569 n.n.** *to* **n.n. [extract from the** *New Orleans Delta***] n.d. n.p.** Describes the magnificent view near Chicoy in Mexico. 18 March 1847. p.4, c2.

**3570 n.n.** *to* **SIR. [from the** *London Economist***] n.d. Leamington.** Relates his conversation with Cobbett in 1826, when the latter predicted the Irish potato famine. 18 March 1847. p.4, c2.

**3571 n.n.** *to* **n.n. [from the** *New York Commercial Advertiser***] n.d. n.p.** Praises a pamphlet by Mr. George Combe advocating a comprehensive program of national education in England. 18 March 1847. p.4, c3.

**3572 C. C. BURLEIGH** *to* **FRIEND. 19 March 1847. Chester County Jail, West Chester.** Gives account of his arrest, trial, and imprisonment for buying and selling books on the Sabbath. 25 March 1847. p.2, c1.

**3573 n.n.** *to* **MESSRS. GALES AND SEATON. [from the** *Intelligencer***] 15 March 1847. New Orleans.** Reports that, contrary to popular rumors, Matamoras has not been taken by the American army. 25 March 1847. p.2, c4.

**3574 PLAIN SPEAKER** *to* **n.n. 23 March 1847. New York.** Reports on speeches by George F. White and B. Rush Plumly at a meeting of Quakers; denounces White's "tirades against temperance." 25 March 1847. p.2, c5.

**3575 NO. IV** *to* **n.n. 20 March 1847. Boston.** Reports that the Massachusetts legislature has been petitioned by 3,000 citizens to withdraw from the republic; states that the cause of temperance has been strengthened by a ruling of the Supreme Court sustaining the license laws of Massachusetts; comments on the Democratic victory in New Hampshire. 25 March 1847. p.3, c1.

**3576 n.n.** *to* **n.n. [extract] n.d. Ohio.** Requests that C. C. Burleigh visit the state of Ohio during the coming summer. 25 March 1847. p.3, c2.

**3577 n.n.** *to* **n.n. [extract from the** *Journal of Commerce***] n.d. London.** Comments on the influence of Dr. Cox at the Evangelical convention. 25 March 1847. p.3, c4.

**3578 GEORGE SHAW** *to* **REV. DR. BOOTH. 15 February 1847. Annaduff, Ireland.** Describes misery in Ireland caused by famine. 25 March 1847. p.3, c4.

**3579 n.n.** *to* **n.n. [from the** *London Herald*] **27 February 1847. Dublin.** Questions the Irish government's claim that conditions are improving; reports starvation by the hundreds and a high rate of emigration to the United States. 25 March 1847. p.3, c5.

**3580 THE DUKE OF PORTLAND** *to* **n.n. n.d. n.p.** States that the potato blight in Ireland has reappeared, putting an end to hopes for a crop in the coming summer. 25 March 1847. p.3, c5.

**3581 MR. SECRETARY BUCHANAN** *to* **MR. REJON. [extract] 24 July 1846. Washington.** Informs the minister of foreign relations of Mexico that the American government deems it useless to discuss the causes of the current war. 1 April 1847. p.1, c2.

**3582 MR. REJON** *to* **MR. SECRETARY BUCHANAN. [extract] 31 August 1846. n.p.** Replies, on behalf of the president of Mexico, that since the causes of the existing war cannot be discussed with the American government, they will be considered "a thing that is past, and belongs to history." 1 April 1847. p.1, c2.

**3583 MR. SECRETARY BUCHANAN** *to* **MR. REJON. 26 September 1846. Washington.** Informs the foreign minister of Mexico that the United States government does not wish to withdraw from a discussion of the causes of the present war, as this would ignore the just claims of injured American citizens. 1 April 1847. p.1, c2.

**3584 W. L. MARCY** *to* **MAJ. GEN. Z. TAYLOR. 4 June 1846. Washington.** Encloses copies of a proclamation in Spanish, addressed to the people of Mexico, which General Taylor is directed to sign and circulate. 1 April 1847. p.1, c3.

**3585 C. C. BURLEIGH** *to* **FRIEND. 30 March 1847. Philadelphia.** Reports on a well attended anti-slavery meeting at Little Elk. 1 April 1847. p.2, c3.

**3586 RACHEL H. BROSIUS** *to* **THE EDITORS OF THE** *FREEMAN*. **n.d. n.p.** Forwards a resolution of the Union Free Produce Society. 1 April 1847. p.2, c3.

**3587 n.n.** *to* **n.n. [extract] n.d. n.p.** Contends that it is the perfection in manners characteristic of Southern gentlemen which accounts for the fact that Southerners are usually chosen for the presidency. 1 April 1847. p.2, c5.

**3588 n.n.** *to* **n.n. [extract] n.d. n.p.** Proposes, in response to the suggestion that the Southerner strives for perfection in manners while the Northerner strives for perfection in morals, that when the millennium arrives, "the North will produce her due proportion of Presidents, and Vermont . . . will wear her morality as 'a diadem of beauty.' " 1 April 1847. p.2, c5.

**3589 n.n.** *to* **n.n. [extract] n.d. n.p.** Recounts how his aid in teaching a Negro youth to read and write eventually led to the boy's freedom; predicts eventual rebellion among American slaves. 1 April 1847. p.3, c1.

**3590 PLAIN SPEAKER** *to* **n.n. 29 March 1847. New York.** Describes the concern of the London Evangelical Alliance at learning that Dr. Patton of New York assigned colored worshippers in his church to a "Jim Crow" pew; describes the subsequent visit of the Rev. Ebeneezer Davies to Patton's church; summarizes a discourse by Davies on the condition of emancipated slaves in British Guiana and the evils of the system of "coolie" emigration in that country. 1 April 1847. p.3, c2.

**3591 n.n.** *to* **n.n. [extract] n.d. Macomb, McDonough County, Il.** Doubts that efforts to alter the constitution of Illinois to permit the introduction of slavery into the state will meet with success. 1 April 1847. p.3, c4.

**3592 SANTA ANNA** *to* **SIR. [from the** *Tampico Sentinel*] **23 February 1847. Camp near Buena Vista.** The Mexican commander reports on the heavy casualties of his late encounter with the American forces. 1 April 1847. p.3, c5.

**3593 EDWARD N. KIRK** *to* **MESSRS. GILBERT, LOVEJOY, AND OTHERS. 20 February 1847. Boston.** Praises the American Bible Society's plan to place Bibles in the households of Southern slaves. 8 April 1847. p.2, c4.

**3594 C. M. BURLEIGH** *to* **n.n. 27 March 1847. Williamsport.** Reports on his speaking tour through Warren County. 8 April 1847. p.2, c5.

**3595 A CITIZEN OF CHESTER COUNTY** *to* **MR. EDITOR. n.d. n.p.** Denounces the editor of the *Philadelphia Daily Sun* for his support of the Mexican war. 8 April 1847. p.3, c1.

**3596 n.n.** *to* **n.n. [from the** *United States Gazette*] **11 March 1847. U. S. Schooner** *Petrie,* **Off Vera Cruz.** Reports the landing of American troops at Vera Cruz, and minor encounters with Mexican forces; believes that if the war is not carried on with greater vigor, it may last another several years. 8 April 1847. p.3, c3.

**3597 n.n.** *to* **MR. W. N. HALDEMAN. [from the** *Louisville Courier*] **29 March 1847. St. Louis.** Reports a victory of the American army in a battle at Santa Fe. 8 April 1847. p.3, c4.

**3598 n.n.** *to* **n.n. [extract from the** *New York Tribune*] **n.d. Washington.** States that the liquidation of all financial claims resulting from the Mexican war would amount to $100 million. 8 April 1847. p.3, c4.

**3599 PLAIN SPEAKER** *to* **n.n. 5 April 1847. New York.** Criticizes a pro-slavery letter published in the *Western Continent;* denounces the recent statement of 100 Methodist ministers on the subject of the Mexican war; criticizes the appointment of a Presbyterian clergyman, Mr. Sprole, as chaplain and professor of ethics at West Point. 15 April 1847. p.2, c5.

**3600 GEORGIA** *to* **MASSACHUSETTS. [extract from the** *Western Continent*] **n.d. n.p.** Maintains that biblical authority sanctions slavery; denounces the hypocrisy of Northern states, particularly New York and Ohio, regarding the treatment of Negroes. 15 April 1847. p.2, c5.

**3601 GEORGIA** *to* **MASSACHUSETTS. [extract from the** *Western Continent*] **n.d. n.p.** Criticizes Pennsylvanians who profess abolitionism while maintaining a lucrative slave trade. 15 April 1847. p.2, c5.

**3602 ROBERT GOVER** *to* **FRIEND. 16 March 1847. Hartford County, Md.** Intends to persevere in the cause of anti-slavery, despite being seventy-eight years old and threatened with being jailed. 15 April 1847. p.3, c1.

**3603 n.n.** *to* **SIR. 31 March 1847. Hartford County, Md.** Responds to an inquiry, discussing the situation of Mr. Robert Gover, a member of the Society of Friends and "a good abolitionist," who is charged with sedition for distributing copies of the *Freeman.* 15 April 1847. p.3, c2.

**3604 MARY T. STICKNEY** *to* **MESSRS. EDITORS. 10 April 1847. n.p.** Encloses a resolution of the Committee of Ladies on Capital Punishment. 15 April 1847. p.3, c2.

**3605 n.n.** *to* **n.n. [extract] n.d. [Vera Cruz.]** Describes the devastation resulting from the American shelling of Vera Cruz. 15 April 1847. p.3, c4.

**3606 SANTA ANNA** *to* **GEN. DON CIRCIACO VASQUEZ. [from the** *Matamoras Flag***] 25 February 1847. Agua Nueva.** Reports on the state of his army after two days of intensive fighting. 15 April 1847. p.3, c4.

**3607 SANTA ANNA** *to* **HIS EXCELLENCY D. RAMON ADAME. [from the** *Matamoras Flag***] 26 February 1847. Agua Nueva.** Reports that his army is falling back to points where supplies might be obtained, and that the treason of a Mexican informer prevented his complete victory over the Americans. 15 April 1847. p.3, c4.

**3608 n.n.** *to* **n.n. [extract] n.d. Vera Cruz.** An American witness to the shelling of Vera Cruz describes the scene and expresses sympathy for the people of the city. 15 April 1847. p.3, c4.

**3609 MR. KENDALL** *to* **THE** ***PICAYUNE.*** **28 March 1847. Vera Cruz.** Reports that Santa Anna has put down the rebellion of Gomez, Farias, and Sallas, has joined forces with the clergy, and is anxious for peace. 15 April 1847. p.3, c4.

**3610 A PROTESTANT EPISCOPALIAN [WM. JAY]** *to* **THE RIGHT REV. L. SILLIMAN IVES. n.d. n.p.** Criticizes the pro-slavery stand of the Episcopal bishop of North Carolina as set forth in a recent address to a convention of his diocese. 22 April 1847. p.1, c1.

**3611 GEORGE WASHINGTON** *to* **LAFAYETTE. [extract] 10 May 1786. n.p.** Praises Lafayette's decision to emancipate the slaves of an estate he has lately purchased; wishes that a like spirit would prevail among all Americans. 22 April 1847. p.1, c2.

**3612 JAMES MADISON** *to* **THE ACS. [extract] 29 December 1831. n.p.** Characterizes slavery as a "dreadful calamity"; expresses his hope for its gradual removal from American society. 22 April 1847. p.1, c2.

**3613 PATRICK HENRY** *to* **A. BEN[E]ZET. [extract] n.d. n.p.** States that slavery is at variance with the Christian religion. 22 April 1847. p.1, c2.

**3614 n.n.** *to* **n.n. [extract from the** *New York Commercial Advertiser***] 12 March 1847. n.p.** An American officer in the fleet off Vera Cruz writes of his sympathetic reaction upon hearing the contents of a letter taken from a dead Mexican officer. 22 April 1847. p.1, c4.

**3615 n.n.** *to* **BROTHER. [from the** *North American***] 2 April 1847. Off the Balize.** An officer on board the steamship *Princeton* relates details of the siege of Vera Cruz and the surrender of some 4,000 Mexican soldiers. 22 April 1847. p.1, c5.

**3616 C. M. BURLEIGH** *to* **FRIEND. 16 April 1847. Bear Gap, Northumberland County.** Relates account of his lectures in Wellsborough, centering on debates over the validity of the Mexican war. 22 April 1847. p.2, c1.

**3617 n.n.** *to* **n.n. [extract] n.d. n.p.** Reflects on the explosion of a powder mill, and thinks that many more persons might have suffered and died had the same materials reached their destination on the battlefield. 22 April 1847. p.2, c5.

**3618 n.n.** *to* **n.n. [extract] n.d. Pottsville.** Considers a murder recently committed in the area, remarking that the murderer, had he enlisted in the army and perpetrated the same deed upon a Mexican, would be considered a hero in the popular mind. 22 April 1847. p.2, c5.

**3619 PLAIN SPEAKER** *to* **n.n. 19 April 1847. New York.** Expresses hostility toward the formation of a new temperance society, which claims to be founded on Christian principles, as an instance of clericalism; hopes that Horace Greeley will not endorse General Taylor if the latter is nominated the Whig candidate for the presidency. 22 April 1847. p.3, c1.

**3620 n.n.** *to* **n.n. [extract from the** ***Cincinnati Herald*****] n.d. New York.** Reports the streets of New York are in horrid condition; encloses a poem commenting on the fact. 22 April 1847. p.3, c3.

**3621 n.n.** *to* **n.n. [from the** ***North American*****] 16 April 1847. Pittsburgh.** Reports an unsuccessful attempt to kidnap an alleged fugitive slave. 22 April 1847. p.3, c3.

**3622 OBSERVER** *to* **n.n. [from the** ***Public Ledger*****] 18 April 1847. Washington.** Denies rumor that, in order to avoid the consequences of the Wilmot Proviso, the administration intends to give up all territory conquered from Mexico which lies south of the sixth degree of latitude. 22 April 1847. p.3, c4.

**3623 MONTGOMERY** *to* **n.n. [from the** ***Sun*****] 30 March 1847. Vera Cruz.** Considers a special mission to distribute money to the Mexican government unwise, as this would support an unpopular military regime and dampen the desire of the Mexican people for peace with the United States. 22 April 1847. p.3, c4.

**3624 MONTGOMERY** *to* **n.n. [from the** ***Sun*****] 29 March 1847. Vera Cruz.** Reports on the "plan of La Playa," a scheme of several Mexican states to withdraw from the central government and negotiate separate peace treaties with the United States. 22 April 1847. p.3, c5.

**3625 A PROTESTANT EPISCOPALIAN [WM. JAY]** *to* **THE RIGHT REV. L. SILLIMAN IVES. n.d. n.p.** Continues his letter to the episcopal bishop of North Carolina, criticizing the exoteric and esoteric doctrines of slavery and Christianity held by certain Southerners who would deceive people of the North. [continued from 22 April 1847] 29 April 1847. p.1, c1.

**3626 PLAIN SPEAKER** *to* **n.n. 26 April 1847. New York.** Comments on Professor McClintock's view that the duty of the Christian Church is to direct its influence toward the extirpation of slavery; ridicules the indictment of the *Christian Advocate and Journal* as an incendiary publication; criticizes the *New York Observer*'s justification of the Mexican war. 29 April 1847. p.2, c5.

**3627 A PROTESTANT EPISCOPALIAN [WM. JAY]** *to* **THE RIGHT REV. L. SILLIMAN IVES. n.d. n.p.** Argues that the form of Christianity represented to the slave is necessarily repugnant to him; attacks the bishop's contention that the widespread suffering of American slaves is "imaginary." [continued from 29 April 1847] 6 May 1847. p.1, c1.

**3628 THE REV. J. CABLE** *to* **n.n. 20 March 1846. [Virginia.]** Condemns the "worst kind" of slavery, the practice of hiring out slaves on a yearly basis. 6 May 1847. p.1, c2.

**3629 FREDERICK DOUGLASS** *to* **FRIEND. [from the** ***Liberator*****] 21 April 1847. Lynn.** Describes the prejudicial treatment he received at the hands of the agent of the Cunard steamship lines while procuring his passage to America. 6 May 1847. p.2, c1.

**3630 PLAIN SPEAKER** *to* **n.n. 3 May 1847. New York.** Ridicules the coming meeting of the Evangelical Alliance in London, which will discuss a proposition regarding slavery which is offensive to all factions; criticizes a clergyman in Pittsburgh who proposed a public discussion of the propriety of funerals on the Sabbath; denounces Park Benjamin's attempt to start a newspaper in New York City; comments on dissension within the Liberty Party. 6 May 1847. p.2, c5.

**3631 n.n.** *to* **FRIEND. April 1847. Boston.** Comments on the late session of the Massachusetts legislature, which passed resolutions condemning the Mexican war and expressing gratitude to General Taylor; reports new ownership of the *Boston Atlas*; reports on a meeting of colored citizens interested in aiding Frederick Douglass; recommends a book by the Rev. Mr. Hague, which discusses why slavery was not specifically condemned by Christ and the apostles. 6 May 1847. p.3, c1.

**3632 n.n.** *to* **n.n. [extract from the** ***Pittsburgh Mystery*****] n.d. Philadelphia.** Regrets having observed two of his colored friends illuminate their houses in celebration of American victory in Mexico. 6 May 1847. p.3, c5.

**3633 n.n.** *to* **n.n. [extract from Saunder's** ***News Letter,*** **Dublin] 1 January 1847. Ascension Island.** A naval officer describes a massacre which took place on the coast of Africa, where 2,000 slaves were killed by their owners when it was realized that the coast was too well guarded to ship them. 6 May 1847. p.3, c5.

**3634 n.n.** *to* **n.n. [from the** ***Lynn Pioneer and Herald*****] n.d. n.p.** Praises Charles Mackay, editor of the *Glasgow Argus.* 6 May 1847. p.4, c3.

**3635 A PROTESTANT EPISCOPALIAN [WM. JAY]** *to* **THE RIGHT REV. L. SILLIMAN IVES. n.d. n.p.** Concludes the open letter to the Episcopal bishop of North Carolina, attacking the bishop's contention that the English factory system is more oppressive than American slavery. [continued from 6 May 1847] 13 May 1847. p.1, c1.

**3636 H. C. WRIGHT** *to* **FRIEND. 13 April 1847. Glasgow.** Remonstrates with the Relief Committee of the Society of Friends, in Dublin, for rejecting the contribution of a theatre while accepting contributions from American slaveholders. 13 May 1847. p.2, c1.

**3637 n.n.** *to* **n.n. [extract] n.d. Vera Cruz.** Reports that two privates in the American army at Vera Cruz were found guilty of theft, sentenced to one month in prison, and fined one month's pay. 13 May 1847. p.2, c4.

**3638 n.n.** *to* **n.n. [extract] n.d. Vera Cruz.** Reports that General Scott has issued a proclamation to the Mexican people, declaring himself and the American army the friends of all peaceable Mexicans and the guardians of their civil and religious liberties. 13 May 1847. p.2, c4.

**3639 PLAIN SPEAKER** *to* **n.n. 10 May 1847. New York.** Declares the conference for the formation of the American Evangelical Alliance a failure. 13 May 1847. p.3, c1.

**3640 NO. IV** *to* **n.n. 13 April 1847. Boston.** Laments the recent American victories in Mexico, the failure of Northern legislators to stand firmly against the slave powers, and the exaltation of General Taylor by both major political parties. 13 May 1847. p.3, c2.

**3641 DR. SNODGRASS** *to* **n.n. [extract from the** ***National Era*****] n.d. n.p.** Criticizes the *Pennsylvania Freeman* for its report that he has become editorially connected with the *National Era.* 13 May 1847. p.3, c3.

**3642 C. C. BURLEIGH** *to* **C. W. GARDNER. 1 May 1847. n.p.** Regretfully informs his friend that he cannot be present at a Thanksgiving meeting celebrating the late repeal of the slave statutes of Pennsylvania. 13 May 1847. p.3, c4.

**3643 n.n.** *to* **n.n. [extract from the** ***Courier and Enquirer*****] n.d. Paris.** Introduces a translation of a note from M. de Chateaubriand, the French man of letters, to a M. Martin. 13 May 1847. p.4, c1.

**3644 M. DE CHATEAUBRIAND** *to* **M. MARTIN. [from the** *Courier and Enquirer*] **n.d. n.p.** Addresses a poet who had dedicated some lines to him, upholding the value of religion. 13 May 1847. p.4, c1.

**3645 n.n.** *to* **n.n. [from the** *New Orleans Delta*] **n.d. n.p.** Comments on the kindness displayed by Mexican women toward American soldiers during the siege of Monterey. 13 May 1847. p.4, c2.

**3646 n.n.** *to* **n.n. [extract from the** *New York Evening Post*] **n.d. n.p.** Commemorates Alexander Kunze, late private in the United States Army and a German immigrant of extraordinary intellectual ability, who died on the battlefield at Buena Vista. 13 May 1847. p.4, c2.

**3647 n.n.** *to* **n.n. [from the** *National Intelligencer*] **n.d. Paris.** Announces the publication of a new monthly journal, the *French Abolitionist.* 13 May 1847. p.4, c3.

**3648 THO. CORWIN** *to* **SIR. [from the** *Lafayette Journal and Free Press*] **4 April 1847. Lebanon, Oh.** A United States senator thanks a constituent for a letter supporting his opposition to the government's war policy. 20 May 1847. p.1, c5.

**3649 JOSEPH DUPTON AND THOS. HARVEY** *to* **THE EDITORS OF THE** *LEEDS MERCURY.* **n.d. n.p.** Appeal for contributors to raise 500 pounds for the purchase of a printing press for Frederick Douglass. 20 May 1847. p.3, c4.

**3650 E. MORTIMER** *to* **FRIEND McKIM. 11 May 1847. Oxford, Pa.** Reports on a recent anti-slavery meeting at Eastland Hall. 20 May 1847. p.3, c5.

**3651 n.n.** *to* **n.n. [from the** *Anti-Slavery Reporter*] **25 February 1847. Bucharest.** Reports that a resolution has passed the Diet of Wallachia granting emancipation to 60,000 gypsy slaves held by the state, the church, and the clergy in that country. 20 May 1847. p.4, c3.

**3652 E. CURTISS HINE** *to* **THE** *AUBURN ADVERTISER.* **n.d. Vera Cruz.** Describes the devastation of the city of Vera Cruz in the wake of the American bombardment. 20 May 1847. p.4, c3.

**3653 PLAIN SPEAKER** *to* **n.n. 26 May 1847. New York.** Ridicules Trinity Church in New York for erecting a monument to the memory of two naval heroes; criticizes the American clergy for its failure to oppose the Mexican war; reports that the *Christian Advocate and Journal* has ceased publication of Professor McClintock's articles on slavery; reports that Lucretia Mott has addressed two Quaker meetings on behalf of the cause of freedom. 27 May 1847. p.2, c3.

**3654 NO. IV** *to* **n.n. 22 May 1847. Boston.** Summarizes the history of the temperance movement in Massachusetts, rejoicing in the recent action by the city of Boston which prohibits the retail sale of alcohol. 27 May 1847. p.2, c4.

**3655 n.n.** *to* **n.n. [from the** *Journal of Commerce*] **4 May. Washington.** Reports that the consensus of opinion among American officers in Mexico is that peace is not to be expected in the near future, and perhaps not for several years. 27 May 1847. p.3, c1.

**3656 ANTONIO CANALES** *to* **THE ADJUTANT INSPECTOR OF THE NATIONAL GUARDS. 4 April 1847. Camp in San Augustin.** Directs him to declare martial law; declares that any able-bodied Mexican who has not taken up arms within eight days of the decree will be considered a traitor. 27 May 1847. p.3, c1.

**3657 n.n.** *to* **n.n. [from the** *Picayune***] 8 May. Vera Cruz.** Encloses a list of fifty-five American soldiers killed lately in Mexico; comments on the high mortality prevailing at Vera Cruz. 27 May 1847. p.3, c2.

**3658 WENDELL PHILLIPS** *to* **MR. OLIVER DYER. 14 May 1847. New York.** Attests to the accuracy of phonographic reports of speeches by himself and Frederick Douglass. 27 May 1847. p.3, c2.

**3659 JOHN W. TAYLOR** *to* **HON. CHARLES HUDSON. [from the** *Boston Atlas***] 15 May 1847. Cleveland, Oh.** A retired congressman commends a current member of the House of Representatives for a recent speech on the "three million bill"; recalls his own efforts to arrest slavery in Missouri and Arkansas; denounces the war with Mexico and calls upon the Northern states to stand firm in the struggle against Southern usurpation. 3 June 1847. p.1, c4.

**3660 JOHN W. TAYLOR** *to* **HON. CHARLES HUDSON. [from the** *Boston Atlas***] n.d. n.p.** Grants permission to publish his letter of 15 May 1847, and criticizes the usurpation by Southern slaveholders of powers not given in the Constitution. 3 June 1847. p.1, c5.

**3661 n.n.** *to* **n.n. [extract from a New Orleans paper] n.d. n.p.** Reports that Senator Thomas Corwin was burned in effigy by a "large and respectable convocation" of soldiers in an American military camp. 10 June 1847. p.2, c4.

**3662 NO. IV** *to* **n.n. 5 June 1847. Boston.** Compares the recent anniversary week in Boston to those in the past; praises the recent New England Anti-Slavery Convention; criticizes the selfishness of those in Massachusetts who are greatly alarmed at the influx of refugees from the famine in Ireland. 10 June 1847. p.2, c5.

**3663 THOMAS H. BENTON** *to* **WADE M. JACKSON, ESQ. 27 May 1847. St Louis.** Expresses regret that the Northern states have produced but one president in fifty years, and indignation at Southerners who would perpetuate this situation. 17 June 1847. p.1, c2.

**3664 n.n.** *to* **n.n. [from the** *Ledger***] n.d. Washington.** Comments on the illegitimate birth and sympathies for the African race of General Almonte of Mexico, former minister plenipotentiary in Washington. 17 June 1847. p.2, c2.

**3665 ALGERNON** *to* **n.n. [extract from the** *Philadelphia Sun***] n.d. n.p.** Believes that General Taylor will be the next presidential candidate supported by slaveholding interests; speculates on a possible Northern opponent. 17 June 1847. p.3, c2.

**3666 OBSERVER** *to* **n.n. [extract from the** *Ledger***] n.d. n.p.** Reports that the *Charleston Mercury* has endorsed General Taylor for the presidency. 17 June 1847. p.3, c2.

**3667 n.n.** *to* **THE EDITORS OF THE** ***DELTA*****. 29 May 1847. Vera Cruz.** An American soldier at Vera Cruz decries the waste of public funds in the course of the Mexican war, providing illustrations from slave vessels anchored in the local harbor. 17 June 1847. p.3, c4.

**3668 S. M.** *to* **MR. CHANNING. [from the** *Boston Christian World***] n.d. n.p.** Criticizes the *New York Evangelist,* which labelled a speech by Wendell Phillips as "warfare against the Church." 24 June 1847. p.1, c4.

**3669 B. RUSH PLUMLY** *to* **J. GRIMES. 1 June 1847. Trenton, N.J.** Declares that both the church and state are wrong to support the war with Mexico; demands of abolitionists an increased effort for the overthrow of slavery in America. 24 June 1847. p.3, c1.

**3670 n.n.** *to* **n.n. [extract from the** *Times and Keystone***] 26 June 1847. Washington.** Reports that General Taylor is inferred to be, beyond doubt, a free trade man. 1 July 1847. p.2, c4.

**3671 GEORGE BRADBURN** *to* **n.n. [extract from the** *Cleveland American***] n.d. n.p.** Criticizes the recent editorial course of the *National Era* regarding the United States Constitution. 1 July 1847. p.2, c5.

**3672 n.n.** *to* **n.n. [extract] n.d. Delaware.** Comments on the ineffectiveness of the Delaware law against selling slaves to persons outside the state. 1 July 1847. p.3, c1.

**3673 C. J. INGERSOL** *to* **THE** *NATIONAL INTELLIGENCER.* **[extract] n.d. n.p.** Criticizes the newspaper's "sentimental, poetical, and common idle denunciations" of the Mexican war. 1 July 1847. p.3, c2.

**3674 n.n.** *to* **n.n. [extract] n.d. n.p.** An anonymous abolitionist asserts the guilt of Northern states for their participation in the crime of slavery. 1 July 1847. p.3, c4.

**3675 O. N. H.** *to* **SIR. n.d. n.p.** Encloses for publication an extract from a letter written by an unnamed abolitionist to a friend who had attempted to apologize for slavery and deny the North's guilt. 1 July 1847. p.3, c4.

**3676 F. P. DE R.** *to* **FRIENDS. [from the** *New York Tribune***] 22 May 1847. Mexico.** Comments on the present state of affairs in Mexico, discussing popular sentiment against Santa Anna, the desire for peace among all but the military, and the self-serving actions of the clergy. 1 July 1847. p.4, c1.

**3677 n.n.** *to* **n.n. [from the** *Journal of Commerce***] 20 January 1847. Constantinople.** Compares and contrasts slavery in Turkey with slavery in the western hemisphere. 8 July 1847. p.1, c1.

**3678 n.n.** *to* **n.n. [extract] n.d. n.p.** A gentleman who volunteered for military service in Mexico advises his fellow Pennsylvanians against doing the same. 8 July 1847. p.3, c2.

**3679 n.n.** *to* **n.n. [extract from the** *Daily News***] 28 July 1847. Rome.** Reports that the urn containing the heart of Daniel O'Connell has arrived in Rome, and has been deposited in the Church of St. Agatha dei Goti. 8 July 1847. p.3, c5.

**3680 n.n.** *to* **n.n. [from the** *Paris Univers***] 5 July 1847. Rome.** Reports on funeral services for Daniel O'Connell, held at the Church of St. Agatha of the Irish College in Rome. 8 July 1847. p.3, c5.

**3681 n.n.** *to* **BROTHER. [from the** *Pittsburgh Mystery***] n.d. Carlisle.** Reports on a recent riot in Carlisle, prompted by an attempt to capture a woman and child alleged to be fugitive slaves. 15 July 1847. p.1, c4.

**3682 n.n.** *to* **THE** *LEDGER.* **[extract] n.d. New York.** Notes with disapproval that several anti-war sermons were preached by Presbyterian clergymen in New York on the preceding day. 15 July 1847. p.3, c2.

**3683 G. W.** *to* **MESSRS. EDITORS. [from the** *Christian Repository***] n.d. n.p.** Declares that abolitionism and fanaticism are identical, citing a letter recently published in the *National Anti-Slavery Standard* in support. 22 July 1847. p.1, c2.

**3684 L. T.** *to* **MESSRS. EDITORS. [from the** *Christian Repository***] n.d. n.p.** Refutes the contention of "G. W." that abolition and fanaticism are identical. 22 July 1847. p.1, c2.

**3685 n.n.** *to* **n.n. [from the** *Journal of Commerce***] n.d. Washington.** Denies rumors that an official peace treaty with Mexico has been concluded; condemns the disgraceful situation in that country. 22 July 1847. p.1, c5.

**3686 n.n.** *to* **n.n. [extract from the** *York Gazette***] n.d. Pennsylvania.** Considers the war with Mexico an enterprize "under the direction of divine Providence, to civilize and Christianize . . . a most ignorant, indolent, wicked, and unhappy people." 22 July 1847. p.2, c2.

**3687 O. N. H.** *to* **MESSRS. EDITORS. n.d. n.p.** Summarizes the history of the Indian tribes in Mexico from the Spanish conquest to the present day, concluding that the various Mexican races are swiftly amalgamating under a democratic model of government; denounces the American invasion of Mexico and atrocities committed by Americans against the Indians in their own land. 22 July 1847. p.2, c2.

**3688 EN. LOCKE** *to* **ESTEEMED FRIEND. 13 July 1847. Lockport, N.Y.** Reports an incident at Niagara Falls, where a woman's attempt to escape from slavery terminated in a mob brawl. 22 July 1847. p.2, c4.

**3689 NO. IV** *to* **n.n. 15 July 1847. Boston.** Discusses a recent meeting of the Boston Prison-Discipline Society, which awakened much interest in the community; reports on the cool reception given President Polk on his visit to Boston; comments on the late Fourth of July celebration in that city. 22 July 1847. p.3, c2.

**3690 C. M. BURLEIGH** *to* **McKIM. 17 July 1847. Pleasant Height, Plainfield, Ct.** Comments on the progress of the anti-slavery cause in Connecticut. 22 July 1847. p.3, c3.

**3691 n.n.** *to* **n.n. [from the** *North American***] n.d. n.p.** Discusses the proposal of Dr. Lang, member of the legislative council of New South Wales, to send destitute persons of Scotland to raise cotton in Australia, thus providing ample free labor cotton for British manufacturers, and sufficient competition for the American market to render slavery unprofitable. 22 July 1847. p.3, c4.

**3692 n.n.** *to* **n.n. [from the** *New York Herald***] n.d. n.p.** Provides figures of the cost of the Mexican war in men and dollars. 22 July 1847. p.3, c4.

**3693 THOMAS WHIPEMWELL** *to* **HON. HENRY CLAY. [from the** *Anti-Slavery Bugle***] 4 July 1847. Negropen, Va.** Satirical letter presents Henry Clay with the gift of "a likely young negro of the best Virginia breed"; praises the Missouri compromise and the prohibitory tariff which have greatly enhanced the enterprise of Negro-breeding. 29 July 1847. p.1, c4.

**3694 HENRY CLAY** *to* **THOMAS WHIPEMWELL, ESQ. [from the** *Anti-Slavery Bugle***] 12 July 1847. Ashland.** Fictitious letter expressing gratitude for the gift of a young slave and acknowledging his sympathy for the oppressed peoples of Greece and Poland, his efforts on behalf of human liberty in general, and his opposition to such sentimental philanthropy as would uproot the institutions of his beloved South. 29 July 1847. p.1, c4.

**3695 n.n.** *to* **GREELEY. [from the** *Tribune***] 12 July 1847. Ashtabula County, Oh.** Reports solid opposition to the nomination of General Taylor for the presidency among the Whigs of Ohio. 29 July 1847. p.1, c4.

**3696 n.n.** *to* **SISTERS. 18 May 1847. Bucks County, Pa.** Donates articles of needlework to the annual fair sponsored by the Pennsylvania AS. 29 July 1847. p.2, c3.

**3697 NO. IV** *to* **n.n. 22 July 1847. Boston.** Recounts events surrounding an alleged conspiracy of slaves to revolt in Charleston in 1822, and the consequent formation of the South Carolina Association. 29 July 1847. p.2, c4.

**3698 E. CAREW** *to* **MR. H. L. TOOMER. [from the** ***Charleston Courier*****] 16 July 1847. n.p.** Laments the death of his black servant, Mary, promising to undertake an investigation of the incident when he regains his composure. 29 July 1847. p.3, c1.

**3699 GEO. F. HORTON** *to* **FRIEND McKIM. 16 July 1847. Terrytown, Pa.** Encloses his subscription to the *Freeman*; calls on abolitionists to persist in the fight against slavery and the war with Mexico. 29 July 1847. p.3, c4.

**3700 J. C. CALHOUN** *to* **SAMUEL A. WALES, ESQ. [date and place illegible.]** Acknowledges receipt of a resolution by the Whigs of Putnam County, Georgia, supporting his opposition to the Wilmot Proviso. 5 August 1847. p.1, c5.

**3701 C. M. BURLEIGH** *to* **McKIM. 30 July 1847. Plainfield, Ct.** Reports a railroad accident near Oxford, Connecticut; comments on a man awaiting execution in Rhode Island; reflects on changed sentiments toward slavery in Canterbury, Connecticut. 5 August 1847. p.2, c5.

**3702 n.n.** *to* **n.n. [extract from the** ***Charter Oak*****] n.d. n.p.** Contrasts the pleasures of life by the sea with the misery of summer in the city. 12 August 1847. p.4, c1.

**3703 JOHN RANKIN** *to* **BRETHREN. [from the** ***National Era*****] n.d. n.p.** Denounces the decisions of both Presbyterian bodies in the United States to sustain slaveholders in their respective communions; urges anti-slavery Presbyterians to unite in the formation of a third faction. 19 August 1847. p.1, c5.

**3704 JAMES N. BUFFUM** *to* **n.n. [extract] n.d. n.p.** Reports on a meeting of the colored people of New Bedford to commemorate the emancipation of 800,000 slaves in the West Indies. 19 August 1847. p.3, c2.

**3705 n.n.** *to* **SIR. 9 August 1847. Harrisburg.** Reports on a meeting in Harrisburg where Frederick Douglass and William Lloyd Garrison were harassed by mobocrats. 19 August 1847. p.3, c2.

**3706 JOHN D. OLIN** *to* **n.n. n.d. n.p.** A member of the committee of arrangements for the recent reception of Frederick Douglass and William Lloyd Garrison praises the two men. 19 August 1847. p.3, c5.

**3707 ABBY HUTCHINSON** *to* **MRS. HOWITT. [from** ***Howitt's Journal*****] 5 May 1847. Plymouth.** Informs her friend in England of recent events affecting her celebrated family; hopes that she may soon visit them in America. 26 August 1847. p.3, c4.

**3708 n.n.** *to* **n.n. [from the** ***New York Tribune*****] n.d. Boston.** Announces plans for the publication of a new quarterly review which will be devoted to political matters, particularly the condemnation of the Mexican war. 26 August 1847. p.3, c5.

**3709 HOSEA BIGLOW** *to* **THE** ***BOSTON COURIER*****. n.d. n.p.** Encloses for publication a lengthy poem on the life of a soldier in the Mexican war, written by a volunteer from his town. 2 September 1847. p.1, c2.

**3710 BIRDOFREDOM SAWIN** *to* **n.n. [from the** ***Boston Courier*****] n.d. Saltillo.** A volunteer in the Mexican war sends home a poem contrasting the harsh realities of military life with his earlier fantasies of glory. 2 September 1847. p.1, c2.

**3711 ALBERT CULBERT** *to* **J. M. DAVIS, ESQ. 19 July 1847. Boston.** An escaped slave informs his former master of his new life in Boston, enclosing the bill of fare of the restaurant where he is currently employed. 2 September 1847. p.2, c5.

**3712 FREDERICK DOUGLASS** *to* **READERS. [from the** ***Ram's Horn*****] n.d. n.p.** Describes his current tour of western Pennsylvania, made in the company of William Lloyd Garrison. 2 September 1847. p.3, c2.

**3713 FREDERICK DOUGLASS** *to* **FRIEND. [from the** ***Ram's Horn*****] 20 August 1847. Austinburgh, Oh.** Gives further account of his western tour with William Lloyd Garrison, now progressing in Ohio. 9 September 1847. p.1, c1.

**3714 n.n.** *to* **MR. EDITOR. [from the** ***New York Sun*****] n.d. n.p.** Discusses outrages committed on the people of Mexico by American soldiers, particularly the violation of women, and the minor acts of courtesy officially demanded of the troops by their superiors. 9 September 1847. p.1, c3.

**3715 E. MORTIMER BYE** *to* **FRIEND. n.d. n.p.** Describes an anti-slavery meeting in Cecil County, Maryland, which was successful in spite of harassment of mobocrats. 9 September 1847. p.1, c5.

**3716 SIMMONS COATES** *to* **n.n. n.d. n.p.** Encloses a copy of the resolution of the latest anti-slavery meeting at Clarkson. 9 September 1847. p.2, c1.

**3717 HENRY C. WRIGHT** *to* **THE EDITOR OF THE** ***FREEMAN*****. 7 September 1847. Philadelphia.** Relates his ambivalent feelings upon his return to America after an absence of five years. 9 September 1847. p.2, c1.

**3718 n.n.** *to* **n.n. [extract from the** ***Christian Observer*****] n.d. n.p.** Recalls his visit to a Louisiana plantation where slaves were being educated for colonization; reflects on the awesome responsibility resting on the American nation and the church, having at hand the means to prepare the entire continent of Africa to receive the Christian religion. 9 September 1847. p.2, c3.

**3719 n.n.** *to* **THE** ***LOUISVILLE EXAMINER*****. [extract] n.d. Georgia.** Expresses the opinion that Kentucky, should she enact emancipation measures, would give impetus to Tennessee and western Georgia to do the same. 9 September 1847. p.3, c2.

**3720 n.n.** *to* **n.n. [extract] n.d. Jonesboro.** Speculates that if Kentucky were to abolish slavery, his state would follow suit. 9 September 1847. p.3, c2.

**3721 n.n.** *to* ***TENNESSEE EAST*****. [extract] n.d. Jefferson, N.C.** Reports widespread anti-slavery sentiment in North Carolina. 9 September 1847. p.3, c2.

**3722 n.n.** *to* **n.n. [from the** ***Sun*****] n.d. Carlisle.** Reports on the sentencing of the defendants in the case concerning the Carlisle riots. 9 September 1847. p.3, c2.

**3723 WM. L. ROY** *to* **n.n. [extract from the** ***True Wesleyan*****] n.d. n.p.** Discusses fugitive slaves who have settled in Canada. 9 September 1847. p.3, c3.

**3724 n.n.** *to* **n.n. [extract from the** ***Standard*****] n.d. Paris.** Reports growing abolitionist sentiments among the populace of France. 16 September 1847. p.1, c1.

**3725 n.n.** *to* **n.n. [extract from the** ***Standard*****] n.d. Paris.** Comments on efforts on the part of the governments of Sweden, Denmark, and Holland to liberate the slaves in their respective dominions. 16 September 1847. p.1, c1.

**3726 n.n.** *to* **n.n. [from the** *Standard*] **n.d. Paris.** Reports on a bill recently passed by the General Assembly of Wallachia, providing for the emancipation of 60,000 Bohemian serfs. 16 September 1847. p.1, c1.

**3727 J. I. ALEXANDER** *to* **n.n. [from the** *Michigan Signal of Liberty*] **21 August 1847. Niles, Berrien County, Michigan.** Recounts an unsuccessful attempt by a band of Kentuckians to capture and enslave a number of persons in Michigan. 16 September 1847. p.1, c2.

**3728 FREDERICK DOUGLASS** *to* **n.n. September 1847. Austinburgh, Oh.** Reports great progress in the anti-slavery cause in Ohio, where he is lecturing with William Lloyd Garrison, Stephen Foster, and others. 16 September 1847. p.1, c2.

**3729 J.** *to* **n.n. 6 September 1847. Salem, Oh.** Reports on the Ohio Yearly Meeting of Friends, recently held at Salem, at which William Lloyd Garrison, Frederick Douglass, and Stephen Foster were guests. 16 September 1847. p.2, c1.

**3730 n.n.** *to* **n.n. [extract from the** *Emancipator*] **n.d. n.p.** A lady in Virginia reports on a recent meeting of an undesignated presbytery in that state; remarks the neglect of religious instruction among slaves as well as white children. 16 September 1847. p.3, c1.

**3731 n.n.** *to* **n.n. [extract from the** *Emancipator*] **n.d. n.p.** The Virginia woman relates an episode to illustrate the slaves' fear of their masters. 16 September 1847. p.3, c1.

**3732 n.n.** *to* **n.n. [from the** *Tribune*] **4 September 1847. Hartford.** Calls for passage of a proposed amendment to the state constitution guaranteeing suffrage to all men in Connecticut regardless of color. 16 September 1847. p.3, c2.

**3733 HENRY C. WRIGHT** *to* **THE EDITORS OF THE** *PENNSYLVANIA FREEMAN.* **19 September 1847. Philadelphia.** Denounces Stephen H. Gloucester, pastor of the Central Presbyterian Church of color in Philadelphia, who is repudiating American abolitionism on his present tour of Scotland. 23 September 1847. p.2, c1.

**3734 n.n.** *to* **JAMES N. BUFFUM. [extract] 19 August 1847. Glasgow.** Denounces the Rev. Stephen H. Gloucester as "infinitely contemptible, and deserving of scorn from every honest man," for criticizing American abolitionists while in Scotland. 23 September 1847. p.2, c2.

**3735 E. F. PENNYPACKER** *to* **FRIEND. 20 September 1847. Schuylkill.** Reports on the recent meeting at Westchester, which examined the subjects of peace, war, and human brotherhood. 23 September 1847. p.2, c3.

**3736 n.n.** *to* **HENRY CLAY. [extract from the** *Boston Atlas*] **n.d. Boston.** A committee of Boston Whigs praises the "comprehensive intellect and warm heart" of Henry Clay. 23 September 1847. p.3, c2.

**3737 n.n.** *to* **HENRY CLAY. [extract from the** *Boston Atlas*] **n.d. Boston.** The committee of Boston Whigs expresses sorrow over the death of Henry Clay's son, who was killed in the war in Mexico. 23 September 1847. p.3, c2.

**3738 J. M. McKIM** *to* **n.n. 12 September 1847. Isabella Furnace.** Reports that he has recovered his health after a vacation in the country; rejoices in the return of H. C. Wright to America; criticizes an article in the *National Era* which favored the annexation of Mexico. 23 September 1847. p.3, c2.

**3739 A. J.** *to* **FRIEND MATTHEWS. [from the** *Cincinnati Herald***] 22 August 1847. Dayton.** Argues against the plan of Dr. Bailey, editor of the *National Era*, to annex the Mexican states. 23 September 1847. p.3, c3.

**3740 n.n.** *to* **MR. EDITOR. [from the** *Massachusetts Spy***] n.d. n.p.** Encourages Whigs to resist any attempt to annex conquered Mexican territory. 30 September 1847. p.1, c1.

**3741 WINFIELD SCOTT** *to* **HON. M. FILLMORE. [from the** *New York Tribune***] n.d. Headquarters of the Army.** Discusses the case of James Thompson, a man seeking dismissal from military duty on the grounds of conscience. 30 September 1847. p.1, c4.

**3742 JOHN O. WATTLES** *to* **THE EDITORS OF THE** *PENNSYLVANIA FREEMAN.* **n.d. n.p.** Refers to a community in Ohio founded upon the principles of universal brotherhood; expresses confidence in the ultimate triumph of the causes of temperance, anti-slavery, moral reform, and non-resistance. 30 September 1847. p.2, c2.

**3743 n.n.** *to* **n.n. [extract] n.d. n.p.** A Southerner who recently emancipated four of his slaves informs a friend in the North of the tense political climate in the South, where both parties favor General Taylor as a presidential candidate. 30 September 1847. p.2, c3.

**3744 MR. DAVIS** *to* **SIR THOMAS READE. 20 March 1846. Rufsa.** Reports to the consul general of the British government at Tunis of the success of measures adopted by the Bey of Tunis to abolish slavery in that country. 30 September 1847. p.2, c5.

**3745 SIR THOMAS READE** *to* **THE RIGHT HON. THE EARL OF ABERDEEN. 31 March 1846. Tunis.** Reports the success of the campaign of the Bey of Tunis to abolish slavery in his dominions. 30 September 1847. p.3, c1.

**3746 THE COLONEL [***sic***] COUNCIL OF GUADALOUPE** *to* **SIR [THE KING OF FRANCE]. [extract] n.d. n.p.** Appeals to the king to abolish slavery in the French colonies. 30 September 1847. p.3, c1.

**3747 n.n.** *to* **n.n. [from the** *National Era***] n.d. n.p.** Reports that the Rev. Mr. Todd stated, before a meeting of the American Board of Commissioners for Foreign Missions, that benevolence toward the heathen who groan under the superstitions of the Old World demands that American Christians "slide over" the sufferings of slaves in this land. 30 September 1847. p.3, c3.

**3748 HENRY WILLIAM HERBERT** *to* **THE EDITOR OF THE** *NEWARK DAILY ADVERTISER.* **6 September 1847. Newark, N. J.** Reports the death of a Negro woman who was hit by a train and expired, in his opinion, as a consequence of the negligence of the bystanders. 7 October 1847. p.1, c1.

**3749 L.** *to* **WM. LLOYD GARRISON. [from the** *Liberator***] 15 August 1847. Kirkaldy, Scotland.** Considers the election of George Thompson to Parliament a triumph of the principles of anti-slavery and peace; discusses Alexander Campbell and J. Henshall, two Virginians touring Scotland in support of American manstealers, and the steps being taken to warn the public against them. 7 October 1847. p.2, c2.

**3750 NO. IV** *to* **n.n. 28 September 1847. Boston.** Comments on the exhibition and fair of the Massachusetts Charitable Mechanic Association, which provides ample illustrations of the creative skill that can arise only in the context of free labor. 7 October 1847. p.3, c1.

**3751 n.n.** *to* **MR. WHITE. [extract from the** *National Intelligencer***] 10 September 1847. Puebla.** An American officer reports that General Scott's dispatches from the capital have been cut off, and that the country is filled with guerrillas. 7 October 1847. p.3, c3.

**3752 GEN. SCOTT** *to* **GEN. SANTA ANNA. [extract] 6 September 1847. Tacubaya.** Warns that if he does not answer certain allegations regarding violations of the armistice with the United States, said armistice shall be considered void as of noon the following day. 7 October 1847. p.3, c4.

**3753 ANTONIO LOPEZ DE SANTA ANNA** *to* **GEN. SCOTT. [extract] n.d. n.p.** Responds to the American general with counter-allegations of American violations of the present armistice; charges that General Scott's threats of renewed hostilities are due to Santa Anna's refusal to sign a treaty which would decrease Mexico's territory considerably. 7 October 1847. p.3, c4.

**3754 n.n.** *to* **n.n. [extract from the** ***Ledger*****] n.d. Washington.** Declares that the offers of peace made by the American government in its negotiations with Mexico are "historical monuments of our candor, moderation, and forebearance, and will justify our conduct with posterity." 14 October 1847. p.1, c1.

**3755 FREDERICK DOUGLASS** *to* **FRIEND. [from the** ***National Anti-Slavery Standard*****] 26 September 1847. West Winfield.** Relates news of his present speaking tour and facts surrounding the illness of William Lloyd Garrison. 14 October 1847. p.1, c3.

**3756 THOS. CORWIN** *to* **THE EDITOR OF THE** ***CINCINNATI ATLAS*****. 23 September 1847. Lebanon.** Clarifies remarks he made at the recent convention of the Whig Party in Ohio on the Wilmot Proviso; opposes any new annexation of territory to the United States, but maintains that the Wilmot Proviso must apply in the event that annexation occurs. 14 October 1847. p.1, c4.

**3757 n.n.** *to* **n.n. [from the** ***Lowell Courier*****] n.d. Charleston, S. C.** Describes his visit to a work house where slaves waited to be taken to market, and where he witnessed the flogging of an adolescent boy. 14 October 1847. p.1, c5.

**3758 n.n.** *to* **BROTHER LEE. [from the** ***Wesleyan*****] n.d. n.p.** Describes the savage beating of a female slave in Mississippi. 14 October 1847. p.1, c5.

**3759 THE COUNCIL OF GUADALOUPE** *to* **THE KING OF FRANCE. n.d. n.p.** Pleads for the abolition of slavery in the French colonies. 14 October 1847. p.2, c1.

**3760 HIRAM WILSON** *to* **n.n. [extract] n.d. n.p.** Announces that at least twenty fugitive slaves have passed safely into Canada in the past three days. 14 October 1847. p.3, c4.

**3761 n.n.** *to* **THE EDITOR OF THE** ***EXAMINER*****. [extract] n.d. n.p.** A native of Alabama expresses affection for the country and sorrow that he was compelled to leave by his moral objection to slavery. 21 October 1847. p.1, c1.

**3762 n.n.** *to* **THE EDITOR OF THE** ***EXAMINER*****. [extract] n.d. n.p.** A former resident of Alabama states his opinion that anti-slavery sentiment is more extensively felt among the Southern middle class than is commonly supposed. 21 October 1847. p.1, c1.

**3763 n.n.** *to* **THE EDITOR OF THE** ***EXAMINER*****. [extract] n.d. Western Virgina.** Expresses the opinion that an emancipation representative might be elected from his county and from surrounding counties, if someone would take the lead. 21 October 1847. p.1, c1.

**3764 n.n.** *to* **THE EDITOR OF THE** ***EXAMINER*****. [extract] n.d. n.p.** A Southerner praises the *Examiner* and calls for the abolition of American slavery. 21 October 1847. p.1, c1.

**3765 n.n.** *to* **THE EDITOR OF THE** ***EXAMINER*****. [extract] n.d. North Carolina.** Advocates the decentralization of power to abolish slavery and recommends that it be put into the hands of counties and townships. 21 October 1847. p.1, c2.

**3766 n.n.** *to* **THE EDITOR OF THE** ***EXAMINER*****. [extract] n.d. Maryland.** A Marylander praises the *Examiner*, but despairs of loosening the slaveholders' grip on the Southern states. 21 October 1847. p.1, c2.

**3767 n.n.** *to* **THE EDITOR OF THE** ***EXAMINER*****. [extract] n.d. Kentucky.** Issues a call to action to Kentuckians sympathetic to the cause of emancipation. 21 October 1847. p.1, c3.

**3768 ROBERT SEARS, ESQ.** *to* **n.n. [extract from a London monthly journal] n.d. New York.** Advocates the perpetual alliance of England and America in an agreement which would settle all disputes through arbitration, and unite both nations in a mission of benevolence toward the entire human race. 21 October 1847. p.2, c1.

**3769 JOSEPH A. DUGDALE** *to* **EDITORS. 10 October 1847. Clark County, Oh.** Reports that the anti-slavery cause in Ohio is gaining strength. 21 October 1847. p.2, c2.

**3770 S. W. P.** *to* **n.n. [from the** ***Syracuse Star*****] n.d. New York.** Comments on a Turkish gentleman who immigrated to America with his three wives, and the legal dilemma surrounding the division of property after his death. 21 October 1847. p.2, c5.

**3771 n.n.** *to* **THE** ***NEW YORK COURIER AND ENQUIRER*****. n.d. London.** Bemoans the election to Parliament of Mr. George Thompson, whom he considers "one of the most verbose and enthusiastic fanatics that ever lived." 21 October 1847. p.3, c2.

**3772 MAJOR LALLY** *to* **n.n. [extract] 11 September 1847. Jalapa, Mexico.** Reports robbery and wanton destruction committed by American forces in Mexico. 28 October 1847. p.1, c1.

**3773 DR. SNODGRASS** *to* **THE** ***NATIONAL ERA*****. [extract] n.d. n.p.** Reports the escape of a number of slaves owned by a member of the Maryland legislature, the subsequent accusations brought against two persons thought to have aided them, the beating of one of the accused (a slave), and the imprisonment of the other (a freeman). 28 October 1847. p.1, c3.

**3774 DR. SNODGRASS** *to* **THE** ***NATIONAL ERA*****. [extract] n.d. n.p.** Comments on the preachers he heard at the Yearly Meeting of Orthodox Friends in Baltimore, whose discourses he describes as tending toward "doctrinalism." 28 October 1847. p.2, c5.

**3775 n.n.** *to* **THE** ***NATIONAL ERA*****. [extract] n.d. Buffalo.** Discusses the statement of the Rev. Mr. Todd, made at the recent meeting of the American Board of Commissioners for Foreign Missions, that the sufferings of 3 million American slaves must be overlooked in favor of aiding the 150 million heathen who groan under oppressive superstitions of the Old World. 28 October 1847. p.3, c2.

**3776 n.n.** *to* **n.n. [extract] n.d. London.** Reports on anti-slavery movements abroad, discussing Mr. Scoble's tour of Holland, the likely prospect of the abolition of slavery in the French colonies, the partial abolition of slavery in the Dutch West Indies, and the increasing demand for slaves in Cuba and Brazil due to economic incentives from the British government for the products of their labor. 28 October 1847. p.3, c3.

**3777 T.** *to* **n.n. [from the** ***National Intelligencer*****] 15 October. n.p.** Praises the courage and integrity of Francisco Olaguibel, the governor of Mexico; denounces the American invasion of Mexico; predicts failure for the efforts of the United States to procure funds from the Mexicans to pay the expenses of the war. 4 November 1847. p.1, c1.

**3778 n.n.** *to* **n.n. [extract from the** ***New York Tribune*****] n.d. n.p.** A Southern statesman discusses the possibility of annexation of Mexican territory; argues against the propriety of a congressional act introducing slavery there. 4 November 1847. p.1, c4.

**3779 FIAT JUSTITIA** *to* **McKIM. n.d. n.p.** Criticizes an undesignated Philadelphia editor who had asserted that the United States "must *exact* and not *ask for* Peace" with Mexico. 4 November 1847. p.2, c2.

**3780 C. D. C.** *to* **n.n. [extract from the** ***New York Evangelist*****] n.d. n.p.** A woman writes of the rescue of her two daughters from slavery. 4 November 1847. p.2, c3.

**3781 n.n.** *to* **n.n. [extract from the** ***Christian Observer*****] n.d. n.p.** Condemns the actions of a woman who rescued her two daughters from slavery as "an outrage against the precepts of religion and the peace of society." 4 November 1847. p.2, c4.

**3782 n.n.** *to* **n.n. [extract from the** ***National Intelligencer*****] n.d. California.** An American soldier in California expresses disappointment at the extreme aridity of that land. 4 November 1847. p.3, c2.

**3783 n.n.** *to* **n.n. [extract from the** ***National Intelligencer*****] 4 September 1847. Buena Vista.** An American officer from Virginia writes of the barrenness of the Mexican land, concluding that such a country could never be "the fit abode of the Anglo Saxon race." 4 November 1847. p.3, c2.

**3784 HENRY C. WRIGHT** *to* **ELIZABETH PEASE. [extract] 18 October 1847. n.p.** Comments on William Lloyd Garrison's recuperation from a recent illness. 4 November 1847. p.3, c3.

**3785 n.n.** *to* **THE** ***LOUISVILLE EXAMINER*****. [extract] n.d. n.p.** Encloses statistics illustrating the decline of slavery in the western counties of Virginia, noting the strong sentiments in favor of freedom there. 4 November 1847. p.3, c4.

**3786 n.n.** *to* **THE** ***MOBILE DAILY ADVERTISER*****. [extract] n.d. Mexico.** Condemns the disgraceful conduct of American troops in Mexico, as illustrated by the recent murder of a Mexican for refusing to sell his daughter as a prostitute. 4 November 1847. p.3, c4.

**3787 J. SCOBLE** *to* **LEWIS TAPPAN. [extract from the** ***National Era*****] 4 October 1847. London.** Reports on the progress of the anti-slavery cause in Holland and France; rejoices in hearing that two provinces in India have abolished slavery. 11 November 1847. p.2, c4.

**3788 n.n.** *to* **THE** ***PENNSYLVANIA FREEMAN*****. [extract] n.d. Western Virginia.** Asks that the *Freeman* publish Dr. Ruffner's address to the people of western Virginia which advocated the gradual abolition of slavery. 18 November 1847. p.1, c5.

**3789 n.n.** *to* **THE EDITOR OF THE** ***UNION*****. [extract] n.d. n.p.** Proposes that a physician be appointed to journey to Mexico for the purpose of recording the medical and surgical knowledge that has been gained as a result of the recent military campaign. 18 November 1847. p.3, c1.

**3790 n.n.** *to* **n.n. [extract from the** ***Richmond Republican*****] n.d. Mexico.** An army surgeon describes the scene at his hospital in the aftermath of a battle. 18 November 1847. p.3, c1.

**3791 MR. KENDALL** *to* **n.n. [extract] n.d. Tacubaya.** Praises the conduct of Mr. McCarty, a chaplain in the American army. 18 November 1847. p.3, c1.

**3792 n.n.** *to* **n.n. [from the** *Journal of Commerce***] 5 November. Washington.** Discusses the likely impact of the New York election on the settlement of the Mexican war. 18 November 1847. p.3, c2.

**3793 RICHARD ALLEN** *to* **n.n. [extract from the** *Liberator***] n.d. Dublin.** Describes the reaction of the British House of Commons to the passage of a resolution outlawing the apprenticeship system in the West Indies colonies. 25 November 1847. p.1, c2.

**3794 n.n.** *to* **n.n. [from the** *New York Herald***] 30 October. Washington.** Discusses a law recently enacted in the District of Columbia requiring every free colored person to pay $1000 as security for his good behavior for one year. 25 November 1847. p.1, c3.

**3795 n.n.** *to* **SIR. [from the** *Boston Christian World***] n.d. Meadville, Pa.** Describes a lecture delivered by one Professor S. which compared the condition of the American slave favorably to that of the heathen in Siam. 25 November 1847. p.1, c3.

**3796 n.n.** *to* **n.n. [extract from the** *National Era***] n.d. Columbus, Oh.** Discusses the trial of a man in Ohio for harboring fugitive slaves, which will also involve the question of whether blacks and mulattoes may testify in court. 25 November 1847. p.1, c4.

**3797 J. S. PEACOCKE** *to* **n.n. [from the** *American Agriculturalist***] 27 July 1847. Belgrade, La.** Advises Southern farmers to become more self-sufficient by diversifying their crops and raising their own pork. 25 November 1847. p.2, c1.

**3798 LEWIS HAYDEN** *to* **THE** *NEW YORK TRIBUNE***. [extract] n.d. n.p.** A former slave of Henry Clay relates instances of his master's cruelty, refuting a *Tribune* correspondent's contention that Mr. Clay is a friend of the slave and advocate of emancipation. 25 November 1847. p.2, c5.

**3799 H. PASSY** *to* **THE PRESIDENT OF THE BRITISH AND FOREIGN AS. [extract] n.d. n.p.** The vice president of the French AS expresses sympathy with its allies in Britain, and reports that prospects are hopeful for the abolition of slavery in the French colonies in the near future. 2 December 1847. p.1, c1.

**3800 REV. B. T. KAVANAUGH** *to* **THE** *COLONIZATIONIST***. [extract] n.d. Kentucky.** Reports growing sentiments favorable to emancipation in Kentucky. 2 December 1847. p.1, c4.

**3801 n.n.** *to* **n.n. [extract from the** *Public Ledger***] n.d. Washington.** Defends Mr. Buchanan against charges that he is "behind the age" regarding his prosecution of the Mexican war. 2 December 1847. p.1, c5.

**3802 LIEUTENANT BELL** *to* **n.n. [extract] n.d. n.p.** The commander of the U. S. brig *Dolphin* comments on the practice of carrying slave cargoes under Brazilian colors, in vessels owned by Americans. 2 December 1847. p.2, c4.

**3803 SECRETARY BANCROFT** *to* **COMMODORE SLOAT. [extract] 12 July 1847. n.p.** Informs of the objective of the United States government "to possess itself entirely of Upper California." 2 December 1847. p.2, c5.

**3804 WASHINGTON CORRESPONDENT** *to* **THE** *BALTIMORE SUN***. n.d. Washington.** Comments on the progress of efforts to introduce a uniform system of cheap postage in the United States. 2 December 1847. p.3, c2.

**3805 THE REV. C. H. A. DALL** *to* **n.n. [extract from the** ***Liberator*****] n.d. n.p.** Estimates that there are hundreds of schools which present opportunities for instruction among the slaves and free colored people of the South. 9 December 1847. p.1, c1.

**3806 n.n.** *to* **THE** ***NATIONAL ERA*****. [extract] n.d. Baltimore.** Considers the success of a petition for freedom presented before the Baltimore County Court an indication that slavery's hold on public sentiment in Maryland is weakening. 9 December 1847. p.1, c2.

**3807 PEACE AND LIBERTY** *to* **THE EDITORS OF THE** ***FREEMAN*****. n.d. n.p.** Criticizes them for their reprobation toward Henry Clay. 9 December 1847. p.1, c4.

**3808 n.n.** *to* **n.n. [extract from the** ***Tribune*** **at Syracuse] n.d. Syracuse.** Discusses sermons preached in three churches in Syracuse on Thanksgiving Day, all of which spoke boldly on the evils of the Mexican war, slavery, and intemperance. 9 December 1847. p.3, c2.

**3809 G. B. STEBBINS** *to* **FRIEND GAY. [extract from the** ***National Anti-Slavery Standard*****] 8 November 1847. Rochester, N.Y.** An agent of the AAS, having been in the field for three years, welcomes the increased readiness of the people to hear the doctrines of the abolitionists. 9 December 1847. p.3, c4.

**3810 n.n.** *to* **n.n. [extract] 5 December 1847. Mount Holly, N.J.** Reports on a recent meeting in Mount Holly to take measures to protect the colored citizens of New Jersey. 9 December 1847. p.3, c4.

**3811 FREDERICK DOUGLASS** *to* **HENRY CLAY. [extract from the** ***North Star*****] n.d. n.p.** Comments on Mr. Clay's late speech at Lexington, appealing to the senator to emancipate his slaves. 16 December 1847. p.1, c1.

**3812 n.n.** *to* **n.n. [extract from the** ***Tribune*****] n.d. Hayti.** Comments on the many admirable and social qualities of the people of Haiti, and the shameful prejudice which has prevented the United States from officially recognizing that republic. 16 December 1847. p.3, c1.

**3813 H.** *to* **THE EDITORS OF THE** ***PENNSYLVANIA FREEMAN*****. 13 December 1847. Philadelphia.** Notes the Southern tendency to increase the production of cotton without any corresponding addition to the demand for it; predicts the eventual bankruptcy of the South and Southwest. 16 December 1847. p.3, c2.

**3814 ARNOLD BUFFUM** *to* **n.n. [extract from the** ***National Anti-Slavery Standard*****] n.d. n.p.** Reports that his assertion before the World's Anti-Slavery Convention that there were no colored members of the Society of Friends in Philadelphia was upheld, despite objections by Isaac Collins. 23 December 1847. p.1, c4.

**3815 n.n.** *to* **n.n. [extract from the** ***Louisville Examiner*****] n.d. n.p.** Compliments Henry Clay's recent speech at Lexington. 23 December 1847. p.1, c5.

**3816 n.n.** *to* **n.n. [from the** ***Commercial Advertiser*****] n.d. London.** Comments on the late Dr. Andrew Combe, noted British physician and author. 23 December 1847. p.4, c2.

**3817 G. W. J.** *to* **FRIEND ROBINSON. [from the** ***Pioneer*** **and** ***Herald of Freedom*****] 20 October 1847. Schuylerville.** Suggests quick-lime as a preventive for potato rot. 23 December 1847. p.4, c3.

**3818 J. W.** *to* **MESSRS. EDITORS. 10 December 1847. Lower Merion Township.** Urges the advocates of emancipation to exercise a charitable forbearance toward all who disagree with them. 30 December 1847. p.1, c3.

**3819 HENRY BOWMAN** *to* **THE** ***PENNSYLVANIA FREEMAN*****. 22 December 1847. Byberry.** Reports on the controversy surrounding a colored child's attempt to matriculate at a public school in Byberry County. 30 December 1847. p.1, c4.

**3820 HENRY GREW** *to* **FRIENDS. n.d. n.p.** Criticizes the *Freeman*'s opposition to "schemes for giving the slaves the Bible," and comments on the appropriateness of such an action. 30 December 1847. p.2, c1.

**3821 n.n.** *to* **n.n. [extract] n.d. Delaware.** Reports efforts to improve the state of colored persons in Delaware, and growing sentiments favorable to emancipation in that region. 30 December 1847. p.2, c2.

**3822 ALLAN AGNEW** *to* **H. C. WRIGHT. [extract from the** ***Liberator*****] 20 November 1847. Pennsbury, Delaware.** Describes the debate at a meeting of the local Sons of Temperance over admission of colored men to their organization. 30 December 1847. p.2, c4.

**3823 JOSHUA L. FUSSELL** *to* **H. C. WRIGHT. [extract from the** ***Liberator*****] 21 November 1847. Hamorton, Pa.** Discusses the exclusion of a colored man from membership in a Pennsylvania chapter of the Order of the Sons of Temperance. 30 December 1847. p.2, c4.

**3824 JOHN G. PALFREY** *to* **R. C. WINTHROP. 5 December 1847. Washington.** Questions Winthrop, a Whig candidate for Speaker of the House, concerning his position on the Mexican war, the extension of slavery in United States territories, and the right of slaves to trial by jury. 30 December 1847. p.3, c1.

**3825 ROBERT C. WINTHROP** *to* **HON. J. G. PALFREY. 5 December 1847. Washington.** Responds to Palfrey's inquiry, stating that as a candidate for the position of Speaker of the House, he feels it inappropriate to answer such specific questions, or to pledge himself to any particular line of action. 30 December 1847. p.3, c1.

## [1848]

**3826 J. E. SNODGRASS** *to* **THE** ***PENNSYLVANIA FREEMAN*****. 26 December 1847. Baltimore.** Encloses for publication an article on the trial of Robert Gover, accused of circulating incendiary publications in Maryland. 6 January 1848. p.1, c1.

**3827 CASSIUS M. CLAY** *to* **THE SUBSCRIBERS OF THE** ***TRUE AMERICAN*****. 18 December 1847. Lexington, Ky.** Announces that the *True American* has ceased to exist, being succeeded by the *Examiner*; expresses faith in the progress of mankind, anticipating the day when all Americans shall be free. 6 January 1848. p.2, c4.

**3828 RICHARD MENDENHALL** *to* **THE** ***NATIONAL ERA*****. [extract] 30 October 1847. Indian Territory.** Reports on a slaveholding missionary establishment among the Indians of the Northwest Territory. 6 January 1848. p.2, c5.

**3829 n.n.** *to* **n.n. [extract from the** ***Tribune*****] n.d. Washington.** Notes that Mr. Holmes of South Carolina retired from the House of Representatives on the last ballot for Speaker, thus permitting the election of Mr. Winthrop of Massachusetts; characterizes the procedure as an act of "high-minded courtesy" on the part of Mr. Holmes and his state. 6 January 1848. p.3, c1.

**3830 n.n.** *to* **n.n. 16 December. Richmond, Va.** A resident of Maine visiting Virginia reflects on the difference in manners and customs between the two states, a painful illustration of which is found in the slave auctions. 6 January 1848. p.3, c3.

**3831 LEGGETT** *to* **n.n. [extract] October 1838. n.p.** Cites the swift tide of anti-monopoly reform in New York state in the previous three years, confidently predicting the triumph of the abolitionist cause in the years ahead. 13 January 1848. p.2, c1.

**3832 RUSSELL JARVIS** *to* **THE EDITORS OF THE** ***PENNSYLVANIA FREEMAN*****. 11 January 1848. Philadelphia.** Announces a course of lectures against the extension of slavery to the new states and territories, and comments upon the causes which have served to enlarge the institution to its present scope. 13 January 1848. p.2, c1.

**3833 JOHN O. WATTLES** *to* **BROTHER. [extract from the** ***Cincinnati Herald*****] n.d. n.p.** Comments on the great flood in Clermont County, Ohio, in which the Community House was swept away, and seventeen lives were lost in the ruins. 13 January 1848. p.3, c4.

**3834 CAPTAIN TOBIN** *to* **THE** ***NEW ORLEANS DELTA*****. [extract] n.d. n.p.** Muses over the possibility of a premature close to the Mexican war, in which case he is at a loss to say how he and his fellow soldiers would make a living. 13 January 1848. p.4, c3.

**3835 MR. BOOTH** *to* **THE** ***CHARTER OAK*****. [extract] n.d. n.p.** A Liberty Party lecturer describes a portion of his late tour through Connecticut, where he found a large number of churches opposed to the cause of the slave. 20 January 1848. p.1, c4.

**3836 n.n.** *to* **n.n. [extract from the** ***Tribune*****] n.d. n.p.** A traveller in the South relates some scenes from his experience of slavery there, expresses his disdain for the institution, and lauds the Wilmot Proviso. 20 January 1848. p.1, c4.

**3837 n.n.** *to* **n.n. [extract from the** ***Tribune*****] n.d. n.p.** Recounts the flogging of a marine on board a United States ship, the action allegedly taking place more than a fortnight after the man's enlistment had expired. 20 January 1848. p.1, c5.

**3838 HON. JOSHUA R. GIDDINGS** *to* **THE** ***CLEVELAND HERALD*****. [extract] n.d. n.p.** Explains that his vote against Mr. Winthrop for Speaker of the House of Representatives was based on the latter's support for the Mexican war. 20 January 1848. p.1, c5.

**3839 n.n.** *to* **n.n. [from the** ***Picayune*****] 9 December 1847. Vera Cruz.** A soldier in Mexico states his opinion that the worst of the Mexican war is yet to come, and that it will require a longer time and a larger army to secure the land for the United States. 20 January 1848. p.1, c5.

**3840 n.n.** *to* **n.n. [from the** ***Tribune*****] n.d. Baltimore.** Reports great enthusiasm among the Whigs of Baltimore, occasioned by the visit of Henry Clay. 20 January 1848. p.3, c1.

**3841 FREDERICK DOUGLASS** *to* **n.n. [extract from** ***Howitt's Journal*****] n.d. n.p.** Acknowledges a gift of books and pictures from some friends in England. 20 January 1848. p.3, c2.

**3842 EDWARD EVERETT** *to* **THE ITALIAN DEMONSTRATION MEETING, NEW YORK. [extract] n.d. n.p.** Asserts the imperative of a free nation to provide inspiration to other peoples through the exhibition of public virtue. 20 January 1848. p.4, c3.

**3843 MR. HULL** *to* **n.n. [extract from the** ***Ohio Clarion of Freedom*****] n.d. Morgantown, Va.** The editor of the *Ohio Clarion of Freedom*, travelling in Virginia, reports that slavery is the dominant topic of discussion in the area, being utilized even by schoolboys in their forensic disputations. 27 January 1848. p.1, c4.

**3844 MR. HULL** *to* **n.n. [extract from the** *Ohio Clarion of Freedom***] 20 December 1847. Knottsville, Va.** The editor of the *Clarion* reports on an unsuccessful attempt to silence him in Virginia, a subsequent debate between himself and a pro-slavery man, and a lengthy sermon in which the author preached abolitionism before a crowded congregation. 27 January 1848. p.1, c4.

**3845 n.n.** *to* **n.n. [extract from the** *Christian Watchman***] n.d. [Kentucky].** Reports growing strength for the cause of emancipation in Kentucky. 27 January 1848. p.1, c5.

**3846 MR. CROOKS** *to* **n.n. [extract from the** *True Wesleyan***] n.d. North Carolina.** Reports progress for the cause of anti-slavery in North Carolina to the degree that some predict the state would side with the North in the event of a dissolution of the Union. 27 January 1848. p.2, c3.

**3847 n.n.** *to* **n.n. [extract from the** *Albany Atlas***] n.d. Cortlandville.** Rejoices in the unanimous vote of a local meeting in favor of a resolution opposing the further extension of slavery. 27 January 1848. p.3, c1.

**3848 HORACE WELLS** *to* **THE EDITOR OF THE** ***JOURNAL OF COMMERCE*****. n.d. New York.** An eminent dentist and pioneer in the use of ether, who is jailed in New York for assaulting two females by throwing vitriol on their dresses, recounts the exact circumstances surrounding the event and confesses his derangement resulting from the excessive use of ether. 27 January 1848. p.3, c4.

**3849 HORACE WELLS** *to* **THE EDITOR OF THE** ***JOURNAL OF COMMERCE*****. Saturday Evening. New York.** Expresses his anguish at the recent events which have labeled him a villain, and his increasing derangement from the use of ether; reveals his intention to take his own life. 27 January 1848. p.3, c5.

**3850 HORACE WELLS** *to* **EDITORS. n.d. New York.** Requests that those who shall report his suicide do so in a manner considerate of his family. 27 January 1848. p.3, c5.

**3851 HORACE WELLS** *to* **WIFE. n.d. New York.** At the precipice of an act of suicide, the author bids his wife farewell. 27 January 1848. p.3, c5.

**3852 HORACE WELLS** *to* **MR. DWIER. n.d. New York.** On the verge of suicide, the author gives instructions regarding his burial and the manner in which his wife is to be informed of the fact. 27 January 1848. p.3, c5.

**3853 HORACE WELLS** *to* **MESSRS. DWIER AND BARBER. n.d. New York.** The writer, anticipating death by his own hand, requests that Mr. T. W. Storrow, of Paris, be informed of the incident. 27 January 1848. p.3, c5.

**3854 A COLORED CITIZEN** *to* **THE** ***LIBERATOR*****. [extract] n.d. n.p.** Assails a plan of some colored citizens of Boston to form a separate AS. 3 February 1848. p.2, c5.

**3855 JOHN McLEAN** *to* **SIR. [from the** *Cincinnati Gazette***] 7 January 1848. Washington.** Calls upon Congress to take a strong initiative in ending the Mexican war. 3 February 1848. p.2, c5.

**3856 n.n.** *to* **n.n. [extract from the** *Christian Watchman***] n.d. Washington.** Reports that opposition to slavery in Texas has become widespread, causing some to believe that it may soon become a free state. 3 February 1848. p.3, c1.

**3857 HENRY CLAY** *to* **MR. H. R. ROBINSON. 24 December 1847. Ashland, Ky.** Acknowledges the gift of a lithographic print depicting the Battle of Buena Vista. 3 February 1848. p.3, c2.

**3858 n.n.** *to* **n.n. [extract from the** *Ledger***] n.d. Washington.** Predicts defeat for the "Ten Regiment Bill" in the House of Representatives. 3 February 1848. p.3, c3.

**3859 n.n.** *to* **n.n. [extract from the** *Portland Advertiser***] n.d. Fryeburg, Me.** Comments on the cold weather in Fryeburg, on one day ranging from thirty-six to thirty-nine degrees below zero. 3 February 1848. p.4, c3.

**3860 n.n.** *to* **n.n. [extract] 11 January 1848. Franconia, N.H.** Reports Franconia's coldest day on record, with the mercury frozen in the thermometer at thirty-nine degrees below zero. 3 February 1848. p.4, c3.

**3861 POPE PIUS IX** *to* **THE EMPEROR OF AUSTRIA. [extract] n.d. n.p.** Acknowledges the emperor's superior strength in men and arms, and states that his own strength lies in public opinion and the assurance of moral right. 10 February 1848. p.1, c3.

**3862 n.n.** *to* **n.n. [extract from the** *Charlestown Courier***] n.d. Washington.** Praises the Speaker of the House of Representatives, Mr. Winthrop, for his behavior towards Southern congressmen and his late assignment of certain abolitionists to committees where they will not deal directly with the issue of slavery. 10 February 1848. p.1, c4.

**3863 n.n.** *to* **n.n. [extract from the** *Ledger***] n.d. New York.** Reports that two Democratic Party organizations in New York, the General Committee and the Young Men's General Committee, have lately voted to sustain the Wilmot Proviso. 10 February 1848. p.1, c4.

**3864 HENRY GREW** *to* **MESSRS. EDITORS. n.d. n.p.** Discusses the value of personal narratives in the battle against slavery, the need for the American nation to open its eyes to its own guilt, and the inappropriateness of a slave's committing either suicide or murder in order to escape his bonds. 10 February 1848. p.2, c1.

**3865 ROBT. PURVIS** *to* **MESSRS. EDITORS. 7 February 1847 [sic]. Byberry.** Reports on the case of two teachers accused of assaulting students in the Byberry public school system; states that although the teachers were not indicted by the grand jury, a school law in question throughout the case will likely be challenged in the Supreme Court. 10 February 1848. p.2, c2.

**3866 JOHN G. FEE** *to* **THE** *NATIONAL ERA***. [extract] n.d. n.p.** Reports a revolution in public sentiment, upon returning from a lecture tour in Ohio, and appeals to all good men to work diligently for the cause of freedom. 10 February 1848. p.3, c1.

**3867 CASSIUS M. CLAY** *to* **THE EDITORS OF THE** *CHRISTIAN REFLECTOR***. 14 January 1848. Lexington, Ky.** Defends the principles that prompted him to volunteer for military service in the Mexican war. 10 February 1848. p.3, c3.

**3868 C. D. JACKSON, M.D.** *to* **THE** *BOSTON ATLAS***. [extract] n.d. Boston.** Considers the desirability of chloroform as a substitute for ether in surgical operations. 10 February 1848. p.4, c2.

**3869 G. G. L.** *to* **n.n. [extract from the** *Boston Atlas***] n.d. Paris.** A sketch of the character and residence of Alexandre Dumas, the popular French author who is a mulatto. 17 February 1848. p.1, c5.

3870 **ALEXANDRE DUMAS** *to* **HON. J. C. C. 1 April 1847. Paris.** Writes to an eminent American statesman John C. Calhoun, expressing his desire to visit America, the apprehensions of his friends who say his African blood would subject him to inconveniences there, his disbelief of these assertions, and his desire for a clarification of the matter by the statesman he addresses. [The *Freeman* labels this a "fancied correspondence."] 17 February 1848. p.1, c5.

3871 **J. C. C.** *to* **ALEXANDRE DUMAS. 1 August 1847. Charlestown.** Fictional response to the correspondence of Dumas, in which the American statesman John C. Calhoun confirms the allegation that Dumas's genius would afford him no protection from abuse in the slave states of the Union; characterizes slavery as an institution favorable to civilization and ordained by Divine Providence. 17 February 1848. p.2, c1.

3872 **A BALTIMORE CLERGYMAN** *to* **THE** *NATIONAL ERA*. **[extract] n.d. n.p.** Transcribes a portion of a Thanksgiving sermon denouncing the institution of slavery. 17 February 1848. p.2, c2.

3873 **n.n.** *to* **n.n. [extract from the** *National Era*] **n.d. London.** Supplies information concerning the slave trade in the Sahara Desert. 17 February 1848. p.2, c2.

3874 **VISCOUNT GODERICH** *to* **n.n. [extract] 5 November 1831. n.p.** The British colonial secretary, writing three years before West Indian emancipation, refers to the severe commercial distress of that society, the source of which he perceives to be the institution of slavery. 17 February 1848. p.2, c4.

3875 **S. W. W.** *to* **n.n. [from the** *Liberator*] **5 February 1848. Providence, R.I.** Reports that an act providing for the protection of fugitive slaves has passed both houses of the Rhode Island legislature. 17 February 1848. p.3, c1.

3876 **CALEB ATKINSON** *to* **FRIEND McKIM. December 1847. Medford Township.** An aged friend of the anti-slavery cause reports that he has persuaded another person to subscribe to the *Freeman*. 17 February 1848. p.3, c4.

3877 **n.n.** *to* **SIR. [from the** *Tribune*] **15 January 1848. Washington.** Introduces an extract from a letter by Col. William Grayson, then a Southern member of Congress, in which the latter speaks of the political reasons for the South's agreement to the banning of slavery in Ohio, Michigan, Iowa, Illinois, and Wisconsin. 24 February 1848. p.1, c5.

3878 **COL. WILLIAM GRAYSON** *to* **n.n. [extract] 8 August 1787. New York.** A Southern member of Congress states that the reason he and his Southern colleagues accepted the provision excluding slavery in the territory northwest of the Ohio River was the desire to prevent tobacco and indigo from being grown in that area. 24 February 1848. p.1, c5.

3879 **n.n.** *to* **n.n. [extract from the** *National Era*] **3 February 1848. n.p.** A Democratic member of Congress from New York reports a growing spirit favorable to emancipation among members of his party, likely to be reflected at the upcoming state convention. 24 February 1848. p.1, c5.

3880 **CHARITY** *to* **THE EDITORIAL COMMITTEE. n.d. n.p.** Criticizes the *Freeman* for what the author considers undue harshness in its treatment of Henry Clay, referring specifically to an article of 27 January. 24 February 1848. p.2, c1.

3881 **n.n.** *to* **n.n. [from the** *Ohio True Democrat*] **24 January. Washington.** Illustrates the cruelty of slavery in the District of Columbia by recounting an incident involving Joshua Giddings and a colored man seeking his aid. 24 February 1848. p.3, c2.

**3882 GEN. ZACHARY TAYLOR** *to* **GEN. R. JONES. [from the** *Public Ledger***] 28 July 1839. Fort Brooke.** Comments on the subject of procuring bloodhounds to aid the army in ascertaining the whereabouts of Indian parties in Florida. 24 February 1848. p.3, c3.

**3883 S. H. DE K.** *to* **LIZZ. [from the** *Rochester Advertiser***] 25 November 1847. Lake Cottage.** A young woman, blind and widowed, reflects on the transitory nature of human existence and the enduring love of God. 24 February 1848. p.4, c1.

**3884 A TEXAN** *to* **n.n. [from the** *Tribune***] n.d. n.p.** Disputes the assertion made in a recent speech by General Houston that the government of Texas maintained authority over the strip of land lying between the Neuces and the Rio Grande from the time of its declaration of independence. 24 February 1848. p.4, c3.

**3885 DEMOCRITUS** *to* **THE EDITOR OF THE** *MORNING HERALD***. 10 February 1848. Washington.** Reports on the senatorial debate over the "Ten Regiment Bill." 2 March 1848. p.1, c1.

**3886 J. S. GREEN** *to* **n.n. [from the** *American Missionary***] May 1847. n.p.** Comments on polygamy, and asserts that the practice is not to be tolerated by Christian missionaries. 2 March 1848. p.1, c2.

**3887 MICAH 6:8** *to* **THE** *CHRISTIAN CITIZEN***. [extract] 31 December 1847. n.p.** Criticizes an article in the *Vermont Chronicle* by one who denounced Mr. J. G. Palfrey as a Sabbath-breaker for having written a letter on Sunday. 2 March 1848. p.1, c3.

**3888 LOUISA CATHERINE ADAMS** *to* **HON. ROBERT C. WINTHROP. 29 February 1848. Washington.** Expresses gratitude for the resolutions of the House of Representatives honoring her deceased husband. 9 March 1848. p.1, c4.

**3889 n.n.** *to* **n.n. [extract from the** *Examiner***] n.d. Warren County.** A man in Kentucky expresses his desire to bring up his children in such a way that they value labor, and laments the impossibility of doing so in a slave state. 9 March 1848. p.1, c5.

**3890 n.n.** *to* **THE** *EXAMINER***. n.d. Kentucky.** A native South Carolinian praises the anti-slavery stance taken by the *Examiner*; speaks of Arkansas, whose natural resources he judges shall be of little use until slavery is abolished. 9 March 1848. p.3, c1.

**3891 n.n.** *to* **THE** *EXAMINER***. [extract] n.d. n.p.** Expresses his desire to see a society in Kentucky organized for the purpose of distributing tracts and articles addressed to the issue of slavery. 9 March 1848. p.3, c1.

**3892 n.n.** *to* **n.n. [from the** *Ledger***] 7 March. Washington.** Reports that a treaty with Mexico is approaching ratification in the Senate. 9 March 1848. p.3, c3.

**3893 JESSE WALTON** *to* **MR. EASTMAN. [from the** *Western Citizen***] 28 December 1847. Alton, Il.** A native Georgian offers a picture of the effects of slavery on both the servant and the master, drawn from his personal experience. 16 March 1848. p.1, c2.

**3894 D. L. DIX** *to* **MRS. WHEAT, MRS. RUTLEDGE, MRS. WASHINGTON, AND OTHER LADIES WHOSE NAMES ARE ATTACHED TO A COMMUNICATION RECEIVED THROUGH MRS. WHEAT. 27 January 1847. Nashville.** Expresses gratitude to ladies of Nashville who, as a token of their respect, had asked her to sit for her bust. 16 March 1848. p.1, c3.

**3895 n.n.** *to* **n.n. [extract from the** *Charleston Evening News*] **n.d. Washington.** Comments on the fictional correspondence between Alexandre Dumas and John C. Calhoun recently published in the *Boston Atlas*, which the author considers to have been in poor taste. 16 March 1848. p.1, c3.

**3896 M.** *to* **THE** *NEW ORLEANS COMMERCIAL TIMES*. **13 February. Mexico.** States the terms of the peace treaty lately signed by representatives of the governments of Mexico and the United States. 16 March 1848. p.1, c5.

**3897 n.n.** *to* **THE** *EXAMINER*. **[extract] n.d. n.p.** Praises the anti-slavery sentiments of the *Examiner* and exhorts the friends of emancipation to work for its increased circulation. 16 March 1848. p.1, c5.

**3898 D. W. MARVIN** *to* **MR. MORRIS. [extract from the** *True Wesleyan*] **10 January 1848. n.p.** Discusses the discrepancy between the popular religion of the age and true biblical Christianity, illustrated by the Church's various alliances with slaveholders. 16 March 1848. p.2, c1.

**3899 J. F. L.** *to* **n.n. [from the** *Christian Citizen*] **23 February. Harveysburg, Oh.** Comments on the expulsion from an academy in Harveysburg of a young woman with a trace of African blood in her lineage, effected at the command of an Orthodox Quaker superintendent. 16 March 1848. p.2, c1.

**3900 n.n.** *to* **n.n. [extract from the** *Massachusetts Spy*] **6 March 1848. Baltimore.** Reports on a lecture by C. M. Clay before the Mercantile Library Association of Baltimore, concerning the subjects of Mexico and American slavery. 23 March 1848. p.1, c4.

**3901 n.n.** *to* **n.n. [extract from the** *Liberty Standard*] **n.d. New York.** A faculty member of a theological seminary in New York indicates increased anti-slavery sentiments in every entering class; cites an improvement in the condition of the black population in the South and expresses faith in a coming day of universal emancipation. 23 March 1848. p.2, c4.

**3902 DR. SNODGRASS** *to* **THE** *NATIONAL ERA*. **[extract] n.d. Dover, De.** Informs of the action which prevented him from delivering an anti-slavery lecture in Dover, and its ironic consequence of rousing the citizens of that community to earnest inquiry and debate. 23 March 1848. p.2, c5.

**3903 n.n.** *to* **n.n. [extract from the** *Christian Citizen*] **n.d. n.p.** Discusses oaths of office, which many persons consider a grave problem; maintains that "A form of words is nothing in itself, and imposes no moral obligation, other than the intended and understood meaning." 30 March 1848. p.3, c1.

**3904 HAMPDEN** *to* **THE EDITOR OF THE** *ALBANY PATRIOT*. **19 February 1848. Washington City.** Comments on the venerable widow of President James Madison and her design to sell certain slaves in her possession for the purpose of alleviating a dubious penury. 6 April 1848. p.1, c4.

**3905 WILLIAM JAY** *to* **MR. MOSES PIERCE. [from the** *Liberty Press*] **9 October 1847. Bedford.** Upholds the duty of abolitionists to use all lawful means necessary to prevent the capture of fugitive slaves. 6 April 1848. p.1, c5.

**3906 n.n.** *to* **n.n. [extract from the** *National Era*] **n.d. South Hadley, Ma.** States the rationale for the early nomination of a presidential candidate by the Liberty Party at its convention in Buffalo the previous fall. 6 April 1848. p.3, c2.

**3907 n.n.** *to* **n.n. [extract from the** *National Era*] **n.d. South Hadley, Ma.** Urges members of the Liberty Party to reconsider their policy favoring an early presidential nomination, believing this course of action to be a disastrous mistake. 6 April 1848. p.3, c2.

**3908 D. W. B.** *to* **THE** *CHRISTIAN CITIZEN.* **[extract] n.d. n.p.** Reports on the Free Trade Meeting lately held in Manchester, England; on a proposal of General Narvaez, the Spanish Minister of State, to reduce his country's armed forces; on a speech of Mr. Sheil in the British Parliament, favoring total benefits of citizenship for Jews; and on the efforts of the grand duke of Tuscany to grant greater freedom to the press. 6 April 1848. p.3, c3.

**3909 A LADY IN VIRGINIA** *to* **THE** *EMANCIPATOR.* **[extract] n.d. Virginia.** Reports the increased sale of slaves in Virginia due to the overstocking of plantations and the depletion of the soil; notes the irony of protracted religious revivals among the state's slaveholders. 13 April 1848. p.2, c4.

**3910 DR. SNODGRASS** *to* **n.n. [extract from the** *National Era*] **n.d. n.p.** Illustrates the difference in the results of free and slave labor by contrasting two farms with which he is familiar, one in Pennsylvania and the other in Virginia. 13 April 1848. p.2, c5.

**3911 n.n.** *to* **n.n. [extract from the** *Columbia Daily Telegraph*] **n.d. South Carolina.** Contrasts the economic condition of South Carolina with that of the Northern states, concluding that the latter's inferiority results from a lack of exertion; calls upon his fellow South Carolinians to industrialize. 20 April 1848. p.2, c2.

**3912 FREDERICK DOUGLASS** *to* **THE** *NORTH STAR.* **[extract] n.d. Steuben County, N.Y.** Comments on an encounter with a pro-slavery Methodist minister. 20 April 1848. p.3, c1.

**3913 HENRY WATSON** *to* **MR. GARRISON. [from the** *Liberator*] **28 February 1848. Westerly, R.I.** A fugitive slave reports on his activities in Rhode Island, which have included some fifty lectures in the course of two months. 20 April 1848. p.3, c2.

**3914 C. M. CLAY** *to* **HON. HENRY CLAY. 13 April 1848. New York.** Severely criticizes Henry Clay for putting himself forward for the Whig nomination for the presidency. 20 April 1848. p.3, c4.

**3915 HORACE MANN** *to* **n.n. [extract] n.d. n.p.** Accepts the nomination of his party for the congressional seat lately held by John Quincy Adams; discusses the impending annexation of Mexican territory and the importance of preserving for all men their inalienable rights. 27 April 1848. p.1, c4.

**3916 n.n.** *to* **THE** *CINCINNATI HERALD.* **[extract] n.d. Washington.** Rejoices in the unexpected action of Judge Wick of Indiana, who lately gave notice of a bill to prohibit the importation of slaves into the District of Columbia. 27 April 1848. p.1, c5.

**3917 MARY B. THOMAS** *to* **FRIEND. 19 April 1848. Downington.** Describes the kidnapping of a colored girl who was residing in her household. 27 April 1848. p.3, c2.

**3918 MARY B. THOMAS** *to* **n.n. [extract] n.d. n.p.** Expresses her deep sorrow over the recent kidnapping of Martha, a colored girl living with the Thomas family. 27 April 1848. p.3, c3.

**3919 I. S. F.** *to* **FRIEND. 16 April 1848. Wilmington, De.** Discusses a recent meeting of sympathizers with the French revolution, held in Wilmington, which provided the author with evidence of increased knowledge of and support for the cause of freedom among the people of Delaware. 4 May 1848. p.2, c2.

**3920 A CONSTANT READER OF YOUR VALUABLE PAPER *to* FRIENDS. 20 April 1848. Phenixville.** Accuses the *Freeman* of an undue prejudice against C. M. Clay, and an unmerited bias in favor of Henry Clay, both of which were reflected in an editorial preface to a letter of the former gentleman to the latter which appeared in the last issue. 4 May 1848. p.2, c3.

**3921 CONSISTENCY *to* MESSRS. EDITORS. n.d. n.p.** Comments upon the slogan, "No Union with Slaveholders," as professed by the Annual Meeting in New York, and proposes a conditional clause preserving commercial union; this, he maintains, would be a more accurate reflection of the popular attitude. 4 May 1848. p.2, c3.

**3922 n.n. *to* n.n. n.d. n.p.** Comments on Stephen N. Taylor, a young man forced to flee his native Virginia for circulating anti-slavery publications. 4 May 1848. p.2, c5.

**3923 n.n. *to* THE *TRIBUNE*. 1 April 1848. London.** Predicts that the revolutionary spirit which recently dissolved the monarchy in France will spread to Ireland and Great Britain. 4 May 1848. p.3, c4.

**3924 C. M. BURLEIGH *to* THE *FREEMAN*. 9 May 1848. New York.** Reports on the late anniversary meeting in New York, which included speeches by Theodore Parker, Lucretia Mott, Wendell Phillips, and Frederick Douglass. 11 May 1848. p.3, c1.

**3925 JOHN I. SLINGERLAND *to* FRIEND WEED. [from the *Albany Evening Journal*] 22 April. Washington.** Describes the scene at a railroad station where a number of slaves are being readied for transport. 11 May 1848. p.3, c1.

**3926 n.n. *to* THE *NATIONAL ERA*. [extract] n.d. Louisville.** Reports on a speech by one Mr. Thurston, who strongly denounced the institution of slavery and met with a sympathetic response. 11 May 1848. p.3, c3.

**3927 WILLIAM BAILEY COATES *to* THE *PENNSYLVANIA FREEMAN*. 8 April 1848. Chester Springs.** Discusses Mr. Green, a missionary in the Sandwich Islands, and his departure from the American Board of Commissioners for Foreign Missions. 11 May 1848. p.3, c5.

**3928 n.n. *to* n.n. [extract from the *North Star*] n.d. Oberlin.** Informs of a prosperous school for colored persons at Oberlin. 18 May 1848. p.1, c3.

**3929 H. B. *to* THE *TRIBUNE*. 17 April 1848. Paris.** Discusses the provisional government of France, and how it survived a general demonstration by workmen in Paris. 18 May 1848. p.1, c3.

**3930 n.n. *to* THE *TRIBUNE*. 18 April 1848. Paris.** Observes a new sense of security in Paris as a result of the triumph of the provisional government over the workmen's demonstration earlier in the week; informs that transactions in the money market with America are very low; reports socialist tendencies within the new government. 18 May 1848. p.1, c4.

**3931 R. W. H. *to* THE *FREEMAN*. n.d. n.p.** Comments on the recent message of President Polk to the Congress, in which he put forth the possibility of the annexation of Yucatan by the United States. 18 May 1848. p.1, c5.

**3932 J. G. PALFREY *to* DR. BAILEY. [from the *National Era*] 8 May 1848. Washington.** Encloses for publication an open letter to the signers of petitions forwarded to Palfrey. 25 May 1848. p.1, c2.

**3933 JOHN G. PALFREY** *to* **THE SIGNERS OF PETITIONS FORWARDED TO THE SUBSCRIBER, FOR PRESENTATION IN THE HOUSE OF REPRESENTATIVES. [from the** ***National Era*****] 8 May 1848. n.p.** States that most of the petitions he has received since January remain in his hands, and explains the rules and orders of the House which have engendered this situation. 25 May 1848. p.1, c2.

**3934 FERDINAND MENDEZ PINTO** *to* **THE** ***NEW YORK EVENING MIRROR*****. n.d. Paris.** Satirizes the American position that one can be a good republican and a slaveholder simultaneously, in this fictional letter purportedly written from the scene of the recent revolution in France. 25 May 1848. p.2, c4.

**3935 JOSEPH A. DUGDALE** *to* **JOSHUA R. GIDDINGS AND JOHN P. HALE. 14 March 1848. Green Plains, Clark County, Oh.** Writes on behalf of a number of citizens in Clark County, Ohio, expressing praise and gratitude for the moral courage displayed by the two men in their outspoken opposition to the Mexican war. 25 May 1848. p.3, c2.

**3936 JOHN I. SLINGERLAND** *to* **THE** ***ALBANY EVENING JOURNAL*****. [extract] n.d. n.p.** Describes the scene at a railway depot where slaves are being prepared for transport. 25 May 1848. p.3, c3.

**3937 JOHN I. SLINGERLAND** *to* **REV. HENRY SLICER. [from the** ***Tribune*****] 10 May 1848. Washington.** Chastizes the chaplain of the United States Senate for his friendly conduct toward a notorious slave-dealer in Washington. 25 May 1848. p.3, c3.

**3938 n.n.** *to* **THE** ***CHRISTIAN CITIZEN*****. [extract] n.d. n.p.** Responds to the *Freeman*'s remarks on a prior letter about the propriety of members of the League of Universal Brotherhood taking oaths of office; maintains that oaths should be abolished, but allows that one is justified in voting for a man who would take an oath to support the Constitution "under the express promise, publicly given, that he would disregard it." 1 June 1848. p.2, c3.

**3939 n.n.** *to* **THE** ***COMMERCIAL ADVERTISER*****. [extract] n.d. Pittsburgh.** Discusses petitions from Southern Methodists to the General Conference meeting in Pittsburgh requesting the protection of that body in the aftermath of a Southern secession; notes the awkward position in which the General Conference is thus placed with regard to the issue of slavery. 1 June 1848. p.2, c4.

**3940 FREDERICK DOUGLASS** *to* **THE** ***NORTH STAR*****. 25 March. Penn Yan.** Reports on a series of anti-slavery meetings in Penn Yan, led by himself and Messrs. Hathaway and Remond; comments that the Rev. Silas Hawley, pastor of the local Congregational church, had circulated prejudicial reports against them prior to their arrival. 1 June 1848. p.3, c2.

**3941 n.n.** *to* **THE** ***NEW YORK HERALD*****. [extract] n.d. Washington.** Criticizes Levi Woodbury's recent proposal, which would prevent legislation banning slavery from a given United States territory prior to its admission as a state. 1 June 1848. p.3, c2.

**3942 GEO. W. CLARK** *to* **n.n. [extract from the** ***Albany Patriot*****] 29 March 1848. Victor.** Comments on the case of Samuel R. Ward, a colored man whose controversial admission to the Sons of Temperance in Cortlandville occasioned the dissolution of that local chapter. 8 June 1848. p.3, c3.

**3943 SAMUEL R. WARD** *to* **GEO. W. CLARK. 20 March 1848. Cortlandville.** Provides information pertinent to his admission to a division of the Sons of Temperance in Cortlandville and the conflict engendered by the act. 8 June 1848. p.3, c3.

**3944 S. P. CHASE** *to* **THE** *CINCINNATI GAZETTE.* **n.d. n.p.** Calls attention to a proposal made by Thomas Jefferson in 1784 to exclude slavery from all territory thereafter ceded to the United States. 15 June 1848. p.1, c5.

**3945 n.n.** *to* **THE** *NEW YORK EVENING POST.* **[extract] n.d. n.p.** Declares that the anti-slavery cause is making notable progress in the Southern states, as is evidenced by the opinions on the subject expressed by certain public officials and newspaper editors. 22 June 1848. p.1, c3.

**3946 JAMES M. PENDLETON** *to* **THE** *LOUISVILLE EXAMINER.* **[extract] n.d. Bowling Green, Ky.** Asserts that the vast majority of Southern Christians admit that the force of Christianity will ultimately abolish slavery, inferring the impossibility of a rational appeal to the New Testament in support of the institution. 22 June 1848. p.1, c4.

**3947 HON. E. S. HAMLIN** *to* **THE** *CLEVELAND TRUE DEMOCRAT.* **n.d. n.p.** Recounts a railway journey during which he sat next to Frederick Douglass, for whom he offers high praise. 22 June 1848. p.2, c1.

**3948 n.n.** *to* **n.n. [extract from the** *National Intelligencer***] 21 May 1847. City of Mexico.** Reports the ratification of the proposed American peace treaty by the Mexican Chamber of Deputies. 22 June 1848. p.3, c2.

**3949 JOHN MITCHEL** *to* **n.n. [extract from the** *United Irishman***] n.d. n.p.** Denounces the monarchy and institutions of Great Britain—"from the topmost crown jewel to the meanest detective's notebook"—and calls for the establishment of an Irish Republic. 22 June 1848. p.3, c3.

**3950 n.n.** *to* **THE** *LOUISVILLE EXAMINER.* **[extract] n.d. n.p.** Reports a growing sentiment favorable to emancipation in Kentucky. 22 June 1848. p.3, c4.

**3951 JOSEPH A. DUGDALE** *to* **THE** *FREEMAN.* **11 June 1848. Selma, Clark County, Oh.** Reacts against the pro-slavery intolerance of the Indiana Yearly Friends Meeting, announcing that he and a proscribed group of dissidents are planning their own yearly meeting to be held at Green Plain. 22 June 1848. p.3, c4.

**3952 n.n.** *to* **THE** *NATIONAL INTELLIGENCER.* **[extract] 8 May 1848. Franklin, N.C.** A government agent forwards anecdotes about the coercive removal of the Cherokee Indians from their homes in the Allegheny Mountains. 22 June 1848. p.4, c2.

**3953 W. H. BARNWELL** *to* **THE REV. AND HON. J. G. PALFREY, M.C. n.d. Charleston.** Criticizes Palfrey's alignment with the abolitionist cause as ill conceived; discusses the question of whether a federal anti-slavery law would be constitutionally binding on the Southern states; considers the possibility of the federal government purchasing the freedom of American slaves; cites Mr. Palfrey's hypocrisy with reference to racial equality. 29 June 1848. p.1, c1.

**3954 n.n.** *to* **THE** *TRIBUNE.* **[extract] n.d. Baltimore.** Reports that Hope H. Slatter, the noted Baltimore slave-dealer, has abandoned his business and closed his slave prison. 29 June 1848. p.2, c3.

**3955 n.n.** *to* **THE** *TRIBUNE.* **[extract] n.d. Baltimore.** Discusses the case of Stephen Redden, found guilty of possessing anti-slavery pictures by a Maryland court, and the 1835 statute under which he was convicted. 29 June 1848. p.2, c5.

**3956 C. M. BURLEIGH** *to* **THE** ***FREEMAN*****. 26 June 1848. Worcester, Ma.** Expresses dismay over the recent nominating conventions of the major political parties; praises the "Barnburners" and the *New York Daily Globe*; reports on prominent Whig newspapers in New England whose editors are opposed to the nomination of Taylor; reports on a speech by Charles Allen, a Whig who opposed Taylor's nomination at the party's convention; reports on a ratification meeting held in Worcester to endorse the nomination of Taylor, which displayed little support for the candidate. 6 July 1848. p.2, c3.

**3957 C. M. BURLEIGH** *to* **THE** ***FREEMAN*****. 28 June 1848. Worcester, Ma.** Reports on a "people's convention" in Worcester, comprised mainly of anti-Taylor Whigs. 6 July 1848. p.2, c4.

**3958 n.n.** *to* **THE** ***NATIONAL INTELLIGENCER*****. 20 April 1848. Dahlonega, Ga.** Comments on the working gold mines of Georgia. 6 July 1848. p.4, c1.

**3959 SIMON BARNARD** *to* **THE EDITOR OF THE** ***PENNSYLVANIA FREEMAN*****. 6 July 1848. Chester County, Pa.** Denounces the Rev. W. H. Barnwell of South Carolina, and his contention that slavery is an "experiment for the improvement of the African race"; encloses for publication an address on the subject of slavery issued by the Sadsbury Monthly Meeting of the Society of Friends. 13 July 1848. p.2, c2.

**3960 ALPHA** *to* **THE** ***FREEMAN*****. 12 June 1848. n.p.** Recounts an escaped slave's portrayal of his life in captivity. 13 July 1848. p.2, c3.

**3961 JOHN G. PALFREY** *to* **HON. CHARLES ALLEN, HON. HENRY WILSON, AND CHARLES SUMNER, ESQ., COMMITTEE OF INVITATION, &C. 24 June 1848. U.S. House of Representatives.** Regrets that he cannot attend the upcoming convention at Worcester, expressing his unhappiness with the actions of the late Whig national convention. 13 July 1848. p.3, c1.

**3962 n.n.** *to* **THE** ***TRIBUNE*****. n.d. n.p.** Expresses his indignation at a recent incident on a train, where a young colored gentleman was turned out of a car. 13 July 1848. p.3, c3.

**3963 n.n.** *to* **THE** ***ROCHESTER AMERICAN*****. n.d. Augusta, Ga.** Discusses Frank Shadwick, who in the course of fifteen years has purchased from slavery himself, his wife, and several children; Shadwick is held in high esteem in Augusta, and has recently departed for Pennsylvania in order that his children might enjoy a lawful education. 13 July 1848. p.3, c3.

**3964 LEWIS CASS** *to* **A. O. P. NICHOLSON, ESQ. 24 December 1847. Washington.** States his reasons for opposing the Wilmot Proviso. 20 July 1848. p.1, c4.

**3965 JESSE CHICKERING** *to* **FREEMAN HUNT, ESQ. [from the** ***Globe*****] 4 July 1848. Boston.** Cites various statistical data, concluding the inevitability of emancipation due to the steadily increasing political power of the free states. 20 July 1848. p.1, c5.

**3966 G. S. D.** *to* **FRIENDS. n.d. n.p.** Proclaims that the granting of suffrage to citizens on the basis of sex or color constitutes "taxation without representation" and is thus contrary to the true principles of republican government. 20 July 1848. p.2, c3.

**3967 HON. DAVID WILMOT** *to* **n.n. [extract] n.d. n.p.** Pledges his support to the presidential campaign of Van Buren. 20 July 1848. p.3, c1.

**3968 B.** *to* **THE** ***TRIBUNE*****. 12 July 1848. Washington.** Encloses for publication a letter from Mr. Trist, an American diplomat at the peace negotiations in Mexico, to Mr. Buchanan, the secretary of state. 20 July 1848. p.3, c1.

**3969 MR. TRIST** *to* **MR. BUCHANAN. [extract] 4 September 1847. n.p.** An American delegate to the peace negotiations with Mexico informs the secretary of state of the revulsion of the Mexican commissioners at the prospect of the introduction of slavery into any territory ceded to the United States, and of his assurances to them that this would not be the case. 20 July 1848. p.3, c1.

**3970 ISAAC S. FLINT** *to* **FRIEND. 16 July 1848. Wilmington.** Remarks that Fanny Lee Townsend, a lecturer of the National Reform movement, has been maligning certain prominent abolitionists on a tour through Delaware. 20 July 1848. p.3, c1.

**3971 n.n.** *to* **THE** *NEW YORK COURIER AND ENQUIRER*. **n.d. London.** Provides biographical data on Louis Napoleon, pretender to the throne of France. 20 July 1848. p.4, c2.

**3972 THE ANAK OF THE CLAPHAM COMMON SCHOOL** *to* **MISS BUXTON. 14 February 1834. Devonshire Street.** Describes a luncheon with the "eminent Jew," Mr. Rothschild. 20 July 1848. p.4, c2.

**3973 HENRY RUFFNER** *to* **THE EDITORS OF THE** *EXAMINER*. **n.d. n.p.** Expresses his happiness over the gradual shift in the popular sentiment of Kentucky which favors the eventual emancipation of slaves; pronounces slavery an anomaly in a free country; looks with confidence to the ultimate triumph of the cause of liberty. 27 Juy 1848. p.1, c3.

**3974 n.n.** *to* **THE** *NEW YORK COURIER*. **n.d. n.p.** Reports on the current popularity of Cavaignac among the people of France, and on a movement to name him president of the Republic. 27 July 1848. p.1, c5.

**3975 JAMES MOTT** *to* **FRIEND. 2 July 1848. Auburn.** Relates his interviews with colored citizens residing in Canada and finds that their condition is good and that most are comfortable and content. 27 July 1848. p.3, c3.

**3976** *CINCINNATI HERALD to* **GENERAL TAYLOR. n.d. n.p.** Asks if Taylor opposes the use of the executive veto or other measures to restrict slavery. 27 July 1848. p.3, c4.

**3977 C. M. BURLEIGH** *to* **THE** *FREEMAN*. **29 July 1848. East Douglas.** Expresses disappointment at continued ill health, and looks forward to death as an end to his pain and suffering. 6 August 1848. p.2, c2.

**3978 JURIST** *to* **THE** *EVENING BULLETIN*. **29 July 1848. Washington.** Discusses a fugitive slave case in Washington, in which the defense rests upon the admission that the defendant assisted slaves to escape but did not engage in theft. 6 August 1848. p.3, c4.

**3979 JACOB LYBRAND** *to* **MESSRS. EDITORS. 17 July 1848. Monroe, Wi.** Urges an anti-slavery constitutional amendment. 10 August 1848. p.1, c4.

**3980 A. C. C. THOMPSON** *to* **THE** *DELAWARE REPUBLICAN*. **n.d. Wilmington, De.** Attempts to discredit the narrative by Frederick Douglass, claiming Douglass was too ignorant to write such a narrative; accuses Northern rhetoric of hardening the South; opposes slavery but defends the integrity of slaveholders. 10 August 1848. p.2, c2.

**3981 FREDERICK DOUGLASS** *to* **THE EDITOR OF THE** *LIBERATOR*. **27 January 1846. Perth (Scotland).** Assails A. C. C. Thompson's attack on his narrative as cruel, murderous, infernal, and full of myths about the equity of the institution of slavery. 10 August 1848. p.2, c3.

**3982 CORRESPONDENT** *to* **THE** ***TRIBUNE*****. 5 August 1848. Washington, D.C.** Cites the Drayton case as establishing the precedent that helping slaves escape constitutes theft; comments on the slow progress of proceedings against Drayton. 10 August 1848. p.3, c2.

**3983 C. ELLET, JR.** *to* **n.n. [extract from the** ***Baltimore American*****] 29 July 1848. Niagara Falls.** States that he designed the bridge over Niagara River and describes his fear and excitement upon being the first person to ride in a buggy across it. 10 August 1848. p.4, c3.

**3984 CORRESPONDENT** *to* **THE** ***EVENING BULLETIN*****. 12 August 1848. Washington.** Transcribes the Senate debate on the Oregon Bill and an unsuccessful attempt to extend provisions of the Ordinance of 1787. 24 August 1848. p.1, c1.

**3985 JUDGE McLEAN** *to* **JAMES A. BRIGGS. 28 July 1848. Columbus.** Believes the free states can prevent the extension of slavery by utilizing the principles of the Constitution and the judiciary. 24 August 1848. p.2, c5.

**3986 G. F. HORTON** *to* **FRIEND. 10 August 1848. Terrytown, Pa.** Distrusts Free-Soilers as compromisers; praises the abolitionists and believes that the country needs them now more than ever. 24 August 1848. p.3, c1.

**3987 G. B.** *to* **MESSRS. EDITORS. n.d. n.p.** Mourns the death of a colored girl, Harriet Shadd, who was an outstanding student and a self-reliant young woman. 24 August 1848. p.3, c3.

**3988 n.n.** *to* **n.n. [extract] n.d. Eldridge's Hill, N.J.** Rejoices that the North is standing firm against slavery; repudiates the story that many escaped slaves are returning voluntarily to slavery. 31 August 1848. p.2, c5.

**3989 ZACHARY TAYLOR** *to* **GEORGE LIPPARD, ESQ. 24 July 1848. Baton Rouge, La.** Asserts that he is not a "party" candidate, and that if elected president, he will be the president of all the people. 31 August 1848. p.3, c2.

**3990 Z. TAYLOR** *to* **n.n. [extract] n.d. n.p.** Affirms his desire to be president of the whole nation, not a president of one party or section. 31 August 1848. p.3, c2.

**3991 EPHRAIM WILCOX** *to* **MR. BOOTH. 20 July 1848. Salem, Racine County.** Relates an attempt to kidnap two colored men and expresses thanks that the community protected them and sent the kidnappers to jail. 31 August 1848. p.3, c4.

**3992 JAMES HANWAY** *to* **MESSRS. EDITORS. n.d. n.p.** Praises a colored school in which the Randolph Negroes are enrolled, noting that their education and ability are equal to that of white children. 31 August 1848. p.3, c4.

**3993 JOHN P. HALE** *to* **HON. S. LEWIS. [extract] n.d. n.p.** Withdraws his candidacy for the presidency and urges support for Van Buren. 7 September 1848. p.3, c2.

**3994 LEWIS CASS** *to* **R. S. WILSON. [from the** ***True Democrat*****] 19 February 1847. Washington.** Opposes the Wilmot Proviso as harmful to prosecution of war efforts and hostile to the president and Southern interests. 7 September 1848. p.3, c5.

**3995 CALHOUN** *to* **THE** ***CHARLESTON MERCURY*****. [extract] 1 September 1848. n.p.** Takes no position on the presidential race, seeing "much to condemn and little to approve" in either candidate. 14 September 1848. p.3, c1.

**3996 JOHN GAYLE** *to* **C. C. LANGDON, ESQ. [from the** ***Mobile Daily Advertiser*****] 30 August 1848. Mobile.** Encloses letter in which Fillmore addresses Southern claim that he is an abolitionist. 14 September 1848. p.3, c3.

**3997 MILLARD FILLMORE** *to* **HON. JOHN GAYLE. 30 July 1848. Albany, N.Y.** Explains his view that slavery is an evil but that the national government has no jurisdiction over it since it is the province of the individual states. 14 September 1848. p.3, c3.

**3998 FREDERICK DOUGLASS** *to* **MY OLD MASTER. [from the** ***North Star*****] n.d. n.p.** Explains that his motives for running away were based on his belief that all men are equal and slavery negates that truth. 21 September 1848. p.1, c1.

**3999 LEWIS CASS** *to* **A. O. P. NICHOLSON, ESQ. 24 December 1847. Washington.** Opposes exerting congressional influence over either the extension or prohibition of slavery in the territories; advocates popular sovereignty. 21 September 1848. p.2, c1.

**4000 GRACE GREENWOOD** *to SATURDAY EVENING POST.* **[extract] n.d. n.p.** Believes that outmoded clothing has prevented many women from receiving proper exercise; favors reform in this area. 21 September 1848. p.4, c2.

**4001 SAMUEL M. JANNEY** *to* **THE** *LOUDON WHIG.* **8 September 1848. Springdale, Loudon County, Va.** Declines the Free-Soil nomination for office; supports the party's opposition to the extension of slavery as a degrading institution. 28 September 1848. p.1, c1.

**4002 SAMUEL WILLISTON** *to* **REV. R. ANDERSON, D.D. 12 September 1848. Easthampton.** Relays report on ownership of slaves among "Christianized" Cherokee and Choctaw Indians, urging the Church to disassociate itself from slavery. 28 September 1848. p.2, c2.

**4003 C. F. ADAMS** *to* **n.n. [extract from the** ***Boston Republican*****] n.d. n.p.** Explains his reasons for supporting the presidential candidacy of Martin Van Buren and his reasons for not doing so in the last election. 28 September 1848. p.3, c4.

**4004 n.n.** *to* **n.n. [extract from a New York paper] n.d. Paris.** Reports that a Negro colonel is in command of "the largest and finest battalion of Garde Mobile" in the French army. 28 September 1848. p.3, c4.

**4005 CORRESPONDENT** *to* **THE** *LOUISVILLE COURIER.* **[extract] n.d. Frankfort.** Predicts that the issue of gradual emancipation will be the key topic at the proposed constitutional convention in Kentucky. 5 October 1848. p.1, c4.

**4006 REV. JOHN G. FEE** *to* **THE** *NATIONAL ERA.* **[extract] n.d. Kentucky.** Advocates publication of anti-slavery tracts in an inexpensive form for gratuitous circulation throughout the South. 12 October 1848. p.3, c2.

**4007 C. C.** *to* **THE EDITORS OF THE** *PENNSYLVANIA FREEMAN.* **28 September 1848. n.p.** Defends his proposal which would encourage emancipation by means of pecuniary compensation to the slaveholder. 12 October 1848. p.3, c4.

**4008 FREDERICK DOUGLASS** *to* **H. G. WARNER, ESQ. [from the** ***North Star*****] n.d. n.p.** Denounces Warner for opposing the admission of Douglass's daughter to a girls' school in Rochester. 19 October 1848. p.1, c1.

**4009 HAMPDEN** *to* **PRESTON KING. [from the** ***Daily Globe*****] 25 August 1848. Washington.** Details facts concerning the case of the schooner *Pearl*, whose officers are in jail pending an appeal; provides illustrations of slavery in the District of Columbia. 19 October 1848. p.1, c2.

**4010 D. D. TAPPAN** *to* **MESSRS. EDITORS. 12 September 1848. North Marshfield.** Encloses for publication a resolution of certain members of the Trinitarian Congregational Church in North Marshfield, stating that they will not knowingly vote for any slaveholder or abettor of slavery. 19 October 1848. p.1, c5.

**4011 ZACHARY TAYLOR** *to* **THE SECRETARY OF STATE. [extract] n.d. n.p.** Writes in the course of the Florida Indian campaign, expressing his unwillingness to deprive the Indians of their Negro slaves. 19 October 1848. p.2, c5.

**4012 CORRESPONDENT** *to* **THE** ***NEW YORK RECORDER*****. [extract] n.d. Baltimore.** Reports that the people of Baltimore are becoming increasingly anxious to arrest the extension of slavery. 19 October 1848. p.2, c5.

**4013 n.n.** *to* **SIR. [from the** ***Ohio Standard*****] 4 August 1847. New Orleans.** Transmits a copy of the deed of sale of a plantation and slaves by John Hagard to Zachary Taylor. 19 October 1848. p.3, c1.

**4014 HARRISON GRAY OTIS** *to* **n.n. [extract] n.d. n.p.** An enemy of the cause of emancipation sketches the progress of abolitionists in Boston. 19 October 1848. p.3, c3.

**4015 CORRESPONDENT** *to* **THE** ***BUFFALO ADVERTISER*****. 2 October 1848. Niagara Falls.** Provides an account of a man who went to his death over Niagara Falls. 19 October 1848. p.4, c2.

**4016 n.n.** *to* **MESSRS. EDITORS. n.d. n.p.** Encloses for publication an extract of a letter from Boston assessing the merits of the Free-Soil Party. 26 October 1848. p.2, c1.

**4017 n.n.** *to* **n.n. [extract] n.d. Boston.** Discusses the merits and defects of the Free-Soil Party. 26 October 1848. p.2, c1.

**4018 MARTIN VAN BUREN** *to* **THE UTICA CONVENTION. [extract] n.d. n.p.** Justifies his past actions which served to sustain slavery in the United States. 26 October 1848. p.2, c5.

**4019 GERRIT SMITH** *to* **THE EDITOR OF THE** ***RAM'S HORN*****. 2 October 1848. Peterboro'.** Explains why he cannot in good conscience vote for Martin Van Buren. 26 October 1848. p.3, c3.

**4020 JOSHUA DUNGAN** *to* **THE** ***PENNSYLVANIA FREEMAN*****. n.d. n.p.** Argues in support of his position, recently the object of the *Freeman*'s editorial derision, which favors the presidential candidacy of Zachary Taylor. 2 November 1848. p.2, c1.

**4021 GERRIT SMITH** *to* **THE** ***MODEL WORKER*****. [extract] n.d. n.p.** States that his hope for good effects from the Free-Soil movement has diminished due to the wide range of abolitionists who are drawn to it. 2 November 1848. p.2, c5.

**4022 WILLIAM SLADE** *to* **MR. GIDDINGS. [extract] n.d. n.p.** Criticizes the Whig Party for its nomination of Zachary Taylor. 2 November 1848. p.3, c2.

**4023 BENJ. STANTON, ON BEHALF OF THE INDIANA YEARLY MEETING OF ANTI-SLAVERY FRIENDS** *to* **THE GENERAL CONFERENCE OF THE WESLEYAN METHODIST CONNECTION OF AMERICA. [extract] n.d. Indiana.** Comments on the importance of boycotting the products of slavery. 2 November 1848. p.3, c2.

**4024 DANIEL WORTH, ON BEHALF OF THE GENERAL CONFERENCE OF THE WESLEYAN METHODIST CONNECTION OF AMERICA** *to* **THE INDIANA YEARLY MEETING OF ANTI-SLAVERY FRIENDS. [extract] 4 October 1848. New York City.** Acknowledges the inconsistency of opposing slavery and purchasing products of slave labor. 2 November 1848. p.3, c3.

**4025 n.n.** *to* **n.n. 26 October 1848. Towanda.** Refutes an article in the *North American* claiming that Mr. David Wilmot had compromised his position on slavery. 2 November 1848. p.3, c3.

**4026 ENOCH PRICE** *to* **EDMUND QUINCY, ESQ. 10 January 1848. St. Louis.** Comments on the *Narrative of William W. Brown*, written by his former slave; offers free papers to Brown for the sum of $325. 2 November 1848. p.3, c4.

**4027 A PROMINENT ORTHODOX FRIEND** *to* **FRIEND. 30 October 1848. n.p.** States that he is appalled by the number of Quakers who intend to vote for General Taylor. 9 November 1848. p.1, c1.

**4028 JAMES BUCHANAN, SECRETARY OF STATE** *to* **SAMUEL H. HEMPSTEAD, U.S. ATTORNEY FOR THE DISTRICT OF ARKANSAS. 30 August 1848. Washington.** Warns that certain American citizens are believed to be preparing a military expedition into Mexico, thus violating the recent treaty signed by the two governments. 9 November 1848. p.1, c2.

**4029 DAVID PLUMB** *to* **THE** *MODEL WORKER*. **[extract] 31 October 1848. Troy.** Reports on a Free-Soil meeting lately held in Troy, at which John Van Buren welcomed the Liberty Party's abandonment of fanatical measures for effecting emancipation. 9 November 1848. p.1, c5.

**4030 HANNAH L. STICKNEY** *to* **THE EDITORS OF THE** *FREEMAN*. **n.d. Philadelphia.** Encloses for publication a circular stating the principles of the Industrial Group of the Philadelphia Union. 9 November 1848. p.2, c1.

**4031 THOMAS BORTON** *to* **FRIENDS. [extract] n.d. n.p.** Relates the events surrounding the death of his wife. 9 November 1848. p.2, c2.

**4032 JOHN M'CLEAN** *to* **CHARLES H. MORSE, ESQ. 26 October 1848. Cincinnati.** States that he is compelled to refrain from any active effort regarding the current presidential contest; declares that the American government can be preserved only by rousing the moral energies of the people and prompting them to political action. 9 November 1848. p.3, c1.

**4033 DAVID WILMOT** *to* **WM. ELDER. [from the** *Daily Republic***] 30 October 1848. Towanda.** Denies that he has endorsed the presidential candidacy of General Cass; affirms his support for Van Buren. 9 November 1848. p.3, c3.

**4034 CORRESPONDENT** *to* **THE** *[DETROIT] TRIBUNE*. **n.d. n.p.** Reports widespread disgust in the Northwest with the spirit of the Northern subservience prevalent in Washington. 16 November 1848. p.1, c3.

**4035 JOHN C. CALHOUN** *to* **n.n. [extract] n.d. n.p.** Expresses his feeling that the current presidential election affords no hope for arresting the abolitionist cause. 16 November 1848. p.1, c5.

**4036 J. E. SNODGRASS** *to* **THE EDITOR OF THE** *FREEMAN*. **13 November 1848. Baltimore.** Confirms a report that Mr. Hope H. Slatter has officially retired from the slave trade, though he has evidenced no change of heart in the matter. 16 November 1848. p.2, c1.

**4037 GEORGE P. DAVIS** *to* **THE** *FREEMAN*. **[extract] n.d. n.p.** Reports on a speech of Thaddeus Stevens at a Whig meeting in Kennett, characterizing it as "one of the best abolition speeches I ever heard, bating the miserable daubing he gave it of Taylorism." 16 November 1848. p.2, c2.

**4038 CORRESPONDENT** *to* **THE** *NEW YORK JOURNAL OF COMMERCE*. **[extract] n.d. Washington.** Reports that Thaddeus Stevens is pledged to introduce a bill in the next session of Congress which would abolish slavery in the District of Columbia. 16 November 1848. p.3, c1.

**4039 n.n.** *to* **n.n. n.d. n.p.** Reports on the Baltimore Yearly Meeting of the Society of Friends, where considerable sympathy for the slave was evidenced. 16 November 1848. p.3, c3.

**4040 DE GRASSE AND RAY** *to* **THE EDITOR OF THE** ***TRIBUNE*****. 30 October 1848. New York.** Express indignation at their exclusion from publicly advertised university lectures on the basis of color. 16 November 1848. p.3, c5.

**4041 AMERICAN OFFICER IN THE PACIFIC SQUADRON** *to* **n.n. [extract from the** ***Buffalo Courier*****] n.d. n.p.** Relates his experience in hunting seals. 16 November 1848. p.4, c3.

**4042 n.n.** *to* **n.n. [extract from the** ***Boston Chronotype*****] n.d. n.p.** Relates an incident at a slave auction in New Orleans. 23 November 1848. p.1, c4.

**4043 CORRESPONDENT** *to* **THE** ***CONCORD DEMOCRAT AND FREEDMAN*****. n.d. Georgia.** Describes whipping of Negroes for gambling on the Sabbath; comments upon the detrimental effects of slavery in Georgia and Florida. 23 November 1848. p.1, c3.

**4044 CORRESPONDENT** *to* **THE** ***INDEPENDENT DEMOCRAT*****. n.d. Atlanta, Ga.** Describes the scene of a Georgia slave market. 23 November 1848. p.2, c1.

**4045 n.n.** *to* **n.n. [extract] n.d. Indiana.** Derides Quakers who support the presidential candidacy of General Taylor. 23 November 1848. p.2, c5.

**4046 n.n.** *to* **n.n. [extract from the** ***Toledo Blade*****] n.d. Wabash Valley.** Comments on the agricultural productivity of the Wabash Valley. 23 November 1848. p.4, c3.

**4047 CORRESPONDENT** *to* **THE** ***PUBLIC LEDGER*****. [extract] n.d. n.p.** Criticizes Daniel Kaufman of Carlisle, recently found guilty of aiding fugitive slaves; denounces the "false philanthropy" of abolitionists. 30 November 1848. p.2, c5.

**4048 n.n.** *to* **n.n. [from the** ***New York Commercial Advertiser*****] 3 November 1848. London.** Reports that President Roberts of Liberia has arrived in London to negotiate a commercial treaty and recognition of his government. 30 November 1848. p.3, c2.

**4049 CORRESPONDENT** *to* **THE** ***NEW YORK TRUE SUN*****. n.d. Washington.** Discusses the likely policy of Senate Democrats regarding confirmation of General Taylor's political appointments. 30 November 1848. p.3, c3.

**4050 CORRESPONDENT** *to* **THE** ***LOUISVILLE PRESBYTERIAN*****. n.d. n.p.** Reports on a subterranean fire in eastern Texas. 30 November 1848. p.4, c3.

**4051 SAMUEL C. ELAN, R. B. FOSTER, AND W. A. ERWINE** *to* **J. W. GRAY. 2 November 1848. Cumming, Ga.** Denounce the Free-Soil opinions expressed in Gray's paper, the *Campaign Dealer*. 7 December 1848. p.1, c2.

**4052 J. W. WALKER** *to* **THE** ***ANTI-SLAVERY BUGLE*****. [extract] n.d. Ohio.** Relates the story of the Rev. Mr. P., a Baptist minister highly critical of abolitionists, who was recently exposed as a scoundrel. 7 December 1848. p.1, c4.

**4053 J. M. McKIM** *to* **WM. ELDER, ESQ. 1 December 1848. Philadelphia.** Conveys facts concerning the case of Daniel Kaufman, a Carlisle man accused of aiding fugitive slaves. 7 December 1848. p.1, c5.

**4054 n.n.** *to* **n.n. [extract from the** ***Buffalo Commercial Advertiser*****] n.d. n.p.** Praises the moderation of the Whig Party evidenced by the election of Taylor; expresses his hope that the election has put an end to serious threats of disunion. 7 December 1848. p.2, c5.

**4055 n.n.** *to* **n.n. [extract] 15 November 1848. Louisville, Ky.** Comments on the impending battle to alter the constitution of Kentucky and allow gradual emancipation. 7 December 1848. p.3, c1.

**4056 THE REV. MR. COOKE** *to* **THE** ***TRUE WESLEYAN*****. [extract] n.d. n.p.** Reports a serious lack of educational and religious instruction in western Virginia. 7 December 1848. p.3, c2.

**4057 FREDERICK DOUGLASS** *to* **THE** ***NORTH STAR*****. [extract] n.d. Lynn, Ma.** Characterizes Daniel Webster as a "house divided" between his words, which justify slavery, and his moral convictions, which demand its annihilation. 14 December 1848. p.3, c4.

**4058 HENRY GREW** *to* **MESSRS. EDITORS. n.d. n.p.** Challenges the assertion of J. W. Walker, stated in a recent letter to the *Freeman*, that a scoundrel whom he describes is typical of ministers who speak out against abolitionists. 14 December 1848. p.3, c4.

**4059 CORRESPONDENT** *to* **THE** ***TRIBUNE*****. 5 December 1848. Washington.** Relates facts surrounding the case of Daniel Drayton, who is currently appealing his conviction for stealing slaves before the circuit court in Washington. 21 December 1848. p.1, c5.

**4060 MARTIN VAN BUREN** *to* **THE REV. CALVIN PHILLIO. [from the** ***Bureau Advocate*****] 17 October 1848. Lindenwald.** Sympathizes with those who would halt the extension of slavery. 21 December 1848. p.3, c4.

**4061 CORRESPONDENT** *to* **THE** ***PUBLIC LEDGER*****. n.d. Washington.** Predicts that the extension of the Missouri Compromise will not be approved by Congress; discusses the increasing political power of the western states. 28 December 1848. p.1, c1.

**4062 CORRESPONDENT** *to* **THE** ***NATIONAL INTELLIGENCER*****. [extract] n.d. London.** Comments on the excessive income enjoyed by the clergy of the established church. 28 December 1848. p.4, c3.

## [1849]

**4063 W. R. G.** *to* **MR. EDITOR. 18 December. Florence, N.Y.** Reports on the progress of the new town of Florence, a colored settlement being constructed on land donated by Gerrit Smith. 4 January 1849. p.1, c5.

**4064 HORACE GREELEY** *to* **THE** ***NEW YORK TRIBUNE*****. [extract] n.d. Washington.** Supports a bill before the United States Senate which would allow the question of slavery in California and New Mexico to be decided by the voters in those territories. 4 January 1849. p.2, c5.

**4065 INDEPENDENT** *to* **THE** ***NORTH AMERICAN*****. [extract] n.d. Washington.** Expresses indignation at the temperament of Northern congressmen instrumental in passing a House resolution calling for a ban on slavery in the District of Columbia. 4 January 1849. p.3, c2.

**4066 A SUBSCRIBER** *to* **THE** ***PENNSYLVANIA FREEMAN*****. n.d. n.p.** Criticizes an article in the *Daily Republic* for referring to "Labor—the Immanuel, the God with us in the flesh." 4 January 1849. p.3, c3.

**4067 CORRESPONDENT** *to* **THE** ***PROVIDENCE JOURNAL*****. n.d. n.p.** Offers an account of a horse that is strongly attracted to piano music. 4 January 1849. p.4, c2.

**4068 JOHN QUINCY ADAMS** *to* **WILLIAM SLADE. August 1847. Quincy, Ma.** Commends his friend's alignment with the anti-slavery cause; reflects on the great struggle faced by the advocates of freedom. 11 January 1849. p.1, c3.

**4069 MR. ROBERTS, PRESIDENT OF THE REPUBLIC OF LIBERIA** *to* **MR. PHELPS. [extract from the** *Commercial Advertiser*] **n.d. n.p.** Informs an official of the New York CS of the success of Roberts's recent mission to Europe. 11 January 1849. p.1, c4.

**4070 H. G.** *to* **MESSRS. EDITORS. n.d. n.p.** Challenges the logic of Adin Ballou's defense of persons who purchase products of slave labor. 11 January 1849. p.2, c1.

**4071 JOSEPH GIBBONS** *to* **THE EDITORIAL COMMITTEE. 18 December 1848. Enterprise, Pa.** Accuses the *Freeman* of unfairly stating the case of the Friends at Lampeter who refused the use of their meetinghouse to Isaac S. Flint. 11 January 1849. p.2, c1.

**4072 THE REV. DR. BULLARD** *to* **n.n. [extract from the** *Christian Observer*] **n.d. n.p.** Reports a growing sentiment in favor of gradual emancipation among the slaveholders of Missouri. 11 January 1849. p.2, c4.

**4073 CORRESPONDENT** *to* **THE** *TRIBUNE*. **6 January 1849. Washington.** Reports on the congressional debate over the claims of Antonio Pacheco of Florida, who seeks government compensation for the loss of a slave. 11 January 1849. p.3, c3.

**4074 CORRESPONDENT** *to* **THE** *EXAMINER*. **n.d. n.p.** Reports a Missouri slaveholder's willingness to emancipate his slaves if the state line can be amended in such a way as to place his lands in Iowa. 18 January 1849. p.1, c5.

**4075 CHARLES J. INGERSOL** *to* **BENJAMIN FITZPATRICK, ALVIN A. McWHORTER, SETH P. STORRS, REUBEN HILL, AND N. S. GRAHAM, COMMITTEE OF INVITATION. 1848. Philadelphia.** Accepts an invitation to a meeting and barbecue sponsored by a Democratic association in Alabama; denounces the Whig Party for its lack of principle; upholds traditional Democratic positions on slavery and currency. 18 January 1849. p.3, c4.

**4076 C. M. CLAY** *to* **THE EDITORS OF THE** *EXAMINER*. **25 December 1848. Madison County, Ky.** Calls for a convention of the friends of emancipation in Kentucky. 25 January 1849. p.1, c4.

**4077 OBSERVER** *to* **THE** *LEDGER*. **19 January 1849. Washington.** Summarizes the contents of a recent report of the United States Patent Office. 25 January 1849. p.2, c1.

**4078 JACOB T. STERN** *to* **FRIENDS. 8 January 1849. Cochranville.** Comments on the prejudice against colored persons in every department of society, with special reference to education. 25 January 1849. p.2, c2.

**4079 THOS. E. LONGSHORE** *to* **FRIENDS. 12 January 1849. Attleboro'.** Reports on a recent meeting held in Attleboro' by William W. Brown. 25 January 1849. p.2, c2.

**4080 HUMANITAS** *to* **THE EDITORS OF THE** *PENNSYLVANIA FREEMAN*. **n.d. n.p.** Offers a character sketch of Emaline B., a widow renowned for her beneficence. 25 January 1849. p.2, c2.

**4081 CORRESPONDENT** *to* **THE** *TRIBUNE*. **[extract] 18 January 1849. Washington.** Reports that the United States House of Representatives has voted to abolish flogging in the navy. 1 February 1849. p.3, c1.

**4082 CORRESPONDENT** *to* **THE** *BALTIMORE SUN.* **[extract] n.d. Washington.** Outlines a measure introduced in Congress by Mr. Douglas of Illinois proposing conditions for admitting California into the federal Union. 1 February 1849. p.3, c3.

**4083 ROBERT WALSH** *to* **LITTLE'S [*sic*]** *LIVING AGE.* **[extract] n.d. n.p.** Comments on the popular attitude toward colored persons in France. 1 February 1849. p.4, c3.

**4084 HORACE BUSHNELL** *to* **THE CHURCHES OF WISCONSIN. n.d. n.p.** Predicts a great revival of religion. 1 February 1849. p.4, c3.

**4085 EDWARD WEBB** *to* **THE** *FREEMAN.* **3 February 1849. Wilmington, De.** Reports indignation among influential citizens of Delaware whose anti-slavery petitions have been ignored by the state legislature; relates facts of a case in Maryland involving the imprisonment of three colored men. 8 February 1849. p.2, c3.

**4086 ENOS PRIZER** *to* **THE** *FREEMAN.* **29 January 1849. Gause's Corner.** Complains of unfair treatment by the *Village Record* in its account of an anti-slavery petition forwarded to Congress. 8 February 1849. p.2, c4.

**4087 ISAAC S. FLINT** *to* **FRIEND. 28 January 1849. Wilmington.** Comments on the Delaware legislature's refusal to consider anti-slavery petitions. 8 February 1849. p.2, c4.

**4088 CORRESPONDENT** *to* **THE** *NEWS.* **31 January 1849. Harrisburg, Pa.** Reports on the defeat of a resolution before the Pennsylvania senate which would amend the state constitution to grant suffrage to persons of color. 8 February 1849. p.3, c4.

**4089 A MEMBER OF THE NATIVE CHURCH AT HILO** *to* **GEORGE C. BECKWITH, SECRETARY OF THE AMERICAN PEACE SOCIETY. [extract] n.d. n.p.** Expresses admiration for the principles and operations of the American Peace Society. 15 February 1849. p.1, c1.

**4090 JOSEPH GIBBONS** *to* **MR. EDITOR. n.d. n.p.** Challenges the fairness of the *Freeman*'s commentary on a previous letter regarding the Friends at Lampeter who refused their meetinghouse to Isaac S. Flint. 15 February 1849. p.2, c1.

**4091 JOHN DOVE** *to* **MESSRS. ALLEN AND PAXSON. 23 December 1848. Richmond.** Requests that the New York police be advised to search several vessels on which his slave may have escaped from Richmond. 15 February 1849. p.3, c1.

**4092 MESSRS. ALLEN AND PAXSON** *to* **DR. JOHN DOVE. 26 December 1848. New York.** State that they cannot in good conscience assist their correspondent in his effort to recapture a fugitive slave. 15 February 1849. p.3, c1.

**4093 CORRESPONDENT** *to* **THE** *COURIER AND ENQUIRER.* **January 1849. London.** Lists the various expenditures of the British monarchy. 15 February 1849. p.4, c2.

**4094 CORRESPONDENT** *to* **THE** *TRIBUNE.* **8 February 1849. Washington.** Encloses for publication a petition presented to Congress by a war widow seeking compensation for her husband according to the principle established in the recent Pacheco case. 22 February 1849. p.1, c1.

**4095 AN AMERICAN RESIDENT IN HAVANA** *to* **THE** *NEW YORK EVENING POST.* **[extract] n.d. n.p.** Reports substantial anti-slavery sentiment in Cuba. 22 February 1849. p.2, c3.

**4096 CORRESPONDENT** *to* **THE** *BOSTON ATLAS.* **[extract] n.d. Washington.** Reports that a Washington resident has recently departed for California with eight slaves in his possession. 22 February 1849. p.2, c5.

**4097 CORRESPONDENT** *to* **THE** ***TRUE DEMOCRAT*****. [extract] n.d. Columbus, Oh.** Comments on the disillusionment experienced by idealistic men who are introduced into political circles. 22 February 1849. p.2, c5.

**4098 CORRESPONDENT** *to* **THE** ***PHILADELPHIA NORTH AMERICAN*****. 29 November 1848. St. Petersburgh.** Reports plans for a bridge in St. Petersburgh, the largest of its kind in Europe, to be constructed by American mechanics. 22 February 1849. p.4, c1.

**4099 FRANCIS JACKSON** *to* **THE CHAIRMAN OF THE MASSACHUSETTS CHARITABLE ASSOCIATION. 15 December 1848. Boston.** Protests the association's investment in a Boston hotel dealing in ardent spirits. 1 March 1849. p.1, c4.

**4100 n.n.** *to* **THE** ***NEW YORK EVENING POST*****. [extract] n.d. Havana, Cuba.** Relates the substance of a conversation between two Cuban slaveholders on the beneficial effects of emancipation in Jamaica. 1 March 1849. p.1, c5.

**4101 A. DE LAMARTINE** *to* **M. PROSPER GUICHARD. [extract] n.d. n.p.** Explains his decision to publish an autobiography of his early life. 1 March 1849. p.4, c1.

**4102 RUFUS ANDERSON, SELAH B. TREAT, SWAN L. POMROY, SECRETARIES OF THE AMERICAN BOARD OF COMMISSIONERS FOR FOREIGN MISSIONS** *to* **THE EDITOR OF THE** ***CHRISTIAN OBSERVER*****. 20 February 1849. Boston.** Define the position of the American Board of Commissioners for Foreign Missions on the question of slavery in mission churches. 8 March 1849. p.2, c2.

**4103 CORRESPONDENT** *to* **THE** ***PENNSYLVANIA FREEMAN*****. [extract] n.d. n.p.** Comments on a recent execution in Delaware. 8 March 1849. p.2, c4.

**4104 CORRESPONDENT** *to* **THE** ***PENNSYLVANIA FREEMAN*****. [extract] n.d. Princeton, N.J.** Reports a substantial number of abolitionists at Princeton Seminary; predicts a corresponding change in the position of the Presbyterian church regarding slavery in the next decade. 8 March 1849. p.2, c4.

**4105 A SOUTHERN GENTLEMAN** *to* **n.n. [extract] 26 February. n.p.** Expresses confidence that Congress will take no effective action against slavery. 8 March 1849. p.2, c5.

**4106 HENRY CLAY** *to* **RICHARD PINDELL, ESQ. [from the** ***Lexington Observer and Reporter*****] 17 February 1849. New Orleans.** Outlines a program for gradual emancipation in Kentucky. 15 March 1849. p.1, c1.

**4107 A LADY IN NASHVILLE** *to* **n.n. [extract from the** ***Cleveland True Democrat*****] 25 December 1848. Nashville, Tn.** Condemns the widespread drunkenness and violence exhibited in Nashville on Christmas Day. 15 March 1849. p.1, c4.

**4108 CORRESPONDENT** *to* **THE** ***NEW YORK EVANGELIST*****. 22 February 1849. Washington.** Reports a reversal by the circuit court of the verdict in the Drayton case, which had judged Drayton guilty of larceny for transporting escaped slaves. 15 March 1849. p.1, c5.

**4109 CORRESPONDENT** *to* **THE** ***COMMERCIAL ADVERTISER*****. n.d. Washington.** Reports "fights and personal collisions" on the floors of both houses of Congress. 15 March 1849. p.1, c5.

**4110 FREE COLORED CITIZENS OF NEW JERSEY** *to* **THE SENATE AND HOUSE OF ASSEMBLY OF THE STATE OF NEW JERSEY. n.d. Princeton, N.J.** Petition for the right of elective franchise. 15 March 1849. p.2, c1.

**4111 JOHN G. FEE** *to* **MESSRS. EDITORS. [from the** ***Examiner*****] 20 February. Calvin Creek, Ky.** Reports on a recent meeting of friends of emancipation in Maysville, Kentucky; argues against colonization. 15 March 1849. p.2, c2.

**4112 MARTHA HAYHURST, SIDNEY PIERCE, HANNAH PENNOCK, FOR THE WOMEN'S TEMPERANCE CONVENTION** *to* **THE SENATE AND HOUSE OF REPRESENTATIVES OF THE COMMONWEALTH OF PENNSYLVANIA. n.d. n.p.** Urge passage of a law prohibiting the sale of intoxicating liquors. 22 March 1849. p.1, c5.

**4113 GEO. P. DAVIS** *to* **READER. n.d. n.p.** Encourages friends of emancipation to circulate petitions. 22 March 1849. p.2, c1.

**4114 A SLAVEHOLDING CORRESPONDENT** *to* **A SOUTHERN PAPER. [extract] n.d. n.p.** States that if slavery is in fact evil, it shall nevertheless continue in the United States due to a lack of religion and virtue in both the North and the South. 22 March 1849. p.2, c5.

**4115 MARTIN VAN BUREN** *to* **THE** *OHIO STANDARD.* **29 January 1849. Boston.** Praises resolutions of a Free-Soil Convention in Ohio. 22 March 1849. p.3, c1.

**4116 CORRESPONDENT** *to* **THE** *TRIBUNE.* **28 February 1849. Maysville, Ky.** Expresses hope that the convention to draft a new constitution for Kentucky will adopt a safe and practicable plan for the removal of slavery. 22 March 1849. p.3, c3.

**4117 n.n.** *to* **n.n. [extract from the** ***National Era*****] 5 March. Lexington, Ky.** Reports favorable prospects for the cause of emancipation in Kentucky. 29 March 1849. p.1, c1.

**4118 ERNEST LACAN** *to* **MR. BURRITT. [from the** ***Christian Citizen*****] 8 January 1849. Paris.** Describes an audience with M. de Lamartine. 29 March 1849. p.4, c1.

**4119 WILLIAM LLOYD GARRISON** *to* **HENRY CLAY. [extract] n.d. n.p.** Criticizes Clay's plan for the gradual emancipation and colonization of the slaves of Kentucky. 5 April 1849. p.1, c2.

**4120 H. W. D.** *to* **THE** *NATIONAL ERA.* **12 February 1849. Kingston, Jamaica.** States that the economic problems of the West Indies are not the result of emancipation. 5 April 1849. p.1, c3.

**4121 AMOS GILBERT** *to* **n.n. [extract from the** ***Liberator*****] n.d. Oakland, Oh.** Stresses the importance of active involvement in the anti-slavery movement. 12 April 1849. p.2, c1.

**4122 CORRESPONDENT** *to* **THE** *LIBERATOR.* **n.d. n.p.** Rebukes the *Emancipator and Republican* for its lack of critical comment on Henry Clay's plan for the gradual emancipation and colonization of the slaves of Kentucky. 12 April 1849. p.2, c1.

**4123 A MEMBER OF THE SOCIETY OF FRIENDS** *to* **n.n. [extract] n.d. n.p.** Reports on the attitude of slaveholders in his state toward Northern immigrants and the anti-slavery cause. 12 April 1849. p.3, c1.

**4124 n.n.** *to* **FRIEND. [extract] April 1849. Bristol.** Asserts that strength of character and depth of affection are things not measured by color; praises C. C. Burleigh. 19 April 1849. p.2, c1.

**4125 UNITED STATES REPRESENTATIVE IN MADRID** *to* **THOMAS CAUTE REYNOLDS. [extract] 12 July 1847. Havre.** Instructs a member of the American delegation in Madrid on the proper course of action in light of a British plan to obtain Cuba from the Spanish government. 19 April 1849. p.3, c1.

**4126 THOMAS CAUTE REYNOLDS** *to* **n.n. [extract] n.d. Madrid.** Relates a scene from a diplomatic conference between representatives of Spain and the United States regarding a British plan to obtain Cuba. 19 April 1849. p.3, c1.

**4127 THOMAS CAUTE REYNOLDS** *to* **MR. SAUNDERS. [extract] n.d. Madrid.** Expresses a lack of confidence in Mr. Buchanan, the American secretary of state. 19 April 1849. p.3, c1.

**4128 H. G.** *to* **FRIENDS. n.d. n.p.** Comments on an anti-slavery resolution offered by R. J. Breckinridge at a meeting of the citizens of Fayette County, Kentucky. 26 April 1849. p.2, c2.

**4129 MR. BOTTS** *to* **THE** ***RICHMOND REPUBLICAN.*** **[extract] n.d. n.p.** States his opposition to the Wilmot Proviso and his commitment to defend the United States Constitution. 26 April 1849. p.2, c4.

**4130 BRUTUS** *to* **CITIZENS OF SOUTH CAROLINA. n.d. n.p.** Advocates a state convention to draft a new constitution which would rectify the disproportionate political power allotted to slaveholders. 26 April 1849. p.3, c1.

**4131 MR. BRYANT** *to* **THE** ***NEW YORK EVENING POST.*** **[extract] n.d. n.p.** Reports on a cotton mill in Augusta, Georgia, which employs free white laborers. 3 May 1849. p.2, c2.

**4132 J. B. PECK** *to* **MR. EDITOR. 24 April 1849. Steam Ship** ***Columbus.*** Defends his actions in returning a runaway slave who had hidden himself aboard Peck's ship. 3 May 1849. p.2, c3.

**4133 G. F. HORTON** *to* **FRIENDS. n.d. n.p.** Admits his inability to "see clearly the identity of the old Liberty party and the Free Soil party"; calls for either the abolition of slavery under the federal Constitution, or a dissolution of the Union. 3 May 1849. p.3, c1.

**4134 JOHN WENTWORTH** *to* **THE** ***CHICAGO DEMOCRAT.*** **[extract] n.d. n.p.** Cites statistics to illustrate the disproportionate number of congressional districts allocated to the Southern states as a result of slave representation. 3 May 1849. p.3, c3.

**4135 CORRESPONDENT** *to* **THE** ***TRIBUNE.*** **n.d. n.p.** Reports on the activities of various men of letters in Boston. 3 May 1849. p.4, c1.

**4136 CORRESPONDENT** *to* **THE** ***NATIONAL INTELLIGENCER.*** **[extract] n.d. London.** Comments on the beneficial effects of physical exercise evident in English women. 3 May 1849. p.4, c3.

**4137 CORRESPONDENT** *to* **THE** ***NEW YORK EVENING POST.*** **n.d. Wilmington, N.C.** Comments on the discomfort of Southern Whigs who are uncertain of the new administration's party line on slavery. 10 May 1849. p.1, c5.

**4138 C. M. B.** *to* **THE** ***FREEMAN.*** **8 May 1849. New York.** Reports on the anniversary meeting of the AAS. 10 May 1849. p.2, c2.

**4139 CORRESPONDENT** *to* **THE** ***PHILADELPHIA INQUIRER.*** **n.d. Paris.** Reports that Mr. Henry Wickoff of the United States has recently contracted to supply the French army with all such India rubber articles as they may require. 10 May 1849. p.3, c3.

**4140 REV. T. D. HUNT** *to* **THE** ***NEWARK ADVERTISER.*** **[extract] 1 March 1849. San Francisco.** Comments on the "moral desolation" induced by "gold fever" in California. 10 May 1849. p.3, c4.

**4141 n.n.** *to* **THE** ***CINCINNATI CHRONICLE.*** **[extract] n.d. Washington.** Relates an anecdote concerning Judge Collamer, the postmaster general, illustrating his commitment to the cause of temperance. 10 May 1849. p.4, c3.

**4142 n.n.** *to* **n.n. [extract] n.d. Ohio.** Relates a prison conversation with Richard Dillingham, a young Quaker convicted of aiding fugitive slaves. 17 May 1849. p.3, c3.

**4143 MR. THOMPSON** *to* **n.n. [extract from the** ***American Missionary*****] 13 October 1848. Mendi Mission.** Reports on a law recently passed by the chiefs at the mission providing that a man caught stealing may either be shot or be sold into slavery. 17 May 1849. p.3, c3.

**4144 CORRESPONDENT** *to* **THE** ***ANTI-SLAVERY BUGLE.*** **n.d. Lake County.** Expresses sympathy with disunionists. 24 May 1849. p.1, c3.

**4145 A CLERGYMAN IN THE SOUTH** *to* **THE** ***GEORGIA CONSTITUTIONALIST.*** **n.d. n.p.** Disputes Henry Clay's assertion that slavery is not a divinely sanctioned institution. 31 May 1849. p.1, c2.

**4146 NORTH CAROLINA YEARLY MEETING OF FRIENDS** *to* **THE DIFFERENT SOCIETIES AND THEIR INDIVIDUAL MEMBERS, PROFESSING THE RELIGION OF OUR LORD AND SAVIOUR JESUS CHRIST. November 1848. Guilford County.** Appeals to fellow Christians to examine the institution of slavery in the light of the gospel. 31 May 1849. p.1, c3.

**4147 C. W. G.** *to* **MR. EDITOR. n.d. n.p.** Encloses for publication an extract from the minutes of a preparatory anti-slavery convention at Salem, New Jersey. 31 May 1849. p.1, c5.

**4148 A READER** *to* **MESSRS. EDITORS. 4 May 1849. n.p.** Challenges the assertion that "voting makes the voter a party in the views sanctioned by the Constitution." 31 May 1849. p.1, c5.

**4149 JOHN QUINCY ADAMS** *to* **DR. FRANCIS BACON. [extract] 31 March 1845. n.p.** Criticizes Whig acquiescence to slaveholding interests. 31 May 1849. p.2, c2.

**4150 CORRESPONDENT** *to* **THE** ***NEW YORK EVENING POST.*** **n.d. Washington.** Reports a possible rupture of diplomatic relations between the United States and Mexico. 31 May 1849. p.3, c5.

**4151 CORRESPONDENT** *to* **THE** ***NEW YORK COMMERCIAL ADVERTISER.*** **n.d. London.** Reports on a case of blindness which was cured through mesmerism. 31 May 1849. p.4, c2.

**4152 CORRESPONDENT** *to* **THE** ***CHRONOTYPE.*** **[extract] n.d. n.p.** Describes the scene of a hanging at Haverhill, New Hampshire. 7 June 1849. p.1, c4.

**4153 ELWOOD FISHER** *to* **THE** ***NEW YORK TRIBUNE.*** **[extract] n.d. n.p.** Denies the statement that he "was a Quaker, but was turned out; was a Whig, but turned Democrat; and was once an abolitionist, but has now run into an opposite extreme." 7 June 1849. p.2, c5.

**4154 JOSEPH STURGE** *to* **THE EDITORS OF THE** ***BRITISH FRIEND.*** **16 May 1849. Birmingham.** Encloses for publication a letter from Sarah Pugh and Mary Grew to Samuel Rhoades, with an introductory note by Rhoades. 14 June 1849. p.1, c1.

**4155 SAMUEL RHOADES** *to* **JOSEPH STURGE. n.d. n.p.** Introduces a letter from Sarah Pugh and Mary Grew regarding the work of the Pennsylvania AS. 14 June 1849. p.1, c1.

**4156 SARAH PUGH AND MARY GREW** *to* **SAMUEL RHOADES. n.d. n.p.** Appeal to British abolitionists for aid on behalf of the Pennsylvania AS. 14 June 1849. p.1, c1.

**4157 n.n.** *to* **THE** ***PENNSYLVANIA FREEMAN.*** **5 June 1849. Alexandria, Va.** Comments on an enclosed article reporting on two cases where the death penalty has been imposed for theft. 14 June 1849. p.2, c2.

**4158 CORRESPONDENT** *to* **THE** ***BOSTON CHRONOTYPE.*** **[extract] n.d. Athens, Ga.** Describes the scene of an election day in Georgia, where many were drunk and prone to violence. 21 June 1849. p.1, c4.

**4159 REVILO** *to* **THE** ***TRIBUNE.*** **[extract] 7 June 1849. Waterloo, Seneca County, N.Y.** Reports on the Yearly Meeting of Congregational Friends at Waterloo, New York. 21 June 1849. p.2, c2.

**4160 THE YEARLY MEETING OF CONGREGATIONAL FRIENDS** *to* **ALL EARNEST AND DEVOTED LABORERS IN THE VARIOUS HUMANITARY REFORMS. June 1849. Waterloo, N.Y.** Expresses sympathy with all who labor for humanitarian reforms. 21 June 1849. p.2, c3.

**4161 MR. BELSER** *to* **n.n. [extract] n.d. n.p.** Declares his opposition to a national bank, protective tariffs, and the Wilmot Proviso. 21 June 1849. p.2, c4.

**4162 S. D. MARSHALL** *to* **THE** ***SANGAMON JOURNAL.*** **[extract] n.d. n.p.** Comments on the regular trade in kidnapping carried on in northern Illinois. 21 June 1849. p.3, c1.

**4163 RICHARD D. WEBB** *to* **THE** ***STANDARD.*** **n.d. n.p.** Lauds Joseph Barker as "one of the most remarkable and one of the ablest men in England." 21 June 1849. p.3, c2.

**4164 EDMUND QUINCY** *to* **THE** ***STANDARD.*** **[extract] n.d. Boston.** Deplores the execution of a possibly innocent black man in Boston. 21 June 1849. p.3, c2.

**4165 J. R. GIDDINGS** *to* **JOHN CROWELL. [extract from the** ***True Democrat*****] 29 May 1849. Jefferson.** Cites evidence leading to the conclusion that General Taylor has effectively used his influence to undermine congressional support for the Wilmot Proviso. 28 June 1849. p.1, c4.

**4166 J. COOPER** *to* **HON. JOSHUA R. GIDDINGS. 7 May 1849. Pottsville.** Corroborates Giddings's testimony regarding General Taylor's opposition to the Wilmot Proviso. 28 June 1849. p.2, c2.

**4167 B. B. THURSTON** *to* **HON. J. R. GIDDINGS. 18 April 1849. Hopkinton, R.I.** Quotes General Taylor regarding his hope for passage of the Walker amendment, a measure designed to undercut the Wilmot Proviso. 28 June 1849. p.2, c2.

**4168 JOHN M. CLAYTON** *to* **EDWARD HURST, ESQ. 9 June 1849. Washington.** Denies a passport to Hurst's client, Henry Hambleton; informs him that the State Department does not issue passports to persons of color. 28 June 1849. p.2, c5.

**4169 ROBT. H. STONE** *to* **MADAM [THE MOTHER OF C. M. CLAY]. [from the** ***Lexington Observer*****] n.d. Foxtown, Ky.** Informs that her son has received a serious knife wound in the lungs, and urges her to come to Foxtown at once. 28 June 1849. p.3, c2.

**4170 A LEADING CASS DEMOCRAT OF IOWA** *to* **THE** ***OHIO STATESMAN.*** **[extract] n.d. n.p.** States that the South has proved traitor to Northern Democrats, and urges a Northern platform founded on Free-Soil principles. 28 June 1849. p.3, c4.

**4171 CORRESPONDENT** *to* **THE** ***TRIBUNE*****. 12 June 1849. Washington.** Compares the irrationality of the Salem witchcraft trials to contemporary justifications of slavery; illustrates the cruelty and greed of slaveholders in the District of Columbia. 5 July 1849. p.1, c1.

**4172 CORRESPONDENT** *to* **THE** ***AMERICAN STATESMAN*****. 4 May 1849. Washington.** Comments on the inhumanity of the slave traffic in Washington and Maryland, and its deleterious effect on the area's economy. 5 July 1849. p.1, c4.

**4173 S. S. FOSTER** *to* **THE EDITOR OF THE** ***LONG ISLAND FARMER*****. 15 June 1849. Rocky Hill.** Reports on a mob's disruption of an anti-slavery meeting in Hempstead. 5 July 1849. p.2, c1.

**4174 n.n.** *to* **THE** ***NEW YORK HERALD*****. [extract] n.d. Nashville.** Portrays the scene of the baptism received by former President Polk on his deathbed. 5 July 1849. p.3, c4.

**4175 ADAM CROOKS** *to* **THE** ***TRUE WESLEYAN*****. 7 June 1849. Big Creek, Stokes County, Va.** Chronicles the trial of the Rev. Jarvis C. Bacon, charged before the court in Grayson County, Virginia, with circulating an anti-slavery sermon and the *Narrative of Frederick Douglass.* 12 July 1849. p.1, c1.

**4176 n.n.** *to* **n.n. [extract from the** ***Baltimore Sun*****] 18 June 1849. Parish of Ascension, La.** Reports that an epidemic of cholera is sweeping through the black population of the area. 12 July 1849. p.2, c1.

**4177 A SAVANNIAN** *to* **THE** ***SAVANNAH REPUBLICAN*****. n.d. Savannah.** Objects to the ostentatious manner in which a company of Negroes departed from Savannah for Liberia. 12 July 1849. p.3, c2.

**4178 M.** *to* **THE** ***TRIBUNE*****. 27 June 1849. Bourbon County, Ky.** Reports a strong popular sentiment in favor of gradual emancipation in Kentucky. 19 July 1849. p.1, c1.

**4179 A DISTINGUISHED PREACHER** *to* **M. [extract] n.d. n.p.** Affirms his commitment to gradual emancipation in Kentucky. 19 July 1849. p.1, c2.

**4180 OBSERVER** *to* **THE** ***HARTFORD REPUBLICAN*****. n.d. n.p.** Reports on a recent meeting of the General Association of the Congregational Churches of Connecticut. 19 July 1849. p.2, c2.

**4181 MR. FOOTE** *to* **n.n. [extract] n.d. n.p.** Denounces Senator Benton of Missouri for his vote against Walker's compromise bill. 19 July 1849. p.3, c1.

**4182 OBSERVER** *to* **THE EDITOR OF THE** ***NATIONAL ERA*****. 24 April 1849. Washington.** Depicts the slave traffic and the "slave pens" of the District of Columbia. 19 July 1849. p.3, c2.

**4183 A GENTLEMAN ON THE COAST OF BRAZIL** *to* **THE** ***ANTI-SLAVERY REPORTER*****. n.d. n.p.** Reports on the Brazilian slave trade. 19 July 1849. p.3, c4.

**4184 MRS. SWISSHELM** *to* **COUNTRY GIRLS. [from the** ***Pittsburg Saturday Visiter*****] n.d. n.p.** Discusses the importance of hand and skin care and a healthy diet. 19 July 1849. p.4, c1.

**4185 MARTIN VAN BUREN** *to* **THE FREE SOIL CONVENTION AT CLEVELAND. [extract] n.d. n.p.** Comments on the significance of the Ordinance of 1787, which prohibited slavery from extending into the Northwest Territory. 26 July 1849. p.1, c2.

**4186 CHARLES FRANCIS ADAMS** *to* **THE FREE SOIL CONVENTION AT CLEVELAND. n.d. n.p.** Expresses his support for the Free-Soil movement, continuous in principle with the celebrated Ordinance of 1787. 26 July 1849. p.1, c2.

**4187 HENRY CLAY** *to* **GENTLEMEN. 16 June 1849. Ashland, Ky.** Explains why he must decline an invitation to attend the Free-Soil Convention at Cleveland. 26 July 1849. p.1, c3.

**4188 HORACE MANN** *to* **MESSRS. J. C. VAUGHAN AND THOMAS BROWN, COMMITTEE. 9 July 1849. West Newton, Ma.** Expresses regret that he cannot accept an invitation to the Cleveland convention; characterizes the Ordinance of 1787 as "one of the grandest moral events in the annals of mankind." 26 July 1849. p.1, c4.

**4189 C. M. CLAY** *to* **MESSRS. JOHN C. VAUGHAN AND THOMAS BROWN, COMMITTEE. 5 July 1849. Madison County, Ky.** Expresses sympathy with the principles of the Free-Soil Convention at Cleveland; denounces American slaveholders. 26 July 1849. p.1, c4.

**4190 B.** *to* **THE** *SYRACUSE STAR*. **[extract] n.d. Memphis, Tn.** Describes a slave market in Memphis. 26 July 1849. p.2, c1.

**4191 WM. H. PRAY** *to* **THE** *KILLINGLY AURORA*. **[extract] n.d. Rio de Janeiro, Brazil.** Depicts the cruelty of Brazilian slavery, but notes the absence of color prejudice among free citizens of the country. 26 July 1849. p.2, c1.

**4192 CORRESPONDENT** *to* **THE** *SPIRIT OF THE AGE*. **[extract] n.d. n.p.** Reports the torture and execution of a runaway slave. 26 July 1849. p.2, c3.

**4193 n.n.** *to* **n.n. [extract] n.d. Civita Vecchia.** Reports on the victory of the French army over the Italians at Rome. 26 July 1849. p.3, c4.

**4194 M. DE CORCELLES** *to* **THE MINISTER OF FOREIGN AFFAIRS. 3 July 1849. Marseilles.** Reports that Roman authorities are prepared to capitulate to the French forces and seek a pacific resolution to the present conflict. 26 July 1849. p.3, c4.

**4195 n.n.** *to* **n.n. [from the** *Boston Journal***] 14 July 1849. St. John.** Offers an account of the recent riot at St. John, in Ireland. 26 July 1849. p.3, c5.

**4196 REV. G. W. PERKINS** *to* **THE GENERAL ASSOCIATION OF CONNECTICUT. n.d. n.p.** Proposes resolutions remonstrating with the General Assembly of the Presbyterian Church for its intercourse with slaveholders. 2 August 1849. p.1, c1.

**4197 A CAROLINIAN** *to* **THE EDITOR OF THE** *NATIONAL ERA*. **n.d. n.p.** Quotes a speech of Mr. McDuffie, who argued that the comparative poverty of the Southern states is attributable to slavery. 2 August 1849. p.2, c1.

**4198 CORRESPONDENT** *to* **THE** *AUGUSTA REPUBLIC*. **[extract] n.d. n.p.** Defends slavery as a "holy, wise and merciful work of the beneficent Creator." 2 August 1849. p.2, c5.

**4199 J. F. G. MITTAG** *to* **n.n. [extract from the** *Charleston Courier***] n.d. n.p.** Regrets the absence of a clear moral basis to the American federal system in which the justness of slavery is readily acknowledged. 2 August 1849. p.2, c5.

**4200 n.n.** *to* **THE** *INDEPENDENT*. **[extract] n.d. Vermont.** Reports strong anti-slavery sentiment in Vermont. 2 August 1849. p.3, c1.

**4201 S. P.** *to* **THE *FREEMAN*. n.d. n.p.** Encloses an editorial response from the *Anti-Slavery Bugle* defending the salaries paid by the Western AS to its agents. 2 August 1849. p.3, c2.

**4202 CORRESPONDENT** *to* **THE *NEW YORK POST*. [extract] n.d. n.p.** Describes the arrival of a ship of gold seekers in California, the speculation in coastal real estate, and the physical hardships to which miners are subject. 2 August 1849. p.3, c5.

**4203 MARIA WESTON CHAPMAN** *to* **MRS. GARRISON. 15 April 1849. Paris.** Discusses the rights of women in France. 2 August 1849. p.4, c2.

**4204 n.n.** *to* **n.n. [extract] 14 March 1849. Pisa, Italy.** Reports the publication of three different editions of the Bible in Italy. 2 August 1849. p.4, c3.

**4205 JEANNE DEROIN, EDITOR OF THE *OPINION DES FEMMES*** *to* **THE ELECTORS OF THE DEPARTMENT OF THE SEINE. n.d. n.p.** Announces her candidacy for the national legislative assembly. 2 August 1849. p.4, c3.

**4206 THE YEARLY MEETING OF CONGREGATIONAL FRIENDS, HELD AT WATERLOO, N.Y.** *to* **ALL PEOPLE, AND ESPECIALLY TO RELIGIOUS PROFESSORS OF EVERY NAME. [extract] n.d. n.p.** Urges an end to economic injustice, slavery, war, racial prejudice, and the oppression of women. 9 August 1849. p.1, c3.

**4207 R. W. EMERSON** *to* **W. L. GARRISON. 24 July 1849. Concord.** Accepts an invitation to an anti-slavery meeting at Worcester. 9 August 1849. p.2, c3.

**4208 CORRESPONDENT** *to* **THE *DAILY NEWS*. 12 July 1849. Berlin.** Reports the rumored insanity of the Russian Czar. 9 August 1849. p.3, c4.

**4209 JOHN M. CLAYTON** *to* **EDWARD HURST, ESQ. 9 June 1849. Washington.** Denies a passport to Hurst's client, Henry Hambleton; informs him that the State Department does not issue passports to persons of color. 16 August 1849. p.1, c1.

**4210 CORRESPONDENT** *to* **THE *JOURNAL OF COMMERCE*. [extract] n.d. n.p.** Reports on his travels through Virginia; reflects on the injustice of slavery; speculates on the possibility of emancipation. 16 August 1849. p.1, c2.

**4211 n.n.** *to* **n.n. [from the *New York Sun*] n.d. Cuba.** Reports the reestablishment of large-scale African slave traffic in Cuba. 16 August 1849. p.1, c3.

**4212 THOMAS STURGE** *to* **FRANCIS JACKSON. 23 June 1849. Northfield, near Gravesend, England.** Encloses a contribution of 100 pounds to aid the anti-slavery cause in America. 16 August 1849. p.1, c5.

**4213 WM. LLOYD GARRISON, FRANCIS JACKSON, WENDELL PHILLIPS, AND H. I. BOWDITCH, COMMITTEE** *to* **REV. THEOBALD MATHEW. 26 July 1849. Boston.** Extend an invitation to an anniversary celebration of emancipation in the British West Indies. 16 August 1849. p.2, c1.

**4214 DANIEL O'CONNELL, THEOBALD MATHEW, AND SEVENTY THOUSAND OTHER INHABITANTS OF IRELAND** *to* **COUNTRYMEN AND COUNTRYWOMEN IN AMERICA. 1842. n.p.** Declare that slavery is a sin against God and man; urge unification with the abolitionists. 16 August 1849. p.2, c2.

**4215 GEO. F. HORTON** *to* **THE *PENNSYLVANIA FREEMAN*. 21 July 1849. Terrytown, Pa.** Discusses the question of the pro-slavery character of the United States Constitution; concludes that the act of voting is not in itself supportive of slavery. 16 August 1849. p.2, c3.

**4216 A CITIZEN OF WESTON, MO.** *to* **n.n. [extract from the** *Examiner*] **n.d. n.p.** Expresses his belief that emancipation will prevail in Missouri within a short time. 16 August 1849. p.3, c3.

**4217 DR. CHANNING** *to* **n.n. [A LADY IN ENGLAND]. [extract from the** *London Inquirer*] **n.d. n.p.** Solicits his friend's opinions concerning female education. 16 August 1849. p.4, c3.

**4218 THE FREE PRESBYTERIAN SYNOD** *to* **MEMBERS. [extract] n.d. n.p.** Directs member churches not to tolerate persons who deal in intoxicating liquors in the communion of the church; urges members to testify against slavery at the ballot box. 23 August 1849. p.1, c1.

**4219 CORRESPONDENT** *to* **THE** *NATIONAL ERA*. **[extract] n.d. n.p.** Draws a distinction between abolitionists and Free-Soilers. 23 August 1849. p.1, c3.

**4220 SPIRIT OF '76** *to* **MR. EDITOR. [from the** *Louisville Courier*] **n.d. n.p.** Encloses for publication an anti-slavery editorial from the *Palmyra Whig*. 23 August 1849. p.1, c3.

**4221 JOHN G. PALFREY** *to* **SAMUEL MAY, JR. 27 June 1849. Cambridge.** Declines an invitation to address the Worcester Convention for the Celebration of the Anniversary of West Indian Emancipation; argues against dissolution of the Union. 23 August 1849. p.1, c5.

**4222 CHARLES SUMNER** *to* **WILLIAM LLOYD GARRISON. 1 August 1849. Boston.** Regrets that he cannot be present at the Worcester Convention for the Celebration of the Anniversary of West Indian Emancipation. 23 August 1849. p.1, c5.

**4223 ELDER CHESIMAN** *to* **n.n. [extract] n.d. n.p.** Expresses disappointment with the lack of moral improvement evident among the natives of Grand Bassa County, Liberia. 23 August 1849. p.3, c1.

**4224 JOHN M. CLAYTON** *to* **THE** *SALEM REGISTER*. **13 August 1849. Washington.** Denies that the refusal of the State Department to issue passports to persons of color is the result of a new policy initiated since he became secretary of state. 23 August 1849. p.3, c3.

**4225 ROBERT B. ROGERS** *to* **FRIEND GARRISON. [from the** *Liberator*] **13 August 1849. Boston.** Laments recent statements by the Rev. Theobald Mathew which indicate to the writer a betrayal of anti-slavery principles. 30 August 1849. p.1, c5.

**4226 B. COATES** *to* **J. M. McKIM. 29 June 1849. Philadelphia.** Criticizes the *Freeman* for publishing articles unfavorable to officials of the Liberian government. 30 August 1849. p.2, c1.

**4227 COMMODORE JOEL ABBOT, U.S.N.** *to* **THE SECRETARY OF THE MASSACHUSETTS CS. [extract] 5 May 1846. Warren, R.I.** Commends J. J. Roberts, governor of Liberia, and John B. Russwurm, governor of Cape Palmas, for their moral and Christian characters. 30 August 1849. p.2, c3.

**4228 SIR CHARLES HOTHAM** *to* **THE SECRETARY OF THE ADMIRALTY. 7 April 1847. St. Helena.** Reports that the rumors linking Governor Roberts of Liberia to the slave trade are without foundation. 30 August 1849. p.2, c3.

**4229 GERARD BALSTON** *to* **ELLIOT CRESSON. 1 September 1848. London.** Reports a cordial reception for President Roberts of Liberia among European dignitaries. 30 August 1849. p.2, c3.

**4230 THOMAS GARRET** *to* **FRIEND. 20 August 1849. Wilmington.** Reports a recent incident in Elkton, Maryland, where two colored men were harassed by a local constable. 30 August 1849. p.2, c3.

**4231 AN OFFICER OF THE AMERICAN SQUADRON** *to* **n.n. [extract from the** *New York Evening Post*] **n.d. n.p.** Estimates that the American squadron has decreased the number of slaves usually imported on American vessels by at least 20,000. 6 September 1849. p.1, c5.

**4232 WENDELL PHILLIPS** *to* **JAMES HAUGHTON, ESQ. [from the** *Liberator*] **20 August 1849. Boston.** Laments Father Mathew's decision to remain silent on the subject of slavery during his tour of America. 6 September 1849. p.2, c1.

**4233 DR. SNODGRASS** *to* **THE CLEVELAND [FREE-SOIL] CONVENTION. [extract] n.d. n.p.** Criticizes Northerners who speak against the cause of freedom. 6 September 1849. p.3, c3.

**4234 BOSTON CORRESPONDENT** *to* **THE** *NEW YORK HERALD.* **[extract] n.d. n.p.** States that the secret of Yankee prosperity is "universal, incessant, persevering, calculating, well-directed labor." 6 September 1849. p.3, c3.

**4235 COMMODORE CHAS. STEWART** *to* **n.n. [extract] n.d. n.p.** Expresses his opposition to flogging in the United States Navy. 6 September 1849. p.3, c4.

**4236 WASHINGTON CORRESPONDENT** *to* **THE** *NEW YORK HERALD.* **[extract] n.d. n.p.** Speculates on the division of cabinet members over the question of buying and admitting Cuba into the Union as a slave state. 6 September 1849. p.3, c4.

**4237 MICHAEL DOHENEY** *to* **THE** *TRIBUNE.* **[extract] n.d. n.p.** Expresses his belief, as a Roman Catholic, that the pope should not be regarded as a temporal prince. 6 September 1849. p.3, c5.

**4238 FREDERICK DOUGLASS** *to* **THOMAS AULD. [extract] n.d. n.p.** States that he has received word that Auld is no longer a slaveholder. 13 September 1849. p.2, c5.

**4239 JOSEPH A. DUGDALE** *to* **THE** *NEW YORK TRIBUNE.* **[extract] n.d. n.p.** Reports on the proceedings of the Ohio Yearly Meeting of Friends. 20 September 1849. p.2, c1.

**4240 AFRICANUS** *to* **MESSRS. EDITORS. [from the** *Albany Atlas*] **3 September 1849. n.p.** Challenges the contention that he is not legally a citizen of the United States. 20 September 1849. p.2, c6.

**4241 J. W. C. PENNINGTON** *to* **SIR. [from the** *New York Tribune*] **24 June 1849. London, England.** Relates the story of a fugitive slave in England. 27 September 1849. p.1, c4.

**4242 DANIEL O'CONNELL** *to* **T. D. DISNEY, ESQ., W. HUNTER, ESQ., PATRICK CROSKEY, ESQ., P. CODY, ESQ., T. CONNOLLY, ESQ., AND STEPHEN BONNER, ESQ. [extract from the** *Liberator*] **11 October 1843. Dublin.** Responds to their recent apology for the institution of American slavery. 27 September 1849. p.1, c4.

**4243 MR. CUTTING** *to* **THE EDITORS OF THE** *ALBANY ARGUS.* **[extract] n.d. n.p.** Denies that he has ever been a slaveholder. 27 September 1849. p.4, c3.

**4244 EDWIN H. NEVIN** *to* **THE ANTI-SLAVERY MINISTERS AND MEMBERS OF THE PRESBYTERIAN CHURCH, (O.S.). [from the** ***National Era*****] 7 September 1849. Mount Vernon, Oh.** Renounces his affiliation with the Old School Presbyterian Church due to that body's strong pro-slavery stance. 4 October 1849. p.1, c3.

**4245 WASHINGTON CORRESPONDENT** *to* **THE** *NEW YORK OBSERVER*. **[extract from the** ***Liberator*****] n.d. n.p.** States that Mr. Gurley is a government agent making an official investigation into the state of the government in Liberia. 4 October 1849. p.1, c4.

**4246 GEORGE BRADBURN** *to* **THE EDITOR OF THE** *PENNSYLVANIA FREEMAN*. **n.d. n.p.** Defends himself against the *Freeman*'s accusation that he had published false statements regarding the Pennsylvania AS. 4 October 1849. p.2, c2.

**4247 WASHINGTON CORRESPONDENT** *to* **THE** *BALTIMORE CLIPPER*. **n.d. n.p.** Reports a disturbance at Pendleton, South Carolina, where a mob raided a post office in order to destroy anti-slavery circulars. 4 October 1849. p.3, c2.

**4248 CINCINNATI CORRESPONDENT** *to* **THE** *BOSTON REPUBLICAN*. **n.d. n.p.** Relates two instances of the cruelty of slavery, one concerning a free colored woman who justified her right to beat her child on the grounds that her offspring had been purchased at a great price, and the other case involving a free colored barber who was seized and confined in New Orleans. 11 October 1849. p.1, c4.

**4249 CORRESPONDENT** *to* **MR. EDITOR. [extract from the** ***Choctaw Journal*****] 10 September 1849. Butler.** Reports on a public meeting in Choctaw, where Mr. P. P. Gaines spoke in favor of the Wilmot Proviso. 11 October 1849. p.1, c5.

**4250 GEORGE WASHINGTON** *to* **ROBERT MORRIS. [extract] n.d. n.p.** Expresses his desire for the abolition of slavery through the exercise of proper legislative authority. 11 October 1849. p.2, c1.

**4251 GEORGE WASHINGTON** *to* **LAFAYETTE. [extract] n.d. n.p.** Praises Lafayette for his purchase of an estate with a view toward emancipating the slaves there; expresses his desire for the abolition of slavery in America. 11 October 1849. p.2, c1.

**4252 GEORGE WASHINGTON** *to* **JOHN F. MERCER. [extract] n.d. n.p.** States his intention never to purchase another slave unless compelled by circumstance; expresses his wish to see slavery abolished by law. 11 October 1849. p.2, c1.

**4253 GEORGE WASHINGTON** *to* **SIR JNO. SINCLAIR. [extract] n.d. n.p.** Concludes that slavery is the cause for the low value of land in Maryland and Virginia relative to Pennsylvania; expresses his belief that the former states will eventually provide for emancipation. 11 October 1849. p.2, c1.

**4254 AMOS GILBERT** *to* **THE** *PENNSYLVANIA FREEMAN*. **n.d. n.p.** Sympathizes with the sufferings of the American slave; exhorts anti-slavery men to an even greater dedication to abolishing the system. 11 October 1849. p.2, c2.

**4255 LONDON CORRESPONDENT** *to* **THE** *NATIONAL ERA*. **[extract] n.d. n.p.** Comments on the most popular speakers at the Paris Peace Conference. 11 October 1849. p.3, c4.

**4256 JAMES HAUGHTON** *to* **THE** *LIBERATOR*. **[extract] 9 September 1849. Dublin.** Expresses sorrow at Father Mathew's refusal to speak out against slavery during his American tour. 18 October 1849. p.1, c2.

**4257 W. WELLS BROWN** *to* **REV. WM. ALLEN, D. D. 2 September 1849. London.** Responds to Allen's recent apology for American slavery; cites examples of slavery's extreme cruelty. 18 October 1849. p.1, c3.

**4258 JOHN M. CLAYTON** *to* **EDWARD HURST, ESQ. 9 June 1849. Philadelphia.** Informs Hurst that the State Department does not grant passports to persons of color. 18 October 1849. p.1, c4.

**4259 CORRESPONDENT** *to* **THE** *WILMINGTON CHICKEN.* **[extract] n.d. n.p.** Reports an effort on the part of some men in Wilmington to drive off or have arrested a colored man who is an expert at shooting birds, for fear that their sport will be ruined. 18 October 1849. p.3, c2.

**4260 JOSEPH BARKER** *to* **n.n. [extract from the** *North Star***] n.d. n.p.** States that he is considering moving his family from England to America. 18 October 1849. p.3, c3.

**4261 A SUBSCRIBER** *to* **THE** *AUGUSTA CONSTITUTIONALIST.* **[extract] n.d. n.p.** Expresses his desire to hang an abolitionist before he dies. 18 October 1849. p.3, c3.

**4262 AMASA WALKER** *to* **THE** *BOSTON REPUBLICAN.* **[extract] n.d. Frankfurt.** Offers his impressions of the German people. 18 October 1849. p.4, c2.

**4263 D. R. ATCHISON** *to* **MR. BENTON. n.d. n.p.** Declares "open war" upon Senator Benton, Free-Soilism, and abolitionism. 25 October 1849. p.3, c3.

**4264 PARIS CORRESPONDENT** *to* **THE** *TRIBUNE.* **n.d. n.p.** Reports that Kossuth, Bem, Dembinski, and Mazzini are likely to travel to New York in November. 25 October 1849. p.3, c4.

**4265 HENRY DOHERTY** *to* **THE** *TRIBUNE.* **n.d. Paris.** Declares that a nation must be industrialized before it can be civilized; advocates the reduction of armies and the increase of the "productive arts of peace." 1 November 1849. p.1, c3.

**4266 CORRESPONDENT** *to* **THE** *CHRISTIAN CHRONICLE.* **n.d. n.p.** Reports that the Rev. J. M. Pendleton of Bowling Green has decided to leave the state of Kentucky. 1 November 1849. p.1, c5.

**4267 W. FARMER** *to* **W. L. GARRISON, ESQ. [extract] n.d. n.p.** Reports that W. W. Brown has held a highly successful meeting in Worcester, England; reports that popular sentiment in England is against Father Mathew for his refusal to take an active part in the anti-slavery movement in America. 1 November 1849. p.2, c1.

**4268 GEORGE BRADBURN** *to* **THE EDITOR OF THE** *PENNSYLVANIA FREEMAN.* **8 October 1849. Lynn, Ma.** Denies that he has made false statements concerning the Pennsylvania AS. 1 November 1849. p.2, c2.

**4269 n.n.** *to* **THE** *TRIBUNE.* **n.d. Washington.** Expresses indignation at the sight of a wagon full of slaves on the way to the Southern market. 1 November 1849. p.3, c2.

**4270 CORRESPONDENT** *to* **THE** *DAILY NEWS.* **[extract] n.d. n.p.** Reports a strong public sentiment favoring disestablishment of the Church of Ireland. 1 November 1849. p.3, c4.

**4271 MRS. FOLLEN** *to* **THE READERS OF THE** *CHILD'S FRIEND.* **[extract] n.d. n.p.** Describes her feeling upon sighting a butterfly at sea. 1 November 1849. p.4, c3.

**4272 CORRESPONDENT** *to* **THE** *NEW YORK EVENING POST*. **[extract] n.d. n.p.** Reports on the major debates of the recent Kentucky constitutional convention. 8 November 1849. p.1, c1.

**4273 CORRESPONDENT** *to* **THE** *POST*. **[extract] n.d. n.p.** Comments on the "overweening pride" displayed by Kentuckians in the debates of their recent constitutional convention. 8 November 1849. p.1, c1.

**4274 WM. WELLS BROWN** *to* **FRIEND GARRISON. [from the** *Liberator***] 12 October 1849. London.** Recounts highlights of his journey to the Paris Peace Congress. 8 November 1849. p.1, c2.

**4275 JAMES B. CONGDON** *to* **A MEMBER OF THE BOSTON SCHOOL COMMITTEE. 10 August 1849. New Bedford.** States that there is no separate school for colored children in New Bedford, despite an attempt to establish one seventeen years earlier; commends the New Bedford system, where colored children enjoy the advantages of the public schools equally with whites. 8 November 1849. p.1, c4.

**4276 J. M. BARRETT** *to* **MR. EDITOR. [from the** *Era***] 8 October 1849. Spartanburg.** Announces that he has been released from prison in South Carolina. 8 November 1849. p.1, c4.

**4277 A TRAVELLING CORRESPONDENT** *to* **THE** *CHRONOTYPE*. **[extract] n.d. Georgia.** Comments on the degradation of the white laboring class in the South. 8 November 1849. p.1, c5.

**4278 E. J. W.** *to* **THE EDITOR OF THE** *PENNSYLVANIA FREEMAN*. **n.d. n.p.** Criticizes Mr. J. J. G. Bias for assailing the Quakers before the Norristown convention. 8 November 1849. p.2, c1.

**4279 G. WASHINGTON SIMONDS** *to* **MESSRS. EDITORS. 2 October 1849. East Lexington, Ma.** Argues that the preamble to the United States Constitution necessarily nullifies those sections which uphold slavery. 8 November 1849. p.2, c1.

**4280 DELAWARE CORRESPONDENT** *to* **THE** *BLUE HEN'S CHICKEN*. **[extract] n.d. n.p.** Reports the arrest and subsequent release of two free colored men who travelled to Maryland. 8 November 1849. p.2, c4.

**4281 BALTIMORE CORRESPONDENT** *to* **THE** *TRIBUNE*. **29 October 1849. n.p.** Reports that over 200 slaves have absconded from their masters in Maryland within the past five months. 8 November 1849. p.2, c5.

**4282 WASHINGTON CORRESPONDENT** *to* **THE** *CLEVELAND TRUE DEMOCRAT*. **[extract] n.d. n.p.** Recounts a discussion with Thomas C. McDonald, U. S. Consul at St. Catharines, concerning the deep involvement of American Christians in the Brazilian slave trade. 8 November 1849. p.3, c1.

**4283 WILLIAM JAY** *to* **n.n. n.d. n.p.** Criticizes Free-Soilers in New York who have allied themselves with the regular Democratic Party. 8 November 1849. p.3, c2.

**4284 n.n.** *to* **n.n. 5 November 1849. Quincy, Il.** Reports the escape and subsequent capture of approximately fifty slaves from Missouri. 8 November 1849. p.3, c3.

**4285 CONSTANTINOPLE CORRESPONDENT** *to* **THE** *COURIER AND ENQUIRER*. **n.d. n.p.** Assesses the character and customs of the Turks. 8 November 1849. p.4, c2.

**4286 n.n.** *to* **n.n. [extract from the** *Examiner***] n.d. Baltimore.** Reports an effort is underway in Maryland to call a constitutional convention to provide for emancipation. 15 November 1849. p.1, c3.

**4287 TRUMAN CASE** *to* **THE** *ANTI-SLAVERY BUGLE.* **[extract] 8 October 1849. Randolph.** Relates the story of a slave who received 300 lashes for requesting permission to visit his wife at Christmas. 15 November 1849. p.1, c5.

**4288 J. B. PINNEY** *to* **MR. EDITOR. 12 October 1849. New York.** Appeals for funds to help liberate a slave named Dickinson and his family, who wish to become colonists in Liberia. 15 November 1849. p.2, c4.

**4289 THOMAS AMOS** *to* **THE EDITORS OF THE** *PENNSYLVANIA FREEMAN.* **n.d. n.p.** Encloses a resolution of the Hosanna AS. 15 November 1849. p.3, c3.

**4290 CALIFORNIA CORRESPONDENT** *to* **THE** *NEW YORK TRIBUNE.* **[extract] n.d. n.p.** Reports that the Sandwich Islands have been taken by the French. 15 November 1849. p.3, c3.

**4291 CORRESPONDENT** *to* **THE** *MORNING CHRONICLE.* **n.d. Paris.** Announces that the Austrian government has officially recognized the Bey of Tunis. 15 November 1849. p.3, c3.

**4292 n.n.** *to* **n.n. [extract from the** *Norfolk Co. Democrat***] n.d. Providence.** Praises the colored population of Providence. 15 November 1849. p.3, c4.

**4293 JOSEPH BARKER** *to* **THE EDITOR OF THE** *STANDARD.* **16 October 1849. New York.** Regrets that he could not attend an anti-slavery meeting at Norristown; states that men's worth should be measured by their efforts to serve their race. 22 November 1849. p.1, c5.

**4294 GEO. BRADBURN** *to* **THE EDITOR OF THE** *PENNSYLVANIA FREEMAN.* **10 November 1849. Lynn.** Retracts a misstatement concerning Patrick Henry's view of the constitutional power of the federal government to abolish slavery. 22 November 1849. p.2, c1.

**4295 n.n.** *to* **WM. HARNED. 13 September 1849. n.p.** Encloses a fifty-dollar contribution in response to a vigilance committee circular. 22 November 1849. p.2, c3.

**4296 CORRESPONDENT** *to* **THE** *NEW YORK JOURNAL OF COMMERCE.* **14 November 1849. Washington.** Discusses Senator Calhoun's plan to resist the admission of California as a state into the Union so long as its organization restricts slavery. 22 November 1849. p.3, c1.

**4297 CORRESPONDENT** *to* **THE** *LONDON DAILY NEWS.* **[extract] n.d. n.p.** Reports that the Italian cardinals have suspended work on the railway from Naples to Rome. 22 November 1849. p.3, c2.

**4298 LOUIS NAPOLEON BONAPARTE** *to* **n.n. 31 October 1849. n.p.** Explains his reasons for choosing a new cabinet. 22 November 1849. p.3, c3.

**4299 A MECHANIC** *to* **MR. EDITOR. [from the** *Investigator***] n.d. n.p.** Forwards an article on the Conway Bridge in England. 22 November 1849. p.4, c1.

**4300 LONDON CORRESPONDENT** *to* **THE** *CHRONOTYPE.* **n.d. n.p.** Reports on conditions in the model lodging houses of London. 22 November 1849. p.4, c3.

**4301 S. P. CHASE** *to* **HON. JOHN G. BRESLIN. October 1849. Cincinnati.** Denounces slavery as the worst form of despotism; declares that the Democratic Party must repudiate slavery as a matter of principle. 29 November 1849. p.1, c2.

**4302 CORRESPONDENT** *to* **THE** ***PUBLIC LEDGER*****. 11 November 1849. Washington.** Surveys the volatile issues facing the next session of Congress. 29 November 1849. p.1, c5.

**4303 BENJAMIN FISH** *to* **THE FRIENDS OF THE SLAVE AND OF THE** ***NORTH STAR*****. 23 October 1849. Rochester.** Appeals to each subscriber of the *North Star* to send an extra dollar with his yearly subscription and to procure at least one additional patron. 29 November 1849. p.1, c5.

**4304 MR. MAHAN** *to* **THE** ***OBERLIN EVANGELIST*****. n.d. London.** Exhorts American clergymen to examine the question of slavery in light of the gospel; encloses a letter from W. E. Whiting published in an English periodical. 29 November 1849. p.2, c2.

**4305 W. E. WHITING, ESQ.** *to* **n.n. 24 May 1849. New York.** Criticizes the Church for its failure to take a stand against slavery. 29 November 1849. p.2, c2.

**4306 A MARYLAND SLAVEOWNER** *to* **n.n. 12 November 1849. n.p.** Offers a $300 reward for his escaped slave; believes that the fugitive is in his correspondent's vicinity. 29 November 1849. p.2, c2.

**4307 WASHINGTON CORRESPONDENT** *to* **THE** ***LEDGER*****. n.d. n.p.** Reports agreement that the question of slavery in the territories must be settled in the upcoming congressional session; cautions against disunion. 29 November 1849. p.3, c1.

**4308 CORRESPONDENT** *to* **THE** ***PITTSBURGH DISPATCH*****. n.d. n.p.** Describes the valley of the Great Salt Lake. 29 November 1849. p.3, c2.

**4309 NOTA BENE** *to* **THE** ***CONCORDIA INTELLIGENCER*****. n.d. New Orleans.** Reports that Mr. James A. Campbell has patented an improved printing press which will print 5,000 sheets per hour more than the best presses currently in use. 29 November 1849. p.3, c2.

**4310 MARIA W. CHAPMAN** *to* **MR. GAY. [from the** ***Standard*****] 31 October 1849. Paris.** Encloses her translation of an article in *La Reforme*. 6 December 1849. p.1, c5.

**4311 JUDGE LUMPKIN** *to* **REV. THEOBALD MATHEW. 12 October 1849. Athens, Ga.** States his opinion that a visit by Father Mathew to the South, in light of his publicized association with Irish abolitionists, would be productive of evil and do harm to the cause of temperance. 6 December 1849. p.2, c2.

**4312 CORRESPONDENT** *to* **THE** ***CHRISTIAN CHRONICLE*****. n.d. n.p.** Reports that the Rev. J. M. Pendleton of Bowling Green is leaving Kentucky with his family, due to increased alienation on account of his anti-slavery sentiments. 6 December 1849. p.2, c4.

**4313 C. M. BURLEIGH** *to* **THE** ***FREEMAN*****. 24 November 1849. Plainfield, Ct.** Reports on the anniversary meeting of the Rhode Island AS. 6 December 1849. p.2, c5.

**4314 LONDON CORRESPONDENT** *to* **THE** ***MANCHESTER GUARDIAN*****. n.d. n.p.** Comments on *Shirley*, the new novel by the author of *Jane Eyre*. 6 December 1849. p.3, c3.

**4315 M. R. TEWKSBURY, M.D.** *to* **MR. EDITOR. [from the** ***Boston Herald*****] n.d. n.p.** Describes the land and people of California. 6 December 1849. p.4, c2.

**4316 WASHINGTON CORRESPONDENT** *to* **THE** *BALTIMORE SUN.* **[extract] n.d. n.p.** Reports that a compromise is at hand in Congress regarding the admission of California to the Union. 13 December 1849. p.2, c1.

**4317 A MISSIONARY OF THE BAPTIST BOARD** *to* **MESSRS. EDITORS. [from an American journal] 27 October 1846. Mergui.** Worries that his missionary work among the wild Karens will be imperiled once they learn of the American slave system. 13 December 1849. p.2, c4.

**4318 [LEWIS] CASS** *to* **n.n. [extract from the** *Western Citizen***] n.d. n.p.** Asserts that Congress has no right to exclude slavery from any given territory. 13 December 1849. p.2, c4.

**4319 JOS. T. BUCKINGHAM** *to* **n.n. [extract] 9 November 1849. Cambridge, Ma.** Asserts that the Whig Party has abandoned its principles by nominating General Taylor for the presidency. 20 December 1849. p.1, c1.

**4320 GEO. THOMPSON** *to* **WILLIAM L. GARRISON. 23 November 1849. Edinburgh.** Bemoans the "dark cloud" of slavery which lies over America; implores Americans to make haste in their efforts to rid their country of its shame. 20 December 1849. p.2, c1.

**4321 WASHINGTON CORRESPONDENT** *to* **THE** *PENNSYLVANIA INQUIRER.* **13 December 1849. Washington.** Reports on a heated debate in the House of Representatives over the selection of a Speaker. 20 December 1849. p.2, c5.

**4322 BURKE** *to* **n.n. [extract from the** *Macon Journal and Messenger***] n.d. n.p.** Warns that allowing slaves to become master mechanics would serve to undermine the institution of slavery. 20 December 1849. p.3, c3.

**4323 CORRESPONDENT** *to* **FRIEND. [from the** *Bugle***] 28 October 1849. Philadelphia.** Characterizes the recent annual meeting at Norristown as "the very best ever held in Pennsylvania." 27 December 1849. p.1, c1.

**4324 n.n.** *to* **THE EDITOR OF THE** *NATIONAL ERA.* **24 September 1849. St. Louis.** Describes the sale of three slaves at a public auction. 27 December 1849. p.1, c3.

**4325 DANIEL B. ANDERSON** *to* **MESSRS. EDITORS. 19 December 1849. Wilmington, De.** Challenges an article in the *Freeman* which falsely accused the Rev. Isaac Barney of censuring an abolitionist and of not sympathizing with the cause of the oppressed. 27 December 1849. p.1, c5.

**4326 JOSEPH HARLAN** *to* **FRIEND McKIM. 1849. Chester County.** Reports a more favorable attitude toward abolitionists in his area than in the past; commends the work of W. L. Garrison and Dr. Bailey. 27 December 1849. p.2, c1.

## [1850]

**4327 CORRESPONDENT** *to* **THE** *PUBLIC LEDGER.* **20 December 1849. Washington.** Reports on a debate in the United States Senate over a resolution admitting Father Mathew to a seat within the bar of the Senate chamber. 3 January 1850. p.1, c5.

**4328 EDWIN H. NEVIN** *to* **MR. EDITOR. [from the** *Ohio Times***] n.d. n.p.** Reports that a branch of the Free Presbyterian Church has been organized in Mount Vernon, Ohio. 3 January 1850. p.2, c2.

**4329 W. A. P.** *to* **MESSRS. EDITORS. 17 December 1849. Bart.** Criticizes teachers for their failure to combat prejudice in the public schools. 3 January 1850. p.2, c2.

**4330 JOSEPH HARLAN** *to* **THE EDITOR. 29 December 1849. Chester County.** Comments on a previous communication concerning the quarrel between William Lloyd Garrison and Dr. Bailey; asserts that "an honest man is doing right when he sincerely *believes* he is doing right." 3 January 1850. p.2, c3.

**4331 L. A. GODEY** *to* **THE EDITORS OF THE** *TELEGRAPH.* **1 December 1849. Philadelphia.** Denies that his periodical, the *Lady's Book*, has contained articles maligning Southern institutions. 3 January 1850. p.3, c1.

**4332 AN OCCASIONAL CORRESPONDENT** *to* **THE** *DAILY NEWS.* **2 January 1850. Washington.** Declares that disunion is preferable to the continued fostering of black slavery by Northern forbearance. 17 January 1850. p.2, c3.

**4333 N. RAMIREZ** *to* **THE SECRETARY OF STATE. [from the** *Tribune***] 6 October 1849. Santiago de Manegua [***sic***], Nicaragua.** Declares that Nicaragua will adhere to the principle of absolute exclusion of foreign powers from the domestic or international affairs of American states. 24 January 1850. p.1, c4.

**4334 A WILMINGTONIAN** *to* **FRIENDS JEANDELL AND VINCENT. [from the** *Blue Hen's Chicken***] n.d. n.p.** Relates the story of an escaped slave from Georgia. 24 January 1850. p.1, c5.

**4335 G. B.** *to* **FRIEND. 7 January 1850. n.p.** Encloses the narrative of "Le Grand," a freed slave who was kidnapped into bondage once again and eventually proved his status before a St. Louis court. 24 January 1850. p.2, c1.

**4336 WASHINGTON CORRESPONDENT** *to* **THE** *LEDGER.* **16 January 1850. n.p.** Comments on the potential conflicts in the new session of Congress; reports that some Southern members believe that General Taylor will veto the Wilmot Proviso and oppose all legislation regarding the territories. 24 January 1850. p.3, c2.

**4337 HENRICO** *to* **THE** *WASHINGTON BULLETIN.* **19 January 1850. Washington.** Reports that Mr. Calhoun of South Carolina is suffering from a severe attack of pneumonia which may prove fatal; speculates on imminent changes in the cabinet. 24 January 1850. p.3, c2.

**4338 CORRESPONDENT** *to* **THE** *TRIBUNE.* **[extract] n.d. Fort Nisqually, Or.** Reports that slavery is prevalent among the Oregon Indians. 31 January 1850. p.2, c5.

**4339 J. M. McKIM** *to* **FRIEND. n.d. n.p.** Reports on the annual meeting of the Massachusetts AS. 31 January 1850. p.2, c5.

**4340 WASHINGTON CORRESPONDENT** *to* **THE** *PUBLIC LEDGER.* **n.d. n.p.** Characterizes the South as a "powder magazine" ready to explode over the issue of slavery; predicts that there will be no significant legislation of any kind until the slavery question is settled. 31 January 1850. p.3, c5.

**4341 GASSAWAY WINTERTON, SELBY PARKER, AND J. E. SNODGRASS** *to* **THE FRIENDS OF TEMPERANCE THROUGHOUT THE UNION. 1 January 1850. Washington.** Announce a National Temperance Convention to be held in Washington. 7 February 1850. p.3, c5.

**4342 GRACE GREENWOOD** *to* **THE** *NATIONAL ERA.* **n.d. n.p.** Praises the speakers she heard at anti-slavery meetings in Philadelphia. 14 February 1850. p.1, c2.

**4343 WASHINGTON CORRESPONDENT** *to* **THE** *TRIBUNE.* **[extract] n.d. n.p.** Dismisses arguments against the admission of California into the Union. 14 February 1850. p.1, c4.

**4344 CORRESPONDENT** *to* **THE** *EVENING BULLETIN.* **n.d. Washington.** Commends the Whigs in the House of Representatives who were instrumental in tabling a resolution of Mr. Root regarding the organization of California and New Mexico; reports the tabling of a resolution of Mr. Giddings to guarantee the rights of all persons regardless of color. 14 February 1850. p.2, c1.

**4345 WM. HARNED** *to* **THE EDITOR OF THE** *TRIBUNE.* **n.d. n.p.** Encloses three letters, all regarding the sale of the daughters and grandchildren of Mrs. Nancy Cartwright, a colored woman who has purchased her own freedom and now resides in New York. 14 February 1850. p.3, c2.

**4346 EMILY RUSSELL** *to* **NANCY CARTWRIGHT. 22 January 1850. Alexandria.** Informs her mother that she is in jail and expects to be sold within a short time; asks her to visit as soon as possible. 14 February 1850. p.3, c2.

**4347 WM. HARNED** *to* **MR. JOSEPH BRUIN. 28 January 1850. New York.** Inquires into the price at which Bruin will sell Emily Russell to her mother, and how long she might have to make up the amount, as well as the price of Emily's sisters and their children. 14 February 1850. p.3, c2.

**4348 BRUIN AND HILL** *to* **WM. HARNED, ESQ. 31 January 1850. Alexandria.** Quote the price at which they will sell Emily Russell, her sisters, and the sisters' children. 14 February 1850. p.3, c2.

**4349 GRACE GREENWOOD** *to* **GENTLEMEN. [from the** *Saturday Evening Post***] 22 January 1850. New Brighton.** Responds to Mr. Saxe's reply to her criticism of his volume; defends the rights of women in general and literary women in particular. 14 February 1850. p.4, c2.

**4350 AN AMERICAN IN BERLIN** *to* **THE** *BOSTON DAILY ADVERTISER.* **[extract from the** *Tribune***] n.d. n.p.** Condemns the conduct of an American minister in Germany, Mr. Hannegan, whom he characterizes as "the most mannerless and utterly vulgar man I ever met." 21 February 1850. p.1, c1.

**4351 ROBERT BARCLAY** *to* **THE** *TRIBUNE.* **9 February 1850. Washington.** Reports on a senatorial debate prompted by an anti-slavery memorial of certain Pennsylvania Quakers; defends the right of petition; anticipates further attempts in Congress to extend and secure the domestic slave traffic. 21 February 1850. p.1, c2.

**4352 WASHINGTON CORRESPONDENT** *to* **THE** *NORTH AMERICAN.* **10 February 1850. n.p.** Reports that Mr. Calhoun is recovering from his recent illness, and openly advocates disunion and the establishment of a Southern confederacy; reports that Mr. Buchanan is said to favor a scheme to extend the Missouri line to the Pacific. 21 February 1850. p.1, c5.

**4353 WASHINGTON CORRESPONDENT** *to* **THE** *LEDGER.* **[extract] n.d. n.p.** Laments the state of affairs in Congress, where the issue of slavery is preventing action on a number of important bills. 21 February 1850. p.2, c5.

**4354 CORRESPONDENT** *to* **THE** *PENNSYLVANIAN.* **[extract] n.d. n.p.** Relates a portion of a conversation with a pro-Southern Pennsylvania man. 21 February 1850. p.2, c5.

**4355 C. M. BURLEIGH** *to* *FREEMAN.* **9 February 1850. Weymouth, N.J.** Provides an account of his activities on a recent lecture tour. 21 February 1850. p.3, c1.

**4356 CORRESPONDENT** *to* **THE** *TRIBUNE.* **12 February 1850. Washington.** Comments on the question of the right of the people to petition Congress; reports that only three senators—Seward, Chase, and Hale—voted to uphold the right of petition. 21 February 1850. p.3, c4.

**4357 n.n.** *to* **n.n. [extract] 20 December 1849. Lisbon.** Reports the wreck of a ship, supposed to be an American vessel, discovered off Cape Finisterre. 21 February 1850. p.3, c4.

**4358 CORRESPONDENT** *to* **THE** *NORTH AMERICAN.* **n.d. n.p.** Summarizes the majority and minority reports issued by a committee of the Pennsylvania legislature appointed to inquire into the existing federal relations of that state; criticizes the majority opinion which claims that Congress has no legitimate power to restrict slavery in the territories. 28 February 1850. p.3, c2.

**4359 CORRESPONDENT** *to* **THE** *NORTH AMERICAN.* **25 February 1849 [sic]. Harrisburg.** States that two of the three signers of the majority report on the slavery question submitted to the Pennsylvania House of Representatives have repudiated certain positions assumed therein, and that the report will not be adopted. 28 February 1850. p.3, c3.

**4360 HENRY GREW** *to* **THE EDITOR OF THE** *LEDGER.* **n.d. n.p.** Argues for a dissolution of the Union. 28 February 1850. p.3, c4.

**4361 WILLIAM JAY** *to* **HON. WILLIAM J. NELSON. [from the** *New York Evening Post*] **11 February 1850. New York.** Discusses the eight resolutions lately placed before the Senate by Henry Clay; concludes that they do not constitute a compromise, but rather a surrender to slaveholding interests. 7 March 1850. p.1, c1.

**4362 A WHIG POST MASTER** *to* **MESSRS. EDITORS. n.d. n.p.** States that he would be willing to accept the authority to grant certificates to slaveholders or their agents for the return of escaped slaves, since his interpretation of the Constitution would not oblige him to utilize this power. 7 March 1850. p.2, c1.

**4363 HENRY GREW** *to* **SIR. n.d. n.p.** Commends the *Freeman*'s declared hostility to slavery in all forms, but argues that this stance is inconsistent with the paper's policy of support of the Constitution. 7 March 1850. p.2, c1.

**4364 THE EXECUTIVE COMMITTEE OF THE PENNSYLVANIA AS** *to* **THE READERS OF THE** *FREEMAN.* **7 March 1850. Philadelphia.** Appeal for subscriptions to the *New York National Anti-Slavery Standard.* 7 March 1850. p.3, c2.

**4365 OBSERVER** *to* **THE** *LEDGER.* **[extract] n.d. n.p.** Comments on a speech of Mr. Calhoun in the Senate, in which he argued against the admission of California as a state. 7 March 1850. p.3, c4.

**4366 Z. S. WALLINGFORD** *to* **HON. JEREMIAH CLEMENS. 6 February 1850. Dover.** Responds to questions regarding the condition of factory laborers in New England. 14 March 1850. p.1, c1.

**4367 TRIM** *to* **MR.** *FREEMAN.* **n.d. n.p.** Summarizes recent debates in his region over the issues of slavery and disunion. 14 March 1850. p.2, c3.

**4368 R. THOMASON** *to* **MR. EDITOR. n.d. n.p.** Announces that the Emigrant's Friend Society of Philadelphia is in operation, providing the services of foreign laborers. 14 March 1850. p.2, c4.

**4369 C. M. BURLEIGH** *to* **THE** *FREEMAN.* **21 February 1850. Weymouth.** Reports on his lecture tour of New Jersey. 14 March 1850. p.3, c1.

**4370 HENRY CHARLES** *to* **n.n. [extract from the** ***Non-Slaveholder*****] n.d. n.p.** Reports that in every section of the South there is a widespread sentiment in favor of a dissolution of the Union. 14 March 1850. p.3, c1.

**4371 CORRESPONDENT** *to* **n.n. [extract from the** ***Non-Slaveholder*****] n.d. n.p.** Expresses his feelings after visiting a man imprisoned in Nashville for aiding fugitive slaves. 14 March 1850. p.3, c2.

**4372 CORRESPONDENT** *to* **THE** ***EVENING BULLETIN*****. [extract] 5 March 1850. Harrisburg.** Reports that a bill has been introduced in the Pennsylvania senate which calls for the expulsion of all Negroes from the state and the repeal of the 1847 act protecting fugitive slaves. 21 March 1850. p.1, c4.

**4373 CORRESPONDENT** *to* **THE** ***NORTH AMERICAN*****. 11 March 1850. Washington.** Praises Senator Seward of New York as "the prompt and efficient defender of popular liberty and the rights of man." 21 March 1850. p.2, c2.

**4374 CORRESPONDENT** *to* **THE** ***NORTH AMERICAN*****. [extract] n.d. n.p.** Considers the probability for passage of the compromise legislation before Congress. 21 March 1850. p.2, c2.

**4375 WASHINGTON CORRESPONDENT** *to* **THE** ***NORTH AMERICAN*****. [extract] n.d. n.p.** Reports that the French government has announced to Great Britain its intention to withdraw from the stipulations of the treaty of 1845, which required the French to maintain a fleet off the African coast to aid in preventing the slave trade. 21 March 1850. p.3, c2.

**4376 C. M. BURLEIGH** *to* **THE** ***FREEMAN*****. 26 February 1850. Weymouth.** Continues an account of his lecture tour in New Jersey. 21 March 1850. p.3, c3.

**4377 WASHINGTON CORRESPONDENT** *to* **THE** ***NORTH AMERICAN*****. [extract] n.d. n.p.** Comments on Daniel Webster's proposal to compensate for the admission of California as a free state by admitting a slave state. 21 March 1850. p.3, c5.

**4378 WASHINGTON CORRESPONDENT** *to* **THE** ***NEW YORK EVENING POST*****. [extract] n.d. n.p.** Reports rumors that an expedition is being organized for the purpose of invading and revolutionizing Cuba. 21 March 1850. p.3, c5.

**4379 WILLIAM JAY** *to* **HON. WM. NELSON, MEMBER OF CONGRESS. 16 March 1850. New York.** Criticizes Daniel Webster's reversal of his position regarding the Wilmot Proviso. 28 March 1850. p.1, c1.

**4380 CORRESPONDENT** *to* **THE** ***CLEVELAND TRUE DEMOCRAT*****. n.d. n.p.** Recounts his unsuccessful attempt to purchase the slave Emily Russell on behalf of the girl's mother. 28 March 1850. p.1, c4.

**4381 n.n.** *to* **THE** ***NEW YORK EVENING POST*****. [extract] n.d. n.p.** Comments on the large percentage of colored barristers and legislators in Jamaica. 28 March 1850. p.1, c5.

**4382 GRACE GREENWOOD** *to* **THE EDITOR OF THE** ***NATIONAL ERA*****. 12 February 1850. New Brighton, Pa.** Criticizes Henry Clay's recent speech in support of conciliatory resolutions before Congress. 28 March 1850. p.1, c5.

**4383 WM. F. JOHNSTON** *to* **THE SENATE AND HOUSE OF REPRESENTATIVES OF PENNSYLVANIA. 22 March 1850. Executive Chamber.** Transmits certain resolutions of the legislatures of Virginia and Georgia pertaining to the preservation of the Union and alleged Northern encroachments upon the rights of the slaveholding states. 28 March 1850. p.2, c1.

**4384 HARRISBURG CORRESPONDENT** *to* **THE** *NORTH AMERICAN.* **[extract] n.d. n.p.** Criticizes the members of the Pennsylvania legislature who opposed the distribution of Governor Johnston's message regarding the resolutions on slavery transmitted by the legislatures of Virginia and Georgia. 28 March 1850. p.3, c2.

**4385 ISAAC A. PENNYPACKER** *to* **THE EDITORS OF THE** *PENNSYLVANIA FREEMAN.* **16 March 1850. Phoenixville.** Contests the *Freeman*'s account of his recent debate with Mr. McKim at the Schuylkill Lyceum. 28 March 1850. p.3, c3.

**4386 CORRESPONDENT** *to* **THE** *NEW ORLEANS PICAYUNE.* **19 February 1850. Havana.** Reports that many are responding to a rumor that Cuba will be invaded in May; discusses the possibility of a civil war to overthrow Spanish rule, and the prospects for emancipation. 4 April 1850. p.1, c3.

**4387 PAUL SEYMOUR** *to* **J. M. McKIM, ESQ. 22 March 1850. Louisville, Ky.** Thanks McKim for forwarding a contribution to the *Louisville Examiner*; reports that the adoption of the new constitution in Kentucky is questionable. 4 April 1850. p.2, c5.

**4388 A MEMBER OF THE LEGISLATURE** *to* **SIR. 1 April 1850. Harrisburg.** Reports that the bill to repeal portions of the act of 1847 (regarding fugitive slaves) will probably pass the House, but cannot pass the Senate. 4 April 1850. p.2, c5.

**4389 W. BURTON** *to* **FRIEND. 12 March 1850. Penns Meinter, N.Y.** Cautions readers against a colored man named John Bostick, who is soliciting money from the benevolent under false pretenses. 4 April 1850. p.3, c1.

**4390 WASHINGTON CORRESPONDENT** *to* **THE** *BOSTON COURIER.* **n.d. n.p.** States that he is unable to find any Northern Whig member of Congress who concurs with Mr. Webster's assertion of the propriety of establishing a territorial government in New Mexico without the Wilmot Proviso. 4 April 1850. p.3, c4.

**4391 LONDON CORRESPONDENT** *to* **THE** *NATIONAL INTELLIGENCER.* **n.d. n.p.** Comments on Charlotte Brontë, author of *Jane Eyre*, and her late sisters, all of whom wrote under the assumed name of Bell. 4 April 1850. p.3, c5.

**4392 DANIEL WEBSTER** *to* **COMMODORE STOCKTON. n.d. n.p.** Praises Stockton for his capacity for unbiased judgment in political matters. 11 April 1850. p.2, c4.

**4393 COMMODORE STOCKTON** *to* **DANIEL WEBSTER. [extract] n.d. n.p.** States that a great crisis faces the republic; advances arguments in defense of American slavery. 11 April 1850. p.2, c4.

**4394 THE BOSTON UNION** *to* **THE PHILADELPHIA UNION ASSOCIATION. n.d. n.p.** Express greetings and best wishes on the occasion of the third annual festival of the Philadelphia Union Association. 11 April 1850. p.3, c3.

**4395 CALVIN FAIRBANK** *to* **CITIZENS OF BOSTON. 19 March 1850. Boston.** Expresses gratitude to those who procured his release from a Kentucky prison following a confinement of four and one-half years. 18 April 1850. p.1, c1.

**4396 C. M. BURLEIGH** *to* **THE** *FREEMAN.* **12 April 1850. n.p.** Sketches his recent activities on a lecture tour of New Jersey. 18 April 1850. p.3, c2.

**4397 CORRESPONDENT** *to* **THE** *TRIBUNE.* **10 April 1850. Washington.** Provides a verbatim account of a Senate debate on the census bill. 18 April 1850. p.3, c3.

**4398 T. D.** *to* **THE** ***TRIBUNE*****. 24 March 1850. Pittsburgh, Pa.** Reports the formation of a Working-Men's Congress in Pittsburgh; reports on the organization of local unions in various trades. 18 April 1850. p.3, c5.

**4399 NATHAN THOMAS AND HENRY CHARLES** *to* **THE** ***NON-SLAVEHOLDER*****. [extract] 3 January 1850. n.p.** Relate their conversation with a Southern pro-slavery man aboard a train. 25 April 1850. p.1, c1.

**4400 NATHAN THOMAS AND HENRY CHARLES** *to* **THE** ***NON-SLAVEHOLDER*****. [extract] 5 January 1850. n.p.** Report on an agreeable voyage on the Alabama River; relate an incident with a Georgia man with whom one of the correspondents read from the Bible. 25 April 1850. p.1, c1.

**4401 NATHAN THOMAS AND HENRY CHARLES** *to* **THE** ***NON-SLAVEHOLDER*****. 7 January 1850. Selby County, Al.** Report that they have found a settlement occupied principally by nonslaveholders, where most of the cotton is raised by free labor. 25 April 1850. p.1, c1.

**4402 NATHAN THOMAS AND HENRY CHARLES** *to* **THE** ***NON-SLAVEHOLDER*****. 11 January 1850. n.p.** State that they have found a good deal of free labor cotton, but no free labor gins; note the suspicion of a local merchant. 25 April 1850. p.1, c1.

**4403 NATHAN THOMAS AND HENRY CHARLES** *to* **THE** ***NON-SLAVEHOLDER*****. 13 January 1850. n.p.** Summarize a conversation with their landlord, an anti-slavery Southerner. 25 April 1850. p.1, c1.

**4404 NATHAN THOMAS AND HENRY CHARLES** *to* **THE** ***NON-SLAVEHOLDER*****. [extract] 18 January 1850. Walker County, Al.** Describe conditions in Walker County, where the cotton is raised and the gins operated almost entirely by free labor; report that the proportion of Southerners who refrain from holding slaves is about equal to the number of Northerners who refrain from purchasing the fruits of slavery. 25 April 1850. p.1, c2.

**4405 CLERICUS** *to* **MESSRS. EDITORS. [from the** ***Charleston Mercury*****] n.d. n.p.** Suggests that all persons who have received copies of Mr. Seward's speech in the mail forward the same to Mr. Seward. 25 April 1850. p.1, c3.

**4406 JANE G. SWISSHELM** *to* **MR. GREELEY. 17 April 1850. Washington.** Provides an account of a Senate debate on the California question, which culminated in Mr. Foote drawing a pistol on Mr. Benton. 25 April 1850. p.1, c5.

**4407 A WHIG POSTMASTER** *to* **MESSRS. EDITORS. n.d. n.p.** Defends his prior assertion that he, as an abolitionist, is justified in holding the position of postmaster, since his oath to support the Constitution relates only to the duties of that particular office. 25 April 1850. p.2, c4.

**4408 A VENERABLE AND BELOVED PASTOR** *to* **THE** ***CHRISTIAN OBSERVER*****. n.d. n.p.** Expresses hope that the state legislature will not do battle over the question of slavery during the coming session. 25 April 1850. p.3, c1.

**4409 HARRISBURG CORRESPONDENT** *to* **THE** ***SPIRIT OF THE TIMES*****. 10 April 1850. n.p.** Reports that a select committee of the Pennsylvania Senate has advised against the House bill to repeal certain sections of the act of 1847 relative to kidnapping. 25 April 1850. p.3, c2.

**4410 DR. CHARLES BELL GIBSON** *to* **THE EDITOR OF THE** ***RICHMOND REPUBLICAN*****. [extract] n.d. n.p.** States that the "shower of flesh" experienced in the locality has been subjected to analysis and has been found to be of some species of fish dropped in distant places by a water spout. 25 April 1850. p.3, c4.

**4411 JANE G. SWISSHELM** *to* **THE** ***NEW YORK TRIBUNE*****. [extract] n.d. n.p.** Comments critically on congressional speeches by Mr. Ross of Pennsylvania and Mr. Harris of Tennessee; discusses the tendency of congressmen to glorify the Constitution in their orations; expresses her feelings upon encountering a slave woman who had just been sold away from her family. 2 May 1850. p.1, c5.

**4412 EIGHT HUNDRED CITIZENS OF BOSTON** *to* **THE HONORABLE DANIEL WEBSTER. 25 March 1850. Boston.** Concur with the sentiments expressed in Webster's recent speech in the United States Senate on the subject of slavery. 2 May 1850. p.2, c2.

**4413 A LEARNER** *to* **THE** ***AMERICAN MISSIONARY*****. n.d. n.p.** Denounces an enclosed statement by the Board of Foreign Missions of the Presbyterian Church on the subject of polygamy. 2 May 1850. p.2, c4.

**4414 HENRY CHARLES** *to* **THE** ***NON-SLAVEHOLDER*****. [extract] n.d. n.p.** States that the cause which gave rise to the Union Literary Institute may be traced to those laws which deprived the colored people of the Western states of the benefit of the free school system. 2 May 1850. p.3, c2.

**4415 CARDINAL ANTONELLI** *to* **n.n. 12 March 1850. Royal Palace of Portici.** Announces that the pope will return to his temporal dominions in April; expresses trust in governments with which the Holy See maintains amicable relations to ensure the independence of the Church. 2 May 1850. p.3, c4.

**4416 n.n.** *to* **LUCRETIA MOTT. [extract] n.d. n.p.** Criticizes the "nauseous sentiments" advanced in a lecture by Mr. Dana on the nature and role of woman. 2 May 1850. p.4, c2.

**4417 THE LADIES OF BOLTON** *to* **WILLIAM WELLS BROWN. [from the** ***Manchester Examiner and Times*****] 22 March 1850. n.p.** Express their affection for Brown and their sympathy for the anti-slavery cause. 9 May 1850. p.1, c3.

**4418 M. G.** *to* **READERS. n.d. n.p.** Announces her temporary withdrawal from the editorial staff of the *Freeman*. 9 May 1850. p2, c3.

**4419 C. M. B.** *to* **THE** ***FREEMAN*****. 7 May 1850. New York.** Reports on the anniversary meeting of the AAS. 9 May 1850. p.3, c2.

**4420 n.n.** *to* **THE** ***PROVIDENCE REFORMER*****. [extract] n.d. Washington, D.C.** Reports widespread alarm among Washington slaveholders that the District of Columbia slaves will be emancipated. 9 May 1850. p.3, c3.

**4421 WASHINGTON CORRESPONDENT** *to* **THE** ***PHILADELPHIA NORTH AMERICAN*****. n.d. n.p.** Lists the major points of the treaty recently concluded between the United States and Great Britain. 9 May 1850. p.3, c4.

**4422 CORRESPONDENT** *to* **THE** ***TRIBUNE*****. [extract] n.d. n.p.** Comments on the appearance of Daniel Webster, quoting Milton's description of the fallen Lucifer. 9 May 1850. p.3, c4.

**4423 GEORGE WASHINGTON** *to* **ROBERT MORRIS. [extract from the** ***Louisville Examiner*****] 12 April 1786. n.p.** States that there is not a man living who wishes more sincerely than he for the abolition of slavery through legislative means. 16 May 1850. p.1, c3.

**4424 GEORGE WASHINGTON** *to* **LAFAYETTE. [extract from the** *Louisville Examiner*] **10 May 1786. n.p.** Praises Lafayette for his purchase of an estate, in the Colony of Cayenne, with a view toward emancipating the slaves there; expresses his desire to see gradual emancipation of slaves in the United States. 16 May 1850. p.1, c3.

**4425 GEORGE WASHINGTON** *to* **JOHN F. MERCER. [extract from the** *Louisville Examiner*] **9 September 1789. n.p.** States his resolve never to purchase another slave, and his wish to see the abolition of slavery in America. 16 May 1850. p.1, c4.

**4426 A CITIZEN OF SOUTH CAROLINA AND A SLAVEHOLDER** *to* **THE EDITOR OF THE** *TRIBUNE*. **n.d. n.p.** Challenges the official statement of the New York chief of police regarding the disturbances of the recent anti-slavery meetings there; accuses the mayor and the police of an "outrageous disregard of duty." 16 May 1850. p.3, c5.

**4427 HENRY W. SMITH** *to* **MR. GREEL[E]Y. [from the** *New York Tribune*] **10 May 1850. New York.** Accuses the New York police of making an inadequate attempt to preserve the peace at the recent meeting of the AAS. 16 May 1850. p.3, c5.

**4428 n.n.** *to* **THE** *ATHENAEUM*. **[from the** *New York Evening Post*] **25 July. Tungu, N. E. Sikkim.** Provides an account of Dr. Hooker's scientific expedition in Tibet. 16 May 1850. p.4, c1.

**4429 S. H. GAY** *to* **THE EDITOR OF THE** *TRIBUNE*. **n.d. 142 Nassau Street.** States facts concerning the recent riot at the AAS meeting in New York; denies that the mob was present by invitation and that Mr. Garrison declined police protection. 23 May 1850. p.1, c5.

**4430 WM. LLOYD GARRISON** *to* **THE EDITOR OF THE** *TRIBUNE*. **13 May 1850. Boston.** Disputes the account of the disturbances at the AAS meeting offered in an anonymous letter to the *Tribune*; criticizes the city officials for their failure to preserve peace. 23 May 1850. p.2, c1.

**4431 ISAAC T. HOPPER** *to* **THE EDITOR OF THE** *TRIBUNE*. **16 May 1850. n.p.** Offers his account of the violence attending the late meeting of the AAS; records his interview with the mayor on the subject. 23 May 1850. p.2, c1.

**4432 ISAAC S. FLINT** *to* **FRIEND. 12 April 1850. Easton, Md.** Discusses the effects of the competition between slave and free labor. 23 May 1850. p.2, c2.

**4433 PARKER PILLSBURY** *to* **FRIEND. 15 May 1850. Newtown.** Reports on his tour of Bucks County; criticizes local Friends for their lack of zeal for the anti-slavery cause and their support of Zachary Taylor. 23 May 1850. p.2, c3.

**4434 LONDON CORRESPONDENT** *to* **THE** *NORTH AMERICAN*. **[extract] n.d. n.p.** Reports indignation in the British Parliament over a South Carolina law which allows foreign black sailors to be seized and sold while in port there. 23 May 1850. p.2, c5.

**4435 JOHN G. WHITTIER** *to* **FRIEND GARRISON. [from the** *Liberator*] **13 May 1850. Amesbury.** Sympathizes with Garrison in the matter of the late disturbances at the annual meeting of the AAS. 23 May 1850. p.3, c3.

**4436 HAVANA CORRESPONDENT** *to* **THE** *CINCINNATI ENQUIRER*. **[extract from the** *New York Evening Post*] **n.d. n.p.** Reports that several Kentuckians aboard his vessel are bound for California with their slaves, having promised them freedom in return for two years of work in the mines. 23 May 1850. p.3, c4.

**4437 HORACE MANN** *to* **n.n. [extract] n.d. n.p.** Affirms his dedication to the anti-slavery cause; compares the friends of freedom in Congress to Jacob wrestling with the angel; characterizes Clay's compromise resolutions as the kind that "the wolf offers to the lamb, and the vulture to the dove"; criticizes at length the recent speech of Mr. Webster before the Senate on the subject of slavery in the territories. 30 May 1850. p.1, c1.

**4438 AQUILA BARRETT** *to* **DR. BRISBANE. 30 March 1850. Dublin, In.** Reports the death of her son, J. M. Barrett, from an illness attributable to his confinement in prison. 30 May 1850. p.1, c4.

**4439 SEVENTY LADIES** *to* **HON. WM. H. SEWARD. [from the** *Syracuse Journal*] **18 April 1850. Syracuse.** Commend Seward for his efforts on behalf of the anti-slavery cause. 30 May 1850. p.1, c4.

**4440 WM. H. SEWARD** *to* **LADIES. [from the** *Syracuse Journal*] **29 April 1850. Washington.** Expresses gratitude for their recent letter of praise for his devotion to the cause of freedom. 30 May 1850. p.1, c5.

**4441 THE HON. ANDREW STEVENSON** *to* **n.n. [extract] n.d. n.p.** Declares his devotion to the federal Union, but states that he will choose the side of the South if a separation must occur. 30 May 1850. p.1, c5.

**4442 MILWAUKEE CORRESPONDENT** *to* **THE** *HARTFORD COURANT.* **n.d. n.p.** Describes a large cave near Madison which was explored recently by an expedition headed by Howe Lumley. 30 May 1850. p.4, c3.

**4443 HORACE MANN** *to* **HIS CONSTITUENTS. [extract] n.d. n.p.** Continues his critical analysis of Daniel Webster's recent speech before the Senate; appeals to Northern businessmen not to sacrifice moral right for pecuniary gain; warns against further concession to the slaveholding powers. [continued from 30 May 1850] 6 June 1850. p.1, c1.

**4444 WM. LLOYD GARRISON** *to* **THE EDITOR OF THE** *BOSTON TRANSCRIPT.* **[extract] 17 May 1850. Boston.** Responds to "Sigma," an anonymous correspondent of the *Transcript*, who has called for Garrison's indictment for the crime of blasphemy. 6 June 1850. p.1, c6.

**4445 WM. LLOYD GARRISON** *to* **THE EDITOR OF THE** *BOSTON TRANSCRIPT.* **[extract] n.d. n.p.** Disputes the representation of his recent New York speech by "Sigma," a correspondent of the *Transcript*. 6 June 1850. p.2, c1.

**4446 DANIEL WEBSTER** *to* **CERTAIN CITIZENS OF NEWBURYPORT. [extract from the** *National Intelligencer*] **n.d. n.p.** Criticizes laws which forbid the employment of state facilities for the recapture or imprisonment of fugitive slaves; denounces abolitionist presses and societies; commends Pennsylvanians, particularly the Friends, for opposing slavery without seeking to overthrow or undermine the Constitution. 6 June 1850. p.2, c2.

**4447 T. M.** *to* **J.C. n.d. New Orleans.** States that if J. C. does not retract certain remarks made earlier in the day regarding money owed to him by T. M., T. M. will demand "personal satisfaction." 6 June 1850. p.3, c4.

**4448 J. C.** *to* **T. M. n.d. New Orleans.** Refers to remarks he made earlier in the day, and to the money owed by T. M., and declares he is prepared to "take it all back." 6 June 1850. p.3, c4.

**4449 R. D. WEBB** *to* **THE** *STANDARD.* **n.d. n.p.** Describes the reluctance of the American artists Risley and Smith to depict the truth about American slavery when exhibiting their works abroad. 6 June 1850. p.3, c4.

**4450 A. G. CAMPBELL** *to* **MR. EDITOR. 11 May 1850. Lowell.** Encloses a letter of the secretary of state of Michigan regarding the abolition of capital punishment in that state. 6 June 1850. p.4, c3.

**4451 C. H. TAYLOR** *to* **ALFRED GIBBS CAMPBELL, ESQ. 6 May 1850. Lansing, Mi.** States that Michigan has not reinstated the death penalty, as was reported, and that a majority of citizens do not favor such an action. 6 June 1850. p.4, c3.

**4452 CORRESPONDENT** *to* **THE** *CLEVELAND TRUE DEMOCRAT*. **[extract] n.d. n.p.** Upholds John G. Fee, who has established a free church in a slave state, as an example to Northern abolitionists. 13 June 1850. p.3, c2.

**4453 EPES SARGENT** *to* **THE** *BOSTON TRANSCRIPT*. **[extract] n.d. n.p.** Describes the scene at the late meeting of the AAS, where Frederick Douglass responded to the theory of racial inequality. 20 June 1850. p.1, c3.

**4454 HORACE MANN** *to* **THE EDITORS OF THE** *BOSTON ATLAS*. **[extract] 6 June 1850. Washington.** Responds to Webster's charges of "personal vituperation" and "confused legal apprehensions"; challenges Webster's assertion that the Bible contains no injunction against slavery; laments that Webster has wandered onto such a devious path. 20 June 1850. p.1, c4.

**4455 AN ANTI-SLAVERY EPISCOPALIAN** *to* **MESSRS. EDITORS. 3 June 1850. Philadelphia.** Questions the consistency of the Episcopal Diocese of Virginia, whose canons admit slaveholders to the Lord's Supper while withholding the Sacrament from persons who attend theatres or public balls. 20 June 1850. p.2, c2.

**4456 CAROLINE W. HEALEY DALL** *to* **WM. LLOYD GARRISON. [extract] n.d. n.p.** Praises Garrison for his courageous stand against slavery; denounces the city officials of New York for their conduct at the recent disturbance of the AAS meeting; laments the course lately adopted by Daniel Webster; appeals to God for strength to endure in the right cause. 20 June 1850. p.3, c3.

**4457 REV. JOHN G. FEE** *to* **THE** *CLEVELAND TRUE DEMOCRAT*. **[extract] n.d. n.p.** Asserts that it is a Christian's duty to separate himself from any ecclesiastical body whose members sanction the sin of slavery. 20 June 1850. p.3, c4.

**4458 GERRIT SMITH** *to* **MR. EDITOR. [from the** *Liberty Party Paper***] 22 April 1850. Peterboro'.** Requests publication of the latest report of the managers of the Massachusetts AS, and recommends it to all Liberty Party members. 20 June 1850. p.3, c4.

**4459 J. B. VASHON** *to* **THE** *NORTH STAR*. **[extract] n.d. Pittsburgh.** Declares that any colored man who allows himself to be colonized is an enemy to the slave and a traitor to the anti-slavery cause. 27 June 1850. p.1, c5.

**4460 n.n.** *to* **THE** *OHIO STATESMAN*. **[extract] 1 April 1850. San Francisco.** Reports a case of Southern emigrants abusing their slaves in California; calls for more Northern emigrants "to establish law and order." 27 June 1850. p.1, c5.

**4461 n.n.** *to* **THE** *NEW YORK TRIBUNE*. **[extract] n.d. Baltimore.** Reports on a slave case in Maryland involving a woman who was claimed as a slave after being permitted to go at large for twenty years; reports that a large number of slaves have absconded from their owners during the spring. 27 June 1850. p.1, c5.

**4462 A VIRGINIAN** *to* **COUSIN. 18 May 1850. Lee County, Va.** Criticizes the Taylor administration and Henry Clay's compromise resolutions; proclaims the duty to place God's laws above the laws of men; characterizes the Southern church as "a mockery." 27 June 1850. p.2, c1.

**4463 SIMON BARNARD** *to* **FRIEND. 4 June 1850. Huntington, Ia.** Extends his subscription to the *Freeman*; relates an encounter with slaveholders in Maryland; assesses the progress of the anti-slavery cause in his vicinity. 27 June 1850. p.2, c2.

**4464 WASHINGTON CORRESPONDENT** *to* **THE** *JOURNAL OF COMMERCE.* **n.d. n.p.** Reports that there is reason to believe that the United States will become involved in the Haitian conflict on the side of the Dominicans; speculates on the consequences of a Dominican victory. 27 June 1850. p.3, c1.

**4465 ALFRED WOOD** *to* **EDITORS,** *PENNSYLVANIA FREEMAN.* **12 June 1850. Philadelphia.** Provides details of an assault inflicted on him while passing through Maryland. 27 June 1850. p.3, c1.

**4466 MARTIN LUTHER** *to* **A FRIEND. [extract] n.d. Coburg.** Illustrates the nature of faith through a metaphorical reflection on the stars. 27 June 1850. p.4, c3.

**4467 OBSERVER** *to* **THE** *LEDGER.* **[extract] n.d. n.p.** Speculates on the possibility of Southern secession; concludes that the Southern states could not write a viable and enduring constitution. 4 July 1850. p.3, c1.

**4468 CHAS. W. SLACK, WM. R. STACY, DANIEL BAXTER, EDWIN P. HILL, JOSHUA NYE, JR., AND EDWARD STACY** *to* **THE NATIONAL DIVISION, SONS OF TEMPERANCE, OF NORTH AMERICA. 14 June 1850. Boston.** Protest an official report of the Committee of Appeals of the Sons of Temperance, which opposed the admission of Negroes. 4 July 1850. p.3, c1.

**4469 n.n.** *to* **THE** *PENNSYLVANIA FREEMAN.* **[extract] n.d. n.p.** A young merchant in Europe expresses disgust at the servility displayed by Northern editors and politicians to the slave powers; denounces Henry Clay and the Fugitive Slave Bill; comments on the political situation in France. 4 July 1850. p.3, c2.

**4470 TWO INTELLIGENT LADIES** *to* **FRIENDS. 25 June 1850. Milton.** Enclose fifteen dollars to further the work of the Pennsylvania AS. 4 July 1850. p.3, c3.

**4471 HON. JOSEPH T. BUCKINGHAM** *to* **THE** *BOSTON COURIER.* **[extract] n.d. n.p.** Corrects certain misrepresentations by the press concerning the late New England Convention, particularly the charge of blasphemy against H. C. Wright. 11 July 1850. p.1, c3.

**4472 PRISCILLA STEWART** *to* **FRIEND. 25 May 1850. Woodbury, N.J.** Expresses disdain for those who characterize abolitionists as insurrectionists; decries the evils of the slave system; expresses faith in God and the eventual triumph of liberty. 11 July 1850. p.2, c2.

**4473 SAMUEL R. THURSTON** *to* **HORACE MANN. [extract] n.d. n.p.** Predicts that slave labor will become a part of the producing capital of New Mexico, Utah, and California, unless prohibited by legislation. 11 July 1850. p.3, c3.

**4474 WASHINGTON CORRESPONDENT** *to* **THE** *TRUE AMERICAN.* **22 May. n.p.** Details the assault of two constables upon a slave woman in Washington, and her violent abduction. 11 July 1850. p.4, c2.

**4475 RICHARD D. WEBB** *to* **THE** *ANTI-SLAVERY STANDARD.* **n.d. n.p.** Describes his acquaintance, Mr. Brown, who is an eminent example of one who has sought knowledge under difficult circumstances. 11 July 1850. p.4, c2.

**4476 J. C.** *to* **H. GREELEY, ESQ. [from the** ***Tribune*****] 30 May 1850. San Francisco.** Criticizes a California law barring the testimony of Negroes, mulattoes, and Indians in legal cases involving white persons. 18 July 1850. p.1, c3.

**4477 HENRY COLEMAN** *to* **n.n. [extract] 4 March 1848. Paris.** Comments on the hypocrisy of American slaveholders in offering their congratulations to the French provisional government for the attainment of liberty. 18 July 1850. p.1, c5.

**4478 REV. SAMUEL J. MAY** *to* **THE** ***ANTI-SLAVERY STANDARD*****. n.d. n.p.** Relates facts surrounding the late Indiana slave case involving a number of colored persons seized in Cass County, Michigan; criticizes Judge McLean, who presided. 18 July 1850. p.2, c5.

**4479 LEWIS D. CAMPBELL** *to* **HON. DANIEL R. TILDEN. [extract] n.d. n.p.** States that since the Wilmot Proviso cannot pass the Congress, the prudent policy is that of "non-action" with regard to the territories. 18 July 1850. p.3, c1.

**4480 DANIEL R. TILDEN** *to* **HON. LEWIS D. CAMPBELL. [extract] n.d. n.p.** States that the "non-action" policy of President Taylor is a virtual veto of the Wilmot Proviso; criticizes Campbell and other Free-Soilers who have fallen into the Taylor ranks. 18 July 1850. p.3, c1.

**4481 D. WILMOT** *to* **HON. L. D. CAMPBELL. [extract] n.d. n.p.** Declares that the advocates of liberty must rest on the righteousness of their cause and refuse to compromise their principles. 18 July 1850. p.3, c2.

**4482 GEORGE THOMPSON** *to* **MR. W. W. BROWN. 30 May 1850. Chelsea.** Excuses himself from attendance at an anti-slavery meeting in London, due to ill health. 18 July 1850. p.3, c2.

**4483 A SUBSCRIBER** *to* **THE** ***HARTFORD REPUBLICAN*****. [extract] n.d. n.p.** Commends the *Republican* for its sound editorial judgment; states that he must discontinue his subscription. 18 July 1850. p.3, c2.

**4484 n.n.** *to* **n.n. 16 July 1850. Washington.** Reports that the members of the cabinet have refused the new president's request that they retain their offices for thirty days. 18 July 1850. p.3, c3.

**4485 CORRESPONDENT** *to* **n.n. 16 July 1850. Washington.** Lists members of President Fillmore's new cabinet. 18 July 1850. p.3, c4.

**4486 INDEPENDENT** *to* **THE** ***NORTH AMERICAN*****. [extract] 15 July 1850. n.p.** Comments on the significance of the new administration's policy concerning the disputed boundary between Texas and New Mexico; states that President Taylor fully intended to hold possession of New Mexico. 18 July 1850. p.3, c4.

**4487 INDEPENDENT** *to* **THE** ***NORTH AMERICAN*****. [extract] 15 July 1850. n.p.** Reports that official intelligence from Captain McKeever of the U. S. frigate *Congress* indicates that the Contoy prisoners will be released in a few days. 18 July 1850. p.3, c4.

**4488 JAMAICA CORRESPONDENT** *to* **THE** ***NEW YORK EVENING POST*****. [extract] n.d. n.p.** Reports that all parties in Jamaica attribute the decline of the country's economy to free trade and not to the abolition of slavery, and that color is becoming less important in Jamaica, unlike the United States. 25 July 1850. p.1, c3.

**4489 G. W. ALEXANDER** *to* **n.n. [extract from the** ***Tribune*****] n.d. Kingston, Jamaica.** Reports on economic condition of Jamaica, which is generally good despite the trial imposed by the Sugar Act of 1846; states that the situation of the common laborer is encouraging. 25 July 1850. p.1, c4.

**4490 MILLARD FILLMORE** *to* **HON. JOHN GAYLE. 31 July 1848. Albany, N.Y.** States that he supports the right of citizens to petition Congress; expresses his belief that slavery is an evil, but that Congress has no power to interfere with it. 25 July 1850. p.1, c4.

**4491 MILLARD FILLMORE** *to* **HON. JOHN GAYLE. 13 September 1848. Albany.** Denies that he considers it within Congress's power to interfere with the interstate transportation of slaves; cites an opinion of Supreme Court Justice McLean issued in 1841 as a statement of his own policy. 25 July 1850. p.1, c5.

**4492 A DISTINGUISHED MEMBER OF THE ORDER IN NEW YORK STATE** *to* **THE EDITOR, MR. A. WHITE. [from the** *New Englander***] n.d. n.p.** Approves of White's protest against the exclusion of colored persons from the Sons of Temperance by the order's national division. 25 July 1850. p.2, c1.

**4493 A MEMBER IN MASSACHUSETTS** *to* **n.n. [from the** *New Englander***] n.d. n.p.** Expresses indignation at the National Division of the Sons of Temperance, which invalidated the admission of Negroes. 25 July 1850. p.2, c1.

**4494 DR. ACWORTH, REV. F. CLOWES, W. WHITEHEAD, AND JOHN COOKE** *to* **THE BAPTISTS IN THE CITY AND COUNTY OF PHILADELPHIA, AND IN THE FREE STATES OF NORTH AMERICA GENERALLY. n.d. n.p.** Appeal on behalf of the Baptist churches of Yorkshire, England, for the emancipation, education, and social elevation of colored persons. 1 August 1850. p.1, c4.

**4495 J.** *to* **FRIEND. 1 July 1850. New York.** Reports on the late Yearly Meeting of Friends in New York. 1 August 1850. p.1, c5.

**4496 THOMAS CHANDLER AND ABIGAIL LAPHAM** *to* **THE NEW YORK YEARLY MEETING OF FRIENDS. 8 October 1849. Livonia, Mi.** Appeal on behalf of the Michigan Yearly Meeting of Friends for "those measures of Christian benevolence which aim at the restoration of the rights of man, and at the raising up of the down trodden image of God." 1 August 1850. p.2, c1.

**4497 E. P. GOFF** *to* **FRIENDS. 1 July 1850. Clearfield County.** Criticizes the "Regular Baptists" for their indifference to the causes of temperance and abolition; relates an incident at a recent Baptist meeting in Clearfield County, where he introduced an anti-slavery resolution. 1 August 1850. p.2, c2.

**4498 GEO. W. SIMONDS** *to* **THE EDITOR OF THE** *FREEMAN.* **22 July 1850. Lexington.** Requests publication of a report of Gerrit Smith's remarks at a recent Liberty Party Convention; challenges the *Freeman* to show where Smith errs in his argument demonstrating that the Constitution is anti-slavery. 1 August 1850. p.2, c3.

**4499 WASHINGTON CORRESPONDENT** *to* **THE** *MADISON DEMOCRAT.* **[extract] n.d. n.p.** Reports that Washington is in a "frightful confusion." 1 August 1850. p.3, c1.

**4500 n.n.** *to* **THE** *DUBLIN UNIVERSITY MAGAZINE.* **n.d. n.p.** Encloses a communication from G. P. R. James. 1 August 1850. p.3, c2.

**4501 G. P. R. JAMES** *to* **L. n.d. n.p.** Encloses a poem; characterizes Americans desirous of Irish aid in a war with England as "insolent" and "mad." 1 August 1850. p.3, c2.

**4502 n.n.** *to* **THE** *BALTIMORE PATRIOT.* **[extract] n.d. Washington.** Regrets the action of certain Southern Democrats who left the Senate chamber in a body when Mr. Seward began to speak. 1 August 1850. p.3, c5.

**4503 JOHN G. FEE** *to* **FRIEND EDITORS. [from the** *True Democrat***] 26 June 1850. Cabin Creek, Ky.** Relates facts pertaining to the case of Brother Haines, a local Bible distributor charged with the attempted theft of slaves; reports that Fee was recently assaulted on the highway. 8 August 1850. p.1, c2.

**4504 CORRESPONDENT** *to* **THE** *OHIO STATESMAN.* **[extract] n.d. Santa Fe, N.M.** Condemns the system of "peon slavery" recognized by the New Mexico constitution; cites the case of a man who has been held under the system for eighteen years as a result of a ten-dollar debt. 8 August 1850. p.1, c3.

**4505 EDITOR** *to* **THE** *FREEMAN.* **31 July 1850. Plainfield, Ct.** Relates scenes of his journey from Philadelphia to New England. 8 August 1850. p.2, c5.

**4506 MILLARD FILLMORE** *to* **SIR. 17 October 1838. Buffalo.** States that he believes anti-slavery petitions should be received and considered by Congress, that he opposes the annexation of Texas as long as slaves are held in that area and that he favors abolition of interstate slave trade and immediate legislation for the abolition of slavery in the District of Columbia. 8 August 1850. p.3, c1.

**4507 HILLTOWN** *to* **MR. EDITOR. n.d. n.p.** Affirms abolitionist principles; condemns the recent legislative proposals of Henry Clay; criticizes extremists who call for disunion; chides abolitionists for their lack of cooperation with those who differ with them on inconsequential matters. 8 August 1850. p.3, c4.

**4508 GRACE GREENWOOD** *to* **THE** *SATURDAY EVENING POST.* **[extract] n.d. n.p.** Describes the oratorical styles of Senators Benton, Webster, and Hale. 15 August 1850. p.1, c1.

**4509 EDITOR** *to* **THE** *FREEMAN.* **1 August 1850. Worcester, Ma.** Reports on the anniversary celebration of West Indian emancipation in Worcester; perceives strong public reaction against Daniel Webster and the Rev. Moses Stuart. 15 August 1850. p.2, c2.

**4510 EDITOR** *to* **THE** *FREEMAN.* **10 August 1850. On the Wing.** Continues his report on the anniversary celebration of West Indian emancipation in Worcester. 15 August 1850. p.2, c4.

**4511 n.n.** *to* **MR. EDITOR. n.d. n.p.** Inquires concerning a cure for rattlesnake and copperhead bites. 15 August 1850. p.4, c2.

**4512 PARIS CORRESPONDENT** *to* **THE** *ST. LOUIS REPUBLICAN.* **2 May 1850. n.p.** Relates a story regarding the charity of an escaped galley slave. 15 August 1850. p.4, c3.

**4513 WASHINGTON CORRESPONDENT** *to* **THE** *NORTH AMERICAN.* **[extract] n.d. n.p.** Alleges that a secret plan for the organization of a Southern confederacy was submitted to the Mexican cabinet for its approval in April, and was honorably rejected by that government; contends that the British minister was cognizant of the proceedings. 22 August 1850. p.1, c1.

**4514 BALTIMORE CORRESPONDENT** *to* **THE** *TRIBUNE.* **[from the** *New York Evening Post***] n.d. n.p.** Reports an increase in the number of runaway slaves in Maryland and Virginia, and a corresponding increase in the rewards for their recapture. 22 August 1850. p.1, c2.

**4515 H. N. G.** *to* **MR. EDITOR. [from the** *Ohio State Journal***] 12 July 1850. Quaker Bottom, Lawrence County, Oh.** Details an armed conflict which took place in Lawrence County, Ohio, involving six runaway slaves and eight or ten white citizens. 22 August 1850. p.1, c3.

4516 **WM. STILL** *to* **MR. J. M. McKIM. 8 August 1850. Philadelphia.** Relates the story of how he discovered that a stranger was his own brother; sketches his family's history and the circumstances effecting the separation. 22 August 1850. p.2, c1.

4517 **CORRESPONDENT** *to* **THE** *EXPRESS.* **7 August 1850. Washington.** Reports an incident which has excited much sympathy in Washington, involving the sale of the wife, daughters, and grandchildren of William Williams, the coachman of Presidents Polk, Taylor, and Fillmore. 22 August 1850. p.2, c4.

4518 **P. H. BELL** *to* **HIS EXCELLENCY ZACHARY TAYLOR, PRESIDENT OF THE UNITED STATES. 14 June 1850. Austin, Tx.** Inquires whether the military officers of the United States stationed at Sante Fe, having acted to prevent the extension of the boundary of Texas, meet with the approval of the president. 22 August 1850. p.2, c5.

4519 **DANIEL WEBSTER** *to* **P. H. BELL. [extract] n.d. n.p.** Reviews events leading to the establishment of a military government in New Mexico and its subsequent designation as a United States territory; maintains that a late order issued by the military governor, which prevented the extension of the Texas boundary into New Mexico, was justified. 22 August 1850. p.3, c1.

4520 **WASHINGTON CORRESPONDENT** *to* **THE** *BULLETIN.* **n.d. n.p.** Reports widespread dysentery and cholera in Washington. 22 August 1850. p.3, c4.

4521 **CORRESPONDENT** *to* **THE** *ALBANY EVENING JOURNAL.* **9 July 1850. Clayton.** Records impressions of a journey on the St. Lawrence River, and of his companion, Capt. Bill Johnston. 22 August 1850. p.4, c1.

4522 **MISS _______** *to* **MR. BALY. n.d. n.p.** Apologizes, in semi-literate style, for her inability to complete a prescribed course of study at a teachers' institute; expresses hope that she can receive her teaching certificate nonetheless. 22 August 1850. p.4, c2.

4523 **LORD EXMOUTH** *to* **n.n. [extract from the** *United Service Journal***] n.d. n.p.** Relates the wreck of the *Dutton*, in which Lord Exmouth displayed great courage. 22 August 1850. p.4, c3.

4524 **FREDERICK DOUGLASS** *to* **SIR. [from the** *London Times***] n.d. n.p.** Expresses his gratitude to the paper for certain timely remarks on American slavery, and for animadversions on the assault he recently sustained in New York. 29 August 1850. p.1, c3.

4525 **A SOUTHERNER** *to* **THE** *TRIBUNE.* **[extract] n.d. n.p.** Disputes the accounts presented in the Washington papers of the case of Mr. Chaplin, who unsuccessfully attempted to aid several fugitive slaves. 29 August 1850. p.1, c4.

4526 **A GENTLEMAN OF BOSTON** *to* **DANIEL WEBSTER. [from the** *Boston Bee***] n.d. n.p.** Advises Webster to ignore a recent letter of Horace Mann. 29 August 1850. p.2, c4.

4527 **DANIEL WEBSTER** *to* **A GENTLEMAN OF BOSTON. 27 July 1850. Washington.** States that he will not answer Horace Mann's letter; cites St. Jude and Archbishop Tillotson on the subject of dealing with the devil. 29 August 1850. p.2, c4.

4528 **MILLARD FILLMORE** *to* **SIR. 17 November 1848. Albany.** Expresses concern over the illness of Henry Clay; and his gratitude to Clay for vindicating him from the charge of abolitionism. 29 August 1850. p.2, c5.

**4529 PROGRESSIVE** *to* **THE** *SPIRIT OF THE TIMES.* **25 August 1850. Harrisburg.** Reports on the trial of three fugutive slaves charged with stealing horses, and an outbreak of violence which followed; reports the kidnapping of a colored boy on the Gettysburg turnpike. 29 August 1850. p.3, c2.

**4530 CORRESPONDENT** *to* **THE** *NEW YORK EVENING POST.* **[extract] n.d. n.p.** Comments on the conditions of slavery in the District of Columbia and the factors which encourage escape; denounces the slave trade carried on in the city and the upper slave states. 5 September 1850. p.1, c1.

**4531 CHARLES SUMNER** *to* **n.n. [extract] n.d. n.p.** Disparages the spirit of compromise pervading the anti-slavery movement; appeals for bold action among the friends of human rights. 5 September 1850. p.1, c3.

**4532 S. P. A.** *to* **THE** *TRIBUNE.* **26 August 1850. Washington.** Reports the passage of the Fugitive Slave Bill in the Senate; describes the character and circumstances of William L. Chaplin, now in jail on the charge of aiding the escape of slaves. 5 September 1850. p.1, c3.

**4533 BALTIMORE CORRESPONDENT** *to* **THE** *TRIBUNE.* **26 August 1850. Baltimore.** Reports great indignation among slaveholders in Maryland and Virginia over the rash of slave abductions from those states; reports a movement to force the free black population to leave the state or be removed to Liberia. 5 September 1850. p.1, c4.

**4534 GRACE GREENWOOD** *to* **THE** *PHILADELPHIA POST.* **n.d. Washington.** Describes three "remarkable and distinguished women": Dorthea Dix, Fredrika Bremer, and Appollonia Jagello. 5 September 1850. p.1, c5.

**4535 A FREEMAN** *to* **THE EDITORS OF THE** *TRIBUNE.* **28 August 1850. Washington.** Relates facts in the case of Andrew Lewis, a free colored youth recently seized in Washington; reports the capture of two slaves belonging to W. F. Colcock, and their courageous refusal to reveal the whereabouts of a third. 5 September 1850. p.2, c2.

**4536 WILMINGTON CORRESPONDENT** *to* **n.n. [from the** *National Anti-Slavery Standard***] n.d. n.p.** Reports that the coachman of Presidents Polk and Taylor, whose family was unexpectedly sold, has succeeded in raising the funds necessary to procure their freedom. 5 September 1850. p.2, c4.

**4537 MARY GREW** *to* **THE** *FREEMAN.* **28 August 1850. Boston.** Expresses disappointment at Fredrika Bremer's tribute to the memory of General Taylor. 5 September 1850. p.2, c5.

**4538 A. B.** *to* **THE** *NEW YORK EVENING POST.* **n.d. n.p.** Cites various sources to support the contention that the breeding of slaves is an integral part of Virginia's economy. 12 September 1850. p.1, c1.

**4539 ARMISTEAD BURT** *to* **HON. F. W. PICKENS AND COL. DRAYTON NANCE. [from the** *Fairfield Herald***] 13 May 1850. Washington City.** States that since he entered Congress in 1843, "Abolition has moved forward with fearful and unfaltering strides"; despairs of passage of a compromise resolution on the admission of California; predicts increasing conflict between North and South. 12 September 1850. p.1, c2.

**4540 WASHINGTON CORRESPONDENT** *to* **THE** *TRIBUNE.* **[extract] n.d. n.p.** Comments on the punishment inflicted on two captured slaves of Hon. William Colcock in order to compel them to reveal the whereabouts of another. 12 September 1850. p.2, c3.

**4541 A FRIEND** *to* **n.n. [extract from the** *Non-Slaveholder*] **n.d. England.** Reports that J. W. C. Pennington of New York is lecturing to large audiences in England in support of the free produce movement. 12 September 1850. p.3, c1.

**4542 WASHINGTON CORRESPONDENT** *to* **THE** *TRIBUNE.* **n.d. n.p.** Reports on the debate in the United States Senate over Mr. Seward's bill for the abolition of slavery in the District of Columbia. 19 September 1850. p.1, c1.

**4543 n.n.** *to* **THE** *NEW YORK EVENING POST.* **[extract] n.d. Chester County.** Denounces Senator Cooper as a traitor to the anti-slavery cause, due to his speech against the advocates of disunion; reports widespread contempt for the senator throughout the state. 19 September 1850. p.1, c5.

**4544 SAMUEL MAY, JR.** *to* **THE EDITORS OF THE** *EVENING POST.* **6 September 1850. Leicester.** Criticizes the choice of Isaiah Rynders as a delegate to the New York Democratic Convention. 19 September 1850. p.2, c1.

**4545 n.n.** *to* **n.n. [from a New Orleans paper] n.d. Brownsville, Tx.** Details the case of a female slave and her child who escaped to Mexico, and their master's unsuccessful attempt to reclaim his property. 19 September 1850. p.3, c2.

**4546 PARIS CORRESPONDENT** *to* **THE** *LEDGER.* **n.d. n.p.** Lists resolutions passed at the annual session of the World's Peace Congress at Frankfurt am Main. 19 September 1850. p.3, c3.

**4547 CALIFORNIA CORRESPONDENT** *to* **THE** *BOSTON TRAVELLER.* **[extract] n.d. n.p.** Reports the presence of a large number of slaves among the Mormons of the Salt Lake Valley, introduced by Southerners who have been connected to the community at various times. 19 September 1850. p.3, c4.

**4548 AUNT FANNY (FRANCES D. GAGE)** *to* **n.n. [extract from the** *Ohio State Journal*] **n.d. n.p.** Discourses on the proper attitude toward one's daily tasks, which need not be a source of drudgery. 19 September 1850. p.4, c2.

**4549 CORRESPONDENT IN LONDON** *to* **THE** *TRIBUNE.* **n.d. n.p.** Reports on "vinesipathy," a system which treats diseases by employing external motions of the body which affect the internal organs. 19 September 1850. p.4, c3.

**4550 BOSTON CORRESPONDENT** *to* **THE** *TRIBUNE.* **11 September 1850. n.p.** Describes a silver pitcher ordered by a committee of ladies in western New York, to be presented to William L. Chaplin. 26 September 1850. p.1, c3.

**4551 BALTIMORE CORRESPONDENT** *to* **THE** *TRIBUNE.* **n.d. n.p.** Expresses indignation at the Baltimore slave trade; reports a plan to test provisions of the Fugitive Slave Law in the courts of Pennsylvania and New York. 26 September 1850. p.1, c3.

**4552 WASHINGTON CORRESPONDENT** *to* **THE** *NEW YORK EVENING POST.* **[extract] n.d. n.p.** Reports great excitement among the Southern senators resulting from Mr. Winthrop's late remarks on the imprisonment of free Negro seamen in the South, and Mr. Seward's proposal to abolish slavery in the District of Columbia. 26 September 1850. p.1, c5.

**4553 ALEXANDER HUTCHISON** *to* **SIR. [from the** *Liberator*] **12 March 1850. Edinburgh.** Announces that the late Mrs. Margaret Sanson has bequeathed a portion of her estate to the AAS. 26 September 1850. p.2, c1.

**4554 CORRESPONDENT** *to* **THE** *ANTI-SLAVERY BUGLE.* **n.d. Ohio.** Reports that local churches are horrified that "Infidel books" were offered for sale at a recent anti-slavery anniversary, though the bookseller in question had no connection with the meeting. 26 September 1850. p.2, c2.

**4555 SOUTHRON** *to* **THE** *CHICAGO WESTERN CITIZEN.* **n.d. n.p.** Denounces the "National Kidnapping Law" recently passed by Congress; urges circumvention of the measure. 3 October 1850. p.1, c3.

**4556 A GENTLEMAN** *to* **THE** *ANTI-SLAVERY BUGLE.* **[extract] n.d. n.p.** Acknowledges a change in his view of disunion advocates as a result of a lecture by Mrs. Foster. 3 October 1850. p.1, c4.

**4557 THOMAS M'CLINTOCK AND RHODA DE GARMO** *to* **THE WOMEN OF THE STATE OF NEW YORK. 5 June 1850. Waterloo, N.Y.** Address the question of women's rights, on behalf of the Yearly Meeting of Congregational Friends. 3 October 1850. p.4, c1.

**4558 CORRESPONDENT** *to* **THE** *NEW YORK JOURNAL OF COMMERCE.* **[extract] n.d. n.p.** Describes the condition of poor whites in the pine woods of Georgia. 10 October 1850. p.1, c4.

**4559 A FRIEND** *to* **THE** *TRIBUNE.* **[extract] n.d. n.p.** Urges escaped slaves residing in New York City to travel further North to avoid the danger posed by slave catchers. 10 October 1850. p.1, c5.

**4560 SENATOR CLEMENS** *to* **n.n. [extract] n.d. n.p.** States that it must be established that Texas has given up land to the territory of New Mexico in order to create an argument for the extension of Texas law and slavery into the region. 10 October 1850. p.3, c2.

**4561 SENATOR BERRIEN** *to* **n.n. [extract] n.d. n.p.** Explains to constituents his vote in favor of the Texas boundary bill. 10 October 1850. p.3, c2.

**4562 DIDIMUS JONES** *to* **MR. HORACE GREELEY. 14 September 1850. Mayslick, Ky.** Reports the sale of two Negro youths on a local plantation and quotes their respective prices; approves the recent assault on Frederick Douglass in New York. 10 October 1850. p.3, c3.

**4563 PEDESTRIAN CORRESPONDENT** *to* **THE** *INDEPENDENT.* **n.d. England.** Describes his visit to Birmingham and the new church established by George Dawson; reflects on the life and influence of Dr. Arnold. 10 October 1850. p.4, c2.

**4564 CORRESPONDENT** *to* **THE** *ROCHESTER DAILY AMERICAN.* **n.d. n.p.** Cites Lardner's lectures on the temple at Jerusalem and how it was protected from lightning by the application of modern scientific principles. 10 October 1850. p.4, c3.

**4565 O. J. WHEELER** *to* **THE EDITOR OF THE** *TRIBUNE.* **[extract] 5 October 1850. Syracuse.** Reports on a meeting in Syracuse of citizens opposed to the Fugitive Slave Law; encloses resolutions of the meeting. 17 October 1850. p.1, c1.

**4566 REV. HENRY WARD BEECHER** *to* **THE** *INDEPENDENT.* **[extract] n.d. n.p.** Comments on the progress of free blacks in the North; denounces the Fugutive Slave Law; urges aid to fugitive slaves. 17 October 1850. p.1, c3.

**4567 R. R. CORSON** *to* **FRIENDS. 9 October 1850. Norristown.** Encloses resolutions of a meeting of colored people held the preceding evening. 17 October 1850. p.2, c4.

**4568 CHARLES A. RANLETT** *to* **HON. R. C. WINTHROP. 29 August 1850. Charlestown, Ma.** Testifies to the large number of free black seamen seized and imprisoned in Southern ports. 17 October 1850. p.3, c2.

**4569 THE COLORED PEOPLE OF BOSTON** *to* **THE CLERGY OF MASSACHUSETTS. n.d. n.p.** Urge opposition to the Fugitive Slave Law recently adopted by Congress. 17 October 1850. p.3, c3.

**4570 MOSES A. CARTLAND** *to* **THE** ***INDEPENDENT DEMOCRAT.*** **[extract] n.d. n.p.** Expresses his abhorrence of all manner of slave catchers. 17 October 1850. p.3, c4.

**4571 BALTIMORE CORRESPONDENT** *to* **THE** ***TRIBUNE.*** **n.d. n.p.** Despairs of General Chaplin receiving justice from a Maryland court; reports that Edward Burke has purchased the *Washington Union* in conjunction with Mr. Overton, one of the present editors. 17 October 1850. p.3, c4.

**4572 TEXAS CORRESPONDENT** *to* **THE** ***NEW ORLEANS PICAYUNE.*** **[extract] n.d. n.p.** Reports a rapidly expanding population of Free-Soilers in western Texas; predicts a longitudinal division of the state. 17 October 1850. p.3, c4.

**4573 FRANCIS JACKSON** *to* **J. MILLER McKIM. 10 October 1850. Boston.** Regrets his inability to attend the annual meeting of the Pennsylvania AS; offers encouragement to abolitionists everywhere. 24 October 1850. p.1, c5.

**4574 D. W. BARTLETT** *to* **THE** ***HARTFORD REPUBLICAN.*** **n.d. London.** Reports on a new invention in churches and lecture halls for the aid of partially deaf persons. 24 October 1850. p.4, c2.

**4575 ROBT. PURVIS** *to* **MESSRS. EDITORS. n.d. n.p.** Encloses a declaration of citizens of Byberry Township, Philadelphia County, regarding the Fugitive Slave Law. 31 October 1850. p.2, c1.

**4576 WILLIAM JAY** *to* **MESSRS. GEO. T. DOWNING AND WILLIAM P. POWELL. 2 October 1850. Bedford.** Expresses his opinion regarding the "constitutionality and binding force" of the Fugitive Slave Law. 31 October 1850. p.4, c2.

**4577 JOHN G. WHITTIER** *to* **n.n. [extract] n.d. n.p.** States that he will not cooperate in any manner with the Fugitive Slave Law recently approved by Congress. 7 November 1850. p.1, c1.

**4578 S.** *to* **THE** ***TRIBUNE.*** **n.d. Trenton, N.J.** Reports the death of a colored man named William Gordon, who entered a state of paralysis upon hearing a rumor that slave catchers were in the area. 7 November 1850. p.1, c3.

**4579 CHARLES GIBBONS** *to* **ROBERT C. GRIER. [extract] n.d. n.p.** Inquires concerning the Garnett case, in which Judge Grier clarified the rights of one who is accused of being a fugitive slave. 7 November 1850. p.1, c4.

**4580 R. C. GRIER** *to* **CHARLES GIBBONS, ESQ. 25 October 1850. Philadelphia.** Explains that while an alleged fugitive slave may not testify for himself, evidence on his behalf may be accepted from disinterested parties. 7 November 1850. p.1, c4.

**4581 J. M. McKIM, JAMES MOTT, AND C. M. BURLEIGH** *to* **THE PUBLISHERS OF THE** ***EVENING BULLETIN.*** **18 October 1850. Anti-Slavery Office.** Challenge the accuracy of the *Evening Bulletin*'s account of the annual meeting of the Pennsylvania AS at West Chester. 7 November 1850. p.2, c1.

**4582 J. M. McKIM, JAMES MOTT, AND C. M. BURLEIGH** *to* **THE PUBLISHERS OF THE** ***EVENING BULLETIN.*** **21 October 1850. Anti-Slavery Office.** Correct inaccuracies published in the *Evening Bulletin* regarding resolutions passed at the annual meeting of the Pennsylvania AS. 7 November 1850. p.2, c1.

**4583 CORRESPONDENT** *to* **THE** ***TRIBUNE.*** **31 October 1850. Boston.** Reports on the unsuccessful attempt of slave hunters to arrest William and Ellen Craft in Boston. 7 November 1850. p.3, c1.

**4584 BOWEN AND McNAMEE** *to* **THE PUBLIC, INCLUDING THE** ***NEW YORK JOURNAL OF COMMERCE.*** **26 October 1850. New York.** Maintain that their goods and not their principles are on the market; repudiate the attempt to punish them as merchants for their political and moral beliefs. 14 November 1850. p.1, c2.

**4585 HENRYS, SMITH, AND TOWNSEND** *to* **THE EDITORS OF THE** ***DAY-BOOK.*** **n.d. n.p.** Acknowledge that they subscribe to and advertise in the *Courier and Enquirer* and the *Journal of Commerce*, but deny that this implies approval of the papers' editorial policies; repudiate the views of Mr. Seward and the course pursued by the *Tribune*; express solidarity with the South. 14 November 1850. p.1, c2.

**4586 THE COLORED WOMEN OF PHILADELPHIA** *to* **THE FRIENDS OF HUMANITY. n.d. n.p.** Appeal for the restoration of their "right to life, to liberty, and to the pursuit of happiness." 14 November 1850. p.2, c2.

**4587 H. G.** *to* **MR. EDITOR. n.d. n.p.** Accuses the *Ledger* of inconsistency regarding its ethic of civil disobedience; states that the determining question concerning adherence to the Fugitive Slave Law must be whether or not it is in accordance with the law of God. 14 November 1850. p.2, c3.

**4588 L. H. GAUSE** *to* **MR. EDITOR. n.d. n.p.** Argues that the Fugitive Slave Law is unconstitutional. 14 November 1850. p.2, c3.

**4589 JOHN GRIMES** *to* **FRIEND. 1 November 1850. Boonton.** Encloses resolutions adopted at a meeting of citizens in Boonton regarding the Fugitive Slave Law. 14 November 1850. p.2, c4.

**4590 GEORGE THOMPSON** *to* **MR. GARRISON. [extract] n.d. n.p.** Implores Americans to make haste in ridding their land of the curse of slavery. 14 November 1850. p.3, c1.

**4591 HON. SAMUEL A. ELLIOT** *to* **n.n. [extract] n.d. n.p.** States that there was no provision for trial by jury under the old law pertaining to fugitive slaves, and the new law is therefore not a deprivation of this right; denies that the new law suspends the operation of the writ of habeas corpus. 14 November 1850. p.3, c3.

**4592 EDWARD NEEDLES, JOSEPH LINDSAY, AND PASSMORE WILLIAMSON** *to* **THE PEOPLE OF COLOR IN PENNSYLVANIA. [from the** ***Friends' Intelligencer*****] n.d. n.p.** Appeal, on behalf of the old Pennsylvania Abolition Society, for peaceful opposition to the late act of Congress governing fugitive slaves. 14 November 1850. p.3, c4.

**4593 HORACE MANN** *to* **n.n. [extract] n.d. n.p.** Discusses the Fugitive Slave Law; argues for repeal of the measure. 21 November 1850. p.1, c1.

**4594 AMOS GILBERT** *to* **THE** ***PENNSYLVANIA FREEMAN.*** **n.d. n.p.** Comments on the efficacy of public meetings in influencing Congress to repeal the Fugitive Slave Law. 21 November 1850. p.2, c3.

**4595 A FRIEND IN NEWBERRY** *to* **THE** *PENNSYLVANIA FREEMAN.* **[extract] n.d. n.p.** Reports that a circus was refused permission to perform in Newberry after an employee was discovered with a number of copies of the *New York Atlas*, a paper of strong abolitionist sentiments. 21 November 1850. p.3, c2.

**4596 HARRISBURG CORRESPONDENT** *to* **THE** *TRIBUNE.* **[extract] n.d. n.p.** Expresses outrage at the recent kidnapping of four colored men in the area; reports that the Taylor trial will begin the following week, involving charges of rioting which resulted from an earlier attempt to recapture fugitive slaves. 21 November 1850. p.3, c2.

**4597 CORRESPONDENT** *to* **THE** *BOSTON ATLAS.* **[extract] n.d. n.p.** Describes the conferral of the degree of Doctor of Divinity upon the Rev. J. W. C. Pennington by the University of Heidelberg. 21 November 1850. p.3, c4.

**4598 W. L. MACKENZIE** *to* **THE** *NEW YORK TRIBUNE.* **n.d. Toronto.** Reports a large and courteous colored population in Toronto, composed largely of fugitive slaves. 21 November 1850. p.3, c4.

**4599 COTTON POLITICS** *to* **THE** *NEW YORK TRIBUNE.* **[extract] 14 November 1850. Castle Garden, N.Y.** Comments on a window in the dining room of a British steamer depicting an "Angel of Light" descending to liberate a group of African slaves. 28 November 1850. p.3, c3.

**4600 EAST INDIAN CORRESPONDENT** *to* **THE** *NEW YORK EVENING POST.* **[extract] n.d. n.p.** Describes the Upas tree found in Malaysia. 28 November 1850. p.4, c3.

**4601 DAVID PAUL BROWN** *to* **n.n. [extract from the** *Tribune*] **n.d. n.p.** States his reasons for judging the Fugitive Slave Law to be unjust and unconstitutional. 5 December 1850. p.1, c3.

**4602 M. J. THOMAS** *to* **THE EDITOR OF THE** *NATIONAL ERA.* **28 October 1850. Philadelphia.** Encloses a letter from a slave catcher. 5 December 1850. p.1, c3.

**4603 REUBEN B. CARLLEY** *to* **JOHN C. LAUNDERS. 24 March 1831. Poolsville, Montgomery County, Md.** Reports the capture of a fugitive; requests information on runaway slaves. 5 December 1850. p.1, c4.

**4604 A METHODIST PREACHER IN VIRGINIA** *to* **THE** *TRUE WESLEYAN.* **[extract] n.d. n.p.** Describes a group of slaves being transported to an unknown destination. 5 December 1850. p.1, c4.

**4605 A GENTLEMAN** *to* **n.n. [extract from the** *Mobile Tribune*] **n.d. n.p.** States that the South is on the verge of revolution; predicts the secession of South Carolina from the Union, unless a convention of the Southern states advises delay. 5 December 1850. p.1, c5.

**4606 HUMANITAS** *to* **MESSRS. EDITORS. 18 November 1850. Phoenixville.** Describes a meeting of a "Teacher's Institute" where an unnamed gentleman spoke against agitation and for preservation of the Union; bemoans the spirit of Northern subservience exemplified there. 5 December 1850. p.2, c1.

**4607 P. LESTER** *to* **FRIEND. 13 October 1850. San Francisco.** Expresses his desire to be present at West Chester for the annual meeting of the Pennsylvania AS; reports a large number of slaveholders with their slaves in California; comments on the defeat of a local abolitionist in a contest for the state legislature. 5 December 1850. p.2, c1.

**4608 FABRICUS** *to* **THE EDITOR OF THE** ***PENNSYLVANIA FREEMAN*****. 30 November 1850. Harrisburg.** Reports the acquittal of Mr. Taylor of Virginia, and his companions, on charges stemming from their attempt to recapture fugitive slaves earlier in the year. 5 December 1850. p.2, c2.

**4609 CORRESPONDENT** *to* **THE** ***HARTFORD REPUBLICAN*****. [extract] n.d. n.p.** Reports on a meeting held in Killingly, Connecticut, to protest the Fugitive Slave Law. 5 December 1850. p.3, c1.

**4610 DAVID PAUL BROWN** *to* **MESSRS. EDITORS. 7 December 1850. n.p.** Corrects misstatements by the *Freeman* concerning a letter of Brown's read before the Union Meeting in Philadelphia by Josiah Randall. 12 December 1850. p.2, c3.

**4611 THOMAS JEFFERSON** *to* **DR. PRICE. 7 August 1785. Paris.** Commends Price for his anti-slavery pamphlet; anticipates its reception in various sections of America; suggests that he address an exhortation on the subject to the students at the College of William and Mary. 19 December 1850. p.1, c5.

**4612 CORRESPONDENT** *to* **THE** ***EMANCIPATOR*****. n.d. n.p.** Relates the case of a Northern freeman who was taken from a Boston merchant vessel and imprisoned in the Carolinas; ridicules the spirit of the Union men who, had they been true to their professed beliefs, would have risen to the individual's defense. 19 December 1850. p.2, c2.

**4613 AN OFFICER OF A SHIP ON THE AFRICAN STATION** *to* **n.n. [from the** ***Boston Journal*****] n.d. n.p.** Reports that a large number of slave ships avoid British seizure by sailing under the American flag; suggests modification of treaty restrictions in order to rectify the situation. 26 December 1850. p.1, c5.

**4614 ALBERT H. CLARKE** *to* **GRACE GREENWOOD. [from the** ***Boston Transcript*****] 13 September 1850. San Francisco.** Recounts his struggle to survive after his yacht was capsized and his companion drowned. 26 December 1850. p.4, c2.

**4615 SPRINGFIELD CORRESPONDENT** *to* **THE** ***HARTFORD REPUBLICAN*****. n.d. n.p.** Relates the prayer of a fugitive slave. 26 December 1850. p.4, c4.

**4616 CORRESPONDENT** *to* **THE** ***NEW YORK COMMERCIAL*****. [extract] n.d. On board the steamer** ***Pacific*****, in St. George's Channel.** Comments on the giant icebergs off the coast of Nova Scotia and Newfoundland. 26 December 1850. p.4, c4.

## [1851]

**4617 DAVID PAUL BROWN** *to* **J. M. McKIM, ESQ. 28 December 1850. n.p.** Declines a contribution for his services on behalf of Adam Gibson, an alleged fugitive slave. 2 January 1851. p.3, c5.

**4618 n.n.** *to* **n.n. n.d. n.p.** Reports that there are over 25,000 tailors in London, of which 3,000 are unemployed and plan to travel to America with the aid of the benevolent societies. 2 January 1851. p.4, c3.

**4619 H. M. DARLINGTON, M. P. WILSON, AND S. F. PEIRCE** *to* **THE PEOPLE OF CHESTER COUNTY. 21 November 1850. Doc Run Meeting House.** Appeal, on behalf of the Women's Temperance Convention, for complete prohibition of intoxicating liquors. 9 January 1851. p.1, c5.

**4620 J. D.** *to* **REV. JOHN CHAMBERS. 15 December 1850. Philadelphia.** Disputes ideas presented in a Thanksgiving sermon of Chambers; asserts the superiority of conscience over human law; criticizes Chambers's remarks concerning George Thompson; declares the incompatibility of slavery with the doctrines of the New Testament. 9 January 1851. p.2, c1.

**4621 GRACE GREENWOOD** *to* **n.n. [extract from the** ***National Era*****] n.d. Boston.** Describes her visits to the Asylum for the Blind and the School for Idiots, both in Boston. 9 January 1851. p.4, c2.

**4622 A MERCANTILE HOUSE IN PORT-AU-PRINCE** *to* **A MERCANTILE HOUSE IN PHILADELPHIA. [extract] n.d. n.p.** Expresses disappointment over the delay of coffee crop deliveries; reports that American dry goods are taking precedence in the Haitian market. 9 January 1851. p.4, c4.

**4623 CORRESPONDENT** *to* **THE** ***TRIBUNE*****. [extract] n.d. n.p.** Describes the homage paid by the president and Mr. Webster to Jenny Lind at a Washington concert. 16 January 1851. p.1, c3.

**4624 JOHN BROWN, FERRYMAN** *to* **THE** ***NEW YORK EVENING POST*****. 27 December 1850. Jersey Ferry.** Reports that Daniel Webster was "tight" at a recent concert of Jenny Lind in Washington, and suppression of this news was his motive for an evangelical speech before the New England Society; reports on Webster's efforts to defeat Charles Sumner's bid for the United States Senate. 16 January 1851. p.1, c3.

**4625 JUSTICE** *to* **THE EDITORS OF THE** ***EVENING POST*****. n.d. n.p.** Disputes a correspondent's interpretation of Professor Agassiz's theories regarding the Negro; maintains that Agassiz's view does not support African slavery. 16 January 1851. p.1, c4.

**4626 GEO. THOMPSON** *to* **GARRISON. [from the** ***Liberator*****] 3 October 1850. Matlock, Derbyshire, England.** Announces his intention to visit America in order to renew old friendships and offer a series of lectures. 16 January 1851. p.2, c1.

**4627 CORRESPONDENT** *to* **THE** ***EVENING BULLETIN*****. [extract] 5 December 1850. Paris.** Reports the French National Assembly's denunciation of laws in the Southern United States providing for the imprisonment of all colored persons on vessels entering their ports. 16 January 1851. p.2, c2.

**4628 n.n.** *to* **THE** ***PENNSYLVANIA FREEMAN*****. 29 December 1850. Gum Tree.** Provides an account of the unlawful entry of slave hunters into the house of N. Green, a free colored man, and the fight that ensued. 16 January 1851. p.2, c3.

**4629 ROBT. PURVIS** *to* **J. M. McKIM. 11 January 1851. Byberry.** Suggests a series of anti-slavery meetings at Exeter Hall coinciding with the World's Convention. 16 January 1851. p.2, c4.

**4630 WASHINGTON CORRESPONDENT** *to* **THE** ***NORTH AMERICAN*****. n.d. n.p.** Commends the "good sense, ability and patriotic sentiments" expressed in the late message of Governor Johnston regarding slavery and the Union. 16 January 1851. p.2, c5.

**4631 THE** ***BOSTON CHRONOTYPE*** *to* **THE BAR OF THE UNITED STATES. n.d. n.p.** Announces the publication of 20,000 copies of the first chapter of the appendix of Spooner's *Defence for Fugitive Slaves*, to be distributed among all lawyers whose names appear in Livingston's *Lawyers Directory*. 16 January 1851. p.2, c5.

**4632 LONDON CORRESPONDENT** *to* **THE** ***TRIBUNE*****. [extract] n.d. n.p.** Comments on the preparations for the World's Fair and the moral benefits which may arise from the project. 23 January 1851. p.2, c1.

**4633 W. S.** *to* **MESSRS. EDITORS. 20 January 1851. Philadelphia.** Reports the arrival in Philadelphia of 50 emancipated slaves formerly held by William H. Fitzhugh of Virginia, who died leaving 295 slaves to be liberated in 1850. 23 January 1851. p.2, c1.

**4634 HENRY H. GARNET** *to* **FRIEND. 5 December 1850. Hitchin, England.** Comments on the progress of the anti-slavery movement in England, notably the increased interest in free labor cotton goods; encloses resolutions of a public meeting at Hitchin regarding the Fugitive Slave Law. 23 January 1851. p.2, c2.

**4635 C. M. BURLEIGH** *to* **n.n. [extract] n.d. n.p.** Sketches his current lecture tour of rural Pennsylvania. 23 January 1851. p.2, c5.

**4636 THE PUBLISHERS OF THE** ***ATLANTA REPUBLICAN*** *to* **MERCHANTS AND BUSINESSMEN GENERALLY. n.d. n.p.** Propose the *Atlanta Republican* as an advertising medium for Northern merchants who desire Southern trade and can provide evidence of their good intentions regarding the restoration of fugitive slaves. 23 January 1851. p.2, c6.

**4637 A FRIEND IN PORTSMOUTH** *to* **n.n. [extract from the** ***Anti-Slavery Bugle*****] n.d. n.p.** Reports favorable public reception of a series of lectures by Sarah Coates. 23 January 1851. p.2, c6.

**4638 B.** *to* **THE** ***LEDGER*****. 18 January 1851. Richmond, Va.** Reports the sale of Henry Long, the fugitive recently apprehended in New York. 23 January 1851. p.3, c1.

**4639 HARRISBURG CORRESPONDENT** *to* **THE** ***SPIRIT OF THE TIMES*****. 5 January 1851. n.p.** Reports the arrest of a constable and an assistant on charges of kidnapping four colored men in Lebanon County. 23 January 1851. p.3, c2.

**4640 J. W.** *to* **MESSRS. EDITORS. [from the** ***Public Ledger*****] 16 January 1851. Sadsbury Township.** Describes the recent kidnapping of John Williams, a colored man of the neighborhood, who had generally been regarded as free. 23 January 1851. p.3, c2.

**4641 CORRESPONDENT** *to* **THE** ***TRIBUNE*****. 5 January 1851. Baltimore.** Relates facts surrounding the case of William Moore and his sisters, who were claimed as slaves after openly exercising the rights of free persons for sixteen years. 23 January 1851. p.3, c5.

**4642 CONSERVATIVE** *to* **THE** ***EVENING POST*****. 18 January 1851. Richmond, Va.** Describes the sale of Henry Long, a fugitive returned to Virginia after being captured in New York. 30 January 1851. p.1, c2.

**4643 GEORGE B. MATHEW** *to* **HIS EXCELLENCY, THE GOVERNOR AND COM.-IN-CHIEF OF S. CAROLINA. 14 December 1850. Columbia.** Requests amendment of a South Carolina law which dictates the imprisonment of colored seamen who enter the ports of that state. 30 January 1851. p.2, c1.

**4644 J. H. MEANS** *to* **H. B. M.'S CONSUL, GEORGE B. MATHEW, ESQ. 16 December 1850. Columbia, S.C.** Acknowledges Mathew's letter concerning the imprisonment of British seamen; assures the consul of his state's amicable feelings toward the British government; states that Mathew's request will be forwarded to the legislature. 30 January 1851. p.2, c1.

**4645 n.n.** *to* **MR. McKIM n.d. Harrisburg.** Appeals for funds to purchase the freedom of Henry Long who was recently imprisoned in Virginia and sold into slavery. 30 January 1851. p.2, c3.

**4646 A FRIEND IN WILLISTOWN** *to* **n.n. n.d. n.p.** Reports success in the circulation of a petition for the repeal of the Fugitive Slave Law; comments on the need for perseverance in the abolitionist cause. 30 January 1851. p. 2, c5.

**4647 JAMES H. HOUSTON** *to* **MESSRS. EDITORS. [from the** *Ledger***] 24 January 185[1]. Gap.** Disputes a portion of an account of a kidnapping recently published in the *Ledger*. 30 January 1851. p.3, c3.

**4648 WASHINGTON CORRESPONDENT** *to* **THE** *EVENING POST*. **[extract] n.d. n.p.** Reports that a large number of Southern emigrants are holding slaves in the Utah territory. 30 January 1851. p.3, c5.

**4649 HERBERT MOORE** *to* **MARGARET NEALE. [from the** *National Era***] n.d. n.p.** Explains his decision to volunteer for service in the Mexican war and terminate his betrothal. 30 January 1851. p.4, c2.

**4650 MARGARET NEALE** *to* **HERBERT MOORE. [from the** *National Era***] n.d. n.p.** Bids farewell to Moore as he prepares to serve in the Mexican War; criticizes his decision to participate "in this most unholy war against a sister Republic." 30 January 1851. p.4, c2.

**4651 HUGH McDONALD** *to* **CAPT. ELLISTON. [from the** *National Era***] n.d. n.p.** Encloses a check for $1,000, to be used for the relief of Herbert Moore in the event of an emergency. 30 January 1851. p.4, c3.

**4652 CONSCIENCE** *to* **MESSRS. EDITORS. [from the** *Independent***] n.d. n.p.** Relates the story of his children's escape from Bedouin slavery; considers a sermon of Dr. Adams on obedience to the law and the Constitution, and questions the morality of his children's act. 6 February 1851. p.1, c1.

**4653 C. M. BURLEIGH** *to* **THE** *FREEMAN*. **2 February 1851. Lancaster.** Reports on his anti-slavery activities in Pennsylvania and Maryland. 6 February 1851. p.3, c1.

**4654 PHILADELPHIA** *to* **MESSRS. EDITORS. [from the** *Public Ledger***] 30 January 1851. Philadelphia.** Inquires whether the "slave" referred to in an article published the preceding day is the statue of the Greek slave recently sold in New Orleans. 6 February 1851. p.3, c2.

**4655 WASHINGTON CORRESPONDENT** *to* **THE** *LEDGER*. **n.d. n.p.** States that the "cheap postage bill" has been so amended by the Senate that it bears little resemblance to the version passed by the House; predicts that it will not pass the present session of Congress. 6 February 1851. p.3, c3.

**4656 HARRISBURG CORRESPONDENT** *to* **THE** *NEW YORK TRIBUNE*. **[extract] n.d. n.p.** Cites the *Daily American*'s laudatory comment on the compliance of Pennsylvanians with the Fugitive Slave Law. 6 February 1851. p.3, c3.

**4657 HERBERT MOORE** *to* **MARGARET NEALE. [from the** *National Era***] n.d. n.p.** Expresses his love for Margaret and his shame for past sins of pride. 6 February 1851. p.4, c3.

**4658 JOHN SCOBLE** *to* **THE RIGHT HON. LORD PALMERSTON. 20 December 1850. Anti-Slavery Office.** Complains, on behalf of the British and Foreign AS, of the laws existing in the Southern slave states which allow the imprisonment of colored British sailors in Southern ports; cautions against increasing pressure to extradite fugitive slaves in Canada. 13 February 1851. p.1, c1.

**4659 STANLEY, OF ALDY.** *to* **JOHN SCOBLE, ESQ. 31 December 1850. Foreign Office.** Acknowledges Viscount Palmerston's receipt of Scoble's letter complaining of the injustice of the laws of certain Southern states in America regarding colored seamen; assures Scoble of the concern of Her Majesty's government. 13 February 1851. p.1, c2.

**4660 CORRESPONDENT** *to* **THE EDITOR OF THE** *NATIONAL ERA*. **[extract] n.d. The Great Salt Lake, Utah.** Describes the character of the Mormon settlement in Utah; reports that slavery is not legally recognized in the colony. 13 February 1851. p.1, c3.

**4661 JAMES MOTT AND HAWORTH WETHERALD** *to* **THE MINISTERS OF RELIGION IN PENNSYLVANIA. 1 January 1851. Philadelphia.** Appeal to ministers, on behalf of the Pennsylvania AS, to exert their influence against the Fugitive Slave Law. 13 February 1851. p.3, c4.

**4662 n.n.** *to* **THE** *SATURDAY VISITER*. **[extract] n.d. n.p.** A recently married gentleman expresses his opposition to the extension of the elective franchise to women. 13 February 1851. p.4, c4.

**4663 C. M. BURLEIGH** *to* **THE** *FREEMAN*. **8 February 1851. Columbia.** Continues the account of his current lecture tour of Maryland. 20 February 1851. p.2, c6.

**4664 C. M. BURLEIGH** *to* **THE** *FREEMAN*. **10 February 1851. Columbia.** Relates events in Columbia, where he was denied the opportunity to lecture with the excuse that it would incite a mob. 20 February 1851. p.3, c1.

**4665 LIEUTENANT SHUFELDT** *to* **THE** *NEW YORK HERALD*. **[extract] n.d. n.p.** Narrates the late voyage of the steamer *Atlantic*, which was imperiled by engine trouble. 20 February 1851. p.3, c2.

**4666 THOMAS JEFFERSON, SAMUEL ADAMS, JOHN HANCOCK, [AND SEVEN OTHERS]** *to* **OUR GOOD AND TRUE LIEGES OF OUR GOOD OLD TOWN OF BOSTON. [from the** *Commonwealth*] **15 February 1851. n.p.** Fictitious letter calls for the release of Shadrach Sims, lately apprehended under the Fugitive Slave Law, by order of the "Supreme Tribunal of the Right of Man." 27 February 1851. p.1, c1.

**4667 MILLARD FILLMORE** *to* **THE SENATE OF THE UNITED STATES. 21 February 1851. Washington.** Responds to Mr. Clay's resolution requesting that the president submit to the Senate any information he might possess concerning a recent case of forcible resistance to federal law in Boston; reviews the laws of Massachusetts designed to circumvent federal ordinances, and the power of the president to repel insurrections and enforce the law. 27 February 1851. p.1, c3.

**4668 WASHINGTON CORRESPONDENT** *to* **THE** *NORTH AMERICAN*. **n.d. n.p.** Comments sarcastically on members of Congress who give social obligations priority over legislative responsibilities. 27 February 1851. p.3, c1.

**4669 RACHEL C. DEACON** *to* **THE EDITOR OF THE** *PENNSYLVANIA FREEMAN*. **n.d. n.p.** Encloses a resolution of the Acting Committee of the Northern Association for the relief and employment of poor women. 27 February 1851. p.3, c1.

**4670 n.n.** *to* **THE** *MEMPHIS EAGLE*. **[extract] n.d. Jackson, Ms.** Reports a common effort among the executive, legislative, and judicial authorities of Mississippi to drive the state from its loyalty to the federal government. 27 February 1851. p.4, c5.

**4671 CORRESPONDENT** *to* **THE** *NEW YORK EVENING POST*. **n.d. n.p.** Notes the ironic fact that Capt. John Smith, the founder of the Jamestown colony, was a fugitive slave who killed his mother in order to attain liberty; encloses an extract from a biography of Smith, published in 1629, relating the story of his escape from Turkish slavery. 6 March 1851. p.1, c6.

**4672 C. M. BURLEIGH** *to* **THE** *FREEMAN.* **1 March 1851. n.p.** Criticizes the town of Columbia, where a mob gathered against him; reports further difficulties in the town of York, and notes successful anti-slavery meetings at Lewisbury and Warrington. 6 March 1851. p.2, c6.

**4673 BALTIMORE CORRESPONDENT** *to* **THE** *TRIBUNE.* **[extract] n.d. n.p.** Reports on the discussion and passage of an article of the Reform Convention of Maryland authorizing the legislature to expel free colored persons from the state. 6 March 1851. p.3, c2.

**4674 E. B.** *to BURRITT'S CHRISTIAN CITIZEN.* **21 December 1850. Hamburg, Germany.** Describes the Rauhe Haus, an institution for delinquent boys in Hamburg. 6 March 1851. p.4, c2.

**4675 SAM S. ABBOTT, LEWIS CHAPPELL, A. M. BAKER, [AND SEVENTEEN OTHERS]** *to* **THE FREEMEN OF MADISON COUNTY. [from the** *Madison County Journal***] 21 January 1851. Hamilton.** Urge fellow citizens to petition Congress for repeal of the Fugitive Slave Law. 13 March 1851. p.1, c3.

**4676 HORACE MANN** *to* **THOMAS H. TALBOT, ESQ. 25 January 1851. Washington.** Argues for repeal of the Fugitive Slave Law. 13 March 1851. p.1, c4.

**4677 GRACE GREENWOOD** *to* **THE** *NATIONAL ERA.* **n.d. n.p.** Describes the members of a weekly Free-Soil soirée in Washington. 13 March 1851. p.2, c1.

**4678 n.n.** *to* **n.n. [from the** *Boston Commonwealth***] 19 February 1851. Whitehall, Ky.** Reports on the abuse suffered by an agent of the American Baptist Emancipation Society at the hands of local ruffians. 13 March 1851. p.3, c1.

**4679 A FRIEND OF EMANCIPATION IN KENTUCKY** *to* **n.n. n.d. n.p.** Announces plans for a convention in Frankfort to nominate anti-slavery candidates for Kentucky offices; expresses hope for the establishment of an anti-slavery paper for that state. 13 March 1851. p.3, c2.

**4680 CORRESPONDENT** *to* **THE** *NEW YORK INDEPENDENT.* **[extract] n.d. Germany.** Comments on the interest taken by Germans in the conflicts attending American slavery; considers that American institution more oppressive than any system imposed by the tyrants of Europe. 13 March 1851. p.3, c2.

**4681 INHABITANTS OF THE CITY OF PERTH** *to* **THE CITIZENS OF THE UNITED STATES OF AMERICA. [extract] n.d. n.p.** Chastise Americans for their participation in human slavery; denounce the Fugitive Slave Law; urge citizens to put pressure on Congress to end the "wretched system." 13 March 1851. p.3, c3.

**4682 CORRESPONDENT** *to* **THE** *FREE PRESBYTERIAN.* **[extract] n.d. n.p.** Predicts that church historians will judge the mid-nineteenth century as an era of "unvarnished infidelity" to Christian principles. 13 March 1851. p.3, c4.

**4683 BOSTON CORRESPONDENT** *to* **THE** *TRIBUNE.* **n.d. n.p.** Reports the flight of thirty-one fugitive slaves from Portland, Maine, to St. John's, New Brunswick, despite promises of protection from the citizenry. 13 March 1851. p.3, c5.

**4684 WM. HOPKINS** *to* **THE** *HORTICULTURALIST.* **n.d. n.p.** Suggests that fruit growers raise poultry and attract wild birds in order to combat worms. 13 March 1851. p.4, c4.

**4685 SAMUEL H. COX** *to* **THE REV. JOHN MORRISON, D.D. [extract from the** *New York Evening Post*] **15 April 1835. New York.** Encloses an edition of William Jay's *Inquiry*, which addresses the subject of slavery; denies that slavery is sanctioned by the Bible; praises the work of W. L. Garrison and George Thompson. 20 March 1851. p.1, c1.

**4686 CORRESPONDENT** *to* **THE** *MERCER PRESBYTERIAN*. **n.d. Ripley, Oh.** Reports the shooting death of a man named Gilbert by a fugitive slave he was attempting to recapture. 20 March 1851. p.1, c5.

**4687 GEORGE ATCHESON** *to* **n.n. [extract from the** *Mercer Presbyterian*] **n.d. n.p.** Reports the probable kidnapping of a free colored boy from Harrisburg. 20 March 1851. p.1, c5.

**4688 E. D. HUDSON** *to* **THE** *LIBERATOR*. **25 February 1851. Springfield, Ma.** Praises Mr. Simmons, a local Unitarian minister, for his sermon denouncing the instigators of a recent riot against abolitionists; summarizes a lecture by Henry Ward Beecher; reports that a petition calling for the return of George Thompson is being launched. 20 March 1851. p.1, c5.

**4689 GENERAL JACKSON** *to* **THE FREE PEOPLE OF COLOR. 18 December 1814. New Orleans.** Praises the conduct and enthusiasm of the colored soldiers in his army; anticipates their valor in the approaching battle. 20 March 1851. p.2, c1.

**4690 LIBERTAS** *to* **MR. EDITOR. [from the** *National Era*] **n.d. n.p.** Expresses his disgust with the pro-slavery sentiments of the *Literary World*; calls for the establishment of a literary magazine sympathetic to the cause of liberty. 20 March 1851. p.2, c2.

**4691 J.** *to* **MESSRS. EDITORS. [from the** *Ledger*] **16 March 1851. West Caln Township, Chester County.** Reports the kidnapping of a black man named Thomas Hall. 20 March 1851. p.3, c1.

**4692 CORRESPONDENT** *to* **THE** *COMMONWEALTH*. **[extract] n.d. n.p.** Proposes the Bunker Hill Monument as a site for a barracoon. 20 March 1851. p.3, c3.

**4693 CORRESPONDENT** *to* **THE** *NEW YORK EVENING POST*. **[extract] n.d. Washington.** States that knowledgable sources consider it a settled point that neither Mr. Fillmore nor Mr. Webster can capture the Whig nomination for president. 20 March 1851. p.3, c3.

**4694 TORONTO CORRESPONDENT** *to* **THE** *TRIBUNE*. **[extract] n.d. n.p.** Reports on an anti-slavery meeting in Toronto. 20 March 1851. p.3, c4.

**4695 PARIS CORRESPONDENT** *to* **THE** *NATIONAL INTELLIGENCER*. **n.d. n.p.** Reports the completion of an eighteen-year effort to drill an artesian well at Kissengen, in Batavia. 20 March 1851. p.4, c3.

**4696 CORRESPONDENT** *to* **THE** *BUFFALO COMMERCIAL ADVERTISER*. **n.d. n.p.** Describes a volcano in the vicinity of the Great Salt Lake. 20 March 1851. p.4, c3.

**4697 DR. J. V. C. SMITH** *to* **n.n. n.d. Antwerp.** Comments on the custom in Belgium and Holland of lining the roadways with trees. 20 March 1851. p.4, c4.

**4698 EDWARD MATHEWS** *to* **BRO. WALKER. [from the** *American Baptist*] **20 February 1851. Bryantsville.** Describes the abusive treatment he received at the hands of ruffians in Kentucky. 27 March 1851. p.1, c1.

**4699 EDWARD MATHEWS** *to* **BRO. WALKER. [from the** *American Baptist***] 22 February 1851. Madison, In.** Continues the account of his harrassment by Kentucky ruffians; chronicles his retreat to Indiana. 27 March 1851. p.1, c2.

**4700 FAIRFAX L. SUTHERLAND** *to* **ELIZUR WRIGHT, ESQ. 19 February 1851. Baltimore.** Denounces Wright for his part in the rescue of the slave Shadrach; warns Wright that he will be murdered if he shows his face south of Mason and Dixon's line. 27 March 1851. p.1, c3.

**4701 CORRESPONDENT** *to* **THE** *NEW YORK EVENING POST.* **15 March 1851. Elkton, Cecil County.** States that slavery has decreased markedly in his county in the past decade, and that this has given rise to increased productivity and wealth. 27 March 1851. p.1, c5.

**4702 n.n.** *to* **THE EDITOR OF THE** *PENNSYLVANIA FREEMAN.* **17 March 1850. n.p.** Assesses popular sentiment in Massachusetts regarding the Fugitive Slave Law. 27 March 1851. p.2, c1.

**4703 THOMAS GARRETT** *to* **FRIEND. 17 March 1851. Wilmington.** Reports the kidnapping of a free colored man, William Brown, outside Wilmington. 27 March 1851. p.2, c3.

**4704 B. T. C.** *to* **FRIEND. 23 March 1851. West Chester, Pa.** Reports the release of Stephen N. Taylor from a prison in Lee County, Virginia. 27 March 1851. p.2, c4.

**4705 DANIEL WEBSTER** *to* **FRIENDS. [extract] n.d. n.p.** Remarks that only a rich man or a bachelor can afford to be secretary of state; states that a "golden opportunity" lies before them with the establishment of Mr. Fillmore's administration. 27 March 1851. p.2, c5.

**4706 DANIEL WEBSTER** *to* **GENTLEMEN. [from the** *Boston Commonwealth***] n.d. n.p.** Offers to champion his friend's tariff cause in exchange for financial backing for his presidential campaign, in the *Commonwealth*'s interpretation of the above letter. 27 March 1851. p.2, c5.

**4707 n.n.** *to* **n.n. [extract] n.d. n.p.** Describes a slave market near his home; bemoans the fate of the colored children commonly lured from Philadelphia to be sold there. 27 March 1851. p.3, c2.

**4708 WM. W. BROWN** *to* **n.n. [extract from the** *North Star***] n.d. n.p.** Comments on antislavery speeches by Dr. Thomas Dick and the Rev. George Gilfillan at a meeting in Dundee, Scotland; describes a subsequent visit to Dr. Dick's residence. 27 March 1851. p.4, c3.

**4709 GEO. THOMPSON** *to* **GARRISON. [from the** *Liberator***] 12 March 1850. Rochester.** Reports on his highly successful lecture in Rochester. 3 April 1851. p.1, c4.

**4710 AN OCTOGENARIAN** *to* **THE EDITOR OF THE** *PENNSYLVANIA FREEMAN.* **n.d. n.p.** Refers to the late kidnapping of Thomas Hall; criticizes the inconsistency of those members of the press who simultaneously denounce kidnapping and uphold the Fugitive Slave Law; ridicules the "Mawkish attempt" of Congress to ban the slave trade in the nation's capital. 3 April 1851. p.2, c1.

**4711 CORRESPONDENT** *to* **THE** *NEW YORK EVANGELIST.* **[extract] n.d. n.p.** Discloses that Henry Clay volunteered his services to a Kentucky court to argue the case against a man accused of being a fugitive slave. 3 April 1851. p.2, c4.

**4712 REV. ADAM CROOKS** *to* **THE** *TRUE WESLEYAN.* **[extract] n.d. n.p.** Refuses the demand of pro-slavery citizens that he leave North Carolina; compares such tactics to the cruelties imposed on the Protestant reformers. 3 April 1851. p.2, c6.

**4713 n.n.** *to* **THE** *NEW YORK SUN.* **[extract] n.d. n.p.** Questions the integrity of Daniel Webster in light of his alleged acceptance of a large financial gift from Boston businessmen. 10 April 1851. p.1, c2.

**4714 PARIS CORRESPONDENT** *to* **THE** *INDEPENDENT.* **n.d. n.p.** Cites a speech by General La Hitte before the French Assembly in which he criticized American laws allowing the incarceration of colored seamen, regardless of nationality, in her ports. 10 April 1851. p.1, c3.

**4715 THOMAS R. CHESTER** *to* **n.n. [extract from the** *Nashville American***] n.d. n.p.** Advises slave owners whose property has fled to the North to capture it by force rather than rely on the aid of the region's officers or people. 10 April 1851. p.1, c5.

**4716 BOSTON CORRESPONDENT** *to* **THE** *NEW YORK EVENING POST.* **4 April 1851. Boston.** Informs of the arrest of "Thomas Symmes," an alleged fugitive slave from Georgia. 10 April 1851. p.1, c6.

**4717 HILLTOWN** *to* **MR. EDITOR. n.d. n.p.** Praises the anti-slavery work of C. M. Burleigh; urges the public to elect men to Congress who have "honesty and moral courage enough" to carry out their anti-slavery views. 10 April 1851. p.2, c3.

**4718 R. C. F.** *to* **THE EDITOR OF THE** *PENNSYLVANIA FREEMAN.* **3 April 1851. Hamorton.** Queries why the *Freeman* inserted the word 'colored' into the title of an article he wrote, "Thoughts on the death of a young woman who died in Kennett, Chester County." 10 April 1851. p.3, c4.

**4719 THE EDITOR OF THE** *PENNSYLVANIA FREEMAN* *to* **R. C. F. n.d. n.p.** Replies that the insertion of the word 'colored' into R. C. F.'s article was a typographical error. 10 April 1851. p.3, c4.

**4720 ASA FAIRBANKS** *to* **THE** *COMMONWEALTH.* **[extract] n.d. n.p.** States that the governor elect, Mr. Allen, was a "decided" Free-Soil Democrat in 1848 and is hostile to the Fugitive Slave Law. 10 April 1851. p.3, c5.

**4721 THE LADIES OF THE GLASGOW FEMALE ASSOCIATION FOR THE ABOLITION OF SLAVERY** *to* **THEIR CHRISTIAN SISTERHOOD IN THE UNITED STATES OF AMERICA. [from the** *Tribune***] 12 March 1851. Glasgow.** Entreat them to bring about the abolition of slavery in America. 17 April 1851. p.1, c2.

**4722 OBSERVER** *to* **THE** *LEDGER.* **[extract] n.d. n.p.** Reports that Mr. Brown of Tennessee, the present minister plenipotentiary to St. Petersburg, has obtained a leave of absence and will probably resign; states that Josiah Randall may take his place. 17 April 1851. p.1, c5.

**4723 CORRESPONDENT** *to* **THE** *ERA.* **2 April. Louisville.** Reports on C. M. Clay's meeting in a Louisville courthouse in which he discussed emancipation in Kentucky. 17 April 1851. p.1, c5.

**4724 n.n.** *to* **n.n. 11 April. Boston.** Gives an account of the proceedings of the trial of the fugitive slave Thomas Sims. 17 April 1851. p.2, c2.

**4725 n.n.** *to* **n.n. 13 April. Boston.** Reports that another attempt was made to capture the fugitive slave Thomas Sims, who is on board the brig *Acorn.* 17 April 1851. p.2, c4.

**4726 AN OCTOGENARIAN** *to* **THE** *PENNSYLVANIA FREEMAN.* **n.d. n.p.** Believes that it is the duty of Christian ministers to oppose slavery. 17 April 1851. p.2, c5.

**4727 SECRETARY GRAHAM** *to* **COMMODORE READ. [extract from the** *Washington Republic***] n.d. n.p.** Informs that the services of the United States Navy may be utilized to enforce the Fugitive Slave Law. 17 April 1851. p.3, c2.

**4728 SECRETARY GRAHAM** *to* **THE SLAVE HUNTING MARSHAL OF BOSTON. [extract from the** *Washington Republic***] n.d. Devens.** Informs that while Massachusetts does not allow the use of her jails for the enforcement of the Fugitive Slave Law, the Navy's services can be used to "take care that the laws be faithfully executed." 17 April 1851. p.3, c2.

**4729 HANCOCK** *to* **HON. SAMUEL A. ELLIOT. n.d. n.p.** Condemns Elliot for voting for the Fugitive Slave Bill. 17 April 1851. p.3, c3.

**4730 DANIEL WEBSTER** *to* **MASTER JAMES TAPPAN. 26 February 1851. Washington.** Thanks him for his letter; recounts the days when Tappan was his schoolmaster. 17 April 1851. p.4, c2.

**4731 BETSY SIMPKINS** *to* **MR. EDITOR. n.d. n.p.** Forwards a letter she received from Jeremiah Swamscot. 17 April 1851. p.4, c2.

**4732 JEREMIAH SWAMSCOT** *to* **AUNT BETSY. March 1851. Mashmedders.** Thanks her for the letter; recounts the days when Betsy was his school-marm. 17 April 1851. p.4, c2.

**4733 DANIEL WEBSTER** *to* **NURSE TABITHA. 1 April 1851. Washington.** Thanks her for caring for him as an infant. 17 April 1851. p.4, c3.

**4734 n.n. [MISSOURI CORRESPONDENT]** *to* **n.n. [extract] n.d. n.p.** Believes that Missouri would prosper more from the abolition of slavery than from "a thousand fugitive slave laws." 24 April 1851. p.1, c4.

**4735 BALTIMORE CORRESPONDENT** *to* **THE** *TRIBUNE***. n.d. n.p.** Reports that many Negroes have fled Baltimore, fearing that their fate would be similar to that of the captured fugitive slave Thomas Sims. 24 April 1851. p.1, c5.

**4736 n.n.** *to* **THE** *NATIONAL ERA***. n.d. n.p.** Informs that the League of Freedom, an anti-slavery group, has been formed in Washington. 24 April 1851. p.1, c6.

**4737 DAVID GRIFFITH** *to* **FRIEND JOHNSON. [from the** *Anti-Slavery Bugle***] 3 April 1851. West Pike Run, Washington County, Pa.** Reports on an unsuccessful kidnapping attempt on a black man in West Pike Run. 24 April 1851. p.1, c6.

**4738 RALPH WALDO EMERSON** *to* **FRIEND. [from the** *Liberator***] 18 March 1851. New York.** Regrets that he is unable to attend the Middlesex County AS meeting. 24 April 1851. p2, c1.

**4739 MRS. SARAH GRAHAM** *to* **n.n. [extract from the** *Belfast Republican Journal***] n.d. n.p.** Hopes that God gives Daniel Webster a new heart, "as he did Nebuchadnezzer when he was transformed from a beast back to the capacity of man." 24 April 1851. p.2, c2.

**4740 ENGLISH CORRESPONDENT** *to* **THE** *INDEPENDENT***. n.d. n.p.** States that the efforts of George Thompson to "expose the injustice of the East India Company towards the Rajah of Satara, have borne fruit." 24 April 1851. p.2, c3.

**4741 REV. E. E. PARRISH** *to* **THE** *WESTERN RECORDER***. [extract] n.d. Oregon.** Gives measurements of vegetables growing in his garden. 24 April 1851. p.4, c3.

**4742 BOSTON CORRESPONDENT** *to* **THE** *NEW YORK INDEPENDENT.* **n.d. n.p.** Discusses discrepancies in opinion over the laws involved in the court case of fugitive slave Sims. 1 May 1851. p.1, c3.

**4743 JOSEPH K. HAYES** *to* **THE FRIENDS OF MR. WEBSTER. n.d. n.p.** Informs that a Temple of Liberty is open to them, at a reasonable charge, for their meetings. 1 May 1851. p.1, c6.

**4744 n.n.** *to* **MR. FENN. [from the** *Pennsylvania Telegraph***] n.d. n.p.** Forwards slave sale advertisements. 1 May 1851. p.1, c6.

**4745 SPECIAL CORRESPONDENT** *to* **THE** *HERALD.* **[extract] 14 April. Charleston.** Claims that South Carolina favors seceding from the Union. 1 May 1851. p.2, c1.

**4746 CORRESPONDENT** *to* **THE** *LEDGER.* **22 April. Harrisburg.** Reports that two fugitive slaves have been arrested in Columbia, Pennsylvania. 1 May 1851. p.2, c3.

**4747 JUDGE WADE** *to* **n.n. [extract] n.d. Ohio.** States that he opposes slavery, but does not intend to interfere with it. 1 May 1851. p2, c5.

**4748 CHARLES SUMNER** *to* **GEN. WILSON. [from the** *Commonwealth***] 22 February 1851. Boston.** States that "personal regrets mingle with gratitude" upon learning of his nomination as candidate for United States senator of Massachusetts. 8 May 1851. p.1, c5.

**4749 PEDRO** *to* **MR. EDITOR. [from the** *Boston Commonwealth***] n.d. n.p.** Discusses the duty of gentlemen to abide by the Fugitive Slave Law. 8 May 1851. p.1, c6.

**4750 S. BARNARD** *to* **THE** *PENNSYLVANIA FREEMAN.* **n.d. n.p.** Reports on the western quarterly meeting of the Society of Friends; gives an account of Joseph A. Dugdale's anti-slavery remarks at the meeting. 8 May 1851. p.2, c1.

**4751 HENRY D. MOORE** *to* **MESSRS. BOWEN AND McNAMEE. 7 May 1851. Philadelphia.** Encloses extracts of a letter from Rev. Henry Ward Beecher. 8 May 1851. p.3, c1.

**4752 REV. HENRY WARD BEECHER** *to* **n.n. [extract] n.d. n.p.** Asserts that Messrs. Bowen and McNamee are not only merchants, but also philanthropists and Christians. 8 May 1851. p.3, c1.

**4753 n.n.** *to* **n.n. 3 May 1851. Vicksburg.** Informs of the burning of the steamboat *Webster*, and of the loss of forty passengers. 8 May 1851. p.3, c6.

**4754 JOHN B. RACON AND M. S. D'LYON** *to* **THE CITIZENS OF BOSTON. [from the** *Savannah Republican* **via the** *Commonwealth***] n.d. n.p.** Thank the citizens of Boston for their courteous aid in helping them find a fugitive slave. 15 May 1851. p.1, c3.

**4755 G. W. P.** *to* **THE** *TRIBUNE.* **7 May. Syracuse.** Gives an account of the seventeenth annual meeting of the AAS. 15 May 1851. p.1, c6.

**4756 CORRESPONDENT** *to* **THE** *COMMONWEALTH.* **[extract] n.d. n.p.** Gives an account of Ralph Waldo Emerson's lecture in Concord, Massachusetts, on the evils of slavery. 15 May 1851. p.3, c4.

**4757 J. S. P.** *to* **MR. EDITOR. n.d. n.p.** Disproves by logical argument Henry Clay's statement, "that is property which the law says is property." 15 May 1851. p.3, c5.

**4758 GENERAL ISRAEL PUTNAM** *to* **COLONEL DAYTON. [extract from the** ***National Intelligencer*****] 16 November 1775. Cambridge.** Advises the governments of New Jersey and Connecticut "to take care and secure the Tories in New York" and see that "all advocates of slavery were taken care of." 15 May 1851. p.3, c5.

**4759 LAUREN WETMORE** *to* **WM. LLOYD GARRISON. 3 May 1851. New York.** Pledges $200 to the AAS for the coming year. 22 May 1851. p.1, c3.

**4760 THOMAS HENNING** *to* **REV. S. J. MAY. 5 May 1851. Toronto.** Regrets that delegates from the Canada AS are unable to attend the annual meeting of the AAS. 22 May 1851. p.1, c3.

**4761 ROBERT M. BRENT** *to* **n.n. [from the** ***Washington Union*****] n.d. n.p.** Discusses the laws governing whether a state can refuse to comply with the warrant from another state for a felon. 22 May 1851. p.1, c4.

**4762 GOV. E. LOUIS LOWE** *to* **GOV. JOHNSTON. [from the** ***Washington Union*****] n.d. n.p.** Refuses to issue a warrant for the arrest of Mr. Mitchell, a kidnapper residing in Maryland. 22 May 1851. p.1, c5.

**4763 S. BARNARD** *to* **THE** ***PENNSYLVANIA FREEMAN*****. 15 May 1851. West Chester.** Praises Samuel R. Ward's anti-slavery lectures. 22 May 1851. p.2, c1.

**4764 J. S. P.** *to* **MR. EDITOR. n.d. n.p.** Criticizes the *North American*'s editorial which denounced the anti-slavery convention in Syracuse as "treasonable." 22 May 1851. p.2, c1.

**4765 CHARLES SUMNER** *to* **THE LEGISLATURE OF MASSACHUSETTS. [extract] n.d. n.p.** Accepts his election as a senator of the United States. 22 May 1851. p.2, c6.

**4766 DANIEL WEBSTER** *to* **MESSRS. H. B. ROGERS AND OTHERS OF THE COMMITTEE. 23 April 1851. Boston.** States that he does not intend to speak in Faneuil Hall during his stay in Boston. 22 May 1851. p.3, c3.

**4767 HORACE WHEATON AND L. L. ALEXANDER** *to* **THE EDITOR OF THE** ***NEW YORK TRIBUNE*****. 13 May. Syracuse.** Refute the printed statement that Syracuse authorities granted the use of the city hall to the AAS only after they had received $10,000. 22 May 1851. p.3, c4.

**4768 REV. J. McBRIDE** *to* **n.n. [extract from the** ***True Wesleyan*****] 30 April 1851. Randolph, N.C.** Discusses the persecution to which he has been subjected for daring to preach against slavery. 29 May 1851. p.1, c5.

**4769 AN ALABAMIAN SLAVEHOLDER** *to* **n.n. [from the** ***Tribune*****] 13 May 1851. Mobile.** Reports on a meeting of the Union Southern Rights Association. 29 May 1851. p.1, c6.

**4770 ELIHU BARNARD** *to* **THE** ***PENNSYLVANIA FREEMAN*****. 20 May 1851. n.p.** Testifies that five years earlier, Joseph Dugdale said that he "did not consider himself a member of any religious society in the world." 29 May 1851. p.2, c3.

**4771 JOSEPH KENT** *to* **THE EDITORS OF THE** ***PENNSYLVANIA FREEMAN*****. 20 May 1851. n.p.** Testifies that Joseph Dugdale had said that "he did not consider himself a member of any religious society in the world." 29 May 1851. p.2, c3.

**4772 WM. KENT** *to* **THE EDITORS OF THE** ***PENNSYLVANIA FREEMAN*****. 20 May 1851. n.p.** Testifies that Joseph Dugdale had denied that he was a member of any religious society. 29 May 1851. p.2, c3.

**4773 ELIHU BARNARD** *to* **ESTEEMED FRIENDS. 20 May 1851. n.p.** Encloses testimonies from those who heard Joseph Dugdale say that he did not belong to a religious society. 29 May 1851. p.2, c3.

**4774 JOSEPH A. DUGDALE** *to* **RESPECTED EDITOR. 26 May 1851. Marlboro', Chester County.** Refutes the testimonies by Barnard, Kent, and Kent stating that he did not belong to a religious society. 29 May 1851. p.2, c3.

**4775 n.n.** *to* **n.n. 27 May. Boston.** Gives an account of the trial of James Scott, a colored man who "rescued" a fugitive slave from the Boston Court House. 29 May 1851. p.3, c1.

**4776 RODNEY FRENCH** *to* **MR. EDITOR. [from the** ***Boston Journal*****] n.d. n.p.** Refutes the rumor that he is to be sheriff of New Bedford. 29 May 1851. p.3, c3.

**4777 S. W. PALMER** *to* **THE EDITOR OF THE** ***FREE PRESBYTERIAN*****. 10 May 1851. South Bend.** States that his possessions are to be sold because he did not deliver a slave to his master. 5 June 1851. p.3, c2.

**4778 n.n.** *to* **THE** ***SAVANNAH NEWS*****. [extract] 7 May. St. Jago de Cuba.** Reports the arrest of revolutionaries in Cuba. 5 June 1851. p.3, c5.

**4779 MR. McBRIDE** *to* **n.n. [from the** ***True Wesleyan*****] 6 May. Guilford.** Gives an account of the insults and outrages to which he has been subjected for preaching opposition to slavery. 12 June 1851. p.1, c1.

**4780 THIRTY-TWO PERSONS** *to* **MR. J. McBRIDE. 6 May 1851. n.p.** Advise him not to fulfill his appointment as preacher. 12 June 1851. p.1, c2.

**4781 A MISSIONARY** *to* **A GENTLEMAN IN MANCHESTER. [extract from the** ***Manchester Guardian*****] April 1851. Freetown, Sierra Leone.** Reports that there is an increase of cotton cultivation in Africa. 12 June 1851. p.1, c5.

**4782 COMMANDER FORBES** *to* **n.n. [from the** ***London Morning Herald*****] 8 April. Army and Navy Club.** Encloses a letter he wrote to Mr. Thomas Hodgekin. 12 June 1851. p.1, c6.

**4783 F. E. FORBES** *to* **MR. THOMAS HODGEKIN. 26 March. Forest, Windsor.** Informs that he knows of Liberian citizens who are involved in the slave trade. 12 June 1851. p.1, c6.

**4784 JAMES MOTT AND J. M. McKIM** *to* **n.n. n.d. n.p.** Appeal for monetary contributions for an AS. 12 June 1851. p.2, c5.

**4785 CORRESPONDENT** *to* **THE** ***NEW YORK EVENING POST*****. n.d. n.p.** States that Fillmore, an Irishman, was "very much disgusted" with his western trip, on which he had to "work his passage" on the canal from Albany to Utica. 12 June 1851. p.3, c4.

**4786 BALTIMORE CORRESPONDENT** *to* **THE** ***TRIBUNE*****. 3 June. n.p.** Reports that Mr. James L. Bowers has been arrested on the charge of giving a forged pass to a slave of Dr. Davidson and enticing him to run off. 12 June 1851. p.3, c5.

**4787 LONDON CORRESPONDENT** *to* **THE** ***COMMERCIAL ADVERTISER*****. n.d. n.p.** Describes the steps involved in the production of flax cotton. 12 June 1851. p.4, c4.

**4788 n.n.** *to* **n.n. [from the** ***New York Evening Post*****] 26 May 1851. Savannah.** Informs that Thomas Sims's master, Potter, is having difficulty selling him because few would wish to risk buying a Negro who has been free for so long. 19 June 1851. p.1, c5.

**4789 J. E. SNODGRASS** *to* **THE SECRETARY OF THE DELAWARE AS. [extract] n.d. n.p.** Condemns Delaware and Pennsylvania for complying with the Fugitive Slave Law; stresses that freedom is more precious than the Union. 19 June 1851. p.2, c2.

**4790 JOSEPH KENT** *to* **THE** *PENNSYLVANIA FREEMAN.* **12 June 1851. n.p.** Queries why Joseph Dugdale denied saying that he was not affiliated with any religious society. 19 June 1851. p.2, c2.

**4791 JOHN CAMPBELL** *to* **n.n. [from the** *New York Herald* via the *Pennsylvanian*] **n.d. n.p.** Protests the admission of Negroes to the Industrial Convention at Albany. 19 June 1851. p.2, c5.

**4792 n.n.** *to* **n.n. [from the** *Tribune*] **15 June. Philadelphia.** States that an abolition meeting in Franklin Hall was disrupted by a mob. 19 June 1851. p.2, c6.

**4793 CORRESPONDENT** *to* **THE** *NEW YORK HERALD.* **[extract] n.d. n.p.** Relates a conversation with a Virginian who charged Daniel Webster with being inconsistent in his dedication to the South. 19 June 1851. p.3, c3.

**4794 TOBEY** *to* **ELIZUR WRIGHT. [from the** *Boston Commonwealth*] **4 June 1851. Wellsboro', Tioga County.** Informs that the *Tioga Banner* has ceased publication. 19 June 1851. p.3, c3.

**4795 n.n.** *to* **n.n. 9 June. Boston.** Informs that "many influential citizens" have nominated Daniel Webster for president of the United States. 19 June 1851. p.3, c4.

**4796 MR. FRY** *to* **THE** *TRIBUNE.* **n.d. Paris.** Reports that opinion of American character has fallen in Europe due to the poor display of American industrial, manufactured, and artistic goods at the World's Exhibition. 19 June 1851. p.4, c3.

**4797 E. B. PHILLIPS** *to* **MR. EDITOR. [from the** *American Baptist*] **n.d. n.p.** Informs of the death of Joseph P. Purvis. 26 June 1851. p.3, c4.

**4798 CORRESPONDENT** *to* **THE** *LONDON MEDICAL GAZETTE.* **[extract] n.d. n.p.** Informs of methods of preventing coughing and sneezing. 26 June 1851. p.4, c3.

**4799 HORACE GREELEY** *to* **n.n. n.d. London.** Describes the production of flax cotton, which he believes will prove profitable. 3 July 1851. p.1, c1.

**4800 CORRESPONDENT** *to* **THE** *AMERICAN BAPTIST.* **[extract] n.d. n.p.** Describes the death of an old, faithful slave belonging to a kind Virginia slaveholder. 3 July 1851. p.2, c1.

**4801 n.n.** *to* **n.n. 20 June. Angelica, N.Y.** Reports that the military and the Irish are of differing opinions as to whether Matthew Carrigan's sentence of hanging will be carried out. 3 July 1851. p.3, c4.

**4802 MR. GREELEY** *to* **n.n. n.d. London.** Reports that M. Claussen, the inventor of the flax cotton process, has also invented the circular loom. 3 July 1851. p.3, c4.

**4803 n.n.** *to* **n.n. n.d. England.** Expresses surprise that so many English people have read Emerson. 3 July 1851. p.3, c5.

**4804 CORRESPONDENT** *to* **THE** *LONDON BUILDER.* **[extract] n.d. n.p.** Details a method of preventing dampness in walls. 3 July 1851. p.3, c5.

4805 **CORRESPONDENT** *to* **THE** *NEW YORK HERALD.* **n.d. n.p.** Describes the "sandhillers" of South Carolina, who are poverty-stricken due to slavery's effects on labor; laments that most of them spend their earnings on whiskey. 3 July 1851. p.4, c2.

4806 **MRS. ELIZABETH CADY STANTON** *to* **THE AKRON WOMAN'S RIGHTS CONVENTION. May 1851. Seneca Falls, N.Y.** Regrets that she is unable to attend the convention; urges education and freedom for the "girls of today." 3 July 1851. p.4, c2.

4807 **CHIEF JUSTICE HORNBLOWER** *to* **SENATOR CHASE. [extract] April 1851. Newark, N.J.** Believes that the Fugitive Slave Law is unconstitutional. 10 July 1851. p.1, c5.

4808 **AN OCTOGENARIAN** *to* **THE** *PENNSYLVANIA FREEMAN.* **June 1851. n.p.** Illustrates, with numerous examples, the influence of slavery upon the North. 10 July 1851. p.2, c2.

4809 **n.n.** *to* **n.n. 2 July. Washington.** Hints that Governor Johnston of Pennsylvania may not be reelected. 10 July 1851. p.3, c2.

4810 **n.n.** *to* **n.n. 3 July. Chicago.** Reports on the Christian Anti-Slavery Convention at Chicago. 10 July 1851. p.3, c2.

4811 **n.n.** *to* **THE** *COURIER.* **n.d. Charleston, S.C.** Reports that there are 100,000 slaves in South Carolina and Georgia who speak English but have "never heard of the plan of salvation by the Redeemer." 10 July 1851. p.3, c5.

4812 **CHAS. BILDERBACK** *to* **n.n. 20 June 1851. Salem, N.J.** Requests money to help him pay off a fine he incurred for aiding the escape of a slave. 10 July 1851. p.3, c5.

4813 **GEN. SCOTT** *to* **T. P. ATKINSON. [extract] 9 February 1843. Washington.** Favors gradual emancipation but does not advocate interference with slavery. 17 July 1851. p.1, c2.

4814 **CAPT. ELISHA CARD** *to* **BENJAMIN T. SANDFORD. 23 June 1851. Portsmouth, Va.** Requests that Sandford ask Thomas Scott Johnson's mother for Johnson's certificate of freedom in order to prevent his being sold as a slave. 17 July 1851. p.1, c4.

4815 **MARIA WESTON CHAPMAN** *to* **THE EDITOR OF THE** *NATIONAL ANTI-SLAVERY STANDARD.* **2 June 1851. London.** Reports on the progress of the anti-slavery cause in France. 17 July 1851. p.2, c1.

4816 **CORRESPONDENT** *to* **THE** *BULLETIN.* **[extract] n.d. n.p.** Gives an account of the Fourth of July address given by Commodore Stockton at Elizabethtown, New Jersey. 17 July 1851. p.2, c3.

4817 **G. W. RICHARDS** *to* **n.n. [from the** *Manchester Democrat***] n.d. n.p.** Criticizes both the Whig and Democratic parties for complying with the Fugitive Slave Law. 17 July 1851. p.2, c3.

4818 **ASA WALTON** *to* **THE** *PENNSYLVANIA FREEMAN.* **10 June. Bart.** States why it is wrong for abolitionists to be involved in the purchase and use of slave labor products. 17 July 1851. p.2, c3.

4819 **B.** *to* **THE** *PENNSYLVANIA FREEMAN.* **30 June 1851. n.p.** Believes that abolitionists would gain support from the working white man if they strived "to burst the shackles of the working white man" who is chained to the "urgent demands" of everyday life. 17 July 1851. p.2, c5.

**4820 C. M. B.** *to* **THE** *PENNSYLVANIA FREEMAN.* **13 July 1851. Worcester, Ma.** Describes his journey through New England; reports on the Providence Annual Anti-Slavery Fair. 17 July 1851. p.2, c6.

**4821 CORRESPONDENT** *to* **THE** *BOSTON TRAVELLER.* **20 June. Bradford, Vt.** Gives an account of the Vermont convention of Congregational ministers. 17 July 1851. p.3, c1.

**4822 E. S. DUNCAN** *to* **GENTLEMEN. [extract from the** *Richmond Enquirer***] 2 June 1851. London.** Describes the World's Fair in London; denounces Horace Greeley as the "rankest abolitionist." 17 July 1851. p.3, c5.

**4823 THE EDITOR** *to* **THE** *NEWARK DAILY ADVERTISER.* **[extract] 15 June. Florence.** Reports numerous political arrests in Italy. 17 July 1851. p.3, c5.

**4824 CORRESPONDENT** *to* **THE** *TRIBUNE.* **n.d. Washington.** Reports that Mr. Webster has resigned as secretary of state. 17 June 1851. p.3, c6.

**4825 HORACE MANN** *to* **THE YOUNG MEN'S DEBATING SOCIETY. 16 June 1851. West Newton.** Counsels the Young Men's Debating Society to choose topics which are both theoretical and practical, and urges them to strive for truth, not triumph. 17 July 1851. p.4, c3.

**4826 CORRESPONDENT** *to* **THE** *BUGLE.* **[extract] n.d. n.p.** Reports that a new Baptist Theological School has been established in Cincinnati; adds that it intends to teach abolitionist principles. 24 July 1851. p.1, c2.

**4827 EVAN M. JOHNSON** *to* **HON. GULIAN C. VERPLANCK. [from the** *New York Evening Post* **via the** *Standard***] n.d. Brooklyn, N.Y.** Agrees with the charge made at a Syracuse meeting that the clergy and members of the Church are "indifferent to the wrongs inflicted upon the African race in this country." 24 July 1851. p.1, c3.

**4828 CORRESPONDENT** *to* **THE** *BOSTON TRANSCRIPT.* **n.d. n.p.** Reports that General Morehead intends to take over Guyanas in the Gulf of California and erect a new slave state. 24 July 1851. p.1, c5.

**4829 n.n.** *to* **n.n. [extract from the** *National Era***] n.d. n.p.** States that during the Revolutionary War, the slave states contributed considerably fewer soldiers to the army than the nonslaveholding states. 24 July 1851. p.1, c6.

**4830 HON. J. T. BUCKINGHAM** *to* **THE COMMITTEE OF THE FREE SOIL FOURTH OF JULY CELEBRATION. n.d. Boston.** Proclaims his confidence that freedom shall be victor over slavery. 24 July 1851. p.2, c3.

**4831 THOMAS GARRETT** *to* **THE** *PENNSYLVANIA FREEMAN.* **8 July 1851. Wilmington.** Reports on a scandal involving the attempted illegal sale of two Negroes, Elizabeth Williams and John Kinnard. 24 July 1851. p.2, c4.

**4832 DANA A. WALKER** *to* **n.n. [from the** *Boston Traveller***] 28 June 1851. Boston.** Asserts that as a juryman, he makes decisions according to law. 24 July 1851. p.3, c1.

**4833 MR. GREELEY** *to* **n.n. n.d. Paris.** Reports that Charles Hugo's sentence of six months' imprisonment for writing a "strong" article is making a "profound sensation" in Paris. 24 July 1851. p.3, c6.

**4834 CORRESPONDENT** *to* **MESSRS. EDITORS. [from the** *Cleveland True Democrat***] 7 July 1851. Chicago.** Reports on the Chicago convention. 31 July 1851. p.1, c4.

**4835 SANTA FE CORRESPONDENT** *to* **THE** *NATIONAL ERA.* **n.d. n.p.** Discusses the scheme of the slave party in New Mexico to defeat Hugh H. Smith in his nomination to the territorial senate. 31 July 1851. p.1, c5.

**4836 GEORGE THOMPSON** *to* **GARRISON. [from the** *Liberator*] **8 July 1851. London.** Wishes him well; states that he is going to attend a debate in the House of Commons on Mr. Hume's reform motion. 31 July 1851. p.2, c3.

**4837 MR. WM. FARMER** *to* **n.n. [from the** *Liberator*] **8 July. London.** Informs that George Thompson has arrived home in England; encloses a letter to George Thompson from passengers on board *America.* 31 July 1851. p.2, c3.

**4838 PASSENGERS OF THE B. R. M. S.** *AMERICA* *to* **GEORGE THOMPSON. n.d. n.p.** Request that he deliver a lecture on British India. 31 July 1851. p.2, c3.

**4839 CORRESPONDENT** *to* **MR. GORDON. [from the** *Free Presbyterian*] **8 July. New Athens, Oh.** Reports on the unsuccessful escape attempt of a slave family in southern Ohio. 31 July 1851. p.2, c4.

**4840 C. M. B.** *to* **THE** *PENNSYLVANIA FREEMAN.* **28 July 1851. Plainfield, Ct.** Praises the citizens of Worcester, Massachusetts, for their strong anti-slavery and anti-slave-hunting sentiment; comments on Daniel Webster's dwindling support. 31 July 1851. p.2, c5.

**4841 BALTIMORE CORRESPONDENT** *to* **THE** *TRIBUNE.* **n.d. n.p.** Reports that free Negroes in Baltimore oppose the CS. 31 July 1851. p.2, c6.

**4842 CORRESPONDENT** *to* **THE** *CONGREGATIONAL JOURNAL.* **28 June. Richmond, Va.** Discloses the contents of William Ragland's will, which liberates his ninety slaves and gives them his plantation. 31 July 1851. p.3, c3.

**4843 FITZ HENRY WARREN** *to* **SIR. 18 July 1851. n.p.** Informs that a new postage act entitles publishers of pamphlets, periodicals, magazines, and newspapers to exchange their publications free of postage. 31 July 1851. p.3, c6.

**4844 HORACE MANN** *to* **n.n. [extract from the** *Boston Commonwealth*] **n.d. n.p.** Defends his speech on the evils of slavery and how the North is an active participant in slavery by virtue of its compliance with the Fugitive Slave Law. 7 August 1851. p.1, c1.

**4845 WM. W. BROWN** *to* *FREDERICK DOUGLASS' PAPER.* **[extract] n.d. London.** Advises fugitive slaves not to come to England, where they would be "beggars." 7 August 1851. p.1, c4.

**4846 G. P.** *to* **THE** *LOUISVILLE JOURNAL.* **13 July 1851. Louisville.** Describes a Negro raffle he attended in Mississippi. 7 August 1851. p.2, c2.

**4847 C. M. B.** *to* **THE** *PENNSYLVANIA FREEMAN.* **3 August 1851. Hopkinton, Ma.** Asserts that slaveholders influence the Church and Northern industries; gives an account of the First of August celebration in Worcester. 7 August 1851. p.2, c4.

**4848 REV. GEO. ARMSTRONG** *to* **n.n. [extract] n.d. n.p.** Condemns the passage of the Fugitive Slave Bill. 7 August 1851. p.3, c2.

**4849 GEORGE THOMPSON** *to* **THE** *LONDON DAILY NEWS.* **[extract from the** *New York Evening Post*] **n.d. n.p.** Explains that his absence from parliamentary duties is due to his efforts in behalf of abolition. 7 August 1851. p.3, c4.

**4850 P. AND E.** *to* **MR. H. LEVY. [from the** *Buffalo Republic***] 7 July 1760. Schenectady.** Request that "wampum, pipes, moons, and blacks" be sent to Detroit as soon as possible. 14 August 1851. p.1, c2.

**4851 P. AND E.** *to* **MR. JAMES STIRLING. [from the** *Buffalo Republic***] 22 August 1769. Schenectady.** Inform of the cost of Negro "lads and wenches." 14 August 1851. p.1, c2.

**4852 P. AND E.** *to* **MR. LEVY. [from the** *Buffalo Republic***] 13 August 1770. Schenectady.** State that they have received two Negro youths; ask whether bills of sale are necessary with "those African gentlemen." 14 August 1851. p.1, c3.

**4853 P. AND E.** *to* **MR. CARPENTER WHARTON. [from the** *Buffalo Republic***] 22 March 1771. Schenectady.** Ask him whether he can purchase two Negro "lads." 14 August 1851. p.1, c3.

**4854 P. AND E.** *to* **MR. JOHN PORTEOUS. [from the** *Buffalo Republic***] 6 June 1771. n.p.** Inform that they have signed a contract with a New England gentleman for some "green Negroes" to be delivered on the first of August. 14 August 1851. p.1, c3.

**4855 PETER BESTES, SAMBO FREEMAN, FELIX HOLBROOK, AND CHESTER JOIE** *to* **THE REPRESENTATIVES OF THE DISTRICT OF STOUGHTONHAM. 20 April 1773. Boston.** A committee of slaves in Massachusetts express their desire that the legislature grant them their freedom. 14 August 1851. p.1, c3.

**4856 CORRESPONDENT** *to* **THE** *NEW YORK EVENING POST.* **n.d. n.p.** Reports that Mr. Winthrop, who was once an advocate of the Mexican war, is now in favor of peace. 14 August 1851. p.1, c4.

**4857 CORRESPONDENT** *to* **THE** *ERA.* **n.d. Toronto, Canada.** Reports on the annual meeting of the Congregational Union at Toronto. 14 August 1851. p.2, c1.

**4858 WM. FARMER** *to* **n.n. [extract from the** *Liberator***] 16 July. London.** Asserts that all of England opposes slavery; describes the warm welcome which George Thompson received upon arriving home in England after his journey to America. 14 August 1851. p.2, c3.

**4859 GEORGE THOMPSON** *to* **SIR. [from the** *Liberator***] 8 July 1851. London.** Announces his return home; affirms his devotion to the anti-slavery cause. 14 August 1851. p.2, c3.

**4860 WM. L. GARRISON** *to* **MRS. THOMPSON. [extract from the** *Liberator***] n.d. n.p.** Bears testimony to Mr. Thompson's usefulness to the anti-slavery cause. 14 August 1851. p.2, c4.

**4861 MR. FARMER** *to* **n.n. [from the** *Liberator***] n.d. n.p.** Gives further details on the reception George Thompson received in London. 14 August 1851. p.2, c4.

**4862 J. H. PICKFORD** *to* **MR. FARMER. [extract from the** *Liberator***] n.d. n.p.** States that he feels certain that George Thompson would win if an election took place. 14 August 1851. p.2, c5.

**4863 VICTOR HUGO** *to* **MRS. M. W. CHAPMAN. [from the** *Paris Evènement***] 6 July 1851. Paris.** Proclaims that he is sure that the United States will renounce slavery. 14 August 1851. p.2, c5.

**4864 C. M. B.** *to* **THE** *PENNSYLVANIA FREEMAN.* **10 August 1851. Plainfield, Ct.** Praises Nature's beauty; reports on the Emancipation Jubilee in Worcester. 14 August 1851. p.2, c6.

**4865 GEORGE SUMNER** *to* **A FRIEND AT PROVIDENCE. [extract] n.d. Paris.** Foresees improved political conditions in France. 14 August 1851. p.3, c5.

**4866 MR. GREELEY** *to* **n.n. 25 July 1851. London.** Reports on the fourth annual World's Peace Congress in London. 14 August 1851. p.4, c2.

**4867 WILLIAM P. POWELL** *to* **THE EDITORS OF THE** *JOURNAL OF COMMERCE.* **n.d. n.p.** States that colonization of American slaves in Africa is unfeasible due to the enormous amount of money it would necessitate. 21 August 1851. p.1, c1.

**4868 SAMUEL S. MARTIN** *to* **THE PUBLIC. 16 June 1851. Chicago.** The attorney repents ever having defended Crawford E. Smith, a kidnapper. 21 August 1851. p.1, c2.

**4869 CORRESPONDENT** *to* **THE** *CLEVELAND TRUE DEMOCRAT.* **n.d. Lewis County, Ky.** Reports on C. M. Clay's speeches in Kentucky; believes that slavery in Kentucky will eventually be overthrown. 21 August 1851. p.1, c5.

**4870 J. S. DONOVAN** *to* **n.n. [from the** *New York Tribune***] 7 October 1850. Philadelphia.** Deplores the passage of the Fugitive Slave Bill. 21 August 1851. p.1, c5.

**4871 J. S. MITCHELL** *to* **DAVID PAUL BROWN. 16 September. Cecilton, Md.** States that he would have captured and returned his female slave and her child to her husband sooner had Brown not interfered. 21 August 1851. p.1, c6.

**4872 DAVID PAUL BROWN** *to* **J. S. MITCHELL. 10 September 1850. Philadelphia.** Condemns Mitchell not for capturing his fugitive female slave, but for kidnapping her freeborn child. 21 August 1851. p.1, c6.

**4873 CORRESPONDENT** *to* **THE** *NEW YORK STANDARD.* **n.d. n.p.** Narrates incidents which occurred on his journey through the South; urges the abolition of slavery. 21 August 1851. p.2, c1.

**4874 C. M. B.** *to* **THE** *PENNSYLVANIA FREEMAN.* **18 August. Plainfield, Ct.** Describes New England; praises her improved institutions for education and criminal justice; lauds the anti-slavery work of Prudence Crandall. 21 August 1851. p.2, c6.

**4875 n.n.** *to* **n.n. 15 August 1851. Buffalo.** Reports that a fugitive slave on board the *Buckeye State* was arrested. 21 August 1851. p.3, c3.

**4876 n.n.** *to* **n.n. 15 August. Buffalo.** Reports on the arrest of a fugitive slave on board the *Buckeye State;* informs that his claimant, Mr. Moore, has been charged with assault and battery for beating the slave. 21 August 1851. p.3, c3.

**4877 MONTREAL CORRESPONDENT** *to* **THE** *CLEVELAND TRUE DEMOCRAT.* **n.d. n.p.** Reports that the fugitive slave Shadrach Minkins is residing in Canada and runs a saloon. 21 August 1851. p.3, c4.

**4878 BUCKEYE STATE** *to* **THE** *NEW YORK EVENING POST.* **7 August 1851. Ohio.** Explains why the "Hunker politicians" in Ohio will not be allowed to "engraft the Fugitive Slave Law into the platform of the Democratic State Convention." 28 August 1851. p.1, c4.

**4879 RICHARD G. MORRIS** *to* **n.n. 10 October 1849. Amherst County, Va.** Estimates the cost and profit per annum of keeping an adult slave. 28 August 1851. p.1, c4.

**4880 AMERICAN RESIDENT OF CUBA** *to* **THE** *JOURNAL OF COMMERCE.* **16 August 1851. Havana.** Gives an account of the invasion of Cuba by General Lopez and his men. 28 August 1851. p.2, c6.

**4881 n.n.** *to* **n.n. 24 August. New Orleans.** Reports that Lopez and his party have been captured by the Spanish troops in Havana. 28 August 1851. p.3, c3.

**4882 PARIS CORRESPONDENT** *to* **THE** *NEW YORK HERALD.* **n.d. n.p.** Reports that a *train de plaisir* filled with Americans will travel through Paris. 28 August 1851. p.4, c3.

**4883 J. E. CALDWELL** *to* **THE GOVERNOR OF NEW YORK. 14 August 1851. New Orleans.** Requests advice regarding where the slaves liberated by Elihu Creswell's will should be moved. 4 September 1851. p.2, c1.

**4884 J. D.** *to* **THE EDITOR OF THE** *FREEMAN.* **n.d. n.p.** Assails the CS for its unfair treatment of colored people. 4 September 1851. p.2, c2.

**4885 DANIEL DAVIS** *to* **THE COLORED POPULATION OF BUFFALO. n.d. Kentucky.** Regrets ever having run from his master; states that he will advise slaves in Kentucky not to run away. 4 September 1851. p.2, c5.

**4886 GILMAN A. COOK** *to* **n.n. [extract from a New Orleans paper] 16 August. Havana.** States that "Lopez the scoundrel" has deserted many of his party. 4 September 1851. p.3, c4.

**4887 THE EDITOR OF THE** *SAVANNAH NEWS* *to* **n.n. 1 September 1851. Savannah.** Reports that General Lopez has been successful in every battle he has fought in Havana. 4 September 1851. p.3, c4.

**4888 JOHN BROWN** *to* **THE** *NEW YORK EVENING POST.* **[extract] n.d. n.p.** Reports that Charles Allen has information which could convict Daniel Webster, whom he believes will resign from the cabinet before this information is made public. 4 September 1851. p.3, c4.

**4889 J. R. GIDDINGS** *to* **THE** *CLEVELAND TRUE DEMOCRAT.* **29 August 1851. Jefferson.** Refutes the statement made in the *True Democrat* that he would promote the election of General Houston to the presidency. 11 September 1851. p.1, c2.

**4890 CORRESPONDENT** *to* **THE** *ESSEX* **(MA.)** *FREEMAN.* **[extract] n.d. Montreal.** Gives an account of his interview with the fugitive slave Shadrach. 11 September 1851. p.2, c2.

**4891 n.n.** *to* **HON. HENRY CLAY. 5 August 1851. New York.** Expresses concern that some Americans are reluctant to uphold the compromises in the Constitution. 11 September 1851. p.2, c6.

**4892 THOS. GARRETT** *to* **FRIENDS. 2 September 1851. Wilmington.** Encloses a notice placed by a Delaware sheriff advertising a Negro for sale; condemns the State of Delaware for sanctioning such injustices. 11 September 1851. p.3, c2.

**4893 n.n.** *to* **THE EDITOR OF THE** *COMMONWEALTH.* **[extract] n.d. Kentucky.** Reports that many emancipationists did not vote in the last election in Kentucky. 18 September 1851. p.1, c1.

**4894 C. M. CLAY** *to* **n.n. [extract from the** *Tribune***] n.d. n.p.** Informs that he has not been elected governor of Kentucky. 18 September 1851. p.1, c1.

**4895 ELLEN BROWN [THE MOTHER OF A SLAVE]** *to* **SIR [THE OWNER]. 25 July 1851. Washington.** Pleads that he free her child from prison or let her buy her child. 18 September 1851. p.1, c2.

**4896 THE EDITOR** *to* **THE** *NEW YORK EXPRESS.* **n.d. Washington.** Reports that apparently General Lopez's invasion of Cuba was partially supported by Southern stocks. 18 September 1851. p.1, c4.

**4897 CORRESPONDENT** *to* **THE** *TRIBUNE.* **6 September 1851. Saratoga, N.Y.** Discusses a fugitive slave woman who married a free colored man in Glen Falls but was pursued by her master and forced to flee to Canada alone. 18 September 1851. p.1, c4.

**4898 HON. WM. WEMYSS ANDERSON** *to* **THE EDITORS OF THE** *NEW YORK EVENING POST.* **[extract] n.d. n.p.** Informs that the legislature of Jamaica sent him to America to determine whether the free colored inhabitants of America could be induced to emigrate to Jamaica. 18 September 1851. p.1, c5.

**4899 JOHN CADWALADER, R. SIMPSON, JOHN SMITH, [AND TWELVE OTHERS]** *to* **THE GOVERNOR OF PENNSYLVANIA. n.d. n.p.** Request that the chief executive of Pennsylvania respond to the assasinations committed by a band of outlaws in a neighboring state. 18 September 1851. p.1, c5.

**4900 WM. F. JOHNSTON** *to* **JOHN CADWALADER, R. SIMPSON, JOHN SMITH, [AND TWELVE OTHERS]. 14 September 1851. Philadelphia.** Informs that the band of outlaws who committed the assasinations have been apprehended and are awaiting their trial. 18 September 1851. p.1, c5.

**4901 WILLIAM P. PADGETT** *to* **EDWARD GORSUCH. 28 August 1851. Lancaster County.** Arranges the details of a slave hunt. 18 September 1851. p.3, c5.

**4902 J. S. GORSUCH** *to* **MESSRS. EDITORS. [from a Baltimore paper] 17 September 1851. Christiana.** A slaveholder gives an account of the Christiana slave hunt. 25 September 1851. p.1, c1.

**4903 n.n.** *to* **n.n. [extract from the** *Chicago Western Citizen*] **n.d. n.p.** Believes that a "deep and growing abhorrence" of slavery is in the mind of Christians. 25 September 1851. p.3, c4.

**4904 n.n.** *to* **n.n. 23 September. Lancaster.** Reports on the Sadsbury Township murder case. 25 September 1851. p.3, c6.

**4905 CHARLES HUGO** *to* **THE PRESS OF GREAT BRITAIN AND IRELAND. 20 August 1851. Prison of the Concergerie [*sic*].** Thanks them for their address of sympathy; condemns capital punishment. 25 September 1851. p.4, c2.

**4906 O. S. LEAVITT** *to* **n.n. 16 August. New York.** Corrects popular misconceptions concerning the manufacture of linen from flax, in order to prepare the way for linen manufacturers in America. 25 September 1851. p.4, c3.

**4907 WM. D. ANDERSEN** *to* **THE PUBLISHER OF THE** *TRUE WESLEYAN.* **30 August 1851. Guilford County, N.C.** Discontinues his subscription to the *True Wesleyan* because he is moving West to avoid mobocracy in North Carolina. 2 October 1851. p.1, c2.

**4908 E. W.** *to* **THE** *PENNSYLVANIA FREEMAN.* **9 September 1851. Wilmington.** Informs that Thomas Garrett is being sued for naming the magistrate who imprisoned Thomas Stuart, a colored man. 2 October 1851. p.2, c5.

**4909 JAS. M. WILSON** *to* **MR. EDITOR. n.d. n.p.** States that the Reformed Presbyterian church is an abolitionist church. 2 October 1851. p.2, c5.

**4910 LENTZ** *to* **THE** ***ART UNION BULLETIN.*** **[extract] May 1851. Dusseldorf.** Thanks them for the copy of *The Scarlet Letter;* states that he saw a painting of Hester Prynne in a portrait gallery in the castle Schwarzald. 2 October 1851. p.4, c2.

**4911 FRIAR LUBIN** *to* **GENTLEMEN. [from the** ***Evening Post*****] n.d. n.p.** Discusses the origin of the phrase "thereby hangs a tale." 2 October 1851. p.4, c3.

**4912 C. M. B.** *to* **THE** ***PENNSYLVANIA FREEMAN.*** **7 October 1851. West Chester.** Reports on an anti-slavery meeting held in West Chester. 9 October 1851. p.2, c4.

**4913 n.n.** *to* **n.n. 1 October. Syracuse, N.Y.** Informs of the arrest of an alleged fugitive slave named Jerry and of his subsequent rescue by a mob. 9 October 1851. p.3, c1.

**4914 CORRESPONDENT** *to* **THE** ***TRIBUNE.*** **n.d. Syracuse, N.Y.** States that abhorrence of the Fugitive Slave Law is growing in Syracuse. 9 October 1851. p.3, c2.

**4915 CORRESPONDENT** *to* **THE** ***TRIBUNE.*** **n.d. n.p.** Reports on the rescue of the fugitive slave Jerry. 9 October 1851. p.3, c2.

**4916 CORRESPONDENT** *to* **THE** ***TRIBUNE.*** **n.d. n.p.** Denies that any firing was done by the crowd which rescued the fugitive slave Jerry. 9 October 1851. p.3, c2.

**4917 E. K. KANE** *to* **n.n. n.d. n.p.** Reports that he has found traces of Sir John Franklin's expedition near Port Innis, Wellington Channel. 9 October 1851. p.4, c2.

**4918 CORRESPONDENT** *to* **THE** ***NEW BEDFORD MERCURY.*** **31 July. San Francisco.** Describes a farm in Santa Cruz managed by Mrs. Farnham and Miss Brice. 9 October 1851. p.4, c2.

**4919 n.n.** *to* **n.n. 14 October. Syracuse.** Reports that the government has issued warrants for the arrest of those who participated in the "fugitive slave riot" in Syracuse. 16 October 1851. p.3, c5.

**4920 n.n.** *to* **n.n. 15 October. Auburn.** Reports that twenty prominent citizens have been arrested on the charge of treason for aiding the escape of the fugitive slave Jerry. 16 October 1851. p.3, c5.

**4921 R.** *to* **THE** ***PENNSYLVANIA FREEMAN.*** **n.d. n.p.** Informs that James Ramage of Norristown has died by the "accidental discharge of a revolver." 16 October 1851. p.3, c6.

**4922 JUSTICE** *to* **THE** ***HARRISBURG TELEGRAPH.*** **[extract] n.d. n.p.** Describes the officers deputized to arrest those connected with the Christiana riot. 23 October 1851. p.1, c1.

**4923 R.** *to* **THE EDITOR OF THE** ***TRIBUNE.*** **[extract] n.d. n.p.** Advocates education for slaves and gradual emancipation by colonization "and other means." 23 October 1851. p.1, c2.

**4924 BALTIMORE CORRESPONDENT** *to* **THE** ***TRIBUNE.*** **8 October 1851. Baltimore.** Reports on the court case of James D. Johnson who was arrested on the charge of transporting slaves from Africa to Brazil. 23 October 1851. p.1, c3.

**4925 n.n.** *to* **n.n. [extract] n.d. n.p.** States that the governor of Vermont declares that all laws must be enforced, even the Fugitive Slave Law. 23 October 1851. p.1, c5.

**4926 AUGUSTE VACQUERIE** *to* ***L'EVENEMENT.*** **n.d. Paris.** Disguises political statements in a menagerie of non sequitor paragraphs. 23 October 1851. p.1, c6.

**4927 CORRESPONDENT** *to* **THE** *TRIBUNE.* **19 September 1851. Toronto.** Reports on the meeting of the national convention of the people of color at Toronto. 23 October 1851. p.1, c6.

**4928 WM. LLOYD GARRISON** *to* **J. M. McKIM. 4 October 1851. Boston.** Regrets that illness prevents him from attending the annual meeting of the Pennsylvania AS; urges abolitionists to follow the guidance of God, not man. 23 October 1851. p.2, c1.

**4929 THEODORE PARKER** *to* **FRIEND. 7 October 1851. Boston.** Regrets that he is unable to attend the annual meeting of the Pennsylvania AS; states that slavery must be uprooted from the South before freedom in the North is secure; criticizes Boston for having but few citizens who dare to defend the principles of God. 23 October 1851. p.2, c4.

**4930 HENRY GREW** *to* **THE PENNSYLVANIA AS. 6 October 1851. Philadelphia.** Regrets that he cannot attend the annual meeting of the Pennsylvania AS; expresses confidence that freedom will be the victor. 23 October 1851. p.2, c5.

**4931 C. M. BURLEIGH** *to* **THE READERS OF THE** *FREEMAN.* **n.d. n.p.** Ends his term as editor of the *Pennsylvania Freeman.* 23 October 1851. p.2, c5.

**4932 CORRESPONDENT** *to* **THE** *TRIBUNE.* **n.d. Auburn.** Discusses the opposition in Syracuse to the Fugitive Slave Law. 23 October 1851. p.3, c3.

**4933 GEORGE THOMPSON** *to* **n.n. [extract] n.d. n.p.** States that he has been elected to serve in Parliament; reports on the revival of anti-slavery sentiment in England. 23 October 1851. p.3, c4.

**4934 WM. FARMER** *to* **THE** *LIBERATOR.* **[extract] n.d. London.** Informs of the death of George Thompson's fifteen-year-old son, William Lloyd Garrison. 23 October 1851. p.3, c5.

**4935 A TRAVELLER** *to* **n.n. n.d. n.p.** Quotes an inscription on a bridge over the Ocmulgee River connecting Georgia and South Carolina. 23 October 1851. p.3, c6.

**4936 HON. GEO. M. DALLAS** *to* **n.n. [extract] n.d. n.p.** Suggests that a prohibitory amendment be added to the Constitution which would crush any anti-slavery activity. 30 October 1851. p.1, c1.

**4937 FRIEND** *to* **THE** *NEW YORK TRIBUNE.* **[extract] 20 October 1851. Syracuse.** An ex-Southerner condemns Negro stealing. 30 October 1851. p.1, c2.

**4938 NEW YORK CORRESPONDENT** *to* **THE** *BURLINGTON COURIER.* **n.d. n.p.** States that he met a fifteen-year-old girl who could recite any page of the *New York Sun* from memory if given twenty-four hours. 30 October 1851. p.1, c5.

**4939 OLIVER JOHNSON** *to* **THE READERS OF THE** *PENNSYLVANIA FREEMAN.* **n.d. n.p.** Introduces himself as the new editor of the *Pennsylvania Freeman.* 30 October 1851. p.2, c3.

**4940 FATHER MATHEW** *to* **A BOSTON FRIEND. [extract from the** *New York Independent***] 12 January 1850. n.p.** Declares that he is entirely free from debt. 30 October 1851. p.2, c4.

**4941 n.n.** *to* **THE EDITOR OF THE** *FREEMAN.* **n.d. n.p.** Reports on a meeting in Sadsbury Township, Lancaster County, of Christians friendly to the abolitionist cause; encloses resolution adopted. 30 October 1851. p.2, c5.

**4942 A FRIEND TO THE SLAVE** *to* **n.n. 22 October 1851. n.p.** Laments the death of Nelly, a Negro woman 130 years old. 30 October 1851. p.2, c6.

**4943 REV. EDWARD SMITH** *to* **THE** *TRUE WESLEYAN.* **[extract] n.d. Greensboro', In.** Reports on the Indiana Conference. 30 October 1851. p.2, c6.

**4944 A MEMBER OF THE NEW YORK EAST CONFERENCE** *to* **THE EDITORS OF THE** *NEW YORK TRIBUNE.* **n.d. n.p.** Condemns the *Christian Advocate and Journal*'s memoir of the slave catcher George Gorsuch, which praised him as a "consistent, meek, and holy Christian." 30 October 1851. p.3, c2.

**4945 CORRESPONDENT** *to* **THE** *TRIBUNE.* **n.d. n.p.** Reports that a friend visited a farm near Santa Cruz that was managed by Mrs. Farnham and Miss Brice. 30 October 1851. p.3, c4.

**4946 CORRESPONDENT** *to* **THE** *TRIBUNE.* **n.d. n.p.** Criticizes discourses by E. Buffum on the Whig candidate for California state senate, John A. Collins. 30 October 1851. p.3, c4.

**4947 CORRESPONDENT** *to* **THE** *TRIBUNE.* **n.d. n.p.** Reports that a tree with a nine-foot base was felled in northern California. 30 October 1851. p.3, c4.

**4948 HARRIET MARTINEAU** *to* **n.n. 3 August 1851. Cromer, England.** Regrets that she is unable to attend the Worcester convention; emphasizes that people should be judged individually, rather than by color or sex. 30 October 1851. p.4, c1.

**4949 ELIZABETH C. STANTON** *to* **PAULINA. 11 October 1851. Seneca Falls.** Urges support of woman's rights. 30 October 1851. p.4, c2.

**4950 n.n.** *to* **THE** *UNIVERS.* **n.d. Hong Kong.** Details the execution of M. Schoeffler, a missionary priest. 6 November 1851. p.1, c1.

**4951 THOMAS L. CARSON** *to* **n.n. [from the** *Syracuse League***] n.d. Jordan, Cayuga County, N.Y.** Informs that two prominent colored citizens in Jordan have left for Canada because they feared for their safety. 6 November 1851. p.1, c3.

**4952 HENRY WARD BEECHER** *to* **n.n. [from the** *Oberlin Evangelist* **via the** *N. Y. Independent***] n.d. n.p.** Discusses the *Oberlin Evangelist*'s retraction of its statement that Parker Pillsbury administered the sacrament of the Lord's Supper to dogs. 6 November 1851. p.1, c5.

**4953 THE EDITOR** *to* **THE** *RICHMOND WHIG.* **n.d. n.p.** Praises the virtues of New Englanders; believes that Southerners have a distorted view of New Englanders. 6 November 1851. p.1, c6.

**4954 A FREE SOILER** *to* **n.n. [extract] n.d. Stark County, Oh.** Praises the violent resistance to the Fugitive Slave Law in Christiana and Syracuse. 6 November 1851. p.2, c5.

**4955 EX-MEMBER OF CONGRESS** *to* **THE** *NEWARK DAILY ADVERTISER.* **[extract] n.d. Marseilles.** Reports that Kossuth, the Hungarian exile, was incensed with Captain Long of the U.S. frigate *Mississippi* for refusing to convey him to England. 6 November 1851. p.2, c6.

**4956 REV. GEORGE WHIPPLE** *to* **n.n. n.d. n.p.** Reports that the colored people of Canada do not want charity. 6 November 1851. p.3, c3.

4957 **WM. STILL, EBENEZER BLACK, SAMUEL NICKLESS, DR. J. J. G. BIAS, AND JAMES McCRUMMILL** *to* **BRETHREN. 10 October 1851. Philadelphia.** Urge attendance of the county convention of colored people. 6 November 1851. p.3, c5.

4958 **PROTEUS** *to* **THE** *NEWARK DAILY ADVERTISER*. **[extract] n.d. New York.** Criticizes the expensive clothes adorning the body of a dead woman, the wife of a man of means and daughter of a wealthy citizen. 6 November 1851. p.4, c1.

4959 **CORRESPONDENT** *to* **THE** *SUSSEX REGISTER*. **n.d. New York.** States that the chief of police informed him that there are 800 known "houses of ill-repute" in New York, but believes that there are probably 1500 such houses. 6 November 1851. p.4, c1.

4960 **WASHINGTON CORRESPONDENT** *to* **THE** *NEW YORK TRIBUNE*. **[extract from the** *National Era***] n.d. n.p.** Inquires what the purpose of aiding the revolution in northern Mexico is. 13 November 1851. p.1, c2.

4961 **CORRESPONDENT** *to* **THE** *NEW YORK TRIBUNE*. **[extract] n.d. Syracuse.** Informs that the Fugitive Slave Law is about to be vindicated in Syracuse. 13 November 1851. p.1, c4.

4962 **J. R. GIDDINGS** *to* **THE** *CLEVELAND TRUE DEMOCRAT*. **28 October. Jefferson.** Explains that his reason for remaining one of the New School Presbyterians was to try to exert an anti-slavery influence within the church. 13 November 1851. p.3, c1.

4963 **VICTOR HUGO** *to* *L'EVENEMENT*. **[extract] n.d. n.p.** Criticizes those who turn from the truth. 13 November 1851. p.3, c4.

4964 **ITALIAN CORRESPONDENT** *to* **THE** *LONDON DAILY NEWS*. **n.d. n.p.** Describes a sculpture by Mr. Powers and the social message it conveys. 13 November 1851. p.4, c4.

4965 **J. W. ADAMS AND JOHNSON WOODLIN** *to* **THE EDITOR OF THE** *PENNSYLVANIA FREEMAN* **[OLIVER JOHNSON]. 10 November 1851. n.p.** Stand by their statement that the editor of the *Pennsylvania Freeman* advised colored people who felt endangered to go to the West Indies or Canada. 20 November 1851. p.1, c1.

4966 **J. G. F.** *to* **THE EDITOR OF THE** *NEW YORK TRIBUNE*. **5 September 1851. Nantucket, Ma.** Condemns Indiana for preventing people of color from becoming citizens of the state; urges the Church to take a stand against slavery. 20 November 1851. p.1, c3.

4967 **THADDEUS STEVENS** *to* **A FREE SOIL MEETING IN BOSTON. 14 October 1851. Lancaster.** Regrets that he cannot attend the Free-Soil meeting; fears that Daniel Webster's efforts will serve to increase the power of slavery. 20 November 1851. p.1, c5.

4968 **n.n.** *to* **n.n. [from the** *Tribune***] n.d. n.p.** Describes how fugitive slave Bolding obtained his freedom. 20 November 1851. p.3, c3.

4969 **CORRESPONDENT** *to* **THE** *TRIBUNE*. **n.d. n.p.** Believes that California's attempt to prohibit the immigration of free Negroes will fail due to the "dubious complexion" of immigrants from Mexico, South America, and China. 20 November 1851. p.4, c4.

4970 **J. G. FEE** *to* **n.n. n.d. n.p.** Appeals to Northern abolitionists for financial aid in erecting a free church in Kentucky. 27 November 1851. p.1, c4.

4971 **REV. SAMUEL J. MAY** *to* **n.n. [extract from the** *Syracuse Star***] n.d. n.p.** Explains why he participated in the rescue of fugitive slave Jerry in Syracuse. 27 November 1851. p.1, c4.

**4972 n.n.** *to* **n.n. 23 November 1851. Baltimore.** Reports that two fugitive slaves from Baltimore were arrested in Columbia, Pennsylvania, and that one managed to escape. 27 November 1851. p.2, c3.

**4973 CORRESPONDENT** *to* **THE** *CHRISTIAN OBSERVER.* **[extract] n.d. n.p.** Reports that the Evangelical Alliance of southern New York and northern Pennsylvania openly declare their opposition to the Fugitive Slave Law. 27 November 1851. p.2, c5.

**4974 BAPTIST MINISTER** *to* **n.n. [extract from the** *Christian Chronicle***] n.d. Meadville.** Testifies that a Swiss Baptist minister near Meadville is opposed to slavery. 27 November 1851. p.3, c1.

**4975 CORRESPONDENT** *to* **THE** *ALEXANDRIA GAZETTE.* **[extract] 10 September. n.p.** Reports that the Mormons have denounced the president and the government of the United States. 27 November 1851. p.4, c3.

**4976 CORRESPONDENT** *to* **THE** *TRIBUNE.* **n.d. n.p.** Reports on the "national depression" of Hungary. 27 November 1851. p.4, c4.

**4977 AN IRISHMAN** *to* **THE** *NEW YORK TRIBUNE.* **[extract] n.d. n.p.** Discusses the treatment of Africans in Ireland. 27 November 1851. p.4, c4.

**4978 M. G.** *to* **n.n. n.d. n.p.** States that the present crisis in the anti-slavery enterprise requires that abolitionists of eastern Pennsylvania, New Jersey, and Delaware be strongly represented at the fair in Philadelphia. 4 December 1851. p.2, c5.

**4979 MARGARET JONES AND MARY GREW** *to* **n.n. n.d. n.p.** Request that friends procure evergreens to be used at the fair. 4 December 1851. p.2, c5.

**4980 M. G.** *to* **n.n. n.d. n.p.** Invites all to attend the Fourteenth Annual Anti-Slavery Fair of Pennsylvania. 11 December 1851. p.2, c5.

**4981 EDWARD M. DAVIS AND HAWORTH WETHERALD** *to* **n.n. n.d. n.p.** Present the prospectus of the *Pennsylvania Freeman* for 1852. 11 December 1851. p.3, c2.

**4982 ABBOT LAWRENCE** *to* **LORD PALMERSTON. 6 April 1852. Office of Legation of the United States of America.** Requests that England free the Irish citizens it has imprisoned. [letter submitted as a predicted communication] 18 December 1851. p.1, c5.

**4983 LORD PALMERSTON** *to* **ABBOT LAWRENCE. 15 April 1852. Foreign Office, Downing St.** Replies that Britain will free the imprisoned Irish citizens if America allows those imprisoned for violation of the Fugitive Slave Law to live in England. [letter submitted as a predicted communication] 18 December 1851. p.1, c5.

**4984 LEWIS TAPPAN, JOSHUA LEAVITT, GEORGE WHIPPLE, WILLIAM F. WHITING, AND SAMUEL E. CORNISH** *to* **HIS EXCELLENCY, LOUIS KOSSUTH &C. &C. 9 December 1851. New York.** State that they do not desire to link Kossuth with any political party in the United States. 18 December 1851. p.2, c2.

**4985 J. I. ZUILLE, T. J. WHITE, PHILIP A. BELL, [AND TEN OTHERS]** *to* **LOUIS KOSSUTH. n.d. n.p.** Agree that Kossuth's anti-slavery mission might be impeded by an affiliation with a political party. 18 December 1851. p.2, c3.

**4986 NEW YORK CORRESPONDENT** *to* **THE** *OSWEGO ADVERTISER.* **n.d. n.p.** Discusses the extremes to which women will go in order to be fashionable. 18 December 1851. p.4, c1.

**4987 PARIS CORRESPONDENT** *to* **THE** *TRANSCRIPT.* **[extract] n.d. n.p.** Informs of the death of Lord Byron's sister, Mrs. Lee. 18 December 1851. p.4, c4.

**4988 A NORTHERN MAN AND A FRIEND OF THE UNION** *to* **THE** *SOUTHERN PRESS.* **n.d. n.p.** Comments on the perseverance and spirit of the abolitionists. 25 December 1851. p.3, c5.

**4989 A SOUTHERN SCHOOL TEACHER** *to* **THE** *MT. STERLING DEMOCRAT.* **[extract] n.d. n.p.** Asks questions as to the duty of a school teacher. 25 December 1851. p.4, c2.

**4990 CORRESPONDENT** *to* **THE** *TRIBUNE.* **n.d. n.p.** Describes the state of Iowa. 25 December 1851. p.4, c4.

## [1852]

**4991 D. Y.** *to* **THE** *NATIONAL ANTI-SLAVERY STANDARD.* **[extract] n.d. Boston.** Relates a story he heard about a member of the Boston bar who wept because the sentence given the Christiana traitors was not harsh enough. 1 January 1852. p.1, c4.

**4992 JOSHUA HUTCHINSON** *to* **n.n. 28 December 1851. West Chester.** Describes Joshua R. Giddings's address to an anti-slavery meeting in Agricultural Hall. 1 January 1852. p.3, c3.

**4993 JAMES WADE, JR.** *to* **JOHN McCORKIE, ESQ. [from the** ***Frankfort*** **(Ky.)** ***Yeoman*** **via the** ***True Democrat*****] 30 October 1851. Cleveland.** A lawyer gleefully informs McCorkie that the fugitives he seeks are safe in Canada. 1 January 1852. p.2, c6.

**4994 JUDGE WILLIAM JAY** *to* **GERRIT SMITH. [from** ***Frederick Douglass' Paper*****] 5 December 1851. New York.** Suggests that Smith publish his scathing letter to Mr. J. C. Spencer; discusses the harmful effects of the Fugitive Slave Law. 8 January 1852. p.5, c3.

**4995 AN AMERICAN GENTLEMAN** *to* **n.n. [extract] 12 December 1851. London.** Reports on Lord Paget's account of the violence of the revolution occurring in Paris. 8 January 1852. p.5, c6.

**4996 KOSSUTH** *to* **MR. EDITOR [OLIVER JOHNSON]. 1 January 1852. Lancaster.** Reports on the treatment of the nine colored Christiana prisoners who arrived in Lancaster with United States Marshal A. E. Roberts. 8 January 1852. p.6, c5.

**4997 S.** *to* **THE** *PENNSYLVANIA FREEMAN.* **4 January 1852. Baltimore.** Narrates the details of the kidnapping of Rachel Parker, a colored girl, and the death of Joseph S. Miller. 8 January 1852. p.6, c6.

**4998 WASHINGTON CORRESPONDENT** *to* **THE** *NEW YORK TRIBUNE.* **1 January 1851. Washington.** Describes the effects of Kossuth's visit to Washington. 8 January 1852. p.7, c2.

**4999 CORRESPONDENT** *to* **THE** *LEDGER.* **n.d. n.p.** Describes the influence of Mr. Meade of Virginia upon the decision of the House to pass the Senate resolution of courtesy to Kossuth. 8 January 1852. p.7, c2.

**5000 CORRESPONDENT** *to* **THE** *NORTH AMERICAN.* **n.d. n.p.** Discusses the interview between Kossuth and the president. 8 January 1852. p.7, c4.

**5001 n.n.** *to* **n.n. 2 January 1852. Washington.** Reports that Kossuth defended his friendship with Seward when confronted by a deputation of Southerners. 8 January 1852. p.7, c4.

**5002 CORRESPONDENT** *to* **THE** *LONDON NEWS.* **16 December 1851. France.** Reports on the status of Louis Napoleon's usurpation. 8 January 1852. p.7, c5.

**5003 CORRESPONDENT** *to* **THE** *DAILY NEWS.* **n.d. Paris.** Analyzes Louis Napoleon's chances for success; opposes Napoleon's election. 8 January 1852. p.7, c5.

**5004 W. B. REED, ATTORNEY GENERAL** *to* **HON. LOUIS KOSSUTH. 23 December 1851. n.p.** Warns that he will report any "incendiary" statements by Kossuth to the grand inquest of Philadelphia County. [letter is forged] 15 January 1852. p.9, c7.

**5005 WASHINGTON CORRESPONDENT** *to* **THE** *NEW YORK MIRROR.* **n.d. Washington.** Reports that even Mr. Webster's presumed friends and supporters secretly favor General Scott for president and Secretary Graham for vice-president. 15 January 1852. p.10, c5.

**5006 CORRESPONDENT** *to* **THE** *CLEVELAND TRUE DEMOCRAT.* **n.d. n.p.** Relays facts he learned while visiting the neighborhood of Christiana. 15 January 1852. p.11, c3.

**5007 n.n.** *to* **n.n. [extract] 1 January 1852. Pesth, Hungary.** Reports that Kossuth's mother and sisters are under police surveillance and that his tutor is in irons. 15 January 1852. p.11, c5.

**5008 CORRESPONDENT** *to* **THE** *NEW YORK TRIBUNE.* **n.d. n.p.** Reports that a deserter was branded and flogged severely at West Point before being "drummed off the Point." 15 January 1852. p.11, c5.

**5009 n.n.** *to* **THE** *JOURNAL OF COMMERCE.* **[extract] 30 October 1851. Ophir, Placer County, Ca.** Describes the mob hanging of a young Mexican woman who had killed a man. 15 January 1852. p.12, c4.

**5010 n.n.** *to* **THE** *NEW YORK TRIBUNE.* **n.d. Havana, Cuba.** Reports the arrival of African slaves at Cuba; explains that the slaves will be leased for seven years before they are transported to Jamaica. 22 January 1852. p.14, c1.

**5011 CASSIUS M. CLAY** *to* **HON. HORACE GREELEY. n.d. n.p.** Forwards a check for $100 to be added to the Kossuth loan; expresses his commitment to the fight against tyranny. 22 January 1852. p.14, c5.

**5012 HENRY GREW** *to* **THE EDITOR OF THE** *PENNSYLVANIA FREEMAN.* **n.d. n.p.** Argues that the *Pennsylvania Freeman*'s criticism of Mr. Wadsworth, a Presbyterian clergyman, was too harsh. 22 January 1852. p.14, c6.

**5013 E. PUGH** *to* **THE** *PENNSYLVANIA FREEMAN.* **12 January 1852. Nottingham.** Describes Joseph C. Miller's funeral. 22 January 1852. p.14, c7.

**5014 C. M. BURLEIGH** *to* **FRIEND JOHNSON. 15 January 1852. Upper Providence.** Describes his anti-slavery lecture tour in Pennsylvania; reports that he solicited subscriptions for the *Pennsylvania Freeman* and the *Standard.* 29 January 1852. p.17, c2.

**5015 ALFRED G. CAMPBELL** *to* **MR. EDITOR [OLIVER JOHNSON]. 11 January 1852. Paterson, N. J.** Charges that America's sympathy for the oppressed is confined to those in other countries; demonstrates the hypocrisy of a meeting for "the promotion of the cause of freedom throughout the world" which rejected resolutions against slavery. 29 January 1852. p.17, c3.

**5016 WENDELL PHILLIPS** *to* **SIR. [from the** *Liberty Bell***] November 1851. Boston.** Responds to a correspondent's claim that the language and style of the anti-slavery advocates have hindered their effectiveness in the slave states; argues that the anti-slavery movement has been extraordinarily successful. 29 January 1852. p.17, c4.

**5017 n.n.** *to* **THE** ***TRIBUNE.*** **n.d. n.p.** Observes that no single issue occupies the Congress at present and that parties are disintegrating; predicts the effect of this situation on the forthcoming presidential election; reports that President Fillmore intends to run again. 29 January 1852. p.17, c6.

**5018 n.n.** *to* **THE** ***LONDON TIMES.*** **1 January 1852. Paris.** Describes Louis Napoleon's inauguration at Notre Dame. 29 January 1852. p.18, c1.

**5019 FRANCIS JOSEPH, EMPEROR OF AUSTRIA** *to* **THE** ***LONDON MORNING ADVERTISER.*** **19 December 1851. Vienna.** Offers $1 million for the return of Louis Kossuth to the emperor. 29 January 1852. p.18, c2.

**5020 J. S. P.** *to* **THE** ***TRIBUNE.*** **[extract] n.d. Washington.** Examines the disagreement between Daniel Webster and President Fillmore over Fillmore's decision to run for reelection. 29 January 1852. p.18, c4.

**5021 CORRESPONDENT** *to* **THE** ***TRIBUNE.*** **n.d. Washington.** Reports that Mr. Hale is postponing his speech on reform of naval discipline until the subject is discussed in the Senate. 29 January 1852. p.18, c7.

**5022 MRS. SARAH H. ERNST, MRS. ELIZABETH COLEMAN, MRS. JULIA HARWOOD, [AND NINE OTHERS]** *to* **FRIENDS OF FREEDOM. 5 January 1852. Cincinnati, Oh.** Invite readers to an anti-slavery convention in Cincinnati commencing 27 April. 29 January 1852. p.19, c7.

**5023 JUDGE WILLIAM JAY** *to* **THE AMERICAN PEACE SOCIETY. [extract] n.d. n.p.** Argues against accepting Kossuth's proposition to condemn Russia so long as the United States upholds slavery. 5 February 1852. p.21, c3.

**5024 JOHN S. C. ABBOTT** *to* **n.n. [from the** *New York Evangelist***] January 1852. Brunswick, Me.** Describes the worst effects of the Fugitive Slave Law, including separation from family and friends, homelessness, and exposure to harsh weather. 5 February 1852. p.21, c6.

**5025 A. J. G.** *to* **THE** ***NEW YORK TRIBUNE.*** **28 January 1852. Boston.** Reports the proceedings and resolutions of the Massachusetts AS annual meeting in Boston. 5 February 1852. p.22, c1.

**5026 HENRY GREW** *to* **FRIEND EDITOR [OLIVER JOHNSON]. n.d. n.p.** Continues his criticism of Oliver Johnson's decision to compare Mr. Wadsworth with Judas. 5 February 1852. p.22, c5.

**5027 JOSHUA HUTCHINSON** *to* **FRIEND. 30 January 1852. Christiana.** Reports that his concert in Christiana's new woolen factory was warmly received; adds that some of the released prisoners attended. 5 February 1852. p.22, c7.

**5028 CORRESPONDENT** *to* **THE** ***LEDGER*** **[extract] n.d. Washington.** Reports that Southern secessionists are split in their support of Buchanan and Butler; guesses that Buchanan has more support, even though Jefferson Davis supports Butler. 5 February 1852. p.23, c1.

**5029 CORRESPONDENT** *to* **THE** ***LEDGER.*** **[extract] n.d. Washington.** Predicts that General Scott will be nominated for president. 5 February 1852. p.23, c2.

**5030 S. SWAIN, JR.** *to* **FRIEND JOHNSON. January 1852. Bristol, Bucks County.** Encloses a temperance petition which has been circulated throughout Bucks County; calls for abolitionists to assist with the temperance movement. 5 February 1852. p.23, c2.

**5031 P. T. BARNUM** *to* **THE** *TRIBUNE.* **[extract] n.d. n.p.** Argues that alcoholic drinks are at least as dangerous as unmuzzled dogs, yet the law permits the former and kills the latter. 5 February 1852. p.23, c4.

**5032 MRS. PAULINE W. DAVIS, N. R. GREENE, MRS. R. R. NEAL, [AND ELEVEN OTHERS]** *to* **THE AMERICAN PUBLIC. n.d. n.p.** Protest insulting treatment of women wearing the short "Bloomer Dress"; ask protection of their inalienable right to wear decent, practical clothing. 5 February 1852. p.24, c3.

**5033 HOMO.** *to* **MR. EDITOR [OLIVER JOHNSON]. 30 January 1852. Norristown, Pa.** A colored man opposes colonization and African emigration; advocates emigration to British soil. 12 February 1852. p.25, c3.

**5034 E. H.** *to* **MR. EDITOR [OLIVER JOHNSON]. n.d. n.p.** A woman condemns two bills introduced into the Pennsylvania legislature which would do harm to the cause of the slave; appeals to readers on behalf of oppressed slaves. 12 February 1852. p.25, c4.

**5035 J. S. P.** *to* **THE** *TRIBUNE.* **2 February 1852. Washington.** Explains how the Fugitive Slave Law hampers the process of electing a Whig president. 12 February 1852. p.25, c7.

**5036 CORRESPONDENT** *to* **THE** *NEW YORK HERALD.* **1 February 1852. Washington.** Discusses the political prospects of the Whig Party; predicts that General Scott will be nominated and adds predictions about the Democratic Party. 12 February 1852. p.26, c1.

**5037 n.n.** *to* **THE** *NEW YORK TRIBUNE.* **5 January 1852. St. Croix.** Describes New Year festivities among free Negroes at St. Croix. 12 February 1852. p.26, c1.

**5038 C. M. BURLEIGH** *to* **FRIEND JOHNSON. n.d. n.p.** Reports on his investigation of the case of a kidnapping and subsequent murder in Nottingham; substantiates the *Pennsylvania Freeman*'s account. 12 February 1852. p. 26, c6.

**5039 REV. SAMUEL AARON** *to* **THE EDITOR [OLIVER JOHNSON]. 1 February 1852. Norristown, Pa.** Urges colored people of Pennsylvania to present a signed memorial to members of the state legislature protesting an oppressive measure which might be passed in order to prove to the South that James Buchanan represents the entire nation. 12 February 1852. p.27, c1.

**5040 n.n.** *to* **n.n. 28 January 1852. Albany, N.Y.** Reports that the Albany temperance demonstration was the largest held in many years. 12 February 1852. p.27, c2.

**5041 NATH'L W. DEPEE, SECRETARY OF THE VIGILANCE COMMITTEE** *to* **n.n. 10 February 1852. n.p.** Reports on the committee's efforts to aid the Christiana prisoners; thanks clothing dealers for their contributions. 12 February 1852. p.27, c2.

**5042 SULPHUR** *to* **MR. EDITOR [OLIVER JOHNSON]. n.d. n.p.** Replies to the editor's intimation that Commissioner McAllister had outdone Satan in impudence. 12 February 1852. p.27, c3.

**5043 CORRESPONDENT** *to* **THE** *NATIONAL INTELLIGENCER.* **[extract] 6 January 1852. Yazoo County, Ms.** Opposes aiding the Hungarians; supports a senator's decision to vote against inviting Kossuth to Washington. 12 February 1852. p.27, c3.

**5044 n.n.** *to* **THE** ***TRIBUNE.*** **n.d. Washington.** Reports that one of Mr. Fillmore's New Mexico judges, Judge Baker, is buying slaves in Washington for mining in New Mexico. 12 February 1852. p.27, c4.

**5045 n.n.** *to* **n.n. n.d. Washington.** Reports that the president will replace Brigham Young, governor of Utah, with Colonel Doniphan. 12 February 1852. p.27, c6.

**5046 n.n.** *to* **n.n. [from the** ***Tribune*****] 15 January 1852. Paris.** Explains Louis Napoleon's proposed constitution. 12 February 1852. p.27, c7.

**5047 CORRESPONDENT** *to* **THE** ***RAVENNA*** **(OH.)** ***WHIG.*** **n.d. Western Virginia.** Reports on a series of fires in Clarksburg, believed to be started by Jacques and his wife, a female slave, two hired boys, and a free Negro. 12 February 1852. p.27, c7.

**5048 C. M. BURLEIGH** *to* **FRIEND JOHNSON. 8 February 1852. Westchester.** Describes his anti-slavery lecture tour; comments on temperance activities. 19 February 1852. p.29, c1.

**5049 J. S. P.** *to* **THE** ***TRIBUNE.*** **n.d. n.p.** Argues that "the Fugitive Slave Law is not in the way of electing a president by Northern votes." 19 February 1852. p.29, c7.

**5050 JOHN S. C. ABBOTT** *to* **n.n. [from the** ***New York Evangelist*****] January 1852. Brunswick, Me.** Narrates the true story of a fugitive slave in Boston who was persecuted under the Fugitive Slave Law and forced to live in exile. 19 February 1852. p.30, c1.

**5051 W. H. JOHNSON** *to* **OLIVER JOHNSON. 3 February 1852. Buckingham.** Commends Dr. Joseph Moyer's conduct in his ongoing debate with John Chambers over the Fugitive Slave Law in the *Olive Branch.* 19 February 1852. p.30, c7.

**5052 JAMES GADSDEN** *to* **n.n. [extract from the** ***Southern Press*****] 10 December 1851. Charleston, S. C.** Hopes that the California legislature will vote to "introduce domestics and our Southern cultivation" into California. 19 February 1852. p.31, c4.

**5053 n.n.** *to* **n.n. [extract from the** ***Boston Liberator*****] n.d. Ohio.** Relates a humorous anecdote about Kossuth's arrival at Quaker-dominated Salem; includes a pun on Hungary. 19 February 1852. p.31, c4.

**5054 CORRESPONDENT** *to* **THE** ***SAVANNAH GEORGIAN.*** **n.d. Washington.** Relates anecdote concerning Mr. Clay's authorship of the reply Lafayette gave to Clay's speech at Kossuth's reception in the House of Representatives. 26 February 1852. p.33, c7.

**5055 J. A. DUGDALE** *to* **THE EDITOR [OLIVER JOHNSON]. 17 February 1852. E. Marlboro', Pa.** Commends the *Pennsylvania Freeman* on its editorial policy; encloses an extract from a letter written by Castner during his final trial at Lancaster; warns colored people against colonization schemes; reports that the Kennett meeting of Friends wrote a memorial against the Fugitive Slave Law. 26 February 1852. p.34, c6.

**5056 CASTNER** *to* **n.n. [extract] n.d. Lancaster.** Comments on a Marylander who had remarked to a stranger that Hanway ought to be hanged, not knowing that the stranger was in fact Hanway. 26 February 1852. p.34, c6.

**5057 n.n.** *to* **FRIEND JOHNSON. 21 February 1852. Ashville, Pa.** Asks for Johnson's help in investigating the disappearance of Gibbons, a colored man; relates the details of his probable kidnapping. 26 February 1852. p.34, c7.

**5058 ROBERT HARE** *to* **HON. MR. BLAIR. [from the** *Philadelphia Inquirer***] n.d. n.p.** Suggests an alternative to Blair's bill preventing Negroes and mulattoes from settling in Pennsylvania; prefers a system of redemption with eventual emigration to Africa. 4 March 1852. p.37, c1.

**5059 JOHN JACKSON** *to* **n.n. [from the** *Pennsylvania Inquirer***] 28 January 1852. Darby, Pa.** Labels Robert Hare's recommendation of a system of redemption for slaves a plan to reestablish slavery in Pennsylvania; argues that free labor is better suited to agriculture than slavery. 4 March 1852. p.37, c1.

**5060 REV. ALBERT BARNES** *to* **REV. S. C. AIKEN, D. D. [from the** *Cleveland True Democrat***] n.d. n.p.** Explains that he does not recommend that opponents of slavery separate themselves from churches with pro-slavery members; prefers that they work against slavery from within the organizations. 4 March 1852. p.37, c4.

**5061 JUDGE WILLIAM JAY** *to* **WILLIAM HARNED. 4 September 1851. Bedford.** Grants the American Missionary Association permission to list him as a life member; praises the association for opposing slavery and rejecting "Cotton Divinity," the belief that God's commandments do not apply to the white man's treatment of the black man. 4 March 1852. p.37, c6.

**5062 n.n.** *to* **THE EDITORS OF THE** *INDEPENDENT.* **9 February 1852. Albany.** Discusses the line of defense which may be used in the trial of the fugitive Jerry. 4 March 1852. p.38, c1.

**5063 n.n.** *to* **GENTLEMEN. [from the** *Cleveland True Democrat***] 16 February 1852. Washington City.** Describes his visit to Drayton and Sayres, who are imprisoned for an attempt to rescue eighty Negroes from slavery which was followed by three days of mob violence. 4 March 1852. p.38, c2.

**5064 n.n.** *to* **n.n. [from the** *Ledger***] 5 February 1852. Paris.** Decries the lack of freedom of speech and press in France under the new "Prince-President." 4 March 1852. p.39, c5.

**5065 HENRY GILES** *to* **MR. EDITOR. [from the** *Boston Commonwealth***] n.d. n.p.** Praises a sculpture entitled "Drowned Mother," by Brackett. 4 March 1852. p.40, c2.

**5066 GERRIT SMITH** *to* **GOVERNOR HUNT. 20 February 1852. Peterboro'.** Attempts to enlighten Hunt about the ACS, in the belief that Hunt cares about the oppressed people of color. 11 March 1852. p.41, c1.

**5067 JOHN JACKSON** *to* **ROBERT HARE. [from the** *Delaware County Republican***] 11 February 1852. Darby, Pa.** Clarifies his objections to Hare's suggestion that slaves be introduced into Pennsylvania as "redemptioners"; fears that such a plan would degrade labor and harm the state. 11 March 1852. p.42, c6.

**5068 IDA IRVINE** *to* **THE EDITOR OF THE** *FREEMAN.* **7 March 1852. Philadelphia.** Lauds the Hutchinson's dedicated work, on the occasion of their departure from Philadelphia. 11 March 1852. p.42, c4.

**5069 CORRESPONDENT** *to* **THE** *FREEMAN.* **7 March 1852. Baltimore.** Attacks notice from "Southern Rights" urging Baltimore citizens to boycott the Hutchinson concert; copies an advertisement from the *Sun* warning that police and the mayor will be needed to protect the right to free speech of several anti-slavery lecturers; asserts Rachel Parker's innocence. 11 March 1852. p.42, c6.

**5070 MISS MINER** *to* **n.n. [extract from** *Frederick Douglass' Paper***] n.d. n.p.** Commits herself to work toward the elevation of colored people to equal status with whites. 11 March 1852. p.43, c2.

**5071 CORRESPONDENT** *to* **THE** *EVENING POST* **[extract] n.d. n.p.** Describes the aurora borealis. 11 March 1852. p.44, c3.

**5072 D. M.** *to* **n.n. [from the** *Knickerbocker***] n.d. Ontario County.** A nearly illiterate writer requests a copy of a new book, *The New York Justice,* in order to learn how to qualify himself for the position of squire. 11 March 1852. p.44, c3.

**5073 n.n.** *to* **n.n. [extract] n.d. Washington.** Asserts that the government must not condone polygamy among the Mormons. 18 March 1852. p.45, c3.

**5074 WILLIAM JAY** *to* **THE EDITORS OF THE** *EXPRESS.* **1 March 1852. New York.** Denies that John Jay, William Wilberforce, and Thomas Clarkson supported the ACS. 18 March 1852. p.45, c4.

**5075 CORRESPONDENT** *to* **THE** *TRUE WESLEYAN.* **n.d. Guilford County, N. C.** Reports that a travelling Quaker was interrupted by a member of the governor's council as he preached at a local church, resulting in a scuffle and injuries to an innocent black bystander. 18 March 1852. p.45, c4.

**5076 SAMUEL H. COX** *to* **ANSON G. PHELPS, ESQ. 21 February 1852. Brooklyn.** Regrets he cannot attend a party in honor of Daniel Webster; praises Webster and the Liberian enterprise. 18 March 1852. p.45, c5.

**5077 n.n.** *to* **THE** *TRIBUNE.* **9 March. Washington.** Presents the suit brought by a United States marshall to reclaim financial losses incurred in the government's war on the Suwanees, among whom four of his slaves had taken refuge. 18 March 1852. p.45, c5.

**5078 n.n.** *to* **THE** *FREEMAN.* **28 February. Matanzas.** Reports that the brig *Hanover* brought 800 African slaves to the island. 18 March 1852. p.45, c5.

**5079 PARKER PILLSBURY** *to* **FRIEND GAY. 26 February 1852. Albany.** Notes the evil appearance and odor which tobacco gives to the mouth. 18 March 1852. p.45, c6.

**5080 JAMES APPLETON** *to* **n.n. 5 March 1852. Portland.** Reports that the Maine Liquor Law has reduced crime and pauperism; suggests prohibition for all. 18 March 1852. p.45, c7.

**5081 C. C. FOOTE** *to* **FREDERICK DOUGLASS. [extract] n.d. n.p.** Relates that a man who returned recently from Liberia witnessed battles between colonists and natives while there. 18 March 1852. p.46, c6.

**5082 n.n.** *to* **THE** *TRIBUNE.* **n.d. Washington.** Cites greedy motives on the part of congressmen and others in Washington. 18 March 1852. p.47, c1.

**5083 S.** *to* **THE** *FREEMAN.* **14 March 1852. Baltimore.** Describes a concert by the Hutchinsons, who avoided abolitionist songs due to threats of mob violence; criticizes the editor of the *Picayune* for contributing to the mobocratic spirit. 18 March 1852. p.47, c4.

**5084 n.n.** *to* **THE** *TRIBUNE.* **[extract] n.d. Washington.** Discusses a congressional bill which would allocate interest on United States bonds for the transportation of free slaves to Liberia or improvement of conditions there. 18 March 1852. p.47, c5.

**5085 n.n.** *to* **THE** *TRIBUNE.* **[extract] n.d. Washington.** Gives an account of a heated debate in the House between two congressmen from Mississippi, one a secessionist and the other a Union man. 18 March 1852. p.47, c5.

**5086 n.n.** *to* **THE** *CLEVELAND TRUE DEMOCRAT.* **n.d. Washington.** Denounces the current proceedings of the Fillmore administration. 25 March 1852. p.49, c3.

**5087 J. S. P.** *to* **THE** *NEW YORK TRIBUNE.* **16 March 1852. Washington.** Denounces the methods used by Washington politicians to win support of their candidates for president. 25 March 1852. p.49, c5.

**5088 WILLIAM H. SEWARD** *to* **S. HART, J. TARDY, AND P. CULLEN, COMMITTEE. 12 March 1852. Washington.** Declines an invitation to attend an anniversary celebration of the Seward Association of Brooklyn. 25 March 1852. p.50, c2.

**5089 GRACE GREENWOOD** *to* **THE** *NATIONAL ERA.* **n.d. Washington.** Commends the Hutchinson family on their concert in Washington. 25 March 1852. p.50, c6.

**5090 SARAH M. GRIMKE** *to* **THE EDITORS OF THE** *CHRISTIAN ENQUIRER.* **10 February. Belleville, N. J.** Urges that the rights of women be respected, and that they be educated in order to become the intellectual equals of men. 25 March 1852. p.51, c3.

**5091 EDITOR OF THE** *MERCHANT'S MAGAZINE* *to* **CONTRIBUTORS. n.d. n.p.** Requests that contributors to his newspaper follow certain rules of style. 25 March 1852. p.51, c7.

**5092 C. L.** *to* **THE** *INDEPENDENT.* **9 March 1852. Hartford, Ct.** Compares the European way of life favorably to the American way. 1 April 1852. p.53, c4.

**5093 PARKER PILLSBURY** *to* **FRIEND GAY. 8 March 1852. Litchfield County, Ct.** Criticizes the extensive use of tobacco in New York. 1 April 1852. p.53, c6.

**5094 n.n.** *to* **THE** *HARTFORD REPUBLICAN.* **n.d. Washington.** Describes an appearance by Daniel Webster. 1 April 1852. p.54, c4.

**5095 MARY MIDDLETON** *to* **THE** *FREEMAN.* **n.d. Philadelphia.** Commends Mrs. M. A. W. Johnson's lectures. 1 April 1852. p.54, c5.

**5096 C. M. BURLEIGH** *to* **FRIEND JOHNSON. 22 March 1852. Adams County.** Describes his travels, his efforts against the Fugitive Slave Law, and his debate with a local Presbyterian minister. 1 April 1852. p.54, c6.

**5097 S.** *to* **THE** *FREEMAN.* **28 March 1852. Baltimore.** Expresses concern at the forced colonization of Liberia; discusses the Rachel Parker case; encloses a letter from "a Union man" to the *Argus* in Baltimore. 1 April 1852. p.55, c1.

**5098 n.n.** *to* **THE** *ARGUS.* **n.d. n.p.** Calls on the South to demand the release of the remaining prisoner held for kidnapping a slave in Pennsylvania. 1 April 1852. p.55, c1.

**5099 HAVANA CORRESPONDENT** *to* **THE** *NEW YORK TRIBUNE.* **13 March 1852. Havana.** Expresses the concern of the Cubans over an invasion by American troops. 1 April 1852. p.55, c4.

**5100 J. S. P.** *to* **THE** *NEW YORK TRIBUNE.* **29 March 1852. Washington.** Rejects both Webster and Fillmore as presidential candidates because of their lack of integrity. 8 April 1852. p.57, c3.

**5101 BAYARD TAYLOR** *to* **n.n. n.d. n.p.** Describes a journey by dromedary across the Nubian Desert. 8 April 1852. p.58, c2.

**5102 CORRESPONDENT** *to* **THE** *CLEVELAND TRUE DEMOCRAT.* **n.d. Washington.** Rejects slavery as an inefficient system for farming. 8 April 1852. p.58, c4.

5103 **FEMALE CORRESPONDENT** *to* **n.n. [extract from a New York newspaper] n.d. n.p.** Condemns the employment of women at making shirts for a sixpence a dozen. 8 April 1852. p.58, c5.

5104 **J. M. N.** *to* **THE EDITOR OF THE *FREEMAN* [OLIVER JOHNSON]. n.d. n.p.** Observes increasing decay of buildings as he travels South. 8 April 1852. p.58, c6.

5105 **VAUGHAN** *to* **THE *CLEVELAND TRUE DEMOCRAT*. n.d. Boston.** Describes the appearance, manner, and personality of Theodore Parker. 8 April 1852. p.58, c7.

5106 **n.n.** *to* **THE *FREE PRESBYTERIAN*. n.d. n.p.** Condemns Judge Grier, both as a judge and as a Presbyterian, because of his stand on abolition. 8 April 1852. p.59, c2.

5107 **WASHINGTON CORRESPONDENT** *to* **THE *LEDGER*. n.d. n.p.** Denounces flogging in the Navy and the attitudes which maintain it. 8 April 1852. p.59, c4.

5108 **JOHN G. WHITTIER** *to* **THE *SALEM FREEMAN*. n.d. n.p.** Praises *Uncle Tom's Cabin* as a work of art and as an anti-slavery instrument. 8 April 1852. p.59, c5.

5109 **n.n.** *to* **THE *BOSTON JOURNAL*. n.d. n.p.** Declares that the gold rush is not at all profitable. 8 April 1852. p.59, c7.

5110 **n.n.** *to* **THE *NASHVILLE BANNER*. n.d. n.p.** Describes the stand of General Scott on the preservation of the Union. 15 April 1852. p.61, c5.

5111 **n.n.** *to* **THE *LEDGER*. 5 April 1852. Washington.** Details the passage of a compromise resolution. 15 April 1852. p.61, c6.

5112 **n.n.** *to* **THE *NEW YORK TRIBUNE*. 3 April 1852. Washington.** Describes the speech of Representative Cleveland to Congress. 15 April 1852. p.61, c7.

5113 **n.n.** *to* **THE *WEST CHESTER REPUBLICAN*. n.d. Harrisburg.** Comments on the pardon of Alberti. 15 April 1852. p.62, c3.

5114 **J. M. E.** *to* **THE *FREEMAN*. n.d. n.p.** Recounts his journey through Virginia; describes an auction of slaves. 15 April 1852. p.62, c6.

5115 **MRS. H. M. TRACY** *to* **THE *PITTSBURGH SATURDAY VISITOR*. n.d. n.p.** Praises the work of Anne Knight. 15 April 1852. p.63, c3.

5116 **GEORGE H. NICHOLS** *to* **THE *PLOUGHMAN*. n.d. West Amesbury, Ma.** Suggests an improved method for growing potatoes. 15 April 1852. p.64, c3.

5117 **THEODORE D. WELD** *to* **WENDELL PHILLIPS. 3 April 1852. Belleville, N. J.** Declines an invitation to attend an anniversary commemoration of the return of Thomas Sims to slavery; conveys his support of their actions. 22 April 1852. p.65, c4.

5118 **CASSIUS M. CLAY** *to* **WENDELL PHILLIPS. 5 April 1852. White Hall P. O., Madison County, Ky.** Declines to attend a conference on the Fugitive Slave Law. 22 April 1852. p.65, c4.

5119 **JOSHUA R. GIDDINGS** *to* **n.n. 3 April 1852. Jefferson, Oh.** Declines an invitation to a Fugitive Slave Law conference; supports opposition to the law. 22 April 1852. p.65, c5.

5120 **G. B. B.** *to* **THE *TRIBUNE*. n.d. n.p.** Explains the chemical nature of grain alcohol. 22 April 1852. p.65, c7.

**5121 B. M. HALL** *to* **WILLIAM REESE. 12 April 1852. Schenectady, N. Y.** Condemns Reese for changing his mind about freeing his slaves. 22 April 1852. p.66, c1.

**5122 JAMES W. WALKER** *to* **n.n. n.d. n.p.** Describes his nocturnal journey to a friend's house. 22 April 1852. p.66, c4.

**5123 J. M. E.** *to* **THE** *FREEMAN.* **April 1852. Philadelphia.** Expresses concern over the insensitive treatment of slaves; describes his travels through Virginia to Washington. 22 April 1852. p.66, c5.

**5124 J. S. P.** *to* **THE** *TRIBUNE.* **7 April 1852. Washington.** Urges Congress not to compromise on the issue of slavery. 22 April 1852. p.66, c7.

**5125 n.n.** *to* **THE** *LEDGER.* **n.d. n.p.** Reports on a Congressional bill to aid emigration to Liberia. 22 April 1852. p.67, c4.

**5126 G. B. STEBBINS** *to* **THE** *PENNSYLVANIA FREEMAN.* **n.d. n.p.** Supports a meeting of the AAS. 29 April 1852. p.70, c3.

**5127 ROBERT PURVIS** *to* **FRIEND JOHNSON. 24 April 1852. Byberry.** Expresses concern over Stowe's beliefs in colonization as articulated in *Uncle Tom's Cabin.* 29 April 1852. p.70, c4.

**5128 HENRY D. MOORE** *to* **FRIEND JOHNSON. n.d. n.p.** Praises *Uncle Tom's Cabin;* encloses a letter to the editor of a pro-slavery paper in defense of Stowe's work. 29 April 1852. p.71, c1.

**5129 HENRY D. MOORE** *to* **THE** *PENNSYLVANIAN.* **n.d. n.p.** Attacks a *Pennsylvanian* correspondent who criticized H. B. Stowe for her beliefs. 29 April 1852. p.71, c1.

**5130 J. R.** *to* **THE** *NEW YORK INDEPENDENT.* **15 March 1852. Panama.** Discloses a scheme for the emigration of slaves to California, for the purpose of making it a slave state. 29 April 1852. p.71, c2.

**5131 HENRY GREW** *to* **THE EDITOR [OLIVER JOHNSON]. n.d. n.p.** Discusses women lecturers. 29 April 1852. p.71, c3.

**5132 S.** *to* **THE** *FREEMAN.* **26 April 1852. Baltimore.** Informs of the postponement of Rachel Parker's trial; criticizes the handling of her case. 29 April 1852. p.71, c4.

**5133 n.n.** *to* **THE** *LONDON TIMES.* **n.d. n.p.** Relates that the Kossuth family is in dire need of money. 29 April 1852. p.71, c5.

**5134 n.n.** *to* *BOSTON TRANSCRIPT.* **n.d. Naples.** Reports on his discovery of a Yankee at Vesuvius. 29 April 1852. p.71, c5.

**5135 GENERAL SCOTT** *to* **ATKINSON. [extract] n.d. n.p.** States that he supported gradual emancipation while a student at William and Mary College. 6 May 1852. p.73, c4.

**5136 n.n.** *to* **THE** *CLEVELAND TRUE DEMOCRAT.* **19 April 1852. Washington.** Lauds the efforts of the Democrats and Whigs who oppose the Compromise. 6 May 1852. p.74, c1.

**5137 n.n.** *to* **THE** *CLEVELAND TRUE DEMOCRAT.* **20 April 1852. Washington.** Decries the use of factionally supported printers for government business. 6 May 1852. p.74, c1.

**5138 RIDGELEY** *to* **n.n. n.d. Baltimore.** Defends his actions as an officer of the law in the murder of the fugitive slave William Smith. 6 May 1852. p.74, c3.

**5139 SAMUEL EVANS** *to* **THE** *TRIBUNE.* **n.d. Columbia.** Presents evidence against Ridgeley; believes that the fugitive slave William Smith was murdered in cold blood. 6 May 1852. p.74, c3.

**5140 n.n.** *to* **THE** *FREEMAN.* **n.d. n.p.** Reports on the attendance at the Christian Anti-Slavery Convention in Cincinnati. 6 May 1852. p.74, c4.

**5141 M. R. DELANY** *to* **THE** *PENNSYLVANIA FREEMAN.* **30 April 1852. Philadelphia.** Denounces the *Freeman* for its review of his book on Negroes in America. 6 May 1852. p.74, c5.

**5142 n.n.** *to* **THE** *LONDON NEWS.* **n.d. n.p.** Discusses the removal of General Concha from his command in Cuba by Queen Christiana. 6 May 1852. p.74, c5.

**5143 STEPHEN F. WEAKLEY** *to* **OLIVER JOHNSON. 26 April 1852. Near Carlisle.** Corrects an article on a slave case appearing in the *Freeman* of 22 April 1852. 6 May 1852. p.74, c7.

**5144 n.n.** *to* **n.n. [extract] n.d. n.p.** Professes a belief in abolition and the repeal of the Fugitive Slave Law; attacks those who oppose slavery but support the Fugitive Slave Law. 13 May 1852. p.77, c4.

**5145 JOHN BROWN** *to* **THE** *NEW YORK EVENING POST.* **24 April 1852. Jersey Ferry.** Informs of a gift of horses offered to a Whig Congressman; expresses concern over the demise of a pro-Union paper. 13 May 1852. p.77, c7.

**5146 C. W.** *to* **GREELEY. 8 May 1852. Providence.** Congratulates Rhode Island on the passage of the Maine Prohibition Law. 13 May 1852. p.78, c1.

**5147 DR. JONAS KING** *to* **THE** *NEW YORK EVANGELIST.* **3 March 1852. Prison of Athens, called Madrese.** Relates his arrest, trial, and imprisonment in Greece. 13 May 1852. p.78, c1.

**5148 X** *to* **THE** *NEW YORK TRIBUNE.* **24 April 1852. St. Louis.** Describes the Plains Indians, fur trade, and the migration of whites to California. 13 May 1852. p.78, c2.

**5149 n.n.** *to* **THE** *FREEMAN.* **9 May 1852. New York.** Laments the death of Isaac T. Hopper. 13 May 1852. p.78, c3.

**5150 n.n.** *to* **THE** *TRIBUNE.* **n.d. n.p.** Laments the death of Isaac T. Hopper, a supporter of the abolitionist movement. 13 May 1852. p.78, c3.

**5151 L. MARIA CHILD** *to* **THE** *NEW YORK TRIBUNE.* **n.d. n.p.** Expresses sorrow at the death of philanthropist Isaac T. Hopper. 13 May 1852. p.78, c3.

**5152 J. R. GIDDINGS** *to* **THE** *PENNSYLVANIA FREEMAN.* **4 May 1852. The House of Representatives.** Proposes a monument in honor of William Smith, who was slain while trying to preserve his freedom. 13 May 1852. p.78, c4.

**5153 FORMERLY A SOUTHERNER** *to* **THE** *EDITOR* **[OLIVER JOHNSON]. n.d. n.p.** Attacks the institution of slavery and those clergymen who support it; quotes from the Bible. 13 May 1852. p.78, c7.

**5154 ROBERT PURVIS** *to* **GERRIT SMITH, ESQ. 23 March 1852. Byberry, Philadelphia County, Pa.** Commends Smith on his report concerning the iniquities of colonization. 13 May 1852. p.79, c1.

**5155 AUSTIN** *to* **THE** ***NORFOLK ARGUS.* 25 April 1852. Pensacola.** Complains about the inhuman punishment of marines and sailors. 13 May 1852. p.79, c3.

**5156 n.n.** *to* **n.n. 9 May 1852. Baltimore.** Reports that both Houses of the Maryland legislature have directed the governor to investigate the murder of a fugitive slave by Ridgeley. 13 May 1852. p.79, c4.

**5157 n.n.** *to* **THE** ***TRIBUNE.* 17 April 1852. Sterling, Il.** Details the exodus to California through Illinois and Missouri. 13 May 1852. p.79, c4.

**5158 CASSIUS M. CLAY** *to* **THE ANTI-SLAVERY CONVENTION. 15 April 1852. White Hall P.O., Madison County, Ky.** Declines an invitation to speak at the Cincinnati Anti-Slavery Convention; praises their efforts. 13 May 1852. p.79, c5.

**5159 WILLIAM G. ALLEN** *to* **FREDERICK DOUGLASS. 19 April 1852. McGrawville, N.Y.** Defends Thomas Jefferson as a believer in the intellectual equality of the blacks; uses Jefferson's correspondence with Benjamin Banneker as evidence. 13 May 1852. p.81, c2.

**5160 THOMAS JEFFERSON** *to* **BENJAMIN BANNEKER. 31 August 1791. Philadelphia.** Praises Banneker's *Almanac*; hails Banneker's efforts as proof that blacks can achieve intellectual equality with whites. 13 May 1852. p.81, c2.

**5161 n.n.** *to* **THE** ***NATIONAL ANTI-SLAVERY STANDARD.* 10 May 1852. Boston, Ma.** Compares Kossuth's visit to Boston with Thompson's visit. 13 May 1852. p.81, c6.

**5162 CHARLES C. BURLEIGH** *to* **THE** ***LIBERATOR.* 30 April 1852. Cincinnati.** Describes his journey to, and the proceedings of, the Christian Anti-Slavery Conference in Cincinnati. 13 May 1852. p.82, c1.

**5163 GERRIT SMITH** *to* **WILLIAM LLOYD GARRISON. 6 May 1852. B---.** Praises the common sense demonstrated by the AAS and the Liberty Party in avoiding internal conflict injurious to the abolitionist cause. 20 May 1825. p.82, c5.

**5164 PARIS CORRESPONDENT** *to* **THE** ***INDEPENDANCE BELGE.* n.d. n.p.** Reports that Europe worried that Kossuth might return. 20 May 1852. p.83, c6.

**5165 PERMILLA SHAW** *to* **MADAM. n.d. n.p.** Inquires about the fitness of a house servant she is about to hire. 20 May 1852. p.84, c1.

**5166 N. P. WILLIS** *to* **n.n. n.d. St. Thomas, West Indies.** Analyzes the physiognomy of the intermixed races of St. Thomas. 27 May 1852. p.85, c4.

**5167 REV. LEWIS RAYMOND** *to* **n.n. 5 April 1852. Chicago.** Informs of the death of David Kennison, the last survivor of the Boston Tea Party. 27 May 1852. p.87, c5.

**5168 n.n.** *to* **THE** ***CLEVELAND TRUE DEMOCRAT.* n.d. Cincinnati.** States that an observer at the anti-slavery convention in Cincinnati reported having freed five slaves. 27 May 1852. p.87, c5.

**5169 MR. WEED** *to* **n.n. 19 March 1852. Naples.** Describes his ascent of Mt. Vesuvius. 27 May 1852. p.88, c4.

**5170 n.n.** *to* **MISS LOWESES. 15 April 1852. Pine Grove.** An illiterate gentleman offers a letter of courtship to a lady. 27 May 1852. p.88, c4.

**5171 ONE** *to* **THE EDITOR OF THE** ***ANTI-SLAVERY STANDARD.* 20 April 1852. New York.** Notes the seating discrimination in Northern churches. 3 June 1852. p.89, c4.

**5172 J. S. P.** *to* **THE** *NEW YORK TRIBUNE.* **24 May 1852. Washington.** Admires self-reliance; denies the "greatness" of men. 3 June 1852. p.89, c5.

**5173 n.n.** *to* **THE** *PENNSYLVANIAN.* **27 May 1852. Harrisburg.** Supports the actions taken to return James Phillips to slavery. 3 June 1852. p.90, c3.

**5174 S. SWAIN, JR.** *to* **FRIEND JOHNSON. May 1852. Bristol.** Lauds *Uncle Tom's Cabin* for portraying the reality of slavery. 3 June 1852. p.90, c6.

**5175 THE** *CHRISTIAN OBSERVER to* **n.n. [extract] n.d. Washington.** Comments upon the remarks of Rev. Albert Barnes made at the Presbyterian General Assembly in Washington. 3 June 1852. p.90, c7.

**5176 n.n.** *to* **THE** *DOYLESTOWN INTELLIGENCER.* **n.d. n.p.** Informs of the proper size for Quaker gravestones. 3 June 1852. p.91, c1.

**5177 n.n.** *to* **THE** *NEW YORK HERALD.* **n.d. San Francisco.** Reports on the influx of slaves into California, and its divisive effect on the state. 3 June 1852. p.91, c2.

**5178 REV. DANIEL FOSTER** *to* **n.n. n.d. Fall River.** Uses the example of a barkeeper to demonstrate that the Church is as corrupt as the slaveholders. 3 June 1852. p.91 c2.

**5179 PARKER PILLSBURY** *to* **THE** *FREEMAN.* **29 May 1852. Boston.** Summarizes the mood of the recently adjourned New England Anti-Slavery Convention. 3 June 1852. p.91, c3.

**5180 BAYARD TAYLOR** *to* **THE** *TRIBUNE.* **n.d. Central Africa.** Describes a welcoming ceremony at a village of Hassaniyehs. 3 June 1852. p.92, c1.

**5181 J. H.** *to* **FRIEND GARRISON. 17 May 1852. Plymouth, Ma.** Contrasts the attitudes of Daniel Webster in 1820 and 1852, citing excerpts from a speech given at Plymouth Rock in 1820 and his present stand on the Fugitive Slave Law. 12 June 1852. p.93, c1.

**5182 n.n.** *to* **THE** *NEW YORK TRIBUNE.* **21 May 1852. Niagara Falls.** Complains that the Americans are ruining their side of Niagara Falls; compares its present state and its appearance fifty years earlier. 12 June 1852. p.93, c4.

**5183 n.n.** *to* **THE** *LOWELL JOURNAL.* **n.d. Mobile.** Reflects on the economic impact of slavery on the South. 12 June 1852. p.93, c5.

**5184 n.n.** *to* **THE** *FREE MISSION VISITOR.* **[extract] n.d. Canada.** Reports on her school for colored people. 12 June 1852. p.94, c6.

**5185 REVILO** *to* **THE** *NEW YORK TRIBUNE.* **25 June 1852. West Chester, Pa.** Reports on the Pennsylvania Women's Rights Convention. 12 June 1852. p.94, c1.

**5186 DR. ELIZABETH BLACKWELL** *to* **MRS. DARLINGTON. 27 May 1852. New York.** Approves the selection of "women's educational equality" as the topic of the Pennsylvania Women's Rights Convention; apologizes for being unable to attend. 12 June 1852. p.94, c3.

**5187 EDWARD WEBB** *to* **n.n. 31 May 1852. Wilmington.** Reports on a motion that was made to the Delaware AS to purchase one copy of *Uncle Tom's Cabin* for every public library in the state. 12 June 1852. p.95, c4.

**5188 HIRAM WILSON** *to* **BROTHER BIBB. 25 May 1852. St. Catharines, Canada West.** Introduces William Briggs, a participant in the Christiana incident. 12 June 1852. p.95, c7.

**5189 n.n.** *to* **THE EDITORS OF THE** *INDEPENDENT.* **31 May 1852. Bay State.** Records anecdotes of Jenny Lind's visit to the Connecticut River Valley of Massachusetts. 12 June 1852. p.96, c5.

**5190 COL. WILLIAM R. KING** *to* **C. H. DONALDSON. 26 July 1851. Tuscaloosa, Al.** Condemns the Democratic abolitionists for causing a breach in the party between the North and the South. 19 June 1852. p.97, c3.

**5191 B. S. J.** *to* **THE** *NEW YORK TRIBUNE.* **27 May 1852. Massillon, Oh.** Describes the proceedings of the Ohio Women's Rights Convention of 27 May 1852. 19 June 1852. p.97, c6.

**5192 n.n.** *to* **THE** *NEW YORK TRIBUNE.* **10 June 1852. Boston.** Reports on the trial and acquittal of Elizur Wright; describes the machinations of the judge in attempting to obtain a conviction. 19 June 1852. p.98, c1.

**5193 BENJAMIN FRANKLIN** *to* **PROFESSOR BARNES. n.d. n.p.** An alleged spirit communication from Franklin informs of the discovery of a northwest passage to the Bering Straits by the missing Sir John Franklin. 19 June 1852. p.98, c2.

**5194 n.n.** *to* **n.n. 6 March 1852. Frysenburg, Denmark.** Relates his meeting with Hans Christian Anderson in Copenhagen. 19 June 1852. p.100, c4.

**5195 BEVERLY CORRESPONDENT,** *VERMONT CHRONICLE* *to* **THE** *PENNSYLVANIA FREEMAN.* **[extract] n.d. Beverly.** Informs of a new way to improve berries. 19 June 1852. p.100, c4.

**5196 JOHN MOSHER** *to* **THE OHIO** *A. S. BUGLE.* **n.d. n.p.** Describes a portion of a Quaker catechism which attacks the abolitionists. 26 June 1852. p.101, c4.

**5197 PROFESSOR CHARLES D. CLEVELAND** *to* **THE CINCINNATI CHRISTIAN ANTI-SLAVERY CONVENTION. 15 March 1852. Philadelphia.** Approves the concept of this convention, but regrets that he is unable to attend. 26 June 1852. p.101, c5.

**5198 S. SWAIN, JR.** *to* **FRIEND JOHNSON. June 1852. Bristol.** Supports the actions of Judge Thompson in regard to the trafficking of liquor on the Sabbath. 26 June 1852. p.102, c7.

**5199 MRS. FRANCES D. GAGE** *to* **THE** *CLEVELAND TRUE DEMOCRAT.* **n.d. n.p.** Discusses the value of labor-saving machinery in industry. 26 June 1852. p.103, c3.

**5200 GENERAL WINFIELD SCOTT** *to* **T. P. ATKINSON, ESQ. 9 February 1843. Washington.** Supports the gradual elimination of slavery over a period of time to be determined by each state. 26 June 1852. p.103, c4.

**5201 HENRY GREW** *to* **FRIEND EDITOR [OLIVER JOHNSON]. n.d. n.p.** Supports some aspects of women's rights and equality, but maintains his belief in other aspects of male superiority. 26 June 1852. p.103, c5.

**5202 n.n.** *to* **THE** *NEW YORK MIRROR.* **n.d. n.p.** Stresses that women should not be protected from seeing how the real world operates. 26 June 1852. p.104, c2.

**5203 n.n.** *to* **THE** *CALAVERAS CHRONICLE.* **n.d. n.p.** Describes one of the many limestone caves in Calaveras County. 26 June 1852. p.104, c3.

**5204 SALLIE HOLLEY** *to* **n.n. [extract] 7 June 1852. Canastota.** Praises the character and work of Gerrit Smith. 3 July 1852. p.105, c4.

**5205 PETER PRUDENT** *to* **BRETHREN. 28 April 1852. Washington, D.C.** Satirizes the church leaders for disregarding American slavery while worrying about foreign missions. 3 July 1852. p.106, c1.

**5206 JAMES PHILLIPS** *to* **MARY PHILLIPS. 20 June 1852. Richmond.** Pleads to be bought by friends in Harrisburg in order to return to his family. 3 July 1852. p.106, c5.

**5207 MRS. FRANCES D. GAGE** *to* **THE** *ANTI-SLAVERY BUGLE.* **n.d. n.p.** Attacks the Quakers for their behavior during the Marlborough incident. 3 July 1852. p.106, c7.

**5208 E. PUGH** *to* **THE EDITOR OF THE** *FREEMAN* **[OLIVER JOHNSON]. n.d. n.p.** Describes the Virginians' attitudes toward the North, and conditions of the slaves in Clark and Frederick counties. 3 July 1852. p.107, c1.

**5209 GENERAL WINFIELD SCOTT** *to* **HON. J. G. CHAPMAN. 24 June 1852. Washington.** Accepts the nomination of the Whig Party and the platform of the convention. 3 July 1852. p.107, c2.

**5210 REV. J. S. GREEN** *to* **THE** *BOSTON COMMONWEALTH.* **n.d. n.p.** Describes the eruption of Mauna Loa in Hawaii. 3 July 1852. p.107, c4.

**5211 W. D. PORTER** *to* **GALES AND SEATON. n.d. n.p.** Describes in detail the cities of Japan. 3 July 1852. p.108, c3.

**5212 MR. WEED** *to* **n.n. n.d. Italy.** Describes the practice of feeding the doves and pigeons in Venice. 3 July 1852. p.108, c5.

**5213 BAYARD TAYLOR** *to* **THE** *NEW YORK TRIBUNE.* **n.d. Khartoum, Soudan, Central Africa.** Discusses the slackening of the slave traffic. 10 July 1852. p.109, c2.

**5214 JAMES BUCHANAN** *to* **A MEMBER OF CONGRESS. 8 June 1852. Wheatland.** Declares himself an optimist; pledges to support both Pierce and the Democratic Party. 10 July 1852. p.109, c4.

**5215 A REPUBLICAN** *to* **THE** *NEW YORK EVENING POST.* **19 June 1852. New Orleans.** Praises the writings of Harriet Beecher Stowe as factual and representative of the slaves' position. 10 July 1852. p. 110, c2.

**5216 PARKER PILLSBURY** *to* **FRIEND. 30 June 1852. Concord, N.H.** Mocks the Quakers and their behavior in the Marlborough incident; remarks briefly on the character of Franklin Pierce. 10 July 1852. p.110, c7.

**5217 SENATOR SEWARD** *to* **A FRIEND. n.d. n.p.** Declines an appointment to national office. 10 July 1852. p.111, c3.

**5218 n.n.** *to* **THE** *NEW YORK TIMES.* **1 July 1852. Washington.** Speculates on the annexation of Puerto Rico, Santo Domingo, Cuba and Central America by the Democrats. 10 July 1852. p.111, c1.

**5219 JAMES BUCHANAN** *to* **LEWIS CASS. 5 June 1852. Wheatland.** Laments his cruel fate. [The *Freeman* does not vouch for the authenticity of these letters.] 17 July 1852. p.113, c7.

**5220 LEWIS CASS** *to* **JAMES BUCHANAN. 7 June 1852. Washington.** Consoles the dejected Buchanan. 17 July 1852. p.114, c1.

**5221 CORRESPONDENT** *to* **THE** *CLEVELAND TRUE DEMOCRAT.* **n.d. n.p.** Praises Joshua R. Giddings's recent anti-slavery speech before the House of Representatives. 17 July 1852. p.114, c4.

**5222 CORRESPONDENT** *to* **THE** *ESSEX COUNTY FREEMAN.* **n.d. n.p.** Commends Garrison's dedication to philanthropy. 17 July 1852. p.114, c7.

**5223 C. D. BERRY** *to* **PETER BRUCKMAN. 17 June 1852. Lowell.** Informs a colored truckman from Lowell that he is not welcome to ride with the Lowell Truck Company. 17 July 1852. p.115, c3.

**5224 CORRESPONDENT** *to* **THE** *NEW YORK TIMES.* **3 July 1852. Toronto.** Reports on the violence caused by rioting whites after rumors that Negroes had killed a fireman. 17 July 1852. p.115, c6.

**5225 D. N. WHITE** *to* **THE** *PITTSBURGH GAZETTE.* **[extract] 21 June 1852. Baltimore.** Denounces the behavior of the crowd at the Baltimore Whig Convention; criticizes the actions of the Southern delegates and their attitudes toward the Northern delegates. 24 July 1852. p.117, c5.

**5226 MRS. E. OAKES SMITH** *to* **THE EDITOR OF THE** *NEW YORK TRIBUNE.* **n.d. n.p.** Argues that a woman's interests and accomplishments need not be confined to the home. 24 July 1852. p.117, c6.

**5227 n.n.** *to* **THE** *CLEVELAND TRUE DEMOCRAT.* **n.d. n.p.** Reports that there should be equal education for males and females in the same classroom. 24 July 1852. p.118, c5.

**5228 CASSIUS M. CLAY** *to* **THE** *NATIONAL ERA.* **n.d. n.p.** Declines to be considered as a candidate for vice-president by the Pittsburgh Convention. 24 July 1852. p.118, c5.

**5229 n.n.** *to* **n.n. 17 June 1852. Turin, Italy.** Criticizes the lack of religious tolerance in Italy. 24 July 1852. p.119, c3.

**5230 MR. WEED** *to* **THE** *PENNSYLVANIA FREEMAN.* **n.d. n.p.** Discusses the current European rage for antique lace. 24 July 1852. p.119, c5.

**5231 CORRESPONDENT** *to* **THE** *COURRIER DES ETATS UNIS.* **19 June 1852. London.** Reports that Jenny Lind will not be appearing on stage. 24 July 1852. p.120, c3.

**5232 PARIS CORRESPONDENT** *to* **THE** *ST. LOUIS REPUBLICAN.* **n.d. n.p.** Informs of a gas developed by a Parisian horticulturist, Herbert, which causes plants to bloom almost instantaneously. 24 July 1852. p.120, c4.

**5233 CHARLES JARED INGERSOLL** *to* **THE NEW YORK DEMOCRATS. [extract] n.d. n.p.** Reports that the Whig and Democratic conventions are attempting to vindicate slavery by citing the guarantee of the treaty for independence that the system be allowed to exist free from foreign interference. 31 July 1852. p.121, c2.

**5234 JOHN G. WHITTIER** *to* **W. S. ROBINSON, ESQ. 13 July 1852. Amesbury.** Declines an invitation to attend the Convention of Free Democracy of Massachusetts, due to ill health; commends their aims as well as those of the forthcoming national convention. 31 July 1852. p.121, c3.

**5235 FRANCES D. GAGE** *to* **THE** *CLEVELAND TRUE DEMOCRAT.* **n.d. n.p.** Describes a visit to Independence Hall, Philadelphia; presents a commentary on the current interpretation of the Declaration of Independence. 31 July 1852. p.121, c4.

**5236 INQUIRER** *to* **THE EDITORS OF THE** *CLEVELAND TRUE DEMOCRAT.* **n.d. n.p.** Challenges the American Tract Society and similar groups to respond to the charges of the Christian Anti-Slavery Convention at Ravenna. 31 July 1852. p.121, c5.

**5237 P. S. M.** *to* **FRIEND EVANS. 17 July 1852. Baltimore.** Relates the story of Elizabeth Parker, a free colored girl who was abducted and then rescued by anti-slavery friends. 31 July 1852. p.121, c6.

**5238 HIRAM WILSON** *to* **THE** *TRIBUNE.* **6 July 1852. St. Catharines.** Presents the story of a black girl who had been freed on the death of her master, but risked being captured and sold back into slavery. 31 July 1852. p.121, c7.

**5239 BROTHER J. McBRIDE** *to* **THE EDITOR OF THE** *TRUE WESLEYAN.* **11 June 1852. Medina County, Oh.** Condemns the activities and resolutions of a pro-slavery group in Grayson, Virginia. 31 July 1852. p.122, c1.

**5240 E. A. L.** *to* **THE** *ST. LOUIS INTELLIGENCER.* **10 May 1852. Cincinnati.** Attacks Charles C. Burleigh as a "traitorous fanatic"; criticizes the presence of blacks and whites in the same audience. 31 July 1852. p.122, c2.

**5241 WILLIAM LLOYD GARRISON** *to* **J. M. M'KIM. 15 July 1852. Boston.** Accepts an invitation to the forthcoming anniversary of the Pennsylvania AS. 31 July 1852. p.122, c3.

**5242 FREDERICK DOUGLASS** *to* **THE** *PENNSYLVANIA FREEMAN.* **n.d. n.p.** Corrects certain statements by Oliver Johnson in reference to Garrison, the AAS, and himself. 31 July 1852. p.122, c4.

**5243 n.n.** *to* **MR. BRUNER. 23 June 1852. Washington.** Relates an interview with General Scott by the Mississippi delegation to the Whig Convention. 31 July 1852. p.122, c5.

**5244 J. B. W.** *to* **THE** *NEW YORK OBSERVER.* **8 April 1852. Rome.** Describes the "Miserere of Allegro" at the Sistine Chapel. 31 July 1852. p.124, c4.

**5245 MR. LOCKE** *to* **THE** *SAVANNAH REPUBLICAN.* **n.d. n.p.** Describes the visit of General Haynau to Graefenburg. 31 July 1852. p.124, c4.

**5246 GERRIT SMITH** *to* **WILLIAM SMITH. 16 June 1852. Peterboro'.** Laments that the W. L. Chaplin affair is still with him; comments on his expenditure of funds for the sake of "wronged humanity." 7 August 1852. p.124 [126], c2.

**5247 REV. W. H. FURNESS** *to* **FRIEND. n.d. Huntingdon, Montgomery County, Pa.** Declines an invitation to attend a picnic to celebrate emancipation in the West Indies; praises the benefits of abolition. 7 August 1852. p.124 [126], c3.

**5248 SENATOR B. F. WADE** *to* **HON. D. R. TILDEN. n.d. n.p.** States that General Scott has told him he will not support slavery. 7 August 1852. p.124 [126], c5.

**5249 J. H. FAIRCHILD** *to* **MESSRS. EDITORS. [from the** *Cleveland True Democrat***] 21 July 1852. Oberlin.** Corrects statements made by correspondent L. A. Hines in an earlier article. 7 August 1852. p.124 [126], c5.

**5250 PARKER PILLSBURY** *to* **FRIEND JOHNSON. 29 July 1852. Concord, N.H.** States that Websterism is slowly dying; faults the Northern Whig press for attempting to keep Websterism alive. 7 August 1852. p.124 [126], c6.

**5251 EDWARD WEBB** *to* **THE** *FREEMAN.* **28 July 1852. Wilmington.** Attacks the Delaware law enslaving free colored men entering the state; defends the character of Delaware's citizens. 7 August 1852. p.127, c2.

**5252 WILLIAM H. JOHNSON, JOSEPH FELL, S. H. POTTS, [AND TWENTY-SEVEN OTHERS]** *to* **FELLOW CITIZENS. n.d. n.p.** Describe the early history of the *Olive Branch*, a temperance paper, and its acceptance; praise the efforts of the editor; solicit new subscriptions. 7 August 1852. p.128, c2.

**5253 WEBSTER LANG AND MARY ANN McCLINTOCK** *to* **THE SALEM MONTHLY MEETING OF FRIENDS IN OHIO. 20 June 1849. New York State.** State that Oliver Johnson is a member of their meeting and request that he be taken into the Salem meeting. 7 August 1852. Extra, c1.

**5254 SUNDERLAND P. GARDNER, ELIJAH P. QUIMBY, AND WILLIAM S. BURLING** *to* **THE MEETING FOR SUFFERINGS OF THE OHIO YEARLY MEETING OF FRIENDS. 11 June 1850. Farmington.** State that Oliver Johnson was never a member of the Genesee meeting, and cannot be considered a member of the Society of Friends. 7 August 1852. Extra, c1.

**5255 OLIVER JOHNSON** *to* **THE EDITOR OF** *FRIENDS' WEEKLY INTELLIGENCER*. **22 July 1852. Philadelphia.** Presents the basis of his claim to membership in the Society of Friends; refutes point by point the charges brought against him by the *Intelligencer*. 7 August 1852. Extra, c1.

**5256 OLIVER JOHNSON** *to* **THE SALEM MONTHLY MEETING OF FRIENDS. n.d. n.p.** Offers to allow the meeting to reconsider his membership and to withdraw his membership if it is deemed necessary. 7 August 1852. Extra, c2.

**5257 THOMAS M'CLINTOCK, MARY ANN M'CLINTOCK, AZALIAH SCHOOLEY, [AND NINE OTHERS]** *to* **OLIVER JOHNSON. 21 April 1850. Waterloo, Seneca County, N.Y.** Detail the split within the Society of Friends which created the Junius Monthly Meeting; cite precedents for their action, and endorse the membership of Oliver Johnson. 7 August 1852. Extra, c4.

**5258 WILLIAM S. SPEER** *to* **HORACE GREELEY. 22 July 1852. Cornersville, Tn.** Commends Greeley's efforts as editor; expresses his support of abolition, and calls for the removal of all blacks from the country. 14 August 1852. p.129, c1.

**5259 JOHN P. HALE** *to* **G. G. FOGG, ESQ. 4 August 1852. Dover, N.H.** Protests the attitudes of the Democratic and Whig conventions; calls for renewed support of the "Independent Democracy." 14 August 1852. p.128 [130], c1.

**5260 JUDGE LOWELL** *to* **THE** *NATIONAL A.S. STANDARD.* **[extract] n.d. Massachusetts.** Relates an experience of his with the Royal Society of Great Britain to demonstrate British support for the anti-slavery movement. 14 August 1852. p.128 [130], c3.

**5261 CORRESPONDENT** *to* **THE** *OHIO BUGLE.* **n.d. Ripley, Brown County.** Condemns the behavior of Ohio River residents who aid in the capture of fugitive slaves. 14 August 1852. p.128 [130], c5.

**5262 n.n.** *to* **THE** *PENNSYLVANIA FREEMAN.* **10 August 1852. Pittsburgh.** Reports the resolution of the Pennsylvania Free-Soil Convention; supports abolition of slavery and election of the president, vice-president and senators by popular vote. 14 August 1852. p.131, c1.

**5263 n.n.** *to* **THE** *PENNSYLVANIA FREEMAN.* **11 August 1852. Pittsburgh.** Reports on the proceedings of the recent National Free-Soil Convention in Pittsburgh. 14 August 1852. p.131, c2.

5264 **N. P. W.** *to* **MORRIS. June 1852. Mammoth Cave.** Describes in detail the journey of five people and a guide into Mammoth Cave. 14 August 1852. p.132, c1.

5265 **M. WILLIS, D. D., THOMAS HENNING, AND ANDREW HAMILTON** *to* **n.n. 15 July 1852. Toronto, Canada West.** Defend the good intentions of the Canadians toward the escaped slaves; describes the latter's living conditions. 21 August 1852. p.133, c1.

5266 **REV. GEORGE THOMPSON** *to* **THE** *OBERLIN EVANGELIST.* **n.d. n.p.** Contrasts two groups of concerned citizens in Canada and the picture they paint of the progress of the blacks; attacks the "agent system" used to raise money. 21 August 1852. p.133, c2.

5267 **HIRAM WILSON** *to* **FRIEND GARRISON. 20 July 1852. St. Catharines, Canada West.** Encloses a statement clipped from the *Toronto Globe* complaining of the way in which the colored population is described by certain charitable organizations. 21 August 1852. p.133, c3.

5268 **KORNER** *to* **THE** *NEW YORK TRIBUNE.* **9 August 1852. Washington.** Alerts the reader to the threat of slavery's being introduced in the Sandwich Islands, should annexation come about; dismisses the danger of a French or English takeover. 21 August 1852. p.133, c4.

5269 **BOSTON CORRESPONDENT** *to* **THE** *NEW YORK HERALD.* **n.d. n.p.** Reports that Horace Mann is sending angry letters to Free-Soilers regarding their treatment of General Scott; suggests he might run for Congress as the Whig candidate. 21 August 1852. p.134, c6.

5270 **RUFUS ELMER** *to* **THE** *SPIRITUAL TELEGRAPH.* **n.d. Springfield, Ma.** Reports that a keeper of a public house heard "sounds" which convinced him to reform. 21 August 1852. p.135, c5.

5271 **G. C.** *to* **THE** *BOSTON DAILY EVENING TRANSCRIPT.* **23 July 1852. Boston.** Describes a visit to the institution for the blind in South Boston, where he met with Laura Bridgeman, a blind, deaf, and mute woman. 21 August 1852. p.136, c5.

5272 **OLIVER JOHNSON, EDITOR** *to* **THE** *PENNSYLVANIA FREEMAN.* **23 August 1852. Salem, Oh.** Reports on the proceedings of the anniversary of the Western AS at Salem, Ohio. 28 August 1852. p.138, c4.

5273 **P. G.** *to* **THE** *NEW YORK EVENING POST.* **July 1852. Among the Clouds.** Describes in detail his ascent of Mount Washington by foot; complains of the lack of imagination in naming these peaks. 28 August 1852. p.140, c1.

5274 **N. P WILSON** *to* **MORRIS. April 1852. Martinique.** Extols the uplifting influences of Catholic church services. 4 September 1852. p.142, c1.

5275 **OLIVER JOHNSON, EDITOR** *to* **THE** *PENNSYLVANIA FREEMAN.* **25 August 1852. Salem, Oh.** Concludes his report on the anniversary of the Western AS. 4 September 1852. p.142, c3.

5276 **CLINTON GILLINGHAM** *to* **FRIEND JOHNSON. 10 August 1852. Aysgarth, Yorkshire, England.** Informs Johnson that slavery is very much the local topic of conversation; believes that the English Parliament is not truly representative; reports on Elihu Burritt's campaign for universal brotherhood, and the success of the *Olive Leaves*, his publication; encourages Olive Leaf societies in America. 4 September 1852. p.142, c5.

5277 **n.n.** *to* **THE** *ST. LOUIS REPUBLICAN.* **23 July 1852. n.p.** Provides additional information on the explosion aboard the steamboat *Dr. Franklin.* 4 September 1852. p.143, c5.

**5278 A. D.** *to* **THE** *NEW ORLEANS TRUE DELTA.* **n.d. n.p.** Relates the story of a visit to Japan told to him by Captain Welsh of the Indiaman Ship *Merlin.* 4 September 1852. p.144, c4.

**5279 EUPHROSYNE** *to* **THE** *SATURDAY VISITOR.* **17 July 1852. Gatesville, N.C.** Describes the burial services of an elderly Negro lady. 11 September 1852. p.148, c2.

**5280 N. R. JOHNSTON** *to* **FRIEND JOHNSON. n.d. n.p.** Corrects information about the Western AS anniversary which Johnson forwarded to the *Pennsylvania Freeman.* 18 September 1852. p.151, c2.

**5281 E. W.** *to* **n.n. 13 September 1852. Wilmington.** Reports on resolutions of gratitude passed by those present at the lectures on anatomy, physiology and hygiene given by Ann Preston, M.D.; endorses Preston and her lectures. 18 September 1852. p.151. c4.

**5282 BOSTON CORRESPONDENT** *to* **THE** *NEW YORK HERALD.* **n.d. n.p.** Reports that Daniel Webster commented that he made a mistake in supporting the South on the 1850 question; informs of Webster's desire to retire from public life. 18 September 1852. p.151, c5.

**5283 HON. JOHN P. HALE** *to* **HON. HENRY WILSON. September 1852. Dover, N.H.** Reiterates his desire to stay out of politics, yet yields to the opinion of his friends and accepts their nomination. 18 September 1852. p.151, c6.

**5284 N. M. G.** *to* **THE** *CHRISTIAN PRESS.* **n.d. n.p.** Defends the depiction of slave life in Harriet Beecher Stowe's *Uncle Tom's Cabin;* relates a corroborating story from the *Richmond Republican.* 25 September 1852. p.153, c7.

**5285 H. W. G.** *to* **THE** *FREEMAN.* **30 August 1852. London.** Describes the conversation he had with three Southerners on his voyage to England; tells of his meeting with Thompson; states that Thompson's defeat was not related to his abolitionist beliefs. 25 September 1852. p.154, c3.

**5286 FRANCES D. GAGE** *to* **FRIEND JOHNSON. 17 September 1852. Cleveland, Oh.** Describes the state fair and praises its progressive benefits; reports on a dinner given for Hale at which there was no liquor, and to which ladies were invited; informs of a women's rights meeting in Dr. Nevin's church. 25 September 1852. p.154, c5.

**5287 O. K.** *to* **THE** *NEW YORK INDEPENDENT.* **[extract] n.d. n.p.** Attacks a scheme whereby ministers would forward their sermons through the mail to other ministers, who would use them as their own. 25 September 1852. p.154, c6.

**5288 HORACE MANN** *to* **n.n. [extract] n.d. n.p.** Asks Northerners what they have gained by "yielding the Compromise measures to Southern slaveholders." 25 September 1852. p.154, c7.

**5289 LEWIS TAPPAN** *to* **MR. EDITOR [O. JOHNSON]. n.d. n.p.** Protests Johnson's article on the Pittsburgh Convention for misrepresenting the facts. 25 September 1852. p.155, c1.

**5290 n.n.** *to* **THE EDITOR OF THE** *OLIVE BRANCH.* **15 September 1852. Norristown.** Writes to support liberty and temperance, Hale and Julian. 25 September 1852. p.155, c3.

**5291 J. W. C. PENNINGTON** *to* **THE EDITORS OF THE** *INDEPENDENT.* **n.d. n.p.** Illustrates that Negroes are discriminated against in the North by describing his frustrated attempt to use omnibuses to go about his ministerial duties. 2 October 1852. p.157, c6.

**5292 CORRESPONDENT** *to* **THE** *NEW YORK TRIBUNE.* **[extract] n.d. n.p.** Forwards an extract from a Southern paper that advertises a small revolver as capable of killing large numbers and especially useful to slaveowners. 2 October 1852. p.157, c7.

**5293 n.n.** *to* **n.n. 27 September 1852. Maysville, Ky.** Describes the escape of thirty-one slaves to Ohio, where authorities refused to grant warrants to their pursuers to search a house in which it was believed the slaves hid. 2 October 1852. p.158, c1.

**5294 GERRIT SMITH** *to* **LEWIS A. HINE. 21 September 1852. Peterboro'.** Responds to Hine's allegation in the *New York Tribune* that Smith held on to large quantities of land while professing support for land reform. 2 October 1852. p.159, c1.

**5295 P. T. BARNUM** *to* **THE EDITORS OF THE** *NEW YORK MUSIC WORLD.* **18 September 1852. American Museum.** Corrects their figures regarding the Jenny Lind concert tour; claims the actual proceeds will exceed the reported $610,000. 2 October 1852. p.159, c5.

**5296 HON. C. J. INGERSOLL** *to* **MESSRS. HORN R. KNEASS, WM. BADGER, WM. CURTIS, WM. STRONG, WM. HEIDENRICH, AND HENRY A MUHLENBURG, COMMITTEE. 1 September 1852. Philadelphia.** Attacks involvement by Europeans, particularly the British, in the abolition movement; believes Pierce will win the election. 9 October 1852. p.161, c1.

**5297 MISSIONARY** *to* **n.n. [extract] 12 December 1851. Africa.** Reports that emancipated slaves are still being sent to Liberia, and that some have not survived the climate there. 9 October 1852. p.161, c6.

**5298 PASTOR** *to* **THE** *CHRISTIAN PRESS.* **17 September 1852. Connecticut.** Reports on the high mortality rate of Liberia. 9 October 1852. p.161, c6.

**5299 JOHN RANKIN** *to* **BRO. BOYNTON. [from the** *Christian Press***] n.d. n.p.** Compares the whites and blacks of Philadelphia and finds them equal; condemns those who consider blacks inferior, noting that this mode of thought furnishes support to Liberian emigration. 9 October 1852. p.161, c7.

**5300 PARKER PILLSBURY** *to* **FRIEND GAY. 15 September 1852. Jefferson, Ashtabula County, Oh.** Reports on a meeting of friends of freedom and encloses resolutions; complains of the behavior of the Free-Soilers when J. R. Giddings and others declined to be present. 9 October 1852. p.161, c7.

**5301 JOSEPH BARKER** *to* **MR. GARRISON. [extract] n.d. n.p.** Finds comfort in the fact that abolitionism is "a power as well as a principle." 9 October 1852. p.162, c5.

**5302 DANIEL RICKETSON** *to* **THE** *LIBERATOR.* **n.d. New Bedford, Ma.** Praises the efforts of Sallie Holley in behalf of the anti-slavery movement. 9 October 1852. p.162, c6.

**5303 CONSTANCE** *to* **THE** *CLEVELAND TRUE DEMOCRAT.* **[extract] n.d. n.p.** Describes the women she met at the Syracuse Convention; praises the efforts of women like Elizabeth Oakes Smith, Lucretia Mott, and Lucy Stone. 9 October 1852. p.162, c6.

**5304 E. Q.** *to* **THE** *STANDARD.* **[extract] n.d. n.p.** Reports that Websterism is falling off throughout Massachusetts, since Webster has been "disgraced and degraded." 9 October 1852. p.162, c6.

**5305 PARKER PILLSBURY** *to* **FRIEND OLIVER [JOHNSON]. 22 September 1852. Cleveland, Oh.** Speaks of the progress of Ohio due to free labor and the decline of Virginia caused by slave labor; discusses the growth of agriculture and industry in Ohio; mocks the nominations of Pierce and Hale. 9 October 1852. p.162, c7.

**5306 RICHARD D. WEBB** *to* **THE** *NATIONAL ANTI-SLAVERY STANDARD.* **[extract] n.d. n.p.** Notes that the English press is "infested" with American pro-slavery writers who defame *Uncle Tom's Cabin.* 9 October 1852. p.163, c2.

**5307 CORRESPONDENT** *to* **THE** *UTICA GAZETTE.* **[extract] 10 September 1852. Norfolk, Va.** Describes the battleship *Pennsylvania,* which was recently converted to an officer's ballroom. 9 October 1852. p.163, c5.

**5308 COMPROMISE** *to* **THE** *NEW YORK TRIBUNE.* **31 August 1852. San Francisco.** A correspondent reports on a California state supreme court decision which supported the Fugitive Slave Law. 16 October 1852. p.165, c7.

**5309 JOEL PARKER** *to* **HARRIET BEECHER STOWE. n.d. n.p.** Requests an interview with Mrs. Stowe to discuss certain statements which were wrongly attributed to him in *Uncle Tom's Cabin.* 16 October 1852. p.166, c3.

**5310 HARRIET BEECHER STOWE** *to* **JOEL PARKER. n.d. n.p.** Apologizes for the error she made; explains the reasons for her believing that certain pro-slavery statements were made by Parker; offers to assist in restoring Parker's good name. 16 October 1852. p.166, c3.

**5311 JOEL PARKER** *to* **HARRIET BEECHER STOWE. n.d. n.p.** Thanks her for her letter of correction; states that the publication of her letter will set the matter right. 16 October 1852. p.166, c4.

**5312 JOEL PARKER** *to* **HARRIET BEECHER STOWE. [extract] n.d. n.p.** Condemns her for attributing certain pro-slavery remarks to him. 16 October 1852. p.166, c5.

**5313 PROFESSOR WM. G. ALLEN** *to* **THE EDITOR OF THE (PA.)** *FREEMAN.* **6 October 1852. McGrawville, N.Y.** Reports on the Jerry Rescue celebration and on speeches given on the occasion by renowned abolitionists. 16 October 1852. p.167, c1.

**5314 PARKER PILLSBURY** *to* **THE** *BUGLE.* **[extract] n.d. n.p.** Discloses the enthusiasm of Northern citizens for hiding fugitive slaves. 16 October 1852. p.167, c4.

**5315 M. A. BRONSON** *to* **THE** *PITTSBURG VISITER.* **n.d. n.p.** Discusses the poor treatment of women in medical colleges and programs. 16 October 1852. p.168, c3.

**5316 GERRIT SMITH** *to* **SAMUEL AARON AND T. B. HUDSON. 16 September 1852. Peterboro'.** Comments on equality between races and sexes at the Central College of New York; commends the founding principles of the Church of McGrawville. 16 October 1852. p.168, c4.

**5317 REV. J. P. THOMPSON** *to* **THE** *INDEPENDENT.* **n.d. Edinburgh.** Informs of the success of *Uncle Tom's Cabin* in Great Britain. 23 October 1852. p.169, c2.

**5318 ANGELINA J. KNOX** *to* **THE** *LIBERATOR.* **September 1852. Hyannis.** Praises the quick-acting conscience of a Southern slaveholder who was converted when his son was awarded a tract in school. 23 October 1852. p.169, c3.

**5319 A.** *to* **THE** *NEW YORK EVANGELIST.* **n.d. n.p.** Gives an account of a visit to a slave auction at Richmond, Virginia; examines the attitudes of slaveowners toward their slaves. 23 October 1852. p.169, c.4.

**5320 JOHN G. FEE** *to* **THE** *NATIONAL ERA.* **n.d. Cabin Creek P.O., Lewis County, Ky.** Reports on the speeches of C. M. Clay and George Julian before a calm and somewhat receptive audience in Kentucky. 23 October 1852. p.169, c6.

**5321 GEORGE THOMPSON** *to* **GARRISON. 21 September 1852. London.** Reports on the loss of his seat in Parliament and other election results; states that *Uncle Tom's Cabin* has been well received; ridicules the manner in which the Duke of Wellington's funeral is being handled. 23 October 1852. p.169, c7.

**5322 THEODORE PARKER** *to* **SAMUEL J. MAY. 25 September 1852. West Newton.** Declines an invitation to the Jerry Rescue celebration; declares that the Fugitive Slave Law is a violation of universal law; decries the actions of those Boston citizens who supported the Fugitive Slave Law. 23 October 1852. p.170, c1.

**5323 PARKER PILLSBURY** *to* **THE** ***BUGLE*****. [extract] n.d. Michigan.** Reports that Michigan holds much promise as an anti-slavery state. 23 October 1852. p.170, c2.

**5324 JOHN THOMAS** *to* *FREDERICK DOUGLASS' PAPER*. **[extract] n.d. n.p.** Describes the actions of a group of people in Syracuse about to protest the reported arrest of Rev. J. W. Loguen, a fugitive slave. 23 October 1852. p.170, c4.

**5325 REV. R. R. RAYMOND** *to* **JOHN THOMAS. [extract] n.d. Syracuse.** Protests Thomas's implications of violence in the matter involving Reverend Loguen; commends the nonviolent methods of participants in the Jerry Rescue. 23 October 1852. p.170, c4.

**5326 WM. THOMPSON** *to* **THE EDITOR OF THE** ***FREEMAN*****. 19 October 1852. Danville, Pa.** Forwards an account given in the *Ledger* of the kidnapping of a free Negro youth. 23 October 1852. p.170, c5.

**5327 CORRESPONDENT** *to* **THE** ***TRIBUNE*****. n.d. Boston.** Reports that Webster is gravely ill, and that his physician fears he is incurable. 23 October 1852. p.170, c7.

**5328 LEWIS TAPPAN** *to* **THE EDITOR OF THE** ***FREEMAN*** **[O. JOHNSON]. n.d. n.p.** Responds to Johnson's criticism of Tappan's political and patriotic attitudes in a recent issue of the *Freeman*. 23 October 1852. p.171, c1.

**5329 n.n.** *to* **n.n. 30 August 1852. Catania, Italy.** Describes the flow of lava from Mount Etna. 23 October 1852. p.171, c3.

**5330 CALIFORNIA CORRESPONDENT** *to* **THE** ***LEDGER*****. n.d. California.** Reports on the lack of opportunity in the California gold fields; notes that many people have been ruined. 23 October 1852. p.171, c6.

**5331 WILLIAM JAY** *to* **THE EDITOR OF THE** ***NATIONAL ERA*****. n.d. n.p.** Encloses an extract of a letter to Reverend Mr. Manning. 30 October 1852. p.173, c4.

**5332 GRANVILLE SHARPE** *to* **REV. MR. MANNING. [extract] 11 December 1785. Old Jewry.** Praises Manning for his support of the abolition of slavery; encloses an argument which supports and defends those people who feel it their duty to defend and protect runaway slaves. 30 October 1852. p.173, c4.

**5333 X** *to* **THE EDITORS OF THE** ***CLEVELAND TRUE DEMOCRAT*****. 4 October 1842 [sic]. Ripley, Browns County, Oh.** Reports on the behavior and habits of those engaged in searching out runaway slaves; informs of a plot to trap one of the escaped. 30 October 1852. p.173, c5.

**5334 M. D.** *to* **THE EDITOR OF THE** ***OHIO STATE TIMES*****. 23 September 1852. Cincinnati.** Relates the story of a slave named Henry, who escaped to the North disguised as one "Aunt Hannah," in order to demonstrate that "colored people can take care of themselves." 30 October 1852. p.173, c6.

**5335 HARRIOT K. HUNT** *to* **FREDERICK U. TRACY. 18 October 1852. Boston.** Protests the fact that women must pay taxes yet have no say in how they are allocated. 30 October 1852. p.173, c7.

**5336 JAMES L. HILL** *to* **THE EDITOR OF THE** *NEW YORK EVANGELIST.* **17 September 1852. Springfield, Il.** Relates two stories of slave life which corroborate Harriet Beecher Stowe's portrayal in *Uncle Tom's Cabin.* 30 October 1852. p.174, c2.

**5337 RICHARD D. WEBB** *to* **GAY. [extract from the** *NATIONAL ANTI-SLAVERY STANDARD*] **1 October 1852. Dublin.** Encloses a copy of the *Anti-Slavery Advocate*; announces his intention to publicize the evils of American slavery. 30 October 1852. p.174, c5.

**5338 MARY HOWITT** *to* **THE** *TRIBUNE.* **[extract] n.d. England.** Reports on the widespread popularity of *Uncle Tom's Cabin.* 30 October 1852. p.174, c6.

**5339 n.n.** *to* **n.n. 21 October 1852. Pittsburgh.** Informs that a number of fugitive slaves ready to cross from Sandusky, Ohio, to Canada were apprehended by slave catchers and subsequently liberated by citizens. 30 October 1852. p.175, c1.

**5340 n.n.** *to* **THE** *AMERICAN UNION.* **n.d. n.p.** Describes an evening's entertainment aboard a boat going from Fall River to New York. 30 October 1852. p.175, c5.

**5341 J. McBRIDE** *to* **THE EDITOR [O. JOHNSON]. 4 October 1852. C.O.** Describes a collection taken at a colored church to aid a fugitive slave en route to Canada; confirms the success of the Underground Railroad. 6 November 1852. p.177, c7.

**5342 CORRESPONDENT** *to* **THE** *NEW YORK DAILY TIMES.* **21 August 1852. City of the Great Salt Lake.** Describes the city of the Mormons, including its location and layout. 6 November 1852. p.180, c1.

**5343 FRANCES D. GAGE** *to* **OLIVER JOHNSON. n.d. n.p.** Reports on her return home by train; mentions fairs in Morgan and Washington counties. 11 November 1852. p.183, c1.

**5344 E. W.** *to* **n.n. 1 November 1852. Wilmington, De.** Discusses moral and religious aspects of anti-slavery lectures by Miss Holley. 11 November 1852. p.183, c7.

**5345 MISS MARTINEAU** *to* **THE** *DAILY NEWS.* **[extract] n.d. n.p.** Describes the island and people of Achill, in Ireland; reports on one priest's efforts to drive out the Protestants. 11 November 1852. p. 184, c4.

**5346 W. H. FURNESS** *to* **THE EDITOR OF THE** *PENNSYLVANIA FREEMAN* **[O. JOHNSON]. n.d. n.p.** Encloses an article which illustrates statements made by Harriet Beecher Stowe in *Uncle Tom's Cabin.* 18 November 1852. p.185, c4.

**5347 GERRIT SMITH** *to* **THE VOTERS OF THE COUNTIES OF OSWEGO AND MADISON. 5 November 1852. Peterboro'.** Sets forth political creeds which he will bring with him to Washington. 18 November 1852. p.185, c7.

**5348 THOMAS HENNING** *to* **n.n. 27 October 1852. Toronto.** Declares that the Refugee's Home Society is honest and legitimate; cautions about other societies which misappropriate funds. 18 November 1852. p.186, c3.

**5349 E. C. D.** *to* **THE EDITOR [O. JOHNSON]. 27 October 1852. Lancaster.** Reports on the slave-hunting party headed by the owner, Mr. Cheney, who was subsequently arrested for disorderly conduct. 18 November 1852. p.187, c1.

**5350 REV. W. L. JUDD** *to* **THE** *BOSTON TRAVELLER.* **n.d. Hayti.** Commends the character of the Haitians and the quality of life in Haiti. 18 November 1852. p.187, c5.

**5351 REV. FREEMAN YATES** *to* **THE** *PENNSYLVANIA FREEMAN.* **[extract] n.d. Providence, R. I.** Reports that Rhode Islanders are receptive to the Maine Liquor Law; informs that its opponents, though still busy, are becoming discouraged. 18 November 1852. p.187, c6.

**5352 RICHARD HILL** *to* **HON. EDWARD JORDAN. 30 September 1852. Spanishtown.** Explains why productivity has declined since the emancipation of slaves in the British West Indies colonies. 25 November 1852. p.189, c5.

**5353 LONDON CORRESPONDENT** *to* **THE** *NEW YORK TIMES.* **n.d. London.** Notes that Lord Carlisle's preface to an edition of *Uncle Tom's Cabin* has swelled its reception in England; criticizes the literary attitudes of English reviewers. 25 November 1852. p.189, c6.

**5354 PARIS CORRESPONDENT** *to* **THE** *NEW YORK INDEPENDENT.* **n.d. n.p.** Reports that *Uncle Tom's Cabin* is now being translated; anticipates its widespread acceptance. 25 November 1852. p.189, c7.

**5355 n.n.** *to* **THE** *NEW YORK POST.* **[extract] n.d. New Orleans.** Defends the veracity of *Uncle Tom's Cabin*; hopes that more writers will present slavery as it is; plans to work against slavery, although he is a slaveowner himself. 25 November 1852. p.189, c7.

**5356 REV. EDWARD MATHEWS** *to* **THE** *AMERICAN BAPTIST.* **[extract] n.d. England.** Hopes that termination of church support for slavery will bring down the system; describes the upcoming *Uncle Tom's Cabin Almanac, or Abolition Memento for 1853.* 25 November 1852. p.190, c3.

**5357 LONDON CORRESPONDENT** *to* **THE** *NEW YORK INDEPENDENT.* **n.d. England.** Considers the sight of Ambassador Lawrence walking arm in arm with President Roberts of Liberia as an example to all. 25 November 1852. p.190, c4.

**5358 DANIEL WEBSTER** *to* **JOHN TAYLOR. 7 March 1852. n.p.** Argues that slavery should be decided by the individual states; believes it wrong to try to turn one part of the country against another. 25 November 1852. p.90, c6.

**5359 L.** *to* **THE EDITOR OF THE** *PENNSYLVANIA FREEMAN* **[O. JOHNSON]. November 1852. Lionville.** Encloses a description of Sallie Holley's speech at the Lionville Friends Meeting House; notes the difficulty encountered in securing a place for the lecture. 25 November 1852. p.190, c7.

**5360 REV. EDWARD KELL** *to* **SAMUEL MAY, JR. [extract from the** ***Liberator*****]. n.d. Newport, England.** States that America should worry about slavery at home before worrying about oppression overseas, and that England should help America in abolishing this evil. 2 December 1852. p.193, c3.

**5361 A. HOGEBOOM** *to* **THE EDITOR OF THE** *TRIBUNE.* **21 November 1852. Erieville.** Discusses the effects of the Fugitive Slave Law and the Baltimore Whig platform on support for Gerrit Smith and the Whig Party in Erieville. 2 December 1852. p.194, c1.

**5362 n.n.** *to* **n.n. n.d. n.p.** Describes the effect Sallie Holley had upon the people in attendance at her meeting at Goodwill. 2 December 1852. p.194, c6.

**5363 J. G.** *to* **THE EDITORS. October 1852. Salt Lake City, Utah Territory.** Describes the conditions in Utah; reports on an interview with an elder and one of his wives. 2 December 1852. p.195, c2.

**5364 DAVID THOMAS** *to* **n.n. [extract] n.d. n.p.** Protests the debasement of slaves; considers the Fugitive Slave Law a betrayal of the principles embodied in the Declaration of Independence. 9 December 1852. p.197, c2.

**5365 REVEREND DR. J. W. C. PENNINGTON** *to* **THE** *NEW YORK TIMES.* **[extract] n.d. n.p.** Reports a growing acceptance of the colored people as citizens. 9 December 1852. p.197, c3.

**5366 EARL OF SHAFTESBURY** *to* **THE** *LONDON TIMES.* **n.d. n.p.** Encloses an address on slavery from women of England to their American sisters; comments on the powerful role of the press. 9 December 1852. p.197, c6.

**5367 J. E.** *to* **n.n. [extract from the** *National Era***] n.d. n.p.** Announces the establishment of Antioch College at Yellow Springs, Ohio, with Horace Mann as president; describes the environs of the school. 9 December 1852. p.197, c7.

**5368 n.n.** *to* **THE** *NATIONAL ERA.* **2 November 1852. Chatham County, N.C.** Reports that a printer who was to print tickets for the Free-Soil Party of Greensboro, North Carolina, received threats because of this affiliation; believes Hale might have won if he had been on the ticket. 9 December 1852. p.198, c3.

**5369 ENGLISH CORRESPONDENT** *to* **THE** *PITTSBURGH COMMERCIAL JOURNAL.* **[extract] n.d. n.p.** Describes the furor caused by *Uncle Tom's Cabin* in England; informs of Shaftesbury's efforts to raise funds to start a free Negro colony. 16 December 1852. p.202, c1.

**5370 AMERICAN GENTLEMAN** *to* **THE** *NEW YORK TIMES.* **n.d. n.p.** Reports on the reception of the five French translations of *Uncle Tom's Cabin* in Paris. 16 December 1852. p.202, c2.

**5371 BUCHANAN** *to* **MR. SAUNDERS, MINISTER AT THE COURT OF SPAIN. [extract] n.d. n.p.** Informs Saunders that President Polk would be willing to offer up to $100 million for the purchase of Cuba. 16 December 1852. p.202, c4.

**5372 n.n.** *to* **THE** *NEW YORK EVENING POST.* **n.d. Cuba.** Describes the brutish appearance of the slaves; suggests that using Chinese as indentured servants may be a good way to eliminate slavery. 16 December 1852. p.202, c5.

**5373 SPECIAL WASHINGTON CORRESPONDENT** *to* **THE** *NEW YORK TIMES.* **n.d. n.p.** Presents a case brought before the Supreme Court of the United States involving the powers of the state and federal government in enforcing the Fugitive Slave Law; notes that in *Eells* v. *Illinois*, the constitutionality of the Fugitive Slave Law might be called into question. 23 December 1852. p.206, c1.

**5374 AN OBSERVER** *to* **THE EDITOR [O. JOHNSON]. 16 December 1852. New York.** Relates the history of the Five Point House of Industry in New York. 23 December 1852. p.207, c4.

**5375 ELLEN CRAFT** *to* **THE** *ANTI-SLAVERY ADVOCATE.* **26 October 1852. Ockham School near Ripley, Surrey, England.** Denies the rumor that she wishes to return to slavery in Georgia; claims she would rather die of starvation in England than live comfortably in slavery. 23 December 1852. p.207, c5.

**5376 WILLIAM CRAFT** *to* **SAMUEL MAY, JR. 10 November 1852. Ockham School, England.** Informs May and his friends of the birth of his first freeborn child; comments on the health of the child and mother; denies rumors of his wife's desire to return to bondage. 23 December 1852. p.207, c6.

**5377 CALIFORNIA CORRESPONDENT** *to* **THE** *NATIONAL ERA*. **[extract] n.d. Sacramento.** Informs of a plot to introduce slavery into California; notes that Southerners seek a foothold for slavery in California, while Northerners there are concerned only with making money and leaving. 30 December 1852. p.209, c3.

**5378 CORRESPONDENT** *to* **THE** *NATIONAL ERA*. **n.d. Springfield.** Calls attention to legislation already adopted which promotes slavery in California. 30 December 1852. p.209, c3.

**5379 DANIEL WEBSTER** *to* **ROBERT M. WALSH. [extract] n.d. n.p.** Encloses a copy of the English minister's instructions to the English consul at Haiti; instructs Walsh to make the Haitian Emperor aware of the consequences of a rejection of American terms of peace. 30 December 1852. p.210, c6.

**5380 ENGLISH MINISTER** *to* **THE ENGLISH CONSUL AT HAYTI. [extract] n.d. n.p.** Urges the consul to threaten the Emperor with a blockade or similar action, to ensure acceptance of English terms of peace. 30 December 1852. p.210, c7.

**5381 M.** *to* **MR. EDITOR [O. JOHNSON]. n.d. n.p.** Discusses the Moyamensing House of Industry in Philadelphia, including its benevolent activities and the benefits it provides to the community. 30 December 1852. p.210, c7.

**5382 JOHN NEEDLES** *to* **FRIEND. 14 December 1852. Baltimore.** Requests financial aid for the defense of accused runaways; informs that Rachel Parker is doing well in prison, and is respected by other prisoners because of her education. 30 December 1852. p.211, c3.

**5383 R. D. WEBB** *to* **THE** *ANTI-SLAVERY STANDARD*. **[extract] n.d. Ireland.** Describes a visit by Father Gavazzi, an Italian priest who does not speak English, yet is able to communicate his feelings with his intonation and gestures. 30 December 1852. p.212, c4.

## [1853]

**5384 MARIA WESTON CHAPMAN** *to* **n.n. [from the** *Liberty Bell***] 6 October 1852. Paris.** Tells of a conversation with the first mate of a vessel who, despite his professed hatred of "niggers," admitted to being in love with a Haitian girl. 6 January 1853. p.1, c6.

**5385 CORRESPONDENT** *to* **THE** *CINCINNATI HERALD*. **n.d. n.p.** Describes the unhappy state of an eighteen-year-old colored youth he met on board a steamboat on the Mississippi. 6 January 1853. p.2, c1.

**5386 A FRIEND** *to* **GREELEY. n.d. n.p.** Writes of the defeat of his party in the recent elections, declaring that he has forsaken politics for farming. 6 January 1853. p.2, c2.

**5387 SAMUEL R. WARD** *to* **A FRIEND IN PHILADELPHIA. 13 December 1852. Toronto.** Opposes the Refugees Home Society, referring to its land policy and its misrepresentation of blacks in Canada. 6 January 1853. p.2, c3.

**5388 AN OBSERVER** *to* **THE** *PENNSYLVANIA FREEMAN*. **30 December 1852. New York.** Discusses the "Union for the Moral, Mental, and Physical Improvement of the Youth of this City, of the State, the Country and the World" and describes the designation of its new headquarters. 6 January 1853. p.2, c5.

**5389 CORRESPONDENT** *to* **THE** *TRIBUNE*. **n.d. n.p.** Discusses the deterioration of Webster's health prior to the onset of his fatal illness. 6 January 1853. p.2, c5.

**5390 CORRESPONDENT** *to* **THE** *NEW YORK EVENING POST*. **4 November 1852. San Francisco.** Writes that Southern influence in the affairs of California is increasing because of the acquiesence of Northern interests. 6 January 1853. p.2, c6.

**5391 MARCUS SPRING, ESQ.** *to* **n.n. [extract from the** *Tribune*] **n.d. n.p.** Gives an account of the rescue of the crew of the Scottish bark *Jessie Stevens* by the steamer *Pacific*. 6 January 1853. p.4, c1.

**5392 CORRESPONDENT** *to* **THE** *KNICKERBOCKER*. **n.d. Seneca County.** Tells the story of a stranger from the Prairie who offered his toothpick to another gentleman. 6 January 1853. p.4, c3.

**5393 TEXAS CORRESPONDENT** *to* **THE** *KNICKERBOCKER*. **n.d. n.p.** Relates a humorous story involving several men who boasted of their boxing prowess in the presence of a minister. 6 January 1853. p.4, c4.

**5394 WILLIAM ELDER** *to* **JOHN ASHTON, JR., THOMAS L. KANE, JOHN SARTAIN, ALEXANDER HARRISON [ET AL.]. 24 December 1852. Philadelphia.** Acknowledges that he will soon deliver three lectures on "Societary Science." 13 January 1853. p.7, c1.

**5395 CORRESPONDENT** *to* **THE** *PITTSBURGH GAZETTE*. **[extract] n.d. Washington.** Reports that the only claims for damages approved by Congress are those awarded to Southerners. 13 January 1853. p.7, c1.

**5396 MR. KINNEY** *to* **THE** *NEWARK DAILY ADVERTISER*. **[extract] n.d. Genoa.** Notes that *Uncle Tom's Cabin* is producing "a mischievous influence against the U.S. all over Europe." 13 January 1853. p.7, c2.

**5397 DAUPHIN** *to* **MR. HOPE. n.d. n.p.** Protests the prospective appointment of the Hon. Richard McAllister as governor of Minnesota; accuses McAllister of being "a pretended Democrat." 20 January 1853. p.9, c6.

**5398 EDITORIAL CORRESPONDENT** *to* **THE** *ONEIDA* **(N.Y.)** *TELEGRAPH*. **n.d. On board a Mississippi Riverboat.** Tells of a slave who committed suicide upon learning that he was to be separated from his family. 20 January 1853. p.9, c7.

**5399 CHARLES LANMAN, GEORGE J. ABBOTT, AND BENJAMIN PERLY POORE** *to* **SIR. 1 January 1853. Washington City.** Solicit funds to purchase Daphne, the slave wife of Daniel Webster's free servant William, in order to prevent her being sold away from her husband. 20 January 1853. p.11, c6.

**5400 SARAH HELEN WHITMAN** *to* **HORACE GREELEY, ESQ. 7 December 1852. Providence.** Claims knowledge of a communication to Mrs. Simmons from the spirit of her deceased son. 20 January 1853. p.12, c4.

**5401 C. R. B.** *to* **THE** *TRIBUNE*. **n.d. n.p.** Reports on the continued popularity of *Uncle Tom's Cabin* and on George Sand's tribute to Harriet Beecher Stowe. 27 January 1853. p.13, c5.

**5402 HENRY WARD BEECHER** *to* **WILLIAM LLOYD GARRISON. 20 October 1852. Brooklyn.** Requests a subscription to the *Liberator*, noting that its fairness of reporting, more than its editor's views, influenced his choice. 27 January 1853. p.14, c2.

**5403 B.** *to* **OLIVER JOHNSON. 13 January 1853. Salem, Oh.** Discusses recent events in Salem, Ohio, including a controversy between the treasurer of Columbiana County and officials of the Farmers' Bank of Salem which resulted in an armed confrontation. 27 January 1853. p.14, c7.

**5404 LONDON CORRESPONDENT** *to* **THE** *INDEPENDENT*. **n.d. n.p.** Comments on seeing a man engrossed in *Uncle Tom's Cabin* while walking home from work. 27 January 1853. p.14, c7.

**5405 n.n.** *to* **THE *LILY*. n.d. Wellsville, Oh.** Discusses the lengths to which a woman went to prevent her husband from consuming a jug of whiskey. 27 January 1853. p.15, c1.

**5406 n.n.** *to* **n.n. 18 January 1853. Columbia, Pa.** Details the kidnapping of a free colored man and his subsequent release. 27 January 1853. p.15, c1.

**5407 GEORGE P. FISHER, ESQ.** *to* **THE *BOSTON CONGREGATIONALIST*. n.d. Germany.** Reports on the interest of the Germans in the subject of Negroes, Indians, and Mormons. 27 January 1853. p.15, c5.

**5408 REV. MR. THOMPSON** *to* **THE *NEW YORK INDEPENDENT*. n.d. Paris.** Reveals the existence of the Secret Order of the Society of the Tenth of December, a group which assembles to applaud Louis Napoleon at public occasions wherever he goes. 27 January 1853. p.15, c6.

**5409 n.n.** *to* **n.n. 31 December 1852. London.** Reports the death of Kossuth's mother on 28 December; criticizes the Belgian government for refusing to allow Kossuth to see his dying mother. 27 January 1853. p.15, c6.

**5410 WILLIAM CULLEN BRYANT** *to* **THE *EVENING POST*. n.d. Marseilles.** Comments on the ability of the French to forget Napoleon's past wrongs, and issues a warning to French rulers that idleness and famine among the citizenry give rise to revolution. 27 January 1853. p.16, c4.

**5411 WATCHMAN** *to* **THE EDITORS OF THE *INDEPENDENT*. 3 December 1852. Manchester, England.** States that an address from the ladies of England to the ladies of the United States should have arrived; commends the address and its arguments against slavery. 3 February 1853. p.17, c4.

**5412 C. WEBSTER** *to* **THE *FREEMAN*. n.d. n.p.** Questions whether justice prevailed in the Rachel Parker case; inquires about the lack of an abolitionist daily in Philadelphia and offers to support such an enterprise. 3 February 1853. p.19, c3.

**5413 CONESTOGA** *to* **n.n. 22 January 1853. Lancaster, Pa.** Describes the kidnapping trial of F. John Anderson, the first of its kind in Lancaster. 3 February 1853. p.19, c5.

**5414 CORRESPONDENT** *to* **THE *LEDGER*. n.d. Norfolk, Va.** Writes of the lethargic nature of Virginians; censures them for allowing a natural harbor like Hampton Roads to go to waste. 3 February 1853. p.20, c4.

**5415 STERNE** *to* **DR. ----. 1760. n.p.** Questions the current practice of eulogizing the dead; favors publication of the whole truth. 3 February 1853. p.20, c5.

**5416 QUIC NUNC.** *to* **THE *PENNSYLVANIAN*. 29 January 1853. Harrisburg.** Reports on the settlement between the Pennsylvania Railroad and the Canal commissioners; comments upon McAllister's rumored appointment as a United States commissioner. 10 February 1853. p.22, c2.

**5417 CASPAR MORRIS** *to* **n.n. n.d. n.p.** Forwards additional material pertaining to the case of Richard Neal. 10 February 1853. p.22, c4.

**5418 F. W. CHESSON** *to* **THE *LONDON MORNING ADVERTISER*. n.d. n.p.** Addresses the problem of whether or not the AAS is a legitimate representative of the abolitionist movement; defends Garrison and the goals of his movement. 17 February 1852. p.25, c1.

**5419 LORD DENMAN** *to* **HARRIET BEECHER STOWE. 1 December 1852. Nice.** Praises Stowe's work in behalf of abolition; informs of the growing awareness of the problem in England and on the Continent. 17 February 1853. p.25, c4.

**5420 ROSE MADIAI** *to* **FRANCISCO MADIAI. n.d. Florence.** Professes her love for her husband; urges him to maintain high spirits. 17 February 1853. p.25, c6.

**5421 HENRY CLAY** *to* **GENTLEMEN. 8 January 1845. Ashland.** Addresses himself to the problems involved in freeing his slaves. 17 February 1853. p.25, c7.

**5422 FOREIGN CORRESPONDENT** *to* **THE** ***NORTH AMERICAN*****. 14 January 1853. Dublin.** Details the life of crime led by Kirwin, who was lately accused of the murder of his wife. 17 February 1853. p.28, c4.

**5423 CORRESPONDENT** *to* **THE** ***TRIBUNE*****. n.d. n.p.** Cites the success of *Uncle Tom's Cabin* in France, which he attributes to the emotional temperament of the French. 24 February 1853. p.30, c7.

**5424 REV. T. W. HIGGINSON** *to* **THE** ***LIBERATOR*****. n.d. n.p.** Praises the oratory of Lucy Stone, as demonstrated by her lectures on women's rights. 24 February 1853. p.31, c2.

**5425 CORRESPONDENT** *to* **THE** ***TRIBUNE*****. 12 January 1852. Grass Valley.** Informs of the harsh winter weather on the Pacific Coast, and the flooding of Sacramento. 24 February 1852. p.31, c6.

**5426 PARIS CORRESPONDENT** *to* **THE** ***NEW YORK TRIBUNE*** **n.d. n.p.** Discusses entertainment and fashions of the French elite. 24 February 1852. p.32, c4.

**5427 n.n.** *to* **n.n. n.d. Harrisburg.** Reports a delay by the governor of Pennsylvania in delivering an indictment against the men who kidnapped Rachel Parker; attacks the governor's bill to allow slaves to pass through the state without becoming emancipated. 3 March 1853. p.34, c2.

**5428 n.n.** *to* **n.n. n.d. n.p.** Reports Gerrit Smith's denunciation of Judge Hall and his behavior at the rescue trials. 3 March 1853. p.34, c7.

**5429 BOSTON CORRESPONDENT** *to* **THE** ***STANDARD*****. n.d. n.p.** Describes a meeting called in Boston to determine the fate of some 'Fugitives from labor.' 3 March 1853. p.35, c1.

**5430 CORRESPONDENT** *to* **THE** ***INDEPENDENT*****. n.d. New York.** Describes a meeting held for vagrant boys in New York to keep them off of the streets. 3 March 1853. p.35, c2.

**5431 LONDON CORRESPONDENT** *to* **THE** ***TRIBUNE*****. n.d. n.p.** Informs that Kossuth had nothing to do with an insurrection in Italy and that Mazzini was involved, but had not wanted to be. 3 March 1853. p.35, c3.

**5432 WASHINGTON CORRESPONDENT** *to* **THE** ***TRIBUNE*****. 22 February 1853. n.p.** Relates the escape of President-Elect Pierce from the clutches of supporters and office-seekers at the Washington depot. 3 March 1853. p.35, c5.

**5433 SOUTHERN CORRESPONDENT** *to* **THE** ***NEW YORK TIMES*****. [extract] n.d. n.p.** Tells of the poor quality of their livestock; describes how Northerners moving to Virginia have transformed the area into fruitful farms. 3 March 1853. p.35, c5.

**5434 FRIEND** *to* **THE** *DELAWARE COUNTY REPUBLICAN*. **n.d. n.p.** Attacks the attitudes which the Fugitive Slave Law has encouraged; criticizes Governor Bigler in his handling of the Neal affair. 3 March 1853. p.35, c6.

**5435 H. B. STOWE** *to* **DR. WARDLAW. 4 December 1852. n.p.** Expresses her amazement at the success of her works; accepts his invitation on behalf of a Scottish abolitionist group. 3 March 1853. p.36, c1.

**5436 CORRESPONDENT** *to* **THE** *TRIBUNE*. **7 February 1853. Paris.** Describes Mardi Gras festivities in Paris. 3 March 1852. p.36, c4.

**5437 JOHN L. THOMPSON** *to* **EDWARD McPHERSON. 22 February 1853. Lancaster, Pa.** Sets forth the circumstances affecting the state's actions in the Ridgeley murder trial. 10 March 1853. p.37, c3.

**5438 A NORTHERNER** *to* **MR. EDITOR [O. JOHNSON]. n.d. n.p.** Describes life in slavery and in freedom, concluding that slavery is the more beneficial condition for blacks. 10 March 1853. p.37, c5.

**5439 FRIEND** *to* **THE** *POST*. **[extract from the** ***Boston Commonwealth*****] n.d. Paris.** Writes to say that *Uncle Tom's Cabin* will do the United States great harm in Europe. 10 March 1853. p.37, c6.

**5440 HON. HORACE MANN** *to* **WILLIAM LLOYD GARRISON. 21 February 1853. Washington.** Writes to correct false impressions conveyed in the speech of Wendell Phillips published in the *Liberator*. 10 March 1853. p.38, c1.

**5441 WENDELL PHILLIPS** *to* **WILLIAM LLOYD GARRISON. 1 March 1853. Boston.** Responds to Horace Mann's attack upon his speech published in the *Liberator*; gives evidence to support his statements. 10 March 1853. p.38, c2.

**5442 WILLIAM GOODELL** *to* **OLIVER JOHNSON. 4 November 1853 [sic]. Bristol Center, Ontario County, N.Y.** Replies to criticism of his work by Johnson. 10 March 1853. p.38, c6.

**5443 WASHINGTON CORRESPONDENT** *to* **THE** *TRIBUNE*. **n.d. n.p.** Reports that Capt. Isaiah Rynders has arrived in Washington seeking appointment as a United States marshal. 10 March 1853. p.39, c2.

**5444 MELISSA** *to* **THE** *HOME JOURNAL*. **n.d. n.p.** Inquires as to the propriety of bloomers and French boots, considering the conditions of the streets. 10 March 1853. p.40, c2.

**5445 n.n.** *to* **THE** *NEW YORK TRIBUNE*. **3 March 1853. Richmond, Va.** Tells of the brutality of slave auctions; describes one bidder who nearly attacked a man sketching the scene, believing him to be an abolitionist. 17 March 1853. p.41, c6.

**5446 PUNCH** *to* **MRS. LEGREE, MRS. JONATHAN JEFFERSON LEGREE, AND THE MISSES LEGREE. n.d. n.p.** Replies satirically to the Legrees' failure to condemn slavery. 17 March 1853. p.41, c7.

**5447 W.** *to* **THE** *NEW YORK EVENING POST*. **22 February 1853. n.p.** Reports having seen a black man in chains being paraded through New York City; inquires if it is known whether the man was a fugitive slave. 17 March 1853. p.41, c7.

**5448 CORRESPONDENT** *to* **THE** *CHICAGO DAILY TIMES*. **n.d. Memphis.** Describes the Memphis slave market. 17 March 1853. p.41, c7.

**5449 HARRIET BEECHER STOWE** *to* **WENDELL PHILLIPS. n.d. n.p.** Defends her father's actions regarding an incident at the Lane Theological Seminary. 17 March 1853. p.42, c1.

**5450 WENDELL PHILLIPS** *to* **THE** ***LIBERATOR*****. 4 March 1853. Boston.** Claims that Mrs. Stowe's defense of her father is no defense at all, but rather an affirmation of his statements. 17 March 1853. p.42, c1.

**5451 CYRUS M. BURLEIGH** *to* **OLIVER JOHNSON. 2 March 1853. Bacon's Neck, Greenwich, N.J.** Describes his travels through New Jersey canvassing for the *Pennsylvania Freeman* and promoting the aims of the abolitionists and the temperance movement. 17 March 1853. p.42, c4.

**5452 S. R. WARD** *to* **THE EDITOR [O. JOHNSON]. n.d. n.p.** Thanks the editor for his support; discloses more information on Canadian land dealings relating to blacks. 17 March 1853. p.42, c7.

**5453 ABBY KELLEY FOSTER, LUCY STONE, THOMAS W. HIGGINSON, [AND TWENTY-FOUR OTHERS]** *to* **FELLOW CITIZENS. n.d. n.p.** Announce a convention for equal rights for all in Massachusetts. 17 March 1853. p.44, c2.

**5454 CORRESPONDENT** *to* **THE** ***NEW YORK TRIBUNE*****. 29 January 1853. Rock Bend, Mn.** Describes a frontier courthouse and its first day's proceedings in Rock Bend. 17 March 1853. p.44, c3.

**5455 BAILE** *to* **THE** ***DAILY REGISTER*****. 1 March 1853. New York.** Relates the details of a $13,000 swindle perpetrated by a phony clairvoyant medium. 17 March 1853. p.44, c4.

**5456 CORRESPONDENT** *to* **THE** ***NEW YORK TRIBUNE*****. 4 December 1852. Chihuahua.** Describes the Indian enslavement of the Mexicans in the area between Missouri and Mexico; informs that most captives are children and are well treated. 24 March 1853. p.45, c3.

**5457 PARKER PILLSBURY** *to* **THE** ***BUGLE*****. n.d. n.p.** Tells of his lack of success as a preacher. 24 March 1853. p.45, c4.

**5458 A. H. B.** *to* **n.n. n.d. n.p.** Describes the dwellings and occupations of the colored people of Philadelphia. 24 March 1853. p.45, c5.

**5459 JUSTICE** *to* **THE** ***INDEPENDENT WHIG*****. March 1853. Columbia.** Doubts the veracity of John L. Thompson's story; provides evidence for his views. 24 March 1853. p.45, c6.

**5460 D. F. N.** *to* **BROTHER BOYNTON. [from the** ***Christian Press*****] n.d. n.p.** Discusses corruption in the slaveholding churches, noting the various forms of intemperance which are tolerated. 24 March 1853. p.45, c7.

**5461 HON. J. R. GIDDINGS** *to* **THE** ***ASHTABULA SENTINEL*****. [extract] 4 March 1853. Washington.** Condemns Congress for suspending procedural rules in order to deal with a seventy-year-old claim for lost Negroes; considers it ironic that damages were awarded in this case, while Northerners ruined by financing the Revolutionary War went uncompensated. 24 March 1853. p.46, c1.

**5462 C. M. BURLEIGH** *to* **THE READERS OF THE** ***FREEMAN*****. n.d. n.p.** Bids Johnson farewell as editor; pledges his best efforts to the *Freeman*. 24 March 1853. p.46, c2.

**5463 BEN FRANKLIN** *to* **THE** *PENNSYLVANIA FREEMAN.* **14 March 1853. Harrisburg.** Reports on the recent local elections, and the resounding defeat of the "Union savers." 24 March 1853. p.46, c5.

**5464 GEORGE F. HORTON** *to* **FRIEND McKIM. 26 February 1853. Terrytown, Pa.** Informs McKim that the progress of the anti-slavery movement has slowed; encloses a donation and the names of three new subscribers to the *Pennsylvania Freeman.* 24 March 1853. p.46, c5.

**5465 N. R. JOHNSTON** *to* **WILLIAM STILL. [extract] n.d. n.p.** Warns of the danger of purchasing the freedom of slaves; commends the job of the *Freeman.* 24 March 1853. p.46, c7.

**5466 A. H. B.** *to* **THE** *INDEPENDENT.* **n.d. n.p.** Discusses the occupations and status of the colored women of Philadelphia. 31 March 1853. p.49, c1.

**5467 HON. HORACE MANN** *to* **WM. L. GARRISON. 14 March 1853. West Newton.** Responds to Phillips's accusations against Mann; attacks Garrison for taking sides in the matter. 31 March 1853. p.49, c4.

**5468 WENDELL PHILLIPS** *to* **WM. L. GARRISON. 21 March 1853. Boston.** Defends himself against Mann's latest response. 31 March 1853. p.49, c7.

**5469 MISSOURI CORRESPONDENT** *to* **THE** *NEW YORK EVENING POST.* **[extract] n.d. n.p.** Criticizes the state of Illinois for its new "Black Law." 31 March 1853. p.51, c2.

**5470 KENT** *to* **THE EDITORS OF THE** *HOME JOURNAL.* **n.d. n.p.** Reports on a candle factory in Vauxhall, London which has slowly developed a school and recreation program benefitting all of its employees. 31 March 1853. p.52, c2.

**5471 A. H. B.** *to* **THE** *INDEPENDENT.* **n.d.n.p.** Discusses in detail the health conditions of Philadelphia's racial groups. 7 April 1853. p.53, c1.

**5472 CORRESPONDENT** *to* **THE** *TRIBUNE.* **[extract] n.d. Toronto, Upper Canada.** Reports on a free Negro who sold his wife into slavery after finding that his father-in-law would not make a dowry available suitable to his wants. 7 April 1853. p.54, c6.

**5473 n.n.** *to* *GRAHAM'S MAGAZINE.* **[extract] n.d. n.p.** Lauds the merits of Edwin P. Whipple in a "rhapsody of adjectives." 7 April 1853. p.54, c6.

**5474 n.n.** *to* **THE EDITOR OF THE** *FREEMAN* **[C. M. BURLEIGH]. n.d. n.p.** Discusses the takeover of the Philadelphia Methodist Episcopal Conference staged by the Pennsylvania CS; presents their views on colonization. 7 April 1853. p.54, c7.

**5475 n.n.** *to* **n.n. n.d. n.p.** Writes in reply to a dunning epistle from a city creditor. 7 April 1853. p.56, c3.

**5476 A. H. B.** *to* **THE** *INDEPENDENT.* **n.d. n.p.** Describes the poor blacks of Philadelphia, the sections they inhabit, and the assistance made available to them by the city. 14 April 1853. p.57, c1.

**5477 HON. JOSHUA R. GIDDINGS** *to* **n.n. 8 March 1853. Jefferson.** Bids farewell to his district; describes the changes in attitudes since his first term in Congress. 14 April 1853. p.57, c3.

**5478 CORRESPONDENT** *to* **THE** *INDEPENDENT.* **n.d. n.p.** Extracts quotes from Rev. Dr. Spring's text, "First Things," in which he supports the Fugitive Slave Law; demonstrates the inhumanity of this belief with a hypothetical example. 14 April 1853. p.57, c5.

**5479 CORRESPONDENT** *to* **THE** *NATIONAL ERA.* **15 March 1853. St. Louis.** Informs that *Uncle Tom's Cabin* convinced H. D. Bacon to emancipate his two slaves. 14 April 1853. p.57, c6.

**5480 VIENNA CORRESPONDENT** *to* **THE** *LONDON TIMES.* **n.d. n.p.** Describes the performance of Ira Aldridge, the colored tragedian, at a Vienna theater. 14 April 1853. p.57, c7.

**5481 SOUTHERN CORRESPONDENT** *to* **THE** *BOSTON COMMONWEALTH.* **[extract] n.d. n.p.** Describes a railroad journey through the South with a man from Salem who now lives in the South and condones slavery. 14 April 1853. p.58, c2.

**5482 JNO. S. MANN** *to* **C. M. BURLEIGH. 2 April 1853. Coudersport, Potter County.** Defends the actions of the political anti-slavery advocates in forwarding the causes of abolition and temperance; believes the *Freeman* has been too harsh in its criticism of these people. 14 April 1853. p.58, c5.

**5483 n.n.** *to* **n.n. n.d. n.p.** Expresses continued concern for the colored people of the South; discusses slaveholding in his part of the South. 14 April 1853. p.59, c3.

**5484 JAMAR DAVIS** *to* **THE** *BOSTON INVESTIGATOR.* **n.d. n.p.** Tells of the maltreatment of a ten-year-old Negro boy by his master, a Presbyterian minister. 14 April 1853. p.59, c4.

**5485 HON. HORACE MANN** *to* **WENDELL PHILLIPS, ESQ. n.d. n.p.** Continues his debate with Phillips; cites seventy-five errors in Phillips's latest response, several of which he corrects. 21 April 1853. p.61, c1.

**5486 WENDELL PHILLIPS, ESQ.** *to* **W. L. GARRISON, ESQ. 7 April 1853. Boston.** Responds to Horace Mann's latest communication. 21 April 1853. p.61, c7.

**5487 ENOCH E. CAMP** *to* **P. T. BARNUM, ESQ. 2 April 1853. New York.** Encloses an address given by Camp one year earlier; expresses remorse at the error of his ways, and vows to repent and forward the cause of temperance. 21 April 1853. p.63, c5.

**5488 A. H. B.** *to* **THE** *INDEPENDENT.* **n.d. n.p.** Discusses education, beneficial societies, and religion of the colored people of Philadelphia. 28 April 1853. p.65, c2.

**5489 LIBERIAN RESIDENT** *to* **MY DEAR SISTER. 11 July 1852. Beeley, Bassa County.** Describes the harsh conditions and high rate of mortality in Liberia. 28 April 1853. p.65, c5.

**5490 REV. J. McBRIDE** *to* **THE** *WESLEYAN.* **11 March 1853. Sylvania, Oh.** Discusses the progress of Wesleyans; mentions John Cornett, who defied a mob and freed his slaves. 28 April 1853. p.65, c6.

**5491 n.n.** *to* **THE** *BUGLE.* **n.d. Linesville, Crawford County, Pa.** Inquires how great an evil would be required to offend Southern Christians; reports that two letters in which his son expressed opposition to slavery nearly provoked a riot in Memphis. 28 April 1853. p.65, c6.

**5492 LONDON CORRESPONDENT** *to* **THE** *DAILY REGISTER.* **[extract] n.d. n.p.** Reports that *Uncle Tom's Cabin* has had a profound effect on England. 28 April 1853. p.66, c4.

**5493 E. W.** *to* **THE** *PENNSYLVANIA FREEMAN.* **18 April 1853. Wilmington, De.** Encloses a copy of the resolutions adopted by the Constitutional Convention at Dover regarding slavery; attacks Senator James A. Bayard for his views on slavery and his influence on the proceedings. 28 April 1853. p.67, c2.

**5494 JUDGE JAY** *to* **MR. COOK. [extract] n.d. n.p.** Presents his reasons for declining to donate to Cook's tract society; attacks the society for its hypocrisy and its disregard of the issue of slavery. 28 April 1853. p.67, c5.

**5495 BOSTON CORRESPONDENT** *to* **THE** *NEW YORK CHRISTIAN INQUIRER.* **[extract] n.d. n.p.** Comments on Josiah Quincy's dedication and civic-mindedness. 28 April 1853. p.68, c1.

**5496 A VIRGINIAN** *to* **THE EDITOR OF THE** *NEW YORK TRIBUNE.* **n.d. n.p.** A slaveholder states that the Southerners should decide how to aid in setting the slaves free, as only they know the needs of the slaves; admits that slavery is wrong. 5 May 1853. p.69, c1.

**5497 n.n.** *to* **THE** *NEW YORK TIMES.* **n.d. Havana.** Details further measures to stop the slave trade and the illegal importation of slaves. 5 May 1853. p.70, c3.

**5498 n.n.** *to* **THE** *PENNSYLVANIA FREEMAN.* **n.d. Ireland.** Writes hopefully on the anti-slavery movement in Ireland; informs of the archbishop's interest in the movement. 5 May 1853. p.70, c4.

**5499 E. W.** *to* **THE EDITOR OF THE** *FREEMAN* **[C. M. BURLEIGH]. 2 May 1853. Wilmington, De.** Reports that the pro-slavery amendments submitted by Bayard to the constitutional convention were defeated in his absence; encloses a transcript of the proceedings. 5 May 1853. p.70, c6.

**5500 SOUTHERN MAN** *to* **n.n. n.d. n.p.** Writes of his conversion to the anti-slavery cause, which resulted from witnessing the mistreatment of a slave by his owner. 5 May 1853. p.70, c6.

**5501 H. W. G.** *to* **THE** *PENNSYLVANIA FREEMAN.* **28 March 1853. Florence.** Describes his travels through Florence; tells of the Catholics' general contempt for the Pope and his authority. 5 May 1853. p.70, c7.

**5502 CORRESPONDENT** *to* **THE** *NEW YORK TRIBUNE.* **n.d. n.p.** Describes in a vivid manner the cruelty of corporal punishment in the army. 5 May 1853. p.71, c5.

**5503 AUNT FANNY GAGE** *to* **MY DEAR NIECES. n.d. n.p.** Bids her nieces farewell as she leaves Ohio for Missouri. 5 May 1853. p.72, c1.

**5504 HON. HORACE MANN** *to* **W. L. GARRISON, ESQ. 19 April 1853. West Newton.** Responds once again to the latest charges by Wendell Phillips. 12 May 1853. p.73, c1.

**5505 WENDELL PHILLIPS, ESQ.** *to* **THE EDITOR OF THE** *LIBERATOR.* **29 April 1853. Northampton.** Continues his debate with Mann, accusing him of failure to address the points of criticism adequately. 12 May 1853. p.73, c6.

**5506 EDMUND JACKSON** *to* **MR. GARRISON. 2 May 1853. Boston.** Questions the sincerity of Mann's denunciation of caste schools in his continuing controversy with Wendell Phillips. 12 May 1853. p.74, c4.

**5507 CORRESPONDENT** *to* **THE** *NEW YORK TIMES.* **2 April 1853. Matanzas.** Discusses the taking of slaves in Cuba, including kidnappings, bribes, and the murder of those who protest their enslavement. 12 May 1853. p.74, c4.

**5508 CORRESPONDENT** *to* **THE** *CHRISTIAN INDEX.* **n.d. n.p.** Condemns the denial of representation to colored churches by the various Baptist associations. 12 May 1853. p.75, c2.

**5509 n.n.** *to* **n.n. n.d. n.p.** Reports on Free-Soil speeches given at a dinner for Hon. John P. Hale in Boston. 12 May 1853. p.75, c3.

**5510 YEOMAN** *to* **THE** *NEW YORK TIMES.* **n.d. Virginia.** Describes the cities of Richmond, Petersburg, and Norfolk, arguing that the genteel pace of life has limited Virginia's growth. 19 May 1853. p.77, c1.

**5511 HON. WILLIAM JAY** *to* **THE TREASURER OF THE AMERICAN MISSIONARY SOCIETY. 8 March 1853. New York.** Complains that certain missionaries have promoted support of slavery among the Choctaws and Cherokees; encloses a check for $100 to support the society. 19 May 1853. p.77, c5.

**5512 n.n.** *to* **THE** *NEW YORK JOURNAL OF COMMERCE.* **n.d. Havana.** Reports on recent incidents of slave smuggling in Cuba. 19 May 1853. p.77, c6.

**5513 HON. HORACE MANN** *to* **W. L. GARRISON, ESQ. 9 May 1853. West Newton.** Continues his debate with Phillips, accusing him of failure to address the issues involved. 19 May 1853. p.78, c1.

**5514 C. M. CLAY** *to* **C. DONALDSON, ETC. COMMITTEE. 25 March 1853. Madison County, Ky.** Apologizes for his late response to their letter; tentatively accepts their invitation to attend the Cincinnati Anti-Slavery Convention; praises Garrison and his methods. 19 May 1853. p.78, c5.

**5515 REV. SAMUEL J. MAY** *to* **FRIEND. 4 May 1853. Syracuse.** Invites the AAS to hold a meeting in Syracuse; reports on the anniversary of the Rescue of Jerry; apologizes for not being present at their convention in New York. 26 May 1853. p.82, c7.

**5516 HON. WILLIAM JAY** *to* **SIR. 9 May 1853. Bedford.** Declines an invitation to attend the AAS convention; supports the convention and the cause of abolition. 26 May 1853. p.82, c7.

**5517 HON. SALMON P. CHASE** *to* **SIR. 8 May 1853. Cincinnati.** Declines an invitation to attend the New York AAS convention; sends his best wishes to the convention. 26 May 1853. p.82, c7.

**5518 JOHN WILBUR** *to* **S. H. GAY. 10 May 1853. North Easton.** Declines an invitation to attend the AAS meeting in New York due to illness. 26 May 1853. p.83, c1.

**5519 S. S. GRISWOLD** *to* **S. H. GAY. 9 May 1853. Mystic Bridge, Ct.** Declines an invitation to attend the AAS convention in New York; wishes them well. 26 May 1853. p.83, c1.

**5520 JUSTICE** *to* **W. L. GARRISON, ESQ. 3 May 1853. Boston.** Requests the names of the colored persons to whom Horace Mann referred in one of his replies; praises the efforts of Wendell Phillips in behalf of colored people and abolition. 26 May 1853. p.83, c1.

**5521 CORRESPONDENT** *to* **THE** *NEW YORK OBSERVER.* **n.d. Italy.** Complains of a seeming conspiracy to plunder travellers in Italy, where every type of service is rendered for a fee. 26 May 1853. p.83, c5.

**5522 BOSTON CORRESPONDENT** *to* **THE** *ANTI-SLAVERY STANDARD.* **n.d. n.p.** Describes the reception given Garrison at Hale's festival. 2 June 1853. p.86, c3.

**5523 CORRESPONDENT** *to* **THE** *ESSEX COUNTY FREEMAN.* **n.d. n.p.** Acclaims Garrison's speech as one of the best at the Hale festival, lauding his "liberal and conciliatory" tone. 2 June 1853. p.86, c3.

**5524 WASHINGTON CORRESPONDENT** *to* **THE** *TRIBUNE.* **n.d. n.p.** Describes a conflict between Miss Dix and the doctors of Washington concerning the superintendent of construction at the District's lunatic asylum; congratulates President Pierce for supporting Miss Dix. 2 June 1853. p.86, c5.

**5525 CORRESPONDENT** *to* **THE** *TRIBUNE.* **17 May 1853. Portsmouth, Oh.** Tells of an incident whereby the protector of a runaway slave was knifed by the owner, who quickly fled. 2 June 1853. p.87, c2.

**5526 A SOUTHERN WOMAN** *to* **THE DUCHESS OF SUTHERLAND AND OTHER WOMEN OF ENGLAND. n.d. n.p.** Responds to "The Affectionate and Christian Address of many thousands of women of Great Britain and Ireland to their sisters, the Women of the United States of America." 9 June 1853. p.89, c1.

**5527 RECTOR GEORGE G. BEADON AND 1400 CITIZENS OF THE AXEBRIDGE, ENGLAND LOCALITY** *to* **THE PEOPLE OF THE UNITED STATES. n.d. n.p.** Plead for the people in bondage in America, and for their immediate emancipation. 9 June 1853. p.89, c3.

**5528 C. C. BURLEIGH** *to* **BROTHER. 29 May 1853. Plainfield, Ct.** Relates the proceedings of the recent New England AS Convention in Boston. 9 June 1853. p.90, c5.

**5529 HENRY GREW** *to* **C. M. BURLEIGH. n.d. n.p.** Cites scripture in defense of the exclusion of women from the World Temperance Convention in New York. 9 June 1853. p.90, c7.

**5530 C. C. BURLEIGH** *to* **n.n. [extract] n.d. n.p.** Describes his visits to a temperance convention, to the Five Points House of Industry, and to the Tombs' prison following the New York anniversaries. 9 June 1853. p.91, c1.

**5531 n.n.** *to* **n.n. n.d. n.p.** Tells of a young lady who apprehended a man who stole her mother's purse as they walked near the Boston depot. 9 June 1853. p.91, c3.

**5532 CHINESE CORRESPONDENT** *to* **n.n. n.d. n.p.** Tells of a conversation with Lumgua, a Chinese artist. 9 June 1853. p.92, c3.

**5533 IMAUM ALI ZADI** *to* **[MR. LAYARD]. n.d. [Turkey.]** Responds to Layard's request for demographic and economic data, stating that it would be "both difficult and useless" to answer his questions; advises him that there is no wisdom equal to the belief in God, and that he should not seek those things which he does not require. 9 June 1853. p.92, c4.

**5534 n.n.** *to* **THE EDITORS OF THE** *NEW YORK EVENING POST.* **8 May 1853. Alabama.** Commends *Uncle Tom's Cabin*, which he feels will prove influential in the debate on the slavery question. 16 June 1853. p.93, c3.

**5535 J. A. O.** *to* **THE** *NEW YORK TRIBUNE.* **n.d. St. Joseph, Mo.** Deplores slavery and abolitionists equally; encloses fifteen subscriptions to the paper. 16 June 1853. p.93, c4.

**5536 BOSTON CORRESPONDENT** *to* **THE** *NEW YORK EVENING POST.* **n.d. n.p.** Relates an ongoing debate at Harvard Law School regarding slavery, demonstrating a decline in conservatism and "Hunkerism" at this institution. 16 June 1853. p.94, c1.

**5537 OBSERVER** *to* **THE** *PENNSYLVANIA FREEMAN.* **30 May 1853. Philadelphia.** Details the visit of Dr. Miles, an impostor who sells abdominal supporters. 16 June 1853. p.94, c6.

**5538 T. C.** *to* **THE** *PENNSYLVANIA FREEMAN.* **n.d. n.p.** Discusses the life of Arthur Spring, the condemned murderer recently executed. 16 June 1853. p.94, c7.

**5539 CORRESPONDENT** *to* **THE** *GERMANTOWN TELEGRAPH.* **n.d. n.p.** Suggests the application of finely ground oyster shell compost for barren fruit trees. 16 June 1853. p.96, c4.

**5540 G. JACOB HOLYOAKE, RICHARD MOORE, AND COLMAN BURROUGHS** *to* **THE EDITOR OF THE** *NEW YORK TRIBUNE.* **May 1853. London.** Enclose an address from the Democrats of England to the Democrats of the United States; hope to add credibility to the previously released address at Stafford House. 23 June 1853. p.97, c1.

**5541 DEMOCRATS OF ENGLAND** *to* **THE DEMOCRATS OF THE UNITED STATES. n.d. n.p.** Praise the United States for instituting many English principles; call upon the United States to abolish slavery, as it is inconsistent with these principles. 23 June 1853. p.97, c1.

**5542 EARL OF SHAFTESBURY** *to* **THE** *LONDON TIMES.* **16 May 1853. n.p.** Defends his earlier remarks on the sinfulness of slavery, in response to a reply by the editor of the *Times*. 23 June 1853. p.97, c2.

**5543 n.n.** *to* **THE** *WILLIAMSBURGH* **(N.Y.)** *TIMES.* **[extract] n.d. Aiken, S.C.** Describes the activities of men involved in tracking down runaway slaves and trailing thieves. 23 June 1853. p.97, c4.

**5544 PETER GORDON** *to* **THE EDITOR OF THE** *LONDON ANTI-SLAVERY ADVOCATE.* **10 May 1853. 1 Bedford Place, Brighton, England.** Informs readers of the *Advocate* of a great lack of knowledge among both rulers and ruled in India regarding the issues and methods of abolition. 23 June 1853. p.97, c6.

**5545 DAVID PAUL BROWN** *to* **n.n. 26 April 1853. Philadelphia.** Declines an invitation to attend Hale's public dinner. 23 June 1853. p.97, c7.

**5546 ELLIS GRAY LORING** *to* **THE** *LONDON EXAMINER.* **14 February 1853. Boston.** Apologizes for placing America and England side by side; praises England's slow but steady progress toward equal rights of men, and accuses America of backsliding. 23 June 1853. p.98, c2.

**5547 S. W.** *to* **THE** *PENNSYLVANIA FREEMAN.* **12 June 1853. n.p.** Calls for an end to the purchase of slave-labor products. 23 June 1853. p.98, c6.

**5548 M. M. BALDWIN, REV. ALBERT BARNES, W. J. A. BIRKEY, M.D., [AND SIXTEEN OTHERS]** *to* **CITIZENS OF PHILADELPHIA. June 1853. Philadelphia.** Solicit donations for the endowment of the Female Medical College of Pennsylvania. 23 June 1853. p.99, c2.

**5549 C. H.** *to* **THE** *PENNSYLVANIA FREEMAN.* **10 June 1853. Upper Oxford.** Gives an account of a discussion between Charles C. Burleigh and Edward E. Orvis of the question, "Are the American Church and Ministry a Brotherhood of Thieves?" 23 June 1853. p.99, c3.

**5550 n.n.** *to* **THE** *LONDON ANTI-SLAVERY ADVOCATE.* **[extract] n.d. Ohio.** Informs that he has been converted to "ultra anti-slavery views" by H. C. Wright; believes in taking a firm stand on the issue. 23 June 1853. p.99, c6.

**5551 REV. WM. L. M'CALLA** *to* **n.n. [extract] n.d. n.p.** Writes in defense of *Uncle Tom's Cabin,* relating his own experiences with slavery; attacks the Fugitive Slave Law; praises the efforts of Mrs. Stowe. 30 June 1853. p.101, c1.

**5552 A FUGITIVE SLAVE** *to* **THE EDITOR OF THE** *NEW YORK TRIBUNE.* **n.d. n.p.** Answers "Mrs. Tyler's Reply to the Ladies of England"; describes the suffering endured by her sister at the hands of a ruthless master. 30 June 1853. p.101, c4.

**5553 E. LOUIS LOWE** *to* **WM. BIGLER. 2 May 1853. Annapolis, Md.** Declines to issue a warrant for the arrest of M'Creary and Merritt, who are charged with the kidnapping of Rachel Parker. 30 June 1853. p.102, c2.

**5554 WM. BIGLER** *to* **E. LOUIS LOWE. 26 May 1853. Harrisburg.** Takes issue with Lowe's refusal to arrest M'Creary and Merritt; explains why these indictments are important. 30 June 1853. p.102, c3.

**5555 JACOBUS** *to* **THE** *NEW YORK TRIBUNE.* **9 June 1853. Columbus, Oh.** Reports that the Black Law of Ohio convinced most of its residents of the evil of slavery; discusses the subsequent repeal of the law. 7 July 1853. p.106, c4.

**5556 MR. BROOKS** *to* **n.n. n.d. Georgia.** States that the average Southerner feels that slavery is beneficial to colored people, and sees the piety of the slaves as evidence. 7 July 1853. p.106, c5.

**5557 CORRESPONDING SECRETARY OF THE N.Y. STATE TEMPERANCE SOCIETY** *to* **THE EDITOR OF THE** *PENNSYLVANIA FREEMAN.* **2 July 1853. Albany.** Corrects statements made by the *Freeman* concerning the society's annual meeting; recommends a visit to the society's semiannual meeting. 7 July 1853. p.107, c1.

**5558 NEW YORK CORRESPONDENT** *to* **THE** *LEDGER.* **28 June 1853. n.p.** Reports on the latest rum licenses issued in New York's fifth ward. 7 July 1853. p.107, c2.

**5559 CORRESPONDENT** *to* **THE** *CLEVELAND TRUE DEMOCRAT.* **4 May 1853. Rome.** Describes the rooms in Rome formerly occupied by Margaret Fuller; discusses the impact of Fuller and her work. 7 July 1853. p.108, c1.

**5560 CORRESPONDENT** *to* **THE** *NATIONAL ERA.* **10 May 1853. Near Cardenas, Cuba.** Describes plantation life of Cuba; fears that an uprising of the slaves would be disastrous, as they outnumber the whites. 14 July 1853. p.109, c5.

**5561 CORRESPONDENT** *to* **THE** *NEW YORK TRIBUNE.* **28 June 1853. Havana.** Reports on the illegal trafficking of slaves in Cuba and the arrest of two wealthy Cuban slave importers. 14 July 1853. p.109, c7.

**5562 A MERCHANT** *to* **THE** *DAILY REGISTER.* **[extract] n.d. n.p.** Informs of the discriminatory practices of one omnibus line, and commends the courtesy of another. 14 July 1853. p.110, c6.

**5563 REV. EDWARD MATHEWS** *to* **THE** *AMERICAN BAPTIST.* **n.d. n.p.** Describes the zeal for abolition in England; comments on Mrs. Stowe's Exeter Hall speech. 14 July 1853. p.109 [111], c4.

**5564 J. M. M'KIM** *to* **THE EDITOR OF THE** *LONDON INQUIRER.* **14 June 1853. London.** Corrects certain erroneous statements made by Rev. Edmund Squire regarding the anti-slavery movement in America. 21 July 1853. p.113, c2.

**5565 C. E. STOWE** *to* **G. W. SIMONDS. 30 July 1853. Andover.** Responds to a question of Simonds, published in the *Liberator,* regarding American consumption of slave-labor produce; corrects Simonds's interpretation of his words. 21 July 1853. p.113, c4.

**5566 CORRESPONDENT** *to* **THE** *ERA.* **n.d. n.p.** Discusses the life of Richard Stanop, who is 106 years of age and the last surviving member of President Washington's Revolutionary War staff. 21 July 1853. p.113, c4.

**5567 BOSTON CORRESPONDENT** *to* **THE** *NEW YORK INDEPENDENT.* **n.d. n.p.** Exposes the American Sunday School Union's use of false advertising to draw a crowd to its anniversary; condemns the continuance of such practices by other groups. 21 July 1853. p.113, c5.

**5568 HENRY T. TUCKERMAN** *to* **THE EDITORS OF THE** *HOME JOURNAL.* **n.d. n.p.** Announces the death of Pierre Toussaint, a Negro hairdresser from Santo Domingo. 21 July 1853. p.113, c7.

**5569 CORRESPONDENT** *to* **THE** *NASHVILLE UNION AND AMERICAN.* **[extract from the** *National Era***] n.d. n.p.** Rejoices that a Nashville bookseller returned an invoice for *Uncle Tom's Cabin,* but laments that such a book no longer causes such a stir as it did in the past. 21 July 1853. p.114, c1.

**5570 PROFESSOR WILLIAM G. ALLEN** *to* *FREDERICK DOUGLASS' PAPER.* **[extract] n.d. n.p.** Tells of his and his wife's reception in England, commending the English lack of prejudice against racially mixed marriages. 21 July 1853. p.114, c2.

**5571 F. W. CHESSON** *to* **THE EDITOR OF THE** *LONDON MORNING ADVERTISER.* **n.d. n.p.** Refutes Dr. Lang's contention that the abolitionists have furthered the cause of slavery, and asks Lang to support all anti-slavery activities. 21 July 1853. p.114, c3.

**5572 n.n.** *to* **THE** *PENNSYLVANIA FREEMAN.* **12 July 1853. Plumstead.** Purchases subscriptions to the *Pennsylvania Freeman* and the *National Anti-Slavery Standard* for two families who cannot afford the papers. 21 July 1853. p.114, c4.

**5573 H. W. G.** *to* **THE** *PENNSYLVANIA FREEMAN.* **18 May 1853. Florence, Italy.** Characterizes Italian society, noting the growing dissatisfaction with the Pope, the indecision of the Vatican regarding Napoleon, the absence of prejudice against color, the lack of education for the peasants and other classes, and the continual presence of French soldiers. 21 July 1853. p.114, c7.

**5574 A FRIEND TO THE RIGHT** *to* **THE** *LANCASTER INDEPENDENT WHIG.* **[extract] n.d. n.p.** Takes issue with a preacher who delivered a pro-slavery sermon based on the injunction, "Render unto Caesar the things which are Caesar's." 21 July 1853. p.115, c2.

**5575 n.n.** *to* **n.n. 2 July 1853. Liverpool, England.** Informs of the arrival of 12,000 Russian troops at Jasey on 25 June. 21 July 1853. p.115, c7.

**5576 CORRESPONDENT** *to* **THE** *BAY STATE.* **n.d. n.p.** Suggests a method for converting the common fluid lamp into a safety lamp. 21 July 1853. p.116, c1.

**5577 WASHINGTON CORRESPONDENT** *to* **THE** *NEW YORK JOURNAL OF COMMERCE.* **n.d. n.p.** Reports on a scarcity of labor in Virginia; foresees a decrease in field slave labor in the near future, with most slaves becoming domestics. 28 July 1853. p.117, c3.

**5578 REV. DR. J. PERKINS** *to* **PROFESSOR C. E. STOWE, D.D. 16 April 1853. Ooroomiah.** Encloses a letter from Chevalier N. Khanikoff to R. W. Stevens, and comments on the life of the former. 28 July 1853. p.117, c6.

**5579 CHEVALIER N. KHANIKOFF** *to* **R. W. STEVENS, ESQ. [extract] n.d. n.p.** Praises *Uncle Tom's Cabin* and discusses its reception in England and in France; requests an English or American edition of the work. 28 July 1853. p.117, c6.

**5580 CHRONICLE** *to* **n.n. [extract] n.d. n.p.** Protests amalgamation in New Orleans; speaks out against the development of black institutions such as schools and churches. 28 July 1853. p.117, c7.

**5581 CORRESPONDENT** *to* **THE** *CINCINNATI CHRISTIAN PRESS.* **[extract] n.d. n.p.** Describes a slave-holding Methodist class leader from Kentucky and warns against trusting such a fellow. 28 July 1853. p.118, c1.

**5582 TRAVELLING CORRESPONDENT** *to* **THE** *TRIBUNE.* **[extract] n.d. n.p.** Tells of finding a well-read copy of *Uncle Tom's Cabin* in the greenhouse during a visit to the farm and tomb of Daniel Webster at Marshfield. 28 July 1853. p.118, c1.

**5583 n.n.** *to* **n.n. [extract] n.d. n.p.** Informs the *Boston Commonwealth* through a New Bedford gentleman that he and his family are doing quite well in a suburb of Liverpool. 28 July 1853. p.118, c1.

**5584 THE SUFFOLK BAPTIST HOME MISSIONARY UNION** *to* **THE BAPTIST MINISTERS AND CHURCHES THROUGHOUT THE UNITED STATES OF AMERICA. 9 June 1853. Botesdale, Suffolk, England.** Pleads for the elimination of slavery, warning against slavery's effect upon master and servant and deploring its widespread practice by church members. 28 July 1853. p.118, c2.

**5585 KENT AND SUSSEX ASSOCIATION OF BAPTIST CHURCHES** *to* **THE AMERICAN BAPTIST FREE MISSION SOCIETY. n.d. n.p.** Pleads for the abolition of slavery in the United States; condemns the actions of the slaveholding churches. 28 July 1853. p.118, c2.

**5586 CORRESPONDENT** *to* **THE** *NEW YORK ORGAN.* **n.d. n.p.** Describes the efforts of the ladies of Leoni and other Michigan towns, which resulted in the passage of a Maine [Liquor] Law in that state. 28 July 1853. p.118, c3.

**5587 CORRESPONDENT** *to* **THE** *BOSTON BEE.* **n.d. n.p.** Describes a railroad safety car with ejection seats designed to remove passengers from the cars in the event of a disaster. 28 July 1853. p.120, c1.

**5588 YEOMAN** *to* **THE** *NEW YORK TIMES.* **n.d. n.p.** Refutes the view aired in Hunt's *Merchant's Magazine* that "slavery is the (only) true, speedy, and successful method for civilizing and christianizing the heathen!" 4 August 1853. p.121, c1.

**5589 FREDERICK DOUGLASS, J. M. WHITFIELD, H. O. WAGNER, REV. A. N. FREEMAN, AND GEORGE B. VASHON** *to* **THE PEOPLE OF THE UNITED STATES. n.d. n.p.** Report on a convention of free colored citizens which met to inquire into the general condition of the colored people and seek to aid their improvement and education. 4 August 1853. p.121, c4.

**5590 LONDON CORRESPONDENT** *to* **THE** *NEW YORK TRIBUNE.* **[extract] n.d. n.p.** Tells of an interview in which Thackeray praised America; compares Thackeray's view of slavery with that of Mrs. Stowe. 4 August 1853. p.122, c4.

**5591 CORRESPONDENT** *to* **THE** *PORTLAND* **(ME.)** *INQUIRER.* **[extract] n.d. n.p.** Commends the anti-slavery lectures of Rev. J. W. Loguen, a fugitive slave involved in the Jerry Rescue incident. 4 August 1853. p.122, c5.

**5592 S. S.** *to* **FRIEND BURLEIGH. 26 July 1853. Bristol.** Informs Burleigh of a number of reform meetings occuring in town, including Van Wagner speaking against rum, Lucretia Mott speaking on Christ, and Sojourner Truth speaking against slavery. 4 August 1853. p.122, c5.

**5593 DR. BAILEY** *to* **THE** *NATIONAL ERA.* **[extract] n.d. London.** Tells of the success of *Uncle Tom's Cabin* and *The Wide, Wide World,* two American works sweeping Europe; suggests that Stowe's work has won favor for American literature in general. 4 August 1853. p.123, c3.

**5594 A FRIEND** *to* **THE** *BUGLE.* **n.d. Linesville, Crawford County, Pa.** Reports on a visit by J. F. Selby; tells of the good he is doing for the cause; informs of the success of the anti-slavery movement in the region. 4 August 1853. p.123, c4.

**5595 PETER GORDON** *to* **n.n. [extract from the** *London Anti-Slavery Advocate***] n.d. n.p.** Tells of the unfair practices of the East India Company; protests the serfdom imposed upon the Indians. 11 August 1853. p.125, c1.

**5596 GLASGOW FEMALE AS** *to* **HARRIET BEECHER STOWE. 14 April 1853. Glasgow.** Welcomes Stowe to Scotland; thanks her for *Uncle Tom's Cabin*; tells her of their desire to see all anti-slavery efforts united; promises to keep up their efforts until universal emancipation is achieved. 11 August 1853. p.125, c7.

**5597 HARRIET BEECHER STOWE** *to* **THE COMMITTEE OF THE GLASGOW FEMALE AS. 17 April 1853. Glasgow.** Thanks the society for its letter of 14 April; regrets she cannot meet with them; hopes they will continue their fine work. 11 August 1853. p.125, c7.

**5598 FRANKLIN** *to* **THE** *NEW YORK EVENING POST.* **22 July 1853. Cleveland.** Reports on Giddings's efforts at uniting the anti-slavery Whigs and the Free-Soilers; informs that the anti-slavery Whigs will likely join with the Democrats; tells of various issues which will come out of the upcoming election campaigns. 11 August 1853. p.126, c3.

**5599 CORRESPONDENT** *to* **THE** *NEW YORK DAILY TIMES.* **7 July 1853. Havana, Cuba.** Reports on the illegal activities of slave traders and American vessels operating between Cuba and Sierra Leone. 11 August 1853. p.126, c6.

**5600 MAZZINI** *to* **n.n. [extract] n.d. n.p.** Praises the work of Mott, Garrison and other abolitionists; compares his efforts at eliminating white slavery to the abolitionists' goal of eliminating black slavery. 11 August 1853. p.127, c2.

**5601 A FUGITIVE** *to* **THE EDITOR OF THE** *NEW YORK TRIBUNE.* **n.d. n.p.** Describes an incident in which a runaway slave was beheaded and no action was taken against the murderers; notes that the slave was owned by a New York merchant. 18 August 1853. p.129, c4.

**5602 NEW YORK CORRESPONDENT** *to* **THE** *DAILY REGISTER.* **n.d. n.p.** Informs of a rumor circulating that the theatergoers at the National Theater will tar and feather any slave catchers they might find. 18 August 1853. p.130, c2.

**5603 n.n.** *to* **THE EDITOR OF THE** ***PENNSYLVANIA FREEMAN*** **[C. M. BURLEIGH]. n.d. n.p.** Corrects a New Orleans correspondent of a Natchez journal on several facts; defends the late Bishop Allen against allegations made in this article. 18 August 1853. p.130, c5.

**5604 CORRESPONDENT** *to* **THE** ***NEW YORK TIMES.*** **n.d. Burlington, Vt.** Reports on the effectiveness of the Maine [Liquor] Law. 18 August 1853. p.131, c2.

**5605 R. T. BROWN** *to* **GOVERNOR WRIGHT. n.d. Crawfordsville, In.** Encloses samples of flax cotton and discusses H. L. Ellsworth's success in producing this cotton. 18 August 1853. p.132, c4.

**5606 THOMAS JEFFERSON** *to* **DR. PRICE. 7 August 1785. Paris.** Informs Dr. Price of the reception which his ideas on the abolition of slavery would be likely to receive in the various parts of America. 25 August 1853. p.134, c3.

**5607 A.** *to* **MR. EDITOR [C. M. BURLEIGH]. 14 August 1853. Chester County, Pa.** Reports on a convention of lyceums held in Chester County on 13 August; describes the activities and the people of this convention; praises the efforts of the lyceums. 25 August 1853. p.135, c2.

**5608 n.n.** *to* **n.n. [extract from the** *Western Christian Advocate***] n.d. n.p.** Reports additional information on the case of Freeman; details his identification of one Mr. Patillo from Monroe, Georgia, and Patillo's recognition of Freeman. 1 September 1853. p.318 [138], c1.

**5609 CORRESPONDENT** *to* **THE** ***TRIBUNE.*** **n.d. Indianapolis.** Expresses opposition to the Fugitive Slave Law; feels confident that Freeman will be acquitted. 1 September 1853. p.139, c3.

**5610 CORRESPONDENT** *to* **THE** ***SCIENTIFIC AMERICAN.*** **n.d. n.p.** Reports on the success of the steamboat law in reducing casualties in accidents; recommends similar measures for the railroad industry. 1 September 1853. p.139, c4.

**5611 SOUTHERN CORRESPONDENT** *to* **THE** ***NEW YORK DAILY TIMES.*** **n.d. n.p.** Describes how the task system reduces slaves' productivity; compares systems of labor in North and South, criticizing the misapplication and waste of labor in the South. 8 September 1853. p.141, c1.

**5612 NEW YORK CORRESPONDENT** *to* **THE** ***NATIONAL ERA.*** **[extract] n.d. n.p.** Notes the stir caused in New York by the staging of the Drama of Uncle Tom. 8 September 1853. p.141, c4.

**5613 WILLIAM WHITEHEAD** *to* **SIR. 24 August 1833. West Chester.** Informs of the controversy in his area regarding African colonization; criticizes the rude manner of Pease and those in favor of colonization. 8 September 1853. p.141, c5.

**5614 A. CAMBERTON** *to* **MR. EDITOR [C. M. BURLEIGH]. 26 August 1853. n.p.** Expresses his views on the debates inspired by Rev. Pease concerning African colonization; mentions the impressions made by Whitehead and Pugh in speaking against colonization. 8 September 1853. p.141, c6.

**5615 n.n.** *to* **SIR. 19 June 1853. Pine Woods, Randolph County, Ga.** Relates first-hand experiences with slavery which prove the veracity of "The Key to Uncle Tom's Cabin." 8 September 1853. p.141, c7.

**5616 JAMES BIRNEY** *to* **THE EDITORS. [from a Cincinnati paper] 18 August 1853. Cincinnati.** Criticizes the decision of Judge McLean in a fugitive slave case; argues that McLean failed to consider all the evidence before reaching his decision. 8 September 1853. p.142, c1.

**5617 NEAL DOW** *to* **SIR. 26 August 1853. Portland.** Declines to attend the World's Temperance Convention, due to his recent travels and desire to be with his family. 8 September 1853. p.142, c5.

**5618 HON. S. P. CHASE** *to* **R. T. TRALL, C. B. LE BARON, &C. 28 August 1853. Steubenville, Oh.** Regrets he cannot attend the World's Temperance Convention. 8 September 1853. p.142, c5.

**5619 HORACE MANN** *to* **REV. T. W. HIGGINSON. 21 May 1853. West Newton, Ma.** Regrets that he is unable to attend the World's Temperance Convention. 8 September 1853. p.142, c5.

**5620 JAMES RUSSELL LOWELL** *to* **SIR. 31 August 1853. Cambridge, Ma.** Regrets that he is unable to attend the World's Temperance Convention. 8 September 1853. p.142, c5.

**5621 JAMES HAUGHTON** *to* **SIR. [extract] n.d. Dublin.** Wishes he could send a delegation from Ireland to the World's Temperance Convention; tells of Mrs. Carlisle, an aged woman who travels through England and Ireland lecturing on teetotalism. 8 September 1853. p.142, c5.

**5622 C. M. B.** *to* **THE** ***PENNSYLVANIA FREEMAN.*** **5 September 1853. New York.** Praises the World's Temperance Convention; considers it a rousing success. 8 September 1853. p.143, c2.

**5623 G. W. SIMONDS** *to* **THE EDITOR OF THE** ***FREEMAN*** **[C. M. BURLEIGH]. 19 August 1853. East Lexington, Ma.** Reveals that Thackeray's new novel, *Henry Esmond,* which was written during his United States visit, ends with the hero's becoming a Virginia slaveholder. 8 September 1853. p.143, c5.

**5624 n.n.** *to* **n.n. [extract from the** ***American Baptist*****] n.d. Racine, Wi.** Describes how a man tried to kidnap a woman he claimed as his property; tells of the efforts of the townspeople to resist. 15 September 1853. p.145, c1.

**5625 SITRUCCIO** *to* **MR. EDITOR [C. M. BURLEIGH]. n.d. n.p.** An Englishman describes his shock at finding segregation in America; calls for a new breed of citizen who will rise up to defend freedom everywhere. 15 September 1853. p.145, c2.

**5626 JOHN B[E]LTON O'NEALL** *to* **THE EDITOR OF THE** ***NEW YORK TRIBUNE.*** **23 July 1853. Springfield, S.C.** Corrects several statements in Mrs. Stowe's "Key to Uncle Tom's Cabin"; believes that the South will reform itself if let alone. 15 September 1853. p.145, c3.

**5627 DANIEL DEVINNE** *to* **THE EDITOR OF THE** ***NEW YORK TRIBUNE.*** **16 August 1853. Newtown, L.I.** Responds to Judge O'Neall's letter to the *Tribune*; states that Mrs. Stowe underestimated the sufferings of the slave in her "Key." 15 September 1853. p.145, c4.

**5628 JOSEPH TREAT** *to* **MARIUS. [from the** ***Anti-Slavery Bugle*****] 13 August 1853. n.p.** Relates how he came to despise slavery; describes the escape of a mother and child from Kentucky into Canada. 15 September 1853. p.145, c5.

**5629 T. S.** *to* **THE** *NEW YORK TRIBUNE.* **3 September 1853. Wilkesbarre.** Describes the attempted kidnapping of a mulatto, Bill, at Wilkesbarre; deplores those who uphold the Fugitive Slave Law. 15 September 1853. p.145, c6.

**5630 FRANKLIN** *to* **THE** *NEW YORK EVENING POST.* **1 September 1853. Columbus.** Gives an account of the efficiency of the Underground Railroad; tells of the kindness of the people of Ohio toward the fugitives. 15 September 1853. p.145, c7.

**5631 MRS. J. S. GRIFFING** *to* **THE** *BUGLE.* **n.d. n.p.** Tells of her dinner with Mr. H---, a former slaveholder who is now an active anti-slavery man; relates a story of his regarding a violent Southern minister who whipped a female slave to death. 15 September 1853. p.146, c2.

**5632 CORRESPONDENT** *to* **THE EDITOR OF THE** *GREEN MOUNTAIN FREEMAN.* **n.d. n.p.** Informs of the recent successful speaking tour of Lucy Stone. 15 September 1853. p.147, c2.

**5633 NEW YORK CORRESPONDENT** *to* **THE** *NATIONAL ERA.* **[extract] n.d. n.p.** States that there are no discriminatory practices at Crystal Palace in New York regarding the privileges of admission or exhibition. 22 September 1853. p.149, c2.

**5634 n.n.** *to* **n.n. 24 August 1853. Niagara Falls.** Tells of the capture of a fugitive slave charged with murder in Savannah, Georgia. 22 September 1853. p.149, c2.

**5635 WENDELL PHILLIPS** *to* **NEAL DOW. 12 September 1853. n.p.** Attacks Dow and the behavior and attitudes of those involved with the World's Temperance Convention. 22 September 1853. p.150, c1.

**5636 JOHN G. FEE** *to* **FRIEND GREELEY. 5 September 1853. Glenville, Lewis County, Ky.** Describes the upright character of C. M. Clay. 22 September 1853. p.150, c3.

**5637 PASSMORE WILLIAMSON** *to* **THE** *PENNSYLVANIA FREEMAN.* **19 September 1853. Philadelphia.** Warns of a black female swindler in Philadelphia who preys on the sympathies of anti-slavery supporters. 22 September 1853. p.151, c1.

**5638 n.n.** *to* **THE EDITOR OF THE** *ANTI-SLAVERY BUGLE.* **29 August 1853. Indianapolis.** Details the events of Freeman's release from jail after the dismissal of charges against him. 22 September 1853. p.151, c3.

**5639 C. D. C.** *to* **THE EDITOR OF THE** *NEW YORK TRIBUNE.* **n.d. n.p.** Condemns publishers who remove anti-slavery passages from readers destined for use by Southern children, citing one such volume advertised as the work of Dr. Porter. 29 September 1853. p.153, c2.

**5640 JAMES M'CUNE SMITH** *to* **THE EDITOR OF THE** *NEW YORK TRIBUNE.* **8 September 1853. New York.** Protests his exclusion on false grounds from the World's Temperance Convention. 29 September 1853. p.153, c5.

**5641 WENDELL PHILLIPS** *to* **NEAL DOW. 7 September 1853. New York.** Protests the voting procedures involved in a motion to allow Miss Antoinette L. Brown to speak before the World's Temperance Convention. 29 September 1853. p.153, c5.

**5642 PETER GORDON** *to* **THE EDITOR OF THE** *ANTI-SLAVERY ADVOCATE.* **[extract] 8 August 1853. Nantes, France.** Reports on the dissolution of the East India Company in 1852; informs that slavery still might exist in India under the sovereign's rule, citing the complex character of the slave emancipation laws. 29 September 1853. p.154, c1.

**5643 SOUTHERN CORRESPONDENT OF A NORTHERN NEWSPAPER** *to* **n.n. n.d. n.p.** Describes the iron collar worn by a slave boy of a Presbyterian elder in Louisville, Kentucky; tells of his slaves' lack of "moral or mental culture." 29 September 1853. p.154, c3.

**5644 JOHN A. DIX** *to* **DR. I. P. GARVIN. 31 August 1853. New York.** Denies being an abolitionist; declares his support of the Fugitive Slave Law, as well as the Compromise and the Baltimore platform. 29 September 1853. p.154, c5.

**5645 H. W. G.** *to* **n.n. 27 August 1853. Zurich.** Describes his travels in Venice and Switzerland. 29 September 1853. p.155, c1.

**5646 ROBERT PURVIS** *to* **GARRISON. 22 August 1853. Byberry, Philadelphia County.** Defends himself against an article in *Frederick Douglass' Paper.* 29 September 1853. p.155, c4.

**5647 NEW YORK CORRESPONDENT** *to* **THE** *LEDGER.* **[extract] n.d. n.p.** States that the citizens of New York look upon the World's Temperance Convention as an outrage. 29 September 1853. p.155, c5.

**5648 F. W. CHESSON** *to* **THE EDITOR OF THE (***LONDON***)** *LEADER.* **n.d. n.p.** Criticizes "Ion" for his scathing review of Wendell Phillips's speech. 6 October 1853. p.157, c5.

**5649 W. C. N.** *to* **n.n. September 1853. n.p.** Encloses extracts from a letter from Amy Post. 6 October 1853. p.158, c2.

**5650 AMY POST** *to* **W. C. N. [extract] n.d. Rochester.** Tells of a black family she helped en route to Canada. 6 October 1853. p.158, c2.

**5651 CORRESPONDENT** *to* **THE** *NEW YORK EVENING POST.* **n.d. Cincinnati.** Details the lack of success of the slave catchers in Cincinnati, who recently became emboldened by a ruling of Judge McLean concerning a fugitive slave. 6 October 1853. p.158, c2.

**5652 n.n.** *to* **n.n. 15 September 1853. St. Johns, N.B.** Telegraphic dispatch informs of the sod-turning ceremony for the European and North American Railroad. 6 October 1853. p.158, c3.

**5653 REV. J. S. GREEN** *to* **THE** *CHRISTIAN PRESS.* **[extract] n.d. n.p.** Opposes annexation of the Sandwich Islands; fears for the natives, who risk being reduced to bondage. 6 October 1853. p.158, c6.

**5654 PARKER PILLSBURY** *to* **THE** *LIBERATOR.* **[extract] n.d. Ohio.** Criticizes the petty bigotry invading the Free-Soil Party; fears this will cause the self-destruction of true humanitarian reform. 6 October 1853. p.158, c7.

**5655 F. W. CHESSON** *to* **THE** *WESLEYAN.* **[extract] n.d. n.p.** Mocks Campbell's belief that the true purpose of abolitionism is to overthrow Christianity; observes that the newest target of Campbell's spite is temperance reform. 6 October 1853. p.159, c1.

**5656 JOHN G. FEE** *to* **THE** *NEW YORK TRIBUNE.* **4 October 1853. Cabin Creek, Lewis County, Ky.** Corrects a statement by C. M. Clay, informing that A. G. W. Parker worked for the American Missionary Association, an anti-slavery group. 13 October 1853. p.163, c3.

**5657 SALLIE HOLLEY** *to* **FRANCIS JACKSON. 17 September 1853. Jonesville, Mi.** Reports on the anti-slavery and women's rights activities of herself and others. 13 October 1853. p.163, c4.

**5658 W. E. HERRENDON** *to* **JOHN LAWRENCE. n.d. Glenville, Va.** Explains to Lawrence, editor of the *Religious Telescope,* that his paper has been destroyed due to his abolitionist sympathies, in accordance with the Virginia state statutes, and that a copy of the paper has been retained and will be presented to the next grand jury. 13 October 1853. p.164, c1.

**5659 HENRY WARD BEECHER** *to* **THE** *INDEPENDENT.* **n.d. n.p.** Describes a walk to the mountains in the Taconic range. 13 October 1853. p.164, c2.

**5660 LOOKER ON IN BALTIMORE, A BOSTON CORRESPONDENT** *to* **THE EDITOR OF THE (***BOSTON***)** *COMMONWEALTH.* **18 September 1853. Baltimore.** Details the life and death of Hope H. Slatter, a slave trader. 20 October 1853. p.165, c4.

**5661 CORRESPONDENT** *to* **THE** *NEW YORK TRIBUNE.* **[extract] 26 September 1853. Havana.** Informs of the vast numbers of slaves brought into or near Trinidad de Cuba; asserts that officials knew these slaves were being landed. 20 October 1853. p.165, c7.

**5662 HENRY MILES** *to* **ESTEEMED FRIEND. 2 September 1853. Monkton, Vt.** Proposes an American Free Produce Association to boycott and counter the sale of slave-grown cotton; hopes to be able to supply free-labor cotton at comparable costs. 20 October 1853. p.166, c7.

**5663 JACOB WESTON** *to* **AN EMANCIPATED SLAVE OF SOUTH CAROLINA. 26 May 1853. Charleston.** Responds to her letter asking why her slave husband had remarried; condones the remarriage of separated slaves, and gives her permission to do the same. 20 October 1853. p.167, c1.

**5664 n.n.** *to* **n.n. [extract from the** *New York Evening Post***] n.d. n.p.** Telegraphic dispatch compares Judge Grier to Judge Jeffreys, a tyrannical magistrate serving James II. 20 October 1853. p.167, c2.

**5665 J. R. GIDDINGS** *to* **JAMES FULLER, M.D. 22 September 1853. Jefferson, Oh.** Proclaims his hatred of the Fugitive Slave Law; calls upon others to voice their contempt for the law. 20 October 1853. p.167, c3.

**5666 CORRESPONDENT** *to* **THE** *NEW YORK INDEPENDENT.* **[extract] n.d. n.p.** Tells of the apparently harmonious annual meeting of the American Board of Commissioners for Foreign Missions. 20 October 1853. p.167, c3.

**5667 JOSEPH BARKER** *to* **FRIEND. 13 October 1853. Salem.** Asks that his *Freeman* subscription be sent to his home address; informs of the Women's Rights National Convention held in Cleveland. 20 October 1853. p.167, c5.

**5668 n.n.** *to* **n.n. [extract from the** *New Orleans Christian Advocate***] n.d. n.p.** Tells of an overseer's desire to bring missionaries in to preach to the slaves. 20 October 1853. p.167, c5.

**5669 CORRESPONDENT** *to* **THE** *HOME JOURNAL.* **n.d. Rome.** Informs of the progress of Miss Hosiner, a Bostonian studying sculpture in Rome. 20 October 1853. p.168, c4.

**5670 A NEW ORLEANS PHYSICIAN** *to* **THE** *BOSTON MEDICAL JOURNAL.* **n.d. New Orleans.** Speculates that the wave of yellow fever spreading in New Orleans is the result of intemperance. 20 October 1853. p.168, c4.

**5671 JAMES HAUGHTON** *to* **THE EDITOR OF SAUNDERS'** *DUBLIN NEWS LETTER.* **6 September 1853. 33 Eccles Street.** Attacks a letter from a Virginian which claimed that America is a land of "civil and religious rights"; exposes the hypocrisy of the statement. 27 October 1853. p.169, c3.

**5672 JOHN R. NEILL** *to* **THE EDITOR OF THE** *LIBERATOR.* **[extract] 6 September 1853. Belfast, Ireland.** Relates the visit of J. Miller McKim to his house; praises McKim and his supporters. 27 October 1853. p.171, c4.

**5673 INDIANA CONGREGATIONAL CLERGYMAN** *to* **n.n. [extract from the** ***Hartford Republican*****] n.d. n.p.** Reports on the condemnation of the Fugitive Slave Law by the North Indiana Conference. 4 November 1853. p.173, c2.

**5674 MATTHEW S. CLAPP** *to* **H. M. ADDISON. 21 September 1853. Mentor.** Writes to voice his support of an anti-slavery convention of the Campbellite Church. 4 November 1853. p.173, c2.

**5675 SOUTHERN CORRESPONDENT** *to* **THE** *NEW YORK TIMES.* **[extract] n.d. n.p.** Relates his conversation with a Louisiana slave. 4 November 1853. p.173, c3.

**5676 JAMES HAUGHTON** *to* **MY COUNTRYMEN. n.d. n.p.** Relays the message of McKim to his fellow countrymen, calling on them to come to the aid of colored men by convincing those Irish men and women in America to support emancipation. 4 November 1853. p.173, c7.

**5677 CHIEF JUSTICE HORNBLOWER** *to* **THE FREE DEMOCRATIC MEETING IN NEW YORK. [extract] n.d. n.p.** Condemns the Fugitive Slave Law as oppressive and contrary to the common law of the land. 4 November 1853. p.175, c5.

**5678 DR. B. FRANKLIN** *to* **MISS HUBBARD. n.d. n.p.** Discusses death as birth into immortal life. 4 November 1853. p.176, c3.

**5679 BAYARD TAYLOR** *to* **THE** *TRIBUNE.* **[extract] n.d. n.p.** Expresses his eagerness to return to America from his expedition to China and Japan. 4 November 1853. p.176, c4.

**5680 CORRESPONDENT** *to* **THE** *NEW YORK TRIBUNE.* **24 October 1853. Adrian, Mi.** Reports on the state anti-slavery convention. 10 November 1853. p.177, c5.

**5681 HAVANA CORRESPONDENT** *to* **THE** *NEW YORK JOURNAL OF COMMERCE.* **n.d. n.p.** Informs of a Negro who was born of free parents in Charleston, South Carolina, but was kept in bondage for thirty years. 10 November 1853. p.177, c5.

**5682 n.n.** *to* **n.n. n.d. n.p.** A Presbyterian clergyman explains how slaves are educated and cared for by members of his church. 10 November 1853. p.178, c4.

**5683 ROBERT PURVIS** *to* **FRIEND BURLEIGH. 5 November 1853. Byberry.** Encloses a letter he drafted to the collector of taxes after seeing many of his rights denied. 10 November 1853. p.179, c1.

**5684 ROBERT PURVIS** *to* **JOSEPH J. BUTCHER. 4 November 1853. Byberry.** Refuses to pay the school tax because his children were denied admission to the town's schools. 10 November 1853. p.179, c1.

**5685 CORRESPONDENT** *to* *FREDERICK DOUGLASS' PAPER.* **n.d. n.p.** Informs that many of the Bourbon heirs are of African ancestry, due to a liaison between Comte Charles D'Artois, later Charles X, and a quadroon. 10 November 1853. p.180, c4.

**5686 C. CUSHING** *to* **HON. R. FROTHINGHAM, JR. 29 October 1853. Washington.** Attacks certain Democrats for uniting with the Free-Soilers in Massachusetts; warns against being threatened by the abolitionists. 17 November 1853. p.181, c1.

**5687 PARKER PILLSBURY** *to* **THE** ***LIBERATOR.*** **n.d. Ohio.** Tells of the controversy over the Maine Liquor Law and its effect on Maine elections; sees whiskey manufacture as a drawback to the spreading of temperance; denies that the Fugitive Slave Law was intended by its designers to promote the recapture of runaway slaves. 17 November 1853. p.181, c6.

**5688 CHARLES FRANCIS ADAMS** *to* **n.n. [extract] n.d. n.p.** Replies to an invitation to attend a Free Democratic meeting in New York; explains how thinking men must soon come to act. 17 November 1853. p.181, c7.

**5689 W. WELLS BROWN** *to* **REV. S. MAY, JR. [extract] 3 October 1853. London.** Describes the recent events concerning his family; sends his regards to his "old coadjutators." 17 November 1853. p.182, c7.

**5690 HENRY GREW** *to* **THE EDITOR OF THE** ***PENNSYLVANIA FREEMAN*** **[C. M. BURLEIGH]. n.d. n.p.** Responds to several remarks made against his resolution on the use of slave products at the anniversary meeting; defends free labor as more profitable than slave labor, but adds that there would be a financial loss to the slave owner if the slaves were emancipated. 17 November 1853. p.183, c2.

**5691 CORRESPONDENT** *to* **THE** ***TRIBUNE.*** **n.d. Grass Valley, Ca.** Informs of the rapid spread of temperance through California; states that several Maine Law advocates have been elected to the state legislature. 17 November 1853. p.183, c4.

**5692 HENRY GREW** *to* **THE EDITOR OF THE** ***PENNSYLVANIA FREEMAN*** **[C. M. BURLEIGH]. n.d. n.p.** Disagrees with published remarks by McKim concerning Garrison; believes certain aspects of Garrison's doctrine are of a principle which is "skeptical and infidel." 17 November 1853. p.183, c5.

**5693 n.n.** *to* **n.n. [extract from the** ***New York Tribune*****] n.d. n.p.** Tells of the admission of colored children to the public schools of Nantucket. 24 November 1853. p.185, c2.

**5694 CORRESPONDENT** *to* **THE EDITORS OF THE** ***OHIO COLUMBIAN.*** **n.d. n.p.** Relates the history of an emancipated slave, James Edwards, including his seizure and confinement under the Fugitive Slave Law; calls upon the government to come to his aid as it came to the aid of the slaveowners in the Shadrach case. 24 November 1853. p.185, c5.

**5695 EDWARD MATHEWS** *to* **n.n. 30 September 1853. Bristol, England.** Corrects statements made by Professor Stowe regarding slavery and the Congregational Church; states that Congregationalists not only condone slavery, but they hold slaves as well. 24 November 1853. p.185, c5.

**5696 CORRESPONDENT** *to* **THE** ***NEW YORK TRIBUNE.*** **11 November 1853. New Albany, In.** Describes the impact of Lucy Stone's lectures on the people of the town. 24 November 1853. p.185, c6.

**5697 MINTHORNE TOMPKINS** *to* **THE** ***EVENING POST.*** **n.d. n.p.** Attacks John Van Buren for his criticism of Tompkins and the Free-Soil Party; wonders if Van Buren assumes that the Fugitive Slave Law deprives citizens of New York of freedom of speech. 24 November 1853. p.186, c5.

**5698 C. CUSHING** *to* **PRESIDENT PIERCE. 14 November 1853. Washington.** Delivers a legal opinion that the suit brought by Freeman against Marshall Ellington cannot be taken to a United States court, but must be heard in Indiana, and that the government may supply counsel for Ellington; defines more clearly the administration of the Fugitive Slave Law. 1 December 1853. p.189, c5.

**5699 CORRESPONDENT** *to* **THE** *NEW YORK EVANGELIST.* **[extract] n.d. n.p.** Encloses resolutions adopted by the New School Presbyterian Synod at Albany condemning the Fugitive Slave Law. 1 December 1853. p.190, c4.

**5700 H. W. G.** *to* **THE** *PENNSYLVANIA FREEMAN.* **9 October 1853. Heidelberg, Germany.** Describes his travels through Switzerland. 1 December 1853. p.190, c6.

**5701 FRENCH CONSUL OF BUCHAREST** *to* **M. DE BOURQUENAY. 18 November 1853. Bucharest.** Details the Turkish invasion and the gradual Russian retreat. 1 December 1853. p.191, c5.

**5702 HENRY FITZROY** *to* **n.n. 19 October 1853. Whitehall.** Comments upon the causes of cholera, and explains how it can be stopped. 1 December 1853. p.192, c1.

**5703 REV. JOHN G. FEE** *to* **n.n. [extract from the** *Christian Press***] 14 November 1853. Bethesda Ch., Bracken County, Ky.** Relates how a free black was jailed when incriminated by a drunken white man. 8 December 1853. p.193, c2.

**5704 GERRIT SMITH** *to* **GARRISON, QUINCY, PHILLIPS, AND GAY. 13 November 1853. Peterboro'.** Declines to attend the twentieth anniversary of the AAS due to poor health. 8 December 1853. p.194, c2.

**5705 REV. E. H. CHAPMAN** *to* **W. L. GARRISON, WENDELL PHILLIPS, EDMUND QUINCY, AND S. H. GAY. 24 November 1853. New York.** Expresses sympathy with the cause; declines to attend the twentieth anniversary of the AAS due to previous engagements. 8 December 1853. p.194, c2.

**5706 CASSIUS M. CLAY** *to* **WM. LLOYD GARRISON, PRESIDENT; WN. PHILLIPS, E. QUINCY, S. H. GAY, SECRETARIES. 21 November 1853. Cincinnati, Oh.** Expresses his support of the AAS on its twentieth anniversary. 8 December 1853. p.194, c2.

**5707 HON. GEORGE W. JULIAN** *to* **WM. LLOYD GARRISON. 20 November 1853. Centerville, In.** Explains why he will not be able to attend the twentieth anniversary of the AAS. 8 December 1853. p.194, c3.

**5708 HENRY C. HOWELLS** *to* **MY BELOVED FRIENDS IN THE CAUSE OF UNIVERSAL RIGHTEOUS FREEDOM. 28 November 1853. Rosedale, near Allegheny, Pa.** Praises the efforts of the AAS; regrets that he cannot attend its twentieth anniversary. 8 December 1853. p.194, c3.

**5709 n.n.** *to* **n.n. [extract from the** *Cincinnati Christian Press***] n.d. Locust Grove, Adams County, Oh.** Details the seizure of alleged runaway slaves by five ruffians. 8 December 1853. p.195, c6.

**5710 C. C.** *to* **THE** *FREEMAN.* **28 November 1853. Wilmington, De.** Corrects the *Louisville Democrat* on the subject of a watch which was found and assumed to be over 400 years old; explains the 1431 was its serial number, and not the year in which it was manufactured. 8 December 1853. p.195, c6.

5711 **CORRESPONDENT** *to* **THE** ***INQUIRER*****. n.d. San Francisco.** Gives an account of a new race of people discovered in a fertile oasis in the heart of the Great Desert. 8 December 1853. p.196, c2.

5712 **BROOKLYN CORRESPONDENT** *to* **THE** ***TRIBUNE*****. [extract] n.d. n.p.** Relates the story of a stranded Jamaican servant who was refused a ride to her boat because of her color. 15 December 1853. p.197, c4.

5713 **LORD HOWDEN** *to* **F. P. CORBIN. 14 November 1853. Paris.** Describes to Corbin his efforts toward ending slavery in Cuba. 15 December 1853. p.197, c5.

5714 **MELANCTHON** *to* **THE** ***NEW YORK INDEPENDENT*****. [extract] n.d. n.p.** Condemns the corruption of the clergy; calls on lay persons to take a stand against slavery. 15 December 1853. p.198, c1.

5715 **HENRY GREW** *to* **THE EDITOR OF THE** ***PENNSYLVANIA FREEMAN*** **[C. M. BURLEIGH]. n.d. n.p.** Corrects an interpretation of his remarks which appeared in the previous issue of the *Freeman*. 15 December 1853. p.199, c6.

5716 **G.** *to* **THE** ***NEW YORK TRIBUNE*****. 10 December 1853. Washington.** Hypothesizes about a shift in Southern attitudes toward slavery; traces a growing liberality in beliefs. 22 December 1853. p.201, c1.

5717 **WILLIAM G. W. LEWIS** *to* **WENDELL PHILLIPS, EDMUND QUINCY, AND S. H. GAY. 29 November 1853. Cincinnati.** Answers an invitation to the Decennial Meeting of the AAS for his father, Samuel Lewis, who is ill and will not be present. 22 December 1853. p.201, c2.

5718 **T. W. HIGGINSON** *to* **WENDELL PHILLIPS, EDMUND QUINCY, AND S. H. GAY. 2 December 1853. Worcester, Ma.** Commends the anti-slavery movement, but declines an invitation to the twentieth anniversary of the AAS due to previous engagements. 22 December 1853. p.201, c2.

5719 **LUCY STONE** *to* **THE GENERAL AGENT OF THE MASSACHUSETTS AS. [extract] 18 November 1853. Louisville, Ky.** Reports on her women's rights lectures in Kentucky; believes that emancipation would receive more support if the people were assured that the slaves would not be a burden to the state. 22 December 1853. p.201, c4.

5720 **J. M. McKIM** *to* **BURLEIGH. n.d. n.p.** Encloses several speeches given at the first meeting of the AAS in 1833. 22 December 1853. p.203, c1.

5721 **STEPHEN F. WEAKLY** *to* **n.n. 19 November 1853. Carlisle.** Informs that he has paid off Kauffman's judgment; tells how he raised the money. 22 December 1853. p.203, c3.

5722 **ANTI-SLAVERY CALVINIST MINISTER** *to* **THE EDITORS OF THE** ***PRESBYTERIAN WITNESS*****. n.d. n.p.** Attacks the Synod of New York and New Jersey (New School) for its views on religion and slavery. 29 December 1853. p.205, c1.

5723 **VELASCO** *to* **n.n. 8 December 1853. Havana.** Discusses the value of the sugar crop and the land in Cuba; describes the overworking of the slaves at harvest time. 29 December 1853. p.205, c3.

5724 **W. H. C.** *to* **THE** ***NEW YORK TRIBUNE*****. 20 December 1853. Washington.** Describes the speech of Gerrit Smith on the higher law and universal liberty; commends the sincerity of Mr. Preston of Kentucky. 29 December 1853. p.206, c2.

**5725 WASHINGTON CORRESPONDENT** *to* **THE** *TRIBUNE.* **n.d. Washington.** Commends Gerrit Smith for his performance in the House of Representatives regarding the Koszia affair. 29 December 1853. p.206, c2.

**5726 REV. EDWARD MATHEWS** *to* **THE** *AMERICAN BAPTIST.* **[extract] n.d. n.p.** Provides evidence of a revival of anti-slavery sentiments in England; encloses resolutions calling for an end to American slavery. 29 December 1853. p.206, c5.

## [1854]

**5727 W. L. GARRISON** *to* **ESTEEMED FRIEND. 30 November 1853. Boston.** Defends the *Liberator* against the charge that "it will take from poor Uncle Tom his Bible, and give him nothing in its place." 5 January 1854. p.1, c1.

**5728 n.n.** *to* **n.n. [extract from the** *Hartford Republican***] n.d. Princeton, Il.** Reports on a reward of $3,000 offered for thirteen fugitive slaves who could not be caught. 5 January 1854. p.1, c3.

**5729 GEORGE THOMPSON** *to* **n.n. [extract from the** *Anti-Slavery Standard***] n.d. Manchester.** Reports on his movements and the action of the anti-slavery party in Great Britain. 5 January 1854. p.1, c5.

**5730 WM. C. NELL** *to* **THE** *BOSTON COMMONWEALTH.* **n.d. n.p.** Informs that M. Jullien of the Music Hall apologized to the colored persons who were proscribed from his concerts and promised they would have the same facilities in the future as other ticket holders. 5 January 1854. p.1, c5.

**5731 JOSEPH BARKER** *to* **FRIEND. [from the** *Liberator***] 15 December 1853. Salem, Oh.** Sends a donation of ten dollars to prevent Daniel Kauffman from being "reduced to want." 5 January 1854. p.3, c1.

**5732 G. B. STEBBINS** *to* **FRIEND BURLEIGH. 26 December 1853. Phoenixville, Pa.** Reports on his anti-slavery work in Kennett Square and Wilmington; praises a speech by Rev. Antoinette L. Brown, "the first and only clergywoman in the world." 5 January 1854. p.3, c4.

**5733 G. B. STEBBINS** *to* **FRIEND BURLEIGH. 30 December 1853. Pottstown.** Reports on his anti-slavery lectures in Coventry and Lawrenceville. 5 January 1854. p.3, c5.

**5734 CORRESPONDENT** *to* **THE** *NEW YORK DAILY TIMES.* **22 December 1853. Havana.** Forwards translation of a notice published in an official paper which decrees "the superseding of the cause pending against Don Pantaleon L. Aillon." 12 January 1854. p.6, c3.

**5735 CORRESPONDENT** *to* **THE** *NEW YORK DAILY TIMES.* **12 December 1853. Havana.** Avers that Don Pantaleon L. Aillon is guilty of aiding the landing of the Bozal Negroes; condemns the African slave trade. 12 January 1854. p.6, c3.

**5736 MR. PRESTON** *to* **GERRIT SMITH. [extract from the** *Massachusetts Spy***] n.d. Kentucky.** Asserts that Southerners hold slaves because "we are not willing to amalgamate any more than the people of New York, with the negroes." 12 January 1854. p.6, c3.

**5737 G. B. STEBBINS** *to* **FRIEND BURLEIGH. 7 January 1854. Norristown.** Condemns the German Baptists for closing their doors to reform speakers; reports on anti-slavery meetings in Valley Forge and Penn's Square. 12 January 1854. p.7, c2.

**5738 JOHN SHEDDEN** *to* **THE EDITOR OF THE** *FREEMAN* **[C. M. BURLEIGH]. n.d. n.p.** Satirizes the hypocrisy of Alexander Campbell, who asserts that slavery is Christian, and believes his Christian mission to Africa will "enlighten its darkness." 12 January 1854. p.6, c3.

**5739 SAMUEL AARON** *to* **FRIEND. 8 January 1854. Norristown, Pa.** Encloses five-dollar donation for Messrs. Kauffman and Weakley. 17 January 1854. p.11, c1.

**5740 WM. WRIGHT** *to* **FRIEND. 10 January 1854. York Springs.** Denounces the slave laws and encloses twenty dollars for Kauffman and Weakley. 17 January 1854. p.11, c1.

**5741 JOSEPH BARKER** *to* **FRIEND. n.d. n.p.** Laments that John Mitchell, the Irish repealer and republican of 1848, is "in heart a tyrant, a despot, and a slaveholder." 17 January 1854. p.11, c3.

**5742 n.n.** *to* **THE** *NEW YORK INDEPENDENT.* **[extract] n.d. n.p.** An American missionary in Asia notes the inconsistency of Americans who donate Bibles to foreign missions yet deny them to their own slaves. 17 January 1854. p.11, c4.

**5743 CORRESPONDENT** *to* **THE** *TRIBUNE.* **n.d. Kingston, Jamaica.** Observes the material gains made by ex-slaves in Jamaica; relates his visit to a wealthy black man's home. 17 January 1854. p.11, c6.

**5744 n.n.** *to* **THE** *TRIBUNE.* **[extract] n.d. New Bedford.** Relates a tale of a fugitive slave who escaped to New Bedford; notes that the colored population in New Bedford is large and consists of many fugitive slaves. 26 January 1854. p.13, c5.

**5745 S.** *to* **THE EDITOR OF THE** *NEW YORK TRIBUNE.* **n.d. n.p.** Encloses an advertisement for the return of a stolen white servant girl, as a commentary on the American slave system. 26 January 1854. p.13, c6.

**5746 J. M. McKIM** *to* **n.n. 23 January 1854. n.p.** Announces Joseph Barker's pledge of $50, in the expectation that others will make up the balance of a fund of no less than $2,000. 26 January 1854. p.15, c5.

**5747 JOSEPH BARKER** *to* **FRIEND. 21 January 1854. n.p.** Raises his contribution for Stephen Weakley from ten to fifty dollars. 26 January 1854. p.15, c5.

**5748 LUCY STONE** *to* **MR. BIRNEY. n.d. n.p.** Protests the exclusion of colored people from her lecture on woman's rights. 26 January 1854. p.15, c5.

**5749 L. W. GAUSE** *to* **MR. EDITOR [C. M. BURLEIGH]. n.d. n.p.** Condemns merchants who purchase sugar, molasses and rice produced by slave labor in Cuba, yet call themselves abolitionists. 2 February 1854. p.17, c1.

**5750 CORRESPONDENT** *to* **THE** *TRIBUNE.* **[extract] n.d. Athens County, Oh.** Reports on the success of the Underground Railroad in Ohio. 2 February 1854. p.17, c2.

**5751 THE REPRESENTATIVES OF OHIO** *to* **FELLOW CITIZENS. 19 January 1854. Washington.** Entreat their constituents to oppose a new Nebraska Bill that proposes to open Nebraska to slavery. 2 February 1854. p.18, c3.

**5752 n.n.** *to* **C. M. BURLEIGH. 26 January 1854. n.p.** Queries whether the advertisement appearing in the 26 January *Freeman* regarding a celebration of Thomas Paine's birthday was actually paid for. 2 February 1854. p.18, c6.

**5753 E. E. ORVIS** *to* **MR. EDITOR [C. M. BURLEIGH]. n.d. n.p.** Defends Mr. Campbell's approval of the Fugitive Slave Bill and disapproval of the AAS. 2 February 1854. p.19, c2.

**5754 n.n.** *to* **n.n. n.d. Lancaster.** A farmer sends five dollars for the relief of Weakley. 2 February 1854. p.19, c5.

**5755 G. B. STEBBINS** *to* **FRIEND BURLEIGH. 28 January 1854. Philadelphia, Pa.** Reports that he has met with little "open opposition" during his anti-slavery tour through Pennsylvania. 2 February 1854. p.19, c5.

**5756 AN ARTIST** *to* **FRIEND BURLEIGH. n.d. n.p.** Corrects a typographical error referring to Miss E. M. Gove as Grover; praises Miss Gove's portrait of John P. Hale. 2 February 1854. p.19, c6.

**5757 YEOMAN** *to* **THE** *NEW YORK TIMES*. **n.d. n.p.** Observes the effect of slavery on various classes of Southern people. 9 February 1854. p.21, c1.

**5758 ALEXANDER HOLINSKI** *to* **JOHN MITCHEL. [from** *Le Republicain* **of New York]. n.d. n.p.** A Polish refugee reprimands Mitchel for refusing to condemn slavery. 9 February 1854. p.21, c4.

**5759 J. A. DUGDALE** *to* **CYRUS. 1 January 1854. Kennett.** Reports on the Quarterly Meeting of Progressive Friends; supports Weakley. 9 February 1854. p.23, c7.

**5760 JOHN MITCHEL** *to* **H. W. BEECHER. [extract] n.d. n.p.** Defends his support of slavery, citing Washington's and Jefferson's possession of slaves. 16 February 1854. p.25, c3.

**5761 HENRY WARD BEECHER** *to* **JOHN MITCHEL. [from the** *New York Independent*] **n.d. n.p.** Replies to John Mitchel's arguments in favor of slavery, accusing him of taking "an amateur survey of Moses and the prophets." 16 February 1854. p.25, c4.

**5762 CORRESPONDENT** *to* **THE** *TRIBUNE*. **n.d. n.p.** Reports on enthusiasm manifested at an anti-slavery meeting addressed by Rev. H. W. Beecher, Dr. Edward Beecher, Mr. and Mrs. Stowe, and others. 16 February 1854. p.27, c2.

**5763 THE VOICE OF MANY** *to* **THE EDITOR OF THE** *FREEMAN* **[C. M. BURLEIGH]. 16 January 1854. Wilmington, De.** Reports on the Delaware State CS meeting, where Rev. Bishop Scott spoke to colored citizens about Liberia. 16 February 1854. p.27, c6.

**5764 L.** *to* **THE** *FREEMAN*. **n.d. n.p.** Encloses a prayer of Emperor Joseph, in the hope of enlightening readers about the dangers of intolerance. 16 February 1854. p.28, c2.

**5765 TAZEWELL TAYLOR, M. COOKE, H. WOODIS, WM. G. DUNBAR, SIMON S. STUBBS, WM. T. HENDREN, JOHN S. LOVETT, AND P. P. MAYO** *to* **RICHARD H. BAKER. 10 January 1854. n.p.** Enclose a copy of the judgment in a case in which a woman was imprisoned for teaching slaves to read. 23 February 1854. p.29, c2.

**5766 HIRAM WILSON** *to* **GARRISON. 14 January 1854. St. Catharine's, Canada West.** Comments on the intellectual, moral, and physical improvement of Afro-Americans living in Canada. 23 February 1854. p.29, c5.

**5767 REV. DANIEL DEVINNE** *to* **THE** *TRIBUNE*. **n.d. n.p.** A Methodist clergyman relates an act of "legalized murder" he witnessed in the South; narrates his meeting with a Negro slave who was hanged for resisting his master. 23 February 1854. p.30, c5.

**5768 WESTERN CORRESPONDENT** *to* **THE** *NATIONAL ERA*. **[extract] n.d. n.p.** An Irishman gives a brief biographical sketch of John Mitchel; discusses Ireland's view of American slavery. 23 February 1854. p.31, c2.

**5769 WASHINGTON CORRESPONDENT** *to* **THE** *NEW YORK JOURNAL OF COMMERCE*. **4 February. Washington.** Predicts that the Nebraska Bill will split parties into non-intervention and abolition factions. 23 February 1854. p.31, c3.

**5770 PARKER PILLSBURY** *to* **THE** ***LIBERATOR*****. n.d. Dublin.** Announces his safe arrival in Great Britain and remarks on his two-week voyage across the ocean. 23 February 1854. p.31, c4.

**5771 WASHINGTON CORRESPONDENT** *to* **n.n. [extract] n.d. n.p.** Comments on the corruption in the different departments of government. 23 February 1854. p.31, c5.

**5772 MRS. HARRIET BEECHER STOWE** *to* **THE WOMEN OF THE FREE STATES OF AMERICA. n.d. n.p.** Appeals to women to sympathize with the slaves; urges them to use any means available, including writing letters to legislators, to block pro-slavery legislation; tells of anti-slavery views held by Europeans. 2 March 1854. p.33, c3.

**5773 CORRESPONDENT** *to* **THE** ***NEW YORK EXPRESS*****. [extract] n.d. n.p.** Reports on Mr. Chase's reply in the Senate to Mr. Douglas; describes Chase's early life. 2 March 1854. p.34, c4.

**5774 OBSERVER** *to* **THE** ***LEDGER*****. n.d. Washington.** Praises the eloquence of Sumner's speech on the Nebraska question; foresees ill consequences for the Nebraska Bill as a result of the speech. 2 March 1854. p.35, c2.

**5775 E. E. ORVIS** *to* **THE** ***PENNSYLVANIA FREEMAN*****. n.d. n.p.** Defends Mr. Campbell and his "brethren" from allegations in the *Freeman* of pro-slavery opinions; attacks the anti-slavery movement for its unchristian leaders, citing Mr. Garrison. 2 March 1854. p.35, c4.

**5776 BOARD OF MANAGERS** *to* **THE FRIENDS OF IMPARTIAL FREEDOM. n.d. Cincinnati, Oh.** Urges all of anti-slavery opinion to attend the fourth annual anti-slavery convention in Cincinnati; condemns an Ohio judicial decision which holds that colored citizens are considered slaves unless able to prove otherwise. 2 March 1854. p.35, c6.

**5777 LUCRETIA MOTT, WENDELL PHILLIPS, ERNESTINE L. ROSE, LUCY STONE, AND T. W. HIGGINSON** *to* **THE FRIENDS OF THE CAUSE OF WOMEN. 15 January 1854. n.p.** Request information on the educational and business opportunities of American women for essays on these subjects to be prepared at the request of the Cleveland Women's Rights Convention. 2 March 1854. p.35, c7.

**5778 CLINTON GILLINGHAM** *to* **THE** ***SATURDAY EVENING POST*****. [extract] n.d. n.p.** Praises the moral, religious and physical qualities of the inhabitants of Tyrol, which he witnessed on a journey there. 2 March 1854. p.36, c1.

**5779 J. S. P.** *to* **THE** ***TRIBUNE*****. [extract] n.d. Washington.** Discusses the attitudes of pro-slavery factions toward their opponents; paraphrases a taunting speech of Mr. Stephens in the House; foresees the victory of slavery as a consequence of the Nebraska Bill. 9 March 1854. p.37, c7.

**5780 RICHARD MENDENHALL** *to* **THE EDITOR OF THE** ***NATIONAL ERA*****. 19 February 1854. Plainfield, In.** Responds to Douglas's 30 January speech before the Senate concerning slave owning on the part of missionaries in Nebraska; distinguishes between the Methodist Church of the South and that of the North in their respective attitudes toward slavery. 9 March 1854. p.38, c1.

**5781 CORRESPONDENT** *to* **THE** ***TRIBUNE*****. [extract] n.d. Harrisburg, Pa.** Reports on the prevalence of anti-slavery sentiments in Harrisburg and the inability of the Loco Focos to secure passage of a resolution in favor of the Nebraska Bill. 9 March 1854. p.38, c6.

**5782 CORRESPONDENT** *to* **THE** ***NORTH AMERICAN.*** **n.d. Washington.** Reports a debate between supporters and opponents of the Nebraska Bill, in particular an exchange between Senators Badge of North Carolina and Wade of Ohio. 9 March 1854. p.39, c2.

**5783 OLIVER JOHNSON** *to* **SARAH B. DUGDALE. 16 February 1854. n.p.** Praises Sarah Dugdale in a poem on the occasion of her sixty-seventh birthday; praises her trust in God, her sympathies for mankind, and her support of the battle against slavery. 9 March 1854. p.39, c4.

**5784 HOWARD W. GILBERT** *to* **n.n. 9 February 1854. London.** Commends the moral and cultural qualities of the English people which he observed on a sojourn in England; praises the struggle of the English people against slavery and an "outrageous" church system; comments on the imminence of war between Russia and an alliance of England and France. 9 March 1854. p.39, c5.

**5785 BOARD OF MANAGERS** *to* **THE FRIENDS OF IMPARTIAL FREEDOM. n.d. Cincinnati, Oh.** Urges all of anti-slavery opinion to attend the fourth annual anti-slavery convention in Cincinnati; condemns an Ohio judicial decision which ruled that colored citizens are considered slaves unless able to prove otherwise. 9 March 1854. p.39, c6.

**5786 LUCRETIA MOTT, WENDELL PHILLIPS, ERNESTINE L. ROSE, ET AL.** *to* **THE FRIENDS OF THE CAUSE OF WOMEN. 15 January 1854. n.p.** Request information on the educational and business opportunities of American women for essays on these subjects to be prepared at the request of the Cleveland Women's Rights Convention. [reprint of letter first appearing 2 March 1854] 9 March 1854. p.39, c7.

**5787 n.n.** *to* **n.n. 25 February 1854. Harrisburg, Pa.** Reports a resolution passed opposing the Nebraska Bill at a meeting organized by the state administration for the purpose of endorsing the bill. 16 March 1854. p.41, c2.

**5788 W.** *to* **THE** ***TRIBUNE.*** **4 March 1854. Washington.** Reports on Senate speeches concerning the Nebraska Bill, including Douglas's speech in favor of the measure and Fessenden's speech opposing it. 16 March 1854. p.41, c4.

**5789 JNO. M. WAINWRIGHT, STEPHEN H. TYNG, G. T. BEDELL, [AND 144 OTHERS]** *to* **THE SENATE AND HOUSE OF REPRESENTATIVES. n.d. New York City.** Protest the Nebraska Bill, which they consider a violation of previous guarantees of freedom in the region. 16 March 1854. p.42, c2.

**5790 GEORGE L. LLOYD** *to* **JOHN MITCHEL. n.d. Peterboro', Madison County, N.Y.** Challenges John Mitchel to debate the question of whether or not slavery is a crime. 16 March 1854. p.42, c2.

**5791 OBSERVER** *to* **THE** ***LEDGER.*** **n.d. Washington.** Foresees the defeat of the Nebraska Bill in the House. 16 March 1854. p.42, c2.

**5792 CORRESPONDENT** *to* **THE** ***PENNSYLVANIA FREEMAN.*** **[extract] n.d. Texas.** Sends the professional card of a slave-catcher; comments on the use of dogs by slave-catchers. 16 March 1854. p.43, c1.

**5793 WOMEN OF HOLLIDAYSBURG** *to* **THE JUDGES OF BLAIR COUNTY COURT OF QUARTER SESSIONS. [extract] n.d. Hollidaysburg.** Appeal to judges against granting licenses for the sale of liquor. 16 March 1854. p.43, c1.

**5794 CORRESPONDENT** *to* **THE** ***BOSTON COMMONWEALTH.*** **[extract] n.d. n.p.** Contends that slaveholders refuse to sell their lands out of fear that "grog-shops" will be introduced, and that this situation contributes to the perpetuation of slavery. 16 March 1854. p.43, c1.

**5795 AN IRISHMAN** *to* **THE** *PEOPLE'S JOURNAL*. **[extract] n.d. Ireland.** Condemns John Mitchel's pro-slavery stance; affirms the anti-slavery position of Irishmen in Ireland. 16 March 1854. p.43, c2.

**5796 n.n.** *to* **C. M. BURLEIGH. n.d. n.p.** Encloses a letter from Georgia colonists to General Ogelthorpe opposing the introduction of slavery into the colony in 1739. 16 March 1854. p.43, c4.

**5797 A GROUP OF GEORGIAN COLONISTS** *to* **GENERAL OGELTHORPE. 3 July 1739. New Inverness, Darien, Ga.** Oppose the introduction of slavery into Georgia for moral and economic reasons. 16 March 1854. p.43, c4.

**5798 CLINTON GILLINGHAM** *to* **THE** *PENNSYLVANIA FREEMAN*. **22 January 1854. Vienna.** Reaffirms support for the anti-slavery cause; supports gradual reform in Europe but not revolution, on the basis of his observation of conditions in Europe. 16 March 1854. p.43, c5.

**5799 WIVES, MOTHERS, AND DAUGHTERS OF STARK COUNTY, OH.** *to* **SENATOR DOUGLAS. 1 March 1854. Alliance, Oh.** Liken Douglas's support of the Nebraska Bill to Judas's betrayal of Jesus; present Douglas with thirty pieces of silver. 16 March 1854. p.43, c6.

**5800 CORRESPONDENT** *to* **THE** *TRIBUNE*. **n.d. Washington.** Foresees that future developments will establish the Nebraska Bill as part of a conspiracy to settle Mexico, Central America, and Cuba and to convert them into slave states. 16 March 1854. p.43, c7.

**5801 CLERGYMEN OF DIFFERENT RELIGIOUS DENOMINATIONS IN NEW ENGLAND** *to* **THE HOUSE OF REPRESENTATIVES. 1 March 1854. Boston, Ma.** Protest the Nebraska Bill on moral and political grounds. 23 March 1854. p.45, c1.

**5802 CORRESPONDENT** *to* **THE** *TRIBUNE*. **[extract] n.d. Washington.** Relates a Southerner's views on the ineffectiveness of Northern opposition to the Nebraska Bill. 23 March 1854. p.46, c2.

**5803 HOWARD W. GILBERT** *to* **THE** *PENNSYLVANIA FREEMAN*. **21 January 1854. Heidelberg.** Reports on relations between the Catholic church and the state in Germany; warns against the growing influence of Catholicism in the United States. 23 March 1854. p.47, c1.

**5804 W. H. FURNESS** *to* **THE EDITORS OF THE** *ANTI-SLAVERY STANDARD*. **9 March 1854. Philadelphia.** Recommends *The Narrative of Solomon Northup, or Twelve Years a Slave* as a book which will contribute to the strength of the anti-slavery movement. 23 March 1854. p.47, c4.

**5805 R. B. F.** *to* **THE** *PENNSYLVANIA FREEMAN*. **n.d. Hartsville, Bucks County.** Warns against the overvaluation of political power; praises William Lloyd Garrison as one who values moral power above all else. 23 March 1854. p.47, c5.

**5806 n.n.** *to* **THE FRIENDS OF IMPARTIAL FREEDOM. n.d. Cincinnati, Oh.** Urges all of anti-slavery opinion to attend the fourth annual anti-slavery convention in Cincinnati; condemns an Ohio judicial decision which holds that colored citizens are considered slaves unless able to prove otherwise. 23 March 1854. p.47, c7.

**5807 CORRESPONDENT** *to* **THE** *NORTH AMERICAN*. **n.d. London.** Describes the departure of English troops from London to fight the Russians in Constantinople. 23 March 1854. p.48, c1.

**5808 CORRESPONDENT** *to* **THE** *NEW YORK TIMES.* **[extract] n.d. Paris.** Describes experiments with machines using gas to increase running speed and jumping ability. 23 March 1854. p.48, c4.

**5809 SAML. E. FOOTE** *to* **THE EDITOR OF THE** *NEW YORK TRIBUNE.* **10 March 1854. New Haven, Ct.** Calls for a convention to consider the possibility of the separation of the free states from the slave states; asserts that such a separation would bring no harm to the free states. 30 March 1854. p.49, c5.

**5810 GERRIT SMITH** *to* **FREDERICK DOUGLASS. 6 March 1854. Washington.** Explains that he voted against the Homestead Bill because of an amendment to the bill restricting the benefit of its provisions to white people only. 30 March 1854. p.49, c6.

**5811 EX-SENATOR CLEMENS** *to* **n.n. [extract from the** *Huntsville* **(Al.)** *Advocate***] n.d. n.p.** Relates a conversation with President Pierce in which the latter declared that the Nebraska Bill would promote freedom. 30 March 1854. p.50, c7.

**5812 CORRESPONDENT** *to* **THE** *SYRACUSE REPUBLICAN.* **[extract] 24 March 1854. Auburn, N.Y.** Reports unrest in Auburn aroused by the approaching release of a fugitive slave from prison. 30 March 1854. p.51, c1.

**5813 REPRESENTATIVE COMMITTEE OF THE RELIGIOUS SOCIETY OF FRIENDS OF PENNSYLVANIA, NEW JERSEY, DELAWARE AND ADJACENT PARTS OF MARYLAND** *to* **THE SENATE AND HOUSE OF REPRESENTATIVES. 17 February 1854. Philadelphia, Pa.** Protests the Nebraska Bill on religious grounds. 30 March 1854. p.51, c3.

**5814 C. L. R.** *to* **FUGITIVE SLAVES AND THEIR FRIENDS. 1 March 1854. Philadelphia, Pa.** Urges that no letters concerning escape from slavery be written to colored persons in the South for fear that the letters will be opened and read by others. 30 March 1854. p.51, c3.

**5815 HOWARD W. GILBERT** *to* **THE** *PENNSYLVANIA FREEMAN.* **24 December 1853. Heidelberg.** Describes the scenery around Heidelberg and comments on German society. 30 March 1854. p.51, c4.

**5816 PARKER PILLSBURY** *to* **GARRISON. [extract from the** *Liberator***] n.d. Bristol, England.** Explains that his failure to write was due to a recent illness. 30 March 1854. p.51, c5.

**5817 LUCRETIA MOTT, WENDELL PHILLIPS, ERNESTINE L. ROSE, ET AL.** *to* **FRIENDS OF THE CAUSE OF WOMAN. 15 January 1854. n.p.** Request information on the educational and business opportunities of American women for essays on these subjects to be prepared at the request of the Cleveland Women's Rights Convention. [reprint of letter first appearing 2 March 1854] 30 March 1854. p.51, c6.

**5818 CORRESPONDENT** *to* **THE** *CLEVELAND HERALD.* **[extract] n.d. n.p.** Describes the method used to transport mail in the Lake Superior copper region. 30 March 1854. p.52, c1.

**5819 YEOMAN** *to* **THE** *NEW YORK DAILY TIMES.* **n.d. Austin, Tx.** Describes life in Austin with particular attention to German immigrants in Texas. 6 April 1854. p.53, c5.

**5820 A GENTLEMAN** *to* **n.n. n.d. n.p.** Relates a conversation with Archbishop Hughes on the subject of Cuba, in which Hughes showed a desire for the island's annexation. 6 April 1854. p.54, c1.

**5821 n.n.** *to* **THE** *NORTH AMERICAN AND UNITED STATES GAZETTE.* **[extract] 29 March 1854. Washington.** Reports various events concerning the anticipated duel between Representatives Cutting and Breckinridge; comments on past congressional duels. 6 April 1854. p.54, c4.

**5822 DAVID JEWELL, JR.** *to* **WILL. March 1854. County Prison, Pittsburgh, Pa.** Urges Will to refrain from drinking liquor. 6 April 1854. p.55, c3.

**5823 BELL SMITH** *to* **n.n. [extract from the** *National Era***] n.d. Paris.** Relates impressions of a visit to the house of Marat; gives a friend's account of an interview with Marat's sister. 6 April 1854. p.56, c3.

**5824 YEOMAN** *to* **THE** *NEW YORK DAILY TIMES.* **[extract] n.d. Texas.** Relates impressions of a visit to the German town of New Braunfels, Texas. 13 April 1854. p.57, c1.

**5825 CORRESPONDENT** *to* **THE** *NORTHERN CHRISTIAN ADVOCATE.* **[extract] n.d. New England.** Condemns the Baltimore Conference for failing to oppose slavery decisively. 13 April 1854. p.58, c3.

**5826 CORRESPONDENT** *to* **THE** *NEW YORK TIMES.* **[extract] n.d. The South.** Discusses the religious conditions of Negroes in the South. 13 April 1854. p.58, c3.

**5827 HOWARD W. GILBERT** *to* **n.n. 9 March 1854. London.** Describes the conditions of the miners in Cornwall. 13 April 1854. p.59, c1.

**5828 CORRESPONDENT** *to* **THE** *REGISTER.* **[extract] n.d. n.p.** Cites an advertisement in the *New York Republican* announcing the opening of a store by the sisters of Kossuth; subjoins the comments of the *Brussell's Nation* upon it, praising the sisters for their noble poverty and Kossuth for not having plundered Hungary while ruling it. 13 April 1854. p.59, c2.

**5829 CORRESPONDENT** *to* **THE** *POST.* **[extract] 4 April 1854. Boston, Ma.** Reports Edward Everett's claim to authorship of the Hulsemann letters, which were previously attributed to Daniel Webster; tells of the excitement this claim has aroused in Boston. 13 April 1854. p.59, c4.

**5830 CORRESPONDENT** *to* **THE** *POST.* **[extract] 6 April 1854. Boston, Ma.** Reports the successful effort by friends of Daniel Webster to persuade Edward Everett to abandon his claim to authorship of the Hulsemann letters. 13 April 1854. p.59, c4.

**5831 CORRESPONDENT** *to* **THE** *NEW YORK TRIBUNE.* **[extract] 8 April 1854. Washington.** Reports on the meeting of an ecclesiastical council to install the Reverend Alex. Duncanson as pastor of the First Congregational Church. 13 April 1854. p.59, c4.

**5832 CORRESPONDENT** *to* **THE** *NEW YORK TRIBUNE.* **[extract] 9 April 1854. Washington.** Reports on a sermon of Mr. Beecher on the duty of the Church to fight oppression. 13 April 1854. p.59, c4.

**5833 OBSERVER** *to* **THE** *LEDGER.* **[extract] n.d. n.p.** Comments on Mr. Campbell's introduction of a resolution in the House favoring the opening of negotiations with England for the annexation of Canada; cites the benefits annexation would bestow upon England, the United States, and the cause of freedom. 13 April 1854. p.59, c5.

**5834 THIRTY WOMEN OF NEW LEBANON SPRINGS, N.Y.** *to* **STEPHEN ARNOLD DOUGLAS. 29 March 1854. New Lebanon Springs, N.Y.** Cite Douglas's betrayal of human freedom; enclose thirty pieces of silver, likening him to Judas. 20 April 1854. p.61, c3.

**5835 THE REV. MR. CRUMMELL** *to* **n.n. [extract from the** *Calendar***] n.d. Monrovia, Africa.** Reports favorable conditions in Liberia for agricultural and commercial development. 20 April 1854. p.61, c6.

**5836 n.n.** *to* **n.n. [extract] n.d. Newcastle upon Tyne, England.** Reports on William Wells Brown's criticism of J. B. Gough; notes efforts to raise funds to purchase Brown's freedom and enable Brown to return to America. 20 April 1854. p.62, c4.

**5837 CORRESPONDENT** *to* **THE** *NORTH AMERICAN***. [extract] n.d. n.p.** Reports a conversation with a Southern friend who told of the "astonishment and indignation" in the South over the protests in the North against the Nebraska Bill. 20 April 1854. p.62, c6.

**5838 CORRESPONDENT** *to* **THE** *ALTON* **(IL.)** *COURIER***. [extract] n.d. Marine, Il.** Relates Rev. Mr. Robbins's account of government efforts to promote slavery in the Kansas-Nebraska region. 20 April 1854. p.62, c6.

**5839 CORRESPONDENT** *to* **THE** *TRIBUNE***. [extract] n.d. Washington.** Informs that the Nebraska Bill is occupying all of Congress's efforts; mentions Senator Gwin of California, who, like others, has eliminated his chances for reelection by voting in favor of the bill. 20 April 1854. p.62, c6.

**5840 CORRESPONDENT** *to* **THE** *TRIBUNE***. [extract] n.d. Chicago.** Reports resolutions approved by a clerical body of Chicago condemning the Nebraska Bill; notes the strength of anti-slavery sentiment in Chicago. 20 April 1854. p.62, c6.

**5841 n.n.** *to* **n.n. [extract] n.d. Chicago.** Describes the efforts in Illinois to secure passage of the Maine Law. 20 April 1854. p.63, c2.

**5842 ELIZUR WRIGHT** *to* **THE** *NEW YORK TRIBUNE***. [extract] n.d. n.p.** Denies authorship of Hulsemann's reply to Webster's letter; speculates on how the letter would have been received in the Austrian cabinet, had it been transmitted to that body. 20 April 1854. p.63, c3.

**5843 n.n.** *to* **BROTHER BOYNTON. [extract from the** *Cincinnati* **(Oh.)** *Christian Press***] n.d. Lexington, Ky.** Describes a journey by stage in the company of a slave woman and her master. 27 April 1854. p.65, c6.

**5844 CORRESPONDENT** *to* **THE TRIBUNE. [extract] n.d. Toronto, Canada.** Denies that Canadians are either dissatisfied with English rule or desirous of union with the United States. 27 April 1854. p.65, c7.

**5845 n.n.** *to* **n.n. [extract from the** *Tribune***] n.d. Richmond, Va.** Declares the concurrence of a large proportion of Virginians with Northern opposition to the Nebraska Bill. 27 April 1854. p.66, c5.

**5846 B. S. J.** *to* **FRIEND. n.d. n.p.** Describes the lifelong anti-slavery activities of the recently deceased James W. Walker. 27 April 1854. p.66, c6.

**5847 CORRESPONDENT** *to* **THE** *ANTI-SLAVERY BUGLE***. [extract] n.d. Steuben County, In.** Tells of Madison Moss, who caused the arrest of Barry, Clark and F. Fox for aiding fugitive slaves. 27 April 1854. p.67, c3.

**5848 JAS. M. BUSTILL** *to* **THE VISITING COMMITTEE OF PUBLIC LIBRARY IN THE INSTITUTE FOR COLORED YOUTH. 1 April 1854. Philadelphia, Pa.** Describes the books in the library and indicates those most widely read. 27 April 1854. p.67, c6.

**5849 FRANKLIN** *to* **n.n. [extract] 1771. England.** Describes the importance of developing domestic industry rather than relying on imports. 4 May 1854. p.69, c1.

**5850 MR. BIGELOW** *to* **n.n. [extract from the** *New York Evening Post***] n.d. Hayti.** Comments on the neatness of the Haitians. 4 May 1854. p.71, c3.

**5851 n.n.** *to* **n.n. [extract from the** *Newark Advertiser***] n.d. Florence, Italy.** Describes the activities of several English authors residing in Florence. 4 May 1854. p.72, c1.

**5852 CORRESPONDENT** *to* **THE** *NEW ENGLAND FARMER.* **[extract] n.d. n.p.** Describes cures for bites. 4 May 1854. p.72, c4.

**5853 YEOMAN** *to* **THE** *NEW YORK DAILY TIMES.* **March 1852. San Antonio de Bexar, Tx.** Describes the educated upper-class German immigrants in Texas, who fled Germany after the collapse of the revolution in 1848 and are now living as farmers and manual laborers. 11 May 1854. p.73, c1.

**5854 WILLIAM WALKER** *to* **S. BLOCKER. [extract from the** *Cleveland Daily Herald***] n.d. Indian Territory, at Junction of Missouri and Kansas Rivers.** Reports the existence of slavery in Nebraska and a Missouri court decision confirming this situation. 11 May 1854. p.73, c2.

**5855 J. BIGELOW** *to* **THE** *NEW YORK EVENING POST.* **[extract] n.d. Hayti.** Remarks upon the politeness of the Haitians. 11 May 1854. p.73, c5.

**5856 n.n.** *to* **n.n. 8 May 1854. Washington, D.C.** Reports proceedings in the Senate and House relating to the Nebraska Bill; recounts Stephen Douglas's response to a letter from clergymen protesting the bill, and a debate in the House on the consequences of the bill. 11 May 1854. p.74, c4.

**5857 n.n.** *to* **n.n. [extract] 13 April 1854. Madrid, Spain.** Relays information concerning the affair of the *Black Warrior* and its effect on Spanish-American relations. 11 May 1854. p.75, c6.

**5858 CORRESPONDENT** *to* **THE** *LONDON TIMES.* **[extract] n.d. Madrid, Spain.** Reports recently promulgated decrees designed to discourage slavery. 11 May 1854. p.75, c6.

**5859 CHARLES GAVAN DUFFY** *to* **JOHN MITCHEL. 13 April 1854. Black Rock, Dublin, Ireland.** Protests against Mitchel's slanders, attacking Mitchel for his actions as a political prisoner and as editor of the *Citizen.* 18 May 1854. p.77, c3.

**5860 E. A. NESBIT** *to* **SENATOR JOHN WALES. 5 May 1854. Macon, Ga.** Informs Wales of the death of Ned Davis; declares that he would be willing, were Davis still alive, to undertake his case. 18 May 1854. p.79, c4.

**5861 n.n.** *to* **n.n. [extract] n.d. n.p.** Reports Mr. Cooper's presentation to the Senate of a petition by Hanway which requested indemnification for fees incurred by Hanway in his trial on charges arising from the Christiana riots. 18 May 1854. p.79, c4.

**5862 HENRY GREW** *to* **THE** *PENNSYLVANIA FREEMAN.* **13 May 1854. Philadelphia, Pa.** Defends Capt. Charles Stuart from charges presented in the *Freeman* that he attacked woman's rights; seeks to define the true rights of woman according to the Bible. 18 May 1854. p.79, c7.

**5863 T. D. W.** *to* **H. B. S. 15 February 1832. Mifflin Township, Oh.** Desribes an escape from drowning in Alum Creek. 18 May 1854. p.80, c2.

**5864 SAMUEL JONES** *to* **WASHBURN ASHBY. 5 April 1824 [1854]. New York.** Discusses financial and other arrangements concerning the escape of slaves. 25 May 1854. p.82, c3.

**5865 n.n.** *to* **THE** ***NEW YORK TIMES*****. [extract] n.d. n.p.** Describes Mike Walsh being brought into the House, "disgracefully besotted," during the vote on the Nebraska Bill. 25 May 1854. p.83, c2.

**5866 GILES B. STEBBINS** *to* **J. M. McKIM. 16 April 1854. Ann Arbor, Mi.** Describes anti-slavery activities in Ypsilanti, Michigan; reports on a debate between Samuel Aaron and John Pease in Norristown, and on speeches favoring and opposing reform in Rochester. 25 May 1854. p.83, c4.

**5867 GILES B. STEBBINS** *to* **J. M. McKIM. 19 April 1854. Port Huron, Mi.** Describes Port Huron; reviews unfavorably a speech given in Detroit by Horace Mann. 25 May 1854. p.83, c4.

**5868 CORRESPONDENT** *to* **THE** ***LONDON TIMES*****. n.d. Spain.** Speculates, on the basis of conversations with Spaniards, on the probable consequences of a war between Spain and the United States. 25 May 1854. p.83, c5.

**5869 n.n.** *to* **n.n. [extract from the** ***Tribune*****] n.d. Havana, Cuba.** Describes the attitudes of the various sectors of the Cuban population toward the measures adopted by the governor general threatening the existence of slavery. 25 May 1854. p.83, c5.

**5870 MARIUS R. AND EMILY ROBINSON** *to* **THE READERS OF THE** ***BUGLE*****. n.d. n.p.** Mourn the death of daughter Cornelia, citing her opposition to slavery. 25 May 1854. p.83, c6.

**5871 JOHN W. HOWE** *to* **JAMES POLLOCK. 22 March 1854. Meadville, Pa.** Questions Pollock, Whig candidate for governor of Pennsylvania, concerning his views on the Nebraska Bill. 1 June 1854. p.85, c1.

**5872 A LOUISIANIAN** *to* **THE EDITORS OF THE** ***NEW ORLEANS CRESCENT*****. n.d. n.p.** Comments on the moral character and loyalty of the free colored people of Louisiana; condemns those who favor colonization. 1 June 1854. p.85, c1.

**5873 TWENTY-EIGHT MEMBERS** *to* **THE NEW SCHOOL GENERAL ASSEMBLY. n.d. n.p.** Protest the lack of active opposition to slavery on the part of the Church. 1 June 1854. p.86, c3.

**5874 E. A. NESBIT** *to* **JOHN WALES. 18 May 1854. Macon, Ga.** Retracts his earlier report of Edward Davis's death, and declines to undertake Davis's case. 1 June 1854. p.86, c5.

**5875 JOSEPHINE BROWN** *to* **MR. MAY. 27 April 1854. East Plumstead School, East Plumstead, Woolwich, England.** Describes the lack of prejudice shown to black people in England. 1 June 1854. p.87, c6.

**5876 OBSERVER** *to* **THE** ***NEW YORK TRIBUNE*****. 25 May 1854. Kennett Square, Chester County, Pa.** Reports on the second Yearly Meeting of the Pennsylvania Society of Progressive Friends, and discusses the origins and doctrines of the society. 1 June 1854. p.87, c7.

**5877 YEOMAN** *to* **THE** ***NEW YORK DAILY TIMES*****. April 1854. San Antonio de Bexar, Tx.** Describes the German immigrants to Texas, noting their strong commitment to education. 1 June 1854. p.88, c2.

**5878 n.n.** *to* **THE** ***RICHMOND WHIG*****. [extract] n.d. n.p.** Describes Samuel Hairston as "the richest man in Virginia" and, perhaps, "the largest slaveholder in the world." 1 June 1854. p.88, c4.

**5879 W. S.** *to* **THE EDITOR OF THE** ***TORONTO PROVINCIAL FREEMAN.*** **1 May 1854. Philadelphia, Pa.** Describes various matters relating to the escapes of slaves. 8 June 1854. p.89, c6.

**5880 D. Y.** *to* **THE** ***ANTI-SLAVERY STANDARD.*** **30 May 1854. Boston, Ma.** Reports the events relating to the capture of Anthony Burns and the protests against his treatment as a fugitive slave. 8 June 1854. p.89, c7.

**5881 A LOUISIANA PLANTER** *to* **A LOUISIANA CONGRESSMAN. [extract] 15 May 1854. Louisiana.** Opposes the annexation of Cuba on the grounds that such annexation would be economically harmful to Louisiana. 8 June 1854. p.90, c1.

**5882 RICHARD MENDENHALL** *to* **n.n. [extract from the** ***National Era*****] 14 May 1854. Friends' Shawnee Mission, Kansas Territory.** Reports on slaveholding among members of the Methodist Church South; condemns Thomas Johnson, delegate to Congress from Nebraska, for his efforts to induce Indians to sell their land. 8 June 1854. p.90, c3.

**5883 CORRESPONDENT** *to* **THE** ***RICHMOND DAILY MAIL.*** **[extract] n.d. Washington.** Refutes the notion that passage of the Nebraska Bill signals the end of debate on slavery in Congress. 8 June 1854. p.90, c7.

**5884 n.n.** *to* **THE EDITOR OF THE** ***PENNSYLVANIA FREEMAN.*** **[extract] n.d. n.p.** Encloses an appeal to the controllers of the public schools. 8 June 1854. p.91, c3.

**5885 n.n.** *to* **THE CONTROLLERS OF THE PUBLIC SCHOOLS. [extract] n.d. n.p.** Deplores the absence of physiology classes in the schools. 8 June 1854. p.91, c3.

**5886 CORRESPONDENT** *to* **THE** ***POTTSVILLE*** **(PA.)** ***REGISTER AND DEMOCRAT.*** **[extract from the** ***Union*****] n.d. Washington.** Praises representative Straub's speech on the Nebraska-Kansas Bill. 8 June 1854. p.91, c5.

**5887 JACOB H. GROVE** *to* **J. W. C. PENNINGTON. 27 May 1854. Baltimore, Md.** Offers to sell Stephen Pembroke. 8 June 1854. p.91, c6.

**5888 STEPHEN PEMBROKE** *to* **J. W. C. PENNINGTON. 30 May 1854. Sharpsburg, Md.** Appeals to Pennington to arrange the purchase of his freedom. 8 June 1854. p.91, c6.

**5889 J. W. C. PENNINGTON** *to* **n.n. n.d. New York, N.Y.** Appeals for contributions toward the purchase of Stephen Pembroke's freedom. 8 June 1854. p.91, c6.

**5890 BELINDA MARDEN PRATT** *to* **LYDIA KIMBALL. [extract from the** ***Boston Commonwealth*****] n.d. Utah.** Upholds the Mormon practice of polygamy, citing her experience with the custom. 8 June 1854. p.92, c3.

**5891 THOMAS JEFFERSON** *to* **JOHN ADAMS. [extract from the** ***National Intelligencer*****] 1 June 1822. Monticello.** Comments on the impending war between Russia and Turkey, commending the peaceful ways of the Quakers. 8 June 1854. p.92, c3.

**5892 CASSIUS M. CLAY** *to* **THE EDITOR OF THE** ***NEW YORK TRIBUNE.*** **n.d. n.p.** Urges all possible measures against slavery, including economic and political pressure. 15 June 1854. p.93, c3.

**5893 "'76"** *to* **THE EDITOR OF THE** ***NEW YORK TRIBUNE.*** **n.d. n.p.** Urges condemnation of the Fugitive Slave Law and efforts to aid fugitives. 15 June 1854. p.93, c5.

**5894 HAMILTON WILLIS** *to* **THE EDITOR OF THE** ***ATLAS.*** **3 June 1854. Boston, Ma.** Describes United States District Attorney B. F. Hallet's obstruction of arrangements for the purchase of Anthony Burns's freedom. 15 June 1854. p.94, c2.

**5895 B. F. HALLET** *to* **SIDNEY WEBSTER. n.d. Boston, Ma.** Asks whether funds are available for the payment of troops needed to extradite Anthony Burns, who is on trial as a fugitive slave. 15 June 1854. p.94, c3.

**5896 FRANKLIN PIERCE** *to* **B. F. HALLET. 31 May 1854. Washington.** Tells Hallet to incur any necessary expense for the execution of the law in the case of Anthony Burns. 15 June 1854. p.94, c3.

**5897 B. F. HALLET** *to* **SIDNEY WEBSTER. 31 May 1854. Boston, Ma.** Informs Webster that there are adequate military forces for the preservation of peace after the decision in the Anthony Burns case. 15 June 1854. p.94, c3.

**5898 B. F. HALLET** *to* **SIDNEY WEBSTER. 2 June 1854. Boston, Ma.** Reports the decision in the Anthony Burns case; states that the military force is sufficient for the peaceful execution of the decision. 15 June 1854. p.94, c3.

**5899 THIRTY WOMEN OF WOBURN** *to* **COMMISSIONER EDWARD GREELEY LORING. 3 June 1854. Woburn.** Condemn Loring for his decision in the Anthony Burns case; enclose thirty pieces of silver as payment for his betrayal of liberty. 15 June 1854. p.94, c3.

**5900 GEORGE L. WILLIAMS, B. L. ALLEN, W. WASHBURN, TISDALE DRAKE, AND A. B. MUNROE** *to* **n.n. n.d. Boston, Ma.** Aldermen of Boston deny complicity in the mayor's decision to use the military to deliver Anthony Burns to a slave vessel. 15 June 1854. p.94, c3.

**5901 CITIZENS OF RHODE ISLAND** *to* **THE GENERAL ASSEMBLY OF RHODE ISLAND. 3 June 1854. Rhode Island.** Ask the general assembly to pass a law rendering all complicity in the capture of fugitive slaves illegal. 15 June 1854. p.94, c4.

**5902 CORRESPONDENT** *to* **THE** ***TRIBUNE*****. [extract] n.d. n.p.** Sees war with Spain and the annexation of Cuba as the goal of the president's policies. 15 June 1854. p.94, c5.

**5903 HENRY GREW** *to* **THE EDITOR OF THE** ***PENNSYLVANIA FREEMAN*****. n.d. n.p.** Protests Mr. Furness's slighting of the Christian doctrine of atonement in a sermon. 15 June 1854. p.94, c7.

**5904 CORRESPONDENT** *to* **THE** ***RHODE ISLAND FREEMAN*****. [extract] n.d. n.p.** Calls for the arrest of "Southern kidnappers" who arrive in the North in pursuit of fugitive slaves. 15 June 1854. p.95, c2.

**5905 GOVERNOR BIGLER** *to* **THE STATE CONVENTION OF THE FRIENDS OF A PROHIBITORY LIQUOR LAW. [extract] n.d. Pennsylvania.** Deplores the evils of intemperance; declines to support a prohibitory liquor law before studying it carefully. 15 June 1854. p.95, c3.

**5906 JUDGE JAS. POLLOCK** *to* **THE STATE CONVENTION OF THE FRIENDS OF A PROHIBITORY LIQUOR LAW. 30 May 1854. Milton, Pa.** Proclaims his willingness to execute a prohibitory liquor law, should such a law be enacted. 15 June 1854. p.95, c3.

**5907 F.** *to* **THE** ***NEW YORK TRIBUNE*****. 15 June 1854. Boston, Ma.** Describes the opposition of New England to slavery. 22 June 1854. p.98, c6.

**5908 J. W. C. PENNINGTON** *to* **THE EDITOR OF THE** ***NEW YORK TRIBUNE*****. 15 June 1854. New York, N.Y.** Details negotiations with Jacob Grove, Stephen Pembroke's owner, for the latter's release from slavery. 22 June 1854. p.98, c7.

**5909 CORRESPONDENT** *to* **THE** *NEW YORK DAILY TIMES.* **[extract] June 1854. New Orleans, La.** Describes agitation for the annexation of Cuba; reports plans to take Cuba with a private raiding party led by General Quitman. [partially illegible] 29 June 1854. p.101, c4.

**5910 CORRESPONDENT** *to* **THE** *NEW YORK INDEPENDENT.* **[extract] n.d. n.p.** Refutes Senator Douglas's claim that the Nebraska Bill would not promote the expansion of slavery, pointing to its expansion after the annexation of Texas. 29 June 1854. p.101, c5.

**5911 DELPHI** *to* **THE** *MIDDLETOWN* **(N.Y.)** *WHIG PRESS* **[?]. [extract] 17 May 1854. Charlotte, N.C.** Describes the beating of a slave in Winneborough, North Carolina. 29 June 1854. p.101, c7.

**5912 A PROMINENT LOUISIANA PLANTER** *to* **A LEADING MERCHANT OF PHILADELPHIA. [extract] 2 June 1854. New Orleans, La.** Discusses the desire of sugar planters for the emancipation of slaves in Cuba, which would lead to the economic ruin of Cuba and the end of its competition in the sugar trade. 29 June 1854. p.102, c1.

**5913 EVAN PUGH** *to* **ESTEEMED FRIEND. 24 April 1854. Leipsic, Germany.** Compares America's inventiveness favorably with Europe's traditionalism; condemns slavery and the Nebraska Bill. 29 June 1854. p.103, c2.

**5914 JAMES HAUGHTON** *to* **THE EDITOR OF THE** *NATION.* **8 May 1854. n.p.** Condemns the pro-slavery position of John Mitchel and T. F. Meagher as a betrayal of the true cause of Ireland. 29 June 1854. p.103, c4.

**5915 CORRESPONDENT** *to* **THE** *OHIO STATE JOURNAL.* **[extract] 10 June 1854. Council Bluffs, Ia.** Relates impressions of a journey through Kansas, Nebraska, Missouri, and Iowa. 29 June 1854. p.103, c4.

**5916 A PRESBYTERIAN CLERGYMAN** *to* **FRIEND K. 30 May 1854. Philadelphia, Pa.** Relates impressions of a visit to Philadelphia. 29 June 1854. p.104, c4.

**Hallowell (Me.)**
*Advocate of Freedom*

**Figure 5. Austin Willey**

# Austin Willey

## [Editor, *Advocate of Freedom*]

Fifty years ago, slavery had the entire control of the nation, the church, the press, the general public sentiment, and the conscience of the people. To question the divinity of slavery was to subject one to the charge of infidelity, and as being in opposition to the welfare of the church and state, and the progress of civilization. "Darkness, gross darkness, covered the people," and the cries, groans, and bitter tears of more than three millions of slaves were going up to Heaven unheeded by both church and state; and yet there was a remnant left who would not bow the knee to Baal. There were men and women who believed the Bible, and who gave full credence to its unqualified condemnation of slavery in all its forms.

Pre-eminent among the few who occupied this position of uncompromising hostility to slavery, was Rev. Austin Willey, the author of *The History of the Antislavery Conflict in Maine and Nation*. Mr. Willey is a native of New Hampshire, of Puritan stock, and wields a powerful pen in defence of truth and righteousness as connected with the cause of temperance in the country. On graduating from Bangor Seminary he was called by the friends of the slave in Maine to assume the editorship of the antislavery paper, which had then been in existence about a year, under the supervision of the late and greatly lamented Professor William Smyth, of Bowdoin College. On commencing his labors, he adopted as his motto, *"Immediate Abolition of Slavery is the duty of the Master and the right of the Slave."* On this platform he labored for the space of sixteen years with signal ability, and with a persistent, unconquerable zeal worthy of all praise until the victory was gained, and the principles and labors of the friends of the slave culminated in the organization of a new political party that absorbed all the antislavery element in both the old political parties. The victory was complete. Maine was morally, religiously, and politically revolutionized, and lifted up from abject bondage to slavery to a noble Christian civilization, by the force alone of God's truth upon the minds and hearts of the people. This was done as in no other state. The conflict was desperate with both religious and political forces, and was prosecuted with inadequate means, but with uncompromising persistence and faith in God. And not this alone, but Maine marched in the front line with other states, and at last that pagan despotism was annihilated, and our country was saved from ruin. During this long-continued and bitter contest, Mr. Willey, by reason of the position he occupied as editor of the chief paper in the state that dared to speak in defence of the slave, denouncing slavery and all complicity with it on the platform as well as in the press, became the target at which were aimed the deadliest missiles of pro-slavery ingenuity and wrath. Amid it all he stood erect and firm, and without fear, in defence of the cause of God and humanity, manifesting always the distinguishing characteristics of a Christian gentleman. As an editor, he was one of the ablest in the antislavery field, enjoying the confidence and esteem of such men as Salmon P. Chase, Joshua Leavitt, Lewis Tappan, Charles Sumner, and other able leaders in the antislavery cause. As a public speaker, Mr. Willey was far above mediocrity. He met the people as one of them, and came before his audience with plain words addressed to the hearts and consciences of men, and presented them so clearly and forcibly that the common people could understand them and feel their force. In this way his hearers and readers were instructed and convinced of their duty. No one complained of his bold Saxon bluntness and plain dealing but the enemies of truth and the half-hearted and timid.

No one was ever known to doubt the honesty and integrity of Austin Willey and his ability to wield the truth with terrible effect against the "sum of all villainies," and it is but justice to say that few men, living or dead, did more for the correction of public opinion, for the elevation of the people to the standard of a noble Christian civilization, and to a proper estimation of the value of liberty; and no man has a stronger claim on the people of Maine and the country for gratitude and good will, than has Mr. Willey. There is cause for devout gratitude to the Author of all good for the preservation of the only man living who has a personal knowledge of the facts, and the material and the ability to furnish for future generations a correct though condensed history of the most important and remarkable revolution of modern times.

C. C. Cone, letter in Austin Willey,
*The History of the Antislavery*
*Cause in State and Nation*
(Portland, 1886), p.1-3.

# ADVOCATE OF FREEDOM.

"All Men are born equally Free and Independent."—Maine Declaration of Rights.

VOL. I. BRUNSWICK, MAINE, THURSDAY, MAY 10, 1838. NO. 5.

ADVOCATE OF FREEDOM.
Semi-Monthly.
PUBLISHED UNDER THE DIRECTION OF THE EXECUTIVE COMMITTEE OF THE MAINE ANTI-SLAVERY SOCIETY.
THOMAS W. NEWMAN, Printer,
No. 2, Forsaith's Block.

## Anti-Slavery.

**Anti-Slavery Meeting in Edgecomb.**

Agreeably to previous notice, a meeting was held in the Freewill Baptist meeting house in Edgecomb on the 7th inst. to discuss the subject of slavery. The meeting was called to order by Rev. S. Fairfield, and organized by choosing Stephen Parsons, Esq. moderator, and J. Penness scribe. The exercises were commenced with singing a hymn, after which Rev. A. Caldwell led in prayer. A committee of arrangements, consisting of Messrs. Caldwell, Fairfield, and Hawes, reported the following resolutions which were severally discussed and unanimously adopted.

1. *Resolved*, That to admit that the spread of the gospel will overthrow slavery, and yet to contend for slavery as a divine institution and right in itself, is to bring against the gospel the infidel charge that it is opposed to God, and truth, and righteousness.

2. *Resolved*, That the rapid spread and strong influence of our principles both at the North and South, is evidence of God's blessing upon our measures, and should draw forth the most sincere gratitude and thanksgiving, and encourage to new and more vigorous exertions.

3. *Resolved*, That we at the north are deeply involved in the guilt of slavery; that the northern States and northern churches are corrupted by its influence; and to effect a radical cure, slavery must be exterminated from the South.

4. *Resolved*, That as we believe the slave-holder to be a *great sinner*, no duty is plainer than that we should remind him in the spirit of kindness and brotherly love, yet with solemn earnestness, how abhorrent his character must be to God.

5. *Resolved*, That we would, however, by no means be understood to express hostility to the slaveholder; we deeply pity his wickedness, and aim not less at his welfare and salvation, than at the liberty and improvement of the slave.

6. *Resolved*, That for abolitionists to give their suffrages to elect men to our National and State legislatures, who they have reason to believe will support slavery, if elected, is glaringly inconsistent with their professions.

7. *Resolved*, That the permanent prosperity of the northern States in their civil privileges, and northern churches in their great work of saving men from their sins, depends to a great extent, upon the diffusion of right views upon the subject of slavery.

8. *Resolved*, That the christian religion can not flourish in its purity among a people who claim and exercise exclusive control over the persons of their fellow-men; who require the performance of arduous daily tasks and appropriate the *fruits* of labor thus extorted, to their own benefit, regardless of these scriptural declarations—"The laborer is worthy of his hire"—"Render unto all their dues"—"Wo to him that buildeth a house by unrighteousness, and his chambers by wrong; that useth his neighbor's service without wages, and giveth him not for his work."

9. *Resolved*, That the Bible is the great charter of this world's liberties; and that slavery as it exists in this land, receives no countenance from that source.

10. *Resolved*, That as it is admitted by those who "dislike our measures," that the gospel will ultimately do away slavery, this admission is evidence of the Anti-slavery power of the gospel, and that the only reason why slavery has existed to this day, is that the gospel has not been fully applied and honestly lived up to. The single precept, "whatsoever ye would that men should do unto you, do ye even so to them," would, if brought home to the heart and conscience, be certain death to that system which holds men to involuntary servitude, and compels them to labor generation after generation, that others may eat the fruit of their toils; while the amount of labor, and the kind of toil, and of the time allowed for rest, and the food to eat, and the raiment to put on, both as to quantity and quality are dictated by irresponsible masters.

11. *Resolved*, That we base our abhor- [illegible] property in the bodies and souls of men, should, like any other sin, be instantly relinquished;—that every husband should have his own wife, and every wife her own husband;—that the power with which the master is now vested to punish his slave to any extent which his pleasure or caprice may dictate, should be taken away;—that the laws which prohibit the instruction of slaves should be repealed; that masters should employ their slaves as *free* laborers, and pay them for their services; and that the same power which repeals the unrighteous slave laws should make all necessary provisions to prevent pauperism and vagrancy, and secure the general welfare.

14. *Resolved*, That as the above is what we mean by immediate emancipation, we feel injured when we are denounced as "fanatics and incendiaries," and that the cause we love—the cause of God and of bleeding humanity, is injured by those who urge a *gradual* breaking off from slavery, and thus afford a palliative to the slaveholder's conscience.

15. *Resolved*, That in our view, immediate and universal emancipation, instead of producing the amalgamation of the white and black races, would in a great measure retard that amalgamation which is now going on at a rapid rate, and which grows out of the *condition of the slave*, rather than out of the *character of the black*.

16. *Resolved*, That *if* it be true, that "the agitation of the subject of slavery tends to rivet the chains of the slave," this very fact shows that the time is hastening when the sufferings of the slave will be past all endurance; that merciless slaveholders will hasten the work which they wish to retard, just as the Egyptians did, when they made the Israelites to serve with greater rigor, because God, by the mouth of his servant Moses, said, "*let my people go that they may serve me.*"

It will be perceived that the above resolutions were passed with the design of meeting objections, and removing them. To those who were present, the meeting was one of uncommon interest. It seems to me, all that is necessary to bring over the mass of our people, is a correct understanding of our principles and our measures. The great difficulty is, many people "know all about the subject" before they know anything, and hence we cannot gain a hearing—they are too wise to be taught. Others "know nothing about it, and wish to know nothing," so they cannot be instructed. They "never knew any good to come from the discussion of this subject, and never expect to." But we must "be patient towards all men, instructing those that oppose themselves." Our cause will go forward—it is "the cause of God, and of bleeding humanity" and must succeed—"the oppressions that are done under the sun" have an end. That this end may be hastened, may the number of those who "open their mouths for the dumb in the cause of all such as are appointed to destruction," be multiplied till the land is filled with them. May all who know the way to the throne of grace, open their mouths in prayer for such as are "oppressed and have no comforter." And may they not forget to pray for the oppressor, that his heart may relent, and he be led to say with Joseph's brethren—"we are verily guilty concerning our brother," before he is constrained to add, "therefore is this evil come upon us." O slavery must cease. Every attribute of God declares it. The whip must fall from the grasp of the driver. The light of science and religion must shine on the dark-hearted slave. The song of jubilee must be heard throughout our coasts. When that day arrives—and I cannot believe it to be very far distant—those who have pleaded the cause of the oppressed, will feel that they have a right to join that jubilee, while those who have held their peace, or opened their mouths only to object and complain, and misrepresent and vilify, will know that "deliverance has come from another quarter."

By order of the meeting,
J. T. HAWES.

SPIRIT OF LIBERTY. The following resolution was recently passed at a [illegible]

*From the Youth's Cabinet.*

**The Slaves can't take care of themselves.**

PORTLAND, (ME.) March, 1838.

*Mr. Editor*,—I have just witnessed the completion of a bargain between a wealthy farmer of this region, and a man who a little while ago was a slave, the terms of which were, work for wages. It was the young man's first bargain on his own account, and his glistening eyes told the joy of his heart, as he acceded to these (to him) novel terms.

After great hardship and many difficulties, which called into exercise all his shrewdness and caution, as well as his bodily vigor, he succeeded in reaching this place, having made his escape from the unrighteous bondage in which he had been held for more than twenty years. During at least one half of this time, he has been robbed of the first fruits of his labor. I pitied him when he said to me "O, 'tis hard to work so many years, and get no benefit from it." He receives now, I think, 12 dollars a month, besides his board. Let us calculate of how much money he has been defrauded during his past life. I will call the time ten years, and his wages six dollars a month. Ten years make 120 months, and his pay at six dollars would be 720 dollars—enough to procure for him a small farm. This sum has been *stolen* from him. But this is only a trifling part of the robbery that a slaveholder has committed. [illegible] less soul has been robbed of that moral and intellectual culture which was its right, and has sustained a loss which can never be repaired. When he came here, three months ago, he did not know a letter of the alphabet, and he states that when he attempted to learn to read, his book was taken from him and burnt. Now he can read the Bible without assistance. His disposition is kind and affectionate, and he blesses God for having delivered him from slavery.

He has of late been quite restless for want of employment, often saying, "I don't feel right. I want work." He is probably a fair specimen of those "lazy, ignorant, saucy, shiftless creatures who can't take care of themselves."

You may ask, "Is he not afraid of being carried back into slavery?" No: there is now no danger. The judiciary committee of our legislature have just reported that "the existing laws of the State secure a trial by jury to every human being," and their report has been accepted. Henceforth the runaway slave has nothing to fear from man-hunters.

WHAT IS SLAVERY. The following just picture of American slavery, is from the pen of James G. Birney, Esq. who is well acquainted, by experience and personal observation, with "southern institutions." It needs no comment. Can a relation, [illegible] such principles, be innocent?

1. The slaves are deprived of all their wages, from the beginning of life to the end of it. There is not a slave in the South, that possesses a right that is available to him, to one dollar of the proceeds of his toil.

2. The slave trade is carried on with a system as complete as the trade in any other merchantable commodity. Vessels freighted only with slaves are regularly cleared from the custom house in the District of Columbia, and other places for more southern ports—where their cargoes are offered for sale in *the market*. Coffles of slaves are driven through the country, by land, in *chains*, without any necessity for concealment, and without exciting astonishment, *to the same market*.

3. Among slaves there is no such thing as legal marriage. A husband acquires no rights in the wife, nor the wife in the husband. Neither do they, jointly or severally, acquire any right to the superintendence of their children, nor to their services. Every master can sell his slave at discretion. Any relation in which the slave may [illegible]

*colored people*, and he is in no danger of punishment, or even of being questioned for the offence, for they are by law, *incompetent to testify against a white man*. It is not known that a master has suffered the penalty of death, *in a single instance*, for the murder of his slave.

5. The slaves are forbidden the acquisition of letters, in the most elementary form. It is made penal even in the masters to teach their slaves to read or write.

They are forbidden to attend the preaching of *colored* men—and that they do not, in any numbers, attend the preaching of *white* men is also well known.

**Foundation of the Right of Property.**

What, sir, is the foundation of the right of property? Is it not a grant, expressed or implied, from the great original Proprietor? Nothing can give a higher title than creation; and, as man is the noblest work, so is he, in the highest sense, the property of the Creator.

Now, sir, show me the grant of a right of property in men. Every thing else is granted. There is nothing upon earth, that can be rightfully held as property, the dominion of which, is not the subject of express grant from the Creator. Read the sublime description of the Creation in the first chapter of Genesis. Having given being to the vast universe of matter, [illegible]

"[illegible] MAN IN OUR IMAGE, AFTER OUR LIKENESS."

[illegible]

So God created man in his own image, in the image of God created he him; [illegible]

slavery cannot stand the ordeal of discussion: "Where and when did it ever happen, that slavery was not abolished, after a convention was once called to consider the subject?"

*From the Herald of Freedom.*

**The Slave sick of Liberty.**

It is sometimes said that the slave, after enjoying liberty awhile, becomes displeased with his condition and sick of its cares, and prefers to return to a state of bondage where he is relieved from the trouble of providing for himself, or his family. To show how near the truth such sayings approach, we give in evidence the following anecdote told in an interesting conversation at a public meeting in Peterborough, State of New York, by Mr. Wilson, agent of the American A. S. Society in Upper Canada, in answer to the question, whether masters were sometimes successful in flattering their slaves back to slavery when they find them in Canada? Mr. Wilson said, he had never known of but one instance:—

A slaveholder had followed a very valuable slave from one of the slave states, (I think Kentucky,) to Malden in Upper Canada, at the Head of Lake Erie. He found him, and accosted him very kindly, and asked him if he had not got almost sick of Canada, and if he did not want to go back with him. The slave answered he had become disgusted with the place, and with his brethren of Canada, and would take it as a very great favor to get back again, and would willingly do so, if his master would promise not to punish him. The promise was quickly made, and they were soon on their way to the land of the Patriarchs—the slave frequently expressing his delight at his good fortune once more to be permitted to return in quiet to his old master, and to enjoy once more the society of his wife and children. They arrived in safety—and it was announced in triumph that here was one instance where a man chose slavery rather than the freedom and society of the colored people—the slave in the mean time was vehement in his denunciations of Canada, it was a miserable, cold, desert country—the colored people a poor, ignorant mass of wretchedness, &c. Nothing was now too good for him, the master's confidence was unbounded almost, and as he had served the cause of slavery so well, he allowed him greater privileges than is usual to slaves. But mark the sequel. There was to be a camp-meeting some distance off.—The slave got permission to go and take his family—a couple of horses were saddled, and the slave and his wife with each a little one mounted behind them, put off for the camp-meeting to be absent several days. But somehow or other they missed their way to the camp-meeting, till they found themselves in sight of the Ohio river—they crossed it—and still the North seemed to have great attractions for them, and they could not stop. By and by the Detroit river hove in sight; they dismounted their horses, leaving them for their master on the American side, and crossed over to that same poor, inhospitable clime of Canada, and are settled and doing well, in that province: free and unfettered, as is the case with about 10,000 others, who have escaped from the horrors of southern slavery. This, said Mr. Wilson, was the only case he had ever known when the fugitive from slavery had become tired of Canada, and sick of Liberty.

*Legislative progress in Ohio.*—The Legislature of Ohio have closed their session. The editor of the Philanthropist thus sums up and reports the progress that has been made by the cause of human rights.

WHAT HAS BEEN GAINED.—The Legislature adjourned, Monday, 19th inst. We congratulate abolitionists on the success of their efforts, in moving this body. "Why? Have the 'Black laws' been repealed, or the right of jury trial been secured by law to persons claimed as fugitives from service?" No—but prejudice has been softened, obstacles have been lessened, friends have been multiplied, the right of petition has been sacredly regarded, legislators have been taught to feel their responsibilities on the great subjects brought before them by abolitionists; the current which last year flowed strongly in favor of oppression, this year has set in favor of the cause of human rights, there has been plenty of discussion on abolition [illegible]

Figure 6

# Journal Data

TITLE: *Advocate of Freedom*

MOTTO: All Men are Born Equally Free and Independent—Maine Declaration of Rights

INCLUSIVE DATES OF PUBLICATION: 8 March 1838–12 June 1841

PLACES OF PUBLICATION: Brunswick, Maine (8 March 1838–21 February 1839); Augusta, Maine (25 April 1839–11 April 1840); Hallowell, Maine (18 April 1840–12 June 1841)

FREQUENCY OF PUBLICATION: Semi-Monthly (8 March 1838–21 February 1839); Weekly (25 April 1839–12 June 1841)

DAY OF WEEK PUBLISHED: Thursday (8 March 1838–25 July 1839); Saturday (3 August 1839–2 May 1840); Thursday (7 May 1840–29 April 1841); Saturday (12 June 1841)

AVERAGE NUMBER OF PAGES PER ISSUE: 4

NUMBER OF COLUMNS PER PAGE: 5 (8 March 1838–21 February 1839); 4 (25 April 1839–12 June 1841)

EDITOR: Austin Willey (5 October 1839–12 June 1841)

PUBLISHER: Executive Committee, Maine Anti-Slavery Society

PRINTERS: Thomas W. Newman (8 March 1838–21 February 1839); William Noyes (25 April 1839–12 June 1841)

FEATURES: letters; editorials; local, national and foreign news; poetry

PRICE: Annual subscription paid in advance: $.50 (1838–39); $1.00 (1839–41)

LANGUAGE: English

PERSPECTIVE: Abolitionist

REPOSITORY: Harvard University Library. 8 March 1838–12 June 1841.

# Prospectus

Many friends of immediate emancipation in Maine, have long desired the establishment of an Anti-Slavery paper in this State. The time, we think, has come when this desire should be gratified, and a medium of communication opened, through which they may freely and fully expound their principles, state their views, and urge their measures for the speedy and peaceful removal of slavery "the foulest blot and direst curse of our country."

The power of the press in directing public sentiment, is universally admitted. We wish to bring more fully into operation the resources of this mighty engine, in diffusing correct information, and creating an enlightened public sentiment upon the momentous subject of slavery. Let the truth, spoken in love, the spirit-stirring truth relating to slavery, be spread out before the whole community. Let our true principles be known, our approved measures be understood, and see if misapprehensions cannot be removed, prejudices be obviated, and the co-operation of all the wise and the good be secured. The speedy attainment of this end, seems to require increased facilities for communication with the public.

The talents and piety already enlisted in the Anti-Slavery cause in this State, are without doubt, amply sufficient to sustain more than one periodical of the highest order. Yet for the want of some official organ of communication, these gifts have thus far, but to a very limited extent, been brought into requisition. We wish to present new inducements to those who sympathise with the slave, and desire that his wrongs may be redressed, to wield the pen in his behalf. By the establishment of a new paper, we would open a broader and deeper channel, through which, from full hearts, they may pour forth their earnest pleadings for the oppressed and the dumb.

A separate paper seems to be required, in order to meet, to better advantage, the peculiar wants of our own State. The general principles of abolition are the same in all parts of the country. To establish or inculcate them, nothing local or peculiar is needed. But slavery exerts some influences of a local nature, excites prejudices and raises objections, somewhat confined to places. Its effects, for example, can not fail to be somewhat different upon our extended sea coast, from what they are upon the inland inhabitants of New Hampshire and Vermont. Our ship owners, the masters and mariners employed in the carrying trade, forming a most important part of our population, have an interest to be on good terms with southern planters, not felt by those whose ordinary business concerns do not bring them into immediate contact with the South.

Our extensive commercial intercourse with the Southern States, renders it exceedingly important that our whole community should be truly enlightened upon this momentous subject. Questions of a grave character, vitally affecting our rights, and the cause of freedom, grow out of this intercourse. A recent transaction has forcibly reminded us of this.—The Governor of Georgia has demanded of the Governor of this state two of our citizens, to be dragged from their homes, and taken to Savannah, there to be tried as common felons to the peril of life.—Why is this demand made? Because, a slave impelled by that desire for liberty, which can never be extinguished in the human breast, had secreted himself on board their vessel, and came to Maine, to escape from the horrors of slavery. Many others might be made the subjects of a similar question. While the lives and property of our citizens are thus put in jeopardy, do we not need one paper, at least, in which this system of usurpation may be freely and fully examined?

The State Society requires a paper, in which the entire proceedings of its public meetings, and the documents which from time to time it may have occasion to put forth, may be published. The doings of town and other auxiliary societies, the proceedings of the county conventions proposed to be held, will furnish a large amount of matter for publication, adapted, it may be presumed, to exert a most happy influence, in promoting mutual emulation and zeal among the friends of the cause, and exciting them to more vigorous efforts in its promotion. Much of this matter can not well be urged upon exisiting papers, and, as matter of fact, but a small portion of it can be brought before the public, without a paper devoted to the object.

The Society is in want of some representative before the public, by which its existence may be known, an organ through which its voice may be continually heard. We want a paper to which reference may be had, for a correct exposition of our doctrines and measures, and which shall be the standard of abolition in Maine.

We would deprecate the unnecessary multiplication of Anti-Slavery periodicals. In addition, however, to the *Emancipator,* the organ of the parent society, and the common property of abolitionists generally, one Anti-Slavery paper to each State can not surely be more than the exigencies of the cause require. Maine has already suffered, we believe, from the want of such a paper. The Anti-Slavery cause found in this State some of its earliest and most efficient advocates. The mass of the community are not, however, yet awakened to this great subject. Some of our sister states, in which the true doctrines began to be disseminated at a later period, are already in advance of us. – How much their local papers have contributed to this result, deserves serious consideration. We can not admit that the soil of New Hampshire is better adapted to the growth of Anti-Slavery principles than that of Maine. But she has had her *Herald of Freedom* to proclaim the glad truths of abolition. Its trumpet tones have aroused her hardy sons, and they have come up to the work in numbers and with an energy, that reproves our faultering [*sic*] pace, and tardy footsteps. In Ohio, the work was commenced late, and under circumstances of peculiar trial and difficulty. But her *Philanthropist* has been abroad in the State, pleading in unaffected tones of kindness the cause of the slave. Gathering strength from opposition, and renewed zeal from every effort to destroy it, it has increased the number of its friends, and multiplied converts to the cause, until the whole state has been aroused to an extent that excites our admiration, while it puts our own supineness to the blush.

Abolitionism in Maine, is however, on the advance. The power of truth; and the blessing of God upon the feeble instrumentality employed, have produced most important and favorable changes. The evidence is most cheering, that the true principles of abolitionism, are taking a deep and strong hold on the mass of unperverted, unsophisticated minds, "the bone and muscle of the country," the strength and energy of the church. Upon this class of persons, under God, we mainly rely for success in this mighty moral enterprise. In their bosoms the love of liberty has not been choked by the noxious atmosphere which slavery has been diffusing over the country. In them it still burns, a pure flame. Among them the spirit of inquiry is awake, demanding increased means of information, and promising to sustain a well conducted paper, which, on moderate terms, may widely disseminate the truth.

It is not part of the design in establishing this paper, to divert matter from other mediums of communication with the public, already accessible to the friends of emancipation. When the Anti-Slavery movement commenced in Maine, the religious periodicals, with the exception of the *Christian Mirror*, were closed against the discussion of the subject. They are now, it is believed, without exception, open to it. Every friend of the cause should avail himself of this method of coming before the public, as fully and as far as may be consistent. Although some of the political bearings of slavery, as well as some of the controversies growing out of its discussion, and the mere details of the doings of local societies, may be regarded by some as not coming within the proper sphere of our religious newspapers, yet as a great moral and religious question, slavery must be admitted by all to have a strong claim upon their attention. In this point of view, they can with no more propriety be silent in reference to it, than they can with respect to intemperance, or licentiousness, or any other great sin with which the world is afflicted. Nor will the religious part of the community be satisfied without instruction, through the medium of their newspapers, upon this as well as upon other subjects, in which the interests of religion and morality are concerned. Relieved by the establishment of this paper, of much which might be considered, at least, as a tax upon their space, the moral bearings of slavery, and these are by far the most important, may, we trust, be discussed in their columns to a greater extent than heretofore, and in a manner the best adapted to promote the great object we have in view.

The political press will ere long, we believe, be open to the discussion of this subject. The establishment of this paper, may not be without its influence in producing this desirable result. We shall urge upon abolitionists, to use all the avenues to the public mind which may be opened, and to the extent that propriety will admit. We hope this paper will furnish much matter, which will be transferred to the columns of the common newspapers of the day.

There are many individuals, not connected with Anti-slavery Societies, who, it may be presumed, would look with some degree of interest upon an Anti-slavery paper published in our own State, and who would be induced to read and perhaps to sustain it, if from no other reason, at least from the desire of general information, and the wish to correctly understand the views and purposes, of a large and rapidly increasing body of their fellow citizens, upon one of the most important and vitally interesting questions, upon which the public mind is now agitated.

The question of establishing a paper, has repeatedly been discussed, at the annual meetings of the State Society. Arrangements were made about a year since to commence a paper in Portland, under the title "The Rights of Man," to be under the editorial charge of J. G. Whittier Esq. The commercial embarrassments of the country arrested the movement. Since that time, a paper has been issued under the same title, by a few individuals who have taken a deep interest in the subject. It was continued for about three months, when its further publication was suspended, until the State Society should have opportunity, again to take some action on the subject. At the recent meeting the whole subject, as it will be seen by reference to the votes passed by the Society, was left with the Executive Committee. This committee, after mature deliberation, have determined to proceed with the publication of a paper, provided that a subscription can be obtained sufficient to defray the expense of printing.

The paper if established, will be under the direction of the Executive Committee, and will be conducted by an Association of gentlemen of different religious denominations. It will be exclusively an Anti-slavery paper, and will carefully avoid every thing sectarian in its character and influence. Its object will be to diffuse a knowledge of the truth in respect to the character of American Slavery, to awaken a deeper interest in the cause of our enslaved countrymen, to arouse our fellow-citizens to a sense of the peril to our own liberties arising from the existence of slavery in our land, to rectify public sentiment on the subject, and to bring the whole moral influence of Maine to bear, as it ought, upon the annihilation of the mind-depressing, soul-destroying system of American, republican bondage. It will labor to unite the efforts of the philanthropist, the patriot, and the christian, the wise and the good, for the speedy accomplishment of this great object. Especially will it call upon the church, the purchase of a Savior's blood, "to remember those that are in bonds as bound with them" to "open her mouth for the dumb and to plead the cause of the poor and needy." It will preach "deliverance to the captives, the opening of the prison to those that are bound." It will proclaim, thus saith the Lord "undo the heavy burdens and let the oppressed go free." It will call upon the slave to be "obedient to his master" and to the master to "give unto his servants that which is just and equal."

The present is designed as a specimen number of this paper. The Committee do not deem it proper to pledge the funds of the Society for its support. If the paper proceeds, it must be therefore upon the strength of its subscription list. That the paper may be thus easily sustained, there can be no reasonable doubt, if the friends of the object will make suitable exertions in its behalf. With them, we leave the question, whether it shall proceed or stop. We will merely add our decided conviction, that the best interests of the Anti-slavery cause in the State, require that we go forward.

*Advocate of Freedom,* 8 March 1838,
p.2, c4. [Title supplied.]

## [1838]

**5917 REV. J. HAWES** *to* **THE AAS. [from the** *Bangor Journal*] **n.d. n.p.** Asserts his Christian opposition to slavery. 8 March 1838. p.4, c3.

**5918 n.n.** *to* **THE** *ADVOCATE OF FREEDOM.* **[extract] n.d. n.p.** Expresses her and her husband's commitment to the cause of abolitionism. 29 March 1838. p.7, c1.

**5919 HON. WILLIAM JACKSON** *to* **FRANCIS JACKSON. 11 April 1835. Washington.** Describes the trial and acquittal of Dr. Reuben Crandall, who was charged with abolitionist activity. 29 March 1838. p.8, c3.

**5920 R. G. WILLIAMS** *to* **SIR. 24 February 1838. Maryville, Tn.** Requests that abolitionist literature be sent to him. 29 March 1838. p.8, c4.

**5921 A FRIEND OF THE SLAVE** *to* **MISS GRIMKE. 13 March 1838. Boston.** Discusses his conversion to abolitionism. 12 April 1838. p.9, c4.

**5922 J. S. GREEN** *to* **BROTHER LEAVITT. 29 May 1837. Honolulu, Sandwich Isles.** Supports anti-slavery work in the United States. 12 April 1838. p.9, c5.

**5923 A SPECTATOR** *to* **THE** *ADVOCATE OF FREEDOM.* **7 March 1838. Albany.** Describes the rise of anti-slavery activity in Albany. 12 April 1838. p.12, c4.

**5924 REV. THOMAS T. STONE** *to* **THE** *ADVOCATE OF FREEDOM.* **24 March 1838. East Machias.** Discusses his conversion to abolitionism. 26 April 1838. p.14, c5.

**5925 CHEVALIER DE ST. ANTHOINE** *to* **ELIZUR WRIGHT, JR. [extract] 22 February 1838. Paris.** Discusses anti-slavery efforts of the French. 26 April 1838. p.15, c3.

**5926 ELIZABETH LOVEJOY** *to* **MRS. M---. 19 March 1838. Orono, Old Town.** Thanks the Female AS for accepting her as a lifetime member. 10 May 1838. p.18, c2.

**5927 EDWARD EVERETT** *to* **EDMUND QUINCY. [from the** *Boston Atlas*] **26 April 1838. Boston.** Speculates on the influence which Thome and Kimball's volume on emancipation in the West Indies could have on Northern and Southern views of slavery. 10 May 1838. p.18, c3.

**5928 J. CODDING** *to* **THE** *ADVOCATE OF FREEDOM.* **3 May 1838. New York.** Gives an account of a recent New York AS meeting. 10 May 1838. p.19, c4.

**5929 n.n.** *to* **THE EDITOR OF THE** *EMANCIPATOR.* **18 November 1837. Kaluaaha.** Believes that all Christians should oppose slavery. 10 May 1838. p.19, c5.

**5930 C. C. CONE** *to* **THE EDITOR OF THE** *ADVOCATE OF FREEDOM.* **11 April 1838. East Machias.** Reports on resolutions adopted at an anti-slavery convention in Washington County. 24 May 1838. p.21, c2.

**5931 THOMAS T. STONE** *to* **n.n. 23 January 1838. East Machias.** Affirms his support of the anti-slavery cause. 24 May 1838. p.24, c2.

**5932 DAVID THURSTON** *to* **CONGREGATIONAL MINISTERS OF MAINE. n.d. n.p.** Appeals to Congregational ministers in Maine to support abolitionism. 7 June 1838. p.26, c3.

**5934 J. N.** *to* **THE EDITORS OF THE** *ADVOCATE OF FREEDOM.* **n.d. n.p.** Criticizes the *Advocate of Freedom*'s coverage of mob violence in Philadelphia. 7 June 1838. p.27, c4.

**5935 BENJAMIN TAPPAN** *to* **THE EDITORS OF THE** *ADVOCATE OF FREEDOM.* **5 June 1838. Augusta.** Discusses the formation and purpose of the Augusta AS. 21 June 1838. p.30, c4.

**5936 CITIZEN OF BRUNSWICK** *to* **THE** *ADVOCATE OF FREEDOM.* **n.d. n.p.** Reports on an anti-slavery meeting held at Rev. G. E. Adams's house. 21 June 1838. p.31, c3.

**5937 JOHN Q. ADAMS** *to* **SAMUEL WEBB AND WILLIAM SCOTT. 19 January 1838. Washington.** Congratulates the Pennsylvania Hall Association for erecting an abolitionist hall in Philadelphia. 21 June 1838. p.32, c4.

**5938 n.n.** *to* **n.n. [from the** *Pennsylvania Freeman***] 20 May 1838. Washington, D.C.** Expresses satisfaction at the destruction of the abolitionist meeting hall in Philadelphia. 21 June 1838. p.32, c5.

**5939 RAY PALMER** *to* **MR. DAVID THURSTON. 14 June 1838. Bath.** States that he opposes slavery but is not convinced that anti-slavery meetings are the correct means by which to abolish slavery. 5 July 1838. p.33, c1.

**5940 P. R.** *to* **THE EDITORS OF THE** *ADVOCATE OF FREEDOM.* **May 1838. Cumberland.** Describes the rise of anti-slavery activity in Cumberland. 5 July 1838. p.33, c5.

**5941 S.** *to* **THE EDITORS OF THE** *ADVOCATE OF FREEDOM.* **n.d. n.p.** Reviews the life of abolitionist William Wilberforce. 5 July 1838. p.34, c2.

**5942 JOHN WESLEY** *to* **WILLIAM WILBERFORCE. 24 February 1791. n.p.** Praises Wilberforce for his anti-slavery work. 5 July 1838. p.35, c3.

**5943 REV. J. EDWARDS** *to* **MR. BIRNEY. 16 June 1838. Andover.** Thanks him for sending an article on emancipation in the West Indies. 5 July 1838. p.35, c5.

**5944 M. R.** *to* **THE EDITORS OF THE** *ADVOCATE OF FREEDOM.* **n.d. n.p.** Reports on resolutions adopted at the New England Methodist Episcopal Conference. 19 July 1838. p.38, c2.

**5945 ICHABOD CODDING** *to* **THE ABOLITIONISTS OF MAINE. n.d. n.p.** Exhorts the Maine abolitionists to continue and escalate their abolitionist work. 19 July 1838. p.38, c4.

**5946 PETER THATCHER** *to* **THE EDITORS OF THE** *ADVOCATE OF FREEDOM.* **14 July 1838. Machias.** Reports on the first annual meeting of the Washington County AS. 19 July 1838. p.39, c5.

**5947 E. GOODNOW** *to* **THE EDITORS OF THE** *ADVOCATE OF FREEDOM.* **n.d. n.p.** Reports on the formation of the Norway and Paris AS. 19 July 1838. p.39, c5.

**5948 A. C. B.** *to* **FRIEND. [from the** *Pennsylvania Freeman***] 25 June 1838. Baltimore.** Encloses an article from the *Baltimore Sun* on the accidental drowning of an unidentified Negro. 19 July 1838. p.40, c4.

**5950 DAVID THURSTON** *to* **BROTHER PALMER. n.d. n.p.** Concurs with Palmer's propositions, but exhorts him to promote abolition more forcefully. 2 August 1838. p.42, c1.

**5951 A.** *to* **THE EDITORS OF THE** *ADVOCATE OF FREEDOM.* **n.d. n.p.** Encloses a narrative of a runaway slave. 2 August 1838. p.43, c1.

**5952 C. C. CONE** *to* **THE EDITORS OF THE** *ADVOCATE OF FREEDOM.* **30 July 1838. n.p.** Describes the controversy surrounding the Pacification Bill. 2 August 1838. p.43, c3.

**5953 R.** *to* **THE EDITORS OF THE** *ADVOCATE OF FREEDOM.* **n.d. n.p.** Describes the rise of abolitionist activity in Bethel. 16 August 1838. p.45, c3.

**5954 F.** *to* **THE** *ADVOCATE OF FREEDOM.* **25 July 1838. South Bridgton.** Describes Fourth of July celebration in Bridgton. 16 August 1838. p.45, c4.

**5955 A FREEMAN** *to* **THE** *ADVOCATE OF FREEDOM.* **5 August 1838. Calais.** Reports on Mr. Codding's anti-slavery lecture in Calais. 16 August 1838. p.46, c1.

**5956 EXECUTIVE COMMITTEE OF THE SOMERSET AS** *to* **GOV. EDWARD KENT. 23 July 1838. Norridgewock.** Wishes to know Kent's position on slavery. 16 August 1838. p.47, c3.

**5957 GOV. EDWARD KENT** *to* **EXECUTIVE COMMITTEE OF THE SOMERSET AS. 27 July 1838. Bangor.** Asserts that slavery is a great evil. 16 August 1838. p.47, c4.

**5958 DAVID THURSTON** *to* **REV. PALMER. n.d. n.p.** Criticizes Palmer's reasons for refusing to join an AS. 30 August 1838. p.49, c1.

**5959 n.n.** *to* **THE** *ADVOCATE OF FREEDOM.* **n.d. n.p.** Describes a successful abolitionist meeting in Machias. 30 August 1838. p.50, c4.

**5960 HON. JOHN FAIRFIELD** *to* **MESSRS. E. COBURN, &C. 15 August 1838. Saco.** Affirms that slavery is a moral and political evil. 30 August 1838. p.51, c3.

**5961 WM. R. HAYES** *to* **n.n. [from the** *New Haven Herald***] 2 August 1838. Barbados.** Describes emancipation celebrations in Barbados. 27 September 1838. p.57, c4.

**5962 RAY PALMER** *to* **MR. THURSTON. 17 September 1838. Bath.** Reaffirms his opposition to slavery, but refuses to abandon his Christian endeavors to labor for the cause. 27 September 1838. p.58, c1.

**5963 J. W. ELLINGWOOD** *to* **THE** *ADVOCATE OF FREEDOM.* **n.d. n.p.** Corrects "T. N. L." 's assertion that pro-slavery sentiment prevailed at a recent meeting of the Lincoln Conference of Churches. 27 September 1838. p.58, c4.

**5964 DANIEL B. RANDALL AND HARRISON B. GOWER** *to* **THE EDITORS OF THE** *ADVOCATE OF FREEDOM.* **8 September 1838. New Sharon.** Enclose resolutions adopted by a meeting of young men of New Sharon calling for an anti-slavery convention. 27 September 1838. p.59, c5.

**5965 JOHN Q. ADAMS** *to* **EDMUND QUINCY. 28 July 1838. Quincy.** Refuses offer of a speaking engagement but encourages Quincy to continue with his abolitionist work. 27 September 1838. p.60, c3.

**5966 JAMES G. BIRNEY** *to* **THE EDITOR OF THE** *ADVOCATE OF FREEDOM.* **n.d. n.p.** Describes atrocities committed by slaveholders. 27 September 1838. p.60, c3.

**5967 D. HART** *to* **n.n. [from the** *Liberator***] 19 July 1838. Kingston, Jamaica.** Denies reports of laziness and irresponsibility in freedmen. 27 September 1838. p.60, c4.

**5968 MR. CUMMINGS** *to* **THE EDITORS OF THE** *ADVOCATE OF FREEDOM.* **n.d. n.p.** Asserts that no portion of the country will be free from the influence of slavery until slavery is abolished. 11 October 1838. p.61, c5.

**5969 C. C. CONE** *to* **THE** *ADVOCATE OF FREEDOM.* **10 September 1838. n.p.** Requests further evidence in support of the Pacification Bill. 11 October 1838. p.62, c1.

**5970 B. F. SPRAGUE AND H. B. GOWER** *to* **MESSRS. EDITORS OF THE** *ADVOCATE OF FREEDOM.* **20 September 1838. M. W. Seminary.** Describe the formation and purpose of the Maine Wesleyan Seminary AS. 11 October 1838. p.62, c2.

**5971 T. N. LORD** *to* **THE EDITORS OF THE** *ADVOCATE OF FREEDOM.* **n.d. n.p.** Reaffirms his assertion that pro-slavery sentiment prevailed at the meeting of the Lincoln Conference of Churches. 11 October 1838. p.62, c4.

**5972 J. T. HAWES** *to* **THE EDITORS OF THE** *ADVOCATE OF FREEDOM.* **n.d. n.p.** Comments on pro-slavery opinions of those attending a recent meeting of the Lincoln Conference of Churches. 11 October 1838. p.62, c5.

**5973 GEORGE W. HATHAWAY** *to* **THE EDITORS OF THE** *ADVOCATE OF FREEDOM.* **26 September 1838. Bloomfield.** Supports a call for a young men's anti-slavery convention in Maine. 11 October 1838. p.63, c4.

**5974 L.** *to* **MESSRS. EDITORS. n.d. n.p.** Reviews the events of Garrison's early adult life, culminating in his establishment of the *Liberator;* encloses a letter from Garrison to Arthur Tappan. 11 October 1838. p.64, c1.

**5975 W. L. GARRISON** *to* **ARTHUR TAPPAN. 14 July 1830. Baltimore.** Thanks Tappan for paying a fine for libel which he incurred while editing the *Genius of Universal Emancipation.* 11 October 1838. p.64, c1.

**5976 T. FOWELL BUXTON** *to* **[JOSEPH] STURGE. 30 July 1838. London.** Rejoices that slavery has been abolished in the West Indies. 25 October 1838. p.65. c1.

**5977 JOHN BOYNTON** *to* **MR. EDITOR. n.d. n.p.** Refutes Rev. Ellingwood's charges of "lawlessness" and "rudeness" for introducing the subject of slavery at a recent meeting of the Lincoln Conference of Churches. 25 October 1838. p.65, c3.

**5978 C.** *to* **THE EDITORS OF THE** *ADVOCATE OF FREEDOM.* **5 October 1838. Norwich.** Gives an account of the proceedings of the Young Men's Anti-Slavery Convention at Worcester. 25 October 1838. p.67, c1.

**5979 W.** *to* **THE EDITORS OF THE** *ADVOCATE OF FREEDOM.* **25 October 1838. Topsham.** Urges attendance at the first anniversary of the Lincoln County AS. 25 October 1838. p.67, c5.

**5980 DANIEL O'CONNELL** *to* **THE EDITOR OF THE** *MORNING CHRONICLE.* **n.d. n.p.** States his intent to inform England and Europe of the cruelty of American slavery. 8 November 1838. p.69, c5.

**5981 A YORK COUNTY ABOLITIONIST** *to* **THE EDITORS OF THE** *ADVOCATE OF FREEDOM.* **n.d. n.p.** Urges attendance at an abolitionist meeting in South Berwick. 8 November 1838. p.70, c2.

**5982 E. C. P.** *to* **MR. EDITOR. [from the** *Liberator***] n.d. n.p.** Encloses an extract of a letter for publication. 8 November 1838. p.72, c2.

**5983 n.n.** *to* **n.n. [extract from the** *Liberator***] n.d. L---.** Describes the assistance given by local residents to fugitive slaves. 8 November 1838. p.72, c2.

**5984 REV. JOHN MITER** *to* **STANTON. [from the** *Emancipator***] 4 October 1838. Knoxville.** Gives an account of the first anniversary meeting of the Illinois AS held at Farminton. 22 November 1838. p.73, c4.

**5985 J. W. ELLINGWOOD** *to* **THE EDITOR OF THE** *ADVOCATE OF FREEDOM.* **n.d. n.p.** Asserts that no efforts were made to prevent prayers for the slaves at the meeting of the Lincoln Conference of Churches. 22 November 1838. p.73, c5.

**5986 GOVERNOR EDWARD KENT** *to* **REV. S. L. POMROY. 5 November 1838. Bangor.** Praises the book by Messrs. Thome and Kimball discussing the success of emancipation in the West Indies. 22 November 1838. p.74, c4.

**5987 REV. JOHN B. MAHAN** *to* **THE** *PHILANTHROPIST.* **n.d. n.p.** Discusses his experiences in Southern jails. 22 November 1838. p.75, c4.

**5988 J. W. ELLINGWOOD** *to* **THE** *ADVOCATE OF FREEDOM.* **n.d. n.p.** Criticizes Hawes's letter alleging strong pro-slavery sentiment at the Lincoln Conference of Churches; reviews the conduct of speakers at the conference. 22 November 1838. p.76, c2.

**5989 JOHN BOYNTON** *to* **THE EDITORS OF THE** *ADVOCATE OF FREEDOM.* **n.d. n.p.** Reports on the first annual meeting of the Lincoln County AS. 6 December 1838. p.77, c1.

**5990 H. K. R.** *to* **THE EDITORS OF THE** *ADVOCATE OF FREEDOM.* **n.d. n.p.** Criticizes the *Advocate of Freedom* for failing to report the views of abolitionists and slaveholders objectively. 6 December 1838. p.78, c2.

**5991 REV. KIAH BAYLEY** *to* **REV. J. T. HAWES. n.d. n.p.** Denounces pro-slavery men who asserted that laborers are not qualified to enter into politics; urges abolitionists to strive for the cause. 6 December 1838. p.78, c3.

**5992 O. SCOTT** *to* **BROTHER LEAVITT. [from the** *Emancipator***] n.d. Pittsburgh.** Reports on a meeting of the AS of Western Pennsylvania. 6 December 1838. p.78, c5.

**5993 S. A. LOVELL** *to* **THE** *ADVOCATE OF FREEDOM.* **n.d. n.p.** Gives an account of the first annual meeting of the Bangor Juvenile AS. 6 December 1838. p.79, c3.

**5994 J. W. ELLINGWOOD** *to* **THE EDITOR OF THE** *ADVOCATE OF FREEDOM.* **n.d. n.p.** Defends the Lincoln Conference of Churches' rules limiting the discussion of slavery at meetings. 6 December 1838. p.80, c1.

**5995 JOHN TITCOMB AND DANIEL SEWALL** *to* **THE** *ADVOCATE OF FREEDOM.* **n.d. n.p.** Give an account of the second meeting of the Franklin County AS. 20 December 1838. p.81, c1.

**5996 O. B. WALKER** *to* **BRO. WASHBURN. 3 December 1838. Baring, Me.** Emphasizes the need for an AS in Baring, Maine. 20 December 1838. p.81, c3.

**5997 O. B. W[ALKER]** *to* **THE** *ADVOCATE OF FREEDOM.* **n.d. Baring, Me.** Emphasizes the usefulness of the *Anti-Slavery Almanac.* 20 December 1838. p.81, c3.

**5998 REV. MERRILL** *to* **MESSRS. EDITORS. 17 October 1838. Alna.** Defends the exclusion of the issue of slavery from discussion at the meeting of the Lincoln Conference of Churches. 20 December 1838. p.82, c2.

**5999 A COLORED MECHANIC** *to* **HIS BROTHER. 23 September. Kingston, Jamaica.** Describes the benefits and difficulties which have resulted from the abolition of slavery in Jamaica. 20 December 1838. p.83, c2.

**6000 LUTHER LEE** *to* **THE EDITOR OF THE** *ADVOCATE OF FREEDOM.* **n.d. n.p.** Encloses a handbill advertising slaves for sale; condemns slavery. 20 December 1838. p.84, c1.

**6001 n.n.** *to* **JAMES G. BIRNEY. 22 November 1838. n.p.** Requests that abolitionist literature be sent to him. 20 December 1838. p.83, c3.

**6002 L. BRADFORD** *to* **n.n. 12 December 1838. Guilford.** Gives an account of the first annual meeting of the Piscataquis County AS. 20 December 1838. p.83, c5.

**6003 LUTHER LEE** *to* **THE EDITOR OF THE** *ADVOCATE OF FREEDOM.* **n.d. n.p.** Denounces slavery and calls for immediate and unconditional abolition. 20 December 1838. p.84, c1.

## [1839]

**6004 HENRY SCOTT** *to* **THE CITIZENS OF WORCESTER. [from the** *Massachusetts Spy***] 4 December 1838. Worcester.** A colored man condemns the existence of slavery. 3 January 1839. p.85, c4.

**6005 I. C.** *to* **THE EDITOR OF THE** *ADVOCATE OF FREEDOM.* **n.d. n.p.** Reports on the success of his anti-slavery lecture tour of Parsonsfield, Limerick, Bridgton, and Waterford. 3 January 1839. p.87, c2.

**6006 DAVID H. LORD** *to* **THE** *ADVOCATE OF FREEDOM.* **10 December 1838. Springvale.** Reports on the proceedings of the York County AS. 3 January 1839. p.88, c1.

**6007 J. Q. ADAMS** *to* **OLIVER JOHNSON. 13 December 1838. Washington.** Proclaims that slavery is contradictory to the principles on which the United States is founded. 17 January 1839. p.89, c2.

**6008 GOV. EDWARD KENT** *to* **GOV. GEORGE R. GILMER OF GEORGIA. 25 June 1838. Augusta.** Refuses to comply with Gilmer's demand for the surrender of Messrs. Philbrook and Kelleran, who are accused of stealing an alleged slave from Georgia. 17 January 1839. p.89, c4.

**6009 C.** *to* **THE** *ADVOCATE OF FREEDOM.* **n.d. n.p.** Reports on the annual meeting of the Piscataquis County AS. 17 January 1839. p.91, c1.

**6010 n.n.** *to* **REV. JOSHUA LEAVITT. [from the** *Emancipator***] 6 December 1838. Kingston, Jamaica.** Expresses optimism for the economic and spiritual future of Jamaica. 17 January 1839. p.91, c5.

**6011 H. E. C. F.** *to* **THE** *ADVOCATE OF FREEDOM.* **10 January. Camden.** Believes that women can play a useful part in the abolition of slavery. 31 January 1839. p.93, c5.

**6012 L. BRADFORD AND C. LENOX REMOND** *to* **THE** *ADVOCATE OF FREEDOM.* **n.d. n.p.** Provide an account of the first annual meeting of the Piscataquis County AS. 31 January 1839. p.94, c1.

**6013 F.** *to* **THE** *ADVOCATE OF FREEDOM.* **n.d. n.p.** Stresses the Christian nature of abolitionism. 31 January 1839. p.94, c5.

**6014 J. R. SHAW** *to* **THE EDITORS OF THE** *ADVOCATE OF FREEDOM.* **26 January 1839. Camden.** Announces the formation of the Camden AS. 31 January 1839. p.95, c3.

**6015 JUSTIN PARSONS** *to* **THE EDITOR OF THE** *ADVOCATE OF FREEDOM.* **[from the** *Voice of Freedom***] 12 January 1839. Jamaica.** Praises the *Advocate of Freedom* for its anti-slavery work. 31 January 1839. p.95, c3.

**6016 J. HAWES** *to* **A. M. COLLINS. 4 December 1838. Hartford.** Emphasizes the importance of abolitionism and speculates about the position of the Negro after freedom. 31 January 1839. p.96, c1.

**6017 REV. I. N. SPRAGUE** *to* **THE PRESIDENT OF THE STATE ANTI-SLAVERY CONVENTION. 4 December 1838. Hartford.** Regrets that poor health will prevent him from attending the state anti-slavery convention at Middletown. 31 January 1839. p.96, c1.

**6018 GERRIT SMITH** *to* **THE EDITOR OF THE** *UNION HERALD.* **1 December 1838. Peterboro'.** Describes the successful escape of the slaves John Williams and John Williams Scott from their master, Samuel Ferguson. 31 January 1839. p.96, c2.

**6019 J. W. ELLINGWOOD** *to* **THE EDITOR OF THE** *ADVOCATE OF FREEDOM.* **n.d. n.p.** Provides further clarification of the Lincoln Conference discussion. 31 January 1839. p.96, c4.

**6020 S. B. G.** *to* **THE EDITOR OF THE** *ADVOCATE OF FREEDOM.* **November 1838. Bath.** States that despite his disagreement with some of the abolitionist principles, he has recently joined an AS. 21 February 1839. p.97, c5.

**6021 W. R. HAYES** *to* **H. G. LUDLOW. [from the** *N. Y. Journal of Commerce***] 26 December 1838. Barbadoes.** Describes the successful emancipation of slaves in Barbados; considers the merits and shortcomings of colonization. 21 February 1839. p.98, c2.

**6022 J.** *to* **THE EDITOR OF THE** *ADVOCATE OF FREEDOM.* **n.d. n.p.** Encloses an account of the escape of a runaway slave. 21 February 1839. p.100, c3.

**6023 REV. E. ROBINSON** *to* **REV. WM. SMYTH. 14 March 1839. Pownal.** Affirms his opinions as an abolitionist. 25 April 1839. p.3, c2.

**6024 S. A. LOVELL** *to* **MR. CODDING. n.d. n.p.** Thanks the Juvenile AS for its financial contribution to the cause. 25 April 1839. p.3, c3.

**6025 I. CODDING** *to* **THE EDITOR OF THE** *ADVOCATE OF FREEDOM.* **n.d. n.p.** Expresses dismay at a speech given by a fugitive slave who claimed to have seen Henry Clay "half drunk"; reports that both Whigs and Democrats accuse Codding of being a member of the opposite party. 25 April 1839. p.3, c3.

**6026 REV. G. W. HATHAWAY** *to* **DR. E. SOUTHWICK. 20 April 1839. Bloomfield.** Declines the appointment as editor of the *Advocate of Freedom* because of opposition from members of his church and other ministers in Bloomfield. 2 May 1839. p.7, c3.

**6027 D. S. INGRAHAM** *to* **BRO. BENEDICT. 17 January 1839. Kingston, Jamaica.** Discusses the reluctance of emancipated slaves in Jamaica to work, due to low wages; comments on the growth of interest in religion since emancipation. 9 May 1839. p.12, c2.

**6028 n.n.** *to* **FRIENDS. 21 February 1839. Paterson's Point, La.** Comments on the increase of violence and decrease of religious sentiment in Louisiana. 16 May 1839. p.14, c3.

**6029 W. T. ALLAN** *to* **BRO. [from the** *Emancipator*] **n.d. n.p.** Gives an account of a pro-slavery speech delivered to the Choctaw Indians in Arkansas by the Methodist missionary M'Kenzie. 16 May 1839. p.16, c3.

**6030 GERRIT SMITH** *to* **MR. GOODELL. [from the** *Friend of Man*] **15 February 1839. Peterboro'.** Encloses an extract of a letter describing slave sales in Richmond. 23 May 1839. p.18, c1.

**6031 A FRIEND** *to* **GERRIT SMITH. [extract from the** *Friend of Man*] **7 February 1839. Washington.** Describes the selling of slaves in Richmond. 23 May 1839. p.18, c2.

**6032 BENJAMIN TAPPAN** *to* **FRANCIS S. KEY. 31 July 1838. Augusta.** Requests information concerning public opinion in the South on slavery. 23 May 1839. p.18, c2.

**6033 H. NYE** *to* **n.n. [extract from the** *Emancipator*] **8 March 1839. Putnam, Oh.** Criticizes the Ohio legislature for passing a pro-slavery law; reports on the growth of anti-slavery sentiment in Ohio. 23 May 1839. p.18, c4.

**6034 O. S. C.** *to* **MR. EDITOR. [from the** *Christian Reflector*] **9 February 1839. Boston.** A former slaveholder describes his experiences with slavery and discusses his conversion to abolitionism. 23 May 1839. p.20, c2.

**6035 JOSHUA COFFIN** *to* **BROTHER. [from the** *Liberator*] **12 March 1839. Philadelphia.** Describes his trip to the South. 23 May 1839. p.20, c3.

**6036 MR. KEY** *to* **DR. TAPPAN. 8 October 1838. Washington.** States that Maryland would favor emancipation if the freedmen were to be colonized, rather than remain in the United States. 30 May 1839. p.21, c1.

**6037 S. D.** *to* **THE EDITOR OF THE** *CULTIVATOR.* **29 April 1839. Wayland.** Requests agricultural advice and information. 30 May 1839. p.23, c1.

**6038 HARLEY BUSHNELL BROWNELL** *to* **HIS UNCLE. [from the** *Zion's Watchman*] **15 March 1839. Centerville, Bibb County, Al.** Describes his lucrative position as an overseer of slaves; believes that slaves should not be pitied. 30 May 1839. p.24, c3.

**6039 J. S.** *to* **THE EDITOR OF THE** *ADVOCATE OF FREEDOM.* **1839. Washington.** Believes that the existence of slavery is a contradiction to the principles on which the United States was founded. 6 June 1839. p.28, c3.

**6040 D. S. INGRAHAM** *to* **S. W. BENEDICT. 3 April 1839. Shortwood.** Encloses a financial contribution to the anti-slavery cause. 6 June 1839. p.28, c4.

**6041 R. F.** *to* **THE EDITOR OF THE** *ADVOCATE OF FREEDOM.* **n.d. n.p.** Commends a letter from W. E. Channing to Jonathan Phillips in which Channing refutes Henry Clay's pro-slavery arguments. 20 June 1839. p.33, c1.

**6042 W. P.** *to* **THE EDITOR OF THE** *ADVOCATE OF FREEDOM.* **7 June 1839. Brewer.** Refutes arguments by Southern ministers who attempt to justify their purchase of slaves. 20 June 1839. p.33, c2.

**6043 DR. [B.] TAPPAN** *to* **F. S. KEY. 30 May 1839. Augusta, Me.** Discusses difficulties encountered by emancipated slaves in the United States; opposes colonization. 20 June 1839. p.33, c5.

**6044 B. TAPPAN** *to* **MR. KEY. n.d. n.p.** Describes the evils of slavery; urges Southern Christians to oppose slavery; abhors colonization. [continued from 20 June 1839] 27 June 1839. p.37, c1.

**6045 A WOMAN** *to* **THE** *ADVOCATE OF FREEDOM.* **n.d. Kennebec County.** Criticizes women who deliver speeches in public. 27 June 1839. p.38, c1.

**6046 ICHABOD CODDING** *to* **BROTHER ADAMS. 23 June. Hallowell.** Encloses contributions made to the Maine State AS. 27 June 1839. p.39, c1.

**6047 C.** *to* **THE** *ADVOCATE OF FREEDOM.* **n.d. n.p.** Believes it proper for Christians to oppose slavery. 4 July 1839. p.42, c1.

**6048 I. CODDING** *to* **BRO. ADAMS. 19 June 1839. Farmington.** Reports on anti-slavery lectures by Randall, Remond, and himself; believes that the anti-abolitionist speeches by Clay and Adams will strengthen support for the anti-slavery cause. 4 July 1839. p.42, c3.

**6049 JOHN S. TENNEY** *to* **ELEAZER COBURN. 27 February 1839. Norridgewock.** Explains why he will not be able to address the Norridgewock AS. 4 July 1839. p.43, c2.

**6050 J. J. FLOURNOY** *to* **DR. BENJAMIN TAPPAN. 15 May 1839. Wellington, Ga.** Disagrees with the theory that Negroes are the children of Ham. 4 July 1839. p.43, c2.

**6051 JOHN TITCOMB** *to* **FRIENDS OF THE SLAVE IN FRANKLIN COUNTY. 2 July 1839. Farmington.** Suggests method of raising money for the anti-slavery movement. 11 July 1839. p.46, c2.

**6052 J. W. D.** *to* **THE EDITOR OF THE** *ADVOCATE OF FREEDOM.* **29 June 1839. Bowdoin College.** Provides fund raising suggestions for anti-slavery organizations. 11 July 1839. p.46, c3.

**6053 ISAAC LIBBY** *to* **THE EDITORS OF THE** *ADVOCATE OF FREEDOM.* **n.d. n.p.** Requests donation for the AAS. 11 July 1839. p.46, c3.

**6054 J. S. P.** *to* **MR. WHITTIER. [from the** *Pennsylvania Freeman***] n.d. n.p.** Praises Weld's pamphlet, "Slavery as it is." 11 July 1839. p.47, c1.

**6055 n.n.** *to* **MR. SLEEPER. [from the** *Mer. Journal***] 24 June 1839. Exeter, N.H.** Notes with satisfaction that it will now be possible to travel from Exeter to Boston by railroad. 11 July 1839. p.47, c3.

**6056 Y.** *to* **THE EDITOR OF THE** *ATLAS.* **11 June 1839. New York.** Discusses the economic and political interests of the South and opposes dominance of Southern interests in the formulation of national policy. 18 July 1839. p.49, c1.

**6057 MARSHAL CRAM** *to* **THE EDITOR OF THE** *ADVOCATE OF FREEDOM.* **6 July 1839. South Bridgton.** Reports on resolutions adopted at a meeting of the AS of Bridgton. 18 July 1839. p.50, c3.

**6058 G. F. TALBOT** *to* **THE** *ADVOCATE OF FREEDOM.* **9 July. East Machias.** Informs of the results of elections held by the Washington County AS. 18 July 1839. p.50, c4.

**6059 J. D. W.** *to* **THE** *ADVOCATE OF FREEDOM.* **10 July 1839. Brunswick.** Discusses conflicting views among colonizationists regarding the rights of the Negroes. 18 July 1839. p.51, c1.

**6060 C. C. BURLEIGH** *to* **THE** *PENNSYLVANIA FREEMAN.* **n.d. n.p.** Encloses an extract of a letter from a friend. 18 July 1839. p.52, c4.

**6061 A FRIEND** *to* **C. C. BURLEIGH. [extract from the** *Pennsylvania Freeman***] n.d. n.p.** Encloses a contribution to the executive committee of the Pennsylvania AS. 18 July 1839. p.52, c4.

**6062 G. C. WATERMAN** *to* **REV. MR. ADAMS. n.d. n.p.** Discusses the financial needs of the Maine AS. 25 July 1839. p.53, c4.

**6063 A. W.** *to* **THE EDITOR OF THE** *ADVOCATE OF FREEDOM.* **28 June. n.p.** Discusses the merits of colonization. 25 July 1839. p.54, c1.

**6064 I. C.** *to* **THE MASSACHUSETTS ABOLITION SOCIETY AND THE EDITOR OF THE** *MIRROR.* **n.d. n.p.** Relates the proceedings of the Anti-Slavery Convention of Congregational Ministers and Laymen at Brunswick. 25 July 1839. p.54, c3.

**6065 J. A. THOME** *to* **BROTHER. [from the** *Oberlin Evangelist***] n.d. n.p.** Encloses a letter from a Jamaican planter. 25 July 1839. p.55, c2.

**6066 A PLANTER IN JAMAICA** *to* **J. A. THOME. [from the** *Oberlin Evangelist***] 13 October 1839. Port Morant, Jamaica.** States that emancipated slaves are unwilling to work because they were mistreated by their masters; wishes to hire American Negro workers for his sugar plantation. 25 July 1839. p.55, c2.

**6067 A MERCHANT** *to* **n.n. [extract from the** *Louisiana Advertiser***] 20 May. Vicksburg.** Describes the lack of law enforcement in Vicksburg. 25 July 1839. p.55, c3.

**6068 Z[ENAS] B[LISS]** *to* **MR. TRACY. [from the** *Vermont Chronicle***] n.d. n.p.** Encloses correspondence between himself and Nathan Lord. 3 August 1839. p.57, c1.

**6069 REV. ZENAS BLISS** *to* **REV. NATHAN LORD. [from the** *Vermont Chronicle***] 16 April 1839. Quechee, Vt.** Criticizes him for sanctioning abolitionist activities by church members. 3 August 1839. p.57, c1.

**6070 REV. NATHAN LORD** *to* **REV. ZENAS BLISS. 30 May 1839. Dartmouth College.** Reaffirms his support of abolitionism but reserves the right to disassociate himself from any action by an individual abolitionist; opposes the claim by some pastors to supreme moral authority. 3 August 1839. p.57, c2.

**6071 I. CODDING** *to* **BRO. ADAMS. 23 July 1839. Waterford.** Gives an account of his anti-slavery lecture tour in Bridgton, Fryburg, Sweden, and Waterford. 3 August 1839. p.57 [59], c1.

**6072 H. B. G.** *to* **THE** *ADVOCATE OF FREEDOM.* **31 July. Brunswick.** Criticizes the young men of Massachusetts for their apathetic response to abolitionism. 3 August 1839. p.57 [59], c2.

**6073 ONE OF YOUR READERS** *to* **THE EDITOR OF THE** *ADVOCATE OF FREEDOM.* **22 July. n.p.** Encloses a copy of a sermon on the immorality of slavery. 3 August 1839. p.57 [59], c2.

**6074 J. C. ASPENWALL** *to* **THE EDITOR OF THE** *ADVOCATE OF FREEDOM.* **22 July 1839. Augusta.** Informs that a runaway slave from Georgia was betrayed by the man who aided his escape. 3 August 1839. p.57 [59], c2.

**6075 S. D. C.** *to* **BROTHER. [from the** *Oberlin Evangelist***] 10 June 1839. Oberlin.** Encloses an extract of a letter containing proof that abolitionists receive support in the South. 3 August 1839. p.58 [60], c3.

**6076 n.n.** *to* **SIR. [extract from the** *Oberlin Evangelist***] 14 May 1839. Arkansas.** Informs that support for abolitionists exists in the South. 3 August 1839. p.58 [60], c3.

**6077 WM. GOODELL** *to* **JOHN Q. ADAMS. n.d. n.p.** Criticizes Adams's opposition to abolitionism. 10 August 1839. p.59 [61], c1.

**6078 UNION** *to* **THE** *ADVOCATE OF FREEDOM.* **n.d. n.p.** Argues that the Constitution need not be construed as a pro-slavery document. 10 August 1839. p.60 [62], c1.

**6079 MANY VOTERS** *to* **THE EDITOR OF THE** *ADVOCATE OF FREEDOM.* **7 August 1839. n.p.** Discuss their criteria for an acceptable gubernatorial candidate. 10 August 1839. p.60 [62], c2.

**6080 G. S.** *to* **THE** *ADVOCATE OF FREEDOM.* **n.d. n.p.** Supports the right of free speech on the subject of slavery. 10 August 1839. p.60 [62], c3.

**6081 R. F.** *to* **THE** *ADVOCATE OF FREEDOM.* **n.d. n.p.** Comments on the hypocrisy of the ACS. 10 August 1839. p.60 [62], c4.

**6082 PROF. LEONARD WOODS, JR., PRESIDENT ELECT OF BOWDOIN COLLEGE** *to* **THE** *ADVOCATE OF FREEDOM.* **n.d. n.p.** Discusses the origins of the human race. 10 August 1839. p.61 [63], c1.

**6083 J. G. PIKE** *to* **BRO. BURR. [from the** *Morning Star***] 6 November 1838. Derby, England.** Encourages American abolitionists to strive for the anti-slavery cause. 10 August 1839. p.61 [63], c3.

**6084 I. CODDING** *to* **BRO. ADAMS. n.d. n.p.** Lists towns from which pledges and money have been received. 10 August 1839. p.61 [63], c3.

**6085 TRUTH** *to* **MR. EDITOR. n.d. n.p.** Asserts that Reverend Hopkins's sermon did not imply opposition to abolitionism. 10 August 1839. p.62 [64], c1.

**6086 WILLIAM KENRICK** *to* **THE EDITOR OF THE** *FARMER'S REGISTER.* **1 April 1839. Portsmouth, Va.** Discusses the effect of slavery on agriculture in Virginia. 17 August 1839. p.65, c1.

**6087 n.n.** *to* **JOSIAH BRACKETT. [from the** *Massachusetts Abolitionist***] 19 July 1839. Westboro'.** Regrets that he cannot accept the appointment as delegate to the National Anti-Slavery Convention in Albany; encourages prudent political action by abolitionists. 17 August 1839. p.65, c3.

**6088 THOMAS MORRIS** *to* **N. SAFFORD, ESQ. 22 July 1839. Cincinnati.** Explains why he cannot attend the National Anti-Slavery Convention at Albany. 17 August 1839. p.66, c1.

**6089 EDWARD C. DELAVAN** *to* **GENTLEMEN. 28 July 1839. Ballston Centre.** Regrets that he is unable to attend the National Anti-Slavery Convention at Albany; reports on English opposition to American slavery. 17 August 1839. p.66, c2.

**6090 DELTA** *to* **THE EDITOR OF THE** *ADVOCATE OF FREEDOM.* **13 August 1839. n.p.** Corrects a biblical quote in "Union" 's letter to the *Advocate of Freedom* and comments on the common practice of misquoting the Scriptures. 17 August 1839. p.66, c4.

**6091 D.** *to* **MR. EDITOR. n.d. n.p.** Disagrees with the correspondent "Truth," who asserted that Rev. Hopkins's sermon did not denounce abolitionists; encloses an extract of a letter from Mathew Wilkis to a lady of his acquaintance. 17 August 1839. p.67, c1.

**6092 MATHEW WILKIS** *to* **n.n. [extract] n.d. n.p.** Introduces a friend to her; encloses a poem. 17 August 1839. p.67, c1.

**6093 A HEARER** *to* **THE EDITOR OF THE** *ADVOCATE OF FREEDOM.* **n.d. n.p.** Reports on Reverend Pomroy's lecture refuting the doctrines of colonization. 17 August 1839. p.67, c1.

**6094 UNION** *to* **THE EDITOR OF THE** *ADVOCATE OF FREEDOM.* **n.d. n.p.** Discusses the importance of temperance among Negroes after emancipation. 24 August 1839. p.69, c2.

**6095 G. S.** *to* **n.n. n.d. n.p.** Discusses the goals of abolitionism. 24 August 1839. p.70, c1.

**6096 n.n.** *to* **THE EDITOR OF THE** *ADVOCATE OF FREEDOM.* **n.d. n.p.** Describes the progress of abolitionism in a region of Maine. 24 August 1839. p.70, c3.

**6097 HIPPOLYTE DE SAINT ANTHOINE** *to* **E. WRIGHT, JR. 13 February 1839. Paris.** Reports that the French Chamber of Deputies will soon consider the enfranchisement of slaves in the French colonies. 24 August 1839. p.71, c2.

**6098 ZADOC HUMPHREY** *to* **THE EDITOR OF THE** *ADVOCATE OF FREEDOM.* **29 July 1839. North Yarmouth.** Encloses materials which he feels reveal the true character of colonization. 24 August 1839. p.72, c1.

**6099 THOMAS JEFFERSON** *to* **JOHN LYND. 21 January 1811. Monticello.** Discusses why he supports colonization. 24 August 1839. p.72, c1.

**6100 A MEMBER OF THE SOCIETY OF FRIENDS** *to* **A MEMBER OF THE MARYLAND LEGISLATURE. [from the** *Essex Patriot***] n.d. n.p.** Describes slavery atrocities in Baltimore. 24 August 1839. p.72, c3.

**6101 WM. DAWES AND J. KEEP** *to* **BROTHER. [from the** *Zion's Watchman***] 6 July 1839. London.** Report on their visit to London and describe the proceedings of anti-slavery meetings they attended; state that the English abhor slavery. 31 August 1839. p.73, c1.

**6102 R. F.** *to* **THE** *ADVOCATE OF FREEDOM.* **n.d. n.p.** Praises the work done by abolitionists and encourages others to become abolitionists. 31 August 1839. p.74, c1.

**6103 A MEMBER OF THE CONFERENCE** *to* **BRO. ADAMS. n.d. n.p.** Reports on the annual meeting of the Lincoln Conference of Churches and gives an account of discussion of slavery at the conference. 31 August 1839. p.74, c2.

**6104 DELTA** *to* **BROTHER. 9 August 1839. Phillips.** Asserts that all Christians should enlist in anti-slavery cause. 31 August 1839. p.74, c3.

**6105 B. F. S.** *to* **THE EDITOR OF THE** *ADVOCATE OF FREEDOM.* **30 August 1839. Belfast.** Believes that there must be a place for morality in politics as well as in religion. 31 August 1839. p.74, c3.

**6106 SUBSCRIBER** *to* **THE** *ADVOCATE OF FREEDOM.* **n.d. n.p.** Requests information regarding slave sales. 31 August 1839. p.74, c4.

**6107 Z. HUMPHREY** *to* **THE** *ADVOCATE OF FREEDOM.* **27 August 1839. North Yarmouth.** States that he made an erroneous reference to the *Essex Patriot* in his last communication; reports on a meeting held to consider the duty of abolitionists at the polls. 31 August 1839. p.75, c1.

**6108 I. CODDING** *to* **BRO. ADAMS. n.d. n.p.** Acknowledges donations for the *Advocate of Freedom* from the Portland Female AS, the Portland AS, and anonymous donors in Windham. 31 August 1839. p.75, c1.

**6109 A.** *to* **THE EDITOR OF THE** *CHRISTIAN WATCHMAN.* **n.d. n.p.** Asserts that the tone of Rev. S. Hopkins's sermon was clearly abolitionist. 31 August 1839. p.75, c2.

**6110 B. M.** *to* **THE EDITOR OF THE** *ADVOCATE OF FREEDOM.* **26 August 1839. Brunswick.** Criticizes abolitionists for denying their opponents a fair hearing. 7 September 1839. p.78, c1.

**6111 n.n.** *to* **FRIEND. [from the** *Liberator***] n.d. n.p.** Describes her conversations with Southerners about their views on slavery; believes that covetousness is the cause of the decline of religious fervor in Southern churches. 7 September 1839. p.79, c1.

**6112 I. CODDING** *to* **BRO. ADAMS. 2 September 1839. Wilton.** Gives an account of his anti-slavery lecture tour in Maine. 7 Septemper 1839. p.79, c3.

**6113 G. D.** *to* **THE EDITOR OF THE** *PHILANTHROPIST.* **27 May 1839. n.p.** Questions the omission of a passage describing a slave auction in Georgia from the new edition of Peter Parley's book. 7 September 1839. p.80, c4.

**6114 S. V.** *to* **THE YOUNG MEN OF MAINE. n.d. n.p.** Encourages youth of Maine to become involved in abolitionist work. 14 September 1839. p.82, c1.

**6115 A. W.** *to* **THE** *ADVOCATE OF FREEDOM.* **n.d. n.p.** Disagrees with the assertion of correspondent "B.M." that abolitionists do not allow their opponents a fair hearing. 14 September 1839. p.82, c2.

**6116 R. F.** *to* **THE** *ADVOCATE OF FREEDOM.* **n.d. n.p.** Discusses beneficial effects which abolitionists have had on the South. 14 September 1839. p.82, c3.

**6117 L. N.** *to* **THE EDITOR OF THE** *ADVOCATE OF FREEDOM.* **2 September 1839. n.p.** Believes that some slaves and slaveholders may go to heaven. 21 September 1839. p.86, c2.

**6118 n.n.** *to* **THE EDITOR OF THE** *ADVOCATE OF FREEDOM.* **n.d. n.p.** Wonders why some Christians who profess to oppose slavery are hesitant to join the ranks of abolitionists. 21 September 1839. p.87, c1.

**6119 G. S.** *to* **THE** *ADVOCATE OF FREEDOM.* **n.d. n.p.** States that when slavery ends, the Negro's rights to be educated, worship God, and protect his family will be acknowledged. 21 September 1839. p.86, c1.

**6120 n.n.** *to* **n.n. [from the** *American Citizen***] 21 August 1839. Augusta.** Describes the beauty of Augusta. 21 September 1839. p.87, c3.

**6121 n.n.** *to* **WM. GOODELL. [from the** *Friend of Man***] 24 August 1839. Toronto.** Discusses the importance of abolitionist work. 28 September 1839. p.89, c4.

**6122 JAMES APPLETON, SAMUEL FESSENDEN, AND JOHN PEARSON** *to* **LEVI CUTTER, MAYOR OF PORTLAND. 20 August 1839. Portland.** Regret that he will not allow the use of Portland City Hall for anti-slavery lectures. 28 September 1839. p.90, c1.

**6123 G. C. W.** *to* **THE EDITOR OF THE** *ADVOCATE OF FREEDOM.* **n.d. n.p.** Urges abolitionists to strive for the cause. 28 September 1839. p.90, c3.

**6124 E. N.** *to* **THE EDITOR OF THE** *ADVOCATE OF FREEDOM.* **n.d. n.p.** Encloses a letter for publication. 28 September 1839. p.90, c3.

**6125 E. NEWJENT** *to* **MR. EDITOR. 16 September 1839. Baring, Me.** Laments that slavery exists in a country which holds freedom in such high regard. 28 September 1839. p.90, c3.

**6126 BENNETT ROBERTS** *to* **THE EDITOR OF THE** *ADVOCATE OF FREEDOM.* **n.d. Watertown, Oh.** Condemns the separation of slave families. 28 September 1839. p.92, c1.

**6127 UNION** *to* **THE EDITOR OF THE** *ADVOCATE OF FREEDOM.* **n.d. n.p.** Warns that there is no middle course between righteousness and sin. 28 September 1839. p.92, c2.

**6128 B. N. G.** *to* **DR. G. BAILEY. [from the** *Philanthropist***] n.d. n.p.** States that in slave states, Negroes are not permitted to testify against white men; discusses the practice of whipping slaves to force them to confess to crimes they did not commit. 28 September 1839. p.92, c2.

**6129 SAMUEL L. ROCKWOOD AND JAMES BIRNEY** *to* **n.n. 22 August 1839. Andover.** Report on an anti-slavery meeting held at the Andover Theological Seminary. 28 September 1839. p.92, c4.

**6130 D. DE VINNE** *to* **MR. MANKIN. [from** *Zion's Watchman***] 8 August 1839. Catskill, N.Y.** Believes that a slaveholding church is incapable of converting slaves to genuine Christianity. 5 October 1839. p.93, c1.

**6131 HENRY CLAY** *to* **GENTLEMEN. [from the** *Baltimore Chronicle***] 25 May 1839. Ashland.** Disapproves of abolitionists who attempt to use their votes to abolish slavery; argues that the Constitution is not invested with the authority to abolish slavery. 5 October 1839. p.93, c4.

**6132 LEWIS TAPPAN** *to* **THE EDITOR OF THE** *EMANCIPATOR.* **22 September 1839. Hartford.** Commends the conduct of the *Amistad* Africans at a religious service. 5 October 1839. p.95, c2.

**6133 WENDELL PHILLIPS** *to* **W. L. GARRISON. [extract] 11 July 1839. London.** Criticizes Gladstone and other English merchants for exploiting Indian laborers. 5 October 1839. p.96, c1.

**6134 HON. WILLIAM JAY** *to* **LEWIS TAPPAN. 7 September 1834 [*sic*]. Bedford.** Encloses a contribution for the legal defense of the *Amistad* prisoners. 5 October 1839. p.96, c2.

**6135 ELIZUR WRIGHT, JR.** *to* **BRO. CODDING. 24 September 1839. Boston.** Regrets that he is unable to attend the Young Men's Anti-Slavery Convention; reaffirms his anti-slavery beliefs. 12 October 1839. p.97, c2.

**6136 N. P. ROGERS** *to* **REV. D. THURSTON. 13 September 1839. Concord.** Regrets that he is unable to attend the Young Men's Anti-Slavery Convention. 12 October 1839. p.97, c3.

**6137 L. B. ALLEN** *to* **THE EDITOR OF THE** *ADVOCATE OF FREEDOM.* **[AUSTIN WILLEY]. 5 October 1839. Thomaston.** Encloses a list of resolutions adopted at the Convention of Baptists held in Sedgwick, Maine. 12 October 1839. p.99, c1.

**6138 C. L. REMOND** *to* **FRIEND WILLEY. 7 October 1839. Hallowell.** Describes the success of his anti-slavery lectures in West Machias, North Yarmouth, Bangor, and Freeport. 12 October 1839. p.99, c2.

**6139 BENJ. CLARK** *to* **THE POSTMASTER OF WORCESTER. 19 September 1839. Fredericksburg, Va.** Reports on the kidnapping of a free Negro boy from Worcester, who was sold to slaveholders in Virginia. 12 October 1839. p.99. c3.

**6140 REV. J. A. JAMES** *to* **THE EDITOR OF THE** *NEW YORK EVANGELIST.* **[extract] n.d. Birmingham, England.** Encourages American abolitionists to remain within the law in their efforts to abolish slavery; hopes that contact between the British and American abolitionists will strengthen ties between Britain and the United States. 12 October 1839. p.100, c3.

**6141 D. DE VINNE** *to* **THE** *ZION'S WATCHMAN.* **n.d. n.p.** Discusses the likelihood that a slaveholding church could convert slaves to genuine Christianity. 19 October 1839. p.101, c1.

**6142 A. S. MADDOX** *to* **REV. DR. COLVER. 15 August 1839. Boston.** Expresses his annoyance at being refused communion in a Baptist church because he is a slaveholder. 19 October 1839. p.101, c3.

**6143 NATHANIEL COLVER** *to* **A. S. MADDOX. 15 August 1839. Boston.** Considers it justifiable to refuse communion to a slaveholder, because slaveholding is a sin. 19 October 1839. p.101, c3.

**6144 GEO. BRADBURN** *to* **WM. JNO. CLARK. 1 October 1839. Boston.** Reports that a free Negro was kidnapped in Boston but later returned to his family; mentions other kidnappings and attempts in the Boston area. 19 October 1839. p.102, c1.

**6145 H. SEWALL** *to* **REV. SAMUEL HOPKINS. 17 October 1839. Augusta.** Stresses one's Christian responsibility to differentiate between right and wrong. 19 October 1839. p.102, c4.

**6146 V.** *to* **THE** *ADVOCATE OF FREEDOM.* **n.d. n.p.** Asserts that if Negroes can be enslaved, then whites should be enslaved as well. 19 October 1839. p.103, c3.

**6147 I. CODDING** *to* **BRO. WILLEY. 12 October 1839. Hallowell.** Acknowledges donations for the Maine AS from the towns of Bridgton, Hallowell, and Farmington, and from the Young Men's Anti-Slavery Convention. 19 October 1839. p.103, c4.

**6148 JOHN H. TREDGOLD** *to* **MR. GARRISON. [from the** *Cradle of Liberty*] **31 July 1839. London.** Describes the progress made by British abolitionists and praises them for their part in the enactment of the law of 1807 which outlawed the slave trade in England. 19 October 1839. p.104, c2.

**6149 GEORGE E. DAY** *to* **THE EDITORS OF THE** *JOURNAL OF COMMERCE.* **8 October 1839. New Haven.** Encloses a narrative by an *Amistad* African describing his enslavement. 26 October 1839. p.105, c3.

**6150 GEORGE S. BULL** *to* **LEWIS TAPPAN. [extract] 23 February 1839. Yorkshire, England.** Queries why slavery exists in a democracy. 26 October 1839. p.106, c1.

**6151 S. D. H.** *to* **THE EDITOR OF THE** *PENNSYLVANIA FREEMAN.* **n.d. n.p.** Sympathizes with the plight of Cinque and the *Amistad* Africans. 26 October 1839. p.107, c2.

**6152 I. CODDING** *to* **BRO. WILLEY. 25 September 1839. Hallowell.** Acknowledges donations received from the towns of Waterville, Bloomfield, Norridgewock, and Topsham for the use of the Maine AS. 26 October 1839. p.107, c4.

**6153 n.n.** *to* **BROTHER GARRISON. [from the** *Liberator***] n.d. n.p.** Informs that a colored man was barred from a train in Lynn. 26 October 1839. p.108, c4.

**6154 T. P. R.** *to* **FRIEND GARRISON. [from the** *Liberator***] 16 October 1839. Fall River.** States that two colored women from New Bedford were refused passage on a stagecoach. 2 November 1839. p.109, c3.

**6155 X.** *to* **THE** *EVENING POST.* **7 October 1839. New Haven.** Encloses a narrative by an *Amistad* African stating the location of his home and describing their capture by the Spaniards. 2 November 1839. p.110, c1.

**6156 C. LENOX REMOND** *to* **WILLEY. 27 October 1839. Bangor.** Describes a lecture tour in Maine. 2 November 1839. p.110, c2.

**6157 H. WHITNEY** *to* **MR. WILLEY. 24 October 1839. Keiths Mills.** Reports on the slow progress of abolitionism in the Keiths Mills area. 2 November 1839. p.111, c1.

**6158 E. N.** *to* **BRO. WILLEY. 12 October 1839. Baring.** Stresses the need to circulate anti-slavery newspapers and pamphlets. 2 November 1839. p.111, c3.

**6159 n.n.** *to* **GENT. [from the** *Whig and Courier***] 27 October 1839. Bucksport.** Informs that the murderers of Judge Carr have been arrested. 2 November 1839. p.111, c4.

**6160 B. G.** *to* **THE ABOLITIONIST. 14 October 1839. New Haven.** Describes the distress of the female *Amistad* captives upon hearing the rumor they were to be returned to their former master. 2 November 1839. p.112, cl.

**6161 DR. MATHESON** *to* **n.n. [extract from the** *New York Evangelist***] n.d. England.** States that three fugitive slaves from Madagascar who recently converted to Christianity received a warm reception at a meeting of missionaries in Birmingham. 9 November 1839. p.113, cl.

**6162 SAMUEL KELLY** *to* **THE EDITOR OF THE** *ADVOCATE OF FREEDOM* **[AUSTIN WILLEY]. n.d. n.p.** Lists resolutions adopted at an abolitionist meeting in Washington County. 9 November 1839. p.113, c4.

**6163 D. THURSTON** *to* **THE** *ADVOCATE OF FREEDOM.* **5 November 1839. n.p.** Appeals to the paper's readers for donations. 9 November 1839. p.114, c2.

**6164 I. CODDING** *to* **WILLEY. 31 October 1839. Pembroke.** Details the proceedings of the anti-slavery convention at Pembroke. 9 November 1839. p.114, c4.

**6165 P.** *to* **WILLEY. n.d. Bridgton.** Describes slavery as an abomination, declaring that he would prefer a monarchy without slavery to a republic with slavery. 9 November 1839. p.114, c4.

**6166 I. CODDING** *to* **BRO. WILLEY. 17 October 1839. Pembroke.** Describes his warm reception at Pembroke and praises the hospitality of his host, Mr. Godfrey. 9 November 1839. p.115, cl.

**6167 I. CODDING** *to* **BRO. WILLEY. 23 October 1839. Baring.** Describes the success of his anti-slavery lectures in East Machias, Dennisville, and East Port. 9 November 1839. p.115, cl.

**6168 I. CODDING** *to* **BRO. WILLEY. 4 November 1839. Calais.** Reports that eggs were thrown at him during his anti-slavery lecture in Calais and that stones were thrown at him afterwards. 9 November 1839. p.115, cl.

**6169 E. ROBINSON** *to* **BRO. WILLEY. 1 November 1839. Kent's Hill.** Encloses donations for the *Advocate of Freedom*. 9 November 1839. p.115, c2.

**6170 JOS. BARRON** *to* **MR. WILLEY. November 1839. Topsham.** Discusses his success in establishing anti-slavery libraries in Topsham, Woolwich, and Phipsburg. 9 November 1839. p.115, c3.

**6171 EDWARD EVERETT** *to* **HON. NATHANIEL B. BORDEN. 24 October 1839. Watertown.** Favors immediate abolition of slavery and believes that all new states should be free. 9 November 1839. p.115, c3.

**6172 BRADFORD SUMNER** *to* **n.n. n.d. n.p.** Believes that Congress has the power to abolish slavery. 9 November 1839. p.115, c3.

**6173 P. H. PIERCE** *to* **n.n. n.d. n.p.** States that he is opposed to slavery. 9 November 1839. p.115, c4.

**6174 JARED WHITMAN** *to* **n.n. n.d. n.p.** States that he is opposed to slavery and favors its abolition. 9 November 1839. p.115, c4.

**6175 SETH SPRAGUE, JR.** *to* **n.n. n.d. n.p.** Believes that slavery should be abolished and that new states should be free. 9 November 1839. p.115, c4.

**6176 SETH SPRAGUE** *to* **GENTLEMEN. 4 November 1839. Duxbury.** Reaffirms his position as an abolitionist. 9 November 1839. p.115, c4.

**6177 JOHN B. OWENS** *to* **BRO. GOODELL. 26 October 1839. Syracuse.** Describes Mr. Davenport's unsuccessful search for a fugitive white female slave. 9 November 1839. p.116, c2.

**6178 n.n.** *to* **SIR. [from the** ***Emancipator*****] n.d. n.p.** Informs that an "ostler" who had been holding a fugitive slave for the slave's master burned to death in a fire while the fugitive slave escaped. 9 November 1839. p.116, c3.

**6179 GERRIT SMITH** *to* **HON. SETH M. GATES. 22 October 1839. Peterboro'.** Criticizes Gates for failing to use his political influence to initiate anti-slavery legislation. 16 November 1839. p.117, cl.

**6180 A FRIEND OF THE COLORED MAN** *to* **BRO. WILLEY. n.d. n.p.** Denies that a Christian can advocate slavery any more than an abolitionist can vote for a candidate who does not oppose slavery. 16 November 1839. p.117, c4.

**6181 FEDERAL DANA** *to* **GERRIT SMITH. 29 October 1839. Cape Vincent.** Informs that Harriet, the white fugitive slave, is safely in the hands of friends. 16 November 1839. p.118, cl.

**6182 L. W.** *to* **BRO. WILLEY. n.d. n.p.** Believes that most Northerners are opposed to slavery. 16 November 1839. p.118, c3.

**6183 G. C. W.** *to* **BRO. WILLEY. n.d. n.p.** Encloses an article about a slaveholder's hiring of free Negroes. 16 November 1839. p.118, c3.

**6184 JOS. BARRON** *to* **MR. WILLEY. November 1839. Topsham.** States that his difficulty in establishing an AS in Wiscasset is due to opposition from colonizationists and religious leaders. 16 November 1839. p.118, c4.

**6185 E.** *to* **BRO. WILLEY. n.d. n.p.** Encloses an extract of a letter from a Baptist minister who offers advice to abolitionists. 16 November 1839. p.119, c1.

**6186 BAPTIST MINISTER** *to* **n.n. 1839. New Hampshire.** Advises abolitonists to take the course which will do the most good for the cause. 16 November 1839. p.119, c1.

**6187 n.n.** *to* **THE EDITOR OF THE** ***ADVOCATE OF FREEDOM*** **[AUSTIN WILLEY]. 9 November 1839. Calais.** Describes anti-abolitionist sentiment encountered by abolitionist lecturers in Calais. 16 November 1839. p.119, c1.

**6188 H. B. STANTON** *to* **WHITTIER. [from the** ***Pennsylvania Freeman*****] 26 October 1839. Cleveland, Oh.** Gives an account of a meeting of the AAS in Cleveland. 16 November 1839. p.119, c3.

**6189 GEO. THOMPSON** *to* **SIR. [from the** ***Liberator*****] 17 September 1839. Manchester, England.** Expresses satisfaction that abolitionism is spreading; believes it necessary to give the "principles and precepts of religion a rigid application to particular and popular practices." 16 November 1839. p.120, c1.

**6190 JOHN CHANEY** *to* **WM. M. HOUSLEY. 5 October 1839. Conneaut, Oh.** Declares that Housley cannot be admitted to the ministry because he is a slaveholder. 16 November 1839. p.120, c3.

**6191 DAVID CHOATE** *to* **GENTLEMEN. n.d. n.p.** Asserts that slavery can be abolished by Congress and that all new states should be free. 16 November 1839. p.120, c4.

**6192 JAMES GILLPATRICK** *to* **THE MINISTERS OF THE BAPTIST DENOMINATION OF MAINE. October 1839. n.p.** Gives an account of the proceedings of an anti-slavery convention at Sedgwick. 23 November 1839. p.121, c1.

**6193 T. P. R.** *to* **GARRISON. n.d. n.p.** Discusses the meaning of Thanksgiving and the proper way for an abolitionist to observe it. 23 November 1839. p.122, c4.

**6194 L. W.** *to* **BRO. WILLEY. November 1839. Brooks.** Asserts that free labor is less costly than slave labor, and is morally acceptable as well. 23 November 1839. p.123, c1.

**6195 I. CODDING** *to* **BRO. WILLEY. 17 November 1839. Bangor.** Condemns the residents of Calais for refusing the use of their town hall to abolitionists. 23 November 1839. p.123, c2.

**6196 MARY S. PARKER** *to* **THE WOMEN OF NEW ENGLAND. n.d. n.p.** Urges women to become involved in the anti-slavery cause. 23 November 1839. p.124, c1.

**6197 J. DAVENPORT** *to* **THE PUBLIC. 26 October 1839. Syracuse.** Holds abolitionists responsible for the escape of his former slave. 23 November 1839. p.124, c3.

**6198 S. HOES** *to* **BRO. SUNDERLAND. [from** ***Zion's Watchman*****] 31 October 1839. Utica.** Describes the condition of slaves in New Orleans and discusses the interest masters take in the spiritual life of their slaves. 30 November 1839. p.125, c1.

**6199 LEWIS TAPPAN** *to* **BRO. LEAVITT. [from the** ***Emancipator*****] n.d. n.p.** Objects to the formation of an anti-slavery party. 30 November 1839. p.126, c1.

**6200 n.n.** *to* **THE EDITOR OF THE** ***ADVOCATE OF FREEDOM*** **[AUSTIN WILLEY]. n.d. n.p.** Encloses an exegesis of the First Book of Timothy. 30 November 1839. p.126, c3.

**6201 B. F. SPRAGUE** *to* **BRO. WILLEY. 28 November 1839. Belfast.** Encloses a contribution for the anti-slavery cause. 30 November 1839. p.127, c1.

**6202 D. N.** *to* **BRETHREN. [from the** ***Emancipator*****] 20 October 1839. n.p.** Relates the story of a slave who chose to remain with her master and move to Texas rather than be sold to another slaveholder in Mississippi. 30 November 1839. p.128, c4.

**6203 ASA CUMMINGS** *to* **THE PRESBYTERY OF TOMBECBEE. 28 December 1838. Portland.** Discusses the appointment of himself and others to a committee to correspond with Southern ecclesiastical bodies on the subject of slavery. 7 December 1839. p.129, c1.

**6204 THOMAS C. STUART** *to* **REV. ASA CUMMINGS, FOR THE COMMITTEE OF GENERAL CONFERENCE OF CONGREGATIONAL CHURCHES IN MAINE. 9 April 1839. Starksville, Ms.** Quotes from the Bible to illustrate that the Bible sanctions slavery. 7 December 1839. p.129, c2.

**6205 J. WILKINSON** *to* **THE** ***JOURNAL OF COMMERCE*****. 31 October 1839. Washington.** States his approval of the navy's decision to send ships to the African coast to protect American commerce. 7 December 1839. p.130, c3.

**6206 NATHANIEL COLVER** *to* **BRO. GROSVENOR. [from the** ***Christian Reflector*****] 20 September 1839. Boston.** Agrees with the Boston Association's view that slavery is a sin. 7 December 1839. p.130, c4.

**6207 T. T. S.** *to* **THE** ***ADVOCATE OF FREEDOM.*** **n.d. n.p.** Considers the uniqueness of American slavery. 14 December 1839. p.135, c1.

**6208 E. N.** *to* **BRO. WILLEY. 16 November 1839. Baring.** States that he is ashamed that slavery exists in America. 14 December 1839. p.135, c2.

**6209 A. HANSCOM** *to* **MR. WILLEY. 4 December 1839. Saccarappa.** Reports the formation of an AS in Saccarappa. 14 December 1839. p.135, c3.

**6210 A FRIEND** *to* **FRIEND WILLEY. 29 November 1839. Bangor.** Discusses the success of his anti-slavery lectures in Prospect. 21 December 1839. p.138, c3.

**6211 S. M.** *to* **MR. EDITOR [AUSTIN WILLEY]. n.d. n.p.** Criticizes the *Advocate of Freedom*'s erroneous reporting of the correspondence between the General Conference of Maine and the Presbytery of Tombecbee. 21 December 1839. p.138, c3.

**6212 n.n.** *to* **THE EDITOR OF THE** ***ADVOCATE OF FREEDOM*** **[AUSTIN WILLEY]. n.d. n.p.** Describes a visit by Mr. Remond. 21 December 1839. p.138, c4.

**6213 S. REDINGTON** *to* **C. REMOND. 8 December 1839. Vassalboro'.** Questions Remond's criticism of the ACS; invites him to his home to discuss the merits of the ACS. 21 December 1839. p.138, c4.

**6214 C. LENOX REMOND** *to* **S. REDINGTON. 5 December 1839. Vassalboro'.** Regrets that he is unable to visit Redington's home to discuss the merits of the ACS. 21 December 1839. p.139, c1.

**6215 A. MOORE** *to* **n.n. 11 December 1839. Vassalboro'.** Lists resolutions adopted by a local meeting of the ACS. 21 December 1839. p.139, c1.

**6216 AMOS STICKNEY** *to* **REMOND. 9 December 1939. n.p.** Encloses payment for a subscription to the *Advocate of Freedom.* 21 December 1839. p.139, c1.

**6217 I. CODDING** *to* **BRO. WILLEY. 14 December 1839. West Prospect.** Comments on the success of his anti-slavery lectures in Hamden, Orrington, Bucksport, and Orland. 21 December 1839. p.139, c1.

**6218 JOHN SMITH** *to* **THE HOUSE OF REPRESENTATIVES. n.d. n.p.** Beseeches officials in Washington to abolish slavery. 28 December 1839. p.141, c4.

**6219 STEPHEN SEWALL** *to* **n.n. [extract] 12 January 1839. Winthrop, Me.** Relates the story of a slave who attempted to drown himself in order to avoid punishment by his overseer; provides numerous examples of masters torturing their slaves. 28 December 1839. p.141, c2.

**6220 S. THURSTON** *to* **BRO. WILLEY. 19 December 1839. West Prospect.** Notes a growing interest in the anti-slavery cause in West Prospect. 28 December 1839. p.142, c2.

**6221 C. L. REMOND** *to* **FRIEND WILLEY. 17 December 1839. Portland.** Reports that a severe snowstorm has temporarily delayed his anti-slavery lecture tour. 28 December 1839. p.142, c4.

**6222 REV. JOHN RANKIN** *to* **THE EDITOR OF THE** *PHILANTHROPIST.* **20 February 1839. Ripley, Oh.** Informs that a slave was beaten by his overseer for being late for work, and that another slave was severely beaten by his master for no apparent reason. 28 December 1839. p.143, c2.

**6223 S. A.** *to* **THE EDITOR OF THE** *EMANCIPATOR.* **n.d. n.p.** Informs that Indian labor is used in Mississippi to alleviate the shortage of slaves. 28 December 1839. p.143, c3.

**6224 GERRIT SMITH** *to* **SETH M. GATES. [extract] n.d. n.p.** Urges abolitionists to become politically active. 28 December 1839. p.144, c1.

## [1840]

**6225 n.n.** *to* **REV. MR. LEAVITT. 15 November 1839. n.p.** Notes an increase in anti-slavery sentiment in the South. 4 January 1840. p.145, c3.

**6226 JAMES D. CHAPMAN** *to* **MR. BIRNEY. 12 December 1839. Walcott, Ct.** Reports that pro-slavery incendiaries burned down an abolitionist meeting hall in Walcott. 4 January 1840. p.147, c3.

**6227 CHARLES STUART** *to* **THEODORE. 10 October 1836. Mt. Charles, Jamaica.** Describes the political and social climate of Jamaica. 11 January 1840. p.149, c1.

**6228 DANIEL LANCASTER** *to* **THE EDITOR OF THE** *CHRISTIAN PANOPLY.* **n.d. n.p.** Criticizes abolitionists of New Hampshire for failing to condemn slavery publicly. 11 January 1840. p.149, c3.

**6229 E. G. L.** *to* **THE EDITOR OF THE** *COURIER.* **n.d. n.p.** Encloses extracts of a letter from John Quincy Adams. 11 January 1840. p.150, c4.

**6230 J. Q. ADAMS** *to* **n.n. [extract from the** *Courier***] n.d. n.p.** Informs that United States' treaties with Spain state nothing about returning fugitive or rebellious slaves to Spain. 11 January 1840. p.150, c4.

**6231 JOS. BARRON** *to* **MR. WILLEY. 2 January 1840. Topsham.** Gives an account of his anti-slavery lecture tour and reports that over $100 was collected for the establishment of anti-slavery libraries. 11 January 1840. p.151, c1.

**6232 I. CODDING** *to* **BRO. WILLEY. 3 January 1840. Sangerville.** Reports on an anti-slavery meeting in Sangerville; announces that he collected $250 for the Maine State AS and obtained seventy-five new subscribers for the *Advocate of Freedom.* 11 January 1840. p.151, c3.

**6233 S. SEWALL** *to* **BRO. WILLEY. n.d. n.p.** Reports that David Doane of Aina witnessed the torturing of a slave. 11 January 1840. p.151, c3.

**6234 LEWIS TAPPAN** *to* **THE COMMITTEE ON BEHALF OF THE CAPTURED AFRICANS. 8 January 1840. New Haven.** Gives an account of the court proceedings of the *Amistad* case. 18 January 1840. p.153, c1.

**6235 JAMES G. BIRNEY** *to* **MESSRS. M. HOLLEY, J. H. DARLING, AND J. ANDREWS. 17 December 1839. New York.** Declines the abolitionists' nomination as candidate for the United States presidency. 18 January 1840. p.153, c3.

**6236 F. JULIUS LEMOYNE** *to* **MESSRS. HOLLEY, DARLING, AND ANDREWS. 10 December 1839. Washington, Pa.** Declines the abolitionists' nomination as candidate for the vice-presidency of the United States. 18 January 1840. p.153, c4.

**6237 SAML. M. POND** *to* **MR. WILLEY. 6 January 1840. Bucksport.** Comments on the enthusiasm generated by a series of anti-slavery lectures by Remond and Codding. 18 January 1840. p.154, c1.

**6238 SILAS McKEEN** *to* **REV. THOMAS C. STUART, CLERK, PRESBYTERY OF TOMBECBEE. [from the** *Christian Mirror***] 20 August 1839. Belfast, Me.** Denies that the Bible sanctions slavery. [continued from 11 January 1840] 18 January 1840. p.156, c1.

**6239 A. CUMMINGS** *to* **BRO. WILLEY. n.d. n.p.** Encloses a letter published in the *Christian Panoply* on the church and slavery. 18 [25] January 1840. p.159, c1.

**6240 A. CUMMINGS** *to* **THE** *CHRISTIAN PANOPLY.* **[extract] n.d. n.p.** Opposes church involvement in the anti-slavery movement. 18 [25] January 1840. p.159, c1.

**6241 ZURY ROBINSON** *to* **FRIEND WILLEY. 19 January 1840. East Sumner.** Provides a copy of the preamble and constitution of the AS recently established in East Sumner. 18 [25] January 1840. p.159, c3.

**6242 I. CODDING** *to* **BROTHER. 13 January 1840. Brownville.** Gives an account of his anti-slavery lecture tour. 18 [25] January 1840. p.159, c3.

**6243 REV. JOHN CROSS** *to* **MR. LEAVITT. 14 December 1839. Joliet, Mill County, Il.** Describes an attempted kidnapping of a free colored man. 18 [25] January 1840. p.160, c3.

**6244 LEWIS TAPPAN** *to* **THE EDITOR OF THE** *EMANCIPATOR*. **n.d. New Haven.** Announces that the court has decided to return the *Amistad* captives to Africa. 1 February 1840. p.161, c2.

**6245 REV. H. G. LUDLOW** *to* **THE EDITOR OF THE** *JOURNAL OF COMMERCE*. **13 January n.p.** Describes the *Amistad* Africans' joyous response to the court's decision to return them to Africa. 1 February 1840. p.161, c2.

**6246 WILLIAM S. SEWALL** *to* **BRO. WILLEY. 20 January 1840. Brownville.** States that there has been an increase in abolitionist sentiment in the Brownville area. 1 February 1840. p.162, c4.

**6247 A. J. W. STEVENS** *to* **BRO. WILLEY. 16 January 1840. Parkman.** Praises the work of abolitionists in Maine. 1 February 1840. p.163, c1.

**6248 CHARLES FITCH** *to* **W. L. GARRISON. [from the** *Liberator*] **9 January 1840. Newark.** Believes that everyone should repent his sins and accept Christ as his savior. 1 February 1840. p.164, c3.

**6249 n.n.** *to* **THE** *MEADVILLE STATESMAN*. **n.d. n.p.** Encloses an extract of a letter about the separation of slave families. 1 February 1840. p.164, c3.

**6250 n.n.** *to* **n.n. [extract from the** *Meadville Statesman*] **n.d. n.p.** Discusses the separation of several slave families whose members were to be sold farther South. 1 February 1840. p.164, c3.

**6251 n.n.** *to* **n.n. [from the** *Emancipator*] **28 December 1839. New York.** Defends abolitionists' right to become involved in politics and approves of their forming political alliances with national parties when it is to their advantage. 8 February 1840. p.165, c1.

**6252 n.n.** *to* **MR. WILLEY. 17 January 1840. Sangerville.** Encloses a report of the Sangerville Female AS. 8 February 1840. p.166, c3.

**6253 I. CODDING** *to* **BRO. WILLEY. n.d. n.p.** Corrects an error in his reporting of donations from Brownville. 8 February 1840. p.167, c4.

**6254 SILAS McKEEN** *to* **REV. THOMAS C. STUART. 20 August 1839. Belfast, Me.** Believes that state authorities should take steps to prevent the separation of slave families. 15 February 1840. p.172, c1.

**6255 n.n.** *to* **n.n. [extract from the** *Boston Patriot*] **8 January. St. Marks, Fl.** Describes the lush vegetation of Florida and reports the arrival of forty Spanish bloodhounds. 15 February 1840. p.172, c2.

**6256 GERRIT SMITH** *to* **E. MACK. [from the** *Morning Star*] **19 January 1840. Peterboro'.** Encloses a donation for the Freewill Baptist Foreign Mission Society. 15 February 1840. p.172, c4.

**6257 JAMES GILLPATRICK** *to* **AUSTIN WILLEY. 3 February 1840. Bluehill.** Stresses the importance of abolitionist work. 22 February 1840. p.173, c1.

**6258 n.n.** *to* **BRO. WILLEY. n.d. n.p.** Praises the work done by the *Advocate of Freedom*. 22 February 1840. p.174, c3.

**6259 W. N.** *to* **THE EDITOR OF THE** *ADVOCATE OF FREEDOM* **[AUSTIN WILLEY]. 29 January 1840. Bethel.** Expresses his indignation that a Negro was not permitted to take communion with the white members of a church in Bethel. 22 February 1840. p.174, c4.

**6260 UNION** *to* **THE EDITOR OF THE** *ADVOCATE OF FREEDOM* **[AUSTIN WILLEY]. n.d. n.p.** Criticizes the unwillingness of the Maine legislature to take an uncompromising stand on slavery. 22 February 1840. p.175, c1.

**6261 A. F.** *to* **FRIEND WILLEY. 6 February 1840. Piscataquis County.** Asserts that Northerners who oppose abolitionism are guiltier than Southern slaveholders. 22 February 1840. p.175, c3.

**6262 D. B. RANDALL** *to* **BRO. WILLEY. 17 February 1840. Kents Hill.** Announces that he will be attending county meetings concerned with anti-slavery literature. 22 February 1840. p.175, c3.

**6263 CHARLES DUNBAR AND DUNCAN DENISON** *to* **BAPTIST ABOLITIONISTS OF THE UNITED STATES. 8 February 1840. New York.** Urge attendance at the Baptist National Anti-Slavery Convention. 29 February 1840. p.177, c3.

**6264 n.n.** *to* **THE EDITOR OF THE** *AMERICAN CITIZEN.* **26 January 1840. Washington.** Criticizes Mr. McLain for failing to mention or condemn slavery in his lecture on colonization. 29 February 1840. p.177, c4.

**6265 G. W. HATHAWAY** *to* **BRO. WILLEY. 21 February 1840. Bloomfield.** Asserts that slavery is inconsistent with Constitutional law. 29 February 1840. p.178, c3.

**6266 S. L. POMROY** *to* **THE EDITOR OF THE** *ADVOCATE OF FREEDOM* **[AUSTIN WILLEY]. 19 February 1840. Bangor.** Praises Brother Cummings's address criticizing the people of New Hampshire as slow to respond to the plight of the slave. 29 February 1840. p.178, c4.

**6267 D. B. RANDALL** *to* **BRO. WILLEY. 24 February 1840. Kents Hill.** Discusses the growth of abolitionism in America. 29 February 1840. p.179, c3.

**6268 n.n.** *to* **FRIEND LEAVITT. [from the** *Emancipator***] 8 February 1840. Albany.** States that the assembly in New York State has declared the tabling of anti-slavery petitions in Congress a denial of the right to petition and a violation of the Constitution. 29 February 1840. p.179, c4.

**6269 n.n.** *to* **SIR. [from the** *Wesleyan Observer***] 23 January 1840. Ludlow.** Describes and condemns the abuse of slaves in New Orleans. 29 February 1840. p.180, c3.

**6270 C. NEWTON** *to* **THE EDITOR. [from the** *Advocate and Baptist***] 18 February 1840. Thomeston.** Believes that colonized American Negroes exert an adverse moral influence on Africans. 7 March 1840. p.183, c1.

**6271 I. CODDING** *to* **BRO. WILLEY. 25 February 1840. Montville.** Discusses the success of his anti-slavery lectures in Montville, noting that he obtained twelve subscribers for the *Advocate of Freedom.* 7 March 1840. p.183, c1.

**6272 ONE OF THE DOZEN** *to* **THE EDITOR OF THE** *ADVOCATE OF FREEDOM* **[AUSTIN WILLEY]. 2 March 1840. Calais.** States that a gift of clothing for slaves came from the town of Calais, not Machias, as was reported. 7 March 1840. p.183, c2.

**6273 A SLAVEHOLDER** *to* **THE HON. HENRY CLAY. 1 October 1839. n.p.** Believes that the slave trade thrives because the United States refuses to comply with the wishes of England and France to abolish slavery. 7 March 1840. p.184, c3.

**6274 STEWARD** *to* **MR. GROSVENOR. n.d. n.p.** Promises to make a large financial contribution to the American and Foreign Bible Society. 14 March 1840. p.185, c4.

**6275 A SPECTATOR** *to* **MR. JOSEPH R. CHANDLER. [from the** *United States Gazette***] 28 January 1840. n.p.** States that because Mississippi slaveholders are able to purchase slaves on credit, they accumulate large debts which they are unable to pay. 14 March 1840. p.186, c1.

**6276 WM. G. COLEBROOKE** *to* **THE MARQUESS OF NORMANDY. [from the** *British Emancipator***] 12 June 1839. Antigua.** Lists statistics on the quantities of sugar, rum, and molasses exported from Antigua from 1824 to 1838. 14 March 1840. p.186, c2.

**6277 UNION** *to* **THE EDITOR OF THE** *ADVOCATE OF FREEDOM* **[AUSTIN WILLEY]. n.d. n.p.** States that he opposes the admission of slave states to the Union. 14 March 1840. p.186, c4.

**6278 C. L. REMOND** *to* **FRIEND WILLEY. 1 March 1840. Gorham.** Gives an account of his anti-slavery lectures in Gorham, Hallowell, and Saccarappa; lists donations received for the *Advocate of Freedom.* 14 March 1840. p.186, c4.

**6279 I. CODDING** *to* **BRO. WILLEY. 28 February 1840. Camden.** Informs of strong opposition to abolitionists in Camden. 14 March 1840. p.187, c1.

**6280 I. CODDING** *to* **BRO. WILLEY. 8 March 1840. Hallowell.** Remarks that despite strong anti-abolitionist feelings in Bath, a large donation was collected there for the Maine AS. 14 March 1840. p.187, c1.

**6281 I. CODDING** *to* **BRO. WILLEY. n.d. n.p.** States that the weather prevents him from attending the Oxford County anti-slavery meetings. 14 March 1840. p.187, c1.

**6282 n.n.** *to* **MR. WILLEY. n.d. n.p.** Calls for increased circulation of the *Advocate of Freedom.* 14 March 1840. p.187, c1.

**6283 HENRY B. TORSEY** *to* **THE EDITOR OF THE** *ADVOCATE OF FREEDOM* **[AUSTIN WILLEY]. 6 March 1840. Monmouth.** Complains about not receiving his paper. 14 March 1840. p.187, c4.

**6284 L. BRAYTON** *to* **n.n. [extract] 23 June 1839. Burma.** Reports that Burma is preparing for war and that Persia has declared war on England. 14 March 1840. p.188, c4.

**6285 JOHN BOYNTON** *to* **THE EDITOR OF THE** *ADVOCATE OF FREEDOM* **[AUSTIN WILLEY]. n.d. n.p.** Believes that the abolitionists in Bath have been neglectful of their duties. 21 March 1840. p.189, c4.

**6286 W. FOX STRANGWAYS** *to* **SIR. 23 December 1839. Foreign Office.** Reports that the British will offer aid to the *Amistad* captives. 21 March 1840. p.191, c3.

**6287 GEO. STORRS** *to* **n.n. [from the** *Emancipator***] 21 February 1840. n.p.** Discusses the advantages and drawbacks of forming an abolitionist party. 21 March 1840. p.192, c1.

**6288 WM. H. PRITCHARD** *to* **THE EDITOR OF THE** *CONSTITUTIONALIST.* **20 December 1836. Aiken, S.C.** Describes the murder of a free colored man who attempted to evade kidnappers. 21 March 1840. p.192, c4.

**6289 G. C. W.** *to* **THE** *ADVOCATE OF FREEDOM.* **March 1840. Litchfield.** States reasons for objecting to abolitionists' involvement in politics. 28 March 1840. p.194, c2.

**6290 D. B. RANDALL** *to* **BRO. WILLEY. 23 March 1840. New Sharon.** Describes a monthly concert of prayer for the slaves. 28 March 1840. p.194, c3.

**6291 CHARLES T. TORREY** *to* **THE EDITOR OF THE** *ADVOCATE OF FREEDOM* **[AUSTIN WILLEY]. 16 March 1840. Worcester, Ma.** Urges the appointment of suitable delegates from Maine for the national convention at Albany. 28 March 1840. p.194, c4.

**6292 T.** *to* **MR. WILLEY. n.d. n.p.** Lists statistics on slave mortality during the journey from Africa to America. 28 March 1840. p.195, c1.

**6293 CHAS. T. TORREY** *to* **BRO. WRIGHT. 8 February 1840. West Medway.** Condemns the members of the Cumberland Congregation of Presbyterians for owning slaves. 28 March 1840. p.196, c1.

**6294 W. H. S.** *to* **THE EDITOR OF THE** *PHILANTHROPIST.* **9 March 1840. Genesee.** Describes the successful escape of a slave from Virginia to Canada. 28 March 1840. p.196, c2.

**6295 WM. HENRY BRISBANE** *to* **EDWARD H. PEEPLES. 4 January 1840. Cincinnati, Oh.** Wishes to buy back slaves sold to Peeples in order to manumit them. 4 April 1840. p.197, c4.

**6296 C. L. REMOND** *to* **FRIEND WILLEY. 21 March 1840. Buxton.** Gives an account of lectures delivered at the meeting of the York County AS. 4 April 1840. p.198, c3.

**6297 WILLIAM ALLEN** *to* **n.n. [from the** *Emancipator***] 15 February 1840. n.p.** Announces the date of the British and Foreign AS Conference. 4 April 1840. p.199, c2.

**6298 POPE GREGORY XVI** *to* **n.n. 3 December 1839. Rome.** Calls for the abolition of slavery. 11 April 1840. p.201, c1.

**6299 D. S. INGRAHAM** *to* **BROTHER SOUTHARD. [from** *Youth's Cabinet***] January 1840. Kingston, Jamaica.** Reports on the British takeover of the Portuguese slave ship *Ulysses* and describes the sufferings of its captives. 11 April 1840. p.201, c4.

**6300 BENJAMIN FENN** *to* **THE EDITOR OF THE** *EMANCIPATOR.* **n.d. n.p.** Favors the formation of a third political party in order to hasten the overthrow of slavery. 11 April 1840. p.202, c1.

**6301 D. B. RANDALL** *to* **A. WILLEY. n.d. n.p.** Reports on an anti-slavery meeting held at Fairfield. 11 April 1840. p.202, c2.

**6302 STANISALUS [***sic***]** *to* **n.n. n.d. Bangor.** Opposes interracial marriages but realizes the futility of laws prohibiting them. 11 April 1840. p.202, c3.

**6303 REV. J. A. JAMES** *to* **A NEW ENGLAND PASTOR. [from the** *New York Observer***] 19 December 1839. Birmingham.** Refutes the accusation that some New England states have not been sufficiently active in abolitionism. 18 April 1849. p.205, c1.

**6304 L.** *to* **THE EDITOR OF THE** *ADVOCATE OF FREEDOM* **[AUSTIN WILLEY]. n.d. n.p.** Encourages continued support of abolitionism. 18 April 1840. p.206, c1.

**6305 WM. B. STONE** *to* **BRO. GARRISON. 21 February 1840. West Brookfield.** Criticizes the Andover Theological Seminary for its ambivalent position on slavery. 18 April 1840. p.208, c1.

**6306 HIRAM WILSON** *to* **A. A. PHELPS. [from the** *Abolitionist***] 7 March 1840. Toronto, Upper Canada.** Describes the success of missionary work among the colored people in Canada. 18 April 1840. p.208, c1.

**6307 DAVID J. WEEKS** *to* **WILLIAM GOODELL. n.d. n.p.** Notes the progress made by abolitionists. 18 April 1840. p.208, c4.

**6308 n.n.** *to* **BROTHER LEAVITT. [from the** *New York Emancipator***] 22 November 1839. Mission Institute.** Relates the story of a female slave whose mistress ordered her to be burned at the stake for being the master's favorite slave. 25 April 1840. p.2, c1.

**6309 G. C. W.** *to* **THE** *ADVOCATE OF FREEDOM.* **April 1840. Litchfield.** Urges the organization of a third political party with an abolitionist platform. 25 April 1840. p.2, c4.

**6310 I. CODDING** *to* **BRO. WILLEY. 6 April 1840. Bristol Centre, Ontario County.** Criticizes Dr. Beman and others at the Albany convention who advocated the formation of an abolitionist party. 25 April 1840. p.3, c1.

**6311 D. B. RANDALL** *to* **BRO. WILLEY. n.d. n.p.** Reports on his anti-slavery lectures in Canaan, Cornville, and South Solon. 25 April 1840. p.3, c2.

**6312 THOMAS P. HUNT** *to* **n.n. 9 March 1840. Port of Spain.** Gives an account of the proceedings at a meeting of the Colored American Emigrants of Trinidad. 25 April 1840. p.4, c3.

**6313 S. McKEEN** *to* **THE EDITOR OF THE** *ADVOCATE OF FREEDOM* **[AUSTIN WILLEY]. n.d. n.p.** Criticizes Willey for misrepresenting portions of an article by Rev. Lancaster on abolitionists. 2 May 1840. p.6, c2.

**6314 D. B. RANDALL** *to* **BRO. WILLEY. n.d. n.p.** Comments on the lack of anti-slavery activity in Anson, Maine, noting that many residents of Anson have moved South and become slaveholders. 2 May 1840. p.6, c4.

**6315 ANTHROPOS** *to* **THE EDITOR OF THE** *ABOLITIONIST.* **n.d. n.p.** Stresses the importance of missionary work in slave communities. 2 May 1840. p.7, c1

**6316 A. K. HOWARD** *to* **BRETHREN. [from the** *American Wesleyan Observer***] n.d. n.p.** Discusses the inherent cruelty of slavery. 2 May 1840. p.8, c2.

**6317 WM. WALKER** *to* **BRO. GARRISON. 11 April 1840. Andover Theological Seminary.** Reports the formation of the Andover Theological Seminary AS. 2 May 1840. p.8, c3.

**6318 J. W. [JEREMIAH WINSLOW]** *to* **THE** *ABOLITIONIST.* **24 December 1839. Havre.** Compares the difference in the treatment of colored students in Paris to the treatment of colored students in Vermont. 7 May 1840. p.9, c3.

**6319 n.n.** *to* **THE** *LIBERATOR.* **1 February 1840. New Orleans.** Criticizes Van Buren's close association with slaveholders. 7 May 1840. p.9, c4.

**6320 D. THURSTON** *to* **THE SUBSCRIBERS OF THE** *ADVOCATE OF FREEDOM.* **n.d. n.p.** Informs that subscribers to the *Advocate of Freedom* must now pay for their subscriptions in advance. 7 May 1840. p.10, c1.

**6321 n.n.** *to* **MRS. E. H. C. n.d. n.p.** Praises her for her abolitionist work. 7 May 1840. p.11, c1.

**6322 J. J. GURNEY** *to* **BENJAMIN LUCOCK. 18 February 1840. n.p.** Reports on his visit to the West Indies. 7 May 1840. p.12, c1.

**6323 HENRY H. CANNON** *to* **THE PUBLIC. [from the** ***Pennsylvania Freeman*****] n.d. n.p.** Denies charges that he is an abolitionist. 7 May 1840. p.12, c2.

**6324 n.n.** *to* **n.n. [extract from the** ***Anti-Slavery Reporter*****] 18 January 1840. Paris.** Approves of de Tocqueville's proposal to abolish slavery in the French colonies, noting that those who oppose it are not politically influential enough to stop it. 7 May 1840. p.12, c3.

**6325 n.n.** *to* **n.n. [from the** ***Emancipator*****] 30 March 1840. New York.** Believes that the South will secede from the Union. 14 May 1840. p.13, c1.

**6326 LEWIS TAPPAN** *to* **THE COMMITTEE ON BEHALF OF THE AFRICANS. [from the** ***Emancipator*****] n.d. n.p.** Reports on the proceedings in the *Amistad* case. 14 May 1840. p.13, c4.

**6327 CLERICUS** *to* **THE EDITOR OF THE** ***ABOLITIONIST.*** **n.d. n.p.** Comments upon the monetary needs of ASs. 14 May 1840. p.14, c3.

**6328 W. H. HARRISON** *to* **THOMAS SLOO, JR. 26 November 1836. Cincinnati.** Asserts that Congress does not have the power to abolish slavery. 14 May 1840. p.14, c4.

**6329 J. M. BERRIEN** *to* **GENTLEMEN. [from the** ***Charleston Courier*****] 11 April 1840. Savannah.** Discloses the contents of a letter in which General Harrison states that Congress does not have the power to abolish slavery. 14 May 1840. p.14, c4.

**6330 J. W.** *to* **n.n. [from the** ***Emancipator*****] 24 December 1839. Havre.** States that there is no evidence of color prejudice in France. 14 May 1840. p.15, c1.

**6331 JOSEPH STURGE** *to* **FRIEND. [from the** ***Emancipator*****] 3 March 1840. Birmingham, England.** Discusses the opposition to the appointment of female delegates to the World's Convention. 14 May 1840. p.16, c3.

**6332 JOHN CLARK** *to* **BRETHREN. n.d. Jamaica.** Encloses a donation for the AAS; reports that the Jamaican economy has prospered since the emancipation of slaves. 21 May 1840. p.19, c2.

**6333 GEORGE S. HALL** *to* **SIR. 25 April 1840. St. Stephen.** Encloses money for two subscriptions to the *Advocate of Freedom.* 21 May 1840. p.19, c3.

**6334 WM. M. CHACE** *to* **n.n. [from the** ***Abolitionist*****] 5 May 1840. Boston.** Announces the anniversary of the AAS. 28 May 1840. p.22, c1.

**6335 JOHN FORSYTH** *to* **n.n. 12 January 1840. Department of State.** Discusses the legal technicalities of the *Amistad* case. 28 May 1840. p.22, c2.

**6336 A. TAPPAN** *to* **THE AAS. 12 March 1840. n.p.** Explains why he will not be attending the annual meeting of the AAS. 28 May 1840. p.23, c1.

**6337 JAMES G. BIRNEY** *to* **MYRON HOLLEY, JOSHUA LEAVITT, AND E. WRIGHT, JR. 11 May 1840. New York.** Explains his reservations about being nominated as candidate for United States presidency. 4 June 1840. p.25, c1.

**6338 D. B. RANDALL** *to* **BRO. WILLEY. 21 May 1840. Baltimore.** Gives an account of an abolitionist meeting in Baltimore. 4 June 1840. p.26, c4.

**6339 DAVID GWYNNE AND JOHN C. WRIGHT** *to* **DR. ALEXANDER. [from the** *Cincinnati Republican* **via the** *Philanthropist*] **10 March 1840. Cincinnati.** Promise to forward material regarding General Harrison's views on slavery. 4 June 1840. p.28, c1.

**6340 M. VAN BUREN** *to* **W. F. LEAKE. 26 March 1840. Washington.** States that his position [on a matter not discussed] remains unchanged. 4 June 1840. p.28, c1.

**6341 JOSEPH A. MERRILL, JOTHAM HORTON, ORANGE SCOTT, [AND SEVENTEEN OTHER] MINISTERS OF THE METHODIST EPISCOPAL CHURCH** *to* **THE AAS. 9 May 1840. Baltimore, Md.** Express enthusiasm about the upcoming AAS meeting. 4 June 1840. p.28, c2.

**6342 I. CODDING** *to* **THE EXECUTIVE COMMITTEE OF THE MAINE AS. 3 June 1840. Hallowell.** Announces his move to Connecticut. 11 June 1840. p.30, c4.

**6343 H. GIBBONS** *to* **n.n. 25 May 1840. Wilmington, De.** Declares that little is being done in Delaware for the anti-slavery cause. 18 June 1840. p.33, c2.

**6344 GEO. S. BROWN** *to* **n.n. n.d. Liberia.** Describes an unprovoked attack on missionaries by Liberians. 18 June 1840. p.34, c3.

**6345 WM. HENRY BRISBANE** *to* **SAMUEL D. HASTINGS. 28 April 1840. Cincinnati, Oh.** Discusses his conversion from slaveholder to abolitionist. 18 June 1840. p.36, c1.

**6346 HIRAM WILSON** *to* **BRO. GOODELL. 25 May 1840. Toronto.** Discusses the progress of a colored mission in Toronto. 18 June 1840. p.36, c2.

**6347 ELON GALUSHA** *to* **THE BAPTIST SLAVE-HOLDERS OF THE SOUTHERN STATES. 29 April 1840. New York, N.Y.** Condemns slavery and informs slaveholders of their responsibility to abolish it. 25 June 1840. p.37, c1.

**6348 ANDREW SPIRLARD** *to* **DR. BAILEY. [from the** *Philanthropist*] **8 May 1840. Wayne County, Ia.** Relates the story of Capt. John Hill, who freed his slaves on his deathbed. 25 June 1840. p.37, c3.

**6349 S. ADLAM** *to* **THE** *ADVOCATE OF FREEDOM.* **n.d. n.p.** Lists resolutions adopted at the Maine Baptist Anti-Slavery Convention. 25 June 1840. p.38, c1.

**6350 D. B. RANDALL** *to* **BRO. WILLEY. 20 May 1840. n.p.** Describes the success of abolitionist lectures at Solon, Bingham, New Portland, Starks, and Norridgewock Village. 25 June 1840. p.39, c1.

**6351 THOMAS EARLE** *to* **MYRON HOLLEY, JOSHUA LEAVITT, AND E. WRIGHT. 30 May 1840. Philadelphia.** Discusses factors supporting and opposing the formation of a third political party with an abolitionist platform. 2 July 1840. p.41, c1.

**6352 n.n.** *to* **BROTHER. 18 June 1840. New Haven.** Lists resolutions adopted at a meeting of the General Association of Connecticut. 2 July 1840. p.41, c4.

**6353 L. N.** *to* **THE EDITOR OF THE** *ADVOCATE OF FREEDOM* **[AUSTIN WILLEY]. 20 June 1840. n.p.** Discusses an article on missionary work in Liberia. 2 July 1840. p.42, c4.

**6354 n.n.** *to* **THE** *ADVOCATE OF FREEDOM.* **n.d. n.p.** Compares the conditions of serfs in Russia with the condition of slaves in the United States. 2 July 1840. p.43, c1.

**6355 GERRIT SMITH** *to* **MR. GOODELL. [from the** *Friend of Man***] 17 June 1840. Peterboro'.** Describes an abolitionist meeting held in New York. 9 July 1840. p.45, c4.

**6356 n.n.** *to* **THE EDITOR OF THE** *CHRISTIAN REFLECTOR.* **n.d. n.p.** Stresses the importance of exercising good judgment at the polls. 9 July 1840. p.45, c4.

**6357 ABOLITIONIST** *to* **THE EDITOR OF THE** *ADVOCATE OF FREEDOM* **[AUSTIN WILLEY]. 30 June 1840. Hallowell, Me.** Requests clarification of an article about an abolitionist conference in Hallowell. 9 July 1840. p.46, c4.

**6358 n.n.** *to* **THE** *ADVOCATE OF FREEDOM.* **n.d. n.p.** Compares the condition of American slaves with the condition of the peasants in Eastern Europe. 9 July 1840. p.47, c1.

**6359 n.n.** *to* **n.n. 24 February 1840. n.p.** Informs that bloodhounds are being imported into Florida to hunt runaway slaves; states that slaveholders are moving out of the South and into Texas in order to improve their prospects. 9 July 1840. p.48, c1.

**6360 J. T. HAWES** *to* **MR. WILLEY. July 1840. New Sharon.** Asks why ministers are not more involved in abolitionist work. 16 July 1840. p.50, c1.

**6361 JUDGE WILLIAM JAY** *to* **J. C. JACKSON. 8 June 1840. Bedford.** Resigns as a member of the AAS because he believes the society is less concerned with the abolition of slavery than with the promotion of equality of the sexes. 16 July 1840. p.52, c3.

**6362 F. F. MANFORD** *to* **THE EDITOR OF THE** *ADVOCATE OF FREEDOM* **[AUSTIN WILLEY]. 17 June 1840. Boston, Ma.** Describes a case of racial discrimination on an omnibus in Charlestown. 16 July 1840. p.52, c4.

**6363 A. D. JONES** *to* **THE** *EVANGELIST.* **8 June 1840. Newark.** Relates the story of slaves who were manumitted and later reenslaved. 23 July 1840. p.53, c1.

**6364 GEO. S. BROWN** *to* **REV. JOHN SEYS. 3 March 1840. Heddington.** Views the commencement of religious revivals in the South enthusiastically. 23 July 1840. p.53, c2.

**6365 D. N.** *to* **BROTHER LEAVITT. [from the** *Emancipator***] 5 May 1840. Mission Institute.** Criticizes slaveholders for keeping their slaves ignorant of the teachings of Christ. 23 July 1840. p.53, c4.

**6366 n.n.** *to* **BRO. WILLEY. n.d. n.p.** Praises Willey for the important work done by the *Advocate of Freedom.* 23 July 1840. p.54, c3.

**6367 AN OLD MAN** *to* **THE EDITOR OF THE** *VOICE OF FREEDOM.* **n.d. n.p.** States that in the event of a national emergency, slaves and free colored people could be used to defend the country. 23 July 1840. p.56, c3.

**6368 P. R.** *to* **MR. SUNDERLAND. [from** *Zion's Watchman***] 15 June 1840. Lenom, Ash County.** Informs that a slave was shot to death for refusing to obey an order. 30 July 1840. p.57, c3.

**6369 JOSHUA COFFIN** *to* **THE EDITOR OF THE** *PENNSYLVANIA FREEMAN.* **n.d. n.p.** Lists the artrocities committed by Thomas Christmas, a slaveholder. 30 July 1840. p.57, c3.

**6370 D. THURSTON** *to* **BRO. WILLEY. n.d. n.p.** Wishes that Americans would be more politically active. 30 July 1840. p.58, c1.

**6371 BROUGHAM** *to* **GENTLEMEN. n.d. House of Lords.** Regrets that poor health will prevent him from attending an abolitionist meeting. 30 July 1840. p.58, c3.

**6372 A SUBSCRIBER** *to* **DR. BAILEY. [from the** *Philanthropist*] **15 July 1840. Cincinnati.** Encloses excerpts of a conversation between an abolitionist and a slaveholder in which the slaveholder favors compensated emancipation. 6 August 1840. p.63, c2.

**6373 ALVAN STEWART** *to* **CHARLES SEXTON. [from the** *Voice of Freedom*] **n.d. n.p.** Praises James Birney's contributions to the anti-slavery cause. 6 August 1840. p.63, c2.

**6374 SENATOR J. RUGGLES** *to* **DR. BENJAMIN AYER. 2 July 1840. Senate Chamber.** Asserts that the abolitionists will support Van Buren, rather than Harrison, because they believe Van Buren will favor them after the election. 6 August 1840. p.63, c3.

**6375 AN ABOLITIONIST** *to* **MR. BIRNEY. [from the** *Emancipator*] **15 July 1839. Maryland.** Condemns slavery and criticizes those who do not work for its abolition. 6 August 1840. p.64, c1.

**6376 MR. GROSVENOR** *to* **THE** *CHRISTIAN REFLECTOR*. **[extract] n.d. n.p.** Describes with satisfaction the warm reception Baptists received at a meeting of abolitionists in London. 6 August 1840. p.64, c2.

**6377 G. C. WATERMAN** *to* **THE** *ADVOCATE OF FREEDOM*. **n.d. n.p.** Encloses the election results and resolutions adopted at the annual meeting of the Litchfield AS. 13 August 1840. p.66, c1.

**6378 ABOLITION** *to* **n.n. [from the** *Christian Witness*] **n.d. n.p.** Relates the story of a slave who refused to accept the Bible as the word of God because it upholds slavery. 13 August 1840. p. 68, c2.

**6379 R.** *to* **THE** *WESLEYAN OBSERVER*. **27 June 1840. n.p.** Informs of a slave who drowned himself after an unsuccessful attempt to run away. 13 August 1840. p.68, c3.

**6380 O. SCOTT AND LA ROY SUNDERLAND** *to* **BRETHREN. 20 July 1840. Lowell, Ma.** Invite abolitionist members of the Methodist Episcopal church to a meeting in New York in order to form an AS. 20 August 1840. p.69, c1.

**6381 MARY MacDOUGAL** *to* **MR. WILLEY. 13 August 1840. Bangor.** Reports on the resolutions adopted at the annual meeting of the Bangor AS. 20 August 1840. p.70, c1.

**6382 WILLIAM WITHEE** *to* **BRO. WILLEY. n.d. n.p.** Lists resolutions debated and passed at a human rights convention in Guilford. 20 August 1840. p.70, c4.

**6383 WILLIAM WARREN** *to* **BRO. WILLEY. 5 August 1840. Windham.** Argues that political action cannot be the only means used to abolish slavery, but fails to offer any new suggestions. 20 August 1840. p.71, c1.

**6384 R. L.** *to* **BRO. WILLEY. n.d. n.p.** Expresses support for the *Advocate of Freedom* and encloses the names of two new subscribers. 20 August 1840. p.71, c2.

**6385 JOHN W. LEWIS** *to* **BRO. PILLSBURY. n.d. n.p.** Describes the favorable reception of his anti-slavery lectures at Dartmouth College. 20 August 1840. p.72, c3.

**6386 J. G. W. P.** *to* **THE** *ADVOCATE OF FREEDOM.* **n.d. n.p.** Asserts that a mother must be more educated than a father because she exerts more influence over the children. 20 August 1840. p.72, c3.

**6387 n.n.** *to* **THE** *ADVOCATE OF FREEDOM.* **n.d. n.p.** Offers advice to the young readers of the *Advocate of Freedom* on how to treat one's friends. 20 August 1840. p.72, c4.

**6388 H. S.** *to* **THE EDITOR OF THE** *ADVOCATE OF FREEDOM* **[AUSTIN WILLEY]. n.d. n.p.** Encloses a note written by Dr. Scott about slavery. 27 August 1840. p. 73, c1.

**6389 DR. SCOTT** *to* **n.n. April 1840. n.p.** Asserts that men should not make distinctions between men since God does not do so. 27 August 1840. p.73, c1.

**6390 JAMES LYONS** *to* **GEN. W. H. HARRISON. [from the** *Cincinnati Philanthropist***] n.d. n.p.** Requests that he clarify his position on slavery and explain his connection with the ASs. 27 August 1840. p.73, c1.

**6391 GEN. W. H. HARRISON** *to* **JAMES LYONS. [from the** *Cincinnati Philanthropist***] 1 June 1840. North Bend.** Replies that he has never and will never become involved in any abolitionist activities. 27 August 1840. p.73, c2.

**6392 GEN. W. H. HARRISON** *to* **GOV. OWEN[S]. [from the** *Cincinnati Gazette***] 16 February 1840. Cincinnati.** Denies any connection with abolitionist organizations and activities. 27 August 1840. p.73, c2.

**6393 ALIQUIUS** *to* **THE EDITOR OF THE** *CHRISTIAN WITNESS.* **30 July 1840. Allegheny.** Favors the formation of the Canadian CS of Pittsburgh and Allegheny because it will aid runaway slaves. 27 August 1840. p.73, c4.

**6394 UNION** *to* **THE EDITOR OF THE** *ADVOCATE OF FREEDOM* **[AUSTIN WILLEY]. n.d. n.p.** Criticizes abolitionists for not voting in accordance with their principles. 27 August 1840. p.74, c1.

**6395 GERRIT SMITH** *to* **F. P. TRACY. 9 June 1840. Peterboro'.** Discusses Mr. Barstow's pro-colonization views. 27 August 1840. p.74, c2.

**6396 THOMAS MORRIS** *to* **G. W. WELLS. n.d. n.p.** Insists that most Americans are opposed to slavery. 27 August 1840. p.74, c3.

**6397 WILLIAM WARREN** *to* **THE** *ADVOCATE OF FREEDOM.* **n.d. n.p.** States that in order for abolitionists to work collectively and constructively, divisions within abolitionist groups must be overcome. 27 August 1840. p.74, c4.

**6398 n.n.** *to* **MR. A. WILLEY. n.d. n.p.** Encourages abolitionists to exercise their political rights at the polls. 27 August 1840. p.75, c1.

**6399 MR. C. FREEMAN** *to* **MR. WILLEY. 19 August. Limerick.** States that slavery is an immoral and destructive system because it dehumanizes both Negroes and whites. 27 August 1840. p.75, c1.

**6400 S. L. POMEROY [***sic***]** *to* **J. C. JACKSON. 7 July 1840. Bangor, Me.** Resigns from the AAS because he no longer concurs with its aims and beliefs. 27 August 1840. p.75, c2.

**6401 BENJ. HARRISON** *to* **GEO. E. BADGER. [from the** *Philanthropist***] 9 June 1840. Berkeley, Charles City County, Va.** Discusses events of General Harrison's early life and his lifelong belief in the legitimacy of slavery. 3 September 1840. p.77, c3.

**6402 GEO. EVANS** *to* **G. C. WATERMAN. 1 September 1840. Gardiner.** Discusses the various powers of Congress, including its power to abolish slavery. 10 September 1840. p.82, c1.

**6403 THOS. H. SANDFORD** *to* **MR. WILLEY. 1 September 1840. Bangor.** Opposes independent political action by abolitionists; criticizes the *Advocate of Freedom* for its uncomplimentary portraits of General Harrison and Van Buren. 10 September 1840. p.82, c2.

**6404 ABBA M. MOODY AND SARAH M. PLUMMER** *to* **MR. WILLEY. 4 September 1840. Bangor.** Comment on the success of a sale held by the AS of Bangor; list the amounts of anonymous donations received. 10 September 1840. p.82, c4.

**6405 n.n.** *to* **THE EDITOR OF THE** *CHRISTIAN WATCHMAN***. n.d. n.p.** Lists resolutions passed by the Baptist Union at its latest session. 10 September 1840. p.83, c3.

**6406 H. P. TORSEY** *to* **THE** *ADVOCATE OF FREEDOM***. n.d. n.p.** Refutes the belief that slaves are in a better position than free laborers; advocates the abolition of slavery. 17 September 1840. p.86, c1.

**6407 J. C.** *to* **J. LEAVITT. [from the** *Emancipator***] 10 August 1840. Washington, D.C.** Describes slave sales in Washington, D.C.; relates the story of a female slave who was put up for sale after bearing her master's child. 17 September 1840. p.86, c1.

**6408 REV. HIRAM WILSON** *to* **BRO. GOODELL. [from the** *Friend of Man***] 19 August 1840. Toronto, Upper Canada.** Praises American abolitionists for their political activism; relates the story of a slave who escaped from Richmond into Canada. 17 September 1840. p.88, c2.

**6409 A FUGITIVE SLAVE** *to* **n.n. n.d. n.p.** Describes his escape from Tennessee into Canada; discusses the success of a Canadian mission for runaways. 24 September 1840. p.89, c4.

**6410 C. P. R.** *to* **MR. WILLEY. 29 August 1840. Bangor.** Offers several reasons why abolitionists should be politcally active. 24 September 1840. p.90, c1.

**6411 HIRAM WILSON** *to* **BRO. LEAVITT. 28 August 1840. Toronto.** Reports that runaways from Richmond and Philadelphia have arrived safely in Toronto and are receiving assistance. 24 September 1840. p.90, c3.

**6412 I. C.** *to* **J. LEAVITT. [from the** *Emancipator***] 5 August 1840. Alabama.** Gives an account of a conversation with a slaveholder who stated that most slaveholders are ignorant of abolitionism, and that abolitionists would be more effective if they were politically more active. 1 October 1840. p.93, c4.

**6413 J. S. GREEN** *to* **BRO. LEAVITT. n.d. Sandwich Island Mission.** Informs of the mysterious death of a fellow abolitionist; reports on the progress made by missionaries on Sandwich Islands. 8 October 1840. p.97, c1.

**6414 n.n.** *to* **THE EDITORS OF THE** *RECORDER* **AND THE** *WATCHMAN***. n.d. n.p.** Lists resolutions adopted at the annual meeting of the Edgefield Baptist Association. 8 October 1840. p.98, c4.

6415 **n.n.** *to* **THE** ***ADVOCATE OF FREEDOM*****. n.d. n.p.** Lists resolutions adopted at an anti-slavery meeting. 8 October 1840. p.98, c4.

6416 **A COLORED MAN** *to* **THE EDITOR OF THE** ***ADVOCATE OF FREEDOM*** **[AUSTIN WILLEY]. 5 October 1840. Bath.** States that he demanded the return of his contributions to a segregated church, and that the church complied with his demand. 8 October 1840. p.99, c1.

6417 **ABIEL PARMELE** *to* **THE EDITOR OF THE** ***EVANGELIST*****. n.d. n.p.** Lists resolutions adopted at a meeting of the Angelica Presbytery. 8 October 1840. p.99, c3.

6418 **WILLIAM STEARNS** *to* **n.n. n.d. n.p.** Lists resolutions adopted during a meeting of the First Congregational Church in Great Falls, New York. 8 October 1840. p.99, c4.

6419 **J. G. BIRNEY** *to* **n.n. [extract from the** ***Anti-Slavery Reporter*****] 23 July 1840. Derby.** Discusses the success of his abolitionist tour to England. 8 October 1840. p.100, c1.

6420 **S. R. HOBBIE** *to* **N. GREENE. 9 September 1840. n.p.** States that the postmaster general has declared the order restricting the conveyance of mail over certain postal routes unjust and has suspended it. 8 October 1840. p.100, c4.

6421 **GERRIT SMITH** *to* **MR. GOODELL. 27 September 1840. Philadelphia.** Stresses the importance of abolitionists' becoming politically active. 15 October 1840. p.102, c4.

6422 **AMMI R. BRADBURY** *to* **n.n. 26 September 1840. Limerick, Me.** Lists resolutions adopted at a meeting of the York County AS. 15 October 1840. p.103, c1.

6423 **JUDGE WILLIAM JAY** *to* **JAMES G. BIRNEY. 28 March 1840. New York.** Regrets that important matters in New York will prevent him from attending the World's Anti-Slavery Conference in London. 22 October 1840. p.105, c1.

6424 **JAMES G. BIRNEY** *to* **SIR. 29 August 1840. London.** Gives a detailed account of the World's Anti-Slavery Conference in London. 22 October 1840. p.105, c3.

6425 **H. B. STANTON** *to* **FRIEND. 31 August 1840. London.** Reports on the success of abolitionist meetings held in towns near London. 22 October 1840. p.105, c4.

6426 **J. T. HAWES** *to* **MR. WILLEY. n.d. n.p.** Argues that the North is as deeply enmeshed in the evils of slavery as is the South. 22 October 1840. p.106, c1.

6427 **KA-LE** *to* **LEWIS TAPPAN. September. Westville.** Thanks Tappan for his support during the *Amistad* trial. 22 October 1840. p.106, c4.

6428 **JOHN G. WHITTIER** *to* **FRIEND SEWALL. [from the** ***Abolitionist*****] 10 October 1840. Amesbury.** Provides a brief biographical sketch of Thomas Earle, vice-presidential candidate on the Liberty ticket. 22 October 1840. p.107, c1.

6429 **JOHN HOLYOKE** *to* **MR. WILLEY. 28 September 1840. Brewer.** Believes that a third party with an abolitionist platform would perpetuate slavery indirectly by lending support to the present administration. 22 October 1840. p.107, c2.

6430 **n.n.** *to* **THE** ***ADVOCATE OF FREEDOM*****. n.d. n.p.** Lists resolutions adopted during a meeting of abolitionists in Somerset County. 22 October 1840. p.107, c3.

**6431 n.n.** *to* **THE EDITORS OF THE** *AMERICAN AND FOREIGN ANTI-SLAVERY REPORTER*. **14 September 1840. East Tennessee.** Encloses names and payments of new subscribers; describes the tarring and feathering of Reverend Kendall. 22 October 1840. p.108, c2.

**6432 C. L. REMOND** *to* **n.n. n.d. n.p.** Discusses the success of a meeting in Glasgow on British exploitation of India. 22 October 1840. p.108, c2.

**6433 S. M. PLUMMER** *to* **MR. WILLEY. October 1840. Bangor.** Lists funds collected during an anti-slavery fair. 29 October 1840. p.110, c4.

**6434 CHARLES** *to* **THE EDITOR OF THE** *ADVOCATE OF FREEDOM* **[AUSTIN WILLEY]. October 1840. n.p.** Expresses amazement at the refusal of ministers to participate in abolitionist activities. 29 October 1840. p.110, c4.

**6435 O. B. WALKER** *to* **BRO. WILLEY. October 1840. Livhe** *Tuscaloosa Flag*] **September 1840. Tuscaloosa.** Condemns abolitionism and asks why abolitionist literature is being mailed to him. 19 October 1840. p.123, c2.

**6436 L. CARY STEVENS** *to* **BRO. WILLEY. n.d. n.p.** Urges abolitionists to exhibit their strength by voting. 29 October 1840. p.111, c2.

**6437 VAN BUREN** *to* **WALTER LEAKE. 27 March 1840. n.p.** Summarizes his position on slavery and the admission of new states to the Union. 29 October 1840. p.111, c3.

**6438 n.n.** *to* **BRO. MURRAY. n.d. n.p.** Reports on an interview with a slaveholder about slavery, color prejudice, and Southern treatment of slaves. 29 October 1840. p.112, c2.

**6439 n.n.** *to* **SIR. 6 June 1840. n.p.** Threatens violence if any more abolitionist papers pass through his office. 29 October 1840. p.112, c3.

**6440 CHARLES B. SMITH** *to* **THE** *ADVOCATE OF FREEDOM.* **2 october 1840. Gorham.** Reports on a meeting of music teachers at the Teacher's Seminary. 29 October 1840. p.112, c4.

**6441 O. B. WALKER** *to* **BRO. WILLEY. 2 November 1840. Livermore Falls.** Clarifies his position on the Van Buren and Harrison tickets. 5 November 1840. p.114, c1.

**6442 D. SEWALL** *to* **BRO. WILLEY. 27 October 1840. n.p.** Praises the abolitionists of Somerset County for selecting and nominating their own presidential candidate. 5 November 1840. p.114, c4.

**6443 n.n.** *to* **THE EDITOR OF THE** *SOUTH CAROLINIAN.* **12 August 1840. Winnsboro'.** Describes the expulsion of an abolitionist preacher from the city of Winnsboro'. 5 November 1840. p.116, c1.

**6444 JAY** *to* **THE EDITOR OF THE** *PHILANTHROPIST.* **n.d. n.p.** Criticizes Andrew Stevenson's narrow, regional position on the Corn Laws. 5 November 1840. p.116, c3.

**6445 LEWIS TAPPAN** *to* **PRESIDENT MARTIN VAN BUREN. 9 September 1840. New York.** Summarizes a letter written to his brother concerning the *Amistad* trial. 12 November 1840. p.117, c2.

**6446 W.S. HOLABIRD** *to* **LEWIS TAPPAN. 5 September 1840. Winchester, Ct.** Claims that he has not received all the information pertaining to the *Amistad* trial. 12 November 1840. p.117, c3.

**6447 JOHN FORSYTH** *to* **LEWIS TAPPAN. 7 September 1840. Washington, D.C.** Reports that information related to the *Amistad* trial has been forwarded to Van Buren. 12 November 1840. p.117, c3.

**6448 JOHN FORSYTH** *to* **LEWIS TAPPAN. 12 September 1840. Washington, D.C.** States that the district attorney of Connecticut has received new materials concerning the *Amistad* trial. 12 November 1840. p.117, c4.

**6449 W. S. HOLABIRD** *to* **LEWIS TAPPAN. 11 September 1840. Winchester.** States that he will attest to the authenticity of the documents alleged to be the decree of the king of Spain of 1817, the ordinance of the queen, and the treaty of 1817 between Spain and Great Britain. 12 November 1840. p.117, c4.

**6450 W. S. HOLABIRD** *to* **LEWIS TAPPAN. 28 September 1840. Winchester.** States that he has been authorized to testify to the authenticity of the Spanish documents. 12 November 1840. p.118, c1.

**6451 LEVESON, ON BEHALF OF LORD PALMERSTON** *to* **THOMAS CLARKSON. 22 August 1840. Foreign Office.** Reports that he has received Clarkson's memorial requesting that the functionaries in the British government neither hold slaves nor hire them, directly or indirectly. 12 November 1840. p.118, c2.

**6452 GOV. WM. PENNINGTON** *to* **THOMAS CLARKSON. 30 July 1840. Newark, N.J.** Acknowledges receipt of a letter calling for the abolition of slavery in the United States. 12 November 1840. p.118, c3.

**6453 THOMAS T. STONE** *to* **BRO. WILLEY. 10 November 1840. Mechisses.** Reports on the successes and failures of his abolitionist tour of Europe. 19 November 1840. p.122, c1.

**6454 MINERVA McDOUGAL, SARAH M. PLUMMER, AND CAROLINE JONES** *to* **THE LADIES OF MAINE. 10 November 1840. Bangor.** Stress the efficacy of petitions to Congress. 19 November 1840. p.122, c4.

**6455 A. P. BAGBY** *to* **HON. SETH M. GATES. [from the** ***Tuscaloosa Flag*****] September 1840. Tuscaloosa.** Condemns abolitionism and asks why abolitionist literature is being mailed to him. 19 October 1840. p.123, c2.

**6456 GOV. CHAS. J. McDONALD** *to* **JUDGE S. M. GATES. 10 September 1840. Milledgville.** Condemns abolitionism and is outraged that abolitionist material is being mailed to him. 19 November 1840. p.123, c2.

**6457 J. RUSSELL** *to* **THOMAS CLARKSON. 21 August 1840. Downing Street.** States that Queen Victoria approves of the resolutions adopted at the World's Anti-Slavery Conference in London. 19 November 1840. p.123, c3.

**6458 THOMAS MORRIS** *to* **MR. BAILEY. [from the** ***Philanthropist*****] n.d. n.p.** Believes that the power of slaveholders is great enough to elect Harrison as president. 19 November 1840. p.123, c3.

**6459 A BAPTIST MINISTER** *to* **BRO. WILLEY. n.d. n.p.** Supports the call for a convention of Baptist ministers to discuss slavery and abolitionism. 19 November 1840. p.123, c4.

**6460 W. H. MURCH** *to* **THE** ***BRITISH AND FOREIGN ANTI-SLAVERY REPORTER*****. 7 October. n.p.** Lists resolutions adopted during a meeting of the Board of Baptist Ministers in London. 26 November 1840. p.125, c4.

**6461 ROBERT NEWTON** *to* **J. H. TREDGOLD. 17 August 1840. Newcastle-upon-Tyne.** Discusses the British and Foreign AS's commitment to the abolition of slavery. 26 November 1840. p.125, c4.

**6462 A. C. TUTTLE** *to* **THE EDITOR OF THE** *NEW YORK EVANGELIST.* **12 November 1840. Fayetteville.** Lists resolutions adopted during the last meeting of the Presbytery of Onondaga. 26 November 1840. p.126, c1.

**6463 R. R. MADDEN** *to* **THE COMMITTEE OF THE BRITISH AND FOREIGN AS. 18 August 1840. Alexandria.** States that the Pasha of Egypt has received the addresses delivered at the anti-slavery convention in London. 26 November 1840. p.127, c1.

**6464 T. D. OXFORD** *to* **CYRUS P. GROSVENOR. 24 August 1840. Henry City.** Objects to abolitionist material which has been sent to him and requests that his name be dropped from the mailing list. 26 November 1840. p.127, c2.

**6465 JAMES R. CAMPBELL** *to* **THE EDITOR OF** *ZION'S WATCHMAN.* **[from the** *Anti-Slavery Reporter***] 14 October 1840. Montrose.** Encloses an address by Ralph Wardlaw presented at the annual meeting of the Congregational Union of Scotland in Dundee. 3 December 1840. p.129, c1.

**6466 E. R. WARREN** *to* **BRO. WILLEY. November 1840. Topsham.** Opposes forming an anti-slavery convention of ministers until further action is taken by the separate denominations. 3 December 1840. p.130, c1.

**6467 JOS. HUTCHINSON** *to* **BRO. WILLEY. 19 November 1840. South Livermore.** Reports on an anti-slavery lecture by Reverend Randall of Readfield. 3 December 1840. p.130, c2.

**6468 n.n.** *to THE ADVOCATE OF FREEDOM.* **25 November 1840. n.p.** Asserts that no man is free until the slave is free; encloses one dollar for the Foreign Missionary Society. 3 December 1840. p.131, c1.

**6469 J. R. DAILY** *to* **n.n. [from the** *Pennsylvania Freeman***] 6 September 1840. Monrovia.** Describes the settlements in Liberia as unfit for residence. 10 December 1840. p.133, c1.

**6470 REMOND** *to* **THE EDITOR OF THE** *LIBERATOR.* **n.d. n.p.** Describes the warm reception of Mr. Gurley in Glasgow, Scotland. 10 December 1840. p.133, c4.

**6471 SIMON PAGE** *to* **BRO. WILLEY. 7 December 1840. Hallowell.** Encloses a sixteen-dollar donation from the Hallowell Sabbath School for the *Amistad* Africans. 10 December 1840. p.135, c1.

**6472 D. B. RANDALL** *to* **BRO. WILLEY. 30 November 1840. New Sharon.** Believes that abolitionists should not be discouraged by apathy in their communities; calls for a convention of abolitionist ministers to discuss a strategy. 10 December 1840. p.135, c2.

**6473 n.n.** *to THE ADVOCATE OF FREEDOM.* **13 December 1840. Union.** Comments on the contradictory nature of the American legal system. 24 December 1840. p.143, c1.

**6474 ALVAN STEWART** *to* **GOV. JAMES K. POLK. 18 November 1840. Utica, N.Y.** Assails Polk's discourteous response to Seth M. Gates, who sent him the report of the World's Anti-Slavery Convention. 31 December 1840. p.145, c2.

**6475 n.n.** *to* **THE EDITOR OF THE** ***ADVOCATE OF FREEDOM*** **[AUSTIN WILLEY]. 16 December 1840. Calais.** Encloses an abolitionist address first published in the *Liberator*, which discusses the physical attacks suffered by abolitionists. 31 December 1840. p.147, c1.

**6476 JOSEPH STURGE** *to* **THE EDITOR OF THE** ***PATRIOT*****. November 1840. Birmingham.** Recommends that Dr. Wayland, president of Brown University, read the pamphlet entitled, "The American Churches, the bulwarks of American Slavery, by an American." 31 December 1840. p.147, c2.

**6477 LIBERTAS** *to* **THE** ***COLORED AMERICAN*****. n.d. n.p.** Reports that residents of Washington, D.C. feel it is unsafe to subscribe to an abolitionist paper. 31 December 1840. p.147, c3.

## [1841]

**6478 W. WILCOX** *to* **THE EDITOR OF THE** ***ADVOCATE OF FREEDOM*** **[AUSTIN WILLEY]. 25 December 1840. East Monmouth.** Criticizes abolitionists who did not vote for the abolitionist nominees for president and vice-president of the United States. 7 January 1841. p.150, c3.

**6479 JAMES M. DODGE** *to* **MR. WILLEY. 1 January 1841. Portland.** Believes that the support of the Liberty ticket was much greater than reported and accuses a local official of tampering with the ballots. 7 January 1841. p.151, c1.

**6480 MANY ABOLITIONISTS** *to* **MESSRS. EDITORS. [from the** ***Albany Argus*****] n.d. n.p.** Explain the nature of abolitionism and the design of abolitionists. 21 January 1841. p.158, c1.

**6481 D. B. RANDALL** *to* **BRO. WILLEY. 19 January 1841. n.p.** Looks forward to attending the coming annual meeting of abolitionists. 21 January 1841. p.159, c1.

**6482 C. CHAUNCY CONE** *to* **THE EDITOR OF THE** ***ADVOCATE OF FREEDOM*** **[AUSTIN WILLEY]. January 1841. Bowdoinham.** Criticizes the "old fashioned abolitionism" which holds that slavery is acceptable under certain circumstances. 21 January 1841. p.159, c1.

**6483 J. CHILD** *to* **THE EDITOR OF THE** ***ADVOCATE OF FREEDOM*** **[AUSTIN WILLEY]. 15 January 1841. Argyle.** Encourages abolitionists to support the *Advocate of Freedom* and other abolitionist publications. 28 January 1841. p.162, c4.

**6484 O. B. WALKER** *to* **BRO. WILLEY. 21 January 1841. Livermore.** Promises to help increase the circulation of the *Advocate of Freedom* by selling subscriptions. 28 January 1841. p.163, c1.

**6485 W. S. SEWALL** *to* **THE** ***ADVOCATE OF FREEDOM*****. 21 January 1841. Brownville.** Lists the election returns and the resolutions adopted during the annual meeting of the Piscataquis County AS. 28 January 1841. p. 163, c1.

**6486 JAMES BROWN** *to* **MR. LEAVITT. 27 November 1840. Jerseyville.** Expresses admiration and support for an unnamed abolitionist. 28 January 1841. p.164, c3.

**6487 LIBERTAS** *to* **n.n. 9 January. n.p.** States that John Quincy Adams is preparing to address the Supreme Court on the *Amistad* case. 28 January 1841. p.164, c3.

**6488 O. MINER** *to* **n.n. [from the** ***Evangelist*****] 19 December 1840. Penn Yan.** Describes the success of the Penn Yan Convention of Abolitionists, and lists resolutions adopted. 4 February 1841. p.166, c3.

**6489 C. P. C.** *to* **BRO. WILLEY. n.d. n.p.** Praises the *Advocate of Freedom* for the firm stand it has always taken against slavery. 4 February 1841. p.167, c1.

**6490 MR. LEAVITT** *to* **MESSRS. PIERCY AND REED. 21 January 1841. Washington City.** Describes the proceedings of the House of Representatives and mentions that the ACS is meeting in Washington. 4 February 1841. p.167, c2.

**6491 SAMUEL FESSENDEN** *to* **THE MAINE AS. 30 January 1841. Portland.** States that he will not be present at the annual meeting of the Maine AS. 4 February 1841. p.170, c4.

**6492 HIRAM WILSON** *to* **THE BANGOR FEMALE AS. [extract] n.d. n.p.** Thanks the Bangor Female AS for its donation to Oberlin teachers. 4 February 1841. p.171, c1.

**6493 W. HALL** *to* **FRIEND WILLEY. 2 February 1841. Hartford, Me.** Describes the rise of anti-slavery sentiment in Hartford. 4 February 1841. p.171, c2.

**6494 JOHN A. JAMES** *to* **n.n. [extract from the** ***New York Observer*****] n.d. Birmingham.** States that the United States will be the great country it pretends to be when slavery is abolished. 4 February 1841. p.172, c1.

**6495 DAVID ROOT** *to* **n.n. [from the** ***Evangelist*****] n.d. n.p.** Lists resolutions adopted at the annual meeting of the Congregational Church of Philadelphia. 4 February 1841. p. 172, c1.

**6496 F. HARRINGTON** *to* **n.n. [from the** ***New York Evangelist*****] December 1840. Franklin.** Lists resolutions adopted during a meeting of the Presbytery of Delaware. 4 February 1841. p.172, c2.

**6497 L. T. BOOTHBY, REV. ASA GREEN, AND FRANCIS MORRILL** *to* **MR. WILLEY. n.d. n.p.** List resolutions adopted during a meeting of abolitionists at the Methodist Meeting House in Livermore. 18 February 1841. p.174, c1.

**6498 HUMPHREY SAUNDERS, JR.** *to* **BRO. WILLEY. 20 January 1841. Waterford.** Reports on the success of anti-slavery efforts in Waterford. 18 February 1841. p.174, c1.

**6499 D. B. RANDALL** *to* **BRO. WILLEY. 15 February 1841. Kent's Hill.** Praises the efforts of abolitionists in Somerset, Fairfield, and New Sharon. 18 February 1841. p.174, c4.

**6500 SIR THOMAS FOWELL BUXTON** *to* **REV. R. R. GURLEY. 9 October 1840. Northrepps Hall, near Aylsham.** Discusses the differences and similarities between the ACS and the African Civilization Society. 18 February 1841. p.176, c1.

**6501 n.n.** *to* **GERRIT SMITH. [extract] 30 November 1840. East Tennessee.** Reports on the growth of anti-slavery sentiment in North Carolina. 4 March 1841. p.177, c1.

**6502 MR. LEAVITT** *to* **n.n. [from the** ***Emancipator*****] n.d. n.p.** Discusses Northern treatment of colored people, the improving relations of Great Britain with the North, and the debate over appropriating $100,000 for the emigration of Florida Indians. 4 March 1841. p.177, c2.

**6503 EDWARD J. PEET** *to* **THE** *ADVOCATE OF FREEDOM.* **15 February 1841. Norridgwock.** Lists resolutions adopted at the fourth annual meeting of the Somerset AS. 4 March 1841. p.178, c1.

**6504 F. MANNING** *to* **SIR. 18 February 1841. South Paris.** Encloses the constitution of the Oxford County AS. 4 March 1841. p.178, c2.

**6505 D. B. RANDALL** *to* **BRO. WILLEY. 26 February 1841. n.p.** Describes the difficulties encountered en route to the Oxford County Convention of Abolitionists; states that many attended the convention. 4 March 1841. p.179, c1.

**6506 EBEN'R CHILDS** *to* **MR. WILLEY. 23 February 1841. Farmington.** Reports on the resolutions adopted during the annual meeting of the New Sharon AS. 11 March 1841. p.181, c2.

**6507 BETH** *to* **THE EDITOR OF THE** *ADVOCATE OF FREEDOM* **[AUSTIN WILLEY]. 24 February 1841. Bangor.** Describes the obstacles to the temperance movement in Augusta. 18 March 1841. p.186, c2.

**6508 J. H. TREDGOLD** *to* **n.n. n.d. n.p.** Criticizes certain steps taken by an unnamed AS. 18 March 1841. p.186, c4.

**6509 J. H. TREDGOLD** *to* **J. A. COLLINS. 16 January 1841. London.** Clarifies the position of the British and Foreign AS on an unspecified internal matter of the AAS. 18 March 1841. p.187, c1.

**6510 C. W. DENNISON [*sic*]** *to* **n.n. [from the** *Free American*] **5 March 1841. Worcester, Ma.** Describes a Union prayer meeting for various leaders of the American people. 18 March 1841. p.187, c3.

**6511 LIBERTAS** *to* **MR. EDITOR. [from the** *Colored American*] **9 March 1841. Washington.** Reports that the Supreme Court has decided to free the *Amistad* captives. 18 March 1841. p.187, c3.

**6512 JACOB SOUTHWICK** *to* **n.n. 5 March 1841. n.p.** Lists resolutions adopted during a meeting of abolitionists in Vassalboro'. 18 March 1841. p.188, c1.

**6513 GERRIT SMITH** *to* **THE EDITOR OF** *ZION'S WATCHMAN.* **[extract] n.d. n.p.** Comments on why he would like to change his church membership. 18 March 1841. p.188, c2.

**6514 C. CHAUNCEY CONE** *to* **THE EDITOR OF THE** *ADVOCATE OF FREEDOM* **[AUSTIN WILLEY]. 14 March 1841. n.p.** Claims that the Methodist Episcopal church has strayed from its commitment to abolish slavery. 25 March 1841. p.190, c1.

**6515 REV. HIRAM WILSON** *to* **n.n. [extract from the** *Friend of Man*] **n.d. n.p.** Reports on the escape of a slave who is the brother-in-law of Col. Richard M. Johnson, vice-president of the United States. 25 March 1841. p.190, c3.

**6516 A GENTLEMAN IN BOSTON** *to* **n.n. n.d. n.p.** Wishes more ministers were involved in anti-slavery work. 25 March 1841. p.190, c4.

**6517 VARNUM CRAM** *to* **THE** *ADVOCATE OF FREEDOM.* **20 March 1841. New Sharon.** Lists resolutions adopted during a meeting of Methodist abolitionists in New Sharon. 25 March 1841. p.191, c2.

**6518 GEORGE WASHINGTON** *to* **n.n. n.d. n.p.** Rejects the idea of a limited monarchy with himself as king. 25 March 1841. p.192, c3.

**6519 KA-LE** *to* **MR. ADAMS. 4 January 1841. New Haven.** Asserts the rights of the *Amistad* captives as human beings, and the importance of setting them free. 1 April 1841. p.194, c4.

**6520 REV. ELIPHA WHITE** *to* **THE ESSEX (MASSACHUSETTS) NORTH ASSOCIATION. n.d. n.p.** States that the association has failed to prove to an audience of Northern men that slavery is not sanctioned by the Bible. 1 April 1841. p.196, c3.

**6521 RICHARD ALLEN** *to* **LORD PALMERSTON. 15 January 1841. Dublin.** Discusses the brutal treatment of slaves and Indians in Texas; comments on Britain's error in recognizing Texas. 8 April 1841. p.200, c1.

**6522 ALVAN STEWART** *to* **THE MASSACHUSETTS LIBERTY CONVENTION. 4 July 1841 [*sic*]. Utica, N.Y.** Regrets that he will not be able to attend the Liberty Convention. 15 April 1841. p.201, c3.

**6523 C. F.** *to* **THE *ADVOCATE OF FREEDOM*. n.d. n.p.** States that Southerners can afford to pay free white laborers more than Northerners can because the South robs the slave of his wages. 15 April 1841. p.202, c1.

**6524 FEMALE CORRESPONDENT** *to* **n.n. [extract] 24 March 1841. Bangor.** Believes that women should use their influence in any way possible to help abolish slavery. 15 April 1841. p.202, c2.

**6525 CYRUS RICKER AND WINSLOW HALL** *to* **THE *ADVOCATE OF FREEDOM*. 26 March 1841. n.p.** List resolutions adopted during an anti-slavery convention in Hartford. 15 April 1841. p.203, c1.

**6526 Z. HUMPHREY** *to* **BRO. WILLEY. 12 April 1841. North Yarmouth.** Cancels the subscription of Asa Humphrey, who died recently, noting that he has found another subscriber to replace him. 15 April 1841. p.203, c1.

**6527 GOV. EDWARD KENT** *to* **THE SENATE AND THE HOUSE OF REPRESENTATIVES. 8 April 1841. Council Chamber.** Informs of the death of William Henry Harrison. 15 April 1841. p.203, c2.

**6528 n.n.** *to* **MESSRS. EDITORS. [from the *Genius of Liberty*] n.d. n.p.** Reports on E. G. Potts's success at raising beets in Putnam County. 15 April 1841. p.203, c4.

**6529 n.n.** *to* **n.n. [extract from the *Richmond Enquirer*] 25 January 1841. Louisville, Ky.** Believes that abolitionists dominate political life in Kentucky. 15 April 1841. p.204, c2.

**6530 SOWADABSCOOK** *to* **BRO. WILLEY. n.d. n.p.** Describes his conversion to abolitionism; insists that abolitionists must support only those political candidates who advocate universal freedom. 29 April 1841. p.206, c1.

**6531 ALVAN STEWART** *to* **THE ABOLITIONISTS OF THE UNITED STATES. n.d. n.p.** Announces that there will be an abolitionist convention in New York to nominate vice-presidential and presidential candidates for the Liberty ticket of 1844. 29 April 1841. p.207, c2.

**6532 JOHN TYLER** *to* **THE PEOPLE OF THE UNITED STATES. 13 April 1841. Washington.** Regrets the death of President Harrison. 29 April 1841. p.207, c3.

**6533 REV. JACOB WESTON** *to* **n.n. [extract] 19 February 1841. Jamaica.** Notes the prosperity and low crime rate in Jamaica since emancipation. 29 April 1841. p.207, c3.

# New York
# *American & Foreign Anti-Slavery Reporter*

**Figure 7. John Greenleaf Whittier**

# John Greenleaf Whittier

## [Editor of The *American and Foreign Anti-Slavery Reporter*, 1841]

John Greenleaf Whittier was a native of Haverhill, Mass., and a descendant of Thomas Whittier, an Englishman, who in 1638, at the age of eighteen years, sailed from Southampton for Boston. Thomas Whittier was not a Quaker. Conversion to that sect did not occur in the Whittier family until the second American generation. At that time Quakers were mercilessly persecuted in the Bay Colony, so that the Whittiers must have been made of the stern stuff with which we are familiar in the career of the poet. Mr. Lowell has remarked that something of heredity appears to have survived in the unswerving adherence of the poet throughout his life to unpopular opinions.

Haverhill at the time of his birth, on Dec. 17, 1807, gave slight promise of becoming the busy manufacturing town it now is. It was only a small village, maintained for the most part by farmers and their needs. Three miles distant from it was the Whittier home, a simple, rude, and lonely farmhouse of the common New-England type of those days. The father was a tall, spare man, and, though he died early, he came of a long-lived race. He saw little promise of any eminence, political or otherwise, in his son John, and probably thought of him only as a future plowman like himself. The boy grew up familiar with the usual duties of the farm lad. He drove the cows afield, spread and raked the hay, carried wood for the household fire, and in Winter tramped away to the neighboring district school.

It was Whittier's mother who first divined that the boy had gifts that fitted him for other usefulness in the world. This mother was named Abigail Hussey and was of French descent. She encouraged his tendency to write verse at an early age, and in all his worthy ambitions gave him her ready sympathy. He has recorded his indebtedness to this mother. "All that the sacred word mother means in its broadest, fullest significance, our dear mother," he says, "was to us—a friend, helper, counselor, companion, ever loving, gentle, and unselfish." The knowledge and discipline which he was acquiring at the district school were necessarily of a limited sort. He must have known this very early and aspired to better things. Shoemaking was in those days a common accomplishment on farms. From a farm laborer young Whittier learned this trade, and he made sufficient money at it to enable him to attend the new academy at Haverhill during six months in 1827. This experience fitted him to become himself a teacher. What is more, it enabled him to earn the money by which he could attend the Haverhill Academy for another six months, and it thus took the place in his economy of shoemaking.

He had had the good fortune in those early days to attract the attention of a traveling Quaker preacher, who gave him the poems of Burns to read. They made a profound impression on the young man's mind, and were destined to influence the development of his genius as did no other English poet. He was then in his fourteenth year, and many years afterward he said his early wonder and delight over Burns still remained as fresh in his mind as if they were of yesterday. "He was the first poet I read and he will be the last." Mr. Lowell has found an intellectual likeness between Whittier and Cowper, but it does not appear from the biographies that Cowper ever made a particularly deep impression on the

New-England poet. Mr. Lowell's words are: "His religion has the sincerity of Cowper's without those insane terrors that made its very sincerity a terror. There are many points of spiritual likeness between the English and the American poet, especially in their unmetaphysical love of outward nature, in their austerity tempered with playful humor, and in that humanity of tone which establishes a tie of affectionate companionship between them and their readers."

On the Haverhill farm books were few. Almanacs and newspapers were read more often than books, save when the boy had walked miles away to borrow something in fiction or biography. Among the books read it is known that Bunyan's immortal work found a place. Along with Burns, Bunyan must hold a place as one of the chief influences in his youth of a literary kind. One of the newspapers which the father subscribed for was a Newburyport journal called the *Free Press*, which had for its editor the famous William Lloyd Garrison. With Garrison, young Whittier was destined to enjoy important association, and the *Free Press* had not been long read in the Whittier home before an acquaintance sprang up. Burns had taught the boy to write verse, and in his eighteenth year he forwarded some of his lines to Garrison, who put them into his poet's corner. Other lines were subsequently sent and printed, though anonymously. They made such an impression on Garrison that he rode over on horseback to Haverhill, a distance of fifteen miles, and called to see the boy who had written them. The boy made his appearance in the house fresh from the fields, without shoes, coat, or waistcoat. Garrison said he ought to be educated in a high school, and praised his verse. It was to raise the money wherewith he might follow this advice of Garrison that young Whittier learned to be a shoemaker.

During his school days in Haverhill Village he boarded with the editor of the *Gazette*, and began to write for that paper. His local fame as a poet had already risen. The academy was opened the year he entered it, and he had written an ode that was sung at its dedication. After completing his studies at Haverhill he became a writer for the *American Manufacturer*, but the pay was small and the work not attractive. He then returned to the farm, where he spent a year, and then for six months edited the *Haverhill Gazette*, a paper for which he was to write more or less for forty years. He became also a contributor to the *Weekly Review* of Hartford, of which George D. Prentice was editor, and when Prentice, in 1830, went to Kentucky to write a campaign life of Henry Clay, he was invited to take his place in Hartford. "I could not have been more utterly astonished," he has since said of this offer, "if I had been told that I was appointed Prime Minister to the Grand Khan of Tartary." Eighteen months was the term of his service in this place. He then went back to the Haverhill farm and remained there five years as its head, his father having died. John Whittier, the farmer, has been described as a hard-working farmer, self-educated, possessed of much practical good sense, and highly esteemed by the community.

While at Hartford the poet had published his first book—the "Legends of New England." His five years on the Haverhill farm were fruitful years in prose and verse as well as in the products of the soil. "Moll Pitcher" and "Mogg Megone" belong to that period, and so does his "Memoir" of J. S. C. Brainard, published with Brainard's poems. His interest in slavery now became active, and led to both prose and verse. Garrison was editing his *Liberator*, and Whittier became one of his strongest adherents. In 1833 he published at his own expense his first striking utterance against slavery. This was "Justice and Expediency; or, Slavery Considered with a View to Its Rightful and Effective Remedy—Abolition." The pamphlet resulted in one very painful incident. He gave a copy to his friend, Dr. Crandall of Washington, in whose office the copy was found by an enemy, who caused his arrest and imprisonment as an abolitionist. Dr. Crandall remained a year in prison, and there contracted consumption of which he afterward died. To this incident Whittier refers in the lines:

"Beside me gloomed the prison cell
  Where wasted one in slow decline
For uttering simple words of mine
  And loving freedom all too well."

To this period belong many anti-slavery poems. By the year 1838 he had written enough to make up two volumes—"Poems, Chiefly Relating to Slavery," and "Ballads, Anti-Slavery, &c." Later years saw others relating to this topic and the war—"Voices of Freedom," (1849,) and "In War Times," (1863.) His early connection with Garrison was attended by an early prominence in anti-slavery circles, and in 1836 he was chosen Secretary of the American Anti-Slavery Society, and was twice (1835 and 1836) elected to the Massachusetts Legislature. Haverhill, like most New-England towns, had a strong pro-slavery element. Samuel J. May was mobbed there while attempting to lecture on a Sunday evening. Whittier himself on the same evening was mobbed in Concord, N. H., and was severely hurt on the shoulder by a stone. He was again mobbed in Philadelphia in 1838, in which year he was editing an anti-slavery paper in that city. His office was sacked and burned. Three years earlier he had visited Washington and been threatened with personal violence, and by advice of friends had gone to Baltimore. His diffusion of anti-slavery sentiment in that city soon roused the antagonism of slaveholders, who threatened him with legal prosecution if he did not depart. After some persuasion by friends he returned to Haverhill. Among other events in his anti-slavery record belong his contributions to the *National Era* of Washington, for which he wrote from 1847 to 1859. It was in the pages of this newspaper that Mrs. Stowe's "Uncle Tom's Cabin" was first published. Here were printed Whittier's "Maud Muller" and "Randolph of Roanoke."

It was not as a poet with literary ambitions that Whittier mainly wrote those days. His verse had another purpose all his own, and hence he said: "I have never thought of myself as a poet in the sense in which we use the word when we speak of the great poets," and the same view of himself he has taken in the following lines from "The Tent on the Beach":

> "And one there was, a dreamer born,
> Who, with a mission to fulfill,
> Had left the muse's haunts to turn
> The crank of an opinion mill,
> Making his rustic reed of song
> A weapon in the war with wrong."

With the outbreak of war his verse almost ceased to have reference to great public events. He would have evaded the conflict had this been possible with honorable means. A surrender, however, was out of the question from his point of view. While the conflict went on he never wrote in a bitter spirit, and when it ended he would have favored a liberal settlement of the difficulties that remained. He now cultivated literature as a profession, and to the years of the war and since belong many of his best-known works. "Snow Bound" appeared in 1862, "The Tent on the Beach" in 1867, "Among the Hills" in 1868, "Ballads of New-England" in 1869, "Miriam and Other Poems" in 1870, "Hazel Blossoms" in 1874, "Mabel Martin" in 1875, "The Vision of Echard" of 1878, "The King's Mission" in 1881, "Bay in Seven Islands" in 1883, "Poems of Nature" in 1885, and "St. Gregory's Guest" in 1886, with a final edition of all his works, revised by himself and including poems by his sister, in 1888-9, in seven volumes.

Most successful of all his writings, in point of sales, was "Snow Bound," which is a truthful picture of his early life on the Haverhill farm, and which Mr. Lowell has characterized as having historical value in being a description of modes of life "now almost as far away as those pictured by Homer." Its sudden popularity was a great surprise to Whittier. Before its publication he had realized only small sums for his writings. He first wrote for any paper that would publish his matter, as he had himself said, and would have wanted for bread had he been forced to depend upon the products of his pen. And yet he was never poor in the sense that the necessaries of life were hard to get. There was the farm for one thing, and for another his wants were few and his mind was a frugal one. When the publisher Muzzey offered him $500 for the copyright of what he had written and a percentage on sales, he was astonished. Muzzey sold pills as well as books, and Whittier suspected the two occupations combined in one person might have had evil effects on his soundness of mind.

The farm at Haverhill was sold by Mr. Whittier in 1840, soon after his return from Philadelphia. He then bought a plain, old-fashioned house at Amesbury, a small manufacturing village four miles from Newburyport, and here he has mainly lived ever since. With him to Amesbury went his mother and his sister, and the sister lived there with him until her death, in 1864. She wrote verse as well as he, and their friendship has more than once been likened to that of Charles and Mary Lamb. Whittier never married, but a story has been told of his affection for a lady in Philadelphia, who declined his proposal because she had not for him that warmth of affection which she deemed necessary in the circumstances. Of late years Whittier often lived at Danvers, Mass., with cousins, his home at Amesbury having been broken up by the death of his sister and that of his brother's daughter, who succeeded his sister as his housekeeper. But he still regarded himself a citizen of Amesbury, and passed a part of each year there, two rooms in his house being reserved for him by its occupants. Some time after "Snow Bound" appeared, a visitor at Amesbury remarked to Whittier that the improved appearance of his house indicated that poetry "had ceased to be a drug in the market." At this the poet smiled only, but on the following morning he excused himself to his guest for a few moments, as he had to call on a collector of taxes, saying: "Since the publication of 'Snow Bound' I have risen to the dignity of paying an income tax."

The *New York Times*,
8 September 1892, p.8, c1.

# ANTI-SLAVERY REPORTER.

PUBLISHED BY THE AMERICAN AND FOREIGN ANTI-SLAVERY SOCIETY.

VOL. II. NEW YORK, SEPTEMBER 1, 1842. NO. 6.

AM. AND FOREIGN ANTI-SLAVERY REPORTER.
PUBLISHED BY S. W. BENEDICT,
No 128 Fulton street, New-York.
Gratuitously. Donations solicited.

### Case of Nelson Hackett,

Application having been made by Mr. Scoble, on behalf of the Committee of the British and Foreign Anti Slavery Society, for the FACTS inconnection with this important case, which was the subject of a parliamentary inquiry, that we lost no time in communicating such information as was at hand, promising to make further inquiry, and communicate the result. CHARLES H. STEWART, Esq. of Detroit, being on a visit to this city, and knowing he was in possession of the material facts, we immediately applied to him on the subject. He very promptly wrote out a narrative of the facts for publication, and we have great pleasure in laying it before our readers. Mr. Stewart is an Irishman by birth, is a lawyer of high respectability in Michigan, and President of the Anti-Slavery Society of that state. The most implicit confidence may be placed in his statements. The circumstances attending this case are of a most important character—Sir Charles Bagot has probably been most ingloriously imposed upon—and the British government will, we doubt not, provide against the recurrence of a similar event.

Hackett was a slave in Arkansas. In the spring or summer of 1841 he was at a race course with his *legal* master, and was desired to take home a race-horse. The home was at a considerable distance, and Hackett finding himself well mounted, under circumstances that permitted absence, directed his course towards liberty—the incessant subject of solicitude with this unfortunate class. At this time he had in care the out-side coat of the master, and he also had his gold watch: in what manner this last was obtained is not known. After many perils, he succeeded in finding and effecting his way through the long route intervening between Arkansas in the remote south-west, to Canada, at its northern frontier: he passed through Detroit in the state of Michigan, and took up his abode at London, or somewhere in the vicinity of Windsor, opposite to Detroit. In the course of the summer or fall, he was followed. A person on behalf of his alleged owner, consulted a lawyer of much respectability, Mr. George F. Porter, whether there was any mode by which Hackett could be recaptured into slavery. Mr. Porter, being an abolitionist, gave no encouragement. The application to him shows the governing motive of the master, and that he desired to repossess himself of the person of Hackett, not so much perhaps on account of his actual value, as that his recaption, and the dreadful punishment that awaits the failing aspirant of liberty, might deter others from a like attempt.

The next thing known, is that the agent went to Canada, and there had Hackett arrested for theft—stealing a coat, gold watch and horse of A. B. (the master). Considerable interest was excited among the colored people, by a proceeding, which they well knew to be but a vindictive persecution for daring to assert self-liberty, but they found that Hackett was in custody, like any other alleged criminal, upon informations sworn in Canada, and that he must abide the due trial of the charge, at the ensuing assizes or circuit, to be held at Sandwich in February or March, 1842. Nothing could be done until then, and Hackett and friends abided patiently the arrival of court.

The arrest was in the fall, probably October or November, 1841. It appears that Hackett was kept a very close prisoner,—a lawyer, Mr. Baby, alone was permitted access to him during his confinement. After Hackett was thus arrested, his claimant had him indicted before a grand jury of Arkansas, for larceny; and procured from the governor of that state, a demand on the governor of Canada for the surrender of Hackett. These papers were sent to the colonial government, and were received by Sir Charles Bagot about the time of his arrival in Canada. It is not known what kind of private applications or representations were made to Sir Charles, but it is probable, nay almost certain, that he was altogether imposed upon,—that Hackett was represented as a great criminal, and that British sense of right was appealed to, to know if their government would screen villany, and reward with impunity the robber,—that Hackett's color, and the strongly extenuating circumstances of his case, were altogether suppressed. That misrepresentation was freely made, I know from the fact that his captors alledged in Detroit that Hackett had committed a rape, under aggravating circumstances, on his master's daughter,—a charge not only without evidence of any kind, but which I ascertained to be false, and to have been suggested for the mere purpose of creating feeling against Hackett. Sufficient discredit is at once given to it, by the fact, that it was not the subject of indictment. Had so aggravated an offence existed, it would readily have been seized on as the groud of demand on a foreign government not bound by treaty or usage to surrender, in place of the light one of larceny. It may also have been represented to Sir Charles, that, along the borders, the magistrates give up to each other those petty criminals who seek, by flight across our dividing line, an impunity from crime. Such is the fact. The surrender is unauthorised by law: it is the exercise of force,—the exchange of neighbors' courtesy, and is winked at all round. There is a great difference between this border surrender of henroost pilferers, and the deliberate official action of the British nation, in its highest and most solemn sanction, forming a precedent in the usage of nations. The American slave-owner had also so managed as to secure the cooperation of those possessed of influence on the Canadian frontier, and poor Hackett became a miserable victim to combined power, skill, wealth, while he lay a captive in British confinement, trusting with implicit confidence to the accused's sacred palladium—that boast of Britain's constitution—a trial by his peers. Neither himself nor a single friend was aware of the measures pursuing: they were prepared for trial, and for nothing else.

At any rate Sir Charles Bagot, deceived or not, ordered the surrender of Hackett, and gave warrant to the jailor at Sandwich to surrender him, and a letter to Col. John Prince, of Sandwich, her Majesty's consul, (a kind of local attorney-general,) and to all British authorities, to aid and assist in the delivery of Hackett, to a man of the name of Davenport, who runs the ferry between Detroit and Windsor.

The mode of executing this warrant, showed the parties' own consciousness of impropriety. It was not done in that open, fearless manner, which imparts dignity to the law, and proclaims its sovereignty; but at 9 or 10 o'clock of a winter's night, in the Canadas, when the severity of the season had housed every person and animal, during the month of February last, a party of men were collected, a boat was prepared, Hackett was seized, without a moment's intimation, and hurried across the Detroit river amid masses of floating ice, and incarcerated in the Detroit jail. Whether or not the demand on the Sandwich jailor had been previously made, is not known; but it probably was, and every arrangement had doubtless been leisurely made, though secretly.

In Detroit, Hackett was immured in a private cell. He was some days there before the fact was known, but it leaked out. I made application to see him: his being there at all was denied. I finally made application to our Supreme Court, and obtained a *habeas corpus*. I was then admitted to see Hackett, and shewn the papers connected with his arrest. Hackett candidly avowed the fact, that he had used the horse as the means of procuring freedom. He had no way of restoring either it, watch, or coat, no demand was made for any of them. At his arrest he still had all of them, and *all were received and used by his captors*, as they admitted.

The papers then consisted only of the letter of Sir Charles Bagot's Secretary, in official form, to Col. Prince and other authorities, and an authenticated copy of the warrant of surrender. The indictment had been left with the colonial government, and its contents were stated to me by the agent and counsel of the captors. Sufficient evidence, however, was afforded, that the colonial government, whether rightly or discreetly, yet, in fact, had duly surrendered Hackett. The question then was,—should we of Detroit contest the matter? We could have done so: a foreign wrrrant was of no validity with us. Hackett was illegally in custody, and being brought *by force* within our jurisdiction, the federal laws made for recapture of fugitives from justice, or from labor, were alike imperative, inasmuch as they require *voluntary* residence as the ground of jurisdiction. On consultation, we deemed it improper to interfere. Great Britain had taken the lead in the assertion of human rights; she had struck the fetters from her own slaves, and was pioneer among the nations of the world in abolishing slavery. She had formally thought proper to surrender an alledged criminal; she had deemed the offence so serious as to justify the exercise of that prerogative about which nations are so jealous that they have oft refused the surrender of even murderers. She had done so on mature deliberation. Would it become us to assume a standard higher than hers? to become the patrons of a crime she had thus markedly denounced as atrocious? We thought not: we were trustees seeking to carry out a great and sacred principle confided to us, and were bound to do so wisely and discreetly. Had we interfered in this case, we would have fought the battle of liberty, not on its own sacred principles, but as protectors of crime; for the prisoner was in custody as a criminal, not as a slave; and that he was an aggravated criminal. Britain's unusual

**Figure 8**

# Journal Data

TITLE: *American and Foreign Anti-Slavery Reporter*

INCLUSIVE DATES OF PUBLICATION: June 1840–April 1846 (last issue available)

PLACE OF PUBLICATION: New York, N.Y.

FREQUENCY OF PUBLICATION: Monthly (irregular)

AVERAGE NUMBER OF PAGES PER ISSUES: 8

NUMBER OF COLUMNS PER PAGE: 2–3

EDITORS: James G. Birney and Henry B. Stanton, Secretaries of the Society (June 1840–1 September 1841?); John G. Whittier (by 1 September 1841–?); Lewis Tappan, Secretary (by June 1842–May 1845?); Rev. Amos Augustus Phelps, Editor and Secretary (May 1845–at least April 1846)

PUBLISHERS: American and Foreign Anti-Slavery Society; S. W. Benedict (by 1 September 1842–?)

PRINTERS: Piercy and Reed

FEATURES: letters; editorials; local, national and foreign news; illustrations

PRICE: $1.00 per volume (1840–42); gratuitous (1842–45); $.50 per volume (1845-46)

AVERAGE CIRCULATION (PER ISSUE): 5,000 (maximum 10,000) in April 1846

LANGUAGE: English

PERSPECTIVE: Abolitionist; official organ of the American and Foreign Anti-Slavery Society

MISCELLANEOUS DATA: List of contents featured on first page of issues by May 1845. Includes a number of "Extra" and special topic issues.

REPOSITORY: Sterling Memorial Library, Yale University, December 1840–12 April 1846.

# Prospectus

We enter upon a new year with profound gratitude to that great Being who watches alike over individuals and communities—who does not permit even a sparrow to fall on the ground without His knowledge and consent, and whose eyes behold the nations. We are grateful for the revelation He has made of his character—that he has styled himself the God of the oppressed; for the consoling promises He has given to mankind that He considers the oppressions done under the sun, and will break in pieces the oppressor; that the anti-slavery cause has taken such deep root in this country, and elsewhere, notwithstanding the errors and faults of many of its advocates and supporters; that He has been propitious to the *American and Foreign Anti-Slavery Society*, and enables us to commence this new year with hope and faith in the ultimate triumph of free principles, and the universal recognition of the rights of our brethren in bonds. While we thus acknowledge our debt of gratitude, and our present views and feelings with reference to the holy enterprise in which we are engaged—while we devoutly invoke the Divine blessing on our labors, and on the labors of our coadjutors throughout the world—we appeal to all those who approve the principles of this Society, and the attempt to advocate the cause in this official organ, to afford their liberal and continued aid, by prayer, subscriptions, donations, the circulation of this paper, and such other means as they may adopt, to up hold the sacred cause of human liberty—the rights of man—and to put down by moral suasion and political action, the arrogant pretensions and usurpations of those who trample upon their fellow-men—and insult their Maker, by defacing His image in our brethren in bondage. The beginning of a new year, while it should fill our hearts with gratitude for all that has been accomplished in this great cause, under the Divine blessing, ought to summon abolitionists to new exertions, greater sacrifices, increased donations, and more fervent prayer. Let it be our constant desire that the Spirit of the Lord may give wisdom and energy to the Executive Committee, and to all their constituents,—persuading them, and all who profess anti-slavery principles, to Christian forbearance and love, and redoubled efforts to carry forward the great cause to a glorious consummation.

*American and Foreign Anti-Slavery Reporter*, January 1841, p.112, c1.

## [1840]

6534 **JUDGE WILLIAM JAY** *to* **LEWIS TAPPAN. 20 October 1840. Bedford.** Provides an account of the *Amistad* case; praises Tappan for his labors in behalf of the Africans seized aboard the ship. December 1840. p.1, c1.

6535 **SETH P. STAPLES AND THEODORE SEDGWICK, JR.** *to* **PRESIDENT MARTIN VAN BUREN. 13 September 1839. New York.** State that the Negroes on board the *Amistad* were carried into Cuba contrary to the treaty between Spain and Great Britain, and therefore Messrs. Ruiz and Montes have no legal claim to them. December 1840. p.6, c1.

6536 **MARTIN VAN BUREN** *to* **n.n. 7 January 1840. Washington.** Orders the federal marshal for the District of Connecticut to deliver the *Amistad* Negroes to Lt. John S. Paine of the United States Navy. December 1840. p.7, c1.

6537 **LEWIS TAPPAN** *to* **PRESIDENT MARTIN VAN BUREN. 9 September 1840. New York.** Encloses correspondence regarding documents from the *Amistad* case; advises Van Buren that his earlier order has not been followed. December 1840. p.7, c2.

6538 **LEWIS TAPPAN** *to* **SENATOR TAPPAN. 24 April 1840. New York.** Asks him to obtain copies of the treaty between Spain and Great Britain prohibiting the slave trade. December 1840. p.7, c2.

6539 **SENATOR TAPPAN** *to* **LEWIS TAPPAN. 25 April. n.p.** States that the president authorized the senator to receive documents requested from the secretary of state, but that when he arrived at the secretary's office, he found it closed. December 1840. p.8, c1.

6540 **J. L. MARTIN, ACTING SECRETARY OF STATE** *to* **LEWIS TAPPAN. 28 August 1840. Washington.** Informs that instructions were given to the United States attorney for Connecticut regarding the documents pertaining to the *Amistad* case. December 1840. p.8, c1.

6541 **W. S. HOLABIRD, DISTRICT ATTORNEY** *to* **LEWIS TAPPAN. 5 September 1840. Winchester, Ct.** States that he never received instructions from the Department of State or any other federal department concerning the requested documents. December 1840. p.8, c1.

6542 **LEWIS TAPPAN** *to* **J. L. MARTIN. 3 September 1840. New York.** Believes that the circumstances of the *Amistad* case justify Tappan's request that immediate attention be given to furnishing the requested documents. December 1840. p.8, c1.

6543 **JOHN FORSYTH** *to* **LEWIS TAPPAN. 7 September 1840. Washington.** Replies that the president of the United States sees no reason to amend his earlier communication to the federal attorney for Connecticut. December 1840. p.8, c2.

6544 **JOHN FORSYTH** *to* **LEWIS TAPPAN. 12 September 18[4]0. Washington.** States that President Van Buren questions whether he has the right to interfere with the decision of the court regarding the *Amistad* documents. December 1840. p.8, c2.

6545 **JOHN FORSYTH** *to* **W. S. HOLABIRD. 30 April 1840. Washington.** Reports that President Van Buren believes that he has no authority in the *Amistad* case. December 1840. p.9, c1.

6546 **W. S. HOLABIRD** *to* **LEWIS TAPPAN. 11 September 1840. Winchester.** Admits the authenticity of the decrees of the king of Spain of 1817, the ordinance of the queen, and the treaty between Spain and Great Britain. December 1840. p.9, c1.

**6547 W. S. HOLABIRD** *to* **LEWIS TAPPAN. 28 September 1840. Winchester.** Expresses astonishment upon locating the unopened communication authorizing Holabird to furnish Tappan with the documents regarding the *Amistad* case. December 1840. p.9, c2.

**6548 PONZOA** *to* **SIR. 2 November 1838. Madrid.** Relays the orders of the queen of Spain that measures be taken to prevent the importation of black slaves into the colonies. December 1840. p.9, c2.

**6549 G. S. S. JERNINGHAM** *to* **HIS EXCELLENCY DON EVARISTO PEREZ DE CASTRO. [from the** *British and Foreign Anti-Slavery Reporter***] 5 January 1840. Madrid.** Directs, on behalf of Her Majesty's government, that the *Amistad* Negroes be granted their freedom. December 1840. p.9, c2.

**6550 YOUNG GENTLEMAN OF THE NEW HAVEN THEOLOGICAL SCHOOL** *to* **n.n. [from the** *Congregational Observer***] n.d. n.p.** Comments on the gratitude, affection, and determination to learn of the *Amistad* Negroes as they await their fate. December 1840. p.11, c2.

**6551 JAMES B. COVEY** *to* **A COMMITTEE MEMBER. 5 November 1840. New Haven.** Requests educational and religious books with which to educate his fellow countrymen when he returns to Africa. December 1840. p.12, c2.

**6552 KA-LE** *to* **A COMMITTEE MEMBER. September. Westville.** Expresses his love for God and the people of the New Haven community. December 1840. p.13.

**6553 S. S. JOCELYN, JOSHUA LEAVITT, AND LEWIS TAPPAN** *to* **THE BOARD OF MANAGERS OF THE AMERICAN BIBLE SOCIETY. 13 November 1840. New York.** Request thirty-six Bibles for the *Amistad* Africans, who are currently imprisoned in New Haven. December 1840. p.14, c1.

**6554 REV. S. W. MAGILL** *to* **n.n. [extract from the** *New Haven Daily Herald***] 23 September 1840. New Haven.** Praises the truthfulness, conduct, and intellectual achievements of the *Amistad* Africans. December 1840. p.14, c1.

## [1841]

**6555 J. H. TREDGOLD** *to* **LEWIS TAPPAN. 5 December 1840. London.** The secretary of the British and Foreign AS explains the nature of two documents condemning Britain for recognizing the Republic of Texas. January 1841. p.105, c2.

**6556 JOSEPH STURGE** *to* **THE EDITOR OF THE** *PATRIOT.* **n.d. n.p.** States that Dr. Wayland, president of Brown University, should be ashamed to support slavery while deeming himself a servitor of Christ. January 1841. p.106, c2.

**6557 E. HUGHES** *to* **THE EDITOR OF THE** *ANTI-SLAVERY REPORTER.* **[from the** *British and Foreign Anti-Slavery Reporter***] n.d. Bryn Lion, Holywell.** Informs that he has presented the resolutions passed at the General Anti-Slavery Convention to his church and congregation. January 1841. p.106, c2.

**6558 JAMES CHURCHILL** *to* **SIR. [from the** *British and Foreign Anti-Slavery Reporter***] 2 November 1840. Thames Ditton, Surrey.** Forwards a declaration to the committee of the British and Foreign AS. January 1841. p.106, c2.

**6559 JAMES CHURCHILL, PASTOR** *to* **J. H. TREDGOLD. [from the** *British and Foreign Anti-Slavery Reporter***] n.d. n.p.** Declares that his congregation opposes slavery. January 1841. p.107, c1.

**6560 JOHN PAIN** *to* **SIR. [from the** *British and Foreign Anti-Slavery Reporter*] **9 November 1840. Horncastle.** Encloses a resolution adopted by a Church of Christ. January 1841. p.107, c1.

**6561 JOHN PAIN, PASTOR** *to* **J. H. TREDGOLD. [from the** *British and Foreign Anti-Slavery Reporter*] **30 October 1840. n.p.** Resolves, on behalf of his parish, to refuse communion with any person who favors slavery. January 1841. p.107, c1.

**6562 W. BREWIS** *to* **THE EDITOR OF THE** *ANTI-SLAVERY REPORTER.* **12 November 1840. Penrith.** Informs that members of the Independent church condemn slavery and will not commune with persons favoring slavery. January 1841. p.107, c1.

**6563 C. STEWART RENSHAW** *to* **BROTHER. 28 November 1840. Oberlin Station.** A missionary in Jamaica writes of the country's economic prosperity, noting that the decrease in profits from sugar and coffee crops was the result of the transfer of labor to other areas of production. January 1841. p.109, c1.

**6564 JULIUS O. BEARDSLEE** *to* **BROTHER. 8 December 1840. Brainerd Station, St. Mary's Parish, Island of Jamaica.** States that he and his Jamaican friends have executed the construction of a church and are currently building a school; informs that many of the former slaves have purchased their own farmland. January 1841. p.109, c1.

**6565 JACOB WESTON** *to* **BROTHER. 25 November 1840. Jamaica, West Indies.** Informs of his success in converting natives of Clarendon to Christianity; hopes that progress in Jamaica will contribute to ending slavery in the United States. January 1841. p.110, c1.

**6566 SIR THOMAS FOWELL BUXTON** *to* **R. R. GURLEY, SECRETARY OF THE ACS. 9 October 1840. Northrepps Hall, near Aylsham.** Discusses the differences between the African Civilization Society and the ACS. January 1841. p.110, c2.

**6567 REV. A. BRONSON** *to* **A FRIEND. n.d. Fall River, Ma.** States that the congregation of the Baptist Church of Fall River has been increasing since the church took an anti-slavery stand five years earlier. January 1841. p.111, c2.

**6568 H. D. GILPIN** *to* **LEWIS TAPPAN. 4 January 1841. Washington.** The United States attorney general informs of the anticipated date of the *Amistad* trial in Washington. January 1841. p.112, c2.

**6569 JAMES G. BIRNEY** *to* **THE EDITORS OF THE** *GLOBE.* **1 January 1841. New York.** Corrects errors in the *Globe* regarding his and Dr. Madden's speeches during an anti-slavery rally. January 1841. p.114, c1.

**6570 JAMES B. COVEY, INTERPRETER FOR THE AFRICANS OF THE** *AMISTAD* *to* **n.n. 14 December 1840. n.p.** States that the *Amistad* Africans are eager to learn to read and write, and wish that he would remain with them. January 1841. p.115, c1.

**6571 CORRESPONDENT** *to* **THE** *AMERICAN AND FOREIGN ANTI-SLAVERY REPORTER.* **n.d. n.p.** States that Noah Webster's essay entitled, "Effects of Slavery on Morals and Industry" is the best history of slavery he has seen. January 1841. p.116, c2.

**6572 n.n.** *to* **GERRIT SMITH. [extract from the** *Friend of Man*] **31 August 1840. East Tennessee.** Comments on the polite attitude of a group of aristocratic South Carolinians who were aware of his anti-slavery sentiments. January 1841. p.117, c2.

**6573 n.n.** *to* **THE** *AMERICAN AND FOREIGN ANTI-SLAVERY REPORTER.* **[extract] n.d. Ohio.** Describes assistance rendered by a landlady which enabled a runaway slave to escape to Canada. January 1841. p.118, c1.

**6574 JOSHUA LEAVITT** *to* **n.n. 15 February. Washington.** States that he is unable to form a judgment, regardless of the length of the argument, in the *Amistad* case. 15 March 1841. p.2, c1.

**6575 P. A. DE ARGAIZ** *to* **HON. JOHN FORSYTH. 20 March 1840. Washington.** Encloses a translation of a confidential memorandum regarding the laws relative to Negro slavery in Cuba. 15 March 1841. p.2, c1.

**6576 H. S. FOX** *to* **THE HON. JOHN FORSYTH. 20 January 1841. Washington.** States that the attention of Her Majesty's government has been directed to the case of the *Amistad* Negroes. 15 March 1841. p.2, c2.

**6577 JOHN FORSYTH** *to* **HENRY STEPHEN FOX. 1 February 1841. Washington.** Informs that the president of the United States has neither the power nor the disposition to intervene in the *Amistad* case. 15 March 1841. p.3, c1.

**6578 ROGER S. BALDWIN** *to* **HON. JOHN FORSYTH, SECRETARY OF STATE. 19 February 1840. New Haven.** Questions whether the United States government will insist on proof from the Africans of the authenticity of the decree of the king of Spain prohibiting the importation of African Negroes. 15 March 1841. p.4, c1.

**6579 JOHN FORSYTH** *to* **ROGER S. BALDWIN. 3 March 1840. Washington.** States that the files of the State Department pertinent to the *Amistad* case will be made available to Baldwin upon his request. 15 March 1841. p.4, c1.

**6580 ROGER S. BALDWIN** *to* **MR. VAN BUREN, PRESIDENT OF THE UNITED STATES. n.d. n.p.** Requests that Van Buren direct the district attorney of the United States to admit the treaty prohibiting slavery in the *Amistad* case. 15 March 1841. p.4, c2.

**6581 ROGER S. BALDWIN** *to* **HON. JOHN FORSYTH, SECRETARY OF STATE. 20 March 1840. New Haven.** Acknowledges receipt of Forsyth's letter; questions Forsyth's statements regarding the availability of the treaty; requests a copy of the treaty between Spain and Great Britain providing for the abolition of slavery. 15 March 1841. p.4, c2.

**6582 JOHN FORSYTH** *to* **ROGER S. BALDWIN. 25 March 1840. Washington.** States that the Department of State does not possess a copy of the treaty between Great Britain and Spain. 15 March 1841. p.4, c2.

**6583 CORRESPONDENT** *to* **THE** *CONNECTICUT CONGREGATIONAL OBSERVER*. **n.d. n.p.** Praises the speech of Mr. Baldwin of New Haven on the *Amistad* case. 15 March 1841. p.7, c1.

**6584 JOHN QUINCY ADAMS** *to* **SIR. 9 March 1841. Washington.** Explains the decision of the Supreme Court in the *Amistad* case, which upheld all aspects of the Connecticut court's decision except that which placed the Africans at the disposal of the president, thus granting them freedom in America. 15 March 1841. p.8, c1.

**6585 SMITH THOMPSON** *to* **THE MARSHAL OF CONNECTICUT. n.d. n.p.** Encloses the mandate requiring that the Africans from the *Amistad* be discharged from custody. 15 March 1841. p.8, c2.

**6586 AMOS TOWNSEND, JUN., ESQ.** *to* **n.n. 11 March 1841. New Haven.** Describes the rejoicing of the Africans of the *Amistad* upon learning that they had been freed. 15 March 1841. p.9, c1.

**6587 S. M. BOOTH** *to* **SIR. 9 March 1841. New Haven.** A Connecticut teacher of the *Amistad* Africans reports on their progress and passion for learning; notes also that they are very devout and abhor dishonesty. 15 March 1841. p.9, c1.

**6588 KA-LE** *to* **JOHN QUINCY ADAMS. 4 January 1841. New Haven.** A ten-year-old *Amistad* African asks why the Americans jailed the Mendis; asserts that they have done nothing wrong, and that they miss Africa and desire their freedom. 15 March 1841. p.9, c2.

**6589 G. W. ALEXANDER** *to* **J. H. TREDGOLD. [from the** *British and Foreign Anti-Slavery Reporter***] 21 December 1840. Madrid.** States that he has been busily occupied in Madrid and is leaving for Valencia. 15 March 1841. p.15, c2.

**6590 GEORGE W. ALEXANDER AND BENJAMIN WIFFEN** *to* **THE DUKE DE LA VICTORIA, PRESIDENT OF THE REGENCY OF SPAIN. n.d. n.p.** Request that the government of Spain intercede in the *Amistad* case. 15 March 1841. p.16, c1.

**6591 JOSEPH STURGE** *to* **THE FRIENDS OF IMMEDIATE EMANCIPATION THROUGHOUT THE UNITED STATES. 7 June 1841. Philadelphia.** Comments on efforts to promote the abolition of slavery. 1 September 1841. p.17, c3.

**6592 JOSEPH STURGE** *to* **THE ABOLITIONISTS OF THE UNITED STATES. 7 June 1841. Philadelphia.** Reports on his visit to Washington, D.C.; describes a slave sale in Alexandria; comments on former President Adams's vain efforts against a discriminatory congressional bill, expressing his hope that one day no slaveholders will hold office. 1 September 1841. p.19, c2.

**6593 CHARLES TYLER** *to* **THE** *LONDON ANTI-SLAVERY REPORTER.* **7 April 1841. n.p.** Addresses the moral issue of the use of the products of slave labor. 1 September 1841. p.20, c3.

**6594 RODRIGO DA FONSECA MAGALHAENS** *to* **THOMAS CLARKSON, PRESIDENT OF THE ANTI-SLAVERY CONVENTION IN LONDON. 15 May 1841. London.** States that the queen of Portugal will continue to cooperate in efforts to eradicate slave traffic. 1 September 1841. p.29, c1.

**6595 ESTERHAZY** *to* **J. H. TREDGOLD. 2 May 1841. Chandos House.** Informs that the emperor of Austria is negotiating a treaty for the abolition of the slave trade. 1 September 1841. p.29, c1.

**6596 REV. JOHN CLARKE** *to* **FRIEND. 5 April 1841. Clarence, Fernando Po.** Discusses the results of colonization in Liberia; states that the Negro colonists are in good health, but that sickness prevails among the white population; reports strained relations between the colonists and natives in some areas; believes that colonization will be successful only if willing native Africans are shipped to Liberia. 1 September 1841. p.29, c2.

**6597 C. W. DENISON** *to* **SIR. 21 August 1841. Syracuse, N.Y.** Describes a gunpowder explosion in Syracuse which killed thirty people; cites the incident as an illustration of divine retribution; mentions his meeting an abolitionist in Middletown, Connecticut, who had been a member of the mob that attacked Denison three years earlier. 1 September 1841. p.30, c2.

## [1842]

**6598 S. S. JOCELYN** *to* **MESSRS. EDITORS. n.d. n.p.** Encloses the minutes of two missionary committee meetings which met to address misconceptions regarding missionary funds. June 1842. p.54, c1.

**6599 JAMES RICHARDSON** *to* **JOHN SCOBLE, ESQ. 2 March 1842. Lazaretto of Malta.** Announces that the bey of Tunis has abolished the slave trade; condemns Christian America for perpetuating slavery, a system which even a Moorish king has seen fit to end. June 1842. p.55, c2.

**6600 SIMEON S. JOCELYN, CORRESPONDING SECRETARY OF THE AMERICAN AND FOREIGN AS** *to* **THE SECRETARY OF THE BRITISH AND FOREIGN AS. 1 April 1842. New York.** Expresses gratitude to the British government for its determination not to surrender the Negroes of the *Creole*; assures that anti-slavery principles are spreading in the North and even in the South. June 1842. p.57, c1.

**6601 n.n.** *to* **GERRIT SMITH. [extract] n.d. East Tennessee.** Believes that one year of free discussion would result in the overthrow of slavery, and that many slaveholders desire the abolition of slavery. June 1842. p.57, c3.

**6602 REV. LORRIN ANDREWS** *to* **LEWIS TAPPAN, TREASURER OF THE AMERICAN AND FOREIGN AS. 17 September 1841. Lahainaluna, Sandwich Islands.** Thanks Tappan for his letter; prays for the success of the anti-slavery movement. June 1842. p.58, c2.

**6603 REV. J. S. GREEN** *to* **LEWIS TAPPAN, ESQ. 27 September 1841. Wailuku, Sandwich Islands.** Questions how those who refuse to sign the Anti-Slavery Constitution can profess to be friends of the slave. June 1842. p.58, c3.

**6604 ROBERT B. DOBBINS** *to* **BROTHER M'ROBERTS. [from the** *Protestant and Herald*] **15 April 1842. Bernadotte, Ky.** Encloses an extract from the Bennington Church records discussing the church's endeavors to abolish slavery. June 1842. p.60, c1.

**6605 CHARLES STUART** *to* **LEWIS TAPPAN. n.d. Bathwick-hill, Bath, England.** Reports that the Parisian Anti-Slavery Convention was hindered by French restrictions of the press and of public gatherings of more than twenty people; states that the French condemn slavery and that America is beginning to stand alone in her pro-slavery stance. June 1842. p.60, c2.

**6606 W. W. ANDERSON** *to* **n.n. 2 May 1842. Kingston, Jamaica.** States that the Jamaican economy has prospered since his visit eighteen months earlier; discusses the educational and social advancement of the blacks; reports that a Kingston riot was caused by police interference in the Christmas tradition of drumming and dancing in the streets. June 1842. p.61, c1.

**6607 MR. STEELE** *to* **n.n. n.d. At sea.** Describes his voyage to Sierra Leone accompanied by Cinque, thirty-four of his countrymen, James Covey, and the Raymond and Wilson families. June 1842. p.61, c3.

**6608 MR. STEELE** *to* **n.n. January, February 1842. Sierra Leone.** Describes their arrival in Sierra Leone; notes that he is to depart on an exploratory expedition. June 1842. p.62, c2.

**6609 MR. RAYMOND** *to* **n.n. February 1842. Sierra Leone.** Informs of the arrival of William Parker; comments on life in Sierra Leone. June 1842. p.63, c1.

**6610 CINQUE** *to* **MR. [LEWIS] TAPPAN. 13 January 1842. At sea, near Sierra-Leone.** One of the *Amistad* Africans rejoices that he is returning home; thanks Tappan, J. Q. Adams, and others for helping them gain their freedom; notes that he and his fellow passengers have been treated well by the non-African crew members and missionary supervisors. June 1842. p.63, c3.

**6611 KIN-NA** *to* **MR. LEWIS TAPPAN. 13 January 1842. Sierra Leone.** One of the *Amistad* Africans thanks God for a safe journey home, and hopes that he will meet Tappan in Heaven. June 1842. p.63, c3.

**6612 WILLIAM FERGUSSON** *to* **LEWIS TAPPAN. 20 April 1842. Sierra Leone.** States that the Mendians were originally from Kosso country, not Timmanec country; reports that only the women and ten men of the *Amistad* Africans have remained together. 20 June 1842. p.66, c1.

**6613 REV. JAMES STEELE** *to* **n.n. 11 April 1842. Fourah Bay.** Comments on his excursion with Cinque and others along the coast, his African fever infection, and his return to America because of illness. 20 June 1842. p.66, c2.

**6614 W. CROWLY** *to* **REV. WILLIAM RAYMOND. 10 March 1842. Waterloo.** Reports that Kim-bo, one of the Africans of the *Amistad* case, was involved in a drunken fight in Waterloo and was nearly shot; returns Kim-bo to him and advises that he prevent him from returning to Waterloo. 20 June 1842. p.69, c3.

**6615 WILLIAM RAYMOND** *to* **MR. CROWLY. 10 March 1842. Freetown.** Thanks him for returning Kim-bo to him; regrets to announce that Kim-bo has escaped again and is apparently en route to Waterloo; requests that he arrest Kim-bo if he appears in Waterloo. 20 June 1842. p.69, c3.

**6616 WILLIAM RAYMOND** *to* **n.n. n.d. n.p.** Announces that he has replaced the Wesleyan missionary at York and that ten of the thirty-three Mendians have moved with him; states that they have been given free use of the land and that the Mendians prefer to work under him rather than procure their own tracts of land. 20 June 1842. p.69, c3.

**6617 JAMES STEELE** *to* **n.n. 14 April 1842. Fourah Bay.** Reports that missionaries for Liberia and Cape Palmas arrived in Fourah Bay from Philadelphia; discusses the best route of correspondence between African missionaries and America; requests money for his return journey to New York. 20 June 1842. p.71, c2.

**6618 JAMES STEELE** *to* **n.n. 19 April 1842. Freetown, Sierra Leone.** Discusses his plan to appeal to the British government to finance the establishment of a colony in Kosso country for those Kossos now settled in Freetown; states that he will need funds for his return trip to New York. 20 June 1842. p.71, c3.

**6619 JAMES STEELE** *to* **BROTHER JOCELYN. 19 April 1842. Freetown, Sierra Leone.** Discusses his disappointment with some of the Mendians; reports that Cinque has left and become a trader, and that some of the others have abandoned Western religion. 20 June 1842. p.72, c1.

**6620 WILLIAM RAYMOND** *to* **n.n. 20 April 1842. Freetown, Sierra Leone.** Believes that it has proved beneficial for most of the Mendians to leave the Americans, and that those Mendians who have remained loyal may be useful in establishing a mission; requests that a plough, planes, and a set of irons be sent to him. 20 June 1842. p.72, c2.

**6621 GEORGE BROWN(FU-LI)** *to* **LEWIS TAPPAN. 15 April 1841. Sierra Leone.** Discusses the occupations and activities of several *Amistad* Africans; prays for his friends in America. 20 June 1842. p.72, c2.

**6622 CHARLES H. STEWART** *to* **THE AMERICAN AND FOREIGN AS. 9 August 1842. New York.** Describes the case of the fugitive slave Nelson Hackett, who escaped from Arkansas into Canada with some of his master's possessions, was arrested for theft, and was returned to his former master; states that he fears for Hackett's welfare. 1 September 1842. p.73, c1.

**6623 DR. NELSON** *to* **FRIEND. 20 June 1842. Quincy, Il.** States that he is an abolitionist, but opposes amalgamation; describes slaves near the Ohio River in Kentucky as less humble than they had been ten years earlier; asks slaveholders to be compassionate toward their slaves. 1 September 1842. p.74, c2.

**6624 DR. NELSON** *to* **n.n. n.d. n.p.** Relates his discussions with slaves and former slaves as he journeys along the Kentucky border. 1 September 1842. p.74, c3.

**6625 WILLIAM ALLEN** *to* **THE FRIENDS OF THE ANTI-SLAVERY CAUSE. 13 June 1842. 27 New Broad Street, London.** Discusses the resolutions of the General Anti-Slavery Convention held in London in June 1840. 1 September 1842. p.75, c2.

**6626 A GENTLEMAN** *to* **n.n. [extract] 15 May 1842. Trinidad.** States that laborers arrive daily from the neighboring islands, so that the prospect of additional labor from the United States is regarded with indifference. 1 September 1842. p.77, c1.

**6627 PARISIAN CORRESPONDENT** *to* **THE** *BRITISH AND FOREIGN REPORTER*. **n.d. n.p.** Provides a discouraging account of the anti-slavery cause in France. 1 September 1842. p.77, c2.

**6628 WILLIAM WEMYSS ANDERSON** *to* **n.n. 10 June 1842. Spanish Town, Jamaica.** Encloses a letter to William Jay; announces that Renshaw has returned to Jamaica; reports on social, political, moral and religious advancement in Jamaica over the past nine years, commenting on the increasing frequency of intermarriage between white males and "brown females." 1 September 1842. p.77, c3.

**6629 WILLIAM W. ANDERSON** *to* **WILLIAM JAY. 25 July 1842. Bedford.** Reports that the riot in Jamaica was precipitated by police interference with emancipated slaves who were attempting to perpetuate a slave tradition of celebrating Christmas in the streets. 1 September 1842. p.78, c1.

**6630 WILLIAM JAY** *to* **n.n. n.d. n.p.** Encloses an article from the *New York Express* stating that the *New Orleans Picayune* had reported rampant arson and murder in Jamaica. 1 September 1842. p.78, c1.

**6631 P. LIVINGSTON** *to* **n.n. [from the** *Journal of Commerce*] **n.d. n.p.** A farmer in Ohio, previously a slaveholder in Jamaica, reports on the beneficial results of emancipation in Jamaica. 1 September 1842. p.78, c3.

**6632 ADAM** *to* **n.n. n.d. n.p.** Details the unpleasant experiences of M. George in America; laments America's poor treatment of people of color in general. 1 September 1842. p.79, c1.

**6633 JAMES STEELE** *to* **MR. LEWIS TAPPAN. 14 May 1842. Freetown, Sierra Leone.** Praises the good behavior of the ten Mendians who remained in York with Raymond; discusses his poor health. 1 September 1842. p.82, c3.

**6634 n.n.** *to* **THE** *AMERICAN AND FOREIGN ANTI-SLAVERY REPORTER*. **[extract] n.d. Cleveland, Oh.** Delights in the honesty of news reports concerning the Mendian mission. 1 September 1842. p.83, c1.

**6635 n.n.** *to* **THE** *AMERICAN AND FOREIGN ANTI-SLAVERY REPORTER*. **[extract] n.d. Old Hampshire County, Ma.** Feels encouraged by the progress of the anti-slavery cause in Old Hampshire County. 1 September 1842. p.83, c1.

**6636 n.n.** *to* **THE** *AMERICAN AND FOREIGN ANTI-SLAVERY REPORTER*. **n.d. Farmington, Ct.** Believes that the Church is the greatest deterrent to the abolition of slavery. 1 September 1842. p.83, c2.

**6637 n.n.** *to* **THE** *AMERICAN AND FOREIGN ANTI-SLAVERY REPORTER*. **n.d. Farmington.** Comments on the need for a purely anti-slavery paper and the failure of the Church to take a stand against slavery. 1 September 1842. p.83, c2.

**6638 JOHN SCOBLE, ESQ.** *to* **THE** *AMERICAN AND FOREIGN ANTI-SLAVERY REPORTER.* **n.d. London.** Details preparations for the coming anti-slavery convention in London. 1 September 1842. p.83, c3.

**6639 JAMES G. BIRNEY** *to* **n.n. n.d. n.p.** Discusses Steele's and Raymond's accounts of the "relapse" of the majority of the Mendians; condemns the religious and political corruption of America. 1 September 1842. p.84, c1.

**6640 ROBERT PURVIS, CHARLES W. GARDNER, AND DANL. A. PAYNE** *to* **THE PUBLIC. n.d. n.p.** Discuss the origin of the riots in Philadelphia which took place 1 August 1842. 1 September 1842. p.86, c1.

**6641 DANIEL A. PAYNE AND SAMUEL NICKLESS** *to* **THE PUBLIC. n.d. n.p.** Inform that the Temperance Hall in Moyamensing had been utilized by both blacks and whites before the commissioner ordered it razed. 1 September 1842. p.86, c1.

**6642 JOHN G. WHITTIER** *to* **FRIEND ALDEN. 6 August 1842. Amesbury.** Gives an account of the Philadelphia riot of 1 August 1842 during which white rioters attacked colored people; cites the poor treatment of the colored inhabitants of Philadelphia as indicative of racism, and charges the press and city officials with negligence in dealing with the issue. 1 September 1842. p.86, c3.

**6643 CHARLES D. GREENE** *to* **THE** *OBERLIN EVANGELIST.* **n.d. n.p.** Encloses preamble and resolutions on the subject of slavery adopted by the High Street Congregational Church in Providence. 1 September 1842. p.87, c2.

**6644 JULIUS O. BEARDSLEE** *to* **LEWIS TAPPAN. 9 March 1842. Brainerd Station, Jamaica, West India.** Describes the location of several missions in Africa; informs that white missionaries in Africa usually survive no longer than five years. 1 September 1842. p.87, c3.

**6645 REV. JOHN J. LAWRENCE** *to* **THE** *AMERICAN AND FOREIGN ANTI-SLAVERY REPORTER.* **4 May 1842. Dindigul, India.** A missionary in India praises the constitution of the American and Foreign AS, and hopes that the day of India's redemption is near. 1 September 1842. p.88, c3.

**6646 n.n.** *to* **THE CONGRESS OF THE UNITED STATES. n.d. n.p.** Protests the slave trade in Washington, D.C. 1 November 1842. p.89, c2.

**6647 A LADY** *to* **n.n. [extract] n.d. Ohio.** Reports on the success of the colored students at Oberlin. 1 November 1842. p.90, c1.

**6648 GERRIT SMITH** *to* **THE EDITOR OF THE** *AMERICAN AND FOREIGN ANTI-SLAVERY REPORTER.* **24 September 1842. Peterboro'.** Discusses the possibility of forming an abolitionist party; declares that a consistent abolitionist cannot belong to any national party; believes that man will "follow a multitude" in committing evils which he would not perpetrate alone. 1 November 1842. p.90, c3.

**6649 ANTI-SLAVERY FRIEND** *to* **THE** *AMERICAN AND FOREIGN ANTI-SLAVERY REPORTER.* **n.d. Cincinnati, Oh.** Wishes that the *Reporter* could publish more frequently; comments on the political climate in Ohio and the immigration of many colored people to Canada. 1 November 1842. p.92, c2.

**6650 n.n.** *to* **THE** *AMERICAN AND FOREIGN ANTI-SLAVERY REPORTER.* **[extract] n.d. East Tennessee.** Informs of the progress of anti-slavery principles in East Tennessee and predicts the downfall of slavery. 1 November 1842. p.93, c2.

**6651 REV. B. F.** *to* **THE** *AMERICAN AND FOREIGN ANTI-SLAVERY REPORTER.* **n.d. New Hampshire.** Proposes that the *Reporter* be published monthly at fifty cents per copy. 1 November 1842. p.93, c3.

**6652 REV. WILLIAM RAYMOND** *to* **n.n. n.d. York, Sierra Leone.** Comments on his health and that of Rev. James Steele; believes that God wants him and his fellow missionaries to establish a mission in Sherbro. 1 November 1842. p.94, c1.

**6653 n.n.** *to* **THE** *CLEVELAND GAZETTE.* **n.d. n.p.** Discusses the disproportionate congressional representation of the slaveholding states. 1 November 1842. p.94, c3.

**6654 A MINISTER** *to* **n.n. n.d. Connecticut.** Details the essence of an anti-slavery tract he proposes to write. 1 November 1842. p.95, c1.

**6655 MERCANTILE FIRM** *to* **THE** *AMERICAN AND FOREIGN ANTI-SLAVERY REPORTER.* **5 August 1842. New Orleans.** Encloses the text of a Louisiana law which will take effect 16 September, preventing free persons of color from entering the state. 1 November 1842. p.95, c1.

**6656 n.n.** *to* **n.n. [from the** *Journal of Commerce***] 16 August 1842. Nassau, N.P.** Informs of the dismissal of charges against Henry Jones of being a slave. 1 November 1842. p.95, c3.

**6657 WM. RAYMOND** *to* **THE** *AMERICAN AND FOREIGN ANTI-SLAVERY REPORTER.* **1 August 1842. Sierra Leone, West Africa.** Informs of the arrival of Captain Brown from New York on the schooner *Atlanta*; discusses monetary difficulties he faces because of the inability of American abolitionists to raise money to support him. 1 November 1842. p.96, c2.

**6658 D. L. BRAYTON** *to* **THE** *AMERICAN AND FOREIGN ANTI-SLAVERY REPORTER.* **5 February 1842. Mergru, Brit. Bur.** Expresses shock and disbelief upon learning that slaves are legally kept from reading the Bible, that Christians are responsible for the perpetuation of slavery, and that there are some who believe that "slaveholders are the only ones who can properly judge slavery." 1 November 1842. p.98, c1.

**6659 RICHARD D. WEBB** *to* **THE** *AMERICAN AND FOREIGN ANTI-SLAVERY REPORTER.* **21 July 1842. Dublin.** Lists anti-slavery publications received in Dublin; praises the *American and Foreign Anti-Slavery Reporter*'s reports on the *Amistad* Africans; expresses doubt that Africa could be converted to Christianity. 1 November 1842. p.99, c1.

**6660 JOSEPH STURGE** *to* **THE AMERICAN AND FOREIGN AS. n.d. n.p.** States that he is pleased that the society has nominated delegates for the following year's anti-slavery convention; claims that he is glad to have been defeated in the elections for the House of Commons, because of the corruption of its current members. 1 November 1842. p.99, c2.

**6661 DR. R. R. MADDEN** *to* **n.n. 12 August 1842. 48 Sloane Square, Chelsea, London.** States that his latest journey to the western coast of Africa has weakened his health; regrets to report the British government's involvement in sustaining the African slave trade. 1 November 1842. p.100, c2.

**6662 CASPAR WISTAR** *to* **THE** *AMERICAN AND FOREIGN ANTI-SLAVERY REPORTER.* **12 September 1842. Philadelphia.** Encloses a donation for the *Reporter*; regrets that he was unsuccessful in obtaining subscriptions from anti-slavery friends. 1 November 1842. p.100, c2.

**6663 CHARLES STUART** *to* **THE AMERICAN AND FOREIGN AS. n.d. Britain.** Describes his surprise, grief, and indignation that slavery still exists in the United States. 1 November 1842. p.100, c2.

**6664 A BLUSHING AMERICAN** *to* **HIS HIGHNESS THE BEY OF TUNIS. 12 October 1842. New York.** Reports having observed a notice in an American paper advertising weekly board for adults at ten dollars, children at five dollars, and horses and colored servants at four. 1 November 1842. p.100, c3.

**6665 VISCOUNT PALMERSTON** *to* **MR. ASTON. 6 March 1841. Foreign Office.** Refers to the demand for the recall of David Turnbull, consul at Havana, for having written an anti-slavery book entitled, *Travels in the West.* 1 November 1842. p.101, c3.

**6666 NAVAL OFFICER** *to* **n.n. [extract] n.d. Mozambique, Africa.** Reports that there is no slave trade in Mozambique. 1 November 1842. p.103, c1.

**6667 CORRESPONDENT** *to* **THE** ***BOSTON COURIER.*** **n.d. n.p.** Compares the populations of slaveholding and nonslaveholding states. 1 November 1842. p.103, c1.

**6668 REV. W. TAYLOR** *to* **n.n. [extract] 22 April 1842. Madras.** Reports that slavery thrives in both Madras and the Malabar coast of East India; informs that people of Madras sell their children into slavery during hard times, that kidnapping is common among them, and that Madras slaves who work the soil receive a portion of the produce. 1 November 1842. p.103, c2.

**6669 CORRESPONDENT** *to* **THE** *NATIONAL ANTI-SLAVERY STANDARD.* **n.d. St. Albans, Vt.** Reports on the stand taken by a church in a neighboring town which, if universally adopted, would help destroy slavery. 1 November 1842. p.103, c3.

## [1843]

**6670 WILLIAM RAYMOND** *to* **THE AMERICAN AND FOREIGN AS. [extract] n.d. n.p.** Comments on his finances, his health, and the need for additional missionaries to help in the establishment of the Mendi mission. 1 January 1843. p.105, c3.

**6671 WILLIAM RAYMOND** *to* **THE AMERICAN AND FOREIGN AS. 28 October 1842. Wesleyan Mission House, Freetown, Sierra Leone.** Discusses his plan to sail with six of his people to Sherbro to find a location for his mission. 1 January 1843. p.107, c1.

**6672 WILLIAM RAYMOND** *to* **THE AMERICAN AND FOREIGN AS. 31 October 1842. York, Sierra Leone.** Announces his decision to go to Kaw-Mendi with Mr. Raston to find a location for the mission, which will be established by the end of the dry season; directs all proceeds from his pamphlet, "The Legacy," to the Mendi fund and requests that temperance literature for children be sent to him. 1 January 1843. p.107, c2.

**6673 WILLIAM RAYMOND** *to* **REV. S. S. JOCELYN. 7 October 1842. York, Sierra Leone, West Africa.** Thanks him for supporting the establishment of a mission; discusses his disappoval of drinking and condemns wakes as a "system of iniquity"; notes signs of moral improvement in York. 1 January 1843. p.107, c2.

**6674 THOMAS BUNYAN** *to* **LEWIS TAPPAN. 7 October 1842. York, Sierra Leone, West Africa.** A Mendian school teacher in York discusses his experiences with some of the *Amistad* Africans; praises Raymond for his success in instilling temperance principles. 1 January 1843. p.108, c1.

**6675 W. HENRY GRAHAM** *to* **LEWIS TAPPAN. 6 October 1842. York, Sierra Leone, West Africa.** Praises Raymond for establishing a temperance society and a regular church service, noting that the previous minister gave sermons only once a year; comments on his earlier life, stating that he was stolen from his parents in A-Ku and sold as a slave to a Spaniard, but was rescued by the English and sent to school in York. 1 January 1843. p.108, c3.

**6676 GEORGE H. DECKER** *to* **THE MENDIAN COMMITTEE. 3 October 1842. York, Colony of Sierra Leone, West Africa.** Reports that he was visited by the Mendians as they were journeying to Sherbro, and comments on their affection for Mr. Raymond; adds that Raymond is the only Westerner he knows who does not drink. 1 January 1843. p.109, c1.

**6677 JOSEPH MAY** *to* **MR. RAYMOND. 5 October 1842. Charles Street, New Town, West Freetown.** A Wesleyan minister praises Raymond's success in organizing a temperance society and sympathizes with his being a "stranger in a strange land." 1 January 1843. p.109, c3.

**6678 REV. B. V. R. JAMES** *to* **THE CORRESPONDING SECRETARY OF THE AMERICAN AND FOREIGN AS. 21 September 1842. West African Mission, Fishtown Station.** Thanks the society for sending him anti-slavery literature; apologizes for not replying earlier. 1 January 1843. p.109, c3.

**6679 REV. ALLEN GRAVES** *to* **THE AMERICAN AND FOREIGN AS. 17 August 1842. Mahabuleshour Hills.** Hopes to make a donation to the CS at the end of the year; proposes that Northerners purchase slaves, ship them to Africa, and furnish Southerners with inexpensive white or free colored servants. 1 January 1843. p.110, c1.

**6680 P. J. GULICK** *to* **THEODORE D. WELD. 20 July 1841. Kauai, Hawaiian Isles.** States that reading "Slavery As It Is" has changed his former apathy to concern; quotes South Carolina's slave laws and expresses his indignation that slaves are prohibited from practicing biblical virtues and are denied the rights of education and trial by jury. 1 January 1843. p.110, c2.

**6681 GEORGE STACEY, CLERK OF THE YEARLY MEETING OF THE SOCIETY OF FRIENDS IN ENGLAND** *to* **n.n. n.d. n.p.** Expresses the society's deep regret and sympathy that slavery exists in European colonies and in America. 1 January 1843. p.112, c3.

**6682 FORMER EDITOR OF THE** ***PHILADELPHIA NATIONAL GAZETTE*** *to* **THE EDITORS OF THE** ***NATIONAL INTELLIGENCER*****. [extract] n.d. Paris.** Informs that M. P. Linstant, a native of Haiti, has published his "Essay on the Means of Extirpating the Prejudices of the Whites against the Color of the Africans and of Mixed Bloods." 1 January 1843. p. p.112, c3.

**6683 R. W., JR.** *to* **THE** ***ANTI-SLAVERY REPORTER*****. n.d. n.p.** Inquires whether the Missionary Committee and the Union Missionary Society at Hartford, Connecticut, have united; asks God's blessings on the American and Foreign AS. 1 January 1843. p.113, c1.

**6684 n.n.** *to* **n.n. [from the** ***Rochester Daily Advertiser*****] n.d. n.p.** Describes how it was possible for a white man to be held in bondage and sold as a slave in the United States. 1 January 1843. p.113, c2.

**6685 WM. B. DODGE** *to* **SIR. 9 November 1842. Salem, Ma.** Praises Mr. Clark's anti-slavery lectures as superior to those given by abolitionists; urges the Church to take part in the overthrow of slavery. 1 January 1843. p.113, c3.

**6686 ISAAC H. HUNTER** *to* **n.n. [from the** ***Brooklyn Star*****] 23 November 1842. Brooklyn, N.Y.** A former slave of Raleigh, North Carolina, thanks those who aided him in purchasing his and his family's freedom; states that he now resides with his family in Brooklyn, New York, and that they are members of the Methodist Episcopal church. 1 January 1843. p.113, c3.

**6687 n.n.** *to* **MR. EDITOR OF THE** ***BROOKLYN STAR*****. n.d. n.p.** Comments on the article by "Justice" describing the mistreatment of colored people; believes that the press and the clergy can be most effective in eliminating discrimination against colored people. 1 January 1843. p.114, c2.

**6688 PHILO-JAMES** *to* **MR. EDITOR. [from the** ***Brooklyn Star*****] n.d. n.p.** Expresses interest in the articles written by "Justice" and by "James" about the "right treatment of colored people"; relates a conversation he overheard about an article by "Justice." 1 January 1843. p.114, c3.

**6689 REV. WILLIAM RAYMOND** *to* **n.n. 7 October 1842. York, Sierra Leone, West Africa.** Describes the country, people, and customs of York, Sierre Leone. 1 January 1843. p.116, c2.

**6690 A FRIEND TO THE INTERESTS OF VITAL RELIGION, AND TO THE ANTI-SLAVERY CAUSE** *to* **MR. EDITOR OF THE** ***ANTI-SLAVERY REPORTER*****. n.d. Massachusetts.** Expresses concern that the American Board of Commissioners for Foreign Missions has not condemned the heresy of the American slave states. 1 January 1843. p.116, c1.

**6691 MR. BARRETT** *to* **n.n. n.d. n.p.** A correspondent from the West Indies forwards an account of a prayer meeting for the world's slaves held in conjunction with the First of August celebration; states that he was able to purchase his and his family's freedom with money lent from friends. 1 January 1843. p.119, c1.

**6692 JOHN SCOBLE** *to* **n.n. [extract] n.d. n.p.** Discusses projected British policies regarding India, which would grant slaves protection under the law, the right to hold property, and freedom for their offspring; states that the British have already abolished slavery in Malacca, Singapore, Penang, and Province Wellesley. 1 January 1843. p.119, c2.

**6693 R.** *to* **THE EDITORS OF THE** ***CINCINNATI GAZETTE*****. 1 September 1842. Liverpool.** Believes that cotton produced in India could supply Britain's needs and compete with American slave-grown cotton, thereby reducing the profitability of slavery and helping to bring about its end. 1 January 1843. p.119, c3.

**6694 REV. JULIUS O. BEARDSLEE** *to* **THE EDITORS OF THE** ***NEW YORK EVANGELIST*****. [extract] 14 October 1842. Brainerd, Jamaica, West Indies.** Relates the Negroes' rejoicing at the First of August celebration; notes that some own the land which they used to work as slaves, and others are given the opportunity to become educated; announces that the Elliot station has paid its debts and that there has been an increase in attendance at the school. 1 January 1843. p.120, c1.

**6695 DR. THOMAS LAFON** *to* **BROTHER TAPPAN. 2 March 1842. Sandwich Islands.** The president of the Sandwich Island AS condemns slavery as the worst vice tolerated by Christians; expresses shame for his previous involvement in the slave trade; regrets that most of his relatives are Christian slaveholders. 1 January 1843. p.120, c2.

**6696 A. L. DONOVAN** *to* **HIS WIFE. [extract from the** ***Maysville*** **(Ky.)** ***Gazette*****] n.d. Mississippi jail.** Proclaims his innocence of any involvement in a Negro insurrection; asks God's blessing on his wife. 1 March 1843. p.136, c1. (2nd ed. p.135, c2.)

**6697 n.n.** *to* **n.n. [from the** *Cincinnati Gazette*] **11 July 1841. Williamstown, Ky.** Assails Governor Lynch of Mississippi for failing to support the Constitution and permitting the heinous massacre of innocent people. 1 March 1843. p.136, c2. (2nd ed. p.136, c1.)

**6698 WILLIAM WILSON** *to* **n.n. 17 June 1836. Lexington, Va.** Advises that a law was passed in Virginia obligating postmasters to report the receipt of all anti-slavery publications. 1 March 1843. p.138, c1. (2nd ed. p.137, c2.)

**6699 W. C. PRESTON AND WILLIE P. MANGUM** *to* **T. EWING, SEC. OF THE TREASURY. n.d. n.p.** Believe Major Noah to be eminently qualified for public office. 1 March 1843. p.141, c2. (2nd ed. p.140, c2.)

**6700 HON. WILLIAM JAY** *to* **THE NEW YORK HISTORICAL SOCIETY. [extract] 20 March 1843 [sic]. n.p.** Describes the contents of the parliamentary documents relating to slavery and the slave trade which he is presenting to the society. 1 March 1843. p.143, c2.

**6701 T.** *to* **MESSRS. EDITORS. [from the** *Journal of Commerce*] **n.d. n.p.** Encloses a letter of John Scoble; informs that slavery has been abolished entirely in Malacca, Singapore, and Penang. 1 March 1843. p.144, c2.

**6702 JOHN SCOBLE** *to* **M. ISAMBERT. 15 March 1843 [sic]. London.** Reports on the amount of sugar and coffee received from the British West Indies; sends cheering news regarding the abolition of slavery in British India. 1 March 1843. p.144, c2.

**6703 WILLIAM H. SEWARD** *to* **THE COLORED CITIZENS. [extract] 4 January 1843. Albany.** Asks God to reward the colored citizens for their kindness to Seward. 1 March 1843. (2nd ed.) p.142, c2.

**6704 HON. J. C. CALHOUN** *to* **REV. ALEXANDER M'CAINE. n.d. n.p.** Praises M'Caine's scriptural defense of slavery. 1 March 1843. (2nd ed.) p. 142, c2.

**6705 WILLIAM RAYMOND** *to* **THE EXECUTIVE COMMITTEE OF THE UNION MISSIONARY SOCIETY. 13 April. n.p.** Gives an account of the journey to search for the Sherbro mission; describes Plantain Island and reports meeting the king of Kaw-Mendi, Henry Tucker; discusses the settlement made for land for the Sherbro mission. May 1843. p.2, c1.

**6706 DR. S. M. E. GOHEEN** *to* **THE EDITOR OF THE** *JOURNAL OF THE AMERICAN TEMPERANCE UNION.* **[extract] 14 February 1843. n.p.** Informs of Mr. Raymond's successful introduction of temperance reform in Sierra Leone. May 1843. p.3, c3.

**6707 JOSEPH MAY** *to* **BROTHER WILLIAM RAYMOND. 3 November 1842. New Town West, Freetown.** States that he was unable to meet Raymond and Raston in Freetown, due to a temperance meeting; informs that he has convinced many to sign the temperance pledge, and requests temperance tracts for distribution at meetings. May 1843. p.4, c1.

**6708 JOSEPH MAY** *to* **BROTHER WILLIAM RAYMOND. 16 November 1842. New Town West, Freetown.** Thanks him for his advice regarding the sin of pride; rejoices that he has conquered "poisonous, intoxicating liquor"; praises the missionaries in Africa. May 1843. p.4, c1.

**6709 WILLIAM E. BELL** *to* **BROTHER JOSEPH MAY. 4 November 1842. Wellington.** Requests copies of the temperance tract; reports difficulties in increasing the membership of the temperance society. May 1843. p.4, c2.

**6710 THOMAS BUNYAN** *to* **n.n. [extract] 1 February 1843. York, Sierra Leone, West Africa.** Discusses his religious experiences and praises the Lord. May 1843. p.4, c3.

**6711 GEORGE H. DECKER** *to* **BRETHREN. 4 February 1843. York, Sierra Leone, West Africa.** States that the "spirit of God began to strive within" in 1836, but it was not until he attended Brother Raymond's sermons that he became truly enlightened by the teachings of God. May 1843. p.5, c1.

**6712 W. HENRY GRAHAM** *to* **BRETHREN. 7 February 1843. York, Sierra Leone, Western Africa.** States that Brother Raymond's guidance enabled him to receive the blessings of the Lord. May 1843. p.5, c3.

**6713 DR. THOS. LAFON** *to* **MR. LEWIS TAPPAN. 18 April 1843. Perth Amboy.** States that he had joined the American Board of Commissioners for Foreign Missions after freeing his slaves, but later withdrew his membership because of the board's connection with slavery. May 1843. p.10, c3.

**6714 LORRIN ANDREWS** *to* **LEWIS TAPPAN. [extract] 17 December 1842. Lahainaluna.** States that he has withdrawn from the American Board of Commissioners for Foreign Missions due to the board's pro-slavery doctrines; informs that he and others have established a new missionary society. May 1843. p.11, c1.

**6715 REV. J. S. GREEN** *to* **LEWIS TAPPAN. [extract] 12 Demember 1842. Wailuku, Maui, Sandwich Islands.** States that he withdrew from the American Board of Commissioners for Foreign Missions because of its affiliation with slavery; believes that God opposes the Board's pro-slavery stance. May 1843. p.11, c2.

**6716 REV. J. S. GREEN** *to* **LEWIS TAPPAN. 14 October 1842. Lahainaluna, Maui.** Requests that Tappan receive Reverend Lafon as a brother to the anti-slavery cause; hopes that his "disconnection" with the American Board of Commissioners for Foreign Missions will not destroy plans to aid the fugitive slaves in Canada. May 1843. p.11, c2.

**6717 JOSEPH S. GREEN** *to* **MR. LEWIS TAPPAN. 22, 23 August 1842. Wailuku, Maui.** Reports on the success of the seminary for young Hawaiian ladies; informs that oppression in the Hawaiian islands has declined; urges abolitionists to help spread the teachings of the Gospel. May 1843. p.11, c3.

**6718 J. S. GREEN** *to* **LEWIS TAPPAN. 27 September 1841. Wailuku, Maui, Sandwich Islands.** Praises the biography of Wilberforce, written by his sons; remarks that although the plights of the Indians and the slaves are similar, the Indians inspire more respect because of their "native dignity of manners and roving state of independence." May 1843. p.12, c2.

**6719 LORRIN ANDREWS** *to* **LEWIS TAPPAN. 17 September 1841. Lahainaluna, Maui, Sandwich Islands.** Thanks him for his letter; commends the work of the American and Foreign AS in foreign countries. May 1843. p.12, c3.

**6720 THOMAS LAFON** *to* **BROTHER LEWIS TAPPAN. 2 March 1842. Sandwich Islands.** Apologizes for not having answered Tappan's letter sooner; condemns slavery as the most malignant vice on earth. May 1843. p.13, c2.

**6721 P. J. GULICK** *to* **BROTHER THEODORE D. WELD. 20 July 1841. Kauai, Hawaii.** Protests that slaves are denied the opportunity to follow Christian practices in marriage and raising families. May 1843. p.13, c2.

**6722 ALLEN GRAVES** *to* **THE TREASURER OF THE AMERICAN AND FOREIGN AS. 17 August 1842. Mahabuleshour.** States that he was previously unaware of the cruelties of slavery, although he lived in Virginia; commends the CS. May 1843. p.14, c2.

**6723 JONAS KING** *to* **LEWIS TAPPAN. 23 February 1841. Athens, Greece.** Acknowledges receipt of anti-slavery literature, which he has placed in the mission library; requests copies of the reports and pamphlets published by the American and Foreign AS for his children's use. May 1843. p.14, c3.

**6724 REV. JOHN J. LAWRENCE** *to* **THE** *AMERICAN AND FOREIGN ANTI-SLAVERY REPORTER.* **[extract] 4 May 1842. Dindigul, India.** Expresses gratitude for a copy of the constitution of the American and Foreign AS; discusses his attempt to love the people of India despite their "villanies"; believes that there is less guilt in "heathen" India than in the "civilized" slave states of America. May 1843. p.14, c3.

**6725 JUSTIN PERKINS** *to* **LEWIS TAPPAN. 22 January 1841. Ooroomiah, Persia.** Thanks him for forwarding the constitution of the American and Foreign AS; informs that although Nestorian Christians were slaves to the Mohammedans, they did not live in the degraded condition that slaves of Christian Americans endure. May 1843. p.15, c1.

**6726 n.n.** *to* **LEWIS TAPPAN. March 1843. Fall River, Ma.** Explains that in 1841 he contributed money to the Committee for the *Amistad* Africans rather than supporting the American Missionary, Bible, Tract, and Education societies, because the latter help to perpetuate American slavery. May 1843. p.15, c3.

**6727 REV. JUSTIN PARSONS** *to* **n.n. [extract] 8 March 1843. North Ridgeville, Oh.** An elderly man thanks his correspondent for copies of the *American and Foreign Anti-Slavery Reporter*, but regrets that he is unable to pay for them; adds that he wishes to send five dollars to Raymond and Wilson in Canada before his death. May 1843. p.16, c1.

**6728 DR. F. JULIUS LEMOYNE** *to* **n.n. [extract] n.d. Washington, Washington County, Pa.** Reports that opposition to the anti-slavery cause has resulted in decreased abolitionist activity in Washington, Pennsylvania; urges abolitionists to strive for the cause; encloses forty dollars for the Mendians. May 1843. p.16, c1.

**6729 n.n.** *to* **n.n. n.d. Yale College, New Haven, Ct.** Informs that Yale College holds a monthly concert at which a collection is taken up for the Mendi mission; asks the Lord to hasten the deliverance of the oppressed. May 1843. p.16, c1.

**6730 n.n.** *to* **n.n. [extract] n.d. Cheshire County, N.H.** Encloses six dollars to aid the Mendi mission. May 1843. p.16, c1.

**6731 D. M. CAMP** *to* **LEWIS TAPPAN. 27 March 1842. Derby, Vt.** States that many friends of missions in Vermont have become dissatisfied with the American Board of Commissioners for Foreign Missions' affiliation with slaveholders and have redirected their donations; encloses five dollars for the Mendi fund from a sabbath school. May 1843. p.16, c2.

**6732 REV. JULIUS O. BEARDSLEE** *to* **n.n. [extract] 7 August 1843. West India.** Discusses the activities of several missionaries in the West Indies; reports on the construction of new chapels in Hermitage and Devon Penn. December 1843. p.1, c3.

**6733 REV. J. S. GREEN** *to* **LEWIS TAPPAN. [extract] 14 July 1843. Sandwich Islands.** A missionary informs that he withdrew from the American Board of Commissioners for Foreign Missions because of its affiliation with slaveholders and declares that abolitionists should sever all ties with slaveholders; discusses the success of his mission and defines the duties of a missionary. December 1843. p.1, c3.

**6734 n.n.** *to* **n.n. [extract] n.d. Amesbury, Ma.** Intends to forward donations for the Mendi mission from the members of the Congregational Church in Amesbury. December 1843. p.7, c3.

**6735 n.n.** *to* **n.n. [extract] n.d. Fitzwilliam, N.H.** Encloses money to be used to sustain the Mendi mission. December 1843. p.7, c3.

**6736 n.n.** *to* **n.n. [extract] n.d. Weston, Van Buren County, Mi.** Encloses ten dollars to aid the Mendi mission. December 1843. p.7, c3.

**6737 n.n.** *to* **n.n. [extract] n.d. Fitchburg, Ms.** Encloses a contribution for the foreign missions. December 1843. p.7, c3.

**6738 n.n.** *to* **n.n. n.d. Philadelphia, Pa.** Praises Dr. Lafon's sermon delivered before the Union Missionary Society on the obstacles to the success of the missions. December 1843. p.8, c1.

**6739 HON. WM. SLADE** *to* **n.n. [extract] n.d. Middlebury, Vt.** States that he will gladly distribute copies of Dr. Lafon's address to persons in different parts of Vermont. December 1843. p.8, c1.

**6740 A MERCHANT** *to* **n.n. [extract] n.d. Syracuse, N.Y.** States that the *American and Foreign Anti-Slavery Reporter* has awakened him to the horrors of slavery. December 1843. p.8, c1.

**6741 HON. SETH M. GATES** *to* **n.n. 16 November 1843. Warsaw, N.Y.** Admires Dr. Lafon's address on the anti-slavery missions. December 1843. p.8, c1.

## [1844]

**6742 n.n.** *to* **n.n. [extract from the** *British and Foreign Anti-Slavery Reporter*] **n.d. Havana.** Describes the brutalities inflicted on persons who had knowledge of an insurrection plot. September 1844. p.3, c2.

**6743 n.n.** *to* **THE** *LONDON MORNING CHRONICLE.* **n.d. Cuba.** Informs of an aborted conspiracy to assassinate all white men and Negro women in Cuba. September 1844. p.3, c2.

**6744 n.n.** *to* **n.n. [from the** *Bangor Gazette*] **n.d. Nashville.** Informs that James K. Polk is a slaveholder. September 1844. p.7, c1.

**6745 JAMES G. BIRNEY** *to* **n.n. n.d. n.p.** Proposes that Northerners decide whether they will be drawn down by the slave states, or be strong and save everyone from destruction. September 1844. p.7, c1.

**6746 HON. THEO. FRELINGHUYSEN** *to* **JOSEPH G. HALL [from the** *Louisville Chronicle*] **11 June 1844. New York.** Asserts that he is not an abolitionist and that he supports the CS; believes that Congress has no right to interfere with slavery, as it is a "domestic concern." September 1844. p.7, c1.

**6747 JAMES G. BIRNEY** *to* **FRIENDS. 1835. n.p.** States that he freed his slaves, and considers compensation for the loss of slaves as justified as compensation for stolen property. September 1844. p.7, c1.

**6748 JAMES G. BIRNEY** *to* **MILLS. July 1834. n.p.** States that he has witnessed the American "anti-republican" tendencies of slavery, and concludes that slavery is contradictory to the founding principles of the United States government. September 1844. p.7, c1.

**6749 JAMES G. BIRNEY** *to* **n.n. 1844. n.p.** Accepts the Liberty Party nomination and asserts that those who fail to live by God's rules can never attain permanent prosperity. September 1844. p.7, c1.

**6750 JAMES G. BIRNEY** *to* **THE PITTSBURGH COMMITTEE. 1844. n.p.** Believes that men have "no more right to enact slavery than they have to enact murder, blasphemy, incest, or adultery"; asserts that Texas should not be admitted as a slave state because this would perpetuate the existence of "chains that we have no right to forge or to impose." September 1844. p.7, c1.

**6751 THEO. FRELINGHUYSEN** *to* **JOSEPH G. HALL. [from the** ***Louisville Chronicle*****] 11 June 1844. New York.** States that he is not an abolitionist, but that he supports the CS; believes that slavery is a domestic problem with which Congress is not authorized to interfere. November 1844. p.9, c1.

**6752 WILLIAM JAY** *to* **THE** *AMERICAN AND FOREIGN ANTI-SLAVERY REPORTER.* **1 October 1844. Bedford.** Believes that Frelinghuysen, a candidate for the vice-presidency, wrote the letter renouncing abolitionism and supporting the CS as an "electioneering document" to gain Southern favor; asserts that the CS's constitution is not adverse to abolition, and accuses Frelinghuysen of misrepresenting abolitionists' intentions regarding congressional legislation on slavery. November 1844. p.9, c1.

**6753 CORRESPONDENT** *to* **THE** *MORNING CHRONICLE.* **n.d. n.p.** Provides an account of the meeting of the General Assembly of the Free Church. November 1844. p.14, c1.

**6754 CORRESPONDENT** *to* **THE** *CHARLESTON OBSERVER.* **n.d. n.p.** Believes that the Negroes in America should be introduced to the teachings of God because they are as uninformed as those in Africa. November 1844. p.14, c1.

**6755 MRS. ALANSON WORK** *to* **n.n. n.d n.p.** Describes the death of one of her children, which occurred while her husband was imprisoned for helping a slave to escape. November 1844. p.14, c2.

**6756 A. P. UPSHUR, SECRETARY OF THE NAVY** *to* **EDWARD FITZGERALD. 26 October 1841. n.p.** Grants Fitzgerald's request to take his servant Robert Lucas on board the frigate *United States.* November 1844. p.15, c1.

**6757 HON. WM. JAY** *to* **THE** *CINCINNATI HERALD.* **[extract] n.d. n.p.** Informs that the Liberty Party papers are now being circulated in the slave states. November 1844. p.15, c2.

**6758 S. P. ANDREWS** *to* **DR. SNODGRASS, EDITOR OF THE** *BALTIMORE SATURDAY VISITER.* **n.d. Baltimore.** Reports on the prevalence of anti-slavery sentiment in the South. November 1844. p.16, c1.

## [1845]

**6759 AMERICAN** *to* **n.n. 4 April. Havana.** States that the governor's proclamation forbidding the landing of slaves in Cuba was issued "to please John Bull," and has already been disobeyed. May 1845. p.38, c1.

**6760 SLAVEHOLDER** *to* **THE** *CINCINNATI HERALD.* **2 January. Kentucky.** States that his strongest desire is that Kentucky become a free state. May 1845. p.38, c2.

**6761 DR. BAILEY** *to* **n.n. n.d. n.p.** Reports that hostility to the discussion of the slavery question is disappearing in parts of Kentucky. May 1845. p.38, c2.

**6762 BALTIMORE CORRESPONDENT** *to* **THE** *ALBANY PATRIOT.* **14 February. n.p.** Explains the difficulty in converting Southern men to the principles of anti-slavery. May 1845. p.39, c1.

**6763 n.n.** *to* **THE *CHARLESTON* (S.C.) *COURIER*. n.d. n.p.** Comments on the degradation of Southern whites resulting from slavery. May 1845. p.39, c2.

**6764 EX-PRISONER** *to* **A FRIEND. 30 January. Theopolis.** Describes his physical and emotional health following his release from a Missouri penitentiary. May 1845. p.39, c2.

**6765 C. E. S.** *to* **THE *BOSTON RECORDER*. n.d. Cincinnati.** States that slavery will continue to agitate Church and state as long as it exists; informs that Dr. Baxter told the students of Lane Seminary that the abolitionists have been banished. May 1845. p.40, c1.

**6766 CORRESPONDENT** *to* **n.n. May 1845. Cincinnati.** Reports on the pro-slavery attitude of the majority at the General Assembly of the Presbyterian Church. July 1845. p.44, c2.

**6767 PROFESSOR GEYER** *to* **n.n. [extract] 11 April. Stockholm.** States that freedom has been secured for four or five hundred slaves in St. Bartholomew. July 1845. p.47, c2.

**6768 JOSHUA TINSON** *to* **JOSEPH STURGE. [extract from the *British and Foreign Anti-Slavery Reporter*] 15 November 1844. Calabar.** Informs of effects of emancipation in Jamaica. July 1845. p.48, c1.

**6769 A. A. PHELPS** *to* **THE SECRETARIES OF THE AMERICAN BOARD OF COMMISSIONERS FOR FOREIGN MISSIONS. February 1845. Boston.** Submits inquiries to the board regarding the election of corporate members, the solicitation of funds from slaveholders, the agencies in the South, the receipt of funds, the missionaries and mission churches, and Dr. Lafon and Rev. Dr. Armstrong. August 1845. p.49, c2.

**6770 A. A. PHELPS** *to* **DR. ANDERSON. 15 January 1845. Boston.** Encloses a list of inquiries about slavery addressed to the American Board of Commissioners for Foreign Missions. August 1845. p.49, c2.

**6771 DAVID GREENE** *to* **REV. AMOS A. PHELPS. 29 January 1845. Missionary House, Boston.** Acknowledges receipt of the inquiries directed to the American Board of Commissioners for Foreign Missions; states that the answers may be found in the board's published proceedings, and that the board's secretaries do not issue statements on the official policy of the board. August 1845. p.51, c2.

**6772 A. A. PHELPS, W. W. PATTON, M. S. SCUDDER, [AND FORTY-TWO OTHERS]** *to* **THE SECRETARIES OF THE AMERICAN BOARD OF COMMISSIONERS FOR FOREIGN MISSIONS. 8 January 1845. Boston.** State that their questions are proposed with sincerity and honesty. August 1845. p.51, c2.

**6773 DAVID GREENE** *to* **REV. AMOS A. PHELPS. 19 February 1845. Boston.** Replies, on behalf of the Prudential Committee, that the American Board of Commissioners for Foreign Missions will postpone answering the list of inquiries about its position on slavery until after the board's official meeting. August 1845. p.52, c1.

**6774 DR. R. ANDERSON** *to* **[ELNATHAN DAVIS]. [extract] 9 December 1836. Missionary Rooms, Boston.** Informs that the American Board of Commissioners for Foreign Missions disapproves of Davis's views on infant baptism; hopes that the matter can be reconciled. August 1845. p.53, c2.

**6775 REV. W. J. ARMSTRONG** *to* **[ELNATHAN DAVIS]. 5 January 1837. Missionary Rooms, Boston.** Informs Davis that he has been dismissed from the American Board of Commissioners for Foreign Missions due to his views on infant baptism. August 1845. p.53, c2.

**6776 ROBERT BURNS, D.D., MODERATOR, AND WILLIAM RINTOUL, SYNOD CLERK *to* THE MODERATOR OF THE GENERAL ASSEMBLY OF THE UNITED STATES PRESBYTERIAN CHURCH. 9 June 1845. Coburg, Canada West.** State that the Presbyterian General Assembly of Canada disapproves of its American counterpart's refusal to discuss slavery at its recent meeting; beseech Americans to consider the sinfulness of slavery. August 1845. p.56, c1.

**6777 B. W. DUDLEY, THO. H. WALTERS, AND JOHN W. HUNT *to* CASSIUS M. CLAY. 14 August 1845. Lexington.** Delegates claiming to represent the Lexington community ask Clay to close down the *True American*, an anti-slavery newspaper, because it is disruptive to the peace of the community; emphasize that they are not threatening him, but warn that his safety may depend on whether or not he grants their request. October 1845. p.66, c2.

**6778 CASSIUS M. CLAY *to* B. W. DUDLEY, THO. H. WALTERS, AND JOHN W. HUNT. 15 August 1845. Lexington.** Denies that they represent the Lexington community; calls their threat contemptible, and accuses them of cowardice for challenging him while he is bedridden. October 1845. p.67, c1.

**6779 CASSIUS M. CLAY *to* THE KENTUCKIANS. 15 August 1845. Lexington.** Requests public support for his refusal to comply with Dudley, Walters, and Hunt's demand that he discontinue publication of the *True American.* October 1845. p.67, c1.

**6780 MR. E. L. MAGOON *to* THE *RICHMOND RELIGIOUS HERALD.* n.d. n.p.** States that the English do not accept the conciliatory attitude of the American clergy toward slavery. October 1845. p.69, c1.

**6781 REV. DR. COX *to* DR. JONATHAN A. ALLEN. 10 February 1836. Auburn.** States that all slaveholders ought to be excluded from the communion of the Church. October 1845. p.69, c2.

**6782 BISHOP ANDREW *to* n.n. n.d. n.p.** Declares that "it is now time to stop the overflowing of these turbid waters, and, in their stead, to bring over the land the healing streams of peace and holiness." October 1845. p.69, c2.

**6783 n.n. *to* THE *CHRISTIAN ADVOCATE.* 27 August. n.p.** Criticizes Bishop Andrew's statement. October 1845. p.69, c2.

**6784 n.n. *to* MR. EDITOR OF THE *RELIGIOUS HERALD.* 1 September 1845. Hartford.** Inquires whether a church has the right to deny communion to a man who has reclaimed his fugitive slave and who is currently a pastor of a congregational church in Connecticut. October 1845. p.69, c2.

**6785 FREDERICK DOUGLASS *to* n.n. n.d. England.** Remarks that he is enjoying London and has experienced no discrimination. November 1845. p.77, c2.

**6786 n.n. *to* REV. A. A. PHELPS. n.d. Massachusetts.** Claims that the American Board of Commissioners for Foreign Missions tacitly agrees with the principles of abolition, and need only bring the principles into practice; quotes from a book, *Fanaticism*, to illustrate that man cannot be free of guilt if he ignores the evil perpetrated by others. November 1845. p.79, c2.

**6787 n.n. *to* REV. A. A. PHELPS. n.d. n.p.** A Southerner who was educated in the North writes that since his return to the South, he has implored his friends to relinquish their slaves, and has rejected jobs which would require silence on the subject of slavery. November 1845. p.80, c1.

**6788 n.n.** *to* **SIR. n.d. Kentucky.** Describes the anti-slavery activities and the spirit of abolitionists throughout Kentucky. November 1845. p.80, c1.

**6789 n.n.** *to* **n.n. n.d. Kentucky.** Believes that Cassius Clay should have accepted the insults thrust at him cheerfully, in order to further the anti-slavery cause. November 1845. p.80, c2.

**6790 GOV. WILLIAM SLADE** *to* **REV. C. W. GARDNER. 10 May. n.p.** Regrets that Middlebury College has denied admission to four young men of color. November 1845. p.80, c2.

**6791 DR. R. S. STEWART** *to* **JOHN L. CAREY. n.d. n.p.** Regrets that Carey was not re-elected to the legislature in Maryland; praises Carey's promotion of gradual emancipation. December 1845. p.82, c1.

**6792 DR. R. S. STEWART** *to* **n.n. n.d. n.p.** Discusses slavery as the primary cause of emigration from Maryland; approves of colonization. December 1845. p.84, c1.

**6793 CORRESPONDENT** *to* **THE** *NATIONAL INTELLIGENCER.* **n.d. Wilton, Va.** Regrets that the people of Virginia have emigrated to the South and West. December 1845. p.84, c2.

**6794 GENTLEMAN** *to* **n.n. [from the** *Cincinnati Herald***] 25 September 1845. Indianapolis.** Informs that sixty families from Washington County, Maryland, passed through Indianapolis en route to their new homes in Illinois. December 1845. p.84, c2.

**6795 CORRESPONDENT** *to* **THE** *PHILANTHROPIST.* **n.d. n.p.** States that several slaveholders in Kentucky have emancipated their slaves. December 1845. p.84, c2.

**6796 LYDIA S. WIERMAN** *to* **THE** *PENNSYLVANIA FREEMAN.* **3 November. York Springs, Pa.** Encloses an extract of a letter concerning a slaveholder in Virginia; states that in some districts in Virginia, expulsory laws against free colored persons are not enforced. December 1845. p.84, c2.

**6797 n.n.** *to* **LYDIA S. WIERMAN. [extract] n.d. n.p.** Informs that John Nixon is deceased and that he provided for the freedom of his slaves in his will. December 1845. p.84, c2.

**6798 REUBEN STARBUCK** *to* **n.n. [extract from the** *Bangor Gazette***] n.d. n.p.** States that there has been a recent increase in anti-slavery sentiment in North Carolina. December 1845. p.84, c2.

**6799 AARON STALKER** *to* **THE BALTIMORE YEARLY MEETING OF FRIENDS. November 1844. n.p.** Gives an account of the Yearly Meeting of Friends of North Carolina, at which the question of slavery was discussed; states that they advocate adherence to Christian laws, rather than state laws. December 1845. p.85, c1.

**6800 CORRESPONDENT** *to* **THE** *BRITISH AND FOREIGN ANTI-SLAVERY REPORTER.* **n.d. France.** Informs of the decision of the Court of Cassation in France to liberate a number of slaves; cites instances of enforcement of the decision. December 1845. p.87, c2.

**6801 CORRESPONDENT** *to* **THE** *NEW YORK EVANGELIST.* **n.d. n.p.** Describes the system of slavery in Brazil. December 1845. p.88, c1.

**6802 CORRESPONDENT** *to* **THE** *NEW YORK EVANGELIST.* **n.d. n.p.** Contrasts slavery in Brazil and slavery in the United States. December 1845. p.88, c1.

**6803 n.n.** *to* **n.n. [extract from the** ***Hampshire Telegraph*****] 30 March 1845. Sierra Leone.** Discusses the passengers of the recently captured slaver, the *Hurican*. December 1845. p.88, c1.

**6804 CASSIUS M. CLAY** *to* **n.n. n.d. n.p.** Emphasizes that freedom of the press is a constitutional right; calls upon Congress to defend this right. December 1845. p.88, c2.

## [1846]

**6805 ARTHUR TAPPAN, WM. BROWN, W. E. WHITING, [AND 109 OTHERS]** *to* **THE FRIENDS OF BIBLE MISSIONS IN THE STATE OF NEW YORK. n.d. n.p.** Invite them to a meeting in Syracuse to consider the biblical methods of propagating the gospel. January 1846. p.94, c1.

**6806 JNO. SCOBLE** *to* **FRIEND. 2 December 1845. London.** Reports that he encountered men on his tour of southern France who promised to help abolish slavery; comments that the AS at Paris failed to take definitive action; hopes that Texas will not be admitted as a slave state. January 1846. p.94, c2.

**6807 SQUADRON OFFICER** *to* **n.n. 26 July 1845. West Coast of Africa.** States that it will be impossible to suppress the slave trade in Africa as long as there is a market for slaves in America. February 1846. p.99, c1.

**6808 n.n.** *to* **n.n. [from the** ***Liverpool Times*****] n.d. Pernambuco.** Informs that the steamer *Cacique* will be fitted with paddles in order to proceed to the coast of Africa to obtain slaves. February 1846. p.99, c2.

**6809 W. L. C.** *to* **CHARLES A. WHEATON. [from the** ***Albany Patriot*****] 30 December 1845. Washington.** Describes the struggle of Sarah Carter for freedom; solicits donations to aid her husband in obtaining her freedom. February 1846. p.100, c1.

**6810 JONATHAN CABLE, S. KITCHRIDGE, J. M. SADD, [AND TWENTY-FIVE OTHERS]** *to* **n.n. 14 October 1845. Logansport.** Issue a call to all opponents of slavery to attend a convention in Philadelphia. February 1846. p.101, c2.

**6811 REV. J. S. GREEN** *to* **n.n. [extract] n.d. Sandwich Islands.** States that while he was a missionary he was sustained by a society that does not acknowledge the duty to preach the gospel to the heathens in America. February 1846. p.102, c1.

**6812 CORRESPONDENT** *to* **THE** ***ALBANY PATRIOT*****. n.d. Oberlin.** Proclaims that Oberlin is the citadel of the anti-slavery spirit in northern Ohio. February 1846. p.102, c2.

**6813 INTELLIGENT PENNSYLVANIAN** *to* **n.n. n.d. n.p** States that slavery is the major deterrent to immigration into Virginia. February 1846. p.103, c1.

**6814 CORRESPONDENT** *to* **THE** ***BALTIMORE VISITOR*****. 24 December. Eastern Shore.** Encourages others in Maryland to join him in voting for anti-slavery candidates. February 1846. p.103, c2.

**6815 n.n.** *to* **THE** ***BALTIMORE VISITOR*****. 26 December. Queen Ann's County, Md.** Reports that slaveholders will hold a meeting to discuss the aggression of the abolitionists. February 1846. p.103, c2.

**6816 A. A. PHELPS** *to* **GOV. THOMAS G. PRATT. 22 August 1845. New York.** Requests information regarding the release of Rev. C. T. Torrey. April 1846. p.105, c1.

**6817 A. A. PHELPS AND C. D. CLEVELAND** *to* **GOV. THOMAS G. PRATT. 20 March 1846. Philadelphia.** State that those who have been fighting for the release of Rev. C. T. Torrey from the Maryland Penitentiary had hoped to obtain his release before his death, but as Governor Pratt has not acted upon their petitions, and Torrey is near death, the money raised will be donated to the support of Torrey's family; ask the governor to allow Torrey to spend his final days with his family. April 1846. p.105, c1.

**6818 MUSHEER AHMED BASHA BEY, PRINCE OF TUNIS** *to* **SIR THOMAS READE, BRITISH CONSUL AT TUNIS. 22 January 1846. n.p.** States that slavery was abolished in Tunis gradually. April 1846. p.108, c2.

**6819 JOHN SCOBLE, SECRETARY OF THE BRITISH AND FOREIGN AS** *to* **THE** *AMERICAN AND FOREIGN ANTI-SLAVERY REPORTER.* **n.d. n.p.** Reports on the favorable outlook for crops and economy in the British colonies. April 1846. p.108, c2.

**6820 JONATHAN CABLE, S. KITCHRIDGE, J. M. SADD, ET AL.** *to* **n.n. n.d. n.p.** Issue a call to all opponents of slavery to attend a convention in Philadelphia. [reprint of letter first appearing February 1846] April 1846. p.110, c1.

**6821 MISSISSIPPI GENTLEMAN** *to* **A PHILADELPHIA CORRESPONDENT. n.d. Mississippi.** Informs that one-fifth of the cotton from northern Mississippi is high quality free-labor cotton and is priced comparably with slave-labor cotton. April 1846. p.111, c1.

**6822 PHILADELPHIA CORRESPONDENT** *to* **MR. STURGE. n.d. n.p.** Comments on the availability of free-labor cotton. April 1846. p.111, c1.

**6823 CORRESPONDENT** *to* **THE** *LONDON TIMES.* **5 January. Trebisond.** Believes that General Budberg, who commands the Russian forts on the eastern coast of the Black Sea, does not interfere with the slave traffic between the Turks and Circassians. April 1846. p.112, c1.

# Index of Correspondents